ABOUT THE AUTHOR

WINNER OF THE Pulitzer Prize in History in 1946 for THE AGE OF JACKSON, Mr. Schlesinger continued his distinguished career with such books as THE VITAL CENTER, THE POLITICS OF HOPE, and the first three volumes of THE AGE OF ROOSEVELT: *The Crisis of the Old Order, The Coming of the New Deal,* and *The Politics of Upheaval.* These three volumes were Book-of-the-Month Club selections.

Please turn the page for the glowing reviews. . . .

If people bring so much courage to this world the world has to kill them to break them, so of course it kills them. The world breaks every one and afterward many are strong at the broken places. But those that will not break it kills. It kills the very good and the very gentle and the very brave impartially.

—HEMINGWAY

Arthur M. Schlesinger, Jr.

A
THOUSAND
DAYS

JOHN F. KENNEDY
IN THE WHITE HOUSE

FAWCETT PREMIER • NEW YORK

in memory of
John Fitzgerald Kennedy

Published by Fawcett Premier Books, a unit of CBS Publications, the Educational and Professional Publishing Division of CBS, Inc. by arrangement with Houghton Mifflin Company.

Book of the Month Club selection, December 1965
Book Find Club selection, January 1966

Cover photo of John F. Kennedy by Morton Tadder-Pictorial

ISBN 0-449-30021-8

Manufactured in the United States of America

First Fawcett Premier Edition: August 1971
Fourteenth Printing: August 1992

CONTENTS

FOREWORD

THIS WORK IS NOT a comprehensive history of the Kennedy Presidency. It is a personal memoir by one who served in the White House during the Kennedy years.

A personal memoir, at best, can offer only a partial view. The Presidency is such a complex institution that only the President himself can fully know his problems and his purposes. John Fitzgerald Kennedy had intended to write the history of his own administration. No one else will ever be able to achieve the central, the presidential, perspective on these years. Even the public official closest to Kennedy, then the Attorney General of the United States, looking at the White House Papers after his brother's death, was astonished at the variety of presidential issues he had not known about before.

A presidential associate, moreover, inevitably tends to overrate the significance of the things he does know about. Grace Tully, who was Franklin D. Roosevelt's personal secretary, acutely observed of the books written by the men around F.D.R., "None of them could know that for each minute they spent with the President he spent a hundred minutes by himself and a thousand more with scores of other people—to reject, improvise, weigh and match this against that until a decision was reached." * This book, for example, deals largely with foreign affairs and only occasionally records President Kennedy's intense feeling about his own country and his deep desire to improve the quality of life and opportunity in the United States. This was an animating purpose of his Presidency, but, as one only irregularly involved in these matters, I have less to say about them. Similarly others will have to describe in greater detail President Kennedy's relations with Congress and with party politics.

The presidential perspective on this administration is now tragically and irretrievably lost. But sometime in the future an historian, today perhaps a very young man, will read the volumes of reminiscences and analysis, immerse himself in the flood of papers in the Kennedy Library and attempt by the imaginative thrust of his craft to recover that perspective. He will not attain it; but he will do the best he can on the basis of the evidence and his own insight to reproduce the form and color and motion of the years as they unrolled before the occupant of the Oval Room. I hope that this and similar books published in the time between may advance his task.

A number of my colleagues in the Kennedy administration helped check and supplement my own recollections as I

* Grace Tully, *FDR, My Boss* (New York, 1949), xi.

worked on this book, and I am deeply grateful for their assistance. But the reconstruction of past events is exceedingly difficult, if not impossible; and, when I have been confronted by diverging judgments and memories, I have had no choice but to consider the evidence as best I could and draw conclusions on my own responsibility. Therefore I am, as author, totally and exclusively accountable for the shape that incidents and people assume in this narrative. I do wish, however, to express special thanks to Nancy Riley Newhouse for valuable assistance on research and to Gretchen Stewart for devoted and unstinting help in every aspect of this undertaking.

This work is based on papers as well as on interviews and recollections. Every statement, I believe, has its warrant; but in order to protect confidential communications it has seemed better not to give a systematic indication of sources at this time. A fully footnoted manuscript will be deposited under seal in the Kennedy Library along with my own White House papers. After an appropriate interval these will be open to scholars.

Many of the quotations come from a journal I kept through these years. At the start of his administration President Kennedy said that he did not want his staff recording the daily discussions of the White House. Remarks tossed off gaily or irritably in conversation, he knew, looked very different in print. He mentioned Henry Morgenthau's solemn chronicling in his diaries of Franklin Roosevelt's jocosities during the gold-buying episode of 1933; and he wished no restraint on his own freedom of expression. Accordingly my White House notes for the first weeks were fragmentary. Then after the Bay of Pigs he said, "I hope you kept a full account of that." I said that I had understood he did not want us to keep full accounts of anything. He said, "No, go ahead. You can be damn sure that the CIA has its record and the Joint Chiefs theirs. We'd better make sure we have a record over here. So you go ahead." I did.

None of this, I fear, can come close to recapturing the exceptional qualities of John F. Kennedy as a man and as a President. But I hope it will suggest something of the way in which he quickened the heart and mind of the nation, inspired the young, met great crises, led our society to new possibilities of justice and our world to new possibilities of peace and left behind so glowing and imperishable a memory.

ARTHUR M. SCHLESINGER, JR.

Washington, D. C.
February 4, 1965

PROLOGUE: JANUARY 1961

IT ALL BEGAN in the cold.

It had been cold all week in Washington. Then early Thursday afternoon the snow came. The winds blew in icy, stinging gusts and whipped the snow down the frigid streets. Washingtonians do not know how to drive in the snow: they slide and skid and spin their wheels and panic. By six o'clock traffic had stopped all over town. People abandoned their cars in snowdrifts and marched grimly into the gale, heads down, newspapers wrapped around necks and stuffed under coats. And still the snow fell and the winds blew.

At eight o'clock the young President-elect and his wife went to the Inaugural Concert at Constitution Hall. An hour later they left at the intermission to go on to the Inaugural Gala at the Armory. The limousine made its careful way through the blinding snow down the Mall. Bonfires had been lit along the path in a vain effort to keep the avenue clear. Great floodlights around the Washington Monument glittered through the white storm. It was a scene of eerie beauty. As stranded motorists cheered the presidential car, the President-elect told his friend William Walton, "Turn on the lights so they can see Jackie." With the light on inside the car, he settled back to read Jefferson's First Inaugural, which had been printed in the concert program. When he finished, he shook his head and said wryly, "Better than mine."

By midnight the city was choked with snow. Workmen labored to clear Pennsylvania Avenue for next day's parade. Soldiers used flame throwers to melt the frozen drifts around the inaugural stand in the Capitol Plaza. At quarter to four in the morning, the President-elect returned to his house in Georgetown from a supper given him downtown by his father after the Gala. His wife, recuperating from the birth of their second child, had gone home hours earlier; but he found her awake, too excited to sleep, and they talked for a moment about the day that had passed and the day yet to come.

Toward dawn the snow began to stop. It covered houses

11

and clung to trees and filled the windswept streets: the white city faintly shimmered in the pale sunrise. The President-elect arose at eight, read over the text of his inaugural address, pencil in hand, and then left to attend mass at a neighboring church. The crowd began to gather in the Capitol Plaza long before noon. At eleven the President-elect and his wife drank coffee with the retiring President and Vice-President and their wives in the Red Room of the White House. They talked formally and inconsequentially. In morning coats and top hats they entered limousines to drive along the snowy streets to the Capitol. The wife of the retiring President said, "Look at Ike in his top hat. He looks just like Paddy the Irishman."

The skies were now blue and cloudless, and the Plaza glistened in the sun, but the wind had not fallen and the temperature was barely twenty degrees above zero. The waiting crowd huddled and shivered. They enveloped themselves in sweaters and mufflers, blankets and sleeping bags. They stamped their feet to keep out the chill. They watched restlessly as the dignitaries slowly took their places on the platform. When the Vice President-elect entered, a man in a ten-gallon hat shouted, "All the way with L.B.J."; the Vice President-elect acknowledged the shout with a slight inclination of his head. Noon passed, and the crowd shuffled with impatience when the ceremony failed to begin. The President-elect, starting to come from the Capitol onto the platform, was instructed to wait. Then, at twenty minutes after twelve, he appeared, and the spectators warmed themselves with applause.

Now they listened with stoicism as the Cardinal boomed out an interminable invocation. They looked with envy as blue smoke thinly curled up from a short circuit in the electric wires underneath the lectern: where there was fire, there must be heat. The Chief of the Secret Service watched the smoke with apprehension, fearful that the whole inaugural stand might go up in flames. Three times he started to give the order to clear the stand, and three times he paused; then the smoke stopped. The Chief mused that his Service would be in for a lively era protecting the athletic and fearless new President.[1]

On the platform, the breath of the old poet congealed in the freezing air; and now, when he stepped forth to speak, the glare from the sun and snow blinded him. He read three lines from a manuscript:

[1] U. E. Baughman, *Secret Service Chief* (New York, 1962), 3, 12.

Summoning artists to participate
In the august occasions of the state
Seems something artists ought to celebrate.

Then he stopped and said, "I'm not having a good light
here at all. I can't see in this light." The Vice President-
elect held out his hat to shield the old man's eyes; Robert
Frost still could not see, could not conclude the poem:

It makes the prophet in us all presage
The glory of a next Augustan age
Of a power leading from its strength and pride,
Of young ambition eager to be tried,
Firm in our free beliefs without dismay,
In any game the nations want to play.
A golden age of poetry and power
Of which this noonday's the beginning hour.

Instead he said, "This was to have been a preface to a
poem which I do not have to read," and from memory he
recited "The Gift Outright"—"The land was ours before
we were the land's"—changing the last line:

Such as we were we gave ourselves outright
(The deed of gift was many deeds of war)
To the land vaguely realizing westward,
But still unstoried, artless, unenhanced,
Such as she was, such as she *will* become.

At nine minutes before one the Chief Justice came forward to administer the oath. The President-elect, without
hat or coat, the old Douay Bible of the Fitzgerald family
open before him, gave his responses in firm tones. At last
he began his inaugural address, his voice ringing out in the
frosty air. "Let the word go forth from this time and place,
to friend and foe alike, that the torch has been passed to a
new generation of Americans—born in this century, tempered by war, disciplined by a hard and bitter peace, proud
of our ancient heritage." And so he continued, striking
notes of strength, conciliation and hope. "Let us begin
anew," he said, "—remembering on both sides that civility
is not a sign of weakness, and sincerity is always subject
to proof. Let us never negotiate out of fear. But let us
never fear to negotiate." The prospect would not be easy.
"All this will not be finished in the first hundred days. Nor
will it be finished in the first thousand days, nor in the life
of this Administration, nor even perhaps in our lifetime on
this planet. But let us begin." The burden of the "long
twilight struggle" lay on this people and this generation.

"And so, my fellow Americans: ask not what your country can do for you—ask what you can do for your country." [2] (That morning, reading over his text, he had scratched out "will" and replaced it by "can.") He concluded: "My fellow citizens of the world: ask not what America will do for you, but what together we can do for the freedom of man."

The applause was strong and sustained. The President left the platform. His young wife joined him in the Capitol, whispered, "Oh, Jack, what a day," and softly touched his face. Then the inaugural parade marched through the freezing afternoon, and the thirty-fifth Presidentiad, as Walt Whitman would say, began.

I

THE ROAD TO THE NOMINATION

THE ELECTION OF Dwight D. Eisenhower to the Presidency in 1952 had signaled a change in the prevailing weather of American politics—a return, in effect, to Republican 'normalcy' after twenty years of Democratic activism. Yet, in losing the 1952 campaign, Adlai Stevenson had left an indelible imprint on the American mind. By giving the tradi-

---

[2] This thought had lain in Kennedy's mind for a long time. As far back as 1945 he had noted down in a looseleaf notebook a quotation from Rousseau: "As soon as any man says of the affairs of the state, What does it matter to me? the state may be given up as lost." In his address accepting the Democratic nomination in 1960, he said of the New Frontier, "It sums up not what I intend to *offer* the American people, but what I intend to *ask* of them." On September 5 at Cadillac Square in Detroit, Kennedy departed from his prepared text to say: "The new frontier is not what I promise I am going to do for you. The new frontier is what I ask you to do for our country." He continued to polish the thought in the back of his mind until he was ready to put it in final form in the inaugural address.

Though this line was clearly Kennedy's own, like all such lines it had its historic analogues. Gilbert Seldes cites the remarks of the mayor of Haverhill at the funeral of John Greenleaf Whittier as quoted by Van Wyck Brooks in *New England: Indian Summer:* "Here may we be reminded that man is most honored, not by that which a city may do for him, but by that which he has done for the city." And James Rowe, Jr., Oliver Wendell Holmes's last law clerk, points out the following lines from a Memorial Day address delivered by Justice Holmes in 1884: "It is now the moment when by common consent we pause to become conscious of our national life and to rejoice in it, to recall what our country has done for each of us, and to ask ourselves what we can do for our country in return."

tion of progressive idealism brilliant and exciting expression, he renewed, even in defeat, the vitality of American liberalism. "A whole new generation," said Edward M. Kennedy in later years, "was drawn to take an interest in public affairs when he came on the scene. They were led by him, taught by him and inspired by him."

By 1956 that new generation of Democrats was preparing to claim national recognition. John Fitzgerald Kennedy had been one of its first members to enter politics. Elected to the House of Representatives from Massachusetts after the war in 1946 and then to the Senate in 1952, he was now a contender for the second place on the national ticket. The vice-presidential contest at the Democratic convention that year brought him for the first time toward the center of the national consciousness—a brief fifty-four months before he took the presidential oath in Washington.

1. CHICAGO: 1956

Kennedy's father, Joseph P. Kennedy, was dubious about his son and the Vice-Presidency. He feared that the Democrats would lose in 1956 and a Catholic running mate would be blamed for the defeat. But the young administrative assistant whom Kennedy had taken on in 1953 at the suggestion of Senator Paul Douglas of Illinois, Theodore C. Sorensen of Nebraska, was all for going ahead. Without finally committing himself, Kennedy decided to let Sorensen test the wind. Through the spring of 1956 Sorensen talked to political leaders, wrote a persuasive memorandum designed to prove from the distribution of the Catholic vote that a Catholic would strengthen the ticket and worked unceasingly to line up support.

In the course of his missionary endeavors Sorensen got in touch with me. I had served on Stevenson's campaign staff in 1952 and, if he were renominated, would presumably do so again. Moreover, I had come to the view that, of the various vice-presidential possibilities, Kennedy would help Stevenson most. I also felt that putting a Catholic on the lower half of the ticket would be the most expeditious way to attenuate the taboo against a Catholic President which had too long disgraced American politics. Accordingly I had told Kennedy in the spring that I wanted to assist in any way I could consistent with my role in the Stevenson campaign. Sorensen came to our place at Wellfleet on Cape Cod early in July to discuss tactics at the convention.

Kennedy already had friends at the Stevenson headquarters in Chicago, notably two Stevenson law partners, William McCormack Blair, Jr., and Newton Minow. But he had opposition within the party, especially from professional Catholic politicians and from the older generation of party leaders. The soft-spoken and sagacious James Finnegan, Stevenson's campaign manager, was convinced that Kennedy would antagonize voters in anti-Catholic areas, as in the rural counties of Finnegan's own state of Pennsylvania. Jim Farley told Stevenson, "America is not ready for a Catholic." And the older party leaders disliked the idea of Kennedy not only because of his religion but because of his youth and independence. Truman dismissed the thought out of hand. Rayburn said to Stevenson, "Well, if we have to have a Catholic. I hope we don't have to take that little —— Kennedy. How about John McCormack?" (Rayburn later changed his mind about Kennedy.) Stevenson was troubled by the reaction of experienced pros like Truman, Farley and Finnegan. On the other hand, he wanted to give the new political generation prominence, and he considered Kennedy its most attractive spokesman. As the Democrats began to assemble in Chicago for the convention, he therefore decided to ask Kennedy to put his name in nomination.

The Stevenson staff had taken on itself to write drafts of all the nominating and seconding speeches in order to make sure that the proper points would be made. Kennedy characteristically rejected his draft, and he and Ted Sorensen set to work to produce a new one. I conducted these negotiations, and it was then that I first saw the Kennedy-Sorensen team in operation. There was no question which was the dominant partner, but there was no question either that in Sorensen Kennedy had found a remarkably intelligent, sensitive and faithful associate. Eventually the two labored together nearly till dawn on the speech.

Kennedy nominated Stevenson the next evening, and Stevenson won on the first ballot. Afterward Stevenson met with Rayburn, Lyndon Johnson, Paul Butler, chairman of the Democratic National Committee, Governor Ribicoff of Connecticut and Governor Battle of Virginia to discuss the Vice-Presidency. Wilson Wyatt and Thomas K. Finletter had already proposed to Stevenson that the nomination be thrown open to the convention. A free choice, they argued, would provide an effective contrast to the 'dictated' renomination of Richard M. Nixon by the Republicans. Moreover, it would obviously liberate Stevenson from the embarrassment of having to pick one of the hopefuls and thereby disappoint the others.

When Stevenson broached this idea in the meeting, Rayburn said vigorously and profanely that it violated all tradition and logic. Butler backed Rayburn, and Johnson was plainly cool. But Finnegan spoke resourcefully for the open convention and finally prevailed. Later Stevenson told me that he regarded it as a gamble, since it might put a weak candidate on the ticket (he named a couple of Democratic politicians, neither of whom in the end was a serious contender), but that, in the circumstances, it was a risk he was willing to run.

Whatever else it did, the move brought the convention to life. The vice-presidential candidates spent the next twelve hours in frantic efforts to organize headquarters, track down delegates and plead for support. Estes Kefauver led on the first ballot, Kennedy was second. Then Lyndon Johnson announced that his state was switching to Kennedy ("Texas proudly casts its vote for the fighting sailor who wears the scars of battle"), and Kennedy went ahead. There were a few moments of pandemonium until Albert Gore arose to say that Tennessee was shifting to Kefauver. This set off the stampede, and Kefauver soon was over the top. A few moments later Kennedy, who had been taking a bath in his headquarters in the Stockyard Inn, made a poised good-loser speech asking that Kefauver be named by acclamation.

The open-convention device left a wake of obscure resentments. Both Kennedy and Senator Hubert Humphrey of Minnesota had expected Stevenson's backing (though neither had solid ground for such hopes), and both now felt let down. Stevenson, in Kennedy's case, thought that, in asking him to make the nominating speech, he had already given a thirty-nine-year-old first-term Senator an unexampled opportunity to impress the convention and the nation and that Kennedy should appreciate this. Kennedy instead began to look on Stevenson as indecisive and elusive. Up to this time, the two men, without knowing each other well and divided by seventeen years, had had the friendliest feelings for each other. Now their relationship began to take on a slight tinge of mutual exasperation. In later years, however, Kennedy rejoiced that he had lost in Chicago. Had he won the nomination for Vice-President in 1956, he might never have won the nomination for President in 1960.

2. KENNEDY AND THE LIBERALS

Eisenhower's personal popularity, replenished by his success in ending the Korean War, proved invincible in the presidential contest; but the Democrats came out with control of both the Senate and House. This Democratic success, however, hastened the division of the party into what James MacGregor Burns has called its presidential and congressional wings. In the years after 1952 Stevenson had sponsored a small brain trust organized by Thomas K. Finletter, who had been Secretary of the Air Force under Truman and was now a leader of the reform Democrats of New York City, and John Kenneth Galbraith, the economist, my Harvard colleague and Cambridge neighbor. The Finletter group now became the basis for a new body, the Democratic Advisory Council, set up after the election by Paul Butler. The DAC, as an agency of the presidential party, was regarded with mistrust by the congressional leaders. Lyndon Johnson and Sam Rayburn both declined to join. Humphrey became a member, however, and so eventually did Kennedy, though Kennedy took no very active part. The DAC pursued an aggressive line both in attacking the Eisenhower administration and in developing new Democratic policies. The congressional party was inclined to work with Eisenhower and accept the national mood of moderation. In the meantime, battle lines began to form for 1960.

Early in 1957 Lyndon Johnson wrote me that he understood I was critical of the congressional leadership and suggested that I call on him when next in Washington. Accordingly I dropped by the majority leader's office on a Saturday noon late in March. Johnson was affable and expansive. He began by saying that he was a sick man (his heart attack had taken place in 1955) with no political future of his own. His main desire, he said, was to live. He had no interest at all in the presidential nomination. He did not even mean to run again for the Senate. He planned only to serve out his present term. Being entirely disinterested, he wanted only to do the best he could for his party and his nation in the three, or two, or one year remaining to him.

He then poured out his stream-of-consciousness on the problems of leadership in the Senate. He described the difficulties of keeping the conservative southerners, whom he called the Confederates, and the liberal northerners in the same harness; he analyzed a number of seemingly insoluble parliamentary situations which he had mastered through unlimited perseverance and craft; and he gave a virtuoso's account of the role which timing, persuasion and parliamentary tactics played in getting bills through. Saying, "I want you to know the kind of material I have to work with," he ran down the list of forty-eight Democratic Senators, with a brilliant thumbnail sketch of each—strength and weakness, openness to persuasion, capacity for teamwork, prejudices, vices. In some cases he amplified the sketch by devastating dashes of mimicry. (My notes report him "highly favorable about Kennedy, but no special excitement.")

He went on to express his annoyance over the unwillingness of the organized liberals to accept him as one of their own. "Look at Americans for Democratic Action," he said. "They regard me as a southern reactionary, but they love Cliff Case. Have you ever compared my voting record with Cliff Case's?" Thereupon he pulled out of a desk drawer a comparison of his voting record with those of five liberal Republicans on fifteen issues. On each, he had voted on the liberal side and Case on the conservative. "And yet they look on me as some kind of southern bigot." He added that maybe he was showing undue sensitivity to liberal criticism. "But what a sad day it will be for the Democratic party when its Senate leader is not sensitive to liberal criticism."

He talked for an hour and a half without interruption. I had carefully thought out in advance the arguments to make when asked to justify my doubts about his leadership; but in the course of this picturesque and lavish discourse Johnson met in advance almost all the points I had in mind. When he finally paused, I found I had little to say. It was my first exposure to the Johnson treatment, and I found him a good deal more attractive, more subtle and more formidable than I expected. After nearly two hours under hypnosis, I staggered away in a condition of exhaustion. Later I gathered that this was part of a broader Johnson campaign to explain himself to the liberal intellectuals. In a few weeks, when Kenneth Galbraith visited him on his Texas ranch, Johnson told him, "I had a good meeting with Schlesinger. I found him quite easy to get along with. The only trouble was that he talked too much."

As for Kennedy, he too was having his problems with the liberal intellectuals. The Chicago convention had made him a national figure; and it was increasingly clear that the vice-presidential nomination would not satisfy him the next time around. In 1958 he came up for his second term in the Senate. His hope was to return to Washington by the largest possible vote in order to lay the basis for a presidential try two years later. His wife later remembered it as "the hardest campaign ever . . . just running, running, running." He won by 875,000 votes, the greatest margin up to that point in Massachusetts history. [1] Now his presidential campaign was starting in earnest.

[1] His younger brother Edward exceeded this margin in 1964.

Many liberal Democrats regarded him with suspicion. In part this went back to the days of Senator Joseph McCarthy in the early fifties. Kennedy at first had not taken the Wisconsin Senator very seriously. "I think that the stories of communism within the executive branch of the government have more or less died out," he had said optimistically on Meet the Press in December 1951, "and I think that determined efforts have been made to rid the executive branch of the government of the communists, and I think it's been done on the whole." But by 1953 it was impossible to dismiss McCarthy any longer. When I mentioned him from time to time those days to Kennedy, he referred to the McCarthy Committee with articulate dislike but showed no interest in saying so publicly. He put this to me on political grounds—"Hell, half my voters in Massachusetts look on McCarthy as a hero"—and the political grounds were, I suppose, compelling. No one in the Senate in 1953, except for Herbert Lehman and, on particular occasions, Estes Kefauver and J. W. Fulbright, showed much courage about McCarthy. Even Senators like Paul Douglas and Hubert Humphrey kept out of McCarthy's way; and the fate of Millard Tydings and William Benton, who had taken him on and lost their seats, presumably in consequence, remained instructive.

One might have hoped that Kennedy, another Irish Catholic Senator and a genuine war hero, would have seen himself in a particularly strong position to challenge McCarthyism. But there were perhaps deeper reasons for his lack of involvement. His family's relations with McCarthy were certainly an important factor. His father liked McCarthy and invited him once or twice to Hyannis Port. The Wisconsin Senator could be engaging in the Victor McLaglen manner, and the Ambassador even perhaps saw the campaign against this fighting Irishman as one more outlet for the anti-Catholic sentiment which had so long oppressed the Irish-American community. Moreover, Robert Kennedy worked for a time on the staff of the McCarthy Committee, though he soon found himself in disagreement with the Committee's procedures and resigned, returning later as counsel for the Democratic minority.

As for John Kennedy himself, McCarthyism simply did not strike him as one of 'his' issues. This diffidence was no doubt related to his exasperation with the ideological liberals of the day and what he regarded as their emotional approach to public questions. A writer in *The Saturday Evening Post* in 1953 quoted him as saying, "I never joined the Americans for Democratic Action or the American Veterans Committee. I'm not comfortable with those people." Liberalism for him still existed mainly in terms of social and economic programs. As he later said to James MacGregor Burns, "Some people have their liberalism 'made' by the time they reach their late twenties. I didn't. I was caught in cross currents and eddies. It was only later that I got into the stream of things."

Still, Kennedy's actual position was no better and no worse than that of most Democrats, including those more clearly in the liberal stream of things. It was always a puzzle why the liberals took so long to forgive him when they forgave Hubert Humphrey immediately for his sponsorship of a bill to outlaw the Communist Party—an act of appeasement in excess of anything undertaken by Kennedy. Certainly, in spite of the whispering campaign against him in 1960, Kennedy never gave the slightest support to McCarthyism. He had no sustained social relations with McCarthy (his wife never even met him), did not question the motives of people who advocated unpopular policies [2] and voted consistently as Senator against McCarthy on matters close to McCarthy's heart, such as the confirmation of Charles E. Bohlen as ambassador to Russia and of James B. Conant to West Germany. He prepared a speech in August 1954 explaining that he would vote for McCarthy's censure, though he planned to rest his case on rather technical grounds; when the vote finally took place in December, he was gravely sick in the hospital, awaiting a critical operation on his back. If he did not join Americans for Democratic Action, he always served as sponsor for ADA's annual Roosevelt Day dinners in Boston. And, if he kept out of the public debate, he did not hesitate to intervene privately. About this time John Fox of the *Boston Post*, who had backed Kennedy for the Senate in 1952, scheduled a series of articles exposing the reds at Harvard. My name was high on Fox's list. Hearing about the series, Kennedy protested on my behalf. "Fox didn't like it much," he told me later. "He probably suspects me of being a Communist now."

Nonetheless, Kennedy's silence on McCarthy contrasted with Stevenson's eloquent defense of civil freedom; and,

[2] Except for a couple of speeches about China which he delivered in 1949 before McCarthy discovered the communist issue. These speeches were out of character and remained on Kennedy's conscience for a long time. As late as 1960 he separately expressed both to Theodore H. White and to me his sorrow that he had ever given them.

if Humphrey had been silent too, he had not made the mistake of writing a book called *Profiles in Courage*. Mrs. Roosevelt was the conscience of the liberal community, and her reproach carried force: "I feel that I would hesitate to place the difficult decisions that the next President will have to make with someone who understands what courage is and admires it, but has not quite the independence to have it." (I once suggested to Kennedy that he had paid a heavy price for giving his book that title. He replied drily, "Yes, but I didn't have a chapter in it on myself.")

Old New Dealers, moreover, cherished an ancient and ardent suspicion of Kennedy's father. And his candidacy touched uglier strains in the liberal syndrome, especially the susceptibility to anti-Catholicism. Most liberals, in addition, already had their hero in Stevenson and continued to hope that he might change his mind about not running in 1960. If Stevenson remained unavailable, then Humphrey, by temperament, record and rhetoric, better fitted liberal specifications than Kennedy. The Minnesota Senator was a man of exuberance, charm, courage and political skill, who had given unstintingly of himself to liberal causes, and his inexhaustible flow of language did not conceal his sharp intelligence and discriminating judgment. Kennedy seemed too cool and ambitious, too bored by the conditioned reflexes of stereotyped liberalism, too much a young man in a hurry. He did not respond in anticipated ways and phrases and wore no liberal heart on his sleeve.

3. KENNEDY AND CAMBRIDGE

To those who knew Kennedy in Massachusetts the liberal mistrust seemed unfair and unwarranted. My main interest in these years, like that of Kenneth Galbraith, was in having a liberal nominee in 1960, whether Kennedy, Humphrey or, if he became a candidate, Stevenson. Kennedy and Humphrey seemed likely to be the active contenders; and we feared that, if the rivalry between them turned into enmity, it might divide the liberals and permit a conservative to seize the prize. When I wrote Kennedy to this effect in the spring of 1959, he replied, "I agree with you, of course, on the principle of avoiding any fratricidal blood-letting between Hubert and myself." Galbraith and I talked the problem over in the winter of 1959–60 and hoped that we might somehow serve as moderating influences in what threatened to become a bitter battle within the liberal family. But, though Humphrey was an old friend and a man we greatly admired, Kennedy, of course, was our Harvard

and Massachusetts Senator. More important, we found ourselves, as we saw more of him, bound to him by increasingly
strong ties of affection and respect.

Kennedy himself was now prepared to go some distance
to propitiate the liberals. After 1956 he made a special effort with issues in the civil liberties field, such as getting
rid of the loyalty oath in the National Defense Education
Act, and he counted on the strong liberalism of his senatorial record to overcome doubts. He was unwilling, however, to engage in retrospective denunciations of McCarthy;
it seemed to him undignified. This reluctance only confirmed his critics in their view that he lacked moral sensitivity.

Galbraith and I resolved to do what we could to combat
the continuing mistrust. We declared our confidence in Kennedy's basic liberalism. We also tried to help recruit people
for his growing brain trust, though we had little or nothing
to do with its actual operations. One day in 1959 Kennedy
phoned that he was feeling increasingly guilty about constantly imposing on Galbraith and Seymour Harris, the other
politically concerned Harvard economist, for economic
counsel and wondered whether there was not an economist
in Massachusetts who could devote steady time to helping
him. I consulted with Galbraith and Harris. Our first choice,
Carl Kaysen of Harvard, was about to leave for a year in
Greece. We then thought of Kermit Gordon, an able economist at Williams. Gordon had had government experience—
I had known him first fifteen years before in the OSS—and
I was confident that he and Kennedy would be temperamentally congenial. But when I called Gordon he was distinctly
cool. Finally he said that I could mention his name to
Kennedy so long as I made it absolutely clear that he was
not for Kennedy in 1960 but for Stevenson. When I reported this to Kennedy, he sighed and said he would try
Gordon anyway; but the negotiations came to nothing at
that time.

There was also concern about the lack of relationship between Kennedy and the reform movement in New York.
Here Mrs. Roosevelt, Governor Lehman, Thomas Finletter
and the other reformers yearned after Stevenson, while
Carmine DeSapio and the Tammany crowd inclined toward
Johnson, and only Charles Buckley and Peter Crotty, old-
line bosses in the Bronx and Buffalo, backed Kennedy. It
seemed useful not only to broaden Kennedy's New York
base but to dispel the suspicions of him entertained by the
liberal group in New York City, so important both as a

source of funds and as a shaper of opinion. Finletter, who was then using his mordant executive capacities in a brave effort to hold together the divergent and adolescent energies of New York reform, was obviously a key figure.

Kennedy and Finletter had a talk in the early spring, but it was followed by trivial misunderstandings. Then in May 1959, Kennedy wrote that he was planning to attend the Harvard Commencement in June, when the Finletters, I knew, would be on their way to Bar Harbor. Accordingly I arranged a dinner on Commencement evening in one of those dark-paneled rooms upstairs at Locke-Ober's to permit Kennedy and Finletter to have a second talk. The Galbraiths were along, and the McGeorge Bundys and one or two others. Finletter and Kennedy were both rational and sardonic men, and they got along well. Finletter thereafter succeeded to some degree in tempering the anti-Kennedy reflexes of the New York reformers.

What stands out from the evening, however, was a discussion of the confirmation of Lewis Strauss, whose name President Eisenhower had recently submitted to the Senate as Secretary of Commerce. It was politically essential for Kennedy, as a liberal Democratic presidential aspirant, to vote against Strauss. But, though he had no use for him, he had a belief, with which I sympathized, that any President was entitled to considerable discretion in naming his cabinet. In addition, though this mattered less, his father, an old friend of Strauss's, strongly advocated confirmation. My impression was that Kennedy was looking for a respectable reason to oppose Strauss. At this point, Mac Bundy, whose ancestral Republicanism had survived Dewey and Eisenhower, suddenly spoke up for rejecting the nomination. The backing of Harvard's Dean of the Faculty may have somewhat reassured Kennedy, who voted against Strauss a few days later. Probably also Kennedy then began to realize that Mac Bundy, in spite of the certified propriety of his background, had an audacious mind and was quite capable of contempt for orthodoxy.

One morning in mid-July 1959, as I was sitting in the sun at Wellfleet, Kennedy called from Hyannis Port to invite me for dinner that night. This was my first visit to the Kennedy compound; and, though I had met Jacqueline Kennedy several times since their marriage, it was really the first occasion for a leisurely chat with her. My wife was not able to come, and there were only the three of us. Jacqueline was reading *Remembrance of Things Past* when I arrived. In the course of the evening I realized that, underneath a veil of lovely inconsequence, she concealed tremendous awareness, an all-seeing eye and a ruthless judgment. As for Kennedy, our relations had hitherto been more political than personal; this was the freest, as well as the longest, talk I had ever had with him. I was struck by the impersonality of his attitudes and his readiness to see the views and interests of others. I was also a little surprised by the animation and humor of his assessment of people and situations. I now began to understand that the easy and casual wit, turned incisively and impartially on himself and his rivals, was one of his most beguiling qualities, as those who had known him longer had understood for years.

Kennedy was fairly optimistic over his presidential chances. He did not think that Humphrey could win the nomination. He supposed that Lyndon Johnson would edge out Symington, and that Johnson could not win either. Stevenson's sleeping candidacy he regarded as his greatest threat. He was inclined toward Humphrey or Governor Orville Freeman of Minnesota as his running mate. And he said that he would have to go into the primaries in order to maintain his momentum.

His greatest need, he thought, was to give his campaign identity—to distinguish his appeal from that of his rivals and suggest that he could bring the country something no one else could. He observed in this connection that he had been stimulated by a memorandum I had written and Finletter had circulated called "The Shape of National Politics To Come." This memorandum had argued that the Eisenhower epoch, the period of passivity and acquiescence in our national life, was drawing to its natural end, and that a new time—a time of affirmation, progressivism and forward movement—impended. This thesis was an extension of the cyclical account of American politics which my father had set forth twenty years earlier in an essay called "Tides of National Politics." He had forecast in 1939 that the then dominant liberal impulse would taper off around 1947. The ensuing conservative period, if the rhythm held, could be expected to run its course about 1961–62.

Invoking this analysis, I had gone on to propose that the approaching liberal epoch would resemble the Progressive period of the turn of the century more than it would the New Deal. The New Deal had taken its special character from the fight against depression; but the Progressive revolt grew out of spiritual rather than economic discontent; and this seemed the situation in 1959. I hazarded the guess that "a revival of a new sense of the public interest will be

central to the new period." Aspects of this argument
—the belief that we stood on the threshold of a new political era, and that vigorous public leadership would be the
essence of the next phase—evidently corresponded to
things which Kennedy had for some time felt himself.

When I asked about the Republicans, he spoke with enthusiasm of John Sherman Cooper of Kentucky and Jacob
Javits of New York. He was caustic about Eisenhower: "I
could understand it if he played golf all the time with old
Army friends, but no man is less loyal to his old friends
than Eisenhower. He is a terribly cold man. All his golfing
pals are rich men he has met since 1945."

He talked too about his senatorial concern with labor. He
was fascinated by Jimmy Hoffa, whom he described as a
man of great vitality and intelligence and, in consequence,
of great danger to American society. The only man in the
labor movement who could deal with Hoffa, he said, was
Walter Reuther; but the Republicans on the Senate Labor
Committee were anxious to use Hoffa to beat Reuther. He
spoke with scorn of Senators Capehart, Curtis and Mundt,
who seemed, he thought, to care about labor corruption
mostly as a way of compromising the trade union movement; they really detested the incorruptible Reuther far
more than they did Hoffa. However, Barry Goldwater, he
said, was a man of decency and character.

Kennedy's candor provoked candor. I asked him about
the rumors that he had Addison's disease and was taking
regular doses of cortisone for adrenal deficiency. He said
that after the war fevers associated with malaria had produced a malfunctioning of the adrenal glands, but that this
had been brought under control. He pointed out that he had
none of the symptoms of Addison's disease—yellowed skin,
black spots in the mouth, unusual vulnerability to infection.
"No one who has the real Addison's disease should run for
the Presidency, but I do not have it."

4. KENNEDY AND THE PRIMARIES

In the next weeks, Kennedy's campaign began to take shape.
My Harvard classmate Theodore H. White has described it
vividly in *The Making of the President: 1960;* and I can
only add a few notes from the outside. With Humphrey's
candidacy now definite and Symington's highly probable,
there remained the enigmas of Stevenson and Johnson.
Stevenson was seizing every opportunity to insist that he
was not a candidate, though he was clearly the favorite of
some politicans and many voters. As for Johnson, Kennedy

told me in July 1959 that he had recently encountered the Majority Leader, who put out his hand, looked him in the eye and said, "As you know, John, I am not a candidate." Kennedy said, "He hasn't done this for nearly two months."

This seemed certain to change. Six months later, Philip L. Graham, the publisher of the *Washington Post* and close to Johnson, outlined the strategy. He predicted that Kennedy and Johnson would be the only candidates to come into the convention with sizable blocs of delegates—about 500 for Kennedy, perhaps 300 for Johnson. But Kennedy would not make it, and Stevenson would emerge as the northern candidate. Then the convention would settle down to a struggle between Johnson and Stevenson. In this fight, the northern pros—Truman, Daley, Lawrence, DeSapio—would go for Johnson partly because, Graham said, they disliked Stevenson and partly because they did not think he could be elected.[3]

This talk took place in December 1959. A few days later a hand-written letter arrived from Kennedy in Palm Beach. He said he was coming to Cambridge on January 2, 1960, to do a television program with Mrs. Roosevelt. (This had been arranged by Galbraith with considerable ingenuity and effort in order to advance the rapprochement with the liberals.) "I shall be finished around 7:30 or 8," he wrote. "Is there any chance you both might be free that evening for dinner? Perhaps we could get the Galbraiths and any one else you think of and go to Locke Ober's."

This turned out to be the day that he announced his candidacy. The Galbraiths joined us in an upstairs room in the old restaurant. I noted of Kennedy later, "He was, as usual, spirited and charming, but he also conveyed an intangible feeling of depression. I had the sense that he feels himself increasingly hemmed in as a result of a circumstance over which he has no control—his religion; and he inevitably tends toward gloom and irritation when he considers how this circumstance may deny him what he thinks his talent and efforts have earned." The religious issue, he said, left him no choice but to go into Wisconsin. It would be a gamble, but his only hope of forcing himself on the party leaders was to carry the primaries. A victory over Humphrey in Wisconsin would make his case irresistible. When someone asked what he considered the main source of his appeal, he said that obviously there were no important differences between Humphrey and himself on issues; it came down to a difference in personalities. "Hubert

[3] He was wrong about Lawrence and Daley, both of whom liked Stevenson.

is too intense for the present mood of the people. He gets people too excited, too worked up." He went on ironically, "What they want today is a more boring, monotonous personality, like me." He added that he anticipated that Symington would emerge as the safe-and-sane candidate of the party professionals.

A week later, I chanced to see Johnson in Washington. He too was gloomy about election prospects. He had recently visited a number of states and did not think the Democrats could carry any of them. The Democratic liberals in the Senate had put over the picture of a divided party with a militant wing of "wasters, spenders and wild men. . . . The country doesn't want this. The country wants to be comfortable. It doesn't want to be stirred up. Have a revolution, all right, but don't say anything about it until you are entrenched in office. That's the way Roosevelt did it." He again defended his strategy as leader. "Congress is not the action arm of the government, and the things we can do are limited. We can't impose policy on the executive. We sought the best and did the possible." He brushed off talk about his own candidacy, implying that he had not made up his mind. Then he said, "I would support Stevenson with enthusiasm. I would support Humphrey with enthusiasm." After a long pause, he added, "I would support Kennedy. I would support Symington."

In late March the Democrats of the Middle West held a conference in Detroit at which I had been invited to speak (the title of my talk was "New Frontiers of American Liberalism"). After the Jefferson-Jackson dinner that night, I drove back to the hotel with Sam Rayburn, who reminisced about the House with great charm. He had begun his service in Congress, he noted, before Jack Kennedy was born, and forty-seven of his "boys"—men who had served with him in the House—were now in the Senate. He said that the one of whom he had the lowest opinion was Nixon. When I got back to the hotel, Kennedy and John Bailey, his senior professional adviser, were just coming in. Bailey signaled me to come up to the Kennedy suite.

Kennedy, though tired, was in excellent spirits. Again one was delighted by the total lack of front. When phones rang, he answered them himself; and when a message was required (he had just received the Democratic nomination at an undergraduate mock convention at Purdue), he sat down and wrote it out. Someone called on behalf of a Knights of Columbus bowling team whose members wanted to shake his hand. Kennedy, who did not answer the phone this time, whispered to Bailey, "Tell them I've gone out. If I don't have *their* votes, I might as well give up." He smiled a good deal about Wayne Morse, who had been affable toward him at the banquet. "Half the time," he said, "Wayne claps me on the shoulder and congratulates me; the other half, he denounces me as a traitor to liberalism and an enemy of the working class. It all reminds me of *City Lights* and the millionaire who, when he is drunk, loads Charlie Chaplin with gifts and insists that he spend the night, but, when he is sober, can't recognize him and throws him out of the house."

After a few moments Kennedy invited me into his bedroom for a private talk. As usual, he was objective and wryly humorous, candid about himself and impressively dispassionate in his judgment of others. He said that he expected to win in Wisconsin but that he hoped, if possible, to avoid a contest in West Virginia. He did not want to expend the energy or the money. In addition, West Virginia was 97 per cent Protestant, and the religious issue was always a risk, though if Humphrey were determined on West Virginia, Kennedy was confident that he could beat him there. And even if he should lose in West Virginia, this would not bring Humphrey any closer to the nomination. He would knock out Kennedy, but the real victor would be a more conservative candidate, probably Symington. On the other hand, if Humphrey withdrew before West Virginia, he would be the logical man for Vice-President. Kennedy added that, if he himself won in West Virginia under present conditions, he would get the nomination on his own without owing anything to anyone. But if other leaders—Humphrey, for example, and Stevenson— came out for him between Wisconsin and West Virginia, he would of course feel under certain obligations to them. He suggested that I talk to Humphrey and Stevenson and mention some of these considerations.

When I talked to Humphrey the next day, he simply said that he was committed to going into West Virginia, whether he won or lost in Wisconsin. As for the Vice-Presidency, he said emphatically, "I have no interest at all in the Vice-Presidency. I would not go on the ticket with Jack. I would not go on with Adlai. I would not go on with Lyndon or Stu or any one of them. If I am knocked out of this presidential fight, I am going back to Minnesota and do my damnedest to win re-election as Senator."

5. KENNEDY AND STEVENSON

A few days later I talked to Stevenson. He said that he

had given his word to all the candidates that he would remain neutral, that he planned to keep his word, and that his great concern was to have a united party. Kennedy did not give up on Stevenson, however, and, as the weeks passed, he became more and more the critical figure in the Kennedy calculations. Though Stevenson continued to maintain that he was not a candidate, his supporters were increasingly active. James Doyle of Wisconsin was now the director of an unofficial Stevenson movement designed to unite the efforts of volunteer groups throughout the country; Mrs. Roosevelt, Tom Finletter and the New York liberals were out for him; and in Washington Stevenson's old friend George W. Ball, along with Ball's law associate John Sharon, Senator Mike Monroney and William Attwood of *Look,* were working on strategy for the convention. A popular demand for Stevenson seemed to be rising steadily.

Relations between Stevenson and Kennedy, while nominally still friendly, had become uneasy. This was unfortunate because, in spite of differences in temperament and disparities in age, they had affinities in background and taste. A relaxed afternoon at Libertyville or Hyannis Port had very much the same mood and tempo—the same sort of spacious, tranquil country house; the same patrician ease of manners; the same sense of children and dogs in the background; the same kind of irrelevant European visitors; the same gay humor; the same style of gossip; the same free and wide-ranging conversation about a variety of subjects; the same quick transition from the serious to the frivolous. Moreover, the two men were in substantial agreement on the great issues of public policy.

And, in a sense, Stevenson had made Kennedy's rise possible. The Democratic party had undergone a transformation in its eight years in the wilderness. In the last days of Truman the party motto had been, "You never had it so good." The essence of the party appeal was not to demand exertions but to promise benefits. Stevenson changed all that. His lofty conception of politics, his conviction that affluence was not enough for the good life, his impatience with liberal clichés, his contempt for conservative complacency, his summons to the young, his demand for new ideas, his respect for the people who had them, his belief that history afforded no easy answers, his call for strong public leadership—all this set the tone for a new era in Democratic politics. By 1960, the candidates for the Democratic nomination, and Kennedy most of all, were talking in the Stevenson idiom and stressing peril, uncertainty, sacrifice, purpose. More than either of them ever realized or admitted, Kennedy was emerging as the heir and executor of the Stevenson revolution.

But by 1960 it was too late for them ever really to know one another. Each felt that the other did not understand his problems. Each doubted whether the other appreciated what had been done for him—Stevenson by giving Kennedy his opportunities in the 1956 convention, Kennedy by campaigning in twenty-six states for Stevenson in the election. And rivalry now made the differences in temperament and age emotionally more important than the affinities. Certainly the contrast between Stevenson's diffidence and Kennedy's determination in the spring of 1960 heightened for each his misgivings about the other. And Stevenson, like all the political leaders of his generation, thought that Kennedy was a young man pushing too hard who should wait his turn.

Yet every day made Stevenson more crucial to Kennedy's hopes; and later in the spring he renewed his efforts to persuade Stevenson, if not to endorse him publicly, at least to assure him private support at some definite point before the convention. He calculated that he lacked about 80 to 100 votes, and that Stevenson could give him what he needed in California and Pennsylvania. "He is the essential ingredient in my combination," he told me in mid-May. "I don't want to have to go hat-in-hand to all those southerners, but I'll have to do that if I can't get the votes from the north. . . . I want to be nominated by the liberals."

When I talked to Stevenson the next day, he said that Bill Blair had been urging him, "as he has for the past year," to come out for Kennedy, but to do so would be inconsistent with his pledges and his personality. "It would look as if I were jumping on the bandwagon. Everybody would say, 'There's the deal we told you about.' It would look as if I were angling for a job. I can't do this sort of thing." As for helping Kennedy before the convention, he said, "On the basis of present alternatives, I would be quite prepared to do it in terms calculated to preserve as much party harmony as possible. To come out now and kick Lyndon and Stuart in the face and demean my own position of neutrality and aloofness would be an error. . . . Maybe I can help to keep the avenue open to Johnson."

A few days later, Kennedy, returning from the Oregon primaries, stopped off to see Stevenson at Libertyville. William Blair and Newton Minow met him at the airport and drove him out to the North Shore. On the way, Kennedy said, "Do you think I ought to offer him the State Department?"

Minow replied, "No. It would be a great mistake. For one thing, he would resent it. For another, you don't want to tie your own hands." When they arrived, Stevenson took Kennedy into his study for a private talk. They first discussed foreign policy. This was just after the Soviet Union had shot down the CIA's U-2 plane engaged in photographic reconnaissance over Russia, and the two men agreed in their assessment of what they regarded as a bungled administration response. Then they turned to the campaign. Kennedy reviewed his situation, state by state, pointing out how much Stevenson, with his strength in the Far West and the East, could help him. Stevenson replied that he wanted to be consistent and therefore could not declare for Kennedy now, but that he would not be a party to any stop-Kennedy movement, nor would he encourage the various draft-Stevenson movements.

Stevenson, who had met with Lyndon Johnson a few days before, then mentioned the importance of Johnson's cooperation if Kennedy were elected. Kennedy, who knew of the meeting, feared that Stevenson had been, as he later put it, "snowed" by Johnson into thinking that, if he stayed neutral, he would be Johnson's second choice. (Kennedy's conjecture was right. Johnson had said that he could not stand to be pushed around by a forty-two-year-old kid, and that he favored Adlai next to himself.) Kennedy told Stevenson, as he later described it to me, that there was only one way to treat Johnson; that was to beat him. "Everyone will come around the day after the convention; and anyone who doesn't come around will be left out and won't matter. The support of leaders is much overrated anyway. Leaders aren't worth a damn: I learned that in the Powers campaign if I hadn't known it before." He was referring to a recent mayoralty campaign in Boston when Kennedy, John McCormack, Leverett Saltonstall and all the dignitaries had endorsed John Powers only to see him go down to defeat.

"The meeting [with Kennedy] was entirely satisfactory from my point of view," Stevenson wrote me later, "and I cannot say he seemed disappointed or surprised about my attitude." He added, "He seemed very self-confident and assured and much tougher and blunter than I remember him in the past." Kennedy also thought the talk pleasant but less satisfactory. He said later, "I guess there's nothing I can do except go out and collect as many votes as possible and hope that Stevenson will decide to come along."

As Minow and Blair took their guest back to the airport, Minow, who could restrain his curiosity no longer, asked

Kennedy, "Well, did you offer him the State Department?" Kennedy answered, somewhat surprised, "No, certainly not. You told me not to bring it up." (Minow later wondered whether he had given the best advice. The next morning he went a little guiltily to Stevenson and told him what he had done. Stevenson at once assured him that he had been right.) As they drove on, they asked Kennedy whom he favored for the nomination if he did not get it himself. He replied, "Johnson," saying cryptically, "he's got talent." When Kennedy got on the plane that would take him to Boston on his way to Hyannis Port, he said to Blair, "Guess who the next person I see will be—the person who will say about Adlai, 'I told you that son-of-a-bitch has been running for President every moment since 1956'?" Blair answered correctly, "Daddy."

6. AFTER WEST VIRGINIA

West Virginia had gone to the polls on May 10. That night, as the returns showed a stunning Kennedy victory, an impassioned debate took place in the Charleston hotel room of Hubert Humphrey.

Humphrey's organization was dominated by two able Washington lawyers, both graduates of Harvard and the Harvard Law School, one a clerk to Justices Cardozo and Frankfurter, the other to Justice Holmes, both paladins of the New Deal, even similar in their names, Joseph L. Rauh, Jr., and James H. Rowe, Jr. From the start of the Humphrey campaign Joe Rauh had made it clear that his interest was in having a liberal nominee and that Jack Kennedy was his second choice. Jim Rowe, on the other hand, was a close friend of Lyndon Johnson's and had gone for Humphrey because in early 1959 Johnson had assured him that he would not possibly be a candidate. Now, with the defeat in West Virginia, Rauh told Humphrey that he could not get the nomination himself, that if he hung on to his delegates and stayed in the race he would only be serving the purposes of the stop-Kennedy movement and that the course of liberalism as well as personal dignity was to announce his withdrawal. Rowe argued that there was no hurry, that Humphrey should take his time about deciding, and that there might be some point in keeping his delegates together till Los Angeles.

Humphrey himself listened somberly to the debate which swayed around him, inserted an occasional question, telephoned supporters in other parts of the country for advice and kept his counsel. Then James Loeb, Jr., who had founded Americans for Democratic Action and worked in the White House for Harry S. Truman and was now a newspaper publisher in Saranac Lake, New York, sat down at a typewriter and wrote out the draft of a withdrawal statement. Loeb's draft brought the discussion to a head. Muriel Humphrey strongly backed Rauh and Loeb. Humphrey read the statement, thought for another moment and finally said OK, he agreed, he would get out of the race.

At that point word came from the hotel switchboard that "Mr. Kennedy" was below and was coming up to the Humphrey suite. The room froze; everyone supposed that Jack Kennedy was back from Washington where he had gone earlier in the day. In a minute the door slowly opened. It was Robert Kennedy, slight and youthful in a raincoat. He walked the length of the silent room to Muriel Humphrey, kissed her, almost to her consternation, then shook Hubert's hand. The two men left the suite together and walked through the gusts of spring rain to Humphrey's campaign headquarters. There Humphrey read his statement of withdrawal before the television cameras. Soon they went on in the night to greet the victor, at last flying in from Washington.

Joseph Rauh now threw himself into the Kennedy campaign, and James Rowe was soon at work for Johnson. Humphrey himself remained enigmatic about his preference. In the meantime, the U-2 incident was putting the contest in a new and grave setting. The collapse of the summit in Paris suddenly reminded the nation that the next President would have to deal with issues of nuclear war. Was the boyish Kennedy the man for this appalling responsibility? The supporters of Johnson began to talk about the need for a man of maturity and experience—a man "with a touch of gray in his hair." And, even more important, there ran through the party a convulsive movement toward the candidacy of Adlai Stevenson. On Memorial Day Joe Rauh called me from Washington to express concern over the recent slowdown of the Kennedy campaign. Why had everything stood still for a week? Why had states on which we had been counting not moved faster toward Kennedy? The answer, Rauh said, was the Stevenson movement. He feared that Stevenson might develop enough strength to stop Kennedy without having enough to nominate himself. The beneficiary of Stevenson, he said, would be Johnson.

But Stevenson, when he came to Cambridge a week later,

still insisted that he was not a candidate. I urged him once
again to consider declaring for Kennedy. He said, "I
don't preclude the possibility of coming out for Kennedy.
But how am I going to do this without letting down Johnson and Symington, whom I have assured I would remain
neutral, and Monroney, Gore, Joe Clark and a lot of others
who have begged me to stay out of this?" Then he observed in a worried way that, if his support became necessary to put a liberal over, this might change things.

By this time, a group of liberals, organized by John L.
Saltonstall, Jr., of Massachusetts, were planning an endorse-
ment of Kennedy. The group included Rauh, Galbraith,
Arthur J. Goldberg of the AFL-CIO, Gilbert Harrison of the
New Republic, the historians Allan Nevins and Henry Steele
Commager, the political scientist James MacGregor Burns,
Congresswoman Edith Green of Oregon, John Frank of
Arizona, myself and half a dozen others. I had wondered whether to mention this to Stevenson during his
Cambridge visit; but, since the statement had not been
drafted and the release date was some time away, it seemed
right to wait until the project was further advanced. Then
word leaked in the newspapers forty-eight hours after
Stevenson's visit. Stevenson had obviously been touched
by the cries through the country for his nomination; and he
could not but have been hurt by the defection of old friends
like Galbraith (who, indeed, had come out for Kennedy
some weeks before) and myself. But he never spoke a
word of reproach, and our relations suffered no permanent damage. He retained in any case the loyalty of my
wife Marian who promptly told the newspapers that she was
still for Stevenson. (A few days later I received a letter
from Robert Kennedy with a scrawled postscript: "Can't
you control your own wife—or are you like me?")

Our statement, as drafted and redrafted by Commager
and Rauh, finally appeared on June 17. "The purpose of
this letter," it read, "is to urge, now that Senator Humphrey has withdrawn from the race and Mr. Stevenson continues to stand aside, that the liberals of America turn to
Senator Kennedy for President. . . . We are convinced that
Senator Kennedy's adherence to the progressive principles
which we hold is strong and irrevocable. He has demonstrated the kind of firmness of purpose and toughness of
mind that will make him a great world leader." On civil
rights, "he has assured us that he favors pledging the
Democratic Party to Congressional and Executive action in
support of the Supreme Court's desegregation decisions and

to whatever measures may prove necessary to make voting a reality for all citizens." As for Stevenson, "all of us supported Adlai Stevenson in 1952 and 1956 and hope that he will be a leading foreign affairs figure in any new Democratic Administration. But he insists he is not a candidate in 1960, and Senator Kennedy, a man of whom liberals can be proud, is an active candidate who has proved his appeal to men and women of all ranks and creeds."

The reaction from several leaders of the Stevenson movement was not unsympathetic. Jim Doyle called immediately to say that he supposed that a lot of Stevensonians would be angry, but that he wanted me to know that he understood and respected the reasons which led me to come out for Kennedy. William Blair and William Attwood expressed similar sentiments; and, though George Ball and Thomas Finletter regretted the statement, they were amiable about it. Other Stevensonians were less tolerant, however, and in the next few days I received a flood of letters and telegrams:

You must indeed be proud this morning. You were among the first to admit that a good man had no chance in this country. You and your historian associates, Henry Steele Commager, etc. were willing to work in the junk heap of defeat, before defeat had happened. Shame to a teacher of the young, who before the fight makes a separate peace with the enemy. I congratulate you—prophets of a bought convention. (Southwest Harbor, Maine)

I've admired your work and everything you stand for for a long, long time. So your defection to the Kennedy camp comes as a particularly brutal blow . . . All I think you are doing is climbing on the well-oiled bandwagon at a time when the bandwagon can be stopped. (Evanston, Illinois)

When first I heard of your switch from Adlai Stevenson to Kennedy I was incredulous. Now that the original report has been confirmed I am perplexed. It would appear to me that the only thing these two gentlemen share is membership in the Democratic Party. (San Francisco)

TO OUR ADA CHAPTER YOU AND THE REST OF THE TURNCOAT OPPORTUNISTS YOUR ACTIVITIES ARE THE MOST IGNOBLE ACTS IN HISTORY (Great Neck, New York)

A few days before the statement finally came out, my wife and I drove to the Cape with Galbraith for luncheon at Hyannis Port. It was a hot, overcast day, and we vainly sought cool breezes on the *Marlin*, the Kennedy power launch. Kennedy kidded Marian mildly about her declaration for Stevenson, though it genuinely puzzled him. He used to ask Jacqueline what magic Stevenson had to account for his devoted female support. (On a later occasion at Hyannis Port, when women at the beach were clustering around his boat, he said to Galbraith, "You see I have my women supporters as well as Adlai.")

He was looking forward to Los Angeles and the convention with apparent confidence. Johnson now seemed to him his serious opponent. We chatted about the discrepancy between Johnson's towering stature in Washington and the dim shadow he cast in the rest of the nation. Kennedy compared him to British politicians like Peel who were omnipotent in Parliament but had no popularity in the country. He talked of Johnson with mingled admiration and despair, calling him the "riverboat gambler" and evoking a picture of the tall Texan in ruffles and a long black coat, a pistol by his side and aces up his sleeve, moving menacingly through the saloon of a Mississippi steamer.

On the Vice-Presidency, Kennedy seemed inclined toward Humphrey. He reported Arthur Goldberg as telling him that Humphrey would accept if he were Kennedy's definite choice. Humphrey would add more to the ticket than anyone else, Kennedy said, but he thought Hubert had campaigned irresponsibly in West Virginia, even though he had been under provocation (he had in mind Franklin Roosevelt Jr.'s attack on Humphrey's war record). He hoped he wouldn't have to spend the campaign explaining away extravagant statements Hubert might make about the Republicans.

On Stevenson he said, "One reason I admire him is that he is not a political whore like most of the others. Too many politicians will say anything when they think it will bring them votes or money. I remember in 1956 when Adlai met with Dewey Stone and some other big contributors in Boston after Suez. They wanted him to endorse the Israeli attack on Egypt. If he had said the things they wanted, he could have had a lot of money out of that room; but he refused. I admired that. You have to stick to what you believe."

Much of the talk concerned organization. Galbraith and I urged him to build his own staff and to avoid people like ourselves who had been identified with Stevenson. The civil rights question was much on his mind, and we discussed that at some length. Galbraith, seeking some way by which Kennedy might dramatize his commitment to the issue, suggested an announcement that, if elected, he would try to prevent Eastland of Mississippi from continuing as chairman of the Senate Judiciary Committee. Kennedy answered quickly, "It wouldn't be in character for me to do that. After all, the Senate is a body where you have to get along with people regardless of how much you disagree. I've always got along pretty well with old Eastland."

We talked a bit about Massachusetts politics and the anticipated senatorial contest between Leverett Saltonstall, the Republican incumbent, and Governor Foster Furcolo, whom Kennedy had detested for many years. When Galbraith said that he would probably vote for Furcolo, Kennedy said, "The thing I like about professors is their party regularity." He then asked me how I planned to vote. When I hesitated a moment, he said, "Say it, say it—of course you're going to vote for Saltonstall. Sometimes party loyalty asks too much." (The Democratic voters of Massachusetts evidently agreed, because Furcolo was denied the nomination in the primaries in September.) He spoke gloomily about the Massachusetts Democratic party: "Nothing can be done until it is beaten—badly beaten. Then there will be a chance of rebuilding." He added, "If I were knocked out of the Presidential thing, I would put Bobby into the Massachusetts picture to run for governor. It takes someone with Bobby's nerve and his investigative experience to clean up the mess in the Legislature and the Governor's Council."

So the Democrats moved on toward Los Angeles. I had a final talk with Kennedy early in July after President Truman had denounced him for being young and others had denounced him for being sick. He said that he was glad that Truman had brought out the youth issue and that India Edwards, who had been vice-chairman of the Democratic National Committee in Truman's day and was now supporting Johnson, had brought out the health issue; this gave him the opportunity to dispose of both matters before the convention. He spoke gratefully of Averell Harriman's rejoinder to the Truman attack and thought he would ask Harriman to second his nomination. "It will be useful for me to have someone who serves as a link to the Roosevelt and Truman administrations; also an older man. I don't want the convention to think that we're just a collection of angry young men." As for the Vice-Presidency, he still leaned toward Humphrey, though he said he had made no commitments because he wanted to preserve flexibility for the convention. He asked what I heard from Stevenson. I said that our relations, though friendly, had probably been rendered less confidential by my coming out for Kennedy. He said, "Yes, but Marian ought to have pretty good relations. Maybe she can serve as that 'bridge' Adlai keeps talking about"—referring to Stevenson's idea of serving as a bridge between Kennedy and Johnson.

II

TRIUMPH IN LOS ANGELES

AMERICAN POLITICS has an occasion to match every mood: ceremony, circus, farce, melodrama, tragedy. Nothing rolls them together more opulently than a presidential convention; nothing else offers all at once the whirl, the excitement, the gaiety, the intrigue and the anguish. But a convention is far too fluid and hysterical a phenomenon for exact history. Everything happens at once and everywhere, and everything changes too quickly. People talk too much, smoke too much, rush too much and sleep too little. Fatigue tightens nerves and produces a susceptibility to rumor and panic. No one can see a convention whole. And no one can remember it with precision later, partly because it is so hard to reconstruct the sequence of events and partly because people always say and do things they wish to forget. At the time it is all a confusion; in retrospect it is all a blur.

Though I had attended and enjoyed every Democratic convention since 1948, I headed toward Los Angeles in July 1960 with distinct foreboding. I was vigorously in favor of Kennedy; but I retained strong personal ties to Stevenson who now, in the last days, evidently against his conscious will, was emerging as the candidate of a growing and impassioned movement. I stopped for a day in San Francisco and, in the Edwardian lobby of the Fairmont Hotel, ran into Oscar Chapman, who had been Truman's Secretary of the Interior and was now working for Johnson. Chapman, a man of vast political experience, shook his head and said, "If Adlai had declared as a candidate, he would be unbeatable now." His remark forecast the mood in Los Angeles where the Stevenson movement had suddenly become the center of emotion. When I arrived there on July 9, the Saturday before the convention opened, Kenneth Galbraith warned me to be on my guard against old friends from earlier Stevenson campaigns. He said that at a party given by Mrs. Eugene Meyer of the *Washington Post* one of "the Stevenson women" had hissed at him that, in coming out for Kennedy, he and I had committed "the worst personal betrayal in American history."

On Monday morning Galbraith and I attended the staff meeting at the Kennedy headquarters in Room 8314 of the Hotel Biltmore. About twenty-five people were present, most of whom were assigned to one or another of the state delegations. After a time Robert Kennedy, his coat off, his tie loose, climbed up on a chair to call the meeting to order. He gave detailed instructions about the demonstration to follow his brother's nomination. Then he discussed the platform, saying crisply: "I want to say a few words about civil rights. We have the best civil rights plank the Democratic party has ever had. I want you fellows to make it clear to your delegations that the Kennedy forces are unequivocally in favor of this plank and that we want it passed in the convention. Those of you who are dealing with southern delegations make it absolutely clear how we stand on civil rights. Don't fuzz it up. Tell the southern states that we hope they will see other reasons why we are united as Democrats and why they should support Kennedy, but don't let there be doubt anywhere as to how the Kennedy people stand on this." It was an impressive performance—in its efficiency, its incisiveness and, in an odd way, in its charm. Afterward Kenneth O'Donnell, Kennedy's appointments secretary, asked me whether I would speak in delegation caucuses. I said that I would be glad to talk privately to delegates for Kennedy but that, in view of my past relations with Stevenson, I did not wish to take part in an anti-Stevenson campaign. O'Donnell did not press me.

In the afternoon, Ken Galbraith and I called on Stevenson, who received us with entire friendliness. His law partners, W. Willard Wirtz, William Blair and Newton Minow, had set up an informal command post in his suite. He still disclaimed interest in the nomination, but Stevenson enthusiasm was rising on every hand. Mike Monroney, the persuasive Senator from Oklahoma, was a whirlwind of activity, doing his best to convince both Stevenson and the delegates that Stevenson had a chance to win. Adlai himself, I think, had few illusions; but he did not wish to let his friends down, and with every passing hour they were becoming more importunate and optimistic. The prospect of his candidacy, moreover, was generating an extraordinary popular response, especially in Los Angeles, his birthplace and long a Stevenson citadel. The makeshift headquarters in the shabby Paramount Building from which James Doyle, George Ball, Thomas Finletter and John Sharon were talking to delegates was soon inundated with telegrams and volunteers. Already Stevenson pickets were gathering around the Sports Arena. In the inner circle only Blair and Minow continued to argue that Kennedy had the nomination and that Stevenson should take no irrevocable steps.

1. CHOOSING A PRESIDENT

One cannot speak with certitude about the motives and actions of politicians in that week of strain and clamor and heat, of vast distances and interminable taxi rides. My own impression is that the Johnson strategy was based on building up Stevenson against Kennedy. Nearly every vote cast for Stevenson, the Johnson people reasoned, would be a vote taken away from Kennedy. If Stevenson denied enough votes to Kennedy to prevent nomination on the first ballot, then the Kennedy strength, held together so precariously by momentum and muscle, might begin to crumble. This was, of course, the reason why the Kennedy people, who knew better than anyone the fragility of the combination they had so laboriously put together, were so determined to win on the first round. If the Kennedy combination began to fall apart, who would be the beneficiary? Stevenson would have needed almost all of Kennedy's first-ballot votes to win, while Johnson needed only about 350, or half. Moreover, if Stevenson became the man who stopped Kennedy, he could not realistically expect to inherit all the Kennedy delegates. With Kennedy fading, the northern pros, as Phil Graham had predicted the previous December, might well have switched to Johnson and put him over. The Johnson strategy was grimly plausible, and the Stevenson people were working enthusiastically to carry it out.

So from Johnson's viewpoint, as from Kennedy's, Stevenson was the key. The Kennedy people continued to hope that Stevenson might be persuaded to place Kennedy's name in nomination. Stevenson's reply was that he might if it were the only way to unify the party, but that, because of his commitments to Johnson and Symington, he could not nominate Kennedy without their concurrence. As late as Tuesday afternoon Robert Kennedy discussed the possibility of Stevenson as nominator with Bill Wirtz and Bill Blair. Their talk was courteous and correct; and a number of emissaries appeared in the Stevenson suite to press the point. But the idea perished as the popular clamor for Stevenson grew.

At this point the Johnson people evidently decided to give the Stevenson bandwagon a further push. Senator Eugene McCarthy of Minnesota, as Humphrey told James Wechsler of the *New York Post* and me on Monday, had come to Los Angeles for Johnson. This was logical because, if Johnson were to get the nomination, it would be sensible for him to seek a running mate who, like McCarthy, was both a northern liberal and an Irish Catholic. As for Humphrey himself, the evidence suggests that he had about decided before Los Angeles to back Johnson against Kennedy. He had told Theodore H. White in West Virginia that, if he could not make it himself, Johnson was the best man to run the country. He thereafter resisted the pressure of his liberal supporters to come out for Kennedy as the most liberal of the candidates remaining after his own withdrawal. Soon after he arrived in Los Angeles, he met Johnson in circumstances carefully concealed from his pro-Kennedy friends and apparently agreed to delay a Kennedy endorsement as long as he could. Though under great pressure to declare for Kennedy from some of his warmest supporters, like Walter Reuther and Joseph Rauh, and though he gave the Kennedys the impression that he was waiting for the right moment to announce, he remained ominously silent on Monday and then on Tuesday.

Minnesota, a center of the liberal Democracy, was a key state. I noted Tuesday morning: "Minnesota is teetering on the edge of a Kennedy endorsement. Apparently Humphrey and [Governor Orville] Freeman were set to go for Kennedy this morning, but overnight a strong Stevenson movement developed within the delegation; and Max Kampelman [an astute Washington lawyer, who has been Humphrey's administrative assistant] told me before the caucus that it had been decided that Freeman should endorse Kennedy immediately, with Humphrey trying to get the dissidents in line and endorsing later in the day." At the request of Geri Josephs, the national committeewoman, I agreed to talk privately to a group of Minnesota delegates. I found them resentful over the intense pressure of the Kennedy people and particularly mistrustful of Bobby Kennedy.

This informal session preceded the meeting of the Minnesota caucus, which Humphrey called to order at ten-thirty. Kennedy and the other candidates had addressed it the day before. This morning Stevenson had agreed to come—an indication of how far he was being moved into active candidacy. Before Stevenson arrived, Mike Monroney made a powerful statement of the case for Stevenson, including a series of well-calculated sideswipes at the Kennedy movement and its tactics ("If they called a meeting of all the people to whom they've promised the Vice-Presidency, they couldn't find a room in Los Angeles large enough to hold it in"). His remarks were brilliantly effective, and the tension grew. Monroney finished with an eloquent appeal to choose the best man and, as Stevenson entered the room, the crowd went wild.

Then Stevenson spoke. It was a painful moment. I stood on the side with William Rivkin of Chicago, who had worked his heart out for Stevenson in 1952 and 1956 and who was now the Kennedy liaison with the Minnesota delegation; and we both found ourselves in tears. Stevenson's talk was polished, graceful, courtly, charming, rather noncommittal; in its substantive passages, it rehearsed the litany of Dulles-Eisenhower foreign policy errors, beginning with the pledge of 1953 to unleash Chiang Kai-shek. Something was holding him back, that old pride which prevented him from giving the audience what it was waiting for. I think the delegates were a bit let down; there was less applause at the end than at the start.

In the afternoon I took part with Mrs. Roosevelt in a panel discussion before the Young Democrats. No one was working harder for Stevenson than Mrs. Roosevelt. But she was an old pro, who had seen nearly forty years of Democratic conventions, and did not take politics personally. She explained to me pleasantly that our liberal statement of June for Kennedy had provoked her into open activity for Stevenson. While these skirmishes were taking place in the thickets, in another part of the forest Johnson and Kennedy were having their duel before the Texas delegation—Johnson laying about with heavy saber strokes, Kennedy mastering him with an urbane and deadly rapier.

Late Tuesday afternoon Stevenson arrived in the convention hall to take his seat as a member of the Illinois delegation. He passed through a crowd of wildly cheering supporters marching around the Sports Arena (and was delighted by the sight of an enormously pregnant woman carrying a large placard inscribed STEVENSON IS THE MAN). The appearance of a candidate on the floor is always risky; it had got Estes Kefauver into trouble when he tried it in 1952. Even if Stevenson were not a declared candidate, it was still a risk. But it produced the first massive outburst of honest emotion in the convention. The galleries went mad, and even on the floor there was pandemonium. Eventually Stevenson was invited to the rostrum. Again he seemed to recoil from the occasion. Instead of speaking two or three sober sentences which might have rallied the convention, he tried a pleasantry ("after going back and forth through the Biltmore today, I know who's going to be the nominee of this convention—the last man to survive"). The demonstration quieted down almost instantly. Leonard Lyons said afterward, "He let out all the air with one bad joke."

On Tuesday evening, the California delegation, in which the Kennedys had invested much energy and hope, split almost evenly. Later that evening, Stevenson met with a group of friendly delegates from New York; the emotions of the day were plunging him, against his intention, into the maelstrom. The next morning Hubert Humphrey declared for him. At eight-thirty that morning Robert Kennedy convened his meeting at the Biltmore. He ran through the states, one by one, to get the rock-bottom Kennedy tally. He was crisp and detached. "I don't want generalities or guesses," he said. "There's no point in fooling ourselves. I want the cold facts. I want to hear only the votes we are guaranteed on the first ballot." He cross-examined his people as they reported, practically insisting on the name, address and telephone number of every half-vote. The result showed 740 delegates—21 short of a majority. Bobby said that if Jack had 720 votes by the time the roll call reached Washington, enough votes would shift for victory. But the outcome was far from certain. California was falling apart. North Dakota was held by half a vote under the unit rule. Idaho might fall away if the governor felt that anyone else was going to become the candidate for Vice-President. At one point Carmine DeSapio had proposed to Bobby that thirty New York votes go to Johnson on the first ballot; they would be definite for Kennedy on the second. Bobby said to hell with that. He concluded his exhortation to the troops: "We can't miss a trick in the next twelve hours. If we don't win tonight, we're dead."

Then on to the Sports Arena, surrounded by lines of men and women chanting for Stevenson. The nominations began: Sam Rayburn for Johnson; Orville Freeman for Kennedy, gallantly improvising when the teleprompter went dead; then Eugene McCarthy, in much the best speech of the convention so far, for Stevenson. The Stevenson demonstration was sustained and riotous. After it had gone on for a long time, Governor Collins of Florida, the permanent chairman, ordered the lights turned off in the auditorium in an effort to bring the clamor to an end. There were a few moments of singular beauty—everything black except for spotlights stabbing into the vast darkness, flashing across the delegates and demonstrators on the floor. This was the last burst of defiance. The balloting began. By Washington, Kennedy had 710 votes; and, as Bobby had forecast, the rush began. In a moment Wyoming made him the nominee.

The hall cheered its choice with enthusiasm. But pools of bitterness remained. Many Stevensonians were unreconciled. The hope of the nation and the labor of a decade, as they saw it, had been crushed by a steamroller operated by tough and ruthless young men. The next morning I started to urge on Robert Kennedy the importance of doing something to conciliate the Stevenson people and to bring them into the campaign. He listened patiently for a moment, then put his hand on my knee and said, "Arthur, human nature requires that you allow us forty-eight hours. Adlai has given us a rough time over the last three days. In forty-eight hours, I will do anything you want, but right now I don't want to hear anything about the Stevensonians. You must allow for human nature."

2. CHOOSING A VICE-PRESIDENT

The next question was the Vice-Presidency. This obviously was not a choice Kennedy could sensibly make before the convention, if only for the reason that he might have to use the second place on the ticket, in the manner of Franklin Roosevelt in 1932, as a counter in his own fight for the presidential nomination. He had nevertheless set forth certain general specifications. On June 9 he had told Joseph Rauh that his preference would be Hubert Humphrey or "another midwestern liberal"—presumably Orville Freeman of Minnesota or Stuart Symington of Missouri. He amplified this publicly on Meet the Press a month later, saying that he wanted a running mate from another section of the country with particular background in the farm problem "which I think to be the major domestic problem the United States is facing at the present time. So that I would say it would be somebody from the Middle West or Far West."

In the meantime, he had held an exploratory talk with Clark Clifford, formerly special counsel at the White House for Truman and now a leading Symington strategist. Kennedy told Clifford that he was going to win in Los Angeles, that in no event was Symington likely to win, but that he was still a few votes short and wished that Symington would throw in with him. "Stuart has run a clean campaign," Kennedy said, "and I'd like to talk with you about having him on the ticket." But Symington, who had considerable secondary strength among the delegates, was playing for a deadlock; and Clifford reported back to Kennedy, first in Washington and again in Los Angeles, that his principal preferred to take his chances and try for the distance.

As the delegates assembled, there was inevitable speculation about the vice-presidential choice. On the weekend be-

fore the convention a group of party professionals—men
like Governor David Lawrence of Pennsylvania, John
Bailey, Mayor Richard Daley of Chicago, Colonel Jacob
Arvey of Illinois, Matthew McCloskey of Philadelphia,
Carmine DeSapio—agreed that, if Kennedy won the nomination, Johnson would add most to the ticket. Many of
Kennedy's liberal supporters, myself among them, hoped it
would be Humphrey. By Wednesday of convention week,
however, Humphrey's endorsement of Stevenson made it
obvious that, if the nomination went to a Minnesota liberal,
it must go to Freeman.

As for the Kennedys, their drive for a strong civil rights
plank suggested a continuing commitment to the strategy
of no-compromise-with-southern-conservatism. Robert Kennedy and Ken O'Donnell repeated to liberal and labor
leaders the candidate's assurance that the vice-presidential
probability remained a "midwestern liberal"—a description
implying Symington or Freeman and, by broad geographic
construction, Senator Henry M. Jackson of Washington, and
also loose enough to keep up the hopes of other governors
and Senators west of the Mississippi whose support might
be needed for the nomination.

Now that the presidential balloting was over, the vice-
presidential speculation engulfed the town. Through Thursday morning and early afternoon we lived in a great swirl
of rumors, many of them mentioning Symington. But Kennedy's intention remained impenetrable. In search of clues,
I stopped by at Stevenson's hotel suite shortly after three
o'clock. Bill Blair told me that Stevenson was taking a
phone call in another room. In a few moments Adlai
emerged, visibly startled. Philip Graham had just told him,
he said, that Kennedy had chosen Lyndon Johnson.

Later Graham wrote a memorandum setting forth his
knowledge of the circumstances leading to Johnson's selection. In trying to put the story together, I have drawn on
this as well as on talks with a number of the participants.
It is first necessary to say a word about Graham himself.
He was one of the brilliant and tragic figures of my generation. He had come to Washington in 1939 as a member of
what might be called the third wave of New Dealers—
after the First New Deal of Moley, Tugwell and Berle,
and the Second New Deal of Cohen, Corcoran and Henderson. A graduate of the Harvard Law School, he became law
clerk to Justice Stanley Reed and then to Justice Frankfurter. After Pearl Harbor, he enlisted in the Air Force,

served in the Far East and ended the war as a major. Returning from the war, he abandoned the law forever and became publisher of the *Washington Post*, owned by his father-in-law Eugene Meyer. In the next years he made the *Post* the keystone in a steadily expanding newspaper-magazine-television empire.

Phil Graham was a man of quite extraordinary vitality, audacity and charm, who charged everything he said or did with an electric excitement. He joined an exceptional gift for intimacy with a restless desire to provoke and challenge his intimates. He knew everybody and was intimidated by nobody. He was fascinated by power and by other men who were fascinated by power. Yet power for its own sake gave him only fleeting satisfaction. He wanted to *do* things. His sense of the general welfare was strong and usually sound; and he was a forceful manager of people and situations in what he conceived as the public interest.

In this mood he had thrust himself into the Little Rock crisis of 1957, talking to everyone from Governor Faubus of Arkansas to Roy Wilkins of the National Association for the Advancement of Colored People and playing an indispensable role in helping avert what might have been a disastrous defiance by the state government of federal authority. It was at this time that he first became close to Lyndon Johnson. They worked together in the fight for the Civil Rights Act of 1957; and Graham came away from this experience intensely admiring of Johnson's shrewdness and sophistication, his incomparable skills in manipulation and his hard instinct for power. In 1958 and 1959 he favored Johnson for 1960. But Graham also saw Kennedy as another man of power; and he was captivated by Kennedy's candor, detachment and intellectual force. He had come, in addition, to know Adlai Stevenson well in the years since 1952. His mother-in-law was an important backer of the Stevenson campaign in 1960.

In Los Angeles Graham thus had an almost unique access to all the key figures. On Monday, with the tide apparently running strongly for Kennedy, Graham and another longtime Johnson admirer, Joseph Alsop, decided that Kennedy must be persuaded to take Johnson as his running mate. At Alsop's urging, Graham accompanied him to Kennedy's suite, where they sent in a message requesting five minutes of his time. When Kennedy appeared, Alsop made a brief argument for Johnson, adding that Senator Herman Talmadge of Georgia thought that Johnson would accept.

Then he fell into unwonted silence and whispered to Graham, "You do the talking." Graham developed the case for Johnson. As Graham remembered the meeting, Kennedy immediately agreed—"so immediately," Graham later wrote, "as to leave me doubting the easy triumph." Graham therefore restated the argument, telling Kennedy he could not assume that Johnson would decline and he must make the offer compelling enough to win Johnson over. "Kennedy was decisive in saying that was his intention, pointing out that Johnson would help the ticket not only in the South but in important segments of the Party all over the country." Alsop does not remember Kennedy's reaction as quite this clear-cut; he went away with the feeling that Kennedy was "about 80 per cent" convinced.

Graham, in any case, was astonished that Kennedy should respond to Johnson at all, especially since Robert Kennedy had told him that Johnson would not be considered. He now called James Rowe and asked him to pass the word on to Johnson. Rowe, reasonably taking Kennedy's remark as a traditional and transparent attempt to coax a rival out of the race, reported the meeting to Johnson with reluctance and skepticism. Johnson dismissed it at once, saying impatiently that he expected the same message was going out to all the candidates.

Graham also authorized his colleagues on the *Washington Post* to write for Tuesday that "the word in Los Angeles is that Kennedy will offer the Vice-Presidency to Lyndon Johnson," forbidding them to make it more specific lest it embarrass Kennedy. It was specific enough, however, to terrify the members of the District of Columbia delegation when, by special arrangement, they received their copies of the *Post* the next morning. The Negro delegates descended on Joseph Rauh, who had been working hard to keep them in line for Kennedy, and demanded an explanation. Rauh went immediately to Robert Kennedy, who said Rauh could assure everyone that Johnson was not in the picture.

Graham had meanwhile arranged to lunch that day with Johnson in the double hope of persuading him to release Stevenson from his neutrality pledge in order to nominate Kennedy and also of persuading Johnson himself to accept the Vice-Presidency. But he found the Senate leader far from Isaiah and in no mood for reasoning together.[1] By

---

1 "Come now, and let us reason together." Isaiah 1:18. L.B.J., *passim*.

some mischance the Kennedy staff had left Texas on the distribution list of a telegram sent routinely under Kennedy's signature to uncommitted delegations requesting a chance to talk to their caucuses. The Johnson people had joyfully seized on this to propose a debate that afternoon before a joint session of the Texas and Massachusetts delegations. Johnson was in a state of mingled fatigue and exhilaration, worn out by his own dogged rounds of the delegations but excited by the idea that he might best Kennedy in face-to-face encounter and put himself back in the race for the nomination.

In this battle atmosphere Graham realized that he could not conceivably ask Johnson about Stevenson or the Vice-Presidency. They talked instead about the debate. Johnson was under evident strain, and his thoughts as to what he should say seemed to Graham "a bit harsh and personal." The Johnson people were already hinting in the corridors that Kennedy had an undisclosed and probably fatal disease and that his father had been pro-Nazi. Fearing an outburst that Johnson might later regret, Graham urged him to avoid *ad hominem* remarks and to use the occasion to present himself as a man of experience and responsibility, especially in world affairs. He also advised Johnson to take a nap. Johnson readily agreed; and, while he slept, Graham wrote out a few notes for him to use "later." During the debate Johnson opened with Graham's "high road" but went on to attempt the personal thrusts which Kennedy parried with such ease and mastery.

That evening Kennedy and Johnson met again before the South Carolina delegation. The South Carolinians were in a private dining room adjacent to the Stevenson headquarters. To avoid the crowds milling in the corridor, the candidates chose to slip into the caucus through the Stevenson office. While Johnson was speaking inside, Kennedy paced about the Stevenson room. After a few moments, Johnson came out, placed his hand on Kennedy's shoulder and his nose next to Kennedy's face and said with great emotion, "Jack, if you don't stop acting the way you are, we're liable to have to support that little fellow we nominated in '56 and '52." A member of the Stevenson staff who witnessed the exchange, told me later, "Johnson's eyes were like flame throwers." Kennedy smiled enigmatically and, without saying a word, entered the other room. The observer's impression was that Johnson "felt that Kennedy's tactics were very unfair and he was ready to do anything to stop his nomination."

At five o'clock Wednesday morning Graham conceived a new idea—a message to the convention from Kennedy to be read by Stevenson on Thursday asking the delegates to draft Johnson for Vice-President. He passed this on to Kennedy later that morning. The two men were driving from the Biltmore to another hotel, where Kennedy was meeting still another caucus. Graham explained that he could leave a draft of the message with Bobby or Ted Sorensen. Kennedy said, "Leave it with me only." He added that he might be twenty votes short on the first ballot and asked if there were any chance of getting Johnson votes out of the Vice-Presidency offer. Graham said he could think of none unless George Smathers could swing some votes in Florida. Kennedy said that the trouble was that Smathers wanted to be Vice-President too. Graham then said that Kennedy could not miss by twenty votes and, dropping into the argot of the Harvard Law School, observed that his nomination was guaranteed by *res ipsa loquitur*. In the midst of the traffic jam and convention hubbub, Kennedy looked up, always ready to learn something new, and said, "What does that mean?"

3. FALLING INTO A DECISION

The week of the convention had been too tense and chancy to give Kennedy time for serious thought about the Vice-Presidency. Now the question could no longer be postponed. During the victory celebrations Wednesday night he observed a little wistfully how terrible it was to have only twenty-four hours in which to make so fateful a choice. But he came that night to a quiet decision to make the first offer to Johnson.

He decided to do this because he thought it imperative to restore relations with the Senate leader. Johnson was the man whose cooperation would be essential for the success of a Kennedy legislative program, and he was in addition the representative of the section of the country which regarded Kennedy with the greatest mistrust. News of the offer, Kennedy hoped, would reunite the Democrats, please the older generation of professionals, now so resentful of the 'angry young men' who had taken over their party, improve the ticket's chances in the South and lay the basis for future collaboration with Johnson. He was certain, on the basis of Johnson's multitudinous declarations and attitudes, that there was practically no chance that Johnson would accept. Very few people in Los Angeles that week imagined for an instant that Johnson would exchange the power of the majority leadership for the oblivion of the Vice-Presidency.

Accordingly he called Johnson's suite at eight forty-five on Thursday morning. Johnson was still sleeping, and his wife answered the phone. Kennedy said that he would like to come down and see the leader. Lady Bird awoke her husband, who nodded assent. As she put down the phone, she burst out, "Honey, I know he's going to offer the Vice-Presidency, and I hope you won't take it."

This was not Johnson's first intimation that the question might be raised. The Johnsons had taken defeat philosophically. When his downcast associates gathered after the balloting in Johnson headquarters in the Sports Arena, Lynda Bird, Johnson's seventeen-year-old daughter, had dispelled their gloom with a cheerful speech, saying that all was not lost and they would live to fight another day. James Rowe, calling on Johnson later that evening at the Biltmore, found him in his pajamas, smiling and good-humored and looking forward to his first tranquil night's sleep in a week. But a few minutes later Sam Rayburn had disturbed the tranquillity. He telephoned Johnson and said, "They are going to try to get you to go on the ticket. You mustn't do it. It would be a terrible thing to do." Johnson expressed great doubt that he would be asked but said he would do nothing without checking with Rayburn.

Kennedy's call now made it highly likely that an offer would be forthcoming, and Johnson, bestirring himself, began the telephone rounds he customarily made when large decisions impended. He was, as one of his associates put it, a "spectrum thinker," consulting a carefully selected panel of advisers from left to right at critical moments. If the adviser gave the expected counsel, Johnson moved on. If the advice differed from what he expected, he would pause and brood.

He first alerted Rayburn, who repeated his dour warnings of the night before. He called a Texas intimate, Congressman Homer Thornberry, whom he caught shaving. Lather on his cheek, Thornberry went to the phone, heard Johnson's story and emphatically advised him not to touch the Vice-Presidency. Johnson, listening silently, finally said, "But what will I say to Senator Kennedy?" A few minutes later, Thornberry, back before his mirror, began to wonder what right he had to tell anyone that he should not become Vice-President of the United States. He returned to the telephone and reported his change of mind to Johnson, who again listened silently and finally said, "But what will I say to Mr. Sam?" Another adviser, Rowe, started out by opposing the Vice-Presidency on the ground that Johnson had more power as leader. When Johnson seemed not a little resistant to this argument, there flashed through Rowe's mind the astonishing thought that Johnson might be considering the idea seriously.

This was, indeed, the case. It is true that a week before Los Angeles, when George Smathers remarked in the leader's office that Kennedy might offer Johnson the Vice-Presidency, Johnson, reflecting that the only duty assigned by the Constitution to the Vice-President was that of presiding over the Senate, had said with feeling, "I wouldn't trade a vote for a gavel." Yet there are reasons to suppose that the idea of the Vice-Presidency had lain for some time in the inner recesses of that infinitely complex and subtle mind. Indeed, in the winter and spring of 1960, he had striven to avoid trouble with Kennedy almost as if he wished to keep the vice-presidential option open. Thus he had shunned confrontations in the primaries, even though he had been under great pressure to enter West Virginia where his southern accent and Protestant faith might have made him a powerful contender. Only toward the end, carried away by the emotions of combat, had he risked personal clashes with the man who seemed most likely to win the nomination.

During the spring Johnson must have thought a good deal about his future if Kennedy and Nixon became the nominees. Whoever won the election, the post of Senate leader would be very different from what it had been under an indifferent and passive President like Eisenhower. Johnson could hardly expect to retain the power he had exerted with such relish and skill in the late fifties. Moreover, it was a taxing job, and he was tiring of it. And he could not but recall the fate of his predecessors, Knowland and McFarland and Lucas, all of whom had become politically vulnerable at home as a result of their absorption in the responsibilities of Senate leadership.

Beyond this, Johnson had long wanted to be a national and not a sectional political figure. But this ambition had always been blocked by his identification with his Texas constituency. The Vice-Presidency had attracted him before as a way of escape from the purely regional role. In 1952 Rayburn had urged Stevenson to take him on the ticket, and for a moment in 1956 Johnson had succumbed to the pleadings of Senator Russell of Georgia and allowed his availability to be reported to Stevenson and James Finnegan. Now he saw what might be a last chance to break out of the Texas trap and become a national leader.

He had, in addition, a deep sense of responsibility about

the future of the South in the American political system. He used to lament the fact that so much southern political energy was diverted from constructive channels to the defense of the past, that a Senator with the manifest abilities of Russell, for example, had wasted his talent and energy in fighting for lost causes. If the Democratic party did not give a southerner a place on the ticket in 1960, it would drive the South even further back on itself and into self-pity, bitterness and futility. He may well have seen in the Vice-Presidency a means of leading the South back into the Democratic party and the national consensus.

Such considerations were doubtless in his mind when Kennedy arrived around ten o'clock, and the two men sat together on a couch in the living room of Johnson's suite.

Kennedy began by telling Johnson, as Johnson later recalled the talk, "that he had said many times that he thought I was the best qualified for the Presidency by experience, but that as a southerner I could not be nominated. He said he felt that I should be the one who would succeed if anything happened to him."

Then, to Kennedy's astonishment, Johnson showed every interest in the project. "I didn't offer the Vice-Presidency to him," Kennedy told a friend later. "I just held it out like this"—here he simulated taking an object out of his pocket and holding it close to his body—"and he grabbed at it."

Having indicated receptivity, Johnson went on to say that his own people—Lady Bird and Sam Rayburn in particular—did not want him to go on the ticket. He asked what alternatives Kennedy had in mind. Kennedy mentioned Freeman, Symington and Jackson, and Johnson had the impression that his thoughts were running toward Freeman. Then Kennedy asked whether Speaker Rayburn had anything against him. Johnson said that he did not; Rayburn simply thought that Johnson should stay as leader—perhaps Kennedy should talk to him. Finally Johnson asked time to think the matter over. Kennedy left, saying, "I'll call you back in two or three hours."

Johnson now resumed his canvass of opinion. Most of the southern leaders who had backed him for the nomination vigorously opposed his taking second place. A parade of southern governors, led by Price Daniel of Texas, insisted that the burden of running in the South with a man who was both a Catholic and a champion of civil rights was too much to carry; one handicap might be tolerable, but not both. Someone suggested that Kennedy might have mentioned the Vice-Presidency on the assumption that Johnson would turn it down; and this thought evidently preyed on Johnson's mind. He paced his suite, made telephone calls around the country (including one to his fellow Texan John Nance Garner, who had served as Vice-President for two terms under Roosevelt and who reminded Johnson of the influence a Vice-President could exercise in critical debates by his power to give or deny Senators the floor), collared his associates and demanded their advice, thought, agonized and paced some more.

In the meantime, Kennedy had returned to his own suite in a state of considerable bafflement. "You just won't believe it," he said. ". . . He wants it!" Still, having started on the Johnson road, he had no immediate choice except to follow it a little further. He accordingly went to Rayburn. He said that he wanted to be the candidate of a united party and that he planned to give the Vice-President significant assignments, especially in foreign affairs. Rayburn listened carefully and, as he later recalled it, replied, "Well, up until thirty minutes ago I was against it, and I have withheld a final decision until I could really find out what was in your heart." The Speaker ruminated a moment about his age—"I am in the twilight of my life, walking down into the valley"—and said that he had wanted to keep Johnson in the legislative end because he needed him there. "Now the way you explain it I can see that you need him more. You are looking at the whole." He mused for another moment about Johnson. "Well, there is always the thought in a fellow's mind that he might get to be President. Lyndon is a good soldier, and he will hear the call of duty. I yield on one condition . . . that you go on the radio or television and tell the people you came to us and asked for this thing." Kennedy agreed.[2]

Rayburn then called Johnson and said, "Lyndon, you've got to go on the ticket." Johnson replied, "But last night you told me that, whatever happened, I should not go on the ticket. What has made you change your mind?" Rayburn said, "I'm a wiser man this morning than I was last night. Besides, that other fellow [Nixon] called me a traitor, and I don't want a man who calls me a traitor to be President of the United States. We've got to beat him, and you've got to do everything you can to help."

[2] C. Dwight Dorough, *Mr. Sam* (New York, 1962), 570. This account has the Kennedy-Rayburn talk taking place on Wednesday night, which is wrong, but it probably can be relied upon as Rayburn's memory of what he told Kennedy.

4. THE NOMINATION OF LYNDON JOHNSON

Back again in his own suite, Kennedy now began to review the situation. The offer to Johnson and the appeal to Rayburn had been more effective than he had anticipated. Contrary to every expectation, Johnson evidently wanted the Vice-Presidency. Kennedy's problem now was whether this was the result he himself, as presidential nominee, wanted, and, if not, whether he could get out of it.

As he discussed the matter with his brother, they saw strong arguments for taking Johnson. He would probably help the ticket more than anyone else because he could bring with him states which Kennedy might not otherwise carry—Texas and possibly other states in the South. Even more important, as the Kennedys talked it over, a Kennedy administration would certainly have a greater prospect of success with Johnson as a collaborator in the executive branch than as a competitor on the Hill. And Johnson, as Kennedy had often acknowledged, was a man of force and decision to whom, in case anything happened, the government could be responsibly consigned.

On the other hand, the designation of Johnson would outrage the liberal wing of the party. While Kennedy, as a realist, had no doubt that he could ride out a liberal revolt, he did not like to make his first act as party leader a repudiation of his earlier assurances nor did he wish to begin his campaign amidst angry accusations of bad faith. And the question of how, if elected, he would work with his Vice-President also troubled him. The Senate leader was a proud and testy man, well known for his sensitivity and his egotism, unlikely to defer easily to a backbencher nine years his junior. He had already shown a strain of bitterness in the convention. Though the Kennedy-Johnson relationship had been affable in the past and even not without a certain affection, the rapport between the self-possessed New Englander, urbane and tough, and the emotional Texan, so expansive one minute, so vulnerable the next, had its distinct limitations.

As he weighed these considerations in his mind, Kennedy began his own process of consultations. The older professionals—Lawrence, Bailey, Daley—were of course delighted at the prospect of Johnson. But most of his own staff was in a state of shock. And late in the morning a delegation commissioned by the labor movement to discuss the Vice-Presidency arrived in the suite. Its members were Walter Reuther, Arthur Goldberg and Alex Rose of the Hatters and the New York Liberal party; and its mission was to tell Kennedy that organized labor would find Humphrey, Symington or Jackson—any one of the three—acceptable. When Kennedy now introduced the "possibility" of Johnson, the labor people, remembering Johnson's support of the detested Landrum-Griffin labor bill as recently as 1959, were startled. Governor G. Mennen Williams of Michigan, informed a little later by a gloomy Robert Kennedy, was equally depressed. The labor-liberal group pointed out that, in order to hold their delegates for Kennedy and stop the movement toward Stevenson, they had guaranteed that Johnson would not be on the ticket—and that, in offering these guarantees, they had cited the assertions of Robert Kennedy. They doubted whether they could hold their own people in line and predicted mutiny in the convention and a fight on the floor. Ken O'Donnell, Ralph Dungan and other members of the Kennedy staff reinforced these warnings privately to Kennedy.

When Reuther and Rose left, Kennedy asked Goldberg to stay behind for a minute. He remarked that Goldberg had been unusually quiet during the discussion. Goldberg replied that he interpreted Kennedy's statement about Johnson as meaning that he had already made his choice. Kennedy did not respond to this, asking Goldberg instead how much trouble the selection of Johnson would create. There would certainly be trouble, Goldberg said, but labor and the liberals had no place else to go; in the end they would have to depend on the candidate's political judgment. Kennedy inquired about George Meany, the president of the AFL-CIO. Goldberg said that Meany would be unhappy; only a short while earlier he had denounced an alleged attempt by Johnson to use his control over labor legislation to cajole the labor movement into neutrality. Kennedy asked Goldberg to try to calm him down. (Goldberg enlisted David Dubinsky in this effort, and in the afternoon they persuaded Meany not to fight the Johnson nomination.)

Goldberg left, and the Kennedys returned to their anxious discussion. Though Johnson had shown every sign of wanting the nomination in the morning, he still had mentioned the opposition of his associates and had asked time for consideration. The obvious next step was to find out how really interested he was. Shortly after one o'clock, John Kennedy sent his brother to the Johnson suite to test the atmosphere. When Robert arrived, he was ushered in to see Rayburn.

A few moments later, Philip Graham, unaware of

the spectacular developments of the morning, wandered into the Johnson suite. Johnson seized him and took him into the bedroom along with Lady Bird. Bobby Kennedy, Johnson said, was in another part of the suite with Rayburn, presumably offering the Vice-Presidency, and he had to make an immediate decision. They sat together in the bedroom, "about as composed," Graham later wrote, "as three Mexican jumping beans." Lady Bird tried to leave, but Johnson would not let her go; this had to be her decision too. He kept asking Graham what he thought, and Graham finally said that he had to take the Vice-Presidency. Johnson said that he did not want the Vice-Presidency, would not negotiate for it, would take it only if Kennedy drafted him and would not discuss it with anyone else.

At this point Rayburn entered to report that Robert Kennedy wanted to see Johnson. Lady Bird intervened, noting that she had never before argued with Mr. Sam but she felt that her husband should not talk to Bobby. Graham had the impression that Rayburn thought both that Johnson should see Bobby and also that he should now turn down the Vice-Presidency. Finally, as Graham wrote, "in that sudden way decisions leap out of a melee," they agreed that Johnson at this point should talk only to the principal. Rayburn left to explain this to Bobby, and Graham was instructed to pass this word directly to the candidate. Graham dragged James Rowe, who had now joined the group, along as a witness, and the two men walked through the crowd of newspapermen in the corridor into a vacant bedroom.

Telephoning is always an ordeal at conventions; reaching the suite of the nominee is almost an impossibility. There would be a delay getting Mrs. Lincoln, Kennedy's secretary; another while the call was switched to Stephen Smith or Sargent Shriver, two Kennedy brothers-in-law guarding access to the candidate; another delay before the candidate himself was free to take the call. This was Phil Graham's signal contribution to the events of that wild afternoon. He had everyone's private phone number; and, in a situation where each of the principals was surrounded by people urging him to back away from the deal, Graham alone was able to force them into contact with each other. He persisted until he reached Kennedy about two-thirty and told him that Johnson was expecting word directly from him. Kennedy replied that he was in a mess because some of the liberals were against Johnson. A meeting was going on at that very moment, and people were urging that "no one had anything against Symington." He then asked Graham to call back for a decision "in three minutes."

Graham took off his wristwatch and placed it by the telephone. He and Rowe agreed that "three minutes" in these circumstances meant ten, and about two-forty Graham called back. Kennedy was "utterly calm" on the phone. He said that it was "all set"; "tell Lyndon I want him and will have [David] Lawrence nominate him." He added that he would be busy getting Lawrence and the seconders and preparing his statement announcing Johnson's selection; he asked Graham to call Stevenson, acquaint him with the decision and enlist his support.

After breaking the news to Stevenson, Graham returned to the main suite about three-twenty and found Johnson "considerably on edge." Robert Kennedy, Johnson said, had been back to see Rayburn some twenty minutes before and had said that his brother would phone directly. No call had come; what was up? Graham, noting the private phone numbers in Johnson's bedroom (the Johnson switchboard had long since broken down), said that he would get in touch with Kennedy. When he reached Kennedy ten minutes later, Kennedy said that he had supposed that his earlier word to Graham would suffice. Graham explained what Bobby had told Rayburn. Kennedy said that he would call Johnson. But he brought up the liberal protests again and asked what Graham thought. Phil replied that southern gains would more than offset liberal losses, and added anyway that it was too late for mind-changing; "you ain't no Adlai." Kennedy inquired how Stevenson had taken the news. Graham said that Stevenson had wondered about the liberal and Negro reaction but that he would be all right. Kennedy told him to ask Stevenson to put out a statement shortly after Kennedy made his own, now scheduled for four o'clock. Then Kennedy promptly called Johnson and read him the text of the announcement he planned to make. Johnson said that, if Kennedy really wanted him, he would be glad to go on the ticket. The arrangement was sealed.

The confusion of that afternoon defies historical reconstruction.[3] But *before* Graham had called Kennedy and Kennedy, Johnson, it had evidently been decided that Robert Kennedy should make one more attempt to talk to Johnson and, if he were still hesitant, offer the gathering liberal revolt as an excuse for his withdrawal. Graham

---

[3] Including this one; my account is based on as careful as possible a collation of the diverging recollections of participants.

reached Kennedy after Bobby had left the Kennedy suite; thus Bobby arrived at the Johnson suite *after* his brother had spoken directly to Johnson and without knowledge of their talk. He went straight to Johnson, and they sat on the same couch where his brother had sat a few hours earlier. In a moment Rayburn joined the conversation.

Robert Kennedy said he was there on behalf of his brother to report that the ugly floor fight in prospect might divide the party and cast a shadow over the whole campaign. If Senator Johnson did not want to subject himself to this unpleasantness, Senator Kennedy would fully understand; but he continued to hope that Johnson would play a major role in the election. Should Johnson prefer to withdraw, the candidate would wish to make him chairman of the Democratic National Committee. The implication was that Johnson, through his control of the party machinery, could thereby lay a basis for his own national future. Rayburn later remembered saying "shit!" at this point, but his interjection passed unnoticed. Johnson said with great and mournful emotion, "I want to be Vice-President, and, if the candidate will have me, I'll join with him in making a fight for it." Robert Kennedy said cryptically, "He wants you to be Vice-President if you want to be Vice-President."

Bobby then walked out of the room, leaving consternation behind. Johnson, assuming that Robert's visit superseded the phone call from the candidate, told Bill Moyers, his appointments secretary, to get Phil Graham. Moyers finally found Graham telephoning in a bedroom down the hall and said that Johnson wanted him at once. Graham said, "I'll be along in just a minute." "That won't do," Moyers said, and, grabbing his arm, propelled him along the corridor through a jam of reporters into the suite.

Johnson, who seemed to Graham "in a high state of nerves," said they must talk alone immediately. Everything in the suite was in confusion. Johnson was giving a party for his supporters. Perle Mesta and others of the faithful were swarming around the living room. Price Daniel, still arguing against the Vice-Presidency, was in the bedroom. Johnson led his wife, Rayburn, Graham and Jim Rowe into an adjoining room. There, to everyone's astonishment, stood a collection of delegates from Hawaii, clad in gay shirts and talking happily among themselves. While the others stopped transfixed at the door, wondering how on earth to account for this apparition at the moment of crisis, Johnson called that he was sorry but he needed the room. As the

Hawaiians solemnly filed out, he chanted, "Thank you, boys. Thank you. Thank you for all you did."

Here John Connally, a leading manager of Johnson's campaign, and Bobby Baker, the secretary of the Democratic majority of the Senate, joined them. Johnson, greatly agitated and, as Graham later wrote, "about to jump out of his skin," shouted to Graham that Bobby Kennedy had just said that the opposition was too great and that Johnson should withdraw for the sake of the party. When Johnson finished, everyone started to speak, until someone's voice —either Rayburn's or Rowe's—pierced the uproar, saying, "Phil, call Jack."

"It took a minute which seemed an hour to get the operator," Graham later wrote, "then another series of hourlike minutes as we got Kennedy's switchboard, then his secretary, and finally Kennedy."

Graham said, "Jack, Bobby is down here and is telling the Speaker and Lyndon that there is opposition and that Lyndon should withdraw."

"Oh!" Kennedy said as calmly as though they were gossiping about the weather, "that's all right; Bobby's been out of touch and doesn't know what's been happening."

Graham said, "Well, what do you want Lyndon to do?"

Kennedy said, "I want him to make a statement right away; I've just finished making mine."

Graham said, "You'd better speak to Lyndon."

Kennedy said, "OK, but I want to talk to you again when we're through."

Graham handed the phone to Johnson, who lay sprawled across the bed. Johnson said, "Yes . . . yes . . . yes," and finally, "OK, here's Phil," handing the phone back to Graham.

Kennedy now chatted along "as though we were discussing someone else's problems." He said that Alex Rose was threatening not to list him on the Liberal Party line in New York because of Johnson, but "this is a problem we'll just have to solve." Graham then said, "You'd better speak to Bobby." Baker went out to find Bobby, who came in looking white and exhausted and took the phone. His brother told him that the party leaders had felt the delay was disastrous, that he had to go through with Johnson or blow the whole business. As Graham walked out of the room, he heard Bobby say, "Well, it's too late now," and half-slam the receiver down. Bobby then leaned his head against the wall and said, referring not to the candidate but to the confusion, "My God, this wouldn't have happened except that we were all too tired last night."

The Johnsons waited in the entrance hall of the suite. In his hand Johnson held a typed statement accepting the nomination. He said, "I was just going to read this on TV when Bobby came in and now I don't know what I ought to do." Graham said, "Of course you know what you're going to do. Throw your shoulders back and your chin out and go out and make that announcement. And then go on and win. Everything's wonderful." Bill Moyers swung open the hall doors and the Johnsons walked out into the white glare of the TV lights and the explosion of flashbulbs.

A short while later, Johnson went over to the Kennedy suite. Kennedy was sitting by the window, gazing out at Los Angeles stretching murkily away in the distance. The two men greeted each other warmly. Johnson quickly pledged his "total commitment" to play his role as part of the Kennedy team.

5. THE NEW FRONTIER

At the Sports Arena, however, the Kennedy team was in considerable disarray. The announcement had stunned the convention. Liberal Democrats were unbelieving and angry. The choice of Johnson was regarded as a betrayal. It seemed to confirm the campaign stereotypes of the Kennedys as power-hungry and ruthless. The word "double-cross" was used. There were signs of open revolt on the floor. Michigan was enraged; so were delegates from Minnesota and California. Joseph Rauh and Robert R. Nathan of the District of Columbia were issuing bitter statements on television.

I was still at this time in the Stevenson suite, where there was indignation too, though Stevenson himself had a considerable respect for Johnson, and the more realistic Stevensonians knew that, if Johnson had come out for Stevenson, they would have been delighted to have him as Stevenson's running mate. As I watched the turmoil on the convention floor, I felt an uncontrollable desire to go out and see what could be done. Almost the first person I saw on arrival at the Sports Arena was Graham. Noting my air of incipient rebellion, Phil with characteristic solicitude drew me into a vacant office at the CBS booth, told me not to be silly and explained why he considered the nomination of Johnson logical and right. I was impressed without being altogether convinced; but, by the time he released me, I was notably more relaxed. Phil also calmed Joe Rauh and dissuaded him from putting Orville Freeman's name into nomination. At Robert Kennedy's behest, Galbraith was moving among the liberal delegations. "This is the kind of political expedient Franklin Roosevelt would never have used," Galbraith explained, "—except in the case of John Nance Garner." Soon emotions were subsiding everywhere. Averell Harriman told me that it was a great ticket and would cause no trouble in New York. William Haddad of the *New York Post,* with whom I had gone to the Arena, reported that everyone was accommodating himself to Johnson. The balloting began and, before the roll call reached Michigan, John McCormack moved that Johnson be nominated by acclamation. A roar came up from the hall, mingling "ayes" and "nays," it seemed to me, in about equal proportions, but Governor Collins promptly declared that the vote had carried.

All emotions did not subside. That evening there was an air of depression at Joe Kennedy's house. Jack and Bobby were sitting gloomily around the swimming pool when their father appeared at the doorway, resplendent in a fancy smoking jacket, and said, "Don't worry, Jack. In two weeks everyone will be saying that this was the smartest thing you ever did." Johnson too found himself unaccountably depressed and thought for a moment that he had made the mistake of his life. He growled accusingly to his aides the next morning, "You talked me into this." As for the liberals, they also had their troubles. Violet Gunther, the executive director of Americans for Democratic Action and a Kennedy supporter, was awakened at four in the morning by embittered Stevensonians demanding to know how many pieces of Joe Kennedy's silver she had got for her work.

My own sense of outrage vanished in forty-eight hours. On Saturday morning I had a talk with Reinhold Niebuhr, who was a few miles away in Santa Barbara, and found him strongly in favor of Johnson's nomination. He pointed out that the Democratic party had pledged itself to the strongest civil rights plank in history. If, in addition, it had nominated a militant northern liberal for the Vice-Presidency, this could only have confirmed the South in its sense of isolation and persecution. But the nomination of a southern candidate who accepted the platform, including the civil rights plank, restored the Democrats as a national party and associated the South with the pursuit of national goals. I noted that weekend, "After reflection, I am reconciled to the Johnson nomination and believe that it may come to be seen as a master stroke. . . . I now think that on balance, from the viewpoint both of winning the election and of governing the country, the decision was brave and wise."

And so we had our ticket. I dropped by Stevenson's suite on Friday morning and found the Stevenson faithfuls—Finletter, Monroney, Doyle, Wirtz, Ball, Blair, Minow and some others. These, along with absent Stevensonians like Mrs. Roosevelt, Lehman, Wilson Wyatt, had kept the liberal spirit of the party alive in the dark years. Stevenson himself, unruffled and witty, acted as if a great burden had been taken from his shoulders. Watching him, one sensed the difference between the old group and the new. Kennedy was in the school of Roosevelt. The thought of power obviously neither rattled nor dismayed him. He did not wish cups to pass from his lips. He displayed absolute assurance about his capacity to do the job; and he had a hard and sure instinct about how to get what he wanted. In Kennedy the will to command and the will to victory were visible and unbeatable. One watched the changing of the guard with a mixture of nostalgia and hope.

Late Friday afternoon, in the shadows of the setting sun, John F. Kennedy appeared before a crowd of eighty thousand people in the Los Angeles Coliseum to record his formal acceptance of the nomination. The speech began conventionally enough with tributes to his defeated rivals, who sat behind him in a circle on the platform. Next came the litany of historical allusions: "Richard I . . . bold Henry II . . . Richard Cromwell . . . Pierce . . . Fillmore . . . Buchanan." Then, in a moment, the speech moved on to a new pitch of gravity and emphasis.

The American people expect more from us than cries of indignation and attack. . . . For the world is changing. The old era is ending. The old ways will not do.

Abroad, the balance of power is shifting. There are new and more terrible weapons, new and uncertain nations, new pressures of population and deprivation. . . . More energy is released by the awakening of these new nations than by the fission of the atom itself. . . .

The world has been close to war before—but now man, who has survived all previous threats to his existence, has taken into his mortal hands the power to exterminate the entire species some seven times over.

Here at home, the changing face of the future is equally revolutionary. The New Deal and the Fair Deal were bold measures for their generations—but this is a new generation. . . . A technological revolution on the farm . . . an urban-population revolution . . . a peaceful revolution for human rights—demanding an end to racial discrimination in all parts of our community life . . . a medical revolution . . . a revolution of automation. . . .

There has also been a change—a slippage—in our intellectual and moral strength. Seven lean years of drought and famine have withered the field of ideas. Blight has descended on our regulatory agencies. . . . Too many Americans have lost their way, their will and their sense of historic purpose. . . .

It is time, in short, for a new generation of leadership—new men to cope with new problems and new opportunities. All over the world, particularly in the newer nations, young men are coming to power, men who are not bound by the traditions of the past, men who are not blinded by the old fears and hates and rivalries, young men who can cast off the old slogans and delusions and suspicions. . . .

He was very tired; his delivery was uncertain and at times almost strident; but his conviction carried him along, and the crowd stirred in response to the words, as the sun continued to sink into the sea.

For I stand tonight facing west on what was once the last frontier. From the lands that stretch 3000 miles behind me, the pioneers of old gave up their safety, their comfort and sometimes their lives to build a new world here in the West. . . . Their motto was not "Every man for himself," but "All for the common cause." . . .

Today some would say that those struggles are all over, that all the horizons have been explored, that all the battles have been won, that there is no longer an American frontier. But . . . the problems are not all solved and the battles are not all won, and we stand today on the edge of a new frontier—the frontier of the 1960s, a frontier of unknown opportunities and paths, a frontier of unfulfilled hopes and threats. . . .

The new frontier of which I speak is not a set of promises—it is a set of challenges. It sums up not what I intend to *offer* the American people, but what I intend to *ask* of them. . . . It holds out the promise of more sacrifice instead of more security. . . . Beyond that frontier are uncharted areas of science and space, unsolved problems of peace and war, unconquered pockets of ignorance and prejudice, unanswered questions of poverty and surplus.

It would be easier to shrink back from that frontier, to look to the safe mediocrity of the past. . . . But I believe the times demand invention, innovation, imagination, decision. I am asking each of you to be new pioneers on that new frontier. . . .

For the harsh facts of the matter are that we stand on this frontier at a turning point in history. . . .

It has been a long road from that first snowy day in New Hampshire to this crowded convention city. Now begins another long journey. . . .

The crowds cheered; they promised their help, their hand, their voice, their vote; then, in a few moments, they began to melt away into the hushed dusk. John Fitzgerald Kennedy's long journey had begun.

III

CAMPAIGN FOR THE PRESIDENCY

EARLY IN AUGUST my wife and I were asked to luncheon at Hyannis Port. It was a shining summer Saturday, sunny, clear and still. But the once placid Cape Cod village had lost its wistful tranquillity. It looked more like a town under military occupation, or a place where dangerous criminals or wild beasts were at large. Everywhere were roadblocks, cordons of policemen, photographers with cameras slung over their shoulders, children selling souvenirs, tourists in flashy shirts and shorts waiting expectantly as if for a revelation. The atmosphere of a carnival or a hanging prevailed. The summer residents, proceeding frostily down the streets, were identifiable by their expressions of disapproval.

A stockade now half surrounded the Kennedy compound, and the approach was like crossing a frontier, with documents demanded every ten feet. Eventually we made our way past the tourists and the children and the roadblocks and approached the house. The first courtyard contained newspapermen, lounging in the sun and waiting for a press briefing. We passed on from the court to the terrace of the Senator's house. Here we encountered a delegation from the Foreign Nationalities Branch of the Democratic National Committee, with Mennen Williams in exuberant command. The delegates carried dolls dressed in vivid native dresses as gifts for Caroline Kennedy. Kennedy, smiling and tan, was shaking their hands; he waved us on into the house. In the first room we ran into Frank Morrissey, a devoted Kennedy retainer from his earliest days in Massachusetts politics, waiting with a potential contributor for a word with the nominee. On we went into the living room, dark behind long curtains. My eyes were still dazzled from the sun on the terrace, so I did not at first make out the figure sitting patiently in the shadows. It was Norman Mailer.

1. OPENING MOVEMENTS

The total astonishment of going through this sequence and finding Norman Mailer at the end summed up, it seemed to me, the gaiety and the unpredictability of the household.

65

Jacqueline Kennedy joined us, and we all chatted over drinks. Soon Kennedy came in from the terrace. It was then that he told Mailer that he had enjoyed his books, saying "I've read *The Deer Park* and . . . the others," a remark which startled an author who had heard people in similar situations say a hundred times, "I've read *The Naked and the Dead* . . . and the others." (It was a faithful expression of an idiosyncratic taste. When Kennedy first met James Michener, he said, "I've always liked your *Fires of Spring*," foregoing the inevitable *Tales of the South Pacific*. When he met Eugene Burdick, he mentioned *The Ninth Wave*, not *The Ugly American*.)

About one o'clock six of us—the Kennedys, Jacqueline's sister Lee Radziwill and her husband and ourselves—took off on the *Marlin*. The waters of the sound glittered in the sun; in the distance we could soon see the shadowy outline of Martha's Vineyard. We swam off the stern of the boat. Afterward Bloody Marys were served, followed by luncheon. We cruised serenely for several hours, returning to the Kennedy pier at the end of the day.

Conversation filled in the interstices of the afternoon. I had never seen Kennedy in better form—more relaxed, funny and free. He had lunched in New York the day before with Henry R. Luce and the editors of *Time* and *Life*. "I like Luce," he said. "He is like a cricket, always chirping away. After all, he made a lot of money through his own individual enterprise so he naturally thinks that individual enterprise can do everything. I don't mind people like that. They have earned the right to talk that way. After all, that's the atmosphere in which I grew up. My father is the same way. But what I can't stand are all the people around Luce who automatically agree with everything he has to say." The Luce people were agitated about Galbraith, he continued, and seemed to regard him as a dangerous radical. "Actually," Kennedy said, "Galbraith is a conservative."

He chatted a bit about healing the wounds of Los Angeles. He had had a successful visit from Lyndon Johnson, and he was full of enthusiasm for Orville Freeman and Mennen Williams. Humphrey's behavior still puzzled him: "Hubert was supposed to come out for me on that Tuesday. I have never understood what happened to him." Stevenson's visit, he thought, had gone all right. Adlai's political counsel, Kennedy said with some surprise, was shrewd and realistic, and his thinking on foreign policy generally congenial. Stevenson had pointed out that Kennedy, after his months of absorption in the campaign, would need to be brought promptly up to date on the main problems of foreign policy if elected; perhaps he should make provision now for a report to be delivered right after the election. Though Kennedy's mind was primarily on politics, he saw the point and immediately asked Stevenson to prepare the report himself. Stevenson had said nothing about his own future, so Kennedy had said nothing either; "however, I would not ask him to help me now if I did not think of him as playing a role in the future." Kennedy went on to remark a little sadly that he wished he had more rapport with Stevenson. He had rapport with Bill Blair, he noted, and Stevenson obviously had it with Jacqueline; but he always was conscious of strain when he and Stevenson were in direct contact. At one point, he asked, "If you were me, would you appoint Stevenson Secretary of State?" I said yes and explained why. He listened with apparent interest but without disclosing his own feelings.

He talked a good deal about Nixon, who had just been making imprudent statements in Honolulu. This pleased Kennedy; he said he was sure he could count on Nixon's capacity to make mistakes. But he was irritated over a rather striking column by Eric Sevareid in that morning's *Boston Globe*. Sevareid had argued that there were no real differences between the two candidates: "The 'managerial revolution' has come to politics and Nixon and Kennedy are its first completely packaged products." Both men, Sevareid said, were sharp, ambitious, opportunistic, devoid of strong convictions and deep passions, with no commitment except to personal advancement. The genius of these "tidy, buttoned-down men" was not that of the heroic leader but of the junior executive on the make. They represented the apotheosis of the Organization Man. Sevareid recalled the thirties and the young men who "sickened at the Republic Steel massacre of strikers . . . got drunk and wept when the Spanish Republic went down . . . dreamt beautiful and foolish dreams about the perfectibility of man, cheered Roosevelt and adored the poor."

I can't find in the record that Kennedy or Nixon ever did, thought or felt these things. They must have been across the campus on Fraternity Row, with the law and business school boys, wearing the proper clothes, thinking the proper thoughts, cultivating the proper people.

I always sensed that they would end up running the big companies in town but I'm damned if I ever thought one of them would end up running the country.

Part of this was true, of course. Kennedy had not been a firebrand of the Student Union at Harvard, though one might question the relevance of the point; it is not in the record either that Franklin Roosevelt or Woodrow Wilson spent much time marching on picket lines in his youth. But the contention that he and Nixon were two peas from the same pod exasperated him. He said that this was the fashionable cliché of the campaign, and he obviously feared that it might have some impact. I think, moreover, that he felt personally insulted by it, for he considered that there was no one he resembled less than Nixon. He scorned the way Nixon opened his speeches with the "Pat and I" greeting and employed what one reporter called the "humble bit." "He has no taste," Kennedy said with contempt. On issues, he added with disarming candor, "Nixon is about as far advanced as I was ten years ago." When I said that a publisher had asked me to do a small book setting forth the differences between Nixon and himself, he encouraged me to go ahead.

These were last interludes before the grinding labor of the election began. I had little to do with the inner workings of the campaign and can supplement Theodore H. White's account only by adding some notes on the relations between Kennedy and the liberals. There had been growing enthusiasm for Kennedy in the liberal community in the weeks from West Virginia to Los Angeles. Then the convention, the Stevenson uprising and the Johnson nomination stopped this movement in its tracks. The acceptance speech and the promulgation of the New Frontier revived it for the moment. But it ebbed again in the doldrums of the special session of Congress.

At the end of August the National Board of Americans for Democratic Action held a meeting to decide its position on the election. The leadership—Rauh, Nathan, Samuel H. Beer, Senators Joseph Clark and Herbert Lehman—called for an all-out endorsement of the Kennedy-Johnson ticket; but the representatives of the local chapters, rising one after another to report the sentiments of their members, expressed quite different views. As summarized in the minutes: Essex County, New Jersey: "No feeling for Kennedy. Strong feeling against Nixon. General feeling wait and see." Dallas: "Think ADA has higher duty than endorsing lesser of two evils. Should endorse Democratic platform but no candidate." East Westchester, New York: "Informal poll showed slight majority in favor of no endorsement by ADA at this point. Thought National Board should hold off." West Side, New York City: "Majority for position we don't trust Kennedy and don't like Johnson but Nixon so bad we have to do something." About half the chapters recommended no endorsement for the time being; the other half recommended endorsement but with marked tepidity (except for Massachusetts and one or two others) and only because of their fear of Nixon. In the end, the leadership prevailed on the Board to endorse Kennedy and "the national Democratic ticket," but it was a struggle. The ADA statement studiously omitted the fact that there was also a candidate for Vice-President. I wrote Kennedy after the meeting, "I was prepared for apathy on the part of grass-roots liberals. I was not prepared for the depth of hostility which evidently exists."

A significant section of the traditional Democratic activists—the liberals, the reformers, the intellectuals: in general, the people who were in politics, not because it was their livelihood, but because they cared about issues—seemed immobilized. Adlai Stevenson had enlisted them in active Democratic affairs, and they were not prepared to forgive the man who had usurped his place. The influence of these issue-minded people far exceeded their numbers because they were crusaders of the party; they were the men and women who by Labor Day should have been arguing with their friends, writing letters to their papers, manning their local organizations, canvassing their neighborhoods, plastering their station wagons with Kennedy stickers and, in general, charging the campaign with emotion and zeal. Instead, many of them were sulking; and, worse, some who would have liked to help felt that the Kennedy people in the regular party organizations did not want them in the campaign. When I reported all this to Kennedy, he replied, "I don't mind criticism at this point. I would rather have you tell me now than to wait until November."

Early in September, as part of his effort to meet this problem, Robert Kennedy asked me to go with James Doyle on a trip through areas of Stevenson popularity in California. Doyle and I did our best to explain to Stevenson supporters in Los Angeles, San Diego and Palo Alto why we thought Kennedy would make a great President. One sensed an awakening of interest in Kennedy, a new readiness to give him a chance; this appeared among the film people in Beverly Hills as well as among the academics at Stanford. Our trip had little effect, however, compared to what Stevenson himself did later.

Kennedy, who had not forgotten those lines of people

surrounding the Sports Arena, asked Stevenson to spend as
much time as he could in California. This Stevenson did
in the next weeks, speaking with his customary grace and
magnanimity. Murray Kempton preserved a glimpse of him
during a Kennedy trip to Los Angeles. Introducing the
young man who had beaten him to the crowds who loved
him, Stevenson said, "Do you remember that in classical
times when Cicero had finished speaking, the people said,
'How well he spoke'—but when Demosthenes had finished
speaking, the people said, 'Let us march.'" So with characteristic style he accepted the succession. "Let us never forget," Kempton wrote, "that if a light still rises above this
dreary land, it is because for so long and so lonely a time
this man held it up." [1]

2. THE TIDE TURNS

While the Stevenson Democrats were coming to terms with
the new order, Kennedy himself was beginning to hit his
stride. On September 12, before the Greater Houston Ministerial Association, he knocked religion out of the campaign
as an intellectually respectable issue; it would persist, of
course, as a stream of rancor underground. And his own
political purpose was gradually coming into focus. He was
developing with emphasis, and more and more often with
eloquence, his distinctive theme—the appeal to get the country moving again. On a hundred platforms, at airports and
in armories, at state fairs and in war memorials and municipal auditoriums, before crowds baked in the sun or
shivering in the autumn's early frost, from the interior valleys of California to the familiar town squares of New
England, he was defining the issue, his voice twanging and
rapid, his sentences punctuated by the staccato movement
of the outthrust arm and the pointed finger, his argument
so intent that his flow of discourse often smothered the
bursts of applause.

"I have premised my campaign for the Presidency," he
said, "on the single assumption that the American people
are uneasy at the present drift in our national course, that
they are disturbed by the relative decline in our vitality
and prestige, and that they have the will and the strength
to start the United States moving again." To start moving
again it was essential to identify the real problems. "The
great trouble with American politics today," he said, ". . . is

that we talk in slogans too often and symbols and we fight
old battles. The sixties are going to be entirely different.
... We are a new generation which science and technology
and the change in world forces are going to require to face
entirely new problems which will require new solutions."
And this revival at home was the necessary foundation for
leadership in the world: Wilson, Roosevelt and Truman
were "successful around the world because they were successful here, because they moved this country ahead, because only in this way could America show a watching
world"—we sit, he liked to say, quoting Burke, "on a most
conspicuous stage"—that communism was not, after all,
the wave of the future and "that the future and the United
States are one."

By mid-September his intelligence and intensity were beginning to command the attention of the electorate—and
then the debates began. In retrospect, September 26 was
surely the turning point. My wife saw the first debate with
Jacqueline at Hyannis Port. I had hoped to join them; but
I had to go to New York that afternoon for the publication
of *Kennedy or Nixon: Does It Make Any Difference?*
By the time I caught the plane back to Boston, the Cape was
lying deep in fog, and the Hyannis airport was closed down.
Marian told me later that Kennedy, calling Jacqueline after
the broadcast, could not suppress his delight. Nixon's key
issue—Kennedy's supposed youth and inexperience—had
been eliminated from the campaign in one stroke.

When I went to San Francisco again in a few days, the
atmosphere had changed. The liberals were now showing
enthusiasm and commitment. A few days later Jacqueline
called to say that her husband wanted Galbraith and me to
come to New York to help in the preparation for the third
debate on October 13. She also said he wanted new ideas
and speeches.

Actually he was in no need of assistance. His speech and
research operations were in excellent shape. Though Kennedy had no time now to do any writing, he was a confident
and skilled improvisor who very often departed from or
even abandoned his prepared manuscript—a practice which
tried the warm affection of the newspapermen for him, since
it required them to listen to every speech and, when he
deviated from the text, to file a second story. As for the
manuscripts themselves, they came mostly from two members of his senatorial staff, Ted Sorensen and a young Harvard Law School graduate and former Frankfurter law
clerk, Richard N. Goodwin. A third member of the senatorial staff, Myer Feldman, helped occasionally in the writ-

ing and presided over problems of research and clearance. In addition, two gifted magazine writers, John Bartlow Martin, who had worked in the Stevenson campaigns, and Joseph Kraft, served as literary advance men, checking on the mood and issues in localities where he was to speak, and sending back references, ideas and language to Sorensen and Goodwin. An office in Washington, directed by Professor Archibald Cox of the Harvard Law School, collected research memoranda from experts across the country and turned them into speech drafts.

All this was working exceedingly well if not without the standard quota of frictions. From his long experience with Kennedy and his superb service for him, Sorensen had come to feel that no one else knew the candidate's mind so well or reproduced his idiom so accurately. Justifiably proud of his special relationship, he tended to resent interlopers. And a chronic tension existed between the Sorensen-Goodwin-Feldman operation and the Cox office, since the men on the road, sensitive to the ebb and flow, the very vibrations, of the campaign, found little sustenance in the weighty and academic material they received from Washington.

Kennedy, who was aware of everything, was aware of all this. At luncheon in New York on October 11, he discussed his staff problems at some length. We were in the duplex apartment on the thirty-fourth floor of the Carlyle, the glass of the skyscrapers to the south shimmering in the sun and the East River sparkling in the distance. He said that the senatorial group resisted the idea that things had to be expanded in a presidential campaign and tended to suspect every new face. He regretted the problems between Sorensen and Cox. Then he said, with great emphasis, "Ted is indispensable to me." As candidate, he would just have to live with the situation.

I had helped in a speech or two early in the campaign, especially the Liberal party speech in New York on September 14, and Ted had asked me to try my hand some more; but one knew from previous elections how impossible it was to prepare drafts from a distance. Kennedy agreed and remarked that in due course his people might start to grow tired and run out of ideas, in which case he might want to send for Galbraith and me. He noted, though, that there were public reactions to be taken into account —Nixon's refrain about the Democrats as "the party of Galbraith and Schlesinger and Bowles," as well as press stories about the Kennedy team collapsing and Stevenson's writers taking over. He said that, if I had anything I wanted to get to him, I should communicate through Jacqueline—a channel designed, I assume, to simplify his relations with his immediate staff.

Regarding Nixon, his attitude continued one of amused scorn. During the second debate, the studio, at Nixon's request, had been cooled to almost sixty degrees. Kennedy, trying out his chair, discovered that four lights were shining in his face as against one shining on Nixon. "When I saw all these lights, I decided that NBC had chosen its candidate." After the broadcast, he had gone over to shake hands with Nixon, and they had a moment or two of inconsequential chat. Then a photographer began to take a picture. Nixon, without altering the subject of his conversation or tone of his voice, started waving his finger in Kennedy's face to give the impression that he was telling off Kennedy as he had told off Khrushchev. Kennedy described this episode with mixed incredulity and contempt.

The next night Kennedy gave one of the most remarkable and least noted speeches of the campaign—a brilliant discussion of the Quemoy-Matsu problem, which he and Sorensen had composed in an afternoon. I heard it on television that night at the house of Marietta Tree, the most charming and tireless of New York Democrats. A couple of English visitors were present—Ian Gilmour, then publisher of *The Spectator*, and Roy Jenkins, the historian and Labour M.P. Both had spent the day going around New York with Kennedy and were ecstatic. Gilmour said that Kennedy was his idea of "the young Lord Salisbury." Jenkins said that a speech he had given in Harlem was the best political address he had heard in ten years. The Kennedy identity was emerging. It was about this time that people began to talk about "the Kennedy style."

Galbraith joined me the following morning. We accompanied Kennedy at noon to the launching of the Committee of Arts, Letters and Sciences for Kennedy. A group ranging from Van Wyck Brooks to Bette Davis was at the reception. Kennedy shook hands all around and held an impromptu press conference. (I had tried to get Robert Frost to come to the meeting, but he said that, though he admired Kennedy, he had never in his life signed anything with a lot of other people, and it was too late to begin. "Ganging up" was contrary to the whole point of his poetry and his life. He added, "My father was a rabid Democrat. I regard myself as a Democrat too—a gold-standard, Grover Cleveland Democrat. My first political memory is shouting for Cleveland in 1892. I hope to vote for Kennedy. I have sent for my absentee ballot. But I don't want to commit myself. I want to listen to every speech in the campaign knowing that it still might change my mind. So I sympathize with you, but I'm sorry, and I can't do it.")

Then we returned to the Carlyle for luncheon, where Sorensen joined us. Kennedy seemed a little nervous about the Quemoy-Matsu issue, and we spent most of our time on that. As we went down in the elevator with him after lunch, he said lightly, "Do you realize the responsibility I carry? I'm the only person standing between Nixon and the White House."

3. THE PEOPLE SPEAK

By now I was embarked on a speaking schedule on behalf of the ticket. This brought me back to New York the next week to talk before university groups and reform clubs. Kennedy had also returned to New York to give his marvelous joshing speech at Cardinal Spellman's Al Smith dinner. The audience had been strongly pro-Nixon, and Kennedy was ironically entertained by the fact that the wealthy Catholics obviously preferred a conservative Quaker to a liberal of their own faith. "It all goes to show," he said to me later, "that, when the chips are down, money counts more than religion."

He felt—this was October 20—that things were going well; as he put it, he had "everything made" except the religious issue, and this remained the great imponderable. He also expressed concern, however, about Cuba. Nixon, aided by Khrushchev's shoe-banging performance at the United Nations, was making inroads among suburban Catholics, to whom anti-communism made a strong appeal, denouncing Kennedy as "soft" on Quemoy-Matsu. As we discussed Cuba, Kennedy remarked that any measures against the Castro regime must of course be taken in concert with the other American republics.

After hearing this reasonable view, I was considerably surprised to read in the afternoon papers a militant Kennedy statement attacking the Republicans for their complacency before communism in Cuba and, while affirming the importance of "collective action," adding the ambiguous proposal: "We must attempt to strengthen the non-Batista democratic anti-Castro forces in exile, and in Cuba itself, who offer eventual hope of overthrowing Castro. Thus far these fighters for freedom have had virtually no support from our Government."

In fact, Kennedy had not seen this statement. Richard Goodwin, who had written it the evening before, had shown it to Sorensen and Salinger. They all agreed that this would be an effective riposte to Nixon's attacks on Kennedy's 'softness.' But, by the time they had finished discussing it, Kennedy himself had gone to bed. No one likes to awaken a sleeping candidate; and, since the staff thought the statement did no more than express compactly the things Kennedy had been saying about Cuba for several days, they decided to put it out without bothering him. (This had not happened before during the campaign; it did not happen again.) In all probability, Kennedy would have approved the text, though he told me later he would have changed the phrase "fighter for freedom" to "forces of freedom."

The statement produced an immediate uproar among his liberal and intellectual supporters. James B. Reston described it in the *New York Times* as Kennedy's first major blunder, and Walter Lippmann wrote a column of measured dismay. Kennedy himself was a little shaken by the reaction, though he reproached no one, contenting himself with a wry remark to Goodwin and Sorensen: "OK, if I win this election, I will have won it myself, but, if I lose, you fellows will have lost it." On October 23, as I was leaving the Boston airport for Chicago, Kennedy phoned from Wisconsin to suggest that I call Reston and Lippmann and explain that, by "support from our Government," he meant only moral and psychological, not military, support, and that he was committed to working within the framework of the Organization of American States. Reston had vanished into the Nixon train and could not be reached. Lippmann, who had given Kennedy powerful support in his columns, said he thought the Kennedy people were trying to play the issue both ways and deserved to be called on it. In any case, Kennedy thereafter dropped Cuba and concentrated for the rest of the campaign on his central themes.

It was late October, with events rushing toward their climax. A Georgia court sent Martin Luther King to jail on October 24. Harris Wofford of the campaign staff, who had been handling civil rights matters for Kennedy, told Sargent Shriver that Mrs. King was pregnant and in a state of near-hysteria and suggested that it might be good if Kennedy made a phone call of sympathy to her. Shriver went immediately to Kennedy's hotel in Chicago. Sure that the political experts would oppose a call lest it alienate the South, he waited until, one after another, Sorensen, Salinger and O'Donnell, left the room. Kennedy, responding with instinctive compassion, phoned Mrs. King at once. Later in the day, before arriving in Detroit, he said casually to Salinger, "By the way, I talked to Mrs. King this morning."

At first, Robert Kennedy shared the politicians' doubt. "You bomb throwers better not do anything more in this campaign," he told Shriver and Wofford. But the more he thought about the jailing of King, the madder he got himself; and soon he put through a call to the Georgia judge asking that King be given bail. Before he did, he alerted Lyndon Johnson. Johnson said, "Tell Jack that we'll ride it through down here some way, and at least he's on the side of right." (After the election, Murray Kempton asked Robert Kennedy whether he was glad he had called the judge. Bobby replied, "Sure I'm glad, but I would hope I'm not glad for the reason you think I'm glad." Kennedy later told Galbraith that he had not known of Bobby's call. He added, "The best strategies are always accidental.") In the meantime, King's father told newspapermen that he never thought he could vote for a Catholic but that the call to his daughter-in-law had changed his mind. "Imagine Martin Luther King having a bigot for a father," Kennedy said—then added quizzically, "Well, we all have fathers, don't we?"

The call to Mrs. King was only one of a number of personal gestures revealing the grace and force of feeling which lay beneath the supposedly cool façade. By mid-October one began to feel that the real Kennedy was coming over. No one could mistake him for Nixon any longer. Even the Stevensonians were responding to his wit and resolve. Young people in particular felt, in many cases for the first time, a connection with politics. Wildly cheering crowds surged around him as he crisscrossed the country. One has an unmistakable feeling when a campaign catches fire: it happened to Stevenson for a time in 1952 but not in 1956. It was plainly happening to Kennedy in the third week in October, 1960.

The surge continued for a number of days. Then, toward the end of the month, as mysteriously as it had begun, it started to wane. It was a strange, impalpable ebbing away. Reporters related it to events: the end of the debates, the intervention of Eisenhower. In retrospect one felt it had deeper roots—that it was almost as if the electorate were having sudden doubts whether it really wanted so intense a leader, so disturbing a challenge to the certitudes of their existence; it was as if the American people commenced to think that the adventure of Kennedy might be too much and that they had better fall back to the safe and familiar Nixon. Some close to Kennedy believed that, if the campaign had gone on three days more, he would have been beaten. The candidate himself knew the tide was shifting. When Nixon at the end went on television for a prolonged

question-and-answer session, an aide told Kennedy that his
opponent could be seen on a set in the next room. Utterly
weary, Kennedy waved him away.

I spent this last week in an air cavalcade organized by
Byron White of the Citizens for Kennedy. We returned to
New York City in time for the big Kennedy rally at the
Coliseum the Saturday before the election. On Monday I
went along for the last swing through New England. The
day was at once beautiful and melancholy. It was clear and
cold, the autumn leaves were falling, and intimations of
winter were in the air. We whirled from one point to another—Springfield, Hartford, Burlington, Manchester—
touching down in four states before we came to rest in
Boston long after sunset.

On election eve Kennedy, exhilarated by the return to
home territory, spoke at the Boston Garden. A chapter of
American history was spread out in the hall that evening
—Kennedy, cool, poised, masterful, a son of Ireland and
of Harvard, surrounded by a conventionally seedy Massachusetts state ticket, which he dutifully endorsed with
breakneck speed and evident indifference, and confronting
an audience of his supporters, from South Boston to Harvard
Yard, shouting their hearts out: it was, as one reporter
wrote, the young prince come home. He summed up the
campaign: "This race is a contest between the comfortable
and the concerned, between those who believe that we
should rest and lie at anchor and drift, and between those
who want to move this country forward in the 1960s.
... War and peace, the progress of this country, the security
of our people, the education of our children, jobs for men
and women who want to work, the development of our
resources—the symbolic feeling of a nation, the image
the nation presents to the world, its power, prestige and
direction—all ultimately will come to rest on the next
President of the United States. . . . I do not run for the
office of the Presidency after fourteen years in the Congress with any expectation that it is an empty or an easy
job. I run for the Presidency of the United States because
it is the center of action. . . . The kind of society we build,
the kind of power we generate, the kind of enthusiasm that
we incite, all this will tell whether, in the long run,
darkness or light overtakes the world. . . . I ask you to
join us tomorrow, and, most of all, I ask you to join us in
all the tomorrows yet to come."

What one noticed most was the transformation of Kennedy himself—from the vigorous but still uncertain figure of early September to a supremely assured and powerful

leader. His growth in the campaign conquered even the most skeptical. Mrs. Roosevelt said to me a few days after the election, "I don't think anyone in our politics since Franklin has had the same vital relationship with crowds. Franklin would sometimes begin a campaign weary and apathetic. But in the course of the campaign he would draw strength and vitality from his audiences and would end in better shape than he started. I feel that Senator Kennedy is much the same—that his intelligence and courage elicit emotions from his crowds which flow back to him and sustain and strengthen him."

On Tuesday the people by an alarmingly narrow margin in the popular vote chose John Fitzgerald Kennedy of Massachusetts as the thirty-fifth President of the United States.

IV

KENNEDY ON THE EVE

MY FIRST KNOWLEDGE OF John F. Kennedy went back to undergraduate days at Harvard twenty-five years before. His older brother, Joseph P. Kennedy, Jr., was one of my classmates, a confident, gregarious young man with a rollicking personality that swept all before it. He seemed destined to be a man of power, though one did not feel in him the inward and reflective quality one later found in his brothers John and Robert. But I never knew him well. He was a brave man and died in the war.

His younger brother John arrived in Cambridge as a freshman when Joe and I were in our third year. In those days the freshman class put on a smoker each spring; and the Freshman Smoker of 1937 shamed the older classes with its prodigies of talent imported from Broadway and Hollywood. One learned that young Jack Kennedy was responsible for this triumph. Even upper-classmen were impressed. I saw him from time to time in the Yard but do not recall that I ever exchanged a word with him. Joe and I finished Harvard in 1938, Jack two years later.

My next memory of Jack Kennedy goes back to London in the summer of 1944 when, as buzz-bombs roared overhead, I read one day in *The New Yorker* John Hersey's quiet account of his adventures in the Pacific. In 1946 I heard that he had returned to Boston to run for Congress. In due course he won the Democratic nomination for the House of Representatives in the 11th district, which included Cambridge, and was elected to the seat vacated by James M. Curley, who had once again become mayor of Boston. Kennedy and I renewed, or began, our acquaintance the following winter in Washington. I saw him from time to time in these years before the Presidency, with increasing frequency toward the end of the fifties, though I was not one of his intimates, if indeed he had real intimates outside his family.

In these years I began to understand better the complexity of mind and emotion which underlay that contained and ironic exterior, but only a little better. Kennedy had to an exceptional degree the gift of friendship and, in consequence, a great diversity of friends; part of his gift was to give each the sense that he alone had a clue to the mystery. The friends came in layers—the Choate and Harvard friends, the friends from the Navy, the social friends from Palm Beach and Newport, the Irish friends, the senatorial friends, the intellectual friends—and each layer considered itself closest to the center. But Kennedy kept the layers apart and included and baffled them all. The ultimate reserve was a source of his fascination and his power.

1. THE KENNEDY FAMILY

How had it all come about? Part of the answer, of course, lay in his upbringing. He was born into a family that was large, warm and spirited. There is no point in idealizing the Kennedys. Like any family, it had its share of tensions. Young Joe Kennedy, the oldest son, was bigger and stronger than the others; he was the leader of the children and occasionally, in discharging his role, something of a bully. No doubt Jack Kennedy was shoved around a good deal by his older brother. But, more than most families, the Kennedys were bound together by a love which gave all the children a fundamental confidence. With its subtle and disparate solidarity, the family nourished a capacity for competition, for individuality and for loyalty.

Moreover, it was an Irish family. Little is more dangerous than to try to explain a man in terms of supposed ethnic traits. In most respects, Kennedy departed considerably from the Irish-American stereotype. He was reticent, patrician, bookish, urbane—much closer, indeed, to a young Lord Salisbury than to a young Al Smith or, for that matter, to a young John F. Fitzgerald. Yet the Irishness remained a vital element in his constitution. It came out in so many ways—in the quizzical wit, the eruptions of boisterous humor, the relish for politics, the love of language, the romantic sense of history, the admiration for physical daring, the toughness, the joy in living, the view of life as comedy and as tragedy.

And it gave him a particular slant on American society. Though the Kennedy family was well established politically and financially—Jack's grandfather had twice been mayor of Boston; his father was a Harvard graduate and a successful businessman—it was still marginal socially in Brahmin Boston; and its folk memories were those of a time, not too far distant, when to be Irish was to be poor and have gates slammed in one's face. Joseph P. Kennedy, a man of driving ambition, was determined to reverse all that. His passion was to break down the barriers and win full acceptance for himself and his family. Business success helped; he soon discovered that money encouraged people to forgive an Irish name, though this was less true in Boston than elsewhere. Money also enabled him to offer his sons the protective coloration of schooling at places like Choate, Milton and Harvard; it enabled him to open doors for them all their lives. But what was more important than money was the training he gave his children—a regimen of discipline tempered and transformed by affection.

Regarding money as a means and not as an end, Joe Kennedy forbade its discussion at the dinner table. Conversation turned, not on business, but on public affairs; no child could doubt the order of priority. "I can hardly remember a mealtime," Robert Kennedy said later, "when the conversation was not dominated by what Franklin D. Roosevelt was doing or what was happening around the world. . . . Since public affairs had dominated so much of our actions and discussions, public life seemed really an extension of family life." The father confronted the children with large questions, encouraged them to have opinions of their own, demanded that their opinions make sense, wrote them endless letters when he was away (which was often), told them they had an obligation to take part in public life and instilled convictions of purpose and possibility. As John Kennedy put it one night at the White House: "My father wasn't around as much as some fathers when I was young; but, whether he was there or not, he made his children feel that they were the most important things in the world to him. He was so terribly interested in everything we were doing. He held up standards for us, and he was very tough when we failed to meet those standards. The toughness was important. If it hadn't been for that, Teddy might be just a playboy today. But my father cracked down on him at a crucial time in his life, and this brought out in Teddy the discipline and seriousness which will make him an important political figure."

Young Jack kept up his side in the competitive world of the Kennedys. But for all his vitality he had both a frailness and a sensitivity which set him somewhat apart from the extroverted and gregarious family. He may even have been a little lonely at times. He passed a surprising amount of his childhood sick in bed—with diphtheria, scarlet fever, acute appendicitis and chronic stomach trouble. He was the only one in the family who liked to read; loneliness and sickness made him read all the more. He spent hours in his room at Riverdale or Hyannis Port absorbed in history and biography—King Arthur, *Scottish Chiefs, The White Company,* Cooper, and later Churchill's *Marlborough* when he was in his teens. History was full of heroes for him, and he reveled in the stately cadences of historical prose. His memory of what he read was photographic. Situations, scenes and quotations stuck in his mind for the rest of his life.

The interior life was a source of identity and of power. Already he was moving beyond his brother Joe, moving beyond his father, and developing distinctive standards and goals. The Kennedys were supposed never to finish second; but Jack could present a favorite quotation from Alan Seeger: "Whether I am on the winning or losing side is not the point with me. It is being on the side where my sympathies lie that matters." (He still, however, preferred to win.) Professor William G. Carleton of the University of Florida recalls an evening of discussion with the Kennedys at Palm Beach in April 1941: "It was clear to me that John had a far better historical and political mind than his father or his elder brother; indeed, that John's capacity for seeing current events in historical perspective and for projecting historical trends into the future was unusual." [1] It used to be said that the older Kennedy 'made' his son Jack President and, if Joe, Jr., had only lived, would have 'made' him President first. I do not believe either of these things for a moment. I doubt whether young Joe, for all his charms and gifts, would have been President. And it was Jack Kennedy

---

[1] W. G. Carleton, "Kennedy in History: An Early Appraisal," *Antioch Review,* Fall 1964.

who, in the existential sense, first made himself and then
made himself President. Out of some fierce, cool inner
passion, he became a man in his own right who grew from
but beyond the family in which he was born, which loved
him so much and which he loved so much.

It is hard to judge how much his formal education mattered. He spent only one year at a Catholic school, Canter-
bury in Connecticut. He then went on to Choate, which he
disliked heartily. During his Presidency his old school unveiled his portrait as Choate's most distinguished alumnus.
He observed of the ceremony, "This is the most ironic
celebration of which I have ever heard." He asked what
use schools like Choate were and answered his own
question in a message to his fellow alumni. "Those of us
who have gone to Choate and comparable schools," he
began, "represent really a very tiny minority." Private preparatory schools, he went on, would merit a place in American education only as they took in people of all classes and
races; and those fortunate enough to go to such schools
had to justify their special opportunities, preferably by entering the service of the nation. He named the Roosevelts,
Harriman, Acheson, Douglas Dillon, Charles Bohlen and,
among Choate alumni, Stevenson and Bowles, and suggested a trifle acidly that the careers of such men had done
more than anything else to persuade the American democracy to accept the preparatory school "even when, or perhaps because, the men themselves do things which appear
on occasion to disappoint a good many of their classmates."

Choate provided no intellectual excitement, and he finished only slightly above the middle of his class. His father sent him that summer to the London School of Economics, hoping to expose him to Harold Laski. Instead Kennedy exposed himself to jaundice and had to delay his
entry into Princeton in the fall. Then a recurrence of
jaundice knocked out the rest of his freshman year. With
his Princeton friends advancing into the sophomore class,
he yielded to his father's preference and shifted the next
autumn to Harvard.

2. THE ENGLISH EXPERIENCE

For a time Kennedy continued in his prep-school mood.
He organized the Freshman Smoker, ruptured a disk in his
back playing football, made the swimming squad and the
Crimson, kept apart from the greaseballs in the Harvard
Student Union and concentrated desultorily in the field of
government.

In the meantime, a summer in Europe between his first and second Harvard years exposed him to wider horizons. With Lemoyne Billings, who had been his roommate at Choate and was now at Princeton, he spent a carefree two months wandering around the continent. His diary of the summer records a growing interest in public affairs. "The general impression," he noted after a few days in France, "seems to be that while they all like Roosevelt, his type of government would not succeed in a country like France which seems to lack the ability of seeing a problem as a whole. They don't like Blum as he takes away their money and gives it to someone else. That to a Frenchman is tres mauvais." He concluded the entry: "Looked around and finally got a fairly cheap room for the night (35 francs)."

A visit to St.-Jean-de-Luz on the Spanish border led him to reflect on the Spanish Civil War. He registered his own view as "rather governmental after reading Gunther [*Inside Europe*] even though St. Jean is rebel stronghold." However, a day of rebel atrocity stories, as he noted the next evening, "turns me a bit from government," and an afternoon at a bullfight "made me believe all the atrocity stories now as these southerners . . . are happiest at scenes of cruelty. They thought funniest sight was when horse ran out of the ring with his guts trailing."

On to Lourdes—"very interesting but things seemed to become reversed as Billings became quite ill after leaving." Carcassonne two days later: "an old medieval town in perfect condition—which is more than can be said for Billings." Then Milan: "Finished Gunther and have come to the decision that Facism [*sic*] is the thing for Germany and Italy, Communism for Russia and Democracy for America and England." In Rome he set down a list of questions:

> If the belligerent foreign troops were withdrawn, how much chance would Franco have?
> If Franco wins, what will be the extent of Mussolini's control, Hitler's? . . .
> Isn't the chance of war less as Britain gets stronger—or is a country like Italy liable to go to war when economic discontent is rife? . . .
> Gunther says "Facism, momentarily powerful, may be the convulsive last agonies of the capitalist cycle, in which case Facism will have been merely the prelude of Communism." Is this true?

These were still the thoughts of a sophomore; but later in the year his father became ambassador to Britain and Jack began spending his holidays whenever possible in London. This speeded his intellectual awakening. He was fascinated by English political society, with its casual combination of wit, knowledge and unconcern. The intelligent young Englishmen of his own age, like David Ormsby Gore, seemed more confident and sophisticated than his Harvard friends. He enjoyed the leisured weekends in the great country houses. It was history come alive for him, and it had a careless elegance he had not previously encountered.

This love of England found its expression later in the delight with which he read books like David Cecil's *The Young Melbourne*. It was especially a love for the Whig England of the early nineteenth century, rational and urbane. But it is too simple to suggest that Kennedy was no more than an American Melbourne. The manner captivated him a good deal more than the matter. Kennedy was enchanted by the Whig zest, versatility and nonchalance; he liked the idea of a society where politics invigorated but did not monopolize life. But Whiggism was a posture, not a purpose. It was too passive for a Kennedy. Where Melbourne was willing to yield to the popular voice, Kennedy hoped to guide and anticipate it. Melbourne was an accommodator; Kennedy wanted to be a leader. He infused the Whig style with Rooseveltian activism. He was socially a Whig but politically something else—probably, if a British analogue is required, a Tory Democrat. He liked the notion of aristocrats and commoners united against the selfishness of laissez faire. His mood in later years was often that of Coningsby: "I would make these slum-landlords skip." He had read Winston Churchill's life of his father and found as much historical sustenance, I believe, in Lord Randolph Churchill as in Lord Melbourne. (He did not meet Winston Churchill for another twenty years. He and Jacqueline had a house at Cannes in the late fifties with William Douglas-Home, the playwright, and his wife. One evening they dined with Churchill on the Onassis yacht. It was not altogether a success; Churchill, now an old man, had a little difficulty in distinguishing which of the group that came aboard the yacht was Jack Kennedy, and, when this was finally sorted out, the conversation was hard going. He had met his hero too late. But Churchill remained his greatest admiration.)

All this was still an inchoate stirring in between afternoons at Lady Cunard's, balls in Belgravia and weekends in the country. But London did give him a sense of the tone in which politics might be approached. It also gave him a rather appalling look at the way democracy responded to crisis. Kennedy was in and out of England in the months when Churchill was calling on his fellow countrymen with such slight effect to rouse themselves against the menace of Nazism. Harvard allowed him to spend the second term of the academic year of 1938–39 abroad, and he traveled through Eastern Europe to Russia, the Middle East and the Balkans, stopping in Berlin and Paris on his way back to Grosvenor Square. When he returned to Harvard in the fall of 1939, the question of British somnambulism before Hitler perplexed him more than ever. Professor Arthur Holcombe of the government department had already aroused an interest in the study of politics; and now, under the guidance of Professors Payson Wild and Bruce Hopper, he set to work on an honors essay analyzing British rearmament policy. After his graduation in 1940, the thesis was published.

Remembering that Churchill had called his collection of speeches *While England Slept*, Kennedy brashly called his own book *Why England Slept*. In retrospect, *Why England Slept* presents several points of interest. One is its tone—so aloof and clinical, so different from the Churchillian history he loved, so skeptical of the notion that the individual could affect events ("personalities," he wrote with regret about the American attitude toward history, "have always been more interesting to us than facts"). This detachment was all the more remarkable midst the flaring emotions of 1940. Though ostensibly writing to prepare America for its own crisis ("in studying the reasons why England slept, let us try to profit by them and save ourselves her anguish"), he remained agnostic about the choices confronting the American President. Kennedy did make the quiet suggestion that "a defeat of the Allies may simply be one more step towards the ultimate achievement—Germany over the world"; but, beyond this, and doubtless out of deference to his father's and older brother's isolationism, he stood aside in the book from the great debate between the isolationists and the interventionists. (At Harvard, however, he wrote to the *Crimson* criticizing the isolationist views of his fellow editors.)

His purpose was to discover how much British unpreparedness could be attributed to the personal defects of British politicians and how much to "the more general weakness of democracy and capitalism"; and he found his answer not with the leaders, but with the system. He declined to pursue guilty men: "Leaders are responsible for their failures only in the governing sector and cannot be held responsible for the nation as a whole. . . . I believe it is one of democracy's failings that it seeks to make scapegoats for its own weaknesses." As long as Britain was a democracy, the people could have turned the leaders out if they disagreed with them. Nor did he put much stock in the notion that a leader could change the mind of the nation; after all, he remarked, Roosevelt had been trying to awaken America since 1937 but Congress was still cutting naval appropriations. The basic causes of the British paralysis in his view were impersonal and institutional. "In regard to capitalism, we observe first that it was obedience to its principles that contributed so largely to England's failure." Democracy, moreover, was "essentially peace-loving" and therefore hostile to rearmament. Both capitalism and democracy were geared for a world at peace; totalitarianism was geared for a world at war. A strong sense of the competition between democracy and totalitarianism pervaded the book—a competition in which, Kennedy believed, totalitarianism had significant short-run advantages, even though democracy was superior *"for the long run."*

3. THE WAR

As war came closer to America, Kennedy, having been rejected by the Army because of his back, succeeded in 1941 in persuading the Navy to let him in. After Pearl Harbor, he pulled every possible string to get sea duty, finally enrolling his father in the cause. In due course there followed the Pacific, PT-109, the Solomon Islands campaign, Talagi and Rendova, and the incredible few days in August 1943 when the Japanese destroyer *Amagiri* sliced his boat in half and plunged Kennedy and his crew into the waters of Ferguson Passage, now suddenly aflame with burning gasoline. Kennedy's calm bravery, his extraordinary feat in towing one of his crew to refuge by gripping the end of the life jacket belt in his teeth, his leadership, resourcefulness and cheer until rescue came—this was one of the authentic passages of heroism in the war, so well described in later accounts by John Hersey and Robert Donovan and so seldom mentioned by Kennedy himself. (In a Person to Person program with Edward R. Murrow in the late fifties, Kennedy called it "an interesting experience." Murrow responded: "Interesting. I should think that would be one of the great understatements." When during the Presidency Donovan proposed doing a book on PT-109, Kennedy tried his best to discourage him, saying that there was no story and that it would be a waste of his time. Donovan went ahead nevertheless and eventually decided that he would have to go out to the Solomons and reswim Kennedy's course. Kennedy, who thought this utter madness, could not get over the idea of anyone's going to such trouble and expense.)

The incident in the Solomons embodied two of Kennedy's deeper preoccupations—with courage and with death. He hated discussing these matters in the abstract, but they were nonetheless enduring themes of his life. Robert Kennedy tells us that courage was the virtue his brother most admired. In the first instance, this meant physical courage—the courage of men under enemy fire, of men silently suffering pain, the courage of the sailor and the mountain climber and of men who stared down mobs or soared into outer space. And, when he entered politics, it came to mean moral courage—the courage to which he later dedicated his *Profiles*, the courage of "a man who does what he must—in spite of personal consequences, in spite of obstacles and dangers and pressures," the courage which, he said, "is the basis of all human morality."

Courage—and death. The two are related, because courage, if it is more than reckless bravado, involves the exquisite understanding that death may be its price. "The education of the average American child of the upper middle class," Norbert Wiener has written, "is such as to guard him solicitously against the awareness of death and doom." But this is less true of children brought up in an orthodox faith. Kennedy's religious upbringing, his illness, his reading about the death of kings—all must have joined to give him an early sense of human mortality. Then death became his intimate during the long hours in the black, streaming waters of Ferguson Passage. Exactly a year later, he was notified that his brother Joe had been killed on an air mission against Nazi submarine bases in western Europe. In another month his English brother-in-law, the Marquis of Hartington, the husband of his sister Kathleen, was killed in France.

In a looseleaf notebook of 1945, filled with fragments about Joe and Billy Hartington—Joe's posthumous citation, a *Washington Post* editorial on his death, Kathleen's letter about her husband's death and letters from Billy Hartington's fellow officers in the Coldstream Guards—he inserted two quotations describing the death of Raymond Asquith in France in 1915—one from Churchill's *Great Contemporaries:*

> The War which found the measure of so many men never got to the bottom of him, and, when the Grenadiers strode into the crash and thunder of the Somme, he went to his fate, cool, poised, resolute, matter-of-fact, debonair.

and another from a favorite book, John Buchan's *Pilgrim's Way:*

> He loved his youth, and his youth has become eternal. Debonair and brilliant and brave, he is now part of that immortal England which knows not age or weariness or defeat.

His wife later said, "The poignancy of men dying young haunted him."

4. IN SEARCH OF SELF

Along with a deep sorrow over the battalions of wasted lives, the war left him with an intense concern about the prevention of such waste in the future. He went to San Francisco in June 1945 as a special writer for the Hearst press to watch the founding of the United Nations. For a young veteran, with stabbing memories of violence and death, it was in a way a disenchanting experience. But for a student of politics it was an indispensable education.

"It would be very easy to write a letter to you that was angry," he observed afterward to a PT-boat friend who had sought his opinion of the conference. "When I think of how much this war has cost us, of the deaths of Cy and Peter and Orv and Gil and Demi and Joe and Billy and all of those thousands and millions who have died with them—when I think of all those gallant acts that I have seen or anyone has seen who has been to the war—it would be a very easy thing to feel disappointed and somewhat betrayed." The conference, he continued, lacked moral force; not idealism but self-interest brought the nations together. "You have seen battlefields where sacrifice was the order of the day and to compare that sacrifice to the timidity and selfishness of the nations gathered at San Francisco must inevitably be disillusioning."

Yet could the conference have achieved more? The hard fact was that nations were not prepared to yield their sovereignty to an international organization. He listened in the corridors to the world government arguments of another young veteran, Cord Meyer, about to head the World Federalists. "Admittedly world organization with common obedience to law would be solution," Kennedy scribbled in a notebook. "Not that easy. If there is not the feeling that war is the ultimate evil, a feeling strong enough to drive them together, then you can't work out this internationalist plan." "Things cannot be forced from the top," he told his PT-boat friend.

The international relinquishing of sovereignty would have to spring from the people—it would have to be so strong that the elected delegates would be turned out of office if they failed to do it. . . . We must face the truth that the people have not been horrified by war to a sufficient extent to force them to go to any extent rather than have another war. . . . War will exist until that distant day when the conscientious objector enjoys. the same reputation and prestige that the warrior does today.

These were the things to be considered "when you consider that Conference in San Francisco. You must measure its accomplishments against its possibilities. What [the] Conference accomplished is that it made war more difficult." He summed up his feelings about the UN in his notebook:

> *Danger of too great a build-up.*
> Mustn't expect too much.
> A truly just solution will leave every nation somewhat disappointed.
> There is no cure all.

This was his mood immediately after the war: don't expect too much: no cure-alls. The next year he wrote succinctly in the six-year report of the Harvard Class of 1940, "I joined the Navy in 1941, served in P.T. Boats in the Pacific and was retired in April, 1945, because of injuries." (The Class Secretary added a footnote: "Kennedy received the Navy and Marine Corps Medal.") Concluding a brief paragraph, Kennedy replied to a question asked all members of the class, "I am pessimistic about the future of the country."

He had expected to become a writer; but the San Francisco experience may have helped persuade him that it was better to sit at the conference table than to wait outside with the press. His brother's death also changed things. The family assumption had been that Joe, who had made his political debut as a delegate at the 1940 Democratic convention (where he cast his vote, as pledged, against Franklin Roosevelt), would be the Kennedy to enter politics. Though Ambassador Kennedy did not, as myth later had it, automatically promote his second son into the slot now so sadly vacant, Jack, like many young veterans, felt the need of doing something to help the world for which so many friends had died. Politics perhaps attracted him less as a means of saving this world than of keeping it from getting worse. In 1946 he returned to Boston to test the political air.

The return to Boston must have involved a form of what

anthropologists call 'culture shock.' While born a Boston Irishman, he had never been a member of the Boston Irish community; and his life had carried him far away from his roots. Now, in the 11th Congressional District, he was back among his own people, yet not quite of them. He liked their toughness and their loyalty, but regretted their anti-intellectualism. Campaigning through the three-deckers of Charlestown and the North End, he fraternized for the first time with the men and women from whom the Kennedys and Fitzgeralds had sprung. In the dimly lit hall of one Charlestown tenement he encountered David Powers, a man of exceptional sweetness and fidelity, who beguiled him with his flow of stories, his knowledge of Irish Boston, and his capacity for affable relaxation. Kennedy, at first a little stiff and shy, soon began to relax himself, though, as the old Boston politician and raconteur Clem Norton (the model for Hennessy in Edwin O'Connor's *The Last Hurrah*) put it, he never quite acquired 'a street personality.'

In the fall of 1947 I returned to Massachusetts myself to teach history at Harvard. A note from Kennedy in January 1948 started "Dear Arthur" (and continued: "I have your letter of January 2nd, relative to your interest in conditions at the Harvard Square Post Office"); but my first distinct recollection is of a political meeting in Harvard Yard during the presidential election that October, where we sat together and chatted while he waited his turn to go to the platform. Thomas H. Eliot, who had represented Cambridge with distinction in the House until he was redistricted and beaten by Curley in the Democratic primary, was speaking. The position of the Yankee Democrat in Massachusetts was not easy; and Eliot appeared to be overcompensating for his suspicious origins by the warmth of his advocacy of Paul A. Dever, the Irish Catholic candidate for governor. Kennedy leaned over and said, "How can a man like Tom Eliot say such things about a man like Paul Dever?" Later my opinion of Dever was higher, and so too, I think, was Kennedy's. Eliot, who is now Chancellor of Washington University in St. Louis, may not have been so wrong as we thought. But at the time I was surprised and impressed by Kennedy's unorthodox reaction.

I should not have been so surprised. He had already shown his independence by his refusal to join his Massachusetts Democratic colleagues in the House in petitioning President Truman to pardon Curley, who, though still mayor of Boston, was by 1948 in Danbury prison for using the mails to defraud. (He was, it used to be said, the only mayor of Boston to serve two terms at once.) Occasional meetings with Kennedy in the next years strengthened the impression of a skeptical mind, a laconic tongue, enormous personal charm, an agreeable disdain for the rituals of Massachusetts politics and a detachment from the pieties of American liberalism. He still looked exceedingly young (actually he was six months older than I), but he was plainly purposeful and his own master.

In 1949, for some reason which now escapes me, perhaps because it might be a first step toward the governorship, I urged him to run for mayor of Boston. He replied, "I am interested in my work here in the House, and feel that there is much good that I can do from here." He was right, of course, to avoid the mayoralty trap; but it was soon evident that he was considering possibilities beyond the House. By 1950 he was making regular weekend visits to Massachusetts, speaking in places remote from his own district. He was plainly preparing to run for senator or governor in 1952. Which it would be depended on whether Paul Dever, now governor, chose to seek re-election or to challenge the incumbent Senator Henry Cabot Lodge, Jr. Kennedy's preference for the Senate was clear. As he said one day, gesturing at the State House, "I hate to think of myself up in that corner office deciding on sewer contracts."

Early in 1952 Senator Paul H. Douglas of Illinois delivered the Godkin Lectures at Harvard. The Douglases came for luncheon one winter Sunday along with Bernard DeVoto, Joseph Alsop, the McGeorge Bundys and Kennedy. Douglas, who seemed to regard the young Congressman with paternal fondness, warned him sternly against trying for the Senate, especially if the Republicans should nominate Eisenhower. Why not accumulate seniority in the House? or would not the governorship be less risky? Kennedy listened quietly and said little. Doubtless he received much advice of this sort. But, almost as if he felt he had little time to lose, he had long since resolved to push ahead. When Dever announced in April that he planned to run again for the governorship, Kennedy promptly declared his candidacy for the Senate.

I was away from the state most of the fall, working on Adlai Stevenson's staff in Springfield, Illinois. When the Stevenson party was campaigning through Massachusetts in October, we were much impressed by the cool efficiency of the Kennedy operation and by Kennedy himself, slim, careless and purposeful against the sodden background of the old-time Boston politicians. He beat Lodge by 70,000 votes. In the gloom of Stevenson's defeat, his success was a consolation. Victory now sent him back to Washington as a junior member of the Democratic minority in the Senate.

War had been a hardening experience, and politics hardened him more. Massachusetts Democrats did not exist as a party in the usual sense of the word. They formed rather a collection of rival tongs, controlled by local chieftains and presided over by an impotent state committee. Kennedy carved out his own domain and pursued his own goals. He showed himself determined, unrelenting and profane, able to beat the pols on their own ground and in their own language.

With his instinct for compartmentalization, he did not often display this part of his life to friends in other layers. His closest associate in these enterprises was his brother Robert, who managed his campaign for the Senate in 1952. Though Robert Kennedy was also a Harvard man, the Cambridge liberals regarded him with marked distrust because of his association with the McCarthy Committee; nor were his expressed views on public policy reassuring. Early in 1954 he sent a letter to the *New York Times* which, among other things, seemed to argue the Republican thesis about the iniquity of the Yalta conference. I was moved to write a forceful but perhaps condescending answer denouncing the letter as "an astonishing mixture of distortion and error." Robert Kennedy came back with a lively rejoinder. The last sentence suggests the tone: "I do not wish to appear critical of Mr. Schlesinger's scholarship for his polemics cover such a wide variety of subjects that it is understandable that he is not always able to read all of the documents he so vigorously discusses." He sent me a copy along with a note to the effect that he hoped his response would "clarify the record sufficiently for you to make the necessary public apology." I replied in like spirit; but the *Times,* bored with the argument, did not bother to print the rebuttals and surrebuttals. This exchange only amused Jack Kennedy, who later said, "My sisters are very mad at you because of the letter you wrote about Bobby."

In the 1956 campaign, Robert Kennedy joined the Stevenson party and accompanied the candidate in his trips around the country. He said very little, and no one quite knew what he was doing. (Actually he was learning how a national campaign should—or should not—be run.) His presence was, to my mind, a bit ominous; and I imagine he regarded mine with equal enthusiasm. One day in October Stevenson addressed a meeting in West Virginia. He was due that night in New York; but fog and rain set in, and only one plane was available to fly the candidate north. Arrangements were made to send the rest of the party on to Pittsburgh by bus. When the buses finally appeared, we all tumbled in and groped for seats in the darkness. In a minute I turned to look at my seatmate and, to our joint annoyance, found Robert Kennedy. For the next several hours, we rode through the storm to Pittsburgh. Having no alternative, we fell into reluctant conversation. To my surprise he was pleasant, reasonable and amusing. Thereafter our relations were amiable and uncomplicated.

Next to his brother, Kennedy's chief lieutenant in Massachusetts was a Springfield public relations man who had once worked for Foster Furcolo, Lawrence O'Brien. O'Brien played a large role in organizing the 1952 campaign for the Senate and subsequently joined the senatorial staff. In 1956 the Kennedys engaged in a bitter fight with John McCormack for control of the Democratic State Committee. For that fracas Bobby added to the group a Harvard classmate and former football captain, Kenneth O'Donnell; in 1960 O'Donnell became John Kennedy's appointments secretary and a key figure in the campaign. O'Brien and O'Donnell were both astute, unruffled, soft-spoken and terse. Both had great humor: Larry's was friendly and genial, while Ken, who looked like one of the young IRA men in trenchcoats in John Ford's film of *The Informer*, had a grim, cryptic wit which could be devastating. Both were liberals in the New Deal tradition—more so at this time than the Kennedys. O'Brien had been an early Massachusetts member of Americans for Democratic Action. Once when Robert Kennedy brought O'Donnell home to dinner in their college days, O'Donnell defended Franklin Roosevelt with such vigor that Ambassador Kennedy, deeply angered, left the table. Nevertheless, both were realistic organization politicians slightly contemptuous of reformers and reform groups. They worked in perfect unison with the Kennedys, shared that common understanding which abbreviates communication to swift phrases and imperceptible changes in facial expression, and filled in a vital part of Kennedy's life. Dave Powers, less involved in politics, kept the whole group happy.

But the Irish Mafia did not possess Kennedy any more than anyone else did. They were his instruments in politics, as Ted Sorensen was his instrument on issues. He admired them all because he admired virtuosity in performance—

"the ability," as he once put it, "to do things well, and to do them with precision and with modesty." The techniques by which people did things fascinated him, whether in politics or statecraft, writing or painting, sailing or touch football. He had an instinctive appreciation of excellence. He liked to cite Aristotle's definition of happiness: "The good of man is in the active exercise of his soul's faculties in conformity with excellence or virtue, or, if there be several human excellences or virtues, in conformity with the best and most perfect of them."

But, if there were several human excellences, faith in virtuosity per se could not be enough. Which would take precedence over the others? *Profiles in Courage* celebrated "grace under pressure" without regard to purpose; obviously Webster, Benton and Houston could not all have been right about the Compromise of 1850. The Kennedy of these years was still undefined. He was a Harvard man, a naval hero, an Irishman, a politician, a *bon vivant,* a man of unusual intelligence, charm, wit and ambition, "debonair and brilliant and brave," but his deeper meaning was still in process of crystallization.

5. MARRIAGE

Then he met Jacqueline Bouvier and leaned across the asparagus at Charles Bartlett's house in Washington to ask her for a date. She was a girl of great beauty, at once wistful and luminous, and also of acute intelligence and exacting expectation. In an essay which won *Vogue*'s Prix de Paris in 1951, she wrote that the three men she would most like to have known were Baudelaire, Wilde and Diaghilev. Her natural habitat was the international world of society and art, though Bernard Berenson admonished her in 1952, "American girls should marry American boys. They wear better." She was a Catholic, but from a securely established French-American family; childhood on Park Avenue and in East Hampton had exposed her to none of the social discrimination visited on the Boston Irish. Her father and mother were divorced, and she had grown up in a rather lonely way. Her loneliness and teachers she had encountered at Miss Porter's and Vassar had given her the capacity to care deeply about life, as the rest of her upbringing had given her the skill to disguise her caring. Her response to life was aesthetic rather than intellectual or moralistic. The intensity of this response attracted Kennedy and perhaps alarmed him; their courtship, Jacqueline said later, was "spasmodic." But they shared the gospel of excellence, and this, as well as more youthful emotions, bound them together.

Kennedy was a new experience for Jacqueline Bouvier. He pursued her with penetrating questions of a sort she had not heard before and, in self-defense, she began to ask questions back. One day she inquired how he would define himself. He said, "An idealist without illusions." And the week before they were married in September 1953 she asked him what he considered his best and worst qualities. He thought his best quality was curiosity, and his worst quality irritability. By irritability he meant impatience with the boring, the commonplace and the mediocre. And by curiosity he meant a good deal more than the purely intellectual trait; he meant that hunger for experience which caused him to demand that life be concentrated, vivid and full. "He lived at such a pace," Jacqueline Kennedy said later, "because he wished to know it all." It was all somehow connected with the precariousness of his health: this seemed to give his life its peculiar intensity, its determination to savor everything, its urgent sense that there was no time to waste.

The shadow had never left him. The shock of the collision with the Japanese destroyer in the Solomon Islands had torn his back, already weakened by the football injury at Harvard half a dozen years before. In his exhaustion after the rescue he came down with malaria. When he returned to the United States, he weighed 127 pounds and was in agony from sciatica. He had a lumbar disc operation at the Chelsea Naval Hospital, relieving the pressure on the nerve fibers. But his spine did not cease to torment him. "At least one half of the days that he spent on this earth," his brother has written, "were days of intense physical pain."

Then he was told that he had Addison's disease—a degeneration of the adrenal glands—and between 1946 and 1949 he went on a regimen of cortisone. One day when Joseph Alsop asked about the occasional greenness of his complexion, Kennedy replied matter-of-factly, "The doctors say I've got a sort of slow-motion leukemia, but they tell me I'll probably last until I'm forty-five. So I seldom think about it except when I have the shots." It developed later that he did not have Addison's disease in the classic sense —that is, as caused by tuberculosis of the adrenal glands— that he had not had tuberculosis in any form and that, with modern methods of treatment, his adrenal insufficiency, evidently induced by the physical strain of the long night of swimming and the subsequent malaria, presented no serious problem. He stopped the cortisone shots, though he continued to take corticosteroid tablets from time to time to assure the best possible protection against excessive physical stress or exertion. During those years, except when his back stopped him, he lived, between politics and athletics, a life of marked and exuberant physical activity.

Still the shadow did not leave him. In 1948 his beloved sister Kathleen was killed in a plane crash. In 1951, traveling in the Far East, he came down with a fever in Japan and was rushed to the military hospital in Okinawa. His temperature rose to more than 106 degrees, and they did not think he would live. He recovered, but then his back troubled him again. Jacqueline remembers him in their courtship as on crutches more often than not. By 1954 the pain became so incessant that he decided to try another operation—this time a lumbar fusion with a steel plate inserted in his spine. The surgeons were not sure it would help and warned it would be risky, but Kennedy, drained by the unceasing torment, said, "I don't care, I can't go on like this." If there were a reasonable chance, he was going to take it. The winter after the surgery was torture. The steel plate led to a staphylococcus infection. His condition grew worse. Last rites were pronounced, and death brushed him again. Finally a second operation removed the plate. He continued weak and in pain, lying miserably in bed, turned by nurses at regular intervals from one side to the other. After a time, he started to walk, but, just as he was beginning, one of his crutches broke, he fell and was back in bed again.

The operations did not help. They left his back weaker than ever, and Kennedy later concluded with recrimination that they had been unnecessary. In the spring of 1955 he heard about Janet Travell, a New York physician who treated certain painful muscular conditions with Novocaine. He came to her deeply skeptical about doctors but more ready than ever to try anything. His infection had not healed; he now had anemia; and the pain was constant. Dr. Travell decided that what was causing the pain was not the spine itself or the discs but the old weakness in the back muscles leading to chronic spasm. Now her Novocaine relaxed the cramps in his spinal muscles and brought quick relief. But, when daily mechanical strain was a factor in spasm, Novocaine might have only a temporary effect. Then Dr. Travell discovered that his left leg was three-quarters of an inch shorter than his right—an obvious mechanical aggravation of the weakness along his spine, but, amazingly, unnoticed by doctors up to this point. Every step he had taken for years had caused a seesaw movement in his back and increased the strain on his spinal muscles. He procured shoes with a lift on the left foot and a lowered heel on the right. He also wore a small 'brace' or belt, and, finding relief in a rocking chair in Dr. Travell's office, acquired one for himself. Various nutritional supplements ended his anemia. Dr. Travell's treatment and gentle counsel changed his life. In a surprisingly short time, he regained his old vitality and strength.

Kennedy endured all this with total stoicism. Dr. Travell found him a model patient—never resentful of his condition, always ready to follow any course which seemed reasonable to him. He once quoted Somerset Maugham—"suffering does not ennoble, it embitters"—but, if he had been embittered, he hid it absolutely. He never liked anyone to ask how he was feeling. When he was in pain, others could tell only as his manner grew a little brusque and his face white and drawn. When the pain became intolerable, he would try to get his mind off it by having friends for dinner or going to a movie—anything not to let himself just sit there suffering. Soon he began to distract himself with a larger project. He had been interested for some time in Edmund G. Ross, the Senator whose vote saved Andrew Johnson at the risk of his own career, and he now started an article on political courage which turned in the next few months into a book.

Some have compared Kennedy's illness of 1954-55 with Franklin Roosevelt's polio and suggested that these crises made them President. This is doubtful. After all, Roosevelt had helped run the Navy during a considerable war and had been a candidate for Vice-President before he came down with polio; and John Kennedy had been elected to House and Senate before he nearly died in 1955. In each case, the will and the ability were always there, and the evolution had been sure and steady. Yet Kennedy's ordeal no doubt accelerated his private crisis of identity. Like Roosevelt, he emerged better focused, more purposeful, more formidable. He conveyed a growing impression of weight and power.

It also increased a certain sense of fatalism about himself. Early in 1959 someone wrote an article—"Will the Spell Be Broken?"—pointing out that since 1840 no President elected in a year ending in zero had left the White House alive and sent a copy to everyone mentioned for the nomination the next year. Kennedy replied that he had never reflected on this bit of Americana; but if everyone took the phenomenon to heart 1600 Pennsylvania Avenue would probably have a "for rent" sign from 1960 to 1964. As for the effect this numerological revelation might have on his own plans, Kennedy wrote, "I feel that the future will have to necessarily answer this for itself—both as to my aspirations and my fate should I have the privilege of occupying the White House." On Cape Cod, in October 1953, when he returned from his wedding trip, he had read his young wife what he said was his favorite poem. She learned it for him by heart, and he used to love to have her say it. It was Alan Seeger's "I Have a Rendezvous with Death."

> It may be he shall take my hand
> And lead me into his dark land
> And close my eyes and quench my breath . . .
>
> But I've a rendezvous with Death
> At midnight in some flaming town,
> When Spring trips north again this year,
> And I to my pledged word am true,
> I shall not fail that rendezvous.

6. POLITICS AND PRIVACY

"No congressional leader of the very first rank save James Madison has been elected Pres.," Kennedy wrote in a notebook he kept during his sickness, "—and apart from Polk, Garfield, McKinley & Truman no parliamentarians of the 2nd rank."

Being a Senator was another obstacle, like being a Catholic, but I suppose that for a man who had survived the Ferguson Passage form sheets were made to be ignored. In any case, he was not investing energy in the laborious process of infiltrating the inner ring of the Senate leadership. He preserved affable relations with the club, but he was not of them. He discharged his party duties with efficiency, indulged his own interests in matters like Indochina, Algeria and the electoral college, and wondered how to pursue larger goals. He had discussed the Vice-Presidency with his father as early as 1953; and after 1956 the Presidency itself no longer seemed so far away. When Joseph Alsop suggested to him in the summer of 1958 that the vice-presidential nomination was now his for the asking, Kennedy quickly replied, "Let's not talk so much about vice. I'm against vice, in all forms."

On issues he showed himself a practical and moderate liberal, who made quiet progress on questions of labor and social welfare without trying to force the pace faster than he thought the times permitted. During the first Eisenhower term there was much discussion within the Stevenson group about national policy. I circulated a memorandum suggesting that our inherited liberalism was dominated by the special experience of the depression, that prosperity raised problems of its own and that, where the New Deal had been necessarily concerned with the stark issues of subsistence and employment, the new period called for not a 'quantitative' but a 'qualitative' liberalism, dedicated to enriching the lives people lived. The problems of qualitative liberalism, the memorandum argued, "have to do with education, medical care, civil rights, housing, civil liberties, city planning . . . with the issues which make the difference between opportunity and defeat, between frustration and fulfillment, in the everyday life of the average person." Our country, the memorandum said, "is richer than ever before, and is getting even richer every moment—but is devoting a *decreasing* share of its wealth to the common welfare."

When I sent the memorandum to Kennedy, he replied a little pessimistically that "any attempts to put forward a very advanced program of social legislation would meet with the opposition of the [Democratic] leadership." This was partly because "many members of the Democratic party in the House and Senate are in agreement on the general lines of Eisenhower's middle-of-the-road program" and partly because of "the desire of the leadership to maintain a unified party on the assumption that the Democratic Party is the stronger political party of the two and that if Eisenhower does not run then victory will be almost assured for us."

He then moved on to the question of the Lodge-Gossett amendment, which proposed that in a presidential election each state's electoral votes be divided in the proportion of the popular vote. While this proposal had a democratic ring, its effect, Kennedy thought, would be to reduce the influence of the large, urbanized states and "increase the influence of the one party states in both Democratic and Republican ranks." Kennedy was far more perceptive than most historians and political scientists in seeing the defects of this amendment; his successful fight against it the next year marked his emergence as a significant figure in the Senate. He concluded his letter by mentioning "an article I am now working on in my spare time. It is on political courage. . . ."

These were his years of concentration on politics, and he soon showed the toughness, adroitness and intuition of a master. Yet while he considered politics—in another phrase he cherished from *Pilgrim's Way*—"the greatest and most honorable adventure," took pride in his political skills, delighted in political maneuver and combat and never forgot political effects for a single second, he stood apart, in some fundamental sense, from the political game. When David Ormsby Gore visited him in the hospital, Kennedy remarked that he was not sure he was cut out to be a politician; he saw the strength of opposing arguments too well; it would be easier if he had divine certitude that he was right. In his preliminary notes for *Profiles in Courage*, he wrote of Robert A. Taft, "He was partisan in the sense that Harry Truman was—they both had the happy gift of seeing things in bright shades. It is the politicians who see things in similar shades that have a depressing and worrisome time of it."

The total politician instinctively assumed a continuum between means and ends. But it was the tension between means and ends which fascinated and bothered Kennedy. His sickness provided an unaccustomed chance to reflect on such questions; and *Profiles in Courage* represented his most sustained attempt to penetrate the moral dilemmas of the political life. "Politics is a jungle," he wrote in his notes, "—torn between doing right things & staying in office—between the local interest & the national interest—between the private good of the politician & the general good." In addition, "we have always insisted academically on an unusually high—even unattainable—standard in our political life. We consider it graft to make sure a park or road, etc., be placed near property of friends—but what do we think of admitting friends to the favored list for securities about to be offered to the less favored at a higher price? . . . Private enterprise system . . . makes OK private action which would be considered dishonest if public action."

How could people survive in the jungle? He thought the answer had something to do with that combination of toughness of fiber and courage which constituted character. In the cases of Taft and Walter George, for example, "it is not so much that they voted in a certain way that caused their influence because others voted the same way—or because of length of service—or because of areas of origin—though all had something to do with it. But mostly it was character—& the impression they gave—which all great

and successful Parl. leaders have given—that they had
something in their minds besides the next election. They
were not cynical." He concluded: "Everyone admires courage & the greenest garlands are for those who possess it."

Gradually there evolved a sense of his own identity as a
political man, compounded of his growing mastery of the
political arts and, even more, of his growing understanding
that, for better or worse, his public self had to be faithful
to his private self. This second point may sound like something less than a blinding revelation. But it takes many
politicians a long time to acquire it. Some never do, always
hoping to persuade the voters that they are different from
what they are. "No man, for any considerable period,"
Hawthorne once wrote, "can wear one face to himself, and
another to the multitude, without finally getting bewildered
as to which may be the true." Kennedy was prepared to
settle for his own face—and no doubt was encouraged to do
so by his own cool evaluation of the alternatives. One day
his father asked him why he wanted to take on the appalling burden of the Presidency. "These things have always been done by men," Kennedy said, "and they can be
done by men now." As he looked around him, the others
who yearned to assume the burden did not seem to him
conspicuously better qualified than himself.

The process of internal definition went on in other ways,
and Jacqueline Kennedy made her own contribution to it.
She must at first have been overwhelmed by the life into
which marriage plunged her. Politics had been for her
corny old men shouting on the Fourth of July, at least
until the advent of Stevenson; his was the first political
voice to whom she listened. And, once in this new world,
she found it hard to get used to the ground rules. Her
husband sometimes came home irritated by the action of
a fellow politician. Jacqueline, concluding that this man
was an enemy, would glare across the room when she met
him. Then Jack would speak agreeably about him, and she
would exclaim, "Are you saying nice things about X? I've
been hating him for three weeks." Her husband would
reply, "No, no, that was three weeks ago. Now he has done
Y." He would tell her that in politics you rarely had friends
or foes, only colleagues, and that you should never get in
so deep a quarrel as to lose all chance of conciliation; you
might need to work with the other fellow later.

The teeming world of the Kennedys was another problem. Jacqueline had to fight to preserve her own identity in
this family of active parents-in-law, athletic, teasing broth-

ers-in-law, energetic, competent sisters-in-law. There often seemed no point in trying to compete in politics, any more than in touch football; and she sometimes carried her self-defense to inordinate extremes, as when she would pretend a total ignorance about politics or impose a social ban on politicians. Like all marriages, this one may have had its early strains. Their life together was almost nomadic, shuttling back and forth from Washington to Boston, from Newport to Palm Beach, living often with parents-in-law. They did not really have a house of their own until they had been married four years and their first child was born. Jacqueline often feared that she was a political liability and that everyone considered her a snob from Newport who had bouffant hair and French clothes and hated politics. Some of Kennedy's supporters did feel this way in 1960, but he never mentioned it to her and never asked her to change. He was never worried; he loved her as she was. More and more she embodied something of increasing value for him—a surcease from daily business, a standard of excellence, a symbol of privacy, a style of life.

This was partly because she proved able to extend his knowledge and sensibility. Before they were married, he had her translate and summarize ten or a dozen French books about Indochina; she was then living in the Auchincloss house in Virginia and labored late into hot summer nights to finish the assignment. When she read aloud passages from de Gaulle's *Memoires*, especially the introductory evocation of his image of France, he seized the idea for his own speeches about America. Whatever concerned her interested him, and often he would soon know more about it than she did. But perhaps her greatest influence was to confirm his feelings about the importance of living his life according to the values he honored most. He was determined not to let his public role stunt or stifle his inner existence. At Hyannis Port in August 1960, after the succession of party leaders had paid their respects to their new candidate for President, Kennedy drew one day at lunch a distinction between the totally absorbed professional, for whom politics was the whole of life, and those who enjoyed the game and art of politics but preserved a measure of detachment from it. Jacqueline remarked of some of their visitors that their private faces were completely suppressed by the public face. She had asked one political wife, "What have you been doing since the convention?" expecting her to say, "Oh dear, I've just been resting up since that madhouse" or something of the sort.

Instead the reply came: "I've been writing letters to all those good people who were so helpful to my husband." "It was," Jackie said, "as if they were on television all the time."

Kennedy's determination to defend his privacy was crucial; for it permitted the inner self, so voracious for experience and for knowledge, so intent on reason and result, so admiring of grace and elegance, to ripen into free and confident maturity—and to renew and replenish the public self. By holding part of himself back from politics, he opened himself to fresh ideas and purpose. I do not mean to imply that he ever condescended to politics. His highest hope was to inspire the young with a lofty sense of the political mission. But politics was not the be-all and end-all; and because, with his wife's complicity, he declined to yield himself entirely to it, he was able to charge it with creativity.

7. THE KENNEDY MIND: I

Kennedy was called an intellectual very seldom before 1960 and very often thereafter—a phenomenon which deserves explanation.

One cannot be sure what an intellectual is; but let us define it as a person whose primary habitat is the realm of ideas. In this sense, exceedingly few political leaders are authentic intellectuals, because the primary habitat of the political leader is the world of power. Yet the world of power itself has its intellectual and anti-intellectual sides. Some political leaders find exhilaration in ideas and in the company of those whose trade it is to deal with them. Others are rendered uneasy by ideas and uncomfortable by intellectuals.

Kennedy belonged supremely to the first class. He was a man of action who could pass easily over to the realm of ideas and confront intellectuals with perfect confidence in his capacity to hold his own. His mind was not prophetic, impassioned, mystical, ontological, utopian or ideological. It was less exuberant than Theodore Roosevelt's, less scholarly than Wilson's, less adventurous than Franklin Roosevelt's. But it had its own salient qualities—it was objective, practical, ironic, skeptical, unfettered and insatiable.

It was marked first of all, as he had noted to Jacqueline, by inexhaustible curiosity. Kennedy always wanted to know how things worked. Vague answers never contented him. This curiosity was fed by conversation but even more by reading. His childhood consolation had become an adult compulsion. He was now a fanatical reader, 1200 words a minute, not only at the normal times and places but at meals, in the bathtub, sometimes even when walking. Dressing in the morning, he would prop open a book on his bureau and read while he put on his shirt and tied his necktie. He read mostly history and biography, American and English. The first book he ever gave Jacqueline was the life of a Texan, Marquis James's biography of Sam Houston, *The Raven.* In addition to *Pilgrim's Way, Marlborough* and *Melbourne,* he particularly liked Herbert Agar's *The Price of Union,* Samuel Flagg Bemis's *John Quincy Adams* Allan Nevins's *The Emergence of Lincoln,* Margaret Coit's *Calhoun* and Duff Cooper's *Talleyrand.* He read poetry only occasionally—Shakespeare and Byron are quoted in the looseleaf notebook he kept in 1945–46—and by this time fiction hardly at all. His wife does not remember him reading novels except for two or three Ian Fleming thrillers, though Kennedy himself listed *The Red and the Black* among his favorite books and, at some point in his life, had read most of Hemingway and a smattering of contemporary fiction—at least *The Deer Park, The Fires of Spring* and *The Ninth Wave.* His supposed addiction to James Bond was partly a publicity gag, like Franklin Roosevelt's supposed affection for "Home on the Range." Kennedy seldom read for distraction. He did not want to waste a single second.

He read partly for information, partly for comparison, partly for insight, partly for the sheer joy of felicitous statement. He delighted particularly in quotations which distilled the essence of an argument. He is, so far as I know, the only politician who ever quoted Madame de Staël on Meet the Press. Some quotations he carried verbatim in his mind. Others he noted down. The looseleaf notebook of 1945–46 contained propositions from Aeschylus ("In war, truth is the first casualty"), Isocrates ("Where there are a number of laws drawn up with great exactitude, it is a proof that the city is badly administered; for the inhabitants are compelled to frame laws in great numbers as a barrier against offenses"), Dante ("The hottest places in Hell are reserved for those who, in a period of moral crisis, maintain their neutrality"), Falkland ("When it is not necessary to change it is necessary not to change"), Burke ("Our patience will achieve more than our force"), Jefferson ("Widespread poverty and concentrated wealth cannot long endure side by side in a democracy"), de Maistre ("In all political systems there are relationships which it is wiser to leave undefined"), Jackson ("Individuals must give up a share of liberty to

preserve the rest"), Webster ("A general equality of condition is the true basis, most certainly, of democracy"), Mill
("One person with a belief is a social power equal to
ninety-nine who have only interest"), Lincoln ("Public opinion is everything. With it nothing can fail, without it nothing
can succeed"), Huck Finn on *Pilgrim's Progress* ("The statements are interesting—but steep"), Chesterton ("Don't ever
take a fence down until you know the reason why it was
put up"), Brandeis ("Unless our financial leaders are capable of progress, the institutions which they are trying to
conserve will lose their foundation"), Colonel House ("The
best politics is to do the right thing"), Churchill ("The whole
history of the world is summed up in the fact that, when
nations are strong, they are not always just, and when they
wish to be just, they are often no longer strong. . . . Let
us have this blessed union of power and justice"), Lippmann ("The political art deals with matters peculiar to
politics, with a complex of material circumstances, of historic deposit, of human passion, for which the problems of
business or engineering do not provide an analogy"), Hindu
proverbs ("I had no shoes—and I murmured until I met a
man who had no feet"), Joseph P. Kennedy ("More men
die of jealousy than cancer") and even John F. Kennedy:

> To be a positive force for the public good in politics one
> must have three things; a solid moral code governing his
> public actions, a broad knowledge of our institutions and
> traditions and a specific background in the technical prob-
> lems of government, and lastly he must have political ap-
> peal—the gift of winning public confidence and support.

There emerges from such quotations the impression of a
moderate and dispassionate mind, committed to the arts of
government, persuaded of the inevitability of change but
distrustful of comprehensive plans and grandiose abstractions, skeptical of excess but admiring of purpose, determined above all to be effective.

His intelligence was fundamentally secular, or so it
seemed to me. Of course, this was not entirely true. As
Mary McCarthy wrote in her *Memories of a Catholic Girl-
hood*, "If you are born and brought up a Catholic, you have
absorbed a great deal of world history and the history of
ideas before you are twelve, and it is like learning a language early; the effect is indelible." Though Kennedy spent
only one year of his life in a Catholic school, he assimi-
lated a good deal of the structure of the faith, encouraged
probably by his mother and sisters. He often adopted the
Catholic side in historical controversy, as in the case of
Mary Queen of Scots; and he showed a certain weakness

for Catholic words of art, like 'prudence,' and a certain aversion toward bad words for Catholics, like 'liberal.' Nor could one doubt his devotion to his Church or the occasional solace he found in mass.

Yet he remains, as John Cogley has suggested, the first President who was a Roman Catholic rather than the first Roman Catholic President. Intellectual Catholicism in American politics has ordinarily taken two divergent forms, of which Senator Thomas J. Dodd of Connecticut and Senator Eugene McCarthy of Minnesota were contemporary representatives. Kennedy was different from either. Unlike Dodd, he lived far away from the world of the Holy Name Societies, Knights of Columbus and communion breakfasts. He discussed the princes of the American Church with the same irreverent candor with which he discussed the bosses of the Democratic party. When a dispatch from Rome during the 1960 campaign suggested Vatican doubts about his views of the proper relationship between church and state, Kennedy said, "Now I understand why Henry VIII set up his own church." His attitude toward life showed no traces of the black-and-white moralism, the pietistic rhetoric, the clericalism, the anti-intellectualism, the prudery, the fear of Protestant society, which had historically characterized parts of the Irish Catholic community in America. On the other hand, he did not, like Eugene McCarthy, seek to rescue Catholic doctrine from fundamentalism and demonstrate its relevance to the modern world. Catholic intellectuals recognized his indifference to the scholastic tradition, and some disdained him for it.

Kennedy's religion was humane rather than doctrinal. He was a Catholic as Franklin Roosevelt was an Episcopalian— because he was born into the faith, lived in it and expected to die in it. One evening at the White House he argued with considerable particularity that nine of the ten commandments were derived from nature and almost seemed to imply that all religion was so derived. He had little knowledge of or interest in the Catholic dogmatic tradition. He once wrote Cogley, "It is hard for a Harvard man to answer questions in theology. I imagine my answers will cause heartburn at Fordham and B. C. [Boston College]." One can find little organic intellectual connection between his faith and his politics. His social thought hardly resulted from a determination to apply the principles of *Rerum Novarum* to American life. He felt an immense sense of fellowship with Pope John XXIII, but this was based more on the Pope's practical character and policies than on theological considerations. Some of his Protestant advisers probably knew the encyclicals better than he did. Once during the 1960 campaign I handed him a speech draft with the comment that it was perhaps too Catholic. He said with a smile, "You Unitarians"—meaning Sorensen and myself —"keep writing Catholic speeches. I guess I am the only Protestant around here."

Still, his basic attitude was wholly compatible with the sophisticated theology of Jesuits like Father John Courtney Murray, whom he greatly admired. In the notebook he kept during his sickness, he wrote down some lines from Barbara Ward: "What disturbs the Communist rulers is not the phraseology of religion, the lip-service that may be paid to it, or the speeches and declarations made in its favor. . . . Religion which is a mere adjunct of individual purpose is a religion that even the Soviets can tolerate. What they fear is a religion that transcends frontiers and can challenge the purpose and performance of the nation-state." This was not in the mid-fifties the typical attitude of American Catholics; but, if Kennedy was not a typical American Catholic, his example helped create the progressive and questing American Catholicism of the sixties. Above all, he showed that there need be no conflict between Catholicism and modernity, no bar to full Catholic participation in American society.

His detachment from traditional American Catholicism was part of the set of detachments—detachment from middle-class parochialism, detachment from the business ethos, detachment from ritualistic liberalism—which gave his perceptions their peculiar coolness, freshness and freedom, and which also led those expecting commitments of a more familiar sort to condemn him as uncommitted. In fact, he was intensely committed to a vision of America and the world, and committed with equal intensity to the use of reason and power to achieve that vision. This became apparent after he was President; and this accounts in part for the sudden realization that, far from being just a young man in a hurry, a hustler for personal authority, a Processed Politician, he was, as politicians go, an intellectual and one so peculiarly modern that it took orthodox intellectuals a little time before they began to understand him.

Another reason for the change in the intellectuals' theory of Kennedy was their gradual recognition of his desire to bring the world of power and the world of ideas together in alliance—or rather, as he himself saw it, to restore the collaboration between the two worlds which had marked the early republic. He was fascinated by the Founding Fa-

thers and liked to harass historians by demanding that they
explain how a small and underdeveloped nation could have
produced men of such genius. He was particularly fascinated by the way the generation of the Founders united
the instinct for ideas and the instinct for responsibility.
"Our nation's first great politicians," he wrote, "—those
who presided at its birth in 1776 and at its christening in
1787—included among their ranks most of the nation's first
great writers and scholars." But today

> the gap between the intellectual and politician seems to be
> growing. . . . today this link is all but gone. Where are the
> scholar-statesmen? The American politician of today is fear-
> ful, if not scornful, of entering the literary world with the
> courage of a Beveridge. And the American author and scholar
> of today is reluctant, if not disdainful, about entering the
> political world with the enthusiasm of a Woodrow Wilson.

His summons to the scholar-statesman went largely unnoticed by the intellectual community in the fifties, perhaps because he chose such improbable forums as *Vogue*
and a Harvard Commencement. Only when he began as
President to put his proposition into practice did the intellectual community take a fresh look at him.

8. THE KENNEDY MIND: II

The character of his reading and quoting emphasizes, I
think, the historical grain of his intelligence. Kennedy was
in many respects an historian manqué. The historical mind
can be analytical, or it can be romantic. The best historians
are both, Kennedy among them. *Why England Slept*, with its
emphasis on impersonal forces, expressed one side; *Profiles in Courage*, with its emphasis on heroes, expressed the
other. But, even in his most romantic mood, Kennedy never
adopted a good-guys *vs.* bad-guys theory of history. He may
have been a Whig,[2] but he was not a Whig historian. He
had both the imagination and the objectivity which enabled
him to see the point in lost causes, even in enemy fana-
ticisms. In a review of Liddell Hart's *Deterrent or Defense*
in 1960, he praised the author's credo: "Keep strong, if
possible. In any case, keep cool. Have unlimited patience.
Never corner an opponent, and always assist him to save his
face. Put yourself in his shoes—so as to see things through
his eyes. Avoid self-righteousness like the devil—nothing

[2] In the English sense, that is; in the American sense of believing in a
strong Congress and a weak executive, he often emphasized to James
MacGregor Burns and others, "I am no Whig!"

is so self-blinding." Liddell Hart was addressing these remarks to statesmen; they work just as well for historians.

Kennedy rarely lost sight of other people's motives and
problems. For all the presumed coolness on the surface,
he had an instinctive tendency to put himself into the skins
of others. Once during the 1960 campaign, Kennedy, returning to New York City on a Sunday night from a visit
with Mrs. Roosevelt in Hyde Park, dropped in at Voisin's
for dinner with a couple of friends. At a neighboring table,
a man obviously drunk, began in a low but penetrating
voice to direct a stream of unprintable comments at him.
Kennedy's companions raised their own voices in the hope
that he would not hear, but to no avail. Finally one made
a motion to call the headwaiter. Kennedy laid a hand on
his sleeve and said, "No, don't bother. Think how the fellow's wife must be feeling." His friend looked and saw her
flushed with embarrassment. He later reacted with comparable dispassion to de Gaulle and Khrushchev.

He liked to quote Lincoln: "There are few things wholly
evil or wholly good. Almost everything, especially of Government policy, is an inseparable compound of the two, so
that our best judgment of the preponderance between them
is continually demanded." When something had enough
steam behind it to move people and make an impression
on history, it must have some rational explanation, and
Kennedy wanted to know what that rational explanation
was. The response of the fifties that it was all a struggle
between good and evil never satisfied him.

But it was not a case of *tout comprendre, tout pardonner*.
Though he saw the human struggle, not as a moralist, but
as an historian, even as an ironist, irony was never permitted to sever the nerve of action. His mind was forever
critical; but his thinking always retained the cutting edge
of decision. When he was told something, he wanted to
know what he could do about it. He was pragmatic in the
sense that he tested the meaning of a proposition by its consequences; he was also pragmatic in the sense of being free
from metaphysics. In his response, too, to the notion of a
pluralist universe, Kennedy was a pragmatist—if one may
make sensible use of this word, which came into political
vogue in the first years of the Kennedy administration and
then was oddly revived in the first years of the Johnson
administration with the implication that the Kennedy years
had not, after all, been pragmatic but were somehow ideological. They were not ideological, though they could perhaps be termed intellectual.

The historical mind is rarely ideological—and, when it

becomes so, it is at the expense of history. Whether analytical or romantic, it is committed to existence, not to essence. Kennedy was bored by abstractions. He never took ideology very seriously, certainly not as a means of interpreting history and even not as part of the material of history. If he did not go the distance with de Gaulle in reducing everything to national tradition and national interest, he tended to give greater weight in thinking about world affairs to national than to ideological motives. Like de Gaulle, but unlike the ideological interpreters of the cold war, he was not surprised by the split between Russia and China.

If historic conflicts infrequently pitted total good against total evil, then they infrequently concluded in total victory or total defeat. Seeing the past with an historian's eyes, Kennedy knew that ideals and institutions were stubborn, and that change took place more often by accommodation than by annihilation. His cult of courage was in this sense ethical rather than political; he saw the courage of "unyielding devotion to absolute principle" as the moral fulfillment of the individual rather than as necessarily the best way of running a government. Indeed, he took pains to emphasize in *Profiles* that politicians could also demonstrate courage "through their acceptance of compromise, through their advocacy of conciliation, through their willingness to replace conflict with co-operation." Senators who go down to defeat in vain defense of a single principle "will not be on hand to fight for that or any other principle in the future." One felt here an echo of St. Thomas: "Prudence applies principles to particular issues; consequently it does not establish moral purpose, but contrives the means thereto."

The application of principle requires both moral and intellectual insight. Kennedy had an unusual capacity to weigh the complexities of judgment—in part because of the complexities of his own perceptions. The contrast in *Profiles* between the courage of compromise and the courage of principle expressed, for example, a tension deep within Kennedy—a tension between the circumspection of his political instinct and the radicalism of his intellectual impulse; so too the contrast between the historical determinism, the deprecation of the individual and the passive view of leadership implied in *Why England Slept* and the demand in *Profiles* that the politician be prepared, on the great occasions, to "meet the challenge of courage, whatever may be the sacrifices he faces if he follows his conscience." All this expressed the interior strain between Kennedy's sense of human limitation and his sense of hope, between his skepticism about man and his readiness to say, "Man can be as big as he wants. No problem of human destiny is beyond human beings."

All these things, coexisting within him, enabled others to find in him what qualities they wanted. They could choose one side of him or the other and claim him, according to taste, as a conservative, because of his sober sense of the frailty of man, the power of institutions and the frustrations of history, or as a progressive, because of his vigorous confidence in reason, action and the future. Yet within Kennedy himself these tensions achieved reunion and reconciliation. He saw history in its massive movements as shaped by forces beyond man's control. But he felt that there were still problems which man could resolve; and in any case, whether man could resolve these problems or not, the obligation was to carry on the struggle of existence. It was in essence, Richard Goodwin later suggested, the Greek view where the hero must poise himself against the gods and, even with knowledge of the futility of the fight, press on to the end of his life until he meets his tragic fate.

9. THE CONTEMPORARY MAN

After Kennedy's death, Adlai Stevenson called him the "contemporary man." His youth, his vitality, his profound modernity—these were final elements in his power and potentiality as he stood on the brink of the Presidency. For Kennedy was not only the first President to be born in the twentieth century. More than that, he was the first representative in the White House of a distinctive generation, the generation which was born during the First World War, came of age during the depression, fought in the Second World War and began its public career in the atomic age.

This was the first generation to grow up as the age of American innocence was coming to an end. To have been born nearly a decade earlier, like Lyndon Johnson, or nearly two decades earlier, like Adlai Stevenson, was to be rooted in another and simpler America. Scott Fitzgerald had written that his contemporaries grew up "to find all gods dead, all wars fought, all faiths in man shaken." But the generation which came back from the Second World War found that gods, wars and faiths in man had, after all, survived, if in queer and somber ways. The realities of the twentieth century which had shocked their fathers now wove the fabric of their own lives. Instead of reveling in being a lost generation, they set out in one mood or another to find, if not themselves, a still point in the turning world. The predicament was even worse for the generation which had been too young to fight the war, too young to recall the age of innocence, the generation which had experienced nothing but turbulence. So in the fifties some sought security at the expense of identity and became organization men. Others sought identity at the expense of security and became beatniks. Each course created only a partial man. There was need for a way of life, a way of autonomy, between past and present, the organization man and the anarchist, the square and the beat.

It was autonomy which this humane and self-sufficient man seemed to embody. Kennedy simply could not be reduced to the usual complex of sociological generalizations. He was Irish, Catholic, New England, Harvard, Navy, Palm Beach, Democrat and so on; but no classification contained him. He had wrought an individuality which carried him beyond the definitions of class and race, region and religion. He was a free man, not just in the sense of the cold-war cliché, but in the sense that he was, as much as man can be, self-determined and not the servant of forces outside him.

This sense of wholeness and freedom gave him an extraordinary appeal not only to his own generation but even more to those who came after, the children of turbulence. Recent history had washed away the easy consolations and the old formulas. Only a few things remained on which contemporary man could rely, and most were part of himself—family, friendship, courage, reason, jokes, power, patriotism. Kennedy demonstrated the possibility of the new self-reliance. As he had liberated himself from the past, so he had liberated himself from the need to rebel against the past. He could insist on standards, admire physical courage, attend his church, love his father while disagreeing with him, love his country without self-doubt or self-consciousness. Yet, while absorbing so much of the traditional code, his sensibility was acutely contemporaneous. He voiced the disquietude of the postwar generation —the mistrust of rhetoric, the disdain for pomposity, the impatience with the postures and pieties of other days, the resignation to disappointment. And he also voiced the new generation's longings—for fulfillment in experience, for the subordination of selfish impulses to higher ideals, for a link between past and future, for adventure and valor and honor. What was forbidden were poses, histrionics, the heart on the sleeve and the tongue on the cliché. What was required was a tough, nonchalant acceptance of the harsh present and an open mind toward the unknown future.

This was Kennedy, with his deflationary wartime understatement (when asked how he became a hero, he said, "It was involuntary. They sank my boat"); his contempt for demagoguery (once during the campaign, after Kennedy had disappointed a Texas crowd by his New England restraint, Bill Attwood suggested that next time he wave his arms in the air like other politicians; Kennedy shook his head and wrote—he was saving his voice—"I always swore one thing I'd never do is—" and drew a picture of a man waving his arms in the air); his freedom from dogma, his appetite for responsibility, his instinct for novelty, his awareness and irony and control; his imperturbable sureness in his own powers, not because he considered himself infallible, but because, given the fallibility of all men, he supposed he could do the job as well as anyone else; his love of America and pride in its traditions and ideals.

Of course there was an element of legerdemain in all this. Every politician has to fake a little, and Kennedy was a politician determined to become President. He was prepared to do many things, to cut corners, to exploit people and situations, to "go go go," even to merchandise himself. But many things he would not do, phrases he would not use, people he would not exploit (never a "Jackie and I"). Even his faking had to stay within character. This sense of a personality under control, this insistence on distancing himself from displays of emotion, led some to think him indifferent or unfeeling. But only the unwary could really suppose that his 'coolness' was because he felt too little. It was because he felt too much and had to compose himself for an existence filled with disorder and despair. During his Presidency, when asked about the demobilization of the reserves after the Berlin crisis, he said, "There is always an inequity in life. Some men are killed in a war and some men are wounded, and some men never leave the country. . . . Life is unfair." He said this, not with bitterness, but with the delicate knowledge of one who lives in a bitter time—a knowledge which stamped him as a son of that time. His charm and grace were not an uncovenanted gift. The Kennedy style was the triumph, hard-bought and well-earned, of a gallant and collected human being over the anguish of life.

His 'coolness' was itself a new frontier. It meant freedom from the stereotyped responses of the past. It promised the deliverance of American idealism, buried deep in the national character but imprisoned by the knowingness and calculation of American society in the fifties. It held out to the young the possibility that they could become more than satisfied stockholders in a satisfied nation. It offered hope for spontaneity in a country drowning in its own passivity —passive because it had come to accept the theory of its own impotence. This was what Norman Mailer caught at Los Angeles in 1960—Kennedy's existential quality, the sense that he was in some way beyond conventional politics, that he could touch emotions and hopes thwarted by the bland and mechanized society. Unlike the other candidates, Mailer wrote, Kennedy was "mysterious." He had "the wisdom of a man who senses death within him and gambles that he can cure it by risking his life." Even his youth, his handsomeness, the beauty of his wife—these were not accidental details but necessary means of inciting the American imagination. With Kennedy, Mailer thought, there was a chance that "we as a nation would finally be loose again in the historic seas of a national psyche which was willy-nilly and at last, again, adventurous." The only question was whether the nation would be "brave enough to enlist the romantic dream of itself . . . vote for the image of the mirror of its unconscious." This was the question, I believe, which frightened the nation when it began to fall away from Kennedy in the last days before the election.

Mailer soon repudiated his portrait when, as he later complained at interminable length, Kennedy personally let him down by declining to become the hipster as President. Yet there can be no doubt that Kennedy's magic was not alone that of wealth and youth and good looks, or even of these things joined to intelligence and will. It was, more than this, the hope that he could redeem American politics by releasing American life from its various bondages to orthodoxy.

No man could have fulfilled this hope, and Kennedy certainly did not. He himself regarded the Mailer essay with skeptical appreciation.[3] He knew that as a President of the United States he had no choice but to work within the structure of government and politics—though he did not yet know how beautifully that structure was organized to pre-

---

[3] Richard Goodwin showed him Mailer's piece after it appeared in *Esquire*. Later he asked what Kennedy thought of it. Kennedy replied enigmatically, "It really runs on, doesn't it?"

vent anything from happening. What Mailer left out was the paradox of power—that the exercise of power is necessary to fulfill purpose, yet the world of power dooms many purposes to frustration. Nonetheless the Mailer rhapsody conveys something of the exhilaration which accompanied the start of the Kennedy Presidency. The Presidency itself would show how national vitality could in fact be released —not in an existential orgasm but in the halting progression of ideas and actions which make up the fabric of history.

V

GATHERING OF THE FORCES

CAPE COD IS NEVER MORE POIGNANT than in the last still blue and gold of autumn. The November sun is luminous, the sky and sea are aquamarine, and the light is the light of Greece. It was one of those translucent days on the third day after election when my wife and I drove down from Cambridge to Hyannis Port for luncheon.

The frenzy of August had gone, though people stood in quiet clusters at each end of the Kennedy block on Irving Avenue. The compound itself was tranquil and secluded in the drowsy sunlight. The Kennedys were out for a stroll on the dunes. In a moment they returned, Jack in tweed jacket, sweater and slacks, hatless and tieless, swinging a cane and looking fit and jaunty, and Jacqueline, her hair slightly blown in the breeze, glowing in beauty from the walk. One could only think: What a wildly attractive young couple. It took another minute to remember that this was the President-elect of the United States and his wife.

We sat in the living room and, except for Kennedy, sipped Bloody Marys while we chatted about the election. Jackie said, "I cast only one vote—for Jack. It is a rare thing to be able to vote for one's husband for President of the United States, and I didn't want to dilute it by voting for anyone else." Kennedy at this stage seemed more perplexed than bothered by the narrowness of his victory. He attributed the thin margin to the prevailing sense of prosperity and peace—people did not realize how precarious both were—and to anti-Catholic sentiment. He was particu-

larly surprised by the result in Ohio. "Cuyahoga County
just didn't produce what we counted on," he said. "I can
carry states like that only when I come out of the cities
with a big margin." As for New York, he declared himself
thoroughly fed up with the organization and especially with
Mike Prendergast, the state chairman, and Carmine DeSapio,
the leader of Tammany Hall. They had refused, despite previous assurances to him, to permit Governor Lehman and
Mrs. Roosevelt to speak at the meeting at the Coliseum the
Saturday before election; and they had done their best to
keep him away from the rally put on that day by the reform Democrats. So far as he was concerned, he said, he
was through with them.

But the campaign did not detain him long. What concerned him as we went in for lunch was the Presidency.
He brandished a collection of memoranda on the issues of
transition prepared, he said, by Clark Clifford and "Professor Neustadt of Columbia." These papers were "shrewd and
helpful," he said, but the hardest problem of all would be
"people"—finding the right men for the right jobs. He
wished Galbraith and me to collect our Cambridge ideas
and send them along to Sargent Shriver, whom he had
asked to take charge of recruitment. He named four men
he particularly wanted in important positions—Orville Freeman and Mennen Williams, Frank Coffin of Maine and
George McGovern of South Dakota. He meant to build up
the job of American Ambassador to NATO and wondered
whether Thomas K. Finletter might be interested. He expressed concern over the downward turn in Latin America:
would Adolf Berle be the man to undertake advance planning on hemisphere policy? (All these names, of course,
were well calculated to appeal to a liberal guest.) He mentioned Stevenson only to say that he looked forward to receiving his foreign policy report. He solicited opinions about
a variety of people without disclosing his intentions toward
them.

The time passed lightly and quickly. The Kennedys were
leaving in the afternoon for Palm Beach. After luncheon
his father and mother came in while the President-elect
and his wife went upstairs to change for the trip. The
Ambassador talked beguilingly about present and past. In a
few moments, the younger Kennedys reappeared, and we
all waved them off to the airfield.

1. PLANNING FOR POWER

Kennedy had a clear view of the kind of President he meant

to be. Early in 1960 in a speech at the National Press Club he had sharply rejected a "restricted concept of the Presidency." The Chief Executive, Kennedy said, must be "the vital center of action in our whole scheme of government." The nature of the office demanded that "the President place himself in the very thick of the fight, that he care passionately about the fate of the people he leads, that he be willing to serve them at the risk of incurring their momentary displeasure . . . [that he] be prepared to exercise the fullest powers of his office—all that are specified and some that are not."

He was determined to be a strong President—and this meant for him, I believe, a President in the manner of Franklin Roosevelt. Kennedy was by no means an F.D.R. idolator. I think that he considered Roosevelt's policies, especially in foreign affairs, sometimes slapdash and sentimental. But he admired Roosevelt's ability to articulate the latent idealism of America, and he greatly envied Roosevelt's capacity to dominate a sprawling government filled with strong men eager to go into business on their own. He had mentioned to me a number of times the account of Roosevelt's fluid administrative methods in the last section of *The Coming of the New Deal*. The interregnum was now to provide a first test of Kennedy's own executive instincts and, in particular, of his skill in defending his personal authority against people striving, always for the best of motives, to contract his scope for choice.

The Twentieth Amendment left him only ten weeks to take command of the machinery of government. George W. Norris had designed this amendment to end the constitutional anomaly which could permit a President and Congress to wield power for a period of four months after the electorate had repudiated them in the November election. By shifting the inauguration from March 4 to January 20, the amendment eliminated the lame-duck Congress and nearly halved the tenure of a lame-duck President. But it also nearly halved the time afforded the incoming President to recover from the campaign, reassure his vanquished opponents, select the top officers of his administration and work out his legislative program.

This effect of the amendment had been obscured by the fact that, between its ratification in 1933 and the election of 1960, only one interregnum had involved the transfer of power from one party to the other. But early in 1960, the Brookings Institution, concerned by the casualness of interregnal procedures and remembering the troubles of

1952, set up a committee to study presidential transitions. James Rowe, who was a member of the Brookings group, wrote Kennedy a fortnight after Los Angeles urging him to anticipate his post-election tasks. "You should—now—'cut' some person 'out of the herd' in whom you have real confidence," Rowe suggested, "who should devote himself to lining up these most difficult budget and staffing problems." Rowe proposed Don K. Price and David Bell of the Harvard School of Public Administration as possibilities. Later, when he went to Hyannis Port with Lyndon Johnson, Rowe discussed the matter with Kennedy, who liked the idea but wanted to assign the responsibility to someone he knew personally. He mentioned James M. Landis. Rowe observed that Landis's experience had been with regulatory agencies rather than with the executive branch. Kennedy then suggested Clark Clifford.

In Washington a few days later, Kennedy asked Clifford out to Georgetown for breakfast. Clifford, who had become an enormously successful Washington lawyer after his years with Truman, was a man of unusual ability and discretion, concealing a sharp and quick mind under a big-man-on-campus exterior. Kennedy had known him for a decade as a friend and also as a lawyer. When Drew Pearson said on television that Kennedy had not written *Profiles in Courage*, Kennedy turned over his collection of notes and drafts to Clifford; and Clifford obtained the retraction. Clifford's support of Symington before Los Angeles had not interrupted his friendship with Kennedy, nor even his services as Kennedy's counsel.

Kennedy began by asking Clifford to describe the campaign of 1948. He had heard enough, he said, about 1952 and 1956; now he wanted to hear about an election which the Democrats won. Clifford obliged, and for two hours they discussed how Truman had passed his miracle a dozen years earlier. Then Kennedy said he had one other thing on his mind: "If I am elected, I don't want to wake up on the morning of November 9 and have to ask myself, 'What in the world do I do now?'" His own experience and that of his staff, he pointed out, had been on the legislative side. He needed someone to analyze the problems of taking over the executive branch, and he thought that Clifford, with his White House background, would be ideal. Clifford, impressed by Kennedy's foresight, promptly accepted the assignment. Kennedy did not mention the matter to him again before the election.

Clifford began to attend the meetings of the Brookings group. He also discussed transition problems with an associate from Truman days, Richard Neustadt, a political scientist who had worked in the Bureau of the Budget and later as a Special Assistant in the White House before becoming a professor at Columbia. Neustadt shared Clifford's concern about the interregnum. Both remembered all too well the lost weeks after the triumph of 1948 when Truman went off to Key West and, in his absence, congressional leaders made bargains with interest groups which deprived him of control over his own legislative program. To his practical experience in government Neustadt added an acute and original approach to the theory of government organization. His interest in the facts rather than the forms of power had already done much to emancipate the study of public administration from its faith in organization charts as descriptions of operating reality. He had summed up his viewpoint in a searching essay on the politics of leadership called *Presidential Power*, published the previous April.

By the time Clifford spoke to him, however, Neustadt had already been tapped by Senator Henry Jackson, the chairman of the Democratic National Committee, for a post-election assignment. Jackson, who was also chairman of the Senate Subcommittee on National Security Staffing and Operations, was alarmed by testimony indicating that Eisenhower, as his bequest to the nation, might propose changes in the organization of the Presidency, especially the institution of a team of grand viziers to be called the First Secretary and the Executive Assistant to the President. In order to combat such proposals, Jackson had asked Neustadt to prepare a memorandum on the problems of change-over for the new President.

Neustadt completed "Organizing the Transition" by September 15. Three days later Jackson took him out to Georgetown to meet Kennedy. Kennedy, sitting in his garden, flipped through the twenty pages of the memorandum in his usual manner. He liked it at once, and it is easy to see why. The presentation was crisp and methodical, with a numbered list of specific problems and actions. It began by questioning campaign talk about "another Hundred Days"—a warning which must have inspired Kennedy, embarrassed by rhetorical excess, with confidence in the sobriety of the memorandum's author. It constantly stressed the importance of flexibility. The President's requirements for his personal staff, for example, *"cannot be fully under-*

stood, or met, until they have been experienced." Kennedy, moreover, was probably pleased to have a professor get into the act. At any rate, he told Neustadt to elaborate his argument in further memoranda. "When you finish," he said, "I want you to get the material back directly to me. I don't want you to send it to anybody else." Neustadt asked, "How do you want me to relate to Clark Clifford?" Kennedy replied quickly, "I don't want you to relate to Clark Clifford. I can't afford to confine myself to one set of advisers. If I did that, *I* would be on *their* leading strings." Once Kennedy said that, the author of *Presidential Power* was thereafter on *his* leading strings.

Neustadt went back to Columbia and set to work. Toward the end of October he received a phone call from Fred Holborn of Kennedy's office asking how he was doing. Kennedy often used Holborn, a Harvard political scientist and the son of a distinguished Yale historian, for contacts he wanted to keep out of the hands of his main staff. A few days later Holborn called again, asking Neustadt to join the Kennedy party at Norfolk, Virginia. On November 4, Neustadt duly appeared and went along on one of those frantic campaign days which began in Virginia, paused in Ohio, and concluded with a great rally at the Chicago Auditorium. In Toledo he was told to come onto the *Caroline*, Kennedy's plane. After a time, Archibald Cox, who was aboard, said that the Senator was ready to see him but cautioned against conversation; "he's saving his voice for Chicago." Neustadt, going back to Kennedy, handed him a bundle of memoranda and said, "You don't have to say anything—here are the memoranda—don't bother with them till after the election." One memorandum listed priority actions from election to Thanksgiving. Another dealt with cabinet posts. Another was called "Staffing the President-Elect"; sensing Kennedy's affinities, Neustadt added to this appendixes discussing Roosevelt's approach to White House staffing and to the Bureau of the Budget. Half an hour later Kennedy bounded out of his compartment in search of Neustadt. Finding him, he said, "That Roosevelt stuff is fascinating." Neustadt said, "You're not supposed to read it now." Kennedy repeated, "It's fascinating."

The day after election, Clifford's memorandum was delivered to Hyannis Port. It was shorter and less detailed than the Neustadt series. Where Neustadt viewed the problem in its administrative and organizational context, Clifford viewed it more in its policy context. But in the main the two advisers reinforced each other all along the line. There was only one transient issue between them. Neustadt in his September memorandum had proposed that Kennedy designate a "Number-One Boy, serving as a sort of first assistant on general operations, day by day," to be called Executive Assistant to the President-Elect. This suggestion was contrary to the precepts of *Presidential Power* as well as to the practice of Kennedy, and by November Neustadt had broken up his Number-One Boy into three or four boys, deciding rightly that, as he put it to Kennedy, "You would be your own 'chief of staff.' " Clifford, confronting the problem directly, had advised Kennedy: "A vigorous President in the Democratic tradition of the Presidency will probably find it best to act as his own chief of staff, and to have no highly visible major domo standing between him and his staff."

These were the memoranda which Kennedy flourished at luncheon in Hyannis Port. He ignored a good many of their recommendations; but the Clifford-Neustadt emphasis on molding the executive machinery to meet the needs of the President was exactly what Kennedy wanted. When Eisenhower proposed the day after the election that Kennedy designate a representative to serve as liaison with the outgoing administration, Kennedy immediately named Clifford.

2. NAVIGATING THE TRANSITION

Kennedy now had seventy-three days to go until inauguration. With all his resilience, the daily barnstorming in the general election added to the months of primary fights, had left him physically exhausted. In earlier times, a President-elect had four months to recover—and less to recover from. Palm Beach now promised him a badly needed respite.

He also had to begin his work of reassuring the losers—a task all the more essential because of the slimness of the victory. He started this even before he left Hyannis Port. On Wednesday night after the election he relaxed at dinner with several friends. The group fell into an animated discussion of what the President-elect should do first. One guest suggested that he fire J. Edgar Hoover of the Federal Bureau of Investigation, another that he fire Allen W. Dulles of the Central Intelligence Agency. Kennedy, listening with apparent interest, egged his friends on. When they opened their papers the next morning, they were therefore a little irritated to read a Kennedy announcement that Hoover and Dulles were staying in their jobs.

This was part of the strategy of reassurance. Hoover and Dulles were still national ikons in 1960. Since the political cost of discharging them would have been considerable, reappointment enabled Kennedy to get full credit with their admirers for something he had no real choice but to do anyway. The same motive led him, soon after he arrived in Florida, to make a well-publicized call on Nixon, who was conducting his own recuperation not far away in Key Biscayne. Someone asked him why in the world he was doing this; Eisenhower would never have dreamed of calling on Stevenson in 1952 or 1956. Kennedy replied realistically, "There are some things Democrats must do which Republicans don't have to do."

In the meantime, Clifford in Washington was beginning his talks with the Eisenhower administration. His opposite number was General Wilton B. Persons of the White House staff. At their first meeting on November 14, the two men began by recalling the disastrous transitions of 1932 and 1952, "both marked by bad will and almost complete lack of communication," and resolved to make 1960 a standard for the future. In short order, they set up a system by which Kennedy appointees would receive quick FBI clearance, Persons would put them in touch with their Eisenhower counterparts and office space could be arranged in their new departments. Thereafter Clifford and Persons remained in almost daily contact.

On November 21 Clifford and Neustadt reported their progress to the President-elect and his staff at Palm Beach. After dinner, Kennedy briskly divided up the group, taking Clifford and Sorensen into one room, asking Neustadt to wait in another room, Shriver in still another. When Neustadt's turn arrived, Kennedy raised questions about some of the things his advisers had told him he must do as President—receiving Congressmen, for example, whenever they requested an appointment. Neustadt said that there were few imperatives in the Presidency; he should feel free to work it out in his own way. He then handed Kennedy a copy of *Presidential Power*, recommending that he read chapters three and seven ("The Power to Persuade" and "Men in Office"). Kennedy, almost as if surprised at the limited assignment, said, "I will read the whole book."

When he did, he found an abundance of evidence and
analysis to support his predilections toward a fluid Presidency.

Early in December, Kennedy and Eisenhower had their
first formal meeting. The President-elect prepared himself
with great care, and the two men talked by themselves
for seventy-five minutes before walking arm-in-arm into
the Cabinet Room where Clifford and Persons were waiting. Persons phoned Clifford later and reported that Eisenhower, who had previously called Kennedy a "young whip-
persnapper," was "overwhelmed by Senator Kennedy, his
understanding of the world problems, the depth of his questions, his grasp of the issues and the keenness of his mind."
The subsequent rapport between the two principals assisted
the transition process.

But Kennedy was concerned throughout not to assume
responsibility until he assumed power. He remembered perhaps Hoover's effort in 1932 to trap Roosevelt into decisions
which, as Hoover privately confessed at the time, would
have forced the incoming President to abandon "90 percent of the so-called new deal" and ratify "the whole
major program of the Republican administration." In the
main, the Eisenhower administration did not try to in-
veigle Kennedy into underwriting its policies. There were
exceptions, however—most notably when Robert Anderson,
the outgoing Secretary of the Treasury, wanted a Kennedy
man to go with him to Bonn and discuss the gold problem
with the Germans. Kennedy instead asked Paul Nitze to
receive Anderson's report on his return. Similarly the State
Department sought Kennedy's advance approval of a proposal for a multilateral nuclear force to be submitted to
the December meeting of the North Atlantic Council; Kennedy again declined, instead asking Nitze and David Bruce
to talk quietly with the NATO Director General, Paul-Henri
Spaak. When the Eisenhower administration terminated diplomatic relations with the Castro regime early in January,
Kennedy was informed but took no part in the decision.

3. CHOOSING THE CABINET: I

The question of "people" became more urgent every day.
The Senate Committee on Post Office and Civil Service had
thoughtfully produced a heavy green volume listing all the
posts which the new President had the power to fill—the
cabinet and agency heads, of course, plus about 1200 so-

called Schedule C jobs, to which presidential appointees could name persons of their own choosing. For the next weeks the Green Book was the favorite reading on the New Frontier. It was known as the shopping list.

The White House staff was easy enough. Kennedy promptly announced Ted Sorensen as his Special Counsel and Pierre Salinger as his press man and made it clear that Ken O'Donnell, Lawrence O'Brien, Richard Goodwin, Myer Feldman and Ralph Dungan would all be Special Assistants. But beyond the White House lay the cabinet, and beyond the cabinet the long, hazy rank-on-rank of Green Book vacancies. Neustadt recalls Kennedy exclaiming at Palm Beach on November 21, as he mixed a batch of daiquiris before dinner, "People, people, people! I don't know any people. I only know voters. How am I going to fill these 1200 jobs? . . . All I hear is the name Jim Perkins. Who in hell is Perkins?" (Perkins, who was then vice-president of the Carnegie Corporation and is now president of Cornell, was a name which automatically bobbed up during the interregnum whatever the post; a year or so later the all-purpose name would be Clark Kerr of the University of California.)

Kennedy's acquaintance had, indeed, certain limitations. He knew most national and many local politicians, Republican as well as Democratic; he knew a number of government officials; he knew Washington newspapermen; he knew labor leaders; and he knew a smattering of college professors, mostly from the Northeast. He had his chums from Harvard, the Navy, Massachusetts politics and Palm Beach. He knew, in addition, a miscellany of writers, theatrical figures and society people. On the other hand, he knew relatively few bankers, industrialists, leaders of the bar, university presidents, deans, foundation officials, generals, farmers, social workers, scientists or engineers. In particular, he was little acquainted in the New York financial and legal community—that arsenal of talent which had so long furnished a steady supply of always orthodox and often able people to Democratic as well as Republican administrations. This community was the heart of the American Establishment. Its household deities were Henry L. Stimson and Elihu Root; its present leaders, Robert A. Lovett and John J. McCloy; its front organizations, the Rockefeller, Ford and Carnegie foundations and the Council on Foreign Relations; its organs, the *New York Times*

and *Foreign Affairs*.[1] Its politics were predominantly Republican; but it possessed what its admirers saw as a commitment to public service and its critics as an appetite for
power which impelled its members to serve Presidents of
whatever political faith. Roosevelt and Truman had drawn
freely upon them, partly to avail themselves of Establishment competence, partly to win protective coloration for
policies which, with liberals in front, would have provoked
conservative opposition. It was never clear who was using
whom; but, since it *was* never clear, each side continued to
find advantages in the arrangement.

The New York Establishment had looked on Kennedy
with some suspicion. This was mostly because of his father,
whom it had long since blackballed as a maverick in
finance and an isolationist in foreign policy. It was perhaps also because the younger Kennedy's main associations
were with Democratic politicians and academic intellectuals, two groups the New York Establishment regarded
with mistrust; and partly too because it had not recovered
from a 1957 speech attacking French policy in Algeria
which had shocked it to the core and even created the myth
that Kennedy was anti-NATO, a cardinal Establishment sin.
Now that he was President, however, they were prepared
to rally round; and, now that he was President, he was
prepared to receive them. This too was part of the strategy
of reassurance. It also might help solve the problem of
people.

The chief agent in the negotiation was Lovett, a man of
great subtlety, experience and charm. Lovett punctiliously
informed Kennedy that he had voted for Nixon, apparently
out of fear of J. K. Galbraith; but Kennedy, with the
election out of the way, was losing much of his interest in
how people voted (an indifference which distressed the academic intellectuals as much as the Mafia). He told Clifford, "Now on those key jobs, I don't care whether a man
is a Democrat or an Igorot. I want the best fellow I can
get for the particular job." After a couple of conversations,
Kennedy found himself captivated by Lovett. No doubt
Lovett's urbane realism was a relief from the liberal ideal-

---

[1] The term Establishment was revived by Henry Fairlie for use in
England in a series for *The Spectator* in September–October 1955.
Anyone who writes on the American Establishment must, of course,
acknowledge his debt to our most brilliant and persevering practition-
er of Establishment Studies, the devoted Hudson River scholar,
Richard H. Rovere. All such inquiries begin with Dr. Rovere's pioneer-
ing monograph, "The American Establishment," in *The American
Establishment* (New York, 1962).

ists, like myself, who were assailing the President-elect with virtuous opinions and nominations. Certainly Lovett opened a new sector of talent for him and exerted a quiet influence on his tastes in the next weeks.

Kennedy was prepared to offer Lovett his choice of the three top cabinet portfolios—State, Defense and the Treasury—and he sent Clark Clifford to New York to make a particularly strong try on the last. Over a three-hour luncheon, Lovett, while protesting how much he would like to serve, explained that he had recently had two bouts with bleeding ulcers and doubted whether his doctor would let him do it. When Clifford reported this to Kennedy, the President-elect wondered whether Lovett could be induced to take Defense for a year with Robert Kennedy as Under Secretary; if not, he might want to retain Eisenhower's Secretary of Defense, Thomas W. Gates, for a year, also with Bobby as his second man. In either case, he would expect to move Bobby up at the end of the year. But his advisers argued strongly against keeping Gates, pointing out that Kennedy, after having made a campaign issue about the inadequacy of our defenses, could hardly anoint the man who bore so heavy a part of the responsibility.

The President-elect talked a good deal about cabinet problems when I saw him in Washington on December 1. "State, Treasury and Defense," he told me, "are giving me the most trouble. I'd like to have some new faces here, but all I get is the same old names. It's discouraging. But I suppose that it will take a little while to develop new talent." He seemed in general much more on the defensive than at Hyannis Port—more oppressed by the narrowness of his victory, by the gravity of the balance-of-payments situation and the flight of American gold overseas, by the urgency of appointing people who would get along with what he was now convinced would be a "rough" and conservative Congress.

He had reached firm decisions on two Cabinet appointments—Governor Luther Hodges of North Carolina for Commerce and Governor Abraham Ribicoff of Connecticut for Health, Education and Welfare. Both appointments fitted into the pattern of reassurance. Hodges was an older man, nearly twenty years the President's senior, a southerner of geniality and presence; his designation would appeal to Congress and to the business community. Ribicoff, too, had been an attractive and prudent governor as well as a man to whom Kennedy was indebted for support in the pre-convention period. To give Health, Education and Welfare to Ribicoff he had to reject the claims of Sargent Shriver and of Mennen Williams. Shriver was, of course, a brother-in-law; and, if he were to risk appointing a member of his family to the Cabinet, it seemed that Robert Kennedy should have the priority. As for Williams, who had long been under attack for supposed prodigality as governor of Michigan, "there were just too many difficulties . . . I just don't think he is the man to go before this Congress and request big spending bills for education and medical care. Abe will be able to do this much more effectively." He had announced Williams's appointment as Assistant Secretary of State for Africa that morning. I asked whether Williams had been unhappy about this. Kennedy said, "He was at first, but I think he is feeling better now. After all, you could hardly ask for a more challenging job."

Kennedy had also by this time substantially decided on two more appointments—Stewart Udall of Arizona as Secretary of the Interior, unless Senator Clinton Anderson of New Mexico wanted it, and Arthur Goldberg of Illinois as Secretary of Labor, if opposition within the labor movement, especially from the building trades, could be overridden. Both appointments were almost inevitable. Udall, young, brisk, literate and a Mormon, not only had a distinguished record in Congress as a defender of the nation's resources but had snatched the Arizona delegation away from Lyndon Johnson and turned it over to Kennedy before Los Angeles. Goldberg was a man of unquestioned ability and drive whom Kennedy had got to know well in the Senate fights over labor legislation in 1958 and 1959. It turned out that Anderson did not want Interior too much and that the building unions could be ignored, so Kennedy was free to go ahead. When Udall was announced, Kennedy heard from Robert Frost: GREAT DAYS FOR BOSTON, DEMOCRACY, THE PURITANS AND THE IRISH. YOUR APPOINTMENT OF STUART UDALL OF AN OLD VERMONT RELIGION RECONCILES ME ONCE FOR ALL TO THE PARTY I WAS BORN INTO.

Our talk had begun at noon in his Senate office. We then drove out to Georgetown for a drink before luncheon. In due course Lovett arrived for lunch, and I took my leave. Actually, after this meeting with Lovett, Kennedy was well on his way to the solution of the Defense problem. During his talk with Clifford in New York, Lovett had mentioned Robert S. McNamara, a Michigan business executive, just a year older than Kennedy, who had been elected president of the Ford Motor Company the day after Kennedy had been elected President of the United States. During the

Second World War, Lovett, then Assistant Secretary of War for Air, had brought to the Pentagon a team of management specialists from the Harvard Business School. McNamara, he told Clifford, was the prize of the lot, and the Kennedy people ought to consider him for either the Treasury or Defense. Though the nation's previous experience with presidents of motor companies as government officials, and particularly as Secretary of Defense, had not been inspiring, Kennedy, impressed by Lovett's recommendation, asked Sargent Shriver to take a look.

The look revealed that McNamara was, indeed, an exceptional figure. A Phi Beta Kappa graduate of the University of California in 1937, he had gone on to the Harvard Business School, where he did so well that on graduation he was appointed an assistant professor of business administration. He was already beginning to display quiet symptoms of heterodoxy. During the 1940 election, a poll of the Business School faculty produced a vote of 98 to 2 in favor of Willkie against Roosevelt. McNamara was one of the heretics; the other was a young colleague named Eugene Zuckert. Ending the war as a lieutenant colonel in the Air Force, McNamara then joined Ford, rising steadily to the top. In Michigan, he continued to show wayward tendencies. He declined, for example, to live with other Ford executives in the suburb known derisively on the New Frontier as Fat Point, preferring the academic environment of Ann Arbor. He exhibited sympathy for such dubious organizations as the American Civil Liberties Union and the National Association for the Advancement of Colored People. He had been tremendously impressed by *Profiles in Courage*, and, though nominally a Republican, had voted for Kennedy and contributed money to his campaign.

Kennedy knew none of these last facts, however, but Shriver reported that one of his associates in the talent search, Adam Yarmolinsky, had met McNamara and had the highest opinion of him. J. K. Galbraith, who had sought McNamara's assistance in the fifties for a book on economic organization, also recommended him. One day late in November McNamara received a call from Robert Kennedy requesting that he see Sargent Shriver. When McNamara asked what about, Kennedy said that he would rather let his brother-in-law say when they met. McNamara responded that he could see Shriver the next week. Kennedy remarked that Shriver was prepared to go out to Detroit that afternoon.

Shriver, arriving later that day, said that the President-

elect had authorized him to offer McNamara an appointment either as Secretary of Defense or as Secretary of the
Treasury. Nothing could have surprised McNamara more.
He quickly declined the Treasury on the ground that he
had had no experience in banking or fiscal affairs. As for
Defense, such experience as he had had was fifteen years
out of date and pre-nuclear. Moreover, he had only just
begun his new job as president of Ford. Shriver asked
whether McNamara would meet personally with the President-elect before reaching a final decision. McNamara
agreed, purely as a matter of courtesy, to come to Washington the next day.

When McNamara repeated his arguments to the President-
elect, Kennedy replied drily that he was not aware of any
school for either cabinet members or Presidents, and that
he considered lack of experience no excuse. Shifting his
ground, McNamara named several other people as better
qualified. Kennedy rejected them all for reasons which Mc-
Namara felt bound to accept. Then McNamara took the
offensive, asking Kennedy whether he had really written
Profiles in Courage. Kennedy assured him that he had. But
McNamara, though pleased by the ease and candor of
their talk, continued to insist that his own appointment
would be a mistake. Kennedy asked him to think about it
some more. and see him again in a few days. McNamara
left under Kennedy's spell, thought about the matter some
more, and, at their second meeting, ascertained that he
would have a free hand in making appointments and accepted the post.

4. CHOOSING THE CABINET: II

The problem of the Treasury was still unresolved, though
the successive approaches to Lovett and McNamara showed
how Kennedy's mind was running. Throughout the autumn he had heard a great deal about the balance of payments and the flight of gold from the country, and since
the election he had heard very little else. A task force on national security headed by Paul Nitze reported to him that
"all those whom we consulted in the New York business
community" had put the gold drain at the top of their list
of issues, and that friends in State and Treasury had told
the task force that the problem was worse than publicly admitted. "The early appointment of a Secretary of the Treasury who enjoys high respect and confidence in the international financial world," the Nitze report declared, "would
do more than anything else that your Committee can think

of to consolidate confidence in the international payments position of the United States."

Even Richard Neustadt conceded that there was much to be said "for bowing to tradition and drawing your secretary out of the financial community. . . . His daily duties cannot help but make him sensitive to the concerns of bankers and investors, their colleagues overseas, and their friends on the Hill. He will end as a 'spokesman' for them. He might as well begin as an effective spokesman to them." Neustadt suggested someone of the type of Lovett, McCloy or Douglas Dillon, Under Secretary of State in the outgoing administration and the son of Clarence Dillon of Dillon, Read and Company. "Since Treasury is a major foreign policy post," Neustadt continued, "you would be advantaged further if your man had had a previous experience in State." If Kennedy followed these specifications, Neustadt conceded, he would probably end up with a Republican; but even this had an advantage—"the symbolisms of 'bipartisanship' and 'fiscal responsibility' rolled into one." But Kennedy, Neustadt warned, could pay too great a price; he had better be sure that the man would wear well as a colleague before taking him into the bosom of the family. "Among Republicans, Stimsons and Lovetts are not met with every day; and superficial resemblances can be deceiving. It would be better to forego the symbolism, and to settle for a Democratic known quantity, than to risk a Martin Durkin case." [2]

This last sentence expressed a widespread feeling among Kennedy's supporters. Even some who accepted the Wall Street-acceptability thesis were dismayed at the prospect of installing a Republican in the economic high command of a Democratic administration. About this time a countermovement started for Eugene Black of the World Bank, a man acceptable to Wall Street but at least a Democrat. Still others, seeing the Treasury as crucial for an expansionist economic policy, challenged the whole criterion of Wall Street acceptability. Admitting that the gold drain was a problem, they feared that a conservative Secretary would apply the conventional remedy—i.e., reduce public spending and increase the interest rate, even at the risk of deflation and unemployment. It seemed essential to have a Secretary committed to the use of fiscal and monetary policy to stimulate economic growth. Thus Senator

[2] Martin Durkin was a trade unionist whom Eisenhower appointed Secretary of Labor but who could find no points of social or intellectual contact with the Eisenhower administration and resigned unhappily after a few months.

Albert Gore of Tennessee contended to Kennedy on November 22 that the Treasury was the key to the success of his Presidency. "The present difficulties with balance of payments . . . are symptoms, really, of the failure of the present administration to keep the United States on the 'move.' . . . Why, then, should you consider for a fleeting moment for appointment to the key post of Treasury one whose chief claim to fame is that he has been a member of a team that failed its most important test? This applies not only to Mr. Dillon, who is an affable easy-goer, but to other conservative Republicans who have been mentioned." Such an appointment "would be a signal that you had given up the goals of a truly Democratic Administration."

We had similar apprehensions in Cambridge, and Kenneth Galbraith, Seymour Harris, Paul Samuelson and I met one day in an effort to come up with a candidate. We thought of Averell Harriman, Senator Gore, Congressman Henry Reuss, Congressman Richard Bolling, all of whom were well qualified for the job but lacked, except possibly for Harriman, the mystic relationship with the lower end of Manhattan Island; even Harriman, we conceded, would probably be rejected there as a renegade. A few days later, Galbraith and I went to Washington to go over the Cambridge slate with Sargent Shriver. Dining that evening with Philip Graham, we were distressed by his impassioned insistence that Douglas Dillon should—and would—be made Secretary of the Treasury. Without knowing Dillon, we mistrusted him on principle as a presumed exponent of Republican economic policies. In addition, as an historian and therefore a conservative, I could recall no precedent for giving a vital cabinet post to a sub-cabinet official of a defeated administration, especially to an official who had contributed to Nixon's campaign and might well have been Nixon's nominee for the same job.

When I mentioned this to the President-elect in Washington on December 1, he remarked of Dillon, "Oh, I don't care about those things. All I want to know is: is he able? and will he go along with the program?" They had first met in Cambridge in 1956 when Kennedy received a Harvard honorary degree and Dillon was the Chief Marshal of the Twenty-fifth Reunion class. After the exercises, they met again as fellow members in the rooms of the Spee Club. In 1959, when Dillon received an honorary degree himself, Kennedy took note of his Alumni Day speech calling for an increase in the national growth rate. In the next years, they came to know each other better, and Joseph Alsop as well as Philip Graham had been eloquently urging Dillon's appointment on the President-elect. But Dillon was still surprised to get a phone call from Salinger in late November saying that Kennedy wanted to come over to his house that evening. Pressing Dillon on the question of economic growth, Kennedy satisfied himself that he had found a man whom bankers would trust but who also would support expansionist policies. He therefore resolved to ignore the liberal protests and go ahead.

One obstacle remained: Robert Kennedy, who kept asking what would happen if Dillon resigned in a few months with a blast against the administration's financial policies. He warned his brother that they were putting themselves in the hands of a Republican who had no reason for loyalty to them and might well betray them. Finally the President-elect consented to Bobby's plea that prior assurances of good behavior be obtained. As Dillon was waiting with the President-elect in the Georgetown house before going downstairs to meet the press, Bobby by prearrangement broke in on them and asked bluntly what Dillon would do if he found himself in disagreement with the policy. Dillon, a little surprised but always the Harvard man, said that, if he felt he had to resign, he would of course go quietly.

The President-elect's judgment turned out to be correct. Indeed, no two people became closer friends in the next years than Dillon and Bobby. When one came later to know the Secretary of the Treasury, the anomaly seemed to be, not that he was willing to join the Kennedy administration, but that he ever could have endured the Eisenhower administration. He used to describe the cabinet meetings— the opening prayer, the visual aids, the rehearsal presentations. "We sat around looking at the plans for Dulles Airport. They had a model and everything, and we would say why don't you put a door there, and they would explain why they didn't. It was great fun if you didn't have anything to do." At the same time, though Dillon was considerably more liberal than the Cambridge group thought, he was still likely to be influenced by Wall Street and Republican associations as well as by the institutional conservatism of the Treasury. Following a balancing principle, Kennedy prepared to give the other key economic posts— the directorship of the Bureau of the Budget and the chairmanship of the Council of Economic Advisers—to liberal Democrats.

Clark Clifford had already proposed David Bell, another of Harry Truman's young men in the White House, for the

Budget. After serving as a Truman Special Assistant, Bell
had worked in the Stevenson campaign in 1952, then spent
some years in Pakistan running an economic mission
backed by the Ford Foundation and had come to the Littauer
School at Harvard in the late fifties. The audacity of Clifford's suggestion can be measured by the fact that the
Cambridge group, admiring Bell's ability but wondering at
his youth, had only dared suggest him as associate director.
Kennedy sent Shriver on the usual tour of inspection, received a highly favorable report and then talked with Bell
himself. He later told me, "He's a quiet fellow, but I liked
him and I think I'll go through with him." Bell was, indeed,
a quiet fellow compared to some of the other Cambridge
economists (and historians), but he had the calmness of
temperament, the openness and precision of mind and the
moderation of judgment which were bound to impress the
President-elect.

For the chairmanship of the Council, the Harvard group,
and doubtless many others, proposed Professor Walter
Heller of the University of Minnesota. Kennedy's first
thought was Paul Samuelson; but Samuelson could not be
lured down from the Massachusetts Institute of Technology
and, in any case, Kennedy was beginning to fear that he
might be overdoing appointments from Cambridge. Hubert
Humphrey had introduced Heller to him in Minnesota
during the campaign. Kennedy, who had instantly subjected
him to a cross-examination on economic policy, remembered him favorably and decided to go ahead. One day in
December, back in Palm Beach, Richard Neustadt handed
Kennedy a memorandum on the Council. Kennedy observed that he had already chosen his chairman and, indeed,
was at that moment waiting to hear from him. In a few
minutes Heller called in from Minnesota. As Neustadt
watched with fascination, Kennedy cradled the phone on his
shoulder, and, while he carried on a detailed conversation
with Heller, flicked through Neustadt's memorandum on the
Council, picked up the morning *Herald Tribune*, looked
at the first page and the editorial page, let it slip
to the floor, picked up the *Times*, looked at the first page
and the editorial page, retrieved the memorandum, read
parts of it aloud to Heller, dropped it on the floor again
and simultaneously completed his business and the morning papers.

For the second place in the Council, Heller suggested
James Tobin who, though he had a Harvard degree, had
fortunately moved on to Yale and was thus not subject

to the Cambridge ban. Tobin was a brilliant economic theorist; and, when Kennedy called him, he tried to set forth what he considered his lack of qualifications for the job, concluding, "I am afraid that I am only an ivory-tower economist." Kennedy replied, "That is the best kind. I am only an ivory-tower President." The deal was promptly consummated. For the third member, Heller wanted Kermit Gordon of Williams. Kennedy, retaining a vague memory of Gordon's reluctance to work for him in 1959, was unenthusiastic, and the decision was delayed until January. Finally Heller called on Kennedy at the Hotel Carlyle in New York, hoping to get the matter settled. While he waited, he discussed the problem with Ken O'Donnell. O'Donnell asked whether Gordon was really the best man for the job. Heller said emphatically that he was. O'Donnell then said that he should stick to his guns and tell the President-elect that he had to have Gordon. Heller did so when he saw Kennedy a few minutes later. Kennedy said, "Oh, all right," picked up the phone and called Gordon in Williamstown. Both appointments proved great successes; and Gordon, who quickly won Kennedy's esteem, eventually succeeded Bell at the Budget.

Two conundrums remained—State and Justice—and two uncertainties—Agriculture and Post Office. Nothing was giving Kennedy more trouble than State. The Democrat with the strongest claim was Adlai Stevenson, and Stevenson fully expected to be offered the job. But when the President-elect returned from Palm Beach in late November he told Stevenson that he had taken too many public positions on prickly issues and would in consequence be too 'controversial' for Congress; given the margin of the election, Kennedy said that he needed most of all a Secretary of State who could get along on Capitol Hill. In addition, Kennedy privately questioned Stevenson's capacity for decision and no doubt also did not want a Secretary of State with whom he feared he might not feel personally comfortable.

In talking to Stevenson, Kennedy went on to say that Stevenson had more international prestige than any other Democrat and, in Kennedy's view, could make his greatest contribution as Ambassador to the United Nations. Though this was a hard blow to Stevenson, he accepted it realistically, saying only that he could not take the UN assignment until he knew who the Secretary of State would be. Kennedy told Stevenson not to worry; as President, he would guarantee any stipulations Stevenson wanted to make about the UN job. But Stevenson insisted that the Secretary would have to be someone with whom he could have a relationship of mutual confidence. He had been told by Walter Lippmann that McGeorge Bundy might be the choice; and, since Bundy had voted against him in two elections, Stevenson doubted whether the required confidence would exist between them; therefore he could not immediately accept the post. Kennedy was nettled at this reaction and strengthened in his belief in Stevenson's indecisiveness.

On December 1, he asked me why Stevenson did not want to take the UN job. I started to explain that Stevenson had been at the UN before and that this time he wanted to help shape foreign policy rather than be at the other end of the telephone. Kennedy broke in, "The UN is different now. I think this job has great possibilities." Then, to my astonishment, he said, "I have another thought. What about Adlai for Attorney General?" I was completely taken aback. Kennedy continued, "I'd like Stevenson for Attorney General and Paul Freund for Solicitor General." That night he sounded out Bill Blair on the possibility of Stevenson for Justice, but word came back that Stevenson thought his greatest usefulness would lie in foreign affairs and preferred the UN.

The political grounds which excluded Stevenson from the Secretaryship applied just as much, or more, in Kennedy's mind to Chester Bowles. But his political indebtedness to Bowles, who had been the first nationally known liberal to support him for the nomination and had served as a nominal 'foreign policy adviser' during the campaign, was very much greater. He therefore decided to make Bowles Under Secretary. With Lovett out of the picture, the leading candidates for the top job were now David Bruce, Senator J. William Fulbright of Arkansas, and Dean Rusk of the Rockefeller Foundation.

When I talked to Kennedy on December 1, it was clear that his thoughts were turning more and more to Fulbright. He liked Fulbright, the play of his civilized mind, the bite of his language and the direction of his thinking on foreign affairs. Moreover, as chairman of the Senate Foreign Relations Committee, Fulbright had considerable influence on the Hill. But there were problems too. Fulbright had not had an executive job since he was president of the University of Arkansas, and some doubted his capacity to control a large organization. More seriously, he had taken the segregationist position on civil rights, even going to the length of filing an *amicus curiae* brief against the government during the Little Rock crisis of 1957; this would hardly commend him to the new African states. And his opposition to an all-out anti-Nasser policy had aroused concern in the Jewish community.

At this point, some of Bowles's backers, acting without his knowledge, began stirring up Negro and Jewish organizations against Fulbright. And people close to the President-elect came to feel that Fulbright's appointment would create unnecessary difficulties with the new nations. If as Secretary of State, for example, he had to take a position against the African states, it might be received, not on its merits, but as an expression of racial prejudice. Kennedy had almost decided on Fulbright; but finally, after rather heated arguments, the President-elect yielded and struck Fulbright's name from the list.

David Bruce now became the leading candidate. Philip Graham, Joseph Alsop and others recommended Bruce. He was one of the most experienced of all American diplomats. He had served with distinction in Paris and Bonn. He had been Under Secretary of State in the last years of the Truman administration. Moreover, he had the gift of attracting and using able young men. But he was sixty-two years old, his orientation was European, Lovett was unenthusiastic, and, though he was respected on the Hill, he had no conspicuous following there. Lovett instead began to argue vigorously for Dean Rusk.

Rusk, who was fifty-one years old, had a plausible background. He had been a Rhodes Scholar and a professor of government before the war. He had served with the Army in the Far East; and, after the war, he had gone to the State Department, heading the Office of United Nations Affairs and ending up as Assistant Secretary for Far Eastern Affairs. At the Rockefeller Foundation he had supervised programs of health, education and technical assistance in the underdeveloped countries. He was a Democrat (in fact, he had been chairman of the Stevenson-for-President Committee in Scarsdale in the spring of 1960). Lovett recommended him for the job as against Bruce or Fulbright. Acheson thought highly of him. Bowles, who was a trustee of the Rockefeller Foundation, spoke of him with enthusiasm. Robert Kennedy believed him the best solution. The Kennedy staff read all his speeches and articles they could find and discovered nothing which would cause trouble on the Hill. Kennedy himself was especially taken with parts of a piece Rusk had written for *Foreign Affairs* in the spring of 1960 entitled "The President." Here Rusk discussed the Presidency as the place from which leadership in foreign policy must flow and emphasized the President's responsibility "to influence and shape the course of events." (Actually, though the article showed a nice appreciation of the Presidency, it also contained another and somewhat contradictory argument that the President should *not* engage in foreign negotiations, above all at the summit, and should leave diplomacy to the diplomats.)

On December 4 the board of trustees of the Rockefeller Foundation was meeting at Williamsburg, Virginia. Lovett, McCloy, Bowles, Ralph Bunche and Rusk—all of whom had been mentioned by now as possible Secretaries—were sitting around the conference table when Rusk was called out of the room for a phone call; it was the President-elect inviting him to Washington. On the night of December 7 Rusk dined at Bowles's house in Georgetown and asked him in detail about Kennedy. They met for the first time the next morning. Kennedy mentioned the *Foreign Affairs* piece but said nothing directly about the Secretaryship. Rusk left certain that he and Kennedy were on different wavelengths and that their meeting had come to nothing. But Kennedy was attracted by the clarity of Rusk's views, the quiet competence of his manner and the apparent solidity of his judgment. Accordingly he offered Rusk the Secretaryship the next day. The appointment was announced on December 12 with Bowles as Under Secretary and Stevenson, who knew and liked Rusk, as Ambassador to the United Nations.

The Department of Justice confronted Kennedy with a problem almost as difficult as State but for different reasons. Abraham Ribicoff, to whom the Attorney Generalship was first offered, turned it down; he thought that it would not help the cause if a Jewish Attorney General were putting Negro children into white schools in the South, and he preferred a less controversial post. Adlai Stevenson was not interested. The President-elect's father meanwhile hoped that Robert Kennedy would become Attorney General. Bobby himself was reluctant. He felt that, after five years as counsel for the Senate Rackets Committee, he had been "chasing people" too long and wanted a different kind of assignment now. Also, he recalled an incident in the campaign when Nixon, passing through South Carolina, had tried to conceal the presence of Attorney General William Rogers on his plane, knowing how unpopular Rogers's civil rights activity had made him in the South. Bobby's view was that, if the new Attorney General were named Kennedy, this inevitable unpopularity would quickly spread to the President himself. Instead, he contemplated the possibility of becoming Under Secretary of Defense or perhaps Assistant Secretary for Inter-American Affairs in the State Department. His father argued forcibly, however, that Bobby obviously had to report directly to the President; if he were in a subordinate post, the position of the official who stood between himself and the President would be impossible. Since Bobby did not want to work in the White House, this left the cabinet. Nonetheless, after a time Bobby decided against Justice, thinking that he might return to Massachusetts and run for governor in 1962.

The President-elect, however, wanted his brother in Washington and also wanted an Attorney General in whom he could repose absolute trust. Though nearly all the advice to both brothers was against the idea, he called Bobby over for breakfast one morning and told him that he would have to take the job. When Ben Bradlee later asked Kennedy how he proposed to announce his brother's appointment, he said, "Well, I think I'll open the front door of the Georgetown house some morning about 2:00 A.M., look up and down the street, and, if there's no one there, I'll whisper, 'It's Bobby.' " When the moment finally came, and the brothers started out the door to face the press, he said, "Damn it, Bobby, comb your hair." Then: "Don't smile too much or they'll think we are happy about the appointment."

I had luncheon with Bobby in Washington the day before his appointment was announced. He seemed both rueful and fatalistic about his prospective eminence. The problem of assuring his brother a sufficiently diversified White House staff was much on his mind. Obviously, he said, the President needed to enlarge his staff beyond the men who had worked for him in the Senate and the campaign, able and loyal as they were. Moreover, some neutral figures ought to be introduced in order to relieve what he feared might be a tension between the Sorensen and O'Donnell groups. Thus he had recruited Fred Dutton of California for the White House and had tried in vain to get Richard Neustadt. As we were chatting, he abruptly asked me what I intended to do for my country. I said that an ambassadorship and the Assistant Secretaryship of State in charge of cultural relations had been mentioned, but that neither prospect attracted me much. He then asked whether it would be agreeable if he suggested to his brother that I come down as a Special Assistant to the President and serve as a sort of roving reporter and trouble-shooter. I said I would be delighted.

Bobby's appointment left Agriculture and the Post Office untenanted. By this time, there was spreading unhappiness among the liberals over the failure of any of their particular favorites, except Arthur Goldberg, to make the cabinet. Stevenson was off in the United Nations; Bowles and Williams were in sub-cabinet posts; George McGovern was slated to head the Food for Peace program, Frank Coffin the Development Loan Fund. When I mentioned this discontent to the President-elect, he said, "Yes, I know, the liberals want visual reassurance just like everybody else. But they shouldn't worry. What matters is the program. We are going down the line on the program." I suggested that what he had in mind was an administration of conservative men and liberal measures. He said, "We'll have to go along with this for a year or so. Then I would like to bring in some new people." He paused and added reflectively, "I suppose it may be hard to get rid of these people once they are in."

Still, one policy position remained—Agriculture and one strong liberal candidate—Orville Freeman. Actually Freeman did not much want Agriculture. He would have preferred to be Attorney General or even, for some reason, Secretary of the Army. A number of other midwestern Democratic governors—Herschel Loveless of Iowa, George Docking of Kansas—as well as George McGovern and farm leaders like Fred V. Heinkel of Missouri were active candidates for Agriculture. Kennedy regarded the appointment with some perplexity. His upbringing was ineradicably urban. He had taken positions on farm policy as a Senator which made trouble for him when he became a candidate for the nomination; and the more he studied the agricultural problem, the more he regarded it with a mixture of distrust and incipient despair. He wanted someone intelligent and tough enough to take the problem off his shoulders and even, perhaps, to find solutions. He talked to Loveless, Docking, Heinkel and others, and his sense of hopelessness mounted. He would have liked to appoint McGovern, but there was strong feeling in the Senate that, as a young Congressman who had just lost a senatorial contest, he lacked sufficient seniority. As time passed, Kennedy decided that Freeman was the man. Freeman had a political base in the Middle West, even if he came from Minneapolis rather than from the farms; he was intelligent and brave; he had an ex-Marine's indomitability before insoluble problems; Galbraith, who in the remote past had been an agricultural economist, recommended him; and his appointment would please the liberals. When the matter was put to him, Freeman cheerfully consented. (Asked how he happened to have received the invitation, Freeman said, "I'm not really sure, but I think it's something to do with the fact that Harvard does not have a school of agriculture.")

Only the Post Office was left. There had been a flurry of newspaper speculation over Congressman William Dawson, a Negro political leader from Chicago. Though Kennedy had not offered Dawson the post and had no intention of doing so, the story caught on quickly and began a comedy of complication. Senator Olin D. Johnston, the chairman of the Post Office and Civil Service Committee, denounced the idea as a conspiracy by political opponents in South Carolina designed to force him to have his picture taken with a Negro Postmaster General and thereby weaken him for his next primary contest. On the other side, Mayor Daley of Chicago was concerned lest an outright repudiation of the story seem a rebuff to Dawson and himself. The President-elect finally hit on a diplomatic solution by proposing an exchange of messages in which he would offer the post to Dawson and Dawson would decline it. This having been done, the search continued. Because the Pacific coast was conspicuously unrepresented in the cabinet, word went out to dig up a California businessman. Someone suggested J. Edward Day of Prudential Insurance. Day, a man of rollicking humor, had been Adlai Stevenson's Insurance Commissioner in Illinois before moving to the West. His credentials appeared good, and his rather hasty appointment on December 17 completed the Kennedy cabinet.

VI

PRELUDE TO THE NEW FRONTIER

THE CABINET WAS only the beginning. There remained those vital levers of power in the policy-making jobs just below the cabinet, and these the new President had to control if he meant to command the executive branch. This was the domain of the Green Book and of Schedule C; here, presumably, 1200 places waited to be filled.

He had given Sargent Shriver the job of spying out the land and carrying through the occupation. Though people were sometimes deceived by Shriver's unruffled courtesy and easy amiability into dismissing him as something of a Boy Scout, the President-elect had confidence in his energy and imagination—a confidence Shriver had justified in the campaign and justified again now. He assembled a small group—Harris Wofford, the law school professor who had been with him during the campaign, Adam Yarmolinsky, a lawyer and foundation executive, Louis Martin, a Negro newspaperman who worked for the Democratic National Committee, Herbert Klotz, a New York businessman, and Thomas Farmer, a Washington lawyer. The Shriver staff immediately got on the telephone, and the great talent hunt began.

1. MANNING THE SHIP

Kennedy, as usual, did not propose to give anyone exclusive authority. He therefore charged Shriver to work with Lawrence O'Brien, Ralph Dungan and Richard Donahue, who represented the political interest in appointments. In a sense, the Shriver group began with the positions and looked for people qualified to fill them, and the O'Brien group began with the people and looked for positions they were qualified to fill; one concentrated on recruitment and the other on placement. But the Shriver group understood the importance of finding people who would be loyal to the administration, and the O'Brien group understood the importance of finding people who would do a good job, so there was not too much friction between them. When disagreements arose, Yarmolinsky and Dungan were generally able to resolve them.

The proportions of the search turned out to be not so great as it had first looked. Of the 1200 Schedule C jobs, nearly four-fifths were presently filled from the career service, and about half the incumbents had competitive Civil Service status. Almost 500 of the Schedule C jobs, indeed, were not "policy-determining" at all but rather personal aides to policy makers—secretaries, chauffeurs, and the like. In the end, the Kennedy administration kept most of the career people, including even some on the subcabinet level. Nevertheless, a considerable number of vacancies remained. To fill these, the Shriver group began to compile what they hopefully described as an index of excellence.

They started from scratch and learned as they went. Shriver hoped for a moment that they might benefit from business methods and obtained the loan of a top personnel man from IBM. But, after suggesting as tests of excellence such standards as the rate at which a man's income had increased or the number of people he supervised—both of which the Shriver group found exceedingly unhelpful— the business expert departed, conceding that he had little to offer. The Shriver people ended by devising their own criteria—judgment, integrity, ability to work with others, industry, devotion to the principles of the President-elect and toughness. (The last provoked considerable jocularity in the press as well as a number of phone calls from office-seekers proclaiming, "I am tough"; what was meant was the ability, as Yarmolinsky later put it, "to make use of the vast resources of government without becoming, as some political appointees have become in the past, merely instruments of the permanent staff.")

They had to learn too much about the government. At the start, assuming that Schedule C was sacred and unalterable, they spent valuable time trying to figure out why a job in the Interior Department, for example, was defined in a particular way and classified at a particular level, not realizing that some hard-pressed Assistant Secretary had probably dreamed it up to take care of the protégé of a powerful Senator. Only later did they discover that the inherited table of organization could be juggled and changed around. They received complete cooperation from Roger Jones of the Civil Service Commission and Robert Hampton, who headed Eisenhower's patronage office, but for a long time did not know enough to take full advantage of their help.

They worked night after night through November and December in offices provided by the Democratic National Committee, striving to make sure that all groups and regions were represented in their recommendations. They cast their net especially for women, for Negroes, for westerners. After a time, to be a Harvard graduate, a member of the Cambridge academic complex or an Irish Catholic was almost a handicap, surmountable only by the offsetting evidence of spectacular excellence. (When McNamara's name first came up, there was concern until it was ascertained that he was a Protestant.) Politics mattered here a little more than in Palm Beach; but, if it was helpful to be a Democrat, it did not prove essential to have been a Kennedy Democrat. For a moment Ted Sorensen suggested a point system—so many points for having been with Kennedy before Wisconsin, so many for having been with Kennedy at Los Angeles, and so on—but the idea soon seemed irrelevant. As each cabinet member was appointed, a representative of the Shriver group provided him with a list of names carefully culled for his consideration. By mid-December, the first stage of the roundup was complete. Shriver now left for a holiday in the West Indies. Ralph Dungan took over the talent hunt, later continuing it from the White House.

Each department presented special circumstances. By the time Rusk was offered the State Department, for example, several crucial appointments in the foreign field—Stevenson, Bowles, Williams—had already been made. The next important place was the Under Secretary for Economic Affairs; and here the leading candidate was William C. Foster, a liberal-minded Republican businessman who had held important jobs in the Truman administration. But the prospect of a Republican appointment in addition to Dillon and McNamara seemed excessive, especially when a well-qualified Democrat was available. The well-qualified Democrat was George W. Ball, the Washington lawyer and long-time friend of Adlai Stevenson's who had been closely associated with Jean Monnet and the European Common Market. John Sharon carried word of Foster's impending designation to Stevenson, who called Senator Fulbright, then vacationing in Florida, and asked him to take the matter up with Kennedy. Fulbright went over to Palm Beach and suggested to the President-elect that giving Republicans so many top posts in State, Treasury and Defense was manifestly unfair to Democrats who had worked hard for his election. He added that this policy would create the impression that the Democratic party lacked men of sufficient stature. The argument proved effective. Kennedy withdrew the offer to Foster and appointed Ball; he later made Foster director of the Arms Control and Disarmament Agency.

The Ball argument also applied to the case of Averell Harriman. Kennedy had not known Harriman well, but he appreciated his staunch support before the convention and recognized that Harriman's record and experience in foreign affairs were unmatched in the nation. Still, both the President-elect and his brother remembered Harriman most as a political leader in New York, where he had not always been at his best, and they feared that, at sixty-nine and slightly deaf, he was too old for active service. When I once urged Harriman on Bobby, he said sympathetically, "Are you sure that giving Averell a job wouldn't be just an act of sentiment?" I said that I thought Harriman had one or two missions left under his belt. For some weeks after the election, Harriman heard nothing from Kennedy. In the meantime, the names of his less distinguished but more conservative contemporaries Lovett and McCloy were constantly in the newspapers as Kennedy advisers or possible Cabinet members. Harriman might well have wondered at this point whether he would not have done better to have stayed a Republican thirty-five years earlier instead of breaking with the New York Establishment and going over to Al Smith. But, if he felt this way, he gave no sign of it.

When I lunched with him in New York on December 11, he was temperate and wise. He understood the need for caution in view of the closeness of the election but added that he hoped Kennedy would not appoint too many businessmen; "people have to be given big jobs when they are young, or else their minds become permanently closed. The men who work their way step by step to the top in business are no good for anything big in government. They have acquired too many bad habits along the way." I remarked that the President-elect seemed especially concerned about his relations with Congress. Harriman said, "Everyone worries about the thing he knows best. Jack knows the Senate better than anything else, so he worries about that. For just the same reason, I worry most about the Russians." During the campaign, he had sent word to Khrushchev to be equally harsh about both candidates lest any leniency toward Kennedy help Nixon. He was pleased by a message he had now received from Khrushchev pointing out that Moscow had taken care to be as critical of the Democrats as of the Republicans. Khrushchev went on to imply that the election had wiped the slate clean and that discussions might now resume with the United States. Harriman thought there might be an opportunity for fresh initiatives in the cold war; but he also feared that the Russians might try something risky somewhere in order to test Kennedy's will and response.

Harriman had many admirers on the New Frontier. In time Kennedy, though still a little skeptical, yielded to their enthusiasm and decided to appoint him as the State Department's roving ambassador. First, however, he asked Bill Walton to make Harriman promise to equip himself with a hearing aid. When Walton accomplished this delicate mission, the appointment went through.

Staffing the rest of the State Department involved complicated negotiations among Kennedy, Rusk, Bowles and the Shriver office. Kennedy wanted McGeorge Bundy somewhere on the top level of the State Department; for a moment in early December he had even wondered whether he might be a possible Secretary. He also thought that Walt W. Rostow, with his force and fertility of thought, should be counselor and chairman of the Policy Planning Council. But Rusk for various reasons resisted both Bundy and Rostow. From the institutional interests of the Department, this was a grievous error. Kennedy promptly decided to take them into the White House, Bundy as Special Assistant for National Security Affairs and Rostow as his deputy. The result was to give the White House an infusion of energy on foreign affairs with which the State Department would never in the next three years (even after Rostow finally got the policy planning job) quite catch up.

One reason for Rusk's opposition to Rostow was his desire to keep the post of counselor for his old colleague from Truman days George C. McGhee, who had served a decade before as Assistant Secretary for Near Eastern Affairs. The new Secretary had a temperamental preference for professionals both in Washington and in the field; and he was also rightly determined to rebuild the morale of the Foreign Service after the shocks of the Dulles-McCarthy era.

For its part, the Foreign Service was moving to take care of its own in the appointment of ambassadors and even of Assistant Secretaries. In late November, Loy Henderson, the dean of the career service and the retiring Deputy Under Secretary for Administration, suggested that the Department clear the appointment of seven senior Foreign Service officers as ambassadors to newly independent African states. Thomas Farmer of the Shriver staff intercepted the proposal and called it to the attention of Robert Kennedy. Africa, Farmer argued, was not a place for tired old men awaiting their pensions but for young officers with a career to make and even for people from outside the Foreign Service; it required an infusion of New Frontier spirit. Kennedy vigorously agreed, and, with the aid of Chester Bowles, the Henderson plan was killed. As for Assistant Secretaryships, the Shriver office did not accept the principle that they should necessarily go to professionals, noting that generals and admirals never dreamed of demanding to be made Assistant Secretaries in the Pentagon; and it darkly suspected that State was holding its Assistant Secretaryships down to the civil service salary level of GS-18 precisely in order to ward off outside appointments.

Rusk did not, however, have a consuming interest in personnel; and a letter just before Christmas from Ted Sorensen, listing twenty-three issues of policy, all of complexity and moment, on which the President wanted his immediate advice, gave him other things to do. Accordingly he relinquished to Bowles, as Under Secretary, the responsibility for filling the top posts. Bowles had considerable respect for the professionals and a particular desire to seek out able men in the lower ranks of the Foreign Service. "If we provide the necessary leadership, sense of direction and sensitivity to individual attitudes and problems," he told Rusk, "I am confident that we can count on a high degree of loyalty, intelligence and competent service from the Foreign Service generally." At the same time, he also wanted to bring people from outside "unhampered by past loyalties" and committed to the New Frontier into the conduct of foreign relations. He canvassed the universities, the foundations, the press and politics and was more responsible than anyone else for the high quality of Kennedy's first wave of appointments in foreign affairs. As a result, Abram Chayes became Legal Adviser, Roger Hilsman Director of Intelligence and Research, Lucius Battle Chief of the Secretariat, Harlan Cleveland Assistant Secretary for International Organization Affairs, Philip Coombs Assistant Secretary for Cultural Affairs, Wayne Fredericks Deputy Assistant Secretary for African Affairs, Arturo Morales-Carrión Deputy Assistant Secretary for Inter-American Affairs, Phillips Talbott Assistant Secretary for Near Eastern Affairs. As a result, too, J. Kenneth Galbraith became ambassador to India, Edwin Reischauer to Japan, George Kennan to Yugoslavia, Teodoro Moscoso to Venezuela, William Attwood to Guinea, William McCormick Blair, Jr., to Denmark, Kenneth Young to Thailand, Philip Kaiser to Senegal and, in due course, Lincoln Gordon to Brazil, James Loeb to Peru and John Bartlow Martin to the Dominican Republic. Bowles was also the strong advocate of the appointment of Edward R. Murrow as head of the United States Information Agency.

In the case of Defense, McNamara organized the personnel effort himself. He came to Washington early in December, set up an office in the Ford Suite at the Shoreham Hotel and began to pursue a staff by round-the-clock telephoning all over the country. The President-elect and the Shriver office had suggested that he consider for Deputy Secretary Roswell Gilpatric, a New York lawyer and Democrat who had been Under Secretary of the Air Force under Thomas Finletter a decade before. After intensive inquiry, McNamara decided that Gilpatric, whom he had not yet met, was the man he wanted. He then began to track his quarry down, finally calling Gilpatric's country house on the eastern shore of Maryland, waking his wife at six-fifteen in the morning and arranging to meet her husband later that day at the Baltimore airport. The two men sat in McNamara's automobile in a snowstorm discussing the terms of the appointment. Gilpatric was easy, resourceful and intelligent, and the partnership was sealed.

For Comptroller—a position which McNamara saw as critical to the control of his amorphous inheritance—he rejected the conventional choice of someone with a background in business or accounting. Instead, he chose Charles Hitch, a Rhodes Scholar and economist whose work in operational analysis at the Rand Corporation had shown an ability to break down complex problems to their essentials with a speed and exactness which matched McNamara's own rapidity of mind. Hitch brought along as his Deputy Assistant Secretary for Systems Analysis another economist and Rhodes Scholar, Alain C. Enthoven. Hitch and Enthoven could invoke all the contemporary resources of mathematics and cybernetics to perfect the managerial magic with which, in its more rudimentary form, McNamara himself had so impressed Lovett during the Second World War. For Assistant Secretary for International Security Affairs, presiding over the intersection of defense and foreign policy, McNamara selected Paul Nitze, a man of trenchant mind and wide experience. For Secretary of the Air Force, he picked his fellow Roosevelt enthusiast from the Harvard Business School, Eugene Zuckert, and for Secretary of the Army, Elvis Stahr, still another Rhodes Scholar and president of West Virginia University.

The Navy Department presented a particular problem. Kennedy hoped that McNamara would accept Franklin D. Roosevelt, Jr., who not only was a close personal friend but had helped so much in the West Virginia primary. The Roosevelt record of association with the Navy was, moreover, long and formidable. Both Theodore Roosevelts, Sr. and Jr., had been Assistant Secretaries of the Navy; so too had been Franklin D. Roosevelt, Sr.; and there would be a pleasant historical symmetry in completing the quadrangle. Young Franklin himself had served with distinction in the Navy during the Second World War. But McNamara did not want him; and Kennedy, though regretful, accepted the decision without further question. (Feeling perhaps a little abashed, McNamara did accept Kennedy's old comrade from PT-boat days Paul Fay as Under Secretary of the Navy.) In the meantime, McNamara's personal talent search had unearthed the name of John Connally of Texas as a possibility for the Secretaryship. Late in December he called Kennedy at Palm Beach to clear an invitation to Connally. In view of Connally's Texas connections, he added, perhaps the appointment should be checked with the Vice President-elect. Kennedy said that Senator Johnson was sitting beside him and put him on the phone. Since Connally was one of Johnson's oldest political associates,

Johnson was, of course, delighted. But this was all a happy coincidence, and, contrary to the speculation at the time, Johnson was not the source of the Connally appointment.

Kennedy played a more direct role in filling the top positions in the Treasury. H. H. Fowler, a Washington lawyer with long government experience and a Democrat, came in as Under Secretary. The two vital tax posts—the Assistant Secretary for Taxation and the Commissioner of Internal Revenue—were assigned to scholars who had advised the Kennedy staff on tax matters during the campaign, Stanley Surrey of the Harvard Law School and Mortimer M. Caplin of the University of Virginia Law School. James A. Reed, another Kennedy friend from PT-boat days, became Assistant Secretary for Law Enforcement. For the critical Under Secretaryship for Monetary Affairs, Paul Samuelson and a number of economists had proposed Robert V. Roosa, a brilliant young economist from the New York Federal Reserve Bank. Samuelson, indeed, praised Roosa so extravagantly that the President-elect, who at that time was still looking for a Secretary, finally said, "Well, if this fellow is so good, why don't we give him the top job?" "You can't do that," Samuelson said. "He is too young." Kennedy, noting that Roosa was only a year younger than himself, was considerably entertained. Later, when Dillon mentioned to Kennedy one day the lack of senior economists in the Treasury (most had left in the Eisenhower years), Kennedy suggested that he ask Seymour Harris to serve as economic adviser. Harris, with his versatility, his resourcefulness on policy matters, his deep commitment to the Kennedy program and his imperturbable good humor, played an invaluable role both in mobilizing economic advice for the Treasury and in tranquilizing relations between the Treasury and the Council of Economic Advisers.

And so, one after another, the departments began to acquire their new leaders. Robert Kennedy assembled a crack group from law schools and law offices to man the Department of Justice. Udall similarly worked out his own appointments for Interior. Hodges and Klotz produced the list for Commerce. Goldberg and Ribicoff consulted closely with Ralph Dungan in staffing Labor and Health, Education and Welfare. As the day of inauguration drew near, the Kennedy administration was beginning to take shape.

2. DRAFTING THE PROGRAM

While Kennedy was choosing the members of his administration, he was engaged in still another, and quite separate, effort to chart the main directions of policy. For this purpose, he set up a series of task forces in both domestic and foreign affairs.

The task force idea was hardly new in the Kennedy operation; Ted Sorensen had experimented with one variation or another in the pre-convention period. But the post-election task forces began with Stevenson's July proposal for a foreign policy report to be submitted early in the interregnum. A week later after he told Stevenson to go ahead, Kennedy asked Stuart Symington to head a task force on the organization of the defense establishment; its members were Clark Clifford, Tom Finletter, Roswell Gilpatric, Fowler Hamilton and Marx Leva, all lawyers with defense experience. Up to this point, the Kennedy task forces seemed, in part at least, exercises in the propitiation of defeated rivals for the Democratic nomination. Then at the end of August he announced a committee to deal with national security policy; its chief members were Paul Nitze, David Bruce and Gilpatric, and it included no prominent politician. The Nitze and Stevenson assignments appeared to overlap, which somewhat irritated Stevenson. But Kennedy, in the mood of F.D.R., did not intend to confer on anyone exclusive rights to advise and perceived positive values in competition. So he placated Stevenson and looked forward to receiving both reports.

Before the election, Kennedy appointed four more task forces—on natural resources, wheat, cotton and the use of the agricultural surplus abroad. Meanwhile, Stevenson found himself more involved in the campaign than he had expected—he ended by delivering eighty-four speeches—and he therefore asked George Ball to work with him on his report. Eventually Ball prepared a first draft, discussed it with Fulbright, Bowles, Bruce and Finletter and brought it out to Libertyville the weekend before the election, where Stevenson put it into final shape. On November 14, John Sharon delivered the report to Kennedy in Palm Beach.

The report revolved in the main around Europe and reflected to a considerable degree Ball's preoccupations with NATO and with Atlantic trade policies. "The document has infirmities in emphasis, is uneven in treatment, and I apologize for its length," Stevenson wrote in a typically self-deprecatory cover letter. He thought there was too much detail on sharing the nuclear deterrent and not enough on disarmament and east-west negotiations, too much on strengthening the Atlantic Community and not enough on the problems of the underdeveloped world.

Yet, within its limits, it is an exceedingly able statement. Part I listed questions requiring immediate attention—the gold drain, the postponement of the discussions of the NATO deterrent, new initiatives in disarmament, assurances on Berlin, support of the Organization for Economic Cooperation and Development. Part II proposed long-term policies in the field of trade, economic development, NATO nuclear cooperation and arms control. Of particular interest was Ball's idea for a comprehensive economic bill which would combine new aid proposals with the delegation to the President of five-year authority to reduce tariffs by 50 per cent across the board. Appendixes dealt with the problems of China, sub-Saharan Africa and the organization of the State Department. The memorandum concluded by recommending the formation of further task forces to deal with Latin America and Africa.

When Sharon handed Kennedy the document over the breakfast table at Palm Beach, he suggested that the President-elect might want to look first at the immediate recommendations. Kennedy promptly read Part I, throwing questions at Sharon as he turned the pages: How many presidential appointments would he have in State? Would Stevenson prepare a list of people whom he thought qualified for key positions? How should the proposed peace or disarmament agency be set up? Were there Republicans who might be considered as head of this agency? ("He said," Sharon later reported to Stevenson, "that when one mentions the names of Rockefeller, Dillon and McCloy one has about exhausted the supply of 'good Republicans' and asked if we would come up with additional Republican names.") What was the OECD doing—that is the kind of thing he had not been able to keep up with during the campaign? What about Cuba? How effective was the embargo? Would there be any chance of a 'rapprochement' with Castro after January 20 (Sharon noted that he asked this "rather rhetorically")? What about the problem of State Department allowances for ambassadors? When he finished Part I, Kennedy closed the volume and said, "Very good. Terrific. This is excellent. Just what I needed." Sharon then mentioned the recommendation for additional task forces, but Kennedy made no comment.

In the next few days, Ball and Sharon prepared answers to Kennedy's supplementary questions. In the meantime, the President-elect received the Nitze report on national security policy. This report provided an incisive analysis of the case for a more diversified defense posture. It then offered useful discussions of the relationship between defense policy and disarmament and of the balance-of-payments problem before concluding with some sketchy paragraphs on foreign policy. Actually the Stevenson and Nitze reports overlapped a good deal less than Stevenson may have feared or Nitze hoped. In any case, the two reports evidently convinced the President-elect that the task force approach would help in the interregnum. He told Sorensen to mobilize a broad range of domestic policy task forces, and on November 18 dictated a letter to Sharon proposing a list of further task forces for foreign policy.

He began with Latin America, saying that he wanted by early 1961 to have new proposals

> dramatic enough to catch the imagination of the people there. I would recommend appropriations called for by the authorization of last summer, $500 million [to carry out the Bogota Agreement] but that is hardly enough. What special steps could we take in the winter of 1961 or what recommendations could we make that would create an atmosphere of sympathy for Latin America? Who should chair the task force—what about Berle?

As for Africa:

> We should set up a similar task force. . . . What special proposals should we make in the winter of '61 in regard to raising the educational level, the fight against disease and improving the available food supply?

In addition:

> We should make a study of the State Department personnel in the field—how many speak the language; what steps can we take to improve that; the length of tenure of the Department personnel in overseas assignments—is it long enough; whether the Ambassador should be given greater or lesser control over the various personnel and missions in his country—a related analysis on the general competence and usefulness of the military aides in foreign service. We ought also to consider how to get more Negroes into the Foreign Service.
> We should study the whole USIA effort . . . How does our effort in the field compare with the Communist effort—Chinese as well as Russian—also Cairo's?
> We should have a study of allowances for overseas personnel, not only in Foreign Service but for our other overseas personnel. How do our allowances compare with the British, French and Russian?
> We should set up a task force on the distribution of our agricultural surpluses abroad. . . . How much more should be bilateral . . . multilateral? How can we put more through the United Nations—maybe Hubert Humphrey could set up a task force on this.

We should prepare to set up an Arms Research Institute and should get this in definite form so that we can send it to the Congress early in the year. . . .

Each of these reports should not merely isolate the problems and suggest generalized solutions, but should incorporate particular suggestions which can be implemented by legislative action. These reports should be completed by the end of December if possible.

He concluded by saying that he was sending copies of this letter to Nitze, Bowles and Rostow. "I think it would be helpful if you four could communicate and arrange for the organization of these groups. I will rely on you, John, to be in touch with everyone."

This letter expressed Kennedy's preliminary thoughts, and in the end he did not send it (by accident, however, a copy went to Bowles). On reflection he evidently decided that a four-headed directorate was too much. Instead, he called Sharon on November 23 and told him to set up task forces for Latin America, Africa, USIA and foreign economic policy. When Sharon asked him whether he wished these task forces to be coordinated with Nitze, Kennedy said emphatically, "No. There is no need to do that." He repeated this two days later, observing that, since Bowles had received a copy of the letter, he might head up one or two of the task forces, but "there is no need to work with Nitze." This was not that he liked Nitze less but that he liked a variety of advice more.

Almost immediately a new problem arose. Kennedy's senatorial staff was fighting an inevitable rearguard action against the horde of outsiders to whom their principal was suddenly yielding so much time and confidence. The staff regarded the Ball-Sharon operation with particular mistrust as a device to gain Stevenson a bridgehead in the midst of the Kennedy camp. Moreover, Sorensen undoubtedly felt that in the interests of order all the task force reports ought to clear through a single point. He therefore gave his own task force directive a broad interpretation and moved into foreign policy. As a result, when Sharon started phoning people for the Latin American and African task forces, he discovered that Sorensen and Goodwin had already signed them up. Fearing duplication and embarrassment, Ball and Sharon suspended their activity.

But, if Sorensen wanted to screen the task forces and their reports in the interests of order, Kennedy wanted the reports without screening in the interests of self-protection. When he learned of the situation, he said to Sharon, "I told Ted to turn all this over to you, that he was far too

busy to take on this additional responsibility. I will see
Ted this afternoon and clear this up with him. You are
the one who has charge of these task forces." As soon as he
had the word, Sorensen gracefully called Sharon and arranged to turn over all the foreign policy groups except
three which were already at work—Latin America, India
and the overseas food program.

The task forces now shot forward in all directions. In
addition to the seven set up during the campaign, nineteen
more were at work by mid-December—eleven in foreign
policy and eight in domestic policy. Three further domestic
policy groups were added in January. Sharon and Sorensen
recruited what they regarded as the best talent in the country—Roosa, Samuelson, Robert Triffin and E. M. Bern-
stein on balance of payments; Galbraith, Rostow, Robert
Nathan, Max Millikan, Harlan Cleveland on foreign economic policy; Berle and Lincoln Gordon on Latin America;
Samuelson, Seymour Harris and Walter Heller on the domestic economy; James M. Landis on regulatory agencies;
Paul Douglas on area redevelopment; Wilbur J. Cohen on
social welfare; and many others. The task force members
volunteered their services; the expenses of the Ball-Sharon
operation were met by a grant from the Edgar Stern Foundation, while the Sorensen operation was paid for by the
Democratic National Committee. By inauguration twenty-
four of the twenty-nine groups had turned in their reports.

Kennedy did not read every word of every report, but he
looked at them all and studied some with care. Though he
sent most along to the cabinet or agency head who would
become responsible after January 20, he clearly considered
the task force effort as above all a service for himself. Thus,
when he appointed Rusk, he had Sorensen pass on word
to Sharon that "although he had designated a Secretary of
State, those working on the foreign policy task forces
were to understand that they had been commissioned by
the President-elect and that their reports and recommendations were to be channeled directly to him for consultation
with the Secretary of State."

The documents varied in length and quality—the ones on
Africa, foreign economic policy and regulatory agencies,
for example, were small books; but, in sum, they represented
an extraordinary canvass of vital issues by some of the
nation's best specialists. The task force effort also equipped
Kennedy with an instrument which he could use on special
occasions during the transition; thus Ball and Sharon prepared the briefing papers which helped Kennedy to dazzle
Eisenhower during their December meeting. It exposed him

to people whom he might want in his administration and
whom he had not met in the campaign (or had met perhaps
only helping his opponents in the primaries); thus Ball and
Gilpatric might not have come to his favorable attention if
if had not been for the task forces. It encouraged his old
staff to accept the necessity of enlarging his circle of advisers. It gave the men of the New Frontier an opportunity
to work together in hammering out new policies. Out of
the task force experience there came—for the President-
elect and for those close to him—a freshened sense of programs, of priorities and of people.

3. PREPARING FOR THE DAY

So the transition proceeded, with Kennedy presiding benignly over this diversity of activities and making sure
that every thread was securely in his own hands. His second child, John, Jr., had been born at the end of November.
The birth was difficult, and Jacqueline was making a slow
recovery. This meant that she had to stay in Palm Beach,
and it meant too that the President-elect spent as much time
as he could there in the days between the election and the
inauguration. The time passed placidly in Florida, punctuated by visitations from political dignitaries, press conferences (with Caroline teetering into the room in her mother's shoes), meetings with the new cabinet members and
with the staff, swimming and golf.

The placidity was not complete. One Sunday morning in
December, a man named Richard P. Pavlick parked his car
in front of the Kennedy house to wait for the President-
elect to drive to mass. He had loaded the car with seven
sticks of dynamite, and his idea was to ram the Kennedy
automobile and pull the switch that would set off the explosion. A letter later found on him said, "I believe that the
Kennedys bought the Presidency and the Whitehouse and
until he really became President it was my intention to
remove him in the only way it was available to me." As
Kennedy prepared to leave his house, Jacqueline and Caroline came to the door with him to say goodbye. Pavlick
suddenly thought that he did not wish to kill him in front
of his wife or children and decided instead to try again
later. Though the Secret Service had received word from
New Hampshire that Pavlick was uttering threats against
the President-elect, they did not know until the following
Wednesday that he had actually gone to Palm Beach. They
immediately searched the town and the next day took him
into custody.

On January 9, Kennedy came to Cambridge to address the Massachusetts Legislature and attend a meeting of the Harvard Board of Overseers. After luncheon he set up headquarters in my house on Irving Street. It was a gray, chilly day, but a good many spectators stood outside to catch a glimpse of the President-elect. He received a stream of visitors through the afternoon. McGeorge Bundy rode over on his bicycle to complete the arrangements which would bring him to the White House as Special Assistant for National Security Affairs. Abram Chayes agreed to go to Washington as Legal Adviser to the State Department. Jerome B. Wiesner discussed his assignment as Science Adviser. The task force on tax policy, with Stanley Surrey and Mortimer Caplin among its members, submitted its recommendations. In the middle of the afternoon, the President-elect decided he could wait no longer to select a chairman of the Atomic Energy Commission. Bundy promptly got Glenn Seaborg, Chancellor of the University of California, on the telephone, and Kennedy offered him the job.

At some point between interviews the President-elect turned to me, mentioned my conversation with Bobby in December and asked whether I was ready to work at the White House. I said, "I am not sure what I would be doing as Special Assistant, but, if you think I can help, I would like very much to come." He said, "Well, I am not sure what I will be doing as President either, but I am sure there will be enough at the White House to keep us both busy." I then asked whether this was firm enough in his mind for me to request leave from Harvard. He said, "Yes—but we won't say anything about this until Chester Bowles is confirmed. I don't want the Senate to think that I am bringing down the whole ADA."

He went south that evening and in the next few days began work on his inaugural address. Morning after morning, puffing a small cigar, a yellow, legal-sized pad of paper on his knees, he worked away, scribbling a few lines, crossing out others and then putting the sheets of paper on his already overflowing desk. Many people submitted suggestions, and Ted Sorensen gave his usual brilliant and loyal cooperation. Kennedy's hope was to strike a series of distinctive notes—to express the spirit of the postwar generation in politics, to summon America to new exertions and new initiatives, to summon the world to a new mood beyond the clichés of the cold war. (Walter Lippmann contributed to the last by suggesting, when he was shown a draft of the speech, that the references to the Soviet Union as the "enemy" should be replaced by "adversary"—a word which expressed Kennedy's intention more precisely and which he employed for the rest of his life.) As time passed, the speech took form. Then one day the President-elect stuffed the papers into his battered black briefcase and went north into the cold and snow.

On January 19 Kennedy held a final meeting with Eisenhower. They talked alone and then met with their advisers in the Cabinet Room. The discussion concentrated on points of crisis, and especially on the mounting difficulties in Laos. Eisenhower said that he had hoped that the Southeast Asia Treaty Organization would take charge of the "controversy" but that the British and French did not want SEATO to act. Christian A. Herter, the retiring Secretary of State, added that he did not think that "the Soviet bloc" intended a major war in Southeast Asia but that they would continue to make trouble up to the brink. The United States, Herter recommended, must convince the communists of our intention to defend Laos, at the same time trying to persuade our allies to move with us in concert. If a political settlement could not be arranged in Laos, then this country must intervene. Eisenhower added that Laos was the key to all Southeast Asia. If the communists took Laos, they would bring "unbelievable pressure" on Thailand, Cambodia and South Vietnam. Laos, he said with solemnity, was so important that, if it reached the point where we could not persuade others to act with us, then he would be willing, "as a last desperate hope, to intervene unilaterally." He wondered for a moment why communist soldiers always seemed to have better morale than the soldiers "representing the democratic forces"; evidently there was something about "the communist philosophy" which gave their supporters "a certain inspiration and a certain dedication." Then he said that it would be fatal to permit the communists any part in a new Laotian regime, citing the experience of China and the Marshall mission.

Kennedy, listening quietly, finally asked how long it would take to put an American division into Laos. Secretary Gates replied: twelve to seventeen days from the United States, less if we used troops already in the Pacific. Gates went on to say that he was "exceedingly sanguine" about American capabilities for limited war; our forces were fully adequate to meet "any forseeable test." Then he added that, while the United States was in excellent shape to meet one "limited war situation," it could not of course meet two limited war "situations" going on at the same time. Secretary of the Treasury Anderson spoke about the balance-of-payments crisis. The erosion of the gold position, he said, was continuing unabated; measures had to be found to reverse the present trend.

The *tour d'horizon* reached Cuba. On November 18 Kennedy had learned for the first time from Allen Dulles and Richard Bissell of CIA that on March 17, 1960, the Eisenhower administration had decided to equip and drill Cuban exiles for possible action against the Castro regime. The outgoing President now said that it was "the policy of this government" to aid anti-Castro guerrilla forces "to the utmost." At present, "we are helping train anti-Castro forces in Guatemala." Eisenhower recommended that "this effort be continued and accelerated."

Twenty-four hours later, as he took the presidential oath in the freezing cold of Capitol Plaza, these became John F. Kennedy's problems.

VII

LATIN AMERICAN JOURNEY

THE KENNEDY PRESIDENCY BEGAN with incomparable dash. The young President, the old poet, the splendid speech, the triumphant parade, the brilliant sky and the shining snow: it was one of the most glorious of inaugurals. And the new President himself obviously savored every moment of it. He watched the parade from beginning to end, saluting the marchers and applauding the floats. Noting that there were no Negroes in the Coast Guard contingent, he demanded an immediate explanation and was shocked to discover that the Coast Guard Academy had no Negro students, a condition he ordered changed forthwith. After the parade he dined with the new cabinet, later made the circuit of inaugural balls, and, finally, after midnight, dropped by Joseph Alsop's.

He slept tranquilly in Lincoln's bed and woke very early the next morning. The sun streamed through the windows while he dressed and contemplated the prospects of the day. Soon he was off with springy step to the presidential office in the West Wing. He sat on the presidential chair, tried out the buttons on his deck, summoning Evelyn Lincoln from one adjacent office and Ken O'Donnell from the other, asked Dave Powers where his mail was and explored the West Wing, seeking out the offices of his staff. He called Ted Reardon, who had been with him since his first days on the Hill, and, mentioning a problem, said, "Phone so-and-so, and tell him the Senator says that he wants it such-and-such a way." Then, remembering that he was senator no longer, they both laughed, and Kennedy said, "Do you think the country is ready for us yet?"

President Truman stopped by to pay his respects; it was his first visit to the White House since he had left it himself eight years before. After a few moments, Kennedy took him back to the Mansion to make a call on Jacqueline. They had a gay talk, the old and the new Presidents and the young wife. Later Kennedy brought Robert Frost over for another talk. It was a happy day.

He turned to his new responsibilities with zest. He issued his first executive order, doubling the rations of surplus food provided by the federal government to four million needy people across the nation; this was a response to his memories of West Virginia and the pitiful food rations doled out to the unemployed miners and their families. And he plunged into the great questions of foreign policy. The afternoon before he had received a message from Moscow, signed N. Khrushchev and L. Brezhnev, expressing the hope that "by our own joint efforts we shall succeed in achieving a fundamental improvement in relations between our countries and a normalization of the whole international situation." Kennedy now replied that he was "ready and anxious to cooperate with all who are prepared to join in genuine dedication to the assurance of a peaceful and more fruitful life for all mankind." This message, a piece of State Department boiler plate, expressed the quality neither of the President's hope nor of his concern. For, at the very moment when Khrushchev and Brezhnev were sending their good wishes, the situation was growing worse in Laos. The central committee of the Chinese Communist Party was putting out a statement affirming its solidarity with the Soviet Union and naming the United States as the great enemy of the workers of the world. And the band of Cuban exiles were training on a plantation in Guatemala.

1. FOOD FOR PEACE

I was among those who froze in the Capitol Plaza on that cold Friday noon. I had arrived in Washington the Tuesday before in time for a party given by Jean and Stephen

Smith, the President-elect's sister and brother-in-law. People sat around tables in a vast heated tent in the garden of their house in Georgetown; after dinner there was dancing. Kennedys were everywhere, and the members of the new cabinet, and a vast miscellany of appointees and friends. The atmosphere was spirited and stylish. Everyone felt a sense of anticipation. It was the first rally of the New Frontier.

Among the guests was a quiet, agreeable man with rimless glasses looking like a college professor. As usual, I failed to catch his name; but he spoke a pleasant word or two about a pamphlet I had written in 1960 arguing for a larger allocation of our resources to the public sector. Later I asked Stephen Smith who he was; Steve said, "That's Bob McNamara." The President-elect was there, his face tanned from his weeks at Palm Beach, moving lightly from one group to another with greetings and banter. He asked my wife whether she had found a house in Washington. The remark gave me some relief because I had heard nothing about my supposed White House appointment since the talk in my house in Cambridge three weeks earlier.

When I returned to Cambridge after the inauguration, silence resumed. At the time, it seemed to continue for weeks; but it was actually only a few days before the Senate voted to confirm Chester Bowles. The next morning I received a call from Andrew Hatcher of the White House press office. He said, "The President wants to announce you this afternoon," and requested biographical information for the press release. I inquired when I should plan to come to Washington. Hatcher said that I should ask Ralph Dungan, who was the Special Assistant in charge of personnel.

I called Dungan, whom I hardly knew, and told him that I gathered that my appointment was about to be announced. He said in an astonished voice, "Your appointment as what?" I said, "As I understand it, Special Assistant to the President." After a pause, Dungan said, "That's the first I have ever heard of it." However, he rallied manfully and told me to come to Washington on the next Monday, January 30.

Dungan received me courteously when I arrived. "Things are happening so fast around here," he said, "that no one knows what is going on." Then Dungan and Richard Neustadt stood up with me while I took the oath. I was assigned the office in the East Wing, where James F. Byrnes had held forth twenty years before as the director of the

Office of War Mobilization. I was also given an extraordinarily able and reliable secretary, Gretchen Stewart, who had served in the White House since the days of Truman.[1]

A few minutes later I went to Capitol Hill with a number of my new colleagues to hear the President deliver his first State of the Union message. Kennedy described his inheritance in grim terms—recession in the economy, deficit in the balance of payments, deficiencies in housing, education and medical care, imbalance in the posture of defense, trouble in Laos, the Congo and Latin America—and then, with heartening eloquence, called for action to stimulate economic recovery, to protect the dollar, to improve the national household, to diversify the means of defense and to establish an alliance for progress in the hemisphere, a Food for Peace program and a Peace Corps. "Life in 1961 will not be easy," he concluded. "Wishing it, predicting it, even asking for it, will not make it so. There will be further setbacks before the tide is turned. But turn it we must. The hopes of all mankind rest upon us." We stood along the back wall in the chamber of the House, welcoming the applause as our President set forth his proposals, and then went back to the White House, exhilarated by the sense of taking part in a great new national adventure.

What precisely my own part would be was not, however, clear. The first days in the White House, as a Special Assistant without a special assignment, were uncertain and confusing. Then at the end of the week the President told me that George McGovern, now director of the Food for Peace program, was going to Latin America to discuss food problems with the governments of Argentina and Brazil. As this would be, he said, the first mission of his administration to Latin America, he wanted to demonstrate his personal concern with hemisphere problems by sending along someone from the White House. Knowing my interest in Latin America, he wondered whether I was not the person to go. Moreover, the Latin American intellectual community had the idea that the United States was a reactionary and materialistic nation; maybe my presence in the mission might persuade somebody that things had changed in Washington. He would be particularly interested, he emphasized, in anything that could be discreetly learned about attitudes toward Castro.

The Food for Peace idea went back to the Agricultural Trade Development and Assistance Act of 1954, better

[1] And to whom I must express deep gratitude for her unstinted assistance during the writing of this book.

known as Public Law 480. This measure had been passed
to ease the problems created by mounting farm surpluses
and storage charges after the Korean War; and the Eisenhower administration had carried it out basically as a program for the disposal of unwanted American surpluses
abroad. Though a good deal of food and fiber went to the
new nations in these years, the surplus-disposal philosophy
had seriously limited the effectiveness of the program both
as an aid to development and as an instrument of national
policy. Some foreign countries mistrusted PL 480 as a disguised dumping operation; others acted as if they were doing the United States a favor by relieving the American
economy of the embarrassment of surpluses.

In the late fifties, liberal Democrats in Congress—especially McGovern in the House and Hubert Humphrey
in the Senate—began to agitate for a reconstruction of the
program. This was one aspect of farm policy to which
Kennedy was immediately and whole-heartedly responsive.
McGovern recalls introducing him for a learned speech
about price supports and supply management before fifty
thousand farmers at the National Plowing Contest in
South Dakota during the campaign. "I felt that he was
not at ease with the prepared manuscript," McGovern later
said, "and the crowd reacted indifferently." But two hours
later at Mitchell, South Dakota, speaking without a note,
Kennedy thrilled a farm audience by a moving discussion
of the surplus difficulty. "I don't regard the . . . agricultural
surplus as a problem," he said. "I regard it as an opportunity. . . . I think the farmers can bring more credit,
more lasting good will, more chance for peace, than almost any group of Americans in the next ten years, if we
recognize that food is strength, and food is peace, and food
is freedom, and food is a helping hand to people around
the world whose good will and friendship we want." [2]

In October Kennedy had appointed a task force, with
Murray Lincoln as chairman and including, among others,
Humphrey, to study new ways of using American agricultural abundance overseas. The report condemned "the
conception, the philosophy and the nomenclature of 'surplus
disposal.'" It called for a transformation of "what is now a
surplus disposal act into a food-for-peace act designed to
use American agricultural capacity to the fullest practicable
extent to meet human needs the world over and to promote
world economic development." Instead of sending overseas whatever happened to be in surplus in the United
States, it envisaged the use of American agritultural abun-

[2] George S. McGovern, *War Against Want* (New York, 1964), xi–xii.

dance to meet specific wants abroad both of nutrition and
of development. This could mean shifts in domestic production from wheat and corn into oils and fats and pro-
tein foods; it could mean the use of food to generate
local currency for productive investment and to check the
inflation of food prices which might otherwise result from
development projects; it could mean the use of food as
capital through direct payment in kind to labor working
on dams, roads, ports or similar projects.

Kennedy in his second executive order put the program
within the Executive Office of the President and named
McGovern as director (after Robert Kennedy had objected
to the title coordinator on the ground that it would mean
nothing in South Dakota, McGovern's home state). Mc-
Govern went swiftly to work. In the past, PL 480 had
existed in a limbo between the Department of Agriculture,
which supplied the food, and the Department of State,
which supplied the policy. Though both Agriculture and
State coveted the program, McGovern argued that it should
have a public identity of its own and that it could be best
run out of the Executive Office of the President. Kennedy
agreed in principle, though he was not sure whether it
might not be wise to appease State by locating the office
physically in the Department. But McGovern, taking advantage of the confusions of the first week, established
himself in a vacant suite in the Executive Office Building
before State or Agriculture knew what was happening. To
further the cause of giving Food for Peace a separate
identity, he sent the President a memorandum urging that
Food for Peace missions be dispatched right away to Latin
America, Asia and Africa—a proposal about which he
heard nothing until the Latin American mission turned up
as a recommendation in the State of the Union message.
As McGovern prepared for his trip, he received one day a
phone call from Kennedy saying that he wanted Arthur
Schlesinger to go along "to look into some things for me."

2. THE LATIN AMERICAN DILEMMA

My interest in Latin America was of long standing. It had
begun twenty years earlier in the office of Strategic Services.
As editor of the weekly intelligence bulletin, I had the job of
summarizing and reprinting reports submitted by the regional desks of the Research and Analysis Branch. These
were mostly detached and scholarly documents; but the reports from the chief of our Latin American section, in my
view, showed a clear communist slant. In order to document my suspicions, I began to follow Latin American

affairs myself and soon was rejecting the party-line reports
in favor of my own notes on Latin American developments.
The showdown came over the interpretation of the Bolivian revolution of 1943. The Latin American reports,
faithful to the current party line, described the MNR
uprising against a conservative, pro-Allied government as
a simple pro-Nazi putsch. It seemed more complicated than
that and, reinforced by talks with Latin Americans around
Washington, I wrote about it rather as a social-revolutionary
explosion against intolerable economic conditions and a
government dominated by the owners of the tin mines. The
chief of the section protested; and I was instructed thereafter either to use the reports from the Latin American
desk or nothing at all. This decision was made on orthodox
bureaucratic grounds, for obviously order could not be
maintained if the editor of the weekly bulletin were free
to second-guess the experts. However, I had the eventual
satisfaction of knowing that Maurice Halperin, the chief of
the Latin American section, was indeed a member of the
Communist Party who, after the war, took refuge behind
the Iron Curtain.

This immersion in hemisphere affairs called my attention
to the conspicuous omission of Roosevelt's Good Neighbor
policy. Roosevelt had, of course, wrought a revolution in
hemisphere relations. His affirmation of 'nonintervention'
and of the juridical equality of the American republics,
as well as his sponsorship of the New Deal at home, had
disposed Latin America for the first time to trust United
States leadership. The evident concern of Roosevelt, Cordell Hull, Sumner Welles, Adolf Berle and others had
created bonds of confidence—almost of affection—unprecedented in the history of the hemisphere. Yet, though
Latin Americans trusted Roosevelt, among other reasons,
as the champion of democratic reform, the Good Neighbor
policy did not, as such, call for an extension of the New
Deal to the hemisphere; it was primarily diplomatic and
legal in its emphasis. Except for the Export-Import Bank,
it lacked an economic dimension. Politically Roosevelt even
found it compatible with personal amiability toward Latin
American dictators.

During the war Nelson Rockefeller, as coordinator of the
Office of Inter-American Affairs, began to develop the economic implications of the Good Neighbor policy, initiating
the first technical assistance programs. It was an imaginative and promising start; but after the war it all lapsed
(at least as a public effort: Rockefeller tried in various ways
to sustain it himself privately). The United States govern-

ment, preoccupied first with the recovery of Europe and then with the Korean War, forgot Latin America—a bipartisan error pursued with equal fidelity by the Truman and Eisenhower administrations. Between 1945 and 1960 the single country of Yugoslavia—a communist country at that—received more money from the United States than all the Latin American countries put together.

I was among those who watched these developments with increasing concern. In 1946 I wrote in a piece for *Fortune*: "All across Latin America the ancient oligarchies—landholders, Church, and Army—are losing their grip. There is a groundswell of inarticulate mass dissatisfaction on the part of peons, Indians, miners, plantation workers, factory hands, classes held down past all endurance and now approaching a state of revolt." What should United States policy be? "Many facets of the complex South American problem," the article suggested, "are not accessible to U.S. policy. One facet is accessible—the economic; and one way in which the U.S. can take action to check *Peronismo* and Communism is to develop and execute coordinated measures of its own to deal with economic unrest in Latin America. . . . We now must improve and extend the wartime achievements in the fields of industrialization, nutrition, public health, and education." I added that "our most reliable support in Latin America" came from progressive democratic parties like APRA in Peru, Acción Democrática in Venezuela and the left wing of the Liberal party in Colombia.[3]

In 1950 the Inter-American Association for Democracy and Freedom invited a number of politicians and intellectuals from North and South America to a conference in Havana. The Assocation was operated out of New York by a devoted woman, Frances Grant, who for years ministered to Latin American democrats (she was fiercely anti-communist and anti-fascist), applauded them in power and sustained them in exile (which was most of the time) and did her best to awaken the American liberal community to the existence of the seething continent to the south. The American delegation, of which I was a member, also included such people as Clifford Case, later Senator from New Jersey, Congressman Chet Holifield of California, Norman Thomas, Walter White of the National Association for the Advancement of Colored People, Serafino Romualdi of the American Federation of Labor, Roger Baldwin of

3 Arthur Schlesinger, Jr., "Good Fences Make Good Neighbors," *Fortune*, August, 1946.

the American Civil Liberties Union and James Loeb, Jr.,
of Americans for Democratic Action.

I was enchanted by Havana—and appalled by the way
that lovely city was being debased into a giant casino and
brothel for American businessmen over for a big weekend from Miami. My fellow countrymen reeled through the
streets, picking up fourteen-year-old Cuban girls and tossing
coins to make men scramble in the gutter. One wondered
how any Cuban—on the basis of this evidence—could regard the United States with anything but hatred. We held
a number of long sessions in the Hotel Nacional marked
by the Latin addiction to interminable oratory; and we had
more profitable talks with Latin American leaders over the
luncheon table or in the bar. It was then that I first
met José Figueres of Costa Rica, who two years before
had repelled the first serious communist attempt to seize
a Latin American government. I also met eminent figures
exiled by their own countries, notably Rómulo Betancourt
and Raúl Leoni of Venezuela and Juan Bosch of the
Dominican Republic. Eduardo Frei and Salvador Allende,
who fourteen years later would compete for the presidency
of Chile, were there; so too was German Arciniegas, the
Colombian historian, and Aprista leaders from Peru.
Though memories of Yanqui imperialism had not died, these
Latin American democrats had by no means given up on
the United States. They cherished the hope that the Good
Neighbor policy of Franklin Roosevelt would someday revive and that the influence of the United States would go
to the support of progressive democracy in Latin America.
A few years later I spent some time with Adolf Berle in
Costa Rica as a guest of President Figueres, an experience
which further strengthened my faith in a progressive democratic solution in the hemisphere.

This view found little support in the United States in
the fifties. The stimulus to raw material prices provided
first by the Second World War and later by the Korean
War made it easy to argue that Latin America had no
basic economic problems. The Eisenhower administration
was thus able to relax in the comfortable doctrine that
private investment by itself would bring about development
in Latin America, as they supposed it had done in the
United States; that government aid should be confined to
military and technical assistance; and that the way to
enable private investment to do its job was to back governments which would foster a 'favorable' investment climate by leaving private business alone, guaranteeing investors, especially foreign investors, full and unrestricted

returns and insuring monetary stability. This meant, of course, right-wing governments; and it was this thesis, rather than an innate preference for dictatorships, which sent Vice-President Nixon to Havana to praise the "competence and stability" of the Batista regime and moved President Eisenhower himself to award the Legion of Merit to dictators like Pérez Jiménez of Venezuela (for, among other reasons, his "sound foreign-investment policies") and Manuel Odria of Peru. (When the Vice-President visited these last two countries in the spring of 1958 after their dictators had been thrown out, he became the victim of Washington's identification with the detested regimes.) The insistence on monetary stability before all else received the ardent support of the International Monetary Fund, which imposed deflation on a number of Latin American states as the condition for IMF loans.

The theory of development as an act of immaculate private conception was founded, among other things, on a considerable ignorance of the history of economic development in the United States itself. In the first half-century of our own history government had played a relatively active role in building the turnpikes, canals, harbors, railroads and schools which made subsequent economic expansion possible. When what economists unhappily term 'social overhead capital' or 'infrastructure' is the great need, public investment becomes a necessity, since private capital will not go into these areas of low return. As for Washington's insistence on fiscal purity, this was perhaps a trifle unseemly on the part of a nation which had financed so much of its own development by inflation, wildcat paper money and state bonds sold to foreign investors and subsequently repudiated. If the criteria of the International Monetary Fund had governed the United States in the nineteenth century, our own economic development would have taken a good deal longer. In preaching fiscal orthodoxy to developing nations, we were somewhat in the position of the prostitute who, having retired on her earnings, believes that public virtue requires the closing down of the red-light district.

The policy of the fifties not only violated our own national practice; it was also manifestly inadequate to the problems of Latin America, and it reinforced the cherished Latin conviction that the essence of the United States purpose was economic imperialism. Its result had been to place our position in extreme jeopardy throughout the hemisphere. And the rise of Fidel Castro in Cuba was transforming a failure of policy into a threat to security. This was the situation which the President feared and into which he was now asking McGovern and me to look.

3. HEMISPHERE RECONNAISSANCE: I

We left Idlewild Airport in New York on the evening of February 12. I had known McGovern only slightly, but I admired his record as a Congressman from South Dakota and had regretted his defeat in the senatorial contest the autumn before. Like everyone else (it seemed) in the Kennedy administration, he was five years younger than I— a fact which continued to disconcert one who had long been accustomed to regarding himself as the youngest man in the room. His training as an American historian—he was a Northwestern Ph.D.—established an immediate bond. His modest and diffident manner concealed deep liberal convictions, a sharp intelligence, an excellent sense of humor, a considerable measure of administrative drive and unusual physical courage.

As we flew south through the night, I managed, through astute cross-examination and over many drinks, to drag from him an account of his experiences as a bomber pilot in the 15th Air Force in Italy. On one mission to bomb the Skoda ammunition works at Pilsen an engine had cut out an hour short of target. McGovern decided to go ahead just the same; then, as they were over target, a second engine failed. After dropping the bombs, the plane—the *Dakota Queen*—headed back to the base six hundred miles away, losing altitude at the rate of 100 feet a minute. When they hit the Adriatic, they were down to 600 feet. The crew threw everything movable overboard to lighten the plane. At this point one of the engines burst into flames. After a moment of total despair, the island of Vis suddenly appeared through the clouds. Though Vis's short airstrip was intended for fighters, not for bombers, McGovern immediately gave the order to prepare for an emergency landing. With the fire getting closer to the wing gasoline tank each second, everyone knew that there would be time for only one pass at the field. While the crew sweated and prayed, McGovern coolly brought the plane in—a feat for which he received the Distinguished Flying Cross. He flew thirty-five missions before the war was over. On his last mission, his plane, crippled by flak over Linz in Austria, limped back to base, its landing mechanism jammed, and finally came down with parachutes flaring out from the stanchions beside the waist hatch to brake the landing, despite which ingenuity it turned over at the end of the runway. Five days later the war ended in Europe, and McGovern went off to graduate school.

Our mission began in Buenos Aires. Though President Arturo Frondizi had been elected as a nationalist and a radical, his administration had become increasingly pro-United States in its foreign policy and pro-laissez faire in its domestic policy. The change in foreign policy was especially striking. Historically Argentina had resisted United States leadership in the hemisphere, always seeking to play off Europe—whether Great Britain, the League of Nations or even Nazi Germany—against Washington's attempts to promote an inter-American system. But the days when Argentina could aspire to an independent role were over. In recent years Brazil had so far outdistanced her in every respect that no realistic Argentine could any longer suppose that his country was competing with Washington for dominance in the hemisphere. Frondizi, relieved of this traditional antagonism, was the most pro-American president in Argentine history.

The shift to laissez faire was more puzzling, though it was in part a response to the economic orthodoxy of the Eisenhower administration and the International Monetary Fund. When we met with Alvaro Carlos Alsogaray, the Minister of Economy, he thundered at us across the conference table about the virtues of his 'free enterprise' policies. These policies had in fact brought Argentine national income down 10 per cent and real wages as much as 30 per cent (as a consequence of the termination of overtime rates and food subsidies) and had produced much stagnation and unemployment—and one wondered at Alsogaray's self-satisfaction. Or, if the performance was for our benefit, one wondered whether he understood that there had been a change of administration in Washington.

We found Frondizi a not unimpressive figure, with large, lustrous brown eyes behind enormous horn-rimmed glasses, giving the impression of much shrewdness, caginess and self-control. He had rather the manner of a sharp Italian lawyer in New York who had been associated with Tammany but was about ready, if it seemed advisable, to join the Reform Democrats. As we talked, a delegation of school girls passed through the office; he apparently appeased his constituents by offering them the privilege of seeing him at work.

Frondizi was skeptical about Food for Peace and, indeed, about 'social investment' in general. This was a com-

mon Latin reaction to the program launched in 1960 at
Bogotá providing for a Social Progress Fund and increased investment in housing, education and other forms
of welfare. Frondizi argued that development required hard
capital investment in heavy industry; if this were done, the
new wealth produced would take care of the social problems. A continent-wide program of basic economic growth,
he said, was the only way to save the hemisphere from
communism.

This observation gave me the opportunity to pursue my
mission for the President and raise the question of Castro.
Frondizi indicated that he regarded the Cuban regime as
essentially communist but added: "Castro is not the fundamental question. The elimination of Castro will not solve
the underlying problem. What is required is an attack on
the conditions which produced him. If he is eliminated and
these conditions are left unchanged, new Castros will arise
all over the continent." We agreed but tried to point out
that social and economic reform, however desirable, would
not counter the existing threat which Castro posed to hemisphere unity. What kind of measures against Castro, we
asked, was the Organization of American States likely to
support? He became exceedingly obscure, saying at last
that it would be hard for the OAS to act because a number
of nations—Mexico, Peru, Colombia, Brazil—would hesitate
to endorse anti-Castro measures for fear of domestic political repercussions. He gave no hint as to what Argentina
might do, though we knew, of course, that Argentina had
declined to go all the way with the OAS sanctions against
the Trujillo dictatorship in the Dominican Republic. In
general, his position was that little could be done about
Castro except to press for long-range development.

Buenos Aires itself was depressing. It seemed characteristic that the remarkable writer, Jorge Luis Borges, whom I
had been particularly eager to meet, should be receiving
$60 a month as director of the Biblioteca Nacional—less, as
he bitterly remarked, than a street cleaner. In general, the
government appeared weary and lacking in imagination or
energy. When we went on to Brazil, the contrast was
spectacular. Under Juscelino Kubitschek, the retiring president, the sheer momentum of growth had charged the
nation with a certain economic dynamism. That growth
could hardly have been more vagrant, disorderly and un-
disciplined; a Brazilian economist described Kubitschek to
us as "the playboy of economic development." Yet Brazil,
while defying the orthodoxies of public finance and de-

frauding the International Monetary Fund, could show as a result not only inordinate inflation and inordinate graft but a solid increase in its industrial base and national output. Wild as it all was, it somehow seemed better than the stagnation of Argentina; but one wondered whether a middle course might not be possible.

The hope was that the new president, Janio Quadros, would provide this middle way. He had been a tough administrator as governor of the state of São Paulo, and his inaugural address of a few days before displayed a clear understanding of the fiscal mess he had inherited from Kubitschek. The atmosphere in the new government was bracing and hopeful. Our Food for Peace discussions elicited a concrete response. It was like meeting a crowd of young New Dealers after talking to the Treasury Department in the days of Andrew Mellon. Following a day of talks in Rio, we went on to Brasília to see Quadros.

On the plane Ambassador John Moors Cabot said, "I get very irritated when people blame the problems of Latin America on the United States policy. Of course, I have had my disagreements with and disappointments over some of the things we have done. But the main trouble does not lie in the United States; it lies in Latin America. The source of the difficulty is that the haves in Latin America do not realize that their day is over. The selfishness and blindness of the oligarchies in these countries is the reason why a storm is brewing."

We drove through the impersonal and sinister streets of Brasília, that terrifying preview of a collectivist future, and stopped at the presidential office. Sitting behind a desk in a room with all curtains drawn was a smallish man with trim, precise features. His popping eyes, heavy glasses and aggressive black mustache made Quadros look disconcertingly like a leaner Jerry Colonna; but he radiated a contained energy, and his reactions were swift and incisive. A steel engraving of Lincoln hung on the wall inscribed by Lincoln himself; it was a gift of Nelson Rockefeller.

Quadros greeted us cordially—we were the first foreign delegation he had received since his inauguration—and showed a lively interest in the new administration in Washington. We had decided not to raise the question of Cuba because Adolf Berle was due to see him in a few days. About Brazil, Quadros said that the financial situation was desperate and that he planned to set forth the facts as bluntly as possible in order to prepare the nation for

drastic remedies. He talked well, but with a certain elusive-
ness. I cannot claim to have detected the instability which
would later produce his dramatic resignation; he struck me
rather as one of the new school of delphic statesmen in
the manner of de Gaulle. He had some of de Gaulle's
gift for sibylline utterance—that is, for the gnomic statement which seems fresh and clarifying but at the same
time leaves policy sufficiently ambiguous to keep hope alive
among all interested parties. "The next months," I later
wrote in my report to Kennedy, "will show whether there
is more to him than ingenious mystification."

From Brasília we flew to Recife in Brazil's desolate
northeast. Here we met Celso Furtado, a young economist
who had worked with Kaldor and Kahn at Cambridge
and was now head of SUDENE, the federal commission
for the development of the northeast. We drove with him
through the humid area along the coast, devoted largely
to sugar cultivation. Then we headed toward the semi-arid
land in the interior. I had never seen such an area of
despair—one bleak, stagnant village after another, dark
mud huts, children with spindle legs and swollen bellies,
practically no old people (Furtado noted that life expectancy, for those who survived their first year, was twenty-
nine years). In one hut a baby, lying helplessly in his
mother's arms, was dying of measles. The rest of the family
of seven was sitting on the dirt floor eating a hopeless meal
of beans and farina. When McGovern and I entered, they
looked up apathetically, except for a naked baby, perhaps
eighteen months old, who rushed cheerily toward us, holding out his arms to be taken up. He was covered with
scabs and pockmarks, and we were reluctant to touch him.
A cameraman, who had come along in order to record
evidence of need sufficient to convince Congressmen, kept
flashing pictures of this terrible scene.

Furtado was realistic in his assessment of possibilities.
Seeing no present hope of doing anything in the semi-arid
zone, he was concentrating on the sugar lands. An emergency food program, he said, would do no good; it might
even disturb the existing dietary balance which kept the
people marginally alive. "Real development," he said, "means
giving man the possibility of being happy in his work.
These people hate their work. They are too weak anyway
to work very long. If you give them food and do nothing
to change their way of life, they will only work less." As
we drove through the desperate countryside, Furtado discussed women as the index of the state of development.

"In the poor areas they no longer have the grace or form of a woman; they become beasts of burden." After nine hours in the hinterland, we returned, tired and depressed, to Recife. As we got out of the car, an enameled Brazilian girl came out of the hotel in high heels and a chic Paris dress. Furtado said drily, "We are obviously back in a developed country."

Furtado himself came from a ranch in the interior. During the fifties the American Embassy regarded him with mistrust as a Marxist, even possibly a communist. But in 1961 Furtado seemed to see the problem of the northeast as a personal race between himself and the agitator Francisco Juliao, who was organizing the peasants in *Ligas Camponeses* and urging them to seize the land. McGovern and I were both appalled by the magnitude of the problem and impressed by the initiatives which Brazil had already taken. We carried the cause of northeast Brazil with us back to Washington.

4. HEMISPHERE RECONNAISSANCE: II

McGovern now returned to the United States, while I went on to Peru to complete my presidential mission in the company of a Food for Peace technical group bound for Bolivia. It was headed by James Symington and Stephen Raushenbush.

The process of revolution in Bolivia, which had begun haltingly with the MNR uprising of 1943, had reached its climax when the MNR returned to power in 1952 and, during the presidency of Victor Paz Estenssoro, carried through one of the few genuine social transformations in Latin America's long history of political upheaval. Despite the nationalization of the tin mines and other offenses against free enterprise, the Eisenhower administration exempted Bolivia from its Latin American canons and actually gave it more grant aid than any other country in the hemisphere—about $150 million. This aid, however, had produced little in the way of economic stimulus or other visible result. Much of it had gone for direct budgetary support; the rest for technical assistance. The Bolivian budget had been about $35 million annually (one-fifteenth that of the University of California), and of this the United States had been paying about one-third. But, as a condition for this subsidy, Washington had insisted that everything else should be sacrificed to the stabilization of prices. In 1960 the Assistant Secretary of State for Inter-American Affairs actually told the House Foreign Affairs Committee with regard to a projected development program, "We had to tell the Bolivian Government that they couldn't put their money into it and we weren't going to put ours into it." This decision to pursue stabilization at the expense of development, along with the decline in tin prices, condemned the country to economic stagnation. As President Hernán Siles, who had faithfully carried out the stabilization program in 1956–60, put it, "The United States has given me just enough rope to hang myself." Paz Estenssoro, whose second term as president had recently begun, was now struggling to get his poor and isolated nation moving again.

The visitor to the Presidential Palace in La Paz must pass by the lamppost, across the street, from which the corpse of President Villaroel dangled in 1946—a chastening reminder to his successors of the uncertainty of political life (and one on which Paz Estenssoro may now muse today from his exile in Peru). Paz, an intelligent and harassed man, began by setting forth the general case for revolution with fluency and candor. The great need in Latin America, he said, was to incorporate the poor people into both the money economy and the political society. But too much of Latin America lingered in a quasi-feudal state, with the very poor, and especially the Indians, living under the domination of a landed oligarchy which thought it was ruling by divine right. The longer the oligarchs resisted change, Paz said, the more violent revolution would be when it came. Peru and Ecuador, he added, were particularly near the point of social explosion.

I responded that many North Americans agreed with this analysis, that even a Republican administration in Washington had provided the margin of financial support which had saved the Bolivian Revolution from disaster. Where revolution meant healthy social change, the Kennedy administration could be depended on to look on it with sympathy, but not so when revolution meant dictatorship, repression and the entry of alien forces into the hemisphere. The leaders of the Bolivian government surely bore a particular responsibility to maintain the integrity of their revolution.

"There is much poverty in my country," Paz replied. "The communists have made themselves the advocates of the just demands of the workers and peasants. That makes it hard for us to oppose them without seeming to oppose what we regard as a just social program." But he gloomily admitted that they might try to take over Bolivia as they had taken over Cuba; ever since the Castro revolution, he added, the communists had proved especially successful in winning adherents and forcing issues.

I seized the opportunity to put the President's question. Paz replied without hesitation, "Castro must be eliminated." I wondered how this might be done. He said that first the economic screws must be tightened against him; then an educational campaign must inform the hemisphere of the true character of the Castro regime; then—but at this point he muttered something about the OAS and trailed off into vagueness. His attitude could be described, I think, as composed in equal parts of a strong fear of Castro, a fervent hope that the United States would rid the hemisphere of him and a profound disinclination to identify himself, except in the most marginal way, with anti-Castro action.

When I returned to Lima, I found Victor Haya de la Torre, the leader of the APRA party, even more outspoken in his condemnation of Castro. A car took me to a hideout on the outskirts of the city to meet this oldest of Latin American radical democrats. He had just returned to Peru after a long absence in Europe; and he was still exuberant from the enthusiasm of 200,000 loyal Apristas who had welcomed him home at a great rally a few hours before. He seemed younger than his sixty-six years, jolly and secure, remarkably free from bitterness in view of his years of frustration and persecution, and touchingly sanguine about the future. As for Cuba, he regarded the Castro regime as the great threat to progressive democracy in the Americas and felt that the OAS might consider invoking the Rio Treaty of 1947 against aggression in the hemisphere.

Haya spoke with great warmth about Kennedy and the references to an alliance for progress in his State of the Union message. The new American President, he said, had an unexampled opportunity to lift the hemisphere to new levels of unity. The Good Neighbor policy had been all right for its day, but, though benevolent, it had been unilateral. What the Latin American republics sought from the United States was a genuine coordination of hemisphere policy through consultation and especially through a willingness to create a hemisphere pool of ideas. Now that Washington had abandoned imperialism, relations between the United States and Latin America were largely a "question of style."

He was optimistic, too, about APRA prospects in Peru and critical of Belaunde Terry and his party for supposed collaboration with the communists. Later, however, when I spent an evening with a group of younger Peruvian intellectuals, they all dismissed APRA as old and tired, the party of a former generation. They agreed that it had little to say to youth, that it had a sense of organization but no sense of mission and that the new and vital spirits were looking to Belaunde. They ridiculed the idea that Belaunde was working with the communists.

My last stop was Caracas. I had not met Betancourt since Havana more than a decade before. Till the end of the fifties he had continued to live the life of a political exile, pursued by the agents of Pérez Jiménez, the brutal Venezuelan dictator, and for a time harried by the United States Department of State—a fact for which he seemed to bear no malice. Returning to Venezuela after the overthrow of Pérez Jiménez, he was in due course elected to the presidency. Now he hoped to be the first president in Venezuelan history to serve out his full term. In 1960 Trujillo had done his best to thwart this hope by sending a group of assassins to kill him. They had loaded a parked automobile with dynamite and exploded it as Betancourt drove past in a parade. When the sheet of flame descended on the presidential car, Betancourt threw up his hands to protect his face. In consequence the backs of his hands were savagely burned, though he escaped unscathed otherwise. The man sitting beside him was killed.

After we sipped fruit juices for a time on the veranda, Betancourt suggested a tour of the city. Entering his car, he kicked a couple of machine guns out of the way. Apart from this, security precautions were unobtrusive. As we drove off, Betancourt began to rub salve on the cracked scar tissue on the hands, saying in English, "This for Trujillo—eh?" and laughing genially. On our return there was an agreeable dinner with a number of Acción Democrática leaders, including Rómulo Gallegos, the novelist and former president. Late in the evening Betancourt, an ardent movie fan, had *Der Blaue Engel* projected on a screen in the garden. We sat pleasantly on, smoking Monte Cristo cigars and watching the young Marlene Dietrich, amidst the fragrance of the bougainvilleas and in the pale light of a full moon.

Betancourt was far the most impressive of the Latin American leaders. Tough and good-humored, he conveyed an impression of strength, authority and inextinguishable vitality. Our talk during eight hours ranged widely. He inquired about the new administration in Washington, mentioning the hope that President Kennedy had already excited through the continent. When I brought up Castro, he repeated a remark Quadros had made to him after visiting Cuba: "Those people have no aim, no purpose, no doctrine, no ideology. It is government by epilepsy." Betancourt himself, however, had no doubt of the Castro regime's ideological drift. The personalism of Latin American politics, he said, was a great source of weakness. Without strong democratic parties, like Acción Democrática, the temptation to rely on the disciplined organization of the communists was hard for a man like Castro—even possibly for one like Quadros—to resist. As for a hemisphere policy toward Castro, Betancourt argued that if the OAS first took action against Trujillo it would be easier to unite the American republics against Castro. Beyond this, it was necessary to use all the resources of progressive democracy to combat poverty, illiteracy and injustice.

VIII

THE ALLIANCE FOR PROGRESS

IN A FAMOUS QUOTATION of 1952 German Arciniegas spoke of two Latin Americas: the visible and the invisible. The visible Latin America was the Yanqui's Latin America of presidents, chancelleries, generals, embassies, business houses, law offices, *estancias* and *haciendas*. The other, the "mute, repressed" Latin America, was a "vast reservoir of revolution. . . . Nobody knows exactly what these 150 million silent men and women think, feel, dream or await in the depths of their being."

By 1961 there were a good deal more than 150 million people; they were no longer silent; and the whole hemisphere was seeming to move in response to their inchoate stirrings. When I came back to Washington in early March, it was with the conviction, more urgent now than ever, that the struggle of the invisible Latin America to join the twentieth century was confronting the United States with a crisis—one which, if ignored, might end by transforming the southern half of the hemisphere into a boiling and angry China, but which, if approached in a strong and comprehensive way, might still not be beyond our power to affect.

1. EVOLUTION OF A POLICY

Here was a continent of 200 million souls, at least two-fifths of whom were under fifteen years of age, nearly 50 per cent of whom were illiterate, 30 per cent of whom would die before their fortieth year—a population multiplying faster than any other in the world—where 2 per cent of the people owned 50 per cent of the wealth and 70 per cent lived in abject poverty; yet here also was a part of the west, permeated and tantalized by democratic ideals of freedom and progress, where the existence of a common ethical and political inheritance might create possibilities of partnership and action which did not exist in Asia or Africa.

Here was a world at once fascinating and appalling in its internal contrasts, where a highly polished nineteenth century civilization coexisted with unimaginable primitivism and squalor, and where a surging passion for modernization now threatened to sweep both aside. Here were free republics with meager traditions of stability or continuity—where, indeed, ninety-three illegal changes of regime had taken place in the last thirty years—but with deep pride in their more than a century of independence. Here was half of the western hemisphere, which, if it turned against the United States, would mock our leadership before the world and create a hard and lasting threat to our national security, but which, if we could work effectively with its people, might provide the world a model in the processes of democratic development.

The old order in Latin America was obviously breaking up. There was no longer any question of preserving the status quo. The only question now was the shape of the future. Here was Fidel Castro, the passionate leader of the Cuban Revolution, behind him the inarticulate woes of generations, and behind him too the thrust of communism from beyond the hemisphere; and here was the new young President of the United States, whose accession to power had already awakened fresh hope in the Americas, and behind him the uneven and uncoordinated energies of reasonable men and of indigenous Latin democracy. Which road into the future? My talks with Betancourt, Haya de la Torre, Paz Estenssoro and others had given me the strong impression that the democratic left in Latin America had turned decisively against Castro and that he would increasingly appear as the symbol not of social revolution but of Soviet penetration. Nonetheless, if the United States were not ready to offer an affirmative program for democratic modernization, new Castros would undoubtedly rise across the continent. This was the nature of the crisis.

President Kennedy knew all this, of course; and, when I reported to him, he proceeded, in the manner that was so characteristic, to ask a series of rapid and specific questions: which countries and social groups gave Castro most support? how capable was Castro of setting off simultaneous and prearranged violence in a number of countries? naturally we sympathized with the leaders of the democratic left, but how really effective in fact were they? what were my impressions of Frondizi, of Quadros, of Betancourt? what about our own ambassadors? how prepared were our embassies to handle a massive aid program? He had no illusions about the difficulty of maintaining the position of the United States in the midst of a social revolution in Latin America, but, as revolution seemed inevitable, he clearly believed we had no choice but to do our best, partly because the loss of Latin America would damage our own security but even more because we had a particular, almost familial, responsibility to help these peoples in their battle for democracy.

I put my answers to these and other questions in a memorandum on the dilemmas of modernization in the hemisphere. The modernization of Latin America, I suggested, was basically a task for Latin Americans, though the United States could make a significant, and possibly decisive, contribution to its fulfillment. But no one should underrate the size of the problem. The memorandum emphasized the following points:

1. Because population has been growing faster than output in recent years, Latin America has begun to lose ground in the struggle for development. . . .

2. The Soviet Union, in association with Cuba, is exploiting the situation and providing the U.S. with unprecedentedly serious competition. . . .

3. Time is running out for the parties of the middle-class revolution. . . . The democratic parties . . . have thus far failed to deliver the goods to the satisfaction of the younger and more impatient members of the middle and working classes.

4. Latin America is waiting expectantly for new initiatives in Washington. . . . The Inaugural Address evoked particular admiration. People are looking on J.F.K. as a reincarnation of F.D.R. To a surprising degree, the slate has been wiped clean of past neglect and error. The atmosphere is set for miracles. There is consequently real danger that the intensity of present expectations may lead to future disappointments.

My report only added one more document to the intensive review of Latin American policy which was already under way. The work of reassessment had had its furtive beginnings in the lower levels of the Eisenhower administration. John Moors Cabot, as Assistant Secretary of State for Inter-American Affairs, fought in 1953 for a hemisphere program of economic assistance and social reform. But George Humphrey and his Treasury Department denounced the whole idea, and Cabot, discouraged, resigned to return to the field. His successor, Henry Holland, better fitted the Dulles–Humphrey mood. A doctrinaire apostle of 'free enterprise,' he passionately opposed, for example, United States loans to public undertakings in Latin America, and he feared that, if the progressive democrats came to power, they would curtail the power and disturb the confidence of businessmen, as they had in the United States under the New Deal. It was Holland who tried to keep Rómulo Betancourt from finding refuge in Puerto Rico. After Holland left the government to take advantage as an international lawyer of contacts he made as Assistant Secretary, he was followed by R. R. Rubottom, Jr., a Foreign Service officer of temperate but cautious views.

In the meantime, Milton Eisenhower was emerging as a beneficial influence on hemisphere policy. His education, it must be confessed, was slow. When his brother sent him on a trip south in 1953, he was still the prisoner of 'free enterprise' orthodoxy. But this trip made him for the first time dimly aware that the modernization process might require some changes in social structure, though, as he later wrote, "Except for an uneasiness and a feeling of compassion, I did not relate this [need for social reform] to what we were doing and should do officially." Nonetheless, education had started; and he gained an able and resourceful ally when Douglas Dillon came back from Paris in 1957 to be Under Secretary of State for Economic Affairs.

Though Dillon knew little about Latin America, he soon received his baptism of fire at a conference of hemisphere finance ministers in Buenos Aires in the fall of 1957. Examining the Treasury position papers before the conference, he was struck by their complacent negativism: Inter-American Bank, NO; commodity agreements, NO; development assistance, NO. The State Department was not much better. Its Latin American experts, supposing the Korean War's boost to raw material prices to be permanent, said that Latin America was too prosperous to require external assistance. Three hard weeks at Buenos Aires convinced Dillon that Washington's diagnosis of the hemisphere was badly wrong. On his return to Washington he began to agitate for new policies.

Plenty of ideas lay at hand. Since 1948 the United Nations Economic Commission for Latin America (ECLA) had conducted studies of Latin American development and, under the inspiration of Raúl Prebisch of Argentina, had worked out a number of far-reaching plans—to all of which, however, the State Department had been systematically hostile. In June 1958 President Kubitschek of Brazil put a set of proposals together in a convenient pacakge under the label Operation Pan America. Operation Pan America laid much emphasis on the old scheme of an Inter-American Bank, and this struck Dillon as a good place to begin. In August 1958 President Eisenhower was slated to speak before the United Nations General Assembly. C. D. Jackson, who came down from Time, Inc., to work on the speech, wanted Eisenhower to advocate a middle eastern bank as a device to propitiate the Arab world. Dillon argued that the United States would be in an untenable position if it favored such an institution for the Middle East while opposing one for Latin America. He managed thereby to outflank the Treasury and induce Eisenhower to end United States resistance to the Inter-American Bank. Dillon also, with the concurrence of Thomas C. Mann, a Foreign Service officer who had come in as Assistant Secretary of State for Economic Affairs, set up study groups to examine the question of stabilizing commodity prices, though United States participation in such agreements was still excluded as a sin against free enterprise.

The combination of Dillon, Milton Eisenhower and, in 1959, Fidel Castro finally began to have its effect. The Cuban Revolution convinced Dillon that the United States simply could not go into another hemisphere meeting without solid recommendations of its own to lay on the table. When President Eisenhower returned from his own Latin American trip early in 1960, Dillon persuaded him in June to take a new step and propose American assistance in establishing a hemisphere fund for social progress. This fund, to be administered by the Inter-American Bank, would in effect create a 'soft loan' window for housing, land settlement and use, water supply, sanitation and similar social purposes, to go along with the 'hard loan' window for economic development. Congress rushed through a bill authorizing a contribution of $500 million to a Social Progress Trust Fund just in time for Dillon to make the offer to representatives of the OAS nations at Bogotá in September. He encountered the usual Latin American skepticism about the idea of 'social development,' but finally induced them to go along.

2. ORIGINS OF THE ALLIANCE

In his effort to get the Social Progress Trust Fund authorization through the Congress before the OAS delegates assembled at Bogotá, Dillon talked individually to the members of the Senate Foreign Relations Committee in the summer of 1960. When he called on John F. Kennedy, he found ready support, tinged perhaps by regret over the loss, or at least dilution, of a promising campaign issue.

Kennedy's Latin American interest went back to a tour of South America twenty years earlier. During most of the fifties he had shared the common Washington preference for the problems of Asia until the ferment at the end of the decade—and especially Vice-President Nixon's disastrous trip—renewed his interest in the western hemisphere. Obviously, if the Vice-President were stoned and spat upon in South America, even if one allowed for Nixon's capacity to arouse personal animosity, the position of the United States had declined a good deal since Good Neighbor days. In a speech in Puerto Rico at the end of 1958, a few days before Fidel Castro entered Havana, Kennedy urged that Latin America be given a new priority in United States foreign policy. He warned against the illusion prevalent in North American discussions "that all Latin American agitation is Communist-inspired—that every anti-American voice is the voice of Moscow—and that most citizens of Latin America share our dedication to an anti-Communist crusade to save what we call free enterprise." And he endorsed a number of specific proposals, including the Inter-American Bank, commodity agreements, loans to encourage land reform and the enlargement of programs of cultural and educational exchange.

Critics of the Eisenhower Latin American policy had been making such points for some time. Perhaps the most influential was Adolf Berle, who, after playing a role in the creation of the Good Neighbor policy, had served Roosevelt as Assistant Secretary of State and as ambassador to Brazil. More than anyone else, Berle provided the link between the Good Neighbor policy and the Alliance for Progress. His experience in Brazil, where he helped in 1945 to set off the train of events leading to the overthrow of the Vargas dictatorship, convinced him that the Good Neighbor policy could not survive as a diplomatic and juridical policy alone. The principle of absolute nonintervention, he felt, did not exhaust the policy; it could only be the first phase in its unfolding. If Good Neighborism did not mean a set of democratic ideas, it would be no more than a policy of sanctifying economic stagnation and political tyranny—a result that would injure the moral position of the United States without furnishing strategic security.

These ideas, in Berle's view, implied not only guarantees against aggression, whether from within the hemisphere or without, but the assurance of basic rights, including the freedoms of expression and political opposition, and the commitment to an economic program which would raise mass living standards. Only these positive elements could create a genuine inter-Americanism based on a community of confidence, not just among governments (which was what nonintervention achieved), but among peoples.

This evolution of the Good Neighbor policy, Berle well understood, required the emergence in Latin America of political leaders and parties committed to democratic objectives. During the forties and fifties, when the State Department was ignoring or harassing Latin American democrats, Berle made it his business to keep in close touch with men like Betancourt and Figueres. In this effort, he worked closely with Luis Muñoz Marín, the remarkable governor of Puerto Rico. Together they developed a network of unofficial relationships with the *partidos populares* of Latin America. Kennedy, whose friendship with Muñoz began with the Puerto Rican trip of 1958, fell heir to these ideas and relationships.

Kennedy's man on Latin America was Richard Goodwin. After graduating from Harvard Law School in 1958, Goodwin came to Washington as law clerk to Justice Frankfurter. He then joined the staff of the House Commerce Committee for its investigation of the television quiz scandals; it was Goodwin who persuaded Charles Van Doren to confess that the quiz shows had been fixed. He went over to Senator Kennedy's office in the fall of 1959 and quickly made himself indispensable. Some, especially in these early years, found his personality, in a favorite Washington word, abrasive. He was certainly driving and often impatient; those whom he overrode called him arrogant. But he was a man of uncommon intelligence, perception and charm. Above all, he had immense facility, both literary and intellectual. He soon proved himself more skilled in writing for Kennedy than anyone but Sorensen; and he also showed himself able to take on any subject, however new and complicated, master its essentials with rapidity and precision and arrive at ideas for action. Kennedy liked his speed, wit, imagination and passion.

Goodwin's friendship with Karl Meyer, who wrote editorials on Latin America for the *Washington Post*, had given him an acquaintance with hemisphere problems and personalities even before he met Kennedy. During the campaign the candidate repeatedly cited Latin America as a signal Republican failure in foreign affairs. When the time approached for a full-dress exposition of Kennedy's own Latin American views, Goodwin was charged with preparing a draft, presumably for delivery at the Alamo. On a campaign bus rolling through Texas in September 1960, he tried to think of a phrase which would express for Kennedy what the phrase Good Neighbor policy had expressed for Roosevelt. As he brooded, his eye happened to catch the title of a Spanish-language magazine which someone had left on the bus in Arizona. The magazine, published by the Alianza Hispano-Americana in Tucson, was called simply *Alianza*. Kennedy agreed that "alliance" should be part of the phrase; but alliance for what? Goodwin telephoned Karl Meyer for suggestions. Meyer then called Ernesto Betancourt, a Cuban who had supported the Castro Revolution but had subsequently broken with Castro and was now working at the Pan American Union. Betancourt proposed two possibilities: *Alianza para el Desarrollo*—Alliance for Development; and *Alianza para el Progreso*—Alliance for Progress. When Meyer reported this, Goodwin laughed and said that Kennedy could not possible pronounce *Alianza para el Desarrollo*. Moreover, "progress" had the advantage of being essentially the same word in both languages.

3. THE LATIN AMERICAN TASK FORCE

Instead of giving the Latin American speech in September at the Alamo, Kennedy gave it in October in front of the county courthouse in Tampa, Florida. Finding himself before a restless outdoor crowd, he did not deliver all the prepared text; but when he finished, he told Goodwin that he considered it a most important speech and wanted it released in full as a statement. The speech reached its climax when Kennedy declared his belief "in a Western Hemisphere where all people—the Americans of the South and the Americans of the North—the United States and the nations of Latin America—are joined together in an alliance for progress—*Alianza para Progreso.*" (In the interest of euphony, Goodwin had excised "el" from the phrase; eventually the grammarians of USIA insisted on its restoration.) The *Alianza* would mean, Kennedy said, "a great common effort to develop the resources of the entire hemisphere, strengthen the forces of democracy, and widen the vocational and educational opportunities of every person in all the Americas." It would also mean "constant consultation" with Latin American nations on hemisphere and world problems.

More specifically, the Alliance would involve a number of departures in United States policy:

—"unequivocal support to democracy" and opposition to dictatorship

—provision of "long-term development funds, essential to a growing economy"

—stabilization of "the prices of the principal commodity exports"

—aid to "programs of land reform"

—stimulus to private investment and encouragement to private business "to immerse themselves in the life of the country . . . through mixing capital with local capital, training local inhabitants for skilled jobs, and making maximum use of local labor"

—expansion of technical assistance programs

—enlargment of information and student exchange programs

—an arms control agreement for the hemisphere

—strengthening the OAS

—the appointment of ambassadors who understood and cared about the problems of Latin America.

The Tampa speech summed up Kennedy's thinking on Latin America before the election. But he himself did not feel that the speech had gone nearly far enough; and his letter of November 18, 1960, to John Sharon had expressed his sense of urgency about the need for dramatic new recommendations. In the meantime, Goodwin had begun the work of setting up a Latin American task force. Berle agreed to serve as chairman; the other members, besides Goodwin, were Arturo Morales-Carrión and Teodoro Moscoso from Muñoz's government in Puerto Rico and three professors—Lincoln Gordon of Harvard, who had worked in the Marshall Plan, Robert Alexander of Rutgers, who was an expert on the democratic left in Latin America (and had attended the Havana conference in 1950), and Arthur Whitaker of Pennsylvania, a sagacious Latin American historian.

The task force submitted its report early in 1961. The problem, it said, was "to divorce the inevitable and necessary Latin American social transformation from connection with and prevent its capture by overseas Communist power politics." The communist objective was obviously "to convert the Latin American social revolution into a Marxist attack on the United States itself." The report gave a somber picture of the communist threat, which, it concluded, "resembles, but is more dangerous than, the Nazi-Fascist threat of the Franklin Roosevelt period and demands an even bolder and more imaginative response."

The task force emphasized the danger of armed rebellion and guerrilla warfare in the Caribbean and Andean countries. Since "good wishes and economic plans do not stop bullets or hand grenades or armed bands," the United States must be prepared to offer the military support necessary to defend, for example, the Betancourt regime in Venezuela. But military action alone could not stop communism. Democracy was weak in Latin America in part because the United States "has stated no clear philosophy of its own, and has no effective machinery to disseminate such a philosophy." It was useless to try to "stabilize the dying reactionary situations." A first task of the new administration must be to formulate a positive democratic philosophy; and, since the United States role could only be supplementary, particular effort must go to working with the indigenous democracy of Latin America—"coordinating and supporting the widespread democratic-progressive movements . . . pledged to representative government, social and economic reform (including agrarian reform) and resistance to entrance of undemocratic forces from outside the hemisphere." Political movements desiring social transformation and intensified cooperation with the United States "should be known to have the good-will and support of the United States, just as every Communist group in Latin America is known to have the support of Moscow or of Peiping." To accomplish this, the report proposed the formation of "a coordinating center for a Latin American democratic-progressive front."

Within the State Department, the principal officer in charge of relations with Latin America should have the rank of Under Secretary. In the economic field, Washington must offer "a long-range economic plan for the whole hemisphere," based on "integrated development programs covering several years in advance, prepared first on a national basis . . . and then combined into a region-wide effort." These programs should contain targets for the basic areas of industrial, agricultural and public development as well as measures for achieving internal financial and external payments balance. While private enterprise "has a major part to play," the United States should give greater relative emphasis to indigenous as against foreign capital and end its "doctrinaire opposition" to loans to state enterprises. The hemisphere is large enough "to have diverse social systems in different countries. . . . Our economic policy and aid need not be limited to countries in which private enterprise is the sole or predominant instrument of development." The government should make clear that private enterprise "is not the determining principle or sole objective of American policy."

The report also offered specific suggestions about emergency situations. Its significance, however, lay in the new elements it brought into official thinking. It saw the communist threat as requiring not just a military response, as the Pentagon believed, or just an economic response, as some Latin Americans believed, but a combination of both. Besides military containment, it urged the systematic and semiofficial promotion of democratic political parties and a new stress on economic development through country development plans. These elements carried the task force program beyond Kennedy's Tampa speech or Dillon's Social Progress Trust Fund. If the recommendations were accepted, the goal of the United States would be not just the limited program of social development envisaged at Bogotá but a long-term program of national and continental development, shielded against communist disruption and aimed at leading the whole hemisphere to self-sustaining economic growth and democratic political institutions.

4. BIRTH THROES OF THE ALLIANCE

This view did not prevail in all parts of the executive branch. A preference for right-wing governments had been implicit in the policy of the early Eisenhower years; and the evolution of the Castro regime in Cuba had persuaded some, especially in the armed services, that the right-wing alternative should now become the explicit object of United States policy. The Cuban experience, it was argued, proved that the United States could never retain control of a Latin American revolution, no matter how plausible it might seem in its first stages. As for attempts to avert revolution through pressure for reform, this would only alienate those who held the real power—the oligarchy (more favorably known as the 'producing classes' or 'those commanding capital resources') and the military—and open the door to incompetent liberals who would bring about inflation, disinvestment, capital flight and social indiscipline and would finally be shoved aside by the communists. The conclusion was that we should oppose revolution and reform in Latin America and concentrate on helping our 'tested friends'—those who gave us economic privileges, military facilities and votes in the United Nations and who could be relied on to suppress local communists, tax and land reformers, and other malcontents and demagogues. If we did not support our true friends, we would only convince Latin America that our friendship was not worth having. It was idle to say that a policy of permanent counterrevolution would not work: military support, anti-guerrilla training and unswerving United States backing would keep any friendly regime in power, and the resulting social stability would attract investment and produce growth. Eventually the Latin Americans might become capable of self-government.

There was a sophisticated case for this policy, and it was made during his visits to Washington by a brilliant former diplomat, John Davies, Jr., who had been drummed out of the Foreign Service by John Foster Dulles and was now running a furniture factory in Peru. Davies argued with cogency in conversation (and later in his book *Foreign and Other Affairs*) that the process of development was so inherently disruptive that the first requirement had to be the maintenance of order: "The basic issue is not whether the government is dictatorial or is representative and constitutional. The issue is whether the government, whatever its character, can hold the society together sufficiently to make the transition." Progressive civilian governments tended to be unstable and soft; military governments were comparatively stable and could provide the security necessary for economic growth. This argument, impressive in the abstract, was perhaps less satisfactory when it got down to cases, because the military who really produced development were rare in Latin America. Elsewhere they were revolutionaries of a sort themselves, like Nasser, and hardly more agreeable to the capital-commanding class than a Castro. In finding examples of military leadership which asserted control without manhandling the oligarchs, Davies had to force his comparisons: "Consider what Ayub Khan achieved in Pakistan against what Nehru did for India, or the slow but orderly development under General Stroessner in Paraguay as against the disheveled, aid-dependent performance of Paz Estenssoro in Bolivia."

In Washington the case for the right-wing alternative seemed to proceed less from thoughtful analysis of the conditions of growth than from unthinking satisfaction with the existing social order. During the Second World War the United States armed services began to become acquainted with Latin America. Our officers naturally associated with members of the oligarchy, who spoke English and invited them to parties, and they naturally developed a fellow feeling for their brother officers south of the border. After the war, the War Department argued that military relations with Latin American governments should be enlarged in the interests of the security of the United States. In 1946 Truman proposed—under Pentagon pressure and over the State Department's objections—"to standardize military organization, training methods, and equipment" throughout the hemisphere with the evident hope of ultimately producing an inter-American army under United States generalship. In the wake of this policy came a program of arms exports to Latin American countries. This program was reinforced by the Pentagon's chronic need to dispose of obsolescent weapons and thereby acquire credits against which new ones could be purchased.

In these years the United States military fell into the habit of conducting their own direct relations with their Latin American counterparts, training them in United States staff schools, sending them on tours of United States military installations, welcoming their arms missions in Washington, showing them the latest available (i.e., most recently obsolescent) 'hardware' and engaging in elaborate return visits of their own—all with minimal notice to the Department of State and minimal coordination with the country's foreign policy objectives. The original rationale for all this was the supposed need to protect the long coastlines of the Americas from foreign attack. In time the notion of a flotilla crossing the ocean to invade Latin America began to lose what thin semblance of probability it might ever have had, and the Pentagon began to cast about for new missions to justify its incestuous relations with the military of Latin America. By 1961 anti-submarine warfare and counterinsurgency were the favorite candidates. The Latin American military naturally responded with delight to all overtures and even, on occasion, were able—as in the case of anti-submarine warfare—to play off the United States Navy against the United States Air Force to get the best possible weapons deal.

All this had political and economic side effects. United States military aid obviously gave the recipient governments prestige and their military forces power. The service attachés in United States embassies often disagreed with the polities of the Department of State and on occasion communicated the impression that Washington would not really object to actions the local American ambassador might be trying to stop. A few days before Kennedy's inauguration, General Lemnitzer, the amiable chairman of the Joint Chiefs of Staff, had signed a letter to General Stroessner of Paraguay thanking him in terms of extravagant personal encomium for the Christmas gift of a table cloth; his language cheerfully endowed the Paraguayan dictatorship with "Christian spirit" and "moral might." Such gestures were somehow inconsistent with the spirit of the task force report.

For their part, democratic Latin American leaders began to use the United States arms program as a means of warding off rightwing coups, appeasing their own military and purchasing time for social reform. Thus Frondizi, who ruled on the sufferance of the Argentine military, hoped to placate his generals and admirals by backing their requests for United States arms. Even Betancourt, confronted by Castro, Trujillo and internal unrest, was determined to make sure of his own army by getting his generals the arms they wanted from the United States. This, of course, encouraged military demands on national budgets: Brazil, Peru, Chile and Argentina were all devoting a quarter or more of their annual expenditures to military purposes.

By 1961 the special interests of the military were threatening to distort United States policy much as the special interests of business had distorted policy thirty-five years earlier. Still, even in the Eisenhower administration, the counterrevolutionary case had been a minority view, and in the new administration it had even less hope. After all, the thesis that force was the only thing the Latinos respected was not exactly untested; it was nothing more than a return to the old policy of the Big Stick; and its chief result when tried before had been to make the United States an object of universal detestation. If that policy had endured through the 1930s, the Nazis would have found widespread support throughout the western hemisphere. Only Roosevelt's renunciation of the Big Stick secured the predominant loyalty of the Latin republics in the Second World War.

Nonetheless, pressure for a revival of the policy stirred beneath the surface. The chief voice of the counterrevolutionary line within the government was Admiral Arleigh Burke, who represented the Navy on the Joint Chiefs. Like Lemnitzer, he was an amiable man, but with less flexibility of mind, and he pushed his black-and-white views of international affairs with bluff naval persistence. He had opposed the decision of the Eisenhower administration to support OAS sanctions against Trujillo, and he took every opportunity to advocate full support for all anti-communist regimes, whatever their internal character. For men of Burke's persuasion, talk of an alliance for progress could only seem bleeding-heart, do-good globaloney.

It was here that Adolf Berle made an essential contribution. For Berle, with all his ardor for democracy and development, comprehended also, in another part of his nature, the shadowy world of intrigue, conspiracy and violence. He had an extensive knowledge of communist movements and a vivid apprehension of communist dangers. He was therefore able to give the new social initiatives an edge of 'toughness' which, while it was kept strictly separate from the Alliance for Progress, was still able to protect the idea of the Alliance from those for whom anti-communism was the only issue (as well as in time protect the operations of the Alliance from the communists who sought to destroy it). This ability to combine awareness of the communist threat with a belief in social revolution was possibly one reason why Kennedy asked Berle to join the administration.

But the revolutionary point remained primary. For Kennedy fully understood—this was, indeed, the mainspring of all his thinking about Latin America—that, with all its pretensions to realism, the militant anti-revolutionary line represented the policy most likely to strengthen the communists and lose the hemisphere. He believed that, to maintain contact with a continent seized by the course of revolutionary change, a policy of social idealism was the only true realism for the United States.

5. THE ALLIANCE LAUNCHED

Berle, believing on principle that the top State Department man on hemisphere affairs should have the rank of Under Secretary, was unwilling to accept the post of Assistant Secretary for Inter-American Affairs. Instead Thomas Mann, whom Dillon had transferred to the hemisphere job in August 1960, stayed on in the new administration, and Berle took a somewhat ambiguous appointment as special adviser on Latin American affairs and chairman of a new and now official Latin American Task Force. This was not an altogether satisfactory arrangement. While Berle knew the State Department well, he had always been something of a loner, and the Foreign Service regarded him with ancient suspicion. Moreover, the professionals mistrusted the new approach to Latin America and were even apprehensive about the phrase "alliance for progress" in the inaugural address. But Mann had played a useful role in helping move hemisphere policy forward in the Eisenhower years; and, though he had an old Latin American hand's skepticism about the grandiose schemes of the New Frontiersmen and, on occasion, even responded a little to the crotchets of Admiral Burke, he was a good bureaucrat and ready enough to go along.

Berle and Mann convened the reconstituted Task Force in February. On February 16, Berle again defined the issue— "to develop policies and programs which would channel the revolution now going on in Latin America in the proper direction and to prevent it from being taken over by the Sino-Soviet bloc." The situation in Latin America, he suggested, resembled that of Western Europe in 1947. The Communists had failed then because the Marshall Plan restored Western Europe economically while their own opposition to European recovery discredited communism politically. The need now was to confront the Latin American communists with a similar dilemma by offering, so to speak, a moral equivalent of the Marshall Plan, but of course a plan for the development of a continent held down by ignorance and poverty rather than for the reconstruction of a continent rich in managerial and labor skills. The development program, the Task Force agreed, should be on a ten-year basis. It also agreed that new machinery would be necessary; the Inter-American Bank hardly seemed the institution to organize a social revolution. It decided to press for the abolition of the bar against United States assistance to government-owned enterprises. And it concluded by recommending that the President deliver a major address on Latin American policy in the near future.

In the next week, Dick Goodwin began the White House review of Latin American policy in preparation for the presidential speech. He summoned representatives from all agencies having anything to do with Latin America to a meeting in the Fish Room (so called because Roosevelt had placed a stuffed fish on the wall; preserving the tradition, Kennedy now had a large stuffed sailfish of his own catching in the room). After a prolonged canvass of possible projects, Goodwin adjourned the meeting with the request that each agency submit its recommendations within a week. When I got back from Latin America on March 4, I found him sitting in his attic office in the West Wing behind a desk piled high with memoranda from all over the government.

He also consulted with Latin Americans in Washington. On March 8 a document of particular interest came in from the group of Latin American economists who had been foremost in the fight for development—Raúl Prebisch of ECLA, Felipe Herrera of the Inter-American Bank, José A. Mora of the OAS, Jorge Sol of the Inter-American Economic and Social Council, José Antonio Mayobre, the Venezuelan Ambassador, and others. "Latin America," the memorandum began, "is in a state of crisis. Deep-running currents are bringing about great changes in the economic and social structure. These changes cannot and should not be stopped for they stem from needs which, in the present situation of Latin America, permit of no delay." But they must be guided "in order that solutions may be reached which are compatible with the strengthening of fundamental freedoms."

"The responsibility for such changes," the memorandum emphasized, "lies with Latin America," but international cooperation was imperative if they were to come about in a democratic way. Such international interest had to be free from any suspicion of economic imperialism. "The Latin American masses must be convinced that the tremendous task of transferring modern technology to underdeveloped areas . . . has no other aim than the improvement of their lot." Nor could it be supposed that the free play of economic forces alone would bring about the required structural change. "Vigorous state action" was necessary; and it would not be easy "to overcome the resistance of private groups without disturbances. The policy of cooperation must take this into consideration." The group concluded in somber tones:

> We know that Latin America cannot go through the same stages which capitalistic development passed in the course of its historic evolution. We are likewise disturbed at the thought of imitating methods which pursue their economic objectives at the cost of fundamental human freedoms. Latin America still has time to avoid this, but not much time.

Goodwin's task now was to reduce the jumble of recommendations to a coherent policy. He finally sought refuge in his house in Georgetown, emerging a day or so later with a draft. Ted Sorensen, to whom he showed it, thought that the program should be formulated in the Kennedy manner as a series of numbered points. Secretary Rusk, reading the next draft, proposed, in the Rockefeller Foundation tradition, a concluding point inviting Latin America to enrich life in the United States through educational and cultural exchange. The Department, in a passing mood of acquiescence, omitted its automatic objection to the use of the word "revolution." Kennedy went over the draft with special care, strengthening some points, toning down others.

On March 13 the Latin American diplomatic corps assembled in the East Room of the White House. One hundred thirty-nine years earlier that week the United States had urged the recognition of the Latin republics fighting for independence against Spain. Kennedy noted that the revolution which had begun in Philadelphia in 1776 and Caracas in 1811 was not yet finished; "for our unfulfilled task is to demonstrate to the entire world that man's unsatisfied aspiration for economic progress and social justice can best be achieved by free men working within a framework of democratic institutions." The United States had made mistakes in the past; for their part Latin Americans had ignored "the urgency of the need to lift people from poverty and ignorance and despair." Now was the time, Kennedy said, to turn away from the failures of the past to a future "full of peril, but bright with hope."

> I have called on all people of the hemisphere to join in a new Alliance for Progress—*Alianza para Progreso*—a vast cooperative effort, unparalleled in magnitude and nobility of purpose, to satisfy the basic needs of the American people for homes, work and land, health and schools—*techo, trabajo y tierra, salud y escuela.*

He pronounced the Spanish manfully, but with a distinct New England intonation.

He went on to outline the program, stressing the need for self-help, for national planning, for regional markets, for commodity stabilization and for hemisphere cooperation in education, technical training and research. "If the countries of Latin America are ready to do their part . . . then I believe the United States, for its part, should help provide resources of a scope and magnitude sufficient to make this bold development plan a success." He emphasized that "to complete the revolution of the Americas . . . political freedom must accompany material progress . . . *progreso sí, tiranía no!*" The task was to create an American civilization "where, within the rich diversity of its own traditions, each nation is free to follow its own path towards progress." His peroration was thrilling:

> Let us once again transform the American continent into a vast crucible of revolutionary ideas and efforts—a tribute to the power of the creative energies of free men and women—an example to all the world that liberty and progress walk hand in hand.

It was an extraordinary occasion. The people in the East Room came suddenly alive as the young President spoke his words of idealism and purpose. There was strong applause. Goodwin and I circulated among the group as it dispersed. One found still a measure of doubt and cynicism, but most people were deeply moved. The Venezuelan Ambassador took my arm and said urgently, "We have not heard such words since Franklin Roosevelt." The future of the hemisphere did seem bright with hope.

IX

THE HOUR OF EUPHORIA

THE FUTURE EVERYWHERE, INDEED, seemed bright with hope. By the time I came back from Latin America in early March, the New Frontier was in full swing. The capital city, somnolent in the Eisenhower years, had come suddenly alive. The air had been stale and oppressive; now fresh winds were blowing. There was the excitement which comes from an injection of new men and new ideas, the release of energy which occurs when men with ideas have a chance to put them into practice. Not since the New Deal more than a quarter of a century before had there been such an invasion of bright young men. Not since Franklin Roosevelt had there been a President who so plainly delighted in innovation and leadership.

Before I went to South America, there had been a White House reception for presidential appointees. We had all wandered around the East Room in an intoxication of pleasure and incredulity. One's life seemed almost to pass in review as one encountered Harvard classmates, wartime associates, faces seen after the war in ADA conventions, workers in Stevenson campaigns, academic colleagues, all united in a surge of hope and possibility. The President himself appeared to share the mood, though in his case it was a response to possibilities rather than to facts. He already had his gallery of anxieties—the sliding situation in Southeast Asia, the gold drain, the stagnation of the economy, the Cuban exiles in Guatemala. Yet anxiety did not disturb his easy composure, and he watched the exhilaration around him with pleasure, even if a skeptical smile played on his lips as he considered its more naïve manifestations.

Now, when I returned to Washington a month later, the New Frontier was hard at work. The pace was frenetic. Everyone came early and stayed late. I soon found myself arriving in the East Wing by eight or eight-thirty in the morning and remaining until seven-thirty or eight at night. Telephones rang incessantly. Meetings were continuous. The evenings too were lively and full. The glow of the White House was lighting up the whole city. Washington seemed engaged in a collective effort to make itself brighter, gayer, more intellectual, more resolute. It was a golden interlude.

1. THE WHITE HOUSE STAFF

Within the White House itself, things were beginning to settle into a pattern. Evelyn Lincoln and Ken O'Donnell guarded the two entrances into the presidential office. Pierre Salinger entertained the press with jocular daily briefings. Larry O'Brien, having won the critical fight to enlarge the House Rules Committee, was now deploying his people all over the Hill in support of the presidential program. Myer Feldman and Lee White were working on legislation and messages. Ralph Dungan was conducting the last stages of the talent hunt and supervising questions of government reorganization. Dick Goodwin was handling Latin America and a dozen other problems. Fred Dutton was Secretary of the Cabinet and dealt with many questions of politics and program.

It was already apparent that the key men around the President, so far as policy was concerned, were Theodore Sorensen and McGeorge Bundy. There had been predictions of conflict between the two. Sorensen, it was supposed, having had a monopoly of Kennedy for so long, would not easily relinquish him to other hands. I myself had been warned that, in entering the White House, I would be plunging into a ruthless scramble for access and power. But this did not seem to be taking place—and, indeed, the Kennedy White House remained to the end remarkably free of the rancor which has so often welled up in presidential households. One reason for this was that staff members had more than enough to do and therefore not much time for resentment or feuding. Another was that the President handled the situation with effortless skill, avoiding collective confrontations, such as staff meetings where everyone might find out what everyone else was up to. He tactfully kept the relations with his aides on a bilateral basis.

Sorensen and Bundy themselves were aware of the dangers and behaved with poise and amiability. I had known Ted for some years but never well; it was hard to know him well. Self-sufficient, taut and purposeful, he was a man of brilliant intellectual gifts, jealously devoted to the President and rather indifferent to personal relations beyond his own family. He had grown up in Nebraska. His father, a progressive Republican, was very close to George W. Norris (Evelyn Lincoln's father, Congressman John N. Norton of Nebraska, had been another Norris associate). The Sorensen family resembled the Kennedy family in certain respects. They were a collection of talented brothers and sisters, spirited and competitive, enraptured by politics and athletics, tough and ambitious. Ted's older brother Tom, a man of marked ability and greater personal warmth, was a career officer in USIA who had recently been named one of Ed Murrow's deputies. But in other respects the Sorensens—midwestern, Unitarian, middle-class, liberal, anti-Establishment, puritanical, pacifist—occupied a world different from the Kennedys'. Of Sorensen and Kennedy themselves, two men could hardly have been more intimate and, at the same time, more separate. They shared so much—the same quick tempo, detached intelligence, deflationary wit, realistic judgment, candor in speech, coolness in crisis—that, when it came to policy and speeches, they operated nearly as one. But there were other ranges of Kennedy's life, and of these Sorensen partook very little.

Contrary to the predictions, Sorensen accepted the new situation in the White House with imperturbable grace. The legislative program, domestic policy and speeches became his unchallenged domain; and speeches, of course, assured him an entry into foreign policy at the critical points. No one at the White House worked harder or more carefully; Kennedy relied on no one more; and Sorensen's suspicions of the newcomers, whatever they may have been, were under rigid control. Underneath the appearance of bluntness, taciturnity and, at times, sheer weariness, he was capable of great charm and a frolicsome satiric humor. His flow of comic verse always enlivened festive occasions at the White House.

For his part, McGeorge Bundy treated Sorensen and his relationship with Kennedy with invariable consideration. Bundy possessed dazzling clarity and speed of mind—Kennedy told friends that, next to David Ormsby Gore, Bundy was the brightest man he had ever known—as well as great distinction of manner and unlimited self-confidence. I had seen him learn how to dominate the faculty of Harvard University, a throng of intelligent and temperamental men; after that training, one could hardly doubt his capacity to deal with Washington bureaucrats. Though professionally a Republican, he had supported Kennedy in 1960. On issues, his mind was trenchant and uninhibited. On personalities, an instinctive commitment to the Establishment, of which he was so superb a product, was tempered by a respect for intelligence wherever he could find it. He had tremendous zest and verve. He never appeared tired; he was always ready to assume responsibility; and his subordinates could detect strain only when rare flashes of impatience and sharpness of tone disturbed his usually invincible urbanity. One felt that he was forever sustained by those two qualities so indispensable for success in government—a deep commitment to the public service and a large instinct for power.

Mac was presently engaged in dismantling the elaborate national security apparatus built up by the Eisenhower administration. The National Security Council had been established in 1947 to give permanent form to the wartime State-War-Navy Coordinating Committee and provide the President with an authoritative advisory body for foreign and defense policy. Truman, concerned as always with defending the presidential prerogative, took care to keep the NSC in what he regarded as its place, attending its sessions only sporadically, except during the Korean War, and never letting it forget that the buck did not stop there. Eisenhower, however, with his interest in institutionalizing the Presidency, sought to give the NSC a more central role. In time, he made it the climax of a ponderous system of boards, staffs and interdepartmental committees through which national security policy was supposed to rise to the top. But the result, instead of strengthening the NSC, was to convert it essentially into a forum for intramural negotiation. The process of what Dean Acheson called "agreement by exhaustion" papered over policy discord. The broad and very often empty NSC formulas obscured rather than clarified issues and alternatives.

In 1959 Senator Jackson's Subcommittee on National Policy Machinery began a long inquiry into the national security system. Its recommendations, which began to come out during the interregnum, substantially coincided with Kennedy's own feeling about the future of the NSC. Jackson thought it should be not an elaborate bureaucratic mechanism perched at the top of "policy hill" but "an intimate forum" in which the President and his chief advisers could squarely confront the real policy choices. When he appointed Bundy, the President-elect praised the Jackson study and said that he hoped to use the NSC and its machinery "more flexibly than in the past." Richard Neustadt had taken great pleasure during the interregnum in introducing Bundy to the Eisenhower White House as the equivalent of five officers on the Eisenhower staff. After the inauguration, Bundy promptly slaughtered committees right and left and collapsed what was left of the inherited apparatus into a compact and flexible National Security Council staff. With Walt Rostow as his deputy and Bromley Smith, a remarkable civil servant, as the NSC's secretary, he was shaping a supple instrument to meet the new President's distinctive needs.

2. THE SPIRIT OF THE NEW FRONTIER

The excitement in the White House infected the whole executive branch. A new breed had come to town, and the New Frontiersmen carried a thrust of action and purpose wherever they went. It is hard to generalize about so varied and exuberant a group; but it can be said that many shared a number of characteristics.

For one thing, like the New Dealers a quarter century earlier, they brought with them the ideas of national reconstruction and reform which had been germinating under the surface of a decade of inaction. They had stood by too long while a complaisant government had ignored the needs and potentialities of the nation—a nation whose economy was slowing down and whose population was overrunning its public facilities and services; a nation where the victims of racism and poverty lived on in sullen misery and the ideals held out by the leaders to the people were parochial and mediocre. Now the New Frontiersmen swarmed in from state governments, the universities, the foundations, the newspapers, determined to complete the unfinished business of American society. Like Rexford G. Tugwell in another age, they proposed to roll up their sleeves and make America over.

For another, they aspired, like their President, to the world of ideas as well as to the world of power. They had mostly gone to college during the intellectual ferment of the thirties. Not all by any means (despite the newspapers and the jokes) had gone to Harvard, but a good many had, though Sir Denis Brogan, after a tour of inspection, remarked that the New Frontier seemed to him to bear even more the imprint of Oxford. Certainly there were Rhodes Scholars on every side—Rostow and Kermit Gordon in the Executive Office, Rusk, Harlan Cleveland, George McGhee, Richard Gardner, Philip Kaiser and Lane Timmons in State, Byron White and Nicholas Katzenbach in Justice, Elvis Stahr and Charles Hitch in Defense, as well as such congressional leaders as William Fulbright and Carl Albert. Many of the New Frontiersmen had been college professors. (Seymour Harris has pointed out that of Kennedy's first 200 top appointments, nearly half came from backgrounds in government, whether politics or public service, 18 per cent from universities and foundations and 6 per cent from the business world; the figures for Eisenhower were 42 per cent from business and 6 per cent from universities and foundations.[1]) A surprisingly large number had written books. Even the Postmaster General had published a novel. They had no fear of ideas nor, though they liked to be sprightly in manner, of serious talk. One day in March Robert Triffin, the economist, and I paid a call on Jean Monnet. We asked him what he thought of the New Frontier. He said, "The thing I note most is that the conversation is recommencing. You cannot have serious government without collective discussion. I have missed that in Washington in recent years."

Another thing that defined the New Frontiersmen was the fact that many had fought in the war. Kennedy and McGovern were not the only heroes in the new Washington. Lieutenant Orville Freeman had had half his jaw shot off by the Japanese in the swamps of Bougainville in 1943. Lieutenant Kenneth O'Donnell had flown thirty missions over Germany as a bombardier for the 8th Air Force; his plane had been shot up, and twice he had made emergency landings. Lieutenants McGeorge Bundy and Mortimer Caplin had been on the Normandy beaches on D-day plus 1, while a few miles away William Walton was parachuted in as a correspondent, accompanying Colonel James Gavin in the fighting for Ste. Mère-Eglise. Lieutenant Nicholas Katzenbach, a B-25 navigator, had been shot down in the Mediterranean and spent two years in Italian and German prison camps; he twice escaped and was twice recaptured. Lieutenant Commander Douglas Dillon had been under Kamikaze attack in Lingayen Gulf and had flown a dozen combat patrol missions. Captain Roger Hilsman had led a

[1] Seymour E. Harris, *The Economics of the Political Parties* (New York, 1962), 25.

band of native guerrillas behind Japanese lines in Burma. Lieutenant Edward Day had served on a submarine chaser in the Solomons and a destroyer escort in the Atlantic. Lieutenant Byron White had fought in the Solomons. Ensign Pierre Salinger had been decorated for a dangerous rescue in the midst of a typhoon from his subchaser off Okinawa. Major Dean Rusk had been a staff officer in the China-Burma-India theater. Major Arthur Goldberg had organized labor espionage for the OSS in Europe. Lieutenant Stewart Udall had served in the Air Force. Lieutenants Paul Fay and James Reed were veterans of the PT-boat war in the Pacific.

The war experience helped give the New Frontier generation its casual and laconic tone, its grim, puncturing humor and its mistrust of evangelism. It accounted in particular, I think, for the differences in style between the New Frontiersmen and the New Dealers. The New Dealers were incorrigible philosophizers—"chain talkers," someone had sourly called them thirty years before—and the New Deal had a distinctive and rather moralistic rhetoric. The men of the thirties used to invoke 'the people,' their ultimate wisdom and the importance of doing things for them in a way quite alien to the New Frontier. The mood of the new Washington was more to do things because they were rational and necessary than because they were just and right, though this should not be exaggerated. In the thirties idealism was sometimes declared, even when it did not exist; in the sixties, it was sometimes deprecated, even when it was the dominant motive.

The New Frontiersmen had another common characteristic: versatility. They would try anything. Most had some profession or skill to which they could always return; but ordinarily they used it as a springboard for general meddling. Kenneth Galbraith was an economist who, as ambassador to India, reviewed novels for *The New Yorker* and wrote a series of pseudonymous satiric skits for *Esquire*. Bill Walton was a newspaperman turned abstract painter. This was especially true in the White House itself. Where Eisenhower had wanted a staff with clearly defined functions, Kennedy resisted pressures toward specialization; he wanted a group of all-purpose men to whom he could toss anything. It seemed to me that in many ways Dick Goodwin, though younger than the average, was the archetypal New Frontiersman. His two years in the Army had been too late for the war, even too late for Korea. But he was the supreme generalist who could turn from Latin America to saving the Nile monuments at Abu Simbel, from civil rights to planning the White House dinner for the Nobel Prize winners, from composing a parody of Norman Mailer to drafting a piece of legislation, from lunching with a Supreme Court Justice to dining with Jean Seberg—and at the same time retain an unquenchable spirit of sardonic liberalism and an unceasing drive to get things done.

Not everyone liked the new people. Washington never had. "A plague of young lawyers settled on Washington," one observer had said of the New Dealers. ". . . They floated airily into offices, took desks, asked for papers and found no end of things to be busy about. I never found out why they came, what they did or why they left." Even Learned Hand complained in 1934 that they were "so conceited, so insensitive, so arrogant." Old-timers felt the same resentments in March 1961. One could not deny a sense of New Frontier autointoxication; one felt it oneself. The pleasures of power, so long untasted, were now being happily devoured—the chauffeur-driven limousines, the special telephones, the top secret documents, the personal aides, the meetings in the Cabinet Room, the calls from the President. Merriman Smith, who had seen many administrations come and go, wrote about what he called the New People: "hoteyed, curious but unconcerned with protocol, and yeasty with shocking ideas . . . they also have their moments of shortsightedness, bias, prejudice and needlessly argumentative verbosity." The verbosity, I have suggested, was marked only in comparison with the muteness of the Eisenhower days; but the rest was true enough, especially in these first heady weeks.

The currents of vitality radiated out of the White House, flowed through the government and created a sense of vast possibility. The very idea of the new President taking command as tranquilly and naturally as if his whole life had prepared him for it could not but stimulate a flood of buoyant optimism. The Presidency was suddenly the center of action: in the first three months, thirty-nine messages and letters to Congress calling for legislation, ten prominent foreign visitors (including Macmillan, Adenauer and Nkrumah), nine press conferences, new leadership in the regulatory agencies and such dramatic beginnings as the Alliance for Progress and the Peace Corps. Above all, Kennedy held out such promise of hope. Intelligence at last was being applied to public affairs. Euphoria reigned; we thought for a moment that the world was plastic and the future unlimited.

Yet I don't suppose we really thought this. At bottom we knew how intractable the world was—the poverty and dis-

order of Latin America, the insoluble conflict in Laos, the
bitter war in Vietnam, the murky turbulence of Africa,
the problems of discrimination and unemployment in
our own country, the continuing hostility of Russia and
China. The President knew better than anyone how hard
his life was to be. Though he incited the euphoria, he did
so involuntarily, for he did not share it himself. I never
heard him now use the phrase 'New Frontier'; I think he regarded it with some embarrassment as a temporary capitulation to rhetoric. Still even Kennedy, the ironist and
skeptic, had an embarrassed confidence in his luck and in
these weeks may have permitted himself moments of optimism. In any case, he knew the supreme importance of a
first impression and was determined to create a picture
of drive, purpose and hope.

I had gone to the White House for dinner a few nights
before leaving for South America. It was a small party for
Sam Rayburn and his sister. The Vice-President and his
wife were there, the Fulbrights, the Arthur Krocks, Mrs.
Nicholas Longworth and myself. The historian looking
around the table could not but be impressed by the conti-
nuities of our national life—Alice Roosevelt Longworth,
who had lived in this house sixty years before; Rayburn,
who had come to Congress fifty years ago; Krock, who had
covered Washington for forty years; Johnson, who had
drawn his inspiration from the second Roosevelt; Fulbright,
who had served the country so well since the Second World
War; and then Kennedy, younger than any of them, courteously enjoying their stories, soliciting their counsel, and
all the while preserving his easy domination of the evening and seeming almost to pull the threads of history together in his hands.

Perhaps the sense of possibility had its gayest image in a
party the Kennedys gave for the Radziwills in the middle
of March. Eighty guests sat around small tables in the Blue
Room, and there was dancing till three in the morning.
Never had girls seemed so pretty, tunes so melodious, an
evening so blithe and unconstrained. The President, who
rarely danced, moved from one group to another, a glass
of champagne in his hand (the same glass most of the evening—he rarely drank either), while the music played lightly
on. The glitter of that night remained in slightly ironic
memory for a long time.

3. THE SHADOW OF CASTRO

In the meantime, the Central Intelligence Agency was training 1200 Cuban exiles at a coffee *finca* high in the

Sierra Madre mountains on the Pacific coast of Guatemala, and Kennedy was confronting the first drastic decision of his administration.

The circumstances which brought these Cubans to alien shores and desperate designs were mixed. In the main, they had not been adherents of Fulgencio Batista. Some had fought with Fidel Castro in the Sierra Maestra, many more had welcomed Castro's entry into Havana. They were less opponents than casualties of the Cuban Revolution.

Much has been written about that revolution, its origins and its objectives. Jean-Paul Sartre and C. Wright Mills, who visited Cuba in 1959–60, later proclaimed that the revolution was a peasant uprising, caused by conditions of intolerable poverty and despair in a wretchedly under-developed country. In fact, as more careful writers like Theodore Draper and Hugh Thomas have pointed out, Cuba was hardly in so hopeless a shape. It was, indeed, the perfect test of the Eisenhower theory that unhampered private investment was Latin America's road to salvation. It stood fourth among Latin American nations in per capita income, fifth in manufacturing, first in per capita distribution of automobiles and radios. It ranked near the top in education, literacy, social services and urbanization. These aggregate statistics, however, concealed shocking disparities in the distribution of wealth, especially as between city and countryside and between white and Negro. There was enough wealth about to reveal to all how agreeable wealth might be. The statistics also—along with the popularity of Havana cigars—concealed the extent to which the Cuban economy depended on a single industry, sugar, which not only was at the mercy of world markets but was itself then in a state of decline. Still, if Cuba had serious economic problems and, compared to the United States, a low standard of living, it was quite well off compared to Haiti or Bolivia. The immediate motives behind the revolution were as much political as economic, and the revolutionaries themselves were members of the middle class rather than peasants or workers.

Cuba's history as an independent republic had been a drama of acute and chronic political frustration. One crowd after another had come to power on promises of progress and regeneration only to go out in orgies of graft and plunder. Dr. Carlos Prío Socarrás, who had presided over a genial regime of social reform and political corruption until Batista overthrew him in 1952, once visited my office in the White House and observed with a certain dignity, "They say that I was a terrible president of Cuba.

That may be true. But I was the best president Cuba ever had." That may be true too. By the late 1950s a feeling was spreading through the intellectual community and the professional and even business classes that life was becoming intolerable—the sugar industry was deteriorating, the educational system was decaying, illiteracy was increasing, and Batista was keeping himself in power only by a mounting use of repression, corruption and violence.

This feeling of political and social disgust produced a passion for change. In its origins, the Cuban Revolution was led by professional men and intellectuals (like the Castro brothers and Ernesto Guevara, the Argentine physician) and subsidized by businessmen and landowners. As Blas Roca, secretary of the Cuban Communist Party, admitted in 1959, "The armed struggle was initiated by the petty bourgeoisie." [2] The avowed aim was to establish a regime pledged to carry out the liberal constitution of 1940, which provided for free elections, civil liberties and agrarian diversification and reform. This aim enlisted wide backing throughout the country. At the start of 1957 Castro had been the leader of a beleaguered band of a dozen men hiding out in the hills; at the end of 1958 he entered Havana in triumph. He did this, not because he defeated Batista's 40,000 soldiers on the battlefield—at the moment of victory, his own force numbered less than two thousand men—but because of the withdrawal of support from Batista's government on the part of most of the people and most of the army. The Havana underground, brilliantly organized by a radical young engineer named Manuel Ray, completed the work Castro had begun in the Sierra Maestra.

To what extent did Castro at this point conceal secret communist purposes? He later said that he hid radical views in order to hold the anti-Batista coalition together, and this was probably true. But, though a radical, there is no conclusive evidence that he was then a Communist or even a Marxist-Leninist. Whatever he later became, he began as a romantic, left-wing nationalist—in his own phrase, a "utopian Socialist." He had tried to read *Das Kapital* at the University of Havana but, according to his own account, bogged down on page 370. When he made his first assault on the regime—the attack on the Moncada barracks on July 26, 1953—the Partido Socialista Popular, the Cuban Communist Party, still had relations with Batista. It should not be forgotten that in 1943 Batista had appointed to his cabinet the first avowed Communists ever to hold cabinet posts in any American government; one of them—Carlos Rafael Rodríguez—was in Castro's government twenty years later. Even when the Communists broke with Batista, they continued to condemn Castro as "bourgeois" and a "putschist," adolescent and irresponsible. They refused to believe the situation 'ripe' for revolution. Javier Pazos, the son of Castro's first head of the Bank of Cuba, who served as an officer on Castro's staff in the Sierra Maestra until he was captured by Batista in early 1958, wrote, "The Fidel Castro I knew . . . was definitely not a Marxist. Nor was he particularly interested in social revolution. He was, above all, a political opportunist—a man with a firm will and an extraordinary ambition. He thought in terms of winning power and keeping it." [3]

Sometime in 1958 the Communists began quietly to co-operate with Castro's 26th of July Movement. When Castro came to Havana in January 1959, the Communists were firmly installed as part of the coalition behind him. The next months were critical. Fidel was accustomed to running a guerrilla band, not a government. He had slogans but no program. He was an exciting figure, with his black beard, his flashing eyes, his inexhaustible flow of pungent and philosophical rhetoric, his sympathy and his audacity, and he had an adoring personal following, but a personal following was no substitute for an organization. Hugh Thomas has pointed out the institutional softness of Cuba—the absence of any body of solid democratic experience, of traditions of political continuity and party responsibility, the vulnerability of the system of justice, the civil service, the army, the trade unions, even the Church.[4] In the clamor and confusion, one group stood out as experienced, disciplined, effective, possessed of both revolutionary ideas and the capacity to execute them. This was the Communist Party. Fidel's younger brother Raúl and Guevara, who had long had close relations with the Communists, no doubt helped move Fidel in this direction. Now that he had won his power, the Communists offered him the means of keeping it and using it.

The next months brought widespread and largely beneficial social cleansing and reform. Castro spoke eloquently about a "humanist" revolution which would avoid the errors of both capitalism and communism. But all the while the

[3] Javier Felipe Pazos Vea, "Cuba—'Long Live the Revolution!'" *New Republic*, November 3, 1962.
[4] Hugh Thomas, "The Origins of the Cuban Revolution," *World Today*, October 1963.

Communists were filling their available vacuum, until the revolution had become in large measure their own. This process can be dated with some precision. In January Castro asked José Figueres of Costa Rica, whose gifts of arms and money had kept him going in the early days in the Sierra Maestra, to come to Havana. Figueres could not accept the invitation until March. On his arrival, he later told me, he found the atmosphere curiously sullen and hostile. Castro put off seeing him, but they finally met at a great mass meeting of the Cuban Trade Union Confederation. When Figueres called on the revolution to keep its independence and not become the instrument of extracontinental powers, David Salvador, the secretary-general of the confederation, rushed to the microphone and denounced him as a lackey of Wall Street. Castro himself followed with a bitter speech against the imperialists. By July Castro forced the resignation of Manuel Urrutia, the president of the provisional government, for having criticized communism in a television speech. In October, when Major Huber Matos, one of the heroes of the Sierra Maestra, warned against communist penetration of the government, he was arrested and, after a heated cabinet meeting dissuaded Castro from having him shot, he was sentenced in December to twenty years in prison. In November, Manuel Ray, now Minister of Public Works, Felipe Pazos, head of the national bank, and other representatives of the democratic wing of the revolution resigned from the cabinet. By the end of the year the Communist Party alone enjoyed freedom of political action. (And in a few months more, David Salvador himself who, though fiercely anti-Yanqui, was not a Communist, was seized while trying to escape from Cuba and sent to one of Castro's prisons.)

It cannot be said that there was a fight between the Marxist and democratic wings of the revolution, because the democrats allowed themselves to be picked off one by one; perhaps, as Hugh Thomas has suggested, some felt half the time that, given the record of betrayal by previous reform regimes, they could not now object to an excess of zeal. Nor can it be said that the fusion of the Communist Party and the Castro Revolution was ever complete. The Communists succeeded in breaking their only organizational rival, the 26th of July Movement; but tensions remained— of generations and of temperaments—between the middle-aged bureaucrats of the party and the youthful beatniks of the revolution. To a degree, these tensions may have come to correspond with the widening gap between Russia and

China. The men of the Sierra Maestra—Che Guevara, for example—could identify themselves more easily with the Chinese Revolution, which like their own claimed a peasant base, utilized guerrilla methods and expelled foreign imperialism, than with the Bolshevik Revolution, which had emerged from a quite different experience. Though Fidel came to boast of his Marxism-Leninism, he himself never joined the Communist Party. As the revolution careened along, the Communists may even at times have served as a restraining force, especially in foreign affairs. Yet, despite the jostling for position between Communists and *Fidelistas*, the year 1959 saw the clear commitment of Castro's revolution to the establishment of a Marxist dictatorship in Cuba and the service of Soviet foreign policy in the world— a commitment so incompatible with the expressed purposes of the revolution as surely to justify the word betrayal.

4. WHO LOST CUBA?

Was all this inevitable? Or was it the result of mistaken United States policy which left Castro no alternative? No legend is more enduring than the notion that Washington 'forced' Cuba into the arms of Moscow. In fact, the revolution was very popular in the United States in the early months of 1959. When Castro visited this country in the spring, his journey had aspects of a triumphal procession. I met him at the Harvard Faculty Club in Cambridge, jaunty in his olive-green fatigues, and heard him speak that evening to several thousand students in the Harvard Stadium. He gave a fluent harangue, memorable chiefly for a disarming ability to make jokes in English. The undergraduates were delighted. They saw in him, I think, the hipster who in the era of the Organization Man had joyfully defied the system, summoned a dozen friends and overturned a government of wicked old men.

Even the Eisenhower administration hoped for a while they could do something with him. Official policy toward Castro, it must be said, had been in a more than usual state of confusion. Eisenhower's first ambassador, Arthur Gardner, was strongly pro-Batista; his successor, Earl E. T. Smith, hoped that Batista would leave quietly; while the State Department was sure that the dictatorship was doomed. Arms deliveries to Batista were stopped as early as March 1958, but the United States military mission remained—a compromise which displeased both sides. When Batista fled the country, Washington gave the revolutionary

government prompt recognition. In March 1959 it sent a
new ambassador to Havana—Philip Bonsal, a skilled and
liberal-minded professional who had earned the deep dislike of the Rojas Pinilla dictatorship in Colombia and then
had won the confidence of the leaders of the Bolivian Revolution. When Castro reached Washington in April, the
State Department set up meetings with the economic members of his delegation to discuss an aid program.

But Castro had instructed these officials, to their astonishment, not to raise the question of assistance. Rufo Ló-
pez Fresquet, his Finance Minister, saw Secretary of the
Treasury Anderson and Assistant Secretary of State Rubottom and, as he later wrote, "feigned polite aloofness" when
economic cooperation was mentioned. Castro himself loftily
informed the American Society of Newspaper Editors that,
unlike other foreign leaders who came to Washington to sell
their souls, "We did not come here for money." As early
as the spring of 1959, Castro seems to have decided to cast
the United States in the role of enemy of the revolution. The
hostility of Washington would provide the all-purpose excuse to cancel elections, eliminate political opposition and
tighten internal controls. It is notable that Castro himself
never then or later used the argument so dear to Castro
sympathizers outside Cuba that rejection in Washington
drove him to Moscow. Che Guevara denied in 1964 that
Castro could ever possibly have been seduced by American
blandishments.

Castro's evident pleasure in shooting *Batistianos* after
circus-like trials shocked opinion in the United States; this
reaction, in contrast to the earlier North American ennui
over Batista's terror, shocked Cubans. The State Department grew obsessed with the problem of getting American
citizens proper indemnification for expropriated land and
business; Havana construed this as the anticipated enmity
of American business to Cuban reform. Washington became disturbed over Castro's nonstop anti-Yanqui orations;
Havana complained about exile bombing raids apparently
launched from private airfields in Florida. These recriminations only confirmed Castro in a course set for other reasons. Bonsal, for all his friendliness to the revolution, had
increasing trouble even getting in to see Castro. On May
8, he requested an interview; the request was not granted till
June 13. On July 23 Bonsal sought another meeting—not
arranged till September 5. By November, when Manuel Ray
and others left the government, Bonsal decided that Castro
had no wish for any sort of understanding. But Bonsal still

advocated a policy of moderation in order to make it more difficult for Castro to rush to the other side. If the United States played the role Castro had cast for it, Bonsal felt, it would only fulfill Castro's purposes.

Others in Washington—especially Vice-President Nixon, who had met Castro during his Washington visit and distrusted him from the start—wanted a more aggressive policy, if only on a contingency basis. But as late as January 1960 the United States government made a new effort to reach an understanding, using Dr. Julio A. Amoedo, the Argentine ambassador to Havana and a personal friend of Castro's, as the intermediary. There appears to have been still another attempt in March through Rufo Lopez Fresquet. On the morning of March 17, 1960, President Dorticós rejected this last United States overture. Lopez Fresquet responded that he had remained as Finance Minister only on the assumption that the Cuban government wanted to compose its differences with Washington; if Castro thought no reconciliation possible, then, Lopez Fresquet said, he wanted to resign. Dorticós immediately accepted his resignation. On the same day in Washington President Eisenhower agreed to a recommendation from the CIA to train a force of Cuban exiles for possible use against Castro.

But Washington still declined to use the weapons of economic pressure which lay so easily at hand. It was not until July 1960, long after Castro had effected the substantial communization of the government, army and labor movement and had negotiated economic agreements with Russia and China, that the United States took public retaliatory action of a major sort. The suspension of the balance of Cuba's 1960 sugar quota (that same quota which Guevara had already denounced in March as "economic slavery") was the conclusion, and not the cause, of Castro's hostility. Or rather it was not quite the conclusion. Washington did not finally break off diplomatic relations until January 3, 1961, and then because of Castro's scornful demand that the staff of the Havana Embassy be reduced to eleven people in forty-eight hours.

Once Castro had taken power, it is hard to see that any different United States policy, short of invasion, could have averted the capture of the revolution. The policy of the Eisenhower administration lacked both imagination and consistency, but it was certainly not one of purposeful hostility. Castro took the revolution east for his own reasons. In doing so, he drove many Cubans who had opposed Batista and still held to the original principles of the revolution from their homeland. Some of these men were now drilling on the coffee plantation in Guatemala.

The perversion of the Cuban Revolution was evident enough to leaders of the democratic left in Latin America, like Betancourt, Figueres and Haya de la Torre. It was less evident, however, to left-wing intellectuals in North America and Europe. In spite of a score of disillusionments in Russia, eastern Europe and China—so many eggs broken and so few omelettes—many still cherished the hope that sometime, somewhere, revolution would at last achieve the dream of a truly just and joyous society. "The facts of life do not penetrate to the sphere in which our beliefs are cherished," Proust has written; "as it was not they that engendered those beliefs, so they are powerless to destroy them; they can aim at them continual blows of contradiction and disproof without weakening them; and an avalanche of miseries and maladies coming, one after another, without interruption into the bosom of a family, will not make it lose faith in either the clemency of its God or the capacity of its physician." Among the pilgrims Cuba for a moment rekindled emotions which had not burned with such purity since the Spanish Civil War.

And it was true that revolutionary Cuba had a reckless and anarchic verve unknown in any other communist state, that it had abolished corruption, that it was educating and inspiring its people, that it had exuberantly reclaimed a national identity, that it was traduced and slandered in the foreign press—and these truths blotted out harsher truths and subtler corruptions. So C. Wright Mills, after stating the revolutionary case in an angry book: "Like most Cubans, I too believe that this revolution is a moment of truth." So Jean-Paul Sartre: "I do not see how any people can propose today a more urgent goal nor one more worthy of its efforts. The Cubans must win, or we will lose all, even hope." As Castro's dictatorship within Cuba was a fact, so too was the faith men of good will outside Cuba vested in him.

5. CASTRO AND KENNEDY

Cuba was not a new issue for Kennedy, nor had his view of Fidel Castro been wholly negative. Early in 1960, writing of the "wild, angry, passionate course" of the Cuban Revolution in *The Strategy of Peace,* he described Castro as "part of the legacy of Bolivar," part too "of the frustration of that earlier revolution which won its war against Spain but left largely untouched the indigenous feudal or-

der." He had no doubt, as he said later in the year, that
"the brutal, bloody, and despotic dictatorship of Fulgencio
Batista" had invited its own downfall; and he freely declared
his sympathy with the motives behind the revolution and
with its expressed objectives. He even raised the question
in *The Strategy of Peace* whether Castro might not have
taken "a more rational course" had the United States government not backed Batista "so long and so uncritically"
and had it given Castro a warmer welcome on his trip to
Washington. But he had no question now that Castro had
"betrayed the ideals of the Cuban revolution" and transformed Cuba "into a hostile and militant Communist satellite."

How much was the Eisenhower administration to blame
for all this? Cuba, of course, was a highly tempting issue;
and as the pace of the campaign quickened, politics began
to clash with Kennedy's innate sense of responsibility.
Once, discussing Cuba with his staff, he asked them, "All
right, but how would we have saved Cuba if we had the
power?" Then he paused, looked out the window and
said, "What the hell, they never told us how they would
have saved China." In that spirit, he began to succumb to
temptation.

He made his most extended statement in a speech at
Cincinnati in early October. He began by appearing to adopt
the thesis that the State Department should have listened
to its pro-Batista ambassadors and recognized the revolution
as a communist conspiracy from the outset. This differed
markedly from his interpretation in *The Strategy of Peace*.
Doubtless it was campaign oratory. Though Earl Smith
was an amiable gentleman and old friend from Palm Beach,
Kennedy did not regard him as an oracle on Cuba. He had
remarked at Hyannis Port in August, "Earl Smith once said
to me that the American Ambassador was the second most
important man in Cuba. What a hell of a note that is! Naturally those conditions couldn't last." (Smith also made
his remark about "the second most important man in Cuba"
publicly, stimulating President Dorticós of Cuba to congratulate a Cuban audience on now having "the privilege of
living in a country where the United States Ambassador
means little.")

The more substantial part of the Cincinnati speech—and
the part which I believe more faithfully reflected Kennedy's
views—condemned the Eisenhower policy toward Cuba on
quite different grounds. In the years before Castro, Kennedy charged, the administration had declined "to help

Cuba meet its desperate need for economic progress"; it had employed "the influence of our Government to advance the interests and increase the profits of the private American companies, which dominated the island's economy"; and it had given "stature and support to one of the most bloody and repressive dictatorships in the long history of Latin America." He concluded: "While we were allowing Batista to place us on the side of tyranny, we did nothing to persuade the people of Cuba and Latin America that we wanted to be on the side of freedom."

What could be done about Castro now? Kennedy had told me at Hyannis Port, "We can't do anything except through the OAS, and most of the members of the OAS don't want to do anything at all. Our best hope is to stop the spread of Castro's influence by helping genuine democracy elsewhere in the continent." This also was his theme in Cincinnati: "For the present, Cuba is gone. . . . For the present no magic formula will bring it back." Only by extending "the hand of American friendship in a common effort to wipe out the poverty and discontent and hopelessness on which communism feeds—only then will we drive back tyranny until it ultimately perishes in the streets of Havana."

Two weeks later, the Kennedy staff, seeking to take the offensive after his supposed 'soft' position on Quemoy and Matsu, put out the provocative statement about strengthening the Cuban "fighters for freedom." These words were no more than a rhetorical flourish. Neither Kennedy nor his staff knew about the secret Cuban army in Guatemala, and they had no enterprise of this sort in mind themselves. Nixon, however, knowing that Allen Dulles had briefed Kennedy about Cuba, assumed that the briefing covered covert operations as well as intelligence. He therefore incredibly concluded—or so he later said—that Kennedy was trying to claim credit for the idea and that the secrecy of the project was now in jeopardy. When the fourth television debate took place the next day, Nixon—in the interests, he suggested subsequently, of national security—accused Kennedy of advocating what was in fact his own plan and went on to attack that plan as "probably the most dangerously irresponsible" recommendation made in the campaign. It would, he said, violate the United Nations Charter and five hemisphere treaties;

> if we were to follow that recommendation . . . we would lose all of our friends in Latin America, we would probably be condemned in the United Nations, and we would not accomplish our objective. . . . It would be an open invitation to Mr. Khrushchev to come in, to come into Latin America.

In his response, Kennedy said nothing more about strengthening the fighters for freedom, only noting that economic sanctions against Cuba, to be successful, would have to be multilateral and that "the big struggle will be to prevent the influence of Castro spreading to other countries." For the rest of the campaign, he left Cuba alone.

Immediately after the election, his concern was with an affirmative program for Latin America rather than with Cuba. On November 14 he asked John Sharon for estimates of the effectiveness of the trade embargo against Cuba and of the possibilities of a rapprochement. Three days later Dulles and Richard Bissell of CIA informed him for the first time about the Guatemalan project.

6. PLANNING IN THE SHADOWS

The Eisenhower decision of March 17, 1960, had two main parts. On the political side, it directed the CIA to bring together a broad range of Cuban exiles, with *Batistianos* and Communists specifically excluded, into unified political opposition to the Castro regime. On the military side, it directed the CIA to recruit and train a Cuban force capable of guerrilla action against that regime.

When Nixon first proposed the use of exiles against Castro in the spring of 1959, United States action would have inevitably been pro-Batista; only *Batistianos* were then available. A year later the situation had improved. Thousands of disenchanted Cubans who had disliked Batista and at first welcomed the revolution were now streaming into Florida and Central America, some flying boldly out on commercial airlines, others stealing onto small boats and disappearing into the Caribbean night. Many were lawyers, doctors and businessmen, accustomed to political expression. By the end of 1959 Miami was alive with anti-Castro political activity of an unorganized and feckless sort. Every time two or three refugees gathered together a new *unión* or *movimiento* was likely to emerge.

The political leaders of this second migration were men who had served neither Batista nor Castro. They were characteristically identified with the old Cuba of the traditional parties, of progressive intent and ineffectual performance. Some were decent men; others were racketeers who had found politics a lucrative way of life. They wanted the restoration of political 'democracy' as they had known it before Batista, but they saw no need for far-reaching social change. Their objectives were compatible with the interests of North American investors and with the prejudices of the Eisenhower administration. If this had not been the case, they would gladly have modified their objectives; for they were men long habituated to automatic deference to the United States. They stood for the Cuba of the past.

The CIA turned first to such men when it began to organize the political front in the early months of 1960. In June five leading groups were cajoled into forming the Frente Revolucionario Democrático. Three of the five members of the new committee represented pre-Batista Cuba; Manuel Antonio de Varona, who had been prime minister under Prío Socarrás, was typical. Varona promptly declared that the post-Castro government would restore properties seized by the Castro regime to their United States and Cuban owners. The other two members of the Frente had briefly served the revolutionary government. Dr. Justo Carrillo, an honorable man of liberal views, had been president of the Bank for Industrial and Agricultural Development under both Prío and Castro and had taken part in a plot to overthrow Batista in 1956. The fifth member, a young lieutenant named Manuel Artime, had joined Castro at the end of 1958 and later worked for Castro's National Institute of Agrarian Reform. Soon after he broke with the regime in November 1959, the CIA brought him out of Cuba. His youth, his military experience, his political inexperience and his personal tractability all recommended him to the CIA field operatives. He became their man on the Frente and soon the only Cuban link between CIA's political and military operations.

The Frente was appropriately named: it was a front and nothing more. While its members talked among themselves, CIA was engaged in a recruiting drive among Cuban refugees in Florida and Central America. It had also persuaded President Ydígoras of Guatemala to permit the establishment of a secret training camp and air base in the Guatemalan mountains. By midsummer the Cubans began to arrive. It was the rainy season, and they had to build their own camp in sticky volcanic mud five thousand feet above the sea. In their spare time, they received training from a Filipino colonel who had organized guerrillas against the Japanese during the Second World War.

The first CIA plan was to form small groups designed to slip into Cuba and establish active centers of resistance. Arms and supplies flown in from outside would enable these bands to enlarge their operations until, like Castro himself, they could enlist enough popular support to challenge the regime. In August President Eisenhower approved a budget of $13 million for this project. It was explicitly stated at this point that no United States military personnel were to take part in combat operations. But in the meantime the military conception was beginning to change. The CIA people began to doubt whether the guerrilla theory would work. It is true that several hundred guerrillas were presently hiding out in the Escambray Mountains and that Manuel Ray was reactivating his underground in the cities; but the CIA found it hard to make contact with the Cuban resistance. Efforts to parachute supplies into the Escambray were not very successful. The CIA people feared that the guerrilla bands had been penetrated by Castro's agents. Certainly Castro, who knew all the tricks himself, was a master at counterguerrilla action. Moreover, his army was being strengthened by Soviet equipment, and his control was tightening over the civilian population: all this made him a far more formidable opponent than the Batista of 1958. For these reasons, as the Escambray resistance began to fade out, CIA now reconsidered its original plan.

This, at least, now seems to me what happened, though it is fair to say that some exiles place a more sinister interpretation on these events. They believe to this day that the CIA disliked the guerrillas and the underground groups on the island because it could not control them, that its efforts to help were never more than nominal, and that it ignored the urban underground and folded up the Escambray resistance in order to make way for the Guatemalan brigade. One representative of Ray's organization who came to Miami said later, "When we began to make the necessary contacts, we were referred immediately to mysterious persons who always turned out to be agents of the CIA, and who had their own plans as to how Castro was to be toppled and who were the ones to do it." [5]

In any case the men of Washington were moving on to a new and drastically different conception: the idea of a direct assault on Castro by landing a force of exiles on the Cuban coast. Since amphibious operations required air cover, it seemed reasonable to equip the prospective invaders with a few B-26 planes left over from the Second World War. Perhaps the memory of the successful CIA coup against the Arbenz regime in Guatemala in 1954 played its part; Castro too might collapse under the shock of an attack in force. By the time of the United States election in 1960,

[5] Raúl Chibas on NBC White Paper, "Cuba: Bay of Pigs," February 4, 1964.

the CIA conception had definitely shifted from guerrilla infiltration to a beachhead assault. The guerrilla exercises came to a virtual stop; the Filipino colonel went away; and a new United States team came in to train the Cubans, now numbering almost 500 men, along conventional lines as a pocket army, complete with artillery and air support.

7. AGENTS AND PATIENTS

In the meantime, a new wave of refugees had begun to arrive in Florida. This third migration was led by men who had done more than passively applaud the revolution. They characteristically had conspired against Batista, fought with Castro and served in the revolutionary government. They opposed Castro not for having brought about a social revolution but for having delivered it to the Communists. They sought not to reverse the revolution but to redeem it. Their inspiration was Huber Matos, now in Castro's jail. Their strongest figure was Manuel Ray, who, after resigning from Castro's government, formed the *Movimiento Revolucionario del Pueblo* (MRP) and spent most of 1960 in Cuba organizing an underground against Castro, as he had done two years before against Batista. The men of this third migration tended to be politically radical and nationalist, personally proud and defiant.

In November Ray himself escaped from Cuba and made his way to Miami. He brought a new thesis to which he hoped the new American government might be responsive: that Castro had to be overthrown from within, that the Cuban people must be the means, and that an uprising would succeed only if its clear purpose was to rescue the revolution from the Communists and resume the revolutionary task of building a new and progressive Cuba. Ray's arrival confronted the CIA with a difficult problem.

It is sometimes essential for a state, even for a democratic state, to undertake clandestine operations, as I learned in OSS during the Second World War. But, when such operations are undertaken, it is important never to forget that the relationship between an intelligence agency and its instruments tends to be a corrupting one. The agency has a natural desire to control its operations as completely as possible and therefore a natural preference for compliant people. If people are not compliant to begin with, they are made so. The very process of recruitment begins the process: Artime, for example, was subjected to hours of interrogation, to psychological testing, even to a lie detector. Exiles are typically friendless, moneyless, jobless in a strange land; often they do not even speak the language. They become increasingly dependent on the agent. They know that, if they refuse to take his orders, he can cut off their income and expel them from their organizations.

The relationship is degrading for them and demoralizing for the agent. CIA's main contact with the exile leaders was a ubiquitous operative who went under the name of Frank Bender. His real name was Droller; he was a German refugee who had come to the United States before the war, entered the Army and moved into intelligence. He knew little Spanish and even less about Latin America (he once horrified Justo Carrillo by describing Haya de la Torre as a Brazilian labor leader). But he had money and authority, and he fell easily into habits of command. His power appears to have gone to his head; he liked to say that he was carrying the counterrevolution around in his checkbook. The older exiles disliked and feared him, but they felt they had no choice but to obey him.

Ray and his people proved different. When Bender told him to bring the MRP into the Frente, he refused. His personality, his politics and his advocacy of the underground thesis posed a threat both to the status of the more conservative exiles and to the control of the CIA. Accordingly the older exiles and the Agency were ready to collaborate in an attempt to discredit him. His policy was denounced as *Fidelismo sin Fidel*—Castroism without Castro. His group was denied access to CIA's secret radio transmitter on Swan Island and other forms of support. The more reactionary exiles called Ray a communist.

But the arbitrary CIA control was beginning to cause resentment even within the Frente itself. Bender, finding it inconvenient to deal with five men, insisted that the Frente appoint a coordinator. When Tony Varona was chosen in September, one member resigned. This was Dr. Sánchez Arango, who had been foreign minister under Prío; he later said, "The CIA wanted to control everything. . . . The members who . . . were willing to accept their commands, their orders, their provisions, such as Artime, who was called the Golden Boy, were the ones in the best kind of relationships with them." [6] Justo Carrillo voted against Varona on the ground that the revolution had made the traditional parties and politicians obsolete. He argued that the Frente should take in people "with a revolutionary background" and declare itself unequivocally on social issues. His arguments were ignored. Requests by the Frente

6 NBC White Paper, "Cuba: Bay of Pigs," February 4, 1964.

to visit the training camp in Guatemala were turned down.

By November 1960 the CIA operation had taken on a life of its own. The agents in the field were shaping it to meet their own needs. In favoring the 'reliable' exiles— those who would take orders—they were conceivably endangering the whole project; for the men most capable of rallying popular support within Cuba against the Castro regime were bound to be more independent, more principled and more radical than the manageable types whom the intelligence agency preferred for operational reasons. As for the nominal Cuban leadership in the Frente, it was growing uneasily aware that it lacked authority; that, as it accepted its instructions and its cash from Bender and his associates, it lacked dignity; that it did not even know what was going on.

Meanwhile in the camps of Guatemala the Cubans were turning with enthusiasm from the idea of a guerrilla operation to the idea of an amphibious invasion. The new training and the new weapons filled them with sudden hope. Their American officers—or so the Cubans later told Haynes Johnson—assured them that they were only one of many such groups, one-tenth of the force, and that they would have all the support they needed.[7] Supposing that everyone they had left behind hated Castro as much as they did, they genuinely believed that a mass landing on the Cuban beaches might set off a general revolt. The CIA and Army officers, knowing less about Cuba, were even more sanguine. Once possessed of this dream, neither the Cubans nor their American colleagues were disposed to retreat to the more modest idea of a guerrilla infiltration. As for demobilizing the operation, this would have been unthinkable.

Macaulay wrote of the followers of the Duke of Monmouth:

> A politician driven into banishment by a hostile faction generally sees the society he has quitted through a false medium. Every little discontent appears to him to portend a revolution. Every riot is a rebellion. He cannot be convinced that his country does not pine for him as he pines for his country. . . .
> This delusion becomes almost a madness when many exiles who suffer in the same cause herd together in a foreign country. . . . They become ripe for enterprises which would at once be pronounced hopeless by any man whose passions had not deprived him of the power of calculating chances.

7 Haynes Johnson, *The Bay of Pigs* (New York, 1964, [Dell edition]), 56.

This was the way matters stood when John F. Kennedy learned of the project on November 17, 1960.

X

THE BAY OF PIGS

ON NOVEMBER 29, 1960, twelve days after he had heard about the Cuban project, the President-elect received from Allen Dulles a detailed briefing on CIA's new military conception. Kennedy listened with attention, then told Dulles to carry the work forward. The response was sufficiently affirmative for Dulles to take it as an instruction to expedite the project.

Dulles understood, however, that interest did not mean commitment. All Kennedy wanted at this point was to have the option of an exile attack on the Castro regime. Let the preparation go on for the time being: there would be ample opportunity after the inauguration for review and reconsideration. In the meantime, there was a legislative program to develop and those 1200 jobs to fill . . . Kennedy saw the Cuban project, in the patois of the bureaucracy, as a 'contingency plan.' He did not yet realize how contingency planning could generate its own momentum and create its own reality.

1. CONFUSION IN THE INTERREGNUM

In the next weeks government floated as in a void. Neither the outgoing nor the incoming administrations wanted to make fundamental decisions, and most matters continued to move along existing tracks. Early in December the new CIA plan went in a routine way before the Special Group, the secret interdepartmental committee charged with the supervision of special operations. The lieutenant colonel in command of the training in Guatemala came along to offer his personal testimony about the Cuban Brigade.

The plan was taking definite shape. Its sponsors said little now about the old ideas of guerrilla infiltration or multiple landings except as diversionary tactics. Instead they envisaged 600 to 750 Cubans coming ashore in a body at a point still to be chosen along the southern coast of Cuba. Air strikes from Nicaragua in advance of the attack would knock out Castro's air force. These strikes, along with supply flights, would continue during the landing. The invaders would also have artillery. The mission would be to seize and hold an area sufficiently large to attract anti-Castro activists, induce defections in Castro's militia and set off a general uprising behind the lines. As for the Brigade itself, the lieutenant colonel assured the Special Group that his charges were men of unusual intelligence and 'motivation' and that their morale was suberb. They would have no trouble, he said, in taking care of much larger numbers of Cuban militia.

The Special Group itself was infected with interregnum uncertainties. Not wishing to anticipate the new administration, it did not formally approve the new scheme or even subject it to very severe scrutiny. Instead, it encouraged the CIA to press on with the training in Guatemala and start work on operational planning in Washington.

In particular, the Special Group seems not to have confronted the dilemma created by the change in military plans—the dilemma of the United States role. So long as the guerrilla thesis prevailed, this had not been a problem. CIA then contemplated an orthodox clandestine operation —an undertaking, in other words, which the United States would be able, if necessary, to disown. This meant, as a 'ground rule' for planning, that the operation had to look to the world like one which the Cuban exiles would be capable of organizing and carrying out on their own. If it failed, only Cubans would be held accountable. Nor was the Eisenhower administration, in observing the ground rule and forbidding United States participation in combat, imposing a restriction likely to handicap seriously what was, after all, no more than an exercise in guerrilla infiltration.

But the new plan raised new questions. It called for an expeditionary force of size, scope and visibility; and it proposed to pit that force in pitched battle against defending armies of vastly superior numbers. Could the United States convincingly deny complicity in an expedition well trained and equipped to conduct an amphibious invasion? And, if it could not escape accountability, could it afford to let such an expedition fail? In short, if the United States kept its role small enough to conceal its responsibility, the operation might not have a fair chance of success; while if it made its role large enough to give the operation a fair chance of success, the responsibility could not be plausibly disclaimed in case of failure. Washington might then face the choice between the political humiliation of defeat and the commitment of United States troops to insure victory.

There was reason to suppose that the CIA ground rule had already been stretched to the point of no return. Someone remarked at the Special Group meeting that the Guatemala base was no longer much of a secret. This was plainly so. A Guatemala City newspaper, *La Hora*, had broken the story as early as October 30, saying that an invasion of Cuba was in preparation and hinting at United States collusion. Articles by Ronald Hilton of Stanford University in the *Hispanic-American Report* and *The Nation* brought the story to the attention of American readers in November. By December a number of North American papers were writing about mysterious happenings in Guatemala. Early in January *Time* said in its knowing way that the Frente was getting generous financial assistance from the United States government, that Manuel Ray and his MRP were denied such assistance and that " 'Mr. B,' the CIA agent in charge, reportedly has suggested that the MRP get help from the Frente."

The publicity might well have raised the question whether the old ground rule was compatible with the new plan; but no one in the interregnum seemed to feel final responsibility, and so matters drifted along. In January the Joint Chiefs of Staff began for the first time to get into the act. A JCS paper, tacitly questioning the ban on United States participation in military operations, discussed possible levels of involvement. The paper went to the office of the Secretary of Defense but was shuffled aside in the confusion of the changeover. The Cuban planners in CIA meanwhile pored over maps of southern Cuba, weighed the merits of alternative landing sites and busied themselves with the operational problems of invasion.

The hiatus in Washington gave the CIA operatives in the field a free hand. Since the force in Guatemala was still too small for the new plan, recruitment now had the urgent priority. The political criteria laid down by the CIA in Washington and demanded by most members of the Frente were abandoned in the rush. Bender gave particular authority to a dubious figure in Miami named Joaquin Sanjenis, and Sanjenis favored men of the Cuban right. If they had been in Batista's army, no matter; *Time* reported that, when one member of the Frente complained about the recruitment of *Batistianos,* a United States officer replied, "They're anti-communists, aren't they?" Unmarked planes picked up the refugees in the supposedly deserted

Opa-Locka airport in Miami and deposited them a few hours later at the Guatemalan base.

The influx of new recruits created problems in the training camp. Men who had taken part in the revolution had a natural hatred of officers who had served Batista. The American advisers, on the other hand, were impatient of what they regarded as political quibbling. They preferred men who had professional military experience (like Pepe San Román, who had received training at Fort Belvoir and Fort Benning in the United States) and could be relied on to follow orders. It is true that most of the *Batistianos* were so called because they had once been in Batista's army, not because they now wanted to return Batista to power. But this did not make the Cubans selected by the United States advisers to command the Brigade any more popular with the rank and file.

In spite of the optimistic reports rendered to CIA in Washington about the splendid morale in the camp, discontent increased. In January it broke out into mutiny. Almost half of the now more than 500 Cubans in the camp resigned. It is hard to disentangle all the motives behind this demonstration; but it seems clear that the mutineers had the support of the Frente. At this point, the United States advisers intervened on behalf of the officers. "I am the boss here," one adviser said, "and the commander of this Brigade is still Pepe San Román." A hundred of the Cubans refused to accept this decision and insisted on seeing representatives of the Frente. When they were promised a visit from the Frente, most agreed to rejoin the Brigade, but a few still held out. In one of the unhappier passages in this whole unhappy story, the CIA operatives arrested a dozen of the ringleaders and held them prisoner under stark conditions deep in the jungle of northern Guatemala.

The CIA now decided to bring in Artime, the most amenable member of the Frente, as one of the military commanders. In the end only two other members of the Frente visited the camp—Tony Varona and Antonio Maceo; the CIA successfully discouraged Justo Carrillo as too friendly to the mutineers. When Varona arrived, he cheered the rebels by a speech to the Brigade critical of the intervention by the United States advisers. Then, after a private conference with the senior American officer, Varona capitulated. In a second speech the next day he wholeheartedly endorsed the American choices for the leadership of the Brigade. The CIA was now in complete command.

This episode had scant impact on Washington. If it was ever reported to the new President, it must have been greatly minimized. The impression given at the White House meetings in March was that life in the Brigade could not be happier.

In the meantime, the CIA planners in Washington had settled on the town of Trinidad as the point of invasion. Trinidad, they pointed out, had the advantages of a harbor, a defensible beachhead, remoteness from Castro's main army and easy access to the Escambray Mountains. They proposed a heavy and concentrated amphibious assault, to take place at dawn and to be supported by paratroop drops on the hills behind the town and by simultaneous (though not advance) strikes against the Cuban air force. Once the landing force had established itself on the beaches, it could expect to rally support from the townspeople and overpower the local militia.

As the expeditionary force enlarged its hold, the CIA men argued, now introducing a new idea, a provisional government could be flown in; and, if the invaders could sustain themselves for ten days or two weeks, this government could receive recognition as the government of Cuba. Once this was done, the new government could request United States aid, though this aid was carefully defined as "logistic" and therefore presumably excluded military intervention. The CIA planners envisaged a continuous build-up and enlargement of the perimeter around the beachhead over a long period, rather like Anzio in 1944. The scheme envisaged victory by attrition rather than by rebellion and no longer assigned a significant immediate role to the internal resistance. As the invaders strengthened their position, this, along with their command of the skies and the acceptance of the new government by other American republics, would produce a steady withdrawal of civil support from Castro and his eventual collapse. And, if by any chance the attack failed, Trinidad was near enough the Escambray for the invaders to disappear into the hills.

About this time the snow began to fall, and John F. Kennedy took his oath as President of the United States.

2. KENNEDY AND THE CUBAN INHERITANCE

The Eisenhower administration thus bequeathed the new President a force of Cuban exiles under American training in Guatemala, a committee of Cuban politicians under American control in Florida and a plan to employ the exiles in an invasion of their homeland and to install the committee on Cuban soil as the provisional government of a free Cuba.

On January 22, two days after the inauguration, Allen Dulles and General Lemnitzer exposed the project to leading members of the new administration, among them Dean Rusk, Robert McNamara and Robert Kennedy. Speaking for the Joint Chiefs, Lemnitzer tried to renew discussion of alternatives ranging from minimum to maximum United States involvement. Six days later President Kennedy convened his first White House meeting on the plan. He was wary and reserved in his reaction. After listening for a long time, he instructed the Defense Department to take a hard look at CIA's military conception and the State Department to prepare a program for the isolation and containment of Cuba through the OAS. In the meantime, CIA was to continue what it had been doing. The ground rule against overt United States participation was still to prevail.

The Joint Chiefs, after brooding over CIA's Trinidad plan for a week, pronounced favorably on the chances of initial military success. The JCS evaluation was, however, a peculiar and ambiguous document. At one point it said categorically, in what would seem an implicit rejection of the Anzio model, that ultimate success would depend on either a sizable uprising inside the island or sizable support from outside. Then later, without restating these alternative conditions for victory, the document concluded that the existing plan, if executed in time, stood a "fair" chance of ultimate success. Even if it did not immediately attain all its goals, the JCS remarked philosophically, it would still contribute to the eventual overthrow of the regime.

There was plainly a logical gap between the statement that the plan would work if one or another condition were fulfilled and the statement that the plan would work anyway. One cannot know whether this gap resulted from sloppiness in analysis or from a conviction, conscious or unconscious, that once the invasion were launched, either internal uprising or external support would follow, and, if not the first, then the second—that, in short, once the United States government embarked on this enterprise, it could not risk the disaster of failure. Certainly this conviction permeated the thinking of the exiles themselves as well as of the United States officers in Guatemala. Since some, at least, of the Joint Chiefs had always been skeptical of the CIA ground rule, that conviction may well have lurked in the back of their minds too.

Late in February the Chiefs sent an inspection team to the Guatemala base. In a new report in early March, they dropped the point about external support and hinged victory on the capacity of the assault to produce anti-Castro action behind the lines. From the viewpoint of the Joint Chiefs, then, the Cuban resistance was indispensable to success. They could see no other way—short of United States intervention—by which an invasion force of a thousand Cubans, no matter how well trained and equipped nor how stout their morale, could conceivably overcome the 200,000 men of Castro's army and militia.

The pace of events was quickening. Roberto Alejos, the Guatemalan planter whose *finca* had been sheltering the Brigade, arrived in Washington in early March with a letter from President Ydígoras to President Kennedy. Ydígoras wrote that the presence of the Cubans was a mounting embarrassment and that he must request assurances that they depart by the end of April. For its part, the CIA reported that the Cubans themselves were clamoring to move; the spirit of the Brigade had reached its peak, and further postponement would risk demoralization. Moreover, the rainy season was about to begin, the ground would turn into volcanic mud, and training would have to stop. And there was another potent reason for going ahead: Castro, the CIA said, was about to receive jet airplanes from the Soviet Union along with Cuban pilots trained in Czechoslovakia to fly them; once the MIGs arrived, an amphibious landing would turn into a slaughter. After June 1, it would take the United States Marines and Air Force to overthrow Castro. If a purely Cuban invasion were ever to take place, it had to take place in the next few weeks.

By mid-March the President was confronted, in effect, with a now-or-never choice.

3. CUBA IN THE CABINET ROOM

On March 11, about a week after my return from Latin America, I was summoned to a meeting with the President in the Cabinet Room. An intimidating group sat around the table—the Secretary of State, the Secretary of Defense, the director of the Central Intelligence Agency, three Joint Chiefs resplendent in uniforms and decorations, the Assistant Secretary of State for Inter-American Affairs, the chairman of the Latin American Task Force and appropriate assistants and bottle-washers. I shrank into a chair at the far end of the table and listened in silence. I had first heard of the Cuban operation in early February; indeed, the day before leaving for Buenos Aires I had sent the President a memorandum about it. The idea sounded plausible enough, the memorandum suggested, if one excluded everything but Cuba itself; but, as soon as the focus was enlarged to include the rest of the hemisphere and the rest of the world, arguments *against* the decision gained strength. Above all, "this would be your first dramatic foreign policy initiative. At one stroke you would dissipate all the extraordinary good will which has been rising toward the new Administration through the world. It would fix a malevolent image of the new Administration in the minds of millions."

It was apparent now a month later that matters were still very much in flux. No final decision had yet been taken on whether the invasion should go forward at all and, if so, whether Trinidad should be the landing point. It fell to Allen Dulles and Richard M. Bissell, Jr., as the originators of the project to make the main arguments for action.

I had known both men for more than fifteen years and held them both in high respect. As an OSS intelligence officer in London and Paris during the war, I had admired the coolness and proficiency of Dulles's work in Bern; and, meeting him from time to time in the years after the war, I had come greatly to enjoy his company. Years in the intelligence business had no doubt given him a capacity for ruthlessness; but he was urbane, courtly and honorable, almost wholly devoid of the intellectual rigidity and personal self-righteousness of his brother. During the McCarthy years, when John Foster Dulles regularly threw innocent State Department officials to the wolves, Allen Dulles just as regularly protected CIA officers unjustly denounced on the Hill.

Richard Bissell, whom I had known as an economist in the Marshall Plan before he turned to intelligence work and became CIA's deputy director for operations, was a man of high character and remarkable intellectual gifts. His mind was swift and penetrating, and he had an unsurpassed talent for lucid analysis and fluent exposition. A few years before he had conceived and fought through the plan of U-2 flights over the Soviet Union; and, though this led to trouble in 1960, it still remained perhaps the greatest intelligence coup since the war. He had committed himself for the past year to the Cuban project with equal intensity. Yet he recognized the strength of his commitment and, with characteristic honesty, warned us to discount his bias. Nonetheless, we all listened transfixed—in this meeting and other meetings which followed—fascinated by the workings of this superbly clear, organized and articulate intelligence, while Bissell, pointer in hand, would explain how the invasion would work or discourse on the relative merits of alternative landing sites.

Both Dulles and Bissell were at a disadvantage in having to persuade a skeptical new administration about the virtues of a proposal nurtured in the hospitable bosom of a previous government—a proposal on which they had personally worked for a long time and in which their organization had a heavy vested interest. This cast them in the role less of analysts than of advocates, and it led them to accept progressive modifications so long as the expedition in some form remained; perhaps they too unconsciously supposed that, once the operation began to unfold, it would not be permitted to fail.

The determination to keep the scheme alive sprang in part, I believe, from the embarrassments of calling it off. As Dulles said at the March 11 meeting, "Don't forget that we have a disposal problem. If we have to take these men out of Guatemala, we will have to transfer them to the United States, and we can't have them wandering around the country telling everyone what they have been doing." What could one do with "this asset" if not send it on to Cuba? If transfer to the United States was out, demobilization on the spot would create even greater difficulties. The Cubans themselves were determined to go back to their homeland, and they might well forcibly resist efforts to take away their arms and equipment. Moreover, even if the Brigade were successfully disbanded, its members would disperse, disappointed and resentful all over Latin America. They would tell where they had been and what they had been doing, thereby exposing CIA operations. And they would explain how the United States, having prepared an expedition against Castro, had then lost its nerve. This could only result, Dulles kept emphasizing, in discrediting Washington, disheartening Latin American opponents of Castro and encouraging the *Fidelistas* in their attack on democratic regimes, like that of Betancourt in Venezuela. Disbandment might thus produce pro-Castro revolutions all around the Caribbean. For all these reasons, CIA argued, instead of turning the Cubans loose, we must find some means for putting them back into Cuba "on their own."

The contingency had thus become a reality: having created the Brigade as an option, the CIA now presented its use against Cuba as a necessity. Nor did Dulles's arguments lack force. Confronted by them, Kennedy tentatively agreed that the simplest thing, after all, might be to let the Cubans go where they yearned to go—to Cuba. Then he tried to turn the meeting toward a consideration of how this could be done with the least political risk. The first step was to form a more liberal and representative exile organization, and this the President directed should be done as soon as possible.

Bissell then renewed the case for the Trinidad plan. Kennedy questioned it as "too spectacular." He did not want a big amphibious invasion in the manner of the Second World War; he wanted a "quiet" landing, preferably at night. And he insisted that the plans be drawn on the basis of *no United States military intervention*—a stipulation to which no one at the table made objection. Thomas Mann seconded these points, stressing the probability of anti-American reactions in Latin America and the United Nations if the American hand were not well concealed. He was especially worried that the air strikes would give the show away unless they could seem plausibly to come from bases on Cuban soil; and the Trinidad airstrip could not take B-26s. The President concluded the meeting by defining the issue with his usual crispness. The trouble with the operation, he said, was that the smaller the political risk, the greater the military risk, and vice versa. The problem was to see whether the two risks could be brought into reasonable balance.

For the next three days the CIA planners canvassed alternative landing sites, coming up with three new possibilities, of which the most likely was about 100 miles west of Trinidad in the Zapata area around Cochinos Bay—the Bay of Pigs. The Joint Chiefs, examining these recommendations on March 14, agreed that Zapata, with its airstrip and the natural defense provided by its swamps, seemed the best of the three but added softly that they still preferred Trinidad. When we met again in the Cabinet Room on March 15, Bissell outlined the Zapata plan. The President, listening somberly, suggested some changes, mostly intended to "reduce the noise level"—such as making sure that the invasion ships would be unloaded before dawn. He then authorized CIA to continue on the assumption that the invasion would occur. But he repeated his decision against any form of United States military intervention and added carefully and categorically that he was reserving his final decision on the plan itself. The expedition, he said, must be laid on in a way which would make it possible for him to call it off as late as twenty-four hours before D-day.

4. THE CUBAN REVOLUTIONARY COUNCIL

In the meantime, the CIA had been carrying out Kennedy's instruction to bring representatives of the new Cuba into the Frente. Bender, reversing his earlier position, told the Frente that it must come to an agreement with Manuel Ray and his MRP. But, though Bender changed his line, he did not change his manner, nor were the more conservative members of the Frente themselves eager to embrace *Fidelismo sin Fidel*. Representatives of the Frente and the MRP engaged in complex and acrimonious negotiations. After persistent CIA pressure persuaded the negotiators to return to their groups with a draft agreement, the Frente rejected the common program as too radical.

The CIA now decided on direct intervention. On March 18 at the Skyways Motel in Miami a CIA operative—not Bender, whom the CIA belatedly concluded was not the man for the job—told the Frente that the two groups must unite, that they must together choose a provisional president for Cuba, and that if these things were not done right away, the whole project would be called off. The Frente finally caved in and reluctantly submitted a list of six possibilities for the presidency. For its part, the MRP was no happier about this coerced alliance. Ray and his people liked neither the CIA control nor the idea of an invasion, but, supposing that United States backing guaranteed success, they wanted both to defend the interests of the Cuban underground and to assure their own part in a post-Castro future. Accepting the list, they chose Dr. Miró Cardona as provisional president.

Miró, a lawyer and professor at the University of Havana, had been a noted leader in the civil opposition to Batista. He had inspired many students to work for the revolution, and Castro made him the first prime minister of the revolutionary regime. Though Miró did not last long in the government, Castro as late as May 1960 designated him ambassador to the United States. But by July, as the process of communization advanced, Miró who had not gone on to Washington, resigned his ambassadorship and sought refuge in the Argentine Embassy. He finally came to the United States as an exile in the winter of 1960–61. He was a man of dignity and force, who faithfully represented the liberal ideals of the Cuban Revolution.

On March 22 Varona for the Frente and Ray for the MRP signed an agreement conferring on Miró Cardona authority to organize the Cuban Revolutionary Council. The document also pledged the Council to give "maximum priority" to the resistance inside Cuba, declared that no one who "held an objectionably responsible position with the criminal dictatorship of Batista" was to be admitted into any armed forces organized outside Cuba and said hopefully that the military command of such forces must pledge "their full deference" to the Council's authority. Miró then held a press conference to announce the formation of the Council as the basis for a provisional government of Cuba once it had gained "a piece of Cuban soil." This was all very well, but the CIA regarded the agreement as no more than a placebo, and the CRC's charter meant very little next to Bender's checkbook. Bender now asked Miró to ratify the selection of Artime as commander of the Brigade. When he did so, Ray, Varona and Carrillo all protested; but Miró wearily explained that he had no alternative: this was what the Americans wanted, and the Americans would make the invasion a success.

While this reorganization was going on, I learned that my assignment was to help clarify the new political objectives by preparing a White Paper on Cuba. The President told me that, *if* the invasion took place (the emphasis was his own), he wanted everyone in the hemisphere to know that its intent was not to bring back the old order in Cuba. "Our objection isn't to the Cuban Revolution," he said; "it is to the fact that Castro has turned it over to the communists."

Setting to work, I buried myself under a mass of papers and came up with a draft in a few days. The paper sought to explain, with documentation, the United States attitude toward the Cuban Revolution and the Castro regime. The thesis was that the first had been betrayed by the second, and that the result offered "a clear and present danger to the authentic and autonomous revolution of the Americas." It endorsed the original aims of the Cuban Revolution and said:

> The people of Cuba remain our brothers. We acknowledge past omissions and errors in our relationship to them. The United States, along with the other nations of the hemisphere, expresses a profound determination to assure future democratic governments in Cuba full and positive support in their efforts to help the Cuban people achieve freedom, democracy and social justice.

The White Paper concluded:

> We call once again on the Castro regime to sever its links with the international Communist movement, to return to the original purposes which brought so many gallant men to-

gether in the Sierra Maestra and to restore the integrity of the
Cuban Revolution.

If this call is unheeded, we are confident that the Cuban
people, with their passion for liberty, will continue to strive
for a free Cuba.

There followed my introduction to one of the ordeals of
bureaucratic Washington—the process of interdepartmental clearance. Actually Berle and Mann in State and Tracy
Barnes in CIA applauded the general tone of the document
and confined themselves to helpful factual suggestions. But
USIA, which Edward R. Murrow had not yet succeeded in
shaking loose from the platitudes of the Eisenhower era,
found the piece altogether too racy and liberal. "We" could
not condemn the Batista regime, they said; after all, "we"
had supported it. I pointed out that the "we" in question
had changed on January 20 and that it surely was not
necessary for Kennedy to identify himself with all the
errors of his predecessor. Similarly, I was told, "we" should
not admit error in our dealings with Latin American countries; it was unbecoming, and they would not respect us in
the future. But I took full advantage of the White House
leverage and the presidential mandate, and the document
emerged from this agony substantially intact.

It went to the President over the weekend, and we discussed it on the following Tuesday, March 28. He was, as so
often, generous in his comment but had a number of
specific suggestions, mostly designed to increase the magnanimity of the text. Where, for example, I had written
that the initial Castro programs were progressive in conception "if not in execution," he wondered whether this last
phrase was not "snide" and proposed its omission.

As we finished, I said, "What do you think about this
damned invasion?" He said wryly, "I think about it as little
as possible." But it was clear, as we talked, that he had of
course been thinking about it a good deal. In his judgment,
the critical point—the weak part of the case for going
ahead—lay in the theory that the landings would touch off
a mass insurrection against the regime. How unpopular was
Castro anyway? I mentioned a series written by Joseph
Newman, who had just visited Cuba for the *New York
Herald Tribune,* citing a piece which reported the strength
of sentiment behind Castro. Kennedy said quickly, "That
must have been the fourth piece—I missed it. Could you get
it for me?" I sent it over that evening. In a short while he
called back to ask that I talk to Newman and obtain, as
hypothetically as possible, his estimate about Cuban responses to an invasion.

We all in the White House considered uprisings behind the lines essential to the success of the operation; so too did the Joint Chiefs of Staff; and so, we thought, did the CIA. It was only later that I learned about the Anzio concept; it certainly did not come across clearly in the White House meetings. And it was much later that Allen Dulles wrote: "Much of the American press assumed at the time that this action was predicated on a mistaken intelligence estimate to the effect that a landing would touch off a widespread and successful popular revolt in Cuba. . . . I know of no estimate that a spontaneous uprising of the unarmed population of Cuba would be touched off by the landing."[1] This statement plainly reflected the CIA notion that the invasion would win by attrition rather than by rebellion. It also, strictly construed, was accurate enough in itself—if due attention is paid to such key words as "spontaneous," "unarmed" and "landing." Obviously no one expected the invasion to galvanize the unarmed and unorganized into rising against Castro at the moment of disembarkation. But the invasion plan, as understood by the President and the Joint Chiefs, did assume that the successful *occupation* of an enlarged beachhead area would rather soon incite *organized* uprisings by *armed* members of the Cuban resistance.

Dulles and Bissell themselves reinforced this impression. When questioned early in April about the prospects of internal resistance, instead of discounting it, which seems to have been their view, they claimed that over 2500 persons presently belonged to resistance organizations, that 20,000 more were sympathizers, and that the Brigade, once established on the island, could expect the active support of, at the very least, a quarter of the Cuban people. They backed up such sanguine estimates by citing requests from contacts in Cuba for arms drops and assurances that a specified number of men stood ready to fight when the signal was given.

My experience in OSS during the Second World War left me with a sad skepticism about such messages. Too often the senders inflated their strength, whether out of hope or despair, or because they wanted guns, ammunition and radios to sell on the black market. Recalling disappointment and miscalculation then, one could not find the CIA assurances satisfying. But mine was a special experience; and the estimates coming, as we all supposed, with the Agency's full authority behind them, impressed most of those around the table. Again it appeared only later that

[1] Allen W. Dulles, *The Craft of Intelligence* (New York, 1963), 169.

the Intelligence Branch of CIA had never been officially apprised of the Cuban expedition and that CIA's elaborate national estimates procedure was never directed to the question whether an invasion would trigger other uprisings. Robert Amory, Jr., the able deputy director for intelligence, himself a veteran of amphibious landings in the Second World War, was not informed at any point about any aspect of the operation. The same men, in short, both planned the operation and judged its chances of success. Nor was anyone at State, in intelligence jargon, 'witting' below Tom Mann, which meant that the men on the Cuban desk, who received the daily flow of information from the island, were not asked to comment on the feasibility of the venture. The 'need-to-know' standard—i.e., that no one should be told about a project unless it becomes operationally necessary —thus had the idiotic°effect of excluding much of the expertise of government at a time when every alert newspaperman knew something was afoot.

The talk with Newman strengthened misgivings about CIA's estimates. He said that, though anti-Castro sentiment had markedly increased since his last visit the year before, Castro still roused intense enthusiasm and faith, especially among the young and among those who had benefited from the social changes of the revolution. These two groups, Newman added, constituted a considerable part of the population. Even a sizable middle group, now disillusioned about Castro, would not be likely to respond with enthusiasm to an invasion backed by the United States because we were so thoroughly identified in their minds with Batista. As much as many Cubans detested the present situation, they still preferred it to a restoration of the old order. "We must understand that from the viewpoint of many Cubans, including anti-Castro Cubans, we come into the ring with exceedingly dirty hands."

5. APPROACH TO A DECISION

The meetings in the Cabinet Room were now taking place every three or four days. The President, it seemed to me, was growing steadily more skeptical as his hard questioning exposed one problem after another in the plans. Moreover, the situation in Laos was at a point of crisis. Kennedy feared that, if the Cuban invasion went forward, it might prejudice chances of agreement with the Soviet Union over Laos; Ambassador Thompson's cables from Moscow reported Khrushchev's unusual preoccupation with Cuba. On the other hand, if we did in the end have to send American troops to Laos to fight communism on the other side of the world, we could hardly ignore communism ninety miles off Florida. Laos and Cuba were tied up with each other, though it was hard to know how one would affect the other. But after the March 29 meeting I noted: "The final decision will have to be made on April 4. I have the impression that the tide is flowing against the project."

Dulles and Bissell, convinced that if the Cubans were ever to be sent against Castro they had to go now, sure that the Brigade could accomplish its mission and nagged by the disposal problem, now redoubled their efforts at persuasion. Dulles told Kennedy that he felt much more confident about success than he had ever been in the case of Guatemala. CIA concentrated particularly in the meetings on trying to show that, even if the expedition failed, the cost would not be excessive. Obviously no one could believe any longer that the adventure would not be attributed to the United States—news stories described the recruitment effort in Miami every day—but somehow the idea took hold around the cabinet table that this would not much matter so long as United States soldiers did not take part in the actual fighting. If the operation were truly 'Cubanized,' it would hopefully appear as part of the traditional ebb and flow of revolution and counterrevolution in the Caribbean.

Moreover, if worst came to worst and the invaders were beaten on the beaches, then, Dulles and Bissell said, they could easily "melt away" into the mountains. This might have been true at Trinidad, which lay near the foothills of the Escambray, and it was more true of the Bay of Pigs than of the other two alternative sites proposed in mid-March. But the CIA exposition was less than candid both in implying that the Brigade had undergone guerrilla training (which had substantially ended five months earlier, before most of the Cubans had arrived in Guatemala) and in suggesting the existence of an easy escape hatch. I don't think we fully realized that the Escambray Mountains lay eighty miles from the Bay of Pigs, across a hopeless tangle of swamps and jungles. And no one knew (until Haynes Johnson interviewed the survivors) that the CIA agents in Guatemala were saying nothing to the Cubans about this last resort of flight to the hills, apparently fearing to lower their morale. "We were never told about this," San Román said later. "What we were told was, 'If you fail we will go in.' " [2]

[2] Haynes Johnson, The Bay of Pigs (New York, 1964 [Dell edition]), 67.

Our meetings were taking place in a curious atmosphere of assumed consensus. The CIA representatives dominated the discussion. The Joint Chiefs seemed to be going contentedly along. They met four times as a body after March 15 to review the Bay of Pigs project as it evolved; and, while their preference for Trinidad was on the record and they never formally approved the new plan, they at no time opposed it. Their collaboration with CIA in refining the scheme gave the White House the impression of their wholehearted support. Robert McNamara, who was absorbed in the endless task of trying to seize control of the Pentagon, accepted the judgment of the Chiefs on the military aspects of the plan, understood the CIA to be saying that invasion would shortly produce a revolt against Castro and supposed in any case that the new administration was following a well-established policy developed by its predecessors. Dean Rusk listened inscrutably through the discussions, confining himself to gentle warnings about possible excesses. When he went to the SEATO conference in late March and Chester Bowles as Acting Secretary sat in his place, Bowles was horrified by what he heard but reluctant to speak out in his chief's absence. On March 31 he gave Rusk a strong memorandum opposing the invasion and asked to be permitted, if Rusk disagreed, to carry the case to the President. Rusk reassured Bowles, leaving him with the impression that the project was being whittled down into a guerrilla infiltration, and filed the memorandum away.

In the meantime, Senator Fulbright had grown increasingly concerned over the newspaper stories forecasting an invasion. The President was planning to spend Easter weekend in Palm Beach and, learning that Fulbright also was going to Florida, invited him to travel on the plane. On March 29 Fulbright, with the assistance of Pat Holt, a member of the Foreign Relations Committee staff, wrote a memorandum which he gave Kennedy the next day.

There were two possible policies toward Cuba, Fulbright argued: overthrow, or toleration and isolation. The first would violate the spirit and probably the letter of the OAS charter, hemisphere treaties and our own federal legislation. If successful, it "would be denounced from the Rio Grande to Patagonia as an example of imperialism." It would cause trouble in the United Nations. It would commit us to the heavy responsibility of making a success of post-Castro Cuba. If it seemed to be failing, we might be tempted to use our own armed force; and if we did this, "even under the paper cover of legitimacy, we would have undone the work of thirty years in trying to live down earlier interventions."

> To give this activity even covert support is of a piece with the hypocrisy and cynicism for which the United States is constantly denouncing the Soviet Union in the United Nations and elsewhere. This point will not be lost on the rest of the world—nor on our own consciences.

Instead, Fulbright urged a policy of containment. The Alliance for Progress provided a solid basis for insulating the rest of the hemisphere from Castro. As for the Cuban exiles, an imaginative approach could find a more productive use of their talents than invading their homeland. Remember always, Fulbright concluded, "The Castro regime is a thorn in the flesh; but it is not a dagger in the heart."

It was a brilliant memorandum. Yet the President returned from Palm Beach more militant than when he had left. But he did ask Fulbright to attend the climactic meeting on April 4. This meeting was held at the State Department in a small conference room beside Rusk's office. After the usual routine—persuasive expositions by the CIA, mild disclaimers by Rusk and penetrating questions by the President—Kennedy started asking people around the table what they thought. Fulbright, speaking in an emphatic and incredulous way, denounced the whole idea. The operation, he said, was wildly out of proportion to the threat. It would compromise our moral position in the world and make it impossible for us to protest treaty violations by the Communists. He gave a brave, old-fashioned American speech, honorable, sensible and strong; and he left everyone in the room, except me and perhaps the President, wholly unmoved.

Kennedy continued around the table. McNamara said that he favored the operation. Mann said that he would have opposed it at the start, but, now that it had gone so far, it should be carried through. Berle wanted the men to be put into Cuba but did not insist on a major production. Kennedy once again wanted to know what could be done in the way of quiet infiltration as against the beachhead assault. The meeting fell into discussion before the round of the table was completed. Soon it broke up.

6. A PERSONAL NOTE

As we were leaving the room, the President called me back and asked for my opinion. I said that I was against the operation and tried to explain why. Listening, he nodded his head once or twice but said little. My explanation seemed to me hurried and disorderly, so the next morning I went to the office at six-thirty and wrote down my views in time to put them on the President's desk before his day began.

I had been thinking about little else for weeks and was clear in my mind that the invasion was a terrible idea. This was not because the notion of sponsoring an exile attempt to overthrow Castro seemed intolerable in itself. As my memorandum said, "If we could achieve this by a swift, surgical stroke, I would be for it." The rigid nonintervention argument had never deeply impressed me. The United States had a proud tradition of supporting refugees against tyranny in their homelands; a student of American history could not easily forget Louis Kossuth nor the fact that revolutions in Ireland, Italy, Russia, China and Palestine had all been nourished in the United States. Few of those who expressed indignation at aid to the opponents of Castro would have expressed equal indignation if in 1958 the American government had given identical aid to Castro against Batista; nor would they have objected in April 1961 to aid for the democratic Dominicans against Trujillo. Moreover, in a world shadowed by communism, the pure theory of nonintervention had even less force. "The doctrine of nonintervention," as John Stuart Mill wrote, "to be a legitimate principle of morality, must be accepted by all governments. The despots must consent to be bound by it as well as the free states. Unless they do, the profession of it by free countries comes but to this miserable issue, that the wrong side may help the wrong, but the right must not help the right."

Nor did I object to the operation because of its possible impact on Moscow. My guess was that the Soviet Union regarded Cuba as our special domain and was surprised that we had not taken action long since to rid ourselves of Castro on the model of their own intervention in Hungary. (I was probably wrong here in not allowing for the possibility of Soviet reprisals against West Berlin.) Nor did the impact on Latin America unduly disturb me. I had reported to the President after my Latin American trip, "Action against Castro would unquestionably produce a calculated sequence of riots, demonstrations, etc., in the post-Lumumba manner; but I do not believe that such chain reaction would convulse the hemisphere, as it might have a year ago, especially if the action were taken in the name of the authentic July 26 revolution." Nor could I well question the military premise advanced by CIA and endorsed by the Joint Chiefs that the Brigade would be able to establish itself on the shores of Cuba.

My opposition (expressed in this memorandum of April 5 and a second one five days later) was founded rather on the implausibility of its two political premises: that, if only Cubans took part, the United States could dissociate itself from the consequences; and that, if the beachhead could be held for a few days and enlarged, there would be defections from the militia and uprisings behind the lines. The memorandum proposed two counter-considerations as fundamental:

    a) No matter how "Cuban" the equipment and personnel, the U.S. will be held accountable for the operation, and our prestige will be committed to its success.

And, because there was no convincing evidence that the invasion would touch off a mass insurrection:

    b) Since the Castro regime is presumably too strong to be toppled by a single landing, the operation will turn into a protracted civil conflict.

If the military estimate was correct that the Brigade could secure its foothold in Cuba, the danger would be "that, if the rebellion appears to be failing, the rebels will call for U.S. armed help; that members of Congress will take up the cry; and that pressures will build up which will make it politically hard to resist the demand to send in the Marines."

Nor would sending in the Marines solve the problem, because the *Fidelistas* could be counted on to fight to the end, retreating, if necessary, to the Sierra Maestra. If the threat to our security were direct and demonstrable, then "the controlled use of force for limited objectives might well enhance respect for the United States." But a great many people around the globe, beginning with the chairman of our own Senate Foreign Relations Committee, "simply do not at this moment see that Cuba presents so grave and compelling a threat to our national security as to justify a course of action which much of the world will interpret as calculated aggression against a small nation in defiance both of treaty obligations and of the international standards as we have repeatedly asserted against the Communist world." Seeing no justification for intervention, other nations would sympathize with David rather than Goliath. A prolonged civil war in Cuba between the Castro regime and an exile army backed by the United States, the memorandum went on, would open us to damaging attack in the United Nations and elsewhere around the globe. The Russians would enlist volunteers in José Martí and probably even Abraham Lincoln Brigades and seek to convert the conflict into another Spanish Civil War.

More than that, a course of bullying intervention would destroy the new image of the United States—"the image of intelligence, reasonableness and honest firmness which has had such an extraordinary effect in changing world opinion about the U.S. and increasing world confidence in U.S. methods and purposes. . . . It is this reawakening world faith in America which is at stake in the Cuban operation." What this stately language meant was that the operation might recklessly expend one of our greatest national assets—John F. Kennedy himself. Nothing had been more depressing in the whole series of meetings than to watch a collection of officials, some of them holdovers from the previous administration, contentedly prepare to sacrifice the world's growing faith in the new American President in order to defend interests and pursue objectives of their own. Dean Rusk was almost alone in recognizing this problem; but his solution was the curious one of suggesting that someone other than the President make the final decision and do so in his absence—someone who could be sacrificed if things went wrong.

The first memorandum concluded by doubting the CIA thesis that time was on the side of Castro and arguing that the risks of the operation outweighed the risks of abandonment; the second by proposing ways to counter the communist political attack.

These memoranda look nice on the record, but they represented, of course, the easy way out. In the months after the Bay of Pigs I bitterly reproached myself for having kept so silent during those crucial discussions in the Cabinet Room, though my feelings of guilt were tempered by the knowledge that a course of objection would have accomplished little save to gain me a name as a nuisance. I can only explain my failure to do more than raise a few timid questions by reporting that one's impulse to blow the whistle on this nonsense was simply undone by the circumstances of the discussion.

It is one thing for a Special Assistant to talk frankly in private to a President at his request and another for a college professor, fresh to the government, to interpose his unassisted judgment in open meeting against that of such august figures as the Secretaries of State and Defense and the Joint Chiefs of Staff, each speaking with the full weight of his institution behind him. Moreover, the advocates of the adventure had a rhetorical advantage. They could strike virile poses and talk of tangible things—fire power, air strikes, landing craft and so on. To oppose the plan, one had to invoke intangibles—the moral position of the United States, the reputation of the President, the response of the United Nations, 'world public opinion' and other such odious concepts. These matters were as much the institutional concern of the State Department as military hardware was of Defense. But, just as the members of the White House staff who sat in the Cabinet Room failed in their job of protecting the President, so the representatives of the State Department failed in defending the diplomatic interests of the nation. I could not help feeling that the desire to prove to the CIA and the Joint Chiefs that they were not soft-headed idealists but were really tough guys, too, influenced State's representatives at the cabinet table.

7. THE PRESIDENT'S DECISION

More than once I left the meetings in the Cabinet Room fearful that only two of the regulars present were against the operation; but, since I thought the President was the other, I kept hoping that he would avail himself of his own escape clause and cancel the plan. His response to my first memorandum was oblique. He said, "You know, I've reserved the right to stop this thing up to 24 hours before the landing. In the meantime, I'm trying to make some sense out of it. We'll just have to see." But he too began to become a prisoner of events. After another meeting on April 6, I noted: "We seem now destined to go ahead on a quasi-minimum basis—a large-scale infiltration (hopefully) rather than an invasion." This change reflected the now buoyant CIA emphasis on the ease of escaping from the beaches into the hills. By this time we were offered a sort of all-purpose operation guaranteed to work, win or lose. If it failed of its maximum hope—a mass uprising leading to the overthrow of the regime—it would at least attain its minimum objective—supply and reinforcement for the guerrillas already on the island.

The next morning Dick Goodwin and I met for breakfast in the White House Mess to consider whether it would be worth making one more try to reverse the drift. Though Dick had not attended the Cuba sessions, we had talked constantly about the problem. Later that morning before departing for an economic conference in Latin America he went to see Rusk. When Goodwin expressed strong doubts about the Cuban operation, Rusk finally said, "Maybe we've been oversold on the fact that we can't say no to this." Afterward Goodwin urged me to send Rusk a copy of my memorandum to the President and follow it up by a personal visit. I arranged to see Rusk the next morning.

When I set forth my own doubts on Saturday, the Secretary listened quietly and somewhat mournfully. Finally he said he had for some time been wanting to draw a balance sheet on the project, that he planned to do it over the weekend and would try to talk with the President on Monday. He reverted to a suggestion with which he had startled the Joint Chiefs during one of the meetings. This was that the operation fan out from Guantánamo with the prospect of retreating to the base in case of failure. He remarked, "It is interesting to observe the Pentagon people. They are perfectly willing to put the President's head on the block, but they recoil from the idea of doing anything which might risk Guantánamo."

I don't know whether Rusk ever drew his balance sheet, but probably by that Saturday morning the President had already made up his mind. When Goodwin dropped into his office Friday afternoon to say goodbye, Kennedy, striding over to the French windows opening to the lawn, recalled Goodwin's fiery campaign statement and said ironically, "Well, Dick, we're about to put your Cuban policy into action." I saw the President myself later that same afternoon and noted afterward: "It is apparent that he has made his decision and is not likely now to reverse it."

Why had he decided to go ahead? So far as the operation itself was concerned, he felt, as he told me that afternoon, that he had successfully pared it down from a grandiose amphibious assault to a mass infiltration. Accepting the CIA assurances about the escape hatch, he supposed that the cost, both military and political, of failure was now reduced to a tolerable level. He added, "If we have to get rid of these 800 men, it is much better to dump them in Cuba than in the United States, especially if that is where they want to go"—a remark which suggested how much Dulles's insistence on the disposal problem had influenced the decision, as well as how greatly Kennedy was himself moved by the commitment of the Cuban patriots. He was particularly impressed by the fact that three members of the Cuban Revolutionary Council had sons in the Brigade; the exile leaders themselves obviously believed that the expedition would succeed. As the decision presented itself to him, he had to choose whether to disband a group of brave and idealistic Cubans, already trained and equipped, who wanted very much to return to Cuba on their own, or to permit them to go ahead. The President saw no obligation to protect the Castro regime from democratic Cubans and decided that, if the Cubans wished to make the try on the categorical understanding that there would be no direct United States military support, he would help them to do so. If the expedition succeeded, the overthrow of Castro would greatly strengthen democratic prospects in the hemisphere; if he called it off, he would forever be haunted by the feeling that his scruples had preserved Castro in power.

More generally, the decision resulted from the fact that he had been in office only seventy-seven days. He had not had the time or opportunity to test the inherited instrumentalities of government. He could not know which of his advisers were competent and which were not. For their part, they did not know him or each other well enough to raise hard questions with force and candor. Moreover, the massed and caparisoned authority of his senior officials in the realm of foreign policy and defense was unanimous for going ahead. The director of the Central Intelligence Agency advocated the adventure; the Joint Chiefs of Staff and the Secretary of Defense approved its military aspects, the Secretary of State its political aspects. They all spoke with the sacerdotal prerogative of men vested with a unique understanding of arcane matters. "If someone comes in to tell me this or that about the minimum wage bill," Kennedy said to me later, "I have no hesitation in overruling them. But you always assume that the military and intelligence people have some secret skill not available to ordinary mortals." The only opposition came from Fulbright and myself (he knew nothing of Bowles's memorandum to Rusk, nor did he know that Edward R. Murrow, the new director of the United States Information Agency, who had learned about the operation from a *New York Times* reporter early in April, was also deeply opposed), and this did not bulk large against the united voice of institutional authority. Had one senior adviser opposed the adventure, I believe that Kennedy would have canceled it. No one spoke against it.

One further factor no doubt influenced him: the enormous confidence in his own luck. Everything had broken right for him since 1956. He had won the nomination and the election against all the odds in the book. Everyone around him thought he had the Midas touch and could not lose. Despite himself, even this dispassionate and skeptical man may have been affected by the soaring euphoria of the new day.

On the following Tuesday the Robert Kennedys gave a party to celebrate Ethel's birthday. It was a large, lively, uproarious affair, overrun by guests, skits, children and dogs. In the midst of the gaiety Robert Kennedy drew me aside. He said, "I hear you don't think much of this business." He asked why and listened without expression as I gave my reasons. Finally he said, "You may be right or you may be wrong, but the President has made his mind up. Don't push it any further. Now is the time for everyone to help him all they can."

8. THE POLITICS OF CLANDESTINITY

And so we were going ahead. If this were so, the next thing was to do what could be done to minimize the damage. It was evident that the political and diplomatic planning was far less advanced than the military planning. And it was evident too that, if the invasion was to win support within Cuba, its sponsor, the Cuban Revolutionary Council, must appear not a counterrevolutionary but a revolutionary movement, offering Cuba not a restoration but a liberation.

The formation of the Council on March 22 was only a first halting step. A few days later Tracy Barnes of CIA sent me the first draft of a proposed Council manifesto— a document so overwrought in tone and sterile in thought that it made one wonder what sort of people we were planning to send back to Havana. Barnes wholly agreed that the Council's program was of no use in its existing form, and we discussed how to go about strengthening it. After some thought, we asked two Latin American specialists from Harvard—John Plank of the Government Department and William Barnes of the Law School—to suggest guiding principles for a sensible and progressive platform.

In the meantime, Berle, Philip Bonsal and I held a conference with Miró Cardona. It took place, as it happened, on the afternoon of the day that Fulbright made his gallant attempt to turn the tide. Miró was a genial man in his late fifties, bald and flushed, his great round face dominated by those inordinately heavy horn-rimmed glasses favored by Latin American politicians. Our purpose was to persuade him to give the Council's program social and economic content. We pointed out that the Council draft was filled with impassioned appeals to the foreign investor, the private banker, the dispossessed property owner, but had very little to say to the worker, the farmer or the Negro. I remarked at one point, "It would be foolish if the Cuban Revolutionary Council turns out to be to the right of the New Frontier." We suggested that the Council must reassure the Cubans that it had no intention of destroying the social and economic gains of the last two years.

Miró threw his hands in the air, heartily agreed, and said that we must understand the situation in Miami: whenever he delivered a speech about social justice, half the audience went away convinced that he was a communist. This gave us the opportunity to make a second point— that the Council should move to New York. This would take it away from the feverish atmosphere of Miami, dominated by Cubans of the right, and put it in a better position to present the exile case to the United Nations. Again Miró acquiesced. We welcomed his agreement, of course, and I have no doubt that he accepted our recommendations with personal relief. But I began to understand the humiliating lot of the exile who wished above all to maintain his political group and the sources of its income and who therefore must permit himself to be buffeted about by all those in a position to open a purse, whether wealthy refugees, CIA spooks or now Washington officials.

In Miami the recruitment effort had reached its last frantic phase. By now all pretense of discretion was gone. Talk was unrestrained in the motels and bars. On March 31 Howard Handleman of *U.S. News and World Report,* returning from ten days in Florida, said to me that the exiles were telling everyone that they would receive United States recognition as soon as they landed in Cuba, to be followed by the overt provision of arms and supplies. A few days later Gilbert Harrison of the *New Republic* sent over the galleys of a pseudonymous piece called "Our Men in Miami," asking whether there was any reason why it should not be published. It was a careful, accurate and devastating account of CIA activities among the refugees, written, I learned later, by Karl Meyer. Obviously its publication in a responsible magazine would cause trouble, but could the government properly ask an editor to suppress the truth? Defeated by the moral issue, I handed the article to the President, who instantly read it and expressed the hope that it could be stopped. Harrison accepted the suggestion and without questions—a patriotic act which left me oddly uncomfortable.

About the same time Tad Szulc filed a story to the *New York Times* from Miami describing the recruitment drive and reporting that a landing on Cuba was imminent. Turner Catledge, the managing editor, called James Reston, who was in his weekend retreat in Virginia, to ask his advice. Reston counseled against publication: either the story would alert Castro, in which case the *Times* would be responsible for casualties on the beach, or else the expedition would be canceled, in which case the *Times* would be responsible for grave interference with national policy. This was another patriotic act; but in retrospect I have wondered whether, if the press had behaved irresponsibly, it would not have spared the country a disaster.

The Council meanwhile transferred its operations to the Hotel Lexington in New York. Soon John Plank joined them there and worked with Miró and the others to reshape their pronouncements along reasonable lines. The members of the Council knew that a climax was imminent even if they did not know how, when or where. As decent men, burning with love for their country, they were eager to do anything to free their homeland. This generated an understandable readiness to subordinate the interests of the United States to those of a free Cuba; and, however understandable this was from a Cuban viewpoint, it presented dangers to the United States—above all, the danger of losing control over our own policy and being pulled by political suction into a greater degree of intervention than we intended. The first protection against step-by-step involvement, I suggested to the President in a memorandum on April 10, would be "to convince the Cuban leaders that in no foreseeable circumstances will we send in U.S. troops . . . We must tell the Revolutionary Council that it cannot expect immediate U.S. recognition; that recognition will come only when they have a better than 50-50 chance of winning under their own steam; that this is a fight which Cubans will have in essence to win for themselves."

Kennedy understood this better than anybody and needed no prodding. Two days later he seized the occasion to say in a press conference: "There will not be, under any conditions, an intervention in Cuba by the United States Armed Forces. . . . The basic issue in Cuba is not one between the United States and Cuba. It is between the Cubans themselves. I intend to see that we adhere to that principle and as I understand it this administration's attitude is so understood and shared by the anti-Castro exiles from Cuba in this country." That afternoon in another meeting in the Cabinet Room he again emphasized the importance of making the operation into an entirely Cuban affair. He inquired sharply whether the Revolutionary Council fully grasped that the provisional government would not receive United States recognition until it was fully established, and that in no case would there be overt military intervention. Lest there be any misunderstanding, he said, he was instructing Berle and Schlesinger to go to New York and make this clear to Miró Cardona. These points, of course, simply recorded the assumptions on which the CIA and the Joint Chiefs had drawn up their invasion plan and predicted its success; and, as they sat around the table, they did not protest now. Did any among them think that events might override the President's stipulations? If so, they might have wished to avoid a discussion which would only tie him all the more definitely to nonintervention.

9. ON THE BRINK

The meeting on April 12 was preceded by a strange incident whose significance even today remains indecipherable to me. I received a request from Georgi Kornienko, the counselor of the Soviet Embassy, for an immediate appointment. Soon a sharp-eyed, moon-faced man appeared, speaking fluent but somewhat formal English. After some preliminary palaver, he said courteously that he did not fully understand the policy of the United States toward Latin America and especially toward Cuba. I referred him to the White Paper, observing that the concern of the United States was not over the fact of revolution in Cuba but over its subsequent betrayal; if the Castro regime had any hostility to fear, it was the hostility of Cubans. When he expressed wonder that the United States cared so much about the emergence of a regime in Cuba with ties to the communist world, I suggested that he might understand if he were to transfer recent events in Havana to, say, Warsaw; I doubted whether the Soviet Union would accept such developments in the case of Poland with the same detachment he now urged on me. By Soviet standards he should be more impressed by American patience than by American impetuosity.

After additional inconclusive talk, Kornienko asked whether we excluded the possibility of further negotiation with Castro. When I inquired what he had in mind, he said that of course all this was fantasy, since he was not under instructions and could not, in any case, speak for the Cubans, but that, if he were Castro, he would wonder whether an effort at negotiation might not be appropriate; after all, Castro had not as yet issued a formal reply to the White Paper. I wondered what issues might be negotiated, citing the President's statement in his State of the Union message about the negotiability of social and economic issues and the non-negotiability of communist invasion of the hemisphere. Kornienko doubted whether

Castro would regard internal Cuban questions as negotiable. He then asked what sort of action Washington might
take as evidence of a serious desire to negotiate. I replied
that a crucial issue was the monopoly of political action
enjoyed by the Communist Party. Speaking in the same
spirit of fantasy which he had earlier invoked, I inquired
whether he thought that the Castro regime would, for example, offer the Revolutionary Council equal freedom of
political action. He evidently did not think so. After a
time the discussion moved on to other areas.

I came to know Kornienko better in time; we used to
lunch together at irregular intervals until he returned to
Moscow at the end of 1963. These luncheons were never
very productive. Kornienko, an exceedingly intelligent and
entirely immovable defender of the current Soviet brief,
whatever it might be, rarely showed any inclination to talk
apart from it. For this reason, I am sure that he was acting
under some sort of instruction in bringing up the possibility
of negotiation. But the instruction could not have been very
urgent. His talk was marked by a total absence of warnings
or threats; his attitude seemed one of polite curiosity. His
visit must have been either exploratory or, more probably,
diversionist; for he had nothing positive to suggest. In any
case, I promptly informed the President and Rusk of the
meeting. Neither saw much in it, Rusk confining himself to
the comment that my memorandum of conversation was
unclassified and should have been stamped "secret."

The next day I flew to New York in a blinding rainstorm for the meeting with Miró. Berle, John Plank and
I lunched with him at the Century. Miró was much irritated
because CIA had not cut him in on the invasion: "There
must be some military plan I don't know about. I would
like to know about it for purposes of coordination. I don't
want to know these things; but I have to know to make our
efforts effective." His particular concern, however, was with
the question of United States military support. He displayed resistance and incredulity at the statement that no
United States troops would be used. He waved the President's news conference disclaimer aside as an understandable piece of psychological warfare and kept pressing us
to say how far the administration really meant to go. Berle
said, "We'll take you to the beaches," but this did not
satisfy him.

Everyone knows, Miró said, that the United States is
behind the expedition. If it should succeed no one will

object to the American role. Berle then said that it could not succeed without an internal uprising, and that, if one came, we would provide the democratic Cubans with the things necessary to make it successful. Once the provisional government was established on the beachhead, we would offer all aid short of United States troops. Miró said that 10,000 Cubans would immediately align themselves with the invading forces. Berle replied that there would be plenty of arms for them. The kind of help we were prepared to give, he repeated, would be enough if, in fact, a revolutionary situation existed within Cuba.

I reproduce this part of the conversation from notes made at the time because Miró told his colleagues and later claimed publicly that Berle had promised the support of 10,000 United States troops. Either Miró's knowledge of English or the translation was sadly at fault. Miró, a driven man, probably heard what he desperately wanted to hear. He went on to tell us that, if the provisional government was established and things then began to go badly, he planned to call for help from all the nations of the hemisphere—including the United States. He said with solemnity, "This help must come." For, if the operation should fail, the American government would have suffered a severe defeat on its very doorstep, communism would be consolidated in Cuba, and Castro would move on to destroy the whole inter-American system. "You must understand what will happen to your own interests if we lose. You must commit yourselves to full support of our efforts."

I returned to Washington considerably depressed. Whatever Miró was told, it was evident he simply would not believe he could not count on United States military support. "He is a serious person," I reported to the President the next morning, "and will not be easily moved from his present position. Nonetheless I think a very tough effort should be made to get him to accept the President's press conference statement . . . as the basis for his future relations with the United States." The President promptly picked up the phone—it was a fragrant morning at the beginning of spring, and we were discussing the speech he was about to give at the Pan American Union—called Dick Bissell and told him that Miró must understand that either he agrees to proceed on the basis of no United States military intervention or else the whole expedition would be called off. Bissell sent Tracy Barnes to New York that day to stress the point. Though Barnes got a formal assent, he too returned to Washington doubtful whether Miró really believed him.[3]

Kennedy's speech that morning was a summons to the Council of the OAS to expedite the work of the Alliance for Progress. Though I had composed drafts for his use, this was my first experience in working directly with him on a speech. I had written a text the night before. Gretchen Stewart came to the office at seven-thirty in the morning, along with Wymberley Coerr, now Acting Assistant Secretary of State for Inter-American affairs (Tom Mann, who was scheduled to become ambassador to Mexico, had resigned early in April lest he arrive in Mexico City bearing the onus of the invasion of Cuba). As I revised the pages, I handed them to Coerr, who passed them on to Miss Stewart, who put them on the speech typewriter. A little before ten o'clock—just an hour before the speech was to be given—Evelyn Lincoln called to say that the President was free and wanted to see the draft. When I took it to his office, he read it carefully and calmly, cut out the two explicit anti-Castro passages on the ground that he did not want to mix up the Alliance for Progress with Cuba, decided that the text was too long, made some other cuts and revisions and then read it again—all in a state of total relaxation. He then asked whether I could not find an appropriate quotation from Franklin Roosevelt. I dug one up in the next few minutes.

It was ten forty-five. He invited me to come along with Jacqueline in the car; and, as we drove over to the Pan American Union, he remarked that he thought he might say something about the importance of using existing institutions, like the OAS, rather than succumbing to the pressure of devising new institutions. I said that this sounded fine to me. A few minutes later, when he began the speech, he went into an apt improvisation along these lines. It was the most effective part of the address and drew the only applause. As a veteran ghost, I felt appropriately chagrined. On the way back, he stopped the car just inside the White House grounds and proposed a walk down to the pond to see Caroline's ducks. Caroline, who came running out of nowhere, joined us for a leisurely fifteen-

---

[3] Later in the day the President returned to me my *aide-mémoire* on the Miró conversation with the scrawled notation: "I informed Bissell that he should have Cardona told that the operation would be cancelled immediately unless Cardona made the decision to go ahead with full understanding of the limitations on U.S. support."

minute stroll in the spring sun. It was a last peaceful moment before the storm broke.

XI

ORDEAL BY FIRE

EVENTS WERE RUSHING toward climax. D-day had originally
been proposed for April 5; at the end of March the President postponed it to April 10; now it was set for April 17.
In Guatemala the Cuban Brigade, now grown to almost
1400 men, waited with growing impatience. A veteran Marine colonel arrived to make a final inspection as the force
prepared to leave its base. The day after the President had
publicly excluded United States military intervention, Washington sent an urgent request for the colonel's evaluation
of the Brigade and its capabilities. The reply came back
in unequivocal language:

> My observations have increased my confidence in the ability
> of this force to accomplish not only initial combat missions,
> but also the ultimate objective, the overthrow of Castro. The
> Brigade and battalion commanders now know all details of
> the plan and are enthusiastic. These officers are young, vigor-
> ous, intelligent and motivated by a fanatical urge to begin
> battle. . . .
> They say they know their own people and believe that
> after they have inflicted one serious defeat upon the opposi-
> tion forces, the latter will melt away from Castro, whom
> they have no wish to support. They say it is a Cuban tradi-
> tion to join a winner and they have supreme confidence they
> will win against whatever Castro has to offer.
> I share their confidence.

This message reached the White House on April 14 shortly
before the hour of what is known in Pentagonese as the
'no-go' decision on preliminary operations. The fervent tes-
timonial confirmed the President in his intention to let
the expedition go ahead.

1. PRELUDE TO TRAGEDY

But I doubt whether anyone in Washington really knew
what was taking place in Guatemala. The top CIA officials
—Dulles, Bissell, Barnes—were civilized and responsible
men; but the CIA operatives in the field and their military

colleagues were a different breed, if, at least, the Cubans
themselves are to be believed. As zero hour approached,
the American advisers told them again (or so they later
informed Haynes Johnson) that their Brigade would not
be the only unit in the invasion. They received the impression that after seventy-two hours they could count on
United States military and air support. At one point, according to Pepe San Román, the chief United States adviser even talked darkly of efforts in Washington to cancel
the operation and said that, if a stop order came through,
"you come here and make some kind of show, as if you
were putting us, the advisers, in prison, and you go ahead
with the program as we have talked about it, and we will
give you the whole plan, even if we are your prisoners." He
went on to hint that this was the desire of his superiors.[1]
(Actually the United States Navy had been briefed to intercept and turn back the invasion in case of a last-minute
decision against it.)

As for the Cubans themselves, their spirit was high.
Many of the new recruits, however, had been at the base
only a few days. Some had not even fired a gun. Of the
1400 men, only about 135 were soldiers. Of the rest, 240
students made up the largest single group. In addition, there
were businessmen, lawyers, doctors, landowners and their
sons, along with fishermen and peasants. At least fifty were
Negroes. The average age was about twenty-nine, though one
man was as old as sixty-one and some were no more than
sixteen. Apart from professionals who had served in Batista's army, few real Batistianos had slipped in, but some
notorious Batista criminals somehow showed up on the
boats on the way to Cuba (to be subsequently displayed by
Castro as representative members of the Brigade). The officers, though not active Batistianos, stood considerably to
the right of the Revolutionary Council. The rank and file
were politically heterogeneous. The only common purpose
was to return home and get rid of Castro.

On April 10 the Brigade began to move by truck from
the Guatemalan base to the point of embarkation at Puerto
Cabezas in Nicaragua. By April 13 the men were beginning
to board the boats. On April 14 the United States advisers finally disclosed the invasion plan—the seizure of
three beaches along forty miles of the Cuban shore in the
Bay of Pigs area, with paratroops dropping inland to control the roads crossing the swamps to the sea. Castro's air

[1] Haynes Johnson, *The Bay of Pigs* (New York, 1964 [Dell edition]),
73-74.

force, the advisers said, would be neutralized in advance, and five hundred guerrillas were waiting nearby to join the fight. The Brigade's mission was to hold the beach for three days, after which, as the chief American adviser put it, "you will be so strong, you will be getting so many people to your side, that you won't want to wait for us. You will go straight ahead. You will put your hands out, turn left, and go straight into Havana." [2] The Cubans, still regarding the Americans with veneration and not used to locker-room pep talks, left the briefing in a state of exaltation.

As the flotilla of seven small ships waited off Puerto Cabezas on the late afternoon of April 14, Luis Somoza, the dictator of Nicaragua, appeared at the dock, his face powdered, bodyguards in his wake. He shouted boldly, "Bring me a couple of hairs from Castro's beard," and waved the patriots farewell. The members of the Brigade trailed their vivid battalion scarves in the wind, and the boats, tinted by the red light of the dying sun, set out for Cuba.

The neutralization of Castro's air force was to be brought about by air strikes from Nicaraguan bases before the landings. This question of air attack had been under debate since January. The State Department had opposed pre-invasion strikes as incompatible with the ground rule against showing the American hand. In the Department's view, there should be no air activity until the invaders secured an airstrip of their own in Cuba and their air power could appear to be something they were mounting out of their own resources. The Pentagon, on the other hand, had contended that pre-invasion strikes were essential to knock out the Cuban air force and protect the disembarkation.

The Trinidad plan had contained no provision for advance strikes; but with the Bay of Pigs plan there had come a compromise—a strike against Cuban airfields two days before the landings, to be carried out, in order to meet State's objections, by Cuban pilots pretending to be defectors from Castro's air force. After an interval to permit U-2 overflights and photographic assessment of the damage, a second strike would follow at dawn on D-day morning. No one supposed that the cover story would hold up for very long; Castro, for example, would obviously know in short order that he was not being attacked by deserters from his own air force. But the planners expected that it would hold at least until the invaders hit the beaches—

long enough to mask the second strike. It was also recognized that the pre-invasion strikes would probably cause Castro to move against the underground; but, since CIA did not put much stock in the underground anyway, its elimination was considered less important than the elimination of Castro's air power. The compromise was not altogether satisfactory, the Joint Chiefs fearing that the strikes would alert Castro without destroying his air power, and even CIA preferring a massive strike concurrent with the invasion; but in the end it seemed the best solution.

As the ships made their slow way toward Cuba, eight B-26s took off from Puerto Cabezas in the night. At dawn on Saturday morning they zoomed down on three main Cuban airfields. CIA had estimated Castro's air strength at about fifteen B-26s and ten Sea Furies; there were also four T-33 jet trainers, but these did not figure significantly in either CIA's or, what is worse, the Joint Chiefs' calculations. The Cuban air force, according to the CIA estimate, was "entirely disorganized," its planes "for the most part obsolete and inoperative," its combat efficiency "almost non-existent."

The pilots returned to Nicaragua with optimistic claims of widespread damage. The overflights the next day, however, showed only five aircraft definitely destroyed. And not all the attacking planes made it back to the base. One developed engine trouble, and its pilot headed for Florida, finally making an emergency landing in Key West. In the meantime, a ninth B-26 had flown straight from Nicaragua to Miami to put the cover plan into operation. The pilot on landing announced himself as a Castro defector who had just bombed the airfields. The unscheduled arrival of the second plane at Key West complicated things somewhat; and the appearance at Jacksonville the day before of a perfectly genuine Castro defector in a Cuban plane compounded the confusion.

In New York Adlai Stevenson was getting ready for a long-delayed debate in the United Nations General Assembly over a Cuban charge of aggressive intentions on the part of the United States. Kennedy, who had been much concerned about the UN aspect of the Cuban operation, told the group in the Cabinet Room that he wished Stevenson to be fully informed, and that nothing said at the UN should be less than the truth, even if it could not be the full truth. "The integrity and credibility of Adlai Stevenson," he had remarked to me on April 7, "constitute one of our great national assets. I don't want anything to be done which might jeopardize that."

In preparation for the debate, Tracy Barnes and I had held a long talk with Stevenson on April 8. But our briefing, which was probably unduly vague, left Stevenson with the impression that no action would take place during the UN discussion of the Cuban item. Afterward, when Harlan Cleveland, the Assistant Secretary for International Organization Affairs, Clayton Fritchey of the United States Mission to the UN, and I lunched with Stevenson at the Century, he made clear that he wholly disapproved of the plan, regretted that he had been given no opportunity to comment on it and believed that it would cause infinite trouble. But, if it was national policy, he was prepared to make out the best possible case.

After the Saturday air strike, Raúl Roa, the Cuban foreign minister, succeeded in advancing the Cuban item, scheduled for the following Monday, to an emergency session of the UN Political Committee that afternoon. In Washington Harlan Cleveland tried to ascertain the facts about the strike. His office called the Bureau of Inter-American Affairs, which in turn called the CIA. Word promptly and definitely came back that it was the work of genuine defectors, and Cleveland passed this information on to Stevenson. A few moments later Stevenson told the UN: "These two planes, to the best of our knowledge, were Castro's own air force planes and, according to the pilots, they took off from Castro's own air force fields." As Stevenson spoke, someone handed him a piece of press ticker containing what appeared to be corroborative detail, and Stevenson read further parts of the CIA cover story into the record.

The 'need-to-know' standard had simply left the Bureau of International Organization Affairs and most of the Bureau of Inter-American Affairs (as well as Ed Murrow and the USIA) ignorant of the operation. Rusk himself, moreover, seems for a while to have confused the phony defector at Key West with the authentic defector at Jacksonville. Apparently it was not till late Saturday afternoon that he understood that the Key West plane was part of the CIA plot. Why CIA should have misled State has never been clear. Possibly the Agency, having worked out its deception plan, felt obliged to deceive even the rest of its own government; or possibly the CIA source, if in the Intelligence Branch, was himself 'unwitting.'

The President had meanwhile gone off to his Virginia retreat at Glen Ora early Saturday afternoon; had he remained, contrary to custom, in Washington, the press would have presumed that something was up. At Sunday noon, the last 'no-go' point, he authorized the expedition to proceed to the beaches. But in Washington newspapermen were starting to call the State Department and ask penetrating questions about the fugitive B-26s in Key West and Miami. It was evident that the CIA cover story was cracking, that Stevenson had been permitted to misinform the UN and that the international repercussions might be extensive. Stevenson was understandably indignant. Rusk, remorseful at the position into which State had thrust its UN ambassador, now resolved that the Cuban adventure should not be permitted further to jeopardize the larger interests of United States foreign policy.

In particular, the collapse of the cover story brought the question of the second air strike into new focus. The President and the Secretary understood this strike as one which would take place simultaneously with the landings and have the appearance of coming from the airstrip on the beach. It had slid by in the briefings, everyone assuming that it would be masked by the cover story. But there could be no easy attribution to defectors now. Nor did the fact that the planes were B-26s flown by Cuban pilots save the situation; despite the great to-do about 'Cubanizing' the operation, they would still be United States planes in the eyes of the UN. Rusk, after his talks with Stevenson, concluded that a second Nicaraguan strike would put the United States in an untenable position internationally and that no further strikes should be launched until the planes could fly (or appear to fly) from the beachhead. Bundy agreed, and they called the President at Glen Ora.

It was now late Sunday afternoon. When Rusk said that the projected strike was one which could only appear to come from Nicaragua, Kennedy said, "I'm not signed on to this"; the strike he knew about was the one coming ostensibly from the beachhead. After a long conversation, the President directed that the strike be canceled. When he put down the phone, he sat on in silence for a moment, shook his head and began to pace the room in evident concern, worried perhaps less about this decision than about the confusion in the planning; what would go wrong next? Those with him at Glen Ora had rarely seen him so low.

Bundy promptly passed on the word to General C. P. Cabell, the deputy director of CIA, and Rusk sent Bundy off to New York to answer any further questions from Stevenson. Soon Cabell and Bissell, deeply disturbed by the decision, arrived at Rusk's office—it was now evening—and tried to reopen the case. They argued that both the flotilla and the landing would be endangered if there were no dawn strike. Rusk replied that the ships could unload in darkness before Castro's planes located them and that after the landing the B-26s could defend the beaches from airstrips on shore. The vigorous discussion gave Rusk the impression that CIA regarded the Nicaraguan strike as important but not vital. He suggested to Cabell and Bissell that, if they wanted to carry their case further, they could appeal to the President, but they declined to do so. Instead, they retired to CIA and dejectedly sent out the stop order, which arrived in Nicaragua as the pilots were waiting in their cockpits for take-off.

At four-thirty the next morning Cabell awoke Rusk with a new proposal—that, if the invasion ships retired to international waters, they receive air cover from a United States carrier nearby. Rusk rejected this as a violation of the ban against United States participation, and Kennedy, to whom Cabell this time appealed at Glen Ora, confirmed the rejection. . . . Already the expeditionary force was at its stations off the Bay of Pigs, and frogmen were beginning to mark the invasion points on shore. The first frogman on each beach was, in spite of Kennedy's order, an American.

2. FIASCO

The frogmen almost immediately encountered a militia patrol, rifle fire shattered the silence, and hope of tactical surprise was gone. On the ships the Cubans watched wild flashes of lights on shore and then began with uncertain hearts to clamber into landing craft. Some of the small boats, as they made their way through black waters, ran against coral reefs, not mentioned in the briefing, and foundered, the men swimming to other boats or toward land. Gradually the invaders gathered on the beaches and pushed inland. After daybreak paratroops dropped from the skies and seized interior points.

Castro's air force, alerted by the first clash, reacted with unexpected vigor against both the ships and the men on the beaches. At nine-thirty in the morning, a Sea Fury sank the ships carrying the ammunition reserve for the next ten days and most of the communications equipment: an inexplicable concentration of treasure in a single hull. Other ships suffered damage, and the rest of the flotilla put out to sea. The Brigade's slow-moving B-26s flew defensive missions over the beachhead, but Castro's forgotten T-33s, fast jet trainers armed with 50-calibre machine guns, shot four of them down. The fighting went on through a hot, clear day, the invaders digging in behind their tanks, bazookas and mortars, while Castro's forces, unable to cross the swamps, massed to move down the highways toward the beaches.

In Havana Castro's police arrested two hundred thousand people, herding them into theaters and auditoriums. Through the island anyone suspected of underground connections was taken into custody. In New York the Cuba Revolutionary Council had become mysteriously inaccessible, for Miró had privately agreed with the CIA that the Council should go into hiding. By Sunday night they were installed in a house in the Opa-Locka airport to await transfer to the beachhead and establishment as the provisional government of a free Cuba. The next morning, as they listened to the radio, they were stunned to hear an announcement "from the Cuban Revolutionary Council" that the invasion had begun. Unknown to them, a New York public relations man who had once worked for Wendell Willkie, Lem Jones, was putting out in the name of the Council press releases dictated over the phone by the CIA.

In Washington President Kennedy arrived back by helicopter from Glen Ora early Monday morning. Dean Rusk told a press conference later that morning, "The American people are entitled to know whether we are intervening in Cuba or intend to do so in the future. The answer to that question is no. What happens in Cuba is for the Cuban people to decide." An angry diplomatic note came in from Khrushchev, denouncing the invasion and pledging "all necessary assistance" to Castro. During the day the news from the beaches was confused and fragmentary as a result of the loss of communications facilities; but Washington could still remain hopeful. In the late afternoon a new bulletin announced in the name of the Council, "The principal battle of the Cuban revolt against Castro will be fought in the next few hours. Action today was largely of a supply and support effort." It concluded by calling for "a coordinated wave of sabotage and rebellion."

That evening José Figueres came to my house for dinner with Berle and Mann. I had never seen him so despondent. Afraid that the invasion would fail, he resented the fact that the United States government had not taken him or Betancourt into its confidence. "How can we have an alliance," he said, almost bitterly, "if even our friends will not believe that we can be trusted with secrets? I may disagree with something, but I still can be trusted to keep quiet about it." It was a glum party, shadowed with apprehension.

By early Tuesday it was clear that the invasion was in

trouble. An attempt to knock out Castro's planes by a B-26 raid that morning had been frustrated by heavy haze over the airfield. I noted later that day: "The T-33s turned out to be far more effective than any of us had been led to suppose. This created havoc. . . . In addition, Castro tanks reached the beachhead sooner than had been expected. And the landings failed to set off mass uprisings behind the lines." The President asked me to luncheon with James Reston. In spite of the news, Kennedy was free, calm and candid; I had rarely seen him more effectively in control. Saying frankly that reports from the beaches were discouraging, he spoke with detachment about the problems he would now face. "I probably made a mistake in keeping Allen Dulles on," he said. "It's not that Dulles is not a man of great ability. He is. But I have never worked with him, and therefore I can't estimate his meaning when he tells me things. . . . Dulles is a legendary figure, and it's hard to operate with legendary figures." As for CIA, "we will have to do something. . . . I must have someone there with whom I can be in complete and intimate contact—someone from whom I know I will be getting the exact pitch." He added, "I made a mistake in putting Bobby in the Justice Department. He is wasted there. Byron White could do that job perfectly well. Bobby should be in CIA. . . . It is a hell of a way to learn things, but I have learned one thing from this business—that is, that we will have to deal with CIA. McNamara has dealt with Defense; Rusk has done a lot with State; but no one has dealt with CIA."

Could anything be done about the invasion? Kennedy seemed deeply concerned about the members of the Brigade. They were brave men and patriots; he had put them on the beachhead; and wanted to save as many as he could. But he did not propose to send in the Marines. Some people, he noted, were arguing that failure would cause irreparable harm, that we had no choice now but to commit United States forces. Kennedy disagreed. Defeat, he said, would be an incident, not a disaster. The test had always been whether the Cuban people would back a revolt against Castro. If they wouldn't, the United States could not by invasion impose a new regime on them. But would not United States prestige suffer if we let the rebellion flicker out? "What is prestige?" Kennedy asked. "Is it the shadow of power or the substance of power? We are going to work on the substance of power. No doubt we will be kicked in the can for the next couple of weeks, but that won't affect the main business."

That afternoon we met in the Cabinet Room to consider

a reply to Khrushchev. Rusk and Bundy were there, with some new faces—Charles E. Bohlen and Foy Kohler, the Soviet experts, and Harlan Cleveland to cover the United Nations. Bohlen wrote the original draft, and the President amended it to his satisfaction. "I believe, Mr. Chairman," the message finally said, "that you should recognize that free peoples in all parts of the world do not accept the claim of historical inevitability for communist revolution. What your Government believes is its own business; what it does in the world is the world's business. The great revolution in the history of man, past, present and future, is the revolution of those determined to be free."

It was a long and grim day—the longest and grimmest the New Frontier had known. The reports from Cuba continued sketchy, but whatever news there was was bad. Hour after hour, hope steadily drained away. By late afternoon we learned that twenty thousand government troops with artillery and tanks were moving toward the water to encircle the invaders. Yet the Brigade fought on, its leaders still sustained by the dream of United States intervention —a dream stimulated, they later said, by assurances from Americans in the ships offshore.[3] We could not rid our minds of the thought of those brave men, running short of ammunition, without adequate air cover, dying on Cuban beaches before Soviet tanks. That morning, when CIA had assured San Román he would be taken off the beach, the Brigade commander replied: "I will not be evacuated. We will fight to the end here if we have to."

At the White House it was the night of the annual Congressional Reception. The President lingered in the West Wing until the last possible minute, still hopeful for a turn in the news, still determined to bring out as many survivors as he could. Then he went somberly back to the Mansion to put on white tie and tails. A few moments later, his head high, he entered the East Room and mingled serenely with the guests.

In the meantime, I had gone home dead tired to Georgetown. Around one in the morning, as I was getting into bed, the phone rang. It was Mac Bundy. He said, "I am in the President's office, and he would like to have you come down here as soon as possible." When I arrived, I found the President, the Vice-President, Rusk, McNamara, Lemnitzer and Burke, all resplendent in full dress, along with Bissell, Bundy and Walt Rostow. They were gloomily read-

[3] Johnson, *The Bay of Pigs*, 139.

ing dispatches from the beachhead. Mac said to me as I
entered: "We have no real news, but we fear that things
are going badly. In any case, the Revolutionary Council is
very upset. Some of its members are threatening extreme
action. The President wants Berle to go down and talk with
them. If we can't find Berle, he wants you."

In a moment the President took charge. He was objective
and trenchant in his questions; but absence of information
made decision difficult. Bissell and Burke were proposing a concealed United States air strike from the carrier
Essex lying off Cuba. This, they said, could knock out the
T-33s and free the Brigade's B-26s to deal with Castro's
tanks. The group discussed this proposal in a desultory and
rather distracted way; it seemed to be a renewal of a debate which had begun before I arrived. Finally the President evolved a compromise. He decided to authorize a flight
of six unmarked jets from the *Essex* over the Bay of Pigs
for the hour after dawn Wednesday morning. Their mission
would be to cover a B-26 attack from Nicaragua. They
were not to seek air combat or ground targets, but could
defend the Brigade planes from air attack; it seemed a
somewhat tricky instruction, since it meant that the Castro
planes would either have to let the B-26s go or invite return fire from the jet convoy. The President probably permitted this single relaxation of his ban against the use of
United States armed force in the hope that it might make
possible the evacuation of the Brigade from the beachhead.
(In Puerto Cabezas, the Cuban pilots were in a state of
exhaustion from 48 hours of nearly continuous runs over
the beachhead. A few now declined to go out on what
seemed a suicide mission. Some American civilian pilots,
under contract to the CIA, agreed, however, to fly sorties.
Both the B-26s and the Navy jets started out later that
night, but through one more mix-up in this doomed adventure—this one as elementary as a mix-up between the
Nicaraguan and Cuban time zones—the B-26s arrived over
the beachhead an hour ahead of their jet support. Without
cover, the B-26s ran into sharp enemy fire, and four Americans were killed.)

In a short while Berle arrived. The President then turned
to the problem of the Revolutionary Council. "One member
is threatening suicide," he said. "Others want to be put
on the beachhead. All are furious with CIA. They do not
know how dismal things are. You must go down and talk
to them." Berle said, "Yes," then added wryly, "I can
think of happier missions." As the meeting broke up around

two in the morning, Kennedy called me over and said,
"You ought to go with Berle." Later that night, when the
group had left his office, the President walked alone in the
desolate silence of the White House garden.

3. MISSION TO MIAMI

A military plane was waiting when Berle and I arrived at
National Airport. In a few minutes we were heading south.
For a while we discussed the strategy of the morrow.
Adolf's voice was low, and I could hardly hear him over the
roar of the engines. Then he went into our berths for fitful
sleep. Very soon we were awakened with word that we
were approaching Miami.

About seven o'clock we debouched into a hot, clear
Florida day. The famous Bender met us and took us with
conspicuous stealth to an automobile parked nearby. We
drove for a while; then stopped at a hamburger stand,
where we met a second car. One began to feel like a character out of a Hitchcock film. Then we started driving
again, through mile after mile of sterile Miami landscape.
Eventually we reached the deserted airbase of Opa-Locka.

We stopped first at an old hangar now serving as headquarters for the CIA contingent. Here we called Washington to get the latest word. As usual, there was nothing—no
report yet, for example, from the air strike scheduled for
seven-thirty. More news, we were told, might be available
at ten o'clock. Then back to the automobile and on for
another two minutes until we came to a stop a few yards
from a nondescript frame house deep in the encampment.
Young American GIs, their revolvers conspicuous in hol-
sters, were patrolling the grounds. We entered the house. It
was about eight-fifteen. A radio was playing in the background. As we stumbled onto the sunporch, a young man
lying asleep on a cot stirred uneasily and got up. It was, I
soon discovered, Manuel Ray.

Our arrival brought the house to life. In a few moments
we were all seated around a plain wooden table. The members of the Council wore khaki fatigues: Miró Cardona,
with a son on the beachhead; Tony Varona, with a son, two
brothers and two nephews; Antonio Maceo, with a son;
Ray; Justo Carrillo; and Carlos Hevia. Bender and two
CIA people joined the group.

Miró Cardona looked ten years older than the man with
whom Berle and I had lunched at the Century a short week
before. He spoke to us with deep earnestness. It was, he
said, a life-and-death struggle and not too late to turn the

tide. He talked of sending in more contract fliers. In any case, he said, the only excuse the Revolutionary Council could now offer the people of Cuba was to be permitted to die with the men on the beaches. "It is this," he said with immense gravity, "which I request, this which I beg."

Miró was followed by Varona. Where Miró was melancholy, Varona was intense, florid and truculent. For five minutes it was hard to make out what he was trying to say. Then there began to emerge from his resonant periods a violent indictment of CIA. CIA, he said, had not consulted with the Council nor coordinated with resistance groups inside Cuba. All it had done was to land 1400 men at the worst possible place. Why no uprisings behind the lines? CIA had entirely disregarded the resistance groups. Why had his own men not been used? (Miró interrupted to say that Manuel Ray's men had not been used either.) As for the B-26s, the Brigade was now running out of pilots, while thirty experienced Cuban pilots were sitting around Miami yearning for an opportunity to fight for their homeland. Varona said vehemently that he had inspected the camps in Guatemala; that the CIA had deceived him; that on returning to Miami he had urged the sons of his friends to enlist. It was evident that he had condemned these young men, the flower of their generation, to a wretched death.

What could be done now? Evacuation was impossible. The only possible course, Varona said, was to put United States planes into the battle and, if this was not enough, to send the Marines. After all, Castro had Soviet planes, Soviet tanks, Soviet technicians. Why could not the United States do as much for its friends? If this were not done, no Cuban would ever trust the United States again. And, if this were not done, then the great United States would have been whipped by Fidel Castro. The Americans, he said grimly, could not hope to escape responsibility. The men dying on the beaches might be Cuban; but the training, the command, the timing, the decision to invade—all were American. Did not Washington understand that its whole future in Latin America turned on whether it could meet the challenge of Castro in Cuba?

Justo Carrillo spoke next. He said soberly that confidence in the United States depended on its capacity to fulfill its democratic professions. Kennedy's social and economic program—the Alliance for Progress and the Cuban White Paper—were right, but he had not yet developed the military foundations for his new course. He had revised State Department policy, but he had not yet succeeded in revising CIA policy. Maceo added that the struggle in Cuba was not between two groups of Cubans but between two ways of life; failure on the beaches would mean a world-wide defeat for democracy. If Castro could successfully defy the United States, more and more of Latin America would move into his orbit.

Manuel Ray was next—soft-spoken, direct, non-rhetorical and exceedingly impressive. His group, he said, had argued that the proper strategy was internal insurrection, not external invasion. He had tried in vain to interest the CIA in this approach. "We could get no support for our proposal. There were guerrillas in the Escambray, but they only received help when it could no longer be used. There has never been any serious attempt to support internal uprisings." Instead, the CIA had gambled everything on invasion. When Miró had communicated this decision to the Council, "we did not like it," Ray said; "but, if that is what the leading nation of the free world wanted, we saw no alternative to going along with it. We did not wish to do anything which would help the communists. For this reason, contrary to our convictions, we accepted the second strategy."

He continued with quiet dignity: "We were told that the landings would be followed up by all necessary support. We were even told that ten to fifteen thousand men would be available. [This was an evident reference to Miró's misunderstanding of Berle on April 13.] But nothing was done to bring our people into the operation. Two weeks ago agents unknown to us tried to make contact with our groups inside Cuba. This confused the whole underground movement. More than three weeks ago, we presented a plan for sabotage, programmed for the whole island, cutting power lines in four provinces, blowing up department stores, a cement factory, a paper factory, an oil refinery. This was accompanied by a request for explosive material. For over a month we have had a tunnel under the Havana electric power installation. But no material was ever delivered.

"We have been brought here," Ray went on, "without any knowledge of the operations. When we arrived, we thought we might have the opportunity to discuss strategy. We have found no one who will discuss it with us. We are not allowed to communicate with anybody. We have the feeling of being in a vacuum; nothing we can do is being coordinated with anything else." He added that his own men had not even been permitted to join the Brigade. "It would have been possible to coordinate landings with internal uprisings, and this could have been done without mentioning dates. But it was not done. . . . The Council has no power. Action is taken in our name without our control, without our clearance and even without knowledge. We are unable to talk to the men on the beaches, to our people in the underground or to our friends throughout Latin America. Our conclusion is that we should abandon the pretense of command, go to Cuba and fight as soldiers. Let those who really run things begin to assume the responsibility." He ended by saying that, in the faith that President Kennedy would not desert them, they would stay with him and his decisions to the end. The knowledge gained in this undertaking may help in future battles. The interior strategy might still be resumed. But defeat would set things back dangerously.

Then came Carlos Hevia, a graduate of Annapolis, once provisional president of Cuba, who had run Cuban price control during the Second World War and was a friend of Kenneth Galbraith's. "This combination of accountability without authority," he said, "makes us feel that, if these boys are to be wiped out on the beachhead, our place is to die there with them. But we are not defeatists. . . . If we have massive air attacks, we can still perhaps convert defeat into victory."

Varona read a list of requests: immediate transportation to the beachhead; immediate air strikes; immediate reinforcements. "Someone placed us in this position—that person will have to get us out of it." He denounced the surveillance under which they were kept. "We don't know whether we are your allies or your prisoners." At noon today, he said, he was planning to leave the house despite the armed guards, go to Miami and hold a press conference. "Let them shoot me down if they dare." He asked to be sent forthwith on a Catalina to the beachhead. Ray spoke up and said that he felt he should be dropped into Havana. The others after some talk seemed ready to settle for the command post in Nicaragua.

It was past ten o'clock, and Berle and I retired for consultation. We were much moved by the power and bitterness of the protests. Our first thought was to get them all to Nicaragua. But, when we returned to the hangar and called Washington, we were informed that the operation was substantially over. The only signal from the beach was a wail of SOS's. When we asked about evacuation, we were told that the time had passed even for that.

Our hearts sank as we walked out for a moment into the

dazzling sun. How could we notify the Cubans that there was no hope, that their sons were abandoned for captivity or death—and at the same time dissuade them from public denunciation of the CIA and the United States government? I said, "Can't we do something to bring the President into it?" Adolf said, "We must take them to Washington and have the President see them." It was clear that only Kennedy could save this situation.

I immediately called the White House, and Evelyn Lincoln put me through to the President's office. Dean Rusk, who answered the phone, agreed that the Council should be brought to Washington, though he seemed uncertain whether they should see the President. He gave the impression that he thought it would be enough if they saw him, or perhaps he wished to protect the President from the meeting.

Returning to the house, we told the Council that we were taking them to Washington. When they inquired about the news from the beaches, we had to say that it was not good. They silently changed into civilian clothes. Before we finally took off for Washington, I called the President to explain why we hoped he would see them himself. He said immediately that he wanted us to bring them to the White House as soon as we arrived.

The trip north was funereal. People murmured in low voices or walked fitfully to and fro. Some slept. I had a long talk with Manuel Ray, who seemed more reasonable and realistic than the others. Then I slept too. Colonel Godfrey McHugh, the President's air aide, who met us at the airport, took us immediately to the White House, where we came in by the East Wing to avoid the press. The Council waited in the Cabinet Room, while Berle and I went in to see the President. Kennedy, exceptionally drawn and tired, was, as usual, self-possessed. We told him about the situation at Opa-Locka: the Council under virtual house arrest, the intensity of their resentment, the probability of public denunciations. He expressed shock at the Council's detention; CIA, he said, had told him nothing of this.

In a few moments the Cubans entered. They sat down on the two couches facing each other in front of the fireplace, with the President in his rocking chair. Commander Tazewell Shepard, the naval aide, gave a report, precise and bleak, on the beachhead. Then Kennedy, speaking slowly and thoughtfully, declared his sorrow over the events of the last forty-eight hours. He explained why he had decided against intervention and why he had supposed that the operation might succeed on its own. Here he paused to read the message from the Marine colonel describing the training and condition of the Brigade. The struggle against communism, he said, had many fronts; leadership in that struggle imposed many responsibilities. The United States had to consider the balance of affairs all around the world. But, however tragic this episode, no one could doubt our commitment to the eventual freedom of Cuba. He added that he had himself fought in a war, that he had seen brave men die, that he had lost a brother, and that he shared their grief and their despair.

Miró and other members of the Council said a few words. After hearing Kennedy, they were far more subdued than in the morning. Discussion continued till six o'clock, when the President had a conference with congressional leaders. As the Cubans prepared to leave, he said, "I want you all to understand that, as soon as you leave the White House, you are all free men—free to go wherever you want, free to say anything you want, free to talk to anyone you want." I had never seen the President more impressive. In spite of themselves, his visitors were deeply moved. Then he asked me to take them back to the family quarters and await him there. There on the second floor of the Mansion, we had tea and sandwiches. After a time Kennedy rejoined us. The talk was about a rescue program for the survivors. United States destroyers, with air cover and orders to fire if fired upon, were already searching the waters off the coast; Kennedy was prepared to run more risks to take the men off the beaches than to put them there.

Later that night Lem Jones issued a final bulletin in the name of the Council. "The recent landings in Cuba," the release said, "have been constantly though inaccurately described as an invasion. It was, in fact, a landing of supplies and support for our patriots who have been fighting in Cuba for months. . . . The major portion of our landing party [has reached] the Escambray mountains."

The routine of Washington life is implacable. The prime minister of Greece was visiting the capital that week, and the Kennedys had to go to a dinner at the Greek Embassy. Once again, the President concealed anguish under a mask of courtesy and composure. So many regrets must have flowed through his mind during these bitter hours—the advice so authoritatively rendered and so respectfully accepted, the unexamined assumptions and the misconceived plans, the blow to the bright hopes of the new administration, the problems at home and abroad; but most of all, I think, it was the vision of the men on the beaches, who had gone off with such splendid expectations, who had fought so bravely and who now would be shot down like dogs or carted off to Castro's prisons. This vision haunted him that week and many weeks and months to come.

4. THE LAST ACT

Thursday, April 20, was the ninetieth day of the Kennedy administration. The gay expectations of the Hundred Days were irrevocably over, the hour of euphoria past. Through the country and the world the debacle was producing astonishment and disillusion.

At home the shock of defeat somewhat muted the voices of criticism. Some on the right, though fewer than one might have expected, were talking about sending in the Marines. But some on the left, more than one might have thought, now saw full vindication of their pre-election doubts about Kennedy. A telegram from Cambridge put the matter to me with sarcastic brevity: NIXON OR KENNEDY: DOES IT MAKE ANY DIFFERENCE? It was signed: GRADUATE STUDENTS. A number of these impassioned liberals convinced themselves that the cult of toughness, the determination to win at any cost or something else they supposed to characterize Kennedy, would now lead him to throw the book at Castro—though why he should do on Thursday what he had declined to do on Tuesday was not clear. The Harvard historian H. Stuart Hughes led seventy academicians in an open letter to Kennedy, imprudently endorsing the thesis that the United States had driven Castro into the arms of the Soviet Union, calling for a restoration of diplomatic and economic relations with Castro and demanding that the government "reverse the present drift towards American military intervention in Cuba." One of the signers, a sociologist named Barrington Moore, Jr., in a separate memorandum pronounced the New Frontier a sham and a fraud and predicted that from now on it would be "a militarist and reactionary government that covers its fundamental policies with liberal rhetoric."

Protest meetings erupted on a dozen campuses. A Fair Play for Cuba rally at Union Square in New York on April 21 drew three thousand people. Five literary magazines and Norman Mailer staged a demonstration; one of the marchers, a tall poetess with black hair down to her waist, carried a sign: JACQUELINE, VOUS AVEZ PERDU VOS ARTISTES. C. Wright Mills wired a Fair Play for Cuba rally in San Francisco on April 22: KENNEDY AND

COMPANY HAVE RETURNED US TO BARBARISM. SCHLESINGER AND COMPANY HAVE DISGRACED US INTELLECTUALLY AND MORALLY. I FEEL A DESPERATE SHAME FOR MY COUNTRY. SORRY I CANNOT BE WITH YOU. WERE I PHYSICALLY ABLE TO DO SO, I WOULD AT THIS MOMENT BE FIGHTING ALONGSIDE FIDEL CASTRO.[4] Pickets demonstrated in front of the White House.

Most Americans of course rallied to their President in the moment of national crisis. Still even many of these had their first harsh doubts about the new administration. The nation was in a state of shock, and no one understood more acutely than Kennedy himself the need to restore perspective. Walt Rostow saw him that day in a pensive moment in his office. Britain had been through something like this, the President said, at the time of Suez—the fiasco had interrupted its political life and distorted its policy; France had been through a similar experience with Algeria. But Britain and France were only 6 or 7 per cent of the free world. The United States was 70 per cent of the free world, and we could not afford a Suez sickness, an Algeria sickness. If we let Cuba obsess our policy and poison our politics, it would damage everybody.

His first problem on Thursday was to contain the political consequences of the debacle. He moved now with sure instinct and remarkable dexterity, showing, as he had shown nearly twenty years earlier in the Solomons, the strength to accept disaster, omit recrimination and pitch in to bring the situation back. The war generation, having survived catastrophe, knew that it was not finality. When Rostow came home early one morning that week in the mingled exhilaration and exhaustion of crisis, his wife said to him, "You know what you all are? You are the junior officers of the Second World War come to responsibility."

Routine remained implacable: the President was scheduled to address the American Society of Newspaper Editors at the Statler Hilton that day. Ted Sorensen had already prepared a draft on another subject. But on April 20 only one subject was possible. After consultation with the President, Sorensen stayed up most of Wednesday night composing a speech on Cuba. Thursday morning we all met for breakfast in the small dining room on the second floor of the White House—the President, Sorensen, Bundy, Bohlen and myself—to consider the new draft.

The President's concern was to head off any outcry with-

4 The Militant, May 1, 1961.

in the United States for violent retaliation against Castro, to reassure the democratic world about the prudence of Washington and at the same time to dissuade the communists from regarding restraint as evidence of weakness. He had not wavered at any point in his determination not to commit American troops; if the United States moved against Cuba, Khrushchev might seize this as a pretext for moving against West Berlin. Even his deep concern over the men on the beaches led him to nothing further than a rescue mission. The speech to the editors offered the opportunity to explain the policy of restraint and to divert the demand for action against Castro into a general strengthening of American purpose.

Unilateral intervention, he told the editors, would have violated our traditions and international obligations. "But let the record show," he added, "that our restraint is not inexhaustible. Should it ever appear that the inter-American doctrine of non-interference merely conceals or excuses a policy of non-action—if the nations of this Hemisphere should fail to meet their commitments against outside Communist penetration—then I want it clearly understood that this Government will not hesitate in meeting its primary obligations which are to the security of our Nation!"

Having uttered this obscure but emphatic warning, he went on to define the lesson of the episode. Communism, he said, was now less interested in arms as the means of direct aggression than "as the shield behind which subversion, infiltration, and a host of other tactics steadily advance, picking off vulnerable areas one by one in situations which do not permit our own armed intervention." This "new and deeper struggle," Kennedy said, was taking place every day, without fanfare, in villages and markets and classrooms all over the globe. It called for new concepts, new tools, a new sense of urgency. "Too long we have fixed our eyes on traditional military needs, on armies prepared to cross borders, on missiles poised for flight. Now it should be clear that this is no longer enough—that our security may be lost piece by piece, country by country, without the firing of a single missile or the crossing of a single border."

He concluded: "We intend to reexamine and reorient our forces of all kinds—our tactics and our institutions here in this community." I was never quite clear what this last phrase meant, unless it referred to the CIA and the Joint Chiefs; but once again obscurity probably helped the impact of the speech. Certainly the occasion reestablished

him in a fighting stance without committing him to reckless action.

The next step was to secure the administration against
partisan attack. The Republicans, of course, were a little
inhibited by their own role in conceiving the operation; but
Kennedy took no chances. Later that day he called in
Richard Nixon (whose advice on Cuba was to "find a
proper legal cover and . . . go in" [5]), and by the weekend
he had talked to Eisenhower, Nelson Rockefeller and
Barry Goldwater. Harry S. Truman, being a Democrat, required only the attention of the Vice-President.

As part of the strategy of protection, he moved to stop
the gathering speculation over responsibility for the project.
When in one discussion the Vice-President ventured a general criticism of CIA, Kennedy turned to him and said,
"Lyndon, you've got to remember we're all in this and that,
when I accepted responsibility for this operation, I took
the entire responsibility on myself, and I think we should
have no sort of passing of the buck or backbiting, however
justified." By Friday, however, the morning papers were
filled with what purported to be 'inside' stories about the
Cuba decision. An impulse for self-preservation was evidently tempting some of the participants in those meetings
in the Cabinet Room to put out versions of the episode
ascribing the debacle to everyone but themselves. Kennedy,
having called a ten o'clock press conference, summoned
Rusk, Salinger, Bundy, Sorensen, Goodwin and myself for
breakfast in the Mansion.

The President remarked acidly that the role of the Joint
Chiefs of Staff was notably neglected in several stories—
an omission which, by Washington exegesis, pointed to the
Pentagon as the source. The best way to turn off the speculation, he said, was to tell the truth: that all the senior
officials involved had backed the operation but that the
final responsibility was his own. Then he added, with unusual emphasis, "There is only one person in the clear—
that's Bill Fulbright. And he probably would have been
converted if he had attended more of the meetings. If he
had received the same treatment we received—discontent
in Cuba, morale of the free Cubans, rainy season, Russian
MIGs and destroyers, impregnable beachhead, easy escape
into the Escambray, what else to do with these people—
it might have moved him down the road too." He punctuated the enumeration of the items with short stabs of his

[5] Richard M. Nixon, "Cuba, Castro and John F. Kennedy," *Reader's Digest*, November 1964.

hand. Bundy reminded him that I had opposed the expedition. "Oh, sure," he said. "Arthur wrote me a memorandum that will look pretty good when he gets around to writing his book on my administration." Then, with a characteristic flash of high sardonic humor: "Only he better not publish that memorandum while I'm still alive. . . . And I have a title for his book—*Kennedy: The Only Years*."

We dispersed to engage in a morning of counterbriefing while the President left for his press conference in the State Department auditorium. Here he dismissed the inside stories: "There's an old saying that victory has a hundred fathers and defeat is an orphan." (I later asked him where he had come upon this felicitous observation. He looked surprised and said vaguely, "Oh, I don't know; it's just an old saying." [6]) He then told the newspapermen: "I'm the responsible officer of the Government." He repeated this more fiercely in a White House statement the next Monday: "President Kennedy has stated from the beginning that as President he bears sole responsibility. . . . He has stated it on all occasions and he restates it now. . . . The President is strongly opposed to anyone within or without the administration attempting to shift the responsibility."

I had been scheduled to leave that Friday for a conference in Italy. When I asked the President whether I should still go, he said, "Yes, you might as well. We are only picking up the pieces here. Maybe you can explain to them over there what we have been doing. Do your best." At the end of the afternoon I dropped by the West Wing to say goodbye. When I stuck my head through the open door from Evelyn Lincoln's office, I saw Lyndon Johnson sitting by the desk; but, as I began to retreat, Kennedy beckoned me in. They were talking again about the CIA. The President said that he could not understand how men like Dulles and Bissell, so intelligent and so experienced, could have been so wrong, but added that nothing could be done about CIA immediately. So long as he kept Dulles there, he said, the Republicans would be disinclined to attack the administration over the Cuban failure. The Vice-President vigorously agreed.

Kennedy looked exceedingly tired, but his mood was philosophical. He felt that he now knew certain soft spots in his administration, especially the CIA and the Joint Chiefs. He would never be overawed by professional mili-

[6] On September 9, 1943, Count Ciano noted in his diary. "As always, victory finds a hundred fathers, but defeat is an orphan."

tary advice again. "We can't win them all," he said. "And I have been close enough to disaster to realize that these things which seem world-shaking at one moment you can barely remember the next. We got a big kick in the leg— and we deserved it. But maybe we'll learn something from it." A few hours later I was over the Atlantic on the way to Rome.

Reactions abroad proved more intense than at home. In Latin America demonstrations were brief, communist-inspired and not very serious; but in Western Europe I found widespread disenchantment. In the brief time from the Inaugural to the Bay of Pigs, Kennedy had come to seem the last hope of the west—a brilliant and exciting hope. He had conveyed an impression of United States foreign policy as mature, controlled, responsible and, above all, intelligent. Western Europe in return had made a heavy political and emotional investment in him. Now he suddenly seemed revealed as a mere continuator of the Eisenhower-Dulles past. The New Frontier looked like a collection not only of imperialists but of ineffectual imperialists —and, what was worst of all, of stupid, ineffectual imperialists. "Kennedy is to be regarded as politically and morally defeated," said the *Frankfurter Neue Presse*. "For the time being, Moscow has not only maintained but strengthened its outpost on the threshold of America." "In one day," said the *Corriere della Sera* of Milan, "American prestige collapses lower than in eight years of Eisenhower timidity and lack of determination."

When I arrived in Bologna for the conference—it was sponsored by the magazine *Il Mulino* with its subject, ironically, "The Foreign Policy of the United States and the Responsibilities of Europe"—the atmosphere was one of gloom. The European participants talked about everything but Cuba; one felt as if there had been a frightful scandal in one's family which friends refrained from mentioning for motives of delicacy. When I tried to explain privately to Dean Acheson, one of my colleagues in the American delegation, what had happened he listened with urban disbelief, expressed his scorn for the CIA and quoted an aphorism from Adenauer, whom he had just seen in Germany: "In view of the fact that God limited the intelligence of man, it seems unfair that he did not also limit his stupidity."

The same sense of shock prevailed in Paris and London. "It was a terrible blow," Lord Boothby said, "and it will take a long, long time for us to recover from it." David

Ormsby Gore told me that British intelligence estimates, which had been made available to CIA, showed that the Cuban people were still predominantly behind Castro and that there was no likelihood at this point of mass defections or insurrections. "It was a great blow," Hugh Gaitskell said. "The right wing of the Labour Party has been basing a good deal of its argument on the claim that things had changed in America. Cuba has made great trouble for us. We shall now have to move toward the left for a bit to maintain our position within the party."

Yet, at the same time, it was clear that the fund of goodwill toward Kennedy, though somewhat dissipated, was far from destroyed, even on the democratic left. Men like Ugo La Malfa of the Republican party and Fabio Cavazza, editor of *Il Mulino*, in Italy, Pierre Mendès-France and Jean-Jacques Servan-Schreiber in Paris, as well as Gaitskell and R. H. S. Crossman in London, were sure that Washington could achieve a quick comeback. "You really have got off very lightly," Crossman said. "If this had taken place under Eisenhower, there would have been mass meetings in Trafalgar Square, Dulles would have been burned in effigy, and the Labour Party whould have damned you in the most unequivocal terms. But because enough faith still remains in Kennedy, there has been very little popular outcry, and the Labour Party resolutions have been the very minimum. But one more mistake like this, and you will really be through."

When I returned on May 3, Kennedy commented wryly on the discrepancy between the European and American reactions. If he had been a British prime minister, he remarked, he would have been thrown out of office; but in the United States failure had increased his charm: "if I had gone further, they would have iiked me even more." At this point, Evelyn Lincoln brought in an advance on the new Gallup poll, showing an unprecedented 82 per cent behind the administration. Kennedy tossed it aside and said, "It's just like Eisenhower. The worse I do, the more popular I get."

5. AFTERMATH

Afterward Kennedy would sometimes recur incredulously to the Bay of Pigs, wondering how a rational and responsible government could ever have become involved in so ill-starred an adventure. He soon designated General Maxwell Taylor, Dulles, Burke and Robert Kennedy as a commission of inquiry into the fiasco. The commission, perhaps because two of its members had been architects of the project, construed its mandate narrowly, concentrating on dissecting the military operation and on thinking up a new interdepartmental agency to coordinate future cold war ventures. The State Department successfully opposed this idea; but the Taylor report did focus the government's attention on the problems of coping with guerrilla warfare and of improving the control of clandestine projects.

What caused the disaster? Too much comment on the Bay of Pigs has fallen into the fallacy of Douglas Southall Freeman, who once wrote a long chapter analyzing the reasons for Lee's defeat at Gettysburg without mentioning the interesting fact that the Union Army was there too. For the reality was that Fidel Castro turned out to be a far more formidable foe and in command of a far better organized regime than anyone had supposed. His patrols spotted the invasion at almost the first possible moment. His planes reacted with speed and vigor. His police eliminated any chance of sabotage or rebellion behind the lines. His soldiers stayed loyal and fought hard. He himself never panicked; and, if faults were chargeable to him, they were his overestimate of the strength of the invasion and undue caution in pressing the ground attack against the beachhead. His performance was impressive.

One reason Washington miscalculated Castro, of course, was a series of failures in our own intelligence. We regarded him as an hysteric. We dismissed his air force and forgot his T-33s. We thought that his troops would defect. We supposed that, although warned by advance air strikes, he would do nothing to neutralize the Cuban underground (either that, or we supposed that the underground, without alert or assistance from us, would find means to protect itself and eventually rise against the regime). And there were tactical errors. We chose an invasion site without a way of escape, and we did not in any case tell the Brigade of the guerrilla option. We put too much precious ammunition and communications equipment in a single ship. We did not give the Brigade enough pilots to keep its planes in continuous action. On the other hand, if one renounced the fall-back plan of flight to the hills, the invasion site was well chosen and easily defensible. The men of the Brigade fought with great bravery against superior force and inflicted far more casualties than they received.

Subsequent controversy has settled on the cancellation

of the second air strike as the turning point.[7] In retrospect, there clearly was excessive apprehension that Sunday evening; it is hard now to see why, the first strike already having taken place, a second would have made things so much worse at the United Nations or elsewhere. Kennedy came later to feel that the cancellation of the second strike was an error. But he did not regard it as a decisive error, for, even on the most unlikely assumption that the second strike achieved total success and wiped out Castro's air force, it would still have left 1200 men against 200,000. The Brigade's air power was already in decline because of the scarcity of pilots; and, once the mass arrests had taken place, there was no hope of uprisings behind the lines. The second air strike might have protracted the stand on the beachhead from three days to ten; it might have permitted the establishment of the provisional government; it might have made possible the eventual evacuation of the invading force. There is certainly nothing to suggest that it could possibly have led to the overthrow of the regime on the terms which Kennedy laid down from the start—that is without United States armed intervention.

If there were no intervention, then only an internal uprising could finally have overthrown Castro; and an internal uprising would have required both an intact underground and a far more potent political purpose than any which animated the CIA project. Kennedy had well defined this purpose in the Alliance for Progress and the White Paper, but the CIA had developed its operation in a different political atmosphere and on different political presuppositions. It had put together a non-political military expedition under conservative leadership, excluding the radical exiles and neglecting the internal resistance. The Kennedy Latin American policy called for a changed conception of the project. But there simply had not been time in ninety days to reconstruct the Eisenhower operation in terms of the Kennedy policy.

The expedition was not only misconceived politically. It was also misconceived technically. If it was to be a covert operation for which we could plausibly disclaim responsibility, it should have been, at most, a guerrilla infiltration. Once it grew into a conventional amphibious invasion, it was clearly beyond the limits of disownability. Unless we were prepared to back it to the hilt, it should have been

[7] Mythologists have even talked about a supposed presidential decision to "withdraw United States air cover." There was never, of course, any plan for United States air cover, and no air cover for the landing forces was withdrawn.

abandoned. When the President made it clear time after time that for the most cogent reasons we would not back it to the hilt, the planners should not have deluded themselves into thinking that events would reverse this decision or that the adventure would succeed on its own. Instead of trying to compromise between the claims of clandestinity and the claims of military impact, we should have chosen one or the other. The President had insisted that the political and military risks be brought into balance: given the nature of the operation, this was impossible, and someone should have said so.

All of us, the President most of all, went through this sequence of thoughts again and again in the months to come. And yet, and yet: for all the utter irrationality with which retrospect endowed the project, it had a certain queer logic at the time as it emerged from the bowels of government. The men were there; they had been armed and trained; something had to be done with them; this was what they wanted to do themselves; and, if the worst happened, they could always turn into guerrillas and melt away in the hills. This sequence spun about in our minds for a long time too.

The President reserved his innermost thoughts and, in the end, blamed only himself. But he was a human being and not totally free of resentment. He would say at times, "My God, the bunch of advisers we inherited. . . . Can you imagine being President and leaving behind someone like all those people there?" My impression is that, among these advisers, the Joint Chiefs had disappointed him most for their cursory review of the military plans. About Dulles and Bissell he said little. I think he had made up his mind at once that, when things settled down, they would have to go. He regretted this because he liked them both. Shortly after the Bay of Pigs, a long-time acquaintance from Palm Beach, who was also an old friend of Dulles's, arrived in Washington and told Kennedy self-righteously that he was not going to see Dulles this visit. Kennedy, disgusted, invited Dulles over for a drink with the Palm Beacher that afternoon. When Dulles came, still troubled and haggard, the President put his arm around him.

His vocal irritation, so far as his staff heard it, was concentrated on those who he thought were trying to dodge responsibility after the fact. He was particularly, and perhaps unjustly, aggrieved over Chester Bowles, whose friends had rushed to the press with the story of his opposition in the days after the disaster. He was also disturbed by what seemed to him—and more drastically to Robert Kennedy

—the feebleness of Bowles's presentation at a National Security Council meeting to consider future Cuban policy. Here again Bowles was in part the victim of circumstance; for he brought with him two hastily prepared State Department papers, one tending toward intervention, the other against, and failed to conceal their inadequacy in his own remarks.

But it was not Kennedy's way to waste energy in repining. He continued the task of political recovery. A Gallup poll early in May showed that 65 per cent of the respondents agreed with his opposition to military intervention; only 24 per cent said that the Marines should be sent to Cuba. He made his only misstep when, in a speech before the American Newspaper Publishers Association on April 27, he told the press that it should be prepared to censor itself in the interests of national security. This went much too far, and he did not urge the point again. Though he was genuinely concerned about the threat of subversive warfare, he was basically philosophical about the impact of the Bay of Pigs itself. He saw it as an episode, not as a cataclysm; and he was sure that the hope and confidence generated by the rest of the ninety days were entirely sufficient to absorb this error, if it were not repeated. He set quietly to work to make sure that nothing like the Bay of Pigs could happen to him again.

The first lesson was never to rely on the experts. He now knew that he would have to broaden the range of his advice, make greater use of generalists in whom he had personal confidence and remake every great decision in his own terms—as, indeed, he had done with the other decisions of the ninety days. He understood too that the prestige of the presidential office had been lightly regarded by men whose primary loyalty was not to him or his administration. Thereafter he took care to make sure that the presidential interest would be represented in the large decisions. He turned from the people he had inherited in government to the people he had brought in himself—the people he had worked with longest, knew best and trusted most. Neither Robert Kennedy nor Ted Sorensen had taken part in the meetings in the Cabinet Room; both were at his right hand at every subsequent moment of crisis for the rest of his Presidency. He charged Dick Goodwin with responsibility for the next steps in policy toward Cuba and the exiles. He chose Maxwell Taylor as his personal adviser on military affairs until the time came when he could make him Chief of Staff.

And he took a new view of the White House staff. While Bundy and I had not performed with distinction, he had not used us as he would use his White House people later; he had not, for example, called us in for a staff discussion of Cuba, away from the inhibiting presence of the grandees in the Cabinet Room. In the future, he made sure that he had the unfettered and confidential advice of his own people. For our part, we resolved to be less acquiescent the next time. The Bay of Pigs gave us a license for the impolite inquiry and the rude comment. In addition, Bundy was moved over from the Executive Office Building to the West Wing of the White House and given new authority as a coordinator of security affairs within the White House. He instituted regular morning meetings for his National Security Council staff, to which he invited other members of the White House group involved in foreign affairs—Goodwin, Dungan and myself—as well as representatives from State, Defense, CIA and USIA. This valuable innovation provided the White House a point of information and control below the top and strengthened Bundy's services to Kennedy. All this helped the President to tighten his personal hold on the sprawling mystery of government. This was in the course of happening anyway, as Kennedy worked to establish control over his administration; it was in line with his theory of the Presidency; but the Bay of Pigs made it happen quickly.

The impact of the failure shook up the national security machinery. It taught every adviser something about the President, the other advisers, himself and his own department. It was a horribly expensive lesson; but it was well learned. In later months the President's father would tell him that, in its perverse way, the Bay of Pigs was not a misfortune but a benefit. I doubt whether the President ever fully believed this; the thought of the men of the Brigade suffering in Cuban prisons prevented easy consolation. But no one can doubt that failure in Cuba in 1961 contributed to success in Cuba in 1962.

XII

NEW DEPARTURES

THE INITIATION had been harsh; but then no one had expected the Presidency to be easy. And, though geography gave the Cuban problem a certain intimacy and intensity, it remained a side issue. The great challenge lay not in Havana but in Moscow. The supreme test lay in Kennedy's capacity to deal not with Fidel Castro but with N. S. Khrushchev.

Kennedy approached the Soviet Union without illusion about the character of Russian polity and purpose but also with considerable weariness over the rhetoric of the cold war. The John Foster Dulles contrast between the God-anointed apostles of free enterprise and the regimented hordes of atheistic communism bored him. Seeing the world as an historian rather than as a moralist, he could not utter without embarrassment the self-serving platitudes about the total virtue of one side and the total evil of the other. In 1958 he had called on Americans to renounce the proposition that "we should enter every military conflict as a moral crusade requiring the unconditional surrender of the enemy." The stereotypes of the fifties, he thought, were not only self-serving, but, worse, they simply did not provide a useful way of thinking about international affairs.

With his historian's perspective, he was disposed to view the conflict in national rather than ideological terms. He tended to discount, at times perhaps unduly, the role of dogma in Soviet policy. Marxism-Leninism impressed him less as a body of doctrine than as a mystique capable of uniting masses of men for disciplined action. He did not take Soviet theoreticians seriously; their function seemed to him no more than to rationalize the aims of the Russian state. While he recognized that ideology gave Moscow a potent international weapon, especially in the developing world, he was sure that the Soviet leaders would always use it in their own national interest. He cared less about the clash of abstractions than about the practical problem of living on the same planet with a great and powerful despotism, ambitious enough to seize all it could but sober enough not to wish to blow up the world.

He was an American, holding that a free democracy was the best form of government, and he was ready to go to war if necessary, to save democracy from extinction. But he saw not a final battle between democratic good and communist evil but an obscure and intricate drama, where men, institutions and ideals, all bedeviled by the sin of self-righteousness, threatened to rush humanity to the edge of destruction, and where salvation lay in man's liberation from myth, stereotype and fanaticism. The cold war was a reality and would remain so as long as the Communists refused to acknowledge the permanence of the non-communist world. But he was determined to take the hysteria out of the cold war and get down to the business at hand.

1. FIRST APPROACHES

The new administration had the benefit of considerable discussion of foreign affairs during the Democratic party's interlude in the opposition. Much of this discussion had taken place in the Democratic Advisory Council, and in the course of the decade two divergent schools had emerged. Both opposed the main aspects of the Dulles policy—its exclusive reliance on nuclear power, its faith in military pacts, its intolerance of neutrals and its conception of diplomacy as a sub-branch of theology. But beyond this common ground they disagreed somewhat in diagnosis and prescription.

Dean Acheson led one school, very often with the support of Paul Nitze and one or two others. Acheson's ideas had grown out of his own brilliant period as Secretary of State, when the Soviet Union first became a nuclear power, a disorganized Western Europe lay under the Soviet guns and the communists were attempting direct aggression in Korea. Those years had demanded, above all, a revival of military will and power in the west. Now, a decade later, Acheson took the view that, in spite of the death of Stalin, very little had changed in the Soviet Union. The communist purpose of world domination through the threat of military showdown seemed to him unalterable; and he was increasingly concerned lest the United States allow itself to be diverted from the main battleground of Europe into sentimental crusades against colonialism and hopeless efforts to democratize the underdeveloped world. Though Acheson himself had been the father of the Marshall Plan and retained a lively interest in the reconstruction of the international monetary system, he tended to regard 'hard' military measures as more significant in the cold war than 'soft' economic programs. He expounded his viewpoint with superb style and scathing wit, contriving to leave the impression that anyone who differed was a muddlehead or a ninny.

Actually most of his colleagues on the Foreign Policy Committee of the Democratic Advisory Council differed a good deal. The other school was led by Adlai Stevenson and included Averell Harriman, George Kennan, Chester Bowles, Thomas K. Finletter, Mennen Williams, J. K. Galbraith and Ben Cohen as well as Senators like J.

William Fulbright and Mike Mansfield. These men believed that the world had indeed changed since 1950, that the conflict between Russia and China was real, that the military threat to Western Europe had receded, that the underdeveloped world was the new battleground and that military measures had to be supplemented if not superseded by vigorous political and economic programs. In short, the policy of 1949–52, however sound at the time, was no longer adequate; a changing world called for flexibility and initiative. There were variations within this group, though more in tone than in substance. Bowles and Williams were particular targets of those who regarded large foreign aid efforts and liberal rhetoric as evidence of 'softness.' Harriman and Finletter, on the other hand, because one had warned against the Soviet Union in 1945 and the other had been Secretary of the Air Force, and because both had a certain unsentimentality of personality, managed to present much the same views while preserving a reputation for toughness.

Though Kennedy had, in the main, stayed aloof from the DAC debates, he was clearly aligned with the Stevenson-Harriman-Bowles position, if more in the Harriman than in the Bowles mood. A sharp critic of the tendency to suppose that all problems had military solutions, he was a strong advocate of economic assistance to the uncommitted world. His reactions in 1960 to the shooting down of the U-2 over the Soviet Union and to the Quemoy-Matsu issue showed his dislike for rigid interpretations of the cold war. He did not suppose that the United States had it within its power to work overnight changes in the Soviet Union; but he did not suppose either that the Soviet Union was fixed forever in its present mold. He therefore favored a policy of reasoned firmness accompanied by a determination to explore all possibilities of reasonable accommodation.

The Soviet Union watched the arrival of the new administration with marked interest. Khrushchev, who had given up on Eisenhower after the U-2 incident and the collapse of the Paris summit in May 1960, seized several opportunities to semaphore his hopes for Kennedy. His messages to Harriman and others after the election were followed by a Pugwash meeting on disarmament in Moscow in December. These gatherings, so called because they had begun with a conference called by the Cleveland financier, Cyrus Eaton, at his summer place in Pugwash, Nova Scotia, brought together disarmament experts from both sides in supposedly unofficial exchanges. Walt Rostow and Jerome B. Wiesner, who were among the Americans at the Moscow meeting, saw V. V. Kuznetsov of the Soviet Foreign Office and urged the release of two American RB-47 fliers, shot down over the Arctic the preceding July. In the course of their talk Kuznetsov mentioned the campaign furore about a 'missile gap' and suggested that, if the new administration went in for massive rearmament, it could not expect the Russians to sit still. Rostow replied that any Kennedy rearmament would be designed to improve the stability of the deterrent, and that the Soviet Union should recognize this as in the interests of peace; but Kuznetsov, innocent of the higher calculus of deterrence as recently developed in the United States, brusquely dismissed the explanation.

Rostow and Wiesner returned from the disarmament talks with the feeling that the Russians might be prepared for action in arms control, though they also warned the President-elect that the Kremlin would give no ground on Berlin and would press its advantages in the underdeveloped world. Later Khrushchev's warm congratulatory message to Kennedy at the inaugural and his release of the RB-47 fliers a few days after—an act deliberately postponed, as Khrushchev made clear to Ambassador Llewellyn Thompson, to benefit the Democrats rather than the Republicans—reinforced the sense that Moscow desired, in the phrase of the moment, a reduction of tensions.

Yet the Soviet Union, as usual, was pursuing a double policy; and Khrushchev disclosed its other face in an elaborate speech in Moscow on January 6. This speech made a conspicuous impression on the new President, who took it as an authoritative exposition of Soviet intentions, discussed it with his staff and read excerpts from it aloud to the National Security Council.

Moscow had its own euphoria in January 1961, and the Khrushchev speech gave it truculent expression. The Soviet leader undoubtedly felt then and for the rest of the year, as he could never feel again, that communism was riding the crest of history. Since the death of Stalin, the end of the Korean War and the relaxation of the western rearmament drive, one event after another had strengthened the conviction of inevitable victory. The Soviet rate of industrial growth had been considerably higher than that of the United States. Success in developing the hydrogen bomb and surpassing America in long-range missiles gave the Soviet leaders confidence in their own technological prowess as well as, for the first time in the history of the Bolshevik

Revolution, assurance against foreign attack. At the same time, the revolutionary ferment in the underdeveloped countries from Vietnam to Cuba seemed to foreshadow the humiliation of the 'imperialist' powers and the passage of the third world into the communist camp. Moreover, the meeting of communist leaders from eighty-one countries the previous November appeared for a moment to have composed the argument between Moscow and Peking. Indeed, Khrushchev's January speech was an interpretation to his own people of the unity statement adopted by the communist parties at the conclusion of the November meeting. Underneath the canonical beat of language, the oration sounded a brutal joy over a world where democracy was everywhere on the retreat and communism everywhere on the march.

Khrushchev began by saying that "analysis of the world situation as it appeared at the beginning of the sixties" showed a state of affairs which "greatly exceeded the boldest and most optimistic predictions and expectations." History and communism were inseparable partners: "there is no longer any force in the world capable of barring the road to socialism." He then reviewed the possible ways to triumph. World wars and "local wars" he categorically rejected as leading directly or progressively to nuclear holocaust. "Wars of liberation or popular uprisings" were quite another matter. He defined "national-liberation wars" as those "which began as uprisings of colonial peoples against their oppressors [and] developed into guerrilla wars." "What is the attitude of the Marxists to such uprisings?" he asked. "A most favorable attitude," he replied. ". . . The Communists support just wars of this kind whole-heartedly and without reservation and they march in the van of the peoples fighting for liberation." He named Cuba, Vietnam and Algeria as examples and added that the "multiplying of the forces of the national-liberation movement" in recent years stemmed largely from the opening of the new front against American imperialism in Latin America. As for "peaceful coexistence," this was, "so far as its social content is concerned, a form of intense economic, political and ideological struggle between the proletariat and the aggressive forces of imperialism in the world arena."

In a significant aside Khrushchev brought up Berlin. "The positions of the U.S.A., Britain and France have proved to be especially vulnerable in West Berlin," he said. "These powers . . . cannot fail to realize that sooner or later the occupation regime in that city must be ended. It is necessary to go ahead with bringing the aggressive-minded imperialists to their senses, and compelling them to reckon with the real situation. And should they balk, then we will take resolute measures, we will sign a peace treaty with the German Democratic Republic."

Kennedy, reading the speech, accepted Khrushchev's rejection of nuclear war as honest enough; any other position in the President's view would have been mad. But the bellicose confidence which surged through the rest of the speech and especially the declared faith in victory through rebellion, subversion and guerrilla warfare alarmed Kennedy more than Moscow's amiable signals assuaged him. The references to Russia and China in his State of the Union message constituted Kennedy's response. "We must never be lulled," he said, "into believing that either power has yielded its ambitions for world domination—ambitions which they forcefully restated only a short time ago. On the contrary, our task is to convince them that aggression and subversion will not be profitable routes to pursue these ends." He added: "Open and peaceful competition—for prestige, for markets, for scientific achievement, even for men's minds—is something else again. For if Freedom and Communism were to compete for man's allegiance in a world at peace, I would look to the future with ever increasing confidence."

He designed these last words to help bring things into proportion. For the Khrushchev speech, though sufficiently tough, confined its bellicosity in the main to the underdeveloped world; and here, as Kennedy understood, the Russians were confronted by opportunities which they could not easily resist. Discussing the speech one day with Lippmann, Kennedy observed that, while Khrushchev sounded like a committed revolutionist, he would not press revolution to the point where it might threaten nuclear war. Kennedy consequently persevered in his task of de-emotionalizing the cold war at home. American admirals and generals, long accustomed to touring the country with ritualistic exhortations against the Soviet Union, were instructed to tone their speeches down. The administration relaxed on a number of minor matters: it sent Moscow an invitation to resume civil aviation talks, broken off a year before; it permitted the import of Soviet crab meat, banned for a decade because it had once been produced by forced labor; it ended post office censorship of Soviet publications in the mails. When the Soviet Union railed against the United Nations and the west after the murder of Lumumba in the Congo in mid-February and the State Department cranked out its usual fustian in response, Kennedy wrote with Adlai Stevenson an equally resolute but less declamatory statement. Most important of all, he ordered a review of the American negotiating position on a test ban agreement in an attempt to break the deadlock in the talks which had been proceeding dilatorily in Geneva since the end of 1958. He described his broad policy to Hugh Sidey of *Time* as one of holding firm but probing around the edges "to see if we can't communicate in some ways."

Ambassador Thompson came home from Moscow in February, and Kennedy soon summoned him along with three former ambassadors to Russia—Harriman, Bohlen and George Kennan—for an extended discussion at the White House of Soviet problems. The new President, saying little himself, threw out questions to stimulate the experts. Finally he wondered aloud whether he should not consider a meeting with Khrushchev. Kennedy had a natural curiosity about Khrushchev; what Isaiah Berlin once called the royal-cousins approach to diplomacy has an allure, sometimes fatal, for all heads of state. Moreover, Kennedy, unlike Rusk, had no doctrinaire opposition to the idea of summitry. "It is far better," he had observed in 1959, "that we meet at the summit than at the brink."

The experts agreed that a face-to-face talk might be a good idea. Thompson in particular felt that it was impossible for the new President to get at second hand the full flavor of what he was up against in the Soviet leader. And Bohlen, who had already watched three Presidents go through the process of learning about the Soviet Union, thought that Kennedy, "like almost every person that I ran into during the course of my specialization in that field, really felt he had to find out for himself. The issues and consequences of mistakes of a serious nature in dealing with the Soviet Union are so great that no man of any character or intelligence will really wholeheartedly accept the views of anybody else." Thompson carried back to Moscow a presidential letter of February 22 suggesting a rendezvous in the late spring at Vienna or Stockholm. When he caught up with Khrushchev in Siberia on March 9, the Soviet leader, though showing no inclination to yield on issues, appeared pleased at the prospect of a meeting.

But already hopes for better relations were beginning to fade. One could have expected Moscow to continue its support for what it considered a national-liberation war in Laos, but the bleak Russian reaction to the new test ban proposals in Geneva was unexpected. When Ambassador Arthur H. Dean set forth the revised Anglo-American position in March, the Soviet representative, instead of welcoming an obvious attempt to resolve outstanding differences, responded by withdrawing Soviet assent to points already agreed upon and by introducing an unacceptable new proposal—that the organization policing the ban be directed by a tripartite board, representing the Soviet Union, the democracies and the neutrals, and required to act in unanimity. The *troika* doctrine meant, in effect, a Soviet veto on the verification process. It would have made the ban a farce, and the proposal ended any immediate prospect of agreement.

2. STATE OF THE NATION'S DEFENSE

The policy of probing around the edges would work in any case, Kennedy believed, only so long as the United States preserved its capacity to hold firm. This meant the existence of military power sufficient to restrain the Soviet Union from aggression. The next problem then was the condition of American defenses and the purpose of American strategy. Here again the new administration had the benefit of past discussions. Robert McNamara, as the new Secretary of Defense, was the residuary legatee of a body of doctrine which had taken form under the Truman administration in the late forties and gained clarity and force in a series of debates within and without the Eisenhower administration through the fifties.

In the years when the United States had a nuclear monopoly, the problem of American strategy did not at first appear very complicated. The atomic bomb and the Strategic Air Command were supposed to insure military supremacy; and, so long as they were adequately nourished, the rest of the military establishment did not much matter. In this belief, defense spending had been dropped to a level of $13 billion in the late forties. By early 1950, the Army had only about ten divisions, few of which were fully manned and equipped.

But once the Soviet Union achieved its first nuclear explosion in 1949, the United States had to face a world where its adversary had the terrible new weapons too. This event accelerated a re-examination of strategy already under way within the Truman administration. Led by Paul Nitze, who was then head of policy planning in the State Department, this process resulted in the adoption by the National Security Council in 1950 of a paper known familiarly thereafter as NSC 68. This paper predicted that by 1954 the Soviet Union would have the capacity to launch a nuclear attack on the United States, that this would sufficiently offset American nuclear power to free the Communists for a variety of types of aggression, and that to discourage sub-nuclear forms of aggression the United States must not only continue to build its nuclear strength but must greatly expand its ability to fight non-nuclear wars.

Through the same winter of 1949-50, a number of members of the Harvard and Massachusetts Institute of Technology faculties had been independently discussing the same issues in regular Sunday-morning meetings. The sessions had taken place at the initiative of two MIT scientists, Jerrold R. Zacharias and Jerome B. Wiesner, who had been involved in weapons problems since the Second World War. What made this more than an academic exercise eleven years later was the fact that, among the members, Wiesner was now Science Adviser to President Kennedy, McGeorge Bundy was now Special Assistant on National Security Affairs and Carl Kaysen was Bundy's deputy for military and strategic matters. Kenneth Galbraith, Seymour Harris and I were also in the group, though this mattered less for the defense policy of the Kennedy administration.

In 1950, it was a dark and fascinating education for the non-scientists; and it resulted in a statement which appeared in the *New York Times* on May 1 of that year. "We believe," the eighteen signers wrote, "that our present strategic position is founded on a misplaced faith in atomic weapons and strategic bombing." This strategy, the statement said, provided the United States with no effective answer to limited aggression except the wholly disproportionate answer of atomic war. As a result, it invited Moscow to use the weapons of "guerrilla warfare and internal revolt in marginal areas in the confidence that such local activity would incur only local risks." In addition, continuing reliance on the bomb indicated to the world that American strategy was based on "the principle of mass destruction of human life," an idea which would lead to a misconstruction of American motives and resentment of American power. And, to the extent that the United States placed reliance on the bomb, an agreement restricting the use of atomic weapons would, in effect, constitute unilateral disarmament; only as we liberated our strategy from its bondage to atomic weapons could we press for international controls. In place of the atom-oriented, all-or-nothing strategy, the signers urged the strengthening of the ground Army, tactical air, air transport, and various specialized forces. "The United States," the statement concluded, "can ill afford a strategy . . . which might doom it to the fearful choice between worldwide mass destruction, on the one hand, and outright military defeat, on the other."

The point became grimly evident with the outbreak of the Korean War a few weeks later; it seemed almost as if the Soviet leaders had reached the same conclusion as the drafters of NSC 68 and the Harvard-MIT group. Our unbalanced defense quite possibly persuaded the Kremlin that it could risk countenancing (or inciting) satellite aggression in an area like Korea, where the assault would be too serious for the conventional forces of the United States and not serious enough for nuclear war. This calculation only omitted Harry S. Truman. Under Truman's leadership the United States rose to the occasion, fought a limited war in Korea and led the west in a great rebuilding of military strength.

Then the end of the Korean War produced another spasm of reappraisal—this time by an administration dedicated to the thesis that the foundation of military strength was economic strength and the foundation of economic strength a balanced budget. "A bankrupt America," President Eisenhower once observed, "is more the Soviet goal than an America conquered on the field of battle." With Secretary of the Treasury George Humphrey zealous to enforce this dictum, something in the defense budget had to go. Since preparation for conventional war cost more than nuclear arms and, if a choice had to be made, contributed less to the nation's security, the Eisenhower administration reverted to the thesis of the Truman administration in the carefree days of the American atomic monopoly and decided to place predominant reliance once again on nuclear weapons. "We can't afford to fight limited wars," said Secretary of Defense Charles Wilson. "We can only afford to fight a big war, and if there is one, that is the kind it will be." The Air Force backed this thesis; indeed, the Air Force had invented it, and, with a vast industry scattered through a number of states dependent on expenditures for air power, it was the most powerful of the services in Congress. Even the Navy, dominated by Admiral Arthur Radford, who became chairman of the Joint Chiefs of Staff, exchanged its ancient belief in limited war for an expanded role in nuclear war.

John Foster Dulles summed up the new policy when he propounded the doctrine of massive retaliation, declaring that the United States had abandoned the "traditional" policy of "meeting aggression by direct and local opposition" and would depend in the future "primarily upon a great capacity to retaliate, instantly, by means and at places of our choosing." This seemed to mean that the United States intended to counter local aggression, not by limited war, but by nuclear strikes against the Soviet Union or China. "We have adopted a new principle," exulted Vice-President Nixon. "Rather than let the communists nibble us to death all over the world in little wars, we will rely in the future on massive mobile retaliatory powers." In 1961 Franz Joseph Strauss, the Defense Minister of West Germany, told officials of the Kennedy administration of assurances from Radford that, if a single communist soldier stepped over the frontier into the west, the United States would respond immediately with all-out nuclear war against the communist bloc. One cannot know to what extent this interesting thought deterred Soviet troops from stepping over the frontier; it is hard to suppose that by 1954 even the most hopeful communists regarded the invasion of Western Europe as a likely prospect. In any case, where the communists did go boldly on the offensive, as in Vietnam, massive retaliation turned out to be an empty threat. President Eisenhower could never find the case of local aggression to which nuclear warfare seemed a sensible response. By 1957 Dulles himself began to back away from the idea of strategic nuclear retaliation in favor of what proved in practice another phantom—the resort to tactical nuclear weapons.[1] But nuclear destruction, in one form or another, remained the center of the Eisenhower strategy; and the massive retaliation thesis continued to govern the Eisenhower defense budget.

The threat of massive retaliation, like Wellington's new recruits, may not have terrified the Russians and Chinese, but it did terrify a good many Americans. For the United States no longer enjoyed its atomic monopoly; this was not the world of 1948. Either massive retaliation would expose American cities to nuclear attack; or else, as Soviet missile strength and retaliatory power grew, it would no longer, in view of a vulnerable America, seem a believable response. As our strategy, in Pentagonese, 'lost credibility,'

[1] The proponents of the limited-war thesis also favored the development of tactical nuclear weapons but hoped never to use them. A few—notably Henry Kissinger in *Nuclear Weapons and Foreign Policy* (New York: Council on Foreign Relations, 1957)—believed for a time in the possibility of limited nuclear war, but Kissinger abandoned this position by 1960, and the predominant feeling among the critics of massive retaliation was always that limited nuclear war would billow up quickly (in the jargon, "escalate") into full nuclear war.

it might well embolden the communists to new experiments in piecemeal aggression. This was the strong view taken by the service whose mission, money and traditions were most threatened by the new doctrine—the Army. Within the Pentagon, two successive Army Chiefs of Staff, Matthew B. Ridgway and Maxwell Taylor, and the Army Deputy Chief of Staff for Plans and Research, James M. Gavin, tried to rehabilitate the idea of limited war. "If we are to assure that the disastrous big war never occurs," as Taylor put it, "we must have the means to deter or to win the small wars." They were grave and responsible men and brave soldiers—all three had been combat paratroopers—but they could never overcome George Humphrey's budgetary taboos. In the end, all three resigned to carry their fight to the public—Ridgway in his memoirs of 1956, *Soldier;* Gavin in *War and Peace in the Space Age* in 1958; and Taylor most directly in *The Uncertain Trumpet* in 1960.

In the meantime critics outside the government were also emphasizing the dangers of the all-or-nothing policy. As early as 1954, John F. Kennedy, leading the fight in the Senate to preserve the Army after the Korean War, said, "Our reduction of strength for resistance in so-called brushfire wars, while threatening atomic retaliation, has in effect invited expansion by the Communists in areas such as Indochina through those techniques which they deem not sufficiently offensive to induce us to risk the atomic warfare for which we are so ill prepared defensively." Within the Democratic Advisory Council Nitze and Acheson revived the thesis of NSC 68. Strategic theorists—Bernard Brodie, Henry Kissinger, W. W. Kaufmann, R. E. Osgood —joined the attack.

In 1958 Kennedy summed up the case in the Senate. The commitment to massive retaliation, he said, was producing a Maginot-line mentality—a "dependence upon a strategy which may collapse or may never be used, but which meanwhile prevents the consideration of any alternative." The most likely threat, he said, was, not nuclear attack, but "Sputnik diplomacy, limited brushfire wars, indirect non-overt aggression, intimidation and subversion, internal revolution . . . a thrust more difficult to interpret and oppose, yet inevitably ending in our isolation, submission, or destruction." Though the capacity for massive retaliation, he declared a year later, provided the only answer to the threat of nuclear war, "it is not the only answer to all threats of Communist aggression." It had not availed in Korea, Indochina, Hungary, Suez, Lebanon, Quemoy, Tibet or Laos; it could not be employed against guerrilla forces or in peripheral wars; it could not stop the erosion of our security by encroachments "too small to justify massive retaliation with all its risks." "We have been driving ourselves into a corner," Kennedy said, "where the only choice is all or nothing at all, world devastation or submission." The way out was to enlarge the range of choice by strengthening and modernizing the nation's ability to wage non-nuclear war.

There developed during the fifties two distinctive approaches to national strategy, which Samuel P. Huntington appropriately terms "strategic monism" and "strategic pluralism." Each was rooted in attitudes toward the domestic economy and toward foreign affairs, and each was associated with a political party. The Republicans, with their traditional dedication to a balanced budget and a unilateral foreign policy, tended to favor the more economical course of strategic monism and rested American security predominantly on American nuclear weapons. The Democrats, with their traditional tolerance of government spending and concern for collective international action, tended to be strategic pluralists and sought a military establishment capable of helping other nations meet a diversity of military threats.[2]

McNamara, as Secretary of Defense in the Kennedy administration, thus inherited a clear-cut strategic perspective—one which, it should be added, he firmly embraced on its merits—when he turned his appraising eye on the state of the national defenses.

3. THE OCCUPATION OF THE PENTAGON

McNamara brought striking gifts to his new responsibility —an inquiring and incisive mind, a limitless capacity for work and a personality which lacked pretense and detested it in others. But, more than this, he brought new techniques of large-scale management. American social prophets— Bellamy, Veblen, Howard Scott, Adolf Berle, James Burnham—had long tried to prepare the nation for the coming of the managers. But none had predicted anything quite like this tough, courteous and humane technocrat, for whom

[2] Not all Democrats espoused the limited-war thesis in the fifties. Stuart Symington, Thomas K. Finletter and Roswell Gilpatric believed, in Finletter's words, that only when the needs of the air-atomic retaliatory force were fully satisfied "would we allocate money to other military tasks." Symington and Finletter had both been Secretaries of the Air Force under Truman and Gilpatric Under Secretary.

scientific management was not an end in itself but a means to the rationality of democratic government.

McNamara appeared at a moment of intellectual and administrative crisis in defense affairs. The military establishment had now grown into a small empire. A third of the states in the United Nations had smaller populations than the American Department of Defense, and only a few had larger budgets. Defense operated enormous complexes of transport, communications, procurement, maintenance and distribution as well as of tanks, ships, planes and men. It made a multiplicity of fateful choices in the determination of strategy, the selection of weapons systems, the design of forces and the level of expenditure. Its decisions affected everything from the economy of San Diego to the destiny of mankind.

It had been, however, an empire without an emperor. Generals, admirals, scientists, administrators and Secretaries of Defense all had tried in vain to catch hold of the defense process as it hurtled along. By now it had acquired a dreadful momentum of its own; its direction, such as it was, was determined by a bewildering mixture of internal intrigues and extraneous pressures; and it was producing a set of unanticipated side effects on domestic and foreign policy. After eight years in the White House, even Eisenhower came to feel that something was wrong and issued his unexpected warning against "the acquisition of unwarranted influence, whether sought or unsought, by the military-industrial complex." Still, the military-industrial complex was more a consequence than a cause of the problem. The cause lay in the feebleness of civilian control of the military establishment; and this feebleness was the result in great part of the absence of rational understanding and hence of rational direction.

While technology and science were creating the problem, they were also creating a hope for its solution, or at least for its mitigation. The Second World War had made the scientist a partner, if for a time a suspect and scorned partner, in the enterprise of defense; the nuclear age made the association irrevocable. But, even though the military came to accept the validity of the scientific role and the scientists the validity of the military mission, it was not a particularly happy partnership; indeed, as the military professionals sensed a decline in status and power, their resentment grew. Eisenhower, again feeling that something was wrong, warned that "public policy could itself become the captive of a scientific-technological elite." Yet, for better or worse, a new generation of military intellectuals was revolutionizing what had once been the art of strategy.

The essence of their effort was the application of systematic quantitative analysis to strategic decisions. Operations research, as it was called, had begun during the Second World War, and its first practitioners were mostly physicists, mathematicians, biologists and engineers. After the war, an invasion of economists gave operations research new scope and vitality. Where the scientists tended to accept the terms of the problem as presented to them, the economists, schooled in the search for the most efficient use of resources, accustomed to the 'substitution' effect and trained in such concepts as 'marginal' utility' and 'opportunity cost,' were more audacious in the pursuit of alternatives. In this new phase, operations research was quick to demonstrate that there could be a variety of ways to achieve a desired end, and this both speeded the pace of innovation and left the military even further behind.

The Rand ("research and development") Corporation, established by the Air Force in California after the war, provided the model of the new military-intellectual establishment. Scientists and economists invented new techniques of systems analysis, linear and dynamic programming and game theory, devising ingenious tools by which to formulate problems, break them down, distinguish alternatives, establish their quantitative equivalents, compare the effects of different decisions and seek the most favorable results in situations characterized by a great mass of variables. The electronic computer became an indispensable part of the machinery of national strategy.

The strategy intellectuals did not claim infallibility for their black arts. As the economist Charles J. Hitch put it after leaving Rand for McNamara's Pentagon, "There will always be considerations which bear on the very fundamentals of national defense which are simply not subject to any sort of rigorous, quantitative analysis." He added, breaking into the patois which was the new elite's lesser contribution to civilization, "The fact that we cannot quantize such things . . . does not mean that they have no effect on the outcome of a military endeavor—it simply means that our analytical techniques cannot answer every question." Yet these techniques gave civil government the means of subjecting the anarchy of defense to a measure of order.

McNamara had been fascinated by the intellectual problem of administering large organizations since his days as a student and teacher of statistical control in the Harvard Business School and his experience as a junior officer in the Pentagon during the war. In the fifties he had confronted a similar challenge, if on a smaller scale, at the Ford Motor Company. His belief was that "the techniques used to administer these affairs of a large organization are very similar whether that organization be a business enterprise or a Government institution or an educational institution or any other large aggregation of human individuals working to a common end." In spite of his critics, he was no believer in the omnipotence of the slide rule. He knew that abstractions were different from realities and that the tolerances of calculation on the great computers were refined far beyond the precision of the assumptions. But the quest for control required in his judgment two things: the use of analysis to force alternative programs to the surface and the definition of the 'options' in quantitative terms in order to facilitate choice.

He had no illusions about the difficulties of his quest. The Department had already balked, thwarted, exposed and broken a succession of able men imprudent enough to accept appointment as Secretary. "This place is a jungle— a jungle," McNamara himself cried in his first weeks. But nothing had ever defeated him yet; and he believed that the only way the Secretary could achieve control was through a new theory of the job—conceiving his responsibility not as that of a judge, reviewing and reconciling recommendations made to him by the services, but of an executive, aggressively questioning, goading, demanding and leading. The emergence during the fifties of the scientific-technological elite now gave him the men with whom to begin the reconquest of the Pentagon. The computer was his ally in making options precise. *The Times Literary Supplement* provided an apt parallel: "The military intellectuals move freely through the corridors of the Pentagon and the State Department rather as the Jesuits through the courts of Madrid and Vienna three centuries ago."

Khrushchev's January speech made emphatic the point often expressed by Eisenhower during his Presidency—the impossibility of total nuclear war as an instrument of rational policy. But Eisenhower allowed himself for political and fiscal reasons to remain the prisoner of the doctrine of strategic monism. When McNamara called for the basic defense plans, he found that they still rested on the assumption of total nuclear war. "The Pentagon is full of papers talking about the preservation of a 'viable society' after nuclear conflict," he once said. "That 'viable society' phrase drives me mad. I kept trying to comb it out, but it keeps coming back." Kennedy now charged McNamara with the problem of devising strategies to deal with a world in which total nuclear war was no longer conceivable. This called for a shift from massive retaliation to a capability for controlled and flexible response, graduated to meet a variety of levels and forms of aggression.

The legacy of armed force bequeathed by the Eisenhower administration followed from the belief that the all-out nuclear response was all that mattered. McNamara found a total of fourteen Army divisions, of which only eleven were ready for combat. Of the eleven, only three were deployed in the United States. Kennedy was appalled to discover a few weeks after the inauguration that, if he sent 10,000 men to Southeast Asia, he would deplete the strategic reserve and have virtually nothing left for emergencies elsewhere. Indeed, the United States could not even have invaded Cuba after the Bay of Pigs without drawing troops from other parts of the world and thereby inviting communist moves on other fronts. Equipment was so low that, when Kennedy inspected the 82nd Airborne at Fort Bragg in October, the division had to borrow men and materiel to bring itself up to complement. The Army could hardly fight longer than a few weeks before running short on ammunition, nor was new production set to remedy the deficiencies. The supply of armored personnel carriers, self-propelled howitzers and recoilless rifles fell far below the required number (and, at the same time, as evidence of the procurement mess, there were three times the required number of 105 mm. cartridges and twice the required number of 81 mm. and 4.2″ mortar shells). The airlift capacity consisted largely of obsolescent aircraft designed for civilian transportation; it would have taken nearly two months to carry an infantry division and its equipment to Southeast Asia. And, if such a division had found itself in the jungles of Laos or Vietnam, it would have been like Braddock's army at the Battle of the Wilderness, since counter-insurgency forces hardly existed.

Tactical air power was also grievously weak. Of the sixteen wings of fighter bombers in the Air Force, over three-quarters were F-100s, a 1955 plane with no all-weather capability. Only about 10 per cent were Mach 2 all-weather fighters. In addition, the planes had very little in the way of modern non-nuclear ordnance; the Air Force had only about one-fourth the desired number of Sidewinder missiles; and air-to-ground weapons were mostly of the kind used in the Korean War. When McNamara demanded a demonstration of tactical air support of ground troops, the Air Force actually had to borrow certain types of ordnance from the Navy.

Even the nuclear striking power hardly constituted an invulnerable deterrent. The Strategic Air Command was almost entirely concentrated on about sixty bases, of which only a few were 'hardened' (i.e., capable of surviving nuclear attack) and only a third were on alert. They were, in other words, highly vulnerable to a surprise missile strike.

4. THE RECONSTRUCTION OF NATIONAL STRATEGY

These discoveries shocked McNamara. The United States, for all its splendid capacity to blow up the world, had, it was obvious, an entirely inadequate amount of what McNamara called "usable power"—military force capable of serving reasonable ends. The President, who was perhaps less surprised, directed him to begin the work of building a military establishment versatile enough to meet the full spectrum of possible threats from guerrilla infiltration to nuclear holocaust. Only such a force, Kennedy believed, could give his foreign policy a solid foundation and liberate diplomacy from the constraints imposed by a rigid military strategy.

As McNamara began his review, one fear which had affected the polemics, though not the essence, of the party debate on defense policy now dropped out of the picture. The idea of a 'missile gap' had been first set forth publicly by Eisenhower's second Secretary of Defense, Neil McElroy, who forecast in 1959 that the Soviet Union would probably have a 3-1 superiority in intercontinental ballistic missiles by the early sixties. This estimate rested on the best intelligence then available and was shared by various military experts who conveyed it to Stuart Symington, Kennedy and other Senators. By 1960 it was a staple of Democratic oratory. But new intelligence methods and sources cast doubt on the estimate in the winter of 1960-61; Jerome Wiesner had long been skeptical, and in February McNamara, in a candid background talk to newspapermen, was ready to dismiss the gap as an illusion.[3]

[3] Another fake issue, much fancied by the Democrats in the Eisenhower period, was the objection that under Eisenhower the budget determined defense needs rather than vice versa. While George Humphrey's antique fiscal views undoubtedly imposed irrational constraints on Eisenhower's defense policy, the Democrats never really believed that the Pentagon's view of its own requirements should be decisive. As Charles Hitch put it in his Rand days, "There is nothing absolute about national security, expecially in this thermonuclear era. Some notion of cost, however imprecise, is implicit in the recognition of any limitation. . . . For the logic of choice demands that alternatives be costed, in some

On March 1, McNamara mounted his first major assault on the Pentagon, firing a fusillade of ninety-six questions, each aimed at a specific area, directed to a specific man and requiring a specific answer by a specific time. He wanted to know what the military were doing, why they thought they were doing it and whether there was not a more economical and efficient way of achieving the same result. No one had asked such questions before; and McNamara's memoranda grew sharp as his patience grew short. "A Japanese general who got a query like this," a recipient observed of one McNamara message, "would commit harakiri." While McNamara was pressing his review, Kennedy in the State of the Union message moved to repair the more obvious defects in America's defenses. He called for an increase in airlift capacity to strengthen conventional power, an acceleration of the nuclear missile program and an expansion of the Polaris submarine program to extend the invulnerability of the American deterrent. "The greater our variety of weapons," he later said, "the more political choices we can make in any given situation."

By March 28 the review had advanced sufficiently for Kennedy to send a special message asking Congress for an additional $650 million for the defense budget. Here he restated the familiar themes. Our objective must be "to increase our ability to confine our response to non-nuclear weapons. . . . Any potential aggressor contemplating an attack on any part of the Free World with any kind of weapons, conventional or nuclear, must know that our response will be suitable, selective, swift and effective." He then proposed a series of measures to improve the national ability to deter or restrict limited wars, including the expansion of guerrilla warfare units, as well as other measures to improve and protect the strategic deterrent and defenses. A third message "on urgent national needs," delivered in

---

appropriate way, prior to choice. It tells us that the choices that maximize military power with given resources are the same choices that minimize the resource cost of attaining that level of power." ("Economics and Military Operations Research," *Review of Economics and Statistics*, August, 1958.) The Kennedy Administration proved to be as concerned as the Eisenhower Administration with the balancing of the defense effort against the other demands of the economy, but it believed—correctly—that the balance could be achieved at a much higher level. The two administrations differed, not in their basic attitude toward the idea of budgetary limits on defense spending, but in their estimates as to how much defense spending the economy could stand. As a party used to spending, the Democrats had fewer inhibitions.

late May, a month after the Bay of Pigs and responding to Soviet success in space—Yuri Gagarin's orbital flight around the planet in early April—called for a vastly enlarged effort in space, including landing a man on the moon by 1970. Kennedy also requested "a further reinforcement of our own capacity to deter or resist non-nuclear aggression"—greater modernization of conventional forces, greater mobility and more training in paramilitary warfare.

The work of reconstructing American defense strategy had only begun. Difficult problems of doctrine remained— the proper composition and function of the nuclear deterrent, for example. Difficult problems of command and control were yet to be solved. Morale in the Pentagon itself was also shaken by the new approach. McNamara was well served at the top civilian level, especially by Roswell Gilpatric, who, in spite of his Air Force background, became an able partner in the reorganization. But the Secretary, well aware that he was cutting his way through a thicket of traditional prides and vested interests, came to recognize what he called the "wrenching strains in the Department as new thought patterns have been substituted for old." General Thomas D. White, a former Chief of Staff for the Air Force, wrote bitterly in 1963: "In common with many other military men, active and retired, I am profoundly apprehensive of the pipe-smoking, tree-full-of-owls type of so-called professional defense intellectuals who have been brought into this Nation's Capital. I don't believe a lot of these often over-confident, sometimes arrogant young professors, mathematicians and other theorists have sufficient worldliness or motivation to stand up to the kind of enemy we face." Congressman F. Edward Hébert of Louisiana took his stand "with the professional military man who has had years of experience, who has faced the enemy on the battlefield . . . in preference to the striplings who are the geniuses in the intellectual community but have never heard a shot fired in anger." There was a good deal of this also in the press, but McNamara nevertheless enjoyed strong political and public support.

Within the White House his directness, intelligence and decisiveness immediately won the complete and lasting confidence of the President. The Secretary also quickly achieved an effective relationship with Jerome Wiesner who had fought hard through the fifties to improve the state of American defense and whose work on the Gaither committee of 1957 had prepared the ground for McNamara's reconstruction of strategy now. McGeorge Bundy also kept an alert eye on the evolution of defense policy; and both

Bundy's and Wiesner's hands were strengthened when Carl Kaysen, a Harvard economist who united cogency as a debater and intrepidity as an operator, joined the National Security Council staff. McNamara, Wiesner, Bundy and Kaysen worked well together (three were old friends from Cambridge). They gave the President confidence that he was in a position to control national strategy.

XIII

LEGACY IN SOUTHEAST ASIA

THE REORGANIZATION OF national defense was not merely a theoretical issue. For the communist challenge was already taking acute form in Southeast Asia. Communist guerrillas —the Viet Cong in South Vietnam, the Pathet Lao in Laos —were conducting savage and elusive warfare against prowestern regimes. When Kennedy had met with Eisenhower just before the inauguration, they spent more time talking about Laos than anything else. The situation in Vietnam was almost as bad. On February 2, Walt Rostow gave the President a memorandum about Vietnam written by Brigadier General Edward Lansdale, an imaginative officer who had worked with Magsaysay in ending the guerrilla action of the Hukbalahaps in the Philippines. Kennedy read it in Rostow's presence and said, "This is the worst yet." Then he added, "You know, Ike never briefed me about Vietnam."

1. KENNEDY AND SOUTHEAST ASIA

He was not unfamiliar with the territory. He had gone to Southeast Asia in 1951 when Laos, Cambodia and Vietnam were all part of French Indochina. In Saigon he discovered an acquaintance in the counselor of the American legation—a Foreign Service officer named Edmund Gullion. They had met four years before in Washington when Kennedy, then a young Congressman, had asked Dean Acheson for someone with whom to discuss foreign policy in preparation for a speech, and Acheson had sent over Gullion, his special assistant. Gullion, though a professional, had managed to preserve a private wryness and independence of mind which appealed to Kennedy, and they now resumed their friendship.

300 A THOUSAND DAYS

The official United States line was uncritical support for the French in their struggle against the Vietnamese nationalists. The Saigon legation, however, was bitterly split about the wisdom of this policy. Gullion and the political section, backed by the economic aid people and the CIA, argued that the French could not organize successful resistance on the basis either of military plans calling for conventional assault or of political plans retaining Indochina as part of France. When Kennedy arrived, fresh from his sickness in Okinawa, looking, Gullion recalls, like a plucked chicken with thin neck and jaundiced color under a tousle of uncut hair, he bridled under the routine embassy briefing and asked sharply why the Vietnamese should be expected to fight to keep their country part of France. This viewpoint irritated the American Minister, and, when they met, it irritated General Jean de Lattre de Tassigny, the war hero in command of the French forces, even more. After an animated argument, de Lattre sent the Minister a formal letter of complaint about the young Congressman.

"In Indochina," Kennedy said on his return to Washington, "we have allied ourselves to the desperate effort of a French regime to hang on to the remnants of empire. . . . To check the southern drive of communism makes sense but not only through reliance on the force of arms. The task is rather to build strong native non-Communist sentiment within these areas and rely on that as a spearhead of defense rather than upon the legions of General de Lattre. To do this apart from and in defiance of innately nationalistic aims spells foredoomed failure." The trip gave Kennedy both a new sympathy for the problems of Asia and a new understanding of the power of nationalism in the underdeveloped world. "Without the support of the native population," he said on Meet the Press, "there is no hope of success in any of the countries of Southeast Asia." He dropped his doubts about Point Four and economic aid and set Jacqueline Bouvier to translating French books about Indochina for him. When Justice William O. Douglas invited Senators interested in the Far East to a luncheon in 1953 for an Indochinese political exile named Ngo Dinh Diem, Kennedy was present. Diem, who had been living in a retreat with the Maryknoll Fathers, made a favorable impression. Senator Mike Mansfield wrote later about his "nationalism, his personal incorruptibility and courage, and his idealistic determination." [1]

[1] Mike Mansfield, "Reprieve in Viet Nam," *Harper's Magazine*, January 1956.

Ed Gullion, now back in Washington, was also present at the luncheon, and from time to time he and Kennedy discussed developments in Southeast Asia. (Gullion was suspected in the Department of contributing to Kennedy's foreign policy speeches. One friend warned him not to risk his career; "if you are going to establish a relationship with a Senator, at least pick one who has a future.") By early 1954 the French, who had persisted in their effort to fight a European war in the jungle, found themselves under siege in the fortress of Dien Bien Phu. When the French commander at Dien Bien Phu pleaded for American support, Dulles, forgetting massive retaliation, proposed an allied air strike at Dien Bien Phu to Sir Anthony Eden, the British Foreign Minister. "I am fairly hardened to crises," Eden wrote later, "but I went to bed that night a troubled man. I did not believe that anything less than intervention on a Korean scale, if that, would have any effect in Indochina." In Washington Vice-President Nixon suggested the possibility of "putting American boys in."

On April 6 Kennedy observed in the Senate that, if the American people were to go to war for the fourth time in the century, "particularly a war which we now realize would threaten the survival of civilization," they had a right to inquire in detail into the nature of the struggle and the possible alternatives. He offered a garland of optimistic statements about Indochina—Acheson in 1952 ("the military situation appears to be developing favorably"), Assistant Secretary of State Walter Robertson in 1953 ("in Indochina we believe the tide now is turning"), Secretary of Defense Wilson (French victory is "both possible and probable") and Admiral Radford ("the French are going to win") in 1954—and contrasted this gush of official optimism with the grim actuality. "I am frankly of the belief," Kennedy said, "that no amount of American military assistance in Indochina can conquer . . . 'an enemy of the people' which has the sympathy and covert support of the people. . . . For the United States to intervene unilaterally and to send troops into the most difficult terrain in the world, with the Chinese able to pour in unlimited manpower, would mean that we would face a situation which would be far more difficult than even that we encountered in Korea." He saw no hope for Indochina until the French granted the Vietnamese their independence.

The opposition of the congressional leaders, of General Ridgway, of the British and eventually of President Eisenhower himself forced Dulles to drop the plan of intervention. "I trust," Kennedy said later, "the United States has learned that it cannot ignore the moral and ideological principles at the root of today's struggles." The French abandoned the fight after the surrender of Dien Bien Phu; and negotiations in Geneva, in which the United States ostentatiously took no part, soon resulted in an agreement to divide Vietnam at the 17th parallel and to ratify the independence of Laos and Cambodia.

Diem returned to Saigon in June as prime minister and within eighteen months was president. The French were skeptical about Diem, nor was he precisely, as Justice Douglas suggested, "revered" by the Vietnamese people. But he was remembered and respected as one of the first Indochinese nationalists. His resignation as Chief Minister of Annam in 1933 had been early challenge to French rule. After the war both Ho Chi Minh, the communist leader, and Bao Dai, the French puppet emperor, sought his endorsement. He refused them both. The United States now offered his government substantial economic assistance, and for the next few years South Vietnam enjoyed a significant measure of growth and reform. Then in the late fifties the guerrilla war began again. In spite of his economic success, Diem, a man of austere and authoritarian temperament who preferred to govern through his immediate family, had failed to develop a solid basis of popular support. By 1961 the Viet Cong guerrillas, backed by Ho Chi Minh's Viet Minh in the north, roamed through large areas of the countryside, sometimes very near Saigon itself, murdering local officials, harassing government troops and placing the Diem regime in jeopardy.

2. THE DILEMMA OF LAOS

Prospects in South Vietnam, however, were favorable compared to those in Laos. This curious land of perhaps two million inhabitants—no one knew how many—lay between Vietnam and Thailand along the east bank of the Mekong River and wandered into mountains farther to the north. It was a state by diplomatic courtesy. Though a royal family sat in Luang Prabang, the Lao, a relaxed and lackadaisical people, lacked the nationalist frenzy; and the hill tribes, untouched by the revolution of rising expectations, hardly knew that they lived in a new nation or cared who their rulers might be. As Buddhists, the Lao favored contemplation and disliked killing. Their ambition was to be let alone to enjoy themselves. Politics was reserved for a small elite, largely related to each other, who had begun a movement for independence at the end of the Second World War. When the French came back in 1946, some of these went into exile. Most returned in 1949, except for Prince Souphanouvong who joined Ho Chi Minh in North Vietnam and formed the Pathet Lao ("Land of the Lao") to free Laos from the imperialists. His half brother Prince Souvanna Phouma soon became head of the regular government at Vientiane. In 1953 the Pathet Lao, with Viet Minh support, occupied two provinces in northeastern Laos. The Geneva Agreement now called for a ceasefire and for the reintegration of the Pathet Lao into what was optimistically termed the 'national community.' Provisions against foreign military aid and bases, even though qualified to permit exceptions for purposes of defense, implied a desire to keep Laos out of the cold war—a policy explicitly avowed by Prince Souvanna as prime minister.

But the Laotian ambition for a quiet life was to be further disturbed. For Laos had an evident strategic importance. If the Communists gained possession of the Mekong valley, they could materially intensify their pressure against South Vietnam and Thailand. If Laos was not precisely a dagger pointed at the heart of Kansas, it was very plainly a gateway to Southeast Asia. As the French prepared to depart, Dulles performed his usual incantations and devised a new military pact—the Southeast Asia Treaty Organization (SEATO)—including three Asian states (Thailand, Pakistan and the Philippines) with the United States, Britain, France, Australia and New Zealand. A special protocol extended the protecting arm of the organization around South Vietnam, Cambodia and Laos. The Dulles plan for military containment required Laos to become a 'bulwark against communism' and a 'bastion of freedom.' As part of this program, Laos was expected to build an army of 25,000 men —a State Department idea which the Defense Department had originally opposed as ridiculous.

In pursuit of this dream, the United States flooded the wild and primitive land with nearly $300 million by the end of 1960. This amounted to $150 for every inhabitant— more aid per capita than any other country and almost double the previous per capita income of the Laotians. Eighty-five per cent of this went to pay the total bill for the Royal Laotian Army, which by 1959 was outfitted in American style with jeeps, trucks and a Transportation Corps (all despite the fact Laos had no all-weather roads), as well as an Ordnance Corps, a Quartermaster Corps and Military Police. When trained at all, and effective training did not begin till 1959, the Laotian troops learned, not counterguerrilla warfare, but conventional maneuvers. Of the $300 million, only $7 million went for technical cooperation and economic development.

It was a misbegotten investment. Laos simply did not have the national or social structure to absorb the remorseless flood of American bounty. Instead of lifting living standards or even producing military force, aid led to unimaginable bribery, graft, currency manipulation and waste. Expensive motor cars thronged the dusty streets of Vientiane. The Laotian officials themselves were demoralized, and the army officers, rejoicing in American patronage, grew increasingly involved in politics and graft. As money flowed into Vientiane, the gap widened between the capital and the countryside. The Pathet Lao, speaking out for virtue and the people, gathered strength in the villages. Prince Souvanna Phouma, seeking the reintegration of the dissidents, conducted long talks with his half brother. In November 1957 they finally negotiated the Vientiane Agreements providing for a neutral Laos under a coalition government. The Pathet Lao were to be incorporated in the army and the cabinet, Souphanouvong himself becoming Minister of Economic Planning (the other Pathet Lao post was Minister of Religion).

The Eisenhower administration watched the developments within its bastion with alarm. "I struggled for sixteen months," the American Ambassador, J. Graham Parsons, later said, "to prevent a coalition." In 1958 Washington decided to install a reliably pro-western regime. CIA spooks put in their appearance, set up a Committee for the Defense of the National Interests (CDNI) and brought back from France as its chief an energetic, ambitious and devious officer named Phoumi Nosavan. Prince Souvanna, who had shown himself an honest and respected if impulsive leader, was forced out of office; a veteran politician named Phoui Sananikoune took his place. In 1959 the State Department backed Phoui, but the CIA preferred Phoumi. The CIA station chief refused to follow the State Department policy or even to tell the Ambassador his plans and intentions. One Laotian leader complained to the Ambassador about American policy, "Since so many voices are heard, it is impossible to tell which has an authoritative ring." When Phoui dismissed a CDNI leader as foreign minister and the CDNI seemed on the verge of falling apart, the CIA moved in to preserve its investment. Phoui was overthrown, and Phoumi now was in control. Prince Souphanouvong was in jail (from which, after winning over his guards, he soon escaped to the north). The Pathet Lao took to the hills and resumed the civil war.

During early 1960 Phoumi dominated non-communist Laos. Recognizing that Defense and CIA were committed to him, he felt free to ignore their advice, rigging the spring elections so blatantly, for example, that the results lacked any color of legitimacy. In August a new figure, who had neither a family tie to anyone nor a name like anyone else's, entered the drama. Kong Le, a young paratroop captain, was a simple man, without ambition for himself, who wanted to end domestic corruption and foreign intervention and bring peace to his people. One day when most of the government was out of town he seized power and asked Prince Souvanna to form a new government. Souvanna's aim as ever was to establish a neutralist regime; and he sought a coalition with the right in order to bargain with the Pathet Lao. Winthrop Brown, who had recently arrived in Vientiane as American Ambassador, supported the idea of bringing Souvanna and Phoumi together. This obviously would mean a return to the Vientiane Agreements of 1957 and the end of the bastion-of-freedom dream. But Brown, a clear-sighted and independent-minded man, doubted on the evidence that it would be possible to build a pro-western state in the jungles and mountains of Laos. The proper strategy, as he saw it, was to associate the neutralists and the anti-communists in the defense of a neutral Laos against the Pathet Lao.

A united embassy, including CIA, followed Brown in recommending that Washington accept the coalition. But Kong Le opposed the inclusion of Phoumi; and Phoumi himself began to play for United States backing. For its part, the Bureau of Far Eastern Affairs in Washington considered Kong Le a probable communist and looked with great dubiety on the neutralist solution. Nowhere was the pure Dulles doctrine taken more literally than in this bureau. In 1953 the Republicans had purged it of the Foreign Service officers they held responsible for the 'loss' of China. Then they confided Far Eastern matters to a Virginia gentleman named Walter Robertson. Robertson, like Dulles, judged Chiang Kai-shek moral and neutralism immoral and established policy on those principles. His successor in 1959 was the J. Graham Parsons who had been applying those principles so faithfully in Laos.

As for the Defense Department, it was all for Phoumi. Possibly with encouragement from Defense and CIA men in the field, Phoumi took the Royal Laotian Army to Svannakhet in September, proclaimed a new government and denounced Souvanna. The Phoumi regime became the recipient of American military aid, while the Souvanna government in Vientiane continued to receive economic aid. Ambassador Brown still worked to bring them together, but the military support convinced Phoumi that, if he only held out, Washington would put him in power.

At the working level in Washington doubts were beginning to rise. Some people in State thought that a 'military' (i.e., Phoumi) solution would work only if in the end we were ready to send in American troops. If we were not ready to do this, then should we not try for a 'political' (i.e., Souvanna) solution? Defense backed away from the idea of American troops but not from Phoumi. The Eisenhower team concept required that State's instructions be cleared through Defense, which led to long delays and sometimes contradictory instructions. As James Douglas, the Under Secretary of Defense, put it, "By the time a message to the field had been composed in Washington, it had ceased to be an operational order and had become a philosophical essay." The British and French favored Souvanna and did not want SEATO involved in a fight to put Phoumi in power. President Diem in Vietnam and Marshal Sarit in Thailand favored Phoumi lest neutralization threaten their own lands; Sarit even imposed a blockade of goods to Vientiane.

In October Eisenhower dispatched J. Graham Parsons to Laos in a strange effort to straighten out the situation. Since Parsons had been identified with the previous humiliation of Souvanna (who regarded him as "the most reprehensible and nefarious of men" and "the ignominious architect of disastrous American policy toward Laos"), he was not perhaps the ideal envoy. He put intense pressure on Souvanna to forsake neutralism, accept Phoumi and make Laos a bastion of freedom again. Souvanna's lack of enthusiasm about these suggestions confirmed Washington's mistrust of him. In late October, a few days before the American election, State and Defense agreed that Souvanna must go, though they disagreed on how this should be accomplished. For his part, Souvanna not unnaturally took the Parsons mission to mean that Washington was preparing to dump him. In a last test, he asked the United States for rice and oil to relieve the needs created by the Thai blockade. When Washington refused, Souvanna turned to the Russians, who established an embassy in Vientiane and instituted an airlift from Hanoi—first rice and oil; later guns.

In December, a few weeks after the election, Phoumi marched on Vientiane and with plans drawn up by his American advisers won the only military victory of his life. Souvanna fled to Cambodia and soon after came to terms with Souphanouvong, while Kong Le and his troops, leaving Vientiane in American trucks loaded with American supplies, joined up with the Pathet Lao in the field. Moscow and Peking continued to recognize the Souvanna regime as the true government of Laos. Winthrop Brown's hope of uniting the neutralists and the right against the communists had been thwarted. Instead, the Eisenhower administration, by rejecting the neutralist alternative, had driven the neutralists into reluctant alliance with the communists and provoked (and in many eyes legitimatized) open Soviet aid to the Pathet Lao. And all this was done without serious consultation with the incoming administration which would shortly inherit the problem.

The British, alarmed by this result, now bestirred themselves, sending a note to the Soviet Union in early January 1961 urging a revival of the International Control Commission in Laos. Prince Sihanouk of Cambodia suggested a fourteen-nation conference. Belatedly aware that the United States was losing all international support (save for Thailand and South Vietnam), the State Department itself receded a little from the decisions of December. Officers down the line had discussed for some time the possibilities of neutralization. Now the Department said publicly that the United States "had no desire to establish a western military position in Laos" and expressed readiness to accept a revived ICC if the Laotians wanted it. In the meantime, in Laos itself the civil war had succumbed to the national indolence. Phoumi's Royal Laotian Army let two weeks go by before taking out after the fleeing Kong Le. By the time of Kennedy's inauguration, Phoumi's men, having managed to cover sixty-five miles in twenty-nine days, were in the outskirts of Vang Vieng. They had successfully avoided contact with the enemy. Their only casualty was a lieutenant who accidentally shot himself in the foot.

3. THE RIDDLE OF INTERVENTION

The new President had a clear historical view of Laos. He thought that this was not a land "worthy of engaging the attention of great powers," that the effort to transform it into a pro-western redoubt had been ridiculous and that neutralization was the correct policy. But he knew that the matter was not that simple any longer. For the effort had been made, American prestige was deeply involved, and extrication would not be easy. To strive now for neutralization it was essential to convince the Pathet Lao that they could not win and to dissuade the Russians from further military assistance. In view of the pacifist inclinations of the Royal Laotian Army, moreover, it would be hard to induce the Pathet Lao to call off the war. And Phoumi himself, still receiving American military assistance, supposed that Washington would back his regime to the end. This made him more defiant and unmanageable than ever. One American official observed that he was behaving like a kid out of *West Side Story*.

In his first press conference Kennedy announced his hope for the establishment of Laos as "a peaceful country—an independent country not dominated by either side." This policy became an engrossing personal concern. In the first two months of his administration he probably spent more time on Laos than on anything else. Determined to lift the problem out of the slow-moving machinery of government, he established a Laos task force and sent word to the first meeting that he wanted daily reports on its progress. The change in Washington was instantly reflected in the instructions to the field. Instead of the confused and murky cables of a short while before, the embassy received straight orders and clear answers; Winthrop Brown later exclaimed with relief and admiration how much help it was "when the President is your desk officer." Soon Brown himself came back for consultation and received the usual rapid-fire Kennedy interrogation. The President asked particularly about the *dramatis personae*—a sound instinct in a country where organization and ideology mattered little and where so much of past American error had arisen from misjudgments of Souvanna, Phoumi and Kong Le.

In early February Phoumi set out on a new campaign. Our military experts assured Kennedy that this would lead to the speedy recapture of the Plaine des Jarres in north central Laos. Instead, the Royal Laotian Army retreated after a series of skirmishes more bloody in communiqué than in fact. This fiasco confirmed Kennedy's impression of Phoumi's singular incompetence. He now decided that Laos must have a coalition of the sort that Eisenhower's State Department had vetoed six months before. Brown still considered Souvanna the only possible leader. But Souvanna, bitter at his treatment by the Americans, had been traveling to Hanoi and later to Peking and Moscow. The State Department, having driven him to the communists, now flourished his itinerary as proof of his perfidy. In fact, Souvanna was pursuing the same neutralist course he had followed for a decade. "The Americans say I am a Communist," he now said. "All this is heartbreaking. How can they think I am a Communist? I am looking for a way to keep Laos non-Communist."

On the international front, Washington worked out an alternative to the ICC proposal, to which Moscow had not replied, in the form of an Asian commission, composed of Burma, Cambodia and Malaya, charged with investigating foreign intervention in Laos. On February 19 the King of Laos, who spent most of his time trying to stay out of politics, issued a statement, drafted in the State Department, declaring a policy of non-alignment, appealing to all countries to respect his nation's independence and neutrality and asking his three neighbors to serve as guarantors. Cambodia (despite a personal letter from Kennedy to Prince Sihanouk) and Burma both declined, however, and in any case Moscow, Peking and Prince Souphanouvong all attacked the plan.

In the meantime, the Soviet airlift was increasing the flow of arms and ammunition to the Pathet Lao. G. M. Pushkin, the Soviet deputy foreign minister, later told Averell Harriman that, apart from the Second World War, this was the highest priority Soviet supply operation since the Revolution. In early March the Pathet Lao were ready to take the offensive. The Royal Laotion Army began a circumspect withdrawal, and the Mekong valley itself was threatened. The Pathet Lao attack put the crisis in bleak outline. The peace plan had failed, the pro-western Laotians were in retreat, the Russians were increasing their military support, the British and French were indifferent to everything except the thought of their own involvement, and the idea of an independent Laos seemed doomed.

There still remained the thin hope that the Russian interest sprang less from a desire to get in themselves than to keep the Chinese out and that they might eventually accept the policy of neutralization. But, as the Pathet Lao moved forward, it became a question whether Moscow could turn the local boys off even if it wanted to. In any case, the United States had no choice but to stiffen its position, whether in preparation for negotiation or for resistance. On March 9 the task force proposed stepping up military assistance to the Royal Laotian Army. On March 15 Kennedy told his press conference that "a small minority backed by personnel and supplies from outside" was trying to prevent the establishment of a neutral Laos; "we are determined to support the government and the people of Laos in resisting this attempt." Three days later Dean Rusk made one more attempt to convince Andrei Gromyko, the Soviet Foreign Minister, of America's earnest desire for neutralization. Gromyko gave no ground, but Rusk may have got through better than he thought at the time. On March 20 Kennedy scheduled a National Security Council meeting on the problem.

He had asked me to join him earlier that day for luncheon with Walter Lippmann. Laos was much on his mind. He remarked a little dourly that the United States was overcommitted in Southeast Asia but that he had to deal with facts as they were. It was indispensable to prevent "an immediate communist takeover." We must hold Vientiane in order to have a basis for negotiation. "We cannot and will not accept any visible humiliation over Laos." On the other hand, Eisenhower's recommendation for unilateral intervention was not militarily feasible on any major scale, and it could not command allied support. Moreover, it was hard to fight for a country whose people evidently could not care less about fighting for themselves. And it was also hard to understand why the United States had to take the responsibility. "I don't see why we have to be more royalist than the king," Kennedy said. "India is more directly threatened than we are; and, if they are not wildly excited, why should we be?" Nor could he see why the U.S.S.R. would not accept neutralization; "they are much better equipped to fight within a neutralized Laos than we are." At one point he said ruefully, "If I decided to do nothing, I could be an exceedingly popular President."

As he thought aloud, it was evident that he hoped to steer the course between intervention and retreat and end up somehow with neutralization. Lippmann and I proved of little help. Later that day the National Security Council discussed the possibility of moving a small number of American troops into the Mekong valley not to fight the Pathet Lao but to deter them by their presence and provide a bargaining counter for an international conference. Walt Rostow argued persuasively for this restricted commitment; but the Joint Chiefs opposed the sending of ground forces to the mainland of Asia, drawing a lurid picture of an all-out communist response, with thousands of Viet Minh pouring into Laos and the ultimate possibility of war with China. Their recommendation was all or nothing: either go in on a large scale, with 60,000 soldiers, air cover and even nuclear weapons, or else stay out.

The President himself was reluctant to order a limited

troop movement into the Mekong. He knew how weak the conventional strength of the United States was, and, with Cuba in the wings, troubles in Vietnam and the Congo and the ever-present problem of Berlin, he did not wish to tie up armed force indefinitely in Laos. Moreover, the diplomatic road was not finally blocked. The British with Kennedy's strong approval were about to reintroduce the ICC plan along with a proposal for a conference in Geneva to be called after verification of a cease-fire in Laos.

Neither the meeting on March 20 nor another session the next day reached a decision. Kennedy's objective remained a political settlement. True, if the Russians remained intransigent, he might have to take the next step—a limited commitment of troops along the Mekong; and this might lead to further steps. But, unless the Russians believed that he was ready to go down this road, there would be no incentive for them to accept a political solution. As for the American people, Kennedy saw contradictions in their feelings between the desire to 'get tough' with the communists and the disinclination to get involved in another Asian war; still, if the worst came, he was confident that they would support intervention.

The problem now, in Kennedy's judgment, was to make Moscow understand the choice it confronted: cease-fire and neutralization on the one hand; American intervention on the other. On March 23 his press conference took place against the unusual background of three maps of Laos illustrating the progress of communist encroachment. The Soviet Union, he said, had flown more than 1000 sorties into the battle area since December. There could be no peaceful solution without a "cessation of the present armed attacks by externally supported Communists." If the attacks do not stop, "those who support a genuinely neutral Laos will have to consider their response." As for the United States, no one should doubt its objective. "If in the past there has been any possible ground for misunderstanding of our desire for a truly neutral Laos, there should be none now." Nor should anyone doubt our resolution. "The security of all of Southeast Asia will be endangered if Laos loses its neutral independence. Its own safety runs with the safety of us all—in real neutrality observed by all. . . . I know that every American will want his country to honor its obligations to the point that freedom and security of the free world and ourselves may be achieved."

His tone was grave; and he backed it up with military and diplomatic action. The Seventh Fleet moved into the South China Sea, combat troops were alerted in Okinawa, and 500 Marines with helicopters moved into Thailand across the Mekong River from Vientiane. In Japan 2000 Marines, performing as extras for the film "Marine, Let's Go!" vanished from the set. On the diplomatic front Kennedy asked Nehru to support a cease-fire, which the Indian Prime Minister promptly did; and he arranged a quick meeting with Prime Minister Macmillan, then in the Caribbean, at Key West, where Macmillan reluctantly agreed that, if limited intervention along the Mekong became necessary, Britain would support it. Dean Rusk went to a SEATO conference at Bangkok on March 27 and secured troop pledges from Thailand, Pakistan and the Philippines, though French opposition prevented the organization as a whole from promising anything more specific than "appropriate" measures. In Washington the President saw Gromyko at the White House, took him to a bench in the Rose Garden and, observing that too many wars had arisen from miscalculation, said that Moscow must not misjudge the American determination to stop aggression in Southeast Asia. Chip Bohlen told me that night that Gromyko was "serious" this time, as he had not been in his talk with Rusk nine days earlier; obviously he had new instructions. The sense of acute tension over Laos appeared to be subsiding. For his part Khrushchev had no desire to send Russian troops to fight in the jungles of Laos and even less to set off a nuclear war. Moreover, he could console himself, and hopefully the Pathet Lao, with the thought which had already occurred to Kennedy and which Khrushchev put to Llewellyn Thompson in an expansive moment: "Why take risks over Laos? It will fall into our laps like a ripe apple." After weighing these various factors, Khrushchev on April 1 expressed readiness in principle to consider the British proposal.

4. THE HUNDREDTH DAY

Kennedy had won his first objective. But Khrushchev was at first unwilling to call for a cease-fire as the condition of an international conference. For more than three weeks the British and the Russians debated this point. It is not clear whether Khrushchev was stalling because he wanted time to explain his policy to the Pathet Lao and the Chinese or because he wanted to give the neutralist and communist forces the chance to occupy as much of Laos as they could: probably for both reasons. Certainly the Pathet Lao and Kong Le continued to make new gains and the Phoumi regime to show new weaknesses.

The fighting in these weeks made it more clear than ever

that a cease-fire would mean little if Laos lacked a government strong and stable enough to deal with the Pathet Lao. Kennedy had come early to doubt the briefings he received about the virtues of General Phoumi. In February, David Ormsby Gore, now a Member of Parliament and an Under Secretary of State in the Foreign Office, stopped by in Washington and, speaking with the bluntness of an old friend, offered a caustic picture of American policy in Laos. The United States, he said, had done its best to destroy Souvanna Phouma, who represented the best hope of a noncommunist Laos, and instead was backing a crooked, right-wing gang; the impression of Washington always rushing about to prop up corrupt dictators in Asia could not have happy consequences.

Then late in March Averell Harriman, on his first assignment as roving ambassador, arranged to see Souvanna Phouma in New Delhi. He did this without authorization from Washington. Accustomed to the informality of Franklin D. Roosevelt's diplomacy, when he would go off on the most delicate missions with a few lines of general guidance, he was not yet used to the postwar State Department and its habit of tethering envoys with pages of minute and comprehensive instruction. His talk with the Laotian prince was friendly. Souvanna said that the people of Laos did not wish to be communist and that Laos could be saved from communism, but that time was running out. He proposed the establishment of a coalition government, including the Pathet Lao, and the guarantee of Laotian neutrality by the fourteen-nation conference. He felt that, with the support of 90 per cent of the people, he had the authority to unite his country.

Harriman was favorably impressed. In addition, he had known Winthrop Brown from wartime days in London and had more confidence in Brown's estimate of Souvanna than in the State Department's inevitable judgment that the beleaguered prince was practically a communist. Washington, or at the least the White House, found Averell's testimony weighty. He was, after all, the most experienced and distinguished of American diplomats. Only his age had disqualified him from consideration as Secretary of State. He had spent much of his life in dealing with the Russians—ever since he had bargained with Trotsky over mining concessions in the twenties. During the Second World War he had worked with Roosevelt, Churchill and Stalin and attended nearly all the war-time conferences. He had served as ambassador to Moscow and London. He had run the Marshall Plan in Europe and had been Truman's national security adviser during the Korean War. In all these years he had not succumbed to illusions either about communism or about the anti-communist crusade.

His world trip had shown him the brilliance of the hopes excited by the new President. Convinced that America had not had such potentialities of world influence since the days of F.D.R., he bounded back to Washington filled with energy, purpose and ideas, looking years younger than he had in his last melancholy days as a New York politician. I remember his coming shortly after his return to a farewell dinner I gave for Ken Galbraith, who was about to depart on his new assignment as Ambassador to India. Harriman, in the highest of spirits, talked everyone down, especially the guest of honor; this last, of course, was no inconsiderable feat. When Harriman reported to the White House, he delighted Kennedy, who had known him in his political rather than his diplomatic role, with his freedom and vigor of mind in foreign matters, his realism of judgment and his unconcealed contempt for received opinion. The President concluded that Washington ought to take a new look at Souvanna, and the prince was encouraged to add the United States to his world tour. Souvanna scheduled his Washington visit for April 19-20 but then canceled it when Rusk said he had a speaking engagement in Georgia and could not receive him. Snubbed again, as he thought, Souvanna returned to Moscow.

In the end Rusk did not keep his Georgia engagement, for this was the week of the Bay of Pigs. On Thursday, April 20, Kennedy, determined not to permit restraint in Cuba to be construed as irresolution everywhere, transformed the corps of American military advisers in Laos, who up to this point had wandered about in civilian clothes, into a Military Assistance and Advisory Group, authorizing them to put on uniforms and accompany the Laotian troops. Later that day, when Nixon saw the President and urged an invasion of Cuba, he also urged "a commitment of American air power" to Laos. According to Nixon's recollection, Kennedy replied, "I just don't think we ought to get involved in Laos, particularly where we might find ourselves fighting millions of Chinese troops in the jungles. In any event, I don't see how we can make any move in Laos, which is 5000 miles away, if we don't make a move in Cuba, which is only 90 miles away." [2]

On April 24 the Russians finally agreed on the cease-

2 Richard M. Nixon, "Cuba, Castro and John F. Kennedy," *Reader's Digest*, November 1964.

fire appeal. They were perhaps impressed by the introduction of MAAG and undoubtedly swayed by the intervention of Nehru. (The Indian leader had been skeptical about the American desire for neutralization until Galbraith assured him that Americans were practical men and did not set military value on the Lao, "who do not believe in getting killed like the civilized races.") The next day the Laotian government gratefully accepted the call. So did Souvanna, still on his travels, and even Souphanouvong. But fighting did not cease; and, according to reports reaching Washington on Wednesday, April 26, the Pathet Lao were attacking in force, as if to overrun the country before the cease-fire could take effect. On Thursday the National Security Council held a long and confused session. Walt Rostow has told me that it was the worst White House meeting he attended in the entire Kennedy administration.

Rostow and the Laos task force, supported by Harriman who was now on a trip of inspection in Laos, still urged a limited commitment of American troops to the Mekong valley. But the Joint Chiefs, chastened by the Bay of Pigs, declined to guarantee the success of the military operation, even with the 60,000 men they had recommended a month before. The participants in the meeting found it hard to make out what the Chiefs were trying to say. Indeed, the military were so divided that Vice-President Johnson finally proposed that they put their views in writing in order to clarify their differences. The President, it is said, later received seven different memoranda, from the four Chiefs of Staff and three service secretaries. (It was about this time that a group of foreign students visited the White House and the President, introduced to a young lady from Laos, remarked, "Has anyone asked your advice yet?")

The military proved no more satisfactory in explaining the proposals they were prepared to make. The President was appalled at the sketchy nature of American military planning for Laos—the lack of detail and the unanswered questions. One day they suggested sending troops into two airstrips in Pathet Lao territory; they could land a thousand troops a day, and there were 5000 enemy guerrillas nearby. Kennedy, after interrogation, discovered that the airstrips could only be used by day and that it would take a week or so for troops to reach them overland. He then asked what would happen if the Pathet Lao allowed the troops to land for two days and then attacked. The military did not seem to have thought of that.

For all their differences, the military left a predominant impression that they did not want ground troops at all unless they could send at least 140,000 men equipped with tactical nuclear weapons. By now the Pentagon was developing what would become its standard line in Southeast Asia—unrelenting opposition to limited intervention except on the impossible condition that the President agree in advance to every further step they deemed sequential, including, on occasion, nuclear bombing of Hanoi and even Peking. At one National Security Council meeting General Lemnitzer outlined the processes by which each American action would provoke a Chinese counteraction, provoking in turn an even more drastic American response. He concluded: "If we are given the right to use nuclear weapons, we can guarantee victory." The President sat glumly rubbing his upper molar, saying nothing. After a moment someone said, "Mr. President, perhaps you would have the General explain to us what he means by victory." Kennedy grunted and dismissed the meeting. Later he said, "Since he couldn't think of any further escalation, he would have to promise us victory."

The Chiefs had their own way of reacting to the Cuban fiasco. It soon began to look to the White House as if they were taking care to build a record which would permit them to say that, whatever the President did, he acted against their advice. This had not yet been identified as a tactic, however, and in April 1961 their opposition to limited intervention had a powerful effect. As Robert Kennedy said, "If even the Marines don't want to go in!" Immediately afterward, the President encountered equally formidable opposition from congressional leaders. In New York that night for a speech, he gathered other opinions. General MacArthur expressed his old view that anyone wanting to commit American ground forces to the mainland of Asia should have his head examined. He added that, if we intervened anywhere in Southeast Asia, we must be prepared to use nuclear weapons should the Chinese enter in force. And there always remained the difficulty of justifying intervention against communism in Laos while rejecting it against communism in Cuba.

General Lemnitzer had already gone to Laos, where he joined Harriman. Once on the spot, Lemnitzer endorsed the case for the more limited commitment. When I returned from my post-Bay of Pigs trip to Europe on May 3, the President said, "If it hadn't been for Cuba, we might be about to intervene in Laos." Waving a sheaf of cables from Lemnitzer, he added, "I might have taken this advice seriously." But he was determined to avert total collapse. He

had, I believe, been prepared to undertake limited intervention in Laos before the Bay of Pigs, and he did not altogether exclude it now. Once again he ordered troops on
the alert. At Okinawa 10,000 Marines were ready to go.
Kennedy told Rostow that Eisenhower could stand the political consequences of Dien Bien Phu and the expulsion
of the west from Vietnam in 1954 because the blame fell on
the French; "I can't take a 1954 defeat today."

The Russians knew about the preparations, and they appeared to have their effect. Certainly the Pathet Lao probe
on Monday seemed less terrifying than it had the preceding
Thursday. On May 1 representatives of the warring factions
negotiated a cease-fire. The International Control Commission arrived on the scene and reported on May 11 "a general and obvious discontinuance of hostilities." The next
day the conference opened at Geneva to lay down the conditions for a neutralized Laos.

April 30 marked the hundredth day of the Kennedy administration. Either Cuba or Laos by itself would have
constituted a sufficient initiation into the horrors of the
Presidency; but Kennedy endured both with customary
composure. I saw him mostly those days in regard to Cuba;
but his occasional comments on Laos were invariably detached and dispassionate. His self-control helped produce
a corresponding calmness of public reaction. The Laos
crisis of 1961 differed greatly from the Dien Bien Phu
crisis of 1954, when vague and menacing statements by the
Vice-President, the Secretary of State and the chairman of
the Joint Chiefs of Staff heightened both popular and international tensions without leading to any useful result. Instead, Kennedy made quiet but hard military preparations,
let the Russians know about them and let them know at
the same time that there was an honorable alternative to
fighting. The outcome was to halt the imminent communization of Laos.

This was a first experiment in Kennedy diplomacy under
pressure, and it was marked by restraint of manner, toughness of intention and care to leave the adversary a way of
escape without loss of face. Khrushchev, for his part, found
himself involved with a group of local communist militants whose actions he could not entirely control and whose
allegiance he sought in the struggle for the international
communist movement. But he did not want war, and, once
he believed that Kennedy would fight if pushed too far, he
retreated to negotiation, confident that history would
eventually deliver what opposition had temporarily denied.

In retrospect, the Laos crisis of 1961 seems in some ways a dress rehearsal for the Cuban missile crisis of 1962.

5. COUNTERINSURGENCY

One quick effect of the Laos crisis was to lead the President to take up an old preoccupation from Senate days, now made more urgent by Khrushchev's January speech—the problem of countering guerrilla attack. If what he liked to call "the subterranean war" were to be the major form of communist aggression so long as the United States retained nuclear supremacy, then the Army must learn how to meet the guerrilla threat. The Philippines, Malaya and Greece showed that guerrilla warfare could be stopped, but not by close-order drill. In the next weeks and months he made anti-guerrilla instruction a personal project. Indeed, it required presidential backing; for the Army had fallen into the hands of 'organization generals' after the departure of Ridgway, Taylor and Gavin who looked on the counterinsurgency business as a faddish distraction from the main responsibility of training for conventional assault. The professionals, infatuated with the newest technology and eager to strike major blows, deeply disliked the thought of reversion to the rude weapons, amateur tactics, hard life and marginal effects of guerrilla warfare.

Guerrillas were also an old preoccupation of Walt Rostow's. When Kennedy read Lansdale's report about guerrilla success in Vietnam, he asked Rostow to check into what the Army was, in fact, doing about counterguerrilla training. He was soon informed that the Special Forces at Fort Bragg consisted of fewer than a thousand men. Looking at the field manuals and training literature, he tossed them aside as "meager" and inadequate. Reading Mao Tsetung and Ché Guevara himself on the subject, he told the Army to do likewise. (He used to entertain his wife on country weekends by inventing aphorisms in the manner of Mao's "Guerrillas must move among the people as fish swim in the sea.") He asked General Clifton, his military aide, to bring in the Army's standard anti-guerrilla equipment, examined it with sorrow and ordered Army research and development to do better. Most important of all, he instructed the Special Warfare Center at Fort Bragg to expand its mission, which had hitherto been largely the training of cadres for action behind the lines in case of a third world war, in order to confront the existing challenge of guerrilla warfare in the jungles and hills of underdeveloped countries. Over the opposition of the Army bureaucracy, which abhorred separate elite commands on principle, he reinstated the SF green beret as the symbol of the new force.

With the President's detailed support, Major General William P. Yarborough made the Special Warfare Center into a vigorous and ingenious seminary in the new methods. Other centers were set up in Panama, Okinawa, Vietnam and West Germany. In Washington, Robert Kennedy, Maxwell Taylor and Richard Bissell pushed the cause. Roger Hilsman, drawing on his wartime experience in the hills of Burma, and Walt Rostow, analyzing the guerrilla problem as part of the pathology of economic development, carried the gospel to the State Department. Eventually Foreign Service officers were even put through courses, sometimes of dubious value, in counterinsurgency methods. By the autumn of 1961 a Counter-Insurgency Committee under General Taylor set itself to developing the nation's capability for unconventional warfare.

There was, to be sure, a faddish aspect to this enthusiasm. Some of its advocates acted as if the delicate arts of blacking one's face and catching sentries by the throat in the night could by themselves eliminate the guerrilla threat. The President was under no such illusion. He insisted that the Special Forces be schooled in sanitation, teaching, bridge-building, medical care and the need for economic progress. I do not think he ever forgot Mao's warning that guerrilla action must fail "if its political objectives do not coincide with the aspirations of the people and their sympathy, cooperation and assistance cannot be gained." The problem of applying this maxim to Southeast Asia never ceased to trouble him.

XIV

ENCOUNTER IN EUROPE

"THE ONLY THING that really surprised us when we got into office," the President said late in May at a Democratic Party dinner in honor of his forty-fourth birthday, "was that things were just as bad as we had been saying they were; otherwise we have been enjoying it very much." The fragrant spring of 1961 found him, in spite of the trials of the first winter, in a cheerful mood. He had survived the crises of Cuba and of Laos. He had begun a reorganization of government which would enable him to meet crisis better in the future. He had watched Captain Alan Shepard improve the American position in space by rocketing 115 miles into the upper atmosphere. He was planning a trip to France to see General de Gaulle. And on May 12, he had received an unexpected reply from N. S. Khrushchev to his letter of February 22, reopening the question, presumed dead after the Bay of Pigs, of a meeting in Vienna in early June.

One event marred his buoyancy. In mid-May he went to Canada to return the visit that Prime Minister John Diefenbaker had paid him in Washington in February. The earlier meeting had not proved a success. Diefenbaker, who felt at home with Eisenhower, had been uneasy with the new President. Kennedy thought the Canadian insincere and did not like or trust him. The round of talks in Ottawa was civil enough, though a confidential memorandum from Walt Rostow to the President setting forth our objectives at the meeting somehow fell into Canadian hands and caused trouble later. At one point the President took part in a tree-planting ceremony in front of Government House. Forgetting to bend his knees and keep the shovel close to his body, he stood erect, held the shovel at arm's length and turned a few spadefuls of soil. A premonitory twinge deepened after a few hours into an acute and nagging ache. He had wrenched his back, severely straining the muscles so carefully restored in the years since he had first gone to Dr. Travell. The pain did not leave him for more than six months, and in the weeks of travel immediately ahead it was often sharp and exhausting.

1. BACKGROUND IN BERLIN

What had led Khrushchev to renew the idea of a meeting with Kennedy? His letter, though noting his objections to the Bay of Pigs, reciprocated Kennedy's February hope for better relations and named Laos, disarmament and Germany as leading topics for an exchange of views. No doubt, like Kennedy, Khrushchev was curious about his adversary and eager to take his measure. No doubt too the Bay of Pigs had left him with an impression of the American President as an irresolute young man, incapable of the sort of drastic action Khrushchev himself had undertaken in Hungary; if this were so, then the Russian leader might hope to bully him in direct encounter as he had bullied

so many other heads of state. More specifically, the occasion would give him a chance to resume the campaign,
begun by Stalin thirteen years before, to drive the west
out of Berlin.

For Khrushchev, the German question had become increasingly exasperating. In his speech of January 6, he had
declared the allied position "especially vulnerable" in West
Berlin, adding ominously that, if the democracies did not
come to their senses and make the required adjustments, the
Soviet Union would sign a peace treaty with the communist state of East Germany—an act which, in Khrushchev's view, would terminate the legal basis for the western presence in Berlin. That basis rested on the wartime
agreements which divided Germany into four zones and established four-power control of the German capital. In 1945
these arrangements were intended only to tide things over
until the wartime allies negotiated a final peace settlement
with a post-Hitler German regime. But, as that hope perished with the spread of the cold war, the democratic allies
and the Soviet Union began to convert their zones into
separate German states—the Federal Republic in the west
and the so-called Democratic Republic in the east. Only
Berlin itself, though split into west and east sectors, retained four-power status. Situated in the midst of the Soviet
zone, West Berlin, with its independent administration and
its allied garrison, was now the last democratic outpost on
the communist side of the Iron Curtain.

From an early point the Soviet Union had regarded the
western presence in Berlin as intolerable. In 1948 Stalin
tried to force the allies out, but his blockade succeeded
only in producing the great western airlift in response.
Moscow knew that it could not raise the bidding to military
action without risking atomic war; and, after 321 days of
stalemate, Stalin, who had no atomic bombs, accepted defeat. For the next nine years West and East Berlin went
their separate ways. In these years, however, the Russians
acquired the bomb themselves and thereby lowered the
probability of a western nuclear response. This gave
Khrushchev freedom for maneuver; and in the late fifties he
began to mount a new world offensive. To immobilize the
west he encouraged ban-the-bomb movements and avowed
his passion for peaceful coexistence; to spread communism
he utilized local subversion, wars of national liberation
and the threat of nuclear war. Like his predecessor, he
found the western presence in Berlin particularly objectionable; with the communist penchant for medical meta-

phor, Khrushchev described West Berlin, according to mood, as a bone in the throat or a cancerous tumor. A few months after the first sputnik sailed through the skies, he took advantage of the changing balance of nuclear force to resume Stalin's 1948 campaign. This culminated in November 1958 in demands that the allied occupation end and West Berlin be made a demilitarized 'free city.' If the west did not accept the Soviet plan within six months, Khrushchev said, Russia would sign its own peace treaty with the Democratic Republic.

A number of motives evidently lay behind Khrushchev's action. Europe constituted the single anomaly in the picture which gave the Soviet leaders such satisfaction everywhere else they looked. In Asia, in Africa, in Latin America, in industrial growth, in space, communism was on the offensive. But in Europe communism had been in retreat ever since the late forties—from the time of the Marshall Plan and the organization of NATO. Not only had Western Europe recovered its economic and political vitality, but communist Eastern Europe had been shaken recurrently by revolts against Moscow—Yugoslavia in 1948, East Germany in 1953, Hungary in 1956. At the very least, Berlin offered the opportunity to consolidate the communist position in East Germany and legitimatize the existing territorial division of Europe. If Khrushchev could force the west to grant East Germany legal recognition, he would not only secure the status quo throughout Eastern Europe but would demoralize the West German government in Bonn, disrupt NATO, stop the momentum of western unification and regain the European offensive. And, if he attained his maximum objective and drove the allies out of Berlin, he would subject the west to a humiliation which would weaken it all around the globe and complete the alteration of the world balance of power.

The western leaders for their part found the 'free city' proposal unacceptable. It applied, of course, only to West Berlin; and it would have meant the introduction of Soviet troops into the non-communist part of the city, as well as the prohibition there of what Khrushchev called "hostile subversive activity"—i.e., criticism of communism. Its practical effect would have been to place West Berlin at the mercy of East Germany and the Soviet Union. When Khrushchev made his American trip in 1959, Eisenhower therefore avoided the 'free city' idea. But he did accept the Soviet description of the Berlin situation as "abnormal" (as indeed it was, though it was not discreet to say so); and his administration soon laid certain concessions on the negotiating table, including limitations on the size of the western garrison as well as on democratic propaganda and intelligence activities. Khrushchev meanwhile postponed his six-month deadline.

Some Democrats, like Stevenson and Harriman, were prepared to trade legal points for definitive guarantees of Allied presence and access. Others, like Acheson, regarded all concessions as dangerous. Berlin, Acheson wrote early in 1959, might offer "the hardest test of the West's will and determination since June 1950, when the Communists attacked in Korea." As a Senator, Kennedy had repeatedly emphasized the gravity of the stakes in Berlin. In July 1960 he predicted on Meet the Press that by the next January or February Khrushchev would "face the next President of the United States with a very difficult decision, perhaps even an ultimatum on Berlin." He added: "We should make it very clear that we are not going to concede our position on Berlin, that we are going to meet our commitment to defend the liberty of the people of West Berlin, and that if Mr. Khrushchev pushes it to the ultimate, we are prepared to meet our obligation."

In the months after the U-2 incident and the collapse of the Paris summit, the Berlin problem seemed to subside. As late as the end of March 1961, a Moscow meeting of the Warsaw Pact countries adjourned without mention of Berlin. But there were portents: first, Khrushchev's menacing remark in his January 6 speech; then his subsequent statements to Ambassador Thompson that he had made commitments about Berlin, his prestige was engaged and he had waited long enough.

It is evident that by 1961 local considerations in East Germany were giving Khrushchev an almost desperate feeling that he had to do something. He was, or claimed to be, afraid that West Germany was about to acquire nuclear weapons; and, as he told Walter Lippmann in the spring, he wanted to fix the status of Berlin and the two Germanys before Bonn, emboldened by possession of the bomb, could take advantage of the unsettled demarcation line to move against East Germany. Even worse was the rising stream of refugees fleeing from East Germany, now on the order of four thousand a week. The contrast between the glum and tacky despotism of East Berlin and the exuberant prosperity of West Berlin, with its gleaming new buildings, blazing lights and spirited intellectual life, was too much; and the resulting exodus not only made propaganda about the superiority of communism look foolish but was fast draining East Germany of the professionals and technicians so vital to its future. Indeed, the total population of East Germany declined by nearly two million between 1949 and mid-1961. If Khrushchev now moved against West Berlin, he could still hope to inflict a world-wide political and moral defeat on the democracies, and, even if he did not do this, he could at least stop the flight to the west and stabilize the territorial status quo in Europe.

He may conceivably too have had some genuine fears about the new American administration. Kennedy himself, with characteristic detachment, used to wonder later what had gone wrong in the spring of 1961. He thought at times that the March and May messages calling for an increased American defense effort might have sounded too threatening. It is possible that the acceleration of the Minuteman and Polaris programs had unintended effects in Moscow and that, as Kuznetsov had warned Wiesner and Rostow at the Pugwash meeting, the Soviet leaders now saw no choice but to match the American build-up. In addition, Harriman in his March debut as roving ambassador had said that "all discussions in Berlin must begin from the start." This was a move to disengage Kennedy from the concessions the Eisenhower administration had made in 1959 and even more from the ones we had been informed Eisenhower was ready to make at the 1960 summit meeting in Paris; but Moscow no doubt read it as a hardening of American policy. Yet at the same time the Soviet signals were not, seen from Washington, very encouraging. Khrushchev's truculent speech of January preceded Kennedy's defense messages by many weeks; and his decision to move against West Berlin had ample explanation in his own problems and ambitions.

As for the President, he saw no sense in meeting Khrushchev unless something of substance was likely to result. When the Attorney General made this point to the Soviet Ambassador, he was given to understand that progress was entirely conceivable on Laos and on the test ban. Beyond these specific problems, the President was attracted by the meeting as offering an opportunity to define the framework for future American-Soviet relations. Kennedy saw the world as in a state of uncontrollable change, rushing in directions no one could foresee. The equilibrium of force, he believed, was now roughly in balance between the United States and the Soviet Union—if not in the sense of numerical parity, at least in the sense that neither could hope to destroy the other and emerge unscathed; and the overriding need, he felt, was to prevent direct confrontations between Russian and American power in the chaotic time ahead. He intended to propose, in effect, a standstill in the cold war so that neither great nuclear state, in the inevitable competition around the planet, would find itself committed to actions which would risk its essential security, threaten the existing balance of force or endanger world peace. In particular, if, as Ambassador Thompson's dispatches forecast, Khrushchev meant to get tough over Berlin, Kennedy wished to make clear, in a favorite Washington phrase that spring, that Khrushchev must not crowd him too much.

With such thoughts in mind, Kennedy prepared to leave for Europe. Jacqueline was to come with him. She still had not altogether recovered from John's birth, but a week in the country at the end of May enabled her to sleep and build strength. When Nicole Alphand, the wife of the French ambassador to Washington, asked her whether there was anything special she wanted to do in Paris, she said only that she hoped to meet André Malraux. The President engaged in a quick round of speeches before their departure. "I go to see Mr. Khrushchev in Vienna," he said in Boston on May 29. "I go as the leader of the greatest revolutionary country on earth." Some people regard the United States as "a fixed society," but "that is not my view." On May 30 he lightly told a dinner of the Eleanor Roosevelt Cancer Foundation in New York, "It is now one-thirty in Paris, and I am due there at ten-thirty, and I do not believe it would be a good start to keep the General waiting."

2. INTERLUDE IN PARIS

The General did not have to wait. He met the Kennedys at Orly and escorted them to their apartments at the Quai d'Orsay. Parisians lined the streets to admire the young couple and cheer the motorcade. As the presidential car moved through the Latin Quarter, American students enthusiastically waved a Harvard banner. On arrival Kennedy took a steaming bath to ease the pain of his back. Then he was almost immediately on his way again for his opening talk with the General.

They had not talked together before. When Jacqueline met de Gaulle at the embassy in Washington during his visit in 1960, Kennedy had been campaigning in Oregon. Now the two men sat alone with their interpreters in the splendid presidential office in the Elysée Palace. De Gaulle had courteously provided American and French cigarettes for his visitor. Kennedy, equally courteous and remembering that tobacco troubled his host's sensitive eyes, refrained from smoking them (and also from smoking the cigars he had in his pocket).

Wasting little time in preliminaries, Kennedy cited Khrushchev's warnings to Thompson about Berlin. He saw two possibilities for the allies in view of the evident Russian determination to press the issue: either to refuse discussions on the ground that the rights of presence and access and the status of Berlin were not negotiable, or to give an appearance of negotiation by opening the future status of Berlin as a subject for discussion. De Gaulle commented that Khrushchev had been threatening action on Berlin and laying down six-month deadlines for two and a half years. Surely if he planned to go to war over Berlin, he would have done so already. He recalled his own remark to Khrushchev that, while it was too bad that Berlin was situated in the Soviet zone, there it was, and its future could be solved only within a framework of general *détente* and disarmament.

The problem, Kennedy said, was whether Khrushchev really believed in the firmness of the west; even President de Gaulle himself had recently questioned whether the United States was ready to defend Paris at the risk of the obliteration of New York. De Gaulle remarked that the west simply could not retreat; it could not withdraw its troops or accept obstacles to access or permit a change in the status of West Berlin. Make it clear, he advised Kennedy, that it was the Russians, and not the west, who sought a change; we were not asking for anything. The allies could not stop Khrushchev from signing whatever he wanted with East Germany, but no internal communist document could alter the status of Berlin. If Khrushchev wanted war, he must understand that he would have it at the first moment he used force against us. De Gaulle added that the west could not win a military victory in Berlin; Khrushchev must be made to recognize that fighting around Berlin would mean a general war. The General insisted again that this was the last thing Khrushchev wanted.

But now it was time for luncheon. Jacqueline sat by the General and engaged him in animated conversation in French about French history—Louis XVI, and the Duc d'Angoulême and the dynastic complexities of the later Bourbons—until de Gaulle leaned across the table and told Kennedy that his wife knew more French history than most French women. (Kennedy, delighted, later said that it was as if Mme. de Gaulle had sat next to him and asked him all about Henry Clay.) It was a gay occasion. At one point, de Gaulle gestured at McGeorge Bundy, who was sitting across the table, and said imperiously, "Qui est ce jeune homme?" Jacqueline explained that he was a brilliant Harvard professor who now ran the National Security Council staff. De Gaulle, with a stately inclination of his head, said something about Harvard to Bundy in elaborately slow French, as if to someone not likely to understand the language. When Bundy responded in easy and fluent French, the Americans felt: Score one for our side.

After luncheon the two Presidents resumed their talk. Kennedy returned to the problem of how to convince the Russians that the west was in earnest. The existing allied military plans, based on the assumption of very limited Russian probes, seemed to him inadequate. What if the Russians sent in not a company but a brigade or a division? Or what if they undertook a series of steps, none of which by itself constituted a sufficient provocation but all of which together would destroy our position? We must make our policy clear by action, Kennedy said, and Khrushchev must understand that, if necessary, we would go to nuclear war. De Gaulle, responding, put special emphasis on preparing for a new western airlift; after all, there could be no ambiguity when a plane was shot down. He also noted that Russia needed western trade and might be vulnerable to economic retaliation. The western position in Berlin, he said, was not so weak as people thought.

Kennedy turned the conversation to Laos. De Gaulle observed that the countries of Southeast Asia did not offer a good terrain for western troops, nor indeed for western politics. Unlike India and Japan, which were "real" nations, these were "fictitious" nations, and neutralization was the best solution. The French experience had been that exerting influence in Southeast Asia and taking military action there were almost incompatible. As for Laos, de Gaulle strongly supported the idea of a neutral coalition under Souvanna Phouma. In no case would the French dream of military intervention; but, when Kennedy argued that the threat of western intervention might be necessary to bring the communists to an agreement, de Gaulle said that he would not oppose the United States publicly. They talked for a moment about the tension between Peking and Moscow. Kennedy expressed doubts that the split would become acute until the west was forced out of the area; the rivalry between Caesar and Pompey, he recalled, came into the open only after they subdued their common enemies. Then they touched briefly on Africa, and de Gaulle reaffirmed French opposition to UN operations in the Congo.

As they prepared to break up, de Gaulle paused, charmingly cited the prerogatives of age and ventured to suggest that the President not pay too much attention to his advisers or give too much respect to the policies he had inherited. In the last analysis, the General said, what counted for every man was himself and his own judgment. He was expounding, of course, the Gaullist philosophy of leadership. His counsel, after the Bay of Pigs, fell on receptive ears.

More ceremony followed—meetings with the diplomatic corps, a visit to the Arc de Triomphe, a state dinner at the Elysée, with treatment for the ailing back in between. Malraux was at the Elysée, white and taut; his sons had been killed in an automobile crash a few days before. Mrs. Kennedy was deeply moved at his appearance, and an enduring friendship began. The Parisians cheered the President, but it was now apparent that, as much as they liked him, it was his wife whom they adored. Her softly glowing beauty, her mastery of the language, her passion for the arts, her perfection of style—all were conquering the skeptical city. This was a good deal more than the instinctive French response to a charming woman. It had the air of a startled rediscovery of America as a new society, young and cosmopolitan and sophisticated, capable of aspiring to the leadership of the civilized peoples.

The next morning the talks resumed. Latin America de Gaulle freely acknowledged as a primary American responsibility, but he asserted that common cultural ties gave France a particular access and role; Kennedy said he welcomed French contributions to Latin American development. They returned to Africa, dealing particularly with Angola, where Portugal was clinging to rigid colonial policies in the face of the native demand for self-government. De Gaulle agreed that the Portuguese attitude was inflexible and obsolescent; but pushing Salazar too hard, he said, might cause a revolution in Portugal and establish a communist state in the Iberian peninsula. Kennedy replied that change in Africa was inexorable and the attempt to block it would only benefit the communists. The United States therefore had determined to take a progressive position on Angola in the UN. De Gaulle agreed to encourage Salazar toward more constructive policies and said that, while he could not support the American position, he would not oppose it.

After luncheon on June 1 Kennedy moved into trickier country and raised the problem of NATO. De Gaulle in a flow of felicitous exposition said that NATO was two things: an alliance and an organization. No one questioned the need for the alliance, but the organization in its present form had outlived its time. Its essence had been the defense of Europe by American nuclear weapons; its occasion, the weakness of the Western European states; its result, the integration under American leadership of European contributions to the American defense of Europe. But the world had changed. Washington no longer possessed its nuclear monopoly, and this fact reduced the value of the American nuclear sword. Moreover, America had commitments in all parts of the world. And in Europe the revival of national pride, especially in France, meant that integrated defense under American command was no longer acceptable. The recent revolt of French generals against their government, de Gaulle said, was perhaps a result of the denationalization of defense; the generals, feeling no responsibility for the protection of France, felt no loyalty to the government of France. And the absence of national defense, he argued, weakened the alliance because only national motives could rally the full support of a population in a prolonged war. While France would do nothing to disrupt the existing organization during the Berlin crisis, the President must understand that it sought a different organization for the future. Since no one could be confident any longer that the United States would use nuclear weapons first, the future security of Europe had to be assured by European countries, not without the United States but not exclusively through the United States.

Kennedy responded with equal bluntness. For the United States, he said, the defense of Europe and of America was the same. American troops were stationed in Europe to remind Moscow that an attack on Europe automatically constituted an attack on America. If the Soviet Union threatened to overrun Western Europe, the United States was prepared to respond with nuclear weapons. The advantages were so great to the side which used nuclear weapons first, Kennedy emphasized, that the United States could not afford to hold back its nuclear arm even if the Russians used only conventional forces. If the European states built separate defense establishments, he added, this would create new problems; those states which had no nuclear weapons would be forced toward resentment and neutralism.

De Gaulle commented that all this would be fine if the Russians really believed that America would use its nuclear

weapons in defense of other states; but he doubted whether
Moscow did; he even doubted whether the Americans believed it. No state could be expected to place atomic weapons at the disposal of another state. That is why he did not
ask the United States for atomic weapons or even for assistance in developing French atomic power. The United
States, in his judgment, would use nuclear weapons only
when its own territory was directly threatened; and why
not? This was the way states behaved. France or Russia
would do no differently. If Kennedy said that Americans
regarded Europe and the United States as the same, "since
you say so, Mr. President, I believe you," but could anyone
be really certain? If he sat in Kennedy's place, de Gaulle
said, he would not be certain himself when or where he
intended to use these weapons. After all, had not the United
States already raised the threshold—that is, postponed the
point at which nuclear weapons were scheduled to come
into play?

Kennedy explained that raising the threshold meant only
making sure that local clashes would not lead to nuclear
war; it meant not a decrease in commitment but an increase in control. Obviously any attack which challenged
NATO would rise above the threshold. The General must
understand that the United States, though isolationist as
late as the Second World War, had changed. The American response to aggression in Korea should reassure our
allies. Only as we strengthened confidence among ourselves
could we convince Moscow that we would stand firm in
Berlin.

At this point they adjourned; and that evening de Gaulle
threw a dazzling dinner in the Hall of Mirrors at Versailles.
Jacqueline, fresh from a fascinating day with Malraux at
the Jeu de Paume and Malmaison, glittered in a Givenchy
gown. At they walked to the Louis XV theater for a ballet
performance, passing down the long hall filled with statuary,
Kennedy stopped and inquired about one statue. Malraux,
impressed, asked the interpreter to tell the President that
he had picked the only one that was not a fake.

During dinner Kennedy talked to de Gaulle about Churchill and Roosevelt. Churchill, the General said, was a fighter,
casual in manner, extremely interesting some days, totally
impossible others. His policy was short-run, designed to
meet immediate problems. Like all Englishmen he was a
merchant, bargaining, for example, with Russia, prepared to
make concessions in the east in return for a free hand elsewhere. Roosevelt, on the other hand, was always charming,
always the aristocrat. He had a long-run policy but was

often mistaken in that policy, as about the Soviet Union. Kennedy wondered whom de Gaulle preferred. The General replied that he had quarreled violently and bitterly with Churchill but always felt a basic accord with him. He had never quarreled openly with Roosevelt but never felt a moment of rapport.

On Friday morning, June 2, Kennedy and de Gaulle, still alone with their interpreters, held their fifth meeting. Kennedy, feeling de Gaulle out some more on the alliance, mentioned the possibility of giving NATO increased control of nuclear weapons—for example, releasing Polaris submarines to NATO countries under an arrangement which would place the decision for their use in an authority to be determined by the United States, Britain and France. Would not such an arrangement remove doubts about American readiness to act? De Gaulle replied that nuclear weapons, even if nominally under NATO control, would be in fact under American control—which was natural enough and nothing for which America could be reproached. But such nominal transfer would not constitute the defense of Europe by Europeans, nor would it answer the question: when would nuclear weapons be used? The need therefore remained for Europe to organize its own defense, in association with the United States, of course, but under its own responsibility. Kennedy reiterated his assurance that either a massive conventional attack or the threat of a nuclear attack would produce a nuclear strike against the Soviet Union. De Gaulle remained dubious. Perhaps the situation would never be clear enough; remember that Hitler took over Europe bit by bit.

Later in the morning de Gaulle and Kennedy joined their advisers in a larger meeting. De Gaulle summed up the talks with customary elegance. At the end he said how pleased he had been to meet the President and to perceive his great future—a future which he himself could not share since he would soon be yielding the reins of power to younger men. He believed that he and the President might be taking dramatic actions together, but of course no one could know exactly what might lie ahead. The atmosphere of the talks had been excellent; never had the common destinies of the two nations been closer. The Franco-American alliance was fundamental to France; all the rest was machinery. Kennedy responded that his most vivid impression of France had been not even the magnificence of Versailles but the force and vitality of the French people.

The President now went off to a luncheon for the press, introducing himself: "I am the man who accompanied

Jacqueline Kennedy to Paris, and I have enjoyed it." He gave a frank appraisal of the changing shape of problems in Europe. The policies of the late forties, he said, were no longer "adequate" for the circumstances of the sixties. "All of the power relationships in the world have changed in the last fifteen years, and therefore our policies must take these changes into account." Europe had grown in strength and unity. America had lost its nuclear monopoly and had become "vulnerable to attack"; this had reinforced our view that "your defense and ours is indivisible." And, because of the extraordinary rebirth of Europe, the struggle had switched to the southern half of the planet, where the threat was "not from massive land armies but from subversion, insurrection and despair"; the time had therefore come for a "concerted attack on poverty, injustice and oppression" in the developing world.

In asides intended for Vienna, he affirmed "strong hopes" for a test ban agreement in Geneva and a cease-fire in Laos. He was going to Vienna, above all, he said, so that he and Khrushchev could understand each other's purposes and interests and therefore avoid the "serious miscalculations" which had produced the earlier wars of the century. In the questioning which followed, someone asked what he would think if he were in Khrushchev's place. He replied that, if he had lived Khrushchev's life, he conceivably would draw Khrushchev's conclusion that communism had the momentum of historical inevitability; but that he himself took "a somewhat different view of the tide of history."

In the afternoon he met alone with de Gaulle for a final talk. Kennedy first proposed the consideration of mechanisms of consultation, both political and military, among France, Britain and the United States. De Gaulle agreed, suggesting that the matter might be discussed after the German elections. They then talked about the question of British membership in the Common Market, which Kennedy had told Macmillan he would raise in Paris. The President noted that, while the Common Market would create economic problems for the United States, he believed that it would greatly strengthen Europe, politically as well as economically, and that for this reason its advantages, even to America, far outweighed its drawbacks. To realize the maximum benefit he hoped that Britain would become a member. De Gaulle's response was reserved though dispassionate. He expressed doubt whether Britain really wanted full membership; the British, he said, always preferred the role of brokers. They could have the Commonwealth preference system or the Common Market but not both. In any case the door was open; but, as for himself, he thought British membership should be full or none.

The two men parted on this slightly inauspicious note. The conversations had nevertheless been candid and searching, and both were pleased with them. The meeting was of course pervaded by the contrast between the imperturbable nationalist, serenely certain that the classical state was the permanent and irreducible unit of international life, conducting a policy of national grandeur and expecting other leaders, if they had any sense, to do likewise; and the reasoned pragmatist, convinced that the world was changing and forever interested in testing out new patterns and possibilities. But the philosophical clash was muted. In 1961 each man was primarily concerned with exploring the mind of the other; and in any case, so long as the Algerian war lasted, de Gaulle was not free to pursue, or even to disclose, his designs for Europe. The talks turned up no insuperable obstacles to cooperation and perhaps left the General with a momentary hope that he was on the verge of achieving the aims he had been seeking since he had proposed a Franco-Anglo-American directorate in 1958: the recognition of France as the spokesman for continental Europe, the establishment of mechanisms for joint political and strategic planning, even possibly a French veto over the use of American nuclear weapons. The General had begun with a benignly avuncular attitude toward a young man not even born until Captain de Gaulle had fought three years on the western front in the First World War. The French leader came away with the impression of the American President as *un homme sérieux*, fully aware of the weight of the responsibilities he had accepted and fully capable of meeting them.

As for Kennedy, he had long been fascinated by the idea of de Gaulle—this great and gloomy figure, pitting himself against the probabilities of history and then recording the results in such eloquent and fastidious prose. The Paris meeting increased his understanding of the clarity and tenacity, though not yet of the ferocity, of de Gaulle's vision of Europe and the world.

3. DISUNION IN VIENNA

And so on to Austria, the great plane touching down at the Vienna airport on a gray and rainy Saturday morning. The presidential party motored through crowded streets to the American Embassy. Khrushchev had arrived the day before, and the talks were scheduled to begin almost at once. At 12:45 the Soviet Chairman came to the embassy. A few moments later they were seated in the music room, the two principals, their interpreters and aides—for the Americans, Rusk, Thompson, Bohlen and Foy Kohler, Assistant Secretary for European Affairs; and for the Russians, Gromyko, Mikhail Menshikov, the Soviet ambassador to Washington, and Anatoly Dobrynin, the chief of the American bureau in the Soviet Foreign Ministry.

Kennedy had met Khrushchev briefly in 1959 with the Senate Foreign Relations Committee during the Soviet leader's visit to the United States. Striking immediately a note at once jovial and edged, Khrushchev recalled that Kennedy had been late and there had been no opportunity to say much more than hello and goodbye. He had told Kennedy then, he remembered, that he had heard of him as a promising man in politics. He was gratified now to meet him as President. Kennedy replied equably that Khrushchev had remarked on his youthful appearance in 1959; he had aged since then. There was more such badinage, Khrushchev observing that he would be happy to split his years with the President or exchange ages with him. (Later, when Khrushchev contrasted the Soviet Union and the United States as young and old nations, Kennedy said, "If you'll look across the table, you'll see that we're not so old.")

Kennedy now expressed his hope that the meeting would lead to a better understanding of common problems. To his mind, the question was how two great nations, with different social systems, confronting each other across the world, could avoid head-on collision in an era of great change. Khrushchev went instantly on the offensive. The Soviet Union, he said, had tried for a long time to develop friendly relations with the United States. But it refused to do so at the expense of other peoples because agreements of this sort would not bring peace. America must understand that communism has won its right to grow and develop. The premise of John Foster Dulles's policy had been the liquidation of communism; this philosophy could never lead to good relations. He would not hope to persuade the President of the merits of communism, Khrushchev said, any more than he expected the President to waste time trying to convert him to capitalism. But de facto recognition of the existence of communism was indispensable.

Kennedy observed courteously that Americans were impressed by the economic achievement of the Soviet Union; it was a source of satisfaction to the whole world. But, as he saw the problem, it was not that the democracies were trying to eliminate communism in areas under communist control, but that the communists were trying to eliminate free systems in areas associated with the west. Khrushchev brusquely rejected this. It was impossible, he said, for the Soviet Union to implant its policy in other states. All the Soviet Union claimed was that communism would triumph; this was not propaganda but a scientific analysis of social development. Communism was superseding capitalism today as capitalism had superseded feudalism in the past. Changes in social systems were bound to come, but they would be brought about only by the will of the people themselves. The Communists believed in their systems, as the President believed in his. In any event, this was a matter for debate, not for war. The Soviet desire for general and complete disarmament proved its intention not to resort to arms.

The great need, Kennedy commented, was for each side to understand the other's views. The American position was that people should have freedom of choice. When communist minorities seized control against the popular will, the Chairman regarded this as historical inevitability; we did not, and this brought our two nations into conflict. Obviously we could not avoid disagreement, but we could avoid the direct confrontation of our military forces. Our interest here was to make clear why we were concerned about what the communists called inevitability.

This led Khrushchev into a sententious discourse on intellectual freedom. Did the United States, he asked, plan to build a dam against the development of the human mind and conscience? The Inquisition had burned people but could not burn their ideas, and eventually the ideas prevailed. History must be the judge in a competition of ideas. If capitalism could insure a better life, it would win. If not, communism would win; but this would be a victory of ideas, not of arms.

To this Kennedy responded that the two powers shared the obligation to conduct the competition of ideas without involving vital national interests. Khrushchev said sharply that he hoped he had misunderstood this remark. Did the President hold the Soviet Union responsible for the development of communist ideas? Did he mean that communism should exist only in countries already communist and that, if it developed elsewhere, the United States would be in conflict with the Soviet Union? This view was incorrect; and, if that was really the way the United States thought, conflict could not be avoided. Ideas did not belong to one nation. Once born, they grew. No immunization was possible against them. The only rule was that they should not be propagated by arms nor by intervention in the internal affairs of other countries. He could guarantee that the Soviet Union would never impose ideas by war.

Kennedy quoted Mao Tse-tung's remark that power came out of the end of the rifle. Khrushchev blandly denied that Mao ever said this, Mao was a Marxist, and Marxists were against war. Kennedy repeated that Khrushchev must understand the American views; if our two nations failed to preserve the peace, the whole world would be the loser. "My ambition," Kennedy said, "is to secure peace." The greatest danger was the miscalculation by one power of the interests and policy of another.

The word "miscalculation" irritated Khrushchev. It was a vague term, he said, and it suggested to him that America wanted the Soviet Union to sit like a schoolboy with hands on the top of the desk. The Soviet Union held its ideas in high esteem and declined to guarantee that they would stop at the Russian frontier. He did not understand the American theory of what Russia had to do to maintain the peace. The Soviet Union was going to defend its vital interests, whether or not the United States regarded such acts as miscalculations; it did not want war, but it would not be intimidated either. Of course war would be fatal; both sides would lose equally and be punished equally. But the west should put the word "miscalculation" into cold storage, for its use did not impress the Soviet Union at all.

By "miscalculation," Kennedy patiently explained, he meant the difficulty of predicting what any country might do next. The United States itself had made misjudgments, as when it failed to foresee Chinese intervention in the Korean War. The purpose of the meeting, as he saw it, was to introduce precision into each side's assessments and thereby minimize the risks of misjudgment. Khrushchev, retreating to jolliness, commented that, if the meeting succeeded, the expenses of bringing it about would be well justified. If it failed, not only would the money be wasted but the hopes of the people of the world would be betrayed.

It was time for lunch. The conversation had been civil but tough. Khrushchev had not given way before Kennedy's reasonableness, nor Kennedy before Khrushchev's intransigence. Badinage took over again at the luncheon table. Noticing two medals on Khrushchev's chest, Kennedy asked what they were. The Soviet Chairman identified them as

Lenin Peace Medals. The American President observed, perhaps a trifle grimly, "I hope you keep them." They traded stories about the problems of sending rockets to the moon. Kennedy asked why the United States and the Soviet Union should not go to the moon together. Khrushchev at first said no, then, reflecting, said, "All right, why not?" Kennedy observed that his wife thought that Gromyko had a nice smile. Khrushchev commented that some people said Gromyko looked like Nixon.

The luncheon ended with toasts. Kennedy said that, having welcomed Khrushchev to the United States in 1959, he was now glad to welcome him to this small piece of the United States in Vienna. Khrushchev rose to his feet in a free-wheeling mood and began reminiscing about Eisenhower. He had respected Eisenhower, he said, and regretted the unhappy development of their relations. He was almost certain that Eisenhower had not known about the U-2 flight but in a spirit of chivalry had decided to take responsibility for it. He was sorry never to have been able to receive Eisenhower in the Soviet Union, and he hoped to receive Kennedy when the time was ripe. The road was open, but a caution was in order. Nixon had hoped to convert the Russian people to capitalism by showing them a dream kitchen, which did not exist and never would exist. He apologized, Khrushchev said, for mentioning Nixon, an American citizen, but only Nixon could have thought of such nonsense.

He rambled on. He objected, he said, to the language of commercial bargaining so often used in dealings with the Soviet Union—'you give this and we'll give that.' What was he supposed to concede? He was blamed for Communist parties in other countries, but he did not even know who their leaders were; he was too busy at home. After all, Marx and Engels had invented communism, so, if anyone was to blame, it was the Germans. He added that that was a joke. More seriously, he wanted to say that Russians admired Americans, especially their technical achievements. We might be at opposite poles ideologically, but that should not stop us from working for a better future for our peoples. He envied the President his youth, Khrushchev said; if he were as young, he would be devoting even more energy to the cause, but at the age of sixty-seven he was still not renouncing the competition.

Kennedy and Khrushchev strolled in the garden for a moment after luncheon. Then they resumed the discussion. Kennedy restated his thesis: change was inevitable, but war would be catastrophic in the nuclear age; both sides must therefore take care to avoid situations which might lead

338 A THOUSAND DAYS

to war. As for miscalculation, every leader had to make judgments; he himself had miscalculated about the Bay of Pigs. He had to estimate what the Soviet Union would do, just as Khrushchev had to estimate about the United States. If we could only reduce the margin of uncertainty in such calculations, then our two nations might survive the period of competition without nuclear war.

All right, said Khrushchev, but how could we work anything out when the United States regarded revolution anywhere as the result of communist machinations? It was really the United States which caused revolution by backing reactionary governments: look at Iran, look at Cuba. Fidel Castro was not a Communist, but American policy was making him one. Khrushchev himself had not been born a Communist; the capitalists had converted him. Kennedy's assumption that revolution was the consequence of intervention was dangerous. And, after all, it was the United States which had set the precedent for intervention.

Kennedy disclaimed any brief for Batista; as for Iran, if the Shah did not improve conditions for the people, change would be inevitable. This, he protested, was not the issue. The issue was the disruption of the existing equilibrium of power. The Castro regime was objectionable, not because it expelled American monopolies, but because it offered communism a base in the western hemisphere. The Soviet Union, he said pointedly, did not tolerate hostile governments in its own areas of vital interest; what would Khrushchev do, for example, if a pro-American government were established in Warsaw? The United States did not object to the Marxist governments of Guinea or Mali. If governments ruled in the interests of wealthy minorities, of course they were doomed; but social changes must take place peacefully and must not involve the prestige or commitments of America and Russia or upset the balance of world power.

He now brought up Laos. Past American policy there had not always been wise. The Pathet Lao had certain advantages: they received supplies and manpower from North Vietnam; moreover, they stood for change. Kennedy noted that he himself had been elected President as an advocate of change. The solution was to let a neutral and independent Laos decide its own future; and the problem was to make the cease-fire work by setting up a mechanism for its verification.

Khrushchev, displaying no great interest in Laos, preferred to revert to the question of reactionary regimes. Our two sides differed, he said, in our understanding of what popular or anti-popular movements were. We should both agree not to interfere and to leave it to the people of the country. The worst thing for the United States to do, he warned, was to start guerrilla warfare against regimes it did not like; no undertaking was more hopeless than guerrilla action instigated from outside and not supported by the people. He did not know, Khrushchev went on, whether the balance of power was exact, but no matter; each side had enough power to destroy the other. That was why there should be no interference. But the United States supported colonial powers, as in Africa, and then was surprised when the people turned against it. Kennedy pointed out that the United States had in fact backed liberation movements in Africa and hoped that the number of independent African states would increase. Khrushchev replied with scorn that the American policy was uneven, its voice timid. It might endorse anti-colonialism for tactical reasons, but its heart was with the colonialists. Why not adopt the Soviet policy of tolerance and noninterference?

Kennedy brought up Khrushchev's pledge to support wars of national liberation in his speech of January 6. Was this noninterference? Obviously both nations were helping groups in other countries. The problem, while we backed our respective movements, was not to clash ourselves. Khrushchev vigorously defended his speech. If subject peoples, promised independence by the United Nations, were still denied their rights, how long were they expected to wait? Wars of national liberation, he said, were "sacred" wars, and the Soviet was certainly going to support them. America itself had rebelled in this manner against Britain. Now it opposed other peoples who followed their example. The Tsars had denied the revolutionary American republic recognition for twenty-six years as an illegitimate regime. Now America refused to recognize China; "things have changed, haven't they?" The realistic policy for the United States would be to recognize China and admit it to the United Nations. Of course, this could not be done so long as Chiang Kai-shek held his position, whether in Taiwan or the UN. If he were in Mao's place, Khrushchev added, he would probably have attacked Taiwan long ago.

Kennedy made once again the point about preserving the existing balance of power. The entry of additional nations into the communist camp, the loss of Taiwan—such developments would alter the equilibrium. But Khrushchev energetically rejected this conception. If some African country were to go communist, he said, it might add a few drops to the bucket of communist power, were the balance of power conceived as a bucket on each side. But it would also be an expression of the popular will; and any attempt to stop it from outside would bring about a chain reaction and possibly war.

Kennedy responded with equal force that, so far as Washington was concerned, countries with varied social systems could pursue independent policies, like India, Burma, Yugoslavia. But changes which altered the balance of world power were different; perhaps the Russians might agree if, for example, Poland should join the west. No doubt America supported some governments which did not represent the will of the people; but could the Chairman be certain about the result if the Poles were given a chance to express their free choice? He felt it time, Kennedy added, to discuss Laos and the test ban in detail.

Khrushchev affected outrage over Kennedy's reference to Poland, contending that Poland's electoral system was more democratic than that of the United States, where parties existed only to deceive the people. As for preserving the existing balance, if this were the premise of American policy, Khrushchev said he must doubt whether the United States really wanted peaceful coexistence or was seeking a pretext for war. After all, he said, the United States might occupy Crimea on the claim that this improved its strategic position. This was the policy of Dulles.

It was also, of course, contrary to Kennedy's thesis, since the occupation of Crimea would change the balance; but Kennedy, perhaps with a growing sense of the futility of the ideological dispute, now tried again to persuade his antagonist to focus on Laos. This time Khrushchev acquiesced. After some talk, both said they might influence their clients in Laos to cooperate with the International Control Commission in policing the cease-fire. Kennedy, with a smile, said that at least they could possibly unite on this, even if they could not unite on the merits of the American electoral system. Khrushchev responded that the latter question was an internal affair of the United States.

They broke up at quarter to seven. It had been a rough day. Kennedy was impressed by Khrushchev's vitality, his debating skill and his brutal candor, depressed by the blank wall of dogma. He said to Llewellyn Thompson, "Is it always like this?" Thompson replied, "Par for the course."

4. PRELUDE TO BERLIN

Kennedy and Khrushchev would both have said that they wanted to preserve the status quo. But they had incompatible conceptions of what the status quo meant.

For Kennedy the status quo was the existing balance of international force. This did not at all mean that he wanted to freeze the world in its social mold. On the contrary, he believed internal political and institutional change to be both inevitable and desirable. But his hope was that it would take place without transferring power from one bloc to the other and therefore without making either side feel threatened and constrained to resist change by force.

For Khrushchev, on the other hand, the status quo was something very different: it was in essence the communist revolution in progress (as he hoped) across the world. From this perspective Kennedy's conception of a global standstill was an attempt not to support but to alter the status quo; it was an attack on the revolutionary process itself. This idea of a dynamic or potential status quo was, of course, deeply imbedded in Leninist analysis. Reminiscing about Vienna three years later, Khrushchev complained to William Benton that Kennedy had "bypassed" the real problem. "We in the USSR," he said, "feel that the revolutionary process should have the right to exist." The question of "the right to rebel, and the Soviet right to help combat reactionary governments . . . is the question of questions. . . . This question is at the heart of our relations with you. . . . Kennedy could not understand this." [1]

Kennedy understood it well enough after Khrushchev's January speech, and he understood it very well indeed after the first day in Vienna. Khrushchev's response left no doubt about the joker in the Soviet doctrine of coexistence: the idea of a dynamic status quo meant simply that the democracies had no right to intervene in the communist world, while the communists had every right to intervene in the democratic world. But Kennedy nevertheless felt that the offer of a standstill was worth the effort. Where he perhaps erred was in beginning by engaging Khrushchev in abstract discussion. Ideological debate was bound to be fruitless; Khrushchev was not likely to forswear the faith of a lifetime. Moreover, Khrushchev was a veteran dialectician. Though Kennedy held his own, he was fighting on his opponent's familiar terrain. He might have done better to seek the realm of concrete fact, the pragmatic rather than the ideological debating ground, and concentrate, as he had tried increasingly to do through the day, on particular situations in particular countries. But even this would prob-

---

[1] I am grateful to Senator Benton for letting me see the memorandum of his interview with Chairman Khrushchev on May 28, 1964.

ably not have made much difference. Khrushchev came to Vienna ready to collaborate on Laos and on nothing else; for the rest, he hoped to unnerve Kennedy and force him into concessions.

That night the Austrians gave their guests a state dinner at the Schönbrunn Palace. Khrushchev, in a clowning mood, turned a heavy, waggish charm on Mrs. Kennedy; it was one gag after another, like sitting next to Abbott and Costello. She had been reading Lesley Blanch's *Sabres of Paradise* and, mentioning her enthusiasm about the horses and the dances, asked him about nineteenth-century Ukraine. When he replied that the Soviet Ukraine had so many more teachers per capita than the Ukraine of the Tsars, she said, "Oh, Mr. Chairman, don't bore me with statistics"— and he suddenly laughed and became for a moment almost cozy. They talked about the Soviet space effort, and Jacqueline, remarking that one of the dogs which had careened in the upper atmosphere had had puppies, said, in banter, "Why don't you send me one?" Khrushchev laughed; but two months later two nervous Russians came with Ambassador Menshikov into the Oval Room at the White House bearing a terrified small dog. The President said, "How did this dog get here?" His wife said, "I'm afraid I asked Khrushchev for it in Vienna. I was just running out of things to say." The jolliness danced on the surface. When I asked the President later what Khrushchev was like, he described him as a combination of external jocosity and "internal rage."

They resumed their talks the next morning. The President began by saying that, if they couldn't agree on everything, at least they might be able to agree on Laos. Here after all was a land without strategic importance to either side but in which the United States had treaty commitments. America wanted to reduce its involvement in Laos, Kennedy said, and he hoped the Soviet Union would wish to do the same. Laos was not important enough to entangle two great nations.

Khrushchev responded that the Soviet Union had no desire to assume responsibilities in remote geographical areas. It was in Laos only at the request of Souvanna Phouma and the legitimate government. When Kennedy spoke of American commitments, he made a bad impression. What business did the United States have claiming special rights in Laos? If the President would pardon his bluntness, Khrushchev said, his policy stemmed from delusions of grandeur, from megalomania. America was so rich and powerful that it asserted rights for itself and denied rights to others. The Soviet Union did not agree and would not desist from helping other peoples to win their independence. If America really wanted to normalize the situation and avoid confrontations, it must renounce its claim to special rights.

Kennedy responded that the commitments had been made before he became President; why they were undertaken was not an issue here. Whatever had happened in the past, the issue now was to decrease commitments on both sides and get a neutral and independent Laos. Khrushchev doubted whether these commitments were altogether a legacy; after all, Kennedy had put the American military advisers into uniform and had ordered a landing of Marines. When Kennedy said that, though there had been speculation about sending Marines, no such order had been issued, Khrushchev replied that he was referring to press reports. The west, he added, was better than the Communists in making this kind of refined threat; and, if the United States sent in Marines, another Korea or worse would result. As for the Soviet Union, it would guarantee to exert every effort to influence the Laotian forces to establish a truly neutral government. We should lock our foreign ministers into a room and tell them to find a solution. Kennedy said that he had been reluctant to send in the Marines. All this could be avoided if there were a genuine cease-fire. Khrushchev agreed to make the cease-fire a priority matter. The two men thus completed the one piece of business transacted at Vienna.

The next question was the test ban. There were two issues here, Khrushchev began: the number of suspicious events to be inspected, and the organization of the machinery of inspection. As for the first, the Soviet Union considered three inspections a year sufficient; any more would constitute espionage. As for the control mechanism, the Soviet Union had originally been ready to accept a commission chaired by a representative of the United Nations. Now, after the unneutral behavior of the UN in the Congo, this was no longer possible. The only fair way was to establish a body made up of representatives of the three world groups—the Communists, the neutrals and the western states—empowered to adopt only decisions agreed upon by all. The work of other international organizations, Khrushchev added, should be organized along similar lines. In any case, Khrushchev continued, the test ban had little importance by itself; it must be linked with the general and complete disarmament. If the west would accept the Soviet disarmament plan, then the Soviet Union would drop the *troika* and the requirement for unanimity and agree to any controls. Let the disarmament negotiations include the test ban. If we pushed ahead, we could have general and complete disarmament in two years.

Kennedy asked whether Khrushchev really thought it impossible to find any person neutral between the United States and the Soviet Union. Khrushchev replied that he did. But the *troika*, Kennedy said, meant a veto over the inspection process; how could either he or Khrushchev assure his people that no secret testing was going on in the other nation? Khrushchev said irrelevantly, "But what about Allen Dulles? Isn't that secret?" Kennedy answered that he wished it were.

To Khrushchev's deprecation of the test ban Kennedy responded that, while by itself it would not lessen the number or the production of nuclear weapons, it would make their spread to new countries less likely. Without a test ban, there would be ten or fifteen nuclear powers in a few years. Surely the Soviet Union must balance the risks of espionage against the risks of proliferation. Khrushchev conceded the logic of this but pointed out that, while the test ban discussions were going on in Geneva, France was carrying its nuclear program forward. Unless the test ban were part of general disarmament, other countries would follow the example of France.

Kennedy replied that general disarmament was exceedingly complex and difficult: why not start with the easy question? They discussed the Soviet disarmament plan for a moment, and Khrushchev made it clear that he did not want to begin with the test ban even as part of the larger effort. Kennedy said again that the test ban, if not the most important measure, was at least a very significant start. He quoted a Chinese proverb, "A thousand-mile journey begins with a single step," and added, "Let us take that step." Khrushchev remarked that Kennedy apparently knew the Chinese well, but he knew them well too. Kennedy suggested that he might get to know them better. Khrushchev said tersely that he already knew them very well. As for the test ban, the Soviet Union would agree only subject to the *troika*.

The conversation, Kennedy said, was now back to where they had started. But, before concluding, he wanted to express the American concern over the protraction of an uninspected moratorium on testing for three years while negotiations had been going on. If the test ban were to be tossed into the general disarmament discussions, the uninspected moratorium would continue for several more years. Therefore we should try again in Geneva for a test ban. Khrushchev answered that the Soviet Union would not accept controls which it considered equivalent to espionage. Kennedy suggested that, if the controls turned out really to threaten Soviet security, the Soviet Union retained the right to abrogate the treaty. As for tying the test ban and general disarmament together, the United States could not accept this without assurance that agreement could be reached speedily on disarmament.

After this unsatisfactory discussion, they turned to Berlin. Here Khrushchev, while still stopping short of bluster, displayed his greatest animation and intensity. The German situation, he said, was intolerable. It was sixteen years after the end of the war, and there was still no peace settlement. In the meantime, a rearmed West Germany had become predominant in NATO. This meant the threat of a third world war. Only the West German militarists would gain from further delay. He wanted to reach agreement with the west on a treaty, Khrushchev said; but, if the United States refused, the Soviet Union would sign the treaty alone. This act would end the state of war and cancel all existing commitments, including occupation rights, administrative institutions and rights of access. The treaty would establish a free city of West Berlin. There would be no interference with its internal affairs or its communications, though agreement on access would have to be reached with the Democratic Republic. Western troops would be acceptable in West Berlin under certain conditions—and, of course, with Soviet troops too.

Kennedy, thanking him for putting the case so frankly, came back with equal frankness. This discussion, he said, raised not only legal questions but practical facts which affect American security. They were not talking about Laos any longer; Berlin was of primary and vital concern to the United States. We were not in Berlin on anyone's sufferance. We fought our way there, and our continuing presence rested on contractual rights. If we allowed ourselves to be expelled, American pledges and commitments would ever after be regarded as scraps of paper. Moreover, if we abandoned West Berlin, it would mean the abandonment of Western Europe, which America had deemed essential to its security in two wars. If Khrushchev agreed that the equilibrium of world power was more or less in balance he must understand the consequences of his demand. America, Kennedy said, would not accept an ultimatum. He had not become President of the United States to acquiesce in the isolation of his country—any more than Khrushchev would acquiesce in the isolation of the Soviet Union.

Khrushchev said that he understood this to mean the United States did not want a treaty. Misinterpreting Kennedy again, he declared that the invocation of national security could mean that Americans would wish to go on to Moscow too, since that would improve their strategic position. Kennedy responded sharply that the Americans did not wish to go anywhere, just to stay where they were. No doubt the current situation in Berlin was not satisfactory; but conditions were unsatisfactory all over, and this was not the time to upset the world balance of power. Khrushchev certainly would not accept a comparable shift in favor of the west. This was the basic question.

Khrushchev regretted that Kennedy did not get his point. All he wanted to do was to tranquilize the situation in the most dangerous spot in the world. The Soviet Union wanted to perform an operation—to excise this thorn, this ulcer —without prejudicing interests on either side. The treaty would not change boundaries; it would formalize them. It would only impede those, like Hitler's generals now in NATO, who still wanted *Lebensraum* to the Urals. No force in the world could stop the Soviet Union from signing the treaty; no further delay was necessary or possible. And thereafter any infringement of the sovereignty of East Germany would be regarded as open aggression with all its consequences.

Kennedy said that the United States opposed any military build-up in West Germany which might threaten the Soviet Union. But Khrushchev's proposal would bring about a basic change in the world situation overnight. This was a most serious challenge. He had not come to Vienna for this; he had come in the hope of improving relations. The United States could not accept the abrogation by one nation of the four-nation agreement.

Khrushchev waved this aside as without juridical foundation and recalled Roosevelt's remark at Yalta that American troops would leave Europe after two years. Why did the United States want Berlin? To unleash a war? Berlin had no military significance. After a treaty, West Berlin would be accessible to all countries with which it wished ties; the United States and the Soviet Union could develop guarantees jointly or call in the UN. But, if the United States tried to maintain its present position after a treaty, this would violate the sovereignty of East Germany and of the communist camp as a whole. Once the Berlin question was out of the way, the road would be clear for an improvement of relations. In any case, the Soviet Union intended to sign the treaty by the end of 1961. If America wanted war over Berlin, there was nothing the Soviet Union could do about it. Maybe he should sign the treaty right away and get it over; that is what the Pentagon had wanted. But madmen who sought war ought to be put in strait jackets.

It was not quite a tirade; it was too controlled and hard and therefore the more menacing. Kennedy replied that the United States did not wish to precipitate a crisis. The Soviet Union was doing so by threatening unilateral changes in the existing situation. Was this the way to achieve peace? If the United States surrendered to the Soviet demand, it would not be regarded as a serious country any longer.

Khrushchev became even harsher. The Soviet Union, he said, would never under any conditions accept American rights in West Berlin after the treaty. After all, the United States itself had signed a unilateral peace treaty with Japan. The Soviet Union was determined to go ahead, and responsibility for subsequent violations of East German sovereignty would be heavy.

Kennedy replied that the United States did not wish to deprive the Soviet Union of its ties in Eastern Europe and would not submit to the loss of its own ties in Western Europe. He had not assumed office to accept arrangements totally inimical to American interests.

It was time for luncheon.

Both men, even after the grimness of the morning, retained their capacity for chaff. Kennedy, responding to Khrushchev's toast, recalled that the Chairman had told him the night before that, when he was Kennedy's age, he had been a member of the Moscow Planning Commission and was looking forward to becoming chairman. The President continued that, when he was sixty-seven, he hoped to be head of the Boston Planning Commission and possibly national chairman of the Democratic party. Khrushchev interjected that perhaps he would like to be head of a planning commission for the whole world. Kennedy replied no, only Boston. Then, in solemn language, the President reaffirmed the responsibility both leaders had to avoid confrontations which might threaten the destruction of civilization.

In between, they had snatches of private talk. Khrushchev said that he had read Kennedy's defense message and thought that in consequence the Soviet Union should perhaps increase its land forces and artillery. America, Khrushchev added, was run by monopolists and could not afford to disarm. Kennedy rejoined by mentioning Walter Reuther and adding that he thought the Chairman had met him in San Francisco in 1959. Khrushchev said unsmilingly, "Yes, I met him. We hung the likes of Reuther in Russia in 1917." As for the moon project, Khrushchev on further reflection advised the United States to go by itself; a joint trip would be impossible without disarmament because the same rockets were used for military and scientific purposes. The Chairman added that he had heard Kennedy was under pressure to resume testing; he was too. However, the Soviet Union would wait for the United States to begin. If America tested, Russia would follow.

After luncheon, Kennedy, making a final effort, asked to talk with Khrushchev alone. Accompanied only by interpreters, they sat together for a last conversation. The President began by expressing hope that in the interest of relations between their two countries the Chairman would not present him with a crisis so deeply involving the American national interest as Berlin. Of course any decision Khrushchev wanted to make about the Democratic Republic was his own. But change was taking place everywhere in the world, and no one could predict its end. At such a time, all decisions had to be carefully considered.

Khrushchev returned unrelentingly to the attack. The United States, he said, wanted to humiliate the Soviet Union. If the President insisted on occupation rights after a treaty and if East German borders were violated, whether by land, sea or air, force would be met by force. The United States should prepare itself for this, and the Soviet Union would do the same.

"I want peace," said Khrushchev, "but, if you want war, that is your problem."

Kennedy said, "It is you, and not I, who wants to force a change."

Khrushchev said again that it was up to the United States to decide on peace or war. The Soviet Union had no choice but to accept the challenge. It must, and it would, respond. The treaty decision was irrevocable. He would sign in December.

Kennedy, parting, said, "It will be a cold winter."

5. AFTERMATH IN LONDON

As Kennedy, carrying Khrushchev's *aide-mémoires* on Berlin and the test ban, left Vienna to see Harold Macmillan in

England, he told a friend in the press that "somber" would be a good word for the meetings. For all the poise and command he displayed in the talks, the experience deeply disturbed him. Bohlen and Thompson, who had been through such conferences before, thought the President overreacted. But Kennedy had never encountered any leader with whom he could not exchange ideas—anyone so impervious to reasoned argument or so apparently indifferent to the prospective obliteration of mankind. He himself had indicated flexibility and admitted error, but Khrushchev had remained unmoved and immovable. Apart from Laos, about which Khrushchev evidently cared little, there was no area of accommodation. The test ban seemed dead. Berlin held the threat, if not the certitude, of war. Filled with foreboding, the President flew on to London. It was a silent and gloomy trip. Arriving at London Airport, on Sunday afternoon, the presidential party drove into the city as a great disarmament rally in Trafalgar Square was beginning to disperse. The streets along the way were filled with black banners marked in white letters BAN THE BOMB.

The pretext for the stop was the christening of Lee Bouvier Radziwill's new baby. But the essential reason was the talk with Macmillan. The two men had met twice since the inauguration—at Key West in March, when they discussed Laos, and a few days later at Washington in April for a general canvass of foreign affairs. In June their relationship was still tentative. Macmillan, indeed, was greatly concerned whether he could develop with the new President the genial relations which he had established with Eisenhower in North Africa during the Second World War and renewed during Eisenhower's Presidency. He had been vaguely aware of Kennedy long before 1961 both as the son of an American Ambassador whom he, like all opponents of Munich, had to regard with suspicion, and also as a friend of Englishmen of a much younger generation, like David Ormsby Gore; and he worried about their differences in age and presumably in outlook. The languid Edwardian, who looked back to the sunlit years before the First World War as a lost paradise, feared that the brisk young American nearly a quarter of a century his junior, would consider him a museum piece. Nor had he been much reassured by their conversations in Washington, when, as he thought, Dean Acheson had been permitted to dominate the proceedings with hard talk about showdowns over Berlin and the President had seemed excessively diffident.

On Monday morning, June 5, Kennedy, tense and

tired, went to 10 Downing Street. A formal conference, with each principal flanked by advisers, had been scheduled. But Macmillan said, with the usual weary fling of his hand, "Let's not have a meeting—the Foreign Office and all that. Why not have a peaceful drink and chat by ourselves?" Kennedy seemed grateful and relieved, and the two men settled down for a talk. The President described his grim impressions of Khrushchev. He and Macmillan then agreed that western proposals for negotiation over Berlin would be taken in Moscow as a sign of weakness unless the situation grew so much worse that there seemed imminent danger of war. Macmillan remarked that the French thought negotiation would be better after a treaty was signed with East Germany than before. In the meantime, Kennedy said, military planning on Berlin had to be stepped up. They would have to decide what the west should do in a series of contingencies—if the Russians signed the treaty but made no changes in the existing arrangements; or if they interrupted the civilian supply of West Berlin; or if they interfered with military traffic. The agenda was full and imperative.

Their talk, though brief, marked the real beginning of what became Kennedy's closest personal relationship with a foreign leader. Macmillan, of course, was a far more serious figure than he liked to appear. He had been the first Conservative M.P. to adopt Keynesianism; he had not only opposed Munich but played a distinguished role in the war; and, underneath his affectations and mannerisms, he had a sharp, disillusioned mind, a vivid sense of history and a strong desire to accomplish certain objectives during his term in office. Possessed of a genuine horror of nuclear war, he was determined to press for a test ban and to search without cease for a *détente* with the Soviet Union. "The East-West conflict," he had said, "cannot be resolved by weakness or moral or physical exhaustion of one side or the other. It cannot, in this nuclear age, be resolved by the triumph of one side over the other without the extinction of both. I say, therefore, we can only reach our goal by the gradual acceptance of the view that we can all gain more by agreement than by aggression." To this general purpose he added two other themes: the desire to bring Britain into Europe, and the hope of reconstructing the international monetary system.

On nearly all these points he and Kennedy made easy contact. More than that, they soon discovered, despite the differences in age, a considerable temperamental rapport. Kennedy, with his own fondness for the British political style, liked Macmillan's patrician approach to politics, his impatience with official ritual, his insouciance about the professionals, his pose of nonchalance even when most deeply committed. Macmillan, for his part, responded to Kennedy's courage, his ability to see events unfolding against the vast canvas of history, his contempt for cliché, his unfailing sense of the ridiculous. They found the same things funny and the same things serious. "It was the gay things that linked us together," Macmillan once told me, "and made it possible for us to talk about the terrible things." They soon discovered that they could match each other's transitions from gravity to mischief and communicate as in shorthand. It was as if they had known each other all their lives.

Refreshed by the stopover in London, Kennedy came back to Washington. Whatever the disappointments of Vienna or the stabbing pain in his spine, he seemed, after forty-eight hours, philosophical about the meeting. He knew how Khrushchev thought and where he stood, and that was invaluable. I think also that he felt he had tested himself and had proven more than equal to the test. The talks with Macmillan and de Gaulle had strengthened his confidence in his ability to rally the west. War was a danger but not an inevitability. In a television report to the American people on the day of his return, he described the Vienna meetings as "a very sober two days . . . no discourtesy, no loss of tempers, no threats or ultimatums by either side; no advantage or concession . . . gained or given; no major decision . . . planned or taken; no spectacular progress . . . achieved or pretended." But he found this meeting, "as somber as it was, to be immensely useful." The channels of communication were opened, and the chances of misjudgment on either side should now be less. Yet "we have wholly different views of right and wrong, of what is an internal affair and what is aggression, and, above all, we have wholly different concepts of where the world is and where it is going." Khrushchev was certain that the tide was "moving his way, that the revolution of rising peoples would eventually be a Communist revolution. . . . I believe just as strongly that time will prove [this thesis] wrong, that liberty and independence and self-determination—not communism—is the future of man."

It took another nine days for Khrushchev to make his own report to the Soviet people. He repeated his Vienna arguments on the test ban and disarmament, reiterated the deadline on Berlin, mentioned the agreement on Laos and discussed his differences with Kennedy over coexistence. (Kennedy in his speech had specifically endorsed Khrushchev's point that serious social upheaval was generally the result, not of communist conspiracy, but of a spontaneous protest against misery and oppression which Communists tried to capture. Ignoring this, Khrushchev once again claimed as Kennedy's position "that if the people of a country want to change their social and political system, this should not be allowed.")

"On the whole," Khrushchev concluded, "I am pleased with these talks." This was apparently true. Thompson gathered on his return to Moscow that Khrushchev had been genuinely impressed by Kennedy. One day a year or so later my occasional luncheon partner in the Soviet Embassy in Washington, Georgi Kornienko, said that Khrushchev, during his 1959 visit to the United States, had asked members of the Embassy about Kennedy. "Of all the people he talked to," Kornienko told me, "I gave the most positive picture. I said that, while Kennedy was not yet another Roosevelt, he was independent and intelligent and could be counted on for new departures. Khrushchev listened. Then came Vienna. Afterward he said to me, 'You were right and the others were wrong.'"

"Neither side," Khrushchev continued in his report to the Soviet people, "evaded bringing up and discussing the most acute questions. . . . We listened with attention to the position of the United States Government and set out in detail the position of the Soviet Government. . . . I have the impression that President Kennedy understands the great responsibility that lies with the governments of two such powerful states. . . . Thank you, dear comrades. Goodby. Good night."

Each man came away from Vienna with greater respect for the mind and nerve of his adversary. Having survived their personal confrontation and defined the impassable difference over Berlin, they now faced their first battle of wills.

XV

TRIAL IN BERLIN

OFTEN DURING THE YEAR, on both public and private occasions, the President set forth his conception of the Amer-

ican stake in Berlin. I think, however, the analysis I heard
him make in the autumn to President Kekkonen of Finland carried particular cogency. For here Kennedy stripped
the case of the legalistic and moralistic arguments so cherished in the west and placed it in terms of geopolitical
realism which he hoped would be understood in Moscow.

Kekkonen, who had recently visited the Soviet Union,
began by reporting what he described as a genuine Russian
fear that Germany might be the cause of a third world
war.

"We do not accept the idea that the Soviet Union is in
danger from West Germany," Kennedy replied. "West Germany is a nation of sixty-five million people in an acutely
vulnerable strategic situation. We have been successful in
tying West Germany into Western Europe through NATO,
the Common Market and so on. We want nothing to happen over Berlin which would weaken the ties of West
Germany to Western Europe and set West Germany off on a
nationalistic and independent course. It is in this possibility
that the real danger lies of Germany setting off another
war."

As we see Soviet policy in Berlin, the President continued, "it is designed to neutralize West Germany as a
first step in the neutralization of Western Europe. That is
what makes the present situation so dangerous. West
Germany is the key as to whether Western Europe will be
free." The pressure on West Berlin was the first move in a
Soviet effort to break up NATO. The Soviet campaign left
the United States no choice but to resist—or to see our position in Western Europe disintegrate. "It is not that we wish
to stand on the letter of the law or that we underestimate
the dangers of war. But if we don't meet our commitments
in Berlin, it will mean the destruction of NATO and a dangerous situation for the whole world. All Europe is at
stake in West Berlin."

1. THE BERLIN DEBATE

The administration had begun to consider its Berlin policy
well before the President went to Vienna. In March Kennedy
had invited Dean Acheson to undertake special studies of
the problems of NATO and Germany. This did not mean
(as Joseph Alsop hoped and Walter Lippmann feared) that
he was handing American policy over to the so-called hard-
liners. But Kennedy considered Acheson one of the most
intelligent and experienced men around and did not see
why he should not avail himself of 'hard' views before
making his own judgments.

When Harold Macmillan came to Washington in early April, Kennedy accordingly asked Acheson to take part in the discussion of Berlin. Acheson proceeded to do this in the session that somewhat distressed Macmillan; and, though he explained that his proposals had not yet been submitted to the administration, his strong personality and program governed the exchange. It looked, he said, as if the Soviet Union planned to force the Berlin issue this year. He did not believe that Berlin could be satisfactorily settled apart from the larger question of Germany; and he saw no prospect of any agreement on either Berlin or Germany compatible with the interests of the west. Therefore, when Khrushchev moved to cut off West Berlin, the allies must instantly demonstrate their determination to stand up to the Soviet challenge. Skipping over possibilities of diplomatic or economic response, Acheson crisply offered a formidable catalogue of military countermeasures, concluding tentatively in favor of sending a division down the *Autobahn*. This, he hoped, would make clear that western interest in preserving access was greater than Russian interest in blocking access. If the Russians repulsed the probe, then at least the west would know where it stood, and it could rally and rearm as it did during the Korean War.

This rather bloodcurdling recital, delivered with the usual Achesonian aplomb, startled the British. Lord Home, the British Foreign Secretary, objected that it would be easy to isolate a single division on the *Autobahn* and tried to turn the discussion from military to political issues. The western position, he said, was negative. We were offering no alternative to Khrushchev's proposal of a peace conference and a treaty. We were in Berlin because of the right of conquest, but the right of conquest was wearing thin. Acheson coolly replied that perhaps it was western power which was wearing thin. Home continued that he was never happy about entering a negotiation without a position. To this a State Department official observed that, since no acceptable agreement was possible, we should do everything we could to avoid negotiation. The President sat poker-faced, confining himself to questions about the adequacy of existing military plans and saying that, if Khrushchev could be deterred only by fear of direct encounter, the allies must consider how to convince him that such an encounter would be sufficiently costly.

This preliminary discussion opened up a number of the themes which ran through the Berlin argument for the next six months. It also suggested the diversity of opinion within the American government. Some of the Americans present, like Adlai Stevenson, were as dismayed as the British by Acheson's concentration on the military showdown. "Maybe Dean is right," Stevenson said later, "but his position should be the conclusion of a process of investigation, not the beginning. He starts at a point which we should not reach until we have explored and exhausted all the alternatives."

Acheson's basic thesis, which he developed in a long and powerful paper delivered to the President three weeks after Vienna, was that West Berlin was not a problem but a pretext. Khrushchev's *démarche* had nothing to do with Berlin, Germany or Europe. His object, as Acheson saw it, was not to rectify a local situation but to test the general American will to resist; his hope was that, by making us back down on a sacred commitment, he could shatter our world power and influence. This was a simple conflict of wills, and, until it was resolved, any effort to negotiate the Berlin issue per se would be fatal. Since there was nothing to negotiate, willingness on our part to go to the conference table would be taken in Moscow as evidence of weakness and make the crisis so much the worse.

Khrushchev had only dared precipitate the crisis, Acheson continued, because his fear of nuclear war had declined. Our problem was to convince him that this complacency was misplaced and that we would, in fact, go to nuclear war rather than abandon the status quo. This called for the build-up—prompt, serious and quiet—of both our conventional and nuclear forces. If Khrushchev signed his treaty with East Germany, we should not quibble about this or about changes in access procedures. But, the moment there was interruption of access itself, we must act: first an airlift—and then, if that could not be sustained against Soviet counter-measures, a ground probe in force too large to be stopped by East German troops alone. Acheson cited a Joint Chiefs of Staff estimate that two Allied divisions could hold out indefinitely inside East Germany against an enemy of three or four divisions. The point would be, not to defeat the communist forces in the field, but to persuade Moscow that we had the resolve to go on, if necessary, to nuclear war. There was a substantial chance, Acheson said, that the necessary military preparations would by themselves cause Khrushchev to alter his purpose; but he added frankly that there was also a substantial possibility that nuclear war might result.

Though the preamble of the paper expressed categorical

opposition to any form of negotiation, the paper itself
was slightly less intransigent. If Khrushchev were to change
his mind, Acheson was willing to offer a formula to cover
his retreat through negotiations launched after the military build-up and before the signing of the treaty with
East Germany. He even sketched the outlines of a settlement,
suggesting that Khrushchev's treaty be accompanied by an
exchange of declarations assuring the western position in
Berlin, along with certain western concessions—perhaps
guarantees against espionage and subversion from West
Berlin, perhaps even recognition of the Oder-Neisse line—
thrown in to make the result more palatable to Moscow.

But this section had somewhat the air of an afterthought.
Acheson's attitude toward negotiation was basically determined by his belief, as he later wrote, that "in making
political and military judgments affecting Europe a major
—often *the* major—consideration should be their effect on
the German people and the German government." It was
understandable that the former Secretary of State, priding
himself on the arrangements of 1949–50 which tied West
Germany so securely into the structure of Western Europe,
should reject any action which he felt might loosen those
ties. But his view came close to endowing the Bonn government with a veto over American policy in Europe; and
it meant that the political planning in his paper mostly
concerned a plausible *casus belli* over Berlin rather than a
forward political strategy. For Acheson the test of will
seemed almost an end in itself rather than a means to a
political end. And the thrust of Acheson's rhetoric, and
especially of his brilliant and imperious oral presentations,
helped fix the debate for a time in terms of a clear-cut
choice between negotiation and a military showdown.

The Acheson case followed logically from his conviction
that the Soviet Union had unlimited objectives in raising
the Berlin question. But others in government, especially
some who knew the Soviet Union best, like Ambassadors
Thompson and Harriman, believed that, on the contrary,
Khrushchev's objectives might well be limited. Thompson
argued after Vienna that the predominant Soviet motive
was the desire to improve the communist position in Eastern Europe rather than to achieve the world-wide political
humiliation of the United States. As evidence, he cited the
'free city' proposal which, he said, Khrushchev really intended as a means of accomplishing his local aims and at
the same time saving face for the allies. While Thompson
favored the policy of quiet military build-up, he also argued
that the west must begin a diplomatic offensive soon after

the West German elections, scheduled for September 17. If this was done, then Moscow and not Washington would be in the position of saying no to a plan which might avert nuclear war.

The State Department itself was divided about the Acheson program. Rusk was circumspect, and no one quite knew where he stood; Foy Kohler, the Assistant Secretary for European Affairs, was a complete Achesonian; while George McGhee, head of the Policy Planning Staff, and Abram Chayes, the Legal Adviser, agreed with Thompson that we should prepare negotiating as well as military alternatives. These questions were before the newly established Berlin Task Force; but this body temporarily put them aside in order to spend most of June and a good part of July composing an answer to the *aide-mémoire* on Berlin which Khrushchev had given Kennedy in Vienna.

No one in the White House, least of all the President, would ever understand why this not very exacting assignment proved so difficult. Kennedy had expected a quick American response capable, among other things, of making some appeal to world opinion. Instead, week followed week with no word from the Department, and the President's exasperation grew. When a draft finally came over in mid-July, nearly six weeks after Vienna, it was a tired and turgid rehash of documents, left over from the Berlin crisis of 1958–59, sounding, as Richard Rovere said, "like the kind of speech Andrei Gromyko might make if he were on our side." By this time it was too late to do anything but put the paper out, which the White House did, though after attaching a more cogent summary of its own.

Meanwhile, opposition to the bleak choices of the Acheson program was mounting. Influential Senators, especially Mike Mansfield (who wanted all Berlin, East and West, to be declared a free city and put under the UN), J. William Fulbright, Hubert Humphrey and Claiborne Pell, were critical. The British were unhappy. As *The Economist* put it on June 24: "Unless Mr. Kennedy takes a decisive grip on the wheel, the West is in danger of by-passing one possible line of compromise after another until it reaches a dead end where neither it nor Russia has any choice except between ignominious retreat and nuclear devastation." And in the White House Carl Kaysen, Henry Kissinger, who was in Washington regularly that summer as a consultant, and I, very much on the fringes, all wanted a more aggressive canvass of diplomatic possibilities. The first phase of the Berlin debate was under way.

Looking back, one can now see that the early terms of

the debate were artificial. On the one hand, Acheson, for all his insistence on military confrontations, was not so implacable a foe of negotiation as, in his irritation with the softheads (Washington was not yet divided into hawks and doves), he liked to imply. On the other, some of us who argued that a diplomatic approach should accompany the military build-up unquestionably had illusions as to what negotiation might accomplish. We hoped that diplomacy could at least settle the future status of Berlin and might perhaps lead to a general resolution of the problems of Germany and even of central Europe. In retrospect, this was an unrealistic hope. Acheson was probably right in suggesting that the preservation of the status quo was the goal we should seek.

Where the debate had value was in determining how best to pursue this goal. Those of us who talked about supplementing the build-up with negotiation had hold, however dimly, of one truth: that insistence on a military showdown, accompanied by the rejection of diplomacy and, in early July, by talk of war mobilization under a proclamation of national emergency, contained the risk of pushing the crisis beyond the point of no return.

2. THE CRISIS GROWS

Khrushchev's testy television report on Vienna in mid-June was soon followed by appropriately belligerent remarks by Walter Ulbricht, the Chairman of the East German Council of State. Ulbricht complained of the flow of refugees to West Berlin and forecast new restrictions, allegedly in the interests of safety, on planes flying along the air corridors from the west. Then early in July Khrushchev himself, citing Kennedy's call for a larger American defense effort, announced a suspension of the partial demobilization of the Red Army and a one-third increase in Soviet military spending.

On Wednesday, July 5, I received a visit from my friend Kornienko of the Soviet Embassy. After the usual preliminaries, Kornienko expressed himself as puzzled by the American attitude toward Berlin, much as he had expressed puzzlement about our policy toward Cuba three months before. This led to a long and fruitless discussion of juridical and political issues. Finally he said, "The real trouble is that you don't believe that we are sincere when we say that we honestly wish to keep things as they are in West Berlin within the new context." I said that I feared that this was true, that experience had made us wary, and that the so-called guarantees which Russia offered guaranteed nothing. To this he replied, "Well, if you do not consider these guarantees adequate, why don't you propose your own guarantees? All we want to do is to have a chance to discuss these things."

While nothing Kornienko said indicated that discussions would lead to agreement, it did look as if the Russians might want to get off a collision course. (One realizes now that, if this were so, it may well have been a result of the supposed supremacy of the Acheson line in Washington.) The next day Abram Chayes, Carl Kaysen and I got together to express a collective concern that the Acheson paper was shaping policy along restrictive and potentially dangerous lines. It all reminded me uncomfortably of the prelude to the Bay of Pigs; and, stimulated by this conversation, I set down my misgivings in a memorandum to the President the next morning.

The Cuban fiasco, the memorandum suggested, had resulted in large part from the "excessive concentration [in our advance planning] on military and operational problems and the wholly inadequate consideration of political issues. This error seems likely to be repeated here." The Acheson paper was excellent in analyzing the issues of last resort; it told us what we could fall back on when other alternatives were used up. But, if it were permitted to define our Berlin choices, there could be no systematic effort to bring these alternatives to the surface.

The memorandum questioned whether the military contingency envisaged by Acheson was the most probable way the situation would develop. "Are we not running the risk of directing most of our planning to the least likely eventuality—i.e., an immediate blockade of West Berlin? . . . If Khrushchev restrains himself [after a peace treaty] from immediate physical violation of West Berlin and keeps saying that he will consider any guarantees for the continued integrity of West Berlin that we wish to propose, we will be very much on the political defensive. We will seem rigid and warlike, while he will seem filled with sweet reason." While he was happily issuing statements, calling peace conferences, proposing interim agreements and so on, we would be sitting sullenly by, preparing a military response to what would be thus far a political threat.

The memorandum concluded by mentioning another Cuban resemblance—the tendency to define the issue, "to put it crudely, as: Are you chicken or not? When someone proposes something which seems tough, hard, put-up-orshut-up, it is difficult to oppose it without seeming soft, idealistic, mushy, etc. Yet, as Chip Bohlen has often said, nothing would clarify more the discussion of policy toward the Soviet Union than the elimination of the words 'hard' and 'soft' from the language. People who had doubts about Cuba suppressed those doubts lest they seem 'soft.' It is obviously important that such fears not constrain free discussion of Berlin."

I had to see the President shortly before luncheon about other matters. As we finished, I handed him the memorandum, saying that he might want to look at it that afternoon on his way to Hyannis Port, where he had scheduled a meeting on Berlin the next day with Rusk, McNamara and General Taylor. But he chose characteristically to read the memorandum at once. His response was immediate. Agreeing that Acheson's paper was far too narrowly directed to military problems, he said with emphasis that Berlin planning had to be brought back into balance. Then he asked me to prepare an unsigned memorandum about the unexplored issues in the Berlin problem which he might use in his talks at the Cape. I immediately sent out calls for Chayes and Kissinger, both of whom had left their offices for luncheon. It was not till after three that I finally got them over to the East Wing, and the President's helicopter was due to depart from the White House lawn at five. We quickly worked up an outline. Then, as Chayes and Kissinger talked, I typed. By furious effort, we got the paper to Hyannis Port in time.

The memorandum first identified certain issues omitted in the Acheson paper:

1. What political moves do we make until the crisis develops? If we sit silent, or confine ourselves to rebutting Soviet contentions (cf. the draft reply to the *aide-mémoire*), we permit Khrushchev to establish the framework of discussion. As we do this, we in effect invite him to demand from us a definition of the guarantees we would find acceptable. This, of course, casts the U.S. as rigid and unreasonable and puts us on the political defensive.

2. The paper indicates no relationship between the proposed military action and larger political objectives. It defines an immediate *casus belli;* but it does not state any political objective other than present access procedures for which we are prepared to incinerate the world. It is essential to elaborate the cause for which we are prepared to go to nuclear war. Where do we want to come out if we win the test of wills? German unification, for example: what is our real intention with regard to this traditional objective?

3. The paper covers only one eventuality—that is, the Communist interruption of military access to West Berlin. Actually

there is a whole spectrum of harassments, of which a full-scale blockade may well be one of the least likely.

4. The paper hinges on our willingness to face nuclear war. But this option is undefined. Before you are asked to make the decision to go to nuclear war, you are entitled to know what concretely nuclear war is likely to mean. The Pentagon should be required to make an analysis of the possible levels and implications of nuclear warfare and the possible gradations of our own nuclear response.

5. The paper does not define the problem of the relationship of the proposed strategy to the Alliance. What happens if our allies decline to go along? Which of them, for example, will go along with the ground probe? Even de Gaulle has indicated his opposition to sending a column through. What about the United Nations? Whatever happens, this issue will go into the UN. For better or for worse, we have to have a convincing UN position.

We concluded by recommending that the President tell the State Department to explore negotiating alternatives and ask Acheson to supply the missing political dimension in his argument.

While we were agitating the political side, McGeorge Bundy and Kissinger were bringing the President comparable questions about the state of military planning. McNamara had informed the White House early in May that existing plans in case of trouble in Berlin assumed almost immediate resort to nuclear war. In a pre-Hyannis Port memorandum of his own, Bundy now commented on the dangerous rigidity of the strategic war plan, pointing out that it called in essence for an all-out nuclear strike against the Soviet Union and left the President little choice as to how he would face his moment of thermonuclear truth. Bundy suggested that Kennedy remand the war plan to McNamara for review and revision.

At the Hyannis Port meeting on July 8 the President made his dissatisfaction with the state of planning abundantly clear. On the diplomatic side, he decided to ask Acheson to try his hand at a "political program" for Berlin and instructed Rusk to produce a negotiating prospectus. On the military side, he asked McNamara for a plan which would permit non-nuclear resistance on a scale sufficient both to indicate our determination and to provide the communists time for second thoughts and negotiation before everything billowed up in nuclear war. The State and Defense papers were to be delivered within ten days.

It did not, of course, prove that easy to reshape policy, but the meeting laid out the lines of battle within the American government for the rest of the summer. At first,

Kennedy gained little ground. When the National Security Council met on Berlin on July 13, Rusk reaffirmed the Acheson argument that we should not negotiate until the crisis became more acute. And Acheson himself, supported by Lyndon Johnson, now argued strongly for a proclamation of national emergency. This declaration became the symbol of the drastic reaction to the crisis. It implied an immediate expansion of the armed forces, an increase in the defense budget of perhaps $5 billion, stand-by price and wage controls and new taxation. Though the proclamation would legally facilitate the calling up of reserves, its essential purpose was psychological. Only a response of this order, Acheson argued, could deter Khrushchev from irretrievable steps and make the American people understand the full gravity of the crisis.

These attitudes disturbed the White House group. On the problem of negotiation, Henry Kissinger observed to Bundy that it was wrong "to have refusal to negotiate become a test of firmness. . . . Firmness should be related to the substance of our negotiating position. It should not . . . be proved by seeming to shy away from a diplomatic confrontation." If Khrushchev would not accept a reasonable proposal, this, in Kissinger's view, was an argument *for* rather than against our taking the initiative. Any other course would see us "jockeyed into a position of refusing diplomatic solutions," and, when we finally agreed to discussion, as we inevitably must, it would seem an American defeat. Diplomacy, Kissinger concluded, was the "necessary corollary to the build-up."

As for the proclamation of national emergency, this encountered a number of objections. Rusk felt that it would have the flavor of mobilization and quoted back at Acheson his own original caution that the build-up take place in low key. McNamara also was skeptical. And the Council of Economic Advisers strongly opposed the proposal to increase taxes. This last idea had appealed at first to the President, who did not wish to risk inflation or unbalance the budget further, as well as to a number of cabinet members of whom some, like the Attorney General, wanted to distribute the national burden in the emergency and others, like the Secretary of Labor, wanted to protect the civilian welfare programs. But, as the Treasury Department prepared recommendations for new taxes, Walter Heller argued that the real inflationary danger lay not in the additional defense spending but in the psychological reactions—scare buying to hedge against inflation—which a proclamation might touch off. In the meantime, as the projected increase in defense spending began to decline in size, the Treasury accepted the Council's position, the tax rise disappeared, and another strong argument was registered against the declaration of national emergency.

Kissinger, in further comment on the proclamation, argued that the Soviet Union would be more impressed by a broad and sustained improvement in American military readiness than by a single dramatic gesture, especially one which made us appear "unnecessarily bellicose, perhaps even hysterical." Moreover, if we declared the emergency now, we used up a measure which would be more effective if taken as a response to clear-cut Soviet provocation. Ted Sorensen, summing up the position of the White House staff in an able memorandum, pointed out that the declaration of national emergency might well "engage Khrushchev's prestige to a point where he felt he could not back down from a showdown, and provoke further or faster action on his part in stepping up the arms race." It would also, Sorensen feared, "arouse those at home and abroad who are fearful of 'rash' and 'trigger-happy' actions by the United States."

3. THE PRESIDENTIAL STRATEGY

The President was meanwhile fighting his way through the thicket of debate to his own conclusions. Cuba and Laos had been side issues. But Berlin threatened a war which might destroy civilization, and he thought about little else that summer. Stewart Udall, trying to talk to him about conservation, remarked, "He's imprisoned by Berlin." One afternoon, after a meeting with the Joint Chiefs of Staff, the President talked at some length with James Wechsler of the *New York Post*. Only "fools," Kennedy said, could cling to the idea of victory in a nuclear war. A once-and-for-all peace seemed equally unlikely. But he still hoped to arrive at a point where both the Soviet Union and the United States would accept the premise that the only alternatives were authentic negotiation or mutual annihilation. What worried him was that Khrushchev might interpret his reluctance to wage nuclear war as a symptom of an American loss of nerve. Some day, he said, the time might come when he would have to run the supreme risk to convince Khrushchev that conciliation did not mean humiliation. "If Khrushchev wants to rub my nose in the dirt," he told Wechsler, "it's all over." But how to convince Khrushchev short of a showdown? "That son of a bitch won't pay any attention to words," the President said bitterly on another occasion. "He has to see you move."

This meant that the United States would not give way and, if the Soviet Union persisted in its determination to destroy the freedom of West Berlin, we would be prepared to go to war, even to nuclear war. But, while Kennedy wanted to make this resolve absolutely clear to Moscow, he wanted to make it equally clear that we were not, as he once put it to me, "war-mad." He did not wish to drive the crisis beyond the point of no return; and therefore, while reiterating our refusal to retreat, he rejected the program of national mobilization and sought the beginnings of careful negotiation. Ted Sorensen now prepared a draft for a Berlin speech along these lines, and Kennedy began to work it over. Then on the night of July 25 television cables were installed in the presidential office, and the President made his report to the people.

"We cannot and will not permit the Communists," Kennedy said, "to drive us out of Berlin, either gradually or by force." To be ready for any contingency, he would seek an additional $3.25 billion for the defense budget, call up certain reserve and National Guard units, procure new weapons and enlarge the program of civil defense. But, if our military posture had to be defensive, "our diplomatic posture need not be. . . . We do not intend to leave it to others to choose and monopolize the forum and the framework of discussion. We do not intend to abandon our duty to mankind to seek a peaceful solution." We recognize, Kennedy said, the historical Russian concern about Central and Eastern Europe, and "we are willing to consider any arrangement or treaty in Germany consistent with the maintenance of peace and freedom, and with the legitimate security interests of all nations." We were determined to search for peace "in formal or informal meetings. We do not want military considerations to dominate the thinking of either East or West. . . . In the thermonuclear age, any misjudgment on either side about the intentions of the other could rain more devastation in several hours than has been wrought in all the wars of human history."

The White House group rejoiced at the speech. But for some reason the press, playing up the military points and almost ignoring the passages about negotiation, made it appear a triumph for the hard line. In Russia Khrushchev read it, or affected to read it, in the same way. He happened at the moment to be at Sochi conferring with John J. McCloy about disarmament. On the day before the speech, he was in a jolly mood, comparing the exchange of diplomatic notes to kicking a football back and forth and adding that this would probably continue until a treaty was signed and the Soviet Union kicked a different kind of ball. The next day he told McCloy emotionally that the United States had declared preliminary war on the Soviet Union. It had presented an ultimatum and clearly intended hostilities. This confirmed, Khrushchev said, the thesis of his January speech that the capitalist world had lost confidence in its capacity to triumph by peaceful means. The President, he added, seemed a reasonable young man, filled with energy and doubtless wishing to display that energy; but, if war occurred, he would be the last President. However, Khrushchev concluded, he still believed in the President's good sense. After thunderstorms, people cooled off, thought problems over and resumed human shape.

The storms were apparently not quite over when Khrushchev replied in a televised broadcast on August 7. Though his tone was considerably higher-pitched than Kennedy's, the two speeches none the less bore curious resemblances of the sort which led the President later to invoke the mirror metaphor in discussing Soviet pronouncements. Like Kennedy, Khrushchev was unyielding on his basic position. Like Kennedy, he talked about calling up reservists. Like Kennedy, he mused about the perils of nuclear war. Like Kennedy, he asked his adversaries to meet round the conference table, clear the atmosphere, "rely on reason and not on the power of thermonuclear weapons."

And so the crisis grew in the first weeks of August. Kennedy, having launched his military build-up, now tried to set his diplomatic offensive in motion. He had been pressing the State Department to prepare negotiating positions ever since the Hyannis Port meeting, but it was uphill work. This was in part because of the very genuine intellectual difficulty of devising a proposal. One day Dean Acheson, after hearing Chayes present the case for negotiation, challenged him to come up with a concrete formula: "You'll find, Abe, that it just won't write." Now Acheson himself, in response to the President's request, made his own recommendations. He suggested that the western foreign ministers be called together at the end of August to concert a stand. This could be followed by negotiations with the Soviet Union after the West German elections in September and lead to a four-power foreign ministers' meeting after the 22nd Congress of the Soviet Communist Party in October. As for the content of our negotiating position, Acheson offered in effect a dressed-up version of the status quo.

Acheson's ideas were more helpful with regard to procedure than to substance. Moreover, his star was beginning to wane. He had disapproved of the conciliatory passages in the President's speeches, and some of his characteristically slashing comments had got back to Kennedy, who regretted them, not because they were critical, but because he did not feel, any more than he had after the Bay of Pigs, that those involved in decisions should make their criticisms public. As for Acheson's timetable, even this seemed a little slow. Bundy, McNamara and Maxwell Taylor all thought that the meeting of western foreign ministers should take place as soon as possible; and Kennedy agreed.

Early in August, Rusk went to Paris to work out a negotiating strategy with his three western counterparts. The hope was to find enough agreement to justify inviting the Soviet Union to a four-power conference. The British wanted this, and the West Germans were more receptive than anticipated. But the Americans still had no solid position to propose, and the French remained flatly hostile to the whole idea. De Gaulle soon wrote to Kennedy that the opening of negotiations would be considered immediately as a prelude to the abandonment, at least gradually, of Berlin and as a sort of notice of our surrender. The Paris gathering consequently broke up without result. One wonders whether, if it had produced an invitation to Moscow to discuss the crisis, the Russians would have dared carry through the drastic action they were preparing for the next weekend.

4. THE WALL

For the Berlin crisis was having its most spectacular effect in East Germany itself. The refugee exodus was growing every day; over thirty thousand fled to West Berlin in July alone. Toward the end of the month the East German regime imposed new measures intended to restrict the flight, but the effect was only to increase it. Escape was fast becoming an obsession.

Remembering 1953, our embassy in Bonn began to report the possibility of a popular uprising in East Germany. In Washington a few people began to speculate about further communist countermeasures. Richard Rovere wrote in *The New Yorker* that Khrushchev had "the means at hand for ending the largest of his problems with West Berlin; the flow of refugees could be sealed off at any time." In a television interview on July 30 Senator Fulbright remarked, "I don't understand why the East Germans don't close their border because I think they have a

right to close it." Early in August the President, strolling
with Walt Rostow along the colonnade by the Rose Garden,
observed that Khrushchev would have to do something
internally to re-establish control over the situation—and
that, if he did, we would not be able to do a thing about it.
Eastern Europe was a vital interest for Khrushchev, and
he could not stand by and let it trickle away. But it was
not a vital interest for the United States. "I can get the alliance to move if he tries to do anything about West Berlin
but not if he just does something about East Berlin."

On August 13, a few minutes after midnight, East German troops and police occupied most of the crossing-
points on the East Berlin side of the dividing line, tore up
the streets and installed roadblocks and barbed-wire bar-
ricades. Despite the presidential and other anticipations,
the action caught the State Department and the CIA by surprise; evidently the test-of-will thesis had diverted attention too long from the local problems of East Germany.
And it was at first hard to decide what the action meant.
For—contrary to the later impression that on August 13 the
East Germans built overnight a great wall, which the allies,
if they had had any guts, should have promptly bulldozed
down—a number of crossing-points remained open, the
construction of a concrete wall did not begin till August
17, and movement between the sectors continued for several
days after that. For all Washington could tell on the thirteenth, the intention might have been to control rather than
to end the refugee flow; and this hardly was a reason for
invading the eastern sector and thereby inviting retaliation
and risking war.

Yet the possibility remained that the intention might be
far more sinister: that the Wall might represent the unfolding of an unalterable Soviet plan, based on a conviction of American irresolution, to drive the west out of
Berlin. Kennedy, remarking that there was one chance out
of five of a nuclear exchange, instantly mobilized the resources of government. These were grim days and nights.
The Berlin Task Force went into continuous session. Rejecting some countermeasures, like cutting off interzonal
trade, as too drastic and others, like changing the system
of interzonal passes, as too trivial, it reached the somewhat impotent conclusion that accelerating the military
build-up in the United States was the most effective response. The Task Force also drafted a formal protest.
But it took four days—four interminable days so far as West
Berlin was concerned—before the protest got to Moscow.
The apparent American passivity not unnaturally alarmed

the West Berliners; and on August 16 Mayor Willy Brandt wrote Kennedy condemning the feeble western reaction and proposing a series of more stringent responses. He did not, however, suggest anything like the dispatch of troops into East Berlin to dismantle the barriers. Kennedy replied that the "brutal border closing" represented a Soviet decision which only war could reverse and that no one had supposed "that we should go to war on this point." Nonetheless, Brandt's letter, reinforced by cables from our Minister in Berlin, made it clear that some American reaction more specific than the general military build-up was necessary to sustain the morale of West Berlin. Kennedy therefore decided to send Vice-President Johnson to carry his answer to Brandt and at the same time to signify to the Russians that Berlin was an ultimate American commitment. He also ordered a battle group of 1500 men to move from West Germany to West Berlin.

Adenauer in the meantime, except for political speeches in preparation for the September election, was relatively quiet. He did not visit Berlin till August 22, and, however bold he became as the situation receded, he did not at the time propose any form of direct action against the Wall. Publicly he emphasized that Bonn and the allies stood together and referred vaguely to a possible NATO embargo of the communist bloc. This was apparently campaign oratory; Bonn's representatives never advanced the blockade as a formal proposal before the inter-allied bodies capable of recommending such action. Indeed, in the midst of the clamor, Adenauer held an affable and well-publicized conversation with Andrei Smirnov, the Soviet Ambassador, and even, in an evident effort to discourage uprisings in the Democratic Republic, cautioned the East Germans "not to undertake anything that could only worsen the situation and not make it better." When the Vice-President stopped off at Bonn, the Chancellor pointed out to him that the only sign in the crowd inscribed "Action, Not Words" was borne by an old woman with whom, he said, he would personally wish neither. While he did write Kennedy on August 29 declaring that acquiescence in future acts of communist force in the manner of August 13 would be "out of the question," he did not record even at this point basic disagreement with western policy toward the Wall. In subsequent messages to Kennedy, both Adenauer and Brandt urged the west to move more speedily toward negotiations with the Soviet Union.

Though Johnson is said to have felt a little gloomy over

the prospect of going to West Berlin, he performed his mission superbly. His speech, with its invocation of the Declaration of Independence and its pledge of American lives, fortunes and sacred honor, was cleared personally by the President. Johnson delivered it with genuine and convincing emotion. There was a weekend of anxiety in Washington while the 1st Battle Group, 8th Infantry, rolled down the *Autobahn* to West Berlin. Similar troop movements had often taken place in the past, but no one could be sure that the Russians might not try to stop this one. However, the column proceeded without interference, and the Vice-President greeted the troops when they arrived. Johnson returned deeply moved to Washington. His visit was a turning point in relieving Berlin's crisis of confidence. Then on August 30 Kennedy appointed as his personal representative in West Berlin General Lucius Clay, remembered from the early postwar days as the great symbol of Western protection. These steps, expressing the clear American determination to honor the allied guarantees, revived the spirit of West Berlin.

The Wall remained, a shabby obscenity straggling across the face of the city. In retrospect it seems to have been a defensive rather than an aggressive action. It represented a solution, at considerable political cost, of the problem which, more perhaps than anything else, had led Khrushchev to reopen the Berlin question earlier in the year. By stanching the blood-flow from East Germany, the Wall secured the most immediate Soviet interest in Berlin. Kennedy's determination to rebuild the military power of the west had shown Khrushchev that he could not obtain his maximum objectives by bluff. Now the Wall, by achieving his minimum objective, released him from the necessity of forcing the issue to a showdown.

5. THE CRISIS FADES AWAY

This was not, however, fully perceived at the time. It is hard now to recall the forebodings of the late summer of 1961, to evoke again the pessimism that shrouded the government. George Kennan came back from Belgrade for a few days in August. "I am expendable, I have no further official career, and I am going to do everything I can to prevent a war," he said to me one afternoon with great earnestness. ". . . We both know how tenuous a relation there is between a man's intentions and the consequences of his acts. There is no presumption more terrifying than that of those who would blow up the world on the basis of their personal judgment of a transient situation. I do not propose to let the future of mankind be settled, or ended, by a group of men operating on the basis of limited perspectives and short-run calculations. I figure that the only thing I have left in life is to do everything I can to stop the war."

These were strange, moody days. Khrushchev told Drew Pearson of his admiration for John Foster Dulles, and this seemed to portend new Soviet experiments in brinksmanship. The Wall was followed on August 24 by an angry Soviet note accusing the west of using the air corridors to import "revanchists, extremists, saboteurs and spies" into Berlin and on August 30 by the Soviet resumption of nuclear testing (in the face of Khrushchev's statement to Kennedy at Vienna that he would not test until we did). When Rusk commented to the President on September 5 that Moscow was showing little interest in negotiation, Kennedy replied grimly, "It isn't time yet. It's too early. They are bent on scaring the world to death before they begin negotiating, and they haven't quite brought the pot to boil. Not enough people are frightened." In this atmosphere, I found myself writing friends abroad, "I feel more gloomy about international developments than I have felt since the summer of 1939."

Given this apparent Soviet desperation, the White House group regarded it as more urgent than ever to speed the military build-up and at the same time to exhaust every diplomatic recourse before Armageddon. On August 14, the day after the first crossing-points were closed, Bundy reported to the President unanimity in his immediate staff for the view that we should take a clear initiative for negotiation within the next week or ten days. The possibility of a revolt in East Germany constituted a further argument for seizing the initiative. The State Department, he added, was more cautious about American action, preferring to keep things within the four-power process. Bundy, doubting whether new ideas would come out of the four-power discussions and noting that we were making very slow headway toward a clear position, suggested that a public deadline might be the only way to galvanize the lumbering machinery into action.

Rusk now proposed that the foreign ministers coming to New York for the UN General Assembly meeting might work out a time and place; and Kennedy thought this a good plan. But the machinery continued to creak. "I want to take a stronger lead on Berlin negotiations," Kennedy finally wrote the Secretary on August 21. We must make it plain to our allies that we plan to issue an invitation to negotiations before September 1; they can then come along or stay behind. As for our negotiating position, the Acheson paper was a good start, but more work remained to be done. In this and in succeeding letters and meetings, Kennedy, almost despairingly, threw out a wide variety of specific ideas in the hope of prodding the Department to action.

In a few days Rusk announced that negotiation with the Soviet Union would definitely take place after the General Assembly convened in mid-September. The problem remained of producing a western, or even an American, position. Rusk wanted to match the Soviet revival of its 1958 position by dusting off the essentials of the western 1959 response—reunification of Berlin and Germany on the basis of free elections, and so on. Obviously each side would reject the other's cherished formula; then Moscow could sign its separate treaty, the East Germans would begin checking papers on the *Autobahn*, the American military posture would discourage interference with access, and things would simmer down to tacit agreement on the status quo. Some of us at the White House, on the other hand, clung to the hope of a real negotiation which might lead, we thought, if at the price of hard bargaining with Bonn, to a new status for West Berlin, new guarantees of western presence and access and perhaps a general arrangement for central European security.

The President took a middle position. He was sure that the traditional western plan was the wrong framework for negotiations and wanted something new. The reunification of Germany seemed to him an unrealistic negotiating objective. But at the same time he had no wish to perpetuate the idea of a divided Germany by recognizing East Germany. Accepting that division as a fact, he told President Kekkonen of Finland in October, "is a different matter from giving it status and permanence. You must be aware of the melancholy state of mind induced in West Germany by the Wall. We do not want to spread that state of melancholy by legitimatizing the East German regime and stimulating a nationalist revival in West Germany. . . . Germany has been divided for sixteen years and will continue to stay divided. The Soviet Union is running an unnecessary risk in trying to change this from an accepted fact into a legal state. Let the Soviet Union keep Germany divided on its present basis and not try to persuade us to associate ourselves legally with that division and thus weaken our ties to West Germany and their ties to Western Europe." Nor did Soviet assurances of fresh guarantees of western presence and access impress him. "The Soviet Union," he told Kekkonen, "is asking us to make concessions in exchange for which they will give us again what we already have. And these concessions, in addition, would insure that West Germany goes nationalistic and becomes a danger to the peace. This is no bargain. We would be buying the same horse twice."

He lost no opportunity to signal his attitude to Moscow. James Wechsler, who had come away from his talk with Kennedy moved by the earnestness with which the President discussed the nuclear peril, proposed in late September that he write a column about Kennedy's thoughts on war and peace and challenge the Soviet press to republish it. Pierre Salinger thought this a good idea, and the President personally approved the Wechsler text. Wechsler noted that Kennedy, as the son of a rich man, was the perfect caricature for communist propagandists who assumed that wealth meant war; but "if that doctrinaire rubbish is what Mr. Khrushchev believes, he is mad, and we are all doomed." After observing that Kennedy would not be shoved around and had achieved "a certain composure about the brutal nature of the choice he may have to face in the solitude of some ghastly night," Wechsler added that nothing in the President's view was non-negotiable except the dignity of free men: "I have no trace of doubt about the authenticity and depth of his desire for rational settlements in a world that has trembled on the brink so long. Russian papers, please copy." Considerably to our surprise the Russian papers did copy in a few days, including even the suggestion that Khrushchev was a madman if he considered Kennedy a Wall Street imperialist.

There were many ways to initiate a dialogue; and in the end the substance of negotiations turned out to matter a good deal less than the willingness to negotiate. It was this which gave Khrushchev the pretext he needed for retreat, once he had stopped the refugee flight to the west. While inconclusive talks began between Gromyko and western officials, Khrushchev took the occasion to report in a six-hour speech to the 22nd Congress of the Soviet Communist Party on October 17 that "the western powers were showing some understanding of the situation, and were inclined to seek a solution to the German problem and the issue of West Berlin." If this were so, "we shall not insist on signing a peace treaty absolutely before December 31, 1961." The crisis was suddenly over.

6. CODA

Four months later I visited West Berlin with Robert and

Ethel Kennedy. We arrived on Washington's Birthday, a freezing, blowy, snowy day. As the Attorney General disembarked, a band launched incongruously into "When the Crimson in triumph flashing/Mid the strains of Victory." Brandt, Clay and Allan Lightner, the American Minister, met us at the airport. Thousands of people endured the chill along the streets into West Berlin to welcome President Kennedy's brother. They waved, they shouted, some wept. Over a hundred thousand stood in the square before the *Rathaus* where Bobby, shivering in the bitter cold, gave an impromptu speech. When balloons bearing red flags floated over from the eastern sector, he said, "The Communists will let the balloons through, but they won't let their people come through," and the crowd mingled defiance and anguish in an animal roar.

That night at the Free University of Berlin he delivered the Ernst Reuter lecture in honor of the great mayor of the airlift crisis. We had discussed this talk on the plane from Rome. Someone in Clay's headquarters had sent him an emotional draft filled with denunciations of communist perfidy and promises of American deliverance. The Attorney General had quickly put it aside. There was no point, he said, in kidding anybody, no point in exciting emotions beyond the possibility of satisfaction. This was not responsible. One had to begin with a realistic understanding of the problem and move on to the only lasting solution, which would come from the superiority, to be demonstrated in practice and over time, of one form of society to another.

Students and faculty crowded every inch of the auditorium. The Attorney General began with the ritual of reassurance about the American commitment to Berlin. Then he added, "We do not stand here in Berlin just because we are against communism. We stand here because we have a positive and progressive vision of the possibilities of free society—because we see freedom as the instrumentality of social progress and social justice—because communism itself is but the symptom and consequence of the fundamental evils, ignorance, disease, hunger and want, and freedom has shown mankind the most effective way to destroy those ancient antagonists." When he finished, the applause was vigorous and sustained.

The next morning he spoke at a breakfast attended by West Berlin dignitaries—editors, ministers and lawyers. He was direct and frank, making no effort to gratify the audience by saying the easy things. He courteously reproached the West Germans for assuming that the United States had abandoned solemn commitments whenever a month went by without some American notable coming to Berlin to reaffirm them. The Wall, he said, was an atrocity, but no miracle was going to bring it down. As for German reunification, this was remote; one could only hope that the processes of history, already having their effect in Eastern Europe, would one day change East Germany and deliver West Berlin. The group listened intently and seemed to appreciate the Attorney General's honesty. One felt a surge of respect for their courage patiently sustained through so many years of trial.

After breakfast we made a tour of the Wall. It was more barbaric and sinister than one could have imagined—the crude, gray concrete blocks, the bricked-in windows of apartment houses along the sector line, the vicious tank traps, the tall picket fences erected to prevent East Berliners from even waving to relatives or friends in West Berlin, the plain white crosses marking places where people had jumped to their death and beside which Robert Kennedy now laid flowers. Then we passed on to an equally repellent sight—the Ploetzensee, where the heroes of the anti-Hitler putsch of 1944 had been executed, the stark, whitewashed room with the bare meat-hooks at the end, compact with an extraordinary sense of evil and fatality.

I asked Willy Brandt whether, looking back, he thought the allies should have done something to halt the Wall or to tear it down. He replied with impressive candor, "If I were to say now that something could or should have been done, it would be inconsistent with what I felt and said at the time. I do believe that the allies should have been much quicker in their condemnation of the action. But that would not have stopped the building of the Wall. On August 13 no one proposed that we stop the Wall. We all supposed that such action would run the risk of war."

Trouble was by no means at an end. Though Khrushchev had once again forsworn his deadline and permitted the situation (with the exception of the Wall) to revert to the status quo, he continued to consider West Berlin, as he explained in typical language to Harriman in 1963, the exposed western foot and planned from time to time to stamp on the corns. The year after Vienna saw sporadic and unpredictable harassments of a more or less petty sort in the air corridors and along the *Autobahn*, presumably designed to test western reactions and, with luck, to nibble at western rights. Worse, the Wall itself remained a haunting relic of the crisis and became, from time to time, the occasion for new tragedy, as in August 1962, when the East German police shot down a young man trying to flee to the west and left him to perish in agony in the full view of West Berlin.

General Clay, now in his second term as proconsul, reacted to provocation with speed and strength in the winter of 1961–62. Some of his initiatives alarmed the State Department and the Foreign Office, but, as Clay later said, "whenever I carried my case directly to the President, I was supported." His stout-hearted leadership left a legacy of valuable precedent. But what some considered his compulsion to force issues led to growing friction with Washington. Having ably accomplished his mission, he took advantage of a lull between harassments and resigned his post in April 1962.

Clay's mood reflected in a restrained form the chronic discontent of the government at Bonn—a discontent which periodically soared into acute exasperation as the United States and the Soviet Union pursued desultory talks about Berlin. Bonn's endless stream of complaints, leaks to the press and demands for reassurance increasingly irritated Washington. It was, the President said once, like a wife who asks her husband every night, "Do you love me?" and, when he keeps repeating he does, nevertheless asks again, "But do you *really* love me?"—and then puts detectives on his trail. The German Ambassador to Washington, Wilhelm Grewe, so bored the White House with pedantic and long-winded recitals that word was finally passed to his government that his recall would improve communication.

Kennedy had begun with great respect for Adenauer, for his historic role in binding West Germany to the Atlantic community and for his undiminished personal vitality; he was amused to figure out when Adenauer came to Washington in 1961 that, if he were President of the United States at the Chancellor's age, it would be the year 2002. "He is a greater man than de Gaulle," he said after dinner at the White House one evening in October 1961, "because his objectives transcend his nation while de Gaulle dedicates himself to the aggrandizement of his nation." But, as time passed and Adenauer looked back with growing nostalgia to the days when John Foster Dulles allowed him a virtual veto over American policy, Bonn's laments and obstructions mounted. Kennedy, though he preserved polite relations, came to feel that the old Chancellor was hanging on too hard. He welcomed the rise of Gerhard Schröder, who became Foreign Minister after the elections in 1961, greatly liked Willy Brandt and had hopes for the younger generation of German leaders.

The Berlin crisis of 1961 represented a further step

beyond Laos in the education of the President in the controlled employment of force for the service of peace. One never knows, of course, what would have happened if Kennedy had ordered full mobilization, or if he had rushed straight to negotiation; but either extreme might well have invited Soviet miscalculation and ended in war. Instead he applied power and diplomacy in a combination and sequence which enabled him to guard the vital interests of the west and hold off the holocaust. The weeks from Vienna to the 22nd Party Congress had nevertheless been cruel and disheartening. The Berlin crisis, along with the Soviet resumption of nuclear tests, left the President no alternative but to forgo his pursuit of a standstill and harden his policy and purpose.

As for the negotiations which had seemed so urgent in the early autumn of 1961, they lost their priority after Khrushchev dropped his deadline and descended from the heads of state to the foreign office bureaucracies. In early 1962 each side tabled its set of proposals in a succession of Rusk-Gromyko talks. But technical formulas were not likely to bridge the gap between the allies' determination to stay in Berlin and the Soviet determination to drive them out. It seemed probable that Khrushchev did not want the gap bridged. He realized after the summer of 1961 that he could not expel the west within the existing equilibrium of military force. But he still cherished his dream of a communist Berlin, and this no doubt led him to ponder in 1962 how he might revise the military equilibrium to permit the renewal of his campaign under a balance of power more favorable to the Soviet Union.

It would take still another and more terrible crisis—the moment of supreme risk which Kennedy had predicted to James Wechsler—before Khrushchev was willing to abandon the politics of intimidation and before Kennedy, two years after Vienna, was able to pick up the threads of his policy and try again to lead the world beyond the cold war.

XVI

THE RECONSTRUCTION OF DIPLOMACY

THE FRUSTRATIONS of the summer over Berlin brought the President's discontent with his Department of State to a climax. One muddle after another—the Department's acquiescence in the Bay of Pigs, the fecklessness of its recommendations after the disaster, the ordeal of trying to change its attitude toward Laos, the maddening delay over the answer to Khrushchev's *aide-mémoire* and the banality of the result, the apparent impossibility of developing a negotiating position for Berlin—left Kennedy with little doubt that the State Department was not yet an instrumentality fully and promptly responsive to presidential purpose.

He well understood the difficulty of converting a tradition-ridden bureaucracy into a mechanism for swift information and decision. But resistance was no less great in Defense, where McNamara was plainly making progress in annexing the Pentagon to the United States government. Other departments provided quick answers to presidential questions and quick action on presidential orders. It was a constant puzzle to Kennedy that the State Department remained so formless and impenetrable. He would say, "Damn it, Bundy and I get more done in one day in the White House than they do in six months in the State Department." Giving State an instruction, he remarked, snapping his fingers with impatience, is like dropping it in the dead-letter box. "They never have any ideas over there," he complained, "never come up with anything new." "The State Department is a bowl of jelly," he told Hugh Sidey of *Time* in the summer of 1961. "It's got all those people over there who are constantly smiling. I think we need to smile less and be tougher."

1. THE INSTITUTIONALIZATION OF FOREIGN POLICY

Kennedy had come to the Presidency determined to make the Department of State the central point, below the Presidency itself, in the conduct of foreign affairs. As Dean Rusk told the Department's policy-making officers a few weeks after the inauguration, there was not "a passive reliance but an active expectation on his part that this Department will in fact take charge of foreign policy." McGeorge Bundy emphasized to the Jackson Subcommittee, which had long been casting a critical eye on the organization of national security policy, that the President wanted no question to arise concerning "the clear authority and responsibility of the Secretary of State, not only in his own Department, and not only in such large-scale related areas as foreign aid and information policy, but also as the *agent of coordination* in all our major policies toward other nations." [1]

[1] My italics.

In embarking on this course, Kennedy was influenced not only by a desire to clarify and concentrate the making of foreign policy but also, I believe, by a basic respect for the skills of the Foreign Service. No doubt his attitude toward professional diplomats was mixed. He probably recalled his father's complaints as ambassador to England (Harold Ickes noted in his diary in 1938 that Joe Kennedy "inveighed eloquently against 'the career boys' . . . insisted that the State Department did not know what was going on . . . that nothing got to the President straight unless he sent it to the President direct"). And his visit to Southeast Asia as a young Congressman in 1951 had left him, as he said on his return, with an impression that Foreign Service officers often knew all too little about the nations to which they were accredited, were indifferent to their language and customs, did not represent contemporary America and spent too much time at tennis and cocktails.[2] Nevertheless there were always the Charles Bohlens, Llewellyn Thompsons and Edmund Gullions; and Kennedy's disappointment about the State Department as President sprang in part, I think, from a special sympathy for the diplomatic enterprise. He expected generals and admirals to be refractory and obtuse, but he was not inclined, like Franklin Roosevelt, to write off professional diplomats as inherently stuffy and wrong. In other circumstances he would have liked to be an ambassador himself. He knew that many of 'the career boys' had resented the Dulles regime, and he had looked forward to fruitful collaboration with the Foreign Service and the Department.

The Foreign Service, after all, was the elite unit of the American government. It was in great measure a self-administered body, selecting, assessing and promoting from within. It had deep pride in its *esprit de corps*. "Foreign Service work," as George Kennan wrote, "breeds its own morale, outwardly undemonstrative, often not externally visible, but inwardly far tougher and more devoted than is generally realized." The typical career officer, Kennan continued, was able and patriotic, anxious to learn, to grow in his work and to serve the nation, only too anxious to give loyalty where loyalty was given in return. The process of 'lateral transfer'—the admission to the upper levels of the Service of men trained in other parts of the government—had somewhat diluted the mandarin character of the Service during and after the war; and it entered the postwar world with new accessions of skill and spirit. Anyone who had seen the Service in action well knew the intelligence, de-

[2] Meet the Press, December 2, 1951.

cency and selflessness of this group of exceptionally devoted men and women. The White House could always win any battle it chose over the Service; but the prestige and proficiency of the Service limited the number of battles any White House would find it profitable to fight.

Still, as his pre-election task forces reminded Kennedy, the Service had its professional deformations. Moreover, both its vast increase in size and the trauma of the Dulles-McCarthy period had had a disturbing impact on its thought and operation. Thus Adlai Stevenson in his foreign policy report mentioned the "tremendous institutional inertial force" in the Department of State "which, unless manipulated forcefully from the outset, will overwhelm and dictate to the new regime. A similar institutional force in the Defense Department has systematically absorbed a series of Secretaries of Defense." With such comments in mind, Kennedy set up after the election a task force on "State Department Operations Overseas and in Washington." "Even such a distinguished career group as the Foreign Service," the new group soon reported, "has failed to keep pace with the novel and expanding demands of a changing world." The Department had to recognize that "the prototype diplomatic officer of the past, the so-called 'generalist' whose experience was largely 'political,' cannot be the apogee of the Service." Reform, the report conceded, would provoke the cry that the morale of the Service was in danger; but "that raises the question of whose morale? The morale of real concern to the country is that of the young, imaginative, all too frequently circumscribed officer." The task force pointed out that, if Kennedy himself had entered the Foreign Service instead of politics, he could at this point barely qualify for appointment to Class II under existing Foreign Service regulations and would have to wait for seven more years before he could even hope to become a Career Minister.

These strictures emerged from the experience of the years since the Second World War. The role of American diplomacy in prewar days had been largely spectatorial and ceremonial. But in the postwar world our diplomats could no longer be merely observers. They were operators in more than a hundred countries around the planet, and they needed regional knowledge and technical skill as well as personal initiative to make their interventions effective. But in many cases the older career men deplored the new tendencies toward specialization, whether functional or (except for the Russia and China services) regional. They continued to see themselves as gentlemen, not players; the political officer remained the Service's beau ideal. Economic, scientific, cultural, commercial and agricultural attachés made up a rather grubby supporting cast. As for regional expertise, the State Department efficiency report as late as 1963 did not even include the heading "Knowledge of Country and Area," long standard in USIA forms; of seventeen items under "Qualities" not one pertained to area specialization. Younger officers feared that the better their qualifications for a particular country, the lower rating they would get under "General Usefulness."

Nearly every problem inherent in the Foreign Service process had been compounded by its prodigious growth. In 1930 the Department of State had a budget of about $15 million, the total membership of the Foreign Service was about 1700, and the telegraphic traffic for the whole year amounted to little more than two million words. By the 1960s State had a budget rising toward $300 million, there were over 9000 in the Foreign Service, and every two months the telegraphic traffic was greater than in all 1930. The Department itself had moved from its pleasant and leisured home beside the White House, with its high ceilings, great fireplaces and swinging doors, to a vast, unlovely building in Foggy Bottom, correctly described by August Heckscher, the President's Special Consultant on the Arts, as a "monument to false functionalism and false grandeur."

As it grew in size, the Department diminished in usefulness. This was in part the consequence of bureaucratization. 'Layering'—the bureaucrat's term for the imposition of one level of administrative responsibility on top of another—created a system of 'concurrences,' which required every proposal to run a hopelessly intricate obstacle course before it could become policy. Obviously clearance was necessary to avoid anarchy, but it often became an excuse for doing as little as possible. The mounting unwieldiness of the procedures drove Kennan to the gloomy conclusion that, in really delicate and urgent situations, "American statesmen will have to take refuge in a bypassing of the regular machinery and in the creation of *ad hoc* devices —kitchen cabinets, personal envoys, foreign offices within foreign offices, and personal diplomacy—to assure the intimacy of association, the speed, the privacy, and the expression of personal style essential to any effective diplomacy."

Franklin Roosevelt and Cordell Hull had started the Department's descent from its traditional place at the summit of the foreign policy process—Roosevelt because he wanted certain things done and Hull because he was not temperamentally able to do them. Thwarted in the Secretary's office, Roosevelt fell into the habit of using other instruments—first Sumner Welles, the Under Secretary; then other Cabinet members, like Secretary of the Treasury Henry Morgenthau, Jr.; and later General George C. Marshall and the Joint Chiefs of Staff, new agencies such as the Office of War Information and the Board of Economic Welfare, and personal envoys, like Harry Hopkins and Averell Harriman. No Secretary of State after the war, not even Acheson or Dulles, was quite able to gather back the vanished powers. By 1961 the State Department was but one of many bodies involved in foreign affairs. The London Embassy, for example, housed representatives of forty-four agencies of the United States government.

Bureaucratization was only part of the explanation for State's malaise when Kennedy came to office. The other part was the shock of McCarthy—or rather the shock of the readiness of Dulles, as Secretary of State, to yield up Foreign Service officers to McCarthyism. The Dulles period was a time of distress and humiliation for the professionals. These years saw the expulsion of experienced and independent-minded diplomats, like John Davies, Jr., and the exile of others, like Charles Bohlen. A proud Service found itself ordered about by Scott McLeod, a coarse straw boss whom Dulles brought in as Security Administrator, and cowering before juvenile comedians like Roy Cohn and G. David Schine. Circumspection had always eased the path to advancement in the Service; now it became a requirement for survival. The McCarthy era, by demonstrating the peril of dangerous thoughts, elevated conformism into a conditioned reflex. Career men stopped telling Washington what they really thought and consecrated themselves to the clichés of the cold war. Some did this more skillfully than others, and the result, as Davies wrote later, was that "many cautious mediocrities rose to the top of the Service," along with those most uncritically committed to the cold-war view of the world.

The Service was not so much an instrument of action as a way of life. And it was a way of life which not seldom divested career officers of strong views of their own. The way to success lay in the faithful support of established policy. The lack of continuity in assignment—Iceland one year, Tanganyika the next—made it difficult to develop an intense interest in new policies. It was no coincidence that the Russia and China services, where the necessity of learning a difficult language compelled continuity, were precisely the services where the professionals were most outspoken on policy matters—and were in consequence most punished in the Dulles-McCarthy years. By the time, moreover, that career officers received independent responsibility, they were often, as Kennan said, too old "to grow in the exercise of it." At times it almost looked as if the Service inducted a collection of spirited young Americans at the age of twenty-five and transmuted them in twenty years into bland and homologous denizens of a conservative men's club. "I have seen, over the decades," Kennan said, "an unduly high percentage of older men in this Service who prematurely lost physical and intellectual tone, who became, at best, empty bundles of good manners and, at worst, rousing stuffed shirts."

2. FOGGY BOTTOM IN 1961

This was the situation which confronted Kennedy in his attempt to make the Department the agent of coordination.

The new administration almost immediately bogged down in the bureaucratic tangle. Men like Harriman and Kennan, who had known the Department as late as the Truman administration, were startled by the transformation of a decade. When a foreign ambassador made a courtesy call on Harriman early in 1961, a junior officer mysteriously appeared to record the conversation. Harriman ascertained that he planned to write an *aide-mémoire*, submit it to Harriman for correction and send copies to all interested bureaus and embassies, where presumably it would have to be read, pondered and filed. Shuddering at the proliferation of paper and the expenditure of energy, Harriman said that, if by chance anything of consequence were said, he would inform somebody, and told the officer to go away.

The machinery was becoming an end in itself. Dean Rusk remarked to the Jackson National Security Subcommittee that he often read in the morning telegrams specific questions to which he knew the specific answer, but each telegram would nonetheless have to go "on its appointed course into the Bureau, and through the office and down to the desk. If it doesn't go down there, somebody feels that he is being deprived of his participation in a matter of his responsibility. Then it goes from the action officer back up through the Department to me a week or ten days later, and if it isn't the answer that I knew had to be the

answer, then I [have to] change it." (We experienced the
results with some exasperation at the other end of the
White House line. The Department had the habit of sending cables over at the end of the day and demanding immediate presidential clearance in the most urgent terms,
when we knew that the document had probably taken three
weeks to move from the country desk into and out of the
top offices on the seventh floor.) And all this involved more
than just the waste of time. "The heart of the bureaucratic
problem," Rusk once observed, "is the inclination to avoid
responsibility." The President used to divert himself with
the dream of establishing a secret office of thirty people
or so to run foreign policy while maintaining the State Department as a façade in which people might contentedly
carry papers from bureau to bureau.

Nor did the Department respond to the President's own
emphasis on the values of specialization. A friend of Kennedy's on a trip to Morocco came upon a young officer
who loved the country and had learned the Berber languages but was about to be transferred to the Caribbean.
When this was reported to the President, he said wearily
that he had sent the Department a memorandum six months
ago saying that it was better to let officers build up expertise
than to rotate them mechanically every two years. An acquaintance of mine in the Service had sixteen years of
Japanese language competence; he never was assigned to a
State Department post in Japan. An officer who spoke and
wrote Korean, served seven years in Korea and published
articles in American and Korean scholarly journals, came
to the conclusion that specialization in countries of small
size constituted a dead end in the Service. In his letter of
resignation, he wrote, "We have been willing to leave
30,000 men on the battlefields of Korea, but we have
seemed unwilling to support with consistency and hope of
ultimate success a single career dedicated to American relations with Korea. . . . The tacit assumption that countries
of medium size can absorb American blood and treasure,
but are somehow unworthy of the sustained interest of an
intelligent mind or an ambitious career is, in these areas,
unhelpful to our interests and repute."

Worst of all, bureaucratization and McCarthyism had
strengthened the most defensive and conservative impulses within the Foreign Service. I remember sitting in
our Georgetown garden on an August night in 1961 when
Harriman came back to Washington during a break in the
interminable Geneva conference on Laos. The Foreign

Service, he said, had been so thoroughly brainwashed by Dulles that it almost required what the Chinese called "thought correction" in order to adjust to the New Frontier. The Service, he added sadly, had declined greatly in purpose, clarity and liberalism since he had last known it. One's own experience documented this resistance to the spirit of the new administration. When José Figueres came to Washington in the spring of 1961, our embassy in San José cabled that it viewed the prospect of his seeing President Kennedy "with consternation"; it feared that a meeting with the former president of Costa Rica would upset the present Costa Rican regime. Naturally Kennedy wanted to talk to a leader of Latin American democracy who had been among the first to endorse the Alliance for Progress and whose knowledge and influence went far beyond the borders of his own small country. The Department in Washington, more sensitive to the new mood, interposed no obstacle, the meeting took place, and the Costa Rican regime survived. But it was a constant struggle.

One almost concluded that the definition of a Foreign Service officer was a man for whom the risks always outweighed the opportunities. Career officers had always tended to believe that the foreign policy of the United States was their institutional, if not their personal, property, to be solicitously protected against interference from the White House and other misguided amateurs; and by 1961 those favored in the Dulles years added to this proprietary instinct an immovable devotion to the attitudes of the past, whether good or bad. The hardest thing of all was to change anything—attitudes, programs, clichés. No one was more annoyed by this fidelity to the past, or more poignant in expressing his annoyance, than Galbraith. "You have no idea," he wrote me from New Delhi in 1961, "how difficult it is to control one's reaction over the smug pursuit of what experience has already shown to be disastrous policies." The situation led Galbraith's more philosophical associate, the social analyst Mark Epernay, to point out that, for the sophisticated man, the wisdom of policy naturally mattered far less than its stability. "Few things more clearly mark the amateur in diplomacy than his inability to see that even the change from the wrong policy to the right policy involves the admission of previous error and hence is damaging to national prestige." This insight stimulated Epernay to design a "fully automated foreign policy" guaranteed to produce the proper response to every crisis. So, if Khrushchev threatened to sign a peace treaty with East Germany, the electronic computer could immediately type out the appropriate reply: "We stand willing to negotiate but we cannot act under threat or pressure and we must not make concessions. The reunification of Germany is essential but we do not thereby concede the existence of East Germany. We support the brave people of West Berlin." [3]

At times, it almost seemed that we had achieved the fully automated foreign policy. Thus I spent three years in the White House in a plaintive and unavailing effort to beg the State Department to stop using the phrase 'Sino-Soviet bloc.' This was a typical Foreign Service expression—barbarous in form (the parallelism would be 'Russo-Chinese' or, if absolutely necessary, 'Sino-Russian') and obsolescent in content. In a memorandum to the State Department Secretariat in January 1963, I wrote:

> Whatever substance [the phrase] might once have had as referring to a unified Russo-Chinese operation has surely been trickling away rather fast in recent months. Today the phrase is in most instances simply absurd. It suggests that those who use it don't know what is going on in the world. I assume that this is not the case.

Again in July, when the feud between Moscow and Peking seemed beyond all possibility of denial:

> In view of what is going on currently in Moscow, could not the Department bring itself to abolish the usage 'Sino-Soviet bloc'? The relationship of that phrase to reality grows more tenuous all the time.[4]

This dedication to the past found its ultimate sanction in what seemed the Service's unshakable determination to protect those who, if wrong, were wrong in the right way and to penalize those who, though right, were right out of channels or out of cadence. The Foreign Service operated as a sort of benevolent society, taking care of its worst as well as —sometimes better than—its best. The promotion system was in effect a conspiracy of the conventional against the unconventional. J. Graham Parsons, having drastically misconceived the situation in Laos, was made ambassador to Sweden. His successor as Assistant Secretary for Far Eastern Affairs, a blameless but unimaginative career officer, having displayed no initiative in Washington, was sent as ambassador to a pivotal Asian state.

On the other hand, zeal for good, but new, policies at the expense of bad, but established, ones was likely to gain an officer the reputation for causing trouble and—under the

---

[3] Mark Epernay, *The McLandress Dimension* (Boston, 1963), 61, 67.
[4] It was a losing fight. As I write—on May 9, 1965–I note Thomas C. Mann, Under Secretary of State for Economic Affairs, running on in a interview with the *New York Times* about "instruments of Sino-Soviet military power" and "orders from the Sino-Soviet military bloc."

system where the challenged officer wrote the 'efficiency reports'—a place at the bottom of his Foreign Service class. When Kennedy ended the unrelenting American opposition to the center-left coalition in Italy, the Deputy Chief of Mission in Rome, who had been single-handedly responsible for the prolongation of that policy long after it had become obsolete, became ambassador to Czechoslovakia; while an intelligent junior officer who had fought prematurely for the new policy in the Rome Embassy was marked down for insubordination, his offense having been that of carrying the case past the D.C.M. to the ambassador. This man was saved only by White House intervention from being 'selected out' (a phrase apparently adapted from Samuel Goldwyn) of the Service. Another young officer had served in an Iron Curtain capital. Visiting his country some years before, I had been impressed not only by his insight into the country but by his skill in the language and his exceptional range of acquaintances among writers, journalists and scholars. I ran into him again in 1962 and noted: "His is the all too familiar story. His independence and originality of mind brought him into conflict with his superior. . . . They denounced him as insubordinate; he was rated in the bottom five per cent of his class by the selection board; and is now slated for a consulship in [an Asian country]—obviously a punitive assignment." As Harriman told the Jackson Subcommittee in 1963, "I have noted that men because they haven't gotten along with one individual have been given very low ratings, when others have given them high ratings. . . . Men with a spark and independence of expression are at times held down, whereas caution is rewarded."

Caution even smothered the Department's relations with its own envoys abroad. In Western Europe after the Bay of Pigs one ambassador after another asked me in varying tones of perplexity and anguish what in hell had happened. On my return I called for the cable files and found that Washington had confined itself to sending around bland official 'explanations' couched in language suitable for public release. For what had really happened American diplomats overseas did better to rely on *Newsweek* and *Time*. Even though the Attorney General interested himself in the problem, we were never able to persuade State to level with its own embassies on this matter. This sort of thing was all too common. Galbraith, after receiving a similarly useless 'explanation' of policy, sent a crisp cable to the Department suggesting that in the future the confidential communications of the State Department not be used for purposes of "internal bemusement." The suggestion was unavailing.

3. A NOTE ON LANGUAGE

The intellectual exhaustion of the Foreign Service expressed itself in the poverty of the official rhetoric. In meetings the men from State would talk in a bureaucratic patois borrowed in large part from the Department of Defense. We would be exhorted to 'zero in' on 'the purpose of the drill' (or of the 'exercise' or 'operation'), to 'crank in' this and 'phase out' that and 'gin up' something else, to 'pinpoint' a 'viable' policy and, behind it, a 'fall-back position,' to ignore the 'flak' from competing government bureaus or from the communists, to refrain from 'nit-picking' and never to be 'counterproductive.' Once we were 'seized of the problem,' preferably in as 'hard-nosed' a manner as possible, we would review 'options,' discuss 'over-all' objectives, seek 'breakthroughs,' consider 'crash programs,' 'staff out' policies—doing all these things preferably 'meaningfully' and 'in depth' until we were ready to 'finalize' our deliberations, 'sign on to' or 'sign off on' a conclusion (I never could discover the distinction, if any, between these two locutions) and 'implement' a decision. This was not just shorthand; part of the conference-table vocabulary involved a studied multiplication of words. Thus one never talked about a 'paper' but always a 'piece of paper,' never said 'at this point' but always 'at this point in time.'

Graceless as this patois was, it did have a certain, if sometimes spurious, air of briskness and efficiency. The result was far worse when the Department stopped talking and started writing. Whether drafting memoranda, cables or even letters or statements for the President, the Department fell into full, ripe, dreariness of utterance with hideous ease. The recipe was evidently to take a handful of clichés (saying something in a fresh way might create unforeseen troubles), repeat at five-minute intervals (lest the argument become clear or interesting), stir in the dough of the passive voice (the active voice assigns responsibility and was therefore hazardous) and garnish with self-serving rhetoric (Congress would be unhappy unless we constantly proclaimed the rectitude of American motives).

After the Bay of Pigs, the State Department sent over a document entitled "The Communist Totalitarian Government of Cuba as a Source of International Tension in the Americas," which it had approved for distribution to NATO, CENTO, SEATO, the OAS and the free governments of Latin America and eventually for public release. In addition to the usual defects of Foggy Bottom prose, the paper was filled with bad spelling and grammar. Moreover, the narrative, which mysteriously stopped at the beginning of April 1961, contained a self-righteous condemnation of Castro's interventionist activities in the Caribbean that an unfriendly critic, alas! could have applied, without changing a word, to more recent actions by the United States. I responded on behalf of the White House:

It is our feeling here that the paper should not be disseminated in its present form. . . .

Presumably the document is designed to impress, not an audience which is already passionately anti-Castro, but an audience which has not yet finally made up its mind on the gravity of the problem. Such an audience is going to be persuaded, not by rhetoric, but by evidence. Every effort to heighten the evidence by rhetoric only impairs the persuasive power of the document. Observe the title: 'The Communist Totalitarian Government of Cuba . . .' This title presupposes the conclusion which the paper seeks to establish. Why not call it 'The Castro Regime in Cuba' and let the reader draw his own conclusions from the evidence? And why call it both 'Communist' and 'totalitarian'? All Communist governments are totalitarian. The paper, in our view, should be understated rather than overstated; it should eschew cold war jargon; the argument should be carried by facts, not exhortations. The writing is below the level we would hope for in papers for dissemination to other countries. The writing of lucid and forceful English is not too arcane an art.

The President himself, with his sensitive ear for style, led the fight for literacy in the Department; and he had the vigorous support of some State Department officials, notably George Ball, Harriman and William R. Tyler. But the effort to liberate the State Department from automatic writing had little success. As late as 1963, the Department could submit as a draft of a presidential message on the National Academy of Foreign Affairs a text which provoked this resigned White House comment:

This is only the latest and worst of a long number of drafts sent here for Presidential signature. Most of the time it does not matter, I suppose, if the prose is tired, the thought banal and the syntax bureaucratic; and, occasionally when it does matter, State's drafts are very good. But sometimes, as in this case, they are not.

A message to Congress is a fairly important form of Presidential communication. The President does not send so many —nor of those he does send, does State draft so many—that each one cannot receive due care and attention. My own old-fashioned belief is that every Presidential message should be a model of grace, lucidity and taste in expression. At the very least, each message should be (a) in English, (b) clear and trenchant in its style, (c) logical in its structure and (d) devoid of gobbledygook. The State Department draft on the Academy failed each one of these tests (including, in my view, the first).

Would it not be possible for someone in the Department with at least minimal sensibility to take a look at pieces of paper designed for Presidential signature before they are sent to the White House?

It was a vain fight; the plague of gobbledygook was hard to shake off. I note words like "minimal" (at least not "optimal") and "pieces of paper" in my own lament. I can only testify with what interest and relief the President and the White House read cables from ambassadors who could write—Galbraith from New Delhi with his suave irony, David Bruce from London with his sharp wit, Kennan from Belgrade with his historical perspective and somber eloquence, John Bartlow Martin from Santo Domingo and William Attwood from Guinea with their vivid journalistic touch.

Theodore H. White summed it all up in a letter he sent me from the Far East in the summer of 1961—a dispatch the President read with great interest. "The State Department and its competitive instruments," White wrote, "have in the years since I worked with them become so tangled as to be almost unfit for any policy-making purpose or decision. . . . Somewhere there exists in the State Department a zone, or a climate, or inertia, which prevents it from thinking in terms of a new kind of politics, new departures in technique, an inertia which binds it rigidly to the fossil routine of conferences, negotiations, frozen positions. What must be changed must be changed first in Washington, at the center."

4. THE WHITE HOUSE AND FOREIGN POLICY

The center, of course, lay not in Foggy Bottom but in the White House. The act of 1789 establishing the Department of Foreign Affairs provided that the Secretary should manage the business of the Department "in such manner as the President of the United States shall from time to time order or instruct." Kennedy saw the White House and the Department as intimate partners in the enterprise of foreign policy.

The operating link in this partnership was McGeorge Bundy and the now streamlined National Security Council staff. The Council itself met far less regularly than in Eisenhower days—sixteen meetings in the first six months of the Kennedy administration—and the President convened it only when he was on the brink of decision. He saw no sense in placing unformulated problems before the miscellaneous body of men designated in the statute; he could not understand, for example, why serious matters of foreign policy should be discussed in the presence of his first director of the Office of Emergency Planning, a garrulous southerner who had a flow of irrelevant opinions on everything. Instead he preferred to set up task forces specifically qualified to deal with particular problems.

The task forces of 1961 were not study groups like those of the interregnum; and they differed from the interdepartmental committees of the Eisenhower administration in being *ad hoc* bodies, destined to disappear as soon as the crisis was over, as well as in vesting responsibility, not in the committee as a whole, but in its chairman. By bringing together working representatives of every agency concerned with the matter and giving one man the job of producing recommendations, the task force could greatly improve the speed and coordination with which policy was made. It was symptomatic of the President's doubts about State that the first two task forces in the spring of 1961 had chairmen from Defense—Gilpatric on Laos and Nitze on Cuba. In time the task force approach led to the formation of the so-called Executive Committee of the National Security Council—a group drawn from the NSC but not including all its statutory members and supplemented by people from outside the NSC as occasion demanded.

But, if the National Security Council played a diminishing role, the National Security Council staff was indispensable. Bundy saw his function as that of the clarification of alternatives set before the President and the recording and follow-up of presidential decisions. Neither he nor the President, as Bundy told the Jackson Subcommittee, wanted to interpose "a large separate organization between him and his Secretary of State." Yet, Bundy added, "if his Cabinet officers are to be free to do their own work, the President's work must be done—to the extent that he cannot do it himself—by staff officers under his direct oversight."

The Bundy staff was a remarkable body of men—and it was a tribute to Bundy's own clarity of intellect and force of character that they so cheerfully deferred to his leadership. Walt Rostow, an economic historian turned social philosopher, served as Mac's deputy. A man of unusual inventiveness of mind and copiousness of expression, he was inexhaustible in his capacity to meet every crisis with a plan and unfailing in his decency and enthusiasm. He had written long and thoughtful books on England, America, Russia and China; and his *Stages of Economic Growth,* though no doubt overschematic in its presentation, offered a stimulating profile of the development process from traditional society through "take-off" into the phase of self-sustaining growth to the age of high mass consumption. His combination of the spacious historical view with a passion for counterguerrilla warfare caused much joking about his being "Chester Bowles with machine guns," all of which he took with gentle tolerance. Carl Kaysen applied his brilliant intelligence to security as well as economic issues. Robert Komer, a government career man who had managed to survive the Eisenhower years with undiminished liveliness of wit and hope, covered the uncommitted world. In 1962, Michael Forrestal, the son of Truman's Secretary of Defense, joined the staff and brought intelligent judgment to the baffling issues of Southeast Asia. Bromley Smith, a great civil servant, presided calmly as NSC Secretary over the flow of documents and decisions. All of these men had easy access to the President and served him invaluably in alerting him to problems and executing his instructions.

Nor was the work of foreign policy at the White House confined to the Bundy staff. The President wanted Ted Sorensen at his right hand every time there was a major crisis or a major speech. Because of his special concern with Latin America, he directed Richard Goodwin and me and later Ralph Dungan to follow hemisphere developments for him. Dungan, in addition, watched the foreign aid program and advised on the selection of top government officials. Jerome Wiesner and his Science Adviser's staff dealt with armament and disarmament. Myer Feldman kept a hand in on the Middle East and on tariff and trade issues. I acquired the United Nations and occasional European matters, especially Italy, as particular problems.

The Bay of Pigs made us all more aggressive in defending the interests of the President and therefore in invading on his behalf what the foreign affairs bureaucracy too often regarded as its private domain. Bundy insisted from the start that the White House get the flow of raw intelligence from State, Defense and the CIA; this generally gave us enough facts to be able to ask the departments the pregnant questions and not be put off by the sterile answers. We tried to become the President's eyes and ears through the whole area of national security, reporting to him the things he had to know—and this would sometimes include things which the department involved did not wish him to know until it had decided for itself what it wanted him to do. At the same time we tried to uncover in the middle levels of government ideas which we believed deserved a hearing at the top before they had been diluted or choked off by interbureau or interagency rivalry. The White House staff, in addition to offering the President independent comment on proposals from the departments, served as a means of discovering whether his instructions were being carried out. On occasions too frequent to record, the staff would have to say that State or Defense were not doing the things in one area or another they had been directed to do; and Kennedy would patiently pick up the phone and renew the pressure. We were the President's men, and the government knew it, in part welcoming it, in part resenting it.

Kennedy's use of his staff provoked much press comment about White House 'meddling'; the very word implied that the White House had no business interfering in the internal affairs of the government. One day in the midst of the Berlin crisis Bundy and I wondered whether we dared ask the Department to rework a draft white paper on Berlin. When we explained to Kennedy our reluctance to incense the now highly sensitive Department further, Kennedy, unmoved, said that they ought to read the Constitution over there and find out who was responsible for foreign affairs and whose government it was anyway. We did not ourselves regard meddling as warfare against the bureaucracy, for we were powerless without allies throughout the permanent government. Our purpose was to seek out the people in the great opaque mechanism who were capable of innovation, to bring them and their ideas forward and to strengthen their hands.

The staff was part of the formal panoply of the White House; but in October 1961 Kennedy acquired a highly informal source of wisdom and support in international matters when his old friend David Ormsby Gore came to Washington as British Ambassador.[5] Many ties had strengthened their relationship since they first met in London in 1938. Kathleen Kennedy had married Ormsby Gore's cousin and was godmother of the oldest Ormsby Gore child. During the 1940s and 1950s the two young men had shared a lively interest in books, history and public affairs. As Kennedy rose in American politics, Ormsby Gore became a progressive Tory Member of Parliament and soon Minister of State for Foreign Affairs with special responsibility for disarma-

[5] On the death of his father in 1964, Ormsby Gore became Lord Harlech.

ment. When Ormsby Gore was in New York for the meeting of the UN General Assembly in 1959, he discussed the test ban negotiations a good deal with Kennedy; and it was from Ormsby Gore that Kennedy first understood the feebleness and inconsequence of American disarmament planning, a point he urged with much force in the 1960 campaign. After the election, Kennedy told Ormsby Gore, back in New York for the UN meeting, that he must come to Washington as ambassador. This message was communicated to Harold Macmillan, to whom Ormsby Gore was related by marriage, and in due course he appeared.

The Kennedys (to the irritation of the rest of the diplomatic corps) enjoyed no couple more than they did the Ormsby Gores. The President found the Ambassador a companion for every mood, whether he wanted to sail in Nantucket Sound or brood over the prospects of nuclear annihilation. Like Kennedy and like Macmillan, Ormsby Gore believed in the realistic pursuit of a *détente* with the Soviet Union, and he steadily reinforced Kennedy's skepticism about the clichés of the cold war. He possessed not only great personal charm but exceptional intelligence and integrity. Indeed, only two men of notable character could have so delicately mingled personal and official relations, for each remained at all times the firm and candid advocate of the policies of his own nation. Their long, relaxed, confidential talks together, whether at Hyannis Port or Palm Beach or on quiet evenings in the White House, gave Kennedy probably his best opportunity to clarify his own purposes in world affairs.

Beyond his staff, his task forces, his friends, there was the President himself, increasingly the day-to-day director of American foreign policy. Though he had faithfully served his domestic apprenticeship in Congress, foreign affairs had long since captured his primary imagination, even before he gained his membership on the Senate Foreign Relations Committee. He had had a considerably more varied and extensive international experience than most men elected President. In his twenties he had talked to Franklin Roosevelt, Chamberlain and Baldwin and in his thirties to Churchill, Nehru, Ben Gurion and Fanfani. He knew Europe well and had traveled in Russia, Latin America and the Far East.

It was not accidental that he chose the Under Secretary of State, the Ambassador to the United Nations and the Assistant Secretary for Africa before he named the Secretary of State; he felt this in some particular sense 'his' department. Nor was his early appearance as, in effect, desk officer for Laos uncharacteristic. He wanted to know everything that was going on and, when matters were critical, he often cleared (and redrafted) messages and instructions himself. In the relationship between the President and the ambassadors, there had been, it is true, a slippage since Roosevelt's day. Roosevelt regarded them correctly as "my" ambassadors and encouraged them to supplement their reports to the Department by personal communications to him. A generation later the bureaucracy, here as elsewhere, had contracted the power of the Presidency. In a circular letter to the ambassadors in May 1961, Kennedy actually retained State Department language reminding them that "your own lines of communication as Chiefs of Mission run through the Department of State." Only Kenneth Galbraith, I believe, systematically ignored this injunction (and Kennedy was delighted that he did). But, in spite of the Department's effort to insert itself between the President and his ambassadors, Kennedy succeeded in displaying what Edmund Gullion once described as a "direct and sometimes disconcerting personal interest in the problems of particular missions." Ambassadors as different as George Kennan in Yugoslavia and Joseph Farland in Panama later told me that they found the President far more understanding of their problems than the State Department.

Averell Harriman, who worked for them both, remarked once that Kennedy was more his own Secretary of State than Franklin Roosevelt had been. He meant that Roosevelt picked out the problems he wanted to handle himself and left everything else to Sumner Welles, who ran the Department, while Kennedy dealt personally with almost every aspect of policy around the globe. He knew more about certain areas than the senior officials at State and probably called as many issues to their attention as they did to his. He wanted particularly to stay ahead of problems; nothing exasperated him more than to be surprised by crisis. It was at his instance in early 1961, for example, that a task force worked out the first long-range program for Iran; and as early as August 1961 he sent out a directive saying that the United States should prepare for a more active role in Cyprus if trouble was to be averted in the eastern Mediterranean. More than anyone in the government, he was the source of ideas, initiative and imagination in foreign policy.

This was partly a matter of temperament and curiosity but partly too of necessity. In the modern Presidency, every chief executive, sooner or later, no matter what his background or predilection, is drawn into a particular concern with foreign affairs. It is not just that foreign ques-

tions are often more interesting or offer Presidents more
scope for personal maneuver and decision; it is above all
that the issues are more fateful. And the nuclear age, as
Richard Neustadt liked to point out, added a dimension of
'irreversibility' to policy—that is, certain choices, once made,
could not be called back. Moreover, the irreversible choices
might be, not the final, dramatic decisions, but rather the
minor and technical steps taken at a low level a long time
back but leading ineluctably to the catastrophic choice.
The Bay of Pigs provided Kennedy the warning and confirmed his temperamental instinct to reach deep inside State,
Defense and the CIA in order to catch hold of policies
before these policies made his choices for him. "Domestic
policy," he used to say, "can only defeat us; foreign policy
can kill us."

5. THE STRUGGLE FOR COORDINATION

While Kennedy had no doubt that the President's exercise
of his seniority in foreign affairs was his constitutional duty,
he earnestly hoped that the State Department would really
serve as his agent of coordination. He wanted to end the
faceless system of indecision and inaction which diffused
foreign policy among the three great bureaucracies of State,
Defense and the CIA. But, to make coordination effective,
it was necessary to strengthen the Department's instrumentalities of control. This was especially important overseas,
where the dispersion of power was most acute, visible and
mischievous. Kennedy's circular letter to the ambassadors
consequently gave them the authority to "oversee and coordinate all the activities of the United States Government"
in their countries, except for military forces in the field
under a United States area military commander.

This was not an entirely popular move. It was resisted
by Defense, the CIA, the Peace Corps and other agencies
which liked to act independently—and even by traditional
Foreign Service officers who did not want to be responsible
for nontraditional operations and preferred not to know,
for example, what the CIA was up to. Within State, however, Chester Bowles ardently championed the new approach.
He had provided the original draft of the President's letter,
and he soon followed it up with a memorandum reminding
chiefs of mission of their obligation to see that all United
States representatives "speak with a common voice and are
not played off one against the other by a foreign government."

These instructions were aimed particularly at the CIA.
Cuba and Laos had already provided the new administra-

tion with horrible examples of the readiness of CIA operatives in the field to go off on policies of their own. This was only the most spectacular expression of the steady growth of the CIA in the 1950s. The CIA's budget now exceeded State's by more than 50 per cent (though it was less than half that of the intelligence operations of the Defense Department). Its staff had doubled in a decade. In some areas the CIA had outstripped the State Department in the quality of its personnel, partly because it paid higher salaries and partly because Allen Dulles's defiance of McCarthy enabled it to attract and hold abler men. It had almost as many people under official cover overseas as State; in a number of embassies CIA officers outnumbered those from State in the political sections. Often the CIA station chief had been in the country longer than the ambassador, had more money at his disposal and exerted more influence. The CIA had its own political desks and military staffs; it had in effect its own foreign service, its own air force, even, on occasion, its own combat forces. Moreover, the CIA declined to clear its clandestine intelligence operations either with the State Department in Washington or with the ambassador in the field; and, while covert political operations were cleared with State, this was sometimes done, not at the start, but after the operation had almost reached the point beyond which it could not easily be recalled. The coincidence that one Dulles brother was head of State and another the head of the CIA had resulted in practical independence for the Agency, because Allen Dulles could clear things with Foster without clearing them with Foster's Department. The lucky success in Guatemala, moreover, stirred dangerous longings for adventure in CIA breasts.

None of this is to suggest that the CIA constituted, in the title of a popular exposé, an "invisible government" or that its influence was always, or often, reactionary and sinister. In my experience its leadership was politically enlightened and sophisticated. Not seldom CIA representatives took a more liberal line in White House meetings than their counterparts from State. A great deal of CIA energy went to the support of the anti-Communist left around the world —political parties, trade unions and other undertakings. None the less, it had acquired a power which, however beneficial its exercise often might be, blocked State Department control over the conduct of foreign affairs.

The President's letter now gave every ambassador for the first time the authority to know everything the CIA people were doing in his country (even if not always the way they were doing it). Some ambassadors, like Galbraith, used this authority more stringently than others; but the directive constituted at least a first step toward bringing secret operations under policy control. In Washington, U. Alexis Johnson, the Deputy Under Secretary of State for Political Affairs and an uncommonly efficient administrator, presided over an interdepartmental committee on intelligence affairs. After the Bay of Pigs, Robert Kennedy took a personal interest in the CIA and became an informal presidential watchdog over covert operations.

The Bay of Pigs, of course, stimulated a wide variety of proposals for the reorganization of the CIA. The State Department, for example, could not wait to separate the CIA's overt from its clandestine functions and even change the Agency's name. The President, consulting closely with James Killian, Clark Clifford and the other members of his Foreign Intelligence Advisory Board, decided not to go that far. The Agency itself suffered from doubt and gloom after Cuba, and it was feared that drastic measures would cause total demoralization. Instead, Kennedy moved quietly to cut the CIA budget in 1962 and again in 1963, aiming at a 20 per cent reduction by 1966. At the same time, anticipating the resignation of Allen Dulles, he began looking for a new director. Under Eisenhower the need had been for an authoritative interpreter of the flow of intelligence; here Allen Dulles, with his perceptive and flexible sense of the political ebb and flow, was ideal. But Kennedy, Bundy and the White House staff preferred to interpret intelligence themselves. They sought, not an intellectual oracle, but a sensible and subdued manager of the government's intelligence business. In addition, the President thought it politically prudent to have a CIA chief conservative enough to give the Agency a margin of protection in Congress.

After a long search, he came up in September 1961 with the name of John McCone, a California Republican who had served Truman as Under Secretary of the Air Force and Eisenhower as chairman of the Atomic Energy Commission. He summoned McCone to the White House on the pretext of asking his views on nuclear testing, sized him up in a two-hour conversation and, when McCone returned a fortnight later with his report, startled him by offering the CIA post. The President did this with notable secrecy, recognizing that the appointment would bring a moment of consternation to the New Frontier. McCone had the reputation of a rigid cold-warrior who viewed the world in moralistic stereotypes. Scientists who recalled his opposition to a test ban were particularly agitated. McCone did lack the expansive personality of his predecessor, but he turned out to be a cautious, realistic and self-effacing head of the CIA. He repaired morale within the Agency, instituted measures to subject venturesome proposals to critical scrutiny and did his best to keep the CIA and himself out of the newspapers. He restored its relations with the State Department and the Congress, if not altogether with the Department of Defense. And, declining to allow his own views to prejudice the intelligence estimates, he showed a fair-mindedness which shamed some of us who had objected to his appointment. Two able professionals, Richard Helms and Ray Cline, became his deputies for operations and intelligence. The result was to make the Agency a more consistently technical service.

As further evidence of his desire to place responsibility in the diplomatic professionals, Kennedy gave the Foreign Service an unprecedentedly large share of ambassadorial appointments. In 1940 career officers held only 47 per cent of the embassy posts, in 1955 they were down to 40 per cent, but by the middle of 1962 they held 68 per cent. Nor did this consist only of 'hardship posts' in primitive countries. In 1938–39, there were fifteen non-career Chiefs of Mission in Europe (including Joseph P. Kennedy) as against twelve Foreign Service officers; in 1962, there were seventeen career men and only seven noncareer. And during the interregnum Kennedy persuaded John Rooney, chairman of the House subcommittee which controlled State Department appropriations, to increase representational allowances so that career officers could afford to take major embassies.

6. THE UNEASY PARTNERSHIP

Yet, in spite of the presidential effort to give the Department the central role in foreign affairs, Richard Neustadt was obliged to testify before the Jackson Subcommittee in 1963: "So far as I can judge, the State Department has not yet found means to take the proffered role and play it vigorously across the board."

Part of the trouble was inherent in the effort, as Neustadt defined it, to make the State Department "at once a department and then something more." The Secretary already had, in the jargon, a 'full plate.' He had to manage and represent the Department and Foreign Service, attend to Congress and public opinion and take part in conferences and negotiations all over the planet. To do all this and serve in addition as the President's agent of coordination would require almost superhuman talent and energy. It was not that the Department failed to produce statements of plans and objectives. If anything, it produced too many —a Basic National Security Program, State Department guidelines, country plans, internal defense plans, national policy papers and so on. But the process of codification tended toward generalization and ambiguity and rarely provided specific guidance on the hard choices.

Part of the trouble too lay in the attitude of the White House toward the Foreign Service. Talk of the need for specialization was all very well; but, as Charles Bohlen used to urge with urbane persuasiveness, the art of diplomacy must also be recognized as a specialization and basic to the others. It was Bohlen who, among Foreign Service officers, saw most of Kennedy in the relaxed moments of his Presidency. The gaiety of Bohlen's mind, the shrewdness of his insight, and the breadth of his experience made him a delightful companion. At the same time, though he was infinitely more independent and irreverent than the typical career officer, the Foreign Service had no more faithful or ingenious companion. Once Kennedy, exasperated over the difficulty of getting action out of State, said, "What's wrong with that goddamned Department of yours, Chip?" Bohlen answered candidly, "You are."

By this Bohlen meant, as he explained to an interested Kennedy, that the President did not make sufficient allowance for the virtues of professionalism. He wanted quick and personal replies to significant questions, not taking into account the fact that any significant question had a bundle of implications which the Department must consider in an orderly way before it could make a responsible answer. He wanted ambassadors to know languages, master technical fields and fraternize with the people of the countries to which they were assigned, forgetting that the chief purpose of the diplomat was the transaction of business between governments and that everything else was supporting and subsidiary. Too much emphasis on diplomatic activism per se might lead people to forget the limits of diplomatic action. Bohlen even argued that the Assistant Secretaryships should be filled from the Service, though, when Kennedy mildly observed that it was not easy to find good Foreign Service officers, Bohlen conceded that this was so.

The aggressiveness of the White House staff no doubt compounded the trouble. Probably most of the Foreign

Service had welcomed Kennedy's accession. Yet a year later many career men were wondering whether they had not exchanged King Log for King Stork. White House 'meddling' struck some of the pros as careless intrusion by impulsive and ignorant amateurs—"crusading activism touched with naïveté." This was John Davies's phrase, and he added: "Bold new ideas and quick decisions were asked of men who had learned from long, disillusioning experience that there were few or no new ideas, bold or otherwise, that would solidly produce the dramatic changes then sought, and whose experience for a decade had been that bold ideas and actions were personally dangerous and could lead to congressional investigations and public disgrace." In his visits to Washington, Davies would talk acidly about the Foreign Service, "purged from the right under Dulles, now purged from the left under Kennedy," and ask, "How can you expect these men to do a good job?"

The question was a real one. The Foreign Service obviously had to carry out the policies of the administration; yet 'thought correction,' even in favor of the New Frontier, presented its problems. The President, commenting on the public service in his first State of the Union message, had said, "Let it be clear that this Administration recognizes the value of dissent and daring—that we greet healthy controversy as the hallmark of healthy change." But what if dissent meant opposition to the neutralization of Laos or to the Alliance for Progress or to the center-left experiment in Italy? This was a riddle which the White House, wishing free minds in the bureaucracy but at the same time demanding commitment to its policies—and the Foreign Service, proclaiming its loyalty to all administrations but at the same time reserving the right to defend old policies against new—never solved. Probably it was insoluble.

These structural factors explained part of the State Department's faltering response to its "proffered role." The partnership seemed chronically out of balance. But Kennedy never ceased hoping that it would work. He tried one thing after another. "I have discovered finally that the best way to deal with State," he said to me one day in August, 1961, "is to send over memos. They can forget phone conversations, but a memorandum is something which, by their system, has to be answered. So let's put as many things as possible in memoranda from now on." Though he licensed an exceptional degree of White House interest in foreign policy, he set up no new authorities which would prevent the Secretary of State from serving as the presi-

dential 'agent of coordination.' Instead, he repressed his
frustrations (at some times more successfully than at others)
and kept supposing that by strengthening the direction of
the Department he would enable it to sustain its side of
the partnership.

7. THE ENIGMA OF RUSK

Kennedy had decided on Dean Rusk as Secretary of State
after a single talk. It was an understandable choice. Rusk
was a man of broad experience and marked ability. He
rarely spoke about himself; but I remember one night, on
a plane rushing south to Punta del Este, his talking with
quiet charm about his boyhood in rural Georgia. He was
delivered by an aged veterinarian whose medical training
had been picked up in the Civil War. Rusk's father was
the only one of twelve brothers and sisters who attended
college. But three of his father's five children went to
college; all the grandchildren would go to college. In the
same way the Georgia back-country, a land of kerosene
lamps and goiter and pellagra when Rusk was growing up,
had been transformed by public health and rural electri-
fication. These memories left him a convinced if undemonstrative liberal on domestic issues. To his social and economic convictions he added an earnest concern for the
rights of Negroes; in the Kennedy years his oldest son
was active in the Urban League.

From Davidson College in North Carolina, Rusk, with
his Rhodes Scholarship, went to Oxford, and from Oxford
to the political science department of Mills College. Here
his moderation and competence inevitably made him dean
of the faculty. War service in the China-Burma-India theater
was followed by government service in the Pentagon and
then in the State Department. He was Assistant Secretary
for United Nations Affairs and then for the Far East
before leaving Washington in 1952 to become president of
the Rockefeller Foundation. This background gave him
expert knowledge of the Atlantic and the Pacific, Defense
and State, the United Nations and the ways that science
and medicine could benefit mankind.

A man of exceptional intelligence, lucidity and control,
he had a tidy and exact mastery of the technical detail of
a bewildering range of foreign problems and a talent for
concise and dispassionate exposition. He had a great ability
to summarize divergent views and put his finger on the heart
of a question. His idealism, if subdued and prosaic, was
authentic: "If a new foreign ambassador in Washington were
to ask me, 'What should I keep my eye on to learn how

American policy would react to a given situation?' I would point out to him the eighteenth-century phrase which has always served as to American policy; that is, the notion that governments derive their just powers from the consent of the governed." Privately he was agreeable, modest and compassionate.

As Secretary of State, he worked as long and as hard as anyone in Washington. In negotiations with foreign countries, he was vigilant, impassive, patient and skilled. He displayed the same qualities in his relations with Congress and proved the most effective Secretary of State on the Hill since Cordell Hull. Within the executive branch, he developed excellent relations with McNamara; indeed, Rusk, having spent more than half his government career with the military, disliked cracks about generals and was pleased to have their esteem. His performance on ceremonial occasions was invariably felicitous. As for the general public, he remained deliberately dim until dimness had its effect, repelling controversy and inspiring confidence. His speeches had the quiet authority of one who knew that he spoke for the foreign policy establishment; unlike Dulles, he did not pretend to speak for God too. Toward the Soviet Union he exhibited a matter-of-fact mistrust which at times seemed automatic inflexibility but still differed from Dulles's conviction of irremediable Soviet evil.

He was, more than anything else, a man bred in the large organizations of mid-century America. But, unlike McNamara, his organizational instinct was for service, not for mastery. Nurtured in the successive bosoms of the university, the Army, the government department, the foundation, he drew reassurance from the solidity of the structure, the regularity of the procedures, the familiarity of the vocabulary. His mind, for all its strength and clarity, was irrevocably conventional. He mistrusted what he called "the flashy or sensational" and rejoiced in the role of "tedium" in diplomacy. "A great deal of our work," he would say without complaint, "is perhaps on the boring side. . . . We can be just as repetitive. We can play the long-playing records just as long as someone else. We don't feel that we need to rush to an answer."

He seemed actually to prefer stale to fresh ways of saying things. One felt that he regarded novelty as an effort to shock or make mischief. Presidential speeches sent over to State for his comment would return with arresting phrases stricken out and weary State Department formulas proposed (but rarely accepted) in their place. He was totally unembarrassed by banality and dropped expressions like "this great struggle for freedom" or "the free world" in his familiar conversation. Concepts like "national sovereignty" and "self-determination" seemed to have the same reality for him that mountains would have for Stewart Udall or wheat fields for Orville Freeman. The stereotypes of diplomacy were his native tongue. At times one wondered whether the harshness of life—the seething planet of revolutionary violence, ferocity and hate, shadowed by nuclear holocaust—ever penetrated the screen of clichés, ever shook that imperturbable blandness. As he would talk on and on in his even, low voice, a Georgia drawl sounding distantly under the professional tones of a foundation executive, the world itself seemed to lose reality and dissolve into a montage of platitudes.

He was a superb technician: this was his power and his problem. He had trained himself all his life to be the ideal chief of staff, the perfect number-two man. The inscrutability which made him a good aide and a gifted negotiator made him also a baffling leader. When Assistant Secretaries brought him problems, he listened courteously, thanked them and let them go; they would often depart little wiser than they came. Since his subordinates did not know what he thought, they could not do what he wanted. In consequence, he failed to imbue the Department with positive direction and purpose. He had authority but not command. One telephone conversation with the President was worth a score of meetings with the Secretary.

He was equally baffling at the White House. Where McNamara and Dillon would forcefully and articulately assert the interests of their departments in impending foreign policy decisions, Rusk would sit quietly by, with his Buddha-like face and half-smile, often leaving it to Bundy or to the President himself to assert the diplomatic interest. If the problem were an old one, he was generally in favor of continuing what Herter or Dulles or Acheson had done before him. If the problem were new, it was generally impossible to know what he thought. Indeed, nearly every time Kennedy faced a major foreign policy decision the views of his Secretary of State remained a mystery. Or so at least was the impression of the White House staff. Doubtless this was unfair, and historians in due course may be able to ascertain what the Secretary wanted the government to do during the great crises of those years. One regretted only that he did not care to disclose his ideas at the time. Inscrutability was splendid as a negotiating stance but inadequate as a principle of life.

The staff's judgment of the Secretary failed, I am sure, to take account of his problems. He was a proud and sensitive man, surrounded in his own Department by figures of greater public note—Stevenson, Bowles, Harriman, Williams —and dominated by a President who wanted to be his own Secretary of State. He lived, no doubt, under threats of humiliation and fears of inadequacy. He sometimes allowed the ceremonial side of his job to take precedence over his harder responsibilities, almost as if he were seeking an escape from decision. And at times his colorlessness of mind appeared almost compulsive, the evenness of tone and temper purchased at inner cost. His feelings were stronger than he permitted them to seem. Some who talked to him late at night over highballs on planes bound for international conferences caught him pouring out not the nostalgia I encountered on the way to Punta del Este but bitter resentment over intolerable "interference" by the White House staff. These moments were rare. Most of the time one felt his decency, dignity, durability.

His relationship with the President remained formal. Kennedy remarked to a friend in State that Rusk was the only cabinet member he did not call by his first name. When this was repeated to Rusk, he said he liked it better that way. Kennedy was always impressed by Rusk's capacity to define but grew increasingly depressed by his reluctance to decide. Conceivably this was the kind of Secretary of State Rusk thought the President preferred. But, while the President was certainly determined to direct the foreign policy of the nation, he nonetheless wanted someone who could not only mass the State Department but be a constant source of definite recommendations and fresh ideas—someone who could serve him, for example, as Acheson had served Truman and Welles, Roosevelt. The Secretary, he would say, "never gives me anything to chew on. . . . You never know what he is thinking." Yet, though often perplexed and disappointed by Rusk, Kennedy liked him personally and was protective of him. Nothing irritated the President more than the suspicion, at times justified, that carping newspaper stories about the Secretary came from the White House staff. When Philip Graham tried in 1962 to persuade Kennedy to send Rusk to the United Nations and Stevenson to London and make David Bruce Secretary of State, the President replied (so Graham said later), "I can't do that to Rusk; he is such a *nice* man." He was also an able and useful man; but most compelling perhaps was Kennedy's feeling that dismissal of his Secretary of State would constitute too severe a comment on his own original judgment.

All this meant that, if the President were going to get at the "bowl of jelly," reorganization would have to start at a lower level.

8. THE SACRIFICE OF BOWLES

Chester Bowles, as Under Secretary, had the second place of responsibility in the State Department. Kennedy liked Bowles, appreciated his help in the months before Los Angeles and sympathized with his efforts to redress the balance of our foreign policy toward the underdeveloped world and toward political rather than military solutions. Moreover, Bowles had important assets for the administration. He had unusual gifts for public persuasion. His personal idealism inspired devotion on the part of many who worked for him. He was identified in the United States and through the world with the affirmative impulses of American foreign policy. He was more responsible than anyone else for the distinguished series of ambassadorial appointments. He had been right on Cuba. He retained a strong following in the liberal community.

Bowles, however, had his vulnerabilities too. His ambassadorial choices, though they pleased everybody else, had outraged the old-line professionals. Foreign Service officers trying to stop the designation of Edwin Reischauer to Japan, for example, had gone to the length of extracting statements from the Japanese Embassy saying that it would be terrible to send to Tokyo an American ambassador with a Japanese wife. The new Under Secretary left behind a covey of unemployed and embittered diplomats who circulated rude stories about him over their second and third martinis at the Metropolitan Club.

Once the appointments were completed, his role was ill-defined. Though he had shown marked executive ability when he headed the Office of Price Administration in the Second World War, he never received clear-cut authority to run the State Department. To Bowles's supporters—and they were as zealous and vocal as his enemies—it seemed that Rusk was unwilling either to manage the Department himself or to let Bowles do it. The relationship between the two men was less close than Bowles had expected. The Secretary appeared reluctant to discuss policy with him and preferred to deal directly with Alexis Johnson, the career Deputy Under Secretary. Rusk's administrative philosophy was that "if a man demonstrates that he is willing to make judgments and decisions and live with the results, power gravitates to him because other people will get out of his way"; and, by this standard, Bowles did not succeed in imposing himself effectively on the Department (nor did Rusk).

At the White House the aftermath of the Bay of Pigs had put Bowles in an exposed position. Nor had Bowles made any effort to exploit a personal relationship to the President. Recognizing that he had a public standing which Rusk lacked and fearing to make the Secretary feel more insecure, the Under Secretary was meticulous in not asking to see the President by himself and, indeed, had no private talks with Kennedy between the interregnum in December and the following July. More access would not necessarily have improved things, though, for there was a fatal difference in tempo between Bowles and the New Frontier. In conversation Bowles was accustomed to the slow wind-up. When asked a question, he tended to catch hold of it a long distance back, to discourse on its relations to the multiple revolutions of our time, to invoke pictures of natives struggling out of mud huts for bread and independence, and to move down to the present with all deliberate speed. Kennedy agreed with nearly everything Bowles would say, but he had generally thought of it before himself, and he grew impatient when people explained to him things he knew already. Bowles spoke the unabashed liberal language of the New Deal; again the junior officers of the Second World War disagreed, not with the sentiment, but with what they considered the sentimentality. The New Frontier put a premium on quick, tough, laconic, decided people; it was easily exasperated by more meditative types. And, when the answer came at the end, it would sometimes seem spacious and vague, lacking the operational specifics sought by the Kennedys. Bowles's command of large issues was unfortunately not matched by a command of small issues. "Chet is a fine fellow," the President said to me one day in early May, "but he's just not doing the job. He was perfect as Ambassador to India. A job like that could use all his good qualities—his intelligence, his sympathy, his willingness to listen to difficult problems. But he is not precise or decisive enough to get things done. Because Chet isn't doing his job, Rusk is spreading himself too thin and is not able to do his job either." He added, "Now George Ball is fine. He gets things done. So does Alexis Johnson."

The situation dragged on unhappily for several weeks. One day early in June, after a meeting with the President on the Dominican Republic, Robert Kennedy asked me to stay behind to discuss the Department. The President observed that the present state of affairs really could not be permitted to continue, that Bowles was oriented toward discussion rather than action and therefore only reinforced the vacillating and dilatory habits of the Department. Someone, he said, would have to be put in Bowles's place who could make the Department work; but "of course it will look as if we were throwing out the one man in the State Department who was right on Cuba." He valued Bowles in two roles, the President said: in getting fresh thinking to the White House and in explaining our policies at home and abroad. What he wanted was to transfer Bowles to another assignment while protecting his title and his dignity. The Attorney General proposed that Bowles be made roving ambassador to the underdeveloped world. The President asked me, "Do you think he would take it?" I was doubtful.

Rusk, it appeared, had his own candidate for Bowles's job. This was Arthur Dean, who had come to the Department as a negotiator on test ban problems. Dean, an engaging man and an able lawyer-negotiator of the old-fashioned type, had no great interest in the political or economic aspects of foreign policy. Moreover, he not only was a former law partner of John Foster Dulles but had no relationship to the President and no commitment to the New Frontier. In mid-June, when I was talking with him on test ban matters, he suddenly said, with genuine or calculated naïveté, "I told Dean Rusk the other day that, if I could get my hands on this Department, I would turn the whole thing over." Robert Lovett and other representatives of the foreign policy establishment were urging Dean's appointment.

The Bay of Pigs experience had provided convincing evidence that the President required people in the State Department whose basic loyalty would be to him, not to the Foreign Service or the Council on Foreign Relations. I discussed this with Abram Chayes, the Department's Legal Adviser and an old friend of Bowles's. We speculated about the possibility of a reallocation of functions within the Department: the chief of staff job to be given to George Ball, while Bowles would retain his relationship to personnel and to policy planning and take on new duties in the area of public persuasion, both in the United States and abroad. I submitted this solution to the President early in July, arguing that Bowles's particular abilities could thus be put to full use and that Ball could be depended on as the President's man in the Department. "He is loyal to you," I said about Ball, "and believes in your policies. It would be a great error, both substantive and political, to replace Bowles by someone who is neutral or Republican in his political orientation. . . . It is indispensable to have as Under Secretary a man who sympathizes with your social and economic objectives in the world. We cannot afford a conservative New York lawyer, however competent, in this spot, unless we want to end up with an intelligent updating of Eisenhowerism. Ball is imaginative, practical and able."

Ball was, indeed, all these things. He had come to Washington from Illinois as a New Deal lawyer in 1933. After a few years, he went back to a law office in Chicago, where Adlai Stevenson was one of his colleagues. During the war he returned to Washington in the Board of Economic Warfare. I met him first in Germany in 1945 when he and Ken Galbraith ran the United States Strategic Bombing Survey in Germany. After the war he practiced law in Washington and Paris, becoming Jean Monnet's American representative in the fifties. A high-spirited, calm and resourceful man, he was never afraid to take chances. I remember a moment in the early fifties when Henry Wallace was called to testify on China policy before the Senate Internal Security Committee. This was the height of McCarthyism, and Wallace wanted a lawyer to go to the Hill with him. Joseph Alsop, who had also appeared in these hearings, and I spent several hours one afternoon trying to find counsel for the former Vice-President of the United States. We called one old New Dealer after another; each advanced some vaguely plausible reason why he could not accompany Wallace. Finally it occurred to us to call Ball, who promptly assented. In 1952 and 1956, Ball took a leading part in the Stevenson campaigns, and in 1960 he was a Stevenson manager in Los Angeles.

Bowles liked the idea of some reallocation of responsibility between himself and Ball; but the President shook his head. "It wouldn't work," he said. "It would just prolong the confusion and the agony. Chet would continue to be frustrated. Everyone would continue to blame Chet for everything. It would be best for everyone if Chet were to make a clean break from his present responsibilities." He thought for a moment and said, "What about Brazil? It is the biggest job in the Americas. It is the India of the hemisphere, and the next few years will be crucial. Chet could do a great job there. That is where he should go. I would think he would much prefer it anyway—better to be first in the American Embassy in Rio than second in the Department of State." He told me to telephone Bowles and ask him whether he would go to Rio.

When I called him, Chet listened in silence, dismissed the idea of Brazil and finally said, "There's no point in this. I guess the fat's really in the fire now. I want the President to know I will do everything I can to make my exit as graceful as possible. He need not worry. I will not say anything to anybody. I will go off to Switzerland where no newspaperman can find me." One felt deeply the personal injustice of administrative decision. I reported to the President: "It is ironic that Bowles is being removed for his failure to overcome the entrenched complacency of the Foreign Service pros—and that these very pros, who are the basic source of State Department inertia, will regard his removal as their victory. . . . The people in the Administration who will be most pleased by his removal are those who are most opposed to the Kennedy policies."

But over the weekend Bowles's friends swung into action. On Monday morning, July 17, the *Times* had a front-page story saying that the President intended to ask for Bowles's resignation that day. Kennedy read that story with a connoisseur's interest on the plane back from the Cape to Washington. "You can tell how that story was written," he said. "You can tell where every paragraph came from. One paragraph is from Bowles or his people. The next paragraph is from someone at State trying to make a case against Bowles." He mused about the situation as he sipped his after-breakfast coffee. "I received a cable from Adlai this morning," he said. (Stevenson, who was in Italy, had been reached by transatlantic telephone.) "Soapy [Williams] has been calling me. . . . This started out as a management problem. But these stories today have transformed it into a political problem. It's no longer a personnel question; now it has become a symbolic question. When it comes to issues, there is no great difference between Chester and me. . . . I've asked Rusk to meet me as soon as I arrive. Chester is coming over later."

The result of the Bowles counteroffensive was a reprieve. The President reassured Bowles and on Wednesday made a nimble and complicated statement at his press conference, expressing his warm personal confidence in the Under Secretary but refraining from any permanent commitment to anyone for any job. With this statement, the excitement subsided.

9. THE STATE DEPARTMENT REORGANIZATION

But the problem was as far as ever from solution. A few days later Bowles, who was about to leave Washington to take part in a series of regional conferences of United States ambassadors, sent the President a thoughtful memorandum on the organizational needs of the Department of State. He argued that Kennedy's approach to foreign affairs was "inadequately understood by many of the able career officers of the Department who have attained senior rank in the last ten years. . . . There has been resistance to fresh thinking and a continuing attachment to the sterile assumptions and negative policies that we criticized so vigorously when we were out of office." His solution was to bring more people "who understand the Kennedy policies and believe in them" into top positions.

There was much sense in this, though the structural problems of the Department were deeper than the memorandum suggested. But Bowles was unable to take advantage of the reprieve. His own position had been weakened; his mandate was still ill-defined; and power did not, in Rusk's phrase, gravitate toward him. Moreover, the July counteroffensive depleted his political ammunition. The President, absorbed in Berlin, made no moves, but continued to ponder how he could strengthen the Department. He accepted, I think, the justice of Bowles's point about needing more New Frontiersmen in top positions. It was this which turned his attention increasingly to Averell Harriman.

The contrast between Bowles and Harriman was instructive to a student of Washington. Both men were experienced in government and politics, and both held much the same view of the world. But where Bowles dissipated his authority by diffusing his energy, Harriman seized hold of one hard problem—Laos—and, by mastering it, re-established himself as a force in foreign affairs. Where Bowles tried to fight every battle on every front at once, Harriman picked the battles he knew he could win, or affect, and for the rest bided his time. He was one to whom power gravitated. Theodore H. White's letter from the Far East suggested the next step. We need, he had written, "an Assistant Secretary of State for the Far East who would be of enough rank and eminence to shake the whole China service out of its sloth, and of enough virility to face [Admiral] Felt, CIA and others as equal in impact and influence." White made no nominations, but there were not many around to fit the specifications.

It was Bowles himself, with his sure instinct for appointments, who first proposed putting Harriman in charge of Far Eastern affairs. One night I tentatively mentioned the idea to Harriman, wondering a little what a man of his

experience would think of being asked to take so modest a
job. But Harriman, always more interested in power than in
status, responded that he would serve wherever the President wished. He stipulated only that he report directly to
the Secretary and not through Foreign Service channels. I
passed this on to Kennedy, who remarked that he was thinking about Averell as Assistant Secretary for European Affairs. Later he discussed this possibility with Harriman. In the
end, however, Dean Rusk called Harriman in Geneva to say
that the President wished after all to appoint him to the
Far East. The announcement was to be delayed until other
changes could be made at State.

That autumn Bowles was abroad a good deal of the time,
and Ball was assuming more and more administrative responsibility within the Department. The final act took place
in November on the weekend of the Harvard-Yale game. I
ran into Bowles between the halves in the crowd swirling
around the Yale Bowl. He said in a puzzled way that Rusk
had phoned him that morning, asking him to come to Washington right away; apparently he wanted to discuss some
personnel problems. Bowles had replied that he had thirty
people coming to his house in Essex for dinner that evening:
surely the business could wait until Monday? "He was awfully insistent, and I have finally agreed to go down tomorrow. All this fuss just to rearrange some ambassadors!"

After the game Richard Goodwin reached me by telephone at a party deep in Fairfield County. The President, he
said, was going to act over the weekend. George Ball would
become Under Secretary; George McGhee would move from
the Policy Planning Council to replace Ball as the second
Under Secretary (though for Political rather than for
Economic Affairs); Harriman would become Assistant Secretary for the Far East; and, from the White House, Walt
Rostow would go over to State as counselor and chief of
the Policy Planning Council, Fred Dutton as Assistant
Secretary for Congressional Relations and Goodwin himself
as Deputy Assistant Secretary for Inter-American Affairs.
As for Bowles, the President wanted him to take a new
assignment in relation to the underdeveloped world. The
next day Rusk broke the news to Bowles. Later Ted Sorensen, after a long talk, persuaded Bowles to become Special
Representative and Adviser to the President for African,
Asian and Latin American Affairs.

Bowles, the hapless victim of the conditions which he had
diagnosed better than anybody else, behaved with characteristic nobility and was soon hard at work in his new

assignment. He wrote wise memoranda about the aid program. He conducted useful inspections of overseas operations. He brought forward new ideas for policy in the underdeveloped world. He gave a series of excellent speeches through the country. But he was outside the chain of command, and the job was doomed to frustration. Kennedy felt that his abilities were wasted and made occasional efforts to give him operating responsibilities. In the summer of 1962, he asked him to take over the Alliance for Progress; but Bowles thought, with considerable justice, that political and economic policies could not be separated and that the chief of the Alliance should also be Assistant Secretary for Inter-American Affairs. Kennedy said he was right, but that no one was ready for this yet; it would create too many problems. Later the President suggested his going as ambassador to Indonesia or Canada. After he declined, Kennedy observed, "If I were Chet, I would rather be first in an Iberian village than second in Rome. I guess he would rather be thirty-fifth in Rome." Finally, in December 1962, Bowles decided that his assignment had not worked out and offered his resignation. Kennedy, who had sent Galbraith to New Delhi for a two-year tour (later somewhat extended), now asked Bowles to take his place. Here, back where he had served so well a decade before, Bowles at last found an outlet for his distinguished abilities.

The purpose of the reorganization of November 1961, and especially of the blood transfusion from the White House, was to revitalize the Department and redress the imbalance in the foreign affairs partnership; it was one more expression of Kennedy's effort to make the Department the fulcrum of foreign policy. As he explained to Rostow, "Over here in the White House we have to play with a very narrow range of choices. We are pretty much restricted to the ideas coming out of the bureaucracy. We can't do long-range planning; it has to be done over there. I want you to go over there and catch hold of the process at the level where it counts."

The upheaval somewhat improved the situation. Though Ball remained a lawyer and not a manager, he had the talents of speed and decision and gave the President at least hope that his questions would be answered and his instructions executed. Rostow, perfectly cast, made the Policy Planning Council a bustle of intellectual activity and helped shape policy on a dozen fronts. Dutton joined policy sophistication with political skill in running congressional relations. Goodwin, until he was eventually cut off and isolated by the bureaucracy, brought new imagination and drive to Latin American affairs. Above all, Harriman not only gave Far Eastern policy a coherence and force it had not had for years but rapidly became the particular champion of the New Frontier within the State Department.

One could not but marvel at the inexhaustible vitality of this man, now in his seventies, the most tested of American diplomats, who, after living at the summit with Roosevelt, Churchill and Stalin twenty years earlier, was now cheerfully settled in a job of lower rank than any he had held for a generation. This was part of his attraction. One felt that here was a free man without personal ambition who said what he believed and cared not a damn for anything but getting the policy right. The downrightness of his reactions stimulated a bureaucracy too long accustomed to postponement and evasion. He became known with affection as 'The Crocodile' for his habit of abruptly biting off proposals which seemed to him stupid or irrelevant. He was the inveterate foe of platitude, rigidity and the conventional wisdom. He had been around too long to be impressed by the generals, tycoons, security officers and legislators who had so long intimidated the Department. He believed in giving good men their head. When long, detailed instructions would come across his desk intended for ambassadors in the field—'scenarios,' in the jargon, designed to deprive envoys abroad of all discretion—Harriman, before clearing the message, liked to add a liberating introductory sentence: "For your guidance, you may wish to consider the following." He tried in particular to bring forward the youthful, bright, audacious people; he thought that, if a person did not have a chance to exercise responsibility before he was forty, he probably would not be much good at it thereafter. He once delighted Walter and Victor Reuther by saying with great emphasis at the age of seventy-one: "Do you know what this damned Department needs? Young blood!" The young, detecting a kindred spirit, looked on him with tremendous admiration and devotion. Inside the government, the New Frontiersmen, within and without the State Department, regarded him as their champion. Perhaps no one else, except the President and the Attorney General, had such a stimulating influence on policy.

Power continued to gravitate toward him. In 1963, when George McGhee went on to become ambassador to Bonn, Harriman took his place as Under Secretary for Political Affairs. At the swearing-in George Ball gave a graceful speech, recalling that he had first met Harriman in the early days of the New Deal when people believed that anything was possible and that whatever had been done before was wrong. Averell picked up the theme in his own remarks. He said that he had lived through four times of great creativity in government—during the early New Deal, the Second World War, the Marshall Plan and the Kennedy years. He talked of the mission of the State Department in carrying the New Frontier to the world. After the ceremony he beckoned me into his office and said, "Of course I had to say all those nice things about the spirit in the State Department today. What I want to do is to give it a little of the crusading spirit of those earlier times. I want to bring it to life." He never quite succeeded, but he enlivened everything he touched.

To the end, the Department remained a puzzle to the President. No one ran it; Rusk, Ball and Harriman constituted a loose triumvirate on the seventh floor and, passing things back and forth among themselves, managed to keep a few steps ahead of crisis. But with all the problems and frustrations, Kennedy had gone far toward infusing a new energy into American diplomacy and a new spirit into the conduct of foreign affairs.

XVII

PERIL IN THE SKIES

KENNEDY HAD COME TO THE White House without illusion about peace in our time with the communist states. But he did hope that the Soviet leaders, as rational men, might at least agree on the value of moderating the cold war. The Vienna meeting shook this hope, and the Soviet announcement on August 30 of a decision to resume nuclear testing in the atmosphere almost shattered it. The President's response was prompt and bitter. The Soviet course, he said, "presents a hazard to every human being throughout the world by increasing the dangers of nuclear fallout." It "indicates the complete hypocrisy" of Soviet professions about disarmament. It increases "the danger of a thermonuclear holocaust." It "will be met with deepest concern and resentment throughout the world."

It certainly was met with the deepest concern in the United States. The next morning, newspapers denounced the Soviet move and Senators demanded that the United

States imitate it. The atmosphere was tense in the White House when the President called the National Security Council together at ten o'clock in the Cabinet Room in preparation for a meeting with the congressional leaders at ten forty-five. The faces around the table—Johnson, Rusk, McNamara, General Taylor, General Lemnitzer, Jerome Wiesner, Allen Dulles, Glenn Seaborg of the Atomic Energy Commission, Edward R. Murrow and a few others —were set and anxious. The time was short, and the Secretary of State quickly submitted a draft presidential statement announcing an immediate American decision to resume tests—essential, he thought, both to demonstrate our resolution on Berlin and to satisfy the domestic clamor.

The President dissented. "Why should we put ourselves into this business right away?" he asked. "Nehru said last year that whoever resumed testing would win the opprobrium of mankind. There may be a storm of exasperation in the United States if we don't announce resumption, but we can stand that for a few days." He looked across the table at the Vice-President and asked about the mood on the Hill. Johnson mentioned the belligerent Senators of the morning. "There will be a lot of talk of this sort," the Vice-President said. "But I personally think it would be a good thing if you let Khrushchev take the heat for a little while. Also, you ought not to give the impression of reacting every time he does something. I think you should say these things to the congressional leaders, while at the same time saying that preparations for the resumption of testing are under way."

The Russians thus far had only said they would resume testing; they had not yet tested. We speculated as to when their series would begin and what they could expect to learn from it. The President summed it up: "If you aren't fully briefed in this area, you have vague fears—that a month will make a difference, that testing would give the Soviet Union a major strategic advantage, that testing might give us great new weapons. But in fact the advantages we would gain from a resumption of testing would be relatively marginal and sophisticated." Meanwhile, pencil in hand, he edited the Rusk statement to make it announce, not a decision to resume, but a decision to begin preparations for resumption.

In the back of the room Ted Sorensen and I whispered to each other that the edited statement would be almost as effective as the original in wasting the political opportunities the Soviet Union had given us. We passed this thought on to Ed Murrow, who said he agreed and was about to say so. Murrow did not often talk in these meetings, and his observations in consequence had particular impact. "If we issue that statement," he said in a moment, "we destroy the advantages of the greatest propaganda gift we have had for a long time." Rusk now supported Murrow. Kennedy said, "The Russians are not fools. They thought they would lose less than they would gain by this decision. They must believe they will gain most by appearing tough and mean." But he put the statement aside.

At this point, Hubert Humphrey entered the Cabinet Room, thinking that the congressional meeting had already started; and we broke up. Later in the day the President in a brief statement characterized the Soviet announcement as "primarily a form of atomic blackmail, designed to substitute terror for reason in the present international scene," and said nothing about American testing.

1. THE TEST BAN TRAVAIL

The idea of a test ban first arose in the early fifties in response to the development of the hydrogen bomb. In the summer of 1952, Dr. Vannevar Bush, who had mobilized American science during the Second World War, proposed to Dean Acheson, then Secretary of State, that, before trying out the new bomb, the United States seek a no-testing agreement with the Soviet Union. Bush's effort failed, and the United States shortly began a series of nuclear explosions in the atmosphere.

The fission bombs dropped at Hiroshima and Nagasaki in 1945 had produced little radioactive debris. But the hydrogen superbombs of the fifties were another matter. The detonation of the first fission-fusion-fission bomb in the Bikini Atoll in 1954 sent great sinister clouds floating over the lonely Pacific; and, when the "ashy rain" fell on the Japanese tuna fishermen of the *Lucky Dragon,* leaving them with charred skins and a terrible sickness, the world suddenly learned about the new horror of radioactive fallout. Labour party members in England and Prime Minister Nehru in India called for a standstill agreement on testing. As scientists analyzed the effects of radioactive contamination on bones, blood and germ plasm, fear of testing grew. In the next years people began to hear more and more about strontium-90, carbon-14, cesium-137 and the other poisons generated by nuclear explosions. And the physiological argument for a test ban was soon reinforced by a political argument: that the only way to crack Soviet resistance to comprehensive schemes, like the Baruch Plan for the international control of atomic energy, was to demonstrate cooperation and create confidence in smaller and more manageable areas. The test ban seemed the ideal 'first step' toward general disarmament.

In the course of 1956 the Eisenhower administration was moving toward this position. But, when Adlai Stevenson called for a test ban in the 1956 campaign, discussions were halted within the government, and Stevenson's proposal was unreservedly attacked by Nixon ("catastrophic nonsense") and by Eisenhower himself ("a theatrical gesture"). Once the campaign was out of the way, however, events resumed their course. By 1958 Eisenhower agreed to join with the British and Russians in a conference in Geneva on the discontinuance of nuclear tests. The meeting opened in November 1958, as the United States and the Soviet Union were completing elaborate test sequences. Washington then announced that, unless Soviet Russia resumed, it would hold no tests for a year. Since then, neither nation, so far as the other knew, had conducted a test.

The object of the conference was to produce a comprehensive test ban treaty—that is, a control system outlawing all nuclear testing, whether in the earth's atmosphere, in outer space, in the oceans or underground.[1] Tests in air or water were readily detectable through a variety of long-distance effects—sound, light, radio waves, radiation and radioactive debris. They were consequently self-policing in the sense that violation could not be concealed. But the only known way to detect underground tests was through the measurement of the seismic waves transmitted through the earth; and seismic measurement by itself was unreliable because earthquakes often gave off signals indistinguishable from those of man-made explosions. This meant that, with the existing state of seismic research, underground testing below a certain level could not be policed without the possibility of inspection at the suspected site.

During 1959 and early 1960, Soviet representatives in Geneva displayed a modest willingness to grapple with the issues. But, while the British earnestly sought agreement, the American government remained divided within itself on the desirability of a treaty. Anti-test ban scientists, like Dr. Edward Teller, showed that it was theoretically

[1] With the exception of underground tests producing signals of less than 4.75 seismic magnitude; it was expected that this threshold would be lowered as seismic research improved detection capabilities.

possible to muffle the seismic signals by setting off bombs in great cavities deep under the earth and so to 'cheat' the control system.[2] Moreover, the responsibility for improving the techniques of seismic detection was entrusted to the Air Force, which, of course, was dominated by opponents of the test ban. The President was not sufficiently informed about the issues, nor the Secretary of State sufficiently concerned, to overcome this resistance. As a result, the American delegation in Geneva played a weak and inglorious role in the negotiations.

"For months on end," Sir Michael Wright of the British delegation wrote sympathetically of his American colleagues, "instructions were doled out to them from Washington much as a Victorian workhouse master might dole out the gruel."[3] It took nine months for the Americans to accept the British idea of an annual quota of veto-free inspections; and the Eisenhower administration could never quite bring itself to abandon a provision, considered "clearly untenable" by the British, denying the Russians parity on the control commission. At the end of 1959, Eisenhower even terminated the formal moratorium and declared the United States free to resume testing—an action which, of course, left the Russians technically free to resume two years later.

Nevertheless an informal moratorium continued, and negotiations in Geneva through 1960 began to narrow the areas of disagreement. In time the conference succeeded in adopting a preamble, seventeen articles and two annexes of a draft treaty. As the discussions proceeded, the treaty was assuming a new dimension: it was becoming a first step not only toward wider arms control but toward a working arrangement by which the nuclear superpowers could express their common interest in preventing wars between themselves and the dispersion of nuclear weapons to new powers. Harold Macmillan regarded this as an historic opportunity to make progress toward a *détente*, and he may have been right. But the opportunity was lost. A year later Macmillan told Kennedy that it was all the fault of the American 'big hole' obsession and the consequent in-

2 In 1960 the Scientists' Committee of the Democratic Advisory Council estimated that the hole required to hide a seventy-kiloton explosion would cost $25 to $50 million and require the excavation of an amount of material greater than the country's annual production of anthracite coal. In the Kennedy administration the Atomic Energy Commission, after several years of effort and at the cost of $20 million, detonated an explosion less than one-tenth that size—and discovered that the signal was enhanced in certain directions. In retrospect, the 'big hole' scare could not seem more dubious.

3 Michael Wright, *Disarm and Verify* (London, 1964), 120.

sistance on a wantonly large number of on-site inspections.

Then Kennedy came to office determined to narrow the differences. He had been sympathetic to the idea of a test ban for some years. During the 1956 campaign his colleague Senator Clinton Anderson had convinced him that, if tests were stopped, the relative weapons position of the United States would be satisfactory. "I think the United States should take the leadership in bringing these tests to an end," Kennedy then said, "And I think we owe it . . . because we are the only country that engaged in atomic warfare in the last war" and also because it would be the best way to stop the spread of the bomb to other countries. David Ormsby Gore renewed Kennedy's interest in the matter in 1959 and gave him a detailed memorandum on the British and Russian positions and the American nonposition. Now as President he sent Arthur Dean to Geneva with a new set of American proposals. These included a reduction in our requirements for annual inspections and for control posts, as well as parity of representation on the control commission between the two sides under a neutral chairman. Unfortunately, as American interest grew, Soviet interest declined. Dag Hammarskjold's role in the United Nations intervention in the Congo had convinced Khrushchev that there was no such thing as a neutral person and turned him against the previously acceptable idea of a neutral chairman. More important perhaps, Soviet generals and scientists were now demanding the resumption of tests in the hope of achieving more compact and efficient warheads. They also probably now feared that inspection within the Soviet Union would expose the myth of the 'missile gap,' which had become so politically beneficial to them, and reveal Soviet missile sites as low in number and high in vulnerability. In any case, by the end of 1960 Moscow had probably begun preparations for a possible test series in 1961.

The Russians at Geneva therefore responded to the Kennedy initiative by repudiating earlier agreements and demanding the *troika*. Under their own new proposals an unidentified earthshock within the Soviet Union could not be inspected at all in the first four years after the treaty came into force; the chiefs of both the control posts and the on-site inspection teams would be Soviet citizens; the teams themselves would be 50 per cent Soviet; and no staff could be hired, no control posts established, no instruments set up, no seismic data interpreted and no inspections undertaken without the consent of the Soviet representative on the *troika*. The Soviet proposals reduced inspection in effect to self-inspection and thus to absurdity.

Some time in 1961, probably after the new American Minuteman and Polaris programs were started and after the Vienna meeting, Khrushchev definitely decided to resume testing. Certainly by that summer he was overflowing with nuclear hints. On June 21 he said publicly, "Quite a few devices requiring practical testing have been developed in the Soviet Union." In early July he remarked to the British Ambassador in his genial way that it would take only six nuclear bombs to destroy England, eight to destroy France. McCloy, visiting Moscow in July, tried to dispose of the standard Soviet charge that the United States was secretly preparing tests in Nevada. We would be happy, McCloy said, for a team of Soviet or neutral experts to visit American proving grounds and determine the situation for themselves, if the Soviet Union would permit comparable visitations. Such a reciprocal arrangement, McCloy said, would go far toward removing suspicion and mistrust. The Soviet officials impassively turned the idea down as impractical. Impractical it certainly was, though how impractical McCloy would not understand for another few weeks.

At the end of July, Khrushchev himself told McCloy that he was under strong pressure to test, especially from his scientists, and that the Berlin crisis had increased the pressure. He had been successful thus far, he said, in holding off the decision; but, the more the United States intensified its threats of war, the more arguments it gave those in the Soviet Union who wanted to resume. His scientists favored a one-hundred-megaton bomb as the most economical, and, though they already had the rockets to lift it, the bomb itself needed to be tested. He had cheered his scientists, he said, by telling them that the United States would resume testing and thus release them to try out their own bomb: "Don't piss in your pants—you'll have your chance soon enough."

2. TO TEST OR NOT TO TEST

There was mounting pressure on Kennedy too; Americans as well as Russians chafed under the moratorium. Some really believed that the Soviet Union was cheating in big holes in Siberia. Others, while doubting that the Russians wanted to go to the enormous expense and difficulty of a clandestine program, nevertheless favored American resumption in the interest of American weapons development. It was argued further that resumption would add verisimilitude to our stance of firmness during the Berlin crisis. The growing demand came not just from the Pentagon but from the Congress, especially from members of the Joint Committee on Atomic Energy, and to some degree also from the public.

On the other hand, resumption would create problems. It would legitimatize renewal by the Soviet Union and therefore accelerate the nuclear arms race; and it would permit the world to blame us for having started the cycle of destruction again. "There can be no question," Galbraith wrote from New Delhi to the President in June 1961, "that a resumption of testing would cause us the gravest difficulties in Asia, Africa and elsewhere. Certainly no other foreseeable problem could cause us quite so much difficulty in India." The informal test ban, Hubert Humphrey said to Kennedy a few weeks later, has been "a ray of hope to millions of worried people. . . . The renewal of testing might well turn the political tides in the world in behalf of the Soviets." Moreover, testing in the atmosphere would bring a new surge of fallout, and this weighed heavily with Kennedy. Jerome Wiesner, his Science Adviser, reminded him one drizzling day how rain washed radioactive debris from the clouds and brought it down to the earth. Kennedy, looking out the window, said, "You mean that stuff is in the rain out there?" Wiesner said, "Yes." The President continued gazing out the window, deep sadness on his face, and did not say a word for several minutes. He hated the idea of reopening the race: "We test and then they test and we have to test again. And you build up until somebody uses them." But as President he could not forget his responsibilities for the national security of the United States. The Soviet about-face at Geneva, he explained to a press conference in late June, "raises a serious question about how long we can safely continue on a voluntary basis a refusal to undertake tests in this country without any assurance that the Russians are not testing." He accordingly asked Jerome Wiesner and the Science Advisory Committee to convene a special panel to take a fresh look at the problem.

If it turned out that our military security required testing, the President was concerned to make it clear to the world that we were resuming only because the Russians would not join us in a treaty. At his direction Murrow and I prepared a set of recommendations designed to leave no doubt about the American preference for test ban. Soviet negativism in Geneva had led to a decision to recess the test ban talks; but we now suggested that Arthur Dean be sent back, if possible with new proposals; that our ambassadors and perhaps even a special envoy (we had David Ormsby Gore in mind) confer with neutral leaders; and that the President himself make a major peace speech, probably at the United Nations. My particular assignment was to prepare a white paper on nuclear testing.

Bundy, Sorensen and I discussed these recommendations with the President on July 20. He immediately asked for a continuation of the Geneva talks, directed Dean to go back and ordered a canvass of neutral states. But he was worried about the growing pressure for testing. It was hard to deal with the Joint Committee on Atomic Energy, he said, "because those fellows think they invented the bomb themselves and look on everyone else as Johnny-come-latelies and amateurs." He himself remained unconvinced that the military gains of resumption would outweigh the political losses; the whole idea of testing obviously left him cold.

Wiesner's special panel, chaired by the physicist Wolfgang Panofsky, met with the President and the National Security Council early in August. They reported in effect that it was feasible for the Soviet Union to have conducted secret tests, that there was no evidence it had done so (or had not done so), and that there was no urgent technical need for immediate resumption by the United States. The Joint Chiefs of Staff, however, filed a paper questioning both the premises and the conclusions of the Panofsky report. My notes of the meeting describe the JCS paper as "assertive, ambiguous, semiliterate and generally unimpressive." In summarizing it, General Lemnitzer said, "I would like to emphasize that we are not advocating atmospheric testing. Our memorandum is at fault if it suggests otherwise [as indeed it appeared to do]. And we have no objection to a reasonable delay in the resumption of testing. But we do see urgency in testing for small-yield weapons development."

As the session continued, one saw the old disagreement in the scientific community, going back to the argument over the hydrogen bomb in 1949 and now institutionalized in the divergence between the two great nuclear laboratories, Livermore and Los Alamos. This was the scientific side of the strategic debate of the fifties between massive retaliation and flexible response. Livermore, in the spirit of Ernest Lawrence and Edward Teller, believed that American security rested on the unlimited development of nuclear striking power; in the jargon, this was 'infinite containment.' Los Alamos, in the spirit of Robert Oppenheimer, believed that nuclear power should be only one component in a varied national arsenal; this was 'finite containment.' The bitterness of the time, early in the Eisenhower administration, when the Livermore group had sought to destroy the Los Alamos position by branding Oppenheimer a security risk had to some degree abated. In the later Eisenhower years, after Lewis Strauss left the government and James Killian and George Kistiakowsky had served in the White House as successive presidential assistants for science and technology, the Los Alamos view had recovered favor. But, though only a minority of the scientific community followed Teller, the Livermore position retained strong allies in the Congress and the press; and the perseverance of its advocates, given emotional edge by their conviction of persecution, had won them access to a formidable sector of public opinion.

With Wiesner as Kennedy's Science Adviser, the doctrines of finite containment and flexible response were clearly in the ascendancy. But, in forming the special panel, Wiesner had taken care to assemble a balanced group, including John Foster, the head of Livermore, as well as Norris Bradbury, the head of Los Alamos. Oddly enough, the Livermore scientists, who a year earlier had discoursed most eloquently on the ease and convenience for the Soviet Union of testing in secret cavities underground, were now most insistent in proclaiming the inadequacy of underground testing for the United States and demanding that we go into the atmosphere as soon as possible. Foster argued vigorously to the President that immediate resumption was necessary in order to develop the neutron bomb—that is, a fissionless bomb killing by neutron rays with very limited blast and radiation effect. Actually the scientists had not solved the problem of achieving a temperature sufficiently high to initiate a fusion reaction without the use of a fission bomb, and this problem, which did not require testing in the atmosphere, seemed likely to occupy them for years to come; nor, indeed, had there been systematic analysis of the specific military uses of such a bomb. The President remarked that he had understood that atmospheric testing was not indicated for the neutron bomb for at least another eighteen months. Wiesner added that the feasibility of the basic idea could be determined in a laboratory. It was the problem of 'staging' which required tests, he said, and going at this problem at once would be like building the body of a car before the motor had been invented.

The President then cross-examined the panel to find out

what else we could hope to learn if we resumed testing. Foster and others outlined possibilities both in staging and in tactical nuclear weapons. "Isn't this all a marginal advantage?" Kennedy said. "The argument that we should test for these reasons does not seem to me overwhelming." He added, "If we test, we will presumably test underground alone. The Soviet Union will resume if we do, and they will test in the atmosphere. If you were satisfied that the Soviet Union was *not* testing, would you favor our resumption underground?" Panofsky: "No." Foster: "Yes." Norris Bradbury, who had hitherto been silent: "No. There is no point in our resuming testing if we only test underground. The Soviet Union will test in the atmosphere and will overtake us." John McCloy, who was in charge of disarmament negotiations, remarked that it would be unwise to resume testing with the UN General Assembly about to meet and that the discussion had satisfied him that the decision could be postponed to the first of the year without impairing national security. This appeared to sum up the sense of the meeting, and we adjourned, the President warning that any indications that we might renew testing would undercut our effort to get a treaty in Geneva.

3. THE SOVIET EXPLOSIONS

I came away with the feeling that, while there was no irresistible short-run case for resumption, everyone regarded a return at least to underground testing as inevitable in the long run if the Russians continued to reject the treaty. Kennedy wrote Macmillan early in August that he was still reviewing the evidence but was not very hopeful that it would be possible to wait much beyond the first of the year. If we did resume, the President continued, it would be underground, unless and until the Soviets resumed atmospheric tests. He also mentioned an idea which Ambassador Thompson had sent from Moscow—that we try once again for a limited ban, outlawing tests in the atmosphere and under water. These were the ones that caused fallout; they did not require inspection; and they were presumably the tests which would help the Russians the most.

This proposal greatly attracted both Bundy and me. But Arthur Dean feared that any retreat from the comprehensive treaty would be taken as a general weakening of our position. When the matter was brought to the President, he readily came up with a compromise—that Dean should fight for the whole treaty in Geneva, but, if nothing happened, we could come out for the limited ban later. In mid-August the President concluded that, when Dean returned from Geneva and the Defense Department had completed its review of weapon requirements, the Atomic Energy Commission might announce contingency preparations for underground testing, though this would not mean that we had actually decided to resume tests.

On August 28, the Foreign Broadcast Information Service recorded a Soviet broadcast warning aircraft to stay out of a designated area over Siberia. This bulletin seemed the result of some slip-up in Moscow, and Wiesner and Kaysen, in a state of high excitement, rushed the item to the President, venturing that this was an indication we were soon to have a Russian test in the atmosphere. Kennedy, who was just getting up from an afternoon nap, read the bulletin, grimaced and said bitterly: "Bitched again." They did not soon forget the look of profound discouragement on his face. Two days later came Moscow's official announcement of its decision to resume.

We were still waiting for the actual tests. At three o'clock on September 1, I was chatting in my office with Richard Wilbur and Peter Viereck, who were leaving that afternoon for the Soviet Union on a mission of cultural goodwill. In a minute Bundy called to say that it looked as if the first Soviet explosion had taken place. "The President is still napping," he said, "and we haven't wakened him. We're trying to figure out what to say. You had better come over."

An argument was taking place in Bundy's office when I arrived. Arthur Dean, who had just returned from Geneva, and McCloy favored an immediate announcement of our own determination to resume. Murrow, Wiesner, Bundy and the others favored a declaration calling on the world to condemn the Russians for their action. After discussion it was decided to bring both statements to the President.

We trooped over to the Mansion. In a moment Kennedy came out of his bedroom in a dressing-gown. He listened a little impatiently to the definition of issues, then asked for the drafts. McCloy argued that the American President had to show now that he was capable of hard and tough leadership—that he could not continue to stand by and let the communists kick us in the teeth. Murrow contended that we had nothing to gain and much to lose by precipitate action. The President was in no mood to listen to prolonged debate. Knowing what each side was going to say, he completed our sentences, slashed each statement to bits and said that, while he was not inclined to announce our resumption at this point, he did not know how much longer he could refrain from doing so. Then he briskly ushered us out.

He still hoped to avert a new sequence of atmospheric testing and spare the world a new rain of radioactivity. The time had now come for the Thompson proposal. On September 3 he joined with Macmillan in offering Khrushchev an agreement not to conduct tests which produced fallout, pointing out that such a pact could rely on existing means of detection and would not require additional controls. But later the same day, while cruising off Hyannis Port, he received word of a second Soviet test. If a Soviet series were to constitute the only answer to the offer of an atmospheric ban, Kennedy saw no choice, given the Berlin crisis, but to order United States resumption. When on Monday our detection system picked up a third Soviet test, Kennedy, back in Washington, immediately announced American preparation for tests "in the laboratory and underground, with no fallout. . . . In view of the acts of the Soviet Government, we must now take those steps which prudent men find essential." He wrote Macmillan that we had to show both our friends and our own people that we were ready to meet our own needs in the face of these new Soviet acts; at this hour the gravest danger was that we might seem less determined than Khrushchev.

On September 9 Khrushchev made his formal reply to the Kennedy-Macmillan proposal. "Cessation of one kind of test only—in the atmosphere," he wrote, "—would be a disservice to the cause of peace." So, in the name of peace, he reopened the nuclear race. Soon he was boasting to the Communist 22nd Congress of his intention to detonate a 50-megaton bomb—2500 times bigger than the one which had killed 100,000 people at Hiroshima and five times larger than the total of all high explosives used in all the wars of human history. Between September 1 and November 4 the Soviet Union carried out at least thirty major tests, nearly all in the atmosphere. By this time, though there had been fewer Russian than western tests since testing began, the Soviet Union had discharged more radioactive poison into the air than the United States, Britain and France together. The total force over the years of Khrushchev's atmospheric explosions was about 170 megatons, equal to 170 million tons of TNT, as against about 125 megatons for the United States and a few megatons for the other two countries. As the new series continued, I noted, "I fear that Khrushchev has decided to make the USSR the embodiment of terror and power in the world in the expectation that all 'lovers' of peace, terrified of war and recognizing the futility of trying to alter Soviet policy, will concentrate their energies on making the west give way over Berlin. This is brinksmanship with a vengeance, and it may get us very close indeed to war."

4. APPEAL TO THE UNITED NATIONS

But the President was not ready to accept the challenge of terror without one more appeal to reason. There still remained the General Assembly of the United Nations, gathering in New York in mid-September for its sixteenth session.

In July Kennedy had asked me to follow United Nations matters for the White House. This put me in the not unfamiliar but still sometimes uncomfortable position of middleman between Kennedy and Stevenson—two men whom I so much admired but whose own rapport was perhaps less than perfect. In this assignment I had the good fortune to work closely with Assistant Secretary of State Harlan Cleveland and the excellent staff of his Bureau of International Organization Affairs.

Cleveland was a man of varied experience: a Rhodes Scholar (like Kermit Gordon, he had had Harold Wilson as a tutor at Oxford), then the Board of Economic Warfare, and UNRRA in Italy and China, then to the Marshall Plan (where in 1950 he invented the phrase, so thrashed to death in later years, "the revolution of rising expectations"), then publisher of *The Reporter* magazine and finally dean of the Maxwell School at Syracuse University before Kennedy and Stevenson brought him back to Washington. His intelligence, imagination, good sense and good humor were indispensable not just in working out our UN policy but in preserving communication and confidence within the eternal triangle of the State Department, the United States Mission in New York and the White House.

Kennedy, who had an essential respect and liking for Stevenson, tried, when he thought of it, to make their relationship effective. He understood Stevenson's standing in the world and his influence on liberal opinion in the United States, admired his public presence and wit, valued his skills as diplomat and orator, and considered him, unlike most of the State Department, capable of original thought. He also respected Stevenson's taste in people. Of the men who had gathered a decade before at the Elks' Club in Springfield to work for Adlai's first campaign, J. Edward Day, Willard Wirtz and George Ball were now in the cabinet or sub-cabinet; Kenneth Galbraith, William Blair, John

Bartlow Martin and William Rivkin were ambassadors; David Bell was director of the Budget, Newton Minow chairman of the Federal Communications Commission, Carl McGowan a federal judge, Clayton Fritchey and Philip Stern were in the State Department, and I was in the White House.

Kennedy fully expected, moreover, that people (including some of his own loyalists who still had not forgiven Stevenson for Los Angeles in 1960) would try to make trouble between Adlai and himself, and generally shrugged off the tales helpfully repeated to him of petulance or discontent in New York. On the other hand, certain of Stevenson's idiosyncrasies did try him; and his own effect on Stevenson in face-to-face encounter was unfortunately to heighten those which tried him most. The relationship was of course harder for Stevenson. He was the older man, and in one way or another Kennedy had denied him his highest hopes. Though Stevenson greatly respected the President's intelligence and judgment, he never seemed wholly at ease on visits to the White House. He tended to freeze a little, much as he used to do in the fifties on television shows like the Meet the Press, and, instead of the pungent, astute and beguiling man he characteristically was, he would seem stiff, even at times solemn and pedantic.

Kennedy consequently never saw Stevenson at his best. Their meetings were always friendly—if Kennedy seldom called Rusk "Dean," he generally called Stevenson "Adlai" —but at times they only confirmed Kennedy's theory of Stevenson's supposed inability to make up his mind. To me and to others who knew Stevenson, this theory seemed exaggerated; Stevenson was occasionally indecisive about himself but rarely about his policies. It was his manner, deliberately self-deprecatory, that conveyed an appearance of indecision which did not really exist. Even here the President, though at times ironic, was not unsympathetic. He once remarked that one could not fairly judge what kind of man Stevenson might have become, for no experience could have been more destructive of self-confidence than to have been twice defeated for President; victory would have changed him in another direction. And, though Kennedy expected a certain softness in Stevenson's recommendations and was occasionally ironic about this too, he knew that his Ambassador to the UN had to be responsive to his constituency and, on balance, welcomed Stevenson's advocacy of the claims of American idealism and of the international community, if only to counterbalance the hard-nosed Europe-obsessed mood of the

State Department. When Stevenson wrote the President a week after the erection of the Berlin Wall, "It would be extremely dangerous for us to allow our attention to be so absorbed by Berlin that we overlook attitudes in Asia, Africa and Latin America, or take decisions or public positions based in the exigencies of our NATO allies rather than the exigencies of those areas," the President, for all his own absorption in the Berlin crisis, recognized the justice of the point.

Quite apart from the amiable but sometimes formal personal contacts, there were problems inherent in the relationship between Washington and any ambassador to the UN. Stevenson was of course invited to meetings of the cabinet and the National Security Council, but he was very often detained at the UN when large decisions impended at the Department or the White House. Though both Kennedy and Rusk tried to remember to keep Stevenson abreast of policy, especially after the Bay of Pigs, consultation over the long-distance telephone never proved enough. To influence the making of policy it was really necessary to be in the room. Nearly every significant decision had a UN angle; and this meant that the ambassador to the UN sometimes had the sense of having to defend a world he never made. Cleveland and I did our best to see that the UN interest was represented in policy discussions, but we were often not in the room ourselves.

Washington, moreover, had an ineradicable tendency to think of foreign policy as a matter between the United States and another nation or, at most, as between the United States and an alliance. The idea of policy as lying between the United States and the mess of a hundred nations in New York was alien and uncongenial. The Foreign Service particularly appeared to regard multilateral diplomacy as somehow inferior and nonprofessional—an attitude reinforced by the fact that service in the U.S. Mission to the UN counted less in advancing a career than a Third Secretaryship in Stockholm or Pretoria.

If the atmosphere in Washington made people think too little about the UN, the atmosphere in the headquarters in New York made people think of nothing else. To outsiders the UN often seemed a vast and picturesque form of make-believe, whose excitements bore little connection with serious issues; but to those who lived every day in the all-enveloping UN environment, it became the ultimate reality. Not until I began making regular visits to the great glass tower glittering above the East River did I start to grasp the intensity of the UN life. It was a world of its own, separate, self-contained and in chronic crisis, where a dozen unrelated emergencies might explode at once, demanding immediate reactions across the government and decisions (or at least speeches) in New York. It had its own ethos, its own rules and its own language: delegates would argue interminably over whether to "note" or to "reaffirm" a past resolution, to "deplore" or "regret" or "condemn" a present action. It had its own social life, an endless and obligatory round of evening receptions, where American nonattendance might be taken as an insult and lose a vote on an important resolution.

Stevenson, presiding over this hectic outpost of American diplomacy, had a far more arduous and exhausting job than most Washingtonians appreciated; and, because he had the grace of making everything look easy and the habit of disparaging his own success, people in Washington did not realize how superbly he was discharging an impossible assignment. In New York, however, his public stature, his exceptional personal charm and his realistic faith in the UN as an institution enabled him to recover quickly from the embarrassments of the Bay of Pigs and to assume a role of leadership. He had a gifted group of associates at the United States Mission, especially Ambassador Charles W. Yost, a superb Foreign Service officer, quiet, reflective and tough. On political and press matters the White House often dealt with Clayton Fritchey, an old friend of the President's and my own, an experienced newspaperman who had been General Marshall's director of public information in the Defense Department and a Special Assistant to President Truman before he joined the Stevenson campaign staff in 1952. In the fifties Fritchey served as deputy chairman of the Democratic National Committee. Now back with Stevenson, he handled a whole range of delicate matters with imperturbable resourcefulness.

Though Kennedy had retained from the founding conference in San Francisco a soberly favorable view of the UN, I do not think he had thought about it intensively before he entered the White House. But the 15th General Assembly resumed its session after the inauguration; and the President was quick to note that, next to himself, his ambassador to the United Nations was the most conspicuous voice of American foreign policy. Day after day, UN stories would dominate the front page of the *New York Times*. This was due partly, no doubt, to Stevenson but even more to the issues which crowded the UN agenda. It was then that Kennedy began to develop his avid interest in how the United States was going to vote on UN resolutions; he hated to learn things about his own government in the press. The Bay of Pigs further emphasized the role of the UN; for, as a result of the Cuban debate and of the parliamentary necessity of using the 'right to reply' without delay, the first statements of United States policy at almost every stage were made at the UN.

Plainly the UN was now as much a fact of international life as NATO or Khrushchev's nuclear tests in Siberia; and this Kennedy fully recognized. I noted in October 1961: "Considering the fact that JFK is surrounded every day by State Department people, who believe essentially in bilateral diplomacy, and by generals and admirals, who don't believe in diplomacy at all, I think he does exceedingly well to keep the UN as considerably in the forefront of his attention as he does." In this he had the assistance of Rusk, who had held Cleveland's post in the Truman administration and retained a sure technical command of UN problems, and very often (though the U.S. Mission to the UN would never believe this) of McGeorge Bundy. Kennedy's interest in the UN, however, was primarily as an instrument of political and economic action. Here and elsewhere, the idea of 'institution-building,' which meant so much to a political scientist like Harlan Cleveland, did not have great reality for him. Since I suffered from this same disability, I was inclined to attribute it to the cast of mind of the historian, who assumes that, if developments did not generate institutions, no amount of institution-building could control developments.

5. STATE OF THE UN

The UN remained a congeries of institutions, and it was now, as it had been since 1945, in a state of constitutional evolution. The San Francisco Charter had envisaged a benign, great-power overlordship, with the Security Council as the organization's executive arm. But it had also given each permanent member of the Security Council a veto, and this could render the Council impotent whenever the permanent members were in serious disagreement (provided that they were in attendance, as the Soviet Union was not at the time of Korea). As for the General Assembly, for all the powers it gained from the Uniting for Peace resolution of 1950, it had proved too divided and unwieldy for executive action; despite the later theories about the dominance of the Assembly in this period, nearly all UN peace-keeping operations continued to be authorized by the Council.

The single clear point in the confusion was the Secretary-

General. Dag Hammarskjöld, especially after his re-election in 1957, disclosed a presidential conception of the Secretary-General's "duty to use his office and, indeed, the machinery of the Organization to its utmost capacity." He considered it his obligation to act on his own, without guidance from the organization or the Charter, if this should seem "necessary in order to help in filling any vacuum that may appear in the systems which the Charter and traditional diplomacy provide for the safeguarding of peace and security." He charged this conception with the quasi-messianic passion of an extraordinary personality. Half international civil servant in the tradition of the League of Nations, half Scandinavian visionary in the tradition of Swedenborg and Kierkegaard, he inscribed in his journal his belief that "in our era, the road to holiness necessarily passes through the world of action." From his lofty eminence as (in a phrase he once used in a talk with W. H. Auden) secular Pope, the proceedings below sometimes seemed empty gabble:

> Words without import
> Are lobbed to and fro
> Between us.
>
> Forgotten intrigues
> With their spider's web
> Snare our hands.

But his sense of mission was invincible. Mysticism carried him nearly to the point of identification with Christ: "I am the vessel. The draught is God's. And God is the thirsty one. . . . He who has surrendered himself to it knows that the Way ends on the Cross." With the resourcefulness of a bureaucrat and the fervor of a saint, he sought to make the UN the chosen instrument of mankind in its quest for salvation.

Keeping out of areas of direct Soviet-American confrontation, like Berlin, he concentrated instead on peacekeeping in the third world—in the Middle East, Southeast Asia and Africa. He saw the new nations, which entered the General Assembly in increasing numbers after 1954, as his special constituency and sought to persuade them that the UN was their fortress. His initiative succeeded brilliantly until his entry into the Congo in 1960. Then Khrushchev, perceiving that UN intervention would prevent a communist victory, reached his conclusion that there was no such thing as a neutral person—above all Hammarskjöld—and opened the campaign first to force Hammarskjöld's resignation and then to replace the single Secretary-General with the *troika*.

The United States strongly backed Hammarskjöld, partly no doubt because we agreed with what he was doing in the Congo, but partly also because of a genuine desire to strengthen the capacity of the UN to keep the peace. From our viewpoint the UN, however much it may have fallen short of the dreams of 1945, had amply vindicated itself as a force for stability in a highly unstable world. The very complexity of its procedures and incoherence of its judgments had often provided an invaluable means of muffling and confusing hostilities. Moreover, in its more purposeful moments it had played an indispensable role in averting clashes between the Soviet Union and the west, both by offering a cover for quiet talks, like those which ended the Berlin blockade in 1949, and by containing local crises before the nuclear powers were irretrievably involved, as in the Suez affair in 1956. And the UN represented the best hope of keeping the newly independent nations from sliding into aggression or collapse and of incorporating them into an order of rational development. Despite the rush of the ex-colonial states into the organization, we remained confident that we could mobilize the one-third plus one of the General Assembly necessary to block action against our interests. The meeting of the 16th General Assembly now offered the new President an opportunity to affirm the American concern for peace and to recall the world to its senses.

6. THE DRIVE FOR DISARMAMENT

"I can think of no better position for the United States in the forthcoming General Assembly," Stevenson had written Kennedy in early July, "than the earnest advocacy of disarmament as our top priority national interest. . . . [We must] seize the initiative in disarmament which the Russians have held too long. . . . The United States must appear second to none in its desire for disarmament."

This theme Kennedy himself had expounded for a long time. "The price of running this arms race to the end is death," he had warned in 1959. ". . . We must design and propose a program that combines disarmament with the strengthening of the United Nations and with world development." Arms control, he wrote in 1960 in a review of Liddell Hart's *Deterrent or Defense*, would not happen "in a romantic moment of human redemption," but it might come with "careful, detailed and well-staffed proposals" because of the "overlapping interest between Russians and Americans" in the prevention of nuclear war. During the campaign he repeatedly condemned the Eisenhower administration on the ground that "in the entire U.S. Government we have had fewer than one hundred men working on the complex problems of arms control." Taking up the Democratic Advisory Council's proposal of a National Peace Agency,[4] Kennedy promised to establish a new organization to work for disarmament and declared that "the fight for disarmament must command the personal attention and concern of the President of the United States."

The quest for disarmament had been long and discouraging. Men of goodwill had preached the perils of the arms race for many years. After the First World War the great powers had engaged in ritualistic disarmament discussions and even completed some treaties; but little had happened. Now nuclear weapons were giving disarmament a new and dreadful urgency. For the first time in history one nation could absolutely obliterate another, and very likely the rest of the world in the process. The arms race, which realists could plausibly dismiss in earlier years as no more than a reflection of international rivalries, had clearly become in the nuclear age a source of tension in itself.

But still little happened. The Russians rejected the Baruch Plan; and the UN Disarmament Commission, established in 1952, degenerated into a sort of gladiatorial combat where the contestants waged unrelenting political warfare, brandishing their schemes and retreating in confusion whenever the other side showed any tendency to accept them. The Soviet Union put forward a grandiose proposal for "general and complete disarmament" and in 1959 even secured the General Assembly's endorsement, not for the details of the plan, but for its title. The Soviet plan, however, was self-evidently a fake, for any scheme proposing to combine total disarmament with the creation of an international police force looked either to world government or to world communism; and world government was obviously the last thing the Soviet Union wanted, as its advocacy of the *troika* showed. As for America, in

---

[4] The idea of a National Peace Agency was first submitted to the DAC by Trevor Gardner, who had served briefly as Assistant Secretary of the Air Force in the Eisenhower administration, and Dr. Harrison Brown of the California Institute of Technology. It was revised and approved by the Advisory Committee on Science and Technology and adopted by the DAC, with Kennedy's specific endorsement, on December 5, 1959.

spite of Harold Stassen's valiant efforts during his time
as disarmament negotiator, our policy remained formalistic,
like the Soviet's—dedicated to developing positions, not
for negotiation, but for propaganda.

The formalism of the fifties produced a spreading frustration about the theory of total disarmament by a single
agreement. At the same time, the development of the intercontinental ballistic missile was introducing a new factor which had to be incorporated into disarmament doctrine.
In the United States especially, the new strategic analysis
carried out in the Rand Corporation and elsewhere was
yielding important insights into the character of the arms
problem. The men who had invented nuclear weapons
now began to give hard thought to the idea, not of abolishing them at one stroke, but of regulating them in the interest of stability. Out of this discussion emerged a new
approach to the arms race under the banner of 'arms control.' The thinking was particularly hard along the banks
of the Charles River, where Jerome Wiesner, Thomas C.
Schelling, Henry Kissinger and others worked out the
strategy of equilibrium in the nuclear age. A series of
seminars and study groups at the end of the fifties culminated in a highly influential paper by Wiesner in
Daedalus magazine in the winter of 1960.

The essence of arms control was 'stable nuclear deterrence'—the view, that is, that the best hope for peace and
for ultimate disarmament lay in creating a situation where,
in Wiesner's words, "a surprise attack by one side cannot
prevent retaliation by the other." The temptation of surprise attack in a nuclear age was the hope of knocking out
the opposing nuclear capability. If each side knew that
both its own and the enemy nuclear forces could survive
any conceivable assaults—through making missile bases, for
example, 'hard' or mobile—then neither side would rationally initiate an attack which would only result in its
own destruction. Stable deterrence had interesting implications—among them that the United States would be better
off if the Russian striking force were invulnerable than if it
were vulnerable—and most of its proponents were prepared
to follow their logic to this conclusion. A stable deterrent
system, they further agreed, would make it possible to
limit the size of the deterrent and thereby end the nuclear
race.

The gospel of stable deterrence enlisted support in the
Navy, which saw an expanded role for its Polaris missiles,
and in the Army, which resented the funds channeled to

the Air Force. But it antagonized those, as in the Air Force, who yearned for unlimited American nuclear supremacy. It also for subtler reasons antagonized some who yearned for total disarmament. An extreme school of 'disarmers' pronounced stable deterrence a dangerous deception. It might be a defense against rational enemy decision, they said, but it was little use against irrationality; so long as missiles rested on launching pads, accident or insanity might still rush the world to nuclear holocaust. This school objected in addition that stable deterrence would make disarmament forever impossible by requiring each side to maintain a sizable nuclear establishment. The argument was that, the smaller the opposing nuclear forces became, the more unstable the equilibrium; for the reason that, as the level of force declined, the capacity of cheating to upset the balance increased. If each side, for example, had five hundred legal missiles, hiding two more from the inspectors would make little difference, but, if each side had only five legal missiles, the extra two might be decisive. On these various grounds the once-and-for-all disarmers condemned arms control as an elegant rationalization for a permanent arms race and proclaimed the need for immediate and total abolition of nuclear weapons.

Some arms controllers did indeed think that stabilization of the arms race was the most the world could realistically hope for. But others, like Wiesner himself, rightly doubted that total disarmament was at the moment politically relevant and saw stable deterrence as the best means of creating the atmosphere in which tensions could be reduced, further agreement achieved and, eventually, total disarmament attained. Walt Rostow coined the term 'transitional deterrent' to make this point. As the experience of agreement developed the habits and techniques of inspection and enlarged mutual confidence, the world could begin to cut back military forces and stockpiles and move toward final disarmament. For the interim period, the arms controllers had a variety of proposals designed to reduce the dangers of surprise attack and accidental war.

The Charles River doctrine, in short, appeared to offer a way of reconciling the objective of comprehensive disarmament with the interim requirements of national security. Its evident practicality appealed to Kennedy, and its emergence in 1960 gave him the opportunity for a new start in disarmament policy.

7. ORGANIZING FOR DISARMAMENT

After the election the President-elect had first to decide

how to organize his disarmament effort in order to give it the power and priority it had lacked under Eisenhower. Knowing he had to protect disarmament against suspicions of softness, idealism, one-worldism and so on, he followed his customary practice of seeking a conservative to execute a liberal policy. The appointment of John J. McCloy as his special disarmament adviser was thus a deliberate effort to prepare the political ground by placing disarmament in charge of a figure whose background unassailably combined the Republican party, the Pentagon, the Ford Foundation, the Chase Manhattan Bank, Cravath, Swaine & Moore, the Brook and the Links.

The next question was the location of the new disarmament agency. Kennedy's "superficial preference," as he told Richard Neustadt, was to put it in the Executive Office of the President; nothing, he felt, could demonstrate more effectively the new status and seriousness of the American purpose. On the other hand, as Neustadt persuasively replied, taking disarmament out of the State Department would conflict with the policy of making State the agent of coordination in foreign affairs; "the Secretary ought to have a run for the money." Moreover, if McCloy headed the staff, the new agency would have independence, access to the President and influence at the Pentagon wherever it was. Neustadt therefore recommended that it be set up as an autonomous unit within the State Department. Kennedy received a similar recommendation from his old friend Edmund Gullion, who had worked on disarmament as a Special Assistant to Acheson in the Truman administration and was now head of a "disarmament administration" hastily improvised in State during the campaign in answer to Kennedy's criticisms.

The disarmament agency accordingly came into being as a semi-detached part of State. Because of his commitments as a lawyer, McCloy could not give full time to Washington; so Adrian Fisher, who had once clerked for Justice Frankfurter and had later been Legal Adviser to the State Department under Acheson, and Gullion became his deputies. In September the new agency received its statutory basis when Congress established the Arms Control and Disarmament Agency; the very title was an attempt to liquidate the quarrel between the two approaches. At this point, McCloy had to return to his private affairs and, in another exercise in protective coloration, William Foster, the public-spirited businessman who had originally been considered for Under-Secretary of State for Economic Affairs, was appointed head of ACDA. Foster had met Wiesner and other scientists and received his initiation into disarmament mysteries when he led the American delegation to the 1958 Geneva conference on the prevention of surprise attack.

During the spring McCloy had concentrated on general disarmament policy, leaving the test ban to Arthur Dean and congressional problems to Fisher. A good many cooks helped stir the broth—Wiesner and Kaysen at the White House; Stevenson at the United Nations; Leland Haworth and Glenn Seaborg at the Atomic Energy Commission; Rusk, Abram Chayes and Cleveland at State; McNamara, Gilpatric, John McNaughton and the Joint Chiefs of Staff at the Pentagon. Periodically a so-called Committee of Principals assembled to wrangle over American policy.

The basic problem was to weld balanced deterrents and total disarmament into a single negotiating proposal. Stevenson, Wiesner and Gullion all felt that arms control by itself would not be enough, that the United Nations and world opinion demanded that the sword of Damocles be not only balanced but eventually lifted. After all, the United States had nominally accepted "general and complete disarmament" in the 1959 UN resolution, even if our actual proposals before and after had suggested that we were interested only in partial measures and unwilling to go the distance. Any retreat from the goal of general and complete disarmament by the new administration, Stevenson warned, would be disastrous, and we had to put forward a strong and convincing plan if we were to strengthen allied unity and beat the Soviet Union in the UN.

The Joint Chiefs of Staff, however, and an extreme faction of arms controllers opposed general and complete disarmament on the ground that it was either Madison Avenue huckstering or else a plan for world government and hence utopian. As for McCloy, his original intention was to work toward a somewhat vague conception of the "rule of law." When he and Stevenson debated disarmament policy before the President in mid-March, Kennedy ruled in favor of general and complete disarmament. McCloy accepted this as the objective but, boggling at the phrase lest it imply an endorsement of the Soviet plan, proposed to substitute "total and universal disarmament."

In the early spring Stevenson and Gromyko agreed that there should be an exchange of views between the United States and the Soviet Union to permit a renewal of disarmament negotiations. In July McCloy went to Moscow and engaged in extensive talks with V. A. Zorin, the Deputy

Foreign Minister of the Soviet Union. Though "total and universal disarmament" was now the accepted government objective, the phrase concealed a good deal of confusion and disagreement. When someone on McCloy's plane to Moscow pointed out that the plan involved the reduction of national forces in the final phase to the level required to maintain internal security and meant therefore the disappearance of all national nuclear establishments, a representative of the Navy objected that this was wrong; a nuclear arsenal would still be necessary "to maintain internal security against the Russians."

For two weeks in Moscow, McCloy and Zorin read back and forth across the table elaborate prepared speeches, each always ending up with a plea to the other to accept "total and universal disarmament" or "general and complete disarmament." The two phrases were, in fact, identical in Russian; and toward the end the punch-drunk Soviet interpreter electrified the conference when he concluded his English translation of Zorin's speech by proclaiming the unalterable Soviet devotion to "total and universal disarmament." Zorin peered at McCloy and, speaking his first words in English during the whole proceedings, said, "You know, Mr. McCloy, it looks as if he is going over to your side." The unfortunate interpreter disappeared, perhaps to Siberia; and the episode illustrated the fatuity of the semantic struggle. After McCloy returned to Washington, Rusk stopped the nonsense by pointing out that the two expressions tended to be the same in most languages; in any case, he said, we weren't going to get absolute disarmament for many, many years and, if there were any difference between the two formulas, it was a metaphysical one which did not comport with the dignity of the United States to insist upon.

For a long time Zorin had declined to entertain the idea of any negotiation at all until both countries agreed on the basic provisions of a specific plan; but in Moscow McCloy finally got the Soviet Union to change its position and consider a statement of principles. When negotiations resumed in New York in September, the Russians resisted the American contention that the verification machinery should cover not only the arms and forces abandoned but those retained. "While being for effective control over disarmament," Zorin said, ". . . the Soviet Union at the same time resolutely opposes establishment of control over armaments." This left a considerable gap in the disarmament design; but nevertheless concurrence became possible on a general statement defining the framework for future multilateral talks. The Americans now accepted the Russian point that disarmament should be "general and complete," leaving nations only the forces necessary to maintain internal order; while the Russians accepted two theses which McCloy had made the center of his argument—that the process should take place in stages "under such strict and effective international control as would provide firm assurance that all parties are honoring their obligations," and that it should go hand in hand with the development of international peace-keeping institutions.

During the spring and early summer, while this was going on, Washington had been involved in a complicated effort to work out the details of a new disarmament plan. Panels were convened, experts summoned from all over the country, studies commissioned, meetings held. Finally Wiesner and Spurgeon Keeney of his staff spent a weekend assembling all the ideas of value, including anything of interest they could find in the Soviet disarmament proposals of the five years preceding, and put together a plan.

The matter was one of fantastic complexity, and the plan was a remarkable intellectual feat. It was based on Wiesner's conviction that arms control and stabilized deterrence offered the way to general and complete disarmament. With immense ingenuity it worked out in three stages the progressive reduction and eventual abolition of all kinds of national armed force. It laid primary stress on the elimination of delivery vehicles for weapons of mass destruction—and also on unilateral and reciprocal measures to lessen the risk of war by accident or miscalculation. It provided for the parallel development and strengthening of peace-keeping institutions. The plan raised the most intricate questions of 'linkage' among the various categories of armaments (nuclear weapons, delivery vehicles, conventional forces) within the several stages, lest the balance of deterrence be altered as the level of arms declined. The multiplicity of variables produced a bewildering scholasticism of discourse, and I was constantly impressed by the sobriety with which the Committee of Principles tackled these entangled and almost impenetrable problems. In its essence, so far as one could judge, it was a serious and realistic proposal, at least in the first two stages.

I found myself, however, in the unaccustomed position of sharing the doubts of the Joint Chiefs of Staff about Stage III. By this time, according to the plan, disarmament and international law would develop to a point where "no State would have the military power to challenge the progressively strengthened United Nations Peace Force and all international disputes would be settled according to the agreed principles of international conduct." I suppose some attempt had to be made to visualize a world without national armaments; but Stage III seemed essentially an exercise in millennial rhetoric, and I tried in vain to persuade McCloy to abandon at least a phrase contemplating the day when the United Nations would be able "to assure peace and the just settlement of differences in a disarmed world." It appeared doubtful whether, short of the millennium, any human contrivance would be able to "assure" justice, but the objection glanced off McCloy's faith in the rule of law.

The plan circulated around the government and was vetted, revised, diluted and supplemented; McCloy, William Foster, Robert Matteson and the disarmament staff came up with a new version; the Principals brooded over it; the Joint Chiefs accepted some of the plan and watered down more; our allies made comments, all favorable except for the French, who felt as usual that this was the wrong time to present anything; and early in August a final meeting of the Principals approved the plan in substance. In mid-August the President cleared it. Early in September the American program for "General and Complete Disarmament in a Peaceful World" was ready for submission to the United Nations.[5]

XVIII

NO TRUCE TO TERROR

AUGUST 5 WAS A gray and dreary Saturday in Hyannis Port when Adlai Stevenson, Harlan Cleveland and I arrived at the Kennedy compound to discuss United States strategy in the impending session of the United Nations General Assembly. We found the President in a blue sports shirt and chinos, determined, despite the sullen weather, to take us all out for luncheon on his boat in the sound. A chilling wind sprang up over the water, and, while Jacqueline and

[5] After further revision, designed mostly to make the political changes between the stages more explicit, the American disarmament plan in its final form was submitted to the eighteen-nation Disarmament Committee in Geneva on April 18, 1962.

two of her sisters-in-law huddled forward, the rest of us talked about the UN in the stern.

The first problem was choosing the major theme of the American presentation. Stevenson renewed his proposal of disarmament. Kennedy observed that disarmament did not seem a popular issue in the United States; he could detect no great congressional ardor, for example, for the bill establishing the Disarmament Agency. On the other hand, he knew how much the hope of disarmament meant to the rest of the world. Moreover, it was an issue on which we could make time against the Soviet Union: "We are ready for inspection; they aren't; and we should take all the advantage of this we can." Stevenson of course agreed but added earnestly, "We can't do this effectively if we ourselves equivocate. Your first decision, Mr. President, must be to make sure that you yourself are genuinely for general and complete disarmament. We must go for that. Everything else in our program derives from it. Only total disarmament will save the world from the horror of nuclear war as well as from the mounting expenses of the arms race. Your basic decision must be to identify yourself with a new approach to disarmament. This must be our principal initiative in the United Nations."

1. STRATEGY FOR THE GENERAL ASSEMBLY

Kennedy listened with interest but also with a slight tinge of skepticism. With his profoundly realistic mind, he saw little present chance of significant progress and therefore looked to disarmament primarily as a measure of political warfare, feeling at the same time that, if the political warfare were to be effective, our plan, unlike its predecessors in the fifties, must offer an honest basis for negotiation. Now he said that he well understood the "propaganda" importance of the disarmament drive.

This casual remark stung Stevenson; he seemed seized for an instant as if by an anguished feeling that Kennedy did not really care about disarmament at all. While Cleveland and I, both anxious to keep our principals together, watched a little helplessly, Stevenson returned to the attack, telling the President in effect that he just had to have faith. This was not an argument likely to move Kennedy, and I never felt so keenly the way these two men, so united in their objectives, could so inadvertently arrive at cross-purposes. Cleveland fortunately intervened at this point. The trouble, he said, had been that the Soviet Union had always talked in the UN about general and complete disarmament, while we had talked about "next steps," thus letting the world feel that the Russians were more devoted to disarmament than we were. If we now accepted general and complete disarmament as the goal, this would cast all subsequent debate in terms of "next steps," and here our specific proposals could test or expose the real Soviet desire for arms reduction. Kennedy readily assented, and the matter passed over.

Next came the question of Communist China—at which point the President, calling forward, said, "Jackie, we need the Bloody Marys now." For several years the United States had been staving off the entry of Peking into the UN, and the question was certain to arise with new intensity this year. Kennedy, who considered the state of our relations with Communist China as irrational, did not exclude the possiblity of doing something to change them in the course of his administration. But he never supposed that admission to the UN would work any miraculous conversion in Peking, and he had no doubt in 1961 that the international gains (if any) of admission would be far outweighed by the uproar it would cause at home. Eisenhower, for example, had told him in their last meeting before the inauguration that he hoped to support the new administration on all foreign policy issues but would consider it necessary to return to public life if Communist China threatened to enter the UN. With his slim majority, Kennedy felt that he could not take on the China problem this year.

As for Stevenson, he had long argued as a private citizen that we must deal with realities and perhaps move toward a solution which would seat both Chinese governments. We now discussed various parliamentary approaches which might stall Peking's admission. When Stevenson objected to one stratagem as "too transparent," Kennedy said, "What do you think we ought to do? If you're not for this policy, we shouldn't try it." Stevenson, a little embarrassed, replied, "I will be for it if you decide it's the policy." Kennedy said, "If we can buy twelve months, it will be more than worth it. We may be preparing the way for the admission of Peiping in another year; but in another year things will be different."

(In another year things were not so different after all. It was ironic that in 1961, as in 1949, when an American President was preparing to reconsider the problem of Communist China, Peking itself should elect a course of militance and declare war—in the one case, on South Korea; in the other, on most of the world. In the next Kennedy years, as the traditional advocates, India and the Soviet Union, lost their crusading zeal for Chinese admission, the matter did not prove so pressing again.)

The strategy of keeping Peking out in 1961 involved the question of Outer Mongolia, a pro-Russian communist state on China's western border. Chester Bowles had argued persuasively that it would be to the American interest to recognize Outer Mongolia, both to gain an observation post in central Asia and to nourish the growing mistrust between Russia and China. But Nationalist China bitterly opposed this idea, as did its Republican allies in the American Congress—so much so that the recognition plan was dropped in midsummer. In addition, however, Outer Mongolia was itself a candidate for admission to the UN. If Nationalist China used its power as a permanent member of the Security Council to veto the application, the Soviet Union would presumably retaliate by vetoing Mauritania, and the African members might in turn retaliate by backing the admission of Communist China. We needed African votes, or at least abstentions, to keep Communist China out, and we therefore wanted Outer Mongolia in.

Kennedy had just discussed these questions in Washington with an emissary from Chiang Kai-shek named General Chen Cheng. "He is the most mysterious Chinese I have ever met," the President told us. "All he did was to repeat instructions. We never had any communication." He had gone as far as he could with General Chen on Outer Mongolia, he said, and he thought there was a reasonable chance of persuading the Chinese Nationalists to withhold their veto—unless, he added, "Chiang's *Götterdämmerung* mood" might lead to a desperate assault on the mainland.

The conversation grew steadily more relaxed through the day. In midafternoon we returned to the compound for tennis and swimming and the Kennedys' Finnish sauna. Dinner in the evening was gay and easy. The President produced a copy of Theodore White's *The Making of the President: 1960* and expressed his admiration for it. The only trouble was, he said, that Teddy made his characters larger than life; this was the occupational defect of historians. Turning to me, he said, "When I read your Roosevelt books, I thought what towering figures those men around Roosevelt were—Moley and Tugwell and Berle and the others. Then I read Teddy's book and realized that they were just Sorensen and Goodwin and you."

2. THE PRESIDENT AT THE UNITED NATIONS

The Soviet resumption of testing four weeks later gave the

September session of the General Assembly even more importance than we had expected. For a moment, Cleveland argued that the resumption itself should be brought before the Security Council, but McCloy and Arthur Dean opposed this on the ground that we would gain nothing and might restrict our own freedom of action. When Cleveland mentioned the effect on world opinion, McCloy exploded: "World opinion? I don't believe in world opinion. The only thing that matters is power. What we have to do now is to show that we are a powerful nation and not spend our time trailing after the phantom of world opinion." This was by now a familiar debate in the councils around the President; and, while the term 'world opinion' was unquestionably glib and the people who invoked it often exaggerated its significance, one could not but reflect that the capacity to move opinion was itself an element of power, a fact well understood by the American Presidents who had wielded most power in the world, Wilson and Roosevelt.

In any case, when I carried this particular UN problem to Kennedy, he was talking over the phone to John McCormack about the most recent setback to the foreign aid bill; one always tended to forget how many problems assailed a President beyond one's own. Finishing his conversation, he listened to the UN question; then, silent in his chair, went through a process of almost visible cerebration, as he thought his way into the issue. Finally he said, "I don't see how we can do it. It would look hypocritical for us to take the question to the Security Council if we have already decided to resume testing. The two things seem to me incompatible."

This decision, of course, was based on a belief in the reality of world opinion. And, because, like Wilson and Roosevelt, he regarded opinion as a basic constituent of power, the President now, after the Russian tests, decided to go to New York and address the General Assembly later in the month. On September 5, the day he ordered the resumption of our own underground tests, he called in Rusk, Stevenson, Cleveland, Bundy, Sorensen and me to consider what he might say.

For a while we discussed Berlin, the President rattling off a series of ideas which might constitute part of a negotiating position. Stevenson then urged that he hold a special press conference to emphasize his interest in Berlin negotiations and at the same time unveil the new American disarmament plan; he feared that the Soviet Union might respond to the Kennedy-Macmillan note on an atmospheric test ban by talking once more about general and complete disarmament and thereby scooping our own disarmament initiative. In a moment he expressed his personal regret at the day's decision to resume testing.

Kennedy quickly said, "What choice did we have? They had spit in our eye three times. We couldn't possibly sit back and do nothing at all. We had to do this." Stevenson remarked, "But we were ahead in the propaganda battle." Kennedy said, "What does that mean? I don't hear of any windows broken because of the Soviet decision. The neutrals have been terrible. The Russians made two tests *after* our note calling for a ban on atmospheric testing. Maybe they couldn't have stopped the first, but they could have stopped the second. . . . All this makes Khrushchev look pretty tough. He has had a succession of apparent victories—space, Cuba, the thirteenth of August [the Berlin Wall] though I don't myself regard this as a Soviet victory. He wants to give out the feeling that he has us on the run. The third test was a contemptuous response to our note. . . . Anyway, the decision has been made. I'm not saying that it was the right decision. Who the hell knows? But it is the decision which has been taken."

The talk then turned to China. The State Department reported that Chiang still seemed determined to veto Outer Mongolia. Rusk asked the President whether Stevenson could be authorized to inform other delegations discreetly that the United States did not exclude the possibility that a study committee might recommend for the consideration of the General Assembly in 1962 an essentially "two China" solution based on the successor state approach—the theory that, if an original UN member broke up into two separate states, each new state would be entitled to a seat in the General Assembly. Kennedy said that Stevenson could proceed along these lines. He then expressed his own sympathy with Stevenson's position: "You have the hardest thing in the world to sell. It really doesn't make any sense —the idea that Taiwan represents China. But, if we lost this fight, if Red China comes into the UN during our first year in town, your first year and mine, they'll run us both out. We have to lick them this year. We'll take our chances next year. It will be an election year; but we can delay the admission of Red China till after the election. So far as this year is concerned, you must do everything you can to keep them out. Whatever is required is OK by me." Stevenson asked, "Do you mean to keep them out permanently or for a year?" Kennedy said, "At least for a year. I am for any strategy which works. You can vote on Outer Mongolia as you think best. I am going to send a new letter to Chiang Kai-shek, based on what is good for us, not what is good for Formosa. We'll get Cabot Lodge to talk to Luce—Adlai, you talk to Roy Howard—I will talk to Walter Judd. We'll have to get all these people to make it clear to Chiang that he can't expect to make a domestic political issue out of our strategy in the UN."

Over the next week we began work on the President's UN speech. But, as the days passed, opposition began to arise to the idea of his going to New York, or, if he did go, to his making disarmament his major theme. Lyndon Johnson argued to the President that he could not demand disarmament in New York and then return to Washington and call out more divisions; the contradiction, the Vice-President believed, would baffle our own people and confuse the world. But others of us questioned whether this was really a contradiction, for obviously disarmament negotiations would be predicated on the resolution of the Berlin crisis. Moreover, we considered it a mistake to identify the President with menacing talk, leaving the ambassador to the UN as the champion of peace, as if the United States Mission in New York were conducting its own foreign policy.

Cleveland sent over a strong memorandum setting forth nine reasons why the President should go to New York; and Robert Komer of Bundy's staff summed up the disarmament argument in a forceful paper. With Russia's test resumption, Komer pointed out, we finally had the Soviets "on the defensive re disarmament, an issue devoid at this point of any practical negotiating possibilities but of tremendous psychological significance, particularly as the world moves closer to the brink on Berlin." And, as apprehension was rising over Berlin, "it is more important than ever to look peaceful as well as resolute, to point out how, in contrast to Soviet threats and truculence, we remain genuinely interested in a disarmed world." Of course we were making a bid for "world opinion"; but "to contend that only power talks, even in a Berlin crisis, is as dangerously narrow as to argue that we must always trim our sails to the prevailing public wind." We could not in any case avoid a UN disarmament debate, Komer concluded, and "we have never been in a better position to win it."

On September 18 the tragic news of Dag Hammarskjöld's death in a plane crash in Africa settled whatever doubts the President may have had about going to New York. Hearing the word while receiving a delegation at the White House, he expressed deep sorrow, adding sadly, "I expect my whole time in office to be filled with dangers and difficulties." The Russians would now undoubtedly use the

struggle over the succession to press their campaign to replace a single Secretary-General with the *troika*. Ted Sorensen, taking drafts from Cleveland and myself, began to
prepare the final version of the speech.

A week later the President went to New York. "Let us
here resolve," he began, "that Dag Hammarskjöld did not
live, or die, in vain." He called on the General Assembly
to reject the *troika*. To install a triumvirate, he said, would
be to "entrench the Cold War in the headquarters of peace."
It would paralyze the United Nations; and in the nuclear
age the world needed the United Nations more than ever
before. For "a nuclear disaster, spread by wind and water
and fear, could well engulf the great and the small, the
rich and the poor, the committed and the uncommitted
alike. Mankind must put an end to war—or war will put
an end to mankind. . . . Let us call a truce to terror."

The goal of disarmament, he continued, "is no longer a
dream—it is a practical matter of life or death. The risks
inherent in disarmament pale in comparison to the risks inherent in an unlimited arms race." He set forth the American plan and asked that negotiations continue "without interruption until an entire program for general and complete
disarmament has not only been agreed but has been actually
achieved." The logical place to begin, he said, was a test
ban treaty. He called further for contributions to a United
Nations peace-keeping force, the improvement of UN machinery for the peaceful settlement of disputes, the extension of world law to outer space and the support of the
UN Decade of Development.

In his conclusion, he reminded the Assembly of its historic opportunity. "We in this hall shall be remembered
either as part of the generation that turned this planet into
a flaming funeral pyre or the generation that met its vow
'to save succeeding generations from the scourge of war.'
. . . The decision is ours. Never have the nations of the
world had so much to lose, or so much to gain. Together
we shall save our planet, or together we shall perish in its
flames. Save it we can—and save it we must—and then we
shall earn the eternal thanks of mankind and, as peace-
makers, the eternal blessings of God."

The President spoke with particular intensity, and the
delegates, many seeing him for the first time in person,
were moved by his handsomeness, spirit and commitment.
They responded with deep and sustained applause. Kennedy himself, as he looked out at the representatives of the

world community, understood more vividly than ever before the power and potentiality of the United Nations. He said later that he was surprised by the majesty of the occasion and the impact of his remarks. His speech, moving beyond the clamors of the day, transcending the crises of Berlin and Southeast Asia, abolishing the memories of the Bay of Pigs, established him as a leader of humanity's party of hope.

The momentum of his words, sustained by Stevenson's effective leadership in New York, continued throughout the session. The *troika* was defeated, and U Thant of Burma became the new Secretary-General with unaltered authority. The application of Communist China for membership was turned back by a decisive vote, and the Assembly resolved that any proposal to make a change in the representation of China was an "important question" requiring a two-thirds majority. Outer Mongolia was admitted, Nationalist China abstaining. The groundwork was laid for new negotiations on disarmament. The Assembly called for a treaty to ban nuclear tests under effective international measures of verification and control and asked the Soviet Union to refrain from exploding its 50-megaton bomb. And, to deal with the financial problems caused by the UN operation in the Congo, the Assembly authorized a $200 million bond issue to be taken up by the member nations.

3. INTERLUDE IN BERMUDA

The urgencies of security, however, remained at war with the dreams of disarmament. Kennedy had felt that the Soviet atmospheric tests left him no choice but to authorize underground testing of our own. Now, as one explosion in the skies above Siberia followed another through the autumn, it became increasingly difficult to hold the line at underground tests. The Joint Chiefs of Staff in particular wanted to resume American tests in the atmosphere as speedily as possible. Early in October they forwarded a paper calling for atmospheric testing in November.

The JCS paper was below their usual level in logic and literacy. When we met to consider it at the State Department, Secretary McNamara, who had obviously not examined it with care before the meeting, quickly perceived its imperfections and abandoned it as a basis for argument. One defense official made an impassioned case for the resumption of atmospheric testing in order to prevent the world from believing that the Communists were gaining so commanding a lead that there was no point in resisting them further. McGeorge Bundy replied that he was against tests for the sake of psychological warfare and insisted on the principle that we never test in the atmosphere unless required by military necessity to do so. Then McNamara made clear that a serious case for resumption existed in terms of military security, and the meeting ended with a recommendation that the United States take an early occasion to reserve its freedom to test above ground.

On the morning of October 30 a call from the White House awakened me to report the largest detonation so far —probably that of Khrushchev's threatened 50-megaton bomb. This proved to be the case, though Khrushchev archly said the next day that his scientists had miscalculated: "Instead of fifty megatons it proved to be more, but we will not punish them for that." Our own scientists told us that, if the Soviet superbomb had had a uranium casing, the explosion would have had the force of one hundred megatons. This final atrocity made it impossible to put off our own preparations for atmospheric testing any longer. Kennedy now directed Ted Sorensen to draft a statement saying that, while we would test in the atmosphere only if required to do so by overriding arguments of national security, contingency preparations should begin at once. Three days after the great Soviet explosion, the paper was laid before the National Security Council.

Shortly after the meeting started, Harry S. Truman, who had dined at the White House the night before, came into the room. Looking white and frail, he made a jocose remark across the table to the Vice-President and then listened attentively to the discussion. The meeting had begun with a preliminary analysis of the Soviet tests. The new Russian series, according to the CIA report, followed logically from its 1958 series; this suggested that, despite the 'big hole' thesis, there had been no cheating in the interim. Then McNamara, after an impressive and dispassionate review of our weapons situation, asked that development and effects test in the atmosphere be authorized at the earliest possible moment. The President inquired about the timing of the projected series and said that, if we had to have the tests, they should be run off rapidly; "we want to do as little as possible to prolong the agony." On this note the meeting adjourned.

At the end of the day the President announced publicly that preparations were under way for atmospheric tests "in case it becomes necessary to conduct them." They would not be undertaken, Kennedy emphasized, "for so-called psychological or political reasons." But if "the orderly and essential scientific development of new weapons has reached a point where effective progress is not possible without such tests," then they would be undertaken "within limits that restrict the fallout from such tests to an absolue minimum."

The machinery of government was thus set for resumption. But preparation was one thing, actual testing another. The President still hoped to avoid further corruption of the atmosphere and further stimulus to the nuclear race. Jerome Wiesner maintained in December that it remained basically a political question: "While these tests would certainly contribute to our military strength, they are not critical or even very important to our over-all military posture." Long hours of debate in the National Security Council and in the privacy of the President's office, involving scientists from Defense, AEC and various bomb laboratories, led the President to the conclusion that Wiesner was essentially right. Yet one began to notice an unconscious hardening through the government, as if a final decision had been made. Those who wanted to delay resumption in the interest of political considerations and 'world opinion' were at the usual tactical disadvantage in debating with the 'realists.'

One day a meeting at the State Department considered the public position we should take on nuclear matters. The discussion assumed that we were about to go into the atmosphere ourselves and must readjust our political warfare accordingly—that we should stop talking, for example, about the menace of fallout. I feebly protested that we should also consider what our information policy should be if we decided not to go into the atmosphere, or else we would be foreclosing the presidential decision. When I later described the meeting to Kennedy, he said, "Personally I hate the idea of resuming atmospheric tests. But it's going to be damned hard to stave off the pressure, especially when the news gets out that the big Soviet explosion was relatively clean. This will show that they have something we don't have, and we will be under intense pressure to test in the atmosphere ourselves. But I have made no final decision, and I have told everybody that I have made no decision."

The critical question, as the matter crystallized in the President's mind, became not the Soviet round of 1961 but the rounds which might follow in 1962 or 1963. It was evident that the current series would not by itself enable Khrushchev to reverse the balance of nuclear power. But if the Russians, on the basis of the knowledge so acquired, were to conduct a new series while the United States refrained from atmospheric testing, the next one might well put them in the lead. We could, in other words, "eat" one Soviet round but not two; and without the treaty we had no assurance that, having completed one sequence, Soviet scientists and generals would not demand another and another. However much Kennedy loathed the idea of atmospheric tests, any President who stood aside and allowed the enemy to achieve nuclear superiority would plainly have taken an unacceptable risk in the face of his constitutional obligations.

This, I believe, was the President's state of mind when, after several weeks of racking contemplation, he discussed the problem with Harold Macmillan in Bermuda on December 21. We needed British support in the decision to go ahead. The British colony of Christmas Island in the central Pacific offered an ideal site for testing in the atmosphere; and, in any case, it would be politically difficult for the United States to resume without British concurrence. But the nightmare of nuclear holocaust stirred more than ever underneath Macmillan's Edwardian flippancies, and he opened the talks by evoking the awful prospects of an indefinite nuclear race.

If all those talented scientists were to continue going about their business, the Prime Minister said, the only result would be more and deadlier bombs. Was this the goal to which the next generation of man should dedicate itself? If these horrible weapons were not fired off, it would be a hopeless economic waste; if they were, it would be the end of civilization. And, while the United States and the Soviet Union were having this sophisticated competition, many other nations in a few years would begin to acquire their own simpler bombs. Berlin, Macmillan said, seemed to him small beer compared to the destruction of humanity. The world could not continue down this path. You and I, he said to Kennedy with emotion, could not sit in an ordinary little room four days before Christmas and talk about these terrible things without doing something about it. Before we went into the atmosphere ourselves, should we not make one more effort to break the cycle? The arms race was a "rogue elephant" against which we all must act.

Perhaps you and I, he told Kennedy, should meet at the summit with Khrushchev and really push for disarmament. We might fail, but we would have lost only a few months. Macmillan added that, after reading Russian novels and everything else he could find about Russia, he felt that they might come around. Moreover, the nuclear effort was costing the Soviet Union ferociously. And the Soviet position itself was changing. The Russians were halfway between Europe and Asia and watching the rise of China with foreboding. The west thought of them as enormously different, but their economic and social structure was not that alien. After all, mines and railroads were nationalized through most of Western Europe, and one saw already in Russia a spread of unequal privileges through society; the children of the ruling class were going to elite schools, as they did in Britain. Without yielding, could we not provide time to allow the forces of humanity to exert their influence?

Macmillan was eloquent, and Kennedy was moved. But he had to face realities. The problem, he pointed out, was what would happen in 1964 if the Russians continued to test and the west didn't. We could not afford to be taken twice. Even though he was himself a "great anti-tester," he saw no alternative but to prepare for resumption and, if there was no progress with regard either to Berlin or disarmament, to resume.

The two delegations were staying together in Government House, sharing meals, taking walks and discussing many things not listed on the agenda; it all had, as the participants recalled it, the atmosphere of a country weekend. The Kennedy-Macmillan relationship, David Ormsby Gore later said, "blossomed very considerably during the course of that meeting, and after that it was almost like a family discussion when we all met." As they chatted over drinks before luncheon the next day Macmillan teased the scientists present about the mischief they had made. One answered with dignity that they were only the innocent victims of the folly of politicians. Someone asked Sir William Penney, the physicist who was serving as Macmillan's scientific adviser, how many bombs it would take to destroy his country. Penney replied, "If you are talking about Australia, it would take twelve. If you are talking about Britain, it would take five or six, but, to be on the safe side, let us say seven or eight and"—without a change in tone—"I'll have another gin and tonic if you would be so kind." This singular statement, uttered in one rush of breath, summed up for the Prime Minister and the President the absurdity of mankind setting about to destroy itself; and the refrain—"I'll have another gin and tonic if you would be so kind"—somewhat lightened their subsequent discussions of the matter.

When the talks resumed, the Prime Minister began by

asking that the final decision be postponed to permit one last try at disarmament. Kennedy replied that a new effort would only enable the Russians to stall things for many more months. Our case would be no better a year from now, and in the meantime the Russians could get ready for a new series of tests. He concluded later in the day by asking whether Macmillan would agree to atmospheric tests on Christmas Island if the situation did not change. Macmillan responded that this was a decision for the cabinet; but Britain and America were partners, we were in this together; he only wished that the announcement would seem less a threat than a hope.

4. MACMILLAN'S LAST TRY

The decision was now almost but not quite, firm. Some of us in Washington still thought after Bermuda that one more effort should be made to avert what Wiesner called the "slide into chaos." After consulting with Wiesner and with John McNaughton, a former Harvard Law School professor who was now a Deputy Assistant Secretary of Defense, I sent a memorandum to the President proposing a two-stage plan: we should announce, first, that in order to keep the arms race from breaking out of control the United States had decided not to resume atmospheric testing; but, second, that we planned to complete all necessary stand-by preparations and, if the Soviet Union exploded one more device in the atmosphere, we would instantly begin a massive series of militarily significant tests.

The weakness in this proposal lay in the assumption that it would be possible to maintain the morale of the laboratories and the pace of technical advance even though the weapons scientists had no assurance they could try out their ideas. Though I still am unconvinced that this assumption was wrong, both the Atomic Energy Commission and the Department of Defense argued that the best people would work on what could be done rather than on what could not be done, and that resumption was necessary to avert a decay in the laboratories. Accordingly I rephrased the proposal in a few days to suggest that we announce a decision to resume but offer to cancel our atmospheric tests if the Soviet Union would sign the Geneva treaty. This, it seemed to me, would either get us the treaty or put the Russians in the position of triggering the American test series.

A week after New Year's, Macmillan returned to the battle. In a deeply personal letter to Kennedy, the Prime Minister argued again that resumption would probably lead the

Russians to carry out their next series; we would be forced to do the same; the contest would intensify; and, as the burden of the race mounted, one side or the other, when it had attained superiority, might be tempted to put the issue to the test. As the test programs of the great powers continued, he went on, there would be no hope of preventing the spread of nuclear weapons to non-nuclear states. If this capacity for destruction ended up in the hands of dictators, reactionaries, revolutionaries, madmen around the world, then sooner or later, possibly by the end of this century, either by error or folly or insanity, the great crime would be committed. It would seem to any ordinary person, Macmillan continued, that humanity was setting out on a path at once so fantastic and so retrograde, so sophisticated and so barbarous, as to be almost incredible. He himself noted the strange irony that he should have spent Christmas Day wondering how to commend to his cabinet colleagues the dedication of Christmas Island for this purpose.

It might be, he concluded, that we were condemned, like the heroes of the old Greek tragedies, to an ineluctable fate from which there was no escape; and that like those doomed figures we must endure it, with only the consolation of the admonitory commentaries of the chorus, the forerunners of the columnists of today. But in his view the situation demanded a supreme effort to break the deadlock. Amplifying the thoughts he had advanced in Bermuda, he proposed that the three leaders—Kennedy, Khrushchev and himself—convert the impending eighteen-power disarmament meeting, scheduled for Geneva in March, into a final try for general disarmament, a test ban treaty and an agreement not to transfer nuclear weapons or information to non-nuclear powers. It was, of course, he said, easy to do nothing. But, on the whole, it was not the things one did in one's life that one regretted but rather the opportunities missed.

The Macmillan letter contained certain ambiguities. It did not make clear, for example, whether the use of Christmas Island was conditioned on our agreement to a disarmament conference at the summit, or whether the resumption of American atmospheric testing was conditioned on the conference's failure. It did make clear, however—and in moving and powerful language—both the extent of Macmillan's anxiety and the magnitude of the decision which confronted us. As Adlai Stevenson promptly wrote the President, "It would be unfortunate and could be tragic if we were to give the Prime Minister a dusty answer."

But the State Department was considerably less moved. On January 12 Bundy and I went over to Rusk's office to examine State's draft reply. The answer could hardly have been dustier. It was an evasive, bureaucratic screed, falling so far below Macmillan in style and tone as to be unresponsive. One high State Department officer said contemptuously about the Macmillan letter, "Why are we taking so much trouble over this hysterical document?" and "We can't let Macmillan practice this emotional blackmail on us."

Rusk, however, agreed that the answer should not be perfunctory. Any reply, he said, must contain three elements: an affirmation that our concern equaled Macmillan's; a rejection of any link between the use of Christmas Island and a new disarmament initiative; and an initiative we might offer ourselves as a substitute for what seemed to us the questionable notion of a grandiose disarmament conference. Bundy then prepared an excellent reply along these lines, concluding: "We are ready to examine with you the possibilities for new efforts toward disarmament on the most urgent basis."

In the meantime, a debate arising from the President's State of the Union message had redirected attention to the idea of a test ban confined to the atmosphere. At Kennedy's instruction, the early drafts promised one last try for such a ban before we resumed testing above ground ourselves. But this thought had aroused such distress in both State and Defense that the President eventually reduced it to a generality about breaking the log jam on disarmament and nuclear tests.

Still the idea persisted. In Defense John McNaughton now argued that the offer of a treaty banning tests in the atmosphere alone would probably work to our advantage, whether accepted or refused by the Soviet Union, unless the Russians accepted the ban for two or three years and then found a pretext to break it. If they took advantage of the ban to prepare secretly for new tests, we might lose nearly a year in the technology race. To guard against this, McNaughton therefore proposed a number of political and legal devices to help make the ban stick. In the White House Carl Kaysen after a careful analysis concluded that an atmospheric ban would not pose unacceptable military risks and might well lead to new and striking gains in arms control.

This debate was not simply a disagreement between virtuous anti-testers and wicked big-bomb men. A wholly intelligent case for atmospheric resumption existed, and Robert Komer of the White House made it in comments on the Kaysen-Schlesinger position. The Russians, Komer suggested, were a few years behind us in the intellectual comprehension of the meaning of nuclear plenty; there was doubtless a cultural lag to be overcome before they would understand that arms limitation would be safer and more advantageous to both sides than continued rivalry. If this were so, then they would not appreciate the value of stable deterrence until they grasped the futility of the arms race. So long as our policy encouraged Moscow to think it might possibly overtake us in nuclear power, the Russians would have less incentive to consider other ways of insuring their security. "It is ghastly to think that we may have to escalate the arms race further (at least technologically) before we can start the curve downward. But what realistic alternative is there?" There might be no other way to drive home to Moscow the strategic realities of the nuclear age. Moreover, incessant American concern about nuclear weapons might signal to the Russians a reluctance to use them and thereby, in a time of crisis over Berlin and Southeast Asia, compromise our nuclear deterrent before we had fully developed adequate defenses of other sorts.

5. THE RESUMPTION OF ATMOSPHERIC TESTING

I had to leave Washington in mid-January for the meeting of the Organization of American States at Punta del Este and then for various missions in Japan, India and Europe; so I missed the concluding phase in the argument. In the course of February Kennedy received an analysis of the Soviet tests by a panel of leading scientists, including so prominent an advocate of the ban as Hans Bethe. Their report disclosed a highly advanced nuclear technology, with new designs and techniques, including some unknown to the west—or at least unexplainable on the basis of the information available—as well as substantial gains in weaponry. The technical basis had evidently been laid for a new series which might enable the Soviet Union to develop bombs whose yield per weight of explosive would be somewhat higher than ours. While this would not give any substantial military advantage to the Soviet Union, the knowledge that the Russians had better weapons would have given them a political and diplomatic advantage the President was disinclined to accept. With a heavy heart, he decided that we would have to resume atmospheric testing. As for the tests themselves, he made it clear he wanted low-yield detonations concentrated in short periods. In the next months, he spent a good deal of time reviewing and revising the proposals for the American atmospheric series.

The next question was when the world should be notified. Kennedy at first thought, and Macmillan concurred, that announcement should be delayed until after the eighteen-nation Disarmament Committee had met in Geneva; this would mean sometime in April. At the same time, the President wanted to rescue Macmillan's suggestion for a new disarmament initiative. Opposition had arisen to the proposal that we make one more offer of an atmospheric test ban before resuming our own tests, partly because it would seem a retreat from our original Geneva position and partly because it provided no insurance against secret preparations and thus against another surprise Soviet series. The President therefore decided to declare his readiness to trade off our atmospheric series, not for a partial, but for a comprehensive test ban treaty.

Late in February I lunched in London with Hugh Gaitskell, who had just come back from a visit to Washington filled with enthusiasm for Kennedy. The President had provided him with a full technical briefing on the testing matter—something which the British government had curiously never given him—and Gaitskell agreed that the United States had no choice but to go ahead. Kennedy later told me that Gaitskell's argument for relating resumption to the Geneva disarmament talks had strengthened his determination to try once more for the Geneva treaty, but that it had also convinced him, contrary to Gaitskell's recommendation, that he should not allow the Disarmament Committee to begin its work under the illusion that the United States was not yet settled in its own mind about the need for testing.

On February 27 Kennedy therefore informed Macmillan that he planned a television talk on the subject to the nation on March 1. The Prime Minister had still hoped somehow to stave off American resumption, and Kennedy's message came as a shock. His leading scientific adviser, coming to see me that day in London, said that Macmillan was "a sad and embittered man," and quoted him to the effect that the American decision would "shatter the hopes of millions of people across the earth." The Prime Minister asked the President again for postponement, but Kennedy could not see his way to delay the announcement for more than another twenty-four hours.

The President himself was hardly in a gay mood about his decision. He told me later that he had phoned Truman and Eisenhower. Truman, he said, was sympathetic and seemed to understand how hard the judgment had been. Eisenhower, cold and grumpy, said, "Well, I thought you should have done this a long time ago."

On March 2, Kennedy made his speech. He described the precautions taken to restrict fallout, adding: "I still exceedingly regret the necessity of balancing these hazards against the hazards to hundreds of millions of lives which would be created by a relative decline in our nuclear strength." The United States, he said, would come to Geneva with a series of concrete plans for a major "breakthrough to peace." In particular, it would once again offer a comprehensive test ban treaty. If the Soviet Union were now ready to "accept such a treaty, to sign it before the latter part of April, and apply it immediately—if all testing can thus be actually halted—then . . . there would be no need for our tests." That action, he added, would be "a monumental step toward peace—and both Prime Minister Macmillan and I would think it fitting to meet Chairman Khrushchev at Geneva to sign the final treaty."

Khrushchev quickly declined the offer. On April 25, as dawn broke over Christmas Island, the United States began a new round of tests in the atmosphere.

6. DISARMAMENT AND THE DEFENSE BUDGET

The rogue elephant was loose again, and neither Kennedy nor Macmillan was content to let him rampage unchecked. In March Dean Rusk went to Geneva with new test ban proposals. But the Russians now insisted that the test ban could not be considered apart from comprehensive disarmament, thereby repudiating their own position of 1958–61 (Khrushchev had said then, "Is there any surer way of sabotaging the suspension of nuclear tests than by such conditions?") and adopting the attitude for which they had so self-righteously denounced the Americans in 1956–58.

As for general and complete disarmament, when Arthur Dean presented the updated American plan in Geneva in April, the Russians lost no time in rejecting it because of its insistence on inspection and a dozen other real or pseudo-reasons. For their part, they put forward a plan demanding abolition in the first stage of all means of delivering nuclear weapons, as well as of all foreign bases. This would mean the immediate unbalancing of the existing equilibrium in favor of conventional force and could hardly be acceptable to the west. In addition, the Russians continued to oppose any serious verification of anything except weapons destroyed until the end of the third stage. The talks, as they dragged on through the summer of 1962, seemed more and more a propaganda minuet, repetitive, pointless and sterile.

Yet Kennedy persisted in the struggle for disarmament. I do not think he quite saw the arms race in the image of Macmillan's rogue elephant; for the race was not in fact so insensate as that. Staggering as defense expenditures were, they remained a relatively small proportion of the total national output in both the United States and the Soviet Union; and of money spent on defense, only a fraction—in the United States, perhaps one-fifth—went to nuclear striking power. Nor was the 'overkill' idea—the notion that each side was compulsively engaged in piling up more and more nuclear bombs—justified, at least in its more nightmarish form. Actually each side (outside the air forces) was coming to realize that it had more than enough; and a good deal of the new expenditure went, not to increase stockpiles, but for replacement, modernization of weapons systems, research into new weapons and the maintenance of a higher state of alert. Nor was Lord Snow's sensational fantasy of 1960—"Within, at the most, ten years, some of these bombs are going off"—necessarily acquiring more validity each passing minute; for the vast effort, in the United States at least, to improve fail-safe controls was reducing the probability of the Dr. Strangelove effect.

In short, if there was an arms race, neither side was galloping as fast or as frantically as it could. But this provided only comparative consolation. Even if it was all not so insane as Lord Russell liked to think, it was still a hell of a way to run a world. For his part, Kennedy was sure that we had enough for nearly any conceivable contingency; he regarded the balance of terror, however ingeniously safeguarded, as deeply fragile; and he used to say that he would consider it "the ultimate failure" if he ever had to order the use of a single nuclear weapon. Moreover he was increasingly concerned about the diversion to armaments of resources which could be better put to other uses. "I don't know why it is," he said at the fiftieth anniversary dinner of the Department of Labor in March 1963, "that expenditures which deal with the enforcement of the minimum wage, that deal with the problem of school dropouts, of retraining of workers, of unskilled labor, all the problems that are so much with us in the sixties, why they are always regarded as the waste in the budget, and expenditures for defense are always regarded as the untouchable item in the budget." All these considerations made him even more determined to lead the world toward arms reduction.

The experience of the spring and summer of 1961, moreover, had convinced him that running faster in the race would only provoke his opponent to run faster too and thereby increase the strain without necessarily altering the gap. He had seen no alternative to higher defense spending in order to liberate American strategy from its predominant reliance on nuclear weapons; but the rise in Washington's defense budget had now produced a comparable rise in Moscow's. Increases and decreases in the two capitals had paralleled each other before, and the administration, as time went on, began to draw a significant conclusion: that the defense budget itself might be used as an instrument of arms limitation. For it was evident that the budget was the most effective means of signaling to the Soviet Union our intentions, whether defensive or first-strike, as well as the kinds of weapons and strategies which might be mutually advantageous and the kinds of limitation that might be mutually possible.[1] These considerations were much in the minds of Kaysen and Wiesner when the first full Kennedy defense budget came under consideration within the government in the late summer and fall of 1961.

There remained for a moment the question of the 'missile gap.' Though disowned by McNamara in February, the gap had persisted as a center of intra-service argument, with the Air Force continuing to claim that the Russians had 600 to 800 ballistic missiles, while the CIA estimated 450 and the Navy 200. But on Thanksgiving weekend, when the President convened his defense experts for a meeting at Hyannis Port, the weight of evidence was plainly against the Air Force, and the issue finally withered away. The budget nevertheless contemplated a sizable increase in missiles; and the White House staff, while favoring a larger Minuteman force than the original Eisenhower proposal, wondered whether the new budget was not providing for more missiles than national security required. But the President, though intimating a certain sympathy with this view, was not prepared to overrule McNamara's recommendation. As for the Secretary, he did not believe that doubling

[1] A number of points in this discussion have been clarified by Thomas C. Schelling; see especially "The State of the Arms Race" in J. E. Doughterty, ed., *The Prospects for Arms Control* (New York, 1965), 52–55.

or even tripling our striking power would enable us to destroy the hardened missile sites or missile-launching submarines of our adversary. But he was already engaged in a bitter fight with the Air Force over his effort to disengage from the B-70, a costly, high-altitude manned bomber rendered obsolescent by the improvement in Soviet ground-to-air missiles. After cutting down the original Air Force missile demands considerably, he perhaps felt that he could not do more without risking public conflict with the Joint Chiefs and the vociferous B-70 lobby in Congress. As a result, the President went along with the policy of multiplying Polaris and Minuteman missiles.

Within the magnitudes of the budget the President, of course, retained a series of choices about weapons systems. He had a profound aversion to weapons which could be used effectively only in a first strike and which for that reason might invite a pre-emptive strike from the other side—like the Jupiters which had been sitting for some years on soft bases in Turkey and Italy. As Bundy remarked later, "he always preferred the system which could survive an attack against the system which might provoke one." The budget communicated this preference to the Soviet Union; and McNamara drove the point home in statements and speeches, especially in an address at Ann Arbor, Michigan, in June 1962. Here he argued forcefully for "a strategy designed to preserve the fabric of our societies if war should occur." By this he meant that the targets of nuclear war should be military forces and installations, not civilian populations. This 'counterforce' strategy required us to have the capacity to hold in reserve, even after a massive surprise attack, sufficient striking power to destroy the enemy society if driven to it; this would give an opponent "the strongest imaginable incentive to refrain from striking our own cities." At the same time McNamara reorganized the control system so that, instead of investing all striking power in a single presidential push button, the command structure could retain after attack the ability to respond in a number of ways besides blowing up the world.

The counterforce doctrine had its ambiguities. A striking force large enough to ride out a nuclear salvo and still concentrate selectively on enemy military targets would have to be larger than a force designed only to retaliate against enemy cities in a single convulsive blow. It would in consequence be quite large enough to strike first itself, possibly even large enough to suppose that it might erase the enemy's retaliatory capacity by a surprise attack; indeed, to be effective against Russian soft-based missiles, our attack would presumably have to be made while their missiles were still on launching pads. Some critics accordingly interpreted the administration's desire for nuclear superiority as an 'overkill' philosophy concealing a first-strike premise. Nor could one ever know what secret thoughts lay in the minds of Air Force generals when they urged bigger defense budgets. Yet there were ambiguities on the other side too; for the anti-overkill theorists preferred a 'cities-only' strategy, which would at once emphasize the horror of nuclear war and guarantee those horrors if war should come.

These ambiguities were partly inherent in the rudimentary state of strategic doctrine. It should never be forgotten that the relatively recent development of the intercontinental ballistic missile had revolutionized the problem of war, that the rethinking of strategy in terms of the ICBM had been going on only for five years in the United States and hardly at all in the rest of the world, that previous military experience offered almost nothing to help this analysis and that thinking about the unthinkable was painful anyway. Everything existed in the shadow world of pure theory; nor could the electronic computers of the systems analysts program the political realities weighing on the policy makers. Moreover, deterrence was in the end not a mathematical but a psychological problem. "A threat meant as a bluff but taken seriously," as Henry Kissinger wrote "is more useful for purposes of deterrence than a 'genuine' threat interpreted as a bluff."

All this made strategic analysis far less exact than the pseudo-precision of its terminology suggested, and it permitted a variety of interpretations of diverse strategic postures. But no one who listened to the anguished musings of Kennedy and McNamara on nuclear weapons could doubt their unalterable opposition to preventive or preemptive nuclear war. The Berlin situation prevented the President from making a public declaration against the first use of nuclear weapons once war had begun; as he had explained to de Gaulle and Macmillan, he was prepared to go to nuclear weapons if Soviet conventional forces began a war in Europe. But Kennedy and McNamara well knew that no American first strike could wipe out the Soviet capacity to retaliate and that retaliation, even from a doomed opponent, would be dreadful beyond imagination. "Our arms," the President had said early in his administration, "will never be used to strike the first blow. . . . We are not creating forces for a first strike against any other nation." "My personal opinion," said McNamara, "is . . . we cannot win a nuclear war, a strategic nuclear war, in the normal meaning of the word 'win.' "

They were seeking a second-strike capacity and, both for deterrent and for political reasons, one large enough to exceed the weight of any first strike directed against the United States. We probably attained this state of beatitude by 1962, but the administration took no chances. The decisions of the Kennedy years gave the United States by 1964 1100 intercontinental bombers, of which more than 500 were on fifteen-minute alert, as against 250 Soviet bombers capable of reaching American shores; more than 800 ICBMs, aimed and fueled, nearly all in hardened and dispersed silos, as against the less than 200 Soviet ICBM's poised in far more vulnerable sites; and 250 Polaris missiles deployed in submarines, as against a much smaller Soviet underwater missile capacity with a much more limited range.

7. THE DISARMAMENT FIGHT GOES ON

Kennedy faced no harder problem of public education than that of convincing both Capitol Hill and the Kremlin that his demands for strength and for disarmament, far from being contradictory, were complementary. His view was that, unless we convinced the Russians we could stay in the arms race as long as they could, we would remove the incentive most likely to make them accept general disarmament; for obviously, if we let them win the arms race, they would see no reason to abandon their military superiority and expose their society to external inspection. Both the securing of a second-strike capacity and the diversification of the defense establishment seemed to him, moreover, vital parts of the strategy of deterrence and arms control.

But the notion that these were all actions for peace and not for war required a more sophisticated analysis of the strategic situation than existed in Moscow—or for that matter in Western Europe. In Russia, given what Robert Komer had called the cultural lag, the Soviet leaders could derive little comfort from the inevitably menacing aspect of American nuclear superiority. And even some in the United States tended to feel there was an inconsistency between building military strength, on the one hand, and working for disarmament, on the other. Some who allowed that the two courses might be logically consistent still con-

sidered them psychologically incompatible. They opposed
the test ban, for example, not because they thought it a
military risk but because, as Roswell Gilpatric put it, "they
feared that any easing of tension would soon find the
western democracies inviting disaster by letting down their
guard." Others argued against a high defense budget, even
for the sake of diversification, because defense spending per
se was supposed to incite the 'cold war mentality.'

If this array of paradoxes bewildered Americans, it
doubtless bewildered the Russians even more. But the budget remained a solid indicator of something; and in the end
budget-watching—what Khrushchev came to call the "policy of mutual example"—may have been the most effective
means of slowing down the arms race in these years, especially as the Soviet analysis of the American budget became more sophisticated. Still, this form of indirect communication and tacit restraint was slow and chancy, and it
did nothing to build the international machinery of peace.
Thus, while Kennedy, McNamara, Kaysen and Wiesner
were always alert to possibilities of reciprocated unilateral
action, they could not settle for it as a substitute for multilateral disarmament.

The President therefore maintained a steady pressure on
the executive branch to keep the negotiating effort alive.
Wiesner and Kaysen, flourishing the White House mandate,
were tireless in needling the bureaucracy and forcing disarmament issues; and Bundy intervened valuably at critical
moments. Wiesner often carried the brunt of the argument
against the Pentagon in meetings before the President.
After one contentious session, he told me that he was afraid
he had talked too much and might be wearing out Kennedy's patience. Later the President asked me about the
meeting. I said it had filled me with gloom, that only
Wiesner had made much sense and that he was afraid he
had done more than his share of speaking. Kennedy smiled
and said, "Sometimes I think Jerry talks too much, but I
didn't think so yesterday. Tell him that I thought he made a
series of excellent points and that I want him to keep it
up."

Next to the President, McNamara, with the able backing
of John McNaughton, probably did more than anyone else
to sustain the disarmament drive. With his sense of the
horror of nuclear conflict, his understanding of the adequacy of existing stockpiles, his fear of nuclear proliferation, his analytic command of the weapons problem and
his managerial instinct to do something about an irrational
situation, he forever sought new ways of controlling the

arms race. His contribution was especially crucial in dealing with the Joint Chiefs of Staff, possessed as they were
by the conviction that they alone understood the requirements of American safety. Nor was the invocation of national security confined to the JCS. Once, at a meeting of
the Committee of Principals, someone from ACDA objected to a proposed arms control measure on the ground
that it might imperil the nation. McNamara said sharply,
"If I'm not afraid of it, I don't see why you should be.
You take care of disarmament. Let me worry about the
national security of the United States."

William Foster, while sensitive to congressional reactions,
proved a calm director of ACDA, and in Adrian Fisher
he had a stalwart and effective deputy. Among the civilians
concerned, the Secretary of State proved the main source of
indifference. This came partly, I think, from his concern
about the Bonn government, which disliked disarmament
since it did not want a reduction of east-west tension until
the problem of German unification was solved; partly because he anticipated that disarmament would cause trouble
on the Hill; and partly because of his chronically cautious
cast of mind. Presiding over the Committee of Principals,
he often gave the impression that he regarded disarmament
as an essay in futility, if not in folly. One participant in
the meetings later reported his impression that Rusk "feared
living in a world in which predominant military power was
not his major tool."

It was easy to understand this skepticism, and a number
of thoughtful people shared it. Senator Fulbright, for example, dismissed "general and complete disarmament" as
"an exercise in Cold War fantasy, a manifestation of the
deception and pretense of the new diplomacy." Yet in retrospect those long, laborious talks at Geneva played, I believe,
a vital role in widening understanding between the United
States and the Soviet Union. We were fortunate in having
Arthur Dean as our negotiator through the endless spring
and summer of 1962. Though Dean was willful, long-winded,
sometimes imprecise, very often tactless, and not a little
vain, he was also an exceedingly able lawyer and a man of
endless patience and enthusiasm. Above all, he deeply
wanted to accomplish something. Once, when receiving instructions in Washington, he said with exasperation to the
timid people from ACDA who, he felt, were putting obstacles in his path, "Do you want to win the case or not?
I want to win the case." He left no doubt that he did want
to win the case, and his conviction and energy perhaps

had more effect on the Russians than he or anyone else thought at the time.

Certainly the disarmament talks forced the Russians to think through the intricate problems of nuclear survival, to examine their own strategic limitations and capabilities, and to ponder the riddle of the nuclear equilibrium. In time they evidently began to master the concept of stable nuclear deterrence and to see that arms control might be a means of approaching rather than avoiding general and complete disarmament. The talks may also have done something to convince them that the Americans honestly wanted to stabilize the weapons situation. Even though so little appeared to be accomplished at the time in the antiseptic conference rooms beside the quiet lake at Geneva, the disarmament negotiations turned out in the end to be a good deal more than exercises in political warfare or theological disputation. They became a form of communication and education, a means of overcoming the cultural lag, an encouragement to parallel voluntary action by the two great nuclear powers and even perhaps a prelude to *détente*.

XIX

NEW DIRECTIONS IN THE THIRD WORLD

THOUGH KENNEDY WAS deeply concerned with the conflict between the United States and the Soviet Union, he did not consider that conflict the source of all mankind's troubles. In 1961 this was still rather a novel viewpoint for an American President. The tendency in the years after the Second World War had been to see the planet as tidily polarized between America and Russia. In the 1950s John Foster Dulles had transmuted this from an assumption into a dogma. The Dulles world rested on unitary conceptions of the opposing blocs: on the one hand, the 'free world,' capaciously defined to include such places as Spain, Paraguay, Batista's Cuba and Mississippi and destined ultimately for the private enterprise of the Secretary of Commerce and the god of the Secretary of State; and, on the other, the 'communist camp,' a monolithic conspiracy with headquarters in Moscow, enslaving captive peoples and orchestrating global crises according to a comprehensive master plan.

Countries which did not fit into one category or the other were regarded as anomalies. Dulles, it is true, was no great believer in the virtues of European colonialism. In certain moods, he even took a missionary's relish in discomfiting the empires of mammon. But, like a missionary, he expected the primitive peoples to accept the true faith, only instead of gathering them down by the river for a mass baptism he tried to herd them into the military pacts he scattered across the face of Asia. If they declined to ally themselves to the United States or went their own way in the United Nations or indulged in tirades against the west or engaged in social revolution, it was due to inherent moral weakness compounded by the unsleeping activity of the minions of a communist Satan. Summing up his creed in 1956, Dulles described neutralism as the principle "which pretends that a nation can best gain safety for itself by being indifferent to the fate of others" and excommunicated its devotees as "immoral." Though the Dulles doctrine was considerably tempered in application, he succeeded in implanting both in American policy and in opinion the idea that those who were not with us around the earth were against us.

Of the various transformations wrought in the Kennedy years none was less noted or more notable than the revolution in American attitudes toward the uncommitted world.

1. KENNEDY AND THE THIRD WORLD

As Senator, Kennedy had come to object to the Dulles doctrine both as morally self-righteous and as politically self-defeating.

Thus, where Dulles saw neutralism as immoral, Kennedy felt that the new states, absorbed in the travail of nationhood, were as naturally indifferent to the 'moral' issues in the cold war as Americans in a comparable stage of development had been to the moral issues in the Napoleonic wars. The spread of neutralism consequently neither surprised nor appalled him. "Oh, I think it's inevitable," he told John Fischer of *Harper's* in 1959. "During the immediate years ahead this is likely to be an increasing trend in Africa and probably also in Latin America. . . . The desire to be independent and free carries with it the desire not to become engaged as a satellite of the Soviet Union or too closely allied to the United States. We have to live with that, and if neutrality is the result of concentration on internal problems, raising the standard of living of the people and so on, particularly in the underdeveloped countries, I would accept that. It's part of our own history for over a hundred years."

He felt, moreover, that the third world had now become the critical battleground between democracy and communism and that the practical effect of Dulles's bell, book and candle against neutralism could only be to prejudice the American case and drive the developing nations toward Moscow and Peking. The battle for Europe, Kennedy believed, had been, except for Berlin, essentially won by the end of the forties. "Today's struggle does not lie there," he told Paul-Henri Spaak of Belgium in the spring of 1963, "but rather in Asia, Latin America and Africa." Where Dulles divided the world on the question of whether nations would sign up in a crusade against communism, thereby forcing the neutrals to the other side of the line, Kennedy, by making national independence the crucial question, invited the neutrals to find a common interest with us in resisting communist expansion.

As for anti-colonialism, which Dulles approved only so long as it remained within the bounds of gentility, Kennedy saw it as inherently non-genteel and probably inseparable from disorder, excess and a certain bitterness toward the west. The issue, he said in 1959, "is one of timing—and whether once that freedom is achieved, they will regard the United States as friend or foe." Even if the new countries declined to adopt the free enterprise system or enlist in the cold war, the strengthening of their independence was still likely to be a positive good for the United States. In the end, the secure achievement of national identity, he thought, could only set back the Soviet conception of the future world order and strengthen the American. "The 'magic power' on our side," he said in 1959 to James MacGregor Burns, "is the desire of every person to be free, of every nation to be independent. . . . It is because I believe our system is more in keeping with the fundamentals of human nature that I believe we are ultimately going to be successful."

It was partly knowledge of these views and partly also his youth and the sense he gave of freedom from preconception which led the third world to take heart from his election in 1960. Even that most irascible of neutralists, Prince Sihanouk of Cambodia, later remarked how the news "was welcomed in Cambodia, where nerves had become somewhat frayed by the obvious determination of the outgoing government to ignore the powerful forces making for change . . . a tendency sometimes to be found among older men, who have failed to keep abreast of the times." This was typical of the sense of relief, curiosity and hope Kennedy's accession to office stirred in neutral capitals.

In Washington the President's desire to give our relations with the uncommitted world a new cast received ardent support from Chester Bowles, Adlai Stevenson, Averell Harriman, Mennen Williams, Harlan Cleveland and Edward R. Murrow as well as from Robert Kennedy. In the White House we were all sympathetic; and Robert Komer, who patrolled the gray areas from Casablanca to West New Guinea, and Walt Rostow gave particular attention to these matters. Still the policy remained peculiarly an exercise in presidential diplomacy. Kennedy became, in effect, Secretary of State for the third world. With his consuming intellectual curiosity, he generally knew more about the Middle East, for example, than most of the officials on the seventh floor of the State Department; and the Assistant Secretaries in charge of the developing areas dealt as much with him as with the Secretary of State. Moreover, he conducted his third-world campaign to an unprecedented degree through talks and correspondence with heads of state. He well understood that personalities exert a disproportionate influence in new states without stable political systems, and he resolved to turn this situation to his own purposes.

The leaders of the new nations, it must be said, did not always make this task any easier. They were often ungenerous and resentful, driven by historic frustrations and rancors and brimming over with sensitivity and vanity. Moreover, anti-American bravado was always a sure way to excite a crowd and strike a pose of national virility. The President, understanding this as part of the process, resolved not to be diverted by pinpricks. He was sometimes greatly tried, and on occasion the dignity of the United States required some form of response. But most of the time he was faithful to the spirit of Andrew Jackson who in 1829 had called on his fellow countrymen, in the event of foreign provocation, "to exhibit the forbearance becoming a powerful nation rather than the sensibility belonging to a gallant people."

And so the new President set out to adjust American thinking to a world where the cold war was no longer the single reality and to help the new countries find their own roads to national dignity and international harmony. But in his own government he immediately ran head-on against a set of inherited policies on colonialism, on neutralism and on foreign assistance, deeply imbedded in the minds of government officials and the structure of the executive branch.

2. KENNEDY AND COLONIALISM: THE ANGOLA RESOLUTION

The first problem was colonialism. This was, in one sense, a dying issue. In the fifteen years of the United Nations some forty countries, containing nearly a billion people, had won their independence. In Africa, the colonial continent par excellence, there were twenty-two new states. Yet these successes had only increased the sense of grievance in Asia and Africa about the dependencies which remained. And anti-colonialism was still the most convenient outlet for the revolt of the rest of the world against the historic domination of the west—that revolt so long suppressed, now bursting out on every side.

Since the time of Franklin Roosevelt American policy had had a nominal commitment to anti-colonialism. But the State Department had been dominated by men who, regarding NATO as our top priority, flinched from anything which might bruise the sensibilities of our European allies, some of whom still had colonial possessions. Even in those parts of the Department presumably devoted to the business of the developing world, the aim of helping the new nations meet their problems jostled uneasily with pressure to defend the sanctity of American overseas investment. Such tensions had prevented the formation of a clear American position.

In the December preceding Kennedy's inauguration, forty-three Asian and African states had submitted to the General Assembly a resolution on "the granting of independence to colonial countries and peoples." The resolution declared that "all peoples have the right of self-determination," that "inadequacy of political, economic, social or educational preparedness should never serve as a pretext for delaying independence" and that "immediate steps shall be taken" in all non-self-governing territories "to transfer all powers to the peoples of those Territories, without any conditions or reservations, in accordance with their freely expressed will."

While the language of the resolution was sweeping, its practical implications, as the debate made clear, were limited. It was less a plea for immediate action than for an affirmation of purpose, and it had actually been worked out by the American delegation with Afro-Asian representatives in order to head off a more demagogic Soviet proposal. Our delegation even had the concurrence of the State Department in Washington in its desire to vote for the resolution. But the British were opposed, and Harold Macmillan called Eisenhower by transatlantic telephone to request American abstention. When an instruction to abstain arrived from the White House, James J. Wadsworth, then our ambassador to the UN, tried to reach Eisenhower to argue the case. Eisenhower declined to accept his call. Wadsworth loyally defended the American abstention in the General Assembly; but, when the resolution passed by 89-0, eight other nations joining the United States in abstaining, an American Negro delegate actually stood up and led the applause. Senator Wayne Morse, another delegate, later condemned the United States decision and declared that "on every major issue of colonialism at the 15th General Assembly, our voting record shows that we rejected our own history, and allowed the Communist bloc to champion the cause of those millions of people who are trying to gain independence."

In February the session of the General Assembly resumed with Adlai Stevenson as ambassador. Almost immediately the new admiinstration was confronted by a new colonial issue. For some time the nationalist forces in Angola had been in revolt against the Portuguese authorities. Of all the classical colonial countries, Portugal was far the most impervious to the winds of change. Indeed, the Salazar government, hopelessly anchored in its medieval certitudes, had been the real if unstated target of the December resolution. Now, as the fighting in Angola grew more fierce and sustained, Liberia placed before the Security Council a resolution calling on Portugal to comply with UN policy against colonialism and proposing a UN inquiry into the situation. This resolution incorporated by reference the anti-colonialism resolution of December.

Stevenson and Kennedy both saw the opportunity to intimate a change in American poilcy. The U.S. Mission to the UN, along with Harlan Cleveland and Wayne Fredericks, the new Deputy Assistant Secretary for African Affairs, laid the groundwork for action. There was token opposition from the Europeanists at State; but Kennedy took care that everything should be done with due concern for the feelings of Portugal and the solidarity of NATO. Salazar was informed of the American intention a week before the vote. Stevenson put the case politely in debate, arguing that America "would be remiss in its duties as a friend of Portugal" if it failed to encourage the step-by-step advancement of all inhabitants under Portuguese administration toward full self-determination. The resolution failed in the Security Council, but the new administration was now free of automatic identification with colonialism.

As troubles mounted in Angola, the same resolution came before the General Assembly a month later and this time passed with American support. Our UN votes produced anti-American riots in Lisbon and a mild surge of criticism in the United States. The New York foreign policy crowd feared that Kennedy was opening a gap in the Atlantic Alliance. Unimpressed by such reactions, Kennedy had authorized a White House statement two days after the first vote pointing out that the decision had not been taken in haste and that our NATO allies had been notified in advance. In the third world the new administration was acclaimed as the friend of oppressed peoples.

For a moment the Bay of Pigs compromised the new American role, but, curiously, only for a moment—partly because it was over so quickly that impressions did not have time to crystallize, and partly because, as Sihanouk said later, hopes were actually "increased by the President's statesmanlike handling of the crisis." Kennedy's "refusal to involve American armed forces directly in an attack on a neighboring country," Sihanouk later said, "despite a great public outcry by reactionary elements urging this course of action, showed him to be a man of rectitude and courage." J. K. Galbraith, our new ambassador to New Delhi, reported the same reaction from India.

3. KENNEDY AND NEUTRALISM: LAOS

While these early moves were showing the third world a new American attitude toward colonialism, Kennedy was demonstrating in Laos a new American support of neutralism.

The Laos talks had started in Geneva following the cease-fire of early May 1961. The conference opened in a contentious atmosphere. The Russians insisted that the Pathet Lao be seated on a basis of equality with the representatives of Prince Souvanna Phouma, the neutralist, and General Phoumi, the protégé of the Eisenhower administration, and the British were ready to go along. But the Americans objected at first, and everything seemed blocked. When Rusk, with Kennedy's approval, finally consented to seating the Pathet Lao, the right-wing delegates walked out. Eventually the three Laotian factions met in Laos and agreed on triple representation.

After a few days Rusk returned to Washington, leaving Averell Harriman in charge. Harriman set to work in characteristic style. He looked first at the American delegation. It consisted incredibly of 126 people, and some of the top officers were evidently out of sympathy with the neutralization idea. Harriman preferred both small staffs and people who agreed with the policy. Finally he reached down to a Class III Foreign Service officer, a young man named William H. Sullivan, whom he had found not only a proficient draftsman but a strong backer of the Kennedy effort, and asked him to recommend how the delegation could be reduced. Sullivan, feeling very bold, suggested that it be cut by half. Harriman told him to cut it by two-thirds and took particular pleasure in collapsing the oversized military complement to a colonel and a sergeant. When Harriman then informed the State Department that he wanted Sullivan as his deputy, State replied that, as a Class III officer, Sullivan could not be put over the Class I and II officers already on the delegation. Harriman's solution was simple: send the men who outranked Sullivan home.

The Geneva meeting recessed while Kennedy and Khrushchev met in Vienna. Laos was, of course, the sole beneficiary of their conversations, and the talks resumed in June, spurred on by the Kennedy-Khrushchev commitment to "a neutral and independent Laos under a government chosen by the Laotians themselves." Harriman now plunged into the serious stretch of negotiation. As he saw it, the neutralization policy confronted several obstacles: the Chinese, who wanted the Pathet Lao to win; the Pathet Lao, who hoped to evade the cease-fire and complete the conquest of the country; General Phoumi, who could not believe that Washington was serious about neutralization; and a few people in the State Department, who still considered neutralization a mistake.

The State Department, in fact, was only beginning to recuperate from John Foster Dulles's attack of pactomania. In July, for example, the Department actually reproved Galbraith in New Delhi for suggesting to Nehru that the United States was not trying to collect new military allies in Southeast Asia. The Department had better understand, Galbraith replied, in his customary vein, that acceptance of neutrality in Laos or for that matter in India *did* represent a change in policy from those days when the United States was forming alliances and proclaiming the immorality of neutralism. To advance this understanding, he helpfully passed along page references to the "winning candidate's" views on SEATO and CENTO [1] in the compilation of Kennedy's foreign policy speeches, *The Strategy of Peace*. He added that military alliances with inefficient and unpopular governments involved grave dangers, especially that of converting legitimate anti-government sentiment into anti-American and pro-Soviet sentiment. "To trade strong neutrality for weak alliances is obviously foolish. . . . At all times we must see the reality and not, as in the manner of our predecessors, be diverted by the words."

In a similar spirit of devotion to the past, the Department refused to let Harriman talk even informally with the Chinese delegates at the Geneva conference. At the end of July Galbraith wrote me from Geneva, where he had made a brief trip to bring himself abreast of the negotiations. The argument against contact with the Chinese Communists, Galbraith said, is "that if Sarit, Diem and Chiang Kai-shek were to hear, these noble men would think they were being undermined. . . . All this makes Harriman's task exceedingly difficult and not a little humiliating. Back of it all is only the mindless reluctance to change—and the wish to see foreign relations as a minuet. . . . He has no way of reassuring the Chinese even on minor points, and of course they are naturally suspicious. This is our most experienced and least illusioned negotiator with Communists from Stalin on." Galbraith concluded: "Harriman is going to talk about [his instructions] with Rusk next Friday in Paris but a word from the White House would be most helpful." When I mentioned the problem to Kennedy, he responded wearily as if to one more example of official idiocy and sent word along that Harriman was responsible enough to talk with whomever he saw fit.

Harriman was determined to keep the talks in low key: he saw no advantage in turning the conference into a shouting match. But the negotiations proved long and tortuous. By mid-September agreement had been reached on only a few of the thirty-three critical items. Then he proposed a series of informal meetings, away from a fixed agenda and daily press briefings. Though the United States had few tangible bargaining assets, Harriman had skill, persistence and cool logic, and he conceived his task in terms not of victory but of settlement. In time, his perseverance began to have effect. G. M. Pushkin, the Soviet representative, finally agreed that Moscow would assume responsibil-

[1] The Southeast Asia Treaty Organization (1954) and the Central Treaty Organization (1959).

ity for the observance of the agreement by the communist signatories; and then both Russia and China agreed that, while recommendations by the International Control Commission had to be unanimous, the minority could not veto majority reports on questions of the violation of the agreement. They agreed further to prohibit the entrance of foreign troops and the use of Laos as a corridor into South Vietnam. By early December the conference completed a draft Declaration on the Neutrality of Laos.

The problem remained of establishing a government of national union. Harriman's belief that Souvanna was the only possible head of a coalition displeased the diehards in Washington. The deputy chief of the Far Eastern Bureau snapped, after reading one Harriman telegram, "Well, I suppose the next one will be signed Pushkin." As late as November, when Harriman was trying to organize the coalition, some of our people actually urged Phoumi to hold out for both key ministries of defense and interior. This only reinforced Phoumi's stubbornness. In December negotiations broke down. Though the Geneva conference persuaded the Laotians to resume talks in January 1962, and Harriman finally got the State Department to say publicly that defense and interior should go to Souvanna, Phoumi continued his resistance.

But Harriman persevered. "He's putting together a New York state balanced ticket," the President said one day. "He's doing a good job." In February 1962 Averell got Washington to suspend the monthly grant of $3 million which enabled the Phoumi regime to meet its military and civilian payrolls, and in March he went to Laos to tell Phoumi personally that he must accept the Souvanna solution. Speaking with brutal frankness, Harriman informed Phoumi that he could not expect American troops to come to Laos and die for him and that the only alternative to a neutral Laos was a communist victory. Phoumi was still unyielding until April, when the Thai government, which had hitherto backed him, accepted the Harriman logic and urged him to join a government under Souvanna.

No sooner had Phoumi declared a readiness to negotiate than the Pathet Lao broke the cease-fire in a major way. On May 6, with North Vietnamese support, they seized the town of Nam Tha, where Phoumi had imprudently deployed a substantial force. The engagement was, as usual, almost bloodless. The Royal Laotian Army fled, and the communists appeared to be starting a drive toward the Thai border. This flagrant violation of the cease-fire brought a prompt reaction in Washington. Harriman now proposed that a contingent of Marines be sent to Thailand. Kennedy was at first reluctant, fearing that once the Marines were installed in Thailand it would be difficult to find an occasion to withdraw them, but decided to go ahead. The commitment of limited force on May 15 had an immediate effect. The Pathet Lao came to a halt, and negotiations started up again. In Washington Harriman called in the Laotian Ambassador and said that, if the coalition were not immediately completed, it would be the end of Phoumi. When this word reached Vientiane, Phoumi, whose power had vanished with his army, capitulated. On June 12 a coalition government was formed with Souvanna as prime minister and Phoumi and Prince Souphanouvong of the Pathet Lao as vice premiers.

The trouble was not yet over. For a moment South Vietnam threatened to walk out of the Geneva conference. When Michael Forrestal, who covered Southeast Asia for the Bundy staff, reported this from Geneva, the President sent a strong letter to Diem saying that this was a decision involving American lives, it was the best possible solution and it would be in the interests of South Vietnam. On July 23 the Declaration on the Neutrality of Laos was finally ratified in Geneva. Kennedy described it as "a heartening indication that difficult and at times seemingly insoluble international problems can in fact be solved by patient diplomacy." If the settlement could be made to work, "it would encourage us to believe that there has been a change in the atmosphere, and that other problems also could be subjected to reason and solution."

The settlement did not 'work' in the sense that the signatories observed the Geneva declaration. Coalition might have had a chance at the time of the Vientiane Agreement of 1957; but the Eisenhower administration had killed the idea then and again in 1960. In 1962 coalition labored under terrific disadvantages which had not existed five years earlier—the Pathet Lao army, no longer an ill-equipped rabble of 1800 men, now had 20,000 soldiers armed with Soviet weapons; Pathet Lao ministers now controlled not just Economic Planning but Information, Transport and Public Works; and there was a Soviet Embassy in Vientiane. In addition, Hanoi was now deeply committed to the policy of supplying the Viet Cong rebels in South Vietnam through the Laos corridor.

As a result, the Geneva settlement on Laos never went into effect. The Pathet Lao representatives soon withdrew from Vientiane and resumed their effort to take over the country by force; the International Control Commission

failed to close the corridor to South Vietnam or otherwise
assure neutralization; and Laos fell into a state of *de facto*
partition. The Soviet Union did not—perhaps could not—
fulfill its pledge to secure compliance by the communist
states. In 1961 and 1962 Kennedy often seized the opportunity in a speech or press conference to remind the world
that Khrushchev had promised his support to the neutralization of Laos, and this intermittent needling had intermittent effect. As late as 1963, when Soviet influence in
Southeast Asia was in decline, Kennedy sent Harriman to
Moscow to recall Khrushchev to his pledge. Khrushchev
seemed bored by the subject and asked Harriman irritably
why Washington bothered so much about Laos. But in
the next weeks the attitude of the Soviet Ambassador in
Vientiane markedly improved.

Yet, despite the systematic violation of the Geneva Agreement, the new policy brought clear gains. The Kennedy
strategy ended the alliance between the neutralists and the
Pathet Lao. Souvanna, Kong Le and other neutralist leaders became, as Winthrop Brown and Harriman had foreseen,
the defenders of Laotian independence no longer against
the United States but now against communism. The result
was to localize the crisis, stop an imminent communist
take-over, place the Pathet Lao in the role of breakers of
the peace, block the southward expansion of China and
win the American position international support. By 1965,
General Phoumi, after the failure of his last intrigue, had
fled the country; William Sullivan was now American Ambassador in Vientiane; and Souvanna Phouma was receiving active American assistance in Laos and stoutly supporting American policy in South Vietnam.

The result expressed Kennedy's ability to see the world
in terms more complex and realistic than total victory
or total defeat. Laos was neither won nor lost, but it was
removed from the area of great-power confrontation. The
Laos experiment illustrated both the advantages and problems of neutrality.

4. KENNEDY AND NEUTRALISM: BELGRADE

Washington's tolerance of neutralism was not based on any
sort of *New Statesman* belief in the moral superiority of
neutrals. The President was entirely unsentimental in this
respect. But in the case of Laos he saw no other way out,
and, with his understanding of the historical inevitability of
neutralist attitudes, he was quite prepared, when feasible, to
build neutralism as an alternative to communist expansion.
Moreover, he had no doubt about the value to the United

States of neutralist support in the various disputes with the Soviet Union.

This led to considerable White House interest in a meeting of unaligned nations, called by Nehru, Tito, Nasser and Sukarno for Belgrade in early September 1961. George McGhee, as head of the State Department's Policy Planning Council, responded to our concern. But elsewhere in State there was the usual indifference, if not opposition, to the whole idea of taking special trouble with the third world. When we suggested a presidential message to the conference, State was very cold. A few days before the conference opened, I learned that the Department was about to inform Belgrade no message would be forthcoming.

With the President's approval, I succeeded in stopping the cable and asked Alexis Johnson at State to call a meeting to reconsider the decision. The meeting later in the day was almost a travesty of those Foggy Bottom séances which haunt one's memory. The men from the Department arrived with a whole series of feeble reasons for doing nothing. As Tom Sorensen of USIA and I knocked one down, they clutched for another, until, as Sorensen said later, he was sure that someone would argue that the cable would cost $12.20 and the Department couldn't afford it.

Finally Carl Rowan, who was then Deputy Assistant Secretary of State for Public Affairs and plainly unsympathetic with his colleagues, scribbled an excellent draft on a yellow pad. At the end of the day, Alexis Johnson called to say that he was prepared to back the message if we would agree on a few changes. Most were trivial and unobjectionable, but, when he suggested that a passing presidential expression of good wishes be deleted, this seemed to carry caution to the point of inanity. Johnson, who was good-natured about these matters, consented not to press for this final excision, and the message went out. It was probably worth the effort—at least Hamilton Fish Armstrong, the sagacious editor of *Foreign Affairs,* who covered the Belgrade meeting, told us later that it had been a success and its omission would have been a serious error.

By this time, Kennedy was deep in the year's troubles with the Soviet Union. As the American fight for a test ban met Soviet resistance in the spring and Khrushchev gratuitously reopened the Berlin crisis in the summer, the President was beginning to wonder why American policy had so little backing, or apparently even understanding, among the neutrals. Therefore, a fortnight before Belgrade, he addressed a series of pointed questions to Stevenson and Bowles, as the chief local champions of the third world policy, and also to Galbraith, as his specialist on Nehru. He asked, in effect, why we were failing to put across our position on Berlin to the third world; why the neutrals seemed to equate our firmness with belligerence, as over Berlin, and our moderation with weakness, as over Laos; and why they appeared to judge American actions with such severity and Soviet actions with such apparent charity.

The replies showed considerable convergence of diagnosis. The trouble with Berlin, everyone agreed, was that it was so far away. "These European quarrels," Galbraith said, "are not for Asia. The outcome short of war has little implication for the Indian national interest." If we seemed more belligerent, it was because our papers reported so much about the agony of decision. "Opinions, or alleged opinions, of Acheson, the Joint Chiefs, Joe Alsop and numerous other statesmen and sages have been exhaustively cited. The lineage from the USSR is infinitely less." Moreover, as Stevenson emphasized, when questions involved the danger of war but not their own interests, "neutrals will almost inevitably favor compromise between Western and Communist positions with little regard for the rights and wrongs of the case." The experts suggested that we could strengthen our case in Berlin if we would say something about negotiation, base our argument on self-determination rather than on legalistic talk about rights of conquest and prove the genuineness of our devotion to self-determination by extending the principle from white men in Berlin to black men in Angola and to Indians in Goa. As for the double standard, we should not be unhappy if the neutrals implicitly expected better behavior from us than from the Russians; and we had no choice but to accept the less agreeable fact that they knew us to be responsive to public criticism as the Russians were not. All this would naturally lead them to concentrate their pressure on us. In general, the consultants concluded, our wealth and power, the color of our skins and our association with the colonial nations of Europe, condemned us to an almost irreducible barrage of heckling, and we should have to grin and bear it.

These remarks coincided, I believe, with Kennedy's own fundamental view. But it was hard to be philosophical in the midst of the Berlin crisis, and even harder when, after the Soviet Union resumed nuclear testing, the neutral leaders gathering at Belgrade reacted with stupefying for-

bearance. We all knew how they would have blackened
the skies with resolutions if we had been the first to resume; and the contrast drove Kennedy to great and profane acrimony. He said in a moment of irritation, "Do
you know who the real losers were at Belgrade? Stevenson
and Bowles."

As it turned out, the Belgrade conference disappointed
Moscow about as much as it did Washington. The Soviet
Union conspicuously failed to win neutral support for
its positions on Berlin, on disarmament and on the *troika*
approach to the UN; there was considerable resentment in
the corridors about the Soviet resumption of nuclear testing; and anti-American speeches and statements were notable for their absence. (Our embassy in Belgrade, summing
up the conference, reported that the patience with which
the United States had recently been treating the neutrals
was evidently having its effect.) Indeed, the Belgrade meeting disappointed everybody, even its sponsors, for it revealed such internal differences among the twenty-eight
participating nations that it destroyed the dream of a neutral bloc as a unified force in world affairs. In their devotion to the principle of non-alignment, the new states were
evidently prepared to apply it to each other.

Their final declaration dealt very largely with colonial
questions, the one great bond which held the very motley
group together. Then Nehru, with Nkrumah of Ghana,
was dispatched to Moscow and Sukarno, with Keita of
Mali, to Washington to carry the Belgrade gospel to the great
powers. Kennedy observed, "Khrushchev certainly drew
the pick of the litter," but he received the emissaries politely
and ended up having a spirited and enjoyable talk with the
African.

For a moment the Belgrade interlude strengthened those
in the State Department who opposed the neutralist experiment, whether because they regarded neutralists as potential communists or because, in the more sophisticated version, they believed that the neutralists would always throw
their weight against the more reasonable party to a conflict.
The White House took the matter more calmly. A few
weeks after Belgrade Walt Rostow sent the President a
memorandum arguing that neutral states, like all other
states, were moved by their own views of their national
interests. As Keita had pointed out to Kennedy, most of
the neutrals were militarily weak; their extremely serious
domestic problems generally determined their foreign policies; and their foreign policy interests were in any case
local and regional. Their attitudes toward the cold war,

Rostow argued, depended on the policies most likely to help them maintain their independence and pursue local advantage.

Our interest, Rostow continued, lay primarily in building this independence, in steering their energies toward internal development and in leading them into long-term assocation with the west. This, he added, was one vital role of foreign aid. Keita and Sukarno had told Kennedy that the unaligned countries, in their positions on international issues, did take into account where the aid came from; and, in analyzing the Belgrade conference, Rostow was able to show that, of the eighteen moderates, the great majority had either received most of their aid from the United States or were hoping for increased American aid, while, of the six extremists, all except Yugoslavia (and including Indonesia) had received substantially more aid from the Soviet Union.

This, I believe, made great sense to Kennedy, and the Belgrade meeting did not deflect him long from his chosen course.

5. NEHRU

Of all the neutral countries, Kennedy was most interested in India, which he had long regarded as "the key area" in Asia. The spectacle of this great nation, weighed down by legacies of centuries, making a brave attempt to achieve economic modernization within a democratic polity captured his imagination. The struggle between India and China "for the economic and political leadership of the East, for the respect of all Asia," he said in 1959, would determine the Asian future. Along with John Sherman Cooper in the Senate and Chester Bowles in the House, both former ambassadors to New Delhi, he had introduced a resolution calling for a joint American-European financial effort in support of India's five-year plan. "We want India to win that race with China," he said. " . . . If China succeeds and India fails, the economic-development balance of power will shift against us." He added characteristically: "It is not enough merely to provide sufficient money. Equally important are our attitude and understanding." Nor should anyone be put off by the Indian commitment to neutrality: "Let us remember that our nation also during the period of its formative growth adopted a policy of noninvolvement in the great international controversies of the nineteenth century."

Yet this desire to aid India coexisted with a certain

skepticism about Indian leadership. When Kennedy had visited New Delhi in 1951, Nehru for some reason—perhaps because all he could see was an unknown young Congressman—treated him with marked indifference. The visitor had been warned that, when Nehru became bored, he would tap his fingers together and look at the ceiling. Kennedy was in the office, he later liked to recall, for about ten minutes when Nehru started to tap his fingers and gaze abstractedly at a spot over his visitor's head. Moreover, Nehru's talent for international self-righteousness led Kennedy in some moods to view him as almost the John Foster Dulles of neutralism. Still, Nehru was unquestionably one of the great men of the century; and, even if he were not, India remained the key area of Asia.

In sending Galbraith as his ambassador to New Delhi, Kennedy deliberately chose a man who could be depended upon to bring to Indian problems his own mixture of sympathy and irony. Kennedy was delighted by Galbraith's wit, effrontery and unabashed pursuit of the unconventional wisdom, and they were now exceptionally good friends. Nor did the President appear to mind Ken's guerrilla warfare against the ikons and taboos of the Department of State. From time to time, the President took pleasure in announcing that Galbraith was the best ambassador he had.

Galbraith went to New Delhi with several advantages: an acquaintance with Nehru, his own prestige as an economic and social philosopher, and the President's strong belief in increased economic assistance to India—this last quickly resulting in a $500 million appropriation for Indian development. But he also had the disadvantage of the Dulles legacy and especially of the policy of American military aid to Pakistan. Soon after his arrival, for example, he learned that Washington was planning a delivery of F-104 airplanes to Karachi—planes which the Indians assumed could only be used against themselves. When Galbraith proposed that he inform the Indian government that there were only twelve planes involved, the State Department refused. Finally—"more or less by physical violence," he later said—he was able to extract permission from Washington to communicate the number of planes to Nehru. "Parliament assembled a week or two ago," he wrote me toward the end of August, "and during the recess two things had happened: We had committed a half billion in aid to India and the twelve F-104 planes to Pakistan. The ratio of questions, words, comment and emotion has been not less than ten to one in favor of the planes. Such is the current yield of the Dulles policy."

Very early Galbraith decided that the best way to erase memories of Dulles was to expose Nehru to Kennedy. The two leaders shared that address, patrician instinct and long historical view which made them, next to Churchill, the two greatest statesmen on the British model of their day. But by 1961 Nehru, alas, was no longer the man he had once been. It had all gone on too long, the fathership of his country, the rambling, paternal speeches to his flock, the tired aristocratic disdain in New Delhi, the Left Book Club platitudes when his face was turned to the world. His strength was failing, and he retained control more by momentum of the past than by mastery of the present.

Galbraith thought that Nehru would prefer no fuss on his visit and that everything should be kept easy and private. The President was dubious, remembering other visitors (he had Prince Sihanouk especially in mind) who said in advance they wanted nothing special and then seemed unhappy when they were taken at their word. But Galbraith insisted that Nehru really would wish to be received in a home. Hyannis Port seemed a little too depressing to the Kennedys, and they decided to invite him to Newport. Nehru arrived in New York on November 5, 1961, was promptly subjected to a sharp and unceremonious inquisition by Lawrence Spivak on Meet the Press, and the next morning departed for Rhode Island.

The President met him at the naval base and brought him back to the Auchincloss residence on the *Honey Fitz*. Along the way, he gestured at the great mansions shining in the sun, their green lawns stretching down to the seawall, and said, "I wanted you to see how the average American family lives." Nehru responded that the American Ambassador had been giving him special instruction in the affluent society. When they arrived at Hammersmith Farm, Jacqueline and Caroline were waiting at the front door. The little girl had picked a flower and now she made a curtsy and presented it to him. He smiled and was briefly gay with Mrs. Kennedy. But when the talk turned to Vietnam during luncheon, he fell into remote silence. It was heavy going, then and later.

They all went back to Washington in the afternoon for a state dinner in the evening. It was the first big affair of the autumn, and the staff had forgotten to open the flue in the fireplace on the first floor. The smoke poured into the room, causing confusion and smarting eyes. My wife and I were among the party of about twenty-five, too many for the family dining room on the second floor but a little too few for the state dining room. During dinner Nehru's daughter, Indira Gandhi, assailed the President about American policy, praised Krishna Menon, the professional anti-American of New Delhi, and otherwise elevated the mood of the evening.

The President, unperturbed, gave one of his graceful and witty toasts. "We all want to take this opportunity to welcome you to America, Mr. Prime Minister," he began, "though I doubt whether any words of mine can embellish the welcome already extended to you by Larry Spivak." Nehru listened without expression. His own toast was discursive and overlong, though rather touching. He spoke about Gandhi and other passages in what he called "life's tortuous course." One or two of his allusions, especially a bit on Ireland, seemed to me a trifle condescending. In conversation he displayed interest and vivacity only with Jacqueline. (When I mentioned this later to the President, he said, "A lot of our visiting statesmen have that same trouble.") The next morning B. K. Nehru, the astute and delightful Indian ambassador to Washington, summoned a group of New Frontiersmen to the Indian Embassy for an audience with the Prime Minister. This session confirmed one's feelings of the night before. I had the impression of an old man, his energies depleted, who heard things as at a great distance and answered most questions with indifference.

The private meetings between the President and the Prime Minister were no better. Nehru was terribly passive, and at times Kennedy was hard put to keep the conversation going. The President talked a good deal more about Vietnam, but the Prime Minister remained unresponsive. At one point Nehru expressed doubt about the American commitment to disarmament, citing Eisenhower's valedictory warning about the "military-industrial complex." Was it not a fact, he asked, that powerful interests would bring enormous pressures to bear against any policy that threatened an end to arms production? Kennedy, instead of indulging in statesmanlike banalities about American hopes for peace, answered frankly that his visitor did not know the half of it, that the pressures were indeed enormous; he named particular Congressmen, generals and industries. But even this candor failed to elicit much response. It was like trying to grab something in your hand, only to have it turn out to be just fog. It was all so sad: this man had done so much for Indian independence, but he had stayed around too long, and now it was all going bit by bit. To

Galbraith he once remarked that Lincoln was fortunate; Nehru by contrast much less so.

The following spring, reminiscing about the meeting, Kennedy described it to me as "a disaster . . . the worst head-of-state visit I have had." It was certainly a disappointment, and Kennedy's vision of India had been much larger before the visit than it would ever be again. Nehru was obviously in decline; his country, the President now decided, would be increasingly preoccupied with its own problems and turn more and more into itself. Though Kennedy retained his belief in the necessity of helping India achieve its economic goals, he rather gave up hope, after seeing Nehru, that India would be in the next years a great affirmative force in the world or even in South Asia.

6. GOA AND AFTER

Five weeks after Nehru left the United States he ordered his army to occupy the ancient Portuguese colony of Goa on the west coast of India. Galbraith, in a valiant last-minute effort to stop the military action, got it put off for three or four days. But Washington only authorized him to offer vague diplomatic pressure on Portugal in exchange for a six-month standstill by India. To be effective he needed more specific assurance that sooner or later we would get the Portuguese out.

In Paris, where NATO was meeting, Dean Rusk conversed with Dr. Franco Nogueiria, the Portuguese foreign minister, on the eve of the invasion. It was not a high point of American diplomacy. At no time did the Secretary express any reservations about permanent Portuguese control of Goa or even acknowledge that the Indians might have a legitimate point in resenting the Portuguese presence. In New Delhi Galbraith read the report of this session with incredulity and then sent what he described as "a surprisingly mild commentary" to Washington. "This job," he later complained to me, "is taking all the edge off my personality." Galbraith's cable argued sensibly that just as we had at all times made clear to the Indians our opposition to aggression, so we must at all times make clear to the Portuguese our opposition to colonialism.

Franco Nogueiria had concluded his talk with Rusk in Paris by warning him that the Goanese would fight to the end; they all might die in the resulting slaughter but not until each had killed ten Indians. At midnight on December 17 the invasion began. It was over in twenty-four hours. Forty-five Portuguese and twenty-two Indians were killed. The historical and political reasons for the invasion were understandable enough; but the contrast between Nehru's incessant sanctimony on the subject of non-aggression and his brisk exercise in *Machtpolitik* was too comic not to cause comment. It was a little like catching the preacher in the hen-house; and it suggested that Harrow and Cambridge, in instilling the British virtues, had not neglected hypocrisy. If such judgments were unfair, it was almost too much to expect the targets of Nehru's past sermons not to respond in kind.

In Washington Harlan Cleveland called a meeting at the State Department to consider the American reaction. Obviously we had to condemn the Indian resort to force in unequivocal language. The only issue was whether we should stop there or go on to say, as Galbraith had recommended and Stevenson now urged, that we regarded the Portuguese enclave as anachronistic and looked forward to a peaceful termination of Portuguese colonialism in India. It seemed obvious that our condemnation of aggression would have greater force if at the same time we dissociated ourselves from the Portuguese empire. But the State Department political officers resisted. It finally turned out that Salazar had requested that we keep things to the narrow issue of aggression and that the Department had assured our ambassador in Lisbon the night before that we would not raise the colonial issue. This commitment, undertaken without White House consultation, tied our hands at the United Nations. The State Department, over Stevenson's protest, insisted that he cut out the allusions in his speech to Portuguese colonialism, and this made the speech when delivered at the Security Council seem all the more unfeeling to the Indians.

It was one of Adlai's most effective efforts. He began with a pleasing picture of Krishna Menon, "so well known in these halls for his advice on peace and his tireless enjoinders to everyone else to seek the way of compromise," standing on the border of Goa rallying his troops at zero hour. Stevenson then called for a withdrawal of the invading forces and concluded that, "if the United Nations is not to die as ignoble a death as the League of Nations, we cannot condone the use of force in this instance and thus pave the way for forceful solutions of other disputes." These remarks infuriated the Indians. Indeed, Stevenson himself in a few days began to feel he might have gone a little far.

In New Delhi Galbraith called on the Foreign Secretary

and observed that India had been utterly callous to American opinion from beginning to end. Stevenson's speech, he said, was a measure of how brilliantly they could alienate a good friend. He noted his own difficulty in seeing precisely how India had advanced its position by creating more troubles for the President on foreign aid, the Congo and the opposition to colonialism. It was a useful session, he informed Washington afterward, and "I greatly enjoyed hearing my points being made."

Nehru himself sent the President a long and plaintive letter at the end of the month. "Why is it," he asked, "that something that thrills our people should be condemned in the strongest language in the United States?" He had been "deeply hurt," he remarked, by the "extraordinary and bitter attitude of Mr. Adlai Stevenson." Then in an unfortunate effort at justification, well calculated to set Kennedy's teeth on edge, he added, "You may be interested to know that even the Cardinal Archbishop of Bombay, the highest dignitary of the Roman Catholic Church in India, who is himself a Goan, expresses his satisfaction with [the Goa action]. So also some other dignitaries of the Catholic Church."

The President took his time about replying. In three weeks he wrote:

> You have my sympathy on the colonial aspects of this issue. . . . Sometimes, perhaps, we are inclined to talk a little too unctuously about the colonial origins of the United States, now nearly two centuries in the past. But, like many others, I grew up in a community where the people were barely a generation away from colonial rule. And I can claim the company of many historians in saying that the colonialism to which my immediate ancestors were subject was more sterile, oppressive, and even cruel than that of India. The legacy of Clive was on the whole more tolerable than that of Cromwell.

But he was much concerned, Kennedy continued, about the possible chain reaction to Goa. "All countries, including of course the United States, have a great capacity for convincing themselves of the full righteousness of their particular cause. No country ever uses force for reasons it considers unjust. . . . I fear that the episode in Goa will make it harder to hold the line for peace in other places." He concluded by suggesting that one difficulty was that the invasion followed so soon after Nehru's visit to the United States. "I confess to a feeling that we should have discussed this problem."

Nehru hastily answered that he had said nothing then because he had no intention of taking action; the Portu-

guese provocations at the end of November had brought
the matter to a head. This seemed a little disingenuous.
On October 23, a fortnight before he departed for America,
he had said in Bombay that "the time has come for us
to consider afresh what method should be adopted to free
Goa from Portuguese rule." The whole episode further
diminished Kennedy's hope that India had a serious role
to play in the struggle for peace.

Yet, with his usual realism, he avoided recriminations;
and, indeed, Indian sensitivity lasted longer than American, as I discovered myself in India in February. I had
gone there on another Food for Peace mission with George
McGovern. We found Goa still the compulsory subject of
conversation; even the obsession with Pakistan was taking
second place. When M. C. Chagla, a former Indian ambassador to Washington, presided over a meeting for us in
Bombay, he began his introduction with a diatribe against
the American refusal to applaud Goa and later assailed us
privately for our attitude. As McGovern and I traveled
around, we sought explanations for the Indian action. We
were particularly pleased by the explanation offered by
Frank Moraes, the talented Bombay journalist. The New
Delhi government, he thought, had wished to show that,
though it was doing nothing about Chinese incursions on
the northern frontier, it could still be tough; "it was a little
like stamping on a mouse in the kitchen when there was a
tiger at the door." G. L. Mehta, another former ambassador
to Washington and considerably more thoughtful than
Chagla, suggested that Nehru was acting to rehabilitate
himself in the anti-colonial world; if the Africans were
taking on Portugal over Angola, the least the Indians
could do was to move against Goa.

Kennedy, in any case, had no desire to protract resentments. In November Nehru had invited Jacqueline to visit
India, and during the winter Galbraith enthusiastically
worked out a long and full schedule. The President was
all for the trip in principle; but, when Galbraith's itinerary
arrived, Kennedy, after one glance, pronounced it worse
than a political campaign. One day he called Ken in New
Delhi from Palm Beach and told him the trip would have
to be cut back: "She's tired. I'm not going to let her do it.
It's too much for her." Again as in a political campaign,
the advance man objected: everyone was expecting the
President's wife; the children at Mysore were weaving garlands; we could not risk disappointment. But the President
persisted; the itinerary was revised to his satisfaction; and

Jacqueline with Lee Radziwill arrived in India in March.

It was a happy journey. Nehru was in a gentle and winning mood, much more himself than he had been in Newport or Washington. He was delighted by his guests, evidently welcomed the relief from pressure and liked to take them for strolls through his gardens. He scrupulously avoided politics and did not lobby about Goa, Kashmir or Pakistan. Jacqueline and Lee then went on to Pakistan as part of Washington's policy of non-discrimination within the subcontinent.

On the first day of April, a few days after Jacqueline's return, Galbraith, my wife and I went out to Glen Ora, the Kennedy weekend retreat in Virginia, to watch the NBC television report on the trip. It was a cool, wet Sunday in early spring. As we drove through the pleasant Virginia countryside, the rain stopped; and by the time we arrived Caroline was cheerfully sloshing around in the puddles by the swimming pool. We had tea in the handsome early-nineteenth-century house and at six-thirty switched on the television set. The President said to Jacqueline, "Well, while you and Ken watch yourselves on television, Arthur can read some of his old books and I will listen to some of my old speeches." After the show, much improved by a running commentary from Jackie and Ken, we finished our drinks and went in for dinner. Just as we sat down, Caroline appeared, her eyes filled with tears and a book clutched under her arm. Jackie said, "Oh, I promised Caroline that I would finish her story," and disappeared for a few moments to complete her assignment.

Jacqueline's trip had been a great success. It disposed of the lingering pique about Goa and re-established the process which was making the President so popular a figure throughout India. In this era of Nehru's decline, with India receding from the world stage, young Indians in particular were fixing their hopes more and more on the American President. Even the communist press treated Kennedy with respect.

Then in the autumn the Chinese themselves provided valuable cooperation by invading India from the north. Nehru, forgetting the virtues of non-alignment, sent a desperate appeal for American help. With Kennedy's strong backing, Galbraith took the opportunity to consolidate the American friendship with India. Acting with great sense and skill, and after the usual arguments with the dilatory Department, he succeeded in working out air defense arrangements and otherwise making clear that, in case the war intensified, India could expect American assistance.

Nehru, now frail and sick, was less and less in active command of his government. But, with Galbraith's expert management, the Chinese invasion and then the soothing ministrations of Chester Bowles, his relations with Kennedy were stabilized by 1963. This became evident in the controversy over American aid to the state-owned Bokaro steel mill. Aid to India came up with awful regularity every year when the general aid bill was under consideration. In 1962 Senator Symington had tried to cut down our assistance, and Kennedy personally intervened to save the Indian appropriation. In 1963 congressional opposition centered on the Bokaro project. "The Congress may have other views," Kennedy said in May, "but I think it would be a great mistake not to build it. India needs that steel." Congress did have other views, and Nehru, more sensitive now to the President's problems, withdrew the project in the summer. Kennedy wrote him an appreciative letter in early September. "I have been a strong supporter of Bokaro, and I am still," he said, but he feared that insistence on it would have eroded support for the aid bill, and he thanked Nehru for making things easier. If India were not to be the positive international force for which Kennedy had hoped, nevertheless it had acquired a sober confidence in the American government and a tremendous admiration for the American President.

XX

TANGLE IN SOUTHEAST ASIA

INDIA REMAINED the most reasonable of the developing nations of Asia: British imperialism had not been in vain. The Dutch and French, however, had not created political traditions or institutions calculated to smooth the transition to self-government; nor were they prepared to retreat from empire with the relative skill and tact of the British after the Second World War. The nationalist reaction in Indonesia and Indochina was in consequence fierce and angry.

Indonesia won its independence in 1949, Indochina, after an especially nasty war, in 1954. At Djakarta President Sukarno proceeded to gather the emotions of nationalism unto himself and used them without scruple to establish his power. In Indochina, Cambodia and Laos went their separate paths; and Vietnam, divided by the Geneva Agreements of 1954, now consisted of two hostile states, with North Vietnam stimulating and supporting a civil war south of the border.

In different ways, Indonesia and Vietnam presented Kennedy with problems to which there were no clear or easy answers and which harassed him throughout his administration.

1. SUKARNO

The 'guided democracy' which Sukarno had proclaimed in the fifties grew more and more every year into a capricious personal despotism. Sukarno was a great nationalist demagogue, adored by his people and basking in their adoration. His deep mistrust of the white west was understandably compounded in the case of the United States by his knowledge that in 1958 the CIA had participated in an effort to overthrow him. His internal problems were complex and multitudinous. He looked on them with insouciance and, in the manner familiar to despots, sought to forget them by seeking international victories. By 1961 he was threatening attack on the Dutch colony of West New Guinea, withheld when the rest of the Netherlands East Indies achieved independence.

The Indoesian legal claim was far from irresistible; it was based essentially on the fact that West New Guinea had been part of the package under the Dutch. The Papuan inhabitants of West New Guinea were barely out of the stone age and had no ethnic or cultural ties to Indonesia. There was no reason to suppose they would be better off under Djakarta than under The Hague. But Sukarno suspected that the Dutch had retained West New Guinea as a point of reentry in case his government might collapse, and, seeing the Dutch presence as an intolerable threat to Indonesian security, he was determined to force them out.

He came to Washington in the spring of 1961 and again in September after Belgrade. The meetings with Kennedy were no great success. The Indonesian leader's vanity was unconcealed, and his interest in reasoned exchange seemed limited. He gave the impression of a clever politician who had squandered the opportunity to promote the development of his country in favor of posturing on the world scene and personal self-indulgence. For all this, though, the President regarded Indonesia, this country of a hundred million people, so rich in oil, tin and rubber, as one of the potentially significant nations of Asia. He was anxious to slow up its drift toward the communist bloc; he knew that Sukarno was already turning to Moscow to get the military equipment necessary for invasion. And he was also anxious to strengthen the anti-communist forces, especially the army, in order to make sure that, if anything happened to Sukarno, the powerful Indonesian Communist Party would not inherit the country. He was therefore immediately responsive when Robert Komer proposed that the United States take the initiative in trying to settle the West New Guinea argument before it blew up into a crisis. Settlement meant persuading the Netherlands to turn West New Guinea over to Sukarno under an appropriate face-saving formula. The only alternative to this was war, and the President was sure that the Dutch, having declined to fight over Java and Sumatra, would hardly go to war over this last barren fragment of their Pacific empire. Nor did he propose to let matters develop to the point of a great-power confrontation in the Banda Sea with Moscow and Peking backing Indonesia while America backed the Dutch; like Laos, West New Guinea did not seem to him a part of the world in which great powers should be rationally engaged.

The State Department at first was hard put to remember that the White House existed in connection with policy toward West New Guinea. The Europeanists at State saw little point in satisfying Sukarno's imperialistic ambitions at the expense of a NATO ally; and through most of 1961 the Department kept threatening to align us with the Dutch against the Indonesians in the UN. Toward the end of the year, however, Harriman became Assistant Secretary for the Far East and began to redress the balance. In December Kennedy wrote Sukarno offering to help find a solution by direct negotiation, and soon he asked Harold Macmillan to persuade the Dutch and the Australians toward a greater flexibility on the issue.

In February Robert Kennedy went to Indonesia, bearing a presidential letter urging the Indonesians to come to the conference table without preconditions. Sukarno and the Attorney General got on surprisingly well. Robert Kennedy's directness and candor made a distinct impression in Djakarta; and, in later years when relations between the United States and Indonesia took a bad turn, he was the American who could talk most effectively to the Indonesian leader.

In the meantime, the Dutch, or at least the Foreign Minister, Dr. Joseph Luns, who took a crusading personal interest in West New Guinea which may have outstripped the considered concern of his government, stubbornly opposed the mediation effort. At one meeting with the President, Luns was so carried away by the injustice of it all that he waved a flabby forefinger in Kennedy's face, a gesture which Kennedy courteously ignored. To all such manifestations Kennedy's response was direct: "Do you want to fight a war about West New Guinea?" He made it clear that the Dutch were free to blame the United States for the outcome if only they would permit the problem to be settled.

Robert Kennedy's pressure on Sukarno and the President's and Harriman's on Luns finally brought the principals reluctantly to the conference table in the spring of 1962. Ellsworth Bunker, one of the wisest of American diplomats, sat in as a third party through interminable meetings in Middleburg, Virginia. There followed five months of negotiation, accusation, interruption and provocation. "Everybody is displeased, really, with our role," Kennedy said in April. ". . . The role of the mediator is not a happy one, and we're prepared to have everybody mad, if it makes some progress." Dean Rusk gave Luns some incautious assurances during another NATO meeting at Athens in May which stiffened the Dutch for a moment and probably resulted in worse terms for them in the end.

But progress was made slowly. The agreement of August 1962, based on an idea of Bunker's, called in the United Nations to provide an interim administration while sovereignty passed, over an eight-month period, from the Dutch to the Indonesians. The agreement provided further that in 1969 the Papuans should be permitted a free choice as to whether they wished to continue as part of Indonesia. Critics could plausibly attack the settlement as a shameful legalization of Indonesian expansion, and indeed it was; but the alternative of a war over West New Guinea had perhaps even less appeal.

Kennedy now moved to take advantage of the improved atmosphere. For a time relations between Djakarta and Washington improved. In an effort to persuade the Indonesians to turn inward and grapple with their development problems, the United States offered aid to the Indonesian stabilization program. When private American oil contracts were up for renegotiation and Sukarno threatened restrictive measures, Kennedy sent out Wilson Wyatt, the former lieutenant governor of Kentucky and manager of Stevenson's 1952 campaign, to conduct negotiations for new contracts, a mission which Wyatt discharged with notable dispatch and success. Sukarno remained slippery and temperamental; but he was flattered by Kennedy's attention and stayed precariously within the orbit of communication.

Only later, after Sukarno determined to make the Federation of Malaysia his next target and after the United States had permitted itself to become identified with Malaysia against Indonesia, did the downward slide of relations resume, leading Sukarno eventually out of the United Nations and into the communist camp. The problem was intractable, but the Kennedy policy succeeded in delaying the slide and preserving for a time a basis of contact within Indonesia.

2. DIEM

Most intractable of all was the problem of Vietnam. In the end this was to consume more of the President's attention and concern than anything else in Asia. The American commitment to the Saigon government was now of nearly seven years' standing. After the Geneva Agreements of 1954 had split Vietnam along the 17th parallel, President Eisenhower had written Prime Minister Ngo Dinh Diem of South Vietnam pledging American support "to assist the Government of Viet-Nam in developing and maintaining a strong, viable state, capable of resisting attempted subversion or aggression through military means." The United States, Eisenhower continued, though without particular emphasis, expected that this aid would be met "by performance on the part of the Government of Viet-Nam in undertaking needed reforms." The object of this American effort, Eisenhower concluded, was to "discourage any who might wish to impose a foreign ideology on your free people."

It was never clear that the people were so free or the ideology so foreign as Eisenhower supposed, but his language defined the mood in which Washington began the Vietnam adventure. That mood was essentially moralistic. The commitment to South Vietnam, like the parallel attempt to make the languid country of Laos a bastion of western power, followed directly from the Dulles conception of the world as irrevocably split into two unified and hostile blocs. In such a world, the threat of communism was indivisible and the obligation to oppose that threat unlimited. The moral imperative was reinforced by a popular construction, or misconstruction, of the Munich analogy, soon reformulated by Joseph and Stewart Alsop for Southeast Asia as the 'domino' theory. "You have a row of dominoes set up," Eisenhower explained to a press conference, "you knock over the first one, and what will happen to the last one is that it will go over very quickly. So you have a beginning of a disintegration that would have the most profound influences." "If . . . Indochina passes into the hands of the Communists," he told a doubting Winston Churchill, "the ultimate effect on our and your global strategic position . . . could be disastrous. . . . We failed to halt Hirohito, Mussolini and Hitler by not acting in unity and in time."

This was a moment of the supremacy of abstract principles (up to the point, of course, when they might lead to large-scale military action, as in the case of Dien Bien Phu). When Franklin Roosevelt had judged the Japanese occupation of Indochina a threat to vital United States interests in 1941, he had in mind, among other things, such a mundane fact as the need to keep open the supply routes which brought rubber from South Asia to the United States. The wartime development of synthetic rubber had long since ended American dependence on Asian rubber plantations; and no specific considerations of this sort seemed to underlie the abstractions of 1954. Nor, indeed, did there appear to have been much consideration of the concrete situation in Vietnam. A more discriminating view might have regarded Ho Chi Minh, the boss of North Vietnam, less as the obedient servant of a homogeneous Sino-Soviet bloc than as a leader of nationalist communism, historically mistrustful of the Chinese and eager to preserve his own freedom of action. It might have taken a more relaxed attitude toward the evolution of Vietnam; and it might have decided to draw the American line on the Siamese side of the Mekong River, where both the political and military foundations for an American position were a good deal stronger. But abstractions prevailed, and the commitment was made. Dulles's anti-colonial mood, moreover, required it to be in the main an American commitment, lest our effort in South Vietnam be tainted by suspicions of European imperialism. And, after Washington accepted Diem's refusal to take part in the all-Vietnam elections promised by the Geneva Agreements for 1956, it became increasingly a commitment to one man.

Whether we were right in 1954 to undertake this commitment will long be a matter of interest to historians, but it had ceased by 1961 to be of interest to policy-makers. Whether we had vital interests in South Vietnam before

1954, the Eisenhower letter created those interests. Whether we should have drawn the line where we did, once it was drawn we became every succeeding year more imprisoned by it. Whether the domino theory was valid in 1954, it had acquired validity seven years later, after neighboring governments had staked their own security on the ability of the United States to live up to its pledges to Saigon. Kennedy himself, who had watched western policy in Vietnam in the early fifties with the greatest skepticism and who as President used to mutter from time to time about our "overcommitment" in Southeast Asia, had no choice now but to work within the situation he had inherited. Ironically, the collapse of the Dulles policy in Laos had created the possibility of a neutralist solution there; but the survival of that policy in South Vietnam, where the government was stronger and the army more willing to fight, left us in 1961 no alternative but to continue the effort of 1954.

It cannot be said that Diem had altogether kept his side of the bargain, especially in the performance of "needed reforms," nor can it be said that the Eisenhower administration brought this omission very urgently to his attention. Diem, a profound traditionalist, ran a family despotism in the oriental manner. He held power in his own hands, regarded opposition as treason, showed disdain for the shallow institutions of western democracy and aimed to restore the ancient Annamese morality. "If we open the window," his sister-in-law, the lovely and serpentine Madame Nhu once said, "not only sunlight but many bad things will fly in." On the other hand, he had kept the country together in difficult circumstances. He had subdued the religious sects, cleaned up Saigon (once a swinging city of nightclubs, gambling houses and opium dens) and, with American aid, brought about a measure of economic growth and social improvement. Living standards, indeed, had risen faster in South than in North Vietnam, where Ho Chi Minh concentrated on investment rather than consumption. And Diem himself seemed a man of rectitude and purpose, devoted and incorruptible.

The civil war had begun the year after the cancellation of the elections. Diem's authoritarianism, which increasingly involved manhunts, political re-education camps and the 'regroupment' of population, produced a spreading resistance. At first the communists hung back, but, as the success of Diem's economic policies convinced Ho Chi Minh that he could not wait passively for the Diem regime to collapse, he sent word to his comrades in the south to join the guerrillas. In March 1960 the Viet Cong, as the rebels were known, initiated a National Liberation Front, and in September the Communist Party of North Vietnam bestowed its formal blessing and called for the liberation of South Vietnam from American imperialism. By this time Ho Chi Minh was supplying the Viet Cong with training, equipment, strategic advice and even men—perhaps 2000 a year by 1960. Nearly all those who came from North Vietnam in the Kennedy years, however, were South Vietnamese who had gone north in 1954; most of the Viet Cong in any case continued to be recruited in South Vietnam; and most Viet Cong arms and equipment were captured from Diem's army.

The Viet Cong unquestionably expressed a strain of fanatic idealism. "We are peasants in soldiers' clothing," they sang, "waging the struggle for a class oppressed for thousands of years. Our suffering is the suffering of the people." Nationalists fought side by side with communists. But the Viet Cong did not precisely represent a movement of rural uplift. They extended their power as much by the fear they incited as by the hope they inspired. Still, the systematic murder of village officials—half a dozen a day by 1960—could be an effective weapon too, especially when the people of the countryside had been given little reason to prefer the government in Saigon to their own survival. It was warfare in the shadows, ambush and murder and torture, leaving behind a trail of burned villages, shattered families and weeping women.

American assistance to Diem in the fifties averaged about $300 million a year. This was mostly economic aid, which South Vietnam, unlike Laos, put to fairly good use, though only a fraction got to the countryside where most of the South Vietnamese lived. On the military side, our advisers, many of them veterans of the Korean War, conceived their mission as that of training a conventional army designed, not to fight guerrillas, but to repel a Korean-style invasion from the north. They accompanied this by a systematic barrage of self-serving reports—all too reminiscent of the French military a few years before—about the commendable efficiency of this army and its capacity to control any situation. Cheered by such bulletins, a Senate committee concluded in 1960, "on the basis of the assurances of the head of the military aid mission in Vietnam, that the U.S. Military Assistance Advisory Group (MAAG) can be phased out of Vietnam in the foreseeable future."

Some officers, like Brigadier General Edward Lansdale, who had fought the Hukbalahaps in the Philippines and whose report on Vietnam Walt Rostow handed Kennedy shortly after the inauguration, dissented with vigor from both MAAG's strategy and its complacency. Lansdale thought that it was essentially a guerrilla war and that it was going very badly. For a long time this was a heretical view. But by the end of 1960 even the professional optimists found it hard to wave aside the Lansdale points. The guerrilla attacks were increasing in audacity and scope; the success of the Pathet Lao had opened up the corridor of assistance from North Vietnam to South Vietnam through Laos; there were now perhaps 15,000 Viet Cong in South Vietnam, and they were overrunning half the country, and more by night.

In Saigon there was increasing dissatisfaction with Diem, his government and the conduct of the war. This included the Vietnamese intellectual community, embittered by Diem's methods of political repression, but it centered in the Vietnamese Army. American training had given the younger officers a sense of modern methods, and they regarded Diem's old-fashioned absolutism with growing resentment. In November 1960 a military coup almost succeeded in overthrowing the regime. Diem rode this out. Once back in control, he cracked down on all varieties or potentialities of opposition. He imprisoned or exiled a number of younger officials and, to guard against future military coups, began a process of pitting one general against another and thereby dividing the army. Trusting no one, he based himself more and more narrowly on his family, especially on his able and aggressive younger brother, Ngo Dinh Nhu.

3. JOHNSON IN SAIGON

Vietnam confronted the new American President, not with an immediate crisis, like Laos, but rather with a situation of deepening military and political shakiness. Kennedy had long believed, and Khrushchev's January speech had confirmed that belief, that the main communist reliance in the coming period would be on neither nuclear nor conventional but on guerrilla war. The battle in Vietnam was obviously not along the frontier but in the villages; and it could be won only by a flexibility and mobility which matched that of the guerrillas themselves. Moreover, it could not be won by military means alone. Guerrilla warfare was essentially political war. Effective counterinsurgency action, for example, depended on swift and sure intelligence from the countryside. The Viet Cong could never be defeated unless the Saigon regime could enlist the support of the peasants. Magsaysay's campaign against the Hukbalahaps in the Philippines provided a model: tough counterguerrilla action, generous provisions for amnesty, real and sweeping political and economic reforms.

Middle-level officials in State and Defense had already reached this conclusion, and Rostow gave their effort new sharpness and support. A counterinsurgency plan for Vietnam, prepared in the winter of 1960 and approved by Kennedy in early 1961, proposed an extensive program of military and social reforms; if these recommendations were carried out, the report said, the war could be won in eighteen months. A Vietnam Task Force, set up in April, reduced the report to forty points; Frederick Nolting, a Foreign Service officer who had served in our NATO mission in Paris, was sent to Saigon as ambassador, his predecessor being accounted too anti-Diem; and in May the Vice-President visited in Saigon as part of a general tour of Southeast Asia.

Johnson was accompanied by Jean and Stephen Smith, the President's sister and brother-in-law, and his primary purpose was to reassure Chiang Kai-shek in Taiwan, Diem in South Vietnam and Sarit in Thailand that the new American policy toward Laos did not signify a general intention to withdraw from the area. After a stop in Taiwan, where he was pleasantly surprised to find Chiang Kai-shek and Madame Chiang talking about social progress like old New Dealers, he went on to Saigon. There, in the interests of reassurance, he somewhat imprudently hailed Diem as the Winston Churchill of South Asia. Privately he discussed the military and economic situation with Diem; and in an address to the National Assembly he urged the importance of meeting the needs of the people in education and rural development.

Before he left the United States, an old friend from New Deal days, Arthur Goldschmidt, then with the United Nations, had called his attention to a UN project for the multi-purpose development of the lower Mekong River. This project would bring together the countries of Cambodia, Laos, Thailand and South Vietnam in a joint effort for electric power, irrigation, navigation and fisheries development for the benefit of the whole area. It strongly appealed to Johnson; as he said when he visited the headquarters of the UN Economic Commission for Asia and the Far East in Bangkok, "I am a river man. All my life I have been interested in rivers and their development." He invoked F.D.R., TVA, Bonneville and Grand Coulee in public speeches; the memory of the Mekong valley project was to stay with him a long time.

From Thailand he went on to India, where he had useful talks with Nehru, and then back to Washington. "Our mission arrested the decline of confidence," he reported to Kennedy on his return. "It did not—in my judgment—restore any confidence already lost. . . . If these men I saw at your request were bankers, I would know—without bothering to ask—that there would be no further extension on my note." Time was running out, and "the basic decision in Southeast Asia," he told Kennedy, "is here. We must decide whether to help these countries to the best of our ability or throw in the towel in the area and pull back our defenses to San Francisco and a 'Fortress America' concept. More important, we would say to the world in this case that we don't live up to our treaties and don't stand by our friends. This is not my concept. I recommend that we move forward promptly with a major effort to help these countries defend themselves."

He did not consider Southeast Asia lost, "and it is by no means inevitable that it must be lost." In each country, he said, it was possible to "build a sound structure capable of withstanding and turning the Communist surge." But this could only be done if the nations of Southeast Asia had "knowledge and faith in United States power, will and understanding." The long-term danger, he added, came not from communism but "from hunger, ignorance, poverty and disease. We must—whatever strategies we evolve—keep those enemies the point of our attack, and make imaginative use of our scientific and technological capacity."

As for Vietnam, he found Diem a complex figure beset by many problems. "He has admirable qualities, but he is remote from the people, is surrounded by persons less admirable than he. The country can be saved—if we move quickly and wisely." The Vice-President did not envisage the commitment of American troops beyond training missions. American combat involvement at this time, he said, was not only unnecessary but undesirable because it would revive anti-colonial emotions throughout Asia. Instead, Johnson favored the reorientation of the military effort along with programs of political and economic reform. "It would be useful," he said, "to enunciate more clearly than we have—for the guidance of these young and unsophisticated nations—what we expect or require of them."

Under the pressure of Johnson and Nolting, Diem agreed in May to a number of points in the task force report in exchange for American support on an increase

in the Vietnamese Army. However, Diem's assurances led
to little or nothing in the way of performance. This was
increasingly the pattern of Washington's relations with the
Diem regime. Indeed, American attempts to advise Diem
became a classical exercise in what anthropologists might
call cross-cultural frustration. The Americans did tend to
regard Vietnam, in the Vice-President's words, as a "young
and unsophisticated" nation, populated by affable little men,
unaccustomed to the modern world, who, if sufficiently
bucked up by instruction and encouragement, might
amount to something. The Vietnamese, regarding their nation as infinitely older and more sophisticated than the
United States, looked on the Americans as impatient, naïve
and childlike, lacking all sense of form or history. Diem
in particular viewed the Americans with a mandarin's disdain and increasingly responded to their advice by the
simple but powerful device of doing all the talking himself. What perhaps began as a tactic soon became a disease. By 1961 Diem's compulsive talking was becoming
legendary: survivors would vie with each other in accounts
of conversations lasting six or seven or twelve hours and
would exchange dodges intended to help trapped victims
extricate themselves from the presidential flow.

Diem seemed unwilling or unable to undertake, for example, the programs of rural reform designed to close the
gap between the president's palace in Saigon and the people
in the villages. Most likely the whole conception of seeking
'popular support' seemed to him one of those western delusions with no relevance to life in Asia. In his view it
was the moral obligation of the people to respect their
government. As for the Vietnamese Army, though it continued to regard Diem's one-man rule with periodic restless-
ness, his divisive strategy kept it from acting against him.
Moreover, the officers had been so well persuaded by
American advisers of the virtues of conventional war that
most had little heart of the chancy life of night patrols,
small-unit action and hit-and-run tactics.

The Johnson trip was followed by an economic mission,
headed by Eugene Staley, and still more recommendations.
But it seemed impossible to stop the disintegration. "The
situation gets worse almost week by week," Theodore H.
White wrote us in August. ". . . The guerrillas now control
almost all the southern delta—so much so that I could
find no American who would drive me outside Saigon in
his car even by day without military convoy." He reported
a "political breakdown of formidable proportions": ". . .

what perplexes hell out of me is that the Commies, on their side, seem to be able to find people willing to die for their cause. . . . I find it discouraging to spend a night in a Saigon night-club full of young fellows of 20 and 25 dancing and jitterbugging (they are called 'la jeunesse cowboy') while twenty miles away their Communist contemporaries are terrorizing the countryside." An old China hand, White was reminded of Chungking in the Second World War, complete with Madame Nhu in the role of Madame Chiang Kai-shek. "If a defeat in South Vietnam is to be considered our defeat, if we *are* responsible for holding that area, then we must have authority to act. And that means intervention in Vietnam politics. . . . If we do decide so to intervene, have we the proper personnel, the proper instruments, the proper clarity of objectives to intervene successfully?"

4. THE TAYLOR-ROSTOW MISSION

In September the Viet Cong seized a provincial capital and beheaded the governor. Morale in Saigon sank even lower. Diem was plainly losing the war, and Theodore White's questions were now more relevant than ever. Kennedy, absorbed as he was in Berlin and nuclear testing, faced a series of inescapable decisions in Vietnam.

The broad alternatives ranged from Lyndon Johnson's recommendation of a major American commitment to Chester Bowles's idea of enlarging the concept of a "neutral and independent Laos" to include Burma, Thailand, South Vietnam, Cambodia and Malaya. Such a neutral belt Bowles thought, could ultimately be guaranteed by Russia, China, India, Japan and the SEATO powers. Russia might well be willing to go along in order to block Chinese expansion into Southeast Asia. And, if the communists tried to use neutralism as a screen behind which to take over the whole area, then we would have, Bowles argued, a better chance of rallying international support in defense of neutralism than in defense of western hegemony.

It was an imaginative proposal, but it seemed either too early or too late. Its opponents contended that it would be taken as a deliberate abandonment of regimes which depended on us and a monumental United States retreat— all in exchange for empty promises from Moscow and Peking. Instead, there seemed a strong case for trying the Johnson approach and making an increased effort to stabilize the situation in South Vietnam. Early in October Kennedy sent General Maxwell Taylor and Walt Rostow on a mission to Saigon to see if this could be done. Reminding them of his own visit to Indochina in 1951, he charged them to find out whether we were better off now than the French had been then—whether Vietnamese nationalism had turned irrevocably against us or still might serve as a basis for the fight against communism.

The very composition of the mission—headed by a general, with a White House aide as deputy and no figure of comparable rank from the State Department—was significant. It expressed a conscious decision by the Secretary of State to turn the Vietnam problem over to the Secretary of Defense. Rusk doubtless decided to do this because the military aspects seemed to him the most urgent, and Kennedy doubtless acquiesced because he had more confidence in McNamara and Taylor than in State. The effect, however, was to color future thinking about Vietnam in both Saigon and Washington with the unavowed assumption that Vietnam was primarily a military rather than a political problem.

The mission went about its work in an orderly way. Its members divided the job up on the way over and, after each had completed his assignment, retired to the cool breezes of Baguio in the Philippines to write the report. Their collective answer to Kennedy's question was that South Vietnam had enough vitality to justify a major United States effort. The trouble, as Taylor and Rostow diagnosed it, was a double crisis of confidence: doubt that the United States was really determined to save Southeast Asia; doubt that Diem's methods could really defeat the Viet Cong. To halt the decline, they recommended increased American intervention—in effect, a shift from arm's-length advice to limited partnership. While only the Vietnamese could finally beat the Viet Cong, Americans at all levels, Taylor and Rostow argued, could show them how the job was to be done.

The report concentrated on military matters. In addition to a variety of recommendations designed to get the Vietnamese Army to take the offensive, Taylor proposed that American troops perform certain tasks, like airlift and air reconnaissance, which the Vietnamese were not prepared to undertake; he even envisaged sending an American military task force—perhaps 10,000 men—capable of conducting combat operations for self-defense and perimeter security and, if the Vietnamese Army were hard pressed, of providing an emergency reserve. As for Diem, the report gave a candid account of his political and administrative idiosyncrasies but rejected any idea that he be replaced. While it outlined a number of desirable political reforms—especially broadened participation in government and more work in the villages—it relied mainly on the expectation that the new system of limited partnership could work *de facto* changes in Diem's methods of government and gradually narrow the gap between the regime and the people.

Taylor and Rostow hoped that this program would suffice to win the civil war—and were sure it would if only the infiltration from the north could be stopped. But if it continued, then they could see no end to the war. They therefore raised the question of how long Saigon and the United States could be expected to play by the existing ground rules, which permitted North Vietnam to train and supply guerrillas from across the border and denied South Vietnam the right to strike back at the source of aggression. Rostow argued so forcibly for a contingency policy of retaliation against the north, graduated to match the intensity of Hanoi's support of the Viet Cong, that "Rostow Plan 6" became jocularly established in the contingency planning somewhere after SEATO Plan 5.

The Taylor-Rostow report was a careful and thoughtful document, and the President read it with interest. He was impressed by its description of the situation as serious but not hopeless and attracted by the idea of stiffening the Diem regime through an infusion of American advisers. He did not, however, like the proposal of a direct American military commitment. "They want a force of American troops," he told me early in November. "They say it's necessary in order to restore confidence and maintain morale. But it will be just like Berlin. The troops will march in; the bands will play; the crowds will cheer; and in four days everyone will have forgotten. Then we will be told we have to send in more troops. It's like taking a drink. The effect wears off, and you have to take another." The war in Vietnam, he added, could be won only so long as it was *their* war. If it were ever converted into a white man's war, we would lose as the French had lost a decade earlier.

Though the Taylor report offered political as well as military remedies, the thrust of its argument and recommendation was that the crisis of confidence was military in its origins and could be ended by the commitment of American troops or at least by American partnership in the conduct of Vietnamese field operations. Not all the specialists concurred in the diagnosis. J. K. Galbraith, who was back in Washington for a few days, and Averell Harriman, who was about to take over as Assistant Secretary for the

Far East, were sure on the contrary that the crisis of confidence was political in its origins and had resulted from Diem's repressive and reactionary policies in face of a communist-managed peasant insurrection. "The trouble with the State Department," Harriman said as we dined with Galbraith one autumn evening before his return to New Delhi, "is that it always underestimates the dynamics of revolution." Someone wondered whether the removal of Diem would not be the answer. "Our trouble," replied Galbraith sagaciously, "is that we make revolutions so badly."

Kennedy, still undecided about next steps, asked Galbraith to stop by in Saigon on his way back to India. Galbraith did so, viewed the scene with dispassionate eye and reported to Washington that the fundamental problem was the total ineffectuality of the Diem regime. If there were effective government in Saigon, the situation would be far from hopeless; for, with support from the countryside and something to fight for, the well-equipped Vietnamese Army of a quarter of a million could deal with the fifteen thousand or so lightly armed irregulars opposing them. How to get effective government? There was not "the slightest practical chance," Galbraith said, that the administrative and political reforms now being pressed upon Diem would result in performance. We had no choice but to play out this course for a little while longer, but he could see no long-term solution which did not involve a change of leadership. Diem, a significant man in his day, had passed the point of rehabilitation. "While no one can promise a safe transition, we are now married to failure." As for the cliché that there was no alternative, this was an optical illusion arising from the fact that eyes were always fixed on the visible figures. "It is a better rule that nothing succeeds like successors."

Reflecting on the situation and reposing particular confidence in McNamara and Taylor, Kennedy prepared to go ahead. Moreover, given the truculence of Moscow, the Berlin crisis and the resumption of nuclear testing, the President unquestionably felt that an American retreat in Asia might upset the whole world balance. In December he ordered the American build-up to begin. General Paul Harkins, as the new American commander in Saigon, and Ambassador Nolting worked closely together. Both saw Diem as the key to success, and both were convinced that attempts to bring pressure on him would be self-defeating. The proper policy in their view was to win Diem's confidence by assuring him unswerving support and then try to steer him gently and gradually toward reform; if Diem felt this backing to be anything less than whole-hearted, the policy would not work. This became known, in the phrase of Homer Bigart of the *New York Times*, as the period of "sink or swim with Ngo Dinh Diem."

The result in 1962 was to place the main emphasis on the military effort. When the social and economic program developed in Washington in 1961 encountered the usual resistance in Saigon, it was soon dropped. In place of a serious attack on the central problems of land and taxation, the regime announced a number of marginal and largely meaningless reforms to placate the Americans and did very little to put even these into effect. The appeal to the peasants was concentrated in the so-called strategic hamlet program, launched by the regime in April.

This idea, adapted from the British experience in fighting the guerrillas in Malaya, called for the relocation of peasants into fortified villages, surrounded by barbed wire fences and ditches filled with bamboo spikes. The theory was that the hamlets would give the peasants protection and a sense of security, control the movement of people and supplies through the countryside and cut the Viet Cong off from their primary sources of food, intelligence and recruits. Village defense units would arise to fight the enemy. Each hamlet would elect its political representatives by secret ballot. And each hamlet would eventually become the unit for education, medical care and the distribution of pigs, fertilizer and low-interest agricultural loans. It was an idyllic conception. Ngo Dinh Nhu made the strategic hamlet program his personal project and published glowing reports of spectacular success, claiming 7 million people in 7000 hamlets by the middle of 1963. One might have wondered whether Nhu was just the man to mobilize the idealism of the villages; but Nolting and Harkins listened uncritically to his reports and passed them back to Washington, where they were read with elation.

In military matters the enlargement of the American presence appeared to have even more encouraging effects. The advisers flocked in with the weapons of modern war, from typewriters to helicopters. They worked with local 'counterparts' in all sections of the government in Saigon. In the field, they lived with the Vietnamese Army, helped plan military actions and sometimes participated themselves. The military assignment was frustrating, because the power to advise was not the power to command. It was also thankless, because as a matter of policy the American role was systematically played down. But the advisers themselves were brave and devoted as well as anonymous; their courage and selflessness were deeply impressive; and they made a difference.

Morale rose in Saigon. Viet Cong activity declined in the countryside. No more provincial capitals were attacked. "Every quantitative measurement we have," Robert McNamara said on his first visit to Vietnam in 1962, "shows we're winning this war." Maxwell Taylor, when he returned for a fresh look a year after his first visit, thought he detected "a great national movement" rising to destroy the Viet Cong. No one could doubt a widespread and substantial improvement in the military situation. In Washington, the President, who had other matters on his mind, accepted the cheerful reports from men in whom he had great confidence. His 1963 State of the Union message summed up the mood at the turn of the year: "The spearpoint of aggression has been blunted in South Vietnam."

XXI

AFRICA: THE NEW ADVENTURE

IN NO PART of the third world did Kennedy pioneer more effectively than in Africa.

Of all the continents this one had stayed longest on the outer fringes of the American consciousness. As late as 1960, our direct interests in Africa, political or economic, military or intellectual, were meager. No traditional doctrines guided our African policies. No alliances committed our troops. Our foreign aid programs made only token contributions to African development. Of our $30 billion of overseas investment, less than 3 per cent was in Africa. Our very sense of the continent below the Mediterranean rim was vague and dim. No historic ties bound us to black Africa except the slave trade; and here we had done our best to repress the memory (and, by a sentimental concern with the state of Liberia, to allay the guilt). Even Americans of African descent were not much interested. I can remember in the campaign of 1956 proposing to one of Stevenson's Negro advisers that we make something of the Eisenhower administration's resistance to UN resolutions against the slave trade, only to be told sorrowfully that the American Negro couldn't care less about such matters.

The explosion of African nationalism after the Second World War had at first only a limited impact. There was a stirring of interest in African studies in the universities. John Gunther insided Africa in 1955. In 1957 the State Department established a Bureau of African Affairs. But that year there were still more Foreign Service personnel stationed in West Germany than in all of Africa. As we considered Latin America primarily our own responsibility, so we considered Africa primarily a Western European responsibility. Now that the European colonial powers were joined with us in the Atlantic Alliance, there seemed all the more reason, in the interests of NATO solidarity, to defer to them in African matters. Our nominal sympathy with the anti-colonial movement did lead us to occasional exhortations about the virtues of orderly transition to self-government; but, when the chips were down, as with the United Nations anti-colonial resolution of December 1960, we gave priority to NATO. Our African policy remained general and perfunctory.

Still African nationalism was now a burning fact in the world—never more than in the months of September and October 1960, when sixteen new African states flocked into the UN. During this year the Congolese leader Patrice Lumumba became the bright symbol of nationalist militance; and Lumumba's murder a few weeks after Kennedy's inauguration set off a reaction of outrage through the continent. Whether or not he was killed at the instigation of Moise Tshombe, the ruler of the province of Katanga in the Congo, Tshombe and through him his white mercenaries and European and American sympathizers were held accountable. The martyrdom of Lumumba at the presumed hands of an imperialist agent raised the mistrust of the west to a sudden frenzy of hatred. In Moscow Khrushchev lost no time in embracing the protest and demanding the punishment of the imperialists, hoping thereby to capture the energies of African nationalism. By March 1961 the Congo was in turmoil; a number of the new states, especially Guinea, Mali and Ghana, seemed well launched on the Marxist road; and most of the rest of Africa was consumed with bitterness toward the west. The Atlantic countries had never stood lower nor the Soviet Union higher in the minds of politically conscious Africans.

1. KENNEDY AND AFRICA

Kennedy arrived in office, however, with a record on Africa unique among American politicians. His broad interest in colonial problems had gone back a long way—to childhood

tales of Ireland's long struggle for independence and, in
the contemporary world, at least to the trip he had taken
as an inquisitive young Congressman to Indochina in 1951.
In the mid-fifties he had begun to see in Algeria the same
pattern of colonial decay he had already inspected in Southeast Asia; and he feared that French intransigence would
have the same outcome of uniting the nationalists with the
communists. In addition, he had just come on the Senate
Foreign Relations Committee and no doubt wanted to move
into foreign affairs in a way that would at once be arresting and useful and demonstrate a basic liberalism.

He therefore thought a good deal in the spring of 1957
about a speech on the Algerian struggle for self-determination. In preparing the speech, he was in discreet touch with
William J. Porter, director of the State Department's Office of North African Affairs, an intelligent Foreign Service
officer who feared that Washington's uncritical commitment
to the French was jeopardizing the whole future of the
west in Africa. Kennedy also evidently talked to the Algerians seeking a hearing for the national liberation movement at the United Nations. (This was more audacious than
it sounds: as late as 1960 Secretary of State Herter bleakly declined to meet with representatives of FLN.) He consulted American experts on North Africa and did considerable reading himself.

Rising in the Senate in July 1957, he pointed out that the
French government was repeating its errors of the past—
above all, in its refusal to accept the reality of nationalism;
and he bluntly criticized the American policy of full support to France in the struggle against the Algerian rebels.
"No amount of mutual politeness, wishful thinking, nostalgia, or regret," he told the Senate, "should blind either
France or the United States to the fact that, if France and
the West at large are to have a continuing influence in
North Africa . . . the essential first step is the independence
of Algeria." The Atlantic nations, he said, must understand
that "this is no longer a French problem alone," and the
United States must use its influence to work for a solution
based on a recognition of "the independent personality of
Algeria."

It is hard now to recall the furor his remarks caused.
The Algerian speech brought Kennedy more mail, both
from the United States and abroad, than any other address
he made in the Senate. It produced great irritation not just
in official circles in Paris and Washington but throughout
the foreign policy establishment in the United States—the
Council on Foreign Relations, the *New York Times*, the

Department of State. Kennedy had criticized an ally; he had imperiled the unity of NATO. Even Democrats drew back. Dean Acheson attacked him scornfully. Adlai Stevenson thought he had gone too far. For the next year or two, respectable people cited Kennedy's Algerian speech as evidence of his irresponsibility in foreign affairs.

But there were other reactions. I was in Paris that July, and, as I wrote him, my main impression was of "the great gap between what people thought privately and were willing to say publicly about Algeria. . . . I found no one (including people in the Quai d'Orsai) ready to defend the present policy." French critics of the official policy were pleased to have their hands strengthened by this evidence of international concern. Jean-Jacques Servan-Schrieber ran the full text in *L'Express* with Kennedy's photograph on the cover. In Europe the speech identified him for the first time as a fresh and independent voice of American foreign policy. And Africans, of course, were deeply excited. In 1961, when Ambassador Philip Kaiser presented his credentials to Ould Daddah, the President of Mauritania, his host spoke of the thrill with which he had read the speech as a student in Paris. This was the reaction among political leaders across the continent.

Soon Kennedy became chairman of the African Subcommittee of the Senate Foreign Relations Committee. In this capacity he warned his colleagues about the new energies bursting forth in the dark continent. "Call it nationalism, call it anti-colonialism, call it what you will," he said in 1959, "Africa is going through a revolution. . . . The word is out—and spreading like wildfire in nearly a thousand languages and dialects—that it is no longer necessary to remain forever poor or forever in bondage." He advocated sympathy with the independence movement, programs of economic and educational assistance and, as the goal of American policy, "a strong Africa."

In 1960, for the first time in American history, Africa figured prominently in a presidential election. Kennedy charged repeatedly (there are 479 references to Africa in the index of his 1960 campaign speeches) that "we have lost ground in Africa because we have neglected and ignored the needs and aspirations of the African people," while Nixon, in a rather tepid response, criticized Kennedy for not having called any meetings of the African subcommittee that year. In the summer, when students in Kenya who had scholarships in American universities could not meet their travel fares and the Eisenhower administration declined to do anything about them, Kennedy arranged through the Kennedy Foundation to bring them over on a well-publicized airlift. He also sent Averell Harriman on a fact-finding mission to West and Central Africa.

Once elected, Kennedy moved forward swiftly to lay the groundwork for a new African policy. His first State Department appointment was G. Mennen Williams as Assistant Secretary for African Affairs. He described this as "a position of responsibility second to none in the new administration," and, while this pleasant exaggeration was no doubt intended in part to assuage Williams's disappointment over not being in the cabinet, it also expressed a new sense of urgency about Africa—and was so received by African leaders. Williams, of course, was well known as a progressive governor of Michigan and battler for civil rights; and his designation expressed Kennedy's desire to take African policy out of conventional channels and give it fresh energy and purpose.

Williams had a clear and strong vision of the American role as the friend of African independence and development. But he turned out, despite his political background, not to be too proficient in the intramural warfare of the Department of State; and he was too much the old-fashioned New Deal liberal for his relations with the President to be entirely comfortable. Yet in a way Kennedy admired Williams's very earnestness; and Williams always felt that he had Kennedy's backing. Though they traveled by different roads—Williams, by explicit moral idealism; Kennedy, who hated to declare his idealism, by expressions of practical concern for the American interest—they generally arrived at the same conclusion. When problems made their painful climb through bureaucratic conflicts to the White House, Kennedy ordinarily decided them Williams's way.

Kennedy, indeed, felt rather protective about Williams. When the Assistant Secretary on his first African trip was quoted at Nairobi as saying that Africa was for the Africans, a comment which caused a brief uproar in London, Kennedy was resolved not to give ground to Williams's critics. Asked about the statement at a press conference, he replied briefly, "I don't know who else Africa should be for." The Nairobi incident amused him, and he used to kid Williams about it. That March at the Gridiron Dinner, Kennedy remarked that he had just received a cable from Williams asking whether he could stay in Africa a few more weeks. "I felt I had better send this reply," the President told the Gridiron audience: " 'No, Soapy. Africa is for the Africans.' "

African policy received another infusion from the outside when Williams acquired a singularly able and imaginative Deputy Assistant Secretary in Wayne Fredericks, whose work at the Ford Foundation had been preceded by long business experience in Africa. Then in March the President seized the opportunity afforded by the Angola resolution in the UN to dramatize the new American attitude toward African colonial questions. And on African Freedom Day in April he told a reception of African ambassadors of his "profound attachment to the great effort which the people of Africa are making in working toward political freedom."

In selecting his own ambassadors for the new African nations, he made a special effort to find men who embodied the spirit of the New Frontier. He used to say that Africa was the exciting place for a diplomat to be; London and Paris hardly mattered any more—everything could be done by telephone from Washington—but in Africa a man was on his own. After Robert Kennedy and Chester Bowles had blocked the dying administration's attempt to equip the new African states with Foreign Service officers on the verge of retirement, the President sent to Africa in the next years a group of younger Foreign Service officers, like his old friend Edmund Gullion (to the Congo), leavened by journalists like William Attwood and Edward Korry of *Look* (to Guinea and Ethiopia), scholars like John Badeau (to Egypt) and liberal Democrats with government experience in Truman days like Philip Kaiser, John Ferguson and James Loeb (to Senegal and Mauritania, Morocco and Guinea). Kennedy's concern with Africa necessarily remained marginal, except when, as in the Congo, problems erupted into crisis. But his curiosity was unremitting. He cared very much, for example, about the performance of his African ambassadors and rarely failed to see them when they came home on consultation. "He was really interested in what they thought," as Ralph Dungan once remarked, "and he always wanted to check their judgment against his."

The President's interest was not widely shared in the United States, except by African specialists and, to an increasing degree, by Negro leaders. No one in Congress, for example, showed the concern for Africa that Kennedy himself had shown as Senator. Though Albert Gore of Tennessee kept the Senate Subcommittee on Africa alive for a time, it lapsed into inactivity after his resignation from the chairmanship early in 1963. As one consequence, Kennedy was not able to increase American assistance to Africa as he would have liked. But, as the magazine *West Africa* later put it, the Africans "considered that Mr. Kennedy's political attitudes were even more important than his efforts to aid their economies." And in communicating these political attitudes Kennedy used a weapon more powerful than the most generous aid programs. That weapon was his own personal contacts with African leaders.

2. PRESIDENTIAL DIPLOMACY

Under Eisenhower presidential meetings with foreign leaders had not ordinarily been for the transaction of business; this was left to the Secretary of State and the pros. They were rather for the purpose of generating goodwill—what came to be called "high-level massage." The briefing books the State Department sent to the White House in the early Kennedy days reflected this theory. They were vacuous documents, devoid of the hard facts on which the new President lived. Kennedy tossed them aside; and it took a little while before McGeorge Bundy could persuade State to start giving the President the operational detail. At times it almost seemed to us as if the Department were resolved to prevent the President from discussing anything of importance.

The purely ceremonial aspects of official visits bored Kennedy. With the help of Angier Biddle Duke, his skillful Chief of Protocol, he cut down on the number of full-dress state visits and devised a new category of less formal meetings. The essence for him was, not the warm hand-clasp and the smiling photograph, but private communication and candor. He wanted to find out how foreign leaders saw their problems, to get them to understand something of his own problems and to establish personal relations which could be continued by correspondence. We had the impression that he was sometimes impatient with his European guests, who could be long-winded and self-important. But he went to endless lengths to be friendly to visitors from Latin America, Asia and Africa. Nowhere did his efforts have more striking success than with the Africans. Beginning with Nkrumah of Ghana in March 1961, African leaders flowed through the White House in what appeared an unending stream: eleven in 1961, ten in 1962 and in 1963, when the supply was nearing the point of exhaustion, seven.

They would arrive at the White House, proud, tense and unsure, not knowing what to expect from the head of the most powerful state in the world. Kennedy, with instinctive charm and consideration, put them instantly at ease. For one thing he conveyed an intimate understanding of the force of African nationalism. This was not just put on for Africans. I heard him once explain to President Kekkonen of Finland, "The strongest force in the world is the desire for national independence. . . . That is why I am eager that the United States back nationalist movements, even though it embroils us with our friends in Europe. Mali and Guinea show the power of nationalism to overcome an initial commitment to communism." He talked to Africans as an American and not as a partner of the European colonial powers; and, at the same time, his insight into the African mood enabled him to see African problems, not as outsiders saw them, but as Africans saw them themselves.

He spoke simply and directly, as one world leader talking in confidence to another. He set forth American policy without apology, even when he knew it might disturb or displease his visitor. He made clear his understanding of their determination to stay out of the cold war and made it just as clear that the United States was going to meet its own commitments in the world. At the same time, he treated his visitors as members of the fraternity of working politicians and did not hesitate to discuss the limitations placed on his own action by the Congress or the balance of payments or public opinion: thus "I hope you'll come along with us on Chinese representation; this can't go on forever, but we have to hold the line for another year." Sometimes his candor made the people from State squirm a little; but he knew what he was doing, and his confidence was never betrayed.

He inquired into his visitors' problems with disarming frankness: "Well, now that you've got your independence, aren't you finding that your troubles are just beginning?" He realized that their internal pressures sometimes forced them to do things—of an anti-American sort, for example —which they might rather not do. Indeed, he was the first American President for whom the whole world was, in a sense, domestic politics. He understood the problems of Sékou Touré and Sukarno as Franklin Roosevelt understood the problems of Robert La Follette or Frank Hague.

His knowledge startled his visitors by its sweep and detail. He would mention personalities and issues, cite facts and statistics and comment on past or present in a way which led some of his guests to say afterward that the American President knew more about their countries than they did themselves. When Borg Olivier, the Prime Minister-designate of Malta, came to the White House, Kennedy

inadvertently embarrassed him by questions about the
Knights of St. John and the great siege of Malta which displayed more knowledge than the Maltese leader seemed to
have of the history of his own island. His humor lightened
awkward moments. When Julius Nyerere of Tanganyika, a
Roman Catholic, waited while the Marine Band with a roll of
drums announced his entry into the reception rooms of the
White House, Kennedy leaned toward him and said, "Well,
Mr. President, how does it feel to go into luncheon with
another religious minority politician who made the grade?"
There were never reprimands or homilies: his respect for
the dignity of his visitors was complete. He did not ask
them to do things they could not do nor promise them
things he could not deliver. He gave the impression that
he was looking for areas where he and they could work
together; where disagreement was unavoidable, then let
each side understand the reasons and respect the differences.

He invited their opinions and, whatever the crises on his
desk, heard them out with undivided attention. The African
leaders responded with astonishingly free and open accounts of their uncertainties and hopes. One after another,
they left his presence with admiration for his "sensibility,"
pride in what they now felt to be a special relationship,
a conviction that Kennedy's America, even if it could not
do everything at once, was basically with them, and, most
of all, a fascination with Kennedy himself. "With Kennedy
there were sparks," said Samuel Ibe, a young Nigerian diplomat. "You would meet him and, 'shoo, shoo,' sparks and
electricity would be shooting all over." Hastings Banda,
back in Nyasaland, delivered a great eulogy of the American President at a party rally. The Prime Minister of Sudan,
cherishing a hunting rifle the President had given him,
constantly expressed the wish that Kennedy would go out on
safari with him. Sékou Touré, who had been for a moment
the great Soviet hope in Africa, repeatedly invited him to
Guinea. Kennedy's personal friends soon encircled the continent.

The President's impact was reinforced by the Attorney
General. Robert Kennedy's interest in Africa began when
he headed the American delegation to the independence
celebration of the Ivory Coast in August 1961. He seized
the occasion to have frank talks with Félix Houphouët-
Boigny, the president of the new republic. Houphouët-
Boigny urged him not to give up on Sékou Touré, though
he doubted whether it was worthwhile spending much energy in an effort to reclaim Nkrumah in Ghana. He also

recommended that President Kennedy consult closely with the African leaders on their economic and political problems. Back in Washington, Robert Kennedy became a ready and effective ally for those advancing the claims of African policy. When Houphouët-Boigny visited Washington in 1962 and received a bored reception at the State Department, the Attorney General arranged a special meeting with the President in which the misunderstandings were speedily cleared up. He even talked to nationalist leaders, like Eduardo Mondlane, the political representative of the insurrection movement in Mozambique, when it would have been thought improper for the White House or the State Department to show official interest. Nor did the family concern stop there. Unable to accept Sékou Touré's invitations himself, the President sent Sargent Shriver to Guinea for a couple of visits. No doubt this warm response by the Kennedy clan had a particular appeal for a culture so largely founded on kinship.

3. AFRICA VS. EUROPE

The problem of balancing the relative claims of our NATO allies and the new African states was always tricky. It especially affected our policy in the United Nations, confronting Adlai Stevenson, the State Department and the President with a series of delicate decisions. The vote on the Angola resolutions in March 1961 had liberated the United States from its position of systematic deference to the old colonial powers. Nonetheless, each new issue had to be met on its merits. Some presented hard choices, and the presidential decision was not made easier by the tendency of both Europeanists and Africanists in the State Department to overstate the dreadful consequences which would follow from favoring the other.

Kennedy was thus considerably concerned in the early months of 1961 with his old problem of Algeria. He watched with sympathy de Gaulle's careful and circuitous effort to bring his nation to the acceptance of Algerian independence. When the French generals in Algeria mutinied at the end of April and there seemed for a panicky moment the prospect of a paratroop attack on Paris, Kennedy promptly offered de Gaulle his assistance. The collapse of the revolt permitted de Gaulle to move forward; but in the next months, as France finally began talks with the Algerian nationalists, Tunisia took the opportunity to try to drive the French out of their military base at Bizerte. When the French responded by a large and bloody attack, the matter came before the United Nations. In August a special session of the General Assembly met to consider an Afro-Asian resolution calling for the withdrawal of French armed forces from Tunisian territory.

De Gaulle, of course, pronounced the debate no business of the UN and declined to let France take part. In New York Stevenson felt that we should vote for the Afro-Asian resolution. In Washington the Bureau of European Affairs recommended abstention. When I brought the matter to the President, he thought for a moment and then said, "Everyone forgets how shaky de Gaulle's position is. . . . If the Tunisian affair goes really sour, it might just start a new military revolt. We don't want the ultras to take over France. With all his faults, the General is the only hope for a solution in Algeria. Tell Adlai that our sympathy is with the anti-colonial nations; but their cause won't be helped by the overthrow of de Gaulle, nor will our position in Berlin. Let's sit this one out."

We abstained without undue damage to our position in Africa. Kennedy then asked the State Department to prepare a letter to Habib Bourguiba, the wise president of Tunisia, in order to "reestablish with you a communication which seems to have been partially interrupted by the incidents of Bizerte." When I brought it to him for clearance, he strengthened it by scribbling on the draft: "Standing as my country does close to a holocaust that could destroy the U.S. as well as Europe and much of the East, I have not found it possible to take a public position on this matter satisfactory to you. I regret this greatly, but I am hopeful that you will recognize our difficulties as well as those of your country in these days." Our relations with Tunisia were soon repaired; in another year France was out of Bizerte, Franco-Tunisian relations were restored and Algeria was independent.

The Portuguese colonies were not so easy. Angola, Mozambique and Portuguese Guinea were all in conditions of incipient revolt, and the new African states were determined to help them gain their freedom. Our own capacity to act in this situation, however, was limited by our dependence, or alleged dependence, on the military and naval installations which Portugal made available to us in the Azores. In the summer of 1961, for example, the Joint Chiefs of Staff declared the Azores base essential to American security in case of trouble over Berlin. The problem led to continuous wrangling in Washington—the Bureau of European Affairs vs. the Bureau of African Affairs; the Mis-

sion to the UN vs. the Pentagon—with occasional inter-
polations by such kibitzers as J. K. Galbraith, who enraged the Europeanists by suggesting that they were trading
off Africa for "a few acres of asphalt in the Atlantic," and
by Dean Acheson, who enraged the Africanists by recommending that the United States stop helping draft resolutions on Angola. The Azores lease was due to expire at
the end of 1962, and this gave these discussions a certain
frenetic quality that autumn until Dr. Salazar finally decided to extend American access to the facilities without
formal renewal of the agreement.

This dilemma left us no choice but a moderating policy
on Portuguese questions in the UN—never enough for the
nationalists in Africa and always too much for the Pentagon and Dr. Salazar. We labored to tone down the Afro-
Asian assaults on Portugal; that was why, as Stevenson
tried to explain to Acheson, we took part in the drafting of
resolutions. Thus in 1961 we succeeded in making "self-
determination" the UN goal rather than "independence."
And we consistently opposed the use of sanctions against
Portugal. At the same time, we used private suasion in
Lisbon as well as public argument in the UN in a constant
effort to induce Portugal to reform its colonial methods.

Portugal yielded only imperceptibly under these various
ministrations, though it did agree in the summer of 1963
to talks with African leaders. In the meantime, the failure
of the nationalist insurrections to make much progress
against Portuguese rule led the African delegates to redouble their verbal onslaughts in the UN. The situation
dragged on inconclusively through the Kennedy years, trailing an aura of general dissatisfaction on both sides. Nevertheless Kennedy's effectiveness in making his African visitors understand the American dilemma over the Azores
base limited the harm that restraint on the Portuguese
colonies did to our general position in Africa.

Though without the Azores problem we would have unquestionably moved faster in our policy toward the Portuguese colonies, the middle course did express substantive
conviction as well as tactical necessity. Kennedy always
mistrusted UN resolutions which promised big things but
could not be carried out. He used to quote a Chinese
proverb: "There is a great deal of noise on the stairs,
but nobody comes into the room." He wanted, not hortatory
rhetoric against colonialism, but realistic resolutions which
could help lay the economic, educational and institutional
foundations for self-government. Jonathan B. Bingham, who

handled colonial questions at the UN in 1961 and 1962, set forth this position to the General Assembly in November 1961:

> We would rather see the leaders and peoples of Africa conquer the realities of independence, with all the exertion that this requires, with all of the institution-building that this requires, than to be satisfied with the hollow and sterile image of independence without the reality. . . .
>
> For a nation to have such freedom, two things are necessary. It must have in its own hands, instead of in alien hands, the *right* to decide. And—no less vital—it must have among its people, and among its leaders, the knowledge and experience which alone confer the *ability* to decide.

Similar language, of course, had long been used by the white man as a pretext to deny the Africans their independence. But again the spirit of Kennedy in his personal talks with African leaders rescued the language from its old context and made it the expression of thoughtful concern and friendly counsel.

4. NORTH AFRICA

Once countries had gained their independence, Kennedy believed that the sensible thing was to try to live with the new nations and their new leaders. Not domination or preachment but adjustment and rapprochement seemed to him the fruitful relationship. He saw this as a long-term investment and was ready in the meantime to put up with a certain amount of nonsense.

On July 3, 1962, five years and a day after Kennedy had given his speech in the United States Senate, Algeria became free; and in due course the President took pleasure in sending his confidential Foreign Service consultant of 1957, William J. Porter, to Algiers as ambassador. If independence had come when Kennedy and Porter first discussed the Algerian question, a free Algeria would have had a moderate national government, a functioning economy and a leaning toward the west. But the long war against France had radicalized the political leadership and ravaged the economic and administrative system. Ahmed Ben Bella, who quickly acquired ascendancy in the new Algeria, was a passionate nationalist and socialist presiding over a turbulent and divided land.

Still, even this wilder Algeria had not forgotten the American who had once championed its cause. The National Liberation Front had saluted Kennedy's election in 1960; and in 1962, when Ben Bella made his first major trip outside Algeria, he went straight to Washington. After a cordial meeting with Kennedy, the Algerian leader left more ardent than ever in his enthusiasm. Ben Bella, Ambassador Porter has suggested, thought Kennedy a really good man and "ascribed to Kennedy everything he thought good in the United States: the fight against the big trusts, against the segregationists." Whenever Porter returned to Washington for consultation, Ben Bella charged him with "fraternal greetings" for the President—a message which always entertained Kennedy.

Unfortunately Ben Bella's almost fanatical admiration for the American President did not extend to American foreign policy. When the Algerian leader left Washington, he went on—to Kennedy's surprise and annoyance—to visit Fidel Castro, toward whom he also evidently had fraternal feelings and with whom he promptly joined in a communiqué exhorting the United States to get out of Guantánamo. Kennedy, who had found Ben Bella sincere and congenial, was perplexed by what seemed either hopeless naïveté or calculated insult. In the next months, the Algerian government, in between Ben Bella's fraternal greetings to the American President, applauded the Cubans and the Viet Cong and fulminated against American imperialism.

With his personal stake in the outcome of the Algerian revolution, Kennedy followed Algerian developments with special care. The President used to quiz Porter closely about Ben Bella, even asking him to describe the expressions on the Algerian leader's face when he said the things reported in the dispatches. But Kennedy's disappointment over Ben Bella's erratic behavior did not divert him from his course. He felt that the anti-imperialist extravagance of Algeria was more the result of mood than of doctrine or discipline; that the present state of affairs was not necessarily permanent; that the United States should maintain a presence and help direct Ben Bella's energies toward the welfare of his own people. When Algeria was threatened by mass starvation in the winter of 1962–63, Kennedy rushed in Food for Peace, which ended by feeding one of every three Algerians; indeed, Algerian emergency relief was the largest PL 480 program. In a variety of ways, despite the pinpricks, Kennedy played for the long term. His policy, as Porter once described it, was "to stay in close, keep working and wait for the breaks."

He pursued this policy throughout North Africa. In Habib Bourguiba, who visited Washington in the spring of 1961, Kennedy had a good friend—a relation reinforced by the comradeship of Habib Bourguiba, Jr., as Tunisian ambassador to Washington, with the young men of the

New Frontier. In the case of Libya, Kennedy entertained both the crown prince and the prime minister, though his limitless equability before African politicians did break down, probably for the only time, when the prime minister, his country brimming with oil, made insistent and repeated requests for American economic assistance throughout their meeting. And it was the President's intention, when political conditions permitted, to invite President Nasser of Egypt to the United States.

The Nasser story is more a part of Middle Eastern than of African policy. I had little to do with the Middle East, except as it occasionally impinged on the UN; and I hope that Myer Feldman and Robert Komer, who watched this troubled region for the President, will someday provide their own accounts of one of Kennedy's most interesting experiments in foreign policy. Very early in the administration Bundy and Rostow placed high in a list of problems for the New Frontier the question of whether better relations were possible with the most powerful leader of the Arab world. John Badeau, who had been president of the American University in Cairo and later of the Near East Foundation, went to Cairo as ambassador with general instructions to test out a course of selective cooperation. In August, when Nasser sent an unexpected and lengthy reply to a circular message Kennedy had sent to the Arab chiefs of state the previous spring, a correspondence sprang up between the two Presidents which went on intermittently through the Kennedy years and served as a substitute for a face-to-face encounter.

Middle Eastern policy was complicated not only by Nasser's dreams of empire and by the decay of medieval oligarchies in states like Yemen and Saudi Arabia but also, of course, by the inordinate Arab hatred of Israel. Kennedy believed strongly in America's moral commitment to Israeli security and took steps to strengthen Israel's ability to resist aggression. But he wished to preserve an entrée to Nasser in order both to restrain Egyptian policy toward Israel and to try to work more closely with the modernizing forces in the Arab world. Thus when he recognized the anti-Nasser government in Syria in 1961 and sent Israel the Hawk anti-aircraft missiles in 1962, he took care to inform Nasser in advance what we were doing and why we were doing it—a courtesy which undoubtedly moderated Nasser's response to what he might otherwise have seen as unfriendly acts.

Kennedy's deeper hope, as with Sukarno and Ben Bella,

was to persuade Nasser to concentrate on making progress at home rather than trouble abroad. As in Algeria, our main tool of economic assistance was Food for Peace. For a time the policy of selective cooperation had an encouraging effect. In June 1962, when Nasser wrote Kennedy expressing his appreciation for the PL 480 aid and for a stabilization loan, he agreed with the President that, though the United Arab Republic and the United States had their differences, they could still cooperate. This tacit acceptance of the American interest in a free Israel marked a considerable advance in mutual understanding.

Then the Imam of Yemen died in September 1962, and in the ensuing confusion Nasser backed a military revolution against the Imam's successor. Saudi Arabia took Nasser's intervention as a preliminary to an attack on itself and supported the royalists. Kennedy, fearful that the civil war in Yemen would lead to a larger war between Egypt and Saudi Arabia—a conflict which might involve the United States because of our interests in Saudi oil—decided to accept the revolutionary regime in the hope that it could stabilize the situation in Yemen and begin the job of modernizing that fifteenth-century country. At the same time, he tried to persuade Nasser to withdraw his troops and thereby reassure Saudi Arabia. The British, with their interest in Aden, feared the consolidation of Egyptian influence in Yemen and therefore opposed the revolutionary regime. The matter soon became incredibly entangled, and Kennedy, to Robert Komer's dismay, used to call it, when it was going badly, "Komer's war." In any case, the Yemen affair dominated American relations with Egypt in 1963 and interrupted Kennedy's effort to turn Egyptian energies inward.

5. BLACK AFRICA: SÉKOU TOURÉ AND NKRUMAH

The policy of staying in close, keeping at work and waiting for the breaks had its most notable success in Guinea. Under the influence of Sékou Touré, a left-wing trade union leader, Guinea alone among the former French colonies had voted in 1958 against de Gaulle's idea of transforming the old French empire into a French community. In a fit of irritation, de Gaulle responded by ordering a total French evacuation. He even placed Guinea on an international blacklist, informing the Eisenhower administration, for example, that, if Washington helped this crowd of malcontents, France would be ready to withdraw from NATO. Washington in consequence did not bother to an-

swer the letters subsequently arriving from Guinea requesting modest amounts of aid. In this situation Sékou Touré,
even if he were not a Marxist, had no choice but to turn
east—and, of course, then considering himself a Marxist,
he found this alternative highly agreeable. The Russians,
delighted at the chance to establish themselves on the Atlantic coast of Africa, obliged with an extensive program
of technical assistance. By 1960 Washington had consigned
Guinea to the communist bloc, and such amateur experts
on world communism as Senator Thomas J. Dodd of Connecticut pronounced Sékou Touré a communist operative
beyond hope of redemption.

Kennedy took another view. The fascination with the
break-up of the French empire, which had already involved him in Indochina and Algeria, as well as a desire to
meet the man who had said no to de Gaulle, had led him
in 1959 to seek out Touré when the Guinean leader visited
the United States. Kennedy, who was then speaking in
California, hired a helicopter and conferred with Touré at,
of all places, Disneyland. During the 1960 campaign he repeatedly criticized the Eisenhower administration for its
delay of eight months in sending an ambassador to
Guinea, pointing out that the Russian Ambassador was
there on Independence Day with offers of trade and aid—
"and today Guinea has moved toward the communist bloc
because of our neglect."

There seemed little question that such a movement had
taken place. Touré even refused to receive Eisenhower's
retiring ambassador for a farewell call; in the torrent of
oratory following Lumumba's death, he tried to suggest that
Kennedy was somehow responsible for this crime against
the African people; in April he accepted the Lenin Peace
Prize; and after the Bay of Pigs he affirmed to Castro on
behalf of the people of Guinea "our complete solidarity
and our total support for the cause of your revolution,
which symbolizes the struggle for liberty of all dominated
peoples." Despite all this, Kennedy felt that Sékou Touré
remained a nationalist at heart; and, before William Attwood departed as his ambassador to Conakry, the President
asked him to verify this as best he could.

Attwood found the American position less hopeless than
it seemed from Washington. The Russian aid program, it
turned out, was a great mess. The materials were poor, the
technicians officious and incompetent, the diplomats insistent and patronizing. Returning to Washington in May, Attwood reported a slow disillusionment and recommended a

small American aid program to show Sékou Touré that the United States was willing to go along with genuine non-alignment. Outside the Bureau of African Affairs, the bureaucracy regarded this with disdain as another gust of New Frontier naïveté. Then Robert Kennedy came back from the Ivory Coast and vigorously backed Attwood. The President said, "Bill, tell the AID people I'm for it if they can find the money."

Fearing that, even with Kennedy's endorsement, it would take AID months of paperwork and preparation before anything happened in Guinea, Attwood persuaded the President to send Sargent Shriver to Guinea in June. Shriver and Touré hit it off immediately. Guinea, which had been attacking the Peace Corps as a CIA subsidiary, now invited it into the country; the government radio stopped reviling the United States; and personal relations between Guineans and Americans began to improve. In December, after a clumsy Russian intervention into Guinean politics, Sékou Touré expelled the Soviet Ambassador. By the spring of 1962, American aid was beginning to arrive: food, teachers, money. And, when Touré came to New York in October for the UN General Assembly, the President asked him down to Washington. Kennedy met him at the airport and took him back to the White House, where they talked over the problems of Guinea for an hour in the Cabinet Room. Then Kennedy brought him over to the Mansion, introduced him to Jacqueline and Caroline and gave him a formal luncheon. On his return to Conakry, Sékou Touré reported to his people:

> At the end of our talks with President Kennedy, I and the Guinean delegation expressed our satisfaction to have found in the United States President a man quite open to African problems and determined to promote the American contribution to their happy solution.
> We took this opportunity to congratulate the American Government for the aid which it has so generously granted to Guinea and to express to him our satisfaction regarding the firmness with which the United States struggles against racial discrimination and for the complete integration of the colored people into American society.

From this time on Touré felt that he had a friend at the White House and sent personal messages at the slightest pretext.

The Attwood-Kennedy policy was able to succeed, of course, because it came at the right time. But, if Washington had persisted in its conviction that Guinea was irreclaimable, we would not have been in the position to take advantage of the Soviet errors. Attwood discharged his mission brilliantly despite personal difficulties sadly caused by an attack of polio. Kennedy, greatly admiring, rated him very high among his ambassadors. When he left Guinea in 1963, later moving on to Kenya, James Loeb went to Conakry and carried forward his work.

In the case of Nkrumah of Ghana, the new American policy, as Houphouët-Boigny predicted to Robert Kennedy, found harder going. Relations between Ghana and the United States had started downhill after September 1960, when Secretary of State Herter ("somewhat unwisely, I think," Kennedy said at the time) described Nkrumah "very definitely as moving toward the Soviet bloc" and when neither Herter nor Eisenhower received Nkrumah who had come to New York for the UN. By the time Kennedy's ambassador arrived in Accra at the end of January, the Ghanian cabinet met to consider whether he should be allowed to present his credentials at all. The murder of Lumumba brought a well-organized outburst of anti-American rioting, following which Nkrumah served as the gracious host for Leonid Brezhnev, the president of the Soviet Union.

At the same time, there remained one great foothold for the west in Ghana, and this was the project, originally conceived by the British colonial administration, for a dam on the Volta River. As Commander Robert Jackson, chairman of the Gold Coast Development Commission, had outlined its possibilities in 1955, a Volta dam would not only create a great lake to help meet internal needs for irrigation, fish and transport, but could generate hydroelectric power and make possible the installation of a smelter to convert Ghana's bauxite resources into aluminum; it would be the key to Ghana's economic future.

The British and Canadian aluminum industry had considered aiding the Volta Dam until the increase in the British bank rate in 1958 made participation too costly. Then Nkrumah appealed to Washington, where Douglas Dillon called the project to the attention of Edgar Kaiser and Chad Calhoun of Kaiser Industries. After study, the Kaiser people pronounced the dam economically feasible. In the course of 1960 the United States government held out for a moment the possibility of participation, and Kaiser and Calhoun tried to put together a consortium of aluminum companies to back the project. But, as relations with Ghana grew worse, most of the group, except Reynolds Metals, withdrew, leaving Kaiser with 90 per cent of the consortium.

In the beginning of 1961, there still remained the hope of getting support from the new administration. Calhoun talked with George Ball and Abram Chayes at State and asked Barbara Ward Jackson, the British economist and wife of Commander (now Sir) Robert Jackson to raise the matter with Kennedy. Lady Jackson, who was herself deeply interested in the economic and political development of Ghana, did so at once. Kennedy was fond of Barbara Ward, and her counsel reinforced his own instinct to go ahead with the project. In the meantime, word arrived that Nkrumah was coming to New York for the UN. Barbara urged the President to see him. She described Nkrumah as temperamental, mercurial and caught in the shifting sands of the cold war, but argued that, if he could be kept neutral and close to the United Nations, much could be gained. "It is worth a risk and could conceivably be a triumph."

Kennedy agreed, and Nkrumah appeared at the White House early in March. The visit was a success. The Kennedys liked him, and Nkrumah was so moved that on the plane to New York he scrawled Kennedy a warm personal note on a yellow lined pad expressing his pleasure at the meeting and his hope for future friendship. In July Kennedy wrote him that the United States planned to go ahead with the Volta project.

In the meantime, Nkrumah had set forth on a swing around the communist circuit. With each statement in each new communist capital he seemed to move further from a position of non-alignment. When he reached Peking in September, his communiqué after a talk with Mao actually included some of the same phrases he had scribbled to Kennedy on the plane in March: the sands of the cold war were indeed constantly shifting. The Iron Curtain tour resulted in so apparently fervent an embrace of the communists as to raise new questions about the Volta Dam at just the moment when Abram Chayes had brought the agreement to the point of signature. Nor did Nkrumah strengthen his case by undertaking new measures of internal repression on his return to Ghana.

Kennedy now began to wonder whether it was appropriate to invest a large share of the limited funds set aside for Africa in a single project in a single country— above all, in a country which was not providing stirring examples either of liberalism at home or non-alignment in the world. Congress was increasingly unhappy; Albert Gore and Kennedy's old African subcommittee were hostile to

American support for the dam. Public opinion was critical; Robert Kennedy was opposed; even Adlai Stevenson suggested that aid to the project be suspended. Only Chayes, Bowles, Williams and Fredericks at State were solidly in favor. On the other hand, Kaiser and Calhoun, whom Kennedy sent to Accra in October for tough talk with Nkrumah, returned with his cordial assurances that Ghana would stay on a course of true neutrality; and a circular inquiry to our other African embassies showed that most African governments, including some of Nkrumah's political enemies, hoped we would go ahead. Kennedy now sent a special mission to Ghana, headed by Clarence Randall, a steel magnate of profound and well-publicized conservatism, and including Chayes. The purpose was partly to tell more home truths to Nkrumah and partly to provide political cover for a decision to proceed with the project. (I noted: "Typical of JFK's administrative methods: if he wanted the mission to veto the project, he would have sent Chester Bowles.")

At the same time, the British weighed in heavily. Macmillan wrote Kennedy in November that he did not believe Nkrumah had yet gone over to the Russians. If the United States were now to pull out, Macmillan said, the Africans would regard it as an attempt to use financial power to dictate the national policy of independent African states; the Russians would move in; and cancellation might have the same consequences in West Africa that John Foster Dulles's repudiation of the Aswan Dam had in Egypt in 1956. But, if the west backed the Volta Dam, it would be convincing proof to the Africans, who were tending to regard the Soviet system as peculiarly well designed to bring about industrialization, that industrial development could be combined with freedom.

The President, as usual, was interested in the long run. He probably had made up his mind early in the year to support the project. He was impressed by Barbara Ward's several interventions, and he had high regard for Edgar Kaiser as an aggressive and intelligent businessman. At the lowest point—in September—Kennedy and Edgar Kaiser even discovered that each had recently received a phone call from his famous father with the same complaint: "What in hell are you up to with that communist Nkrumah?" The President well understood that cancellation of the Volta Dam now would set back his whole African policy, while support would dramatize the new American attitude toward non-alignment throughout Africa. He hoped that this policy would preserve a positive American presence within Ghana and that Nkrumah's nationalism would in the end prevail over his leanings toward the east. He made the final decision to go ahead in November. When the National Security Council was informed of the decision, the President said, "The Attorney General has not yet spoken, but I can feel the hot breath of his disapproval on the back of my neck." The agreement was signed in Accra in January. The total American government investment—all in the form of loans—amounted to somewhat over $40 million.

The policy did not allow for the vagaries of Nkrumah. The Ghanian leader proceeded in the next years to transform his country in the direction less of African socialism than of African totalitarianism. The *Osagyefo* or Redeemer, as he called himself (or "His Messianic Dedication" or "The Nation's Pillar of Fire and Fount of Honor"), established a dictatorship, crushed all opposition, turned violently against the west and set himself up as a virtual deity. Kennedy watched these developments with deepening concern. He followed Ghana with keen interest; one morning a desk officer at State answered his phone to find himself talking directly to the President about the capsid, a blight threatening Ghana's cocoa crop. In 1963 Kennedy evidently wished that he had been tougher in the first place. By this time he instructed AID to extend no more long-term credits to Ghana. Yet even then his view was that the final beneficiaries of the Volta Dam would be not the government of Kwame Nkrumah but the people of Ghana.

6. THE CONGO

Of all the African problems, the one that most commanded the President's attention was the Congo. Independence had descended like a hurricane on the unprepared country in July 1960. In a few days the new state was in chaos: the Force Publique had mutinied; Katanga and other provinces were proclaiming their independence; Belgian paratroopers were coming back to restore order. In desperation Prime Minister Lumumba appealed to the United Nations. On July 14 the Security Council voted to provide the central government with enough military assistance to pacify the country.

Lumumba also cabled N. S. Khrushchev "to watch hourly over the situation"; and Khrushchev responded in his own way. By September several hundred Soviet 'technicians'

were in Leopoldville, Russian military equipment was going
to Lumumba's army, and communist sympathizers were
moving into the central government. Lumumba obviously
preferred this to assistance from the United Nations; and in
consequence President Joseph Kasavubu dismissed him
early in September. In another week Kasavubu, closing the
Soviet and Czech embassies, placed his main reliance on the
UN peace-keeping force. The Russians, having just missed
establishing a powerful military and political presence in
this rich, large and strategic land, now turned savagely
against the UN. Khrushchev, still watching hourly over the
situation, vetoed subsequent Security Council action,
launched violent attacks against Hammarskjöld and soon
advanced the *troika* proposal. He accompanied this barrage by vigorous support for Lumumba and, after Lumumba's arrest and murder, for his heir, Antoine Gizenga.

In January 1961 Kennedy inherited a Congo still in
chaos, divided among the Kasavubu government in Leopoldville, the Gizenga group in Stanleyville and the pro-
Belgian secessionist regime of Moise Tshombe in Elisabethville. Overshadowing everything was the prospect that Soviet
meddling in the chaos might lead to a Russian base in the
heart of Africa. From the start the new President had a
simple and constant view: that, unless the United Nations
filled the vacuum in the Congo, there would be no alternative but a direct Soviet-American confrontation. As
one crisis after another flared up in the months to come,
he used to say that, if we didn't have the UN operation,
the only way to block Soviet domination of the Congo
would be to go in with our own forces. The UN could
not bring the great powers together in the Congo, but at
least it could keep them apart.

This policy would not work, however, unless the central
government in Leopoldville possessed authority. It was here
that the secession of Katanga assumed its significance. Katanga, containing the bulk of the country's mineral wealth,
produced nearly half the tax revenues and foreign exchange earnings of the Congo. In Elisabethville, Tshombe,
a shrewd, humorous and cynical politician, backed by the
Belgian Union Minière du Haut Katanga, was using the revenue from the copper mines to hire white mercenaries and
mount propaganda campaigns in America and Europe.
Moreover, the example of Katanga was stimulating secessionist dreams elsewhere in the Congo.

A unified Congo therefore seemed the condition for the
success of the UN policy. Moreover, the question of Katanga
was becoming a crucial test of American intentions through-

out Africa. Every new state was meticulously scrutinizing our actions to detect evidences of support for Tshombe, whom the rest of Africa regarded as the white colonists' black man. "If we don't have a Congo policy," as Wayne Fredericks remarked, "we don't have an African policy."

In the summer of 1961 the Congolese parliament elected a coalition government under a sober trade unionist named Cyrille Adoula. At the request of the new government, the UN forces now began action to end the secession. UN troops took over key installations in Elisabethville and, as they extended their operations in September, they encountered resistance from Tshombe's forces. Several days of desultory fighting followed.

The outbreak of hostilities brought down a storm of criticism on the UN. Great Britain and France both thought that the UN army had exceeded the charter in conducting what seemed to be offensive operations. In New York an extremely effective lobby, run by a Belgian named Michael Struelens, sent out dramatic accounts of what it called Katanga's fight for self-determination. Soon the American Committee for Aid to Katanga Freedom Fighters described Katanga as "the Hungary of 1961," and a number of Senators, especially Dodd of Connecticut, propagated the gospel in Washington. Hammarskjöld, concerned by the fighting, flew to the Congo to arrange a cease-fire and promote negotiations between Leopoldville and Elisabethville. This was his last mission.

In the meantime, Edmund Gullion arrived in the Congo in August as Kennedy's new ambassador. A Kentuckian, who had grown up amidst family recollections of the American Civil War, he saw the Congo, like the United States a century before, poised between nationhood and disintegration. If the Katanga secession were not ended, then, in Gullion's view, the Congo would break up and the communists would pick up most of the pieces. This was also the fear of Williams and Fredericks in the Bureau of African Affairs and of Stevenson and Cleveland on the UN side. The Bureau of European Affairs, on the other hand, shared the British and French doubts about the UN action. As for the high command of State, it regarded the Congo problem with gloomy suspicion. Rusk, it seemed, thought about it as little as possible; Harriman, who had been favorably impressed by Tshombe after a meeting in Geneva, dissented from the prevailing policy; and, though George Ball defended the policy in an exceedingly able speech—the only sustained exposition of the Congo problem from the seventh floor of the State Department during the thirty months of the crisis—he had moments of wariness and reservation. Nor was the White House staff wholeheartedly in favor of the UN action. But Kennedy, with his old confidence in Gullion, subdued occasional doubts to give consistent support to the UN policy. He was backing the UN, as he once explained to Macmillan, as the best insurance against the conflict of great powers in the Congo. Our own national experience, he added, demonstrated that, if a compact of government was to endure, it must provide the central authority with at least the power to tax and the exclusive power to raise armies; we could not argue with the Congolese to the contrary.

Hostilities continued in the Congo despite a nominal UN cease-fire until in mid-December 1961 Tshombe sent Washington a message requesting the President's help in arranging a meeting with Adoula. Kennedy promptly appointed Gullion his personal representative and dispatched his own plane to fly the antagonists to a 'neutral' site at Kitona. He was determined to shift the conflict from a military to a political context, and his pressure resulted in the signing in January of the Kitona agreement in which Tshombe accepted the authority of the central government.

Gullion, however, remained skeptical. He felt that Tshombe was playing for time and would not abide by the agreement. This forecast turned out to be right. Tshombe, hoping that Struelens, the Belgian mining companies and the British might work a change in American policy, began systematically to evade the accord. He even wanted to lobby in Washington himself, a visit discouraged by the State Department. (This decision roused the ire of Arthur Krock of the *New York Times*. Krock was a mainstay of the Metropolitan Club, notorious for its exclusion of Negroes, and Kennedy offered a deal: "I'll give Tshombe a visa and Arthur can give him a dinner at the Metropolitan Club.")

During the summer of 1962 British, Belgian and American officials worked together on a new unification plan which U Thant put into final form and sponsored in September. Once again Tshombe accepted the plan and once again stalled on its execution. Gullion now began to feel that the solution was to unleash the UN troops and let them destroy Tshombe's army. But Ralph Dungan and Carl Kaysen, who were following the Congo for the White House, had become openly critical of deeper American involvement in the Congo. They doubted whether a communist takeover was still an imminent threat, even if it had been in

1961, and they regarded the conflict as essentially an internal matter; as someone put it, "Every nation has a right to its own War of the Roses." I must confess that I inclined toward this view myself.

But the President was still determined to use American influence to bring about unification. Fearing, however, that neither his European allies nor American public opinion would countenance a renewal of the UN war against Katanga, he bent every effort to achieve a political solution. To this end he persuaded Spaak of Belgium to endorse the U Thant plan and sent George McGhee to the Congo to urge Tshombe to comply and thereby avoid a military confrontation. McGhee found Tshombe contemptuous of the Americans and confident of his own strength. Matters dragged unhappily on, with the Adoula government growing feebler every day, till the time limit which U Thant had attached to his plan expired in December. Tshombe now denounced the plan and declaimed, with flourishes, about a "scorched earth" policy. On Christmas Eve his troops resumed the harassment of the UN forces. After four days of accepting Katangan fire without retaliation, the UN army received U Thant's reluctant permission to respond.

Things were tense in the White House in the few days after Christmas. There was strong pressure throughout Washington to stop the UN forces from taking the offensive, while forceful cables were arriving from Gullion at Leopoldville saying that, if we did so, it would mean the end of American influence in the Congo and drive the central government (even if without Adoula) to accept Soviet assistance. But the fighting around Elisabethville suddenly acquired a momentum of its own. Before we really knew what was happening, Tshombe's resistance collapsed. It all occurred so quickly that it outstripped both instructions from the UN headquarters in New York and any revolt in western public opinion as well as any intervention by Moscow. I do not know what Kennedy would have done if the fighting had stretched out. But he had already decided to lend American fighter planes to the UN force if they were requested; and this suggests that he was ready, if necessary, to go very far down the military road to secure a unified Congo.

The Katanga secession thus came to an end. There remained the problems of reconstruction and these were overwhelming. During 1963 Kennedy kept up his interest both in economic assistance to the Congo and in the extension of the UN military presence; he secured the latter from a

U Thant highly dubious about the continued financial drain on the UN. But, in time, the Adoula government fell, and in another year Tshombe, who had fled the country in June 1963, renounced his secessionism and returned as Prime Minister of the unified Congo. With impressive agility, Tshombe, having lost his principle, at least recovered what he evidently valued a good deal more—his power. It was an ironic denouement—as if, after having been beaten in the Civil War, Jefferson Davis had returned as president of the triumphant American Union.

The Congo policy did more, however, than simply settle a constitutional argument and preserve the Congo as a nation. It gave the United Nations its greatest success in peace-keeping and its greatest effort in technical assistance (though at a cost, for the expense of the Congo operations led to a UN financial crisis, relieved for a moment by the UN bond issue of 1963 but at a later moment threatening the very existence of the organization). More than that, it averted a possible Soviet-American clash in the heart of Africa. Above all, it consolidated the growing confidence of the new African states in the American President.

7. THE STRUGGLE AGAINST APARTHEID

Of all the preoccupations of African nationalism, the most obsessive was with South Africa, where *apartheid*—the policy of systematic exclusion of Africans and Asians from the life of the community—was becoming each year more cruel and abhorrent. Blocked from doing anything about apartheid on the spot, the other African states had long since appealed to the United Nations, which for some years had responded by passing resolutions of exhortation and condemnation. This ritualistic exercise had no effect on South Africa, and by 1961 the other African states were concluding that something more was required. The African resolutions of that year therefore demanded political and economic sanctions against apartheid. But even Asian nations considered this an extreme use of UN power, and the resolution as finally voted left it to individual states to consider such action as was open to them.

As South Africa, far from showing any inclination to abandon its practices, proceeded to tighten its system more each year, the question of sanctions was bound to recur. In the autumn of 1962, after more repression, the African states put in a new resolution calling on UN members to break their political and economic relations with South Africa and even asking the Security Council to consider expelling

South Africa from the UN if it did not change its policies.

The United States had joined regularly in the ceremonial condemnation of apartheid. We also sought through diplomatic channels to persuade the South African government of the hopelessness of its course. An *aide mémoire* to Pretoria in September 1961 thus recorded our inability to cooperate with South Africa in ways which would lend support to apartheid. But a program of UN sanctions presented other questions; and the 1962 resolution embodying this program was one of those unrealistic declarations, at once grandiose and ineffectual, which made Kennedy so impatient. So long as South Africa's major trading partners declined to participate, for example, the call for an economic boycott would be meaningless. I worked with Ambassador Francis Plimpton on the speech he gave to the General Assembly in November explaining our opposition to this resolution, and the following passage was a simple paraphrase of words spoken to me by the President:

Would the passage of a resolution recommending sanctions bring about the practical result we seek?

We do not believe this would bring us closer to our objective—the abandonment of *apartheid* in South Africa. We see little value in a resolution which would be primarily a means for a discharge of our emotions, which would be unlikely to be fully implemented and which calls for measures which could be easily evaded by the country to which they are addressed—with the result of calling into question the whole efficacy of the sanction process.

We doubted, moreover, whether the provisions of Chapter VII of the Charter, on which the appeal for sanctions relied, applied to the South African problem. Because of both the cogency in these arguments and the basic confidence in Kennedy's purposes, our refusal to support sanctions in 1962 was readily accepted by the Africans, though the General Assembly passed the resolution by a heavy majority.

We knew, however, that the matter would come up with fresh intensity in 1963. The first all-African association, the Organization of African Unity, met at Addis Ababa in May and laid plans for a new campaign of pressure against South Africa and Portugal. The OAU called, in effect, for the United States to choose between Africa and the colonial powers. After the meeting, friendly African leaders like Houphouët-Boigny and Nyerere warned us that in the case of South Africa we could no longer rest on purely verbal condemnation of apartheid. Reflecting on these developments, Mennen Williams wrote a memorandum in mid-June arguing that we must now prepare to back up disapproval with action. The indicated area, in his view, was the sale of arms.

In June 1962, in connection with the establishment of a United States military tracking station in South Africa, we had agreed to sell South Africa arms for use against communist aggression; this limitation was meant to exclude arms which could be used to enforce apartheid, but the distinction was not always clear, and the partial embargo had proved ineffective. Williams now recommended that we examine the possibility of moving to a full embargo, pointing out that even this would fall far short of the sanctions voted in 1962 by the General Assembly. A few days later Adlai Stevenson wrote Kennedy in similar vein: "It seems clear that we are approaching a decisive situation from which the Africans will draw conclusions about the long-run nature of our policies."

The proposal of a total arms embargo enountered instant opposition in the upper levels of the State Department. One high official argued that it would gain us only a transitory political truce with the African leaders, who would be satisfied with nothing less than a full economic embargo, and that it would lose us the tangible advantages of our present cooperation with South Africa on a wide range of defense matters. An even higher official suggested that, if we embarked on the policy of sanctions against nations whose internal arrangements we disapproved, we must logically end by severing relations with perhaps half the existing community of states. The question, as this officer saw it, was whether we should precipitate crises in relations with other nations over such issues or work doggedly and persistently toward a decent world community within the existing international structure. We were not, he said, the self-elected gendarmes for the political and social problems of other countries.

These were not easy questions; and they involved, of course, the Portuguese colonies as well as South Africa. The choice seemed almost to be between the military risk of losing the Azores and the South African tracking stations and the political risk of losing Africa. The Portuguese and South African cases were, however, separable; and, of the two, the Portuguese problem was the more difficult.

Kennedy, who hoped to present a test ban treaty to the Senate that summer, had to take into account the possibility that the loss of the Azores, on top of a test ban, might open the way to a Republican attack on the administration for alleged neglect of vital national interests. He made this concern very clear in a meeting in the Cabinet Room on July 18 to consider our African policy in the UN. Why, he asked, should we take the initiative in pressing a resolution on Portugal? What if we hung back, did nothing and let nature take its course? He hated, he said, to have the United States become the scapegoat. We could not afford to lose the Azores with the test ban coming up. Let us not try to shepherd everyone around. Let the Portuguese Foreign Minister find out for himself how bad things were. We should not take the lead nor give the impression that we could do much for him—or would do much against him. He asked Stevenson what the probable French attitude would be, and Adlai said that France, as usual, would seek the best of both worlds. The President said, "Well, let us try that this time."

But South Africa was a different matter; and, indeed, pressure here could do something in African eyes to make up for restraint in the case of Portugal. I had brought the State Department debate to the attention of the Attorney General, and Robert Kennedy had raised the South African problem with Robert McNamara. The question of the choice between the military and political risks had not been presented to McNamara before. He promptly said that the South African decision should be made on political, not on military, grounds—a view which he soon registered formally with Rusk.

Still the prospect of a total UN arms embargo troubled the President and the Secretary of State as setting a precedent for collective sanctions which might lead the UN down a road imperiling its very existence. Instead, the Department favored a call upon UN states to refrain from supplying arms which could be used to suppress the African population. Then Kennedy, in a brilliant stroke, went further and proposed a unilateral declaration that as a matter of national policy the United States would sell no additional arms to South Africa after the first of the year, so long as South Africa practiced apartheid. On August 2 Stevenson announced this decision in the Security Council. Five days later he cast the American vote for a resolution calling on all states "to cease forthwith the sale and shipment of arms, ammunition of all types and military vehicles to South Africa." Britain and France abstained. This action could not long satisfy the insatiable African demand for stronger measures against apartheid; but it preserved the new African faith in American policy.

At the same time, developments within the United States

were further increasing African confidence in Kennedy. The distance between the American and African Negro had narrowed greatly since 1956. By 1962 American Negro leaders were meeting at Arden House to frame their recommendations on African policy, and African politicians were reading bulletins from Oxford and Birmingham as if they were local news. The acceleration of the American civil rights struggle cast Kennedy himself more and more as the champion of the American Negro against his traditional oppressors. The American President's speeches about freedom and justice and his use of American troops to protect Negro rights made a deep impression in Africa. Azikiwe of Nigeria wrote Kennedy in the summer of 1963: "I congratulate you on your efforts to bring peace to your people and wish you God's guidance in the struggle to overcome racial segregation." "I thank President Kennedy, the young and dynamic President of your country," said President Léon M'Ba of Gabon in dedicating a new American chancellery in Libreville, "for the great campaign which he has undertaken—and it is a difficult one—against segregation. . . . The United States cannot do otherwise because it is the defender of liberty, equality and fraternity, and because it is the great friend of all of the nations of the world."

The struggle against segregation at home gave substance to our condemnations of apartheid in the United Nations and helped the Africans accept our reasoned objection to sanctions. But, more than this, it made Africans perceive the United States for a moment as "the defender of liberty, equality and fraternity." The American President's gallant leadership in the civil rights fight sealed the vast regard and affection for him in African hearts.

XXII

THE WORLD OF DIVERSITY

KENNEDY'S THIRD WORLD POLICY—the policy of helping the new nations to strength and independence—involved more than a change in American attitudes toward colonialism and non-alignment. For the travail of nationhood required above all economic and social progress. To throw serious weight behind the independence movement, the President had to redesign our existing programs of economic assistance, devise new instruments of social betterment and infuse the whole effort with a fresh idealism.

American assistance to foreign nations had gone through a number of phases since the Second World War. Immediately after the war, during the UNRRA period, foreign aid went mostly for humanitarian purposes. At the end of the forties, in the era of the Marshall Plan, it went for the reconstruction of developed economies shattered by the war. In the fifties attention shifted to the underdeveloped countries of Asia, and aid went mainly for military assistance. This was for several reasons. The Korean War gave priority to the military aspect of the communist offensive in the third world. John Foster Dulles's diplomacy, moreover, conceived aid in large measure as a means of enlisting allies and establishing strong military positions (as in Laos). And the annual agony of getting the aid bill through Congress was somewhat eased when it could be presented as a hard, anti-communist, military program.[1]

In the meantime, the aid organization had been going steadily downhill since the great days of the Marshall Plan. As the change of venue increased its problems, changes of leadership reduced its capacity to deal with them. Moreover, once the original élan waned, the aid effort began to suffer from bureaucratosclerosis. The Economic Cooperation Administration of 1948–51, so splendidly managed by Paul Hoffman and Averell Harriman, thus passed through a succession of phases, each more pallid than the last—the Mutual Security Administration in 1951, the Foreign Operations Administration in 1953, the International Cooperation Administration in 1955. The aid agency had eight different chiefs in the eight Eisenhower years, one of whom had not even believed in foreign aid, or at least had voted against it in Congress. By 1960 foreign aid policy had been static for nearly a decade, in its conceptions as well as its programs. ICA's main responsibility was a far-flung but random program of technical assistance. This continuation of Truman's Point Four had become a bits-and-pieces operation—help to an agricultural college here, to a rural

[1] This process of letting political necessity shape the aid program had actually begun in the last Truman years. In 1951, Harriman, with whom I had worked in Paris in 1948 on the Marshall Plan, called me to Washington to help on the President's aid message. There I first met David E. Bell, Richard Neustadt and Harlan Cleveland and participated with them in the invention of the concept of 'defense support'—a means of bringing in economic aid which could be justified as militarily essential.

development project there, to a school somewhere else. In addition, ICA occasionally doled out funds to support the budgets of shaky governments or achieve other short-term political results. "They ran it," one New Frontiersman said of ICA, "as if it were a country store." It was a tired organization, going faithfully through assigned motions but lacking coherence or urgency. A vague but perceptible malaise about the whole effort was beginning to infect Congress and the country.

1. NEW DIRECTIONS IN FOREIGN AID

In the meantime, a new analysis of the aid problem was emerging from the universities and the foundations. At the start, development had been seen as a relatively self-contained economic process, calling only for the injection of capital and technical skill [2] into a dormant economy. In time economists began to see that development had to be studied in a broader institutional and cultural context. The substantial increase of output and living standards, it was becoming evident, required the modernization of entire social structures and ways of thought and life—and for this capital was not enough. "It is sometimes easier to build a million-ton steel plant," as Kusum Nair wrote of the Indian experience, ". . . than to change a man's outlook on such matters as the use of irrigation water, fertilizers and contraceptives." [3]

As in the case of military strategy, the new approach was most fully explored along the banks of the Charles River. Here a group of economists at Harvard and the Massachusetts Institute of Technology were evolving a comprehensive development process. They all, for example, had been exposed to Keynesianism in New Deal days. While Keynes himself had written about mature economies, his analysis supplied a framework for an approach to underdevelopment, because it identified strategic relationships within the economy, as between savings and investment and between the national budget and the level of economic activity. Another common experience was wartime work in such agencies as the Office of Strategic Services (Edward S. Mason, Walt Rostow, Carl Kaysen) or the Strategic Bombing Survey (J. K. Galbraith), where economists, whether in order to pick out bombing targets or to assess the signifi-

[2] Odiously termed 'know-how' in the bureaucracy.
[3] Kusum Nair, *Blossoms in the Dust: The Human Element in Indian Development* (London, 1961), xxiii.

cance of the damage wrought, had to think in terms of
leverage points within the economic system. Both depression and war thus forced attention on the dynamics of
whole economies. Some of the Cambridge group later
worked in the Marshall Plan (Lincoln Gordon); others took
part in Ford Foundation and other development missions
in the fifties (Mason, Galbraith, David Bell). By the late
fifties the study of development economics centered in
the seminar organized at Harvard by Galbraith, with the
later collaboration of Mason and Bell, and in the work
carried on by Max Millikan, Rostow, P. N. Rosenstein-
Rodan and others at the MIT Center for International
Studies.

Out of this there came the argument that the true role of
foreign aid was neither military nor technical assistance
but the organized promotion of national development. Millikan and Rostow made an early statement of this viewpoint
in a book of 1957, *A Proposal—Key to a More Effective
Foreign Policy;* and Rostow gave the idea its historical
rationale three years later in *The Stages of Economic
Development.* The Charles River analysis made several
contributions of great significance. First of all, it offered
the aid program what it had long lacked—specific criteria
for assistance. The goal, the Charles River economists
said, was to enable underdeveloped nations, in Rostow's
phrase, to "take off" into self-sustaining economic growth.
This, they believed, was feasible for most countries; and,
when it was reached, the need for special external assistance would end. Next they pointed out that non-economic as well as economic factors determine growth. Thus,
in addition to the familiar range of economic issues—
industrialization, agricultural methods, sources of energy,
the internal market, inflation, balance of payments and so
on—they brought in structural change, land reform, the
roles of the public sector and of private entrepreneurship,
political development and other social and cultural adjustments required, as Millikan put it, "to reduce the explosive-
ness of the modernization process." Both economic and
non-economic factors were to be subsumed under national
development plans. The emphasis on national development
was not intended to divorce foreign aid from the political
interests of the United States. But it looked to long-term
rather than short-term political effects. In this view,
foreign aid, instead of being a State Department slush
fund to influence tactical situations, should aim at the
strategic goals of a stronger national independence, an in-

creased concentration on domestic affairs, greater democracy and a long-run association with the west.

All this, it must be confessed, had occasionally a certain blandness. It sometimes made the process sound a little too easy and continuous. Economic development, for example, did not infallibly make for social stability or political democracy; and, while this was duly noted, one missed in the analysis a sense of the savage tensions in developing countries as traditional structures broke down and released new anxieties and furies. Thus most of the Cambridge thinkers wanted to tame the ordeal of land reform, making it gradual and responsible, accompanying it by supervised credit and agricultural extension services. They declined to recognize that its essential value might come precisely from the revolutionary effect it had on the distribution of wealth and power, even if this meant the discomfiture of landlords or the reduction of output. One missed too a sense of the hopelessly widening gap between the poor and the rich nations which was transforming Harlan Cleveland's revolution of rising expectations into a revolution of raging envies.

There was a sharper feeling for the discontinuities of development in an influential essay which Galbraith published in *Foreign Affairs* in April 1961. Pointing out that capital assistance alone could not do the job, Galbraith laid heavy emphasis on four other things as equally crucial: a substantial degree of education within the country; a substantial measure of social justice; a reliable apparatus of public administration; and a purposeful theory of national planning. The stress on education assumed particular importance in the next years. "A dollar or a rupee invested in the intellectual improvement of human beings," as Galbraith said later in India, "will regularly bring a greater increase in national income than a dollar or a rupee devoted to railways, dams, machine tools or other tangible goods." The stress on country planning and social reform similarly became central, especially in Latin America.

The Charles River approach represented a very American effort to persuade the developing countries to base their revolutions on Locke rather than Marx. Perhaps this was a dream, but it was not impossible of fulfillment in all countries. Certainly it represented an immense improvement over the philosophy of the country store. It gave our economic policy toward the third world a rational design and a coherent purpose. It sought to remove our assistance from the framework of the cold war and relate it to the needs of nations struggling for their own political and economic fulfillment. It laid out fields for research and priorities for action. Its spirit was generous and humane. It may have fallen short of the ferocities of the situation. But, given the nature of our institutions and values, it was probably the best we could do.

2. KENNEDY AND FOREIGN AID

In the late fifties a few people in the Eisenhower administration, influenced partly by the Millikan-Rostow book of 1957 but even more by their own experience, were growing dissatisfied with the technical assistance preoccupations of ICA. Within ICA itself middle-level officials wanted more emphasis on capital for development. The case for change was strengthened in 1957 when Douglas Dillon returned from the Paris embassy to become Under Secretary of State for Economic Affairs. Dillon's energy and imagination, combined with pressure from liberal Democrats in Congress, led in 1958 to the Development Loan Fund (DLF), authorized to offer foreign countries capital assistance for development projects, and, two years later, to the Inter-American Development Bank with its Social Progress Trust Fund. But the DLF received only a limited appropriation, and the Dillon of that day recoiled from such heresies as country planning. Moreover, since the congressional advocates of DLF insisted that it be set up as an independent corporation in order to avoid being dragged down in the ICA quagmire, it had little impact on ICA philosophy or performance.

The Charles River economists had their more direct influence on Kennedy who was, after all, their Senator and accustomed to consulting them on other matters. As the decade progressed. Kennedy's interest in aid problems had steadily increased. His concern with India soon led him to larger reflections about the challenge of modernization. He readily accepted the Cambridge thesis that the American interest would be best served by the development of strong and independent states. He knew that money was essential but insisted repeatedly that it was not enough. "If we undertake this effort in the wrong spirit," he said, "or for the wrong reasons, or in the wrong way, then any and all financial measures will be in vain." Along with capital, he wanted education and social change. The political payoff, in his view, would come in the long run and as a result of other things than aid appropriations. He doubtless agreed with Machiavelli: "The friendship which is gained by purchase and not through grandeur and nobility of spirit is bought and not secured."

He also had a deepening sense of the urgency of the

aid effort. In 1959, after mentioning the national preoccupation with the missile gap, he called attention to another gap which, he said, "constitutes an equally clear and present danger to our security"—the economic gap. By this he meant "the gap in living standards and income and hope for the future . . . between the stable, industrialized nations of the north, whether they are friends or foes, and the overpopulated, under-invested nations of the south, whether they are friends or neutrals."

It is this gap which presents us with our most critical challenge today. It is this gap which is altering the face of the globe, our strategy, our security, and our alliances, more than any current military challenge. And it is this economic challenge to which we have responded most sporadically, most timidly, and most inadequately.

The Eisenhower administration's approach to foreign aid, he said, was helter-skelter, fragmentary and ineffectual. "The heart of any solution," he continued, "must be a substantial, long-term program of productive loans to underdeveloped areas from a fully capitalized central fund." The idea behind the Development Loan Fund was right; but the DLF "has never fulfilled the barest intentions, much less the long-range visions, of its architects here in the Senate." Unless it received sufficient resources and authority, we could expect in our aid undertakings "a continuing of *ad hoc* crisis expenditures—a further diffusion and dilution of our effort—a series of special cases and political loans . . . a lack of confidence and effort in the underdeveloped world—and a general pyramiding of overlapping, standardless, incentiveless, inefficient aid programs."

Kennedy's interregnum task force on foreign economic policy renewed this indictment. George Ball was chairman; and Cambridge, with Millikan and Rostow, Galbraith and Gordon, was well represented among the foreign aid consultants. The task force pointed out that three-quarters of the aid funds for fiscal year 1960 and four-fifths for fiscal year 1961 were for military and short-term political programs; development was assigned only 23 per cent one year and 19 per cent the next. The existing system, it said, "has been designed primarily as an instrument against communism rather than for constructive economic and social advancement."

Three weeks after receiving the report, Kennedy as President faced the task of reorganizing the aid effort. He had inherited an organization, or rather a congeries of organizations; he had inherited a congressional conviction that foreign aid was primarily part of the cold war; and he had to work within that inheritance. His first foreign aid message in late March illustrated his quandary. As originally drafted in terms believed necessary to win maximum congressional support, it was an old-fashioned 'let's beat communism through foreign aid' appeal. But Walt Rostow in the White House and David Bell and his deputy, Kenneth Hansen, in the Bureau of the Budget managed to insert a little of the new philosophy into the text before it was delivered.

"The fundamental task of our foreign aid program in the 1960's," Kennedy finally said, "is not negatively to fight communism: its fundamental task is to help make a historical demonstration that in the twentieth century, as in the nineteenth—in the southern half of the globe as in the north—economic growth and political democracy can develop hand in hand." To meet this challenge, he continued, the effort must base itself on new principles—especially national development planning and long-term authorization and financing. It must also have unified administration and operation; and this meant, Kennedy explained, a single aid administration absorbing not only the International Cooperation Administration and the Development Loan Fund but Food for Peace, the Peace Corps and even certain functions of the Export-Import Bank.

In the meantime, he had appointed Henry Labouisse as head of ICA and Frank Coffin as head of DLF. Labouisse, a civilized and intelligent man, had been scheduled for the ICA job under Eisenhower, only to have the appointment withdrawn when a White House sleuth discovered that he had once registered in Connecticut as a Democrat. Giving him the job now seemed a useful act of moral retribution. Coffin, who had fought for the DLF as Congressman from Maine, was a man of judicious and liberal temperament for whom Kennedy had warm personal regard.[4] At the same time, Labouisse was also made chairman of a task force on foreign economic assistance, with three subsidiary groups—on program (headed by Coffin and Max Millikan), organization (headed by George Gant of the Ford Foundation) and legislation (headed by Theodore Tannenwald, Jr.). The task force worked through the spring and summer to lay the groundwork for the new Agency for International Development (AID).

It was notable that the task force mandate was confined to economic assistance, even though military aid constituted

[4] He is also the author of *Witness for Aid* (Boston, 1964), a sensitive discussion of aid issues.

the bulk of the annual program. In the White House Robert Komer argued for a parallel reappraisal of the military effort. There were strong reasons for this. In some underdeveloped countries the military programs imposed heavy economic burdens. If the United States provided the heavy equipment, the countries themselves had to come up with local funds for pay, quarters, food, uniforms. Moreover, the programs had unanticipated and often questionable political side effects. Kennedy saw the point and set up an interagency steering group to look into it.

In three months the group concluded that the days of Korea were over and that the communist threat in most developing nations was not external aggression but internal disruption and subversion. The way to deal with this, it felt, was to build social and economic health; and it therefore recommended a steady shift from military to economic assistance. Kennedy was in complete agreement. But, when the report went to the National Security Council early in 1962, the Secretaries of State and Defense were resistant, and the Joint Chiefs of Staff aggrieved. Among the swarm of problems assailing a President, this one did not seem sufficiently urgent to justify a wrangle with State and the Pentagon; and the military assistance program, though reduced and revamped in a somewhat haphazard way in the next years, remained a vulnerable point in the aid effort.

The establishment of AID inaugurated a long period of turmoil and frustration. The unification of the aid agencies was the inevitable consequence of the decision to encourage national development planning in the countries aided; but a further consequence had to be the organization of the new agency along regional rather than technical lines in Washington. This posed a mortal threat to the vested ideas, interests and routines of the aid bureaucracy. The functional specialists—agriculture, public health, housing and so on—had long dominated the geographical desks in ICA; and their masterful leader, Dr. Dennis Fitzgerald, an old-time government servant, had gradually gathered to himself the reins of operating authority as one aid director after another had flashed by in the Eisenhower era. Labouisse was a kindly, modest man whose experience in diplomacy and then in UN relief work led him to see aid in political and humanitarian more than in development terms and whose energy was stretched between ICA and the task force. He found it hard to control the ICA bureaucracy, traditionally committed to projects rather than to programs, and, as time went on, yielded more and more to the old-timers. By midsummer Kennedy, who liked Labouisse, began regretfully to feel that he was not the man for AID. Labouisse was offered the embassy in Greece; and Ralph Dungan, the President's agent in these matters, began the search for a successor.

Dungan was looking for someone conservative enough to reassure Congress but liberal enough to carry forward the program—a business image, as it was put, without a business mentality. He finally hit upon George Woods, a progressive-minded investment banker; but the involvement of Woods's firm with the Dixon-Yates scandal of Eisenhower years caused a revolt among liberal Democrats on the Hill; and the invitation had to be withdrawn—a Labouisse case in reverse. Woods later had a chance to display his abilities as head of the World Bank. Then the choice fell upon Fowler Hamilton, a New York lawyer and a Democrat with government experience in the Second World War who had been under consideration for the directorship of CIA.

3. EVOLUTION OF AID

Hamilton was a tough and brisk administrator, well fitted to carry through the job of reorganization; and this he did with expedition. The technical assistance specialists were dethroned. Dr. Fitzgerald was shunted into an administrative limbo, from which he retired in 1962 with a blast against "the fanciful contention that brilliant new policies, bright new administrators, and brand new organization" were likely to improve the aid performance. Hamilton then recruited a group of effective regional directors, especially William Gaud for the Middle East and Teodoro Moscoso, Graham Martin and William Rogers for Latin America.

His recruitment effort concentrated on businessmen. This was on the theory, a recurring cliché in government administration, that appointments from the business world would both disarm Congress and improve the efficiency of the agency. But Operation Tycoon, as it was known, had more failures than successes. The idea was actually born in June, before Hamilton came on the scene, when the Vice-President suggested at a White House meeting that the presidents of the fifty largest companies be asked to provide their best vice-presidents for a year of service in the aid program. "You get all those vice presidents," Johnson said, "and we're in business." Someone asked Robert McNamara, the only businessman present, what he thought of this idea. McNamara responded crisply, "Out of about 10 per cent you will get some good people. But 90 per cent of the ones you get won't be any good at all." In the end, Operation Tycoon did little to falsify McNamara's prediction, saddling the agency with executives whose main contribution was to say at regular intervals: "That's not the way we did it at Proctor and Gamble."

For the rest, Hamilton spent most of his time dealing with Congress. This was a heartbreaking job. Congressman Otto Passman of Louisiana, a fanatical foe of foreign aid, had for years used his strategic position as chairman of the House Appropriations Subcommittee on Foreign Aid to denounce "the spenders, the dreamers, the internationalists," torment successive aid directors and tear the program to pieces. Moreover, Congress was filled with suspicions, many of them justified, about the intelligence and efficiency with which the program had been carried out. But the administration staged a vigorous drive for the new aid bill—it "made the Eisenhower foreign aid propaganda campaigns look amateur," Passman complained—and Congress agreed that the Kennedy recommendations deserved a try. The great exception was the request for five-year borrowing authority, but in later years this issue did not seem so crucial as we thought it in 1961.

There followed a year of disappointment. Changing the direction of an agency while it continues its day-to-day operations is one of the hardest tricks in government; it has been likened to performing surgery on a man while he hauls a trunk upstairs. AID, despite the new legislation and leadership, remained sluggish and appeared ineffectual. The President often grew exceedingly impatient over its seeming inability to act, especially in Latin America. Returning ambassadors would tell of the enthusiasm with which the local governments had proposed one program or another, the excitement of planning, the filing of applications—and then the endless silence, interrupted only by the arrival of new technical missions or the request for further feasibility studies, until the government lost interest in the project and faith in Washington. Loan processing sometimes took as long as a year and a half. This was not entirely AID's fault. Congress, in an honorable desire to protect the funds of the taxpayer, wanted to make sure that the money would be spent efficiently; and the resulting standards inscribed in the legislation made the bureaucratic process even more laborious and rigid.

AID's apparent failure to show significant results during its year of grace gave Passman a chance to return to the battle in 1962. He did this with undiminished zest, even keeping one hapless regional director on the stand for a hundred hours of detailed and derisive interrogation. At the same time, Wayne Morse, Ernest Gruening and other liberal Democrats in the Senate, alienated by the persisting emphasis on military aid, began to fight against the program. All this produced a congressional mood that cut the President's 1962 request from $4.9 to $3.9 billion and reduced development loans by more than 20 per cent.

The President was coming to the conclusion that the basic weakness lay in the program itself and its execution. It was mostly in this respect that he found Hamilton wanting. Hamilton had taken on the assignment as a lawyer takes a case; he even occasionally spoke of the President as "my client." But he had no special knowledge of the technical intricacies of the development effort; and his activities as reorganizer, recruiter and salesman left him little time to worry about the substance of AID's work. Then the congressional debacle of 1962 weakened his standing as the program's attorney. He came to feel, I think, that he was losing the confidence of the White House and failing to score points with the President—as, indeed, he was. We had the sense in the White House that he decided in the autumn to prepare his own exit before anyone else had a chance to ask for it. He finally left in November to the accompaniment of newspaper stories that he was the victim of a campaign by 'liberals' in the White House; one or two of the stories named me. I found this puzzling, since Hamilton was an old friend and I had had little to do with AID; but no doubt it was all part of the strain of life in the bureaucratic jungle.

In any case, Hamilton had presided over the organizational transition with considerable success. Yet at the end the program was substantively no more convincing than before and politically weaker than ever. This situation convinced Kennedy that extreme measures were necessary to get the aid bill through Congress in 1963. He was having difficulties with the business community for other reasons, and he resorted to the familiar device of a blue-ribbon panel of bonded conservatives set up to cast a presumably cold eye on the aid effort and then to recommend its continuance as essential to the national interest. He became convinced for some reason that General Lucius Clay was the man to head the group. He also wanted Robert Lovett and Eugene Black, and Clay himself nominated some quite conservative business friends, including Eisenhower's last Secretary of the Treasury. George Meany was put on as a gesture to the left.

At the same time, the President had to choose a suc-

cessor to Hamilton This time Dungan's search was for someone to do the substantive job, and it centered in government rather than among the tycoons. There was strong feeling in the White House in favor of Sargent Shriver, who
had made such a brilliant success with the Peace Corps,
but Shriver indicated he would rather stay where he was.
The other obvious candidate within the government was
David Bell. Bell had exceptional qualifications. His work
with Galbraith and Mason in the Harvard seminar in the fifties had given him a first-rate technical grasp of development
doctrine; he had the practical experience of having run the
Ford Foundation mission in Pakistan; and his superb record
as director of the Bureau of the Budget had won him the
total confidence of the President. Bell himself was dubious,
arguing to Kennedy that he had no particular talent or experience in influencing members of Congress or carrying the
program with the public. Kennedy responded that, so far as
he was concerned, the best way to put the program over
was to make it work. As someone observed at the time,
"You can't sell Ivory soap if it sinks in the bathtub."

Bell, who did not much like the idea of the Clay committee, proposed that Edward S. Mason at least be added to
it. Dungan had not liked the idea either, and Kenneth
O'Donnell was profane and explicit in pointing out its
danger and futility. But Kennedy had confidence in Clay; and
in January 1963 the committee began its inquiry. It held
extensive hearings and did a conscientious job. But the
group was for the most part narrow in its ideas and negative in its reactions. Of the members who knew anything
about aid problems, Black had never much liked bilateral
programs, preferring his old institution, the World Bank,
and Mason disappeared overseas in the concluding stages.
Lovett's main contribution lay in elegantly sarcastic phrases:
"There had been a feeling that we are trying to do too much
for too many too soon, that we are over-extended in resources and under-compensated in results, and that no end
of foreign aid is either in sight or in mind."

The first draft was sour and niggling. But Clay, despite
his own restricted views, did not want to let down Kennedy
or, for that matter, David Bell who had deeply impressed
him in the hearings. He finally acquiesced in a revision of
the report which, without altering the substance, conveyed
a more positive spirit. The impact of the document as
finally issued in March 1963 (George Meany dissenting)
was to suggest that aid operations had to be improved and
aid magnitudes reduced, but that at the same time aid was
indispensable to national security. The exercise was not, I

suppose, without its benefits. Bell sat through the hearings and received a briefing in his new responsibilities which he could hardly have got elsewhere and which helped him in the future. The report endorsed the development orientation and expressed the hope that military aid could be reduced. It also shaped up certain ideas which later proved useful in AID legislative presentations, notably those of concentrating on the countries which could make effective use of assistance (a proposal for which Chester Bowles had argued within the government in 1962) and of discontinuing programs which were no longer needed.

On the other hand, the committee provided more ammunition to the enemies of AID than to its friends. Otto Passman announced himself "surprised and pleased." And buried in the report was a systematic hostility to forms of development which did not yield private profit. Most of the changes it proposed were intended to promote American private investment. Some abroad read the document as a statement of the thesis that the point of foreign aid was to facilitate the penetration of the development world by American business. Ken O'Donnell could hardly have been more right. The President himself remarked, "I am so busy protecting my flank from right-wing criticism that I sometimes wonder where I am getting anything done."

There was a short debate within the administration whether to accept or reject the report. Those in favor won out on the argument that General Clay would then testify for the program; rejection, it was feared, would deliver him to Passman. The original 1963 request had been for $4.9 billion; but in a background briefing for newspapermen just before the report was released, Clay, contrary to an understanding that he would not talk figures, left the impression in responding to a question that the program might be cut $500 million. Kennedy, who read the story in the Sunday newspapers out at Camp David, was briefly furious. Clay later did his best to hold the line at $4.2–4.3 billion and then at $3.9 billion; but the bill was on the downward slide. Before the slaughter was over, it was saddled with restrictions and then slashed to $3.6 billion.

And this was only the authorization: the eventual appropriation went down even further, to $3.2 billion—the largest cut in the history of the program. By the end of the Kennedy years foreign aid was at its lowest point so far as funds were concerned since 1958. Yet philosophically and operationally the program was in better shape than it had been for some time. A comparison of the 1961 and 1963 messages showed how the ideology of foreign assistance had moved out of the cold war into the context of development. And David Bell gave both conception and execution more stability and purpose than they had had since the time of Hoffman and Harriman. His intelligence and force greatly strengthened AID's morale and performance; and his sober optimism offered hope for the future.

Testifying before the House Foreign Affairs Committee in 1963, he could point out that, of the forty countries which had received the major share of American development aid since 1945, fourteen no longer depended on external assistance and ten others were steadily reducing such dependence. In these twenty-four countries, Bell said, "democratic institutions have been strengthened or less democratic regimes liberalized"; and of the whole lot of forty countries he observed, "Although the possibility of economic progress leading to political backsliding cannot be ruled out, there is no clear case of this phenomenon among the countries to which we have extended substantial amounts of development assistance. The relationship is overwhelmingly in the other direction." He concluded with characteristic precision that, while economic progress could not guarantee democracy, "it seems clear that without economic progress the chances for strengthening democratic processes in the less developed countries would be greatly diminished."

The success of the aid program—both in getting support at home and results abroad—remained as elusive as its continuation seemed imperative. But David Bell more than vindicated Kennedy's confidence. In the end, he stayed longer as aid administrator than anyone else in the history of the effort.

4. DEVELOPMENT VS. POPULATION

The struggle for economic growth encountered more than the well-advertised obstacles of ignorance, disease, corruption and inertia. Even when countries had the will to reshape attitudes and institutions, there was still the constant threat that population would increase faster than output, producing a decline in per capita income and therefore in the savings available for capital formation. Indeed, this threat actually became more acute as nations began to modernize. Improvements in sanitation and public health —from the boiling of water and the swatting of flies to penicillin and DDT—often neutralized the old Malthusian checks before economic growth could take up the slack.

In Venezuela, for example, from 1957 to 1963 the gross

national product, according to the UN, grew at a rate of 4.5 per cent, but population grew at a rate of 3.8 per cent, reducing the net gain in per capita income to .7 per cent; in Uganda, the figures were 3.4 and 2.5 per cent, leaving the per capita gain at .9 per cent.[5] Like a thief in the night," said Asoka Mehta of the Indian Planning Commission, "population growth can rob us of all that we achieve, day after day, in economic growth." One AID economist calculated that in certain countries every dollar invested in birth control would be 200 times as productive as the same dollar invested in foreign aid.

This problem had nagged the consciousness of foreign aid people for some time. In the very long run, industrialization and affluence might bring down the birth rate (though even this was not certain; the United States, after a period of decline in the thirties, now had as high a rate of population growth as India); but in the short run the situation seemed to require a more specific and purposeful attack. In 1959 one of the recurrent blue-ribbon reviews of aid policy, this one chaired by General William H. Draper, courageously recommended that the United States assist birth control programs in developing countries. When the Draper report provoked a strong counterstatement by the Roman Catholic bishops, President Eisenhower quickly said, "This government will not . . . as long as I am here, have a positive political doctrine in its program that has to do with birth control. That's not our business." [6] An ICA directive promptly banned birth control assistance or even consultation.

The election in 1960 of a Roman Catholic President might have been supposed to place population control even further outside the realm of public policy. The President-elect's interregnum task force on economic aid hardly mentioned the problem in its report. When one of its consultants, Richard N. Gardner of Columbia, soon to become Harlan Cleveland's Deputy Assistant Secretary for International Organization Affairs, pointed this out, his intervention only produced pitying smiles from those who assumed the question closed in the Kennedy years.

Actually Kennedy had long been concerned about the implications of population growth for economic develop-

5 I am conscious of the spurious precision of such figures and of all statistics from developing countries (indeed, from developed countries as well); see Oskar Morgenstern, *On the Accuracy of Economic Observations* (2nd edition; Princeton, 1963).
6 Eisenhower abandoned this position in later years.

ment. In 1959, for example, John Cowles made a speech on the population problem, arguing that "unless we want to see the conditions that exist in India and in Egypt spread over the rest of the world, the scientists must find some method of simple, inexpensive and effective fertility control"; and Kennedy inserted it in the *Congressional Record* as "a challenging panorama of the developments abroad which will shape our foreign policy during the next decades." Asked on Meet the Press early in 1960 what he proposed to do about countries where people were multiplying faster than production, Kennedy replied that the solution was "for the United States and other powers to help them get ahead of their population increase. If they make a judgment that they want to limit their population under those conditions, that is a judgment they should make, and economic assistance which we give permits them to make that judgment, if that is their choice." In his first foreign aid message, he noted that "in Latin America, for example, population growth is already threatening to outpace economic growth."

In the summer of 1961 George McGhee confronted the State Department's Policy Planning Council with the problem. One result was a cautious paper saying in effect that the problem was real and that, while the United States could not come out for population control, it ought to do something, though no one was ready to say what. Another result was the designation of Robert W. Barnett as the Department's population adviser. Over the next year Barnett pressed the problem in the Department, with occasional public speeches defining the issues and arguing for government support of demographic research.

In the autumn of 1962 Sweden laid before the UN General Assembly a resolution calling on the Secretary-General to conduct an inquiry on population problems. This meant that, for the first time, the General Assembly would debate population policy. Richard Gardner, whose concern was unabated, volunteered to handle the topic for the U.S. Mission. He thereupon drafted a speech welcoming the Swedish initiative and declaring it "absolutely essential that we be concerned with population trends." American policy, as Gardner went on to state it, opposed "any effort to dictate to any country the means to be employed in dealing with its population problem"; but at the same time "the United States believes that obstacles should not be placed in the way of other governments which, in the light of their own economic needs and cultural and religious values, seek solutions to their population problems." Gardner then

The World of Diversity   555

said that the United States would "upon request" help
other countries "to find potential sources of information
and assistance on ways and means of dealing with population problems." He also affirmed on behalf of his government the need for additional knowledge on these matters, including "more facts about alternative methods of
family planning."

Gardner first submitted his draft to Dean Rusk, who
made no objections, and then to Ralph Dungan. Dungan, a
thoughtful Catholic of the John XXIII school, was the
White House liaison with the dignitaries of the Church
and the resident expert on Catholic doctrine. He was, in
addition, a man of wisdom and experience. He had, I think,
a certain skepticism about the birth control zealots in the
United States; the organized movement had for him a little too much the aspect of a crusade of white Anglo-Saxon
Protestants determined to stop non-WASPs from propagat-
ing lest the WASPs be overwhelmed. (Kennedy may have
had the same feeling; as he once put it, most people think
"that it is other people's families that provide the population explosion.") On the other hand, Dungan had a realistic understanding of population issues; and he gave the
speech prompt White House clearance.

A few days later the United States voted for the Swedish
resolution in the General Assembly, balking only at a section calling for UN "technical assistance" on population
problems; we abstained here because the UN already
had all the authority it needed to give its members technical assistance and the inclusion of this superfluous language might raise fears that the UN was about to go into
the business of distributing contraceptive devices. This action took place, however, during the New York newspaper
strike of the winter of 1962–63, and no one seemed to
notice it. The State Department quietly circulated the
Gardner statement to foreign governments, and AID soon
adopted it as a directive, superseding the Eisenhower ban
against action on population questions. This activity slowly
awakened public interest. In April 1963 someone asked
Kennedy at a press conference whether he thought the
United States should supply funds for international birth
control studies. The President replied: "If your question is:
Can we do more, should we know more about the whole
reproduction cycle, and should this information be made
more available to the world so that everyone can make
their own judgment, I would think that it would be a
matter which we could certainly support."

Kennedy's statement represented a significant revolution

in the attitude of the American government. He affirmed two principles: freedom of research on population matters and freedom of every nation to use the resulting knowledge in determining its own policy. In handling the question this way, he dispelled all doubt, if any remained, about the capacity of a Catholic President to decide public issues on their merits. Actually, with the growing reappraisal within the Church itself, the policy provoked little criticism among his co-religionists. Catholic concern seemed now to narrow to the relatively small point—and one on which they received reassurance—that the government should not ship out contraceptives. The Kennedy years thus further strengthened the American attack on world poverty by preparing the means to keep population growth from nullifying the development effort.

5. FOOD AND PEOPLE

The original plan for aid reorganization had contemplated absorbing both Food for Peace and the Peace Corps into the Agency for International Development. After all, they too provided forms of assistance; and the logic of those who wanted to run government by the book was to put them all in the centralized operation. This logic was not perhaps irresistible. Nothing could take the heart out of new ideas more speedily than an old bureaucracy. If Food for Peace and the Peace Corps were to fulfill expectations, there was an argument that they had to retain their own identity and élan. "These two programs," as I wrote Richard Neustadt shortly after the aid message, "have more political potential than anything else in the foreign aid picture. It seems to me there is a strong argument for holding them close to the President. Would F.D.R. ever have let such programs get out of his immediate grasp?"

The heads of both agencies vigorously shared this view, and each had strong support in his fight for autonomy— George McGovern from the agricultural committees on the Hill, and Sargent Shriver from the Vice-President, as chairman of the Peace Corps's National Advisory Committee. And Kennedy himself held the Rooseveltian view that there were things in life more important than the symmetry of organization charts. I often wondered later how Food for Peace and the Peace Corps would have fared had they been permitted to vanish into the opaque depths of AID.

Food for Peace was the great unseen weapon of Kennedy's third world policy. McGovern's imaginative direction of the program received Kennedy's direct and personal support; and, after McGovern was elected Senator from South Dakota in 1962, the work was carried forward by Richard Reuter of CARE. Shipments under Public Law 480 averaged nearly $1.5 billion annually in the Kennedy years. This assistance not only played a notable humanitarian role in averting mass starvation in India, Egypt, Algeria and other nations; but the use of food as wages carried it beyond a relief program to serve, in effect, as a means of financing development. In addition to its profound impact abroad, the program greatly eased the problems created by American agricultural productivity, reduced surplus storage charges, increased farm income and purchasing power and even, under the stipulation that the food be transported in American ships, helped subsidize the maritime industry. Food for Peace, as Hubert Humphrey once put it, was "a twentieth century form of alchemy."

But the part of the aid effort which best expressed the distinctive spirit of the New Frontier was the Peace Corps. In the late fifties Humphrey and Richard Neuberger in the Senate and Henry Reuss in the House had advanced variations on the general idea of sending volunteers overseas for technical assistance work. Humphrey even occasionally used the phrase "Youth Peace Corps," and in June 1960 he introduced a Peace Corps bill into Congress. General James Gavin urged a similar plan on Kennedy. Kennedy himself advanced the idea a little tentatively during the campaign—it was mid-October and two in the morning—to an audience of students at the University of Michigan. The response was unexpectedly warm. A few days later a Michigan delegation greeted Kennedy at Toledo with a petition signed by several hundred prospective volunteers. Later, in California, Kennedy called for the establishment of a peace corps, broadening it from Humphrey's original conception to include women as well as men and older people as well as young.

In its origins, the Peace Corps was undoubtedly suggested by Franklin Roosevelt's Civilian Conservation Corps of 1933; and the Republicans of 1960 reacted dependably in the manner of their fathers a generation earlier. Hoover's Secretary of Agriculture had described the CCC as "utterly visionary and chimerical"; now Eisenhower called the Peace Corps a "juvenile experiment," and Nixon, with customary taste, observed solemnly that Kennedy "proposed to send as America's representatives to other nations young men whom he calls volunteers but who in truth in many instances would be trying to escape the draft." Even some Democrats thought it a nice but impractical idea thrown out for campaign purposes.

But the response of the young had already touched Kennedy. "I want to demonstrate to Mr. Khrushchev and others," he said toward the end of the campaign in Chicago, "that a new generation of Americans has taken over this country . . . young Americans [who will] serve the cause of freedom as servants of peace around the world, working for freedom as the communists work for their system." These remarks, which were not in the advance release of the speech, expressed, I think, a particular ground for his growing commitment to the Peace Corps. He often envied the communist capacity to mobilize popular idealism, especially of the young. I remember his remarking almost wistfully about Cuba: "Each weekend 10,000 teachers go into the countryside to run a campaign against illiteracy. A great communal effort like this is attractive to people who wish to serve their country." He was sure there was a comparable fund of idealism among the youth of America; and the Peace Corps seemed a means of demonstrating the reality of this idealism to the world.

"President Kennedy picked me to organize the Peace Corps, I was told," Sargent Shriver later wrote, "because no one thought the Peace Corps could succeed and it would be easier to fire a relative than a political friend." There were other reasons. If the Peace Corps was to be a vehicle of American idealism, Shriver was an authentic and energetic idealist, well qualified to inspire both staff and volunteers with a sense of purpose and opportunity. Moreover, he could be both tactful and persuasive in his relations with Congress. Shriver promptly convoked the usual task force, began a systematic analysis of problems of function and recruitment, overrode those who objected to the name "Peace Corps" on the ground that the word "peace" had been expropriated by the communists and on March 1, 1961, submitted a report to Kennedy recommending immediate establishment. The objectives of the Peace Corps, according to the report, were threefold:

It can contribute to the development of critical countries and regions.

It can promote international cooperation and good will toward this country.

It can also contribute to the education of America and to more intelligent participation in the world.

On the same day Kennedy set up the Peace Corps by

executive order and sent a message to Congress requesting legislation. The first reactions to the idea, he said, were "convincing demonstration that we have in this country an immense reservoir of dedicated men and women willing to devote their energies and time and toil to the cause of world peace and human progress." Shriver assembled a remarkable staff, luring Vice-President Johnson's ablest aide, Bill D. Moyers, to become his deputy and eventually annexing Richard Goodwin to head the International Secretariat working with other countries to form peace corps of their own. By the spring of 1961 recruitment and training were well under way. Soon the volunteers began to leave on their assignments.

Having defended the autonomy of the Corps in Washington, Shriver was determined not to let his men become involved in diplomatic or intelligence activities overseas. Their only job, he told them, was to help people help themselves; and in personal visits around the world Shriver convinced mistrustful governments that he meant exactly what he said. Despite communist assertions that Shriver was a "bloodthirsty Chicago butcher and sausage maker" and his organization a "nest of spies," neutral states began to ask for volunteers to aid village development and public health, to improve farming methods and, most important of all, to teach their own coming generations of national leaders. The original authorization of 500 grew to 5000 by March 1963 and to 10,000 in another year, and volunteers were soon working in forty-six countries. Congressional doubt turned into enthusiasm: even Barry Goldwater applauded the Corps.

The Peace Corps in action was an immensely moving sight. Here were young American men and women who had given two years of their lives to serve in unknown places in remote lands, with little recognition or reward beyond their own sense of achievement and growth. I saw them in India in 1962 and again in Venezuela in 1963. In the Punjab they were agricultural specialists, working with the farmers in the villages. In Caracas I was taken deep into a *barrio*, along alleys turned into mud by several days of rain. We finally reached a playground, at one end of which a young Negro from Denver was presiding over twenty-five dead-end kids sawing and hammering away on pieces of lumber. A soap-box derby was impending, and Jerry Page, the Peace Corps man, had dug up some boards and set the boys to work. We talked about the boys and their prospects. He described an alliance he had struck with the local

Catholic priest both to encourage the boys to stay in school and also to make the local school better. Later he drove us in a battered jeep to his quarters. The walls along the way were chalked with amiable slogans—*Muera Betancourt* and *Muera Kennedy* [7]—but Jerry received friendly waves and greetings every few steps. I later asked Allan Stewart, our ambassador in Caracas, about the Peace Corps. He said, "It has been wonderful here. It has worked miracles in changing the Venezuelan image of North Americans. Before the Peace Corps, the only Americans the poor Venezuelans ever saw were riding around in Cadillacs. They supposed them all to be rich, selfish, callous, reactionary. The Peace Corps has shown them an entirely different kind of Americans. It is transforming the whole theory they have of the United States."

This was the point—this, and the extent to which the experience gave the volunteers a new understanding of the world and themselves. Critics said that the few thousand Peace Corpsmen were a handful of sand cast into the vast sea of underdevelopment. They argued that the emphasis on what Peace Corps doctrine in an uncharacteristic lapse into bureaucratese termed "middle-level manpower" was nothing more than a revival of the old creed of technical assistance. They suggested that Eagle Scout good deeds had scant impact on the basic problems of capital investment and social reorganization on which economic growth depended. Yet watching the volunteers as they carried to dark slums and sullen villages examples of modesty, comradeship, hard work and optimism, one wondered whether they were not bringing some inkling of the meaning of a democratic community to places hitherto inaccessible to the democratic idea, and whether future Nyereres and Sékou Tourés, even perhaps future Nkrumahs and Castros, might not catch fire from their liveliness and devotion. One simply could not dismiss what the foreign minister of Thailand called "this important idea, the most powerful idea in recent times, of a Peace Corps, of youth mingling, living, working with youth," nor discount his surprise that this idea

should come from the mightiest nation on earth, the United States. Many of us who did not know about the United States thought of this great nation as a wealthy nation, a powerful nation, endowed with great material strength and many powerful weapons. But how many of us know that in the United States ideas and ideals are also powerful?

[7] "Death to Betancourt," and "Death to Kennedy."

The Peace Corps ideas and ideals were indeed powerful; and the most potent of all was set forth by David Crozier in a letter from Colombia to his parents before he was killed in an airplane accident. "Should it come to it," the young volunteer wrote, "I had rather give my life trying to help someone than to have to give my life looking down a gun barrel at them."

6. DOGMATISM VS. PRAGMATISM

Kennedy's third world policy represented a considerable break from the Washington world view of the fifties, and it foreshadowed a fundamental reconstruction of our total foreign policy. In the Eisenhower years the conduct of foreign affairs had rested on a set of abstract and unitary doctrines—about the uncommitted world, which we regarded as immoral; about the 'free world,' or, as it was known in public documents, the Free World, which we hoped would conform to the principles upon which we fancied American society was based; and about the communist world, which we saw as a centralized conspiracy. Now each of these dogmas was undergoing revision.

As we stopped regarding neutralism as a sin, so we receded from the insistence that nations which received our aid should adopt our economic creed. In the fifties Washington had been deeply convinced of the superiority, not to say sanctity, of the system of free private enterprise. No one seemed to care that this system, as described in the official literature, did not correspond to the reality of our own society, which had long since evolved into a mixed economy and a welfare state, or even to the actuality of our own past, marked in pre-takeoff days by considerable initiative on the part of the so-called public sector. Indeed, the official model had so far departed from contemporary reality that India, styling itself a 'socialist' society, averaged in 1958 and 1959 less than 13 per cent of central government expenditures in the gross national product as against more than 19 per cent in the last Eisenhower years in 'capitalist' America.

Since Democrats had no ancestral hostility to purposeful government and social reform in America, they were less inclined to demand such hostility of foreigners. Kennedy's own views were strictly empirical. Declining to regard the choice between private and public means as a matter of moral principle, he rejected equally the theologians of the private sector and the theologians of the public sector—

those on the right who regarded public enterprise as inherently sinful and those on the left who regarded private enterprise as inherently sinful. In his judgment, the only issue was which means could best achieve the desired end, and this to be answered not by doctrine but by experiment. We were not, in short, to worry too much about the ideological character of economic development. "We do not condemn others for their differences in economic and political structures," Robert Kennedy told the students at Nihon University in Tokyo. In the United States, he said, we had time "to permit the intertwining of many small units into the great systems that the modern age requires, and, under government regulation, time to permit the continuation of private control. In many of the newer nations, government appears to be the only mechanism capable of performing these feats within a reasonable length of time. This we can understand and appreciate. It neither offends us, nor can we deem it hostile."

These views did not command much support or understanding in the Congress. In 1962 the Hickenlooper amendment to the aid bill called for the suspension of aid to nations which expropriated American business without prompt, adequate and effective compensation; the Clay committee endorsed this policy; and this ideological outburst found in the Bokaro steel plant in India a conspicuous casualty. "The simple truth is this," Galbraith protested unavailingly from India, "and we cannot repeat it too often: if our case opposes capitalism to communism, as Clay would have it and as capitalism is regarded in this part of the world, we can hardly win. If our case opposes the widest possible choice of free development to communism, we can hardly lose. That, sirs, is it."

That may have been it, but it was not easy to bring even the executive branch of the government, steeped in ancient habits, to tolerate other economic systems or, at first, to describe our own with much accuracy. The United States Information Agency until well into 1961 dispatched a weekly economic commentary portraying the American economy, as if George Humphrey still reigned in Washington, as a system of rugged individualism unhampered by government control. One such essay, offered for distribution to the local press, affirmed the national commitment to free enterprise by likening the United States to a giant corporation with the people as stockholders, the bureaucracy as management, the Congress as board of directors and the President as chairman of the board. Galbraith sent this prose poem to the President suitably underlined and annotated, concluding with the irreverent suggestion that the nation had elected the wrong Kennedy; obviously it should have been the father rather than the son. The President delightedly read the document, complete with gloss, over the phone to Edward R. Murrow, pausing after every sentence to say, "Is this what you really believe, Ed?"

Murrow did not need prompting, however, to begin his revamping of USIA. He proved a brilliant chief, and in Donald M. Wilson he had an exceptionally able deputy. One felt that Murrow finally came into his own in Washington. In the fifties he had been a solitary voice of courage and reason in commercial television; but there had seemed to be gathering within him a searing disgust with the medium and a sad frustration about his own life. He was a harrowed, gloomy presence at New York dinners, punctuating his incessant cigarettes with brief and bitter cracks and leaving the impression that all idealism in the world had vanished with the Battle of Britain. He had no faith at all at this time in Kennedy. One day in the midst of the 1960 campaign Theodore H. White and I lunched with Murrow at the Century. He told us that, if McCarthyism seemed to Kennedy's advantage, Kennedy would become a McCarthyite overnight. Nothing White or I said could dissuade him from this view.

All this now changed quickly in Washington. Kennedy gave Murrow his full confidence; no government information chief, including even Elmer Davis, had been so close to a President; and Murrow, the professional doubter, at last had found someone since Churchill in whose intelligence and purpose he could wholeheartedly believe. He revitalized USIA, imbued it with his own bravery and honesty and directed its efforts especially to the developing nations, where, instead of expounding free-enterprise ideology, it tried to explain the American role in a diverse and evolving world. USIA became one of the most effective instruments of Kennedy's third world policy; and Murrow himself was a new man, cheerful, amused, committed, contented. When his fatal illness began, he must have had the consolation, after those glittering years of meaningless success, that at the end he had fulfilled himself as never before. Under Ed Murrow the Voice of America became the voice, not of American self-righteousness, but of American democracy.

7. UNIFORMITY VS. DIVERSITY

But what was American democracy to say? USIA could only repeat, not invent, policy. The problem remained of giving substance to our conception of the world. Dulles had talked of the Free World, and the State Department continued to blow on this worn locution like a stuck whistle. The phrase was, I suppose, innocent enough, but, among other things, it was innocent of meaning. When printed in capital letters, it had to my mind a portentous and sleazy appearance; and in my first enthusiastic days in Washington I made a mild bid to abandon this bit of Dullese.

Toward the end of May 1961 Secretary Rusk had to appear before the Senate Foreign Relations Committee. He sent his testimony over to the White House for suggestions; and I proposed an introductory paragraph which, in due course, he spoke to the committee. "We seek, above all," Rusk said, "a world of free choice in which a great diversity of nations, each faithful to its own traditions and its own genius, will learn to respect the ground rules of human survival. We do not wish to make the world over in our own image—and we will not accept that the world be made over in the image of any society or dogmatic creed. Against the world of coercion, we affirm the world of choice."

That, alas, was about the last one heard of the world of choice. The Free World continued to dominate State Department rhetoric. The President, however, always restless with clichés, sought continually for a more exact statement of our issue with communism. At the end of July 1961 Khrushchev put out the draft program for the Soviet Communist Party, a document filled with glowing (and extremely bourgeois) assurances that the Soviet Union would do everything from surpassing the per capita production of the United States by 1970 to abolishing the income tax. Harriman, reading this new Communist manifesto in Geneva, cabled the President proposing a democratic counterstatement. On Averell's return to Washington, Kennedy called him over to discuss the idea and asked me to join them.

The President said he was not interested in an exchange of standard-of-living boasts with the Russians or in an anthology of cold war banalities. What he wanted was a fresh analysis of the conceptions of history and the future implicit in the democratic position. "One object of the document," I noted afterward, "would be to destroy the idea of communist inevitability. But the main point would be to provide an affirmative description of the kind of world we seek and the reason why we believe that the pluralistic world will win out over the monistic world."

This was one of those projects always shoved aside by the daily importunities of the in-box, and I am ashamed to say that I never did anything about it in the form the President originally proposed. But the concept of diversity remained very much in his mind. It seemed the key to so much we were doing. Moreover, it expressed the nation's deeper traditions; for what was the idea of diversity, after all, but the expression in politics of William James's radical empiricism, that most American of philosophies? It was James's vision of the pluralist universe, where free men could find partial truths but where no one could ever get an absolute grip on Absolute Truth. It sprang from the sense that, as James put it, "the issue is decided nowhere else than *here* and *now. That* is what gives the palpitating reality to our moral life and makes it tingle . . . with so strange and elaborate an excitement."

Above all, the concept of diversity seemed more and more vindicated by the movement of events—in the end, paradoxically, by events in the communist world as in our own. For by the spring of 1962 the reality of the quarrel between the Soviet Union and China was beginning to become clear to everyone (except the aficionados of the 'Sino-Soviet bloc' in the Department of State). In traveling around Latin America, Asia and Europe in January and February of 1962, I was struck most of all, as I reported to the President on my return, "by the extent to which, since my last foreign travel, the Russo-Chinese tension has become a dominating issue throughout the world." It was draining away the power of the communist mystique, for one great source of communist appeal had been the belief that it was a universal creed capable of abolishing the contradictions of life and ushering in the brotherhood of man. The communist empire itself was "increasingly dividing between the relatively sedate and conservative communist parties of the developed world and the hungry, angry and revolutionary communist parties of the underdeveloped world." The historic forces of diversity were bursting communist discipline and shattering communist ideology.

The forces of diversity, my report added, were operating on our side of the fence too. "Pluralism is splitting both blocs apart and blurring the old, tidy divisions of the cold war. One could almost say that the process of competitive coexistence has turned into one of competitive disintegration. Still, one basic difference remains, and a difference everlastingly to our advantage. Pluralism is incompatible with the communist system; but it is wholly compatible with —indeed, should be the basis of—our system." The memorandum concluded: "What we must do is both to reempha-

size the fact that our objective is a pluralist world and to
rethink our international relationships in these terms."

All this, of course, corresponded very much with Kennedy's long-time view. The pluralist world, indeed, was inherent in the stand-still thesis he had set forth to Khrushchev in Vienna—a thesis which implied that nations should
be free to seek their own roads to salvation without up-
setting the balance between the superpowers. It also fitted
in with the conviction he had been expressing in recent
months that the power of the United States to prescribe
the arrangements of mankind was strictly limited. "We must
face the fact," he had told an audience at the University of
Washington the previous November, "that the United
States is neither omnipotent nor omniscient—that we are
only 6 per cent of the world's population—that we cannot
impose our will upon the other 94 per cent of mankind—
that we cannot right every wrong or reverse each ad-
versity—and that therefore there cannot be an American
solution to every world problem."

No great power could run the world: variety was the stubborn and irreducible reality. The policy of the two blocs
was played out. And, if the monolithic vision was against
the grain of history, the pluralist universe was of its essence. Kennedy felt more than ever that the time was coming to crystallize a new view of the world. Soon after my
return, he remarked that he had to give the Charter Day
address at the University of California later in the month.
"I am tired," he said, "of the headlines. All they describe is
crisis, and they give the impression that we have our backs
against the wall everywhere in the world. But this is an
optical illusion. Look at it from Khrushchev's viewpoint. He
has China, Albania, agriculture, the intellectuals, eastern
Europe"—ticking them off on his fingers—"and I'll bet he
feels just as harried as we do—probably more so. The fact
is that the world has changed a lot in the last decade, and
most of the change has been in our favor—national independence and all that. I want to talk about these things. Let
me have your ideas."

Meanwhile Ted Sorensen also prepared a Berkeley draft,
this one eloquently devoted to the contrast between the
"age of knowledge" and the "age of hate." The day before
the speech, the President called us both to the Mansion after
luncheon. His luncheon guest, J. Edgar Hoover, was leaving
as we arrived. Kennedy carefully refrained from introducing
us, explaining a moment later that he did not want to upset
Mr. Hoover too much. Then we discussed the two speeches.
Kennedy said he liked the part in the Sorensen draft about

the "age of knowledge" but not the part about the "age of hate"; he found both the idea and the word repugnant. He added that he also liked the passages in the other speech explaining that the pluralistic world and not the monolithic world was the wave of the future. Finally he handed both drafts to me and issued the classic presidential injunction: "Weave them together." Ted and I protested mildly that they were two separate speeches. The President got up and headed toward the bedroom for his nap, kidding us as he went. "I think you fellows have enough to go on," he said. "Just go out and write it up and have a new draft here by five o'clock." He added, "This reminds me of my father. When someone gave him an idea or a memorandum, he would say, 'This is lousy. It's no good.' Then they would ask what he wanted, and he would say, 'That's up to you,' and walk out of the room. That's what I am doing now."

I went back to my office and began to weave together the age of knowledge and the inevitable triumph of the pluralistic world. By five I dutifully returned with a new draft. Kennedy read it with care and made a number of suggestions. I changed the text as he indicated and went off to a banquet given by the Harvard Club of Washington. In a few moments I was told I was wanted on the telephone. It was the President calling from the swimming pool with some new thoughts. I added these later in the evening, and he extensively reworked the text the next day on the plane to California.

"It is the profound tendencies of history," he said at Berkeley, "and not the passing excitements that will shape our future. . . . The long view shows us that the revolution of national independence is a fundamental fact of our era. This resolution will not be stopped. As new nations emerge from the oblivion of centuries, their first aspiration is to affirm their national identity. Their deepest hope is for a world where, within a framework of international cooperation, every country can solve its own problems according to its own traditions and ideals."

This meant a world, he continued, marked by "diversity and independence." Such a world, "far from being opposed to the American conception of world order," expressed "the very essence of our view of the future," and movement toward this world was "the unifying spirit of our policies."

> The purpose of our aid programs must be to help developing countries move forward as rapidly as possible on the road to genuine national independence.

Our military policies must assist nations to protect the processes of democratic reform and development against disruption and intervention.

Our diplomatic policies must strengthen our relations with the whole world, with our several alliances and within the United Nations.

Above all, "this emerging world is incompatible with the communist world order," for the communists rested everything on the idea of a monolithic world, "where all knowledge has a single pattern, all societies move toward a single model, and all problems and roads have a single solution and a single destination." The monolith, he suggested, was doomed by the tides of history. "No one who examines the modern world can doubt that the great currents of history are carrying the world away from the monolithic toward the pluralist idea—away from communism and toward national independence and freedom. . . . Beyond the drumfire of daily crisis, therefore, there is arising the outlines of a robust and vital world community, founded on nations secure in their own independence, and united by allegiance to world peace."

There were indeed grounds for optimism in the spring of 1962. Not only was the communist empire itself faced by incipient crack-up, but the Russians had receded from Berlin and Laos, had made a botch of things in Africa and had their troubles at home. "I'm not so much impressed by the challenge of their system," Kennedy told Stewart Alsop about this time. "The most impressive thing they have done is their achievement in space. But there is a lot that is not so impressive." In the meantime, we had enormously strengthened our military position, we were making substantial progress in the third world, we were watching Western Europe grow every month in strength and vitality and we hopefully discerned a new spirit in our own society.

Vienna had shown that the communist leaders would not be persuaded by logic; but, if we could prove that, contrary to Marxist hypothesis, the democratic nations could maintain their unity, a rising rate of economic growth, a strong military capability, a creative relationship with the new nations and a foreign policy at once firm and restrained, then, in the longer run, we could perhaps expect the Soviet Union to reshape its policy to fit these facts. Moreover—as David Ormsby Gore used to urge on the President and the Attorney General—a new generation was emerging in the Soviet Union with values and aspirations of its own, and with this new generation the dialogue would be easier.

There the unitary American dogma of the fifties had dismayed our allies and, in effect, excommunicated the unaligned nations, Kennedy's doctrine of diversity now offered a common cause which even carried its appeal far beyond the Iron Curtain itself. As no one since Roosevelt, he was identifying the United States with the movement toward national independence and popular democracy and, perhaps even more than Roosevelt, with the hopes and aspirations of distant peoples. He made their longing for bread and schools and dignity his own. Most of all, he was giving the younger generation around the earth, as the foreign minister of Austria, Dr. Bruno Kreisky, later put it, "the courage to test their mettle in a field which had been barred to too many of them too long." Around the earth the young looked to him increasingly as their leader. Always he spoke for reason, recognizing the intractable diversity within the human family, eschewing the moralistic crusade, striving, in an age when war could mean the end of civilization, to move beyond war and offer humanity a chance to control its own destiny.

In seeking to build the world community on the idea, not of uniformity, but of diversity, the President expressed his own sense of the grand dynamic of modern history; and, in summoning history as his witness, he struck hard at the heart of the Marxist case. Moscow seems to have felt the blow. By 1964 *Kommunist*, the theoretical organ of the Soviet Communist Party, had inverted the Dulles doctrine, adopted it for itself and issued an irritable *démarche* to the new nations: "The leaders of young countries who really desire progress for their peoples cannot occupy intermediate positions between contradictory social systems. There are only two paths of development—one path leads to capitalism and the other to socialism. There is no third way."

In his vision of a world of diversity united by allegiance to peace, Kennedy established the basis for a wise and strong American policy—a basis from which he could move with equal ease toward conciliation or confrontation with the Soviet Union. Whichever way circumstances compelled him to move, he could act with the deep conviction he set forth at Berkeley: "No one can doubt that the wave of the future is not the conquest of the world by a single dogmatic creed but the liberation of the diverse energies of free nations and free men."

XXIII

THE COUNTRY MOVING AGAIN

THOUGH FOREIGN AFFAIRS CONSUMED the major share of Kennedy's time and attention, foreign policy, as he conceived it, had to draw its vitality and purpose from the energies liberated and the goals pursued within the United States. The Fourteen Points, he had remarked in the campaign, had been the "logical extension" of Wilson's New Freedom; Franklin Roosevelt had succeeded as a good neighbor in Latin America because he had been a good neighbor in the United States; Truman's Marshall Plan was the international "counterpart" of his Fair Deal. These three Presidents, Kennedy said, had been so notably successful around the world "because they were successful here, because they moved this country ahead, because they demonstrated that here in this country we were still revolutionaries." America, in short, had to start moving at home if it were to move the world.

And in motion the country was certainly not. The fifties had hardly been a notable season of innovation in our national life. The politics of boredom had produced widespread public apathy. National policy had been complacent and lethargic. Young people had become so circumspect that they were known as the 'silent generation.' Economic growth had puttered along at an average rate of 2.5 to 3 per cent a year. There had been recessions in 1954 and 1958. In the early spring of 1960, the economy had begun to sink into another recession. Gross national product stagnated. Unemployment increased by 1.2 million between February and October. If Kennedy were to start the country moving again, he would have to begin with the economy.

1. KENNEDY AND ECONOMICS

Kennedy had received his highest grade and only B in freshman year at Harvard in the introductory course in economics. The course made no deep impression on him. Indeed, he remembered his grade as C, or so at least he liked to tell his economists in later years. Nevertheless it was fortunate that this early exposure to economics came in the later days of the New Deal, when the Keynesian revolution was having its first effect. This saved him from being taught that government intervention in the economy was wicked per se or that a balanced budget should be the supreme goal of economic policy. Unlike F.D.R., he never had to unlearn classical maxims in order to meet contemporary problems.

His experience as a young Congressman watching the fluctuations of the economy in the late forties confirmed him in an incipient Keynesianism. Thus just after the election in 1952, when Sylvia Porter, the financial columnist, asked him on Meet the Press whether he now expected inflation or deflation, he replied, "Deflation is going to be the more serious problem particularly if efforts are made which General Eisenhower and Senator Taft and others have talked about of reducing our federal expenditures. Once we begin to balance the budget or begin to reduce out national debt, then deflation obviously is going to be the major issue." The proper policy, he continued, should be "to build up sufficient consumer purchasing power to absorb our increased productivity," and he was prepared to do this either through maintaining government expenditures or cutting taxes—"anything to put enough consumer purchasing power in the market, and obviously that's both ways." If unemployment continued, "then I'd be in favor of unbalancing the budget, not enough to cause a severe economic dislocation but enough to keep a reasonable level of prosperity." If we went into a recession, "one of the steps to meet the recession obviously is going to be government expenditures as it was in the thirties."

Later on, in the presidential years, it was easy to forget that his pervading congressional concern was with domestic affairs. He recruited his senatorial staff, for example—Sorensen, Feldman, O'Brien, Dungan, Goodwin—as knowledgeable men on national problems; he never had a foreign policy specialist in his Senate office. His House issues were those of urban and industrial liberalism: the minimum wage, social security, unemployment compensation, housing, labor reform. To this roster he now added as Senator a growing concern with the structural problems of his state and region—the decay of older industries, like shoes and textiles; the stagnation of historic mill towns; the losing competition with the low-wage South.

The special character of his New England problems led him in the fifties to think less about fiscal and monetary and more about structural remedies—in other words, direct attempts to strengthen New England's position in the national economy. His membership on the Labor and Education

Committee encouraged the structural approach. (Though he sought appointment to the Joint Committee on the Economic Report, which dealt with fiscal and monetary issues, he did not make it until 1960.) In general, he looked for programs which he thought would at once benefit New England and the nation, like redeveloping depressed areas (he served as floor manager of Paul Douglas's first area redevelopment bill in 1956) or raising the minimum wage (and thereby reducing the South's competitive advantage) or repealing the Taft-Hartley Act (and opening the way for the unionization of the South). On occasion, he would vote against what Massachusetts considered its local interest, as when he supported the St. Lawrence Seaway. On other occasions, he was ready to help New England at possible expense to the general welfare, as when he favored special protection for textiles or, for a while, opposed farm price supports on the ground that they worsened New England's terms of trade with the rest of the country.

To these analytical and political influences on his economic thought, a third must be added, though his advisers were always uncertain when it would come into play and how much weight the President gave it himself. This was the practical business wisdom he had heard so long—and from time to time continued to hear—from his father. The older Kennedy was, of course, far from a conventional businessman. He had been an outsider who made his money because he was more astute, daring and imaginative than the established leaders of business, and he was free in expressing his contempt for business grandees. On the other hand, if Mr. Kennedy had no particular faith in the leaders, he had deep faith in the system and deep mistrust of those who sought to tamper with it. In Henry R. Luce's New York apartment, on the night John Kennedy accepted the Democratic nomination for President, when Luce ventured the remark that of course the candidate would have to be left of center on domestic affairs, Joe Kennedy, in Luce's somewhat refined recollection, said, "Blank, blank, how can you imagine that any son of mine would be any blank blank liberal?" This was a considerable miscalculation, but it suggested the direction of his thought. The elder Kennedy had in particular the business belief in the mystique of 'confidence' and used to warn against actions or appointments which might impair that sacred commodity. And he also had the orthodox business reverence for the Eleusinian mysteries of the international monetary system and was apprehensive that 'lack of confidence' would drain America of its gold. These attitudes had some sort of effect on the President, though when he expressed them, one could never be sure whether he was doing so because he thought there was something to it or because he wanted to know the quick answer.

To this combination of influences, Kennedy added his own devouring curiosity about the way things worked. If at the start of his administration he was sometimes unsure of technical detail, he readily acquired an excellent command of economic analysis. In addition, he had shrewd economic intuitions, though perhaps more on national than on international problems. "He was the most perceptive of critics," Walter Heller later said—"he could pick out a sentence or a paragraph and see its weakness. Even though he might not have understood the analytic bases for its weakness, he had the feel for it, and this was uncanny." His approach to economic and social policy, in short, was that of an experimentalist and activist, restrained by politics and prudence but unfettered by doctrinal fetish or taboo.

As President, he meant to assure himself a wide range of intelligent advice. Having chosen Douglas Dillon as Secretary of the Treasury, he chose Walter Heller as chairman of the Council of Economic Advisers. "I need you both," he told Heller, "for a proper balance in economic matters." Diverging institutional interests created in any case a balance, or at least a tug of war, between the Council, charged by statute with working "to promote maximum employment, production and purchasing power," and the Treasury, primarily involved in taxation, the management of the debt and the protection of the dollar. But Kennedy was further pleased by the personal contrasts: the economics professor vs. the investment banker; the liberal vs. the moderate; the man who worried about deflation vs. the man who worried about inflation; the Democrat vs. the Republican.

Dillon, if to the right of Heller, was by no means an economic conservative. He understood the value of academic advice, restored the economists to the Treasury Department, from which they had been driven out by George Humphrey, made Seymour Harris (at Kennedy's suggestion) his economic adviser and encouraged Harris to set up a panel of outside consultants, whose meetings the Secretary regularly attended. Harris, who had a realistic grasp of the political problems of economic policy, became an effective bridge to the Council. Nevertheless, both Dillon's personal background and the institutional predilections of the Treasury inclined him to a particular solicitude for the business community. He was also an exceptionally skilled operator within the bureaucracy, ready to pull every stop and cut many corners to advance the Treasury view, always (and justifiably) confident that his charm could heal any feelings hurt in the process.

Heller, on the other hand, had the knack of composing breezy memoranda on economic problems—some hundreds in three years—and Kennedy read them faithfully. Both Heller and Dillon were urbane and articulate men; and much of the debate between them was conducted in the President's presence. The directors of the Budget also made significant contributions to the dialogue: David Bell was himself a professional economist, and Kermit Gordon, who succeeded Bell at the end of 1962, had been on Heller's Council. The Treasury, the Council and the Bureau soon constituted an informal national economic committee known as the "troika," meeting every two or three months with Kennedy for discussions of the economic outlook. In addition, Kennedy met more often with the Council as a whole than any of his predecessors, finding in Heller and Gordon a congenial blend of doctrine and practicality and in James Tobin, who was a brilliant theorist sometimes impatient of compromise, an economic conscience. The President also consulted with Galbraith, Harris, Paul Samuelson, Carl Kaysen and other economists and talked regularly with William McChesney Martin, Jr., of the Federal Reserve Board. All these sessions contributed to his growing proficiency in economic matters.

2. THE DEBATE OVER EXPANSION

The first problem was the recession. It had deepened throughout 1960, and Kennedy had made it a central issue in the campaign. Deriding Nixon's errant comments about economic "growthmanship," Kennedy had argued that the resumption of economic progress was "the number one domestic problem which the next President of the United States will have to meet." Growth, he said, was necessary not only to end the recession but to provide for the staggering increase in the national population—20 per cent, nearly 30 million people, in the single decade of the fifties. This increase, he pointed out, "has not been matched in our public plans and programs"; and it called for, he said, 25,000 new jobs a week for the next decade. The economy had to expand at an annual rate of 5 per cent, he told his audiences, "to keep you working and your children working."

He threw out a variety of suggestions during the campaign to bring the growth rate up to 5 per cent: using the budget "as an instrument of economic stabilization"; reversing the tight money policy of the Eisenhower years; providing special assistance to areas hit by economic decline and technological change; making "the public investments which provide a solid foundation for the private investment which is the key to our free enterprise economy"; developing the country's resources; encouraging plant modernization; training manpower for an increasingly automated economy; improving the educational system; assuring equal opportunity for employment.

He believed, of course, that these things were worth doing for their own sakes. But, with his innate skepticism, he was not at all sure they would produce the growth rate he desired. This worried him, and he quizzed every economist he met in the hope of finding out how to bring the expansion rate up to 5 per cent. In August 1960 he summoned Galbraith, Seymour Harris, Archibald Cox, Paul Samuelson of the Massachusetts Institute of Technology and Richard Lester of Princeton to a seminar on the boat off Hyannis Port in an effort to learn the secret. They did their best, but there was no philosopher's stone. In October, when Hubert Humphrey introduced him to Walter Heller before a campaign speech in Minneapolis, Kennedy's first question inevitably was, "Do you really think we can make good on that promise . . . of a five per cent rate of growth?"

Now as President he had to make good. The recession had continued to deepen in the weeks after the election. By February 1961 unemployment reached the astonishing figure of 8.1 per cent of the labor force. In deciding how to set in motion the processes of recovery and re-employment, Kennedy met again in the world of economists the two currents of thought he had already brushed in his own experience—the structural and the fiscal schools.[1]

The first school attributed unemployment below a certain level—say, 4 per cent—to structural transformations in the economy. It argued that, given the pace and progress of automation, the scarcity of educated and skilled labor would constitute a bottleneck in an expanding economy, forcing an expansion stimulated by fiscal and monetary policies

[1] Historians will note that the debate between the structuralists and the fiscalists was a new and more analytical phase of the old New Deal debate between the institutionalists of the First New Deal (Tugwell, Berle, Hugh Johnson), who wanted to restore the economy through reorganization of social structure, and the Keynesians of the Second New Deal (Eccles, Currie, Ben Cohen, Henderson), who proposed to end the depression through deficit spending.

alone to stop short of full employment. Thus there might be a shortage of highly skilled labor in Detroit while there was unemployment in Appalachia; nor would aggregative policies solve the problem of the San Diego aircraft worker displaced in the missile age, or of untrained teen-agers or Negroes in a time of increasing technical demand. Professor Charles Killingsworth of Michigan State University and Gunnar Myrdal of Sweden thus identified a 'manpower drag' to be solved by the modernization of the labor market through better schools, vocational education, manpower retraining, improved labor exchanges, area redevelopment and the like.

The fiscal school, on the other hand, attributed stagnation and unemployment to deficiencies in aggregate demand; and it came to place particular emphasis on the theory, popularized by Heller, of the 'fiscal drag'—the theory, that is, that with rising levels of output high tax rates drained away needed purchasing power and thereby forced expansion to stop short of full employment. To prove the efficacy of budgetary policies, extreme fiscalists liked to cite the experience of the Second World War when heavy government spending lifted the economy to unimagined heights, reduced unemployment by 1944 to 1.2 per cent and brought jobs to precisely the groups deemed on the outer fringes of employability—housewives, youth, Negroes, illiterates.

Very few economists were either pure structuralists or pure fiscalists. The pure structuralist argument, for example, omitted the consideration that, so long as, say, 6 per cent of the labor force was unemployed, there were few vacancies to be filled by retraining and that the only way to create more jobs was through the enlargement of demand. And the pure fiscal argument omitted the consideration that an immense structural apparatus—price and wage controls, material priorities, manpower direction—was required during the Second World War to prevent the massive budgetary injections from producing a runaway inflation.

Most government economists in the end therefore sought a combination of fiscal and structural positions—enough of a deficit to produce new jobs, enough redevelopment or retraining to equip men for the jobs. But a critical issue arose as to the best way to create the deficit. Here fiscalists especially sensitive to political urgencies favored tax reduction on the ground that it would slide down congressional throats more easily. Those especially sensitive to structural deficiencies argued, on the other hand, that the deficit should be brought about by an increase in public spending designed to improve education, labor mobility and so on.

Within the administration the Federal Reserve Board was a stronghold of structuralism, partly in order to head off pressure to unbalance the budget; and the Departments of Commerce and the Treasury, partly for the same reason, and the Departments of Labor and of Health, Education and Welfare, because of the character of the problems with which they dealt, all had structuralist tendencies. Those who wished to unite the structural and fiscal approaches in a single program argued in the spirit of *The Affluent Society* for increased investment in the public sector. The strongly fiscalist Council of Economic Advisers, on the other hand, after some interest in public works in 1961, espoused the tax reduction approach for the next two years.

3. POLICY: 1961

Thus the spectrum of possibilities: but in the President's mind what was theoretically desirable had to be tempered by what was politically feasible. His campaign had emphasized discipline and sacrifice; his victory had been slim; his Congress was conservative; and, at least in the mind of the business community, his party had a reputation for fiscal irresponsibility. As Kennedy told Heller in December 1960, "I understand the case for a tax cut, but it doesn't fit very well with my call for sacrifice." Nor did it fit very well with the need, increased by the shaky balance-of-payments situation, to appear, though a Democrat, a defender of the dollar. The science, so called, of economics had to return to its honorable antecedents and become the art of political economy.

Paul Samuelson, heading an interregnal task force, adjusted his recommendations to fit the presidential and congressional mood. While a believer in deficits and inclined toward social spending, he refrained from recommending investment in the public sector, apart from defense, and mentioned a temporary tax cut only as an emergency weapon. As for the use of monetary policy—the traditional Democratic remedy of lower interest rates—this, he thought, was seriously limited by the international payments problem. All this left structural measures, along with defense spending, as Samuelson's main recommendation and the administration's main resort.

Kennedy's special message to Congress on February 2 therefore concentrated on the extension of unemployment insurance, area redevelopment, the increase of the minimum wage, housing and community development, acceleration of procurement and construction and the like. More novel though hardly more radical was a proposal for special tax incentives to investment. The message even catered somewhat to congressional fears about the budget, promising balance "over the years of the economic cycle." Later messages through the spring called for other institutional measures. And Congress proved responsive to the structural approach. Within six months it passed an area redevelopment bill, an omnibus housing bill, a farm bill, a rise in the minimum wage, the liberalization of social security, temporary unemployment benefits, benefits for dependent children of unemployed parents and a program to combat water pollution—a record of action on the domestic front unmatched in any single sitting since 1935.

Still, this was a program of welfare, perhaps a program to end the recession, but not a program of economic expansion. Kennedy himself restlessly continued to seek the answer to the 5 per cent growth rate. A few weeks after his special economic message, when an Americans for Democratic Action delegation called on him, he singled out Robert R. Nathan, a Washington economist from New Deal days, and asked him the usual question. Nathan replied that the President could get his 5 per cent growth rate, but the price would be a deficit of $5 billion a year for the next ten years. The President said skeptically that would be great if only Nathan would organize the political support for such a policy.

As Kennedy told Walter Lippmann and me at luncheon a few days later, most economists were evasive when he tried to pin them down as to what exactly government could do to stimulate growth, but Nathan had been frank; and an addition of $50 billion to the national debt would of course be very little compared to the extra growth and revenue which could be thus induced. Only the systematic creation of annual deficits, he said, was the one thing which the political situation, short of a depression, precluded his doing. "I don't want to be tagged as a big spender early in this administration," he said on another occasion. "If I do, I won't get my programs through later on."

Thus when Heller argued within the administration for the stand-by public works program which Senator Joseph S. Clark was proposing on the Hill, he encountered opposition both in the White House, where the President and Ted Sorensen felt that the new plans for military and space

spending put further domestic appropriations out of the
question and in the Treasury. Douglas Dillon had made it
clear from the start that in case of depression he would
recommend deficits; and he had cheered the New Frontier
economists in the White House meeting on fiscal policy by
saying, "What the country needs for the coming fiscal
year is the largest deficit that will not frighten foreigners,
say $5 billion." But a deficit of this magnitude was coming
anyway; and Dillon did not wish to increase it, partly
because he hoped to hold out the dream of a balanced
budget to the business community, and partly because he
wanted to use limited tax reduction at some later point to
trade off in Congress for a program of tax reform.

While these circumstances led Kennedy in 1961 to oppose
an increased deficit, I have no doubt that his objections
were political and not intellectual. He believed in 1961,
as he had in 1952, in the general validity of compensatory
fiscal policy; he was unquestionably the first Keynesian
President. His problem throughout was not doctrine but
politics. "That is the one thing Eisenhower has put over to
the American people," he once said to me. "We Democrats
have put over other things. But he has put over the idea
of the sinfulness of spending and the danger of inflation."

Then, as the recession came to an end in the course of
the spring and gross national product shot up 2.8 per cent
in the second quarter of 1961 alone, the pressure for
deficits slackened. Indeed, the first flurry of emotion over
the Berlin crisis even produced a movement, which Heller
and others succeeded in blocking, for a tax increase. This
budgetary circumspection disappointed those who felt that
sustained expansion required the purposeful use of fiscal
policy. Leon Keyserling, who had been chairman of the
Council of Economic Advisers under Truman, launched
one long exhortation after another against administration
timidity. In June, Lippmann said that Kennedy was carrying on "in all its essentials the Eisenhower economic
philosophy. . . . It's like the Eisenhower administration
thirty years younger."

This was extravagant, but Keyserling and Lippmann had
a point. The Treasury, in its pursuit of business confidence,
did indeed seem almost to be endorsing the Eisenhower
theory that a balanced budget was the measure of success
in economic policy. Toward the end of the year, Galbraith, after congratulating Dillon on his part in "perhaps
the best [economic policy] we have ever had," felt constrained to add: "You have had a good performance because

the budget was not balanced. Yet you keep saying that a balanced budget is the test. You have now promised a balanced budget for the next year although there is little chance that in the end it will be balanced. Therefore, though there is a very good chance you will have continued recovery and continued reduction in unemployment, improvement in balance of payments and stable prices, it will still be possible to say that you have failed. You are so bent on your discredit that you plan for it. I am reminded of a courtesan whose conquests have made her the cynosure of all men and the envy of all women and who at any critical moment in the conversation insists on the absolute importance of chastity."

As for the Treasury, beyond its avowals of budgetary orthodoxy, it concentrated in 1961 on the idea of a tax credit to provide incentives for modernization of plant and equipment. This was designed both as a spur to investment and as a signal of favorable intent to the business community. To the administration's surprise, however, businessmen recoiled from the proposal; having counted on a liberalization of depreciation allowances, they considered the investment credit a poor substitute. Actually the administration had depreciation revision in mind too and was postponing it only because it involved too great a revenue loss if enacted apart from general tax revision. Yet, despite Washington's placatory policy, business opposition blocked the investment credit in the 1961 Congress, and the bill was finally postponed to 1962.

4. KENNEDY AND BUSINESS

This miscarriage set the tone for Kennedy's relations with business. The resistance to the investment credit had sprung fundamentally from the inability of businessmen to believe that Democrats would ever do anything for business. "The business community," as Robert Kennedy told one interviewer, "always has greater mistrust of any Democratic administration than of a Republican administration. It is an ideological reflex—obsolete, in my opinion—but that's one of the facts of life, so I don't know that businessmen, the big ones, anyway, no matter what we do, will ever be in love with us." The Attorney General said this in 1963 when the Kennedys were reluctantly accepting business hostility as a fact of life; but in 1961 the President, because he also thought the reflex obsolete, really supposed that the hostility might be overcome. Convinced that the ideological fights of the thirties had been settled and hopeful that modern-minded figures, like his friend Thomas J. Watson, Jr., of International Business Machines, were leading business opinion, he saw no reason why government and business should not work together in rational partnership.

But his first steps were not reassuring to business. His series of distinguished appointments to the regulatory agencies—William L. Cary as chairman of the Securities and Exchange Commission, Newton Minow as chairman of the Federal Communications Commission, Frank McCulloch as chairman of the National Labor Relations Board, Joseph Swidler as chairman of the Federal Power Commission, Paul R. Dixon as chairman of the Federal Trade Commission—expressed the theory that these agencies should respond to the public interest rather than to the industries regulated. This naturally outraged businessmen who, in earlier years, had grown used to regarding regulatory agencies as adjuncts of their own trade associations.

Another episode in the spring of 1961 strengthened business anxieties. For a quarter of a century the Business Advisory Council, a collection of big businessmen, representing in 1961 a large share of the industrial production of the United States, had enjoyed a special relationship with the Department of Commerce. Roosevelt had established the BAC as a channel to the business community and, under such chairmen as Averell Harriman, it had played a modestly useful liaison role. But by 1960 its chairman was Ralph J. Cordiner of General Electric, whose firm in 1961 pleaded guilty to criminal charges of price-fixing and bid-rigging, and the BAC itself in the Eisenhower years had become cozily accustomed to closed meetings with government officials where, according to Hobart Rowen, an able business reporter, its members had access to economic information not available to other private groups.

Business had welcomed the appointment of Luther Hodges as Secretary of Commerce. The former governor of North Carolina, who used to describe himself as the administration's "only tie with the nineteenth century," was not only a generation older than the radical young New Frontiersmen but had been a businessman himself. Nonetheless, Hodges was determined that his department should represent the national interest. "You will never hear from me," he said early on, "that this country should do this or that simply because business wants it. What is good for General Motors may, or may not, be good for the country." Moreover, Hodges had serious reservations about the BAC both because it represented only big business and because he doubted the propriety of the secret meetings. Stimulated by Rowen, he asserted a right as Secretary to appoint or approve new members and also ruled that the meetings be open to the press. After a period of irritated negotiation, the BAC leaders, persuaded that they were no longer to enjoy their status of the Eisenhower years, withdrew from their association with Commerce. If even Luther Hodges acted this way, what could they expect from the young radicals?

This breakdown of an established business-government channel worried Douglas Dillon, who urged the President to repair relations. Kennedy, who needed business help on balance of payments and on his projected revision of trade policy, accordingly dissociated himself from Hodges's excommunication of the BAC and initiated a policy of conciliation. When the President met in August with the presidents of the Chamber of Commerce, the National Association of Manufacturers and the Committee for Economic Development, he began by saying: "Gentlemen, I understand that we're labeled anti-business. Why is that?" In September he received the members of the Business Council, as the BAC now called itself, at the White House; and in October, when the Council went into its annual retreat at Hot Springs, a parade of New Frontier officials assured it of the administration's deep affection.

Kennedy had, I believe, considerable respect for the experience of businessmen. He felt that this experience gave them clues to the operations of the American economy which his intellectuals, for all their facile theories, did not possess. On the other hand, he had no great respect for the ideas of businessmen, and the respect declined the further their ideas moved away from their experience. The President probably agreed with Dr. Johnson: "A merchant's desire is not of glory, but of gain; not of public wealth, but of private emolument; he is, therefore, rarely to be consulted on questions of war or peace, or any designs of wide extent and distant consequence."

And he regarded the pressure to play up to businessmen with recurrent exasperation. At dinner at the White House on the night before his September reception for the Business Council, he observed that he was struck by a "paradox" in his dealings with business and with labor. Labor leaders, he said, were individually often mediocre and selfish, but labor as a body took generally responsible positions on the great issues; while businessmen were often enlightened as individuals but collectively hopeless on public policy. He now better understood Franklin Roosevelt's attitude toward organized business, he continued, and he only wished there were no cold war so he could debate the future of America with the businessmen.

5. STEEL

The debate was to take place in spite of the cold war. The President had been much concerned to keep costs and prices down both to prevent inflation at home and to relieve the balance of payments by promoting exports abroad. Inflation created by excess demand was not very likely in an economy only beginning to emerge from a recession; but 'cost-push' inflation, touched off on occasion in the fifties when wages rose faster than productivity, remained a threat. And steel obviously played a key role in the strategy of price stability because increases in steel prices reverberated so far, wide and fast through the economy. Accordingly Kennedy wrote the presidents of the leading steel companies in September 1961, describing steel as "a bellwether, as well as a major element in industrial costs," and suggesting that the industry "forgo a price increase." He followed this by a letter to David J. McDonald of the United Steelworkers proposing that wage demands be kept "within the limit of advances in productivity." In the 1962 Economic Report this criterion became the basis of what were called the wage-price guide-posts and an essential part of the administration's defense against inflation.

Early in 1962, Secretary of Labor Goldberg, who himself had been the Steelworkers' general counsel, helped negotiate a noninflationary settlement which both the union and the industry accepted in April. Everyone concerned assumed that, in return for what one student has called "the least costly agreement in many years," [2] the industry would never dream of raising prices. Then, on April 10, Roger Blough, chairman of the board at United States Steel, made his famous call at the White House and, without advance warning, handed the President of the United States a four-page mimeographed statement announcing the decision to raise steel prices $6 a ton—a statement which the steel people, in fact, released before Blough completed his conversation with the President.

Blough said later that he had informed the President "in what I hope was as courteous a manner as could be devised under all the circumstances" and that he was sur-

[2] Grant McConnell, *Steel and the Presidency–1962* (New York, 1963), 75.

prised at Kennedy's reaction. He added, "I know nothing about politics." This innocence was a little hard to take in Washington, where Blough had been a familiar figure for years. Even Arthur Krock found it either "an intolerable strain on human credulity or an admission of incurable short-sightedness." Yet Blough's whole demeanor suggested a genuine belief that an increase in steel prices was no more the business of government than an increase in the price of the lemonade a child might sell in front of his house.

Kennedy's reaction was a mixture of incredulity over what he saw as the selfishness and stupidity of the steel industry and anger over what he regarded as its premeditated deceit. Honorable people, he felt, did not behave in this fashion. "We were not asking the steel industry for capitulation," Arthur Goldberg said; "we were asking it for candor." The industry had accepted labor's restraint four days before without the slightest hint that it did not plan to be equally restrained itself; its *démarche* now, from the White House view, seemed a plain and impudent double cross. "My father always told me," Kennedy said, in the remark the business community never forgave, "that all businessmen were sons-of-bitches, but I never believed 'it till now." This proposition, though offered in private, soon reached the newspapers. Kennedy later told a press conference that his father had limited his comment to steel men; "he was involved when he was a member of the Roosevelt administration in the 1937 strike. He formed an opinion which he imparted to me, and which I found appropriate that evening. . . . I quoted what he said and indicated that he had not been, as he had not been on many other occasions, wholly wrong." (A few days later, he remarked to Adlai Stevenson and me, "They *are* a bunch of bastards—and I'm saying this on my own now, not just because my father told it to me.")

Anger was a flash; then he called in his advisers on domestic policy and swung into action. If he accepted the steel decision, it would mean a grave threat to the wage-price guideposts, price stability, the program of economic expansion, the balance of payments, the trust the labor movement had in him and the prestige of the Presidency. He was coldly determined to mobilize all the resources of public pressure and private suasion to force steel to rescind the increase. Soon he had to leave the council of war in order to dress for the annual White House reception for members of Congress and their wives. A year before it had been the Bay of Pigs; "I'll never hold another congressional reception," the President said.

The next morning Bethlehem Steel, the second largest company, announced an increase, and four others quickly followed. At his press conference that afternoon Kennedy described these actions as "a wholly unjustifiable and irresponsible defiance of the public interest by "a tiny handful of steel executives whose pursuit of private power and profit exceeds their sense of public responsibility." He added: "Some time ago I asked each American to consider what he would do for his country and I asked the steel companies. In the last twenty-four hours we had their answer."

In the meantime, he had mounted a campaign of pressure against the steel magnates. Dillon, McNamara, Hodges, Clark Clifford and others were making phone calls all over the country. The Defense Department started shifting its steel purchases from the United States Steel to companies which had not yet raised prices. The Department of Justice began inquiries into whether the steel companies had acted in violation of the anti-trust laws.[3] (It was in this connection that the Attorney General asked the FBI to check newspaper reports of remarks made in a Bethlehem Steel stockholders meeting which might indicate that U. S. Steel had forced Bethlehem into its supporting action. The use of the FBI to make preliminary investigations in anti-trust cases was routine. Unhappily, though the instruction went to the FBI in the afternoon, it was apparently passed on to Philadelphia by Pony Express, for the reporter involved was not called till three the next morning. The FBI's post-midnight rap on the door caused a furor. The President, unmoved, later remarked, "Reporters have called up a good many people in the middle of the night themselves.") The Federal Trade Commission announced an informal investigation to see whether the steel companies had broken regulations against collusive price-fixing. Congressional anti-trust committees promised hearings. Ted Sorensen started work on emergency wage-price legislation. And, despite the FBI episode, public opinion rallied behind the President. William W. Scranton, the Republican candidate for governor of Pennsylvania, wired Blough: "The increase at this time is wrong—wrong for Pennsylvania, wrong for America, wrong for the free world."

[3] In 1965 eight major companies, headed by U. S. Steel, pleaded *nolo contendere* to charges of price-fixing between 1955 and 1961. Each company received the maximum fine under the anti-trust laws.

Walter Heller and Kermit Gordon had argued that, if enough companies held out against the rise—the rule of thumb was 10 per cent of national steel production—then U. S. Steel and the others would be forced in competitive self-defense to bring their prices down. This strategy soon centered on the Inland Steel Company of Chicago. The President also talked to Edgar Kaiser of Kaiser Steel. On Friday, April 13, Inland, Kaiser and the Armco Steel Corporation all let it be known that they were prepared to hold the line. Goldberg and Clifford went to New York to talk to Blough—a conference interrupted by word that Bethlehem had rescinded its price increase. Before the afternoon was over, United States Steel surrendered. It was seventy-two hours after Blough's call on Kennedy. On April 17, exactly a week after his ultimatum, Blough made another visit to the White House. At dinner that night I asked the President how his conversation with Blough had gone this time. He said, "I told him that his men could keep their horses for the spring plowing."

The steel fight confirmed the worst suspicions on each side about the other. Businessmen had grown accustomed in the Eisenhower years to a President who sought their company, reverenced their opinions and treated them as if they were the most weighty group in the nation. Though they doubtless admired Kennedy's intelligence, were impressed by his knowledge and were generally conciliated in his presence, they felt he stood at a distance from them. When he protested that he was pro-business, it was in a sense that many businessmen found hard to understand. It was true that he accepted an economic system founded on private ownership and that his policies were designed, in effect, to lure business into investment and growth. But this was not enough. The fact remained that he was outside the business ethos, that he did not regard the acquisitive impulse as man's noblest instinct nor the pursuit of profit as man's highest calling, that he was unimpressed by great accumulators of wealth, that he did not consider successful businessmen as the best brains or the most enjoyable company, that he saw them as a faction to be propitiated and not as a force to be followed, that he brought few of them into government and that he did not like to have them around in the evening. The business community knew that the President was not 'one of ours'; they felt that business was not understood in Washington; and they construed Kennedy's pro-business efforts as based on the need for economic and political placation and not on the belief that the true business of America was business.[4]

They felt, in short, that they were outsiders again. Many may even have resumed this role with a certain relief. During the Eisenhower years they were somehow implicated in the actions of government and therefore debarred from denouncing Washington whenever anything happened they did not like. Kennedy's election had liberated them. Now they were exempt from responsibility. They had a Democratic administration to blame again and 'that man in the White House' to hate again. It was back to the old rituals and devils, and they spoke out with liturgical fervor. The Republican congressional leadership called the steel fight "a display of naked political power never seen before in this nation. . . . We have passed within the shadow of police-state methods." Barry Goldwater said that Kennedy was trying to "socialize the business of the country." John W. Bricker, resurrecting his prose of a generation before, cried, "The recent display of dictatorial power by President Kennedy has made us realize that freedom in its largest sense is at stake. The Republican party is the last and only remaining bulwark." Kennedy's citation of his father reinforced the comforting sense of continuity. (A cartoon of the day showed two businessmen in their club, one saying to the other, "My father always told me that all Presidents are sons-of-bitches." Kennedy was delighted, and the original hung on a wall in Evelyn Lincoln's office.)

As for the President, the steel fight showed once again his cool understanding of the uses of power. He had, in fact, *no* direct authority available against the steel companies. Instead, he mobilized every fragment of quasi-authority he could find and, by a bravura public performance, converted weakness into strength. And his victory was a durable one. When the administration a year later countenanced selective price increases by Wheeling Steel, some commentators rushed to conclude that Kennedy had thrown away his triumph of 1962. Actually these 1963 increases made no difference. As the Council of Economic Advisers reported in 1965, "On the average, steel prices are essentially unchanged from 1959."

In winning this victory, Kennedy answered the question with which the business community had confronted every

---

[4] The Research Institute of America on June 30, 1962, reported the results of a survey of 6000 business executives. Fifty-two per cent described the administration as "strongly anti-business," 36 per cent as "moderately anti-business," and only 9 per cent as "neutral" or "pro-business."

activist Chief Executive since Jackson: "Who is President anyway?" He delivered his answer at a cost, but the cost of not answering would have been greater. And, if the domestic cost was significant, in foreign policy his triumph over steel was an unmixed gain. Newspapers applauded his action around the globe. Wilson, Roosevelt and Truman had won world confidence in part because their domestic policies had established them as the critics, and not the instruments, of American business. Now Kennedy had left the world no doubt that he was equally independent of the American business community—and in a world indoctrinated with fears of aggressive American capitalism this won new trust for his leadership in foreign affairs.

His conclusion about organized business was impersonal and penetrating. "The problem is," he said one day in July on the plane back from the Cape, "that the business community no longer has any confidence in itself. Whenever I say anything that upsets them, businessmen just die. I have to spend my time and energy trying to prop them up."

6. STOCK MARKETS AND SWIMMING POOLS

He began the labor of propping up immediately after Blough's capitulation. Moreover, the strength of pro-business sentiment in Congress and the need for active business collaboration in economic growth and foreign policy made it expedient to heal the wounds as speedily as possible. And in domestic, as in foreign, affairs, Kennedy never believed in humiliating an opponent or cutting off his retreat. He told his staff that it was "important that we not take any action that could be interpreted as vindictive." When Blough received a citation from the Yale Law School, the President sent him a congratulatory telegram. At the end of April he made a conciliatory speech before the Chamber of Commerce.

But business was not notably responsive to the flag of truce. The president of the Chamber of Commerce, after Kennedy's speech, took the platform himself and made the dark observation: "We should remember dictators in other lands usually come to power under accepted constitutional procedures." (Appearing a few days later before the United Auto Workers, Kennedy said, "Last week, after speaking to the Chamber of Commerce and the presidents of the American Medical Association, I began to wonder how I got elected. And now I remember.") And a tension remained between his own public attitudes and private emotions. He exposed some of them one day when

Hugh Sidey asked if it was to be war with business in the old F.D.R. style. Kennedy said at first, "No, no, we're not going to do that. They're our partners—unwilling partners. But we're in this together. . . . I'm not against business—want to help them if I can." Then he added, "But look at the record. I spent a whole year trying to encourage business. And look what I get for it. . . . I think maybe I ought to get a little tougher with business. I think that may be the way to treat them. They understand it. When I'm nice to them, they just kick me. I think I'll just treat them rougher. Maybe it will do some good."

Publicly he continued to be nice, however. Then on Monday, May 28, the stock market suddenly collapsed—the largest one-day drop in prices since the crash of 1929. Actually speculation on the possibility of inflation had pushed prices up too fast in the winter of 1960–61, and the market had been visibly adjusting, at least since the last week in March, to price stability and the diminished prospect for capital gain. But the sudden descent created deep anxieties. Within the government Seymour Harris's panel of Treasury consultants forecast trouble ahead. One conservative writer, Merryle Stanley Rukeyser, produced a book entitled *The Kennedy Recession*,[5] and business comment freely blamed the stock market troubles on the 'lack of confidence,' engendered by the President's disrespect for United States Steel. Marquis Childs, after talks with businessmen, wrote that their attitude to Kennedy was: Now we have you where we want you. When asked about this at a press conference, the President convulsed the newspapermen by replying, with a nod to his office: "I can't believe I'm where business—big business, wants me." Privately he was increasingly disturbed and baffled by the problem of getting business to face the serious issues of the economy.

One afternoon early in June, he held forth to Sorensen, O'Donnell and me. "I understand better every day," he said, "why Roosevelt, who started out such a mild fellow, ended up so ferociously anti-business. It is hard as hell to be friendly with people who keep trying to cut your legs off. . . . There are about ten thousand people in the country involved in this—bankers, industrialists, lawyers, publishers, politicians—a small group, but doing everything they can to say we are going into a depression because business has no confidence in the administration. They are starting

[5] Oddly not published until February 1963, by which time the prospect of a Kennedy recession was long in the past.

to call me the Democratic Hoover. Well, we're not going to take that."

O'Donnell said, "The worst thing we can do now is to put ourselves in a foot-kissing posture." The President wheeled around and said, "Yes, we tried that after the steel case, and we didn't get anywhere. . . . They are trying to make government responsible for everything on the ground that what we did to steel destroyed business confidence. We have to turn it around. We have to put out the picture of a small group of men turning against the government and the economy because the government would not surrender to them. That is the real issue."

The market decline continued, if at a more stately pace, until the end of June 1962, and the business campaign against the administration intensified. Because Kennedy had great personal popularity through the country, the attacks began, in the classical manner, by concentrating on the more vulnerable of his advisers. Past sins made me an obvious target. A contribution in 1947 to a *Partisan Review* symposium on "The Future of Socialism" was now exhumed as evidence, as Barry Goldwater put it, that "for many years [Schlesinger] has been writing about socialism in America and laying out a blueprint on how to accomplish it. He announces himself as a socialist." Goldwater had obviously never read the *Partisan Review* piece, for the article, following a discussion of capitalism and socialism, said: "After all which system has more successfully dehumanized the worker, fettered the working class and extinguished personal and political liberty? . . . The socialist state is thus worse than the capitalist state because it is more inclusive in its coverage and more unlimited in its power." But the suggestion that I was writing about socialism as an analyst and not as an advocate made little dent on the gathering clamor (though Goldwater, to do him justice, stopped calling me a socialist when the facts were pointed out to him). I also attracted the attention of a columnist named Henry J. Taylor, well known for his belief in the existence of flying saucers.[6] Early in May he cited the *Partisan Review* piece in a column for the Scripps-Howard papers entitled crisply "Schlesinger Should Go." A little later I foolishly accepted a telephone call from him. He was inquiring about a piece I had written for

---

[6] Taylor's extravagance did not flag in later years. Thus on April 17, 1965, "It's astounding, but true, that the Communist Party, U.S.A., actually planned the Johnson administration's Voting Rights Act of 1965."

the *Saturday Evening Post* and what I intended to do with the payment (answer: turn it over to charity); but I seized the occasion to point out that his column on the *Partisan Review* piece had falsified my views. In short order the conversation began to deteriorate. When he made some particularly outrageous accusation, I said, "If you believe that, you're an idiot." Taylor soon wrote a column saying indignantly that my "first words" when he called were, "You are an idiot." Walter Winchell added his contribution: "Schlesinger is haunted by intellectual snobbery, dominated by arrogance . . . as power-mad as he is venomous . . . a threat to fundamental American concepts." A group of patriots in California founded the Organization to Remove Schlesinger from Public Life.

At this point Robert and Ethel Kennedy gave a party to celebrate their twelfth wedding anniversary. It was a gentle summer night at Hickory Hill. The tables were set around the swimming pool, and Ethel was sitting at a table for four on a bridge thrown rather precariously across the pool. Dancing took place between the courses. My partner and I ventured out on the catwalk; it shook under our tread; and to our horror we saw Ethel's chair slide on the wet boards to the edge and then into the water. After a moment, I plunged in after her. We changed our clothes, and the party went pleasantly on. A few days later garbled versions of the swimming-pool episode began to find their way into print.

One afternoon I received a call from Tom Corcoran, who had endured similar attention in another age. He said, "I scent a man hunt. Whenever the market goes down, those fellows demand a human sacrifice, and they have nominated you. The play they gave the swimming-pool story was the tip-off." By this time, I began to suffer from the sense of having brought unnecessary trouble on the administration and increased the President's burdens at a time when he had quite enough on his mind. Accordingly, in a lapse of humor, I solemnly told him that I was ready to leave. He said with great kindness, "Don't worry about it. Everybody knows what Henry Taylor is like. No one pays any attention to him. All they are doing is shooting at me through you. Their whole line is to pin everything on the professors—you, Heller, Rostow. When the market fell, *Time* put Heller on the cover, not Dillon. Don't worry about it. This is the sort of thing you have to expect."

XXIV

THE NATIONAL AGENDA

UNDERNEATH THE CLAMOR the President had been thinking intensively about the problems of communication on economic problems. One Sunday in May 1962 he took André Malraux out to Glen Ora for luncheon, and, as Kennedy later described it, they fell into a discussion of the persistence of mythology in the contemporary world. "In the nineteenth century," Malraux said, "the ostensible issue within the European states was the monarchy vs. the republic. But the real issue was capitalism vs. the proletariat. In the twentieth century the ostensible issue is capitalism vs. the proletariat. But the world has moved on. What is the real issue now?" The real issue today, Kennedy replied, was the management of industrial society—a problem, he said, not of ideology but of administration.

This conversation remained in his mind. A few days later, when he spoke to the White House conference on national economic issues, the "difference between myth and reality" provided the theme for his remarks. The old debates of F.D.R. and Wilson and Bryan, the President observed, were increasingly irrelevant to the complex technical decisions of modern society. Only medical care for the aged still roused "powerful feelings among the general public." For the rest—

> the fact of the matter is that most of the problems, or at least many of them, that we now face are technical problems, are administrative problems. They are very sophisticated judgments which do not lend themselves to the great sort of 'passionate movements' which have stirred this country so often in the past. . . .
>
> How can we look at things as they are, not through party labels, or through position labels, but as they are—and figure out how we can maintain this economy so that it moves ahead?

1. REASON AT YALE

In another few days he decided to make this the theme of a major address at the Yale Commencement. One morning early in June he called me in and outlined very specifically the speech he wanted. My first draft seemed to him too mild; and he asked me to "sharpen" it up, which, with Galbraith's help, I did. The result was too sharp, and Sorensen now produced a new draft. This was not right either; and finally McGeorge Bundy and I turned out still another. The President went over it on Sunday morning, June 10, and suggested still more changes. After these were made, he worked over the text himself on the plane north, adding several more paragraphs.

The central issues of our time, Kennedy said in New Haven, "relate not to basic clashes of philosophy or ideology but to ways and means of reaching common goals." As every past generation had to disenthrall itself from an inheritance of truism and stereotype, "so in our own time we must move on from the reassuring repetition of stale phrases to a new, difficult, but essential confrontation with reality."

> For the great enemy of the truth is very often not the lie—deliberate, contrived and dishonest—but the myth, persistent, persuasive and unrealistic. Too often we hold fast to the clichés of our forebears. We subject all facts to a prefabricated set of interpretations. We enjoy the comfort of opinion without the discomfort of thought.

In particular, the dialogue between government and business was "clogged by illusion and platitude." It failed "to reflect the true realities of contemporary American society."

He then dealt with several prevalent myths. As against the myth that government was growing relatively bigger, he pointed out that, excepting defense and space expenditures, the federal government had expanded less than any other major sector of the economy since the Second World War. As against the myth that federal deficits created and surpluses prevented inflation, he cited the historical record of the postwar years. As against the myth that the national debt was growing at a dangerously rapid rate, he pointed out that it had declined sharply since the war, both per person and as a proportion of gross national product. As against the myth that 'confidence' in the national administration was the condition for economic prosperity, he pointed out that such confidence had not prevented recessions in 1929, 1954, 1958 and 1960, and that corporate plans were "not based on a political confidence in party leaders but on an economic confidence in the nation's ability to invest and produce and consume."

> What is at stake [he concluded] is not some grand warfare of rival ideologies which will sweep the country with passion

but the practical management of a modern economy. What we need is not labels and clichés but more basic discussion of the sophisticated and technical issues involved in keeping a great economic machinery moving ahead. . . .

The debate of the thirties had its great significance and produced great results, but it took place in a different world with different needs and different tasks. It is our responsibility today to live in our own world and to identify the needs and discharge the tasks of the 1960s.

In the course of the speech, Kennedy remarked that the governments of Western Europe were prepared "to face technical problems without ideological preconceptions" and therefore could "coordinate the elements of a national economy and bring about growth and prosperity." Our own nation, he said, should begin "a serious dialogue of the kind which has led in Europe to such fruitful collaboration among all the elements of economic society and to a decade of unrivaled economic progress." This observation reflected his marked interest in the performance of the West European economies. Early in his administration he had charged Heller on his transatlantic trips to report on European planning methods, and he used to cross-examine European visitors to learn the secret of their success. He soon discovered that Western Europe was happily free of the American budgetary obsession. As E. Van Lennep, the Treasurer-General of the Netherlands and a leading figure in the OECD (Organization for Economic Cooperation and Development), said to him a fortnight before the Yale speech, "In Europe one does not understand why in the United States there is still a strong tendency to have a balanced budget as a target [even] for the average of a business cycle." The President learned too about European planning of the indirect or 'indicative' sort—not centralized physical direction of the economy but the technique of laying down projections for major industries and then persuading everybody to do what was necessary to make the projections come true.

Lacking doctrinaire belief in the sanctity of balanced budgets or of unregulated markets, Kennedy found all this a perfectly rational way to run a modern economy. The continuing economic sluggishness in the United States, the persistence of unemployment even as business activity increased, the absence in the Keynesian system of a reliable defense against inflation under conditions of full employment: all these factors predisposed him intellectually toward the idea of combining decentralized decision with national economic targets. McNamara, whose interest in management extended to economic matters, strengthened this concern. The Secretary of Defense was sure that systems analysis could help rationalize the economy within the margin of free choice and used to say to Heller, "Your fellows and mine should get together and see what we can do."

In the aftermath of steel, the problem of achieving full employment without inflation—as Rostow called it, "the chapter Keynes never wrote"—was of particular importance. In essential ways the wage-price spiral was beyond the reach of fiscal and monetary policy. The guideposts had represented a first attempt to master the spiral; but they were evidently inadequate when great corporations or unions lacked public responsibility. An incomes policy, perhaps new institutions assuring a greater public role in wage-price settlements, might be a desirable later step. This could constitute part of a rational economic plan—and, if other things were equal, it was in this direction, I believe, that Kennedy's economic thought, with its pragmatic and managerial instincts, might have moved.

But other things, of course, were not equal. Quite apart from the technical problems of transferring French planning methods to the larger and more complex American economy, there remained the American mythology; and this the Yale speech did little to dispel. The old Elis had listened with acute discomfort. The business community as a whole, regarding the speech as blasphemy against the verities, declined the President's invitation to a dialogue. The President, disappointed, concluded that he would have to bide his time. When Solicitor General Archibald Cox, who had worried about wages, prices and inflation since his term as chairman of Truman's Wage Stabilization Board, suggested publicly two days after the Yale speech that a way had to be found to bring government into wage-price decisions on a regular basis and at "a fairly early stage," Kennedy was disturbed, not at the content, he told me, but at the timing. "We have to give the impression of some discipline here," he said. "I don't want anyone to say anything about the domestic economy except Doug Dillon and myself. In due course I may want to give a fireside chat on the economic situation. In the meantime no one should say anything."

2. DILLON AND HELLER

The expectation lingered into the summer that the stock market decline might set off a general decline. This produced a renewed drive among the administration economists and their academic associates for an expansionist program. Heller and Samuelson, remembering their defeat over Senator Clark's public works bill a year before, now decided that the expenditures route would lead into hopeless political thickets. The Council, Harris's Treasury group and most of the economists agreed that the only practical way to stimulate the economy was through a tax cut.

There was one conspicuous holdout: Galbraith. The expansion produced by tax-cutting, he argued to Kennedy toward the end of 1962, would be an expansion of consumer goods; and these the American people already had in abundance. But it was "in the area of public needs, notably schools, colleges, hospitals, foreign policy that our need for growth is greatest." Tax-cutting, as he later put it, was "reactionary" Keynesianism, providing the things the country least needed at the expense of the things it most needed. "I am not sure," he said, "what the advantage is in having a few more dollars to spend if the air is too dirty to breathe, the water too polluted to drink, the commuters are losing out on the struggle to get in and out of the cities, the streets are filthy, and the schools so bad that the young, perhaps wisely, stay away, and hoodlums roll citizens for some of the dollars they saved in taxes." Moreover, fiscal and monetary policy could not immediately help those who entered the labor market under handicaps—the semi-literate, the undereducated, the unskilled young and the Negro. "No general measures," Seymour Harris added, "are going to solve the problems of the textile, coal, automobile, aircraft and similar towns."

Galbraith conceded that it might be politically difficult to get increased spending for public purposes. "That is because public services, though extremely important for people of moderate incomes, are not nearly so essential for the rich. And the rich pay more [in taxes]. The rich and articulate accordingly oppose public spending. That this policy encounters resistance means only that it is painful to the selfish. We must note that the best leaders have always been called spendthrifts by the worst leaders." As for the argument that the stimulus produced by a tax cut would increase federal revenues available for public use, Galbraith rejected this as a trap: "Those who dislike public spending will move immediately at the next stage for more tax reduction, not more spending."

As between stimulus through social spending or through tax cuts, the President, I believe, political conditions permitting, would have preferred the policy which would enable him to meet the nation's public needs. He had defended *The Affluent Society* in the 1960 campaign. When Samuelson first mentioned tax reduction in his task force report before inauguration, Sorensen, Feldman and the President-elect himself all expressed surprise and concern. Kennedy remained sympathetic to the public sector during his administration. "You know, I like spending money," he once told Heller. "What I want from you are good programs by which money can be spent effectively." The 1962 Economic Report stated his position with clarity: "Growth will require increased public investment, just as it will require increased private investment. . . . We must face the question of public versus private expenditures pragmatically, in terms of intrinsic merits and costs, not in terms of fixed preconceptions."

But political conditions, in his judgment, did not permit further social spending; they even cast doubt upon a tax cut. Of the two legislative guardians of tax matters, Wilbur Mills, the chairman of the House Ways and Means Committee, while strong for tax reform, was opposed to reduction, and Harry F. Byrd, chairman of the Senate Finance Committee, was the greatest balanced-budget fundamentalist in the country. The Gallup pull reported 72 per cent of the people opposed to any form of tax reduction which would even temporarily increase public indebtedness. Moreover, on the economic side, Dillon, who felt that the Wall Street decline represented the pricking of a speculative bubble rather than a basic economic slowdown, doubted the need for emergency stimulus. (The sequel proved him right, though without the agitation by the economists for tax reduction in 1962 Dillon and the administration might well not have been right in 1963.) And the Secretary continued both to hope for a balanced budget sometime before his term expired and to fear that emergency tax reduction would deprive the Treasury of the *quid pro quo*'s it would need to get tax reform through Congress.

No one appreciated the political difficulties more acutely than the President. He told me in mid-July that the real choice was between trying for a tax cut and failing, and not trying at all. But he seemed almost prepared to make the attempt and then carry the case to the country in the fall elections if it appeared as if we were really heading into a depression. Thus he looked eagerly for each new set of economic statistics during the summer. Then, when the July figures showed no intimations of crisis, he decided against an emergency cut. The economic indicators were not desperate enough, and the political indicators too desperate.

The debate, however, had not been in vain. Kennedy emerged from the discussion convinced that if the economy did no more than move upward at its present rather languid pace it would make little dent on the persisting problem of unemployment. This problem worried him more and more. It called, he believed, for new stimulus; and, after the discussions of the summer, he thought that new stimulus might at least be within political possibility. Almost as important, Dillon, who up to this point seemed to regard tax reduction as essentially an adjunct to tax reform, now concluded that there was a case for reduction on its own merits as a spur to production. The Treasury thereafter diminished its insistence on a balanced budget; and Kennedy and Dillon proceeded to get assurances of cooperation from Wilbur Mills on a bill combining reduction and reform. On August 13, when the President announced his decision against a tax cut in 1962, he promised a comprehensive tax reduction bill for 1963.

The growing accord between Heller and Dillon was a source of relief and reassurance. The President's economic advisers, in the midst of their sometimes heated discussions, had preserved amiable relations. Dillon was the man of wider experience and superior bureaucratic authority and skill. Nonetheless, Heller was fluent, resourceful and persuasive; and, on the basic issue of deficit spending, it was the Secretary who gave ground and by 1963 came to accept the position for which the professor had been contending since 1961. Still, if Dillon was moving to the left on doctrine, Heller was moving to the right on associations. He was becoming a familiar figure at business meetings, and his agreeable intelligence and candor were disarming earlier suspicions. Moreover, in July 1962 the Treasury announced, with Heller's concurrence, the liberalization of depreciation allowances, a measure intended to increase capital investment but representing an act of government generosity to business which even exceeded the actions of the Eisenhower administration. By this action, along with Heller's goodwill missions, the enactment in October of the investment tax credit and the President's decision—regretted by some of his associates—to put the communications satellite system under private ownership, the administration sought once more to overcome the mistrust of the business community. This time it was in order to win business support for tax reduction—i.e., to get businessmen to back a measure enormously to their advantage but contrary to their superstitions.

3. THE RIDDLE OF GOLD

Tax policy, now resolved at least in principle, was one great battleground between Heller and Dillon. The other was the question, which haunted all economic discussions, of the balance of payments. It was this question which gave the Treasury its most potent leverage over general economic policy. Beginning in 1958, gold had begun to leave the United States in alarming magnitudes in order to meet the deficit in our international payments. The growing pressure on our reserves encouraged those who wished to apply the classical deflationary remedies—high interest rates, government retrenchment—this in spite of the fact that, as Dillon later put it, "the slow growth of our economy was enhancing the relative attractiveness of foreign investment." A pre-inauguration task force, headed by George Ball, had admonished Kennedy that the payments and reserve problems "are being used in an attempt to frustrate expansionist programs at home and abroad and are giving aid and comfort to resurgent protectionism. As long as they remained unresolved, they may seriously hamper the freedom of action of your administration."

Dillon brought in Robert Roosa, an enormously able economist from the Federal Reserve Bank of New York, to handle the payments crisis. In 1961 the Treasury hoped to control the problem by a wide range of piecemeal measures: tying the bulk of foreign aid to purchases within the United States, reducing overseas military expenditures, offering credit guarantees to promote exports and the like. In due course, the so-called 'twist' provided a middle way in monetary policy between relative tightness internationally and relative ease domestically: it held short-term interest rates high enough to keep fluid funds in the country, while making long-term rates low enough to make credit available for domestic investment. And Roosa, with considerable artistry, organized an intricate strategy in defense of our gold reserves through a series of currency 'swaps' and other bilateral international transactions.

Beyond the measures to reduce the outflow of gold, the Treasury in 1961 saw the problem as basically one of technical manipulation among central banks. But Heller and James Tobin on the Council, George Ball in State and Carl Kaysen in the White House took a different view. While admiring Roosa's virtuosity, they saw in it an artist's pride in making a poor system work when the imperative need was for a new system; it was, they said, as if Roosa actually preferred walking a tightrope without any net. Instead of a policy of dazzling improvisation, they wanted a basic reconstruction of the international payments mechanism.

A variety of views united in the pressure for world monetary reform. From London Harold Macmillan sent doleful warnings about the decline in international liquidity: how, he would ask, could the west expect to move four times as many goods with only twice as much credit? Heller and Kaysen saw the payments problem as distorting both the domestic and foreign policies of the New Frontier. Ball and Tobin particularly stressed the political aspects, and did so in terms which evoked Roosevelt's opposition to the London Economic Conference and Jackson's fight against the United States Bank.

The issue, in their view, was whether the control of high financial policy should rest with central bankers and currency speculators or with responsible governments. Bankers and speculators, they pointed out, did not want too much international liquidity. As long as liquidity was tight, they could threaten any country with 'loss of confidence' and thereby influence its national policies. So long as we had to worry about 'confidence,' we were not masters in our own house. Moreover, the theory of confidence held by European bankers was largely derived from the views propagated in the United States by the natural opponents of a Democratic administration—the financial community and the conservative press. Our own conservatives thus weakened foreign confidence in the dollar—and then used the issue of confidence as a weapon against domestic policies they always opposed anyway.

The presumption of the European bankers filled Ball and Tobin with indignation. After all, they pointed out, the American gold crisis was in great part the result of American expenditures for European recovery and defense. Yet the European bankers, as Tobin put it, "by occasional withdrawals of gold and constant complaints . . . have brought tremendous pressure for 'discipline' upon the United States." The adjustments imposed on our economic policy, he added, "have not served the world economy well. Neither were they essential." He concluded: "International financial policy is too important to leave to financiers."

We could not hope, Tobin and Ball continued, to muddle through on our present course without risk of a gold run or serious damage to the domestic economy. The solution lay not in unilateral action by the Treasury—this only left our gold stock at the mercy of European bankers and speculators—but in international monetary machinery. Ball proposed multilateral agreements among governments designed to insulate the United States from excessive gold losses while working to restore long-term equilibrium. Tobin declared it technically and politically possible to reform the international monetary system by putting the world banking functions, now performed by the United States and Britain, into an international institution. One way or another, the United States had to regain its freedom of action. Once governments had enough liquidity to move around in, they could design their national policies without regard for the international bankers.

Dillon stoutly and powerfully opposed these doctrines. He insisted that there was no problem of international liquidity so long as our own payments deficits kept the world supplied with dollars. He doubted that we would have the bargaining power to negotiate international monetary reform until we had first strengthened the dollar at home. He said that any sweeping reform, like the plan devised by Robert Triffin of Yale, would involve an invasion of sovereignty which no Congress would countenance. And, in the meantime, the short-run remedies were having temporary effect. The gold outflow in 1961 and 1962 was at half the 1960 rate, and our payments position materially improved.

The balance of payments remained a constant worry to Kennedy. Of all the problems he faced as President, one had the impression that he felt least at home with this one. He used to tell his advisers that the two things which scared him most were nuclear war and the payments deficit. Once he half-humorously derided the notion that nuclear weapons were essential to international prestige. "What really matters," he said, "is the strength of the currency. It is this, not the *force de frappe*, which makes France a factor. Britain has nuclear weapons, but the pound is weak, so everyone pushes it around. Why are people so nice to Spain today? Not because Spain has nuclear weapons but because of all those lovely gold reserves." He had acquired somewhere, perhaps from his father, the belief that a nation was only as strong as the value of its currency; and he feared that, if he pushed things too far, 'loss of confidence' would descend and there would be a run on gold. But he was determined not to be stampeded into restrictive domestic measures, and he brought steady pressures for remedies which would not block expansion at home. The problem perhaps constrained him more in foreign affairs. He thought, for example, that the continuing payments deficit gave France, with its claims on American gold, a dangerous international advantage; and at times he even briefly considered doing things which would otherwise run athwart his policy, like selling submarines to South Africa, in the hope of relieving the strain on the balance of payments. While he was intellectually sympathetic to the reformers, it seemed to him, as he once said to Kaysen, that, when they put up their ideas, Dillon regularly and gracefully shot them down. He saw Dillon's continuation in Washington as his best insurance against a gold panic in New York. When he was satisfied that the Treasury recommendations were serious and solid, he would not go against them.

Then toward the end of 1962 the drain spurted again, and the problem began to assume a new character. At that time the gold flight was coming increasingly from the sale of foreign securities on the American market. The Treasury devised new expedients in 1963, such as the interest equalization tax on the purchase of foreign securities. More and more, everyone regarded control of long-term capital outflow as the key to the situation. "The great free nations of the world," Kennedy said in June 1963, "must take control of our monetary problems if these problems are not to take control of us." As the debate continued, the Treasury was beginning to recognize international monetary reform as a need independent of the correction of the American payments disequilibrium. Soon Dillon and Roosa were talking (minus the Jacksonian overtones) somewhat as Heller, Ball and Tobin had talked two years earlier. Once again, Dillon had moved closer to Heller.

In economics, as in politics, timing is of the essence. Because Dillon might agree that Heller was right about a tax cut in 1963 did not prove that Heller was right in wanting one in 1962. What the Secretary's critics called his "dillontory" tactics and his penchant for "dillonbusters" may often have been in accord with political and economic actualities. Restraint was the Treasury's job, as it was one of the Council's jobs to venture out ahead of policy. The President would say to Heller, "I can't say that yet, but you can." The Council's sallies in advance of the administration seemed to Kennedy a useful exercise both in political reconnaissance and in public education. Dillon appreciated this too, knowing that, on the things he cared about most, he could ordinarily get Kennedy's support.

The exchanges between the Treasury and the Council in these years taught the one economic ideas and the other political realities. What had begun between Dillon and Heller as an edgy competition became by 1963 a fruitful partnership. Above all, their agreement on the need for tax reduction in 1963 promised action, so long deferred, to get America moving again.

4. THE NEW SOCIETY

But economic growth was only the first step. The nation at midcentury, urban, industrial, mobile, technologically kinetic, spiritually hyperbolic, contained a swarm of hard and insistent problems. Kennedy used to speak almost with envy of the relatively predictable statecraft of the nineteenth century. Then, as he once said, "great Presidents and great Senators dealt with four, five or six issues which flowed in a gentle stream across the panorama of their lives. What they talked about when they came to Congress they talked about . . . at the end of their congressional terms." Now the United States faced issues "which dwarf in complexity every week the kind of problems which those men dealt with in their lifetimes." And these, he said, were "new problems, entirely different from those that have faced the Eisenhower administration, or that of Harry Truman, or Franklin Roosevelt or Woodrow Wilson . . . new problems, requiring new people, new solutions, new ideas."

The problems, of course, were not all that different, nor were the answers he offered in 1960 all that new—the improvement of the educational system, the strengthening of public provisions for social security and medical care, attention to the decaying cities, a more rational farm program, the conservation and development of natural resources, recognition of the Negro revolution. This was, in effect, the unfinished business of Franklin Roosevelt's New Deal. Yet Kennedy's spirited presentation imbued it with his own intense contemporaneity. The program, taken as a whole, offered a systematic identification of the fundamental problems of modern America in terms of a deeply critical assessment of the moral, intellectual and institutional failures of American society. And, despite his support of economic growth and his concern over persisting privation, the thrust of his preoccupation was less with the economic machine and its quantitative results than with the quality of life in a society which, in the main, had achieved abundance.

This, as he fully realized, was a subtle preoccupation, not easily convertible into the coin of politics. With 94 per cent of the labor force employed and national income steadily rising, it would be difficult to persuade a large conservative Congress and a largely contented people of the need for federal action to improve the quality of society. It would require, as he saw it, a long and patient program of public education. This he promptly began in an extraordinary series of messages to the Congress on domestic affairs in the spring of 1961. In addition to his strictly economic documents, he sent the Hill messages on health and hospital care (February 9), education (February 20), natural resources (February 23), highways (February 28), housing and community development (March 9), agriculture (March 16), regulatory agencies (April 13) and an omnibus message on urgent national needs (May 25). In subsequent years he sent further messages on many of these subjects and added a variety of other issues: civil rights, transportation, public welfare, the protection of the consumer, mental illness and retardation, youth, the elderly.

His intimate acquaintance, of course, was with urban and industrial issues. He approached the farm problem with suspicion, but he liked and trusted Orville Freeman and, in time, developed an authentic intellectual interest in farm matters. In 1960 national agricultural policy was in an evident cul-de-sac. The farmer was the victim of his own fantastic technological efficiency. Production per manhour in American agriculture was increasing at a rate twice as fast as in industry; public storage of surplus agricultural commodities, especially wheat and feed grains, was overflowing every available bin and elevator. Yet at the same time people in the United States and abroad were going hungry; only one American farmer in nine was earning wages comparable to those of skilled factory workers; total farm income was declining; and unemployment and poverty were twice as bad on the countryside as in the cities. Moreover, the farmer himself, in spite of his immense contribution, was increasingly regarded as a cadger and parasite on the rest of the economy.

Freeman tackled the problem with energy and intelligence. He brought back the agricultural economists to the Department, from which they had been expelled under the Eisenhower administration, spent long hours with the agricultural committees on the Hill and traveled around the country engaging in extensive colloquies with farmers and their representatives. Though his recommendations had a mixed reception in Congress, in time the elements of a new agricultural policy began to emerge. The surpluses were put to use through Food for Peace abroad and enlarged distribution of surplus foods to the needy at home, soon accompanied by a revival of the Food Stamp plan of the thirties. The Emergency Feed Grain Act of 1961, continued in later years, initiated an attack on the surpluses piling up for the future. When the wheat farmers rejected mandatory controls in May 1963, the administration began to shift from price to income support, allowing prices to find their own level while income was maintained by direct payments to farmers prepared to accept production controls. These policies both reduced surpluses to the level of a prudent national reserve and increased net farm income by the average of almost $1 billion a year during the Kennedy Presidency. In the meantime, Freeman's rural areas development program began the work of improving and modernizing life on the countryside. The result was a series of changes which re-established the farmer in the national polity and offered for the first time in years the hope of a rational policy for agriculture.

The President approached conservation with a good deal more initial warmth, though with similar abstractness. He had enjoyed pointing out during the presidential campaign that "the two Americans in this century who have done more to develop the resources of the west" were both easterners, Theodore Roosevelt and Franklin Roosevelt (he could have added Gifford Pinchot of Pennsylvania and, by adoption, Bernard DeVoto of Massachusetts); and he was determined to carry on this tradition. Early in March 1961, dedicating the National Wildlife Federation Building, he affirmed the responsibility "to hand down undiminished to those who come after us, as was handed down by those who went before, the natural wealth and beauty which is ours." He was not complacent about the condition of the national estate. In his preface to Stewart Udall's valuable book *The Quiet Crisis* he warned that "the race between education and erosion, between wisdom and waste, has not run its course. . . . Each generation must deal anew with the 'raiders,' with the scramble to use public resources for private profit, and with the tendency to prefer short-run profits to long-run necessities. The nation's battle to preserve the common estate is far from won." He concluded:

The crisis may be quiet, but it is urgent. We must do in our own day what Theodore Roosevelt did sixty years ago and Franklin Roosevelt thirty years ago: we must expand the concept of conservation to meet the imperious problems of the new age. We must develop new instruments of foresight and protection and nurture in order to recover the relationship between man and nature and to make sure that the national estate we pass on to our multiplying descendants is green and flourishing.

These were heartfelt words. Kennedy cared deeply about the loveliness of lakes and woods and mountains and detested the clutter and blight which increasingly defaced the landscape. But, in the pressures of presidential life in the sixties, conservation had a rather low priority. "Intellectually he is fine," Udall said to me one day. "He knows the issues and recognizes their importance. When the problems are brought to him, his response is excellent. But he doesn't raise them himself." He did, however, call the first White House Conference on Conservation in fifty-four years, and he gave Udall's vigorous direction of the Department of the Interior strong support; the annual outlays for natural resources were 16 per cent higher than in Eisenhower years. As one who loved ocean beaches, gulls wheeling in the sky, dunes baking in the sun, gleaming surf and salt spray, he was particularly pleased to establish three national seashores, above all the one covering white beaches and serene inland ponds of his own Cape Cod.

5. YOUTH AND THE FUTURE

Yet, except on holiday, he remained unregenerately a city man, deeply anxious about the mess and tangle of urban America. This could be only in part a matter for the national government; and the Attorney General encouraged a decisive change in the capacity of cities to provide for themselves by supporting apportionment cases in the Supreme Court and challenging the system of rural over-representation in state legislatures. *Baker v. Carr* in 1962 adjudged legislative apportionment as within the jurisdiction of the courts, and *Gray v. Sanders*, which Robert Kennedy personally argued, overturned the Georgia county unit system and dealt another blow to urban disfranchisement. In the meantime, the Housing Act of 1961, the most extensive piece of housing legislation for a dozen years, gave the federal government new weapons and resources in its attack on urban squalor. The President's attempts to persuade Congress to authorize a Department of Urban Affairs failed in 1961 and 1962, in part because of the expectation that he would give the new cabinet post to his Housing Administrator, Dr. Robert C. Weaver, eminently qualified in every way save, in the view of some, by the color of his skin.

But the President's particular concern was how to turn the urban and suburban communities, so often chaotic and demoralized, into places where young people could grow up with a sense of purpose in their lives and a belief in the rationality of their society. When he would say that the key to the American future was its youth, this was not a passing piety. It was a central fact as vividly perceived as Orville Freeman's wheatfields or Stewart Udall's dams. He knew (and would rattle off the statistics) that each year 4 million boys and girls were born in the United States; that one out of three who completed the fifth grade would drop out before graduation from high school; that nearly 3 million in their teens would come every year into the labor market; that workers under the age of twenty-five, though less than one-fifth of the labor force, were one-third of the unemployed; that the social cost in aimless defection from society, like that of the beats, or insensate anger against it, like that of the delinquents, was growing; that arrests of the young had increased 86 per cent in a decade; that juvenile delinquency, as his Secretary of Health, Education and Welfare, Abraham Ribicoff, told Congress in 1961, was not so much criminality as "a system of belief and values with a strong and stable tradition of its own"; and that, as the President summed it up, "youth unemployment poses one of the most expensive and explosive social and economic problems now facing this country." The terror of being young and poor or young and cynical or young and hopeless was much on his mind. He understood the power of a glittering society to tantalize and thwart the deprived young, to give them the world on a television screen and slam the door in their faces, to take people already confused by broken homes, overcrowded schools, hostile communities and fill them with such desperate resentment that, to affirm their own impalpable identities, they could not stop short of violence and murder.

In Robert Kennedy, eight and a half years his junior, who cared, if possible, even more intensely about youth trapped in a careless society, the President had both a passionate ambassador to the young and a determined instrument of action. It was the Attorney General who ran the President's Committee on Juvenile Delinquency and Youth Crime (with his old schoolmate from Milton, David Hackett, as director) and did so not as a cop but as a comrade; it was the Attorney General who headed the cabinet study group in 1962 which devised the National Service Corps, later known as Volunteers in Service to America (VISTA); it was the Attorney General who led the national campaign against school dropouts, roamed the streets of Harlem, fought for schools and playgrounds in Washington and talked to the young at every opportunity. Because of the personal concern of the Kennedys, much of the youth program took place outside the Department of Health, Education and Welfare. But that sprawling and disheveled department played a growing role—its annual expenditures increased from $3.6 to $4.9 million in the Kennedy years—under the direction of two Secretaries, Ribicoff, who finally decided that it was unmanageable and resigned to run for the Senate from Connecticut, and Anthony J. Celebrezze, the quiet and sensible mayor of Cleveland; both were reinforced by the unfaltering sagacity of Assistant Secretary Wilbur J. Cohen, who had specialized in social security and health since New Deal days.

If youth constituted the key to the future, "the most direct, rewarding and important investment in our children and youth," as the President once put it, "is education." Education was essential to employment in a high-technology society where among the unemployed 40 per cent had eight years of schooling or less (and where only 1.4 per cent had college training). More than that, education was essential to the fulfillment of talented individuals. As the war generation of babies now pressed upon the colleges, with their younger brothers and sisters beginning to crowd the schools, little seemed more important than the expansion and improvement of the nation's educational facilities. By 1970 there would be a 25 per cent increase in school children and a 75 per cent increase in college students. Nor would building more schoolrooms help much by itself if teachers and curricula remained mechanical and boring. Little disappointed the Kennedys more in domestic policy than their failure to make significant legislative progress in federal aid to education.

A comprehensive education bill passed the Senate in the spring of 1961 but was beaten in the House by a coalition of Republicans, who objected to federal aid, and Catholics, who objected to the first Catholic President's exclusion of non-public schools from the benefits. In 1962 a bill for aid to higher education perished when the House and Senate were unable to reconcile their differing versions in conference. Abandoning the quest for a general bill in 1963, Kennedy asked for a number of separate measures, most of which were passed but which together fell short of the desired comprehensive program. Blocked in the legislative branch, Kennedy in late 1962 had persuaded Francis Keppel, the Dean of the Harvard Graduate School of Education, to become Commissioner of Education. Keppel brought new authority to the job, played a vital role in the legislative successes of 1963 and laid the foundation for comprehensive school legislation in the years to come.

Underneath all this lay the President's acute sense of the rising issue of generations in American life. By 1966 half the population would be under the age of twenty-five. Having seized power themselves from a resentful older generation, the Kennedys understood the emotions of the young crowding into a capricious and incomprehensible society. Many of the legislative measures of the New Frontier may have been left over from the New Deal. But the generational perception was new and original. It reinforced the President in his determination to transform a wealthy society into a civilized community and gave his program its distinctive design and theme. American politics would never be the same again.

XXV

IN THE WHITE HOUSE

By THE SUMMER OF 1962 Kennedy was well settled in the Presidency. He had changed somewhat physically in this year and a half. The face was more lined and furrowed; the features were heavier, less handsome but more powerful. The first eighteen months is always the period of presidential definition, and for Kennedy the succession of crises had tied an already disciplined personality ever more irrevocably to the responsibilities for which he held himself accountable to the future. The experience deepened him and gave emphasis to a certain somber side of his nature. At the same time, it liberated him. He could at last be himself; the private face, somewhat subdued and withheld during the congressional years, became fully the public face. The force of his intelligence, gaiety and wit, now displayed without inhibition, made people wonder how two years earlier they could possibly have confused him with Richard Nixon.

Uniting head of government and head of state in a single office, the American Presidency has its symbolic as well as its executive aspects. The President's seat is at the center of concentric circles of relationships, moving outward from his family, the White House staff, the cabinet, the civil service, the Congress, the press, to the American people and ultimately to the world beyond. The measure of achievement is in part a President's success in suffusing the web of relationships with his own values and purposes. By this second summer the methods of the Kennedy Presidency were coming into focus.

1. IN THE MANSION

The day began at quarter to eight. George Thomas, his devoted and humorous Negro valet, would knock at the door of the Kennedy bedroom. As he sat down before his breakfast tray, surrounded by the morning papers and urgent cables and reports which may have come in during the night, Caroline and John would rush in, greet their father and turn on the television to watch animated cartoons. Then more presidential reading, with the television going full blast. At nine o'clock a calisthenics program came on, and Kennedy liked to watch the children tumble on the bedroom floor in rhythm with the man on the screen. Then, taking one of the children by the hand, he would walk over to the presidential office in the West Wing.

After a morning of work and a swim, often with David Powers, in the White House pool, he returned to the Mansion for luncheon. He preferred to lunch alone or with Jacqueline; very occasionally he brought guests. After luncheon came the nap. Impressed by Churchill's eloquence in praise of afternoon rest, he had begun this practice in the Senate. It was a genuine sleep, in pajamas and under covers. He went off at once; and in forty-five minutes would awaken and chat as he dressed. This was Jacqueline's hour of the day, as the morning was the children's.

This historian, it must be said, had not realized how constricted the living quarters of an American President were. The first floor of the Mansion was given over to public rooms and reserved for state occasions. The third floor was rarely mentioned. The private life of the Kennedys took place on the second floor under conditions which an average Park Avenue tycoon would regard as claustrophobic. A long dark corridor, brightened by a set of Catlin's Indian paintings, transected the floor. Bedrooms debouched from each side. A yellow oval room, marvelously light and lovely, was

used for tea or drinks before dinner; it had served earlier
Presidents as an office. Another room at the west end of
the corridor was Jacqueline's room by day and the sitting
room in the evening. Dinner guests resorted to the President's own bathroom. It was not a house for spacious living.
Yet, until Theodore Roosevelt persuaded the Congress to
build the West Wing, Presidents not only raised their families in these crowded quarters but ran the country from
them.

It never seemed unduly crowded in these days. The atmosphere was always one of informality. When his family
was away, the President used to have his afternoon appointments on the second floor. But generally he returned to the
West Wing after his nap, where he worked until seven-thirty
or eight at night. Jacqueline liked to guard the evenings for
relaxation, and the President welcomed the relief from the
incessant business of the day. These were the times when he
confided public affairs to his subconscious mind, exposed
himself to new people and ideas and recharged his intellectual energies. One of Jacqueline's charms, Robert Kennedy
once said, was that "Jack knows she'll never greet him with
'What's new in Laos?' " From time to time, of course, she
did, as one crisis or another dominated the headlines, and
he would tell Bundy to show her the cables. But her central
effort was to assure him a sanctuary of comfort and affection.

After the first year, they left the White House very seldom
for private dinners elsewhere, though Kennedy always enjoyed the food and conversation at Joseph Alsop's. Instead,
Jacqueline would arrange small dinners of six, eight or ten
in the Mansion. They were informal and gay, the most agreeable occasions in the world. One memorable evening celebrated Stravinsky's eightieth birthday. The composer,
who had been rehearsing all day, was both excited and
tired. A Chicago newspaper publisher, also present, insisted
on talking across him at dinner to the President about
such issues as Katanga and Medicare. Stravinsky said to
me later, "They were speaking about matters which I did not
understand and about which I did not care. I became an
alien in their midst." But then the President toasted him
and Stravinsky, obviously moved, responded with immense
charm. On less formal evenings Jacqueline would sometimes
put on phonograph records and there might be a moment of
dancing. The President often vanished silently into his
bedroom to work or make phone calls, reappearing in time
to bid his guests goodnight. Occasionally there were films

in the projection room in the East Wing. Kennedy was not a great movie fan and tended, unless the film was unusually gripping, to walk out after the first twenty or thirty minutes.[1]

Private relationships are always a puzzle for Presidents. "The Presidency," Kennedy once remarked, "is not a very good place to make new friends"—or sometimes to keep old ones either. They watched with fascination how White Housitis affected their acquaintances, leading some to grievance and others to sycophancy and discussed a book which might be written called "The Poison of the Presidency." By 1963 the dinners became somewhat less frequent. More and more the President fell back on the easy and reliable company of tried friends—William Walton, the Benjamin Bradlees, the Charles Bartletts, the David Ormsby Gores, the Franklin Roosevelts.

The state dinners were inevitable, but Jacqueline made them bearable by ending the old regimented formality of solemn receiving lines and stilted conversation and changing them into elegant and cheerful parties, beautifully mingling informality and dignity. When asked about White House dinners, people would now say with surprise that they really had a very good time. But the gala occasions were the small dinner dances. Jacqueline conceived them as a means of restoring a larger social gaiety to her husband's life. When several months of unrelenting pressure had gone by, she would feel that the time had come for another dancing party and begin to look for a pretext to give one, whether to say hello or farewell to the Radziwills, welcome Kenneth Galbraith or honor Eugene Black. There were not many such parties—only five in the whole time in the White House—and they were all blithe and enchanting evenings. The President seemed renewed by them and walked with a springier step the next day.

The Kennedys liked to preserve the weekends as much as possible for themselves and the children. In 1961 they took a house at Glen Ora in Virginia; but the President found it confining and in later years preferred to go to Roosevelt's old refuge of Shangri-La at Catoctin Mountain

---

[1] He was interested, however, that one of his staff should contribute film reviews to *Show* magazine, and with his curiosity about everything he would often have suggestions about critiques he thought should be written. Before beginning the assignment, I sent him a memorandum asking whether it would be any embarrassment to him if I became a film critic on my own time. The message came back through Evelyn Lincoln: "The President says it is fine for you to write for *Show* as long as you treat Peter Lawford with respect."

in Maryland, renamed by Eisenhower Camp David after his grandson. In the winter there was Palm Beach, where they went for longer periods at Christmas and Easter, and in the summer Hyannis Port and Newport. Sailing relaxed him most of all—the sun, the breeze, the water; above all, no telephone. He could get along quite happily even without the sun and used to insist on taking his friends out on dark and chilly days. The guests would huddle together against the cold while the President sat in the stern in a black sweater, the wind blowing his hair, blissfully happy with a steaming bowl of fish chowder.

The weekends and holidays, despite his battered black alligator briefcase stuffed with papers, gave him time for the children, but he saw them as much as possible during the week, and his delight in them was unconcealed. He loved children and told Jacqueline before their marriage that he wanted at least five; she had four in seven years. He liked young children in particular and always wanted a baby coming along when its predecessor was growing up. Caroline and John were, as the world came to know, wonderfully spirited and original, and they cast their spell throughout the White House. One often encountered them in the corridors going out to their morning nursery school. One morning I said to Caroline, "Who is your friend?" She replied with dignity, "He's not my friend; he's my brother." They invaded the West Wing, took candies from a box kept for them on Evelyn Lincoln's desk and liked to hide from their father under the cabinet table.

Often at the end of the day the President would leave his desk, throw open the French windows leading into the Rose Garden, walk out on the colonnade and clap his hands. At this signal every child and dog in the vicinity would rush across the green lawn into his arms. He would encourage John to dance, clapping his hands again as the accompaniment. In the evening he made up stories for them about Caroline hunting with the Orange County hounds and winning the Grand National and John in his PT boat sinking a Japanese destroyer. He would tell them about Bobo the Lobo, a giant, and about Maybelle, a little girl who hid in the woods, and about the White Shark and the Black Shark. The White Shark lived off people's socks, and one day, when the President and Caroline were sailing with Franklin Roosevelt, Jr., off Newport, Kennedy pretended to see the White Shark and said, "Franklin, give him your socks; he's hungry." Franklin promptly threw his socks into the water, which made a great impression on Caroline. And her father taught Caroline poetry:

For her part Jacqueline was determined that the children lead as normal lives as possible. This was not an easy goal for the young children of a President, but she did her best, arranging the White House nursery school where they could fraternize with their contemporaries and taking them off in her blue Pontiac station wagon on quiet expeditions to shops or parks. On Halloween evening in 1962, the doorbell rang at my house in Georgetown. When my fourteen-year-old daughter opened the door to the trick-or-treaters, she found a collection of small hobgoblins leaping up and down. One seemed particularly eager to have her basket filled with goodies. After a moment a masked mother in the background called out that it was time to go to their next house. Christina suddenly recognized the voice. It was, of course, Jackie, and the excited little girl was Caroline out with her cousin. They had just rung Joe Alsop's bell; Dean Acheson was the next stop.

Such adventures varied their lives. John and Caroline were not, if their mother could help it, the little prince and princess, any more than she and the President were royalty. She disapproved of the term "First Lady," which had come into semi-official usage in the previous administration. When she heard the servants referring to her by the title, she told them her name was "Mrs. Kennedy." She constantly reminded the children that the White House was their temporary residence, not their permanent home. When Mrs. Longworth or Franklin Roosevelt, Jr., came to dinner, she would explain that they had once lived in the White House too, as Caroline and John were living there now.

The White House was temporary for the Kennedys but permanent for the nation. Mrs. Eisenhower had taken her successor on a trip around the Mansion in December 1960. It was too soon after John's birth, and Jacqueline was desperately weak after the Caesarean operation. She trudged through the historic rooms, long since emptied of the authentic past, now filled with mediocre reproductions; it seemed almost as if this were a house in which nothing had ever taken place. She resolved on the spot to establish the President's residence thereafter as unequivocally the nation's house and transform it into a house of which the nation could be thoroughly proud. She asked the Library of Congress to send books about the historic White House to

her at Palm Beach. Between Christmas and the inauguration she immersed herself in the literature. The restoration
of the White House became her special project.

Her hope was to recover as many as possible of the old
and beautiful objects which past Presidents had cherished
and make the President's house both a distillation of American history and an expression of American excellence.
"Everything in the White House must have a reason for
being there," she said. "It would be sacrilege merely to
'redecorate' it—a word I hate. It must be restored—and that
has nothing to do with decoration. That is a question of
scholarship." Her husband sent Clark Clifford to help her
with her plans. But Clifford, remembering the furor over
the innocuous balcony Truman had added to the south
portico, was dubious; "you just can't make any changes
in the White House," he said. Jacqueline, however, soon
talked him around and with his help set up the White House
Historical Association. She enlisted Henry du Pont, James
Fosburgh and others on a Committee of the Fine Arts
Commission for the White House and procured legislation
designating the White House as a museum and enabling it to
receive gifts. The restoration program went speedily ahead.
Exploring the White While basement herself, she uncovered
a superbly carved desk made of oak timbers from a British
frigate and installed it in the presidential office in the
West Wing. Soon she pushed through the publication of
the first White House guidebook in the nation's history.
It was a formidable executive effort, but she carried it out
with a perfectionist's attention to detail, steely determination and lovely command.

The President gave her his full support, applauded as the
inherited furniture was carted away and watched the transformation with mounting pride. He was rather complacent
about the knowledge of decor he had acquired under her
tutelage and liked to point out to visitors the objects which
she had brought back to their original home. The success
of the guidebook pleased him, and he kidded those on the
staff who had said gloomily that it would never do to sell a
guidebook in the White House. He congratulated her as the
number of people going through the White House steadily
rose: in 1962 the total was nearly two-thirds greater than in
1960. In February 1962, when Mrs. Kennedy took the whole
nation on a television tour of the new White House, the
President viewed the program with great satisfaction. (As
for Jacqueline, when Norman Mailer complained about her
voice in *Esquire* and wrote that she walked through the

program "like a starlet who is utterly without talent," she took no offense and thought he was probably right.)

Her husband's delight in her was visible. His eyes brightened when he talked of her or when she unexpectedly dropped by the office. He was even entertained by her occasional bursts of undiplomatic candor. "Whenever a wife says anything in this town," he remarked in high amusement one night at dinner at the White House, "everyone assumes that she is saying what her husband really thinks. Imagine how I felt last night when I thought I heard Jackie telling Malraux that Adenauer was *'un peu gaga'!*"

He adored her because she remained utterly faithful to herself—and the nation, for all its earlier reservations, came to adore her for the same reason. The things people had once held against her—the unconventional beauty, the un-American elegance, the taste for French clothes and French food—were suddenly no longer liabilities but assets. She represented all at once not a negation of her country but a possible fulfillment of it, a dream of civilization and beauty, a suggestion that America was not to be trapped forever in the bourgeois ideal. She had dreaded coming to the White House, fearing the end of family and privacy. But life for herself and her husband and children was never more intense and more complete. It turned out to be the time of the greatest happiness.

2. IN THE OFFICE

It has been traditional for Presidents to curse the Presidency. Washington said he felt like "a culprit, who is going to the place of his execution." Jefferson called the Presidency a "splendid misery," Buchanan "a crown of thorns"; for Truman the White House was "the finest prison in the country." Such melodramatic lamentations never escaped the lips of John F. Kennedy. He had wanted to become President, he loved being President and at times he could hardly remember that he had ever been anything else. He never complained about the 'terrible loneliness' of the office or its 'awesome burdens.' I do not think he felt terribly lonely; as he once remarked to William Manchester, "In many ways I see and hear more than anyone else." (He regarded his life, I think, as threatened more by confinement than by solitude; occasionally at the end of the day he would say, almost wistfully, "What are you doing tonight?" and then enjoy a moment of gossip about old friends in Georgetown.) As for those 'awesome burdens,' he had asked for them, knowing more or less what he was getting into, and would not repine now.

His presidential life was instinct with action. "He did everything around here today," James Reston wrote of a not uncharacteristic day, "but shinny up the Washington Monument." Once, driving with Ben Bradlee during the interregnum, while a small Bradlee child scrambled between the front and back seats, Kennedy said, "I suppose if you had to choose just one quality to have that would be it: vitality." But his own vitality was under sure control. He had written years before about his brother Joe: "Even when still, there was always a sense of motion forcibly restrained." This was preëminently true of the President himself.

Seated at his desk or in the rocking chair in front of the fireplace, immaculately dressed in one of his two-buttoned, single-breasted suits, he radiated a contained energy, electric in its intensity. Occasionally it would break out, especially during long and wandering meetings. His fingers gave the clue to his impatience. They would suddenly be in constant action, drumming the table, tapping his teeth, slashing impatient pencil lines on a pad, jabbing the air to underscore a point. Sometimes the constraint of the four walls seemed too much, and he would stride across the room, pausing wryly to look at the mass of indentations left on the floor by his predecessor's golf cleats, throw open the doors to the lawn and walk up and down the colonnade. One day, while talking, he rose from his desk, picked up his cane, inverted it and started making golf swings; then, looking up with a smile, he said, "I'm getting to be more like Ike every day!"

He had to an exceptional degree the talent for concentration. When he put on his always surprising horn-rimmed glasses and read a document, it was with total intentness; in a moment he would have seized its essence and returned to the world he had left. He was for the same reason a superb listener. "Whoever he's with," someone said, "he's with them completely." He would lean forward, his eyes protruding slightly, concerned with using the occasion not to expound his own thoughts but to drag out of the talker whatever could be of use of him. Isaiah Berlin was reminded of a remark made about Lenin: that he could exhaust people by listening to them. In this way he ventilated problems in great detail without revealing his own position and without making his visitors conscious that he was holding back.

His manners were distinguished, and the more timid or lowly the people, the greater his consideration. "Mr. Kennedy's almost awesome egalitarianism," Secret Service Chief Baughman later wrote, was "in some ways even greater than Mr. Truman's." His moments of irritation were occasional but short. They came generally because he felt that he had been tricked, or because a crisis caught him without warning, or because someone in the government had leaked something to the press. The air would rock for a moment; his years in the Navy and in Massachusetts politics had not been in vain and, when pressed, his vocabulary was vivid. But, though he got mad quickly, he stayed mad briefly. He was a man devoid of hatred. He detested qualities but not people. Calm would soon descend, and in time the irritation would become a matter for jokes.

"Humour," said Hazlitt, "is the describing the ludicrous as it is in itself; wit is the exposing it, by comparing or contrasting it with something else. Humour is, as it were, the growth of nature and accident; wit is the product of art and fancy." Franklin Roosevelt was a man of humor, Kennedy a man of wit. Irony was his most distinctive mode ("Washington is a city of southern efficiency and northern charm"). Explaining the origins of *Six Crises*, Nixon wrote about his visit to Kennedy after the Bay of Pigs: "When I told him that I was considering the possibility of joining the 'literary' ranks, of which he is himself so distinguished a member, he expressed the thought that every public man should write a book at some time in his life, both for the mental discipline and because it tends to elevate him in popular esteem to the respected status of an 'intellectual.'" Only the solemnity with which Kennedy's remark was received could possibly have exceeded the ambiguity with which it was uttered.

His irony could be gentle or sharp, according to mood, and it was directed at himself as often as at others. It helped him to lighten crises and to hold people and problems in balance; it was an unending source of refreshment and perspective, and an essential part of his own apparatus of self-criticism. Detachment was one of his deepest reflexes. When the first volume of Eisenhower's presidential reminiscences came out, he said drily to me, "Apparently Ike never did anything wrong. . . . When we come to writing the memoirs of this administration, we'll do it differently." And self-criticism was a vital strength in his luminous and rational intelligence, so consecutive and objective, so lucidly in possession of his impulses and emotions.

He came to the Presidency almost without break of

stride. Yet the Presidency, as he once put it, is a "mysterious institution." "There is no experience you can get," he said at the end of 1962, "that can possibly prepare you adequately for the Presidency." He himself came to feel the mystique of the Presidency strongly enough to doubt whether the quality of the presidential experience could be understood by those who had not shared it. My father, who had asked a panel of historians and political scientists in 1948 to rate the Presidents in categories from "great" to "failure," repeated the poll in early 1962 and sent a ballot to the historian who had written *Profiles in Courage* and *A Nation of Immigrants*. Kennedy started to fill in the ballot but, as he thought about it, came to the conclusion that the exercise was unprofitable. "A year ago," he wrote my father, "I would have responded with confidence . . . but now I am not so sure. After being in the office for a year I feel that a good deal more study is required to make my judgment sufficiently informed. There is a tendency to mark the obvious names. I would like to subject those not so well known to a long scrutiny after I have left this office." He said to me later, "How the hell can you tell? Only the President himself can know what his real pressures and his real alternatives are. If you don't know that, how can you judge performance?" Some of his greatest predecessors, he would sometimes say, were given credit for doing things when they could do nothing else; only the most detailed study could disclose what difference a President had made by his own individual effort. War, he pointed out, made it easier for a President to achieve greatness. But would Lincoln have been judged so great a President if he had lived long enough to face the almost insoluble problem of Reconstruction?

For all his skepticism, he read the results of the poll with avidity in the *New York Times Magazine* in the summer. He was greatly pleased that Truman made the "near great" class. He was also interested that Eisenhower rated only twenty-second, near the bottom of the "average" category. He said, "At first I thought it was too bad that Ike was in Europe and would miss the article, but then I decided that some conscientious friend would send him a copy." Later Kennedy, jokingly or half-jokingly, blamed Eisenhower's vigorous entry into the 1962 congressional campaign on the historians' ratings. "It is all your father's poll," he said. "Eisenhower has been going along for years, basking in the glow of applause he has always had. Then he saw that poll and realized how he stood before the cold eye of history—way below Truman; even below Hoover. Now he's mad to save his reputation."

What surprised him particularly in the poll was the high rating given to Wilson—fourth in the list and in the "great" category. Why, he asked, should Wilson have placed ahead of Jackson—number six and only "near great"? He reverted to this question a few days later when I brought in Frank Freidel, the biographer of Franklin Roosevelt. After all, the President said, Wilson had made a botch of the Mexican intervention; while he was right to bring us into the war, he had done so initially for narrow and legalistic reasons; he had messed up the League fight and, though a great speaker and writer, had failed in a number of his objectives. Why did the professors admire him so much? (We suggested that he was, after all, the only professor to achieve the Presidency.) He also wondered about Theodore Roosevelt (number seven and "near great"); he had really got very little important legislation through Congress. Why should either Wilson or Theodore Roosevelt rate ahead of Polk (number eight) or Truman (number nine)? It seemed evident that his measure of presidential success was concrete achievement; thus people who educated the nation without necessarily accomplishing their particular purposes rated, in his judgment, below those, like Polk and Truman, who accomplished their purposes without necessarily bringing the nation along with them. The best, of course, were those who did both, and he agreed with the panel's choice of the top three—Lincoln, Washington and Franklin Roosevelt.

Now he sat in the presidential office himself and knew he was facing the appraisal of future historians. He had come in without illusions about the job; and experience soon reinforced what history had indicated. "Every President," he wrote in his foreword to Ted Sorensen's perceptive essay *Decision-Making in the White House*, "must endure the gap between what he would like and what is possible." He quoted Franklin Roosevelt's remark on Lincoln—"a sad man because he couldn't get it all at once. And nobody can." Yet this insight never threw him. He was a natural President, as other men were natural writers or outfielders or steeplechase riders.

Our last natural President had been Franklin Roosevelt. Kennedy freely acknowledged their affinities. He was endlessly curious about Roosevelt and often demanded Roosevelt quotations for his speeches. Like Roosevelt, he was a naval President and filled his office with maritime pictures and ship models. Reading in the *New York Times* in the summer of 1961 an item about F.D.R.'s remarkable collection of naval prints, he immediately proposed that the National Archives put a selection on exhibition. He directed William Walton and me to follow up for him and displayed an active interest every step along the way. When the show "The Old Navy: 1776–1860" was ready a year later, the President opened it himself and later wrote a piece for *Life* about it.

The coolness with Eleanor Roosevelt had long since vanished. She was proud of Kennedy as President and proud of Jacqueline, with whom she had an affectionate correspondence, as the President's lady. When she died in November 1962, the Kennedys flew to Hyde Park for the funeral. The Harrimans, my wife and I accompanied them on the plane. The day was overcast and somber. We sat in the small stone church and watched them walk in: President Kennedy, sad and silent; President Truman, looking very old, an expression of anguish on his face; President Eisenhower, grave and dignified; Frances Perkins and Henry Morgenthau, Jr., Henry Wallace and James A. Farley, Tom Corcoran and Ben Cohen, Herbert Lehman and Adlai Stevenson. "This is the last assembly," Corcoran whispered to me. "There will never again be an occasion on which all these people will gather together." By the time we reached the grave site a gentle rain had begun to fall. Later we went over to John Roosevelt's. All the Roosevelt children were there. Thinking of the young Roosevelts, lost suddenly in middle age, and of the young Kennedys, so sure and purposeful, one perceived an historic contrast, a dynastic change, like the Yorks giving way to the Tudors.

Roosevelt and Kennedy had so much in common: both were patrician, urbane, playful, cultivated, inquisitive, gallant; both were detached from the business ethos, both skeptical of the received wisdom, both devoted to politics but never enslaved by it, both serene in the exercise of power, both committed to the use of power for the ends of human welfare and freedom; both too had more than their share of physical suffering. Yet, as an historian who had written about Roosevelt, I could not but notice the differences as well as the resemblances.

Roosevelt was born thirty-five years earlier in a different century and a different world. He had grown up in those days of glowing hope which were shattered but not wholly extinguished by the First World War. He remained buoyant, expansive, spontaneous, audacious, theatrical, overflowing with a careless confidence about the future; if life was filled with trouble, action and passion could overcome it. Like Churchill, Roosevelt rallied the certitudes of the nineteenth century to fight the duplicities of the twentieth.

Kennedy, the child of a darker age, was more disciplined, more precise, more candid, more cautious, more sardonic, more pessimistic.[2] His purpose was hardened and qualified by the world of ambiguities and perils. Underneath the casualness, wit and idealism, he was taut, concentrated, vibrating with inner tension under iron control, possessed by a fatalism which drove him on against the odds to meet his destiny. One could only speculate about the roots of this fatalism—the days of danger, the months of sickness, the feeling that life was short, the cool but tormented sense of the importunities and frustrations of the age in which he lived.

Someone once asked him what he regretted most; he replied, "I wish I had had more good times." The shadow was never far from him: that rendezvous at midnight in some gaming town. One never knows to what extent retrospect confers significance on chance remarks; but he said so many things attesting to a laconic sense of the transience of the Presidency, if not to a haunted conviction of human mortality. So when he saw Nixon after the Bay of Pigs he said, "If I do the right kind of a job, I don't know whether I am going to be here four years from now." Nor could anyone interest him much in details of personal protection. "If someone is going to kill me," he would say, "they are going to kill me." Before he left on his trip to Mexico in June 1962, John McCone brought in a CIA report about assassination rumors. It had been a hard few days on the Hill; and Kennedy responded, without a second's hesitation, "If I am to die, this is the week for it." When we were preparing an exchange of letters with Harvard about the transfer of university land to the Kennedy Library whenever "The President" requested, he asked that this be rephrased; after all, "Who can tell who will be President a year from

[2] In the spring of 1962, Alfred M. Landon of Kansas, the Republican candidate for President in 1936 and one of the most likable men in American politics, paid a call on Kennedy. "Our conversation drifted from North to South and from South back to North," Landon later told me, "like the smoke from a hookah." I asked him whether Kennedy reminded him at all of Roosevelt. Landon said, "No. Kennedy is very frank and straightforward. Roosevelt was always on the stage, always giving a performance." He went on to describe Truman: "For the first two years he was too humble. Thereafter he became too cocky. Kennedy is neither humble nor cocky." (Subsequently Kennedy said about Landon, "I liked him. Very Trumanesque.")

now?" [3] When Jim Bishop, the author of *The Day Lincoln Was Shot*, visited the White House in late October 1963, Kennedy chatted about his book. "He seemed fascinated, in a melancholy way," Bishop wrote, "with the accidental succession of events of that day which led to the assassination." President Kennedy never appeared ruffled or hurried. But time was his enemy, and he fought it to the end.

3. IN THE EXECUTIVE BRANCH

As a natural President, he ran his presidential office with notable ease and informality. He did this by instinct, not by theory. He was fond of Richard Neustadt but a little annoyed by the notion that he was modeling his Presidency on the doctrines of *Presidential Power*. He once remarked that Neustadt "makes everything a President does seem too premeditated."

He always shrank from portentous discussions of himself and the Presidency (or anything else). Pressed, he turned questioners aside: "I have a nice home, the office is close by and the pay is good." In the autumn of 1961 Kennedy was sitting on the lawn of his mother-in-law's house in Newport, smoking a fragrant pre-Castro cigar, while in the background the sun was setting and a great aircraft carrier was entering the bay. It was the time of Berlin and the Soviet resumption of testing; in California Nixon was having his troubles with former Governor Goodwin Knight in internal Republican politics. As the warship steamed along, the American flag flying high, a friend felt a patriotic glow and was moved to ask Kennedy: "What do you *feel* at a moment like this? What is it *like* to be President?" The President smiled, flicked the ash from his cigar and said, "Well, it's a lot better than mucking around with Goody Knight in California." Once James Reston asked him what he hoped to achieve by the time he rode down Pennsylvania Avenue with his successor. "He looked at me," Reston later wrote, "as if I were a dreaming child. I tried again: Did he not feel the need of some goal to help guide his day-to-day decisions and priorities? Again a ghastly pause. It was only when I turned the question to immediate, tangible problems that he seized the point and rolled off a torrent of statistics." Reston concluded that Kennedy had no large designs; but I suspect that the Presi-

[3] October 2, 1963.

dent was simply stupefied by what he regarded as the impracticality of the question. He was possessed not by a blueprint but by a process.

In order to get the country moving again, he had to get the government moving. He came to the White House at a time when the ability of the President to do this had suffered steady constriction. The clichés about the 'most powerful office on earth' had concealed the extent to which the mid-century Presidents had much less freedom of action than, say, Jackson or Lincoln or even Franklin Roosevelt. No doubt the mid-century Presidents could blow up the world, but at the same time they were increasingly hemmed in by the growing power of the executive bureaucracy and of Congress—and at a time when crisis at home and abroad made clear decision and swift action more imperative than ever before. The President understood this. "Before my term has ended," he said in his first State of the Union address, "we shall have to test anew whether a nation organized and governed such as ours can endure. The outcome is by no means certain."

Kennedy was fully sensitive—perhaps oversensitive—to the limitations imposed by Congress on the presidential freedom of maneuver. But, though he was well aware of the problem within the executive domain, I do not think he had entirely appreciated its magnitude. The textbooks had talked of three coordinate branches of government: the executive, the legislative, the judiciary. But with an activist President it became apparent that there was a fourth branch: the Presidency itself. And, in pursuing his purposes, the President was likely to encounter almost as much resistance from the executive branch as from the others. By 1961 the tension between the permanent government and the presidential government was deep in our system.

This problem had assumed its contemporary dimensions after Franklin Roosevelt and the enlargement of government under the New Deal. Roosevelt had quickly seen that he could not fight the depression through the Departments of Agriculture, Labor, Commerce and the Treasury (or, later, fight the war through State, War and Navy). He had therefore bypassed the traditional structure, resorting instead to the device of the emergency agency, set up outside the civil service and staffed from top to bottom by men who believed in New Deal policies. This worked well in the thirties. But Roosevelt left his successors a much bigger government, and in due course the iron law of organization began to transform what had served as brilliant expedients for him into dead weights for them.

In the thirties conservatives had bemoaned the expansion of the federal government as a threat to freedom. Instead they should have hailed the bureaucracy as a bulwark against change. The permanent government soon developed its own stubborn vested interests in policy and procedure, its own cozy alliances with committees of Congress, its own ties to the press, its own national constituencies. It began to exude the feeling that Presidents could come and Presidents go but it went on forever. The permanent government was, as such, politically neutral; its essential commitment was to doing things as they had been done before. This frustrated the enthusiasts who came to Washington with Eisenhower in 1953 zealous to dismantle the New Deal, and it frustrated the enthusiasts who came to Washington with Kennedy in 1961 zealous to get the country moving again.

The Eisenhower administration in the end met the problem of the permanent government by accepting the trend toward routinization and extending it to the Presidency itself. This was congenial both to President Eisenhower, accustomed all his life to the military staff system, and to the needs of a regime more concerned with consolidation than with innovation. The result was an effort to institutionalize the Presidency, making it as nearly automatic in its operations and as little dependent on particular individuals as possible. It was a perfectly serious experiment; but in the end it was defeated, both by the inextinguishably personal character of the Presidency, which broke out from time to time even in the case of one so well disciplined to the staff system as Eisenhower, and also by the fact that even the Eisenhower administration was occasionally forced to do new things in order to meet new challenges.

Kennedy, who had been critical of the Eisenhower effort to institutionalize the Presidency, was determined to restore the personal character of the office and recover presidential control over the sprawling feudalism of government. This became a central theme of his administration and, in some respects, a central frustration. The presidential government, coming to Washington aglow with new ideas and a euphoric sense that it could not go wrong, promptly collided with the feudal barons of the permanent government, entrenched in their domains and fortified by their sense of proprietorship; and the permanent government, confronted by this invasion, began almost to function (with, of course, many notable individual exceptions) as a resistance movement, scattering to the *maquis* in order to pick off the intruders. This was especially true in foreign affairs.

The Bay of Pigs was a crucial episode in the struggle. This

disaster was a clear consequence of the surrender of the presidential government to the permanent government. The inherited executive bureaucracy rallied in support of an undertaking which the new administration would never conceivably have designed for itself. The CIA had a heavy investment in this project; other barons, having heavy investments in their own pre-Kennedy projects, doubtless wished to show that the newcomers could not lightly reject whatever was bubbling up in the pipeline, however repugnant it might be to the preconceptions of the New Frontier. But the result, except for leading the President to an invaluable overhaul of his own operating methods, was ironically not to discredit the permanent government; instead, it became in certain ways more powerful than ever. The reason for this was that, one risk having failed, all risks were regarded with suspicion; and, since the permanent government almost never wished to take risks (except for the CIA, where risks were the entrenched routine), this strengthened those who wanted to keep things as they were as against those who wanted to change things. The fiasco was also a shock to the President's hitherto supreme confidence in his own luck; and it had a sobering effect throughout the presidential government. No doubt this was in many ways to the good; but it also meant that we never quite recaptured again the youthful, adventurous spirit of the first days. "Because this bold initiative flopped," I noted in June 1961, "there is now a general predisposition against boldness in all fields." With one stroke the permanent government had dealt a savage blow to the élan of the newcomers—and it had the satisfaction of having done so by persuading the newcomers to depart from their own principles and accept the permanent government's plan.

The permanent government included men and women of marked devotion, quality and imagination. Kennedy knew this, seized many occasions to say so publicly and gave John Macy, the chairman of the Civil Service Commission, every support in improving the morale of the career services. Yet, though a valuable reservoir of intelligence and experience as well as a valuable guarantee against presidential government's going off the tracks, the permanent government remained in bulk a force against innovation with an inexhaustible capacity to dilute, delay and obstruct presidential purpose. Only so many fights were possible with the permanent government. The fighters—one saw this happen to Richard Goodwin when he went over to the State Department—were gradually weakened, cut off, surrounded and shot down, as if from ambush, by the bureaucracy and its anti-New Frontier allies in Congress and the press. At the start we had all felt free to 'meddle' when we thought that we had a good idea or someone else a poor one. But, as the ice began to form again over the government, free-wheeling became increasingly difficult and dangerous. At Wellfleet in the summer of 1962, I wrote that our real trouble was that we had "capitulated too much to the existing momentum of government as embodied and urged by the executive bureaucracy. Wherever we have gone wrong—from Cuba to fiscal policy—has been because we have not had sufficient confidence in the New Frontier approach to impose it on the government. Every important mistake has been the consequence of excessive deference to the permanent government. In too many areas we have behaved as the Eisenhower administration would have behaved." The problem of moving forward seemed in great part the problem of making the permanent government responsive to the policies of the presidential government.

Kennedy could not solve this problem as Roosevelt had by bypassing the bureaucracy. An emergency agency, after all, required an emergency. Kennedy had no depression or war; and in the days since the New Deal the traditional structure had moved to absorb into itself as much as it could of the new functions. It was no accident that the organization which best expressed the distinctive spirit of the New Frontier—the Peace Corps—was almost the only one established as an emergency agency and carefully preserved from the embrace of the bureaucracy.

In the long run, the problem of the permanent government could no doubt be solved by permeation and attrition. "Getting the bureaucracy to accept new ideas," as Chester Bowles once said, "is like carrying a double mattress up a very narrow and winding stairway. It is a terrible job, and you exhaust yourself when you try it. But once you get the mattress up it is awfully hard for anyone else to get it down." But it also required day-to-day direction and control. This was Kennedy's preferred method: hence his unceasing flow of suggestions, inquiries, phone calls directly to the operating desks and so on. This approach enabled him to imbue government with a sense of his own desires and purposes. A Foreign Service officer once remarked on the feeling that "we were all reading the cables together"—the man at the desk, the Secretary of State and the White House. Nothing was more invigorating and inspiring, especially for the imaginative official, than personal contact with the President.

Kennedy tried in a number of ways to encourage innovation in the permanent government. His call for "dissent and daring" in the first State of the Union message concluded: "Let the public service be a proud and lively career." He took particular pleasure in the rehabilitation of government servants who had been punished for independence of thought in the past. Early on, for example, Reed Harris, whom Senator McCarthy had driven from USIA a decade before, came back to work under Edward R. Murrow, who himself had been one of McCarthy's bravest critics. The President looked for an appropriate occasion to invite Robert Oppenheimer to the White House and soon found one. He was vigilant in his opposition to any revival of McCarthyism. One of his few moments of anger in press conferences came when a woman reporter asked him why "two well-known security risks" had been given assignments in the State Department. Kennedy remarked icily that she "should be prepared to substantiate" her charges and unconditionally defended the character and record of the officials involved.

But Kennedy's habit of reaching into the permanent government was disruptive as well as exciting for the bureaucracy. For the permanent government had its own set of stability of procedure, everything within channels and according to the book. These were essential; without them government would collapse. Yet an active President, with his own requirements and expectations, was likely to chafe under the bureaucratic minuet.

Early in 1963 a group of communists hijacked a Venezuelan freighter. The President was vastly, if somewhat amusedly, annoyed by the incapacity of his government to help Caracas cope with the situation. One day he beckoned me into his office while he was phoning the Secretary of the Navy to find out why the Navy had been so slow to send out planes to locate the ship. The Secretary apparently was saying that this was not his responsibility; it was a matter for the Joint Chiefs of Staff; nothing had come down through channels. A few days later President Betancourt arrived for a visit. Preparations had been made for a splendid military reception. Then a terrific rainstorm came, and the show was canceled. An hour later Kennedy looked out of his window and saw a forlorn group of soldiers still in formation in the rain. He immediately called General Clifton, his military aide, and asked why, since the ceremony was off, the soldiers were still there. Clifton replied that they had not yet received their orders through channels. Kennedy instructed him to go out right away and tell them to go home. Then he said acidly, "You can see why the Navy has been unable to locate that Venezuelan freighter."

He considered results more important than routine. "My experience in government," he once said, "is that when things are noncontroversial, beautifully coordinated, and all the rest, it must be that not much is going on." He was not, like Roosevelt, a deliberate inciter of bureaucratic disorder; he found no pleasure in playing off one subordinate against another. But his total self-reliance, his confidence in his own priorities and his own memory, freed him from dependence on orderly administrative arrangements. In any case, the Constitution made it clear where the buck stopped. "The President," he once said, "bears the burden of the responsibility. . . . The advisers may move on to new advice." The White House, of course, could not do everything, but it could do something. "The President can't administer a department," he said drily on one occasion, "but at least he can be a stimulant." This Kennedy certainly was, but on occasion he almost administered departments too.

His determination was to pull issues out of the bureaucratic ruck in time to defend his own right to decision and his own freedom of innovation. One devoted student of his methods, Prime Minister Harold Wilson, later spoke of the importance of getting in on emerging questions "by holding meetings of all relevant ministers at an early stage before the problem gets out of hand. That's one of the techniques the world owes to Kennedy." In this and other respects he carried his intervention in the depths of government even further than Roosevelt.

At luncheon one day Ben Cohen and Tom Corcoran drew an interesting comparison. "One of F.D.R.'s great strengths," Cohen said, "was a certain detachment from the details of his administration. He did not try to run everything himself, but gave his people their head. Sometimes he was criticized for letting them go off too much on their own and squabble among themselves. But this was his way of trying people out." Corcoran interjected, "Also it reduced his responsibility for their mistakes. Since he wasn't directly involved, he could wash his hands of bad policies more easily." Ben went on: "Then, when it mattered, he was always ready to weigh in and settle things. We often wished at the time that he would get involved earlier; but in retrospect I think he was right. I am afraid that your man in contrast tries to run too many things himself. He has too tight a grip on his administration.

He is too often involved in the process of shaping things which should be shaped by others before they are presented to a President. I doubt very much whether the Bay of Pigs decision would have been made if the President had not taken part in the preliminary discussions—if he had been confronted in an uncommitted way with the final recommendation. . . . Kennedy is really a President on the model not of Roosevelt but of Wilson. Wilson also tried to run too much himself."

Cohen had a point, though I think he underestimated the extent to which the hardening of the permanent government since Roosevelt's day required presidential intervention at an earlier stage, as well as the extent to which the irreversibility of decisions in the nuclear age compelled a President to make sure that small actions at a low level would not lead ineluctably to catastrophic consequences. In any case, every President must rule in his own fashion. The President, Richard Neustadt had said, is "a decision-machine." Kennedy's purpose in his time of almost constant crisis was to control and stimulate a vast and unwieldy government in order to produce wise decision and efficient execution. He designed his methods to suit his purpose.

4. THE WHITE HOUSE STAFF

His first instrument was the White House staff. This was a diverse group, and Kennedy wanted it that way. Bundy liked to compare the staff to prisms through which the President could look at public problems; and he knew precisely the angle of each refraction. One of his talents was the capacity to attract natural oppositionists—Galbraith, Kaysen, Murrow and others—and put them to work for government. He had some of these on his staff, along with some who were natural public servants; together they provided the mix which met his needs.

He was infinitely accessible to the Special Assistants. One could nearly always get him by phone; and, while Ken O'Donnell guarded one entrance to the presidential office with a wise concern for the President's time and energy, Evelyn Lincoln presided over the other with welcoming patience and warmth. For the half hour or so before luncheon and then again in the last hour of the afternoon, the door between Mrs. Lincoln's office and the President's room was generally ajar—a signal to the staff that he was open for business. One put one's head in the door, was beckoned in; then the report was made or document cleared briskly

across his desk. Everything was transacted in a kind of
shorthand. Kennedy's mind raced ahead of his words; and,
by the time he was midway in a thought, he was likely to
assume that the drift was evident and, without bothering
to complete one sentence, he would begin the next. In the
early evening, however, after the Huntley-Brinkley news
program, the pressure would be off. Then he would frequently be in a mood to lean back in his chair and expand on the events of the day.

He liked to regard his staff as generalists rather than
specialists and had a distressing tendency to take up whatever happened to be on his desk and hand it to whoever
happened to be in the room. But a measure of specialization was inevitable, and the staff on the whole contrived its
own clandestine structure, taking care to pass on a presidential directive to the person in whose area it lay. He
never forgot anything, however, and he was perfectly capable weeks or months later of demanding to know what one
had done about such-and-such.

He expected his staff to cover every significant sector of
federal activity—to know everything that was going on, to
provide speedy and exact answers to his questions and,
most of all, to alert him to potential troubles. When a crisis
was sprung without notice, there would be ejaculations of
incredulity or despair; "For God's sake, do I have to do
everything around here myself?" These passed swiftly; he
wasted little time in recrimination and always buckled
down promptly to the problem of what to do next. For
those who failed him, remorse was a far sharper spur than
reprimands would have been.

He wanted the staff to get into substance. He constantly
called for new ideas and programs. If a staff member told
him about a situation, he would say, "Yes, but what can I
do about it?" and was disappointed if no answer was forthcoming. The Special Assistants were not to get between
the President and the operating chiefs of the departments
and agencies; but they were to make sure that the departmental and agency recommendations took full account
of the presidential and national interests. When the operating chiefs had business which was important enough for
the White House to be informed but not important enough
to justify a direct call to the President, they had a place
to register their recommendation or make their point.
Above all, the responsibility of the staff, Kennedy said,
was to make certain that "important matters are brought
here in a way which permits a clear decision after alterna-

tives have been presented." He added, "Occasionally, in the past, I think the staff has been used to get a pre-arranged agreement which is only confirmed at the President's desk, and that I don't agree with."

When a decision was in the offing, the next step was to call a meeting. Kennedy disliked meetings, especially large ones, and insisted that they be honed to the edge of action. He convened the cabinet far less even than Roosevelt. "Cabinet meetings," he once told John Sharon, "are simply useless. Why should the Postmaster General sit there and listen to a discussion of the problems of Laos? . . . I don't know how Presidents functioned with them or relied on them in the past." (Very few good ones had.) Instead, he asked for weekly reports from cabinet members outlining their activities and proposals. In consequence, he did not use the cabinet as effectively as he might have either to mobilize the government or to advance public understanding of administration policies. Perhaps the best cabinet meeting was in the midst of the Bay of Pigs when there were genuine exchange and assurances of reciprocal support.

If he had to have a meeting, he preferred a small one with candid discussion among the technicians and professionals who could give him the facts on which decision was to be based. Policy people were less essential because he could supply policy himself. Kennedy would listen quietly to the presentation, then ask pertinent questions and expect precise replies. He had a disconcerting capacity, derived in part from his larger perspective and in part from his more original intelligence, to raise points which the experts, however diligently they had prepared themselves, were hard put to answer. Rambling made him impatient, but his courtesy was unshakable; there were only those drumming fingers. At the end, he would succinctly sum up the conclusions.

Meetings, however, did not by themselves guarantee action, any more than White House staff recommendations did. In the main, action followed deadlines, some set by the calendar, some forced by crisis. And, of the scheduled deadlines, the most important, next to the budget, were the ones created by the need to prepare presidential statements.

5. KENNEDY AND SPEECHES

Dean Acheson once said of presidential addresses, "This is often where policy is made, regardless of where it is supposed to be made." The presidential speech was automatically a declaration of national intent, addressed not only to Congress, the country and the world but also (sometimes equally important) to the executive branch of the government.

Kennedy's speeches covered a whole range of occasions from greeting delegations of foreign students to warning the world of the perils of nuclear war. Though he was a perfectly competent writer, he rarely had time to compose his own speeches any longer (except when he spoke extemporaneously, as he very often did). Ted Sorensen was, of course, his main reliance. They had worked closely together for a decade, and on these matters their minds rolled in unison. I do not know which of them originated the device of staccato phrases ("We shall pay any price, bear any burden, meet any hardship, support any friend, oppose any foe to assure the survival and success of liberty") or the use of balanced sentences ("Never have the nations of the world had so much to lose or so much to gain. Together we shall save our planet or together we shall perish in its flames"); but by the time of the Presidency their styles had fused into one.

Next to Sorensen, Richard Goodwin was Kennedy's best writer. After Goodwin's departure to the State Department, I found myself increasingly involved in speech drafting. The President somewhat mistrusted my efforts, however, as "too Stevensonian," by which he meant too complicated in syntax and fancy in language. He felt that his voice had too narrow a range to permit rhetorical flight and used to envy Stevenson his greater inflection of tone. Actually his own range steadily expanded during the Presidency, and he rapidly became an orator of unusual force and eloquence.

He would begin work on a speech by calling in the writer and sketching out his ideas. When the occasion was serious, he would read the draft with intense care, scribble illegibly on the margin and then go over the result with the writer. Like most politicians, he had little sense of the structure of a speech. He also was an uncertain speller; nor was his grammar infallible. In his impromptu remarks, for example, he often bobbled his compound objects.[4] But he was an excellent editor, skilled at tuning up thoughts and eliminating verbal excess. Above all, he loved pungent expressions. Early one Sunday in December 1962 he woke

[4] One can find even in his *Public Papers* a reference to "the tremendous landslide that swept the Vice President and I into office by one-tenth of one per cent." (1963, 444)

me to read aloud two sentences from a Khrushchev speech in the morning newspapers. One began, "At the climax of events around Cuba, there began to be a smell of burning in the air." The other went: "Those militarists who boast that they have submarines with Polaris rockets on board, and other surprises, as they put it, against the Soviet Union, would do well to remember that we are not living in mud huts either." Kennedy remarked with admiration, "Khrushchev certainly has some good writers." (I said that we could do as well for him if he would only give two-hour speeches.)

If the occasion was political or festive, he would approach the speech with greater casualness, quite often using the prepared text only as a point of departure or, as he had done so often in the 1960 campaign, abandoning it entirely. He gave one of his most sparkling talks at a luncheon in October 1961 marking the publication of the first four volumes of the John Quincy Adams papers. I had prepared a draft. Then his rather detailed suggestions led to a new draft, at which he glanced half an hour before the lunch while conducting conversation with other staff people on unrelated topics. In a few moments we went over to the Statler-Hilton Hotel. During lunch he went calmly over the manuscript, crossing out paragraphs and writing inserts. When he rose to speak, the first half of his remarks was absolutely new (including the felicitous opening: "I want to say to Mr. Adams that it is a pleasure to live in your family's old house"). The second half was a free (and improved) adaptation of the text he had brought with him.

The speech process often brought his miscellany of curious knowledge into play. In September 1962 he asked me to prepare something for a talk he had to make at Newport at the dinner before the America's Cup races. He suddenly said, "I understand that there is about the same amount of salt in the human blood as there is in sea water, and that is a proof of our origin in the sea." This sounded like an old wives' tale to me, but I said I would check into it. I called one of Jerome Wiesner's specialists, who was skeptical too but agreed to look further. In an hour he called back, rather excited, and said, "It seems as if you have got on to something there." Apparently blood does have a certain amount of salt, almost as much as sea water, and Claude Bernard and others had speculated that the need of cells for a salt solution might be related to man's primal origin in the sea. When I later asked Kennedy where in the world he had heard this, he said he couldn't re-member. In Newport he converted it into poetry: "All of us have in our veins the exact same percentage of salt in our blood that exists in the ocean, and, therefore, we have salt in our blood, in our sweat, in our tears. We are tied to the ocean. And when we go back to the sea—whether it is to sail or to watch it—we are going back from whence we came."

XXVI

DOWN PENNSYLVANIA AVENUE

ALL THESE DEVICES—White House staff, meetings, speeches—were familiar presidential tools. But by themselves they were only the beginning of the system of presidential control. Every activist President devises further methods, often peculiar and personal, to reach out beyond the White House into the executive branch and beyond that to the Congress. Kennedy's most efficacious means of management and stimulus had no precedent since the age of Jackson and Taney and did not fully exist then—that is, the use of the Attorney General as a prime presidential agent on policy across the board.

In spite of the eight and a half years' difference in their ages, John and Robert Kennedy had achieved by 1961 an extraordinary partnership. Their communication was virtu-ally telepathic and their communion complete. One is not sure when this all started. Robert, the seventh of the nine Kennedy children, was also, among the brothers, the small-est, lightest and, perhaps in consequence, tensest. One had the impression that the family competition had been hardest on him, forcing him to scramble for everything and giving his character at an early point the style of bantam-cock determination. Possibly because of this, and even though the gap in ages could not have permitted much comrade-ship in the early years, his older brother was obviously fond of him. A letter from the South Pacific after PT-109 when Robert, then seventeen, joined the Navy from Milton Academy suggests the relationship. "The folks sent me a clipping of you taking the oath," Jack Kennedy wrote. "The sight of you there, just as a boy, was really moving par-

ticularly as a close examination showed that you had my
checked London coat on. I'd like to know what the hell I'm
doing out here while you go stroking around in my drape
coat, but I suppose that [is] what we are out here for." He
added lightly: "In that picture you looked as if you were
going to step outside the room, grab your gun, and knock
off several of the houseboys before lunch. After reading
Dad's letter, I gathered that the cold vicious look in your
eye was due to the thought of that big blocking back from
Groton."

1. BOBBY

That "cold vicious look" stayed in Robert Kennedy's photographs for some time; his public role in the fifties was that
of a prosecutor and investigator. After the Navy, he went
on to Harvard and then to the University of Virginia Law
School. After law school he briefly joined Truman's Department of Justice. When the Republicans took over in
1953, he moved on to the staff of the Subcommittee on
Investigations of the Senate Committee on Government Operations, chairman, Senator Joseph McCarthy. Here he
worked primarily on an investigation of trade by allied
nations with Communist China. Though this investigation was considerably disputed, it was less disputed than
McCarthy's other investigations into the alleged disloyalty of
government employees. Partly because he genuinely liked
McCarthy, Robert Kennedy watched the committee steer this
second course with mounting disapproval. After six months,
he told McCarthy that he disagreed with the way the committee was being run, predicted that it was headed for
disaster and resigned. Subsequently he returned as counsel
for the Democrats on the committee—Jackson, Symington
and McClellan—and wrote the minority report condemning
McCarthy's investigation of supposed Communist shenani-
gans at Fort Monmouth. In 1957 he became counsel for
the Senate Rackets Committee in its long and angry investigations into "improper activities" on the part of labor
and management. Here his bitter duel with Jimmy Hoffa
of the Teamsters attracted national attention.

Robert's close working association with his older brother
began in 1952, when he managed the Senate campaign, and
flourished in the Rackets Committee, where John Kennedy
was a leader among the senatorial members. In November
1959, Jack naturally turned to Robert to organize his drive
for the presidential nomination. Bringing along such colleagues from the Rackets Committee staff as Kenneth O'Don-

nell and Pierre Salinger, Bobby took over. In the next year
he mobilized the Kennedy forces, brought pressure on undecided party leaders, gave people orders, blew them up if
the execution was slow or slipshod, became the candidate's
no-man and took on himself the onus for the hard judgment and the unpleasant decision. By the end of 1960 he
had thus embellished the public impression of the remorseless prosecutor by stirring in that of the relentless politician.

When, to the general indignation of the bar and the
press, he was appointed Attorney General, he was widely
regarded as a ruthless and power-hungry young man, devoid of principle or scruple, indifferent to personal freedom
or public right, who saw life in rigidly personal and moralistic terms, divided people between the 'white hats' and the
'black hats' and found his greatest pleasure in harassing his
fellow citizens. A cluster of legends arose to reinforce
this theory: thus his father was supposed to have said with
paternal pride, "Bobby hates the same way I do." And
Bobby's public bearing—the ominous manner, the knock-
the-chip-off-my-shoulder look, the stony blue eyes, clenched
teeth, tart, monosyllabic tongue—did not especially dispel
the picture of a rough young man suddenly given national
authority.

I do not know of any case in contemporary American
politics where there has seemed to me a greater discrepancy between the myth and the man. The public theory
of Robert Kennedy could only appear to those who knew
him, as James Wechsler later described it, a case of mistaken identity. No doubt Robert's first political heroes were
Herbert Hoover and Douglas MacArthur; no doubt he once
considered Yalta a national betrayal; no doubt he regarded
(and continued to regard) professional liberals with suspicion. But in my experience he did not hold grudges,
cherish a black-and-white view of life, scorn issues of personal freedom or believe that anyone who was not with him
was against him. This was true neither of his personal relations nor (as was plainly shown by his leadership in
changing the American line on neutral countries) of his
policy judgments. He was emotionally more intense than his
older brother, but he had all of John Kennedy's laconic
candor and increasing shares of his objectivity and his
deadpan, throwaway wit.

Indeed, as one came to know him better, what seemed
most characteristic were his gentleness, consideration,
sobriety, idealism and, if the word had not been hopelessly
degraded by political oratory, compassion. At home in Hick-

ory Hill, with his happy and spirited wife, surrounded by
multiplying sons, daughters and pets (David Ormsby Gore
once said that he had known Bobby and Ethel so long that
he could remember when the dogs outnumbered the children), or in shirtsleeves in his office, children's drawings
thumbtacked on the wall, a litter of souvenirs from foreign
travel strewn around the room, a large dog somnolent on
the floor, he hardly seemed the demon of the liberal imagination. Most striking of all was what one of his first liberal
friends, William O. Douglas, called his "unique capacity
for growth." Thus at some point Robert Kennedy grew
aware of the world of mind and sensibility in which his
brother had been so long at ease; and he determined to
explore this world for himself. He began reading extensively,
especially history and biography; he started listening to
music and attending ballet; and he was responsible for
organizing one of the pleasantest of the New Frontier exercises, the so-called Hickory Hill seminar.

The purpose here was to remind public officials that a
world existed beyond their in-boxes. The regulars, con-
sisting of about twenty cabinet members, agency chiefs and
lesser government people, plus the Ormsby Gores, met once
a month or so to hear an authority speak on a subject of
his own choosing so long as it didn't involve the day-to-
day business of government. Two of the sessions—with
Isaiah Berlin of Oxford and David Donald of Johns Hopkins
were held at the White House, and Jacqueline occasionally
came to others. The evenings were lively and generally
disputatious. Ethel Kennedy and Eunice Shriver were particularly undaunted questioners. One evening A. J. Ayer,
then of the University of London, came and delivered with
his usual virtuosity an attack on abstract propositions. Midway, Eunice whispered to the person on her right, "I don't
think that Professor Ayer believes in God." When Ayer
finished, Ethel immediately rose and challenged him to explain his rejection of metaphysics. Ayer, resorting to the
oldest of teaching tricks, said, "What do you mean by
metaphysics?" Bobby called his wife a warning from the
back of the room, but after a moment Ethel responded
gamely, "I mean whether conceptions like truth and virtue
and beauty have any meaning." An evening with Dr.
Lawrence Kubie, the psychiatrist, produced a heated debate
over the best way to reach pre-school children from poor
families and a subsequent thoughtful correspondence between Kubie and Walter Heller. The seminars summed up
a good deal of the humane and questing spirit of the New
Frontier.

2. THE ATTORNEY GENERAL

As Attorney General, Robert Kennedy was determined to make the Department of Justice professionally the best department in the government. The quality of appointments had not been so high since the New Deal—Byron White and then Nicholas Katzenbach as Deputy Attorney General, Archibald Cox as Solicitor General and, among the Assistant Attorney Generals, Burke Marshall for the Civil Rights Division, John Douglas for the Civil Division, Louis Oberdorfer for the Tax Division, Herbert Miller for the Criminal Division, William Orrick for Anti-Trust, Ramsey Clark for Lands and Norbert Schlei for the Office of Legal Counsel. In addition, two Pulitzer Prize newspapermen, John Seigenthaler and Edwin O. Guthman, were in charge of public information.

It was an exceptionally able staff, and Robert Kennedy told it to make the Department an example of impartial law enforcement. The Attorney General's readiness, for example, to bring cases against Democratic politicians—two Congressmen, three state judges, five mayors, assorted chiefs of police and sheriffs—confounded his critics of 1960. Along with civil rights and juvenile delinquency, he took a particular personal interest in the fight against organized crime. He recruited ardent young lawyers for the Organized Crime Section and for a special investigative staff headed by Walter Sheridan, another associate from the Rackets Committee, and gave them full support. He worked out with Mortimer Caplin of the Internal Revenue Service arrangements for a corps of anti-racketeer tax investigators. He brought the Federal Bureau of Investigation into the broad war against crime syndicates. There were occasional public relations excesses. Criminologists, for example, were skeptical of the sanction the Department gave to the notion of a centrally organized and all-pervasive Mafia; and J. Edgar Hoover resented the publicity given the testimony of convicted racketeers, especially in the Valachi case. Nonetheless, the anti-crime effort had more élan and effect than it had had for years.

The relationship with J. Edgar Hoover was always a problem for Attorney Generals. For a quarter of a century the FBI had operated as if it were an independent agency, choosing its own cases, nourishing its own relations with the Congress and the press and bypassing its Attorney Generals to report directly to the President. The exceptional proficiency of Hoover's investigations and certainly of his public relations had made him an almost sacrosanct national figure. As Cyril Connolly once put it, "The Federal Bureau of Investigation, the G-men and Mr. J. Edgar Hoover form one of the most important elements of the American myth—symbols of perfection in detective methods, wholesome anti-Communism, ruthless pursuit of gangsters and spies, and of a dedicated, puritanical but unselfseeking chief above and outside politics; the nation's watchdog and the President's counsellor." John F. Kennedy would have agreed with him—and would have said it in much the same tone. He regarded the FBI as an element in the panoply of national power requiring both propitiation and control. While he preserved friendly relations with Hooveer and invited him from time to time to the White House, he also wholeheartedly supported his brother's view that the Bureau be restored to the Department of Justice. For the first time in a generation, communications from the Bureau to the White House went through the office of the Attorney General. Moreover, Robert Kennedy directed the FBI to join the Department by moving not only into the drive against organized crime but also, considerably more alien to the Bureau's folkways, into the enforcement of the civil rights laws.

The question of the indigent defendant was another of Robert Kennedy's personal concerns. In 1961 he appointed a committee to inquire into the quality of justice afforded the needy. That committee found, in effect, two systems of criminal justice in the country—one for the rich, another for the poor. Through legislation and the establishment of an Office of Criminal Justice, he now sought to make sure that poor men charged with crime would have free counsel, reasonable bail and a fair opportunity to prepare a defense; he wanted, as he liked to say, a Department of Justice, not a Department of Prosecution.

Judgeships were a recurring negotiation between Justice and the White House. James Eastland of Mississippi, the chairman of the Senate Judiciary Committee, had his own views about judges, especially in the South. In an effort to placate Eastland, and in preparation for Eastland's acquiescence in the appointment of Thurgood Marshall of the National Association for the Advancement of Colored People to the Second Circuit Court, the Attorney General recommended the appointment early in 1961 of Harold Cox and J. Robert Elliott to district court judgeships in Mississippi and Alabama. Both men had been recommended by the American Bar Association. Cox personally assured Robert Kennedy in a long conversation that he would do his constitutional duty in civil rights matters. Once on the bench, however, both Cox and Elliott turned out to be bitter segregationsts; and two other of the eight appointees to southern district courts showed a marked reluctance to apply the civil rights decisions. The appointments were plainly mistakes and caused trouble in the future.

The first Supreme Court vacancy came in March 1962 with the resignation of Charles Whittaker. Kennedy, on the Attorney General's recommendation, appointed Byron White. The President later told me that it was one of the hardest decisions he had had to make and that he had hesitated a week over it. "I figure that I will have several more appointments before I am through, and I mean to appoint Paul Freund, Arthur Goldberg and Bill Hastie. But I didn't want to start off with a Harvard man and a professor [Freund was a professor at the Harvard Law School]; we've taken so many Harvard men that it's damn hard to appoint another. And we couldn't do Hastie [a Negro judge serving with distinction on the Third Circuit] this time; it was just too early." The President also disliked the thought of losing Goldberg from the cabinet; and when the next vacancy came with Felix Frankfurter's resignation in the summer of 1962, he inclined at first toward Freund. The Attorney General meanwhile urged the case of Archibald Cox, who had taken the job of Solicitor General, which Freund had declined. Unhappy about choosing between these two men of high ability and comparable background, the President eventually went ahead with Goldberg. Again he said philosophically, "I think we'll have appointments enough for everybody."

On civil liberties questions, contrary to liberal fears, Robert Kennedy proved concerned and responsive. Like all Attorney Generals since 1940, he wanted wiretapping legislation; but, after imprudent endorsement of a broad bill in 1961, the Department restudied the problem and came up the next year with a far more careful and confined approach. For the rest, he presided over a quiet and thorough liquidation of the McCarthyite heritage. "I think that the Communist party as a political organization is of no danger to the United States," he said. "It has no following and has been disregarded by the American people for many, many years." Insofar as its relationship to the Soviet Union made it a danger, that was a matter for the FBI. Anti-communist vigilantes, he continued, "perform a disservice to the United States," and he attacked "those who, in the name of fighting Communism, sow seeds of suspicion and distrust by making false or irresponsible charges, not only against their neighbors, but against courageous teachers and public officials." Within the government he argued for the dismissal of unsupported security charges and recommended a pardon for the last Smith Act defendant in federal prison, the ex-Communist Junius Scales; he did this over the opposition not only of Hoover, who insisted that Scales should not be released until he cooperated by naming names, but of his successive Deputy Attorney Generals. "For the first time since the rise of McCarthyism," said Joseph Rauh, Washington's leading civil liberties lawyer, "an Attorney General has refused to treat a man's unwillingness to inform on others as a ground for withholding favorable governmental action in his case."

He was also active on questions of visas and travel restrictions. The basic immigration law excluded politically suspect aliens from the country unless a waiver could be secured from the Department of Justice. The definition of political dubiety was broad and loose, and the result was often the denial of visas to eminent writers and scholars for having committed an offense against American ideas of political propriety at some point in the remote past. Robert Kennedy thought the system injurious to the national interest, granted waivers whenever the State Department asked for them and, if the Department hesitated, often spurred it on to make the application.

The President himself, it must be added, was vigorously of the same mind. When he appointed Abba Schwartz administrator of the State Department's Bureau of Security and Consular Affairs, he told Schwartz that he was tired of the impression of the United States as a sort of police state, obsessed with security and judging every applicant for admission by past political views; he wanted the world to see America as an open society ready to listen to anyone. It continued to enrage him to read in the newspapers that a distinguished foreigner invited to the United States had been turned down by a minor consular official. Schwartz would tip me off when possible controversial cases were pending; and I would take them in to the President, who would say with exasperation, "Of course, get the waiver, give 'em the visa, the country will survive."

The Attorney General also strongly supported the move within the executive branch to remove restrictions on American travel to China, Albania and other forbidden lands. Within the State Department, Schwartz, Averell Harriman and George Ball had recommended that restrictions be lifted for all countries save Cuba; and the President

several times gave instructions that this be done. But the
Secretary of State always felt that it was the wrong time
to do it, whether because a bill was pending in Congress
or a negotiation pending in Moscow; and as a result nothing ever happened. The Attorney General went even
further than the internal State Department proposal and
favored lifting restrictions on travel to Cuba as well. It
seemed to him preposterous to prosecute students who had
a desire to see the Castro regime in action. "Why shouldn't
they go?" he once said. "If I were twenty-one years old,
that's what I would like to do this summer."

In the Washington judgment, he turned out to be the
best Attorney General since Francis Biddle twenty years
earlier. But this was a lesser part of his services to the
President. When he first decided to appoint his brother to
the cabinet, I do not know how much John Kennedy expected Robert to do besides run the Department of Justice
and be available for private advice and commiseration. The
Bay of Pigs, however, changed all that. Thereafter the
President wanted Bobby at every crucial meeting. He did
not necessarily agree with his younger brother; the Attorney General was one more prism which he read like the
others. But the President trusted him more than anyone
else to get to the bottom of an idea or project, to distinguish
what was operational from what was literary, to anticipate
consequences, to ride herd on execution, to protect the
presidential interest and, above all, to be candid.

Within the cabinet, Robert Kennedy became a constant
and steady liberal force, no matter how much it irritated
him to have this pointed out. Whatever the issue, one could
expect a reaction on the merits, without regard to vested
intellectual or administrative interests. One could expect a
reaction on political feasibility also; but the two were kept
carefully separate. Gradually the New Frontiersmen came
to see him as their particular champion, knowing that he
was often free to say and do things which the President, in
the nature of things, could not say or do. Soon he had his
allies scattered throughout the administration. An unfriendly observer wrote, "Kennedy, a student of guerrilla warfare, was applying its techniques to intergovernmental relations." But he did not plant these men; he won them.

He was also increasingly the voice of New Frontier
idealism to young people at home and abroad. His programs for poor children through the President's Committee
on Juvenile Delinquency, with their concern for education
and emphasis on what intellectuals would later call 'par-
ticipatory democracy,' represented a genuine innovation in

American social policy. When he resigned as Attorney General, the children of the Washington public schools organized a mass tribute, presenting him an itemized statement of their reasons for gratitude, concluding:

> FOR having hundreds of school children into his office to dis-
> cuss subjects of interest to Washington students;
> FOR making hundreds of unpublicized calls and writing hun-
> dreds of unpublicized letters in connection with student
> problems and programs;
> AND, most of all, both by personal example and by the strength
> of his interest and affection,
> FOR giving the children of the District pride in themselves and
> hope in their future . . .

Especially in foreign affairs, if a good idea was going down for the third time in the bureaucratic sea, one turned more and more to Bobby to rescue it. His distinctive contribution was to fight unremittingly for his brother's understanding that foreign policy was not a technical exercise off in a vacuum but the expression of a nation's internal policy and purpose. When I met him in India in February 1962 after his visit to Japan and Indonesia, he remarked that he had been most impressed by the fact that America could make contact with the youth and the intellectuals in Asia only as a progressive country. "I kept asking myself," he said, "what a conservative could possibly say to these people. I can talk all the time about social welfare and trade unions and reform; but what could someone say who didn't believe in these things? What in the world could Barry Goldwater say?" He freely attacked the policy of association "with tyrannical and unpopular regimes that had no following and no future." To students coming to his office he would say, "Two thirds of the world today goes to bed hungry. The benefits of the world can't be concentrated on the few. Such a solution would be intolerable. We in the United States have a responsibility to help others." He left his mark in a dozen areas of foreign policy from cultural exchange to counterguerrilla warfare.

The myth of ruthlessness persisted. But the man grew; his horizons enlarged; his identity evolved. "He is an active principle," Norman Mailer wrote. ". . . . Something compassionate, something witty, has come into the face. Something of sinew." He was in these years his brother's total partner and, more than anyone else, enabled the President to infuse the government with the energy and purpose of the New Frontier.

3. THE VICE-PRESIDENT

However surprised John Kennedy had been in Los Angeles when Lyndon Johnson accepted his invitation to go on the ticket as candidate for Vice-President, he soon had reason to rejoice in the selection. In the autumn of 1960 Johnson proved a powerful and tireless campaigner, especially in the South. Indignantly rejecting suspicions of the presidential candidate as a Yankee and Catholic, he would say in the regional idiom, "Kennedy's a man to go to the well with." [1] Employing his whole oratorical range—first hunched over the rostrum, talking in a low, confiding, pleading voice, telling a repertory of stories unmatched since Alben Barkley, then suddenly standing erect, roaring, gesticulating, waving his arms—he carried the message of confidence with panache across the southern states. Without Johnson, Kennedy would have lost Texas and perhaps South Carolina and Louisiana: [2] without these three states, the electoral vote would have been evenly split and the result at the mercy of unpledged electors from Mississippi and Alabama. Kennedy fully appreciated all this and was grateful.

After the inauguration, both Kennedy and Johnson confronted the problem of the vice-presidential role in the new administration. Thirty-four previous Presidents had faced this problem with only indifferent success; the real difficulty lay in the Constitution itself. "My country has, in its wisdom," wrote the first Vice-President, "contrived for me the most insignificant office . . . that ever the invention of man contrived or his imagination conceived." Yet, if the Vice-Presidency was an office without power (the duty of presiding over the Senate, whatever that was worth, derived technically from the constitutional provision assigning the Vice-President another and distinct post as President of the Senate), it remained one of absolute potentiality. "I am Vice-President," John Adams continued. "In this I am nothing. But I may be everything." Like the hooded man at the feast, the Vice-President had little to do but remind the emperor of his own mortality. And in the meantime, as Harry Truman once put it, "the President, by necessity, builds his own staff, and the Vice-President

---

[1] A reference to the hazards of replenishing the water supply when an encampment was under Indian assault in frontier days.

[2] In Louisiana, however, the Catholic and Negro vote seems to have been chiefly responsible for Kennedy's gains over Stevenson in 1956.

remains an outsider, no matter how friendly the two may be. . . . Neither can take the other completely into his confidence." It was in a way a doomed relationship. Probably no President and Vice-President since Jackson and Van Buren had wholeheartedly liked and trusted each other.

Nevertheless one did not have the impression that Kennedy worried unduly about his relations with Johnson. He recognized of course that the former majority leader might have difficulty in reconciling himself to the upward rush of the young back-bencher. "After all," Kennedy remarked to me one day, "I spent years of my life when I could not get consideration for a bill until I went around and begged Lyndon Johnson to let it go ahead." And he was well aware too that the Vice-President was temperamental, edgy and deeply sensitive. Writing a birthday telegram to Johnson, he once said, according to Tom Wicker, was like "drafting a state document." On the other hand, ever since their confrontation on the Tuesday of convention week, Kennedy had no doubt, I think, that Johnson would accept his primacy. Moreover, he liked Johnson personally, valued his counsel on questions of legislation and public opinion and was determined that, as Vice-President, Johnson should experience the full respect and dignity of the office. He took every care to keep Johnson fully informed. He made sure he was at major meetings and ceremonies. Nor would he tolerate from his staff the slightest disparagement of the Vice-President.

As for Johnson, he once said philosophically to Franklin Roosevelt, Jr., that no Vice-President could hope to compete with the President in public impact; all any Vice-President could do was stand aside. "Your daddy," Johnson added, "never let his Vice-Presidents put their heads above water"; and I believe that in this respect he regarded Kennedy as a thoroughgoing Rooseveltian. A draft executive order emerging early on from the Vice-President's office and contemplating the assignment to him of certain executive responsibilities produced a post-inaugural joke comparing his relationship with Kennedy to Seward's with Lincoln at the start of their administration (when Seward had proposed that Lincoln turn over major presidential responsibilities to him). Johnson was wounded by this and complained to the President about it. I am sure that pulling a Seward was not in his mind. His sympathetic friend William S. White has written that Johnson set out "to be first of all a loyal Vice-President." [3]

[3] W. S. White, *The Professional: Lyndon B. Johnson* (Boston, 1964), 228.

This was clearly so, and Johnson clearly succeeded. White suggests that Johnson would have handled certain matters differently—Vietnam, Latin America, the steel crisis—but Johnson rigorously kept disagreement to himself. He cleared all important speeches with the White House, held few press conferences and rarely gave stories to newspapermen. At meetings of the cabinet or the National Security Council, he kept his peace until the President asked his view. Then he would faithfully back the President's policies and reserve his own comment for questions of political or congressional management.

The problem still remained of finding things for the Vice-President to do. As Senator, Johnson had helped shape the space program, and as Vice-President he was now able to carry it forward. Johnson also served as chairman of the President's Committee on Equal Employment Opportunities, as Nixon had before him. Above all, as Kennedy had promised Sam Rayburn in Los Angeles, he sent the Vice-President on trips abroad. In the Kennedy years Johnson visited thirty-three countries and delivered more than 150 speeches. The equal employment and overseas assignments, as Johnson must have noticed, gave him an opportunity to build himself up in areas where he had been conspicuously weak when he had tried for the Presidency in 1960.

Johnson's vice-presidential performance was a triumph of self-discipline, and it exacted its psychic price. Underneath the self-imposed constraint, Johnson remained a proud and imperious man of towering energies and passions. Self-effacement was for him the most unnatural of roles; and the foreign visits became one great escape. He sought his missions abroad, adored them and whirled through his thirty-three countries scattering ballpoint pens, cigarette lighters and general pandemonium in his wake and returning with trunks of gifts for his friends. He was effective in his meetings with foreign leaders and had a bracing impact on the correct young men of the Foreign Service. Once an American diplomat met him at the Rome airport and on the way into the city methodically instructed him, as if he were some sort of uncouth backwoodsman, on how to behave when he met the local dignitaries. Johnson listened to this singular performance with unaccustomed patience. When they arrived at the hotel, the diplomat said, "Mr. Vice President, is there anything else I can do for you?" The Vice-President, looking stonily up and down at his model of diplomatic propriety, replied, "Yes, just one thing. Zip up your fly."

But life in Washington was harder. In later years he

would describe the Vice-Presidency as the most valuable time in his career—the time which enabled him to take over the Presidency with such skill and purpose—and doubtless this was so; but at the time one felt an increasing moroseness and unhappiness. One night at a party at The Elms, his large house in Spring Valley, he sent a Negro chauffeur to collect a guest's car. Johnson said, "Do you see that man? He has driven for every majority leader since Joe Robinson. When I became Vice-President, I asked him whether he would keep on driving for me. He said no, he wouldn't. He said, 'I want to drive for the big man. I don't want to drive for the Vice-President. That's nothing.'" Seizing his guest's arm, Johnson said with great earnestness, "I sure wish I had had him with me in Los Angeles in 1960."

Probably Johnson's greatest frustration lay in his role, or lack of it, in relationship to Congress. Beyond his deep emotional identification with the New Deal, somewhat tempered in the fifties by the conservatism of the country and the politics of Texas, Johnson had displayed no consuming interest in the substance of policies. But, once the substance was given, he was the great legislative prestidigitator of his time. Not since James F. Byrnes had Congress seen a man so skilled in modifying a measure to enlist the widest possible support, so adept at the arts of wheedling, trading and arm-twisting, so persistent and so persuasive. Yet these extraordinary talents went largely unemployed in the Kennedy years.

This was partly his own fault. During the interregnum Johnson acted as if he expected to combine the best of both his old job and his new. He set up for business in the majority leader's suite in the Capitol, picked Mike Mansfield as his successor and convened meetings between committee chairmen and members of the new cabinet. But he went too far when he permitted (or encouraged) Mansfield to propose that as Vice-President he continue to preside over the Democratic caucus. Though a majority of the caucus was willing to have Johnson, seventeen Senators, pronouncing his presence an intrusion from the executive branch, voted to reject the motion. This unexpected repudiation deeply wounded Johnson. Belatedly recalling the jealous rules of his old club, he did not press for victory and thereafter left the senatorial caucus alone. The incident reduced his usefulness on the Hill. Once the necromancer had left his senatorial seat, the old black magic evidently lost some of its power.

There were, however, deeper reasons for steering the energies of the Vice-President in other directions. If Kennedy had allowed Johnson to conduct his congressional relations, he would in effect have made the Vice-President the judge of what was legislatively feasible and thereby have lost control over his own program. This was something no sensible President would do. Kennedy therefore relied on his own congressional liaison staff under Lawrence O'Brien, calling on the Vice-President only on particular occasions. Could Johnson have been used more? He thought so and used to say privately with sad incredulity about one or another administration measure or tactic in Congress, "You know, they never once asked me about that!" But in public he remained cooperative and steadfast.

4. KENNEDY AND THE CONGRESS

As Kennedy's comment on Theodore Roosevelt and Wilson as against Polk and Truman had suggested, he felt that in some sense the real test of a President was his ability to get his program through Congress. In the mood of the early sixties this would be the hardest test of all.

Madison had written of the Congress in *Federalist* No. 48: "Its constitutional powers being at once more extensive, and less susceptible of precise limits, it can, with the greater facility, mask, under complicated and indirect measures, the encroachments which it makes on the coordinate departments." Recent developments had borne out Madison's fear. In the years since the Second World War, Congress, through its enlarged use of its powers of appropriation and investigation, had become increasingly involved in the details of executive administration, thereby systematically enhancing its own power and diminishing that of the President. A comparison, say, of the Emergency Relief Appropriation Act of 1935 and its lump sum appropriation of $4.8 billion to be allocated pretty much at presidential discretion, with the tangle of stipulations and restrictions written into the foreign aid legislation of the sixties made the point. Moreover, the more foreign policy required money, the more Congress acquired a means of veto. In the realm of hemisphere affairs, Monroe could promulgate a Doctrine, Theodore Roosevelt wave a Big Stick and Franklin Roosevelt become a Good Neighbor without reference to Congress; and, if Congress disapproved, there was little it could do. But the Alliance for Progress, since it needed appropriations, was at the mercy of Congress every step along the way. No one wished to change the system; but it was hard to deny that contemporary Presidents, hedged round by an aggressive Congress and an unresponsive bureaucracy, had in significant respects notably less freedom of action than their predecessors.

On top of this, Kennedy's margin in Congress was exceedingly nominal. The figures looked fine—64 Democrats to 36 Republicans in the Senate, 263 to 174 in the House—but were deceptive. For one thing, in a number of states Kennedy had run behind the Democratic candidates for Congress. "The people in Congress do not feel that they owe the President anything," a Democratic Congressman told *U.S. News and World Report*. "A good many of them were elected in 1960 in spite of his presence on the ticket rather than because his name was there. They feel that they have more of a mandate for their point of view than he does for his program." Moreover, the apparent Democratic majorities in both House and Senate included many members of the old anti-New Deal coalition of conservative Democrats and Republicans. "Some Democrats," as the President observed in 1962, "have voted with the Republicans for twenty-five years, really since 1938 . . . so that we have a very difficult time, on a controversial piece of legislation, securing a working majority."

He could never escape the political arithmetic. The Democrats had lost twenty seats in the 1960 congressional election, all from the North, nearly all liberal Democrats, nearly all defeated because of the religious issue. Many times in the next two years Kennedy desperately needed these twenty votes. Without them he was more than ever dependent on the South. The old Confederacy was represented by ninety-nine Democratic Congressmen and twenty-one Democratic Senators. This meant in the House that, if the administration carried every northern, western and border Democratic vote, which it rarely did, it would still require a minimum of fifty-five southern votes to preserve a Democratic majority. It meant that he had hardly more Democratic Congressmen from the northern and western states (132) than from the border states and the South (131). Moreover, the old Confederacy, by virtue of seniority, controlled most of the critical committee chairmanships and thereby had further leverage over legislation. The legislative progress of the New Frontier was thus largely in the hands of aging men, mostly born in another century, mostly representing rural areas in an urban nation (and, indeed, mostly coming from states where less than 40 per cent of persons of voting age had cast ballots in the 1960

election). For an edifying four months in 1962 a feud
between Representative Clarence Cannon (eighty-three
years old; and Senator Carl Hayden (eighty-four years
old), each of whom angrily declined to go to the office
of the other, held up House-Senate agreement on appropriation bills and left a number of government agencies
without money to meet their payrolls.

Nothing brought the precariousness of the administration's position home more grimly than the first congressional battle—the fight in January 1961 to enlarge the
House Rules Committee in order to make sure the administration would have the power to bring its program
to the floor. In spite of Kennedy's victory in the national
election two months earlier, it took twenty-two Republican
votes and a personal plea by Speaker Rayburn from the
well of the House for the administration to squeak through
by five votes. Sixty-four southern Democrats were on the
other side. It was a close and bitter business, and the
memory of this fight laid a restraining hand on the administration's legislative priorities for some time to come.
Every President, moreover, has to husband his bargaining
power for its most effective use. Thus in 1962 Kennedy
decided—perhaps mistakenly—to use his for the trade expansion bill first of all; he thereby had less left over for
other parts of his program.

Kennedy used to quote Jefferson: "Great innovations
should not be forced on slender majorities." Nor was he
one to see great virtue in losing. "There is no sense," he
once said, "in raising hell, and then not being successful.
There is no sense in putting the office of the Presidency
on the line on an issue, and then being defeated." Yet, despite such aphorisms, he did, in fact, submit to Congress
an astonishing number of innovations, doing so less perhaps in the expectation of immediate enactment than in
the knowledge they would never be enacted without a long
campaign of congressional and national education. I doubt,
for example, whether he really counted on getting Medicare in 1961 or 1962. But he knew that if he sent up a
message and a bill, there would be debate and hearings;
Congress would begin to accustom itself to unfamiliar ideas;
the legislation would be revised to meet legitimate objections; the opposition would in time expend itself and
seem increasingly frantic and irrelevant; public support
would consolidate; and by 1964 or 1965 the bill would be
passed. This is not to say that he would not have preferred immediate results, did not fight for them (while
always balancing them against desired results in other

areas) and did not, in many cases, achieve them. But, even if he did not get action on all his requests, the educational processes thus set in motion would make the passage of most of them inevitable in the years to come.

Yet one result of his flow of proposals was very likely to increase congressional anxieties. There were too many new ideas, coming too fast, couched in too cool and analytical a tone and implying too critical a view of American society. Instead of being reassured, many Congressmen felt threatened. And the President himself, despite those fourteen years in Congress, had always been something of an alien on the Hill. This had been especially true in the House, where he had had least contact with the leadership, where his experience was most out of date and which now confronted him with his toughest problems. Even in the Senate, where he was liked and respected, he had never been one of the cloakroom boys. He did not act, talk or look like a Senator, or regard the Senate as the climax of human evolution. Now he had shot up over the heads of his seniors, and the congressional elders, who had been great men when he arrived as a gangling first-termer, were sometimes discomfited by dealing with him as President. A few resented his intellectualism, his wealth and the style of his world. A country Congressman from Tennessee told David Brinkley in 1962, "All that Mozart string music and ballet dancing down there and all that fox hunting and London clothes. He's too elegant for me. I can't talk to him." This was perhaps a bizarre reaction, but it suggested the sense of distance.

On his side, Kennedy cultivated his congressional relations with diligence and cheer, though with a certain fatalism. He enjoyed the Tuesday morning breakfasts with congressional leaders, often had congressional groups at the White House and threw himself with necessary vigor into the congressional battles. He particularly liked and valued Mike Mansfield, approved of Mansfield's announced principles of "courtesy, self-restraint and accommodation" and considered him underrated because he did his job with so little self-advertisement and fanfare. He liked Carl Albert, the House leader, for the same reasons. He also liked and was entertained by Everett Dirksen, the Republican leader in the Senate. He respected the standards and the craftsmanship of the Hill. When Tom Wicker asked him why his effort to establish a Department of Urban Affairs in 1962 had gone down to such dismal defeat, Kennedy replied, "I played it too cute. It was so obvious it made them mad." He spent more of his time than people realized working with Congress. But it cannot be said that this was the part of the Presidency which gave him the greatest pleasure or satisfaction.

This made his congressional liaison staff all the more important, and it served him well. Lawrence O'Brien, a man of great decency and character, assembled a first-class group of people—Henry Hall Wilson, Richard Dona-hue, Mike Manatos, Charles Daly, Claude Desautels—and gave the White House a more organized legislative role than it had ever had before. F.D.R. had avoided a formal White House legislative office, fearing that, if the President's staff went into the liaison business, it would end up a routine service agency for Congressmen and departments alike. This was indeed what happened when Eisenhower established the first White House legislative office in the fifties. But Kennedy was prepared to pay this price if it would increase presidential influence on the Hill. He some-times said himself that in his fourteen years in Congress he had had little useful contact with members of the White House staff, and he wished to change that now.

Moreover, where F.D.R., as part of his looser system of presidential management, did not want the White House accountable for all the proposals of his administration (he would sometimes say to cabinet officers with bills of their own, "It is all your trouble, not mine"), Kennedy, with his taut ship, sought to centralize the organization of legis-lative pressure. While the departments and agencies re-tained primary responsibility for their bills, each gave O'Brien every Monday morning a report on activities and plans. Digested and analyzed, these reports went to the President before the Tuesday breakfasts.

O'Brien did not have the most enviable job in the gov-ernment. From the congressional perspective the White House agents on the Hill were always doing too much or too little. Complaints about absence of presidential leader-ship alternated with complaints about excess of presidential pressure. Larry suffered the constantly shifting winds with equanimity and worked for the program with tact and de-votion. It remained a constant battle. "The Congress looks more powerful sitting here," the President said at the end of 1962, "than it did when I was there in the Congress. But that is because when you are in Congress you are one of 100 in the Senate or one of 435 in the House. So that the power is so divided. But from here I look . . . at the col-lective power of the Congress, particularly the bloc action, and it is a substantial power."

The fact that he accepted his congressional compromises

and defeats fatalistically instead of raging back in the manner of the Roosevelts led some observers to suppose that, if he had only fought harder, he would have had greater success. But Kennedy, knowing the arithmetic of Congress and the entrenched power at that time of the conservative coalition, knew that he just did not have the votes for his more controversial proposals—and that he could not afford to alienate Congressmen gratuitously if he wanted to save his less controversial bills. Nor did he rest great hope in the measures for congressional reform urged by Senator Joseph Clark and others. Not only would these be among the most controversial of all; but Kennedy remembered that the Rules Committee, the committee staffs and the seniority system itself were all offsprings of earlier reform movements. He was ready for minor tinkering, like enlarging the Rules Committee; but he was basically resigned to the existing structure and hoped to make it work by getting better people in Congress. In September 1962, when James MacGregor Burns submitted a resolution to the American Political Science Association proposing a presidential commission to investigate executive-congressional relations, Kennedy remarked that this seemed to him the wrong approach; Congress had to be persuaded to reform itself, and there was very little the executive could do about it. It would help greatly, he added, if we could gain a few seats in the election; but nothing really fundamental could be done until after 1964. "We can make loyalty to the ticket the test in 1964, and then we can deal with those who failed to support the ticket."

Congress remained his great frustration. But the extent of that frustration has been exaggerated. The myth grew up in later years that, for all the loftiness of its design, the New Frontier was unusually ineffective in enacting its proposals. While Kennedy did not get everything he wanted, he knew that in many cases the ground had to be sowed in 1961 and 1962 if the crop were to be harvested in 1964 and 1965. And the things he did get even before the 1962 election constituted a legislative record unmatched in some respects since the days of Roosevelt.[4]

[4] 1961: Peace Corps; Alliance for Progress; Arms Control and Disarmament Administration; area redevelopment; general housing act; extension of unemployment compensation; aid to dependent children of unemployed; increase in minimum wage; water pollution control; juvenile delinquency program; community health facilities.

1962: Trade Expansion Act; UN bond issue; tax bill; investment tax credit; communications satellite; manpower development and

XXVII

THE BULLY PULPIT

THE MOST COMMON CRITICISM of Kennedy during his Presidency was that he had failed as a public educator. It was said that he concentrated on 'selling' himself and his family rather than his ideas; that he was excessively preoccupied with his 'image'; and that he was unwilling to convert personal popularity into political pressure for his program. He was compared invidiously with the Roosevelts, Wilson and other Presidents celebrated for their skill in rallying the electorate behind controversial policies. "He has neglected his opportunities to use the forum of the Presidency as an educational institution," wrote Carroll Kilpatrick of the *Washington Post.* "I think it is the President's fault," said Howard K. Smith of CBS-TV. ". . . Every great President has been also a great teacher and explainer. . . . Today [October 1963], in lieu of really important explanations by the President, the papers of America are full instead of the speeches of Goldwater." "He never really exploited his considerable gifts as a public educator," concluded James Reston of the *New York Times.*

Yet in later years the age of Kennedy was seen as a time of quite extraordinary transformation of national values and purposes—a transformation so far-reaching as to make the America of the sixties a considerably different society from the America of the fifties. And, instead of hearing that Kennedy did too little as a public educator, one heard more often in retrospect that he had tried to do

---

training; accelerated public works; drug labeling; restraints on conflict of interest; federal pay reform; federal assistance for the immunization of children; constitutional amendment abolishing the poll tax in federal elections; farm bill with wheat controls.

The statistics for these two years show 53 total major recommendations in 1961, of which 33 were enacted into law; 54 in 1962, of which 40 were enacted into law. "Summary of the Three-Year Kennedy Record and Digest of Major Accomplishments of the 87th Congress and the 88th Congress First Session," 88 Cong., 1 Sess., Sen. Doc. No. 53, 55–60.

too much too quickly, to put over too many new ideas in too short a time, that he had unnecessarily affronted the national mood and pushed ahead so fast that he lost contact with public opinion. Clearly the paradox of Kennedy and public education deserves examination.

1. PUBLIC EDUCATION: THE CONVENTIONAL THEORY

First impressions often crystallize into lasting stereotypes. It is instructive to recall that Kennedy had been in office for only a few weeks before the proposition about his delinquencies as a public educator was becoming a cliché in the newspapers. I discover a memorandum of mine to the President as early as March 16, 1961:

> There is increasing concern among our friends in the press about the alleged failure of the Administration to do as effective a job of public information and instruction as it should and must. Lippmann had a column about this last week. Joe Alsop has been haranguing me about this over the telephone and plans to do some columns about it soon. Lester Markel is going to do a long piece about it in the *Times Magazine*.

Markel had brought his complaint directly to the President, who called me one afternoon to ask how many fireside chats Roosevelt had given. "Lester has been in here saying that I ought to go to the people more often," the President said. "He seems to think that Roosevelt gave a fireside chat once a week."

Markel's remark suggested part of the problem. Memory had left an impression of F.D.R. as incessantly on the air and of Theodore Roosevelt and Wilson constantly using the White House, in T.R.'s phrase, as a "bully pulpit." Compared to these glowing recollections, Kennedy's efforts seemed meager and perfunctory. In fact, memory considerably improved the record of the past. By the most liberal possible interpretation, Roosevelt had given only thirty fireside chats in his twelve years as President; before the war, he averaged no more than two a year.[1] In three years, Kennedy made nine television reports to the nation from the White House, therefore averaging 50 per cent higher than F.D.R.'s peacetime rate; and he gave far more public speeches each year than the Roosevelts or Wilson had given. He also held frequent private meetings at the White House with editors, businessmen, labor leaders, organization

[1] The breakdown is as follows: 1933, 4; 1934, 2; 1935, 1; 1936, 1; 1937, 3; 1938, 2; 1939, 1; 1940, 2; 1941, 3; 1942, 4; 1943, 4; 1944, 3; 1945, 0.

representatives and other panjandrums of the opinion mafia. And he used television and the press with skill and resource.

Like all modern Presidents, Kennedy found the newspapers a major educational instrument. Only 16 per cent had backed him in 1960; but the working press had been strongly for him. Kennedy liked newspapermen; they liked him; and he recognized that they provided him a potent means of appealing to readers over the heads of publishers. In Pierre Salinger he had an engaging and imaginative press secretary. While Salinger sometimes lacked the total knowledge of high policy which his very able predecessor under Eisenhower, James Hagerty, had enjoyed, and while newspapermen claimed he lacked Hagerty's proficiency in making their technical arrangements, he admirably conveyed Kennedy's own insouciant spirit to the White House press room, bore patiently with Kennedy's occasional outbursts against the press and prescribed an open-door policy for newspapermen in the White House and throughout the government.

The press conferences were the central forum of presidential contact. Kennedy averaged twenty-one a year, far fewer than Roosevelt and somewhat fewer than Eisenhower. Though at times oddly resistant when the time came for another press conference, he was the most skilled presidential practitioner in this medium since Roosevelt. Moreover, while Roosevelt's press conferences were intimate off-the-record sessions around the presidential desk in the oval office, Kennedy's were mass public affairs, often on live television; he achieved his success under far more exacting conditions.

Success was the product of study as well as of art. Salinger organized a meticulous briefing process, drawing in predicted questions and recommended responses from information officers across the government. The President would then convene a press conference breakfast, ordinarily attended by Salinger, Sorensen, Bundy, Heller and Robert Manning, the State Department's Assistant Secretary for Public Affairs. Here the President would try out his answers, often tossing off replies which convulsed the breakfast table but which, alas, could not be diplomatically made on the occasion. Later in the day he would go over to the auditorium of the State Department, and the fun would begin: the forest of hands waving from the floor; the questioner recognized by a brisk jab of the presidential forefinger; then the answer—statistics rolling off the presidential tongue, or a sudden glint in the eye signaling the imminence of a throwaway joke, or, very occasionally, an abrupt frostiness of countenance; then the next questioner recognized almost before the answer to the first was completed—it was a superb show, always gay, often exciting, relished by the reporters and by the television audience.

One felt at times that the President missed chances to make points to the nation for fear of boring the men and women in the room by telling them things he supposed they already knew. F.D.R. had never hesitated to cast elementary statement or homely metaphor—lend-lease and the neighbor's firehose—before the sophisticates of the Washington press corps, knowing that the key phrases would filter through to the people who needed them. In Kennedy's case, the uninitiated, instead of learning something about a public issue, often only witnessed abstract and cryptic exchanges between reporter and President. Nonetheless, the conferences offered a showcase for a number of his most characteristic qualities—the intellectual speed and vivacity, the remarkable mastery of the data of government, the terse, self-mocking wit, the exhilarating personal command. Afterward he liked to relax, watch himself in action on the evening news and chat about the curious habits of the press. Once I asked him why he kept calling on the Texas newspaperwoman who had so offended him by asking about security risks in the State Department. He replied, "I always say to myself I won't call on her. But she gets up every time and waves her hand so frantically that toward the end I look down and she's the only one I seem to see."

His relations with the press, like those of all Presidents, had its ups and downs. Calvin Coolidge is the only President on record who did not seem to care what was written about him. When someone asked him about a savage attack by Frank Kent in the *American Mercury*, he replied philosophically, "You mean that magazine with the green cover? It was against me, so I didn't read it." No other President was this philosophical; and Kennedy was certainly not. He read more newspapers than anyone except perhaps Roosevelt,[2] and very often with appreciation; but like Presidents Hoover, Roosevelt, Truman and Eisenhower—indeed, like most politicians—he retained an evi-

---

[2] And expected everyone else to do likewise. No experience was more frequent for members of his staff than to be called by the President early in the morning for discussion of an item in the papers; in my case the calls regularly came before I had had a chance to read the papers. Averell Harriman once told a congressional committee, "A man cannot serve President Kennedy unless he reads the newspaper carefully. He won't last very long if he doesn't, in this administration."

dently inexhaustible capacity to become vastly, if briefly, annoyed by hostile articles or by stories based on leaks. When this happened there would be complaints to the staff, calls to reporters, searches for the sources of stories and even the cancellation for a time of the *New York Herald Tribune*. (This uncharacteristic act resulted from his irritation over the paper's insistence in playing the congressional investigation of Billie Sol Estes on its front page while, he believed, studiously ignoring a concurrent investigation into stockpiling scandals in the Eisenhower administration.) Nor were relations improved when the information officer of the Defense Department talked imprudently about news as "part of the arsenal of weaponry" and affirmed "the inherent right of the government to lie . . . to save itself when faced with nuclear disaster."

Washington reporters, with their acute sense of contemporaneity, always believe that each new administration is plotting an assault on the freedom of the press with a determination and malignity never before seen in the republic; the iniquities of past Presidents fade quickly in retrospect. So for a time in 1962 they proclaimed a deep sense of grievance over the 'hypersensitivity' of the President and the administration. For its part the administration used to wonder about the hypersensitivity of reporters, who seemed to feel that, if a government official dared disagree with a story, it was an attempt to 'manage' the news. When *Look* came out with a piece detailing the indignities which newspapermen were suffering under the reign of terror, Kennedy laughed and remarked, "This is the best example of paranoia I have seen from those fellows yet."

This guerrilla warfare between press and government was, of course, inherent in the situation; it was also a great bulwark of national freedom. Gilbert Harrison, the editor of the *New Republic*, summed the problem up accurately:

> From the past 10 years in Washington, I have decided that irrespective of party or person, race, creed or color, every public official, elected or not, has the same attitude toward journalists, and it is this: "If you knew what we knew, you would not say what you do." Likewise, the attitude of the journalists is constant, and it is this: "If you knew what we knew, you would not do as you do," which is sometimes revised to read: "If you would *tell* us what you are doing and what you *mean* to do, perhaps we would not say what we say."

> Each attitude is proper to the vocation of the one who holds it. Each is unyielding. If a President has never been known to telephone a critical journalist and tell him how wrong he, the President, has been, no journalist I know confesses *his* mistakes.

This was substantially the President's view. When asked what he thought of the press in the spring of 1962, he said, "Well, I am reading it more and enjoying it less—[*laughter*]—and so on, but I have not complained, nor do I plan to make any general complaints. I read and talk to myself about it, but I don't plan to issue any general statement on the press. I think that they are doing their task, as a critical branch, the fourth estate. And I am attempting to do mine. And we are going to live together for a period, and then go our separate ways." [*Laughter*] The reporters understood this; and, despite the animated exchanges of 1962 and occasional moments of mutual exasperation thereafter, the press corps regarded Kennedy with marked fondness and admiration.

2. PROBLEMS OF THE CONVENTIONAL THEORY

Kennedy thus used the conventional instruments of public education with freedom and skill. But he felt that press conferences and public addresses could not work for him as they had worked for the Roosevelts and Wilson—that hortatory and explicit public education was simply not suited to the mood of the 1960s. For, as a student of history, he understood that public education did not take place in a vacuum. To move a nation, a President had first to have the nation's ear; and there was no quicker way to dissipate presidential influence than to natter away when no one was listening.

Thus a decade of reformers and muckrakers, working in the cities and states, had given the nation's ear to Theodore Roosevelt and Wilson, and a depression touching nearly every family in the country had given the nation's ear to Franklin Roosevelt. The early thirties in particular had been a time when visible and tangible crisis had generated a hunger for national action. With people hanging on every presidential word, public education offered no great problem to a President who had something to say. But no President, not even one of the Roosevelts or Wilson, could create by fiat the kind of public opinion he wanted. Effectiveness in public education required leverage in the nation to begin with.

Kennedy had very little leverage. No muckraking agitation had prepared the way for his Presidency; no national economic collapse was making his constituents clamor for action. His was an invisible and intangible crisis, in some ways more profound than the one which confronted Franklin Roosevelt but bearing infinitely less heavily on the daily lives of Americans. The economy was moving forward, 95 per cent of the labor force had jobs, American troops were not fighting in foreign lands, the country was bathed in physical contentment; and, except for racial minorities, spiritual disquietude floated about without commitment to issues. This acquiescent nation had elected him President by the slimmest of margins; no one could possibly claim his victory as a mandate for radical change. "President Kennedy today," as Richard Rovere perceptively stated his problem, "is attempting to meet a challenge whose existence he and his associates are almost alone in perceiving." The President liked to recall Owen Glendower's boast in *Henry IV, Part I*—"I can call spirits from the vasty deep"—and Hotspur's reply:

Why, so can I, or so can any man;
But will they come when you do call for them?

The possibility that they might not come had even troubled Presidents like the Roosevelts and Wilson. Thus by the spring of 1935 a feeling had arisen that F.D.R. was falling down on the job of public education. My father was one of those urging him then to carry his case to the people as he had done in 1933. Roosevelt replied, "My difficulty is a strange and weird sense known as 'public psychology.' " To others he explained, "People tire of seeing the same name day after day in the important headlines of the papers, and the same voice night after night over the radio. . . . Individual psychology cannot, because of human weakness, be attuned for long periods of time to constant repetition of the highest note in the scale." One had to assume that Presidents had a better sense of "public psychology" than most of their critics; that was one reason why they were Presidents and their critics were critics. Moreover, once in the White House, they were in the exact center of pressure and therefore more likely to have an accurate sense of the balance of conflicting forces. If they wanted to act, as Kennedy clearly did, it was idle to suppose that only a misreading of the political situation or mere indolence was holding them back. The presidential secret was timing. The clamor for action was part of the equation, and activist Presidents were wrong to resent such pressure (though of course they all, including Kennedy, occasionally did, because it was so often voiced by friends from whom they expected sympathy rather than complaint). And sometimes when they succumbed to the pleadings the results were hardly those one might have predicted. Throughout 1961 the *New York Times* demanded that Kennedy carry his program to the people. Then in May 1962 at a great outdoor rally the President called for the enactment of the Medicare bill, which the *Times* itself favored editorially. The speech went to thirty-two other rallies and to millions of homes throughout the country. It seemed a splendid exercise in public education and in mobilizing support for the administration program—exactly the sort of thing the *Times* had been advocating. But the *Times* immediately responded by condemning Kennedy for employing "hippodrome tactics."

Timing remained the key. In the absence of visible crisis Presidents had to wait for some event to pierce the apathy and command the nation's ear; experience was a more potent teacher than exhortation. At moments one felt that it was nearly impossible to change people or policies in advance of disaster, because only disaster could sufficiently intimidate and overcome those with vested interests in existing people and policies. So we read every day in the newspapers about the decay of the Diem regime in Vietnam. But, so long as the Secretaries of State and Defense endorsed the policy of unconditional support of Diem, it was hard for the President to act until some dreadful blow-up made the failure of the policy manifest—and by that time it might be too late. So too in Negro rights: if the President committed his prestige to congressional action before the nation was ready to listen to his arguments, he might squander the hope of later influence. In a sense, things had to get worse before there was a possibility of putting them better. Thus Estes Kefauver's bill for the control of the marketing of drugs lingered in committee to immense public indifference until the thalidomide scandal provoked national anger and congressional action. Francis Keppel, the Commissioner of Education, used to express the hope that Congress would pass federal aid to education before some catastrophe—150 schoolchildren, for example, burned to death in a firetrap—came along to stir overdue national concern. In the fall of 1961 President Eisenhower went on television to deliver a political blast against the administration. A few days later over dinner at the White House Kennedy noted that the Eisenhower telecast had received a rating of only 7 as against 20 each for the programs—cowboys and crime—on competing channels. "People forget this," he said, "when they expect me to go on the air all the time educating the nation. The nation will listen only if it is a moment of great urgency. They will listen after a Vienna. But they don't listen to things which bore them. That is the great trouble."

A further trouble was that a good deal of the public

education doctrine was linked to the idea of bringing pressure on Capitol Hill by appealing 'over the heads' of Congress to the people. Critics recalled Wilson's remark that the President had "no means of compelling Congress except through public opinion." In the broad sense this was indisputable. Kennedy himself used to point out that every member of the House "subjected himself, every two years, to the possibility that his career will . . . come to an end. He doesn't live a charmed life. You have to remember that the hot breath is on him also, and it is on the Senate, and it is on the President, and it is on everyone who deals with great matters."

But the notion that this was the way activist Presidents had managed Congress also sprang from garbled memories of Wilson and the Roosevelts. These Presidents passed their programs much more by party leadership within Congress than by popular pressure against it. Very few of F.D.R.'s early fireside chats, for example, were appeals for the enactment of pending legislation; and, when the coalition of southern Democrats and Republicans was joined together, no amount of his incomparable radio persuasion could thrust it asunder. In any case, the hot breath was not particularly relevant to the arithmetic of Kennedy's Congress. No quantity of fireside chats was likely to change the vote of Representative Howard Smith, of Senator Harry Byrd, or, indeed, of most of the other strategically placed opponents of Kennedy's program. "There's nothing that can be done about a man from a safe district," Kennedy used to say. "He'll vote the way he wants to." Such men did not need the President, the Democratic party or organized labor to keep their seats. For the 10 per cent of swing votes in Congress, quieter forms of suasion seemed more likely to produce the desired results.

Public education in the explicit manner of the Roosevelts and Wilson was thus not, in Kennedy's judgment, particularly well adapted either to the times or to his special congressional dilemma—or to himself. This last is a subtler matter; for a period of visible domestic crisis like 1933 would doubtless have called forth different aspects of his own personality. But a politician lives in continuous interaction with his age; and the chemistry of the sixties confirmed Kennedy in temperamental traits already well marked—an aversion to what he called "highly charged" political positions, a scorn for histrionics, a recoil from corniness, a determination not to become a national scold or bore. These traits were rooted partly, as Richard Neustadt has suggested, in a rationalist's "mistrust of mass emotion as a tool in politics." Kennedy feared overexciting people about public issues, as he came to believe that his call for an air-raid shelter program had done during the Berlin crisis of 1961; and he was embarrassed on the rare occasions when he succumbed to public emotion himself, as he did when the Cuban Brigade, freed from Castro's prisons, presented its flag to him at Miami in December 1962. They were rooted too in that qualified historical fatalism which led him to doubt whether words, however winged, would by themselves change the world.

One other factor entered in, and this I find hardest of all to assess. Contrary to a widespread impression, Kennedy did not perceive himself as a partisan President, nor did he wish the country so to perceive him. He perceived himself rather as a man who, unlike the Trumans and Robert Tafts of American politics, generally saw reason on both sides of complex issues. But he knew that the impression of a highly partisan young Democratic politician ruthlessly on the make had been one reason for the narrowness of his victory in 1960. The strategy of reassurance initiated so promptly after the election represented both Kennedy's natural impulse and the only sensible response to the character of the vote. By taking a non-partisan stance, he aimed at erasing the picture of the power-hungry young careerist and winning the national confidence he felt he lacked. As President, he replenished that strategy whenever he feared that any actions might revive the picture or weaken the confidence: thus his propitiatory course in the aftermath of the steel controversy.

At the time it seemed that Kennedy suffered from the illusion so common to new Presidents (even Roosevelt had it till 1935) that he, unlike any of his predecessors, could really be President of all the people and achieve his purposes without pain or trauma. Some of us, however, thought national argument the best way to break national apathy and communicate the reality of problems. We believed that the educational value of fights in drawing the line between the administration and its opponents would guarantee that, even if we did not have a law, we would have an issue. So we thought him mistaken in 1962 in making the entirely respectable, safe and overrated trade expansion bill his top legislative priority instead of staging a knockdown-drag-out fight over federal aid to education or Medicare. To the President I would cite the Roosevelts, Wilson, Jackson and so on in arguing the inevitability and superiority of the politics of combat as against the politics of consensus. But, while he did not dispute the historical points, he plainly saw no reason for rushing prematurely into battle.

I think now he had deeper reasons for this than I understood at the time—that his cast of mind had a profounder source than a pragmatist's preference for a law over an issue, than a rationalist's distaste for give-'em-hell partisanship, or even than a statesman's need to hoard national confidence against the possibility that foreign crisis might require swift and unpopular presidential decisions. I believe today that its basic source may have been an acute and anguished sense of the fragility of the membranes of civilization, stretched so thin over a nation so disparate in its composition, so tense in its interior relationships, so cunningly enmeshed in underground fears and antagonisms, so entrapped by history in the ethos of violence. In the summer of 1963 Kennedy spoke to Robert Stein of *Redbook* about the destructive instincts "that have been implanted in us growing out of the dust" and added, "We have done reasonably well—but only reasonably well" in controlling them. His hope was that it might be possible to keep the country and the world moving fast enough to prevent unreason from rending the skin of civility. But he had peered into the abyss and knew the potentiality of chaos. On another day in the summer of 1963 he concluded an informal talk with representatives of national organizations by suddenly reading them Blanche of Castile's speech from *King John:*

> *The sun's o'ercast with blood; fair day, adieu!*
> *Which is the side that I must go withal?*
> *I am with both: each army hath a hand;*
> *And in their rage, I having hold of both,*
> *They whirl asunder and dismember me.*

3. THE KENNEDY APPROACH

The fact that neither his time nor his temperament encouraged Kennedy to be a public educator in the explicit manner of the Roosevelts and Wilson did not mean that he renounced the presidential responsibility of public education. On the contrary: he turned out to have an ability unmatched in his age to call spirits from the vasty deep; and they generally came when he called for them. But he did so in his own fashion—a fashion which so subtly permeated national attitudes and so quietly penetrated individual lives that no one realized how much he had changed things until his time was over. The essence of his attack was not admonition and remonstrance, in the earlier style, but example.

It was this which led to the familiar charge that Kennedy and his administration were preoccupied, to use the odious word, with 'image.' Noting the discrepancy between Kennedy's personal popularity and the support for his policies, observers concluded that he was reluctant to spend his popularity for result. Critics compared him to a matinee idol. One Republican Congressman dismissed the enthusiasm in which he was held: "It's like that of a movie actor—it's not related to legislation." Yet the Kennedy image was not, of course, anything like that of a movie actor. It was packed with a whole set of intellectual implications which were preparing the nation for legislative change as surely as Theodore Roosevelt's muckrakers or Franklin Roosevelt's depression. In an age of pervasive contentment, his personality was the most potent instrument he had to awaken a national desire for something new and better. The extraordinary effect with which he used it became apparent only in later years: thus Howard K. Smith in retrospect pronounced Kennedy not a failure in public education but a "brilliant communicator."

Kennedy communicated, first of all, a deeply critical attitude toward the ideas and institutions which American society had come in the fifties to regard with such enormous self-satisfaction. Social criticism had fallen into disrepute during the Eisenhower decade. In some influential quarters it was almost deemed treasonous to raise doubts about the perfection of the American way of life. But the message of Kennedy's 1960 campaign had been that the American way of life was in terrible shape, that our economy was slowing down, that we were neglectful of our young and our old, callous toward our poor and our minorities, that our cities and schools and landscapes were a mess, that our motives were materialistic and ignoble and that we were fast becoming a country without purpose and without ideals. As President, he proceeded to document the indictment. In so doing, he released the nation's critical energy. Self-criticism became not only legitimate but patriotic. The McCarthy anxieities were forgotten. Critics began to question the verities again, and defenders of the status quo no longer had the heart, or nerve, to call them communists. The President, in effect, created his own muckraking movement.

The literature of protest in the Kennedy years poked

freely into sacrosanct or shadowed corners of American society—the persistence of poverty (Michael Harrington, Herman P. Miller, Ben Bagdikian, Edgar May, Harry Caudill and many others), racial inequities (a whole bookshelf), taxation (Philip Stern, Stewart Alsop), the spoiling of land, air, water and environment (Stewart Udall, Peter Blake, Howard Lewis, Lewis Herber, Donald Carr), the drug industry (Richard Harris, Morton Mintz); it even challenged such national ikons as television (Newton Minow, Merle Miller and others), the pesticide (Rachel Carson), the cigarette (Maurine Neuberger) and the funeral parlor (Jessica Mitford). There had not been such an outpouring of self-examination since the New Deal. While Presidents cannot claim entire credit for the social criticism of their day, and while in certain fields, notably Negro rights, schools and cities, the process had begun before Kennedy, nonetheless the presidential stance has a pervasive effect on the national mood. "There wasn't a point," said a writer in the *Village Voice*, "where he didn't upset some preconception of every group in the country." Like the Roosevelts, Kennedy, by his own personal attitude, helped the nation see itself with new eyes.

Facts thus collected were one weapon in the dissolution of the established pretensions. Wit was another. The fifties had constituted probably the most humorless period in American history. A President and Vice-President who might have been invented by H. L. Mencken were viewed with invincible solemnity. Adlai Stevenson, a truly serious man who expressed part of his seriousness in humor, was regarded with suspicion. The zone of the acceptably comic had never been so contracted. In 1952 Al Capp, explaining why he was marrying Li'l Abner to Daisy Mae, said that he had decided to go in for fairy tales because the climate for humor had changed; the "fifth freedom" was gradually disappearing. "Without it," he wrote, "the other four freedoms aren't much fun, because the fifth is the freedom to laugh at each other. . . . Now there are things about America we can't kid." This gloom permeated the decade. As Corey Ford asked in 1958, "What's funny any more? Subjects we could treat lightly once are deadly serious today. Slowly but surely the wellsprings of humor are drying up. Derision is taken for disloyalty."

Part of the narrowing of the zone of laughability was no great loss. Laughing at the powerless—at the spinster or the cripple, at the Irishman or Jew or Negro—had never been wildly funny. But laughing at the powerful was one of the great points of laughing at all; and in the fifties this began to grow risky. Comedians watched one social type or group after another eliminate itself as comic material until in the end the one safe subject was the comedian himself: thus Bob Hope or Jack Benny. Only cartoonists— Jules Feiffer and Herblock especially—kept the satiric faith.

For Kennedy wit was the natural response to platitude and pomposity. He once told me that the political writers he enjoyed most were Murray Kempton and Bernard Levin, who were by way of being the Menckens of their day. His whole personal bearing communicated a delight in satire; and in his wake came an exuberant revival of American irreverence. This had had its underground beginnings at the end of the fifties in small San Francisco and Greenwich Village nightclubs—Mort Sahl and the hungry i, Mike Nichols and Elaine May—but now it flourished, bringing Art Buchwald back to the United States ("There are only four of us writing humor from Washington these days," Buchwald said. "Drew Pearson, David Lawrence, Arthur Krock and myself"), producing skits on the Kennedys themselves—Elliott Reid; Vaughn Meader and "The First Family" —and ending in the murky and ambiguous depths of black comedy. Like muckraking, satire forced the nation to take a fresh look at itself and helped prepare the ground for change.

A third component of the Kennedy image was respect for ideas. The fifties had been a decade of anti-intellectualism. For his belief in the trained intelligence Stevenson was ridiculed as an egghead. Neither ideas nor the men who had them were welcome in the places where respectable men fingered the levers of authority. But Kennedy had long hoped, as he said in January 1960, to "reopen the channels of communication between the world of thought and the seat of power." He felt this, I think, both technically essential in a world imposing novel and complex demands on policy and morally essential to assure civilized government. As President, he carried Roosevelt's brain-trust conception further than it had ever been carried before. The intellectual was no longer merely consultant or adviser but responsible official, even in areas so remote from traditional academic preoccupations as the Department of Defense. Some imports from the campuses worked out better than others; but the reversal of national form in a decade could hardly have been more spectacular. No President had ever made such systematic use of the nation's intellectual resources; and under his tutelage both academics and 'practical' men discovered that they had something to learn from the other.

The combination of self-criticism, wit and ideas made up, I think, a large part of the spirit of the New Frontier. It informed the processes of government, sparkled through evenings at the White House and around town, refreshed and enlivened the world of journalism, stimulated the universities, kindled the hopes of the young and presented the nation with a new conception of itself and its potentialities. From the viewpoint of the fifties, it was almost a subversive conception, irreverent and skeptical, lacking in due respect for established propositions and potentates. Perhaps only a President who was at the same time seen as a war hero, a Roman Catholic, a tough politician and a film star could have infected the nation with so gay and disturbing a spirit. But Kennedy did exactly this with ease and grace; and, in doing so, he taught the country the possibilities of a new national style. If he did not get the results he would have liked at once, he was changing the climate in directions which would, in time, make those results inevitable.

4. THE KENNEDYS AND THE ARTS

He did this only partly by doubting the perfection of existing institutions. His more powerful weapon was his vision of the truly civilized community America might become. This vision animated his efforts to improve the quality of American life. It reached its climax in the unprecedented concern which the President and his wife gave to the place of the intellect and the arts in the national society.

"The artist," William Faulkner had said at the American Academy of Arts and Letters in 1957, "has no more actual place in the American culture of today than he has in the American economy of today, no place at all in the warp and woof, the thews and sinews, the mosaic of the American dream." Perhaps it was not quite that bad. The postwar decades saw the beginning of the so-called cultural explosion which by 1960 was sprinkling the American scene with a fallout of amiable statistics—5000 theater groups, 20,000 dramatic workshops, 700 opera groups, 200 dance companies, 1200 symphony orchestras, $100 million spent annually on classical records, $1.5 billion annually on books, more people attending concerts each year than baseball games, more piano players than licensed fishermen, a quadrupling of museums in a generation. The popular interest in the arts soon exerted its pressure on government.

In 1952 President Truman received a report from the Fine
Arts Commission on "Art and Government"; in 1955 President Eisenhower proposed a federal advisory council on the
arts and in 1958 secured a congressional charter for a National Cultural Center in Washington.

On examination, however, the cultural explosion was less
substantial than it seemed. The statistics confused quantity
with quality. Most of the new activity was amateur; of
the symphony orchestras, only about twenty-five could pay
their members a living wage; of the opera and dance
groups very few could put on a professional performance;
of the books sold, too many were Mickey Spillane, Ian
Fleming and *Fanny Hill*. In the words of the Rockefeller
Panel Report on the Performing Arts, "For the vast majority
of Americans, even those dwelling in cities, a live professional performance of a play, an opera, a symphony, or a
ballet is an altogether uncommon experience." The problem, in the midst of the widening public interest in the
arts, lay partly in the preservation and refinement of standards and partly in the organization of financial support
for professional artistic institutions.

The Kennedys came to the White House with a lively
desire to help meet this problem. They were wholly unaffected in their attitude toward the arts; it was simply, as
their close friend William Walton once put it, that they
were "susceptible to the comfort of the arts. They couldn't
live without them—it is woven into the pattern of their
lives." The President's curiosity and natural taste had been
stimulated by Jacqueline's informed and exquisite responses:
art had become a normal dimension of existence. The art
to which Kennedy responded most deeply and spontane-
ously, I think, was literature; but he had a growing interest
in architecture, and he had acquired some knowledge of
painting—he liked the impressionists, though he was baffled
by non-objective art—and sculpture. He was fond of, for
example, a Greek bronze figurine of "Herakles and the Skin
of a Lion" of about 500 B.C. which he bought in Rome in
1963; at the same time he brought back a Roman imperial
head of a young satyr for Jacqueline. He loved picking out
presents for her: her birthdays would be a profusion of
boxes from Klejman and drawings from Wildenstein. Serious music, it must be said, left him cold. But even here he
believed it important for the President of the United States
to lend his prestige to distinction of creation and performance.

Indeed, the character of his personal interest was less

important than his conviction that the health of the arts was vitally related to the health of society. He saw the arts not as a distraction in the life of a nation but as something close to the heart of a nation's purpose. Excellence was a public necessity, ugliness a national disgrace. The arts therefore were, in his view, part of the presidential responsibility, and he looked for opportunities to demonstrate his concern. Thus when Stewart Udall early in December 1960 suggested that Robert Frost be invited to read a poem at the inauguration, Kennedy instantly responded. (Frost replied: IF YOU CAN BEAR AT YOUR AGE THE HONOR OF BEING MADE PRESIDENT OF THE UNITED STATES, I OUGHT TO BE ABLE AT MY AGE TO BEAR THE HONOR OF TAKING SOME PART IN YOUR INAUGURATION. I MAY NOT BE EQUAL TO IT BUT I CAN ACCEPT IT FOR MY CAUSE—THE ARTS, POETRY, NOW FOR THE FIRST TIME TAKEN INTO THE AFFAIRS OF STATESMEN.) And when Kay Halle of Cleveland and Washington proposed that leading artists and writers be asked to attend the inaugural—an idea which startled and annoyed the politicians hoarding tickets on the Inauguration Committee—Kennedy told her to go ahead. The combination of Frost on the rostrum and W. H. Auden, Alexis Léger, Paul Tillich, Jacques Maritain, Robert Lowell, John Hersey, John Steinbeck, Allen Tate and fifty other writers, composers and painters in the audience did seem to prefigure a new Augustan age of poetry and power. Auden called the invitation "as thrilling as it was surprising." "What a joy," said Steinbeck, "that literacy is no longer prima facie evidence of treason." "Thank you," said Lincoln Kirstein, "for restoring to the United States the pleasures and the powers of the mind." And among those who could not be present—

E. B. White:

> One of the excitements of American citizenship is a man's feeling of identity with his elected President. I never had this feeling hit me so hard as January 20, 1961, when, watching on television from a Maine farmhouse, I saw first the lectern take fire, then so much else—thanks to your brave words. I promise that wherever I can manage I'll blow my little draft of air on the beloved flame.

Archibald MacLeish:

> No country which did not respect its arts has ever been great and ours has ignored them too long. And I should like to add a word of my own about that ceremony. I heard the inaugural address on an uncertain short-wave set in a little cove on the west coast of Santa Lucia in the Windwards. It left me proud and hopeful to be an American—something I have not felt for almost twenty years. I owe you and send you my deepest gratitude.

And, from the Mayo Clinic at Rochester, Minnesota, Ernest Hemingway:

> Watching the inauguration from Rochester there was happiness and the hope and the pride and how beautiful we thought Mrs. Kennedy was. Watching on the screen I was sure our President would stand any of the heat to come as he had taken the cold of that day. Each day since I have renewed my faith and tried to understand the practical difficulties of governing he must face as they arrive and admire the true courage he brings to them. It is a good thing to have a brave man as our President in times as tough as these are for our country and the world.

The inauguration was the first step in the unfolding policy of presidential recognition of the arts. Then came a series of White House dinners. In November 1961, Pablo Casals, who had long declined to play his cello in public as a badge of mourning for Spanish democracy, agreed to perform at the White House on an evening honoring Muñoz Marín. Kennedy said with emphasis in introducing Casals: "We believe that an artist, in order to be true to himself and his work, must be a free man." They had talked together for an hour about world peace before the dinner. "I have never known anyone who listened more carefully than he did," Casals said later. "And I was happy I went. When I played at the White House, I was very happy in my heart." Other dinners followed—for Stravinsky; for the western hemisphere Nobel prize-winners (whom Kennedy called "the most extraordinary collection of talent, of human knowledge, that has ever been gathered together at the White House, with the possible exception of when Thomas Jefferson dined alone"); for André Malraux (when Kennedy began his toast by saying, "This will be the first speech about relations between France and the United States that does not include a tribute to General Lafayette") —all memorable affairs. He encouraged the cabinet to arrange a series of cultural evenings—readings, recitals, dramatic performances. Never before had any President sought to identify the White House with the whole range of the nation's intellectual life. Thornton Wilder, who inaugurated the cabinet series, remarked that the administration had created "a whole new world of surprised self-respect" in the arts.

To complete the process of national recognition, Kennedy rehabilitated the Presidential Medal of Freedom in an effort to honor those "whose talent enlarges the public vision of the dignity with which life can be graced and the fullness with which it can be lived." Though an interdepartmental committee was charged with making the recom-

mendations, Kennedy took a keen personal interest in the
candidates and citations. Thus he himself added Edmund
Wilson's name to the list in 1963. (Knowing Wilson's dislike
of honors on principle, I called him to see whether he
would accept the Medal. He said that he would be greatly
pleased to do so, but that the President should know he
was writing a pamphlet attacking the income tax and the
defense budget. It was not, he said, directed so much
against the Kennedy administration, parts of which he much
admired, as against governments in general; still the President ought to know about it, and he would understand if
we decided not to go ahead with the presentation. When I
reported this to Kennedy, he smiled and said that he didn't
think it would make any difference.)

5. THE ARTS AND GOVERNMENT

Kennedy well understood that honoring the masters would
not solve the problems of the young artist or the elevation
of artistic standards or the economic sustenance of the arts.
Nor did he suppose that these were problems to which
government had the solution. But within its own domain
the national government did all sorts of things, from designing stamps to erecting public buildings, which bore upon
the arts; and these things, the President felt, ought to
serve as an example to the rest of the country. In the busy
summer of 1961 he asked Pierre Salinger and me to consider how the White House might take hold of this problem. We recommended that he commission a special consultant to survey the areas where public policy had impact
on cultural life and to define the elements of a national cultural program.

I had in mind for the assignment August Heckscher of
the Twentieth Century Fund. Heckscher combined artistic
sensibility with an astute practical sense of the way government operated. He had written a thoughtful paper on "The
Quality of American Culture" for President Eisenhower's
Commission on National Goals and was no doubt responsible for the sentence in the Commission's report which
so well expressed part of President Kennedy's concern: "In
the eyes of posterity, the success of the United States as a
civilized society will be largely judged by the creative activities of its citizens in art, architecture, literature, music,
and the sciences." After the success of the Casals dinner,
the President thought it was time to go ahead. Early in
December 1961 he invited Heckscher to conduct an inquiry

"without fanfare" into the resources, possibilities and limitations of national policy in relation to the arts. "Obviously government can at best play only a marginal role in our cultural affairs," Kennedy told Heckscher. "But I would like to think that it is making its full contribution in this role."

Kennedy's caution expressed, as Heckscher later noted, his fear of the vague generalization and the empty gesture. "To assume that the varied, unpredictable, and sometimes oddly expressed cultural life of our country could in any way be dependent on government, or be derived from government, was impossible for him. He was skeptical of any idea that government could do more than sometimes stir things up, and sometimes give recognition and support to what had strangely or wonderfully occurred." Heckscher, Salinger and I all shared this feeling. The notion, proposed by some, of a Department of Fine Arts filled us with apprehension; we agreed with John Sloan who was said to have welcomed the idea because "then we'd know where the enemy is." But Heckscher had a profound conviction, sensitively explained in his book of 1962, *The Public Happiness,* that public support of the creative arts could become an antidote to the boredom and alienation of modern industrial society and the means by which the individual in a world of flickering images could recover a sense of objectivity and reality. The goal, he said, was "participation in a common life which is recognized as being enriched, which is known to be illuminated and made coherent, by the forms of art."

Heckscher began work as part-time Special Consultant on the Arts in 1962. "The statement of a philosophy of government and the arts," Kennedy told him, "won't be enough. We have to go beyond that now." As Heckscher carried forward his survey, he suggested as the first test whether government kept its own house in beauty and fitness. Government was, after all, "the great builder, the coiner, the printer, the purchaser of art, the commissioner of works of art, the guardian of great collections, the setter of standards for good or for bad in innumerable fields." Next he reviewed such questions as the impact of tax and tariff laws on artists and artistic institutions; the establishment of the Advisory Council on the Arts, which he lifted out of the Department of Health, Education and Welfare, to which it had been consigned in the original Eisenhower proposal; and then, as "the logical crowning step in a national cultural policy," the establishment of a National Arts Foundation. In the spring of 1963 he embodied these and other recommendations in a report on "The Arts and the

National Government." A few days later Kennedy set up the Advisory Council on the Arts by executive order and prepared to make the Special Consultancy of the Arts a full-time and permanent office. Since Heckscher wished to return to the Twentieth Century Fund, it was the President's intention to appoint Richard Goodwin to the post.

Kennedy and Heckscher had strong support throughout the government in this effort, especially from two members of the cabinet, Arthur Goldberg and Stewart Udall. Udall, the good friend of Frost, deeply believed that it was "the artists and the men of ideas who have done, and will do, the most to determine our national purpose, to fix our national character, and to shape the American legacy." Under his leadership the Department of the Interior became an active sponsor of cultural activities and vigilant defender of historic sites and structures. Goldberg was thrust into cultural affairs when Kennedy insisted that he settle a strike which threatened to close down the Metropolitan Opera at the end of 1961. This led the Secretary of Labor into a characteristically trenchant inquiry into the financial crisis of the performing arts. "To free our art forms from destructive financial tests," he concluded, "is to protect them from the tyranny of the majority. . . . If the arts are to flourish, they must be relieved of total dependence upon the market place." Najeeb Halaby, the administrator of the Federal Aviation Agency, set up an expert committee to supervise the design and decoration of airports. In the House of Representatives Frank Thompson and John Lindsay and in the Senate Hubert Humphrey, Claiborne Pell, Joseph Clark and Jacob Javits all fought hard for the cultural effort.

The President and the Attorney General had a particular interest in television. As Senator, Kennedy had told a group of broadcasters that politics and television presented the practitioner with similar problems. "Will the politician's desire for reelection—and the broadcaster's desire for ratings —cause both to flatter every public whim and prejudice— to seek the lowest common denominator of appeal—to put public opinion at all times ahead of the public interest? For myself, I reject that view of politics, and I urge you to reject that view of broadcasting." In order to encourage the industry in this course, Kennedy appointed Newton N. Minow, the old associate of Adlai Stevenson's, as chairman of the Federal Communications Commission; and Minow promptly told the National Association of Broadcasters that, if they would ever watch television from morning to night, "I can assure you that you will observe a vast wasteland."

A day or so later Joseph P. Kennedy told Minow that "this was the best speech since January 20—give 'em hell— hit 'em again." The powers of the FCC chairman were limited; but in the next years Minow not only hit them again and again but obtained laws providing federal aid for educational television and requiring that new television sets receive channels in the ultra-high frequency range. "You keep this up," Kennedy told him on one occasion. "This is one of the really important things." The Attorney General had a special concern for the quality of children's programs. When, to the President's great regret, Minow resigned in 1963, E. William Henry, a protégé of Robert Kennedy's, carried forward his work with comparable humor and force.

The President's commitment to the arts reached its climax in the city of Washington itself. Most Presidents since Jefferson had remained astonishingly indifferent to their immediate surroundings. But Kennedy, with his strong architectural instincts, had a consuming interest in the physical appearance of the capital. He had hardly taken his presidential oath when he confronted a plan conceived in the previous administration to replace the graceful old residences on Lafayette Square in front of the White House with enormous modern office buildings. He made William Walton, whom he subsequently appointed chairman of the Fine Arts Commission, his agent in these matters. The President and Walton wanted to preserve the nineteenth-century character of the Square; at the same time, it was essential to provide office space for the overflowing federal establishment. For a time the problem seemed to defy solution. Both Kennedy and Walton gave up and concluded that the old buildings would have to go. Only Jacqueline held out. "The wreckers haven't started yet," she said, "and until they do it can be saved." Then the President, running by chance into John C. Warnecke, the San Francisco architect, asked his advice, and Warnecke came up with a brilliant solution which protected the historic houses and placed new and harmonizing office buildings behind them. Kennedy maintained a steady interest in the development of the Lafayette Square plan. One day Walton apologized for interrupting him when weightier affairs were on his desk. "That's all right," said Kennedy. "After all, this may be the only monument we'll leave."

He laid down as a guiding principle for Washington that the "nation's capital should embody the finest in its contemporary architectural thought." Bernard Boutin, the head of the General Services Administration and the government's chief builder, faithfully executed this directive; Mies van der Rohe, Marcel Breuer and Gropius's Architects Collaborative were soon designing federal buildings. The President's greatest dream was the rehabilitation of Pennsylvania Avenue, that broad boulevard stretching from the Capitol to the White House, conceived by L'Enfant as the "grand axis" of the city but now, on its northern side, decaying into block after block of dingy buildings and cheap shops. Arthur Goldberg had noticed the decay when he rode in the stately procession down the Avenue on Inauguration Day, and he soon discussed with Kennedy whether anything could be done. In June 1962 the President appointed a Council on Pennsylvania Avenue headed by another San Francisco architect, Nathaniel A. Owings. The result was a splendid plan for the re-creation of the central city.

"You sir," said J. Roy Carroll, Jr., the president of the American Institute of Architects, to Kennedy in the spring of 1963, "are the first President of the United States—except, possibly, the first and third ones—who has had a vision of what architecture and its allied arts can mean to the people of the nation, and of what the careful nuturing of the architecture of the city of Washington can mean to the millions who come here to pay homage to the heart of their country." And, in 1964, speaking where Faulkner had spoken exactly six years before, Lewis Mumford described Kennedy as "the first American President to give art, literature and music a place of dignity and honor in our national life."

XXVIII

THE POLITICS OF MODERNITY

THE KENNEDY MESSAGE—self-criticism, wit, ideas, the vision of a civilized society—opened up a new era in the American political consciousness. The President stood, in John P. Roche's valuable phrase, for the politics of modernity. "Liberalism and conservatism," Kennedy remarked one night, "are categories of the thirties, and they don't apply any more. . . . The trouble with conservatives today is that most of their thinking is so naïve. As for the liberals, their thinking is more sophisticated; but their function ought to be to provide new ideas, and they don't come up with any." His effort was to dissolve the myths which had masked the emerging realities in both domestic and foreign affairs. His hope was to lead the nation beyond the obsessive issues of the past and to call forth the new perceptions required for the contemporary world.

1. THE PRESIDENCY OF THE YOUNG

It was no accident therefore that he made his most penetrating appeal precisely to those who were coming of age in this contemporary world and who were most free of the legacies of historic controversy. Indeed, nothing in the Kennedy years was more spectacular than the transformation of American youth.

In the fifties the young men and women of the nation had seemed to fall into two groups. The vast majority were the 'silent generation,' the 'uncommitted generation,' the 'careful young men,' the 'men in the gray flannel suits'—a generation fearful of politics, incurious about society, mistrustful of ideas, desperate about personal security. A small minority, rejecting this respectable world as absurd, defected from it and became beats and hipsters, 'rebels without a cause.' Pervading both groups was a profound sense of impotence—a feeling that the social order had to be taken as a whole or repudiated as a whole and was beyond the power of the individual to change. David Riesman, hearing undergraduate complaints in the late fifties, wrote, "When I ask such students what they have done about these things, they are surprised at the very thought they could do anything. They think I am joking when I suggest that, if things came to the worst, they could picket! . . . It seems to me that students don't want to believe that their activities might make a difference, because, in a way, they profit from their lack of commitment to what they are doing." This was November 1960.

Probably it was all beginning to change; but the coming of Kennedy certainly made it change very much faster. He was the first President since Franklin Roosevelt who had anything to say to men and women under the age of twenty-five, perhaps the only President with whom youth could thoroughly identify itself—and this at a time when there were more young people both in the population and the colleges than ever before. His very role and personality, moreover—his individuality in a homogenized society, his wholeness in a specialized society, his freedom in a mechanized society—undermined the conviction of impotence.

If the President of the United States seemed almost a contemporary, then political action—even picketing—no longer appeared so ludicrous or futile.

The New Frontier gospel of critcism and hope stirred the finest instincts of the young; it restored a sense of innovation and adventure to the republic. The silent campuses suddenly exploded with political and intellectual activity. Young people running for office explained that Kennedy had made politics respectable; what perhaps they more often meant was that he had made it rational. The Civil Service Commission reported a great increase in college graduates wanting to work for the government. The Peace Corps was only the most dramatic form of the new idealism. Some of the energy Kennedy released moved rather quickly beyond him and against him, subjecting his administration to unsparing, often deeply emotional, criticism; but it was nonetheless he who had struck off the manacles.

The very qualities which made Kennedy exciting to the youth made him disturbing to many of his contemporaries and elders. For his message was a threat to established patterns of emotion and ideology. When he would say, as he did to William Manchester, "We simply must reconcile ourselves to the fact that a total solution is impossible in a nuclear age," he was affronting all those on both the left and the right who had faith in total solutions. The politics of modernity was intolerable for the true believers. This accounts, I believe, for the ambiguity with which the radical left regarded Kennedy and the hatred which the radical right came to concentrate on him.

2. KENNEDY AND THE LEFT: IDEAS

From the start of the republic American progressivism had had two strains, related but distinct. The pragmatic strain accepted, without wholly approving, the given structure of society and aimed to change it by action from within. The utopian strain rejected the given structure of society, root and branch, and aimed to change it by exhortation and example from without. The one sprang from the philosophy of Locke and Hume; its early exemplars were Franklin and Jefferson. The other sprang from the religion of the millenarians; its early exemplars were George Fox and, in a secularized version, Robert Owen. The one regarded history as a continuity, in which mankind progressed from the intolerable to the faintly bearable. The other regarded history as an alternation of catastrophe and salvation, in which a new turn of the road must somehow bring humanity to a new heaven and a new earth. The one was practical and valued results. The other was prophetic and valued revelations. The one believed in piecemeal improvements, the other in total solutions. Both were impatient with established complacencies and pieties. Both recognized that the great constant in history was change. But the problem of power split them. The pragmatists accepted the responsibility of power—and thereby risked corruption. The utopians refused complicity with power—and thereby risked irrelevance.

Both strains were much alive in the Kennedy years. The administration itself expressed the spirit of liberal pragmatism; and other liberal pragmatists in Congress and elsewhere urged only that it do so with greater audacity and force. Hence mild tensions sometimes existed between the administration and its logical allies. Kennedy and much of the White House staff retained a suspicion of the ritualistic liberal as someone more intent on virtuous display than on practical result; moreover, criticism was harder to take from friends than from enemies. As for the liberals on the Hill, they were sometimes hurt and resentful, as their predecessors had been toward Roosevelt a quarter-century earlier, when the President seemed to be compromising too much and sticking too close to the southern Democrats in the leadership. Hubert Humphrey was our most effective liberal in Congress; after one bitter debate he said wearily to me, "It's hard for us down here to keep on defending the things we think the White House believes in when the White House seems to spend its time saying nice things about the other side."

But the pragmatic liberals, if they often wished the administration to move faster, had no doubt that it was *their* administration. Humphrey worked closely with the White House, where he was liked and valued, and Paul Douglas's attitude toward Kennedy reminded one of George Norris's attitude toward Roosevelt—a large and serene faith in the President's basic purpose and therefore an unwillingness to draw drastic conclusions from temporary tactics. As for Kennedy, despite occasional annoyance over the refusal of some liberals to understand the constraints on presidential action, he knew at bottom that over the long run pressure from the left increased his freedom of maneuver. In 1963, when I prepared a message for him to the annual convention of Americans for Democratic Action, describing the ADA as having contributed an indispensable ferment to the American politics, the President took out his pencil and scrawled an insert: "and looking back you can take satisfaction that on the whole time has confirmed the rightness of your judgments."

The liberals who did not like power constituted a different problem. Their mood was that of the political philosopher of old Virginia, John Taylor of Caroline, who wrote James Monroe on the eve of his Presidency, "The moment you are elected, though by my casting vote, carried an hundred miles in a snow storm, my confidence in you would be most confoundedly deminished, and I would instantly join again the republican minority." The nuclear age had given the recoil from power new intensity. Since Hiroshima many liberals and intellectuals had been reluctant to identify themselves with anything done by government.

Such people now viewed the Kennedy administration with deep suspicion. The President in their mind was the Tempter, using the allurements of power, charm, wealth and flattery to seduce their brethren into betraying their vocation and becoming the tools of what C. Wright Mills had called "the power elite." Kennedy's air of interest in ideas and the arts seemed only the latest and most diabolical Establishment ruse to defeat dissent by absorbing it. Those who succumbed to the temptation, the critics argued, would pay a heavy price both in weakening that principled opposition to power which was the duty of an intellectual community and in debasing themselves. Some critics, like Mills, were inordinate in their reaction; his companion in the last months before his death reports Mills as "ashamed to be an American, ashamed to have John F. Kennedy as his President." Others, less rabid, felt, as Sidney Hyman wrote, that it was "a poor exchange to trade in first-class intellectuals for second-class politicians," or, as Alfred Kazin concluded in a piece not without some highly perceptive passages, "Kennedy's shrewd awareness of what intellectuals can do, even his undoubted inner respect for certain writers, scholars and thinkers, is irrelevant to the tragic issues and contributes nothing to their solution. To be an 'intellectual' is the latest style in American success, the mark of our manipulable society."

Kazin had told me one July day at Wellfleet that he had written this article, and I suggested he might meet Kennedy. When I mentioned this to the President, he proposed that I bring the eminent literary critic down for luncheon. I thought it a lively and agreeable occasion, the talk ranging from Cooper and Malraux to Khrushchev and Chiang Kai-

shek. We chatted a bit about the role of the writer in
American society. Kennedy said that in the United States
the trouble was that success was construed in individual terms
and thus was ultimately unsatisfying. On the other hand, in
Castro's Cuba, people had the higher satisfaction of working
together in a group; but, since the writer was in the end a
"single individual," he would be even more thwarted in a
collective society. Frustration, the President concluded, was
evidently the writer's destiny. Finally, in a remark which
Diana Trilling later reported was passed around New York
literary circles, he said, "But what has all of this to do
with the papers waiting for me on my desk?"

Kazin manfully resisted seduction. A few months later
he came to dinner and announced that the New York intellectuals considered Kennedy slick, cool and empty, devoid of vision, an expert and calculating pragmatist. When
I observed that the same people had thought the same things
about Roosevelt, Alfred replied, with admirable consistency,
that he thought they were right then too. (As for Kennedy,
he was very funny about Kazin's essay when it appeared
in *The American Scholar*. "We wined him and dined him,"
he said, "and talked about Hemingway and Dreiser with
him, and I later told Jackie what a good time she missed,
and then he went away and wrote that piece!")

Kazin's application of John Taylor's principle expressed
a wholly legitimate belief that one role for intellectuals
was that of unremitting hostility to power. But was that the
only role? It seemed to me that there was also a strong case
for intellectuals so inclined to take part in government if
only to provide a link between the political and the intellectual communities. The process of mediation might well
give the intellectual community more impact on the political process than if it remained in solid and permanent opposition. It seemed hard to argue, moreover, that serious
intellectuals were inexorably corrupted by public responsibility; this had hardly happened to Keynes or to MacLeish
or to Berle in the thirties, to Murrow or Galbraith or Heller
now. That was not to say that intellectuals made a great
deal of difference to government, or that intellectuals in
government always kept faith with their own ideals. Ted
Sorensen, describing government meetings with mordant accuracy, once wrote, "The liberal may seek to impress his
colleagues with his caution; idealists may try to sound
tough-minded. I have attended more than one meeting
where a military action was opposed by military minds and

supported by those generally known as peace-lovers." None-theless, if intellectuals decided to abandon government to non-intellectuals, they would have only themselves to blame for the result. If John Taylor of Caroline had a right to his position, Thomas Jefferson had an equal right to his.

3. KENNEDY AND THE LEFT: POLICIES

Where the utopian left felt more than a generalized mis-trust of power, it objected to both the foreign and domestic policies of the administration. In foreign affairs, some re-garded the cold war as the invention of the military-industrial complex and supposed that, if only Washington changed its course, Moscow and Peking would gladly col-laborate in building a peaceful world. This had been some-what the Indian view—or at least until the Chinese crossed the Himalayas and reality broke out. Others, while seeing communism as a problem and the cold war as a reality, felt that resistance involved too great a risk and were gloom-ily prepared to endure a communist world if that would avert a nuclear holocaust: better red than dead. Both groups condemned the policy of nuclear deterrence. Both identi-fied themselves a bit self-righteously with 'peace' as if every-one who disagreed with them wanted to blow up the world. Both yearned for total solutions. And for both the proper United States policy was unilateral disarmament and neutralism.

Thus Professor Stuart Hughes, the Harvard historian, advised the United States in his book *An Approach to Peace* to seek "a new model for foreign policy in the experience of Sweden or of Switzerland, or even of India." He added that he had "toyed" with the idea that the United States should unilaterally declare itself first among the neu-trals; but "in reality we do not need to go that far. The events of the next generation will doubtless do it for us." The mission of the American intellectual, as Hughes saw it, was to do what the Asians and Africans had thus far failed to do and define neutralism "as a faith and a way of life." In the meantime, the United States should renounce nu-clear weapons (by stages), close down most overseas mili-tary bases and rest national safety on "a territorial-militia or guerrilla-resistance type of defense."

In the domestic affairs, the contribution of the utopian left was unimpressive, except in the civil rights effort, in which its members played a brave and valuable part. Some, like Hughes, called themselves socialists but refrained from specifying what they meant by socialism. Obviously if they meant the supersession of the mixed economy by state ownership of the means of production and distribution, they were committed to a gospel which was politically irrelevant and technically obsolete. If they only meant a change in the mix, they had stopped being socialists. Others, like Paul Goodman, were anarchists, who wrote vaguely of diversifying and decentralizing the economy. Goodman thus summarized his program:

> An occasional fist fight, a better orgasm, friendly games, a job of useful work, initiating enterprises, deciding real issues in manageable meetings, and being moved by things that are beautiful, curious, or wonderful.

Norman Mailer's "existential politics" was more drastic. Existential experience, he said, was

> experience sufficiently unusual that you don't know how it is going to turn out. You don't know whether you're going to be dead or alive at the end of it, wanted or rejected, cheered or derided. . . . The hoodlum is more likely to encounter existential experience than the university man. . . . When violence is larger than one's ability to dominate, it is existential and one is living in an instantaneous world of revelations.

Apart from the whimsy of Goodman's manifesto and the hysteria of Mailer's, one could only say that, as serious programs for a high-technology society, they simply would not do. And on the more relevant issues the left made few original contributions. They acted as if they were crying out great ideas in the wilderness which the political leaders studiously ignored. In fact, the political leaders themselves were begging for usable ideas—and not finding any. Even Michael Harrington's book on poverty came along half a dozen years after Averell Harriman had begun a poverty program as governor of New York.

The utopian critique still had value perhaps in its sheer intransigence, though nothing more infuriated the utopians than to be patted on the shoulder and told that society needed their nonconformity. The crime of 'incorporating the critic into the consensus' was quite naturally regarded as the dirtiest trick of all. Thus Goodman wrote bitterly, "I myself have been urged, by one who has access, to continue my 'indispensable role of dissent.' That is, we are the Jester." The undertone was almost a longing for the good old days of McCarthy when heresy was at least taken seriously enough to warrant persecution. One could sympathize with Goodman's chagrin but still wonder whether he was not offering a heads-I-win-tails-you-lose proposition. If dissent was punished, terrible; if embraced, worse.

The Bay of Pigs had quite understandably thrust the

utopian left into bitter opposition; and a curious episode later in 1961 turned its members even more bitterly against the administration. This was the furor which followed the President's request, made originally in May and repeated with emphasis in his July speech on the Berlin crisis, for a fallout shelter program. The proposal was sensible enough. Any President, living in a world of possible nuclear war and knowing that things could be done to save the lives of twenty or thirty million people if war came, would have been plainly delinquent if he had declined to ask for them. Earlier both Truman and Eisenhower had urged civil defense measures, only to have the nation regard the problem with supreme boredom. Now in the Berlin context it acquired, or seemed to acquire, a frightening reality. Before anyone was aware what was happening, a condition of national panic seemed to be boiling up. Get-rich-quick shelter manufacturers arose on every side. Father L. C. McHugh, a Jesuit priest, suggested that shelter owners had the moral right to repel panicky neighbors by "whatever means will effectively deter their assault." The civil defense coordinator of Riverside County, California, warned his constituents to arm themselves in order to turn back the thousands of refugees who might flee their way from Los Angeles. In Las Vegas a civil defense official similarly wanted the Nevada militia to repulse invaders from California. ("In suburban civil defense," said an air-raid warden in a Feiffer cartoon, "our motto is: If you can't get yourself a Russian, settle for an American.") Many on the utopian left feared that the program, if it were not actual preparation for a surprise nuclear attack on the Soviet Union, would at the very least give the American people a false sense of security and therefore encourage them in reckless foreign adventures. Within the United States itself they perceived it as an incitement to vigilantism if not a means by which the radical right could seize control of local communities. The program, in short, became in their minds a portent of preventive war and fascism.

Civil defense policy, in the meantime, was in a state of unjustifiable confusion. As the Defense Department had first conceived the problem, each family was to dig for itself. To advance the cause the Pentagon hired Madison Avenue specialists to prepare a shelter instruction booklet intended for distribution to every householder. This was a singular document. In the draft submitted to the White House, it did not make clear that American policy was to avoid a holocaust; and it offered a relatively sanguine pic-

ture both of life in the shelter and of the world into which
people would emerge after the attack. Moreover, it seemed
to be addressed exclusively to the upper middle class—to
people owning houses with gardens or basements; there
was nothing in it for those who lived in tenements. When
the President asked Galbraith to take a look at it, he responded, "I am not at all attracted by a pamphlet which
seeks to save the better elements of the population, but in
the main writes off those who voted for you. I think it
particularly injudicious, in fact it is absolutely incredible,
to have a picture of a family with a cabin cruiser saving
itself by going out to sea. Very few members of the UAW
can go with them." Moreover, the tract assigned the protection of the population to private enterprise. "The anticipation of a new market for home shelters," it even said, "is
helpful and in keeping with the free enterprise way of
meeting changing conditions in our lives."

Kennedy, while unshaken in his belief that defense
against fallout was a necessary form of national insurance,
was dismayed both by the booklet and the public reaction.
He remarked ruefully that he wished he had never said the
things which had stirred the matter up and wanted to
diminish the excitement as expeditiously as possible. Carl
Kaysen and I, who were following the problem for the
White House, concluded that the do-it-yourself family shelter theory was a disaster and that the only fair and rational
policy would be one of public community shelters. The Defense Department itself was reaching the same conclusion.
The issue went before the President at the defense budget
meeting at Hyannis Port the Friday after Thanksgiving 1961.
It was a dark, sullen day, interrupted by pelting rain. When
I discoursed on the demoralizing effect of the private shelter
approach with its *sauve qui peut* philosophy, the Attorney
General said grimly, "There's no problem here—we can
just station Father McHugh with a machine gun at
every shelter." The President speedily decided in favor of
the public program. The Defense Program rewrote its pamphlet and, instead of putting it in every mailbox, left copies
at post offices for concerned citizens. Thereafter the shelter
panic subsided. Under the calm direction of Steuart Pitt-
man in the Defense Department, and despite mounting congressional resistance to bills offering matching funds to non-
profit institutions for including shelters in new construction, some progress was quietly made in marking existing
buildings as shelter locations and stocking them with food
and equipment.

This episode, following too soon after the Bay of Pigs,

seemed to many on the left a further horrible revelation of the inner essence of the administration. Stuart Hughes, announcing his candidacy for the Senate in Massachusetts in 1962, attacked "the deadening similarity of the two major parties" and declared it time for "a *new kind of politics in America*." When I talked with him on the Cape that summer, he said he expected this would be the beginning of a nationwide third party dedicated to peace. The apparent response to his candidacy and to similar candidacies in other states gave the radical left a few moments of genuine hope.

Kennedy was well aware of this disaffection among the radical intellectuals. He used to say that Adlai Stevenson could still beat him in Madison, Wisconsin, or in Berkeley, California—even perhaps in Cambridge, Massachusetts. Yet, most of the radicals, even at their most critical, felt a sense of reluctant kinship with the President. Kennedy was too bright, too attractive, too *contemporary* to be wholly disowned. He had fortified their own feelings of self-respect. He had made them feel in some way more at home in their own country. "For the first time in our literary life," Mailer told an English interviewer, "it was possible to not only attack the President, you see, but to attack him as a younger brother, with the intensity of a family quarrel."

4. KENNEDY AND THE RADICAL RIGHT

There was no question of a family quarrel with the radical right—and the fury of the right-wing response to Kennedy was a measure of his impact on the nation. If the intellectuals did not always recognize a friend, the reactionaries lost no time in recognizing an enemy.

The burst of right-wing activity in the early sixties was a predictable historical phenomenon. In conservative periods, like the fifties, the radical right was characteristically disorganized and dormant. Its members were soothed by the eternal hope that a conservative administration might do something they would like. The existence of friends—or at least of nodding acquaintances—in Washington restrained them from major organizational efforts on their own. Thus McCarthy faded away quickly after the end of the Korean War; and the publication of Robert Welch's *The Politician* in 1958, with its concise characterization of President Eisenhower as "a dedicated, conscious agent of the communist conspiracy," and the formation the same year of his John Birch Society passed unnoticed.

But the election of a progressive administration generally has a galvanizing effect on the radical right. It grows desperate, convinced that the nation is in mortal danger, that it is five minutes before midnight, that it must rally and resist before it is too late. This happened in the early thirties under Roosevelt. It happened again under Kennedy in the sixties.

I first heard of the John Birch Society in an early-warning letter in December 1960 from that fine old progressive Republican Alfred M. Landon. One heard a great deal more of it and similar groups in the months following. The radical right appealed especially to the incoherent resentment of the frightened rich and the anxious middle class. It flourished particularly in states like California and Texas, overflowing with raw new money; in states like Arizona and Florida, where older people had retired on their pensions; and in small towns in the mountain states, where shopkeepers felt themselves harassed by big business, big labor and big government. The mood was one of longing for a dreamworld of no communism, no overseas entanglements, no United Nations, no federal government, no labor unions, no Negroes or foreigners—a world in which Chief Justice Warren would be impeached, Cuba invaded, the graduated income tax repealed, the fluoridation of drinking water stopped and the import of Polish hams forbidden.

In domestic policy the philosophy of the radical right was well stated by Senator Strom Thurmond in a speech vindicating the right of the military to conservative political utterance: "If the military teaches the true nature of communism, it must necessarily teach that communism is fundamentally socialism. When socialism, in turn, is understood, one cannot help but realize that many of the domestic programs advocated in the United States, and many of those adopted, fall clearly within the category of socialism." The social changes of the last generation were thus—'objectively,' as the communists themselves would have put it—a communist plot. In foreign policy the radical right, like the radical left, derived much of its early impetus from the Bay of Pigs, though it drew the opposite conclusion. It now rallied behind Senator Barry Goldwater, echoing his opposition to a "no-win" policy and his call for "total victory."

As Senator Thurmond's declaration suggested, an early issue was the existence of right-wing views in the military establishment. This aroused attention in the spring of 1961 when Major General Edwin A. Walker was relieved of his division command in West Germany after having propagandized his troops with ultra-conservative political materials and suggested that Mrs. Roosevelt, Edward R. Murrow and others were under left-wing influence. Though reprimanded, Walker was not discharged; instead he was about to be reassigned to Hawaii as assistant chief of staff for training and operations when he resigned from the Army. Subsequently Senator J. W. Fulbright prepared a memorandum reporting the formation of an alliance between Army officers and right-wing groups under the imprimatur of a National Security Council policy statement of 1958 instructing military personnel to arouse the public to the menace of the cold war. This led to prolonged hearings by the Senate Armed Services Committee in which Fulbright was denounced for trying to 'muzzle the military.' In the meantime, Secretary McNamara quietly reorganized the military education program and terminated the relations between the program and private groups.

President Kennedy felt deep concern at the spread of extremism, right and left. This concern was related, I feel sure, to his sense of the latent streak of violence under the surface of American life: the sun o'ercast with blood, the nation torn asunder and dismembered. "We are a frontier country," James V. Bennett, the federal director of prisons, told the Senate Subcommittee on Juvenile Delinquency, "and we have certain elements in our background and culture that incline us to the use of weapons more than some other countries in the world." The tension and anonymity of urban life had further sharpened the impulse to violence. Every day the television industry instructed the children of the nation how easily problems could be solved by revolver shots. Fortifying the Gunsmoke ethic was a mood of national self-righteousness—the happy conviction of American uniqueness, which smoothed out and washed away the cruelties and sins of the past and which now licensed for Americans acts which, if performed by Russians or Chinese, would have seemed instinct with evil.

It all culminated in an image of free-talking, free-shooting national virility. E. M. Dealey, chairman of the board of the *Dallas Morning News,* said furiously to the President that he was a weak sister; "we need a man on horseback to lead this nation, and many people in Texas and the southwest think that you are riding Caroline's bicycle." (When the editor of the evening paper in Dallas, the *Times Herald,* sent the President a note saying that Dealey did not speak for Texas, Kennedy scrawled a postscript on his acknowledgment: "I'm sure the people of Dallas are glad when afternoon comes.") Early in November 1961 the President chatted in his office about the points he planned to make on a trip to the West Coast. An age of insoluble problems, he observed, breeds extremism, hysteria, a weakness for simple and passionate solutions. "There are two groups of these frustrated citizens," he soon said at the University of Washington in Seattle, one group urging the pathway of surrender, the other the pathway of war.

> It is a curious fact that each of these two extreme opposites resembles the other. Each believes that we have only two choices: appeasement or war, suicide or surrender, humiliation or holocaust, to be either Red or dead.

Against the left he urged the indispensability of strength; against the right, the indispensability of negotiation. But the challenge to the right was the main burden of the speech. "At a time when a single clash could escalate over night into a holocaust of mushroom clouds, a great power does not prove its firmness by leaving the task of exploring the other's intentions to sentries."

Two days later in Los Angeles he returned to the theme. "In the most critical period of our Nation's history," he said, "there have always been those on the fringes of our society who have sought to escape their own responsibility by finding a simple solution, an appealing slogan or a convenient scapegoat." Today such people

> look suspiciously at their neighbors and their leadership. They call for "a man on horseback" because they do not trust the people. They find treason in our churches, in our highest court, in our treatment of water. They equate the Democratic Party with the welfare state, the welfare state with socialism, socialism with communism.

Kennedy delivered his reply. "Let our patriotism be reflected in the creation of confidence in one another, rather than in crusades of suspicion. . . . Above all, let us remember, however serious the outlook, however harsh the task, the one great irreversible trend in the history of the world is on the side of liberty."

5. THE POLITICS OF RESENTMENT

A few days later 1800 delegates attended a meeting of the National Indignation Convention at the Memorial Auditorium in Dallas, Texas. One speaker, to the delight of the crowd, complained that the chairman of the meeting had

turned moderate: "All he wants to do is impeach Warren—
I'm for hanging him." [1] General Walker himself had now
retired to Dallas to advocate the cause of the John Birch
Society. Other right-wing organizations were trundling
their wares across the country, like the Christian Anti-
Communism Crusade of Dr. Fred Schwarz and the Christian Crusade of the Reverend Billy James Hargis. Even further to the right the Minutemen were drilling their members
in guerrilla tactics to deal with Soviet invasion or other unspecified contingencies. In the outskirts of Washington itself, George Lincoln Rockwell was recruiting pimply youths
for an American Nazi party.

The spectrum of the right ran all the way from the amiability of Barry Goldwater to the lunacy of the outer fringe.
The press reported much of this with surprising solemnity.
In the summer of 1962 New York right-wingers, convinced
that Nelson Rockefeller and Jacob Javits were beyond redemption, organized the Conservative Party; like Hughes in
Massachusetts, though on the opposite side, they hoped to
prepare the way for a national movement. When *Life*
ran a skeptical story about Fred Schwarz, the outcry from
Schwarz's backers, some of whom were national advertisers,
induced *Life*'s publisher, C. J. Jackson, to fly to a Schwarz
rally in the Hollywood Bowl and offer a public apology. "I
believe we were wrong," Jackson said, "and I am profoundly sorry. It's a great privilege to be here tonight and align
Life magazine with Senator Dodd, Representative Judd, Dr.
Schwarz and the rest of these implacable fighters against
communism."

Aided by such reverent treatment, the right wing grew,
if not more popular, at least richer. Careful analysis by
Group Research, Inc., indicated that the expenditures of
the thirty basic groups rose from $5 million in 1958 to
$12.2 million in 1962 and $14.3 million in 1963; nor did
this estimate include groups for which no figures were available, such as the very active youth organization Young
Americans for Freedom. (The annual national office budget
of Americans for Democratic Action in 1962 and 1963
was about $150,000.) A large amount of the right-wing
finances, Group Research added, had "some sort of privileged status under the tax laws," and the contributors included a number of leading industrial families and their
family foundations.

[1] The speaker was J. Evetts Haley, whose book, *A Texan Looks at
Lyndon*, was one of the more scurrilous contributions to the 1964 campaign.

The more frenetic right-wing agitation focused more and more directly on the President and his family. Every President, of course, provokes his quota of more or less good-natured jokes, and so did Kennedy. In Texas businessmen passed out cards saying "I MISS IKE" and then, in lower case, "Hell, I even miss Harry." The Kennedy cocktail? Stocks on the rocks. "Caroline Kennedy is certainly a nice kid. But that's the last time we should let her plan a Cuban invasion." The Kennedy rocking chair as the symbol of the New Frontier: you get the feeling of moving but you don't go anywhere. If Jack, Bobby and Teddy were on a sinking boat, who would be saved? The country. "Truman showed that anyone can be President, Ike that no one could be President, Kennedy that it can be dangerous to have a President."

But in the domain of the radical right it all became much sicker and nastier. Not since the high point of the hate-Roosevelt enthusiasm of the mid-thirties had any President been the target of such systematic and foul vilification. Everything about Kennedy fed resentment: his appearance, his religion, his wealth, his intelligence, his university, his section of the country, his wife, his brothers, his advisers, his support of the Negroes, his determination to de-emotionalize the cold war, his refusal to drop the bomb. A widely mimeographed letter called for contributions to erect a Kennedy statue in Washington. "It was thought unwise to place it beside that of George Washington, who never told a lie, nor beside that of F.D. Roosevelt, who never told the truth, since John cannot tell the difference." "It went on:

> Five thousand years ago, Moses said to the children of Israel: "Pick up thy shovels, mount thy asses and camels, and I will lead you to the Promised Land." Nearly five thousand years later, Roosevelt said: "Lay down your shovels, sit on your asses, and light up a Camel; this *is* the Promised Land." Now Kennedy is stealing your shovels, kicking your asses, raising the price of Camels, and taking over the Promised Land.

In Auburn, Alabama, the Tiger Theatre, showing the film of Robert Donovan's *PT-109,* inscribed on its marquee: "See how the Japs almost got Kennedy." Southerners repeated with smacking relish a story about Kennedy's seeking out a medium in order to interview the spirit of Abraham Lincoln. "I need your help on this question of civil rights," Kennedy was represented as saying. "What is your advice?" "The only thing I can tell you," Lincoln replied, "is to go to Ford's Theater." Other stories, often of an unbounded obscenity, must be left to specialists in political pornography. All this crystallized and disseminated the pose of national virility, the Gunsmoke stance; it encouraged the unthinking and the vicious to cherish their threats and hatreds. In the two years after November 1961 the Secret Service investigated thirty-four threats against the President's life from the state of Texas alone.

Kennedy, who disliked the very thought of an 'age of hate,' mobilized the weapons of reason to fight the spreading hatreds of his own land, beginning his education of the public before his first year was over. But he knew that reason by itself could not be enough. Once again, he fell back on his most powerful weapon—himself; on his own willingness to attest by example his faith in American rationality and decency, on his own determination, as Norman Mailer said in a flash of insight, to define "the nature of our reality for us by his actions." Kennedy was in this sense the existential hero, though the term would have amused or depressed him. So in November of 1961 he chose to carry his attack on extremism into the city of Los Angeles where four weeks before the publisher of *Life* had publicly apologized to Fred Schwarz. So in the future he never hesitated to define America by his presence and courage in the heart of the enemy's country.

6. THE TRIAL OF 1962

In this swirling mood of emotion Kennedy prepared to confront his first national electoral test—the congressional elections of 1962. The radical right, despite the Conservative Party of New York, constituted, of course, a tiny minority of the electorate and the radical left, despite Stuart Hughes, a tinier still. The great majority of the voters remained in the orbit of conventional politics. But the probabilities were always against the party in power in a mid-term election. In 1954 Eisenhower, for all his popularity, had lost control of both houses of Congress. Indeed, in the entire century only Theodore Roosevelt in 1902 and Franklin Roosevelt in 1934 had been able to prevent opposition gains in off years. The average loss of House seats by the party in power in mid-term elections, leaving out 1934, had been forty-four; the average in the Senate since the First World War, again excepting 1934, had been seven or eight.

These statistics were gloomy. "History is so much against us," Kennedy mused at a press conference. "[Yet] if we can hold our own, if we can win five seats or ten seats, it would change the whole opinion in the House and in the Senate." No one thought this likely. In August the Gallup poll reported that twenty-four of the thirty-five marginal Democratic seats were in danger. Meanwhile Kennedy pondered his own role in the campaign. A letter from Thomas Storke, the venerable Santa Barbara editor, saying that Wilson had intervened disastrously in the 1914 campaign and hoping that Kennedy would not follow this example in 1962, prompted the President to ask me to check the record on presidential intervention in mid-term elections. Storke's memory was inaccurate about 1914, a contest in which Wilson had taken no part; but the historical inquiry seemed to sustain his general point. I reported back that, while presidential intervention had steadily increased in the course of the century, there was no evidence that it had ever played a significant role. Roosevelt, for example, had made only 'non-political' speeches during the great Democratic triumph of 1934; while Eisenhower's campaigns of 1954 and 1958— the most extensive ever undertaken by a President in mid-term elections—had not succeeded in staving off Democratic victories. My memorandum suggested that "the most fruitful form of presidential participation" was the non-political tour, quoting Theodore Roosevelt: " 'The most effective political speeches are often those that are nominally not political speeches at all.' History," the memorandum concluded, "suggests that it would be a mistake . . . to turn the 1962 mid-term election into a test of personal confidence by actively intervening in the form of personal endorsement or advocacy of (or opposition to) individual candidates."

Kennedy wisely ignored both the memorandum and history. He already planned a non-political tour to dedicate dams in mid-August, and he undertook another in early September. But he plainly felt under wraps. Given his sense of the politics of modernity, he may subconsciously have perceived that he himself was the best argument for his issues and that the best hope was to turn the mid-term election precisely into a test of personal confidence. Campaigning, moreover, was a refreshing experience; he always returned cheerful and rejuvenated. I can remember his coming back enormously invigorated from New Jersey after his last-minute entry into the gubernatorial campaign in 1961, saying that the crowds lining the streets reminded him where his support really lay—and that most of them couldn't care less whether the budget was balanced or not. He acknowledged that in the past "fate usually didn't seem to be affected" by what Presidents had done; but "I've never believed that precedents really mean anything in politics. From my own personal experience as well as for other reasons, just because it happened this way in the past doesn't mean anything. The question really is, can we interest enough people to understand how important the congressional election of 1962 is? And that is my function."

In the end he traveled more miles in the campaign of 1962 than Eisenhower had in 1954 and 1958 put together. His central theme was to establish the difference in domestic policy between the two parties. "We have won and lost vote after vote by one or two or three votes in the Senate, and three, four or five votes in the House of Representatives," he would say, "and I don't think we can find jobs for our people, I don't think we can educate our younger people, I don't think we can provide security for our older citizens, when we have a party which votes 'no.' " He would conclude with sharpening voice and stabbing hand: "And that's why this election is important."

XXIX

BATTLE FOR THE HEMISPHERE

1962 HAD NOT BEEN A BAD YEAR: the Berlin crisis over, a settlement in Laos, aggression checked in Vietnam, the Congo straightening out, favorable developments in the rest of Africa, United States Steel chastened, expansion resuming in the American economy. But the problems of the western hemisphere remained acute. "I regard Latin America," the President said early in 1963, "as the most critical area in the world today." The Alliance for Progress, announced with such hope in the brisk March of 1961, had offered Latin America the possibility of a democratic revolution. But in many countries the practical foundations of the Alliance were shaky. Moreover, since the Alliance by its very existence warned Fidel Castro that he could no longer count on the Latin American states falling to Marxist revolution of their own weight, the *Fidelistas* and their communist allies were redoubling their efforts to disrupt the democratic effort and seize the energies of change for themselves. The struggle for the future of Latin America was well joined— and the outcome thus far indeterminate.

The President sought to place our hemisphere policy in the ablest possible hands. Adolf Berle as chairman of the Task Force on Latin America continued to recommend the creation of the post of Under Secretary of State for Latin American Affairs, controlling both political and economic lines of policy; but this was predictably opposed by the State Department on bureaucratic grounds. When Thomas Mann left Washington shortly before the Bay of Pigs to become ambassador to Mexico, Kennedy wanted to persuade some figure of public consequence to take his place as Assistant Secretary of State for Inter-American Affairs. The search was frustrating and lost many valuable weeks. During this time the daily conduct of Latin American affairs remained in the hands of the permanent government—blasé officials in the State Department and the aid agency who believed that they alone understood the *Latinos* and dismissed the Alliance for Progress as a slogan left over from the presidential campaign.

They were decent and hard-working people. But their uncritical commitment to the conceptions of the fifties—to conservative regimes in politics and to private intiative and technical assistance in economics—hardly equipped them to compete with Fidel Castro for the allegiance of a continent in revolutionary ferment. And, as they began to realize that the new President meant business, they seemed to feel threatened by the new policy, as if they feared it would swallow up their own responsibilities and sense of significance. "To get democratic change in Latin America," one of the few Kennedy appointees to the Bureau of Inter-American Affairs told me in June, "you must have people committed to democratic change. Among this group there is no joy, no purpose, no drive. "What's the headache today?' is their attitude. They form a sullen resistance to fresh approaches. They have no realization of the forces at work in Latin America today. They are uninterested in the intellectual community or the labor movement or the democratic left. All they do is sit around the table discussing things. When something comes up, they talk for hours and end up with ten reasons for doing it and twelve for not doing it. . . . We are striving for a new look in Latin America. But if our operating people exhibit the same old attitudes and use the same old clichés, we are going to look in Latin America like the same old crowd." [1]

---

[1] The contrast between two memoranda sent over to the White House from the State Department on the same day that summer makes the point. One discussed a gift to Kennedy from President Betancourt of

1. THE CHARTER OF PUNTA DEL ESTE

The conviction among the bureaucrats that, if only they sat tight, the Alliance for Progress would go away left the initiative to the White House, to Berle's Task Force, increasingly isolated within State, and to the Treasury Department, where Douglas Dillon's long and enlightened interest in Latin America now had the able support of Assistant Secretary John Leddy. It was this situation which led in the spring to the stream of complaints from the State Department, respectfully reproduced in the *New York Times,* about 'meddling' in hemisphere policy. It can be flatly said that without such meddling there would have been no Alliance for Progress.

The Alliance rested on the premise that modernization in Latin America required not just injections of capital or technical assistance but the breaking of the bottlenecks of economic development through reform of the political and social structure. It was formally organized in August 1961 at an Inter-American Economic and Social Council conference held in Punta del Este, Uruguay. In his message to the conference Kennedy defined his conception of the occasion with great clarity. "We live in a hemisphere," he said, "whose own revolution has given birth to the most powerful forces of the modern age—the search for the freedom and self-fulfillment of man. We meet to carry on that revolution to shape the future." This meant "full recognition of the right of all the people to share fully in our progress. For there is no place in democratic life for institutions which benefit the few while denying the needs of the many, even though the elimination of such institutions may require far-reaching and difficult changes such as land reform and tax reform and a vastly increased emphasis on education and health and housing. Without these changes

---

Venezuela of a specially bound and inscribed collection of his speeches. State recommended against any formal acknowledgment and proposed that the Department convey the President's thanks informally to Betancourt through the Venezuelan Embassy. The second memorandum discussed a gift to the President from a Paraguayan Ambassador of a book which the memorandum described as "essentially an apologia for the current Paraguayan regime." Accompanying the book was a letter from its author stigmatizing the opponents of the regime, some of whom had just signed a statement in support of the Alliance for Progress, as "in league with communism." In this case the Department had composed an effusive letter of thanks to the author, which they wanted someone in the White House to sign. Similarly the Department tried to stop Kennedy from corresponding with Pablo Casals lest it offend General Franco.

our common effort cannot succeed." No President of the United States had ever spoken such words to Latin America before. He concluded with an appeal for the participation "of workers and farmers, businessmen and intellectuals and, above all, of the young people of the Americas."

Douglas Dillon, the head of the United States delegation, struck the same note. "This is a revolutionary task," he told the Latin Americans, "but we are no strangers to revolution. . . . The fruits of the American revolution have not yet been extended to all our people. Throughout the hemisphere millions still live with hunger, poverty and despair. They have been denied access to the benefits of modern knowledge and technology. And they now demand those benefits for themselves and for their children. We cannot rest content until these just demands are met."

Che Guevara was there too, smoothly arguing the case for the competing revolution. Some Latin Americans, indeed, wanted to include Cuba in the Alliance. But others, led by Pedro Beltrán of Peru, the conference's chairman, countered the Cubans with a Declaration to the Peoples of America placing the principles of the Alliance in a firm context of representative democracy and political freedom. Richard Goodwin, who had helped Dillon and Leddy organize the United States position, collaborated in writing the Declaration; and Beltrán, working with Arturo Morales-Carrión and Lincoln Gordon of the United States delegation, marshaled an overwhelming vote in its favor. In the meantime, Leddy negotiated the economic provisions of the Charter with the Latin Americans, and Philip Coombs, whom Kennedy had brought from the Ford Foundation to become Assistant Secretary of State for Cultural Affairs, worked hard in pushing through a crucial resolution on a ten-year education plan. Word soon went round the conference that there were only "two left-wing governments present—Cuba and the United States," and the confrontation between Guevara and Dillon in the last session gave the meeting its moment of drama. Guevara told the Latin Americans that they had Castro to thank for this sudden offer of massive United States aid. Observing that Cuba was in sympathy with many of the Alliance's objectives, he said that, as the instrument of imperialism, the Alliance was bound to fail; Cuba would therefore abstain. Guevara's moderation was itself striking evidence of the Alliance's initial appeal. Dillon was cool and effective in rebuttal. Then twenty American republics pledged themselves to a series of quite startling goals:

To improve and strengthen democratic institutions through application of the principle of self-determination by the people.

To accelerate economic and social development. . . .

To carry out urban and rural housing programs to provide decent homes for all our people.

To encourage . . . programs of comprehensive agrarian reform, leading to the effective transformation, where required, of unjust structures and systems of land tenure and use; with a view to replacing latifundia and dwarf holdings by an equitable system of property. . . .

To assure fair wages and satisfactory working conditions to all our workers. . . .

To wipe out illiteracy. . . .

To press forward with programs of health and sanitation. . . .

To reform tax laws, demanding more from those who have most, to punish tax evasion severely, and to redistribute the national income in order to benefit those who are most in need, while, at the same time, promoting savings and investment and reinvestment of capital. . . .

To maintain monetary and fiscal policies which . . . will protect the purchasing power of the many, guarantee the greatest possible price stability, and form an adequate basis for economic development.

To stimulate private enterprise. . . .

To find a quick and lasting solution to the grave problem created by excessive price fluctuations in the basic exports. . . .

To accelerate the integration of Latin America. . . .

To this end the United States will provide a major part of the minimum of 20 billion dollars, principally in public funds, which Latin America will require over the next ten years from all external sources in order to supplement its own efforts. . . .

For their part, as a contribution to the Alliance for Progress, each of the countries of Latin America will formulate a comprehensive and well-conceived national program for the development of its own economy.

The Charter of Punta del Este was a summons to a democratic revolution—nor was revolution a word feared by the architects of the Alliance, even though it continued to dismay the Department of State. Of course most of the governments endorsing this summons were far from revolutionary. Some no doubt joined because they considered American aid worth a signature; others because, as President Alberto Lleras Camargo of Colombia once put it, "In Latin America, perhaps more than anywhere else in the world, political leaders have the habit of carrying revolutionary statements beyond the point to which they are really prepared to go." The American negotiators had no illusions about the mixture of motives, nor did they suppose that setting fine words down on parchment would have magical effects. But they knew that the commitment of twenty governments to this unprecedented set of goals strengthened those in each country who sought democratic progress.

This included the government in Washington. The trip to Vienna, the Berlin crisis, the debate over nuclear test resumption, the reform of the aid program—all the problems of the summer of 1961 had further slowed the reorganization of our own Latin American management. Failing to find an outsider of sufficient stature as Assistant Secretary for Inter-American Affairs, the President in July appointed Robert F. Woodward, an intelligent and liberal-minded career officer, wholeheartedly devoted to the Alliance, then serving as ambassador to Chile. Berle, his assignment valuably completed, resigned. In the fall Kennedy sent Richard Goodwin over to serve as Woodward's deputy. In the White House the President himself, with some help, after Goodwin's departure, from Ralph Dungan and me, continued to keep an exceedingly vigilant eye on hemisphere developments.

The search for a man to run the United States contribution to the Alliance took an even longer time. It was universally assumed that the effort would be set up within the Agency for International Development. In retrospect, this was very probably a mistake. If the Alliance had been established, like the Peace Corps, as a separate agency, the resulting status and independence would, I believe, have increased its effectiveness. But the proponents of bureaucratic tidiness won out. Finally in November, Kennedy appointed as AID Deputy for Latin America Teodoro Moscoso who had been Economic Development Administrator under Governor Luis Muñoz Marín in Puerto Rico and was now ambassador to Venezuela.

He could have found no one more deeply dedicated to the spirit of Punta del Este. The Puerto Rican experience, indeed, was an important source of the ideas behind the Alliance. Puerto Rico had been the last triumph of Franklin Roosevelt's New Deal. Rexford G. Tugwell, whom Roosevelt sent down as governor in the years when Dr. New Deal was giving way to Dr. Win-the-War in the United States, had lent strong and imaginative support to Luis Muñoz Marín, the statesman of ability and vision who in 1940 led a peaceful democratic revolution in Puerto Rico. From a "stricken land," as Tugwell used to call it, Puerto Rico was being transformed into a thriving community. During the fifties it provided both a refuge and something of an inspiration for democratic Latin Americans exiled by their own countries. Muñoz, convinced that these progressive leaders

offered the best hope for the continent, now argued forth-
rightly that in the long run only the democratic left could
make the Alliance work. They constituted the one group
"which *wants* it to succeed in its entirety . . . the group
which seeks social advances and higher living standards for
all the people in a framework of freedom and consent . . .
the only nontotalitarian element which understands the
depths of the revolutionary ferment in Latin America and
which can provide responsible leadership to shape this revolution into constructive channels." The "well-meaning democratic conservatives," Muñoz added, "men whom we can
often respect, have no real grasp of this revolutionary surge,
and are therefore powerless to compete with the totali-
tarians." This was Moscoso's judgment too, and within the
State Department Arturo Morales-Carrión, an historian who
had been Muñoz's Under-Secretary of State in Puerto Rico
and was now a Deputy Assistant Secretary for Inter-American Affairs, expounded the same viewpoint with discriminating wisdom.

2. THE DEMOCRATIC REVOLUTION

Muñoz's formulation was a succinct statement of the philosophy implicit in the Punta del Este Charter. Though the
Alliance included dictatorial regimes like those of Stroessner
in Paraguay and Duvalier in Haiti, its principles were progressive democratic principles and its affinites were with
progressive democratic governments. Adolf Berle made the
point in his final report as chairman of the Task Force:

> The present struggle will not be won, and can be lost, by op-
> portunist support of transitory power-holders or forces whose
> objectives are basically hostile to the peoples they dominate.
> Success of the American effort in Latin America requires that
> at all times its policy be based on clear, consistent, moral
> democratic principles. I do not see that any other policy can
> be accepted or indeed stands any real chance of ultimate
> success. The forces sweeping Latin America today demand
> progress, and a better life for the masses of their people,
> through evolution if possible, or through revolution if that
> price must be paid. A preponderance of these forces want
> the resulting forms to provide liberty, rejecting tyranny
> whether from the right or from the left.

In Latin America the democratic left comprised two
major strains: the *partido populares,* which had battled for
social democracy in various countries of Central and South
America since the Second World War under far-sighted men
like Rómulo Betancourt of Venezuela and José Figueres
of Costa Rica but which now was becoming a little the

movement of an older generation; and the Christian Democrats, emerging as a significant force in Chile and Venezuela and appealing to younger people in other countries. In Venezuela the two strains combined in support of the Betancourt government. For this and other reasons, some of us in Washington saw Venezuela as a model for Latin American progressive democracy (remembering always that its oil revenues gave it a margin of wealth the other republics lacked). Betancourt, who had spent a good share of his exile in Puerto Rico, had brought back to Venezuela plans and institutions derived from the Puerto Rican experience. A rugged fighter for democracy, he was hated by both right and left: Trujillo's assassins had tried to kill him, and Castro's terrorists were seeking now to destroy his government. For Betancourt the Alliance exactly filled the continent's need. "The communist threat to Latin America," he used to say, "is very serious. What makes it so is the economic plight of the vast majority of the 200 million persons who live below the Rio Grande." The communists, he added, naturally detested his own regime "because we are carrying out the type of social action that strips the communists of support and followers." The reactionaries disliked his type of social action for opposite reasons; and, as Betancourt wrote Kennedy in the spring of 1962, "We are hitting both groups, reactionaries and Communists, in earnest and in depth, in conformity with the constitution and the law. . . . The impatient ones would like us to go beyond the written law—and even beyond the unwritten but overriding law of respect for human dignity. I will not, however, deviate from the course laid down for me by the fundamental law of Venezuela and by my own conscience."

No one in Washington understood this course better than the President. He wholly accepted the thesis of the democratic revolution and therefore on his first presidential trip to Latin America in December 1961 chose to visit two presidents notable for their commitment to progressive reform—Betancourt in Caracas and Alberto Lleras Camargo in Bogotá. A good deal of anxious consideration preceded this journey. People in the State Department, recalling the Nixon tour three years before, wondered whether Kennedy might not be inviting unnecessary risks. Goodwin and Morales-Carrión, however, argued strongly for the trip, and Kennedy himself characteristically shrugged and decided to go ahead. Jacqueline, tuning up her Spanish for the occasion, went with him. When the presidential plane flew into Caracas, Kennedy, remembering Goodwin's assurances, said·drily, "Well, Dick, if this doesn't work out, you might as well keep going south."

No one need have worried. Wildly enthusiastic crowds lined the streets in Caracas and the next day in Bogotá. "Do you know why those workers and *campesinos* are cheering you like that?" Lleras Camargo asked Kennedy. "It's because they believe you are on their side." That night at the San Carlos Palace the American President set forth the promise of the Alliance. "We in the United States," he said, "have made many mistakes in our relations with Latin America. We have not always understood the magnitude of your problems, or accepted our share of responsibility for the welfare of the hemisphere. But we are committed in the United States—and our will and our energy—to an untiring pursuit of that welfare and I have come to this country to reaffirm that dedication." Then he said, "The leaders of Latin America, the industrialists and the landowners, are, I am sure, also ready to admit past mistakes and accept new responsibilities."

Each year he made a Latin American trip, with the democratic revolution his constant theme. On his arrival in Mexico City in June 1962 he saluted the Mexican Revolution and added that "the revolution of this hemisphere" would be incomplete "until every child has a meal and every student has an opportunity to study, and everyone who wishes to work can find a job, and everyone who wishes a home can find one, and everyone who is old can have security." Then he and Jacqueline rode into the city amidst unending cries of "Viva Kennedy" and a pink snowstorm of confetti. The following spring he carried the message to a meeting of the Central American Presidents in Costa Rica. Speaking at the University of Costa Rica (he began his remarks: "It is a great pleasure to leave Washington, where I am lectured to by professors, to come to Costa Rica where I can speak to students"), he reminded his audience of the changes Franklin Roosevelt's New Deal had wrought in the United States and then affirmed a continent-wide "right to social justice," which meant "land for the landless, and education for those who are denied education . . . [and the end of] ancient institutions which perpetuate privilege."

He often wondered how he could strengthen the governments most deeply pledged to these objectives. For a time he even mused about the possibility of a 'club' of democratic presidents—Betancourt, Lleras, Jorge Alessandri of Chile, José Orlich Balmarcich of Costa Rica, José Rivera of El Salvador—which might meet regularly in Palm Beach or Puerto Rico, hoping that this might be an incentive for other chiefs of state to commit themselves to the struggle for democracy; but this idea presented obvious problems, and nothing came of it. In the meantime, he seized every opportunity to signify his respect for men like Betancourt and Lleras. When Betancourt came to Washington in February 1963, Kennedy welcomed him as representing "all that we admire in a political leader."

> Your liberal leadership of your own country, your persistent determination to make a better life for your people, your long fight for democratic leadership not only in your own country but in the entire area of the Caribbean, your companionship with other liberal progressive leaders of this hemisphere, all these have made you, for us, a symbol of what we wish for our own country and for our sister republics.

3. THE SHOWCASE THAT FAILED

The President's emphasis was absolutely correct. Democratic leadership in the Latin countries was fundamental to the success of the Alliance. Without it United States aid and exhortation could do little. If anyone had doubted this proposition, it received full verification in the tribulations of the Dominican Republic. Since 1930 Rafael Trujillo had operated a cruel and efficient dictatorship on the eastern half of the lovely but tragic old Spanish island of Hispaniola. His oppression of his own people was considered beyond the reach of the Organization of American States; but, when he sent his agents to Caracas to kill Betancourt, the OAS rallied and in August 1960 recommended that its members break ambassadorial relations with Trujillo and embargo the import of arms and petroleum. In early 1961 Washington began to hear increasing reports of unrest on the island. In February Adolf Berle predicted a blow-up of some sort within three months. He was astonishingly prescient. On May 30 a group of disgruntled army officers stopped Trujillo's car late one night and shot him down.

The assassination took Washington by surprise. The President, who was then in Paris on his visit to de Gaulle, was confronted on his return by a Dominican regime under Joaquín Balaguer, who had been the nominal president under Trujillo, with Trujillo's son Ramfis still in charge of the armed forces. Kennedy examined the situation realistically. "There are three possibilities," he said, "in descending order of preference: a decent democratic regime, a continuation of the Trujillo regime or a Castro regime. We ought to aim at the first, but we really can't renounce the second until we are sure that we can avoid the third."

The problem was whether a country where potential political leadership had been suppressed, murdered or exiled for more than a generation could easily acquire the instincts and skills of self-government. For the next three months the President endeavored to assess the democratic prospects. He sent Robert Murphy, one of the most experienced of American diplomats, and John Bartlow Martin, one of the best of American reporters, on quiet trips to Santo Domingo. Martin came back with a 115-page report so enthralling that Kennedy read it all with relish one autumn afternoon as he listened to the World Series. The accumulating information suggested that Balaguer was making an honest attempt to bring about a transition to democracy. The presence of young Trujillo remained troubling, however; and his control of the army presumably limited our capacity to do anything about him. Toward the end of August the State Department proposed that we try to induce the army, Balaguer, Ramfis Trujillo and the moderate opposition to stick together in order to lay the foundations for movement toward self-government. Kennedy agreed. "Balaguer is our only tool," he said. "The anti-communist liberals aren't strong enough. We must use our influence to take Balaguer along the road to democracy."

Others at the meeting in the Cabinet Room supported this policy, some in terms that suggested a certain scorn for the democratic opposition. One described the intricate factional differences within the opposition in such vivid language that the Attorney General passed me a note, "This is as bad as New York City." Finally Morales-Carrión, evidently distressed over this part of the discussion, spoke up with sober eloquence. "The democratic opposition," he said, "are the people who represent the only possibility of democratic government in the Dominican Republic. They are the counterparts of the people who made democracy effective in Puerto Rico and Venezuela. Naturally they are not too well disciplined at the moment. They have lived under tyranny for thirty years. Now the lid is off, political life has revived and it is not always under control. But we must understand them and their position and their hopes. Otherwise we will lose all chance of bringing democracy to the Dominican Republic."

The President listened with a mixture of sympathy and doubt. Finally he said, "Yes, yes, but the whole key in all those countries is the emergence of a leader—a liberal figure who can command popular support as against the military and who will carry out social and economic reform—a Nehru or a Muñoz. No such figure has emerged. We don't know who he will be. The great danger in the next six months is a take-over by the army, which could lead straight to Castro. That is the situation we have to deal with now—that is why we must get a modus vivendi among all the forces prepared to commit themselves to democracy, instead of letting them tear themselves apart and let in the far right or the far left. The eventual problem is to find someone who will symbolize the future for the island."

In the Dominican Republic the democratic opposition insisted on the expulsion of Ramfis Trujillo as the condition for any rapprochement with Balaguer. Washington instructed its representatives there to support this view. Finally in mid-November Ramfis agreed to leave the country. But the next day two of his uncles made an unexpected return to the island, Ramfis canceled his departure and the developments seemed to portend a military coup to restore the Trujillo family to power. Washington read the cables with rising concern. The President directed the Secretary of State to put out a statement saying that the United States would not remain indifferent if the Trujillos attempted to "reassert dictatorial domination." Then Kennedy decided on a bold stroke: the dispatch of eight American ships, with 1800 Marines on board, to steam visibly off Santo Domingo just outside the three-mile limit, ready to go in if the Balaguer government asked for them. Given the ingrained Latin American hatred of gunboat diplomacy, this course involved obvious risks. On the other hand, it would be, for once, Yankee intervention to sustain a democratic movement rather than to destroy it, and the President was prepared to take his chance.

We waited with some apprehension until surprising and heartening word came in from Santo Domingo. It must have been a unique moment in Latin American history: the people dancing in the streets, cheering the United States fleet and shouting enthusiastic *vivas* for the *gringos*. The presence of the fleet encouraged General Pedro Rodríguez Echavarría of the air force to rise against Ramfis. The Trujillos quickly fled, this time for good; and Kennedy's action won commendation throughout Latin America. Only Fidel Castro objected. The incident provided striking evidence of the change in Latin American attitudes Kennedy had wrought in the seven months since the Bay of Pigs. But the ordeal of Dominican democracy was just beginning.[2] As Washington saw the problem, transition to democracy required the broadening of the Balaguer government by the incorporation of representatives of the democratic groups opposed to *Trujillismo*. These groups were the Unión Cívica, a miscellaneous collection of factions, under the leadership of Viriato Fiallo, which had steadfastly opposed Trujillo and now enjoyed wide popular support; the 14th of June movement, which had moderate and leftist wings and strongly appealed to Dominican youth; and the Partido Revolucionario Dominicano, under Juan Bosch, with more experienced leadership but as yet incapable of mass action.

Strenuous efforts were made after the Trujillos' downfall to bring these disparate elements together. The American Consul General, John Hill, was reinforced by Morales-Carrión, who for several years had been in touch with the anti-*Trujillista* movement and had friends in all camps. For several weeks, Hill and Morales-Carrión worked hard at getting a consensus among the Dominicans. But the animosities and suspicions engendered by the *Trujillista* period made mediation a thankless task. On December 15 President Kennedy stopped in Puerto Rico on his way to Venezuela. That evening the President, Goodwin, Woodward, Bowles, Hill and Morales-Carrión met at La Fortaleza, the governor's mansion. After carefully considering the situation, President Kennedy decided on a personal appeal to Balaguer and Rodríguez Echavarría. His intervention was the catalyst that made possible the establishment of a Council of State, committed to a program of political democracy and the preparation of elections. When Rodríguez Echavarría, who hated the Unión Cívica, then attempted a coup, the popular reaction defeated him.

The Council, under its chairman, Rafael Bonnelly, was never a strong government; but it brought peace and personal freedom to the Dominican Republic and in December 1962, with the technical assistance of the OAS, it held the only democratic election that the people had known in generations. The election resulted in the victory of Bosch, who had returned the year before from twenty years of exile. An old friend of Muñoz, Figueres and Betancourt, Bosch was strongly in the progressive democratic tradition. "The Alliance for Progress," he said after the election, "is a political and economic ideal for which we, the democratic,

---

[2] John Bartlow Martin, whom Kennedy soon sent to Santo Domingo as United States Ambassador, will tell the story in detail in his book *Overtaken by Events*.

revolutionary leaders of Latin America, have been fighting for a long time." Kennedy instructed our government to give Bosch full support, hoping that the Dominican Republic might become a democratic showcase in the Caribbean.

But Bosch was essentially a literary figure, better as short story writer than as statesman. In spite of the invasion of the islands by swarms of Washington economists and engineers, of foundation experts and private consultants, in spite of grants and loans and blueprints, the Bosch government was not able in 1963 to reduce unemployment or prepare a national development program. In the meantime, Bosch alienated the upper classes by his words without winning over the lower by his deeds, while his faith in civil liberties allowed his foes, especially in the army, to stigmatize him most unjustly as pro-communist. But one must not blame Bosch too much. Even had he been a Nehru or a Muñoz he would have confronted problems of overwhelming difficulty; a nation without democratic tradition or experience, a government without trained administrators, an army dominated by *Trujillistas* and an economy burdened by a staggering inheritance of foreign debt leaving him, he thought, no choice but to pursue orthodox monetary policies.

Kennedy watched the Dominican troubles with disappointment but not with much surprise. It confirmed his sense both of the limited capacity of the United States to work unilateral miracles and of the dependence of the Alliance on Latin American leadership.

4. COMMUNISM IN THE WINGS

The Alliance for Progress represented the affirmative side of Kennedy's policy. The other side was his absolute determination to prevent any new state from going down the Castro road and so giving the Soviet Union a second bridgehead in the hemisphere.

It was idle to suppose that communism in Latin America was no more than the expression of an indigenous desire for social reform. Latin America had long occupied an honored place in Leninist meditations about the future of world politics. Not only were Marxist ideas far more relevant to Latin American feudalism than they were, for example, to African tribalism, but communist success in Latin America would deal a much harder blow to the power and influence of the United States. Communist parties had existed for forty years in the major countries. Latin Americans, regularly summoned to training schools in Moscow or Prague, learning everything from political doctrine to paramilitary warfare, carried their lessons back to their home-lands. Khrushchev himself made no secret of his hopes for the western hemisphere. "Latin America," he said in 1960, "reminds one of an active volcano." And, while the Alliance was the best way of attacking the long-run sources of communist appeal, it could not by itself ward off short-run attempts at disruption and subversion: if I may borrow back a line I once contributed to a speech of Dean Rusk's, "Vitamin tablets will not save a man set upon by hoodlums in an alley."

Communism had both targets of priority and targets of convenience in Latin America. Venezuela and Brazil, for example, seemed to be the chief targets of priority. The main target of convenience in 1961—that is, one which became attractive less for intrinsic desirability than because it was there—was a small country, still an English colony, British Guiana.

British Guiana had a population of about 600,000, almost evenly divided between the Negroes of the towns and the East Indians of the countryside. The people enjoyed a considerable measure of self-government and, if things went according to schedule, were due for full independence in another year or two. An election in September 1961 brought the Indian party, the People's Progressive Party, and its leader Dr. Cheddi Jagan into office. Jagan was unquestionably some sort of Marxist. His wife, an American girl whom he had met while studying denistry in Chicago, had once been a member of the Young Communist League. His party lived by the clichés of an impassioned, quasi-Marxist, anti-colonialist socialism.

Jagan was plainly the most popular leader in British Guiana. The question was whether he was recoverable for democracy. Senator Dodd of Connecticut had pronounced him a communist agent, but then he had said the same thing about Sékou Touré. The British, on the other hand, were not unsympathetic toward Jagan. Though they had earlier imprisoned him more than once, they now claimed it was possible to work with him and that he was more responsible than his rival, the Negro leader Forbes Burnham. Their view, as communicated at the highest level, was that if Jagan's party were the choice of the people, London and Washington should do their best to keep him on the side of the west by cooperating fully with him and giving his regime economic support. Otherwise he would turn to the communist bloc, which would only guarantee Soviet influence in an independent British Guiana.

This was the situation when Jagan, after his election, expressed a desire to come to Washington and talk about assistance for his development program. At that point the State Department saw no real alternative to the British policy. The aid budget made tentative provision for assistance in the magnitude of $5 million. Then in late October 1961 Jagan arrived. He made his American debut, like so many other visiting statesmen, on Meet the Press, where he resolutely declined to say anything critical of the Soviet Union and left an impression of either wooliness or fellow-traveling. This appearance instantly diminished the enthusiasm for helping his government. The President, who caught the last half of the show, called for a re-examination of all aspects of the problem, saying he wanted no commitments made until he had seen Jagan himself.

Jagan talked with the President on the morning of October 25. He turned out to be a personable and fluent East Indian but endowed, it seemed to those of us present, with an unconquerable romanticism or naïveté. He began by outlining the economic circumstances of British Guiana and his own development plans. When he explained that, as a socialist, he felt that only state planning could break the bottlenecks, Kennedy said, "I want to make one thing perfectly clear. We are not engaged in a crusade to force private enterprise on parts of the world where it is not relevant. If we are engaged in a crusade for anything, it is national independence. That is the primary purpose of our aid. The secondary purpose is to encourage individual freedom and political freedom. But we can't always get that; and we have often helped countries which have little personal freedom, like Yugoslavia, if they maintain their national independence. This is the basic thing. So long as you do that, we don't care whether you are socialist, capitalist, pragmatist or whatever. We regard ourselves as pragmatists." As for nationalization, the President said that we would, of course, expect compensation, but that we had lived with countries like Mexico and Bolivia which had carried out nationalization programs.

He then began to draw out his visitor's political ideas. Recalling Jagan's words of admiration for Harold Laski on Meet the Press, Kennedy observed that he himself had studied for a term under Laski at the London School of Economics and that his older brother had visited the Soviet Union with him. Jagan replied that the first book of Laski's he had read was *The American Presidency;* he considered himself, he added, a Bevanite. We all responded agreeably to this, citing Bevan's faith in personal freedom and recalling his belief that the struggle of the future would be between democratic socialism and communism. Jagan, after avowing his commitment to parliamentary government, went on to say that he also admired the *Monthly Review* and the rather pro-communist writings of Paul Sweezy, Leo Huberman and Paul Baran. George Ball and I pressed him on this point, declaring there was a large difference between Bevan and the Sweezy group. Jagan finally said, "Well, Bevanism, Sweezyism, Hubermanism, Baranism—I really don't get those ideological subleties." Kennedy observed later that this was the one time when his exposition rang false.

For the rest Jagan spoke as a nationalist committed to parliamentary methods. When Kennedy asked how he conceived his relations with the communist bloc, Jagan inquired whether the United States would regard a trade agreement with the Soviet Union as an unfriendly act. Kennedy responded that a simple trading relationship was one thing; a relationship which brought a country into a condition of economic dependence was another. Ball described the case of Sékou Touré, who in order to recover his independence was now disengaging himself from the Soviet embrace.

The President avoided any discussion of aid figures. There were special problems here because Jagan was requesting $40 million—a figure all out of proportion to the size of his country, especially in relation to the competing needs of Latin American nations with much larger populations and closer bonds to the United States. For this and other reasons, it was decided after the meeting that no concrete commitments could be made to Jagan and that each project would have to be examined on its merits. Jagan was considerably upset on learning this and asked to see the President again. Taking advantage of the President's usual free half-hour before luncheon, I reported these developments. Kennedy wholly agreed with the staff's recommendation that he not receive Jagan a second time but instructed me to see him myself in view of the great British concern that Jagan not return disgruntled to British Guiana; perhaps a statement could be worked out which would give Jagan something to take home and satisfy the British without committing us to immediate action. Sitting down at his desk, he dashed off a longhand letter to Jagan, explaining that I came with his confidence, and asked Evelyn Lincoln to type it. When he looked at it again, he decided that it was a little cold, told me to "warm it up" and signed the warmed-up letter.

The President went on to express doubt whether Jagan would be able to sustain his position as a parliamentary democrat. "I have a feeling," he said, "that in a couple of years he will find ways to suspend his constitutional provisions and will cut his opposition off at the knees. . . . Parliamentary democracy is going to be damn difficult in a country at this stage of development. With all the political jockeying and all the racial tensions, it's going to be almost impossible for Jagan to concentrate the energies of his country on development through a parliamentary system."

With William Burdett, a careful and intelligent Foreign Service officer, I saw Jagan that afternoon at the Dupont Plaza. He was in a desperate mood at the thought of going home empty-handed but brightened at the prospect of a statement. The final text, worked out after complicated negotiation in the next twenty-four hours, committed Jagan "to uphold the political freedoms and defend the parliamentary democracy which is his country's fundamental heritage" and the United States to send a mission to determine what economic assistance we could give in support of the British Guiana development plan.

The problem was genuinely difficult. Assuming that Jagan would be the leader of an independent British Guiana, we estimated that, if we gave aid, there would be a 50 per cent chance of his going communist, that, if we didn't, there would be a 90 per cent chance, and that we would all catch hell whatever we did. The State Department at first thought we should make the try; then Rusk personally reversed this policy in a stiff letter to the British early in 1962. AID was fearful from the start that assistance to British Guiana would cause congressional criticism and injure the whole aid program. The President, after meeting Jagan, had grown increasingly skeptical, but he was impressed by the British contention that there was no alternative. The British advanced this argument at every opportunity, though one always suspected that their main desire was to get out of British Guiana as quickly as possible and dump the whole problem on us (nor could one begrudge the Colonial Office its sarcasm when Americans, after bringing self-righteous pressure on London to advance the independence timetable in Africa, now kept urging delay in this case). Inside British Guiana the situation continued to disintegrate. In February 1962 frightening race riots broke out in Georgetown. Jagan, forgetting his objection to imperialism, requested British troops to help maintain order.

Thus far our policy had been based on the assumption that Forbes Burnham was, as the British described him, an opportunist, racist and demagogue intent only on personal power. One wondered about this, though, because the AFL-CIO people in British Guiana thought well of him; and Hugh Gaitskell told me that Burnham had impressed him more than Jagan when the two visited Labour party leaders in London. Then in May 1962 Burnham came to Washington. He appeared an intelligent, self-possessed, reasonable man, insisting quite firmly on his 'socialism' and 'neutralism' but stoutly anti-communist. He also seemed well aware that British Guiana had no future at all unless its political leaders tried to temper the racial animosities and unless he in particular gave his party, now predominantly African, a bi-racial flavor. In the meantime, events had convinced us that Jagan, though perhaps not a disciplined communist, had that kind of deep pro-communist emotion which only sustained experience with communism could cure; and the United States could not afford the Sékou Touré therapy when it involved a quasi-communist regime on the mainland of Latin America. Burnham's visit left the feeling, as I reported to the President, that "an independent British Guiana under Burnham (*if* Burnham will commit himself to a multi-racial policy) would cause us many fewer problems than an independent British Guiana under Jagan." And the way was open to bring it about, because Jagan's parliamentary strength was larger than his popular strength: he had won 57 per cent of the seats on the basis of 42.7 per cent of the vote. An obvious solution would be to establish a system of proportional representation.

This, after prolonged discussion, the British government finally did in October 1963; and elections held finally at the end of 1964 produced a coalition government under Burnham. With much unhappiness and turbulence, British Guiana seemed to have passed safely out of the communist orbit.

5. THE SECOND PUNTA DEL ESTE

British Guiana, however, was a marginal problem. The central threat remained Fidel Castro, whose broadcasters were now inveighing daily and agents conspiring nightly against the democratic regimes of Latin America. "The duty of every revolutionary," as Castro's Second Declaration of Havana put it in February 1962, "is to make revolution." Fidel himself, who had talked wistfully in 1960 about converting the Andes into "the Sierra Maestra of the American continent," now predicted in 1962 on the first anniversary of the Bay of Pigs that Betancourt and his regime would be overthrown in a year. Nor were such statements merely exercises in abstract prophecy—as the Venezuelan government learned when it found a great cache of weapons, unquestionably Cuban in origin and provenance, secreted for terrorists at a point along the Caribbean coast.

The Organization of American States had handled all this in 1960 and 1961 in somewhat gingerly fashion. The United States favored some form of collective action, or at least exhortation, against Castro; but when this was proposed at a meeting of foreign ministers at San José, Costa Rica, in August 1960, most of the American republics demurred. Some, like Mexico and Argentina, cherished the principle of non-intervention in the internal affairs of their fellow republics; others, like Bolivia, feared the domestic political repercussions of an anti-Castro stand; still others did not want to antagonize Castro or make him further dependent on the Soviet Union. In some cases, no doubt, there was a furtive sympathy for David against Goliath, especially when Goliath seemed primarily agitated about economic properties he had previously appropriated himself. The tendency was to regard the Cuban matter as a private quarrel between Washington and Havana rather than as an inter-American responsibility. The resolution finally adopted at San José condemned interference by extra-continental powers in the hemisphere but said nothing about Cuba.

Castro's growing fierceness during 1961, however, began to disturb his Caribbean neighbors. Venezuela and Colombia broke off diplomatic relations, and Lleras Camargo, increasingly concerned, called for a new meeting of foreign ministers to consider the Cuban problem. By a vote of 14 to 2, with five nations abstaining, the OAS Council resolved in December to hold such a session in January 1962. Again the resolution did not mention Cuba by name, and the split vote—the fact that such significant nations as Argentina, Brazil, Chile and Mexico all either abstained or were opposed—showed the division in the hemisphere. While Lleras Camargo sought mandatory diplomatic and economic sanctions against Cuba, President Arturo Frondizi of Argentina came to Palm Beach at the end of the month in order to tell Kennedy, in effect, that the Castro problem could not be met head-on, that Washington was obsessed with Cuba at the expense of the long-run needs of the hemisphere and that a public OAS fight over Cuba would only strengthen Castro.

Within the United States government, deLesseps Morrison, our ambassador to the OAS, urged economic and diplomatic sanctions even at the risk of splitting the OAS. He argued that, if we brought enough pressure on the Latin-American countries, they would come along anyway, no matter how unwillingly. The President was less sure. The point, he told Morrison at a White House meeting early in January, was to isolate Castro, not ourselves. The day before the delegation left for Punta del Este, Kennedy held a final strategy meeting with Rusk, Goodwin and me. Rusk was enigmatic about the course we could pursue. Goodwin contended cogently that we should aim for the hardest result consistent with the best possible consensus, but not sacrifice substantial consensus to symbolic hardness. Kennedy agreed. With his appreciation of internal political problems in other countries, he said that he did not want a hard line at Punta del Este to set off a chain reaction of government crises across the continent. Also he expressed concern that the voting of sanctions by a narrow margin made up of small states representing a minority of the population of Latin America would be regarded as a victory for Castro.

And so we flew south through the equatorial night, arriving in Montevideo on January 21. A motorcade took us on to Punta del Este, a placid town dotted with palm trees meandering amiably along a wind-swept beach. In a few hours the tactical problem began to fall into shape. The Central American foreign ministers were committed to a hard line; some were under instruction to walk out if sanctions were not voted. Argentina, Brazil and Mexico were passionately opposed to sanctions. Within the United States delegation, Morrison, Senator Bourke B. Hickenlooper and Congressman Armistead Selden favored an all-out effort for sanctions. Speaking with a certain sour force at the first delegation meeting, Hickenlooper said he saw no point in his trying to talk to delegates from other countries because he did not know what our policy was. "I don't even know that we have a policy. It seems to be like the father who told his son, 'Sell the cow for $25 if you can; but, if you can't sell it for 25, accept 15.' That is no policy. I still don't understand why we can't go all out for sanctions." He later said, "The Washington bureaucracy doesn't understand the depth of public feeling on this matter. But Congress knows how deeply people care. If we do not come back with *very strong* action against Castro, the whole Alliance for Progress will be in trouble." Rusk suggested that fourteen votes—the bare two-thirds necessary—for sanctions might not be enough but, if we could get sixteen, it would be different. Goodwin observed that the meeting had two objectives—to get an immediate condemnation of Castro and to strengthen the future capacity of the OAS to deal with Castro; if we pushed the first objective too far, we might lose the second.

The conference displayed Rusk at his best. Here all his qualities—his intelligence, command of detail, inexhaustible patience and effortless inscrutability—precisely fitted the requirements of the occasion. With members of Congress and the Caribbean foreign ministers harassing him on one side and representatives of the most important South American states harassing him on the other, he strove coolly to work out the best possible combination of condemnation and consensus. There were twelve sure votes for a hard policy; but among the dissenters were the largest countries of the hemisphere—Brazil, Argentina, Mexico, Chile—as well as Bolivia and Ecuador. Uruguay and Haiti hung uncertainly in the middle. The foreign minister of Haiti, recognizing the value of his vote, calmly remarked to Rusk that he came from a poor country in desperate need of aid; obviously this need would affect his vote. If the United States, which had been disengaging from aid to Haiti because of the Duvalier dictatorship, would agree to finance particular projects. . . . Rusk turned away and later sent him a message saying that, while the United States as a matter of policy did not associate economic aid and political performance, now that Haiti itself had made the link, it had to understand that any future aid would be scrutinized in the light of its role at Punta del Este.

In the meantime a new idea was emerging out of the incessant buzz of talk in the lobbies and corridors of the San Rafael Hotel—that the government of Cuba be excluded from the inter-American system. This idea had been informally advanced by Argentines seeking an alternative to mandatory sanctions. It could be done at once at this meeting; it would therefore spare wobbly governments the pain of taking something home which their parliaments would have to debate and ratify. Moreover, if the Argentines liked it, it might appeal to the Brazilians too. This proposition, along with partial economic sanctions and the establishment of a special security committee, now became the heart of the United States resolution. The congressional delegation, after 48 hours' exposure to the atmosphere of the conference, agreed that this was the best we could get and said they would defend it in Washington.

My own particular assignment was to prepare, with Walt Rostow and Goodwin, Rusk's address to the conference. The Secretary's speech, with its social and economic emphasis, provided a relief, welcome even to the Latin Americans, from the juridical disquisitions standard for such gatherings; and it went over very well. Rusk concluded by asking the foreign ministers to recognize that Cuba's alignment with "the Sino-Soviet bloc" was "incompatible" with the inter-American system, to exclude the Castro regime from the organs and bodies of that system, to end trade, especially in arms, between Cuba and the rest of the hemisphere and to seek means to defend the Americas against Castro's indirect aggression.

The problem now was to find the missing votes for the resolution. Uruguay boggled at the proposal that the OAS exclude Cuba since the OAS Charter made no provision for expulsion; then Assistant Secretary Woodward solved these juridical scruples by arguing ingeniously that the declaration of incompatibility would exclude Cuba automatically. As for Haiti, we finally yielded to blackmail and agreed to resume our aid to the airport at Port au Prince.[3] There remained the Carribbean states which still wanted mandatory sanctions; but Kennedy in Washington called Lleras Camargo in Bogotá and asked him to instruct his representative to retreat from the original insistence. The other Caribbean foreign ministers followed Colombia's example.

The result was a substantial success. Though only fourteen nations voted explicitly to exclude Cuba from the inter-American system, all twenty republics—the whole hemisphere except for Cuba itself—supported the declaration of incompatibility and the exclusion of the Castro government from the Inter-American Defense Board; nineteen voted to create a Special Consultative Committee of Experts on Security Matters to combat Cuban subversive activities; seventeen voted to suspend arms traffic with Cuba; and sixteen voted to follow this up with study looking toward further extensions of the trade embargo. The resolution on security, calling on the OAS to take all appropriate steps for "individual or collective self-defense" against "the continued intervention in this hemisphere of Sino-Soviet powers," turned out to be of particular importance. Much more progress was made toward the isolation of Cuba within the hemisphere than could have been anticipated a few months before.

[3] In the end, after new problems, we never built the airport.

6. THE RETURN OF THE MILITARY COUP

Punta del Este I had set in motion the grand project for the democratic modernization of Latin America; Punta del Este II now launched the indispensable supporting policy for the containment of Castro. But the meeting did not avert a political chain reaction. The Frondizi government, after originally floating the idea of excluding Castro from the OAS, had mysteriously glided away from its own formula and finally voted against it. One wondered later whether Frondizi, the artful dodger, may not have thrown out the idea in order to lure us away from sanctions without ever intending to support it himself. So far as his own military were concerned, it was almost the last knot in an overtwisted rope. When the *Peronistas* made impressive gains in the March election, the rope was at the end. The military now arrested Frondizi and installed the president of the senate, the next man in the line of constitutional succession, as the new President of Argentina.

By the usual criteria—literacy, per capita income, racial homogeneity—Argentina should have been the most stable democracy in Latin America. But the landed oligarchy had stunted the country's democratic development for generations; and then after the war Perón, while breaking the grip of the oligarchy, also wrecked Argentina's economy, debauched its politics and corrupted its administration. The military, having first installed and then ejected Perón, had acquired the habit of intervention in civil politics; and their action now confronted Washington with a difficult decision. In the meantime, we had acquired a new Assistant Secretary of State for Inter-American Affairs. His superiors in the Department had come to feel that Robert Woodward's temperate personality was better suited to an embassy than to the rigors of the Department in Washington. As one denizen of the seventh floor put it to me, "We need someone down there to clip Dick Goodwin's wings and keep him in channels." Early in March 1962 Woodward was told to prepare himself for an overseas assignment (he soon became ambassador to Spain, where he did his usual thoughtful job), and Edwin M. Martin, the Assistant Secretary of State for Economic Affairs, was appointed in his place.

Martin, who had been in government since the New Deal and in the State Department since 1945, was an administrator of toughness and ability. Rather liberal in his political views, rather conservative in his economic views, he was determined above all to run his own show. Though he believed deeply in the Alliance, he now allowed himself for bureaucratic reasons to be separated from his natural allies, clipping Goodwin's wings, for example, all too effectively in the next months. Dick bore his situation with quiet dignity, complaining neither to the press nor to the White House; in time he moved on to the Peace Corps. The incident reminded one again of the limits of presidential power because, though Kennedy retained his fondness for Goodwin and often called on him for special jobs, he could not, without cost to other objectives, preserve Goodwin's usefulness in a department which did not want to use him. The government lost, however, the imagination, drive and purpose Goodwin had given so abundantly to the Alliance.

The Argentine coup was Martin's first major crisis. He quickly recommended that the President issue a public condemnation. DeLesseps Morrison opposed this, however, and, unable to persuade the Department, stimulated Senators Hickenlooper and Morse to ask the President to delay comment.[4] (There were other free wheelers than Goodwin in Latin American affairs.) The senatorial intervention worked. Our embassy in Buenos Aires then recommended that we accept the new regime as the constitutional continuation of the Frondizi government. Kennedy, despite his distaste for military coups, had a realist's concern not to place himself in positions from which he could neither advance nor retreat. Since Frondizi's overthrow had been greeted with vast apathy by the Argentine people, the prudent policy seemed to be to accept the constitutional argument, however tenuous. This in due course he did.

Soon, however, a problem at once clearer and harder arose in Peru. Unlike Argentina, Peru, with its high degree of illiteracy, its low per capita income, its unassimilated Indian population and its feudal system of land tenure, seemed destined for upheaval. In Haya de la Torre's APRA party, it had the first of the *partido populares* of Latin America; but, though the *Apristas* were deeply anti-communist, their violent clashes thirty years before with the military had given each an enduring hatred of the other. Moreover, APRA was losing its hold on the young, some of whom were moving toward Fernando Belaunde Terry and his *Acción Popular* party, others of whom were tempted by Marxism. James Loeb, our ambassador to Lima, had been so shocked by the failure of the Peruvian academic community

4 Morrison describes this in his own memoir of the period, *Latin American Mission* (New York, 1965), 225.

to protest the Soviet resumption of nuclear testing that he had addressed an open letter to the Rector of the Faculty of Engineering at the National University, suggesting that the silence was "as deafening, I believe, and as dangerous as the explosions which are being unleashed on the civilized world." In the meantime, an intelligent and well-intentioned but hopelessly orthodox conservative government under Prime Minister Pedro Beltrán was making little progress in meeting the bitter problems of the country.

The next presidential election was scheduled for June 1962. In a series of brilliant and pessimistic dispatches, beginning in December 1961, Loeb predicted that the historic feuds which divided the APRA both from the military and from Belaunde's new party of the democratic left would lead to political impasse. When I saw Loeb in Lima after Punta del Este, he spoke somberly about Peru's political future. APRA, he said, was the strongest anti-communist force and the best means of keeping the working class from communism; but he was disturbed both by the intensity of its internal discipline and by the fancifulness of its economic planning. Nor did he believe that the military would accept an APRA victory. He thought he ought to return to Washington to discuss our policy in the face of various predictable contingencies.

In March, Loeb, coming to Washington, worked out his contingency planning with Edwin Martin and then with the President. At a time when the State Department was constantly being overtaken by events, Loeb's foresight gave us a valuable head start. In a number of ways in the next months the United States sought to convey to the Peruvian army and navy that we could not expect to maintain the principles of the Alliance for Progress and at the same time condone military action against a freely elected, progressive anti-communist regime. But the sequel once again suggested the limitations on American power. Haya de la Torre, while narrowly winning the election, polled only a third of the popular vote. The military, echoing Belaunde's cries of fraud, went into action. In July officers trained in the United States, commanding tanks built in the United States, knocked down the iron gates of the Presidential Palace, arrested President Manuel Prado and set up a military junta.

Washington, in accordance with previous planning, now suspended diplomatic relations. The President issued a strong statement explaining that the military coup had contravened the purposes of the inter-American system. In a second statement the State Department announced the suspension of various assistance programs. A few days later at his press conference, the President said, "We are anxious to see a return to constitutional forms in Peru. . . . We feel that this hemisphere can only be secure and free with democratic governments." Within Peru conditions remained tense. President Prado was in prison, and the APRA leaders in hiding. On July 23 Haya de la Torre called a general strike; its failure implied popular acquiescence in the military regime. Behind the scenes Loeb in Lima and Martin in Washington brought pressure on the junta to return to constitutionalism. Responding to this pressure, the junta guaranteed freedom of the press and of political opposition, even for the *Apristas*, promised free elections for June 9, 1963, and soon released most of those arrested at the time of the coup, including President Prado.

On August 1 I said to President Kennedy that I hoped he had not regretted his statement against the coup. He replied, "Certainly not." But, he added, neither the Latin American governments, most of whom were now preparing to recognize the junta (the Chilean foreign minister had already warned the United States against being more royalist than the king), nor the Peruvian people themselves, as shown by the collapse of the general strike, had given us the support for which we had hoped. His concern, he said, was that we might have staked our prestige on reversing a situation which could not be reversed—and that, when we accepted the situation, as eventually we must, we might seem to be suffering a defeat. The problem now, he said, was to demonstrate that our condemnation had caused the junta to make enough changes in its policy to render the resumption of relations possible.

This demonstration came when representatives of the junta appeared before the Council of the OAS, formally set forth the steps taken to restore civil liberties and promised solemnly to hold free elections within a year and abide by the results. On the basis of these assurances, we soon resumed relations with the Peruvian government. Though Kennedy was criticized at the time for seeming to begin one policy—non-recognition—and then to go back on it, the fact was that the suspension of relations produced exactly the desired result. There were no reprisals, civil freedom was restored, free elections were guaranteed. While most American businessmen in Peru wanted unconditional recognition of the regime, the United States government showed its independence of business pressure and its opposition to military dictatorship. The action further consolidated the confidence of democratic Latin Americans in the progressive purpose of the American President. And the Peruvian election was held, as pledged, in June 1963. This time Belaunde won a clear victory and began to give his country the programs of social reform it had so long needed.

7. TROUBLES OF THE ALLIANCE

On March 12, 1962, the anniversary of his first proposal of the Alliance for Progress, the President spoke again to the Latin American diplomats assembled at the White House.

Our "most impressive accomplishment" in the seven months since Punta del Este, he said, had been the "dramatic shift in thinking and attitude" through the hemisphere. The Charter of Punta del Este had posed the challenge of development in a way that could no longer be ignored, and had laid down the principle of "collective responsibility for the welfare of the people of the Americas." A second accomplishment was the creation of the institutional framework within which development would take place. The United States, moreover, had committed its pledged billion dollars to the first year of the Alliance. But the "ultimate responsibility for success," Kennedy declared with emphasis, "lies with the developing nation itself."

> For only you can mobilize the resources, make the reforms, set the goals and provide the energies which will transform our external assistance into an effective contribution to the progress of our continent. Only you can create the economic confidence which will encourage the free flow of capital. . . . Only you can eliminate the evils of destructive inflation, chronic trade imbalances and widespread unemployment.

The men of wealth and power in poor nations, the President continued, "must lead the fight for those basic reforms which alone can preserve the fabric of their own societies. Those who make peaceful revolution impossible will make violent revolution inevitable. These social reforms are at the heart of the Alliance for Progress."

While he spoke, criticism of the Alliance was already rising on the ground that results thus far had been disappointing both in reform and in development. No doubt the rhetoric which accompanied the birth of the Alliance had excited undue anticipations. But without the rhetoric the Alliance would have been stillborn; and the criticism of 1962 simply overlooked the realities of the situation in Latin America.

In the case of reform, it was unrealistic to expect Latin American governments to enact overnight land and tax reforms revising the basic structure of power in their societies when in our own country, for example, it had taken a strong government several years of savage political fighting to pass the relatively innocuous reforms of the New Deal. As for development, a long period was inevitable before plans and projects, separately initiated in a score of nations, proceeding in different sectors and at different paces, could generate cumulative momentum. The Marshall Plan, with all its resources of experienced entrepreneurs, veteran public administrators and skilled labor, had not wrought miracles in its first few months. P. N. Rosenstein-Rodan, now one of the OAS Panel of Experts, recalled that as late as the third year of the Marshall Plan, when the Organization for European Economic Cooperation asked its member governments to consider the consequences of a 5 per cent growth rate, practical men regarded the projection as absurd; yet all the Common Market countries achieved that rate almost at once. Given the most favorable circumstances, the seeds planted by the Alliance in 1961 and 1962 could not hope to bear visible fruit before 1964 or 1965.

Nor was the Alliance given the most favorable circumstances. In addition to the problems created by the communist threat, by rapid population growth and by internal political instability, the effort was beginning at a time of decline in world commodity prices—and in a continent where most nations depended excessively on one or two commodities as a means of earning foreign exchange. After 1953 Latin American exports (other than oil) had increased in quantity by nearly one-third but were bringing in only about 4 per cent more foreign exchange. By 1961 the price of coffee had fallen to about 60 per cent of the 1953 level. The consequent pressure on the balance of payments meant that some 40 per cent of the Alliance for Progress funds in the first year had to go for direct or indirect balance of payments loans. If, on the other hand, commodity prices had stayed at the 1953 level, Latin American export earnings would have been greater than the billion dollars committed by the United States in 1961. In an attempt to deal with a major part of this problem, the United States in 1962 took the lead in stabilizing coffee prices through a five-year international agreement including both producing and consuming countries.

In these early years, moreover, only Venezuela and Colombia (at least through Lleras's presidential term) and some Central American states, notably Costa Rica and El Salvador, had governments fully responsive to the aims of the Alliance. Brazil, the nation in South America with the greatest potentiality, was the one on which we expended most money and concern; but, after the odd departure of Quadros in 1961, the government had fallen into the hands of his vice-president, João Goulart, a weak and erratic demagogue; and it required all the persuasion of two brilliant ambassadors, Lincoln Gordon in Rio and Roberto Campos in Washington, to preserve any rationality in Brazilian-American relations. Argentina, the second largest nation, remained in melancholy stagnation and disarray.

There were problems too in Washington. Moscoso was unexcelled in communicating the political and social idealism of the Alliance—to the Latin Americans, who had great faith in him, to Congress, where he was well respected, and to his own staff. He deeply believed that the Alliance could succeed only as a revolution and a crusade. But the aid bureaucracy was not accustomed to running revolutions and crusades; and Moscoso, always a little at sea in Washington, was hard put to reconcile the conflicting pressures swirling around him. Though he committed the billion dollars each year in program and project loans, the stipulations and rigidities in the aid legislation held up actual disbursement. Even with successive deputies of unusual ability and devotion to the program, Graham Martin and William Rogers, it was difficult to break the bureaucratic threads tying the effort to the ground. "I would rather," Moscoso once said, "have a warm amateur than a cold professional." Warm professionals were not easy to come by. And the Latins themselves, who were often slow to produce good projects and effective development programs, excused their own delinquencies by blaming everything on the Washington bureaucracy.

Moreover, the North American business community had not been, with notable exceptions, enthusiastic about the Alliance. As foreign private investment in Latin America diminished in 1961 and as Latin America's own private capital continued to flow out of the hemisphere into Swiss banks, the Alliance in Washington was under growing pressure from United States companies doing Latin American business to talk less about social reform and more about private investment. They had a point, since the Alliance's capital requirements presupposed an annual flow of $300 million of United States private funds to Latin America. But the effect was further to belittle the crusade, to at-

tenuate the mystique and zeal of Punta del Este and to
lead Latin Americans to see the Alliance, despite its Latin
origins, not as a great adventure of their own, but as a
bilateral money lending operation, 'made in the U.S.A.', to
serve the interests of North American business. "No money-
lender in history has ever evoked great enthusiasm," wrote
Morales-Carrión in a memorandum to the President after
a Latin American trip in April 1962, adding in a sentence
which delighted Kennedy, "We have yet to see a charis-
matic banker."

As a consequence, the Alliance sometimes seemed
bureaucratic and incomprehensible south of the border.
"The present lingo of economic technocracy," wrote
Morales-Carrión, "simply does not reach the average Latin
American. His slogans come from the world of nationalism, not the world of technocracy." The biggest obstacle the
Alliance faced was "that it had not been wedded to Latin
American nationalism, the single most powerful psychological force now operating in Latin America. . . . Unless the
Alliance is able to ally itself with nationalism, to influence
it in a constructive direction, to translate its abstract
terminology into familiar concepts related to nation-build-
ing, the Alliance will be pouring money into a psychological void."

One sometimes felt that the communists, operating on a
shoestring in city universities or back-country villages, were
reaching the people who mattered for the future—the students, the intellectuals, the labor leaders, the nationalist
militants—while our billions were bringing us into contact
only with governments of doubtful good faith and questionable life expectancy. Latin American democratic leaders themselves began to express increasing concern about
the "degeneration" of the Alliance into a bilateral and
technical program without political drive or continental
vision. In October 1962 the Inter-American Economic and
Social Council proposed that leading Latin American statesmen review the Alliance in the hope of promoting its multilateralization and Latin-Americanization and giving it a
vital political base in the hemisphere.

Yet in our gloom we underestimate the extent to which
things were already stirring underneath the surface. For
imperceptibly the Charter of Punta del Este was transforming the politics of Latin America, imprinting the issues
of modernization on the consciousness of the political and
intellectual community and channeling the energies of both
public and private agencies as never before. All the time,
things were happening: development plans submitted, re-

form laws passed, teachers trained, schoolbooks circulated, roads and houses built, water supplies purified, land redistributed, savings and loan associations organized, economic integration among blocs of countries advanced, embers of hope kindled—never enough but a beginning. The shadows of communism, military adventurism and ancient privilege still obscured a gathering consensus which might in time bring the goals of the Alliance into reach.

Moreover, the President himself was winning in Latin America a faith and affection enjoyed by no other North American leader except Franklin Roosevelt in the long history of the Americas. His policies at home were validating his efforts in the hemisphere. Professor Albert O. Hirschman of Harvard, the expert on Latin American economic development, reported, for example, that his clash with United States Steel made a strong impression south of the border; "if Kennedy took on a real fight with a major segment of the U.S. business community, perhaps he meant what he said when he proposed social reforms for Latin America?" Moreover, the President, with his understanding of the crucial role of the Latin American intellectuals, seized opportunities to meet with academic and artistic groups at the White House—Chilean rectors and deans, Brazilian students, the writers, painters and architects assembled at the annual meetings of Robert Wool's Inter-American Committee for the arts.

In 1900 the Uruguayan writer José Enrique Rodó in his essay *Ariel* had articulated a favorite South American view of the United States: "Titanic in its concentration of will, with unprecedented triumphs in all spheres of material aggrandizement, its civilization yet produces as a whole a singular impression of insufficiency, of emptiness." Now for a moment the United States appeared no longer in the guise of Caliban but as a culture worthy in its own right of the leadership of the Americas.

XXX

AGAIN CUBA

IN 1962 THE ALLIANCE FOR PROGRESS was still an uncertainty. As for Castro, increasingly isolated within the hemisphere, he was more bent than ever on the course he had pursued since 1959. "I am a Marxist-Leninist," he said on December 2, 1961, "and I shall be a Marxist-Leninist until the last day of my life"; nor was there any reason to doubt his word. Within Cuba life had settled into drab routine. Economic planners fumbled ineffectually with agricultural and industrial programs. Popular enthusiasm diminished, even if organized opposition did not materially increase. Toward Latin America the regime maintained tenuous relations with half a dozen states and denounced the rest. Toward the United States invective was undefiled, though there were occasional intimations of a desire for something else.

In an accidental encounter after the first Punta del Este conference, Che Guevara told Richard Goodwin that the revolution was irreversible, that Cubans preferred a single-party state headed by Fidel Castro to any alternative and that Cuba's ties with the east were firmly imbedded in a common ideology. At the same time, though, Guevara discussed Cuban economic problems with surprising freedom —bungled planning, shortages in spare parts, in consumer goods and in hard currency reserves—and said that, while any real understanding with the United States would be impossible, what about some sort of *modus vivendi?* He indicated that Cuba might be prepared to pay compensation in trade for expropriated properties and to forswear formal alliance, though not ideological loyalty, to the east. Goodwin saw this—I am sure, quite correctly—as an attempt to persuade Washington to call off the policy of containment before the Latin American governments generalized that policy, as they were soon to do at the second Punta del Este. Castro stated the limits of a *modus vivendi* more exactly on January 23, 1962: "How can the rope and the hanged man understand each other or the chain and the slave? Imperialism is the chain. Understanding is impossible. . . . We are so different that there are no bonds between us. . . . Some day there will be links—when there is a revolution in the United States."

1. THE GAMBLE

On July 2, 1962, Raúl Castro, the Minister of the Armed Forces, arrived in Moscow. Either before his arrival or very soon thereafter the Soviet and Cuban governments arrived at a startling decision: that Soviet nuclear missiles were to be secretly installed in Cuba in the fall.

The Soviet Union had never before placed nuclear missiles in any other country—neither in the communist nations of Eastern Europe, nor, even in the season of their friendship, in Red China. Why should it now send nuclear missiles to a country thousands of miles away, lying within the zone of vital interest of their main adversary, a land, moreover, headed by a willful leader of, from the Russian viewpoint, somewhat less than total reliability? Castro, with characteristic loquacity, later produced a confusion of explanations. He told a Cuban audience in January 1963 that sending the missiles was a Soviet idea; he repeated this to Claude Julien of *Le Monde* in March 1963; in May he described it to Lisa Howard of the American Broadcasting Company as "simultaneous action on the part of both governments"; then in October he told Herbert Matthews of the *New York Times* that it was a Cuban idea, only to tell Jean Daniel of *L'Express* in November that it was a Soviet idea; in January 1964, when Matthews called him about the Daniel story, Castro claimed again that it was a Cuban idea; and, when Cyrus Sulzberger of the *New York Times* asked him in October 1964, Castro, pleading that the question raised security problems, said cagily, "Both Russia and Cuba participated."

As for the Russians, Khrushchev told the Supreme Soviet in December 1962, "We carried weapons there at the request of the Cuban government . . . including the stationing of a couple of score of Soviet IRBMs [intermediate-range ballistic missiles] in Cuba. These weapons were to be in the hands of Soviet military men. . . . Our aim was only to defend Cuba." The presence of the missiles, Khrushchev continued, was designed to make the imperialists understand that, if they tried to invade Cuba, "the war which they threatened to start stood at their own borders, so that they would realize more realistically the dangers of thermonuclear war." This was all very noble, and the defense of Cuba was certainly a side effect of the Soviet action. But the defense of Cuba did not really require the introduction of long-range nuclear missiles. One may be sure that Khrushchev, like any other national leader, took *that* decision not for Cuban reasons but for Soviet reasons. Pending Khrushchev's reminiscences, one can only speculate as to what these Soviet reasons were.

In a general sense, the decision obviously represented the supreme Soviet probe of American intentions. No doubt a 'total victory' faction in Moscow had long been denouncing the government's 'no-win' policy and arguing that the Soviet Union could safely use the utmost nuclear pressure against the United States because the Americans were too rich or soft or liberal to fight. Now Khrushchev was prepared to give this argument its crucial test. A successful nuclearization of Cuba would make about sixty-four medium-range (around 1000 miles) and intermediate-range (1500-2000 miles) nuclear missiles effective against the United States and thereby come near to doubling Soviet striking capacity against American targets.[1] Since this would still leave the United States with at least a 2 to 1 superiority in nuclear power targeted against the Soviet Union, the shift in the military balance of power would be less crucial than that in the political balance. Every country in the world, watching so audacious an action ninety miles from the United States, would wonder whether it could ever thereafter trust Washington's resolution and protection. More particularly, the change in the nuclear equilibrium would permit Khrushchev, who had been dragging out the Berlin negotiation all year, to reopen that question—perhaps in a personal appearance before the United Nations General Assembly in November—with half the United States lying within range of nuclear missiles poised for delivery across the small stretch of water from Florida. It was a staggering project—staggering in its recklessness, staggering in its misconception of the American response, staggering in its rejection of the ground rules for coexistence among the superpowers which Kennedy had offered in Vienna.

The decision having been made, the next problem was the development of a plan. Moscow evidently saw the operation in two stages—first, the augmentation of Cuban defensive capabilities by bringing in surface-to-air anti-aircraft (SAM) missiles and MIG-21 fighters; then, as soon as the SAMs were in place to protect the bases and deter photographic reconnaissance (a SAM had brought down the U-2 over Russia in 1960), sending in offensive weapons, both ballistic missiles and Ilyushin-28 jet aircraft able to deliver nuclear bombs. The first stage, involving only defensive weapons, required no special concealment. The

[1] The Soviet Union had under construction in Cuba twenty-four launch pads for medium-range and sixteen for intermediate-range missiles. The medium-range launch pads could be re-used. Forty-two medium-range missiles were brought to Cuba; it seems reasonable to presume that at least six more were on the way, so that each pad would have two. Apparently no intermediate-range missiles ever arrived. It took much longer to construct bases for them, and there may have seemed no point in sending the missiles until the bases were nearer completion. At any rate, the Soviet plan seems to have contemplated the installation of a minimum of sixty-four missiles.

second stage called for the most careful and complex program of deception. One can only imagine the provisions made in Moscow and Havana through the summer to ship the weapons, to receive them, unload them, assemble them, erect bases for them, install them on launching pads—all with a stealth and speed designed to confront the United States one day in November or December with a fully operational Soviet nuclear arsenal across the water in Cuba.

2. THE SURVEILLANCE

By late July the Soviet shipments began to arrive. Three weeks later CIA sent an urgent report to the President that "something new and different" was taking place in Soviet aid operations to Cuba. There were perhaps 5000 Soviet 'specialists' now in Cuba; military construction of some sort was going on; more ships were on their way with more specialists and more electronic and construction equipment. The data suggested that the Soviet Union was refurbishing the Cuban air defense system, presumably by putting up a network of SAM sites.

The intelligence community concluded that Moscow, having resolved after a time of indecision that it had a large stake in Castro's survival, had decided to insure the regime against external attack. It could thereby hope to secure the Soviet bridgehead in the western hemisphere, strengthen Castro's prestige in Latin America and show the world Washington's inability to prevent such things at its very doorstep. This all seemed logical enough. Obviously Moscow had calculated that the United States, with the Bay of Pigs still in the world's recollection, could not convincingly object to Castro's taking defensive precautions against another invasion. No one in the intelligence community (with one exception; for the thought flickered through the mind of John McCone) supposed that the Soviet Union would conceivably go beyond defensive weapons. The introduction of nuclear missiles, for example, would obviously legitimatize an American response, even possibly an invasion of Cuba. Our best Soviet experts in State and CIA considered Khrushchev too wary and Soviet foreign policy too rational to court a risk of this magnitude.

Nonetheless, when a U-2 flight on August 29 showed clear evidence of SAM sites under construction, the President decided to put Moscow on notice. On September 4, the Secretary of State brought over a draft of the warning. The President showed it to the Attorney General, who recommended stiffening it with an explicit statement that we would not tolerate the import of offensive weapons. The draft as revised read that, while we had no evidence of "significant offensive capability either in Cuban hands or under Soviet direction," should it be otherwise, "the gravest issues would arise."

On the same day the Soviet Ambassador in Washington gave the Attorney General an unusual personal message from Khrushchev for the President. The Soviet leader pledged in effect that he would stir up no incidents before the congressional elections in November. Then a week later, in the midst of a long and wearying disquisition on world affairs, Moscow said flatly that the "armaments and military equipment sent to Cuba are designed exclusively for defensive purposes." It added:

> There is no need for the Soviet Union to shift its weapons for the repulsion of aggression, for a retaliatory blow, to any other country, for instance Cuba. Our nuclear weapons are so powerful in their explosive force and the Soviet Union has so powerful rockets to carry these nuclear warheads, that there is no need to search for sites for them beyond the boundaries of the Soviet Union.

The statement continued truculently by accusing the United States of "preparing for aggression against Cuba and other peace-loving states," concluding that "if the aggressors unleash war our armed forces must be ready to strike a crushing retaliatory blow at the aggressor." The President responded calmly on September 13 at his press conference that the new shipments did not constitute a serious threat but that if at any time Cuba were to "become an offensive military base of significant capacity for the Soviet Union, then this country will do whatever must be done to protect its own security and that of its allies." In the meantime, he asked Congress for stand-by authority to call up the reserves.

He had also taken the precaution of doubling the frequency of the U-2 overflights of Cuba. The evidence from flights on September 5, 17, 26 and 29 and October 5 and 7, as well as from other sources, indicated a continuing military build-up large in its proportions but still defensive in its character. The government saw no reason as yet to believe that Khrushchev intended anything beyond this; he had not, so far as we knew, lost his mind. Only John McCone had his personal presentiment that he might be planning the installation of offensive missiles. However, given the prevailing complacency on this point, McCone himself did not take this thought seriously enough to prevent his going off now for a three weeks' honeymoon in Europe. The

White House staff worried about this increasingly visible Soviet presence, but it seemed to me much more a political threat to Latin America than a military threat to the United States. I found myself, as I told the President on September 13, relatively a hard-liner and felt that the State Department should tell the Soviet Ambassador in cold and tough fashion that persistence in the arming of Cuba would cause both an increase in our defense budget and a surge of national indignation which would color every other issue between our two countries. But, when I advanced this view at the Bundy staff meeting, I was confronted with the wholly proper question: "OK, but how far would you carry it if they keep on doing what you object to?"

And, across the world, ships were sliding out of Black Sea harbors with nuclear technicians in their cabins and nuclear missiles in their holds. Khrushchev, having done his best to lull Kennedy by public statements and private messages, now in early September put the second stage of his plan into operation. He could hope that the hurricane season might interfere with the U-2 overflights and that the fall political campaign might inhibit the administration from taking drastic action. Moreover, he had an advantage unknown to us: Soviet engineering had enormously reduced the time required for the erection of nuclear missile sites. As Roberta Wohlstetter, the searching analyst of both Pearl Harbor and the Cuba crisis, later wrote, "The rapidity of the Russians' installation was in effect a logistical surprise comparable to the technological surprise at the time of Pearl Harbor."

In the meantime, Washington had been receiving a flow of tales about nuclear installations through refugee channels. Such reports had been routine for eighteen months. No one could be sure whether the sources in Cuba could tell a surface-to-air from a surface-to-surface missile; moreover, this government recalled that it had been misled by Cuban refugees before. Lacking photographic verification, the intelligence community treated the information with reserve. After consideration, it recommended on October 4 a U-2 flight over western Cuba. The recommendation was approved on October 10, and from the eleventh to the thirteenth the pilot and plane waited for the weather to break. Sunday the fourteenth dawned beautiful and cloudless.

Senator Kenneth Keating of New York had also been receiving the refugee reports, and he treated them with no reserve at all. At the end of August he began a campaign to force the government into some unspecified form of action. In October he began to talk about offensive missile bases. If he felt the national safety involved, Keating was plainly right to make his case with all the urgency at his command. Some, however, discerned other motives, especially with the approach of the fall election. As Roger Hilsman, Director of Intelligence and Research at the State Department, later wrote, "The charge that Keating was more interested in personal publicity than in his country's welfare may be extreme. But until the Senator comes forward with a better explanation than he has so far supplied, one of two possible conclusions is inescapable: Either Senator Keating was peddling someone's rumors for some purpose of his own, despite the highly dangerous international situation; or, alternatively, he had information the United States Government did not have that could have guided a U-2 to the missile sites before October 14, and at less risk to the pilot."

Now on the fourteenth the U-2 plane returned from its mission. The negatives went swiftly to the processing laboratories, then to the interpretation center, where specialists pored over the blown-up photographs frame by frame. Late Monday afternoon, reading the obscure and intricate markings, they identified a launching pad, a series of buildings for ballistic missiles and even one missile on the ground in San Cristóbal.

3. THE EXECUTIVE COMMITTEE

About 8:30 that evening the CIA informed Bundy of the incredible discovery. Bundy reflected on whether to inform the President immediately, but he knew that Kennedy would demand the photographs and supporting interpretation in order to be sure the report was right and knew also it would take all night to prepare the evidence in proper form. Furthermore, an immediate meeting would collect officials from dinner parties all over town, signal Washington that something was up and end any hope of secrecy. It was better, Bundy thought, to let the President have a night's sleep in preparation for the ordeal ahead.

The President was having breakfast in his dressing gown at eight forty-five on Tuesday morning when Bundy brought the news. Kennedy asked at once about the nature of the evidence. As soon as he was convinced that it was conclusive, he said that the United States must bring the threat to an end: one way or another the missiles would have to be removed. He then directed Bundy to institute low-level photographic flights and to set up a meeting of top officials.

Privately he was furious: if Khrushchev could pull this after all his protestations and denials, how could he ever he trusted on anything?

The meeting, beginning at eleven forty-five that morning, went on with intermissions for the rest of the week. The group soon became known as the Executive Committee, presumably of the National Security Council; the press later dubbed it familiarly ExCom, though one never heard that phrase at the time. It carried on its work with the most exacting secrecy: nothing could be worse than to alert the Russians before the United States had decided on its own course. For this reason its members—the President, the Vice-President, Rusk, McNamara, Robert Kennedy, General Taylor, McCone, Dillon, Adlai Stevenson, Bundy, Sorensen, Ball, Gilpatric, Llewellyn Thompson, Alexis Johnson, Edwin Martin, with others brought in on occasion, among them Dean Acheson and Robert Lovett—had to attend their regular meetings, keep as many appointments as possible and preserve the normalities of life. Fortunately the press corps, absorbed in the congressional campaign, was hardly disposed or situated to notice odd comings and goings. And so the President himself went off that night to dinner at Joseph Alsop's as if nothing had happened. After dinner the talk turned to the contingencies of history, the odds for or against any particular event taking place. The President was silent for a time. Then he said, "Of course, if you simply consider mathematical chances, the odds are even on an H-bomb war within ten years." Perhaps he added to himself, "or within ten days."

In the Executive Committee consideration was free, intent and continuous. Discussion ranged widely, as it had to in a situation of such exceptional urgency, novelty and difficulty. When the presence of the President seemed by virtue of the solemnity of his office to have a constraining effect, preliminary meetings were held without him. Every alternative was laid on the table for examination, from living with the missiles to taking them out by surprise attack, from making the issue with Castro to making it with Khrushchev. In effect, the members walked around the problem, inspecting it first from this angle, then from that, viewing it in a variety of perspectives. In the course of the long hours of thinking aloud, hearing new arguments, entertaining new considerations, they almost all found themselves moving from one position to another. "If we had had to act on Wednesday in the first twenty-four hours," the President said later, "I don't think probably we would have chosen as prudently as we finally did." They had, it was estimated, about ten days before the missiles would be on pads ready for firing. The deadline defined the strategy. It meant that the response could not, for example, be confided to the United Nations, where the Soviet delegate would have ample opportunity to stall action until the nuclear weapons were in place and on target. It meant that we could not even risk the delay involved in consulting our allies. It meant that the total responsibility had to fall on the United States and its President.

On the first Tuesday morning the choice for a moment seemed to lie between an air strike or acquiescence—and the President had made clear that acquiescence was impossible. Listening to the discussion, the Attorney General scribbled a wry note: "I now know how Tojo felt when he was planning Pearl Harbor." Then he said aloud that the group needed more alternatives: surely there was some course in between bombing and doing nothing; suppose, for example, we were to bring countervailing pressure by placing nuclear missiles in Berlin? The talk continued, and finally the group dispersed for further reflection.

The next step was military preparation for Caribbean contingencies. A Navy-Marine amphibious exercise in the area, long scheduled for this week, provided a convenient cover for the build-up of an amphibious task force, soon including 40,000 Marines; there were 5000 more in Guantánamo. The Army's 82nd and 101st Airborne Divisions were made ready for immediate deployment; altogether the Army soon gathered more than 100,000 troops in Florida. SAC bombers left Florida airfields to make room for tactical fighter aircraft flown in from bases all over the country. Air defense facilities were stripped from places outside the range of the Cuban missiles and re-installed in the Southeast. As the days went by, 14,000 reservists were recalled to fly transports in the event of airborne operations.

In the meantime, the Pentagon undertook a technical analysis of the requirements for a successful strike. The conclusion, as it evolved during the week, was that a 'surgical' strike confined to the nuclear missile bases alone would leave the airports and IL-28s untouched; moreover, we could not be sure in advance that we had identified or could destroy all the missile sites. A limited strike therefore might expose the United States to nuclear retaliation. Military prudence called for a much larger strike to eliminate all sources of danger; this would require perhaps 500 sorties. Anything less, the military urged, would destroy our credibility before the world and leave our own nation in intolerable peril. Moreover, this was a heaven-sent oppor-

tunity to get rid of the Castro regime forever and re-
establish the security of the hemisphere.

It was a strong argument, urged by strong men. But there
were arguments on the other side. The Soviet experts pointed
out that even a limited strike would kill the Russians manning the missile sites and might well provoke the Soviet
Union into drastic and unpredictable response, perhaps nuclear war. The Latin American experts added that a massive
strike would kill thousands of innocent Cubans and damage
the United States permanently in the hemisphere. The Europeanists said the world would regard a surprise strike as
an excessive response. Even if it did not produce Soviet
retaliation against the United States, it would invite the
Russians to move against Berlin in circumstances where
the blame would fall, not on them, but on us. It would
thereby give Moscow a chance to shift the venue to a place
where the stake was greater than Cuba and our position
weaker. In the Caribbean, we had overwhelming superiority
in conventional military force; the only recourse for the
Soviet Union there would be to threaten the world with
nuclear war. But in Berlin, where the Russians had overwhelming conventional superiority, it was the United States
which would have to flourish nuclear bombs.

All these considerations encouraged the search for alternatives. When the Executive Committee met on Wednesday, Secretary McNamara advanced an idea which had
been briefly mentioned the day before and from which he
did not thereafter deviate—the conception of a naval
blockade designed to stop the further entry of offensive
weapons into Cuba and hopefully to force the removal of
the missiles already there. Here was a middle course between inaction and battle; a course which exploited our
superiority in local conventional power and would permit
subsequent movement either toward war or toward peace.

As the discussion proceeded through Thursday, the supporters of the air strike marshaled their arguments against
the blockade. They said that it would not neutralize the
weapons already within Cuba, that it could not possibly
bring enough pressure on Khrushchev to remove those
weapons, that it would permit work to go ahead on the
bases and that it would mean another Munich. The act of
stopping and searching ships would engage us with Russians instead of Cubans. The obvious retort to our blockade
of Cuba would be a Soviet blockade of Berlin. Despite such
arguments, however, the majority of the Executive Committee by the end of the day was tending toward a blockade.

That afternoon, in the interests of normality, the President received the Soviet Foreign Minister Andrei Gromyko. It was one of the more extraordinary moments of an extraordinary week. Kennedy knew that there were Soviet nuclear missiles in Cuba. Gromyko unquestionably knew this too, but did not know that Kennedy knew it. His emphasis was rather grimly on Berlin, almost as if to prepare the ground for demands later in the autumn. When the talk turned to Cuba, Gromyko heavily stressed the Cuban fears of an American invasion and said with due solemnity that the Soviet aid had "solely the purpose of contributing to the defense capabilities of Cuba"; "if it were otherwise," the Russian continued, "the Soviet Government would never become involved in rendering such assistance." To dispel any illusion about possible American reactions, the President read the Foreign Minister the key sentences from his statement of September 13. He went no further because he did not wish to indicate his knowledge until he had decided on his course.

In the evening the President met with the Executive Committee. Listening again to the alternatives over which he had been brooding all week, he said crisply, "Whatever you fellows are recommending today you will be sorry about a week from now." He was evidently attracted by the idea of the blockade. It avoided war, preserved flexibility and offered Khrushchev time to reconsider his actions. It could be carried out within the framework of the Organization of American States and the Rio Treaty. Since it could be extended to non-military items as occasion required, it could become an instrument of steadily intensifying pressure. It would avoid the shock effect of a surprise attack, which would hurt us politically through the world and might provoke Moscow to an insensate response against Berlin or the United States itself. If it worked, the Russians could retreat with dignity. If it did not work, the Americans retained the option of military action. In short, the blockade, by enabling us to proceed one step at a time, gave us control over the future. Kennedy accordingly directed that preparations be made to put the weapons blockade into effect on Monday morning.

The next day the President, keeping to his schedule, left Washington for a weekend of political barnstorming in Ohio and Illinois. In Springfield, Illinois, after a speech at the State Fairgrounds, he paused to lay flowers on Lincoln's tomb.

4. THE DECISION

Kennedy left behind a curiously restless group of advisers.

This became evident when they met at the State Department at eleven on Friday morning. Over Ted Sorensen's protest that a decision had been reached the night before and should not be reopened now, several began to re-argue the inadequacy of the blockade. Someone said: Why not confront the world with a *fait accompli* by taking out the bases in a clean and swift operation? It was a test of wills, another said, and the sooner there was a showdown, the better. Someone else said that it was now or never; we must hit the bases before they became operational. If we took a decision that morning, the planes could strike on Sunday. But, if we committed ourselves to a blockade, it would be hard, if not impossible, to move on thereafter to military action.

Secretary McNamara, however, firmly reaffirmed his opposition to a strike and his support for the blockade. Then Robert Kennedy, speaking with quiet intensity, said that he did not believe that, with all the memory of Pearl Harbor and all the responsibility we would have to bear in the world afterward, the President of the United States could possibly order such an operation. For 175 years we had not been that kind of country. Sunday-morning surprise blows on small nations were not in our tradition. Thousands of Cubans would be killed without warning, and hundreds of Russians too. We were fighting for something more than survival, and a sneak attack would constitute a betrayal of our heritage and our ideals. The blockade, the Attorney General concluded, would demonstrate the seriousness of our determination to get the missiles out of Cuba and at the same time allow Moscow time and room to pull back from its position of peril. It was now proposed that the committee break up into working groups to write up the alternative courses for the President—one to analyze the quarantine policy, the other to analyze the strike. Then everyone dispersed to meet again at four o'clock for a discussion of the competing scenarios.[2]

At the second meeting the balance of opinion clearly swung back to the blockade (though, since a blockade was

---

[2] The Secretary of State took little part in these discussions. John M. Hightower, who covers the State Department for the Associated Press, wrote on August 22, 1965: "Criticism over his role in the missile crisis angered Rusk to the point that he heatedly defended it in talks with newsmen on one or two occasions. He said that the responsibility of the Secretary of State was to advise the President and he did not think he should commit himself before all the facts were in. Therefore he withdrew himself from the argument for several days though Under Secretary of State George Ball, instructed by Rusk to take a free hand, presented the State Department viewpoint."

technically an act of war, it was thought better to refer to it as a quarantine). In retrospect most participants regarded Robert Kennedy's speech as the turning point. The case was strengthened too when the military representatives conceded that a quarantine now would not exclude a strike later. There was brief discussion of a *démarche* to Castro, but it was decided to concentrate on Khrushchev. Then they turned to the problem of the missiles already in Cuba. Someone observed that the United States would have to pay a price to get them out; perhaps we should throw in our now obsolescent and vulnerable Jupiter missile bases in Italy and Turkey, whose removal the Joint Congressional Committee on Atomic Energy as well as the Secretary of Defense had recommended in 1961. After a couple of hours, Adlai Stevenson, who had had to miss the day's meetings because of UN commitments, arrived from New York. He expressed his preference for the quarantine over the strike but wondered whether it might not be better to try the diplomatic route also. We must, he said, start thinking about our negotiating position; for example, a settlement might include the neutralization of Cuba under international guarantees and UN inspection; demilitarization would, of course, include our own base at Guantánamo as well as the Soviet installations. The integrity of Cuba should be guaranteed. He also echoed the suggestion that we might want to consider giving up the Italian and Turkish bases now, since we were planning to do so eventually.

The President, still campaigning, received reports from his brother in Washington. The schedule now called for a speech to the nation on Sunday night. By Saturday morning, however, it was evident that preparations would not be complete in time, so it was decided to hold things for another twenty-four hours. Meanwhile, the President, pleading a cold, canceled the rest of his political trip and returned to Washington. Before leaving Chicago, he called Jacqueline and suggested that she and the children come back from Glen Ora, where they had gone for the weekend.

That afternoon he presided over the Executive Committee and its final debate. McNamara impressively presented the case for the blockade. The military, with some civilian support, argued for the strike. Stevenson spoke with force about the importance of a political program, the President agreeing in principle but disagreeing with his specific proposals. A straw vote indicated eleven for the quarantine, six for the strike. The President observed that everyone should hope his plan was not adopted; there just was no clear-cut answer. When someone proposed that each participant write down his recommendation, Kennedy said he did not want people, if things went wrong, claiming that their plans would have worked. Then he issued orders to get everything ready for the quarantine. On Sunday morning a final conference with the military leaders satisfied him that the strike would be a mistake. His course was now firmly set.

5. THE CRISIS

I knew nothing about any of this until late Friday, October 19, when Adlai Stevenson phoned me, saying casually that he was in Washington and wondered when we could get together. He was staying at the house of his friend Dr. Paul Magnuson across the street from my own house in Georgetown, and we agreed to ride down to the State Department together the next day. When we met after breakfast on Saturday morning, he beckoned me into the Magnuson house. "I don't want to talk in front of the chauffeur," he said; and then in a moment, "Do you know what the secret discussions this week have been about?" I said I knew of no discussions; the President was out campaigning; I had presumed that everything was fine. Adlai, observing gravely there was trouble and he had the President's permission to tell me about it, described the seesaw during the week between the diplomatic and military solutions. The quarantine, he now felt, was sure to win. He would have to make a speech early in the week at the Security Council, and he wanted me to help on it. He outlined the argument and, with due discretion, I set to work.

The secret had been superbly kept. But later in the day, when the President returned from the campaign and Rusk canceled a speech that night, a sense of premonitory excitement began to engulf Washington. Already those whose business it was to sniff things out were on the track. In the British Embassy, where a delegation of intelligence officers had come to Washington for a long-scheduled conference with the CIA, suspicions had been aroused early in the week when the meetings drew a diminishing American representation or were called off altogether. By process of elimination the 007s decided on Friday that it must be Cuba. The *New York Times*, noting the troop movements and other unusual activities, also deduced Cuba by the weekend and even speculated about nuclear missiles. James Reston wrote the story and checked it with the White House. The President himself called Orville Dryfoos, the publisher of the *Times*, to say that publication might confront him with a Moscow ultimatum before he had the chance to put his own plans into effect; once again, the *Times* changed a story about Cuba. By Saturday night the town was alive with speculation and anticipation. A good deal of the government found itself late that evening at a dance given by the James Rowes. Here the gap between the witting and the unwitting could almost be detected by facial expressions—on the one hand, anxiety tinged with self-satisfaction; on the other, irritation and frustration. Henry Brandon, the Washington correspondent of the London *Sunday Times,* who had just returned from a trip to Cuba, began to wonder when a succession of top officials asked him elaborately off-hand questions about the mood in Havana.

On Sunday Stevenson, contemplating the problems of gathering UN backing for the quarantine, wrote down his thoughts about our UN strategy. He saw no hope of mustering enough votes in the UN to authorize action against Cuba in advance; but the OAS offered an opportunity for multilateral support, and OAS approval could provide some protection in law and a great deal in public opinion. As for the UN, he said, we must seize the initiative, bringing our case to the Security Council at the same time we imposed the quarantine. In order to avert resolutions against the quarantine, he continued, we should be ready to propose a political path out of the miliary crisis. His negotiating centered on the removal of Soviet military equipment and personnel—i.e., missiles, installations and the several thousand Russian specialists—under UN observation and the introduction of UN influence into Cuba in the hope of ending communist domination of the Cuban government. He would throw a non-invasion guarantee and Guantánamo into the bargain to evidence our restraint and good faith. Exercising the prerogative freely employed that week by nearly all his colleagues, he now wrote that Turkey and Italy should not be included; this would only divert attention from the Cuban threat to the general issue of foreign bases. That problem might later be considered apart from Cuba in the context of general disarmament.

The President, however, rightly regarded any political program as premature. He wanted to concentrate on a single issue—the enormity of the introduction of the missiles and the absolute necessity for their removal. Stevenson's negotiating program was accordingly rejected. Stevenson, when I saw him that weekend, took this realistically; he felt he had done his job as the custodian of our UN interests in making the recommendation, and the decision was the President's. However, some of his colleagues on the Executive Committee felt strongly that the thought of negotiations at this point would be taken as an admission of the moral weakness of our case and the military weakness of our posture. They worried considerably over the weekend (and some of them vocally thereafter) whether, denied his political program, Stevenson would make the American argument with sufficient force in the UN debate.

I spent all day Sunday till well after midnight working at the State Department with Harlan Cleveland, Joseph Sisco and Thomas Wilson on the UN speech. At ten o'clock on Monday morning the President called me in to instruct me to go to New York and assist Stevenson on the UN presentation. He was in a calm and reflective mood. It was strange, he said, how no one in the intelligence community had anticipated the Soviet attempt to transform Cuba into a nuclear base; everyone had assumed that the Russians would not be so stupid as to offer us this pretext for intervention. I asked why he thought Khrushchev had done such an amazing thing. He said that, first, it might draw Russia and China closer together, or at least strengthen the Soviet position in the communist world, by showing that Moscow was capable of bold action in support of a communist revolution; second, that it would radically redefine the setting in which the Berlin problem could be reopened after the election; third, that it would deal the United States a tremendous political blow. When I remarked that the Russians must have supposed we would not respond, Kennedy said, "They thought they had us either way. If we did nothing, we would be dead. If we reacted, they hoped to put us in an exposed position, whether with regard to Berlin or Turkey or the UN."

I met with him again at eleven to go over the draft of the UN speech with Rusk, Robert Kennedy and others. The President suggested a few omissions, including a passage threatening an American strike if the Soviet build-up in Cuba continued; he preferred to leave that to Moscow's imagination. The Attorney General drew me aside to say, "We're counting on you to watch things in New York. . . . We will have to make a deal at the end, but we must stand absolutely firm now. Concessions must come at the end of negotiation, not at the beginning." Then, clutching the speech, I caught the first plane to New York.

In Washington everything awaited the President's television broadcast that night to the nation. Sorensen had been laboring over the draft since Friday. Kennedy himself was never more composed. At four o'clock he had an appointment with Prime Minister Milton Obote of Uganda. Wholly at ease, he talked for forty-five minutes about the problems of Africa and Uganda as if he had nothing on his mind and all the time in the world. Angier Biddle Duke of the State Department remarked to Obote on their way back to Blair House that a crisis of some sort was imminent; the Ugandan was incredulous and, when he heard Kennedy's speech that evening, forever impressed.

At five o'clock Kennedy saw the congressional leaders, many of whom had flown in from their home states in Air Force planes. He showed them the U-2 photographs and told them what he proposed to do. Senator Russell of Georgia disagreed; the quarantine, he said, would be too slow and too risky—the only solution was invasion. To the President's surprise, Fulbright, who had opposed invasion so eloquently eighteen months before, now supported Russell. The President listened courteously but was in no way shaken in his decision. (Kennedy told me later, "The trouble is that, when you get a group of senators together, they are always dominated by the man who takes the boldest and strongest line. That is what happened the other day. After Russell spoke, no one wanted to take issue with him. When you can talk to them individually, they are reasonable.")

Then at seven o'clock the speech: his expression grave, his voice firm and calm, the evidence set forth without emotion, the conclusion unequivocal—"The purpose of these bases can be none other than to provide a nuclear strike capability against the Western Hemisphere." He recited the Soviet assurances, now revealed as "deliberate deception," and called the Soviet action "a deliberately provocative and unjustified change in the status quo which cannot be accepted by this country, if our courage and our commitments are ever to be trusted again by either friend or foe." Our "unswerving objective," he continued, was to end this nuclear threat to the Americans. He then laid out what he called with emphasis his *initial* steps: a quarantine on all offensive military equipment under shipment to Cuba; an intensified surveillance of Cuba itself; a declaration that any missile launched from Cuba would be regarded as an attack by the Soviet Union on the United States, requiring full retaliatory response upon the Soviet Union; an immediate convention of the Organization of American States to consider the threat to hemisphere security; an emergency meeting of the UN Security Council to consider the threat to world peace; and an appeal to Chairman Khrushchev "to abandon this course of world domination, and to join in an historic effort to end the perilous arms race and to transform the history of man."

He concluded with quiet solemnity. "My fellow citizens: let no one doubt that this is a difficult and dangerous effort. . . . No one can foresee precisely what course it will take or what costs or casualties will be incurred. . . . But the greatest danger of all would be to do nothing. . . . Our goal is not the victory of might, but the vindication of right —not peace at the expense of freedom, but both peace *and* freedom, here in this hemisphere, and, we hope, around the world. God willing, that goal will be achieved."

After the broadcast the President returned to the Mansion, sought out Caroline and told her stories until it was time for dinner. He dined alone with Jacqueline.

6. THE REACTION

We listened to the speech clustered around a television set in Stevenson's office in New York. I had found Adlai unperturbed in the midst of pandemonium. The Mission was a frenzy of activity in preparation for the Security Council. The UN had never seemed so much like a permanent political convention: so many people to be considered and cajoled, so many issues going at once, such an inherent unpredictability about the parliamentary sequence. From the moment of the President's statement, Stevenson had to talk so much to UN delegates from other nations that he had little time left for his own speeches and strategy. Through Monday evening and Tuesday morning he snatched moments to revise and edit his remarks for the Security Council. It was reminiscent of his presidential campaigns: the last part of his address was still in the typewriter at the Mission on Tuesday afternoon when he had already begun to speak across the street at the UN.

The speech began at four o'clock. The OAS had been meeting since nine that morning. Edwin Martin had done a splendid job briefing the OAS ambassadors the night before, and Secretary Rusk, invoking the security resolution of Punta del Este, was now offering a resolution authorizing the use of force, individually or collectively, to carry out the quarantine. No one could doubt the OAS sentiment, but a number of ambassadors had not yet received instructions from their governments. As a result, the resolution establishing the legal basis for United States action was not passed until Stevenson was well into his speech.[3]

[3] It was passed unanimously. Uruguay, still awaiting instructions, abstained on Tuesday but changed its vote to affirmative on Wednesday.

Martin, by prior arrangement, notified Harlan Cleveland the moment the OAS acted, and Cleveland instantly called Sisco in New York. Watching Stevenson on television, Cleveland could see Sisco leave the chamber to take the call, then in a moment return and place the text of the resolution on the desk in front of Stevenson. Stevenson, absorbed in his speech, talked on, apparently unaware of the sheet of paper before him. At this moment Kennedy, with characteristic attention to detail, called Cleveland and asked whether Stevenson knew about the OAS action. Cleveland replied that he had sent a message but feared that Adlai had not seen it. Just then on the screen Stevenson reached for the paper. Kennedy, who was also watching television, said, "I guess he has it now."

In New York Stevenson, who had been speaking with extraordinary eloquence to a hushed chamber, now read the OAS resolution. In another moment he concluded: "Since the end of the Second World War, there has been no threat to the vision of peace so profound, no challenge to the world of the Charter so fateful. The hopes of mankind are concentrated in this room. . . . Let [this day] be remembered, not as the day when the world came to the edge of nuclear war, but as the day when men resolved to let nothing thereafter stop them in their quest for peace." The President immediately dictated a telegram:

DEAR ADLAI: I WATCHED YOUR SPEECH THIS AFTERNOON WITH GREAT SATISFACTION. IT HAS GIVEN OUR CASE A GREAT START. . . . THE UNITED STATES IS FORTUNATE TO HAVE YOUR ADVOCACY. YOU HAVE MY WARM AND PERSONAL THANKS.

And now the tension was rising. In Cuba workmen were laboring day and night to complete the bases. Forty-two medium-range nuclear missiles were being unpacked and prepared for launching pads with desperate speed. IL-28 aircraft were being assembled. On the Atlantic at least twenty-five Soviet merchant ships, some no doubt loaded with intermediate-range missiles, were steaming toward Cuba, their course thus far unaltered after the President's speech. Ninety ships of the American fleet, backed up by sixty-eight aircraft squadrons and eight aircraft carriers, were moving into position to intercept and search the onrushing ships. In Florida and neighboring states the largest United States invasion force since the Second World War was gathering. In Moscow, the Soviet government in a long and angry statement insisted that the weapons in Cuba were defensive, ignored the charges of nuclear missiles and savagely denounced the American quarantine.

The United Nations was only the first step in gaining world understanding of the American position. Africa now assumed vital strategic importance because Soviet flights to Cuba would have to refuel at African airports. Both Sékou Touré in Guinea and Ben Bella in Algeria sent Kennedy their assurances that they would deny Russian aircraft transit rights. (Touré later added that the problem must be kept in a Soviet-American context; if it became a Cuban-American problem, we would lose support in the uncommitted world). Most African states, moved no doubt by their faith in the American President, indicated private sympathy.

In Western Europe support was general, though there were waverings in Britain and Italy. In Paris General de Gaulle received Dean Acheson, the President's special emissary, and, without waiting to see the aerial photographs Acheson had brought along, said, "If there is a war, I will be with you. But there will be no war." De Gaulle went on to wonder whether the quarantine would be enough, and so did Adenauer, but both strongly backed the American position.

The British had received their first notification on Saturday, October 20. At Sunday noon Kennedy called David Ormsby Gore to the White House and outlined the alternatives. Ormsby Gore expressed strong support for the quarantine and, with his knowledge of Macmillan, assured the President of a sympathetic British reaction. Later the same day Kennedy explained directly to Macmillan that he had found it essential in the interests of security and speed to make his first decision on his own responsibility, but that from now on he expected to keep in the closest touch. He added that, if Khrushchev tried anything in Berlin, the United States would be ready to take a full role there as well as in the Caribbean.

Macmillan responded on Monday that Britain would give all the support it could in the Security Council, though he did not then or later offer to take part in specific action on the Atlantic. He added that two aspects of the problem particularly troubled him. European opinion, he said, would need attention, because Europeans had grown so accustomed to living under the nuclear gun that they might wonder what all the fuss was about. The other and more worrying point was that, if it came to a negotiation, Khrushchev might try to trade Cuba for Berlin. The President, no doubt detecting an element of reserve in Macmillan's tone, tried to reassure him that the Cuban decision was not simply a response to aroused public opinion or to private passion against Cuba; he had no interest in a squabble with Castro. This was something very different: a major showdown with Khrushchev, whose action had so contradicted all the Kremlinologists had prophesied that it was necessary to revise our whole estimate of his desperation or ambition or both. Thereafter Macmillan did not falter, and his counsel and support proved constant through the week.

Macmillan's initial caution reflected a peculiar reaction throughout his country. The British had greeted Kennedy's Monday night speech with surprising skepticism. Some questioned whether nuclear missiles really were in Cuba; maybe CIA was up to its old tricks again, or maybe this was a pretext to justify an American invasion. Even Hugh Gaitskell doubted the legality of the quarantine and wondered why Kennedy had not gone first to the United Nations; and the *Economist* as late as Friday warned against "forcing a showdown over the shipment of Russian arms to Cuba." The *Manchester Guardian* said on Tuesday that, if Khrushchev had really brought in nuclear missiles, "he has done so primarily to demonstrate to the U.S. and the world the meaning of American bases close to the Soviet frontier." The *Guardian* added two days later, "In the end the United States may find that it has done its cause, its friends, and its own true interests little good." By Saturday it was suggesting that Britain vote against the United States in the UN. A group of intellectuals—A. J. Ayer, A. J. P. Taylor, Richard Titmuss and others—attacked the quarantine and advocated British neutrality. The *Tribune* wrote, "It may well be that Kennedy is risking blowing the world to hell in order to sweep a few Democrats into office." Among the pacifists, Bertrand Russell, who was already on record calling Kennedy "much more wicked than Hitler," sent messages to Khrushchev:

MAY I HUMBLY APPEAL FOR YOUR FURTHER HELP IN LOWERING THE TEMPERATURE. . . . YOUR CONTINUED [*sic*] FORBEARANCE IS OUR GREAT HOPE.

and to Kennedy:

YOUR ACTION DESPERATE. . . . NO CONCEIVABLE JUSTIFICATION. WE WILL NOT HAVE MASS MURDER. . . . END THIS MADNESS.

There was some of the same in the United States. The followers of Stuart Hughes's peace party denounced the quarantine, sought excuses for Khrushchev and prayed for American acceptance of the missiles.

On Tuesday night Kennedy dined quietly at the White House with English friends. Cuba was hardly mentioned at the table; but after dinner he beckoned David Ormsby

Gore out into the long central hall, where they quietly talked while the gaiety continued in the dining room. The British Ambassador, mentioning the dubious reaction in his own country, suggested the need for evidence: could not the aerial photographs be released? The President sent for a file, and together they went through them picking out the ones that might have the greatest impact on skeptics. In a while Robert Kennedy walked in, bleak, tired and disheveled. He had just been to see Ambassador Dobrynin in an effort to find out whether the Soviet ships had instructions to turn back if challenged on the high seas. The Soviet Ambassador, the Attorney General said, seemed very shaken, out of the picture and unaware of any instructions. This meant that the imposition of the quarantine the next day might well bring a clash.

The three old friends talked on. Ormsby Gore recalled a conversation with Defense Department officials who had declared it important to stop the Soviet ships as far out of the reach of the jets in Cuba as possible. The British Ambassador now suggested that Khrushchev had hard decisions to make and that every additional hour might make it easier for him to climb down gracefully; why not, therefore, make the interceptions much closer to Cuba and thereby give the Russians a little more time? If Cuban aircraft tried to interfere, they could be shot down. Kennedy, agreeing immediately, called McNamara and, over emotional Navy protests, issued the appropriate instruction. This decision was of vital importance in postponing the moment of irreversible action. They soon parted, looking forward with concern to the crisis of the morrow.

And so around the world emotions rose—fear, doubt, incertitude, apprehension. In the White House the President went coolly about his affairs, watching the charts with the Soviet ships steadily advancing toward Cuba, scrutinizing every item of intelligence for indications of Soviet purpose, reviewing the deployment of American forces. At one point the Air Force produced a photograph of planes lined wingtip to wingtip on a Cuban airfield, arguing that only a few bombs could wipe out the enemy air power. The President asked the Air Force to run similar reconnaissance over our own airfields; to the Pentagon's chagrin, the photographs showed American planes also lined up row by row. In this manner he preserved a taut personal control over every aspect of the situation; the Bay of Pigs had not been in vain. He said to someone, "I guess this is the week I earn my salary."

He never had a more sober sense of his responsibility. It

was a strange week; the flow of decision was continuous; there was no day and no night. In the intervals between meetings he sought out his wife and children as if the imminence of catastrophe had turned his mind more than ever to his family and, through them, to children everywhere in the world. This was the cruel question—the young people who, if things went wrong, would never have the chance to learn, to love, to fulfill themselves and serve their countries. One noon, swimming in the pool, he said to David Powers, "If it weren't for these people that haven't lived yet, it would be easy to make decisions of this sort."

In Buenos Aires Billy Graham preached to 10,000 people on "The End of the World."

XXXI

THE GREAT TURNING

WITHIN THE KREMLIN, so far as one could tell, there was confusion. The Russians had obviously anticipated neither the quick discovery of the bases nor the quick imposition of the quarantine. Their diplomats across the world were displaying all the symptoms of improvisation, as if they had been told nothing of the placement of the missiles and had received no instructions what to say about them. Ambassador Anatoly Dobrynin himself gave every indication of ignorance and confusion. As late as Wednesday a message to Robert Kennedy from Mikoyan repeated that Cuba was receiving no weapons capable of reaching the United States. Georgi Bolshakov, who transmitted the message and who had seemed to us all an honest fellow, assured the Attorney General that he believed this himself.

In New York on Wednesday Stevenson was continuing the battle for the American resolution in the United Nations. John J. McCloy, whom the President had summoned from a business trip to Germany to give the UN presentation a bipartisan flavor, was adding his weight to our councils. Then U Thant made an unexpected intervention, proposing that the Soviet Union suspend its arms shipments and the United States its quarantine to allow an interlude for negotiations. Khrushchev accepted this thought at once and with evident pleasure; but, from our viewpoint, it equated aggression and response, said nothing about the missiles already in Cuba, permitted work to go forward on the sites and contained no provisions for verification. Still, while New York and Washington agreed in rejecting U Thant's proposal, the manner of the rejection caused debate. Some in Washington appeared to fear any response which would 'entrap' us in a negotiating process; it seemed to us in New York that they must be bent to clear the road for an air strike and an invasion. Stevenson and McCloy strongly recommended a response to U Thant which would keep the diplomatic option alive.

1. WAITING

On Wednesday night, as we were pondering these matters at the U.S. Mission in New York, I received a telephone call from Averell Harriman. Speaking with unusual urgency, he said that Khrushchev was desperately signaling a desire to cooperate in moving toward a peaceful solution. Harriman set forth the evidence: Khrushchev's suggestion of a summit meeting in his reply to Bertrand Russell; his well-publicized call on the American singer Jerome Hines the night before after a Moscow concert; his amiable if menacing talk with an American businessman, William Knox of Westinghouse International; the indications that afternoon that the nearest Soviet ships were slowing down and changing course. This was not the behavior of a man who wanted war, Harriman said; it was the behavior of a man who was begging our help to get off the hook. Khrushchev had sent up similar signals after the U-2 affair in 1960, Harriman continued, and Eisenhower had made the mistake of ignoring him; we must not repeat that error now. "If we do nothing but get tougher and tougher, we will force him into countermeasures. The first incident on the high seas will engage Soviet prestige and infinitely reduce the chance of a peaceful solution." The key to it all, he went on, lay in Khrushchev's two remarks during the recent visit of Robert Frost and Stewart Udall to the Soviet Union—his observation to Frost that the democracies were too liberal to fight [1] and his observation to Udall that the Soviet Union must be treated as an equal. "We must give him an out," Harriman said again. "If we do this shrewdly,

[1] Actually Khrushchev never made this remark; it was Frost's interpretation in a New York press conference after a transatlantic flight of an anecdote cited by Khrushchev from Gorki's memoirs where Tolstoy described himself as "too weak and too infirm to do it but still having the desire." Khrushchev was applying this to nations: the United States as old, the Soviet Union as young. Frost, yielding to prejudices of his own, transposed it into a remark about liberals. See Franklin D. Reeve, *Robert Frost in Russia* (Boston, 1964), 115, 120–123.

we can downgrade the tough group in the Soviet Union which persuaded him to do this. But if we deny him an out, then we will escalate this business into a nuclear war."

These words from the most experienced of all American diplomats seemed utterly convincing to me. I asked him whether he had made these points at the State Department. He said, "They never ask my advice about anything outside the Far East. I haven't been in on this at all." Accordingly I sent Harriman's views along to the President. Kennedy called him the next morning, and I imagine that Harriman's counsel may have strengthened his own inclination to go further along the diplomatic road. At any rate, his reply to U Thant on Thursday, while stressing that the "threat was created by the secret introduction of offensive weapons into Cuba, and the answer lies in the removal of such weapons," authorized Stevenson to continue discussions on whether satisfactory arrangements could be assured to this end. This was a second vital decision.

In Washington they had meanwhile been seeking to provide for every contingency the quarantine might create. By involving us directly with the Russians, it contained a great variety of potential risks; and the Executive Committee undertook the most intensive consideration of all possible gradations and configurations: where, when and how to stop ships, how much force to use, when to board, whether to disable the propeller and tow the ship to port. Soon they ascertained that Soviet submarines were following the ships; as quickly as possible, we put a destroyer on the tail of every submarine. It was all an amazing naval deployment, conducted with skill and efficiency. Among the destroyers to take part, apparently in the natural line of duty, was the *Joseph P. Kennedy, Jr.*

As they plotted the courses and studied the charts, Thursday seemed to confirm the encouraging signs of Wednesday and to justify Ormsby Gore's suggestion of Tuesday night that the line of interception be drawn closer to Cuba. Half the Soviet ships, the Executive Committee noted with a flood of relief, had put about and were heading home. Others were evidently waiting for further orders. Only one had entered the quarantine zone—a tanker, obviously not carrying nuclear weapons. In Washington some felt that we must react to this challenge with full military vigor; but the President decided to give Khrushchev more time and said that the tanker, once it had identified itself and thereby established the quarantine, should be permitted to proceed without boarding and search—a third vital decision.

There were other portents, and to them our intelligence community turned like Roman haruspices to the entrails of a sacrificial victim. For the first time all that long week Soviet diplomatic behavior across the world was beginning to conform to a pattern; this indicated that Moscow had at last sent out instructions. For one thing—and very odd in view of our own and the British apprehension about Soviet reprisals in Berlin—the Russians appeared to be engaged in a studied effort to dissociate Berlin from Cuba. Gromyko, who spoke at Humboldt University in East Berlin on Tuesday, instead of using the occasion for implied threats, did not even mention Cuba. By Friday V. A. Zorin, the Soviet ambassador to the United Nations, was even assuring other UN diplomats that his government would not fall into the American "trap" of retaliatory action in Berlin.

But the essence of the emerging pattern seemed to be concern for a peaceful settlement. This was what the Soviet ambassadors in London and Bonn were saying to the British and West German governments. Nor was Moscow confining its efforts to orthodox channels. In London on Wednesday, for example, Captain Ivanov of the Soviet Embassy asked a demimondain doctor named Stephen Ward to use his influence to persuade the British government to invite Khrushchev and Kennedy to a summit meeting. Ward thereupon approached Lord Arran, a peer who wrote a column in the *Evening News*, and even sent a letter to Harold Wilson, whom he did not know. Thwarted in these efforts to solve the world's problems, he soon returned to the more relaxed company of Christine Keeler.

But despite these gestures the situation was still loaded with danger. Work continued on the sites; unless this was stopped, the missiles would soon be on their launching pads. Nor had the Soviet Union yet admitted the presence of nuclear missiles in Cuba at all. On Thursday evening at the UN Stevenson returned to the debate in the Security Council. He crisply dismissed the communist argument that the United States had created the threat to the peace: "This is the first time that I have ever heard it said that the crime is not the burglary, but the discovery of the burglar." As for those who thought the quarantine too extreme a remedy: "Were we to do nothing until the knife was sharpened? Were we to stand idly by until it was at our throats? . . . The course we have chosen seems to me perfectly graduated to meet the character of the threat."

Zorin made a cocky but evasive reply. Now Stevenson took the floor again. Ironically regretting that he lacked his opponent's "talent for obfuscation, for distortion, for confusing language and for double-talk," saying sternly "these weapons must be taken out of Cuba," he turned on the Russian with magnificent scorn:

> Do you, Ambassador Zorin, deny that the USSR has placed and is placing medium and intermediate-range missiles and sites in Cuba? Yes or no? Don't wait for the translation. Yes or no?

Zorin muttered something about not being in an American courtroom. Stevenson, cold and controlled:

> You are in the courtroom of world opinion. You have denied they exist, and I want to know if I understood you correctly. I am prepared to wait for my answer until hell freezes over. And I am also prepared to present the evidence in this room—now!

It was a moment of tremendous excitement. At Stevenson's order, aerial photographs were wheeled on easels into the council chamber, showing the transformation of San Cristóbal from a peaceful country spot into a grim nuclear installation. Other pictures added further evidence. Zorin wanly denied the authenticity of the display. Stevenson wondered savagely why the Soviet Union did not test its denial by permitting a United Nations team to visit the sites.

Then, in a moment, Stevenson concluded: "We know the facts and so do you, sir, and we are ready to talk about them. Our job here is not to score debating points. Our job, Mr. Zorin, is to save the peace. And if you are ready to try, we are."

The Stevenson speech dealt a final blow to the Soviet case before world opinion.

2. THE LETTERS

But on Friday work still continued on the sites. In Florida the American army prepared for invasion. In Washington the pressure to attack mounted as each passing moment brought the installations closer to operation. And in Moscow there must have been deep anxiety and bitter debate.

Khrushchev had now evidently abandoned the effort to bring in more nuclear weapons. But some of the men around him—perhaps the Soviet military—were apparently determined to make the missiles already there operational as speedily as possible. Indeed, this group may have gone along with the pacific gestures of Wednesday and Thursday precisely to gain time to complete the sites. In any case, once the missiles were on launching pads, Moscow might be able to drive a better bargain.

Khrushchev himself, however, seems to have reached a

different position. He knew by now that his essential gamble had failed. Whatever he had once supposed, the Americans were ready to fight. His own options were narrowing before his eyes. If he were to strike at Berlin, he would only expose the Soviet Union to nuclear attack. If he did not compose matters quickly in the Caribbean, then the great army, massing so visibly in Florida, would descend on Cuba; "on the morning of [Saturday] October 27," as he told the Supreme Soviet in December, "we received information that the invasion would be carried out in the next two or three days." If an invasion began, Khrushchev either would have to use the rockets he liked to boast about so jovially or else desert the only communist state in the Americas and condemn himself as a *fainéant* before the international communist movement. It was now beyond the realm of tactical maneuver: all roads led to the abyss. The Soviet Chairman and the American President were the two men in the world with ultimate responsibility for nuclear war. Like Kennedy, Khrushchev had peered into the abyss before. "Immediate action," as he later told the Supreme Soviet, "was needed to prevent an invasion of Cuba and to preserve peace."

At one-thirty on Friday John Scali, the State Department correspondent for the American Broadcasting Company, received a call from Aleksander Fomin, a counselor at the Soviet Embassy, insisting on an immediate meeting. Scali, who had lunched occasionally with Fomin in the past, joined him at once at the Occidental Restaurant. The usually phlegmatic Russian, now haggard and alarmed, said, "War seems about to break out. Something must be done to save the situation." Scali replied that they should have thought of that before they put the missiles in Cuba. The Russian sat in silence for a moment. Then he said, "There might be a way out. What would you think of a proposition whereby we would promise to remove our missiles under United Nations inspection, where Mr. Khrushchev would promise never to introduce such offensive weapons into Cuba again? Would the President of the United States be willing to promise publicly not to invade Cuba?" When Scali said he did not know, Fomin begged him to find out immediately from his State Department friends. Then, reaching for a pencil, he wrote down his home telephone number: "If I'm not at the Embassy, call me here. This is of vital importance."

Scali carried the proposal to Roger Hilsman at State, and Hilsman carried it to Rusk. After discussion with the

Executive Committee, Rusk asked Scali to tell the Russian that we saw "real possibilities" for a negotiation but they must understand that time was short—no more than forty-eight hours. At seven-thirty Friday evening Scali passed this word along. They met this time in the coffee shop of the Statler Hilton. Fomin, once he had satisfied himself about the authenticity of Scali's message and after a brief attempt to introduce the idea of UN inspection of Florida as well as Cuba, rose and, in his haste to get the word back, tossed down a five-dollar bill for a thirty-cent check and speeded off without waiting for the change.

Two hours later a long letter from Khrushchev to the President began to come in by cable. The Soviet leader started by insisting that the weapons shipments were complete and that their purpose was defensive. Then he declared his profound longing for peace; let us, he said with evident emotion, not permit this situation to get out of hand. The enforcement of the quarantine would only drive the Soviet Union to take necessary measures of its own. But if the United States would give assurances that it would not invade Cuba nor permit others to do so and if it would recall its fleet from the quarantine, this would immediately change everything. Then the necessity for a Soviet presence in Cuba would disappear. The crisis, Khrushchev said, was like a rope with a knot in the middle: the more each side pulled, the more the knot would tighten, until finally it could be severed only by a sword. But if each side slackened the rope, the knot could be untied.

The letter was not, as subsequently described, hysterical. Though it pulsated with a passion to avoid nuclear war and gave the impression of having been written in deep emotion, why not? In general, it displayed an entirely rational understanding of the implications of the crisis. Together with the Scali proposal, it promised light at the end of the cave. And in New York on Friday we heard that Zorin had advanced the same proposal to U Thant, and that the Cubans at the UN were beginning to hint to unaligned delegates that the bases might be dismantled and removed if the United States would guarantee the territorial integrity of Cuba. The President probably had his first good night's sleep for ten days; certainly the rest of us did.

But when the Executive Committee assembled on Saturday morning, prospects suddenly darkened. The Moscow radio began to broadcast a new Khrushchev letter containing, to everyone's consternation, an entirely different proposition from the one transmitted through Scali and embodied in

Khrushchev's letter of the night before. The Soviet Union now said it would remove its missiles from Cuba and offer a non-aggression pledge to Turkey if the United States would remove its missiles from Turkey and offer a non-aggression pledge to Cuba. The notion of trading the Cuban and Turkish bases had been much discussed in England; Walter Lippmann and others had urged it in the United States. But Kennedy regarded the idea as unacceptable, and the swap was promptly rejected. This proposal was perplexing enough; but, far more alarming, word soon came that a U-2 was missing over Cuba, presumably shot down by the Russians (piloted, indeed, by the brave South Carolinian, Major Rudolph Anderson, Jr., who had first photographed the installations on October 14). American planes had thus far flown over the missile sites without interference. The Soviet action now, some felt, could only mean one thing: that the confrontation was entering its military phase. The bases were becoming operational, and the Russians were evidently determined to use force to maintain them. We had no choice, it was argued, but a military response; and our tactical analysis had already shown that strikes at the bases would be little use without strikes at the airfields, and strikes at the airfields of little use without further supporting action, so, once the process began, it could hardly stop short of invasion.

The President declined to be stampeded. Obviously, if they shot down U-2s, we would have to react—but not necessarily at once. Again he insisted that the Russians be given time to consider what they were doing before action and counteraction became irrevocable. There remained the Khrushchev letters, and the Executive Committee turned to them again with bafflement and something close to despair. It was noted that Defense Minister Rodion Malinovsky had mentioned Cuba and Turkey together as early as Tuesday, and that *Red Star,* the army paper, had coupled them again on Friday. Could the military have taken over in Moscow? Rusk called in Scali and asked him to find out anything he could from his Soviet contact. Scali, fearful that he had been used to deceive his own country, upbraided Fomin, accusing him of a double cross. The Russian said miserably that there must have been a cable delay, that the Embassy was waiting word from Khrushchev at any moment. Scali brought this report immediately to the President and the Executive Committee at the White House (where Pierre Salinger nearly had heart failure when, in the midst of the rigorous security precautions of the week, he suddenly saw the ABC reporter sitting at the door of the President's inner office).

In the meantime a new crisis: another U-2 on a routine air-sampling mission from Alaska to the North Pole had gone off course and was over the Soviet Union; it had already attracted the attention of Soviet fighters and was radioing Alaska for help. Would the Russians view this as a final reconnaissance in preparation for nuclear attack? What if they decided to strike first? Roger Hilsman brought the frightening news to the President. There was a moment of absolute grimness. Then Kennedy, with a brief laugh, said, "There is always some so-and-so who doesn't get the word." (The plane returned safely; but perhaps Khrushchev did interpret the flight exactly as Hilsman feared; perhaps this too, along with the invasion force massing in Florida and an unauthorized statement on Friday by the State Department press officer threatening "further action" if work continued on the bases, reinforced his determination to bring the crisis to an end.)

Later that afternoon the Executive Committee met again. Robert Kennedy now came up with a thought of breath-taking simplicity and ingenuity: why not ignore the second Khrushchev message and reply to the first? forget Saturday and concentrate on Friday? This suggestion may, indeed, have been more relevant than anyone could have known. For, as Henry Pachter has argued,[2] the so-called second letter, from internal evidence, appears to have been initiated as the immediate follow-on of Khrushchev's reply to U Thant; it began with a reference to Kennedy's reply to U Thant on Thursday and took no note of events on Friday. Moreover, its institutional tone suggested that it was written in the Foreign Office. Might it not have been drafted in Moscow on Thursday and Friday with an eye to Saturday morning release in New York? Then the so-called first letter, which reflected the movement of events well beyond the U Thant proposal and which was clearly written by Khrushchev himself, may well have been composed late Friday night (Moscow time) and transmitted immediately to Kennedy while the 'second' letter was deep in the bureaucratic pipelines. Knowing heads of state and foreign office bureaucracies, one could take anything as possible.

[2] In his brilliant essay on the missile crisis *Collision Course* (New York, 1963), 67–68. Mr. Pachter tells me that the disclosure of the Scali intervention has altered his view about the sequence of the letters; but I am still inclined to think his original thesis probable.

At any rate, on October 27 Kennedy now wrote Khrushchev, "I have read your letter of October 26th with great care and welcomed the statement of your desire to seek a prompt solution." As soon as work stopped on the missile bases and the offensive weapons were rendered inoperable under UN supervision, Kennedy continued, he would be ready to negotiate a settlement along the lines Khrushchev had proposed. Then, in a sentence profoundly expressive of his desire to retrieve something out of crisis, he added: "If your letter signifies that you are prepared to discuss a détente affecting NATO and the Warsaw Pact, we are quite prepared to consider with our allies any useful proposals."

And so the message shot inscrutably into the night. Robert Kennedy carried a copy that evening to the Soviet Ambassador, saying grimly that, unless we received assurances in twenty-four hours, the United States would take military action by Tuesday. No one knew which Khrushchev letter superseded the other; no one knew whether Khrushchev was even still in power. "We all agreed in the end," Robert Kennedy said afterward, "that if the Russians were ready to go to nuclear war over Cuba, they were ready to go to nuclear war, and that was that. So we might as well have the showdown then as six months later." Saturday night was almost the blackest of all. Unless Khrushchev came through in a few hours, the meeting of the Executive Committee on Sunday might well face the most terrible decisions.

Sunday, October 28, was a shining autumn day. At nine in the morning Khrushchev's answer began to come in. By the fifth sentence it was clear that he had thrown in his hand. Work would stop on the sites; the arms "which you described as offensive" would be crated and returned to the Soviet Union; negotiations would start at the UN. Then, no doubt to placate Castro, Khrushchev asked the United States to discontinue flights over Cuba. (As for the errant U-2 which had strayed over Russia the day before, he warned that "an intruding American plane could be easily taken for a nuclear bomber, which might push us to a fateful step.") Looking ahead, he said, "We should like to continue the exchange of views on the prohibition of atomic and thermonuclear weapons, general disarmament, and other problems relating to the relaxation of international tension."

It was all over, and barely in time. If word had not come that Sunday, if work had continued on the bases, the United States would have had no real choice but to take action

against Cuba the next week. No one could discern what
lay darkly beyond an air strike or invasion, what measures
and countermeasures, actions and reactions, might have
driven the hapless world to the ghastly consummation. The
President saw more penetratingly into the mists and terrors
of the future than anyone else. A few weeks later he said,
"If we had invaded Cuba . . . I am sure the Soviets
would have acted. They would have to, just as we would
have to. I think there are certain compulsions on any major
power." The compulsions opened up the appalling world of
inexorability. The trick was to cut the chain in time. When
Kennedy received Khrushchev's reply that golden October
morning, he showed profound relief. Later he said, "This
is the night to go to the theater, like Abraham Lincoln."

3. THE ELECTION

The President issued immediate instructions that there should
be no claiming of victory, no cheering over the Soviet retreat. That night he limited himself on nationwide television to a few unadorned words about "Chairman Khrushchev's statesmanlike decision" and the "compelling necessity for ending the arms race and reducing world tensions."

The next morning he told me he was afraid that people
would conclude from this experience that all we had to do
in dealing with the Russians was to be tough and they
would collapse. The Cuban missile crisis, he pointed out,
had three distinctive features: it took place in an area
where we enjoyed local conventional superiority, where Soviet national security was not directly engaged and where
the Russians lacked a case which they could plausibly
sustain before the world. Things would be different, he said,
if the situation were one where they had the local superiority, where their national security was directly engaged and
where they could convince themselves and others they
were in the right. "I think there is a law of equity in these
disputes," he continued. "When one party is clearly wrong,
it will eventually give way. That is what happened in the
steel controversy, and that is what happened here. They
had no business in putting those missiles in and lying to me
about it. They were in the wrong and knew it. So, when
we stood firm, they had to back down. But this doesn't
mean at all that they would back down when they felt
they were in the right and had vital interests involved."

He thought it unfortunate that this had happened in the
midst of the campaign, fearing that some Republicans would
feel obliged to denounce the settlement. "They will attack

us on the ground that we had a chance to get rid of Castro and, instead of doing so, ended up by guaranteeing him against invasion. I am asking McNamara to give me the estimated casualties if we had attempted an invasion. [The estimate, I understood later, was 40–50,000 in the American forces.] . . . One thing this experience shows is the value of sea power and air power; an invasion would have been a mistake—a wrong use of our power. But the military are mad. They wanted to do this. It's lucky for us that we have McNamara over there."

What worried Kennedy particularly was the inconceivable way each superpower had lost hold of the reality of the other: the United States absolutely persuaded that the Soviet Union would never put nuclear missiles into Cuba; the Soviet Union absolutely persuaded that it could do so and the United States would not respond. Remembering Barbara Tuchman's enumeration in *The Guns of August* of the misjudgments which caused the First World War, he used to say that there should be a sequel entitled "The Missiles of October." But he believed that rationality had triumphed; he hoped that Khrushchev's deceit and recklessness signified some awful aberration, and that the consequence would be to end Soviet illusions about American behavior under pressure. And, indeed, the alacrity with which Khrushchev had managed his retreat suggested that Harriman may have been right in surmising that the Cuban adventure was less his own idea than a project pressed on him by his hard-liners. Perhaps, like Kennedy after the Bay of Pigs, he was now sitting in the Kremlin wondering how in the world he could ever have embarked on so crazy an undertaking. One noticed three months later that Marshal M. V. Zakharov, the army chief of staff, was transferred to a footling post in the military school system, his name quietly dropped from the forthcoming edition of the textbook *On Soviet Military Science*.

"There are few higher gratifications," Dr. Johnson once said, "than that of reflection on surmounted evils." Kennedy was well satisfied by the performance of his government. The Executive Committee had proved a brilliant instrument of consideration and coordination. He was particularly proud of his brother, always balanced, never rattled, his eye fixed on the ultimate as well as on the immediate. McNamara, as usual, had been superb. Llewellyn Thompson had provided wise counsel; Edwin Martin had managed the Latin American side with tact and efficiency. If the President was disappointed in others, he was not, I think, especially surprised. As a whole, the government could hardly have performed better. For the rest, life went on. On Tuesday, October 30, he wrote Mrs. Paul Mellon, who had recently finished her rehabilitation of the Rose Garden, "I need not tell you that your garden has been our brightest spot in the somber surroundings of the last few days."

The crisis had for a moment suspended the political campaign. The President, the Vice-President and the cabinet had all canceled their speeches, and so had Truman (though the non-political Eisenhower, to Kennedy's amusement, had kept on). It is hard to estimate the impact of the Cuba week on the election, though foreign crisis usually strengthens the administration in office. Certainly it was a rebuke to extremism on both the left and the right. The anti-quarantine demonstrations by peace groups had exposed the bankruptcy of the unilateral disarmament position; and in Massachusetts Stuart Hughes, after an energetic campaign, polled less than 3 per cent of the vote against Edward Kennedy and George Lodge. In New York the new Conservative party fared little better. Four avowed John Birchers running for the House—three in California, one in Texas—were all defeated. And across the country the Democrats, surpassing any administration in a mid-term election since 1934, gained four seats (among them George McGovern) in the Senate and lost a net of only two in the House. The outcome left the internal composition of the Congress little changed, but, in light of the losses usually suffered by incumbent administrations in mid-term elections, the President's personal mandate was triumphantly refreshed. And Richard Nixon's declaration of hatred of the press and 'withdrawal' from politics after losing the governorship of California gave the White House a special fillip of entertainment.

4. LOOSE ENDS

But the problems of the missile crisis were far from over. In New York Stevenson and McCloy were deep in intricate negotiation. In Havana Castro, unconsulted by Khrushchev, furious over the Soviet idea that the UN should verify the dismantlement and removal of the missiles and determined to hold on to the IL-28 bombers, which he now claimed as Cuban property, was doing all he could to upset the Soviet-American settlement. The Russians themselves seemed less than forthcoming on verification and on the removal of the IL-28s. But on November 20 Khrushchev finally agreed that the IL-28s would go within thirty days, and the United States terminated the quarantine.

Castro's resistance, however, made it impossible to establish the UN inspection Khrushchev had proposed, and the United States therefore never completed the reciprocal pledge not to invade Cuba. Discussions dragged desultorily on till in January 1963 the United States and the Soviet Union, accepting the impossibility of resolving "all the problems which have arisen in connection with this affair," formally removed the Cuban missile question from the Security Council. In the months to come, however, the original Khrushchev-Kennedy plan was in a sense put into effect at one remove. Instead of UN inspection, American aerial reconnaissance served as the means of verification; "the camera," the President said in December, ". . . is actually going to be our best inspector." The Soviet Union tacitly accepted this by instructing the Russians at the SAM sites to leave the U-2s alone. For its part, the United States, without formal commitment, refrained from invasion and, indeed, took measures in the spring of 1963 to prevent hit-and-run attacks by Cuban refugees from United States territory.

Argument continued through the winter. Senator Keating, stimulated by his triumph of the preceding October, began a new campaign designed to shake American confidence in the settlement. His charges that the Russians had failed to dismantle concrete missile sites forced Secretary McNamara to bring photographic evidence on television to refute the allegations. Keating also said that missiles were probably being hidden in caves, though the evidence was clear that every nuclear missile known to have been brought into Cuba had been removed; and he denounced the presence of Soviet troops in Cuba, though, from the viewpoint of United States aerial reconnaissance, it was plainly better to have the SAM sites manned by Russians, politely oblivious of our overflights, than by *Fidelistas*. In the end, as the Soviet Union began a gradual withdrawal of its forces, this controversy subsided.

The President helped restore perspective in March at the Gridiron Dinner, held just after Khrushchev's son-in-law Aleksei Adzhubei had paid a visit to the Holy See. "I have a very grave announcement," the President began.

The Soviet Union has once again recklessly embarked upon a provocative and extraordinary change in the status quo in an area which they know full well I regard as having a special and historic relationship. I refer to the deliberate and sudden deployment of Mr. Adzhubei to the Vatican.

I am told that this plot was worked out by a group of

Khrushchev's advisers who have all been excommunicated from the Church. It is known as "EX-COM."

Reliable refugee reports have also informed us that hundreds of Marxist bibles have been unloaded and are being hidden in caves throughout the Vatican.

We will now pursue the contingency plan for protecting the Vatican City which was previously prepared by the National Security Council. The plan is known as "Vat 69."

5. THE ATTACK ON STEVENSON

In the meantime, another problem had arisen which for a few days created sensation and embarrassment. On December 1, 1962, the President called me over to his office and said, "You know that Charlie Bartlett and Stewart Alsop have been writing a piece on Cuba for the *Saturday Evening Post*. I understand that Chalmers Roberts is planning to do a story on the Alsop-Bartlett piece for the *Washington Post* and that he is going to present it as an attack on Adlai Stevenson. You had better warn Adlai that this is coming." I asked what the article said. The President replied that he understood that it accused Stevenson of advocating a Caribbean Munich. He said, "Everyone will suppose that it came out of the White House because of Charlie. Will you tell Adlai that I never talked to Charlie or any other reporter about the Cuban crisis, and that this piece does not represent my views."

The President and Stevenson had worked harmoniously over the last eighteen months. In December 1961, when Mayor Richard Daley of Chicago had wanted Stevenson to resign from his UN assignment to run for the Senate in Illinois, Kennedy had greatly pleased Stevenson by insisting that he stay. He told Stevenson that he would feel even more frustrated as a junior Senator than he was at the UN and reminded him of Alben Barkley, who, when he returned to the Senate after his Vice-Presidency, was just another freshman at the bottom of the list. "I said we needed him in the UN," Kennedy said to me later, "and that I counted on him to stick around."

There were always minor problems: Stevenson would have liked to be consulted more often on the formation of policy, though this complaint was as much against the State Department as against the White House; Kennedy wished that Stevenson would not discuss his occasional irritations with the press. But the relationship was one of mutual respect. Kennedy in particular had been much impressed by Stevenson's UN performance during the missile crisis. Now the *Saturday Evening Post* story promised trouble. Alsop and Bartlett were intelligent and responsible reporters, and Bartlett, in addition, had been for many years a personal intimate of the President's. There was little doubt that anything they had to say would be blamed on the White House.

Soon after my talk with the President, Clayton Fritchey called me about the article from the UN Mission in New York. As sometimes happens, the magazine's advance publicity and its layout (a photograph of an agonized Stevenson with a caption about Munich) were worse than the text. But the paragraph on Stevenson claimed that he alone "dissented from the Executive Committee consensus." It quoted an "unadmiring official" as saying that Stevenson wanted "a Munich," proposed trading Guantánamo and "the Turkish, Italian and British missile bases for the Cuban bases" and would have been satisfied with "the neutralization of the Cuban missiles." In fact, Stevenson had supported the Executive Committee consensus; though he had talked on Friday about the Turkish and Italian bases (no one apparently ever brought up British bases), so had others, and, like others, he had changed his mind on this by Sunday. Moreover, his concept of neutralization applied, not to the missiles, but to the whole island, involving the removal not only of Soviet weapons but of the troops whose presence would soon so upset Senator Keating—all this in advance of any deal on Guantánamo. On the other hand, his advocacy on Friday and Saturday of a political program, unmentioned in the Bartlett-Alsop piece, had seemed to some out of cadence with the general endorsement of the quarantine, and his persistence in contending for negotiation, even in the framework of the quarantine, had caused worry over the weekend that he might want to make premature concessions.

On Monday noon Pierre Salinger put out a statement, which Stevenson had seen and approved, expressing the President's full confidence in his ambassador to the United Nations and saying, in effect, that nothing which took place in the Executive Committee would be disclosed. This statement caused immediate dissatisfaction among the reporters, who pointed out that it did not explicitly deny the Bartlett-Alsop allegations. They recalled that an earlier Bartlett column had preceded the transfer of Chester Bowles; obviously the pattern was repeating itself; obviously Charlie would never have dared write that way unless he were pretty sure he was saying what Kennedy wanted. What was worse, one or two of his friends in the press convinced Stevenson of this; and, when I talked to him later in the afternoon, he said grimly that, if the President wanted him to go, he did not have to go about it in this circuitous fashion.

Much troubled, I went to Kennedy. After a moment's chat, I said, "Mr. President, everyone in town thinks that the Bartlett article is a signal from the White House that you want to get rid of Stevenson. You know that, if you really want Stevenson's resignation, you have only to say a word now and he will resign immediately without any fuss or controversy." The President, swearing briefly, said, "Of course I don't want Stevenson to resign. I would regard his resignation as a disaster. Look at it logically. What in the world would I have to gain from his resignation? In the first place, where could I possibly find anyone who could do half as good a job at the UN? Look at the alternatives—Adlai would do a far better job than any of the others. In the second place, from a realistic political viewpoint, it is better for me to have Adlai in the government than out. In the third place, if I were trying to get him out, Charlie Bartlett is a good friend, but he's the last medium I would use."

That night at Averell Harriman's, Stevenson seemed profoundly depressed. When I reported what the President had said, he answered shortly, "That's fine, but will he say it publicly?" Later he and Fritchey took the sleeper to New York. The next morning Clayton called to read the headline from the *Daily News*: ADLAI ON SKIDS OVER PACIFIST STAND IN CUBA. Stevenson's morale, Fritchey said, was lower than ever. When I told this to Kennedy, however, he observed, "I'm not impressed by the *Daily News*. They spend all their time attacking us. This goes on all the time. Just tell Adlai to sit tight and everything will subside. This is one of those forty-eight-hour wonders. Tell them about all those fights in the New Deal. Just get them to relax."

But the clamor did not subside so simply. Harlan Cleveland, after a day in New York, told me that public action by the President was essential to restore not only Stevenson's morale but his effectiveness in the UN. Kennedy had already a draft of a personal letter to Stevenson reaffirming his confidence and mentioning the problem of having a friend who was also a reporter: "I did not feel I could tell him or any other friend in the press what subject to write or *not* write about." I was then instructed to deliver the letter personally to Stevenson. By the time I reached New York, the President had decided that the best way to handle the matter was to let the newspapers have the letter. This meant that the references to Bartlett were to be eliminated and the letter to become primarily an expression of confidence in Stevenson. Fritchey and I phoned the President, who edited and strengthened the letter himself, adding that Stevenson's work at the UN was of "inestimable" national importance. If not a forty-eight-hour wonder, the furor died away in the next few days.

6. AFTERMATH

The President had one other item of unfinished Cuban business—this one left over from the Bay of Pigs. He had never forgotten the men his government had put on the Cuban beaches, and he had been determined in one way or another to free them from Castro's prisons. In May 1961, when Castro had proposed an exchange of the surviving members of Brigade 2506 for five hundred bulldozers, or, as he soon said, $28 million, Kennedy had instigated the organization of a private Tractors for Freedom Committee led by Mrs. Roosevelt, Walter Reuther and Milton Eisenhower. But the project soon bogged down in domestic political controversy. Republican congressional leaders denounced it as "another blow to our world leadership." "Human lives," said Richard Nixon in one of his communiqués on public morality, "are not something to be bartered." Dr. Eisenhower retreated under the pressure, and three months later negotiations were broken off.

At the end of March 1962, the captives went on trial in Havana. Members of the Brigade who had escaped to Florida now made a new attempt to seek government support. They found an immediate sympathizer in Robert Kennedy, who, with Richard Goodwin's assistance, set to work to mobilize hemisphere opinion to persuade Castro to spare the lives of the prisoners. Then the possibility of ransoming the Brigade revived in Havana, though Castro now lifted the price to $62 million. This sum seemed beyond hope of raising, and in June the Attorney General recommended that the Cuban exiles ask James B. Donovan of New York, a lawyer who had been general counsel of OSS in the Second World War, to intercede with Castro. Donovan, flying to Havana in late August, persuaded Castro to accept food and drugs instead of money. Negotiations dragged on into October and into the missile crisis; but Donovan persisted and arranged a deal. After the crisis, the Attorney General taking personal command, mobilized the Department of Justice, much of the rest of the government and much of the drug industry to get the men out by Christmas. Time was pressing; for the prisoners themselves, underfed and sick, were beginning to look, as one who had visited them told Robert Kennedy, like animals who were

about to die. It was an undertaking of extraordinary drive
and enterprise, and it succeeded. On December 21 Donovan
and Castro signed a memorandum of agreement. Two
days later the first prisoners arrived in Florida. After Christmas the Brigade leaders, gaunt and wasted, were received by
the President at Palm Beach.

On December 29, 1962, the President went over to Miami
to inspect the Brigade in the Orange Bowl. Pepe San
Román, still pale from prison, presented the President
with the Brigade banner which had flown on the beach on
those bitter April days twenty months before. Kennedy,
deeply moved, said, "I can assure you that this flag will be
returned to this Brigade in a free Havana." Then he spoke
again of the democratic revolution of the Americas:

> Under the *Alianza para el Progreso,* we support for Cuba
> and for all the countries of this hemisphere the right of free
> elections and the free exercise of basic human freedoms. We
> support land reform and the right of every *campesino* to own
> the land he tills. We support the effort of every free nation
> to pursue programs of economic progress. We support the
> right of every free people to freely transform the economic
> and political institutions of society so that they may serve
> the welfare of all.

He added that he believed there were men who held to this
faith "all over the island of Cuba, in the government itself,
in the Army and in the militia."

Then Jacqueline Kennedy, speaking in Spanish, expressed
pride that young John had met the officers of the Brigade.
"He is still too young to realize what has happened here,
but I will make it my business to tell him the story of
your courage as he grows up. It is my wish and my hope
that some day he may be a man at least half as brave
as the members of Brigade 2506."

But the ultimate impact of the missile crisis was wider
than Cuba, wider even than the western hemisphere. To the
whole world it displayed the ripening of an American
leadership unsurpassed in the responsible management of
power. From the moment of challenge the American President never had a doubt about the need for a hard response.
But throughout the crisis he coolly and exactly measured
the level of force necessary to deal with the level of threat.
Defining a clear and limited objective, he moved with mathematical precision to accomplish it. At every stage he gave
his adversary time for reflection and reappraisal, taking
care not to force him into 'spasm' reactions or to cut off
his retreat.

Moreover, despite strong pressure to take action repugnant to our national traditions, he always linked his use of power to the ideals of the country and to the necessities of the world which would have to go on after the conflict. By his own composure, clarity and control, he held the country behind him. It was almost as if he had begun to reshape the nation in his own image, for the American people, so many of whom had been in a frenzy about air raid shelters a year before, so many of whom still longed for total solutions, went through the Cuba week without panic or hysteria, with few cries of "better red than dead" and fewer demands (until the crisis was safely over) for "total victory."

In a toast to Chancellor Adenauer two weeks afterward, Kennedy spoke of "an important turning point, possibly, in the history of the relations between East and West." He meant, as he later explained, that this was the first time that the United States and the Soviet Union had ever directly challenged each other with nuclear weapons as the issue; and in his sense of "a climactic period" he associated the missile crisis with the growing conflict between China and Russia and the Chinese attack on India. All this, he said, was "bound to have its effects, even though they can't be fully perceived now."

He did not exaggerate the significance of the Cuban victory in itself. He recognized that he had enjoyed advantages in this specific contest—because Cuba did not lie within the reach of Soviet conventional power or within the scope of Soviet vital interests, and because the Russians knew they could not sustain this particular course of deceit and irresponsibility before the world. These conditions might not be present the next time. But he hoped that he had made to Khrushchev in the Atlantic in October 1962 the point he had failed to make sixteen months before in Vienna—that neither side dare tamper carelessly with the delicate and complex equilibrium of world power. "If we suffer a major defeat, if they suffer a major defeat," he mused with newspapermen at Palm Beach on the last day of the year, "it may change the balance of power. . . . It also increases possibly the chance of war."

This was why, when Khrushchev backed down, Kennedy refrained from calling the American victory a victory or the Russian rout a rout. "Every setback," Kennedy said later, "has the seeds of its own reprisal, if the country is powerful enough." So the German invasion of Czechoslovakia in the winter of 1939 had led to the British guarantee of Poland. "We tried to make their setback in Cuba not the kind that would bring about an increase in hostility but perhaps provide for an easing of relations."

It was this combination of toughness and restraint, of will, nerve and wisdom, so brilliantly controlled, so matchlessly calibrated, that dazzled the world. Before the missile crisis people might have feared that we would use our power extravagantly or not use it at all. But the thirteen days gave the world—even the Soviet Union—a sense of American determination and responsibility in the use of power which, if sustained, might indeed become a turning point in the history of the relations between east and west.

XXXII

THE NOT SO GRAND DESIGN

YET, EVEN AS THE PRESIDENT had won the most decisive victory of west over east since the start of the cold war and in a style which promised the relief rather than the rise of international tension, he faced a setback within the west itself. The concept of a unified democratic Europe as part of a freely trading Atlantic community had been a basic element of Kennedy's world strategy. In a sympathetic and illuminating book of 1962 called *The Grand Design,* Joseph Kraft had set forth the administration's vision of North America and Western Europe happily joined by policies and institutions in common pursuit of economic expansion and military defense. Now in the moment of triumph the Grand Design was shaken by brusque challenge bursting out of the heart of the western alliance itself.

On January 14, 1963, eleven weeks after his prompt support of the United States during the missile crisis, General Charles de Gaulle held one of his periodic press conferences. In two sharp and elegant strokes, he knocked out the economic and military pillars of Atlantic unity. If Great Britain were admitted to the Common Market, the General said, it would transform the character of the European Economic Community and "finally it would appear as a colossal Atlantic community under American domination and direction." As for a coordinated western nuclear policy, "France intends to have her own national defense. . . . For us, in present circumstances, integration is something which is not imaginable." He concluded suavely about the French nuclear force: "It is entirely understandable that this French enterprise should not seem very satisfactory to certain American quarters. In politics and strategy, as in economics, monopoly naturally appears to him who enjoys it as the best possible system."

1. THE METAMORPHOSIS OF WESTERN EUROPE

The de Gaulle press conference was the ironic result of a series of changes the United States itself had set in motion fifteen years earlier. The Second World War had left Western Europe in a state of spiritual and physical shock: France, Italy and Germany had suffered deep national humiliation, Britain was weary and spent; the smaller countries realized more than ever their helplessness in the modern world. The cradle of western civilization seemed to Churchill in 1947 "a rubble heap, a charnel house, a breeding ground for pestilence and hate." The loss of overseas empires intensified the sense of impotence; so too did Western Europe's knowledge of its absolute dependence on the United States for economic reconstruction and military protection.

The Marshall Plan and the North Atlantic Treaty Organization constituted the two sides of the American response. Behind the NATO shield, the nations of Western Europe with Marshall aid set to work rebuilding and modernizing their economies. In France Jean Monnet laid down the bases for national planning. A man of profound practicality, spacious imagination, infinite patience and total disinterestedness, he looked beyond the restoration of France to the restoration of Europe. The unification of Europe, sooner or later, seemed to him a necessity of history. With quiet American collaboration, Monnet began a step-by-step realization of his vision. The Coal and Steel Community was set up in 1951; Monnet became its first president. The failure of the project of a European Defense Community in 1954 only confirmed his belief that economic integration had to precede political integration. The next year he resigned his official post in order to work for economic unity through the Action Committee for a United States of Europe, whose membership included political and labor leaders from the six nations of the Coal and Steel Community—France, West Germany, Italy, Belgium, the Netherlands, Luxembourg. In 1957 these countries signed the Treaty of Rome, organizing the European Economic Community. The EEC further stimulated the renaissance of Western Europe. Soon the EEC's Common Market became the world's largest importer and greatest trading community.

By 1960 the economic dependence on the United States had largely disappeared. Western Europe had been growing twice as fast as America for a decade; it had been drawing gold reserves from America; it had been outproducing America in coal. Americans were flocking across the Atlantic to learn the secrets of the economic miracle. And, at the same time, the military dependence had taken new and perplexing forms. If the prospect of a Soviet invasion of Western Europe had ever been real, few Europeans believed in it any longer. Moreover, the Soviet nuclear achievement, putting the United States for the first time in its history under threat of devastating attack, had devalued the American deterrent in European eyes. These developments meant that the conditions which had given rise to the Marshall Plan and NATO were substantially gone. The new Europe would not be content to remain an economic or military satellite of America. The problem now was to work out the next phase in the Atlantic relationship.

This problem received much hard thought on both sides of the Atlantic in the late fifties; and the search for a solution began to move in two somewhat different directions. Those concerned with the economic and political aspects of the relationship were thinking more and more in terms of a dual Atlantic partnership resting on two distinct entities, the United States and the European Economic Community.[1] Those concerned with the military aspects were thinking more and more in terms of a single Atlantic community based on NATO and the indivisibility of the nuclear deterrent. The divergence was, in the language of the American civil rights movement, between 'separate but equal' and 'integration.'

2. PARTNERSHIP

The existence of the Common Market and its external tariffs, creating the need for reciprocal tariff adjustments with other nations and areas, made the idea of Atlantic partnership almost irresistible to economists both in Europe and the United States. When Jean Monnet carried the gospel to Washington early in 1961, he found the ground already well tilled in the new administration. George Ball, his as-

---

[1] Hopefully to be enlarged by the addition of Great Britain and other members of the European Free Trade Association. Proponents of this conception mysteriously insisted for a time on calling it the 'dumbbell' theory.

sociate for many years, had begun during the interregnum
to formulate the revision of trade policy required to prepare the American economy to live with a unified Western
Europe. Soon Ball became Under Secretary of State for
Economic Affairs; on entering his impressive new office
in the State Department, he is said to have gaily remarked,
"Monnet isn't everything." But Monnet remained a great
deal. Ball's first move was to secure the ratification of the
convention establishing the Organization for Economic Cooperation and Development. The OECD, Kennedy said,
would become "one of the principal institutions through
which we pursue the great aim of consolidating the Atlantic
community."

The next step was taken in London. When Harold Macmillan came to Washington in April 1961, he informed the
President that Britain had resolved to apply for membership
in the Common Market. This was an extraordinary decision;
it represented, as Hugh Gaitskell later complained, the
reversal of a thousand years of English history. The decision had two main grounds: the economic hope that the
competitive stimulus of continental industry in a larger
market would speed the modernization of British industry;
and the political hope that, in the twilight of empire, Britain
could find a new role of leadership in Europe.

From Washington's viewpoint, the second reason was
more attractive than the first; for the Common Market presented the United States with economic problems which
British membership would only enhance. Some in the administration agreed with J. K. Galbraith that it was foolish
to increase our own balance of payments troubles by promoting a strong high-tariff trading bloc against ourselves.
Kennedy fully understood the economic difficulties British
entry would bring to the United States. But these were, in
his mind, overborne by the political benefits. If Britain
joined the Market, London could offset the eccentricities
of policy in Paris and Bonn; moreover, Britain, with its
world obligations, could keep the EEC from becoming a
high-tariff, inward-looking, white man's club. Above all,
with British membership, the Market could become the basis
for a true political federation of Europe. Accordingly Kennedy raised the matter on Britain's behalf with de Gaulle in
Paris in June 1961; this was when de Gaulle turned him
aside by politely doubting whether Britain really wanted
unconditional membership. Early in 1962, when Hugh
Gaitskell came to Washington, Kennedy mobilized half the
cabinet to tell him that Britain must plunge into Europe.

In the meantime, Kennedy took precautions to protect

American economic interests. When Macmillan revisited Washington in April 1962, the President made it clear that the United States was backing British membership for political, not for economic reasons, that Britain must not expect to take care of everyone in its economic wake—either in the Commonwealth or in the European Free Trade Association —at America's expense. In particular, while we recognized the need for transitional arrangements, we could hardly accept a system which would give Commonwealth farm products a permanent position in the Common Market more favorable than that enjoyed by competing products from the United States.

But agriculture formed only part of the problem which British entry might create. The larger risk was that it might defeat the whole conception of Atlantic partnership by breaking the Atlantic community up into two angrily competitive trading blocks. It was this situation which led Kennedy in early 1962 to request far-reaching authority from Congress to engage in tariff bargaining with an enlarged Common Market, the authority to be used, of course, to bring barriers down and thereby promote world trade. As Monnet's Action Committee declared in June, "Only through the economic and political unification of Europe, including the United Kingdom, and the establishment of a partnership between equals of Europe and the United States can the West be strengthened . . . a relationship of two separate but equally powerful entities, each bearing its share of common responsibilities."

Ball and Robert Schaetzel in the State Department and Howard Petersen as a special White House adviser on trade had prepared versions of a trade expansion act in the course of 1961. Ball, looking toward a basic reconstruction of American commercial policy, wanted to let the existing Trade Agreements Act expire and send a wholly new bill to Congress in 1963. Petersen recommended the amendment of the existing act and, to make this easier, the retention of some of its restrictive features. The President, consulting with his congressional specialists, was urged by Lawrence O'Brien to go ahead in 1962 and decided to do so in the spirit of the Ball approach.

The trade expansion fight became the major legislative issue of 1962. A country-wide campaign was organized, a potent Committee for a National Trade Policy set up; business and labor were enlisted, Congressmen pressed and persuaded. "The two great Atlantic markets," the President told Congress, "will either grow together or they will grow apart. . . . That decision will either mark the

beginning of a new chapter in the alliance of free nations
—or a threat to the growth of Western unity." As the trade
expansion bill mystique grew, it was even argued (most
urgently by Joseph Kraft) that the new policy would provide the means of getting America moving again and become "the unifying intellectual principle of the New Frontier"; if the bill failed, "the United States will have to de-
fault on power, resign from history." Such language, coming from an intelligent and ordinarily detached observer,
suggests the evangelical mood.

Some of us felt all this to be a misdirection of the administration's limited political resources. Getting America
moving again, we thought, required economic stimulus at
home; the impact of foreign trade on employment and business activity was limited. Moreover, a significant part of the
bill hinged on Britain's entry into the Market, which was
still problematic. And purists of the administration opposed an amendment, offered by Henry Reuss of Wisconsin
and Paul Douglas of Illinois and adopted in the Senate,
which would have made the tariff reduction part of the
act fully operative even if Britain did not join the Market.
Their fear, as George Ball suggested in the hearings, was
that this provision would strengthen the hands of the
anti-Common Marketeers in England by enabling them
to say "there was an alternative presented to Britain which
had not been available before." The bill, in short, as Reuss
later put it, was tailored to force Britain in. In addition, one
was not clear whether the advocates of the bill understood that, if the partnership were really to meet the
hopes of many European federalists, it would have to go
beyond tariff reduction to the economically difficult and
politically hazardous realm of common agricultural and
monetary policies.

Nevertheless, though the measure had its defects and
its significance was exaggerated, it represented a wholly
useful revision of commercial policy and a wise signal to
Europe both of our desire for cooperation and of our vision
of a desirable world economic order. Nor could the campaign have been more astutely managed. Among other
things, it offered enlightened New York lawyers and bankers a pleasing sense of virtue and audacity in speaking out
boldly for tariff reform, just as their grandfathers had
done in the Cleveland administration. The thought of consolidating relations with this powerful group may not have
been absent from the President's mind when he embarked
on the fight. In any case, contrary to predictions, the bill

passed rather easily—the House by 298 to 125 and the
Senate by 78 to 8. When the President signed the Trade
Expansion Act in October, he said, "By means of agreements authorized by the act, we can move forward to partnership with the nations of the Atlantic Community."

3. INTERDEPENDENCE

At the same time that economics was prescribing a transatlantic partnership between two separate and equal entities,
defense strategy was arguing for a unified Atlantic military community based on the American nuclear deterrent.
The discrepancy between these two conceptions was not
always clearly recognized. But it led to continuous though
murky debate within the American government and the
west, and it represented a lurking vulnerability within
the Grand Design.

Secretary McNamara laid down the strategic position in his
forthright way at the Athens NATO ministerial meeting in
the spring of 1962 and repeated it publicly in his Ann
Arbor speech in June. "There must not be," he said,
"competing and conflicting strategies to meet the contingency of nuclear war. We are convinced that a general
nuclear war target system is indivisible, and if, despite all
our efforts, nuclear war should occur, our best hope lies
in conducting a centrally controlled campaign against all
of the enemy's vital nuclear capabilities."

The nature of nuclear war, in McNamara's view, thus
made a unified deterrent imperative. He regarded "relatively weak national nuclear forces with enemy cities as
their targets" as perilous in peace, because they might invite pre-emptive first strikes, and disastrous in war. The
rational policy, in his belief, was in peace to avoid "the
proliferation of nuclear power with all of its attendant
dangers" and in war to enforce a no-cities strategy on
the enemy. His conclusion was clear: "Limited nuclear
capabilities, operating independently, are dangerous, expensive, prone to obsolescence, and lacking in credibility as
a deterrent."

In response to wails from London McNamara hastened
to explain that this last sentence was not directed at the
British deterrent since it did not operate independently.
Actually the McNamara doctrine saw little role even for
dependent national deterrents; and the President had
privately urged on Macmillan in February 1962 that a British effort to maintain its deterrent through the sixties might
both confirm de Gaulle in his own course and hasten the

day when the Germans would demand nuclear weapons
for themselves. (He added that he would not raise a matter of this sort with any other head of government and
did so only because he was so confident of their continuing
understanding. Macmillan, surprised but appreciative, responded warmly to the confidence if not to the argument;
he began his next letter "Dear Friend," the salutation he
used for the rest of their association.) The French independent deterrent, weaker and cruder than the British, was
left as the target of American public disapproval, an impression which did not stir pro-American feelings at the
Elysée.

The indispensability of nuclear centralization, as Kennedy told Macmillan, called for a NATO solution in order
to head off independent national aspirations; or, as Mc-
Namara put it at Ann Arbor, it emphasized the "interdependence" of national security interests on both sides of
the Atlantic. With this mellifluous but misleading term
McNamara indicated the line of debate between the strate-
gists and the economists: Atlantic interdependence vs.
transatlantic partnership. "Interdependence" was misleading because what McNamara meant at bottom was precisely
the *dependence* of western security on a nuclear deterrent
under American control. Yet his resort to the word also
suggested his recognition of a problem, even if, in stating
the problem, his ordinarily cogent exposition trailed off into
generality: "We want and need a greater degree of Alliance
participation in formulating nuclear weapons policy to the
greatest extent possible." But what Alliance participation
would be possible, except in marginal and symbolic forms,
so long as the United States retained its veto over the use
of nuclear weapons?—and obviously neither prudence nor
the American Congress would permit the renunciation of
the veto. Still, the European desire for such participation
was deemed real; and, if quasi-solutions were to be found,
they had to come not through partnership with a still
nonexistent and (at least in nuclear strength) inherently
unequal European entity but within the single Atlantic
framework of NATO.

The search for devices to give the NATO allies a greater sense of participating in nuclear decisions had begun
five years earlier. When sputnik dramatized the Soviet
achievements in 1957, Britain, Turkey and Italy accepted
nuclear missiles under an agreement by which the United
States retained custody of the warheads and both the United
States and the recipient could veto their use: these were

the Jupiters which caused such argument during the Cuba crisis. No one liked the Jupiters very much, but the emergence of the Polaris missile at the end of the decade introduced new possibilities. In 1959 Secretary of Defense Thomas Gates considered selling Polaris missiles to interested allies on condition that they be assigned to NATO; and in the same year General Lauris Norstad, the NATO Supreme Commander, proposed that NATO itself become a fourth nuclear power, with its own nuclear force. These suggestions were evidently responsive to sentiment of some sort in Europe; but the nature of this sentiment remained hard to define. Clearly there was no popular pressure for the weapons. But a discontent with the American monopoly was rising in top military and government circles. Given the uncertainties of American politics, the new vulnerability of America to Soviet nuclear attack and the new self-confidence of Western Europe, why should not Western Europe have nuclear resources of its own? There was, in addition, the ever-present problem of tying West Germany firmly into the defense structure of the west.

By 1960 the sharing of nuclear control was thus a live issue. Norstad continued his campaign, now with Bonn's support, for a land-based NATO nuclear force. In Washington a feeling arose that the United States should devise a solution of its own before the demand got out of control. Gerard Smith of the State Department, enlisting Professor Robert Bowie, who had been head of the Policy Planning Council in the early Dulles years and was now at Harvard, began the search for a NATO nuclear formula which would give the allies a sense of participation but would discourage proliferation and could not be unscrambled for individual national use. In a memorandum of 1960 Bowie argued for a force which would be mixed-manned (i.e., the crew of each unit should be drawn from a variety of nations) and seaborne; this would prevent any single nation from claiming proprietary rights. In December 1960 the Eisenhower administration, with due lame-duck tentativeness and in general language, laid before the NATO ministerial meeting in Paris the possibility of giving NATO five ballistic missile submarines with eighty Polaris missiles before 1963 *if* a system of multilateral control could be devised. The *if* was enormous, and the proposal attracted only mild interest. Nevertheless it represented a first step in the direction of nuclear sharing; and, for those trained in the Monnet school, an institution once established could acquire a life of its own.

4. FLEXIBLE RESPONSE VS. NUCLEAR CENTRALIZATION

After reflection, the new administration decided to continue along these lines. In Ottawa in May 1961 Kennedy said that the United States was ready to commit to NATO five or more Polaris atomic missile submarines, "subject to any agreed NATO guidelines on their control and use, and responsive to the needs of all members but [sic] still credible in an emergency"; beyond this, he looked forward to the possibility of a NATO seaborne force, "truly multilateral in ownership and control, if this should be desired and found feasible by our Allies, *once NATO's nonnuclear goals have been achieved.*"

The control problem in this formulation remained, however, as obscure as ever. In any case the last clause (my italics) contained a major catch from the European viewpoint, and therefore the Ottawa proposal elicited no immediate European enthusiasm. The Eisenhower multilateral force had been within the context of massive retaliation, empty as that doctrine had become by 1960. But the Kennedy proposal was within the context of the novel and unfamiliar doctrine of flexible response. This new doctrine made the strengthening of the conventional forces of the Alliance, as Kennedy said at Ottawa, the "matter of the highest priority" if, in McNamara's phrase, western strategy was going to multiply its options. The whole conception of graduated deterrence, however, emerged from a careful and exacting process of strategic analysis in the United States to which Europe, deprived of the tutelage of the new caste of military intellectuals, had not yet been exposed. The incoming administration, assuming that the Europeans were more sophisticated in matters of nuclear strategy than they were, and in any case neglecting to consult them in a systematic way, now presented them with the new strategy as a *fait accompli.*

The Berlin crisis of the summer of 1961 revealed some of the difficulties of the European reaction. McNamara, despite heroic efforts, could not bring the Pentagon and the NATO command to consensus on the western military response. While everyone agreed that a Soviet blockade of West Berlin would have to be countered first by a western thrust along the *Autobahn,* there was disagreement between those, like General Norstad, who wanted the probe in order to create a situation where the west could use nuclear weapons and those, like Kennedy and McNamara, who wanted the probe in order to postpone that situation. And, while everyone agreed that we might eventually have to go on to nuclear war, there was disagreement between those who favored a single definitive salvo against the Soviet Union and those who favored careful and discriminate attack.

These were tricky problems because of their political implications as well as because of their inherent difficulty. Washington had been persuading Western Europe for a decade of the infallibility of nuclear protection. The new American passion for conventional force now led many Europeans to believe, or profess to believe, that, in view of our own vulnerability to nuclear attack, we were no longer prepared to go to nuclear war at all. They contended that the Soviet Union would be far more effectively deterred if it knew the United States had no alternative to instant nuclear retaliation. Building up conventional strength, in their view, only weakened the credibility of the nuclear deterrent. (This seemed mad to McNamara, who did not regard nuclear weapons as things to be dropped lightly; "a credible deterrent," he once said, "cannot be based on an incredible act.") Moreover, conventional forces, it was argued, were expensive; they were politically unpopular; they could never be large enough to defeat the Red Army; their use would convert Europe into a battleground while America and Russia remained privileged sanctuaries; and in any case no one believed in the likelihood of a Soviet invasion of Western Europe unless the Russians thought themselves exempt from nuclear reprisal (and, except for Berlin, not many believed it likely then). Thus Norstad, coming to Washington in October 1961, told Kennedy that every document we submitted stressing conventional warfare cast doubt on our nuclear resolve.

Kennedy tried to counter this current of thought by assuring de Gaulle and others that the United States would use nuclear weapons in case of a massive conventional attack on Western Europe. But de Gaulle, thinking always in terms of the narrow interests of the nation-state, did not see why the United States should do so unless its own territory was under assault; presumably he wouldn't if he were the American President. Believing this, he believed all the more fervently in the necessity of the French independent deterrent. Even the British in early 1962 officially suggested to the Defense Department that a substantial increase in conventional forces in Europe might discredit the deterrent and asked whether the United States contemplated a major conventional battle over a long time and a large area.

The Kennedy-McNamara strategy, brilliantly designed to reduce the threat of nuclear war and to cope with the worldwide nuances of communist aggression, thus caused confusion and concern. In European eyes the question of nuclear control became more crucial than ever. A multilateral force conditioned on the achievement of NATO's non-nuclear goals had no great appeal; but the multilateral force in itself implied an entry into the nuclear club, and this did have appeal, especially for Bonn, so long excluded from membership. Early in 1962 the West Germans responded with a proposal for a rather large mixed-manned fleet of surface vessels equipped with missiles; soon afterward the Belgians expressed similar interest. The Bonn proposal said nothing about meeting NATO's conventional force requirements.

If the Ottawa formula had no widespread impact in Europe outside Bonn, it had dramatic impact in Washington. I doubt whether Kennedy, who supposed he was only mentioning a remote possibility to be considered if conventional needs were ever met, realized the energies he had released. For the idea of a multilateral force—MLF, as it was soon familiarly known—met a number of internal problems in our own policy. Though it served no strictly military function (some military men looked much askance on the idea of mixed-manning and the Joint Chiefs of Staff never liked the MLF), it appealed to the advocates of strategic interdependence as a means of preserving the unity of the deterrent and at the same time of giving NATO allies a nuclear role. Thus very early the MLF acquired a powerful convert in Thomas K. Finletter, our ambassador to NATO, a man of notable strength and clarity of mind and tenacity of purpose. At the same time, the MLF attracted advocates of economic partnership because it brought new and urgent pressure on the European governments to move toward federation. The reason for this was that the only body to which we would possibly yield our nuclear veto was the government of a united Western Europe. So long as the American veto remained, the MLF could never seem much more than a rather transparent public relations attempt to meet a supposed European demand for nuclear equality. But, if the MLF could help bring Monnet's United States of Europe into existence, it would at last bring the strategic and economic strains in our Atlantic thought into harmony.

Thus the Europeanists, whether tending toward interdependence, like Finletter, or toward partnership, like Ball, began to see in the MLF a useful vehicle—in time, *the* vehicle—for resolving the contradictions of our Atlantic policy. The MLF group—those who disagreed called it a cabal—became a resourceful and tireless lobby within the government, turning out a steady flow of well-reasoned documents in support of the proposal and carrying the case with ingenuity and zeal to the Europeans themselves. Though their primary concern was political, they received unexpected support in the summer of 1962 when a Navy study, in which Admiral Claude V. Ricketts was a leading figure, pronounced the MLF technically feasible. The Army and the Air Force, to which the MLF offered no role, continued negative.

In September 1962, however, McGeorge Bundy, striking out in another direction in a speech at Copenhagen, declared that the United States was willing to accept a European nuclear force "genuinely unified and multilateral," provided that it was integrated with the American deterrent; this, unlike MLF, meant a force without American participation. Then in October, Gerard Smith and Admiral John M. Lee headed a combined State-Defense party to brief NATO countries on the technical aspects of the MLF. The Smith-Lee mission, an exercise in salesmanship, found a good reception, as was to be expected, in Bonn and Brussels, polite interest in Rome and a mixed reaction in London—Lord Mountbatten and the Admiralty regarding the project as crazy and Lord Home and the Foreign Office prepared to give it, as Home said, "a fair wind."

Kennedy saw all this, including the Bundy speech and the Smith-Lee mission, as entirely exploratory. He was throwing out a variety of ideas in order to meet what he had been assured was an urgent European interest. But he was always careful not to impose American preoccupations on the Europeans; after all, they had a certain historic experience and were quite capable, in his judgment, of making their own decisions. This view accounted for the fact that the President, despite his strong ties to Europe, had no absolute doctrines about it. Both his collection of pre-1960 campaign addresses, *The Strategy of Peace,* and his 1960 campaign speeches were notable for the absence of particular Atlantic theories beyond general affirmations of the desirability of "a stable, creative partnership of equals." He combined a strong sense of ultimate Atlantic solidarity with a wide tolerance of means.

He simply felt that Europe would work toward unity in its own way. As for the character of this unity, he did not think nationalism altogether a bad thing. He knew that the United States would not lightly renounce its own sovereignty; this made him a bit skeptical of rigid supranational institutions in Europe. Though he had the greatest affection and respect for Jean Monnet, he was not tied to Monnet's formulas—or to those of anyone else. His support of the trade expansion bill did not commit him to the theology of partnership any more than his support of the unified deterrent committed him to the theology of interdependence.

He did think that British entry into the Common Market would increase the likelihood of a strong and sensible Europe; and he was determined to stop nuclear proliferation. As he told Adzhubei, Khrushchev's son-in-law, in November 1961, "The United States, as a matter of national policy . . . will not give nuclear weapons to any country, and I would be extremely reluctant to see West Germany acquire a nuclear capacity of its own." Though under certain pressure from the Pentagon and from some of his ambassadors in Paris to consider helping the French nuclear program, the President came to feel that such action would only legitimatize independent deterrents around the world and, in particular, stir Valkyrian longings in German breasts; in any case, de Gaulle never requested any assistance. "It has proved, perhaps," Kennedy said hopefully in 1963, "somewhat more difficult to split the atom politically than it has been to split it scientifically." Apart from nuclear proliferation and from Berlin—a decisive exception in 1961 but somewhat less thereafter—he regarded much of the talk about European nuclear deterrents, multilateral forces, conventional force levels, American divisions and so on as militarily supererogatory since it was based on the expectation of a Soviet attack on Western Europe "than which nothing is less likely." He understood that the Pentagon's business was to plan for every contingency, but he was not much impressed by its projections—the Soviet Union, for example, embarking on aggression in the Middle East and then for diversionary purposes trying to seize Hamburg.

His basic attitude toward Europe was to do what he could to strengthen the hand of modern-minded Europeans in their quest for unity—not to tell Europe what it ought to do but to adjust American policy to the needs and tempo of rational European self-determination. This was the spirit of his moving address at Independence Hall in Philadelphia on July 4, 1962. Here he mingled the Europeanist themes speaking both of the "Atlantic partnership" which would be made possible when Europe formed "a more perfect union" and of a "Declaration of Interdependence" based on "the indivisible liberty of all." In Europe, where the speech made a deep impression, it was correctly read as an affirmation of the American desire for close relationship with whatever sort of united Europe the genius of its people might evolve.

5. SKYBOLT

The President's Philadelphia speech came at a time of rising optimism about European unity. Macmillan had talked with de Gaulle at the Chateau de Champs in early June; and, though the General explained that British entry would change the character of the Common Market politically as well as economically, he did so in such genial terms that the Prime Minister went away with the impression that he would offer no strong resistance to the British application. The trade bill was about to pass Congress. For a moment prospects gleamed for the Grand Design.

Then in the weeks after the missile crisis the concepts of partnership and interdependence entered into unexpected conflict. The issue was, in its first appearance, technical: the decision of the United States government to cancel an agreement made by President Eisenhower with Macmillan at Camp David in 1960 to provide Great Britain with Skybolt missiles. But the problem very quickly became profoundly political. It involved other things than partnership and interdependence—most notably the relationship between Washington and London. Its solution, however, compelled the President to choose between those in his own government whose main interest lay in transforming Western Europe, including Britain, into a unified political and economic entity and those whose main interest lay in guarding the Anglo-American special relationship and integrity of the deterrent.

Skybolt, a two-stage ballistic missile launched from a bomber, originated as the Air Force's answer to Polaris in our permanent inter-service competition over the strategic deterrent. Though Britain could probably have had Polaris in 1960, it preferred Skybolt, which would prolong the life of the Royal Air Force's V-bombers, while Polaris would force the Royal Navy to divert its resources from aircraft carriers to submarines. Moreover, Skybolt seemed more likely to maintain the 'independence' of the British deterrent; Polaris was already being mentioned in a NATO context. The agreement bound the United States to pay all the costs of Skybolt's research and development. Britain had only to pay for the operational missiles she would eventually acquire. At the same time, Britain opened the Holy Loch naval base to American Polaris submarines. Though provisions were made for terminating the Skybolt agreement and though Skybolt and Holy Loch were nominally separate undertakings, the British left Camp David with the conviction that their loan of Holy Loch obligated the Americans to assist the British deterrent by providing one form of missile or another.

Skybolt was an extraordinarily intricate device, which from the start some in the Pentagon regarded with dubiety. But the British, the Air Force and Douglas Aircraft, to whom manufacture was confided, kept up a steady flow of optimism. In the fall of 1961 McNamara, after a careful review and despite cautions from the scientists as well as from David Bell and Carl Kaysen, decided to let the program go ahead; presumably evidence was incomplete, and he had enough fights on his hands with the Air Force already. One day in January 1962 Kennedy wondered aloud at luncheon with Julian Amery, the British Minister of Aviation, whether Skybolt would ever work. Amery, much upset, responded that it was the basis of British nuclear defense; if anything happened, it could have far-reaching effects on Anglo-American relations. The President assured him that the United States was doing everything possible to make the project succeed. After the Air Force took Amery out to Douglas Aircraft on a tour of inspection, he returned to London well satisfied that Skybolt had a future.

Work on Skybolt in the early months of 1962 involved more money and less progress than anyone had supposed, and by August McNamara's cost-effectiveness studies convinced him that further investment would be a mistake. But he had the usual problems with the Air generals, whom he had just affronted by his fight against the RS-70 manned bomber; and he was also aware of the difficulties cancellation would create for Britain—both for its military future as a nuclear power and for the political future of the Conservative government. Brooding over the matter, he decided to postpone the decision until Congress adjourned and next year's budget came up for review in November. When Peter Thorneycroft, the British Minister of Defense, visited Washington in mid-September overflowing with soulful reminders about the moral commitment to Skybolt, he elicited only guarded responses from McNamara.

By the time of the missile crisis McNamara had substantially concluded to end American support for Skybolt. Rumors began to circulate, some reaching the British. On November 6, election night, an old friend, William R. Hawthorne, professor of engineering at Cambridge University and a close associate of Sir Solly Zuckerman, the Defense Ministry's top scientist, came to our house to listen to the returns. Hawthorne's expression was troubled as he drew me aside for a confidential conversation. He wasted little sympathy on Skybolt—like Zuckerman, he had long questioned the project on technical grounds—but he communicated deep concern about possible difficulties between our two countries and emphasized the importance of our taking the initiative in devising a substitute.

The next day McNamara formally recommended cancellation to the President. Secretary Rusk, who was present, agreed with the decision. There was brief talk about other weapons systems which might be offered in place of Skybolt—possibly Polaris. Then the President, knowing that cancellation would be a heavy blow for the Tories, said that the British should be informed in ample time for them to prepare the ground before the decision was publicly announced. McNamara said he would call Ormsby Gore and also Thorneycroft. Rusk, apparently regarding Skybolt as a military rather than a political problem, made no objection.

When McNamara gave Ormsby Gore the bad news the next day, the Ambassador, startled and appalled, said, as he would continue to say in the next weeks, that it would be "political dynamite" in London. On the following day McNamara called Thorneycroft. The Minister of Defense, alerted by Ormsby Gore's report, was relatively calm and expressed interest in alternatives, especially in Polaris. McNamara offered to go to London at the end of the month to discuss the matter further.

The President told me later (in January) that he was totally unable to understand London's reaction in the days and weeks after November 8. He had expected that the British might propose, for example, a combined committee charged with looking into the situation, rendering a final recommendation and coming up with an alternative. Instead, he said in perplexity, they did nothing, even though the political life of their own government was at stake.[2]

[2] Remaining perplexed, he asked Richard Neustadt in March 1963 to undertake a study designed to find out how two close allies could have miscalculated each other and fallen into a surely avoidable crisis. Neustadt spent the summer on the inquiry and submitted the result to the President on November 15, 1963. The President read it with care and on November 20 told Bundy to tell Neustadt that "I want to see him after I get back from Texas."

The irony was that, while Washington was waiting for London to make its proposals, London was waiting for Washington to recommend its substitutes.

A number of things contributed to passivity. The British may still have hoped that the Air Force or the Joint Chiefs would somehow persuade McNamara to reverse his decision. They counted on the moral obligation, presumably inherited from Camp David, to compensate for Skybolt. The Prime Minister was puzzled by the presidential silence but doubted whether he should be the first to open the matter at the top level; moreover, he faced pressing troubles inside his own party and in Parliament. Our exceptionally able ambassador in London, David Bruce, had been informed of the Skybolt decision only by McNamara and through military channels. Hearing nothing from State, he felt immobilized. When he finally sent warnings to the Department toward the end of the month, he received no instructions. The special relationship was in a strange impasse as each partner lingered by the telephone. At the end of the month London and Washington jointly announced a meeting between the Prime Minister and the President for Nassau on December 18, three days after Macmillan was to meet with de Gaulle in France; but this was for other matters. Skybolt was not even on the original agenda.

McNamara, supposing wrongly that the British were hard at work on contingency planning, had directed his own people to appraise possible substitutes for Skybolt. They fixed quickly on Polaris; for, in the view of those who cared about a unified deterrent, the addition of Polaris to a British nuclear force which, as McNamara had pointed out after Ann Arbor, was for all practical purposes integrated with our own, raised no serious problem. The Europeanists in State, however, were now organizing to defend the conception of transatlantic partnership. They had regretted the cancellation of Skybolt, fearing that it would overthrow the government in London committed to bring Britain into Europe. But, if Skybolt had to go, at least let it carry the special relationship down with it; this would place the British and the Germans on a level of equality in the missile age, make Bonn more manageable and facilitate British entry into Europe. What worried the Europeanists was the thought that the United States by offering a replacement for Skybolt—Polaris, for example—would prolong the British deterrent, intensify Bonn's demand for a nuclear role and prove to de Gaulle that Britain preferred the United States to Europe. Some Europeanists, like Schaetzel, were chiefly concerned with the Common Market, others, like

Walt Rostow and Henry Owen of the Policy Planning Council, with the MLF. But both British entry into the Market and the MLF were now, in their view, at stake, and Skybolt offered the grand opportunity to terminate the special relationship and force Britain into Europe.

But these were still mostly flurries behind the scenes. With no evidence of special concern from London, Washington concluded that the British were not too unhappy, and the Skybolt problem receded from official minds. When a so-called defense policy conference was convened at the end of November, Skybolt received only cursory attention. Rusk said he wished that Hound Dog, one of the alternative missiles under consideration, had been named Skybolt B. McNamara replied that the Secretary of State would have been great in the automobile business. The talk then turned to the problem of persuading NATO to increase its conventional forces.

McNamara's trip to London, postponed because of the annual tussle with the defense budget, was finally set for December 11. It was preceded by five successive failures of Skybolt tests—a fact to which McNamara imprudently drew the attention of the British press when he landed at London Airport. The talks with Thorneycroft were a Pinero drama of misunderstanding: Thorneycroft expecting McNamara to propose Polaris, McNamara expecting Thorneycroft to request it. When McNamara's careful explanation of Skybolt's technical shortcomings failed to conclude in any substitute offer which Thorneycroft thought the British with dignity could accept, the Minister of Defense took the offensive. Waving aside the technical arguments—one could find experts, he said, on either side—he concentrated on the political consequences of cancellation: for the Tory government, for Anglo-American understanding. Those who had always been saying that it was impossible to rely on the United States would be confirmed; those who had argued for that reliance would be betrayed. In the context of the Ann Arbor speech, cancellation would be taken as a deliberate American effort to drive Britain out of the nuclear game. It would tear the heart out of the special relationship. Finally Thorneycroft asked the hard question: if the United States were cancelling Skybolt for technical reasons, would it be prepared to state publicly that it would do everything possible to help Britain preserve its independent nuclear role?

McNamara expressed sympathy but tried to steer the talk back to technical alternatives. After a rejection of other possibilities Thorneycroft brought up Polaris. When Mc-

Namara pointed out legal problems, Thorneycroft, recalling the association of Skybolt and the Holy Loch Polaris base in 1960, claimed that the United States lay under a moral obligation, if it announced the demise of Skybolt, to announce at the same time some other means of sustaining Britain's deterrent. McNamara asked whether, if Britain received Polaris, it would make it part of a multilateral force. Thorneycroft declined this as a condition; Britain would decide this as an independent power. That evening the London newspapers, presumably stimulated by the Defense Ministry, portrayed Thorneycroft in sensational stories as the lion-hearted champion of Skybolt against the American Defense.

By now in Washington the battle lines were forming. When McNamara returned, George Ball, a late arrival on the scene, set forth the Europeanists' case in a debate before the President. Kennedy listened with care, mentioned the British sense of our moral obligation and Macmillan's shaky political position and finally suggested the possibility of relating an offer of Polaris to eventual commitment by the British of their Polaris force to NATO.

And in the December drizzle at Rambouillet the Prime Minister met the General. De Gaulle's mood had changed since their conference in June. The Algerian war was now behind him, the Assembly elections at the end of November had refreshed his mandate, and he spoke with towering and placid self-confidence. He no longer saw how Britain could possibly join the Common Market: better let it apply for association rather than membership. Macmillan valiantly argued the case for Britain in Europe. The Prime Minister also brought up Skybolt and told the General that he planned to maintain the British deterrent, hopefully on the basis of Polaris. This was a point with which de Gaulle, cherishing his own deterrent, would presumably sympathize. But the talks were not a success, and the parting was as chilly as the weather: now on to the sunlight of the Caribbean.

6. NASSAU AND AFTER

As for the President, he was preoccupied in November with the removal of the missiles and the IL-28s from Cuba. No one, except David Ormsby Gore, had told him that Skybolt might cause an Anglo-American crisis: neither Macmillan (Kennedy later said, "He should have warned me of the dangers to him—we would have come up with a solution before publicity—he should have had Gore come in"), nor McNamara, who continued to regard it as a technical problem, nor Rusk.

Shortly before leaving for Nassau the President was asked about Skybolt in a television interview. He said briefly he saw no point in spending $2.5 billion for development when "we don't think that we are going to get $2.5 billion worth of national security." Then he prepared for the Caribbean trip. To the President's surprise, Rusk, claiming an annual ceremonial engagement with the diplomatic corps, said he thought it better to stay in Washington. Ball went in his place, along with McNamara, Nitze, Bruce, William R. Tyler and Bundy. David Ormsby Gore joined them on the presidential plane.

On the plane Kennedy settled down for a long talk with Ormsby Gore. The Ambassador lost no time in bringing up Skybolt. While recognizing that preferential relations with Britain on nuclear matters made difficulties for the United States with its European allies, Ormsby Gore warned Kennedy that these troubles would not compare with the storm of anti-Americanism which would sweep England if the British believed the Americans were letting them down. Kennedy's mind was now in full focus on the problem. Within half an hour, he and Ormsby Gore worked out a proposal based on the assumption, created by the Thorneycroft-McNamara meeting and evidently not dispelled by London's instructions to its ambassador, that Britain still wanted Skybolt. The United States, by this new idea, would abandon the missile for itself but agree to split future development charges evenly with the British. This was a wise and generous offer. Had it come a month earlier, it would have changed the whole atmosphere. The British, faced by the spiraling development cost, might have decided to give up Skybolt anyway, but it would have been their own decision. Only now it was too late; Kennedy's television comment had destroyed any lingering interest Macmillan might have had in Skybolt.

When the presidential plane landed in Nassau, the atmosphere was tense. Henry Brandon of the London *Sunday Times* reported in the British delegation a "resentment and suspicion of American intentions such as I have never experienced in all the Anglo-American conferences I have covered over the past twenty years." Thorneycroft wished to lead a fight against the Americans even at the risk of breaking up the meeting. That evening Macmillan told Kennedy that he wanted Polaris, and it was clear that he felt he had to have it under conditions which would preserve the British claim to a national deterrent.

When the formal talks began the next morning, Macmillan with weary eloquence invoked past glories of the Anglo-American relationship and suggested that a straight switch of Polaris for Skybolt would keep that relationship alive. He dismissed the thought that this would harm Britain's application for the Common Market; agriculture was the stumbling block here; Europe would understand that Britain and the United States had built the bomb together; de Gaulle had seemed sympathetic on the point at Rambouillet. In response Kennedy first brought up the 50-50 offer, but Macmillan made it clear that he had no further interest in Skybolt; the lady had already been violated in public. Then the President mentioned the American commitment to multilateral policies in the nuclear field. More eloquent than ever, Macmillan insisted that Britain was determined to stay in the nuclear club. His nation had a great history and would not give up now. If the United States would not help, Britain would continue on its own at whatever cost, including the inevitable rift with the United States. Instead of pleading that his government would fall, he seemed to be saying that his party would accept anti-Americanism to keep itself in power. But this was not a threat; it was a lamentation. It was evidently a bravura performance.

By now the President had very likely made up his own mind that the British had to have Polaris. The only question was how to reconcile this with the claims of multilateralization and European partnership. Macmillan had suggested at one point a willingness to put his Polaris force in NATO if he retained the right to draw it back in case of an emergency. This formula offered a possibility of harmonizing independence and NATO. The drafters now set to work and outdid themselves in masterly ambiguity. Article 6 of the Statement on Nuclear Defense Systems contemplated a NATO multinational force—that is, allocations from national forces to the NATO command. Article 7 pledged both nations to use their "best endeavors" toward a multilateral force—that is, a mixed-manned force from which national withdrawals would be impossible. Article 8 agreed that the United States would make Polaris missiles (minus warheads) available to the British and that the resulting British force might be included in either the multinational or the multilateral system. "The Prime Minister made clear that, except where H. M. Government may decide that supreme national interests are at stake, these British forces will be used for the purposes of international defence of the Western Alliance in all circumstances." The communiqué concluded by expressing the joint Anglo-American conviction that "the nuclear defense" of the western alliance was "indivisible."

For Macmillan it was a great victory, marred only by the extent to which the Conservative party and the London press had identified the British deterrent with Skybolt. For Kennedy it was a reasonable adjustment to a thorny problem, leaving policy free to move in a number of directions. For our own Europeanists, it was a missed opportunity and bitter defeat: instead of forcing the British to an MLF commitment, we had saved their deterrent, thrust an issue into the hands of de Gaulle and set back the cause of European integration.

For France it might, despite Macmillan's mention of Polaris at Rambouillet, have devastating effect; so it was decided at Nassau to offer de Gaulle Polaris on the same terms as to Macmillan—i.e., assignment to NATO but with the escape clause of emergency withdrawal. This was an entirely genuine proposal, though made publicly, formally and without the ceremony the General might have expected. The President himself and others—Bundy and Tyler especially—hoped that it might throw the French a bridge back to NATO. Though the French Minister of Information promptly pointed out that France had "neither the submarines required for the Polaris missiles nor the warheads," Kennedy and Macmillan did not exclude the thought of a British offer of Polaris warheads to Paris in exchange for French nuclear cooperation. The President called Charles E. Bohlen to Palm Beach directly after Nassau to give him a full briefing on what to say to the General; Hervé Alphand, the French Ambassador to Washington, also talked to Kennedy at Palm Beach and early in January 1963 called at the State Department for further exegesis of the Nassau communiqué. On January 5 in Paris Bohlen told de Gaulle as clearly as he could that all possibilities were open for discussion. While the General showed no passion for Nassau, he showed no acrimony against it, and the Ambassador left thinking that he would want to explore its negotiating implications in due course. During December and the first two weeks of the new year those in Washington who based themselves on Nassua's Article 6 remained quite optimistic about the chance of the French joining a NATO multinational force. The MLF, they hoped, was dead.

But the Europeanists were meanwhile rallying from their post-Nassau gloom to mount a new campaign, based on Nassau's Article 7, to retrieve the MLF and defend the

Grand Design against both de Gaulle and Macmillan. Kennedy, impressed by their contention that Nassau had given Bonn a dangerous sense of exclusion, agreed that a modest refloating of the MLF might pull West Germany back toward the alliance and offset Adenauer's growing fascination with de Gaulle. Accordingly, early in January 1963 George Ball was sent to Europe to reassure the Germans. On his way, he stopped in Paris to discuss Nassau with Couve de Murville, the French Foreign Minister.

Four days later in Washington Kennedy in his State of the Union address hailed the alliance: "Free Europe is entering into a new phase of its long and brilliant history . . . moving toward a unity of purpose and power and policy in every sphere of activity." In Paris the same day de Gaulle held his press conference and declared war against the Grand Design.

XXXIII

TWO EUROPES: DE GAULLE AND KENNEDY

THE BRUTALITY OF DE GAULLE'S ATTACK left an impression that he was overcome by sudden anger and caused much speculation over possible irritants: if only Ball had not laid such stress on the integrationist side of Nassau when he talked to Couve, if only the Polaris offer to France had been pressed harder in December, or (from the other view) if only the Polaris offer had never been made to Britain and Nassau had never taken place—then Britain might be in the Common Market, and the Grand Design would be in business. One day the President pushed this back further: could it have been the decision not to give France nuclear information in 1962? or the refusal to establish de Gaulle's tripartite NATO directorship in 1958? or the treatment of de Gaulle by Roosevelt and Churchill during the Second World War?

My own impression was that de Gaulle, like Andrew Jackson, deliberately used anger as an instrument of authority.[1] It seemed unlikely that the policy of January 14

[1] One observer said of Jackson, "He would sometimes extemporize a fit of passion in order to overwhelm an adversary, when certain of being in the right, but his self-command was always perfect."

was the product of passing annoyance. Its roots, as I endeavored to persuade the President, lay deep in the view of Europe and the world de Gaulle had stated and restated throughout his career. Kennedy asked for a memorandum on this point. My report to him concluded: "There is very little we could have done to divert him from what has plainly been the cherished objective of his life."

1. DE GAULLE'S EUROPE

He had set forth as recently as 1959 in *Le Salut,* the third volume of his magnificent memoirs, what he called "the great plan I have conceived for my country." The elements were clearly stated.

a) Britain and the United States wanted "to relegate us to a secondary place among nations responsible for constructing the peace. But I had no intention of letting this happen."

b) "I intended to assure France primacy in Western Europe."

c) I intended "to prevent the rise of a new Reich that might again threaten the safety" of France;

d) I intended "to co-operate with East and West and, if need be, contract the necessary alliances on one side or the other without ever accepting any kind of dependency";

e) I intended "to persuade the states along the Rhine, the Alps, and the Pyrenees to form a political, economic, and strategic bloc; to establish this bloc as one of the three world powers and, should it become necessary, as the arbiter between the Soviet and Anglo-American camps."

De Gaulle could hardly have made his purpose more solemn or emphatic. "Since 1940," he wrote, "my every word and act have been dedicated to establishing these possibilities; now that France was on her feet again, I would try to realize them."

For the longer run, he supposed that Europe could find equilibrium and peace only by an association among "Slavs, Germans, Gauls and Latins." Charlemagne might have drawn up this list; he too would have omitted the Anglo-Saxons for having turned their backs on Europe and crossed the water to Britain in the fifth century. Memories from the war haunted de Gaulle and confirmed his mistrust of islanders: Churchill saying to him in June 1944, "Here is something you should know: whenever we have to choose between Europe and the open sea, we shall always choose the open sea. Whenever I have to choose between you and Roosevelt, I shall always choose Roosevelt"; Harold Macmillan crying at Algiers, "If General de Gaulle refuses the hand stretched out towards him, let him know that Britain and the United States will abandon him completely

—and he will be nothing any more." De Gaulle noted in his memoirs that he had tried and failed to win Churchill to Europe in 1945—"perhaps the last possible occasion to bring him to a change of heart." The Englishman and the Frenchman had agreed, de Gaulle remembered, that in final analysis "England is an island; France the edge of a continent; America another world." Macmillan might still have demonstrated the required change of heart by accepting the Treaty of Rome without conditions, but under pressure he had shown himself unregenerate. NATO was all right as a coalition of national states; but if the United States and Britain tried to use it as an instrument for the Anglo-Saxon domination of Europe, they must be resisted.

No one had predicted his own course more lucidly than de Gaulle himself. Why then had January 14 astonished so many people? One reason, I discovered to my dismay, was that few people in the State Department appeared to have read de Gaulle. Another surely was that de Gaulle liked to put about an impression of himself as a lonely, unyielding, messianic figure, set in his views, oblivious of tactics, prepared to wait in Colombey-les-deux-Eglises until the great world came round to him. No impression could be more misleading. Actually he was one of the consummate political tacticians of the twentieth century. Only such a man could have so audaciously pressed Churchill and Roosevelt during the war, yet always stopping short of the unforgivable provocation; only such a man, brought to power to keep Algeria French, could purposefully and coldly move to make Algeria independent. Similarly in the case of the Common Market he had concealed his goal for a time behind a screen of cryptic phrases and courtly attitudes, like those which in June had lulled not only Macmillan but our Paris Embassy into reporting that the French were resigned to British entry. They all underestimated the old strategist. As John Randolph said of Van Buren, he "rowed to his object with muffled oars."

De Gaulle, who had perceived for a long time the fatal contradiction within the Grand Design between interdependence and partnership, now was moving to exploit it. But why had he chosen this moment to come into the open? Probably the Cuban missile crisis was a precipitating factor. On the one hand, it showed that the United States in emergencies would act on its own, without NATO consultation or 'integration,' on matters affecting not only American security but world peace. This undoubtedly reinforced the General's old belief that America did not regard Europe as a primary interest; no nation could ever be expected to look out for anything but itself (he liked to quote Nietzsche's description of the state as "the coldest of all the cold monsters"). So de Gaulle said in January 14, "No one in the world . . . can say whether, where, when, how, or to what extent American nuclear arms would be used to defend Europe." At the same time the outcome of Cuba renewed his faith in the broad efficacy of the American deterrent. So he added, "This does not of course prevent American nuclear arms, which are the most powerful of all, from remaining the essential guarantee of world peace." And the outcome also reconfirmed his view that there was no danger of war over Berlin. All this left him free to pursue his own ends in Europe.

In addition, if Cuba were to be followed by a *détente*, de Gaulle wanted to be in on the peacemaking; he could never forget Yalta when in his absence non-Europeans (by his definition) imposed what he considered a wicked settlement on Europe. Moreover, if Western Europe were irrevocably tied to the Atlantic, the division of Europe would become permanent, and de Gaulle's dream of rebuilding "Europe from the Atlantic to the Urals" would be forever frustrated. And within the Common Market Britain was steadily acquiring the votes for admission—a result which, if achieved, would end French primacy in the Economic Community and consolidate Atlantic influence on the continent. Europe must be for the Europeans; action was necessary: Nassau provided the pretext. The explanation for his air of moderation between December 21 and January 14 must await volume four of his memoirs.

My memorandum probably pushed the inexorability thesis too far, and I believe the President could never rid his mind of the thought that, if this or that had been done differently, it might have been possible to avoid the impasse of 1963. His interest in de Gaulle never flagged. The General was one of the heroes: he had rallied the Free French in the war; he had liberated Algeria; he had given unquestioning support at the time of a missile crisis; he was a great writer. Yet, while making due allowance for the bitterness generated by de Gaulle's frustrations during the war, the President also felt that rancor demeaned the man and distorted his policy. Kennedy would ask everyone who knew him—his two ambassadors, James M. Gavin and Charles E. Bohlen, Cyrus Sulzberger of the *New York Times* and particularly Malraux—to explain why so obviously great a man took such incomprehensible and petty positions. Gavin recalls the President's saying from time to time, as though to himself, "What can you do with a man like that?" Kennedy also had contempt for the spitefulness of official French pronouncements, especially those emanating from Alain Peyrefitte and the Ministry of Information, and he was angry at the clandestine French campaigns against the United States in Africa and Asia.

Nevertheless, if he had his troubles with the General, there was, as he said at the Malraux dinner in 1962, an American "tradition in that regard, with Franklin Roosevelt and Dwight D. Eisenhower.[2] . . . I know that there are sometimes difficulties, but I hope that those who live in both our countries realize how fortunate we are in the last two decades to be associated in the great effort with him." He came in the end to feel that de Gaulle was operating out of a consistent, if not convincing, conception of France's interests and that the General evidently believed he *needed* some sort of friction with the United States. Kennedy, however, never regarded him as beyond rational discourse. "If I can put all that effort into the Russians," he once said, "I can put some of it into the French." He hoped to see de Gaulle again; a visit was scheduled for February 1964. In a conversation with Gavin in late October 1963, Kennedy said, rather happily, Gavin thought, "Well, I am going to see the General in the next few months, and I think that we will be able to get something done together."

2. MLF

January 14 unavoidably produced the usual reaction—"what can you do with a man like that?"—but in a short while Kennedy accepted the new reality. "From a strictly economic viewpoint," he said to me somewhat sardonically a few days later, "we have known all along that British membership in the Common Market would be bad for us; so we are now better off. On the political side, our chief object was to tie Germany more firmly into the structure of Western Europe. Now de Gaulle is doing that in his own way." He was referring to the Franco-German treaty of cooperation, which Adenauer had signed on January 22. Asked at a press conference in February whether he intended to take measures of economic or political reprisal against de Gaulle, he said, "No . . . definitely not." At a White House meet-

[2] The tradition was even older. Robert R. Livingston, an American Minister to France under Napoleon, wrote to his Secretary of State in 1802: "There never was a government with which less could be done by negotiation than here. There is no people, no legislature, no counsellors. One man is everything. He seldom asks advice and never hears it unasked."

ing, he said that he thought our best policy was just to let
the dust settle. Dean Acheson, who was present and had
tried letting the dust settle after the communists had taken
over China, observed quickly, "Mr. President, I would not
advise putting it in quite that way."

But the Europeanists did not want to let the dust settle.
Ball, uncharacteristically letting his rhetoric run away with
him, discoursed publicly about unspecified European leaders
dominated "by a nostalgic longing for a world that never
was" and seeking to revive the "vanquished symbols of be-
glamored centuries." In particular, Ball's January visit
to Adenauer had given a new spurt of life to the MLF. If
de Gaulle meant to make Western Germany choose between
France and the United States, the MLF in Washington's
view was the way to make it clear that Bonn would find
greater security in the Atlantic relationship. To strengthen
this point, Kennedy decided in mid-January to visit Germany on a spring trip to Europe. Soon afterward Ambassador Livingston Merchant, an experienced career officer,
was directed to work with Finletter in preparing and negotiating American proposals on the MLF.

Kennedy accepted the need to reassure the Germans and
show NATO that there were alternatives to Gaullism. But
he retained a certain skepticism about the MLF. He felt
first of all that the MLF campaign diverted interest from
more serious problems of the planet. "The whole debate
about an atomic force in Europe," he told Spaak of Belgium in May, "is really useless, because Berlin is secure,
and Europe as a whole is well protected. What really matters at this point is the rest of the world." As for the
MLF per se, he really considered that, so long as the United
States retained its veto (and he never mentioned renunciation as a possibility, though other members of his government did), the MLF was something of a fake. Though he
was willing to try it, he could not see why Europeans would
be interested in making enormous financial contributions
toward a force over which they had no real control.

The MLF advocates replied primarily by talking about
West Germany. Bonn wanted the MLF because it was a
status symbol, marking a form of accession to the nuclear
club; because it gave West Germany an indissoluble nuclear
association with the United States and a sense of nuclear
equality with Britain; because it would avert pressures for
an independent German deterrent; because they hoped that
in a few years the control issue would be re-examined on
its merits; in short, because MLF provided a self-respect-

ing role in nuclear deterrence. If MLF failed, its apostles continued, moderate leadership in Bonn would be undermined, West Germany would start pressing for nationally manned and owned missiles and, if denied them by us, a right-wing government might turn to the French.

All this rested on the premise that the Germans were hellbent on having nuclear weapons and, if they could not get them multilaterally, would seek them bilaterally, even at the expense of the American relationship. Though this proposition had been hackneyed around the American government, it did not seem to some, especially the British, all that self-evident. Macmillan had long deprecated this notion; and, spending a few days in London in early 1963, I encountered general doubt. Jo Grimond, the leader of the Liberal party, who had just returned from a trip to Germany and France, said he had come upon no significant German demand for nuclear weapons.[3] Grimond, George Brown of the Labour party and other British political leaders all feared, however, that the Merchant mission was having the effect of generating such a demand where none existed before? They added ominously that, if such a demand ever came into being, it was not likely to be satisfied by the secondary symbolism of mixed-manning.

"The self-fulfilling prophecy," Robert K. Merton has written, "is, in the beginning, a *false* definition of the situation evoking a new behavior which makes the originally false conception come *true*." This seemed to be the logic of the MLF. Perhaps by 1963 it had awakened the German demand it had premised; perhaps its advocates were right in thinking that the demand was inevitable, that the Germans would never accept second-class nuclear status as a permanent condition. The President asked David Bruce, in whose steadiness of judgment he had great confidence, to return from London in early February and reappraise our European policy. Without associating himself with the MLF mystique, Bruce recommended it as a useful instrument for moving toward our basic objectives in Europe. Kennedy agreed with this pragmatic reaction: MLF was the best available tool to reconcile interdependence—the indivisibility of the deterrent—with partnership—the building of a united Western Europe; moreover, it would fill a vacuum into which, otherwise, Gaullism might seep. He reached one final decision in February. A discussion with Admiral Hyman Rickover persuaded him that making MLF

---

[3] Henry Kissinger similarly reported that he saw "no signs of any domestic pressure in Germany for a national nuclear-weapons program."

a submarine force would raise security problems. As the proposal developed in 1963, it now contemplated twenty-five specially constructed surface vessels equipped with eight Polaris missiles each and carrying crews drawn from at least three different nationalities. The cost would be $5 billion over ten years, the United States paying around one-third. In press conferences Kennedy said, "We think the multilateral force represents the best solution to hold the alliance together," though always emphasizing that if "Europe decides that this isn't what they want, we would be glad to hear other proposals." MLF in his view was not a demarche but a response. When he sent emissaries to discuss it with European leaders, he instructed them not to talk as if they were reflecting a personal preoccupation of the American President.

But our Europeanists, seeing the MLF as the last chance of strengthening allied cooperation and of securing Adenauer against the temptation of de Gaulle, pushed the idea with greater zeal than the President intended. The Merchant mission of March and April evolved mysteriously from a modest and quiet exploratory inquiry into an over-sized thirty-two-man group, charging around Europe in a Convair, giving the impression of a major American campaign and stirring opposition wherever it went. A USIA survey of the West European press reported early in April overwhelming rejection of the MLF. Wits dubbed it the multilateral farce. Moreover, as the campaign roared along, it began to exude the pent-up anti-de Gaulle feeling in State—Gavin remembers a State Department officer calling de Gaulle "a bastard who is out to get us." Apart from Germany, the response was meager; and, as the MLF appeared likely to dwindle into a Washington-Bonn operation, which the President would never have accepted, its supporters had to redouble their efforts elsewhere.

In October 1963 when Lord Home, soon to be translated into Sir Alec Douglas-Home and Prime Minister, visited Washington, he said that the British saw the point of MLF but were bothered by the insistence with which the American government was pushing it. Kennedy, a little taken aback, said he had no desire to bring pressure; the decision was Europe's; where had Alec got this impression? Home replied that it was the impression conveyed by Kennedy's own people. The President reaffirmed his feeling that MLF's basic principle was interesting and important; it would give non-nuclear powers a sense of participation in nuclear decisions without making them nuclear powers.

But in his view we should go at it slowly. The experimental working group, just formed by interested countries, and the proposed mixed-manned ship, would show what the MLF meant practically. These steps would take eighteen months to two years, during which time the whole problem could be talked out. "Bill Tyler may still be around," the President said, referring to the senior State Department official present, "but some of the rest of us might not be."

3. ITALY

By 1963 the MLF zealots had become known in the government as the "theologians." One was indeed sometimes oppressed by the long abstract discussions of partnership and interdependence and by the interminable efforts to make the integrated deterrent and the separate and equal economic entities dance on the head of the same pin. The whole debate, useful as it was, appeared at times to involve an increasingly fruitless preoccupation with architecture at the expense of content. Was the crucial question really whether a united Europe should be federal or confederal, whether it should be a separate partner or absorbed in the Atlantic community? or was it whether the result was to be an authoritarian or democratic Europe? If a line were to be drawn against de Gaulle, might it not be drawn most persuasively, not against his concept of Europe or of Atlantica, but against his concept of freedom?

If anything was clear about the new Europe, it was that the economic revival was transforming the mood and expectations of the working classes. By showing that a free economic system could raise mass living standards, it was attenuating their commitment to classical socialism. At the same time, it was inciting them to demand larger shares of the affluence they saw flowing around them. And meanwhile the very abundance of consumer goods was creating a spiritual disquietude among the intellectuals, fearful of materialism and seeking some higher public purpose. All this was producing a ferment in the broad political zone lying between traditional conservatism on one side and communism on the other.

The two great groups historically inhabiting the center-left were the Christian democrats and the social democrats. Though they had long been at odds over such issues as government aid to church schools, the fellowship of the Resistance during the war had encouraged tentative experiments in collaboration. If they could only work steadily together now, might they not give Western Europe the so-

cial leadership it needed to meet its new problems? At the
moment such a rapprochment seemed most likely in Italy.
If the center-left coalition succeeded there, the alliance
between progressive Catholics and democratic Socialists
might offer a model for other nations—for Germany after
Adenauer, for France after de Gaulle, even for Spain after
Franco. The consolidation of a Western European center-
left would also be the best guarantee against the communist effort to revive the prewar united front with the Socialists.

A united front between Communists and Socialists had
existed for some years after the war in Italy. In the late
forties one wing of the Socialists, objecting to the pro-
Soviet tendency of the majority, had split off and established the Social Democratic party under the courageous
leadership of Giuseppe Saragat. Pietro Nenni, who remained
as the head of the Socialist majority, mingled a rhetorical
maximalism in politics with a genially humane and fundamentally democratic personality. The Soviet intervention in
Hungary in 1956 proved too much for him and many of his
comrades. In 1957 Nenni began to move away from the
Communist party. By 1960 his break was complete, though
Socialist-Communist coalitions still lingered in many localities.

The movement of the Nenni Socialists led some in the
democratic parties to see at last the chance to end the
immobilism which had cursed Italian politics since the
death of De Gasperi. The thesis thus arose among the Christian Democrats of an *apertura a sinistra*—an opening to
the left—calling for a center-left government, composed of
the Christian Democratic, Social Democratic and Republican parties with, initially, 'outside' support (i.e., benevolent
parliamentary abstention) by the Nenni Socialists, to be
followed in due course by active voting support and
eventually by participation in a governing coalition.

The policy of the United States before Kennedy had been
one of purposeful opposition to the opening to the left. The
reasons were clear enough: the Eisenhower administration
did not trust Nenni; it believed him to be a neutralist if not
still at heart a fellow traveler; and it did not want social
and economic reform in Italy. The issue had become so
tense in our embassy in Rome that one younger officer, as
noted earlier, was disciplined in 1960 for carrying the case
for the *apertura* past the deputy chief of mission to the ambassador.

That policy was appropriate for the Eisenhower administration and possibly even for the conditions of the fifties. But by 1961 no one could doubt Nenni's break with the Communists. Moreover, by ingenious reinterpretation, Nenni had defined his party's traditional neutralism as meaning the preservation of the existing European equilibrium; since Italian withdrawal from NATO would threaten that equilibrium, Nenni explicitly opposed such withdrawal as an unneutral act. Moreover, a progressive administration in Washington should certainly not be in the position of discouraging progressive policies in Rome, especially when social reform was required to isolate the Communists, eliminate the conditions which bred them and begin the reclamation of the working class for democracy.

For all these reasons it seemed to me and my White House colleague Robert Komer that the time had come to end the American opposition to the *apertura* and make it clear that the United States welcomed a government in Italy which addressed the social and economic needs of the people. Prime Minister Amintore Fanfani's visit to Washington in June 1961 provided an obvious opportunity to signalize the new departure. President Kennedy, who had some acquaintance with the Italian situation, readily agreed that the United States from now on should indicate discreet sympathy for the opening to the left.

Fanfani and Kennedy had first met at the Democratic convention in Chicago in 1956. Kennedy then had delighted the Italian by saying that he had read his book *Catholicism, Protestantism and Capitalism*. When they met again in 1961, a fortnight after Khrushchev in Vienna and in the midst of the Berlin crisis, Fanfani, as he told me later, found a new Kennedy, strong, grave and stamped with the burden of world responsibility. Their talk was a rather routine canvass of the issues; occasionally it passed to larger questions. Fanfani made one general point which especially impressed the President: "It is an irony that the communists, who believe in dictatorship, are always addressing the masses; while the west, which believes in democracy, is always addressing the leaders." Though the *apertura* was not on the formal agenda, Kennedy told Fanfani privately that, if the Italian Prime Minister thought it a good idea (as he did), we would watch developments with sympathy.

The presidential decision was, of course, at once communicated to the State Department, and this should have ended the matter. In fact, it only marked the beginning of a long and exasperating fight. In the end it took nearly two years to induce the Department of State to follow the Presi-

dent's policy. The stratagems of obstruction and delay were
manifold, and the motives mixed. It was partly, I imagine, the chronic difficulty of changing established policies;
partly the patriotic conviction on the part of certain Foreign Service officers that they owned American foreign
policy and, in any case, knew better than the White
House; partly an innate Foreign Service preference for conservatives over progressives along with a traditional weakness for the Roman aristocracy. Whatever the motives, the
sages on State's Italian desk spent 1961 predicting that the
opening to the left would not come for years. Then, as the
apertura gathered momentum, they produced an alternative
argument: that it was coming anyway and therefore did
not require our blessing. The pervading attitude was that in
no case should we encourage a development which would
constitute a crushing blow to communism in Italy and
throughout Europe; rather Nenni and his party must meet
a series of purity tests before they could qualify for
American approval: as usual risks were more impressive
than opportunities.

I passed through Rome in February 1962 when Fanfani
was about to form a new government, which, contrary to
our experts' prophecies, had the outside support of the Socialists. One afternoon at the house of Tullia Zevi I talked
with Nenni, Ugo La Malfa, the brilliant leader of the Republican party, Ignazio Silone, the novelist, and others—a discussion interrupted by several phone calls from Fanfani to
Nenni and La Malfa to discuss the ministerial list. Nenni
was a charming old man, his style oratorical rather than
conversational. I said that Washington was pleased at the
prospect of forward movement in Italian social policy but
wondered about the implications of the *apertura* for foreign affairs. Nenni responded at considerable length, stressing his dislike of the Communists, the neutralist traditions
of his party, his support of the Common Market and his acceptance of NATO on a *de facto* basis. As for Berlin, he
said that he hoped for a formula which would continue
the present arrangement. But the group seemed little interested in foreign matters. It was evident that they were
wholly absorbed in the problem, not unfamiliar to us, of
getting their nation moving again. In any case, the *apertura*
was on the way. I reported to the President that the Embassy had taken a hands-off attitude—obviously a great
improvement over the previous line—but this after saying
most of the previous year that the chances of an opening
to the left were fading fast, whereas it was evident to
most observers that this was not the case. "The result has

been that the opening has taken place, not against the United States, but without it."

The fight continued. In May 1962, the State Department Italianists, apparently unmoved by anything that had happened since the days of John Foster Dulles, declared that the Nenni Socialists were "not anti-Communist" and that their success would strengthen anti-NATO sentiment in Italy. Soon Komer and I enlisted Robert Kennedy, Arthur Goldberg and Walter Reuther in the effort to cajole the Department into abandoning the legacy of the past. It was an odd situation. We had, of course, the presidential decision and the patient backing of McGeorge Bundy. We had the sporadic sympathy of George Ball and William Tyler, when they were not out reorganizing Europe. As for the Secretary of State, he did not have, so far as I could find out, any views on Italian policy beyond a nervous response when President Segni, an old-time opponent of the *apertura*, told him that American interest in the Socialists would be interpreted as a rejection of our only 'true' friends, the Italian conservatives. But in a time when attention at the top was seized by major crises, policy toward Italy inescapably enjoyed low priority; and this gave the officers on the working level a chance to pursue their own preferences, which they did with assiduity.

It was an endless struggle. Meetings would be called, decisions reached, cables sent; then the next meeting would begin with the same old arguments. One felt entrapped as in a Kafka novel. It was worse than carrying Chester Bowles's double mattress up that winding flight of narrow stairs. A memorandum of mine to Bundy in October 1962, sixteen months after the President had tried to change the policy, began: "As you will recall, the White House has been engaged for about fifty years in an effort to persuade the Department of State that an air of sympathy toward the Nenni Socialists would advance the interests of the United States and of western democracy. . . . During this period, practically *all* the evidence has supported our view that the Nenni Socialists have split irrevocably from the Communists and are determined to bring their party into the democratic orbit. . . . During this period, however, State at every step along the way has resisted proposals to hasten the integration of the Socialists into the democratic camp."

Six weeks later—eighteen months after the Fanfani visit —the State Department offered a new argument against the center-left, this time on the incredible ground that, if the Socialists entered an Italian government, it might encourage the Russians in a miscalculation of the west's determination!—as if Moscow were going to base its estimate of American will on the composition of the government in Rome. By this time it was evident that, if those in State who wanted to block the *apertura* had their way, they might well bring into power a right-wing government with fascist support, like the disastrous Tambroni government of 1960, and force the democratic left into a popular front. In January 1963 Komer and I sent the President a melancholy memorandum recalling his Italian directives, describing the present situation and concluding: "Lest you think you run the United States Government, the matter is still under debate." There is no point in prolonging the agony for the reader; it was bad enough for the participant. It finally came to an end when Averell Harriman became Under Secretary of Political Affairs in the spring of 1963. With his expert knowledge of the Italian situation and his administrative vigor, he turned the bureaucracy around. By the time that Nenni and his party eventually entered the Italian government in December 1963, the Department of State was at last in accord.

Our effort in the meantime had not been entirely wasted. The leaders of the center-left parties had no doubt from mid-1961 on that a change of administration had occurred in Washington; and, if they sometimes found little evidence of it in the Department of State, they knew well enough from their own experience that foreign offices suffered from cultural lags. Kennedy, moreover, appealed greatly to them as both a Catholic and a progressive; the coincidence that he and Pope John came on the world stage about the same time strengthened them both. And the idea of a New Frontier in America was exciting to those who sought new frontiers for their own nation. One leading Nenni Socialist assured me earnestly in the spring of 1962, "So long as we have any influence on the Italian government, you can be sure that there will be no Paris-Bonn-Rome axis against London and Washington." In February 1963 Anthony Sampson reported to the *London Observer* from Rome: "Nenni, the old firebrand Socialist, cannot now contain his praise for Kennedy. . . . There is hardly a word of anti-Americanism, except on the far right."

4. THE EUROPEAN TRIP

The rising confidence in Kennedy among the democratic

left was not confined to Italy. Anti-Americanism, so long epidemic in these circles throughout Western Europe, was suddenly suspended. The American President was becoming a hope, if not a hero, for the Labour Party in England, for the Social Democrats in West Germany, for the followers of Mendès-France and Gaston Defferre in France. In London Hugh Gaitskell greatly admired Kennedy (who in turn found him intelligent and delightful and could never understand why Macmillan and Gaitskell, both of whom he liked so much, disliked each other so intensely; I had the sad task of telling the President of Gaitskell's death in January 1963, and he plainly regretted not only the human loss but the vanished opportunity of their working together in the future). In Berlin, Willy Brandt modeled his political campaigns on Kennedy. In Paris, Jean-Jacques Servan-Schreiber in *L'Express* attacked the idea of eliminating American influence in Europe, accused de Gaulle of adopting the communist slogan "U.S. Go Home" and warned France that the alternative to an Atlantic partnership must be a Russian partnership. Many on the left were not only Kennedyites but McNamaraites: they preferred an American nuclear monopoly and, like the Labour Party, opposed the MLF, not because it promised Europe too little control over nuclear weapons, but because it promised too much; the last thing they wished was for Washington to surrender the veto. Most of these people, outside England, were also sympathetic to the movement for a united Europe. But they were not excited by the technocratic Europe of civil servants, high commissions and supranational bureaucracies. They sought neither the European chauvinism of de Gaulle nor the benign Eurocracy of Monnet but an open and democratic European union, charged with political purpose.

The startling reversal of the democratic left seemed to indicate our real opportunity in European policy—to support the Europe of democracy and freedom against the Europe of paternalistic authoritarianism. To George Ball in February I suggested the usefulness "of shifting at least part of the dialogue from the *structure* to the *content* of the New Europe—that is talking less about the modes of supranational affiliation and more about the substance of life within the new European society"; we must stand for a *Europe des peuples* as against a *Europe des pères*. And to the President in April:

> In spite of de Gaulle, the United States appears to be on an ascending curve in Europe today. Certainly the polls suggest this to be the case. . . . The vital fresh source of pro U.S.

feeling in Europe today is the democratic left—and the democratic left is now pro-American in great part because it feels that, with the Kennedy Administration, Washington is once again offering the world progressive rather than standpat leadership. . . . This should not be underestimated just because it is considered bad manners to mention such things in the discussion of foreign affairs. . . . By encouraging progressive tendencies, we can help counter the Gaullist idea of Europe without seeming to challenge de Gaulle directly. This course also—as in Italy—has the effect of isolating and weakening the Communists.

One remembered Fanfani's remark that democracy was always addressing the leaders: why for once should it not address the masses? The President, his European trip approaching, saw it as an opportunity, with all delicacy, to talk beyond governments to people, especially to the young and idealistic. Early in June he asked me to take a look at the speech drafts prepared by the State Department for the trip. "My general impression," I reported to him, "is of their predominant banality and vapidity. These speeches could have been given just as easily by President Eisenhower—or by President Nixon. They fail to convey any sense of a fresh American voice or distinctive Kennedy approach." Obviously the President had to talk about Germany, Euopean unity, our undying commitment to the defense of Europe, the indivisibility of Europe and the United States, Atlantic partnership, low tariffs, and the other respectable issues. But anything he said about them ought to be stated with "due recognition of the fact that Europe considers itself a big boy now—that Europeans are fed to the teeth with what they regard as the American habit of deciding unilaterally what European policy should be and setting out to impose it regardless of what Europe thinks. For example, energetic public advocacy of the MLF would seem to me an error, whatever the merits," partly because mass audiences couldn't care less about it, partly because the President should not become personally more identified with the proposal than he was already, "partly because our position should be one of inviting an Atlantic dialogue rather than insisting on American solutions." And the most important thing was to take advantage of his own issues—to remember that the reason for the rise of pro-American feeling in Europe was not the MLF or our support for British entry into the Common Market but the fact that a young, vigorous, progressive administration had taken over in Washington and was doing things, not for the few, but for the many. Of course "the State Department (as I have noticed so often in Latin American matters) is con-

stitutionally opposed to exploiting abroad the benefits of
the change in administration in Washington. . . . This attitude denies us one of the most powerful weapons we have
in winning the confidence and the enthusiasm of other
peoples."

The State Department drafts were discarded, and Ted
Sorensen applied his brilliant mind and pen to the European
tour. On June 23 the President left for Germany, and the
triumphal journey began. On June 25 he addressed himself
to European issues at the Paulskirche in Frankfurt. He
multiplied his options, speaking about a "democratic European Community," a "unified free Europe," "a united Europe
in an Atlantic partnership—an entity of interdependent
parts, sharing equally both burdens and decisions." He emphasized the American commitment to Europe: "The United
States will risk its cities to defend yours because we need
your freedom to protect ours." But he also emphasized that
"the choice of paths to the unity of Europe is a choice
which Europe must make. . . . Nor do I believe that there
is any one right course or any single final pattern. It is
Europeans who are building Europe."

Then on to Berlin and the wildest reception of all, three-
fifths of the population of West Berlin streaming into the
streets, clapping, waving, crying, cheering, as if it were
the second coming. Before paying the ordained visit to the
city hall and signing the Golden Book, Kennedy made his
first inspection of the Wall. No one is ever prepared for the
Wall: it shocked and appalled the President, and he was still
angry when he came out of the city hall and faced the
seething crowd in the Rudolf Wilde Platz, compressed into
a single excited, impassioned mass. His words were true
but unwontedly harsh:

There are many people in the world who really don't un-
derstand, or say they don't, what is the great issue between the
free world and the communist world.
Let them come to Berlin!
There are some who say that communism is the wave of
the future.
Let them come to Berlin!
And there are some who say in Europe and elsewhere we
can work with the communists.
Let them come to Berlin!
And there are even a few who say that it is true that com-
munism is an evil system, but it permits us to make eco-
nomic progress.
Lass sie nach Berlin kommen! Let them come to Berlin!
The crowd shook itself and rose and roared like an animal.
Absorbed in his short remarks, Kennedy hurried on. In a
moment he concluded: "All free men, wherever they may

live, are citizens of Berlin, and, therefore, as a free man, I take pride in the words 'Ich bin ein Berliner.'" The hysteria spread almost visibly through the square. Kennedy was first exhilarated, then disturbed; he felt, as he remarked on his return, that if he had said, "March to the Wall— tear it down," his listeners would have marched. He always regarded crowds as irrational; perhaps a German one compounded the irrationality. That afternoon at the Free University he talked thoughtfully about human rights and social progress: "The very nature of the modern techno- logical society requires human initiative and the diversity of free minds. So history, itself, runs against the Marxist dogma, not toward it."

On to Dublin the same night, where he began a blissful interlude of homecoming, at once sentimental and ironic. I imagine that he was never easier, happier, more involved and detached, more complexly himself, than in the next few days. So at Wexford, in the county which his great- grandfather had left on an inexplicable adventure across the Atlantic in the 1840s, when the town presented him with an engraved silver and gold box, John Fitzgerald Ken- nedy said: "I am proud to have connected on that beauti- ful golden box the coat of arms of Wexford, the coat of arms of the kingly and beautiful Kennedys, and the coat of arms of the United States." He paused, then, "That is a very good combination." In Cork, after introducing Larry O'Brien and David Powers, beloved friends from so many wars, "And then I would like to introduce to you the pastor at the church which I go to, who comes from Cork— Monsignor O'Mahoney. He is the pastor of a poor, humble flock in Palm Beach, Florida." After receiving honorary degrees from Trinity College, British and secular, and the National University, Irish and Catholic: "I now feel equally part of both, and if they ever have a game of Gaelic foot- ball or hurling, I shall cheer for Trinity and pray for Na- tional." Speaking before the Irish Parliament, where, as Frank O'Connor later wrote, "previously Joyce's name had never been heard except on some debate on evil literature," he reminded his audience that Joyce had called the Atlantic a bowl of bitter tears. (He also quoted Benjamin Franklin, Lord Mountjoy, Charles Stewart Parnell, Yeats, Henry Grattan, John Boyle O'Reilly and Shaw.) Finally at Limerick he recalled the plaintive old song:

Come back to Erin, Mavourneen, Mavourneen,
Come back aroon to the land of thy birth.
Come with the shamrock and springtime,
    Mavourneen. . . .

"This is not the land of my birth," Kennedy said, "but it is the land for which I hold the greatest affection, and I certainly will come back in the springtime."

Then to Birch Grove in England, where Macmillan said no on the multilateral force and yes on British Guiana; and to Italy for the last lap. One of the President's purposes in going to Europe that summer was to see the venerable Pope; but John XXIII died on June 3, seven weeks after the publication of his noble encyclical *Pacem in Terris* and four weeks before the President arrived in Rome. On June 21 Cardinal Montini, an old friend of the Kennedy family, succeeded as Pope Paul VI; his coronation before 300,000 people in St. Peter's Square on June 30 apparently exhausted the Roman appetite for galas, because, when Kennedy arrived the next day, he encountered the thinnest crowds of his trip. In the evening Kennedy met the Italian political leaders at a reception at the Quirinale Palace. He had a good talk, he told me later, with Nenni (adding "So far as I could see, everyone in Italy is for the opening to the left. I was told that they were blaming it all on Fanfani and on us; but I couldn't find anyone there who was against us"). To Palmiro Togliatti, the astute head of the Communist party, the President said impenetrably, "It's nice to be in your country." To Fanfani, whose government had recently fallen, he said, "We shall meet again at the next Democratic convention."

Naples, in its vivid excitement, more than made up for Rome. In a farewell speech the President summed up his European impressions. "First," he said, "it is increasingly clear that our Western European allies are committed to the path of progressive democracy—to social justice and economic reform attained through the free processes of debate and consent. I spoke of this last night in Rome, as I had earlier spoken of it in Germany. And I cite it again here to stress the fact that this is not a matter of domestic politics but a key to western freedom and solidarity." Later on he spoke of the unification of Western Europe: "the United States welcomes this movement and the greater strength it ensures. We did not assist in the revival of Europe to maintain its dependence on the United States; nor did we seek to bargain selectively with many and separate voices. We welcome a stronger partner . . . The age of self-sufficient nationalism is over. The age of interdependence is here. . . . The Atlantic partnership is a growing reality."

The trip represented President Kennedy's effort to move

the European discussion beyond the technicalities of structure to the realities of life. As he knew better than anyone, the impact of an outsider on a continent at once so ancient and so alive as Europe could only be meager. His objectives were limited, but he attained most of them. He defined a democratic alternative to de Gaulle. He made it clear that Europeans must build European unity. He also made it clear that America was not obsessed with the nuclear issue to the exclusion of the urgent social questions of the new Europe. He surmounted the barriers of diplomacy to carry his message to the people. "He spoke to us for the first time in the language of the present generation," wrote Countess Marion Dönhoff, the acute political commentator for *Die Zeit*; "a man who was able to project a vision of the future without moving an inch away from the reality of our time; a man whose many-faceted intellect grasped the essence of power; a man who knew every trick in the political game without having become a cynic in the process." He left behind an indelible memory of a young, vibrant, tough-minded and idealistic America.

Before the Irish Parliament, he had recalled the lines from *Back to Methuselah*: "You see things; and you say 'Why?' But I dream things that never were; and I say 'Why not?'" Shaking off the splintered fragments of the doctrinaire Grand Design of 1961, he now rescued its essence —the hope of a creative west united in common allegiance to progressive democracy—and gave it new identity and purpose. In the summer of 1963, John F. Kennedy could have carried every country in Europe.

XXXIV

THE PURSUIT OF PEACE

THE PROBLEMS WITHIN THE WESTERN ALLIANCE, as Kennedy well understood, were part of the price the west was paying for a certain ebbing in the cold war. But, unlike some of his colleagues in the American government who looked back with nostalgia to the good old days when Khrushchev could be relied on to maintain discipline in western ranks, Kennedy was rather more impressed by the risks of war than by the risks of *détente*. So his first instinct after the missile crisis had been to restore communication with his adversary and resume the search for areas of common interest.

Though Kennedy did not suppose that the humiliation of the missile crisis would transform the Kremlin overnight, he did hope that his restraint in the aftermath might convince the Russians that the American menace to their security was hardly enough to justify the desperate act which had brought on the crisis. Obviously if the United States had been waiting for an excuse to use its considerable nuclear superiority against the Soviet Union, it could hardly expect a better one than the sneak nuclearization of Cuba. Yet Washington had stayed its hand. Still, with his capacity to understand the problems of others, the President could see how threatening the world might have looked to the Kremlin. Reading Khrushchev's speech to the Supreme Soviet of December 12, 1962, he expressed, as he had before, his wonder that the Soviet leader was making much the same set of charges against the west that the west was making against him: the language was almost interchangeable. Kennedy gave Khrushchev credit for sincerity in this —"I do think," he soon said publicly, "his speech shows that he realizes how dangerous a world we live in"—and the mirror effect reinforced his own refusal to regard the global competition as a holy war. If the Russians would "devote their energies to demonstrating how their system works in the Soviet Union, it seems to me his vital interests are easily protected with the power he has, and we could have a long period of peace. . . . But instead, by these constant desires to change the balance of power in the world, that is what, it seems to me, introduces the dangerous element."

1. INTIMATIONS OF DÉTENTE

This is precisely what they had debated the year before in Vienna, and Cuba, for a moment at least, had settled the debate in Kennedy's favor. Khrushchev's retreat meant a clear victory of the American over the Soviet definition of the status quo. And, by accepting the status quo in the form of the existing equilibrium of power rather than of the communist revolution, Khrushchev swallowed not only the dialectic of Vienna but the rhetoric of his flamboyant speech six months earlier proclaiming the historic inevitability of a communist world. It was not, of course, that he was abandoning his beliefs; like devotees of older religions, he was perhaps beginning to reserve them for heavenly fulfillment.

Indeed, the very Cuban adventure had implied a Soviet conclusion that history was not doing the job fast enough and required some sharp encouragement. For in January 1961 the world had seemed ripe for plucking. Asia, Africa, Latin America were all rising against their western masters and appeared to be running in the communist direction. The existence of the nuclear stalemate reduced the credibility of the American deterrent and freed the Soviet Union for nuclear diplomacy—i.e., terrorizing other nations by the manipulation of the threat of nuclear war. The United States itself seemed militarily vulnerable, politically aimless and economically stagnant. The Soviet Union, reviewing its impressive industrial gains of the fifties, could dream of overtaking and surpassing the American economy by the seventies. The communist empire still cherished the hope of unity. These were to have been the glorious years of the final offensive.

By the summer of 1962 that offensive was in ruins. The third world remained obstinately a third world. Nationalism had proved stronger than Marxism; and communism had encountered one frustration after another in Laos, in the Congo, in Latin America. Kennedy's firmness over Berlin had re-established the credibility of the deterrent (for the Russians, if not for General de Gaulle) and handed Moscow still another frustration. The Cuban adventure represented a bold effort to turn the western flank at Berlin by altering the nuclear balance. At the same time, it was a tacit confession of Soviet nuclear inferiority. Its failure struck from Soviet hands, one hoped permanently, the weapon of nuclear blackmail Khrushchev had brandished so long and so jovially and forced the Russians to re-examine their whole strategic position. In the meantime, while the United States was recovering economic momentum and political purpose, the Soviet Union was sinking into ever more worrying agricultural, industrial and intellectual difficulties. The communist empire itself, after the truce of 1960, was clearly splitting into hostile blocs. The high hopes of January 1961 were giving way to bleak realities.

So on November 19, 1962, a month after his defeat in the Caribbean, Khrushchev, in a 30,000 word report to the central committee of the Soviet Communist Party, implicitly called off the world offensive and demanded concentration on the tasks of the Soviet economy. In January 1963 in East Berlin he said that the erection of the Wall had diminished the need for a separate German peace treaty; in effect, he decided to live with the bone in his throat, thereby again accepting Kennedy's version of the status quo. (The Berlin negotiations eventually trailed off; the west, despite periodic Soviet stamps on the corns, retained its presence and its rights; and the future of West Berlin rested with the larger movements of history.)

Clearly the Soviet leaders had decided on a breathing spell. There was nothing new about this, of course; throughout the history of communism pause had alternated with pressure. Lenin in 1921 and Stalin in 1935 had made departures in policy which for a moment impressed men of goodwill in the west as basic transformations but which turned out to be no more than new tactics for achieving the old goal of world communization. Yet Khrushchev's situation in 1963 differed in important respects from Stalin's in 1935 or Lenin's in 1921.

For one thing, the Soviet Union itself had undergone changes. Half a century had transformed it from a revolution dedicated to overturning the existing order to an establishment with heavy vested interests in the status quo. Moreover, in the last decade the revulsion against Stalinism, against forced labor camps, against arbitrary arrests, against the drabness and meanness of daily life, had coincided with the emergence of technical and managerial groups who insisted on a predictable and comfortable existence and whose active loyalty was indispensable to the power of the state. Those outside the Soviet Union might not be so persuaded as Soviet citizens themselves that this process of normalization was irreversible. Nor was it prudent to confuse normalization, which related to personal security, with liberalization, which related to personal freedom (and there was little enough evidence of the second). Yet the Soviet Union of Khrushchev obviously differed in notable ways from the Soviet Union of Stalin. Without accepting Lord Home's thesis that a fat communist would always be better for the world than a skinny communist, one could hope that further progress toward affluence in Russia would enlarge the sense of having a stake in things as they were, further attenuate the old revolutionary messianism, and end the need for tension with the world as a way to justify tyranny at home.

For another thing, the mystique of Marxism itself was dying. This was in part for internal reasons: Khrushchev's indictment of Stalin had permanently discredited the notion that any individual could be the infallible expositor of the creed. And it was in even greater jeopardy for external reasons: Tito had vindicated the right to heresy in 1948, and by 1963 Mao Tse-tung was establishing a rival church. If Marxism had been anything, it had been a universal ideology overriding all national and ethnic interests and dissolving all historic conflicts. Now it was unveiled as one more ideology which individuals, nations and (if Mao were right) races were using and distorting for their own purposes. This decay of Marxist legitimacy reduced the Soviet Union itself to just another state scrapping for leadership within the communist empire.

These changes both inside the Soviet Union and inside the communist world placed Khrushchev's desire for a breathing spell in a new frame. And the onset of the nuclear age completed the transformation of the context. Sitting on a nuclear stockpile was not the most comfortable position in the world. As statesmen, generals and scientists tried to figure out how irrational weapons could be put to rational use, they were likely—especially when there was a chance that the weapons might be used against themselves—to develop a certain wariness. Prolonged contemplation of the nuclear effect could lead even the most bellicose to the conclusion that mutual incineration was of dubious benefit. Peking could afford to be nonchalant because, having no nuclear weapons, it had not had to work out the calculus of nuclear exchange. But Moscow, like Washington, had had to explore the rigorous and terrible logic of holocaust.

Only two men on the planet had been exposed to the absolute pressure of nuclear decision; and even for them it was not till the missile crisis that what was perceived intellectually was experienced emotionally. Khrushchev recorded his reaction in his poignant personal letter to Kennedy on the Friday night of the second Cuba week. As for Kennedy, his feelings underwent a qualitative change after Cuba: a world in which nations threatened each other with nuclear weapons now seemed to him not just an irrational but an intolerable and impossible world. Cuba thus made vivid the sense that all humanity had a common interest in the prevention of nuclear war—an interest far above those national and ideological interests which had once seemed ultimate.

2. BACK TO THE TEST BAN

Though the United States had resumed atmospheric testing in the Pacific in April 1962, both Kennedy and Macmillan continued to keep the idea of a test ban alive between themselves, exchanging through the year thoughts about the form and timing of a new approach to Moscow. The President was particularly interested in the possibility of lowering the required quota of annual on-site inspections from the existing figure of twenty. Spurred on by presidential concern, scientists worked to refine techniques of detection and identification. The discovery that Russian earthquakes were less frequent than we had supposed and occurred mostly in areas where testing would be extremely difficult also cut down the need for inspection to distinguish between natural and man-made earth shocks.

Opponents of a test ban disputed the new technical evidence. But Arthur Dean, still our ambassador to the disarmament conference in Geneva and still eager to win his case, told reporters at the Geneva airport in July 1962 that it was now possible to make a substantial reduction in the requirement for on-site inspections. He did this without instructions or clearance; perhaps he intended to force the issue in Washington. In any case, that was the entirely useful effect, and Kennedy quickly came down on Dean's side.

The question of on-site inspections was political as well as technical. A test ban treaty required Senate ratification. To win the necessary two-thirds vote, in view especially of the strong military opposition, the treaty would have to give every appearance of safeguarding national security against Soviet cheating: the 'big hole' obsession had not died. But the inspection issue pertained, of course, to a comprehensive test ban. In the meantime, the idea of a limited ban, covering self-policing environments, remained under consideration; indeed, the fact that our resumption of atmospheric testing in April 1962 had produced far more outcry than our resumption of underground testing in September 1961 suggested that the world cared primarily about explosions producing radioactive fallout. At the end of July Kennedy consequently proposed to Macmillan the possibility of offering simultaneous treaties at Geneva: a comprehensive ban with much reduced on-site inspection—this Kennedy preferred because of its greater effect on nuclear proliferation—with an atmospheric test ban as a reasonable second best. The Russians, however, lost no time in turning both down at the end of August—the limited ban because it would allegedly legalize underground testing and thus "raise the nuclear temperature," the comprehensive ban because it called for inspection. They suggested instead an immediate ban on atmospheric tests accompanied by a moratorium on underground tests until a treaty could be worked out. But the west, remembering who had terminated the last moratorium, was not impressed.

No doubt Soviet minds were in the Caribbean at this point; but, when the disarmament conference resumed a month after Cuba, one hoped that the mood might be changing. By this time the Soviet Union was winding up its 1962 series of atmospheric tests. We were also completing our own series; and the President's sense of the meagerness of their results after the clamor about their necessity—all the tests seemed to have proved was the need for more tests—made him more determined than ever to bring the whole thing to an end.[1] Conceivably Khrushchev might have similar feelings. Moreover, the Soviet Union had accepted the principle of international verification in the case of the Cuban missiles. And in November it had supported the election of U Thant to his full term as Secretary General of the United Nations: this presumably meant that we had heard the last of the *troika*.

Hoping that all this might portend comparable progress on the inspection problem, Jerome Wiesner had suggested to the Soviet scientist Yevgenii Federov that, since the American scientists had persuaded their government to go down on the number of inspections, perhaps the Soviet scientists could persuade their government to come up until agreement could be reached. Though Wiesner had been careful to mention no figures, Federov evidently emerged with the impression that the Americans would accept three or four inspections. About the same time V. V. Kuznetsov, the Soviet disarmament negotiator, acquired a similar impression from Dean in a talk in New York. When all this was reported to Moscow, Khrushchev, if one can believe the account he gave to Norman Cousins of the *Saturday Review*, told the Council of Ministers, "We can have an agreement with the United States to stop nuclear tests if we agree to three inspections. I know that three inspections are not necessary, and that the policing can be done adequately from outside our borders. But the American Congress has convinced itself that on-site inspection is necessary and the President cannot get a treaty through the Senate without it. Very well, then, let us accommodate the President." He added to Cousins: "Finally I persuaded them."

[1] He was also dissatisfied with the programs of underground testing, which had advanced nuclear technology little and had been by no means so fallout-proof as advertised. In the year after September 1961 there were seventeen cases of venting—that is, the discharge of radioactive debris, primarily iodine 131, into the atmosphere—at the Yucca Flats Proving Ground in Nevada.

"It seems to me, Mr. President," Khrushchev wrote Kennedy on December 19, 1962, "that time has come now to put an end once and for all to nuclear tests, to draw a line through such tests." We believe, Khrushchev continued, that national means of detection are sufficient to police underground as well as atmospheric tests; but we understand your need for "at least a minimum number" of inspections for the ratification of the treaty. "Well, if this is the only difficulty on the way to agreement, then for the noble and humane goal of ceasing nuclear weapons tests we are ready to meet you halfway." Citing the Kuznetsov-Dean conversations, Khrushchev proposed agreement on two to three annual inspections limited to earthquake areas. If this were accepted, "the world can be relieved of the roar of nuclear explosions."

Kennedy, who received the letter at Nassau, was exhilarated: it looked as if the Russians were really interested in a *modus vivendi*. However, the inspection quota still presented difficulties. Dean told the President that the only numbers he had mentioned in his talks with Kuznetsov were between eight and ten. Moreover, the Soviet figure of two or three represented not a real concession but a reversion to a position the Russians had taken in earlier stages of the negotiation and abandoned in November 1961. In replying to Khrushchev, Kennedy remarked on the "misunderstanding" of Dean's statement, sought to reassure him that inspection could be hedged around to prevent espionage and pointed out the difficulties raised by the confinement of inspection to seismic areas. He concluded: "Notwithstanding these problems, I am encouraged by your letter." The next step, he suggested, might be technical discussions between representatives of the two governments.

The discussions, beginning in New York in January, took place in darkening domestic weather. Governor Nelson Rockefeller of New York, nominally considered a liberal Republican, now denounced the idea of a test ban. "This has become an exercise not in negotiation," said Senator Everett Dirksen, the Republican leader of the Senate, "but in give-away." In the House of Representatives Craig Hosmer of California rallied Dr. Edward Teller, Admiral Lewis Strauss and other traditional foes of the ban for a new campaign. In February Senator Thomas J. Dodd of Connecticut, observing that too many concessions had already been made, condemned the comprehensive ban on the ground that it would stop the development of the neutron bomb and of anti-missile missiles. Within the government, the Joint Chiefs of Staff declared themselves opposed to a comprehensive ban under almost any terms and pronounced six annual inspections especially unacceptable.

Actually, Wiesner and a number of scientists had arrived at the "firm opinion . . . that the possibility of five inspections per year would have provided adequate security against clandestine nuclear testing"; and McNamara was ready in February to settle for six. But with the intense military and partisan opposition and the senatorial battle looming ahead, it seemed impossible politically to go below eight or, at the least, seven. As for the Russians, they not only declined to go above three but showed little curiosity about the way the inspections were to be conducted. In effect, we refused to discuss numbers until they discussed modalities, and they refused to discuss modalities until we accepted their numbers. The conclusion in the State Department and the Foreign Office was that the Kremlin, immobilized by its problems with China, could not conceivably join hands with the nation China hated most in permanently excluding China from the nuclear club. The announcement of a Russo-Chinese ideological conference for Moscow in July convinced the experts that for the time being the ban was out of the question.

But, despite the failure of the New York negotiations and the pessimism of the professional diplomats, Kennedy and Macmillan persisted in their pursuit of a treaty. "I am haunted," the President said in March, "by the feeling that by 1970, unless we are successful, there may be ten nuclear powers instead of four, and by 1975, fifteen or twenty. . . . I see the possibility in the 1970s of the President of the United States having to face a world in which fifteen or twenty nations may have these weapons. I regard that as the greatest possible danger." In March and April the President and the Prime Minister passed back and forth across the Atlantic drafts of a new approach to Khrushchev.

The Soviet leader was not in a receptive mood. When Norman Cousins saw him at his Black Sea retreat on April 12, Khrushchev complained that, after he had induced the Council of Ministers to accept three inspections on the guarantee that it would produce a treaty, the Americans had then insisted on eight: "So once again I was made to look foolish. But I can tell you this: it won't happen again. . . . We cannot make another offer. I cannot go back to the Council. It is now up to the United States. Frankly, we feel we were misled." (This last was a peculiar objection from the government which had denied it was sending nuclear missiles to Cuba.) He went on: "When I go up to Moscow next week I expect to serve notice that we will not consider ourselves bound by three inspections. If you can go from three to eight, we can go from three to zero."

Four days after the meeting with Cousins, the new Kennedy-Macmillan letter arrived in Moscow. The Anglo-American proposal noted that the west had already reduced its inspection quota from twenty to seven and mentioned an idea, backed by the neutral nations at the disarmament conference, of spreading the quota over several years. We all, Kennedy and Macmillan said, owe a duty to our own security, but we also have a duty to humanity, and this requires one more serious attempt to stop testing and prevent the further proliferation of nuclear weapons. The letter concluded by saying that the writers would be ready in due course to send to Moscow very senior representatives empowered to speak for them directly with Khrushchev.

Khrushchev's reply in early May could hardly have been more declamatory and rude. There was no point, he suggested, in going through all these arguments again; we have learned your test ban proposals by heart just as we used to learn "Pater Noster." The Soviet Union, he continued, regarded the western demand for inspection as no more than an effort to introduce NATO intelligence agents into Soviet territory. When he had consented to two or three inspections in December, he said, this was because he wanted to help the President with his Senate, not because he thought inspection necessary or sensible. Instead of a positive reply to this great Soviet concession all he had had since was western haggling over the number of inspections and the conditions for conducting them. To judge your position by your proposals, Khrushchev told the western leaders, the only conclusion could be that you were not serious: one wondered whether you were not going through the motions for domestic political reasons. If there were no real hope for agreement, the Soviet Union had no choice but to take measures to strengthen its own security. In a perfunctory final paragraph, Khrushchev, referring to the notion of sending senior representatives to Moscow, said, in effect, so be it; the Russians were even prepared to try this method of discussion.

Kennedy began to feel that the test ban was slipping away. "I'm not hopeful, I'm not hopeful," he said on the day he received Khrushchev's letter. "There doesn't seem to be any sense of movement since December." And two weeks later: "I have said from the beginning that [it] seemed to me that the pace of events was such in the world that unless we could get an agreement now, I would think the chance of getting it would be comparatively slight. We are therefore going to continue to push very hard in May and June and July in every forum to see if we can get an agreement."

Washington and London meanwhile brooded over the reply to Khrushchev's latest unpromising message. The first draft was a debater's screed, dealing *seriatim* with Khrushchev's points. But David Ormsby Gore, picking up Khrushchev's grudging final paragraph, suggested bypassing the debate and concentrating instead on the special emissaries. Macmillan strongly supported this view, and Kennedy readily agreed. Finally on May 30 a brief letter went to Khrushchev, touching lightly on a couple of the familiar arguments but centering on the proposal that American and British emissaries go to Moscow at the end of June or early in July.

3. APPEAL AT AMERICAN UNIVERSITY

In the meantime, the debate in the United States had been producing a certain clarification of issues. Senator Dodd's attack on the ban in February had led to a thoughtful exchange of letters between Dodd and Adrian Fisher of the Arms Control and Disarmament Agency. The correspondence brought new points to Dodd's attention, and the Connecticut Senator had the grace to change his mind. On May 27 he joined with Hubert Humphrey and thirty-two other Senators in introducing a resolution declaring it "the sense of the Senate" that the United States should again offer the Soviet Union a limited test ban; if the Russians rejected the plan, the United States should nevertheless "pursue it with vigor, seeking the widest possible international support," at the same time pledging no more tests in the atmosphere or under water so long as the Soviet Union also abstained. The President had some concern that this approach might undercut the comprehensive ban; but the effect of the Dodd-Humphreys Resolution was to strengthen the antitesting case. Moreover, a series of hearings in the spring before the Stennis subcommittee of the Senate Armed Services Committee gave the administration a chance to organize its ranks and hold, in effect, a dry run of testimony in case a test ban treaty itself ever came up for ratification. In press conferences and in conversations with leaders of opinion, Kennedy hammered away at the dangers of nuclear proliferation.

One day late in May McGeorge Bundy told several of us that the President had decided the time had come for a major address on peace. He had evidently concluded that a fresh context was required to save the dying negotiation. We were asked to send our best thoughts to Ted Sorensen and to say nothing about this to anybody. The President meanwhile outlined his own views to Ted, who set to work. The speech was scheduled for the American University commencement on the morning of Monday, June 10. On June 7 Bundy convened a small group—Kaysen, Rostow, Tom Sorensen and me—to look at Ted's draft.

It was affirmative in tone, elevated in language, wise and subtle in analysis. Its central substantive proposal was a moratorium on atmospheric testing; but its effect was to redefine the whole national attitude toward the cold war. It was a brilliant and faithful reproduction of the President's views, and we read it with mounting admiration and excitement. Kennedy, in the meantime, had gone to California for a speech at San Diego; on June 9 he was going to Honolulu to address the Conference of Mayors. Kaysen was assigned the job of checking the speech with State and Defense, neither of which had yet been involved, while Sorensen flew to the coast to meet the President on his return from Hawaii.

Then on Saturday morning Khrushchev unexpectedly replied to the proposal about the special emissaries. His letter, ungracious and sulky, still doubted the sincerity of the Anglo-American effort and still complained about inspection. But he said at least that he would receive the emissaries; their success, he observed sullenly, depended on what they brought in their baggage to Moscow. For all the querulousness, he had agreed to let the negotiations begin.

On Monday the President addressed himself in the open air on the American University campus to what he called "the most important topic on earth: world peace." By peace, he said, he did not mean "a Pax Americana enforced on the world by American weapons of war," nor did he mean the peace of the grave or the security of the slave. He meant peace which enabled men and nations to grow and to hope and to build a better life for their children, "not merely peace in our time but peace for all time." In the nuclear age, peace had become "the necessary rational end of rational men." It was said, he continued, that it was idle to dream of peace until the Soviet leaders adopted a more enlightened attitude. "I hope they do. I believe we can help them do it." He added, in a sentence capable of revolutionizing the whole American view of the cold war, "But I also believe that we must re-examine our own attitude—as individuals and as a Nation—for our attitude is as essential as theirs."

Too many Americans, he went on, regarded peace as impossible and therefore war as inevitable. "We need not accept that view. Our problems are manmade—therefore, they can be solved by man." Nor was it correct to suppose that peace would end all quarrels and conflict. It "does not require that each man love his neighbor—it requires only that they live together in mutual tolerance." History taught us, moreover, that enmities between states did not last forever; "the tide of time and events will often bring surprising changes in the relations between nations." [2]

The communists were of course trapped in conspiratorial hallucinations about the United States; but that should warn us "not to fall into the same trap as the Soviets, not to see only a distorted and desperate view of the other side, not to see conflict as inevitable, accommodation as impossible and communication as nothing more than an exchange of threats. No government or social system is so evil that its people must be considered as lacking in virtue." Among many traits Americans and Russians had in common was an abhorrence of war. "No nation in the history of battle," he reminded his listeners, "ever suffered more than the Soviet Union suffered in the course of the Second World War." If world war should come again, all both sides had built, "all we have worked for, would be destroyed in the first twenty-four hours." Yet "we are both caught up in a vicious and dangerous cycle in which suspicion on one side breeds suspicion on the other, and new weapons beget counter-weapons."

In short, both countries had "a mutually deep interest in a just and genuine peace and in halting the arms race. . . . If we cannot end now all our differences, at least we can help make the world safe for diversity. For, in the final analysis, our most basic common link is that we all inhabit this small planet. We all breathe the same air. We all cherish our children's future. And we are all mortal."

So we must re-examine our attitude toward the cold war, "remembering that we are not engaged in a debate, seeking to pile up debating points. We are not here distributing blame or pointing the finger of judgment." Our purpose must be to conduct our affairs so that the Russians would see it in their own interest to move toward genuine peace; "we can seek a relaxation of tensions without relaxing our

---

[2] He repeated this thought more explicitly eighteen days later in his speech before the Irish Parliament: "Across the gulfs and barriers that now divide us, we must remember that there are no permanent enemies. Hostility today is a fact, but it is not a ruling law. The supreme reality of our time is our indivisibility as children of God and our common vulnerability on this planet."

guard." To move toward peace would "require increased understanding between the Soviets and ourselves . . . increased contact and communication." In particular, it would require new progress toward general and complete disarmament. And in the area of disarmament one problem "where the end is in sight, yet where a fresh start is badly needed, is . . . a treaty to outlaw nuclear tests." The President then announced that discussions would soon begin in Moscow "looking toward early agreement on a comprehensive test ban treaty" and that the United States would conduct no atmospheric tests so long as other states did not do so; "we will not be the first to resume." No treaty could provide "absolute security" against deception and evasion; but if it were sufficiently effective in its enforcement and sufficiently in the interests of its signers, it could "offer far more security and far fewer risks than an unabated, uncontrolled, unpredictable arms race."

4. MISSION TO MOSCOW

It had first been supposed that John J. McCloy, with his experience in disarmament negotiations and his friendly associations with Khrushchev, would be the American negotiator in Moscow. But McCloy turned out not to be available in June or July. When Kaysen discussed Khrushchev's acceptance of the emissaries with Secretary Rusk, they had chatted for a moment about possible alternatives. Somewhat tentatively Rusk mentioned Averell Harriman. Kaysen immediately reported this to Kennedy, sending along word at the same time to the entourage that the President had better settle on Harriman before the Department had a chance to change its mind. As anticipated, State developed second thoughts in the next twenty-four hours. But by this time Kennedy had given word to go ahead with Averell.

For reasons which the White House could never understand, or perhaps understood all too well, Harriman, in spite of his almost unsurpassed Russian experience, was rather systematically excluded in the State Department from Soviet affairs. Yet from the viewpoint not only of ability and qualification but of persuading the Russians we meant business, he was the ideal choice. "As soon as I heard that Harriman was going," someone from the Soviet Embassy remarked to me, "I knew you were serious." As Khrushchev said to William Benton the next spring, "Harriman is a responsible man."

Harriman set about his preparations in his usual astute,

detailed and all-encompassing manner. The question whether we should try for a comprehensive or limited ban was still unresolved. The British were in favor of reducing the inspection quota still further, arguing that, even on the unlikely chance that the Russians were disposed to try a few clandestine tests underground, these tests could not possibly affect the balance of military power. As for Harriman, he was sure the Russians would not agree to an inspection quota acceptable to us unless he had, as he liked to put it, "some goodies in his luggage." He thus regretted the fact that we had unilaterally pulled the Jupiters out of Turkey and Italy three months earlier: if only he had them to trade now! (not that the Russians had illusions about their military importance; but it would have given Khrushchev something to show his own people and the Chinese).

The problem of China was increasingly on the President's mind—indeed, on the minds of everyone except those in the Department of State who were still babbling about the "Sino-Soviet bloc." By 1963 Kennedy and Macmillan were reaching the conclusion that China presented the long-term danger to the peace. Kennedy had tried to make this point to de Gaulle through Malraux; but the French, who wanted, like the Chinese, to prevent a Soviet-American *détente*, were not interested. (For de Gaulle, in addition, Chinese hegemony in Siberia was essential if he were to realize his dream of restoring Russia to a Europe "from the Atlantic to the Urals.") Britain, however, grasped the point completely. One day when the President and the Prime Minister were discussing the problem of a new commander for NATO, Macmillan said breezily, "I suppose it should be a Russian."

Harriman and Kaysen had a final meeting with the President before the mission's departure for Moscow. Kennedy said that Harriman could go as far as he wished in exploring the possibility of a Soviet-American understanding with regard to China. Averell responded that he would more than ever need something to sweeten the package. Kennedy mentioned possible concessions. The President added, "I have some cash in the bank in West Germany and am prepared to draw on it if you think I should."

In the meantime, the Russians had had a chance to study the American University speech. One cannot know; but it seems probable that that address gave Khrushchev both personal reassurance and a weapon he could use against the Chinese. Harold Wilson, who saw him immediately afterward, found him deeply impressed and considerably more open-minded about the test ban. Khrushchev himself later told Harriman with evident feeling that it was "the greatest speech by any American President since Roosevelt." At any rate, on July 2 in Berlin, after describing it as "notable for its sober appraisal of the international situation," he offered his answer—a limited ban, outlawing tests in the atmosphere, in outer space and under water. "If the western powers now accept this proposal," he said, "the question of inspection no longer arises." He did not this time insist on a concurrent and unpoliced moratorium on underground tests; but he said that "on the conclusion of a test ban agreement" it would also be necessary "to take another big step toward easing international tension"—a non-aggression treaty between NATO and the Warsaw Pact states. A test ban agreement, "combined with the simultaneous signing of a non-aggression pact," would create a "fresh international climate."

Two days later Khrushchev, turning his face from west to east, said that "only madmen" could hope to destroy capitalism by nuclear war; "a million workers would be destroyed for each capitalist. . . . There are people who see things differently. Let them. History will teach them." The next day the delegation of those who saw things differently arrived in Moscow, and the Russo-Chinese ideological talks began. They dragged on in the greatest secrecy from July 5 to adjournment, without communiqué, on July 20. But a long and emotional statement by the central committee of the Soviet Communist Party on July 14 suggested how things were going. Citing Mao Tse-tung as prepared to sacrifice millions of lives in nuclear war, the Russians replied that they could not "share the views of the Chinese leadership about creating 'a thousand times higher civilization' on the corpses of hundreds of millions of people." Such views were "in crying contradiction to the ideas of Marxism-Leninism." The nuclear bomb "does not distinguish between imperialists and working people: it devastates entire areas."

This was the mood in Moscow when on the following day the American and British delegations began discussion of the test ban. Harriman had a delegation according to his own specifications: small and brilliant. It included Carl Kaysen, Adrian Fisher, William Tyler and John McNaughton. Macmillan had originally wanted David Ormsby Gore to head the British delegation, but the Ambassador felt that, from the Prime Minister's own viewpoint, it would be better to have someone of cabinet rank who could not be considered an American stooge. The choice fell on Quintin

Hogg, then Lord Hailsham, Minister of Science and an accomplished if impetuous lawyer. (Macmillan later confided to newspapermen that he had sent Hailsham because he thought he might amuse Khrushchev.) Hailsham, relying on the British amateur tradition, was ill prepared on the technicalities of the problem and was consumed by a desire to get a treaty at almost any cost.

The first meeting took place with Khrushchev in the Kremlin. The Soviet leader began by talking expansively and irrelevantly about farm policy—"like a county agent," one of the American participants said later—discoursing at particular length about the virtues of investment in chemical fertilizer. Then, turning to the question of a comprehensive test ban, he said the Russians still considered inspection to be espionage; they did not think you could let the cat in the kitchen only to hunt the mice and not to drink the milk. Since the British and Americans disagreed, there was no point in wasting time in further argument. With the comprehensive ban thus dismissed, the limited ban was left on the table. Khrushchev now said nothing about his earlier idea of a concurrent moratorium on underground testing, but he did bring up the non-aggression pact he had mentioned in East Berlin.

Harriman quickly replied that the test ban treaty was something the three nations could complete in a few days in Moscow. The non-aggression pact would require extensive consultation with allies, and it might hold up the test ban for a long time. Moreover, he did not see how such a pact would be possible without assurance that interference with access to West Berlin would be considered aggression —a proposition which obviously irritated the Soviet leader. Assuming that the Americans were opposed because of Bonn's hostility to the idea, Khrushchev observed sarcastically, "You conquered the Germans, and now you are afraid of them." Harriman did assure Khrushchev, however, in accordance with his instructions from Washington, that the United States would consult with its allies in good faith about the possibility of a non-aggression pact.

For his part Harriman presented the idea of a nonproliferation treaty, forbidding the transfer of nuclear weapons from one country to another. Khrushchev drew back from this, arguing that as other nations signed the test ban treaty, it would have an anti-proliferation effect; but a no-transfer treaty should be deferred for future consideration.

The opening talk cleared away a certain number of issues. Then the hard negotiation began. The meetings took place at the Spiridonka Palace, a castellated Gothic structure marked by a weird medley of architectural styles. Gromyko for the Russians and Harriman for the west began a close analysis of the treaty draft. Several issues gave special trouble. One arose from foggy language in the preamble seeming to ban the use of nuclear weapons even in self-defense. Harriman, knowing that this was inconsistent with our own stated policy and would cause trouble on the Hill, demanded that the wording be cleared up. A second problem was that of the withdrawal clause. Khrushchev, in an inadvertent admission of the Leninist view of treaties, had argued that a nation always retained the sovereign right to withdraw from a treaty which no longer served its interest; to include an explicit withdrawal clause in this treaty would therefore imply a diminution of that right in other treaties. Harriman knew that the Senate, faced with the probability that China would refuse to sign and then might become a nuclear power on its own, would insist on such a clause. In the end he flatly told Gromyko that, without a withdrawal clause, there could be no treaty. The result was the curious compromise phraseology in Article IV: "Each Party shall in exercising its national sovereignty have the right to withdraw from the Treaty if it decides that extraordinary events, related to the subject matter of this Treaty, have jeopardized the supreme interests of its country."

A third problem was that of accession to the treaty. The issue here was how to arrange for states not recognized by other states to join them in signing the treaty without thereby receiving implicit recognition. Our concern, of course, was to avoid conferring an inadvertent blessing on East Germany and China. Our first solution was an explicit statement that accession did not mean recognition by signatories of other signatories. The Russians, who wanted to improve the international status of East Germany, naturally objected.

The discussions proved long and difficult. Harriman, who dominated the negotiations on the western side, was evidently at his best—correct, forceful, his restraint masking a capacity for toughness and even anger. A member of the British delegation later called him "the great man of the meeting." He would not give ground; and, as the talks dragged on, Hailsham became increasingly restive and unhappy. Soon he was complaining to London that Harriman's rigidity might lose the whole treaty. His reports disturbed Macmillan, who finally instructed Ormsby Gore to call on the President and register official British anxiety.

Harriman, however, had negotiated with the Russians

before and knew precisely what he was doing. "I am always right when I *know* I am right," he said on his return. "Sometimes I only *guess* I am right, and then I may be wrong. This time I *knew* I was right." When Ormsby Gore arrived at the White House, a call came in from Kaysen in Moscow just as the President initiated a call to Macmillan in London. Kaysen's report was optimistic. The Russians had accepted a revision of the preamble eliminating the language which we had disliked. As for accession, the lawyers Fisher and McNaughton had worked out an ingenious system of multiple depositaries, leaving every signatory free to sign only in association with nations of which it approved. (This idea offended the purists of international law, since it seemed to mean that no one could definitively know who the signatories were, but it did not bother practical minds.) Kaysen recommended that this solution be accepted, and the President nodded his approval to Bundy, who was conducting the conversation. Just at this point, the London call was completed. Macmillan came on the phone with a certain elaborateness: he was terribly sorry, he told the President, but he had had to ask David to express his concern about the progress of the Moscow negotiations. Kennedy, a broad smile on his face, broke in: "Don't worry. David is right here. It's been worked out, and I've told them to go ahead." Macmillan, having accomplished one of the dreams of his life (and at the same time having strengthened his government against the problems of John Profumo, Miss Keeler and Dr. Ward) was deeply moved.

In Moscow, after the treaty had been initialed, Harriman and Khrushchev took up the questions of France and China. The American found the Russian prickly and adamant. China was another socialist country, Khrushchev said, and he did not propose to discuss it with a capitalist. Harriman persisted: "Suppose we can get France to sign the treaty? Can you deliver China?" Khrushchev replied cryptically, "That's your problem." Harriman tried again: "Suppose their rockets are targeted against you?" Khrushchev did not answer.

In due course Khrushchev said, "Let us walk over together to our dinner." They left his office and strolled through the Kremlin, once Stalin's gloomy fortress, now a public park, toward the Old Palace. Harriman remarked that he saw few security men around. "I don't like being surrounded by security men," Khrushchev said. "In Stalin's time we never knew whether they were protecting us or watching us." As they walked, a large crowd collected behind them. Khrushchev turned and said, "This is Gospodin Garriman. We've just signed a test-ban treaty. I'm going to take him to dinner. Do you think he's earned his dinner?" The people applauded and applauded. On his return Harriman went straight to Hyannis Port. The President, without ceremony, said, "Well, this is a good job."

It *was* a good job, and it would not have come about without the intense personal commitment of Kennedy and Macmillan. America and Britain had offered the Soviet Union a limited test ban four times in four years; now it was accepted the fifth time around—two less than Robert Bruce and the spider. Left to itself, the Soviet Union, to judge from Khrushchev's attitude in the spring of 1963, would not have perceived that a test ban was to its own interest and would not have understood its potentialities as a key to the future. Left to itself, the Department of State would not have persevered with the issue, nor would it have ever proposed an American University speech—that speech which, in its modesty, clarity and perception, repudiated the self-righteous cold war rhetoric of a succession of Secretaries of State. Mao Tse-tung was also entitled to credit for his indispensable assistance in making the treaty possible.

One more man deserved mention. When Harriman arrived in Washington on July 28, his Georgetown neighbors staged an impromptu welcome for him. Bearing torches and candles, they marched to his house on P Street, serenading him with "For He's a Jolly Good Fellow" and then one of his old campaign songs, adapted from George M. Cohan, "H-A-double-R-I-M-A-N spells Harriman." Finally Averell, tieless and in shirtsleeves, came out on his front steps and spoke a few quiet words of thanks. One girl with a very small baby in her arms said to him, "I brought my baby because what you did in Moscow will make it possible for him to look ahead to a full and happy life."

5. THE TEST BAN ON THE HILL

Negotiation, however, was only half the problem; ratification remained. The President regarded the test ban treaty as the most serious congressional issue he had thus far faced. He was, he told us, determined to win if it cost him the 1964 election. But the opposition was organized and strong; and, while he felt sure the great majority of the people were for it, he was not sure they could make themselves heard in time. I happened to be with him ten days after the American University speech when someone brought in the mail report. He noted that the mail received in the White House in the week ending June 20 totaled 50,010 letters as compared to 24,888 a year earlier and 9482 in the comparable period of the last Eisenhower year. Then he looked at the breakdown. Of this vast accumulation, the American University speech had provoked 896 letters—861 favorable and 25 hostile. In the same period, 28,232 people had sent letters about a freight rate bill. The President, tossing the report aside, said, with disgust, "That is why I tell people in Congress that they're crazy if they take their mail seriously." [3]

Addressing the nation the day after the treaty was initialed in Moscow, Kennedy recalled mankind's struggle "to escape from the darkening prospects of mass destruction." "Yesterday," he said, "a shaft of light cut into the darkness." He did not exaggerate the significance of the agreement. It was not the millennium: it would not resolve all conflicts, reduce nuclear stockpiles, check the production of nuclear weapons or restrict their use in case of war. But it was "an important first step—a step toward peace—a step toward reason—a step away from war." He concluded with the Chinese proverb he had put to Khrushchev two years before in Vienna: "A journey of a thousand miles must begin with a single step."

The prospective end of radioactive fallout was, of course, an immense boon for humanity. But I think that Kennedy saw the main point of the treaty as a means of moving toward his Vienna goal of stabilizing the international equilibrium of power. After all, both America and Russia knew that each had enough nuclear strength to survive a surprise attack and still wreak fearful destruction on the other: the test ban now indicated a mutual willingness to halt the weapons race more or less where it was. In the Soviet case this meant acquiescence in American nuclear superiority. Though our superiority was not decisive, it was still considerable; in 1964 the Defense Department said that we had twice as many intercontinental bombers on constant alert and at least four times as many intercontinental ballistic missiles. The Russian willingness to accept such margins showed not only a post-Cuba confidence in American restraint but a new understanding of the theories of stable nuclear deterrence. And, in addition to slowing down the bilateral arms race, the treaty held out the hope of preventing the spread of nuclear weapons to new nations.

[3] The following week the American University speech produced 781 pro and 5 con; the freight rate bill 23,646.

Moreover, the effect, both practical and symbolic, of Soviet-American collaboration in stopping nuclear tests and dispersion might well lead to future agreement on more general disarmament issues.

So the supporters of the treaty saw it. But sections of the military and scientific community continued in strong opposition. Some, like General Thomas D. White, a former Air Chief, considered the whole theory of stable deterrence as "next to unilateral disarmament . . . the most misleading and misguided military theme yet conceived." True security, he and others argued, lay in unlimited nuclear supremacy and this required unlimited testing. Much of the dissent focused on the contention that the ban would block the development of an anti-missile missile—this in spite of firm statements by McNamara, General Maxwell Taylor and a number of scientists that the hard problems here were non-nuclear and required analysis in the laboratories, not testing in the atmosphere. Edward Teller predictably called for the immediate resumption of atmospheric testing, though he was willing to ration this to one megaton of radioactivity a year. To the Senators Teller cried: "If you ratify this treaty . . . you will have given away the future safety of this country." Admiral Lewis Strauss said, "I am not sure that the reduction of tensions is necessarily a good thing." Admiral Arthur Radford, a former Chairman of the Chiefs, said, "I join with many of my former colleagues in expressing deep concern for our future security. . . . The decision of the Senate of the United States in connection with this treaty will change the course of world history." General Thomas Power, the chief of the Strategic Air Command, attacked the treaty in secret hearings before the Armed Services Committee.

The assault had its effect, if not on the treaty itself, on the nature of the Senate debate. Given such opposition, ratification would be impossible without the support of the Joint Chiefs of Staff. In the spring the Chiefs had opposed a comprehensive test ban on the ground that the Russians would assuredly cheat; and General Curtis LeMay, the Air Force chief, testified now that he would have opposed the limited ban if the signing of the treaty had not created a situation where its rejection would have serious international consequences. (People sometimes wondered why Kennedy kept on Chiefs who occasionally seemed so much out of sympathy with his policy. The reason was that, in his view, their job was not policy but soldiering, and he admired them as soldiers. "It's good to have men like Curt LeMay and Arleigh Burke commanding troops once you decide to go in," he told Hugh Sidey. "But these men aren't the only ones you should listen to when you decide whether to go in or not. I like having LeMay head the Air Force. Everybody knows how he feels. That's a good thing." He was in addition sensitive to the soldier's role—dangerous in war and thankless in peace. He had copied an old verse in his commonplace book of 1945–46 and often quoted it later:

> God and the Soldier all men adore,
> In time of trouble and no more;
> For when War is over and all things righted,
> God is neglected—the old soldier slighted.[4]

Now the Chiefs, in effect, exacted a price for their support. General Maxwell Taylor, whom Kennedy had appointed Chairman of the Chiefs in August 1962 and who had played a judicious and effective role in bringing his brethren along, told the Senate Foreign Relations Committee that "the most serious reservations" of the Chiefs had to do with "the fear of a euphoria in the West which will eventually reduce our vigilance." The Chiefs accordingly attached "safeguards" to their support: vigorous continuation of underground testing; readiness to resume atmospheric testing on short notice; strengthening of detection capabilities; and the maintenance of nuclear laboratories. The President, determined that the treaty should be ratified, gave his "unqualified and unequivocal assurances" that the conditions would be met. Secretary McNamara, while questioning whether "the vast increases in our nuclear forces" had "produced a comparable enhancement in our security," nevertheless assured the Senate that he would move in the next years further to raise "the megatonnage of our strategic alert forces." Senators, reluctant to be associated with what critics might regard as disarmament, seized with delight on the chance of interpreting the renunciation of atmospheric tests as a green light for underground tests. The effect for a moment, as Richard Rovere put it, was to turn "an agreement intended to limit nuclear testing into a limited warrant for increasing nuclear testing."

The President was prepared to pay this price to commit the nation to a treaty outlawing atmospheric tests. He had called the treaty a "step toward reason." For all the concessions in the presentation to the Senate, his reliance on reason was now being broadly vindicated. For two and a half years he had quietly striven to free his countrymen from the clichés of the cold war. In speech after speech

4 He noted, "Lines found in an old sentry box found in Gibraltar. Based on poem by Thomas Jordan."

he had questioned the prejudices and platitudes of the fifties, cautioned against extreme solutions and defined the shape of terror in the nuclear age. The American University speech was the climax of a long campaign. If it had produced few letters to the White House, this might have been a measure of the extent to which people read it as sheer common sense. The absence of major criticism, whether in Congress or the press, showed the transformation which, despite Berlin and despite Cuba, the President had wrought in the mind of the nation. Public opinion polls indicated a marked swing in favor of the treaty—80 per cent by September. And on September 24 the Senate gave its consent to ratification by the vote of 80 to 19—fourteen more than the required two-thirds. The action, Kennedy said, was "a welcome culmination of this effort to lead the world once again to the path of peace."

6. FURTHER STEPS ON THE JOURNEY

If the treaty were to have its full effect, it would have to include all present and potential nuclear powers. This gave Khrushchev the problem of signing up China, as it gave Kennedy the problem of signing up France. These were not easy assignments. Neither Peking nor Paris shared the Washington-London-Moscow view that the treaty was a noble and selfless act on behalf of humanity. After all, America, Britain and Russia had all the nuclear weapons they needed: now, in effect, they proposed to close down the store. To Mao Tse-tung and de Gaulle, the treaty sounded more like a hypocritical conspiracy by the nuclear monopolists to make their supremacy permanent lest new nations enter the club and challenge their control of world affairs.

One does not know what effort, if any, Khrushchev made to get China to sign, or North Korea, North Vietnam and Albania, or even Cuba, where Castro, still smarting from the missile crisis, took the occasion to make clear that Moscow could not deliver him on the world scene. The rest of Khrushchev's flock ambled in without delay. As for France, Kennedy made a determined attempt to persuade de Gaulle by offering him the technical data atmospheric testing would otherwise give him. He declared France a nuclear power in the terms of the Atomic Energy Act, thereby making it eligible for nuclear assistance without new legislation and, as soon as the treaty was initialed, sent Paris a formal proposal.

The General made his first response four days later via a press conference. After expressing polite pleasure that "the Soviets and the Anglo-Saxons" were discontinuing atmospheric tests, he dismissed the treaty as "of limited practical importance." So long as Russia and America retained their capacity to destroy the world, agreement between them would "not divert France from equipping herself with the same sources of strength." Nor was he impressed by the adhesion of other nations because, as he put it a few days later, "hardly any of them are in a position to carry out tests. It is rather like asking people to promise not to swim the Channel." On August 4 he formally rejected Kennedy's offer, arguing that the treaty and even nuclear cooperation with the United States would violate the apparently infinitely violable sovereignty of France. As Kennedy told Macmillan, de Gaulle's answer made it clear that he wished neither Anglo-American nuclear assistance nor even a serious discussion. But though the President was not surprised, he was nonetheless bitterly disappointed. The French declination, on top of the Chinese, meant that the treaty would fail as a means of stopping major proliferation. "Charles de Gaulle," Kennedy told David Brinkley, "will be remembered for one thing only, his refusal to take that treaty."

Yet, if the test ban was not to stop national nuclear weapons development completely, it still denied at least its signatories—soon more than a hundred—the most convenient means of pursuing the nuclear dream. And it still offered the prospect of a *détente* between the two superpowers.

The Soviet Union obviously had tactical reasons of its own to seek a lull in world tensions. The agreement gave the Kremlin its international breathing spell at very small cost. It held out the hope of keeping Soviet defense spending down and enabling Khrushchev to reorganize his domestic economy, invest in his chemical fertilizers and deal with his restless intellectuals. It might encourage a reduction of western military budgets and political pressures. It would give the quarrels within the west a chance to grow and flourish. It could possibly stabilize the communist position in East Germany and Eastern Europe. Above all, perhaps, it provided Khrushchev's coexistence policy a visible success with which he could move to isolate the Chinese in the communist civil war.

Washington was well aware of these tactical purposes. Yet there were other considerations also. America and Russia appeared now to have developed comparable interests in the preservation both of their own societies and of an international order under their own control: history had made these two once revolutionary nations champions of the status quo in a world where revolution had spun beyond them. And, as Marshall Shulman of the Fletcher School emphasized in the test ban hearings, the new Soviet course might have "unintended effects" broader than the conscious aims of the leadership. "Indeed, the most striking characteristic of recent Soviet foreign policy," Shulman observed, "has been the way in which policies undertaken for short-term, expediential purposes have tended to elongate in time, and become imbedded in doctrine and political strategy." This development could be understood as a process of adaptation to a new "terrain of international politics." The question whether it could lead to a "long-term modification of Soviet policies and the Soviet system in a benign direction," he concluded, depended "upon the effectiveness of our own process of adaptation to this environment."

Khrushchev himself appeared ready for next steps. In statements on July 19 and July 26, he laid out a series of possibilities: the non-aggression pact between the NATO and Warsaw Pact countries; the freezing or "still better" the cutting of defense budgets; measures to prevent surprise attack, including reciprocal observation teams and inspection posts in East and West Germany; and the reduction of foreign forces in both German states. Of all these, the non-aggression pact seemed closest to his heart. Harriman and Kaysen had the impression that it might almost be a precondition to further progress.

They had rigorously kept the non-aggression pact out of the test ban negotiations. But both Harriman and Kaysen returned from Moscow convinced that the idea should be seriously considered. They did not suppose that negotiating a non-aggression pact would be easy. But, if we decided in advance that nothing could be done, negotiations would obviously fail. On the other hand, if we approached the problem with an open mind, some mutually desirable arrangement could be worked out. In any case, we had told the Russians that we would explore it in good faith.

The Russians plainly wanted the pact in order to achieve their old-time goal of consolidating the communist position in East Germany and Eastern Europe. But was this now so self-evidently against our interest? Judging by past experience, stability would lead to a better life with somewhat more independence for the peoples of Eastern Europe. It would reduce the threat of war. In the case of East Germany, it would promote greater intercourse with West Germany not only in trade and cultural exchanges but in personal and family contacts; it might even lead in time to the settlement of the Berlin problem and the replacement of the Ulbricht regime by a government more on the Polish model. As for Eastern Europe, stability would diminish the excuse for Soviet occupation and control, encourage a relaxation of ties to Moscow and allow the satellite countries to look increasingly to the west. This had already happened in Hungary and to some degree in Poland. A non-aggression pact might make it happen elsewhere.

For a moment the treaty seemed to be opening up a whole new range of possibilities. This prospect was deeply disturbing to those accustomed to the familiar simplifications of the cold war. They did not like the idea of swimming in uncharted waters; one felt an almost panicky desire in some parts of the government to return things to pre-test ban normal as speedily as possible. The critical question was whether it was to our advantage to maintain or decrease tension in Europe. The emphasis on the perils of euphoria in the Senate debate strengthened those who took the traditional view that a reduction of tension was a bad thing—bad, if only because Moscow liked it and Bonn didn't. Adenauer, whom the treaty had caught off guard, was now sending out signals of vast discontent; and this too troubled the traditionalists. Since the days of Acheson the relationship with West Germany had been a pivot of our European policy; under Dulles it had often appeared *the* pivot. Outsiders might feel that in the fifties we had permitted the West Germans to use us for their own interests and might wish now to distinguish what was good for America from what was good for Adenauer; but those reared in the pure school doubted whether there was such a distinction and thought the first order of business was to repair relations with Bonn. As for Adenauer, his view was simple and understandable: he did not want any change in east-west relations which did not involve progress toward the reunification of Germany. He particularly did not want a non-aggression pact which might confer status on East Germany as one of the Warsaw Treaty countries.

The President hoped to maintain the momentum generated by the Moscow negotiations; but his primary concern was to get the treaty through the Senate. He did not want new diplomatic steps to be taken before ratification, and he was skeptical whether there was much in the non-aggression pact for the United States. The Secretary of State was certain there was not. Such a pact might induce the euphoria so feared by the Joint Chiefs; in any case, Rusk was well aware of a concern, not confined to Bonn, that Russia and America were trying to settle the questions of Europe in the absence of Europeans. As for next steps, he had told the Senate Foreign Relations Committee, during the test ban hearings, "I cannot report that there is another question which is highly promising at this—as of today." He saw his first obligation, as one understood his view, as not to press forward with Moscow but to reassure NATO.

When Rusk went to Moscow early in August to sign the test ban treaty, Khrushchev tried to explain to him that the non-aggression pact was like mineral water—refreshing, involving no gains or losses and invigorating in its effect. The Secretary evidently replied that it was more like the Kellogg Pact. In any case, he told Khrushchev, it was something to come at the end of the road rather than at the beginning. Rusk then went on to Bonn where Adenauer complained bitterly that the test ban treaty had contributed to the prestige of the East German government. The Secretary patiently answered the legal points until Adenauer finally agreed that West Germany would sign the treaty. But the Chancellor achieved what may have been his essential objective by leaving the vivid impression that a non-aggression pact on top of the treaty would be just too much.

In these weeks foreign offices everywhere, eager to regain their control over foreign affairs, appeared to be moving to seal up the uncertainties, whether risks or possibilities, which the test ban had momentarily opened up. When Rusk and Gromyko held long talks at the UN in New York in the fall, it was a meeting of two professionals with a common interest in tidying up the mess created by amateurs. And in due course the professionals brought things back to normal. The non-aggression pact fell by the wayside. The inspection issue blocked the extension of the ban to underground tests. The Americans, returning to the familiar ground of the multilateral force, set up the MLF working group in October; this enabled the Russians to resume their familiar complaint that the United States was planning to give nuclear weapons to West Germany. Everyone felt more secure in the old rubrics, and foreign policy slipped back from men to institutions.

7. DÉTENTE: POSSIBILITIES AND LIMITS

One cannot know what might have happened in these months if Kennedy and Khrushchev, both of whom had urgent preoccupations of their own—the civil rights crisis in the United States, the agricultural crisis in the Soviet Union, as well as respective troubles with de Gaulle and Mao—had been free to deal with their foreign affairs bureaucracies. But, if opportunities were lost, they were probably not decisive ones. Both sides needed time to digest the test ban before they would be ready for a next large step. What was lost rather was a shaping of the atmosphere, a continuation of the momentum, which might have made the next steps quicker and easier.

This was much on Kennedy's mind, especially as he watched the progress of the test ban debate, and it confirmed his decision to speak for a second time before the UN General Assembly. "The treaty is being so chewed up in the Senate," he said on September 9, two weeks before ratification, "and we've had to make so many concessions to make sure it passes, that we've got to do something to prove to the world we still mean it. If we have to go to all this trouble over one small treaty, people are likely to think we can't function at all—unless I can dispel some doubts in New York."

We had the usual series of meetings to recommend to the President what he might say. The Secretary of State proposed what he called an Alliance for Man designed to show how America, Russia and the rest of the UN could work together on issues beyond politics—health, nutrition, agricultural productivity, resources development. It seemed a promising idea; but, when Richard Gardner of the State Department and I canvassed the scientific and technical agencies of the government, we discovered that specific proposals of American-Soviet collaboration seemed trivial compared to the enormities of the space age. As we began casting about for more dramatic forms of cooperation, there swam into our minds the thought of merging the Russian and American expeditions to the moon.

The proposal of a joint moonshot would be a tangible and impressive offer of cooperation; it would mean a substantial budgetary saving for both countries; and it would be an effective political gesture at home and abroad. Gardner warned me, however, that it would cause trouble in the bureaucracy. Only recently someone in the National Aeronautics and Space Administration had asked for a letter from the State Department requesting a study of the problems and possibilities of a joint moonshot; NASA, it developed, feared to proceed on its own without political clearance. Then State declined to send the letter lest it in turn be held accountable for so subversive an inquiry. One thought, what the hell; and on speculation I wrote the idea into an early draft of the President's UN address. I had forgotten that the President had himself suggested this to Khrushchev in Vienna in 1961, or I would have been better prepared for his quick approval. He discussed it with James Webb, the head of NASA; and, when we went over the draft a few days later with representatives from State, Defense and the Arms Control and Disarmament Agency, no one voiced objection. Then at the UN in New York on September 20, he said: "Surely we should explore whether the scientists and astronauts of our two countries—indeed of all the world—cannot work together in the conquest of space, sending some day in this decade to the moon not the representatives of a single nation but the representatives of all of our countries."

The speech was a sober and effective plea for new steps toward peaceful cooperation. "If this pause in the cold war merely leads to its renewal and not to its end," he said, "—then the indictment of posterity will rightly point its finger at us all." Other moves were meanwhile carrying forward the hope of *détente* in one way or another. Least heralded but perhaps most important was the tacit acceptance of reciprocal aerial reconnaissance from space satellites—the American Samos and the Soviet Cosmos. By supplying a partial substitute for organized international inspection, the satellites provided mutual reassurance and thus strengthened the system of stable nuclear deterrence. The Russians further displayed their new sophistication in the higher strategy when Gromyko at the UN in September modified the Soviet program for general and complete disarmament by abandoning the demand for the elimination of all nuclear weapons and delivery vehicles in the first stage and suggesting instead, in the best arms control manner, that America and Russia retain a limited number of missiles and warheads on their own territory until the end of the disarmament process.

In the meantime, the so-called hot line—an emergency communications link between the White House and the Kremlin—had been installed over the summer. Then, early in October, Kennedy authorized the sale of surplus wheat to the Soviet Union as "one more hopeful sign that a more peaceful world is both possible and beneficial to us all"— a project which, though the Vice-President considered it for a moment as "the worst political mistake we have made in foreign policy in this administration," did not turn out too tragically. Later in the month the UN, with enthusiastic American and Russian support and much mutual self-congratulation, passed a resolution calling on all states to refrain from "placing in orbit around the earth any objects carrying nuclear weapons or any other kinds of weapons of mass destruction" and from "installing such weapons on celestial bodies." This resolution, along with the Moscow treaty's abolition of testing in outer space and the adoption by the General Assembly in December of a Declaration of Legal Principles for Outer Space, represented the bold attempt of the earthlings to keep the nuclear race out of the firmament.

All these things were helpful; but much remained on the agenda: the completion of the nuclear test ban; new measures to restrain nuclear proliferation, to which Robert Kennedy gave special attention in later years; further possibilities in reciprocal/unilateral arms reduction and control, as suggested by Roswell Gilpatric and Jerome Wiesner; the cut-off of production of fissionable materials for weapons use, undertaken by both superpowers in 1964; and the old dream of general and complete disarmament.

Yet, had all these measures and others like them been accomplished, they still would not have produced a true *détente*. For in the end a philosophical gap could not be bridged by technical agreements. The 'mirror image' of American and Soviet societies was valid only up to a point; the mirror reflected common anxieties, not common values. The Soviet Union remained a system consecrated to the infallibility of a single body of dogma, a single analysis of history and a single political party. Khrushchev seized many occasions in 1963 to make it clear that lull abroad did not mean liberty at home. As he admonished a group of Soviet artists and intellectuals on March 8, 1963, "We are against peaceful co-existence in the ideological field."

By this he did not mean anything so simple as the proposition that, whatever the condition of *détente*, the ideological debate between communism and democracy must continue. He meant, indeed, the exact opposite. He meant that the ideological debate must not take place at all—at least not within the Soviet Union. "Soviet society," he warned his intellectuals in March, "has reached the stage now when complete monolithic unity . . . has been achieved." The central committee of the party "will demand from everybody—from the most honored and renowned worker of literature and art as well as from the young, budding artist—unswerving abidance by the Party line." Anyone "who advocates the idea of peaceful coexistence in ideology is objectively sliding down to the position of anti-communism." And so Russia defended its prohibition of non-communist books, magazines and newspapers from the west as well as its censorship not only of books and magazines but of personal mail at home. With all the Soviet talk about peaceful competition, the Communists evidently flinched from such competition where it mattered most: in the realm of ideas.

The President was nonetheless determined to persevere in the search. "Let us exhaust every avenue for peace," he said at the University of Maine exactly a year after the missile crisis. "Let us always make clear our willingness to talk, if talk will help, and our readiness to fight, if fight we must. Let us resolve to be the masters, not the victims, of our history." Yet he warned his listeners to distinguish between hopes and illusions. "Mr. Khrushchev himself has said there can be no coexistence in the field of ideology. . . . The United States and the Soviet Union still have wholly different conceptions of the world, its freedom, its future. . . . So long as these basic differences continue, they . . . set limits to the possibilities of agreement."

All this defined the boundaries of *détente*. Obviously the technical measures were of the greatest value. Obviously a world with increased security against self-destruction, a world slowing down the arms race and moving toward general and complete disarmament, a world enlarging its cooperation in economic and scientific matters, a world collaborating on an expedition to the moon and on the conquest of space—such a world would be far better than the world we had. But it would not be a genuine international community, nor would so tense and dour a form of coexistence constitute, except in the minimal sense, peace.

It was because the President understood this so well that he reacted so sharply in November 1963 when Professor Frederick Barghoorn of Yale, a scholar pursuing his studies in the Soviet Union, was arrested on accusations of espionage. The "reasonable" atmosphere between the two countries, the President said, "has been badly damaged by the Barghoorn arrest. . . . Professor Barghoorn I regard as a very serious matter." "In view," the Soviet authorities explained, "of the personal concern expressed by President Kennedy," Barghoorn was released after a few days. But the charges were not withdrawn, and the incident was a useful reminder not only of the fragility of the *détente* but of the profound differences which separated communism from democracy, the monolithic world from the world of diversity.

"We must never forget," Kennedy had said a few days earlier in making his own comment on society and the arts in a speech at Amherst, "that art is not a form of propaganda; it is a form of truth. . . . In free society art is not a weapon and it does not belong to the sphere of polemics and ideology. Artists are not engineers of the soul. It may be different elsewhere. But democratic society—in it, the highest duty of the writer, the composer, the artist is to remain true to himself and to let the chips fall where they may. In serving his vision of the truth, the artist best serves his nation."

So long as one power insisted that it had exclusive possession of the truth, that it would permit no competing truths within its domain and that it could not wait until its absolute truth obliterated competing truths in the rest of the planet, so long as it declined to accept the permanence of a diverse world, so long the cold war would continue. In the end, peaceful coexistence had to mean the free circulation of ideas among all countries or it would mean very little.

XXXV

THE TRAVAIL OF EQUAL RIGHTS

HISTORIANS OF THE TWENTY-FIRST CENTURY will no doubt struggle to explain how nine-tenths of the American people, priding themselves every day on their kindliness, their generosity, their historic consecration to the rights of man, could so long have connived in the systematic dehumanization of the remaining tenth—and could have done so without not just a second but hardly a first thought.

The answer to this mystery lay in the belief, welling up from the depths of the white unconscious, in the inherent and necessary inferiority of those of a darker color. This belief was fortified by the failure of institutions—the church, the university, the government, the business firm—to live up to their own ideals and by the narrow views of the federal system which could lead a President like William Howard Taft to say with unction in his inaugural address, "It is not the disposition or within the province of the Federal Government to interfere with the regulation by Southern States of their domestic affairs." By such means white America virtuously succeeded in cutting the Negro out of conscience and even, except for servants, entertainers and athletes, out of sight.

"I am an invisible man," cried the hero of Ralph Ellison's novel in 1953. ". . . I am invisible, understand, simply because people refuse to see me. . . . You ache with the need to convince yourself that you do exist in the real world, that you're a part of all the sound and anguish, and you strike out with your fists, you curse, and you swear to make them recognize you. . . . I can hear you say, 'What a horrible, irresponsible bastard!' And you're right. . . . But to whom can I be responsible, and why should I be, when you refuse to see me?"

1. INTO THE LIGHT

In the first decade of the twentieth century outbursts of race rioting in Illinois reminded some white Americans of the existence of outcasts in their midst. In 1909 Arthur B. Spingarn joined white Jane Addams, William Dean Howells, John Dewey and others to form the National Association for the Advancement of Colored People. In the next years the national ethos began slowly to change. Woodrow Wilson was the last progressive President for whom Negroes were outside the scope of human concern. Herbert Hoover the last conservative President for whom having the wife of a Negro Congressman for tea at the White House constituted a crisis. In the thirties Franklin Roosevelt gave the Negroes a sense of national recognition. He did so more in terms of their interests in economic and social justice than of their title to equal rights. Yet he threw open the gate of hope; and the Negroes themselves, who had been stirring restlessly for a generation, now began to shake off the psychological manacles with which white society had so long made them accomplices in their own subjection—the convictions of inferiority and dependence, the manner of shuffling docility and what Ellison once called "the long habit of deception and evasion." The future at last was spreading out before them, and they moved to take history into their own hands.

Then the Second World War offered Negro militants the great opportunity to force the moral issue on the white conscience. For that war called on the American Negro to fight the idea of a master race in defense of rights denied them by their own master race; and the paradox proved too manifest even for the white man to ignore. In 1944 Gunnar Myrdal documented the contradiction between creed and performance in his great study *An American Dilemma: the Negro Problem and American Democracy.* Myrdal insisted on the ultimate power of the creed to alter folkways and institutions; and in a way he was right. After the war, President Truman, abandoning the prejudices of his upbringing, set forth the first comprehensive legislative program for civil rights. In these years segregation disappeared in the armed forces. In 1954 a unanimous Supreme Court, including three southerners, outlawed segregation in public schools.

It should have surprised no one that, as the Negroes began to gain some of their rights, their determination to claim *all* their rights hardened. Revolutions accelerate not from despair but from hope. When barriers began to fall, the Negro leadership, ever more able and aggressive, pressed more and more urgently for full membership in American society. The national creed gave them their moral leverage, and politics increasingly responded to their pressure. By the 1950s the northern Democracy had been firmly committed by Truman and Adlai Stevenson to civil rights. "The Democratic party must not weasel on this issue," John F. Kennedy said early in 1956. ". . . We might alienate southern support, but the Supreme Court decision is the law of the land." Yet this remained more a matter of intellectual and political commitment than of emotional identification. The northern Democratic leaders recognized that historic injustices had to end, but they thought that steady and rational progress step by step over a period of years would suffice to satisfy the victims of injustice and contain their incipient revolution.

The school desegregation decision, now to be carried out, in the delphic words of the Court, with "all deliberate speed," was one such step. The next was the Civil Rights Act of 1957, the first congressional enactment on civil rights for eighty-seven years. The most significant provision of the bill, Title III, giving the Attorney General injunctive powers to enforce school desegregation and other civil rights, had failed in the Senate. Nevertheless the act strengthened the authority of the Attorney General to intervene when Negroes were denied the right to vote; and, in two symbolic gestures, it raised the civil rights section of the Department of Justice to a division and established an independent Commission on Civil Rights. A second act, passed in 1960, gave the Department of Justice additional, though still limited, powers in voting cases. The Supreme Court decision and the Civil Rights Acts

were essentially the result of the strategy of the NAACP
and its executive director, Roy Wilkins, a man of exceptional sagacity and purpose. Regarding law as the most
effective and lasting way of securing Negroes their rights,
Wilkins concentrated on persuading the courts to take a
fresh look at old law (as through Thurgood Marshall and the
NAACP legal bureau) and on persuading Congress to enact
new law (as through Clarence Mitchell and the NAACP
Washington office). Yet progress in the courts and Congress,
though of a sort unimaginable a generation earlier, was
beginning to be slow and abstract for the awakening Negro
militancy. The "deliberate speed" of the desegregation decision seemed to mean no movement at all; by 1960 only
one-sixth of 1 per cent of the Negro students in the ex-
Confederate states were in desegregated schools (and this
was mostly in Texas and Florida). Nor in the first years
did the Civil Rights Act of 1957 or the Civil Rights Commission produce notable federal action.

In the meantime, the experience of a Negro bus boycott in Montgomery, Alabama, in the winter of 1955–56
had suggested another strategy. Martin Luther King, Jr.,
a young Baptist minister precipitated into the leadership
of the boycott, preserved Negro purpose and discipline
during the long weeks by preaching the gospel of non-
violent resistance, derived from his reading of Thoreau
and Gandhi. A superb orator, deeply sensitive to the woe
and weariness of his race, King drew from the religious
traditions of southern Negroes a strength which now enabled them to defy white society without giving it the pretext to respond in customary manner with whip and rope.
The spirituals which had once sustained Negroes in servi-
tude now nerved them for battle. Though in fact King's
approach supplemented and supported that of the NAACP
(indeed, it took an NAACP suit to secure the goal of the
bus boycott), his appeal released new energies in the
struggle. Where the NAACP used legal means to attack
the power points in southern society, King and his Southern Christian Leadership Conference went into the communities, called for mass action and brought the Negroes
into the streets.

Then in February 1960 four Negro students at the Agricultural and Technical College in Greensboro, North Carolina,
were denied service at a lunch counter. Their decision to
stay in their seats until the place closed launched the new
technique of 'sit-ins' across the South and brought another
organization, the Congress of Racial Equality (CORE), into

prominence. A year later James Farmer, who had been program director for the NAACP, became CORE's national director. The sit-ins led to kneel-ins, pray-ins and other forms of non-violent protest and soon to the formation of still another group, intense in its emotions and radical, if often obscure, in its doctrines, the Student Nonviolent Coordinating Committee (SNCC).

By 1960 the Negro was no longer the invisible man. The Negro leadership—Wilkins, King, Farmer, Whitney Young of the Urban League and the veteran head of the Brotherhood of Sleeping Car Porters, A. Philip Randolph, whose threat to march on Washington in 1941 had led Franklin Roosevelt to set up the wartime Fair Employment Practices Commission—were as gifted and impressive a group as one could find in the country. The movement for equal rights was beginning to pierce apathy and overcome fear among Negroes, and it was winning increasing support in the white community. The revolution was rushing along. But no one—certainly not the white politicians, not even the established Negro leadership—could foretell at what pace or with what intensity.

2. KENNEDY AND CIVIL RIGHTS

Kennedy had collaborated with the movement for civil rights in the fifties. In the 1957 fight, he had supported Title III of the civil rights bill, though he had earlier disappointed the Negro groups by declining to take part in the effort to bypass Senator James Eastland of Mississippi and his Senate Judiciary Committee and send the bill directly to the floor. In the late fifties civil rights advocates regarded him as sympathetic—Roy Wilkins sent him a favorable letter which he used during his campaign for re-election to the Senate in 1958—but detached. King, who breakfasted with him in New York a month before the 1960 convention, later said that he displayed at this time "a definite concern but . . . not what I would call a 'depthed' understanding." Most civil rights leaders preferred Humphrey or Stevenson for the Democratic nomination.

Kennedy's sense of his weakness with the Negroes led him in the spring of 1960 to ask Harris Wofford of the Notre Dame Law School, who had joined his campaign staff as an expert on Asian matters, to shift over to civil rights. Father Theodore Hesburgh, the president of Notre Dame and a leading member of the Civil Rights Commission, had brought Wofford to Washington in 1958 as his counsel and chief of the Commission's inquiry into discrimination in housing. This experience had given Wofford the belief that the untapped resources of executive action offered the best immediate hope for new civil rights progress. Kennedy liked this approach both because it fitted his conception of an activist Presidency and because the 1957 and 1960 civil rights debates had left him pessimistic about further progress in Congress.

Wofford now arranged a series of meetings between Kennedy and Negro leaders. Each session advanced the candidate a little in his own commitment. At the convention he insisted on a strong civil rights plank; and after the August special session he joined twenty-three other Democratic Senators in a statement condemning the Republican civil rights record. The Eisenhower administration, the Senators declared, had carefully avoided opportunities for executive action; it had not, for example, issued an order to end discrimination in federal housing programs which "the President could do by a stroke of his pen." The statement concluded: "we pledge action to obtain consideration of a *civil rights bill by the Senate early next session that will implement the pledges of the Democratic platform.*"

In the campaign Kennedy incorporated the plight of the Negro into his general critique of American society. "The Negro baby," he said in Wisconsin in October, "has one-half, regardless of his talents, statistically has one-half as much chance of finishing high school as the white baby, one-third as much chance of finishing college, one-fourth as much chance of being a professional man or woman, four times as much chance of being out of work." "Only a President willing to use all the resources of his office," he said in California, "can provide the leadership, the determination and the direction . . . to eliminate racial and religious discrimination from American society." He emphasized that "the greater opportunity" lay "in the executive branch without congressional action." Here he mentioned the housing order and, repeatedly, the stroke of the presidential pen. He also advocated more vigorous measures to win the Negro the right to vote, the right to employment in companies doing business with the federal government and the right to federal appointments, especially in the Foreign Service, where, he said, there were presently only twenty-six Negro officers.

These proposals probably counted less in the election than his phone call to Mrs. Martin Luther King, Jr. "I am deeply indebted to Senator Kennedy," King soon said, "who served as a great force in making my release possible. It took a lot of courage for Senator Kennedy to do this, especially in Georgia. . . . He did it because of his great concern and humanitarian bent." On election day Kennedy received an overwhelming share of the Negro vote.[1] And, if King thought himself indebted to Kennedy before the election, Kennedy, reflecting on his margin, must have known after the election how indebted he was to King and the Negroes. Had only whites gone to the polls in 1960, Nixon would have taken 52 per cent of the vote. In the electoral college Kennedy could not have carried Illinois and Michigan, not to mention Texas, South Carolina and possibly Louisiana. He needed to lose only the first two of those states to have lost the election.

Setting forth Negro expectations in an article in the *Nation* soon after Kennedy's inauguration, King ascribed the "intolerably" slow progress in civil rights as much "to the limits which the federal government has imposed on its own action" as to the segregationist opposition. In the legislative area, he demanded that the President fight for a "really far-reaching" civil rights program with particular emphasis on the right to vote. In the area of executive action, he called on the President to "give segregation its death blow through a stroke of a pen"—especially by stopping the use of federal funds to support housing, hospital and airport construction in which discrimination was open and notorious. "We must face the tragic fact," King said, "that the federal government is the nation's highest investor in segregation." Describing housing as "the most tragic expression of discrimination," King laid special stress on the necessity for a housing order.

Confronted by such proposals, the new President faced a most difficult problem. He had at this point, I think, a terrible ambivalence about civil rights. While he did not doubt the depth of the injustice or the need for remedy, he had read the arithmetic of the new Congress and concluded that there was no possible chance of passing a civil rights bill. Moreover, he had a wide range of presidential responsibilities; and a fight for civil rights would alienate southern support he needed for other purposes (including bills, like those for education and the increased minimum wage, of direct benefit to the Negro). And he feared that the inevitable defeat of a civil rights bill after debate and filibuster would heighten Negro resentment, drive the civil rights revolution to more drastic resorts and place a per-

[1] Gallup and Harris, the two main polling organizations, give figures ranging from 68 to 78 per cent.

haps intolerable strain on the already fragile social fabric. He therefore settled on the strategy of executive action. No doubt wishing to avoid argument and disappointment, he did not even establish an interregnum task force on civil rights.

He explained his position frankly to Wilkins, King and other Negro leaders. "Nobody needs to convince me any longer," he told King, "that we have to solve the problem, not let it drift on gradualism. But how do you go about it? If we go into a long fight in Congress, it will bottle-neck everything else and still get no bill." So in March, with the Americans for Democratic Action delegation, Kennedy, after encouraging Robert R. Nathan to organize pressure for policies of economic expansion, listened to Joseph Rauh make the case for new legislation—voting rights, Title III, a permanent fair employment practices commission. Then he said with definiteness, "No. I can't go for legislation at this time. I hope you have liked my appointments. I'm going to make some more, and Bobby will bring voting suits. And we'll do some other things." Rauh said, "You told Bob [Nathan] you would like some liberal pressure on the economic side. I take it you would also like some liberal pressure on the civil rights side." Kennedy replied emphatically, banging his hand on the desk: "No, there's a real difference. You have to understand the problems I have here."

What was the difference? Undoubtedly he wanted to keep control over the demand for civil rights and this, unlike the demand for federal spending, might well, if stimulated, get out of hand. Rauh also thought that the President, precisely because he perceived civil rights as a moral issue, may have felt that criticism of the administration, which in the field of economic policy would seem a mere disagreement over tactics, might carry here a suggestion of deficient moral energy.

3. THE STRATEGY OF 1961

Kennedy thus began by hoping that a strong and declared presidential commitment to civil rights, accompanied by the appointment of Negroes to government posts and by vigorous action on behalf of Negro rights by the White House and the Department of Justice, would move things fast enough to hold the confidence of the Negro community.

He seized a variety of small opportunities, beginning with the Coast Guard at the inauguration, to communicate his personal contempt for racial prejudice. When the Civil War Centennial Commission, of all bodies, planned segregated housing for its members during a session in Charleston, South Carolina, the President, very angry, arranged to have the meeting held at an unsegregated naval station. When Robert Kennedy, along with George Cabot Lodge, Charles Bartlett, Angier Biddle Duke and a number of others, resigned from the Metropolitan Club because of its discrimination against Negroes, the President told his press conference, "I personally approved of my brother's action." (Privately Kennedy said he did not see how anyone could stay in the club under those conditions; he was exceedingly scornful of liberals who retained their membership. How, he asked one night, could Senators—he named a couple— make speeches on the floor about civil rights and then retire to the Metropolitan Club for drinks and dinner? He thought that the younger people should get together and found a club of their own with decent practices. Jacqueline broke in at this point and said, "You might use the third floor of the White House." Eventually Bartlett carried through the President's suggestion and organized the Federal City Club.)

He issued a strong executive order against discrimination in federal employment and made a special effort to seek Negroes for high federal jobs. The designation as Housing Administrator of Robert C. Weaver, who a quarter-century earlier had been a member of the 'black cabinet' in the New Deal, placed a Negro in charge of the programs which, as King had observed, had such tragic implications for his race. George Weaver of the AFL-CIO became Assistant Secretary of Labor; two Negro newspapermen—Carl Rowan and Andrew Hatcher—were appointed respectively Deputy Assistant Secretary of State for Public Affairs and Pierre Salinger's deputy in the White House; John Duncan became the first Negro Commissioner of the District of Columbia. In February Clifton R. Wharton, a Negro Foreign Service officer, was made ambassador to Norway, the first of a number of Negro ambassadors Kennedy would appoint. In October Thurgood Marshall was nominated to the Second Circuit Court, the first of five Negroes made lifetime judges in the Kennedy years (when he became President, there were only three Negro lifetime judges—William H. Hastie, whom Truman had named to the Third Circuit Court, and two on the customs courts). Requesting reports from all departments and agencies on Negro employment, especially in the higher grades, he was

appalled by the result and instructed the cabinet in the
spring of 1961 to take immediate steps to improve the
situation. Harris Wofford, who was now his Special Assistant for civil rights, presided over a sub-cabinet group,
intended to impress on all parts of the federal government
their duty to use their full powers in the cause of equal
opportunity. The joke in Washington was that every department was sending posses out to recruit Negroes in order
to avert the wrath of the White House. The number of
Negroes holding jobs in the middle grades of the civil
service increased 36.6 per cent from June 1961 to June
1963; in the top grades, 88.2 per cent.

The President also combined a Committee on Government Employment with the Committee on Government Contracts, which had been headed by Vice-President Nixon in
Eisenhower days, and established a single President's Committee on Equal Employment Opportunity under Vice-President Johnson. William S. White has written that Johnson
"privately flinched" from the assignment, fearing that he
would be blamed as a southerner if the Committee failed
to meet expectations.[2] But Kennedy insisted, and Johnson,
conceivably noting that the assignment would give him a
chance to build a record where he had previously been regarded with mistrust, acquiesced. Actually, though Johnson had regularly voted against civil rights bills till 1957
and had even described Truman's civil rights program in
1948 as "a farce and a sham—an effort to set up a police
state in the guise of liberty," this attitude reflected Texas
politics rather than personal bias. The Vice President was
wholly devoid of racial prejudice, took pride in the support he received from Negroes and Mexicans and wanted
now to do his best for his fellow man. He summoned the
heads of firms doing business with the government and
urged them to join in Plans for Progress providing for the
training and employment of Negroes. The deliberations of
the Committee were on occasion contentious. Johnson
tended toward the cajolery of business; other members,
especially the Attorney General and the Secretary of Labor,
wanted more initiative and more action. But the record
far surpassed that of the Nixon committee; and the experience undoubtedly enlarged Johnson's knowledge of the
problem and deepened his concern.

The Department of Justice, however, was the center of
federal action and in the year of the Bay of Pigs, Laos,

[2] W. S. White, *The Professional: Lyndon B. Johnson* (Boston, 1964),
228.

Berlin and test resumption Kennedy left civil rights policy pretty much to his brother. Robert Kennedy, like the President, had a clear sense of historic injustice and a strong feeling of political obligation; but he was relatively new to the problem. Yet, if some of his southern judicial appointments in 1961 were unfortunate, he rapidly showed his deep belief in the idea of equal opportunity. Discovering fewer than ten Negro attorneys in the Department, he laid on a special recruiting campaign and quintupled the number by the end of the year. He also had appointed at once —and for the first time in history—Negroes as United States Attorneys (in San Francisco and Cleveland). He enlarged the staff of the Civil Rights Division. Going to the University of Georgia for Law Day in May 1961, he bluntly told his audience (and was applauded for it), "We will enforce the law, in every field of law and every region. . . . If the orders of the court are circumvented, the Department of Justice will act."

In Burke Marshall, the Assistant Attorney General in charge of the Civil Rights Division, Robert Kennedy had an aide whose passion for self-effacement could not conceal sharp intelligence, wise judgment and steely purpose. Kennedy and Marshall decided from the start that, before taking situations to the courts, they would first try to negotiate with local officials, thereby giving full respect to the federal system and full opportunity for local self-correction. Indeed, in the field of school integration, where they lacked authority to initiate suits, they had ordinarily no other choice. Marshall and John Seigenthaler, Robert Kennedy's special assistant, accordingly visited a number of southern cities before school opening in the fall of 1961. In September schools were desegregated without violence in Atlanta, New Orleans, Memphis and Dallas. In Prince Edward County, Virginia, where white resistance to integration had closed all the schools, the Department of Justice sought court action to bring about their reopening.

The Department gave first priority, however, to voting rights. Many observers had concluded by 1960 that the franchise was the keystone in the struggle against segregation. Negro voting did not incite social and sexual anxieties; and white southerners could not argue against suffrage for their Negro fellow citizens with quite the same moral fervor they applied to the mingling of races in schools. Concentration on the right to vote, in short, seemed the best available means of carrying the mind of the white South. Then, once Negroes began to go to the polls, politicians would have to temper their views or lose their elections. The Department was not alone in regarding voting as, if not the key to civil rights, at least the indispensable condition for the assertion of other federal rights. Though the NAACP still worried more about school integration, Martin Luther King, Jr., in November 1961, noting that the fight was taking place on many fronts—sit-ins, legal defense, educational opportunities—declared: *"The central front, however, we feel is that of suffrage. If we in the south can win the right to vote it will place in our hands more than an abstract right. It will give us the concrete tool with which we ourselves can correct injustice."*

The denial of Negro suffrage had long been an accepted southern scandal. In at least 193 counties fewer than 15 per cent of eligible Negroes were permitted to register; in Mississippi this was true in seventy-four out of eighty-two counties. In thirteen southern counties not one Negro was on the rolls. The civil rights legislation of 1957 and 1960 had equipped the Attorney General with a measure of authority to intervene in such cases; but the Eisenhower administration had brought only ten suits and none at all in Mississippi. By mid-1963, however, Kennedy and Marshall had filed forty-two suits, eight of them in Mississippi. The Attorney General fully realized that winning suits would not make much difference if apathy, ignorance or fear still prevented the mass of Negroes from registering. Accordingly, in a behind-the-scenes effort reminiscent of the campaign to save the Bay of Pigs prisoners, the administration, with helpful assistance from the Taconic Foundation and collaboration from the Southern Regional Council, persuaded the leading Negro organizations to undertake a drive which in 1963 registered a considerable number of Negro voters across the South.

It was not easy, however, to keep the turbulence of civil rights in the ordered channels of due process, and there were other issues than voting and schools. In the spring of 1961 James Farmer and CORE sent out groups of 'freedom riders' to challenge segregation in interstate bus terminals—in their restaurants, waiting rooms, restrooms. The first band, led by Farmer himself, proceeded through the Carolinas and Georgia, with occasional fights and arrests, but without serious trouble until it reached Alabama. At Anniston a white mob burned up one of the buses. At Birmingham the riders were attacked and beaten. By now SNCC, King's Southern Christian Leadership Conference and other groups had their own riders on the road to Alabama, and there was every prospect of serious violence. The Attorney General and then the President tried to reach Governor John Patterson, who declined their calls. Finally Patterson told John Seigenthaler, whom Robert Kennedy had sent to the scene, that he would protect the riders. But he added in a public statement, "We are not going to escort these agitators. We stand firm on that position." On May 20, when a delegation of agitators arrived in Montgomery, a mob of a thousand persons greeted them with clubs and pipes. A number of freedom riders and local Negroes were beaten; Seigenthaler was knocked unconscious. Since the state of Alabama, despite gubernatorial assurances, obviously could not maintain order, Robert Kennedy sent more than 600 deputy federal marshals to Montgomery. Patterson protested; the Attorney General was heard to say over the telephone, "John, John, what do you mean you're being invaded? Who's invading you, John? You know better than that."

The height of the crisis was over, though the rides continued; in the end over a thousand people were involved. The President, asked about freedom rides in a press conference, said, "The Attorney General has made it clear that we believe that everyone who travels, for whatever reason they travel, should enjoy the full constitutional protection given to them by the law and the Constitution." Robert Kennedy had meanwhile petitioned the Interstate Commerce Commission to issue regulations requiring desegregation of all facilities in terminals used in interstate bus travel. On September 22 the ICC put out such orders. When a few cities pleaded local laws as excuse for noncompliance, the Department of Justice brought suits; and at the same time it proceeded against segregation in airports and railroad stations. In time, in a quiet revolution, travel terminals of all sorts through the South were open on equal terms to white and Negro.

4. MINORITY REPORT

The strategy of executive action was thus proving adaptable to new problems. But it was also producing an undercurrent of criticism both within the government and without.

The Civil Rights Commission had been established in 1957 as a propitiatory gesture to hold off pressure for more far-reaching legislation. Eisenhower's appointment of two southern Democrats and three Republicans as the Commission majority suggested an intention of keeping the body as tame as possible. Its authority was limited to investigation (including the holding of hearings) and recommendation. But facts had a power which no one had foreseen. Among the commissioners were two college presidents, Hesburgh of Notre Dame and John Hannah of Michigan State; and, as they began to understand the dimensions of Negro misery and oppression, they became convinced of the need for strong federal action. The southern members regularly endorsed the findings of fact and went further than anyone expected in supporting the Commission's proposals. Younger men on the staff, like Wofford and Berl Bernhard, whom Kennedy made director in 1961, organized the work of the Commission with intelligence and drive. Increasingly the Commission construed its obligations as not only technical but moral; it saw itself as, in Bernhard's phrase, "the duly appointed conscience of the government in regard to civil rights." Father Hesburgh well summed up its mood in his closing statement in the 1961 report: "Americans might well wonder how we can legitimately combat communism when we practice so widely its central folly: utter disregard for the God-given spiritual rights, freedom and dignity of every human person."

The Commission shared the Department of Justice's concern for voting rights. In 1959, adopting an idea that the civil rights movement had exhumed from Reconstruction days, it had recommended that Congress authorize the President to appoint federal registrars to enroll Negro voters in districts where local authorities declined to do so—a proposal that led to the ineffective federal referee provisions in the Civil Rights Act of 1960 and eventually to the Voting Rights Act of 1965. But the Commission also gave great weight to its inquiries into housing, education, employment and law enforcement. As Bernhard put its view in November 1961, "There can be no single approach which will bring an end to discrimination"; inequalities in political participation, education, employment, housing and the administration of justice all reinforced one another. This meant that, while the Commission applauded Justice's work in the field of voting rights (apart from the Department's evident determination to keep the Commission out of that field), its members began to worry whether the government was concentrating on voting to the neglect of other problems equally vital. Indeed, the Commission became so fearful of the conception of voting as the panacea that, in Burke Marshall's view, it "went out of its way" in its 1961 report to point to twenty-one southern counties where Negroes voted freely with no effect at all on segregation.

The 1961 report's chief recommendation was that the President issue the executive order forbidding discrimination in housing; and that it cover not just federally financed housing—that is, mortgages insured by the Federal Housing Administration and the Veterans Administration—but the conventional mortgage activities of federally assisted financial institutions, such as banks whose deposits were guaranteed by the Federal Deposit Insurance Corporation. In the view of the Commission, housing was as much a key to Negro inequality in the North as voting was in the South; and, as Bernhard said in 1962, though present concern focused on the South, "the last battle for equal rights will be joined in the north" where "the forms of discrimination are often more subtle, and hence harder to combat."

The difficulties between the Commission and the Department of Justice were of no great importance; and they arose essentially from the fact that one was an agency of recommendation and the other of action. The Commission moved out ahead to define new areas and offer new proposals; the Department acted to solve immediate problems. Despite occasional arguments between them, it seemed to the outsider a good combination. If annoying at times, the pressure of the Commission probably enabled the Department to do a better job.

The civil rights groups were meanwhile pressing even harder for the executive order on housing. Recalling Kennedy's campaign assurances about "a stroke of the pen," people began sending pens to the White House in a sarcastic effort to ease the President's task. Kennedy had, I think, intended to put out the order when Congress adjourned in the fall of 1961. But he decided to postpone it because he needed congressional support for a Department of Urban Affairs with Robert Weaver as Secretary, because he sought southern votes for the trade expansion bill in 1962 and perhaps because he feared that the order might slow up business recovery by holding back building starts. The delay aggrieved the civil rights leadership. By declining to issue the order, Martin Luther King, Jr., said, "The President did more to undermine confidence in his intentions than could be offset by a series of smaller accomplishments." While conceding that "the vigorous young men" of the administration had "reached out more creatively" than their predecessors and, undaunted by southern backwardness, had "conceived and launched some imaginative and bold forays," King pronounced the broad record "essentially cautious and defensive," directed toward "the limited goal of token integration." He recalled Lincoln's reluctance a century earlier to issue the Emancipation Proclamation lest he alienate slaveholders in the border states. Kennedy, King thought, "may well be tormented by a similar dilemma, and may well be compelled to make an equally fateful decision." In similar vein Wilkins, while praising the President for "his personal role in civil rights and very plain indications of his concern that conditions be improved," declared his "disappointment with Mr. Kennedy's first year" as a result of the failure to issue the housing order and even more of the "basic error" of the strategy of "no legislative action on civil rights."

Yet, despite the discontent of the leadership, the Negro community on the whole seemed well satisfied, and Kennedy's personal popularity was obviously increasing. The President himself, sensitive to the need of maintaining momentum, observed in his 1962 State of the Union message that there was much more to be done "by the Executive, by the courts and by the Congress." In particular he expressed administration interest in bills to end the use of literacy tests and poll taxes as means of denying Negroes the right to vote. In August 1962 Congress obliged by passing a constitutional amendment declaring that the poll tax could not prevent voting in federal elections.[3] But this was a relatively non-controversial proposal, discreet in its approach and changing the situation in only five states. The bill exempting everyone with a sixth grade education from literacy tests was another matter; and a southern filibuster killed it in the spring. The civil rights forces were unable even to get a majority to vote for cloture. This experience seemed to confirm beyond question the President's judgment about the impossibility of legislation. In the meantime, the courts were about to precipitate a new crisis of equal rights.

5. THE BATTLE OF OXFORD

On January 20, 1961, a veteran of nine years in the Air Force named James Meredith, his spirit quickened by Kennedy's imaugural address, wrote to the University of Mississippi requesting an application for admission. "I am an American-Mississippi-Negro citizen," he explained when he

[3] This became the 24th Amendment to the Constitution in January 1964.

returned his form. "With all of the occurring events regarding changes in our educational system taking place in our country in this new age, I feel certain that this application does not come as a surprise to you. I certainly hope that this matter will be handled in a manner that will be complimentary to the University and to the State of Mississippi. Of course, I am the one that will, no doubt, suffer the greatest consequences of this event."

Ole Miss, as the university at Oxford was known through the state, had never (to its knowledge [4]) admitted a Negro, and now offered complicated academic reasons for rejecting Meredith. But Meredith, encouraged by Medgar Evers, director of the NAACP in Mississippi and represented in court by the NAACP Legal Defense Fund, filed suit on the ground that he had been turned down because of his race. When the federal district judge dismissed Meredith's plea, he appealed, and the Fifth Circuit Court, finding in June 1962 that he had been rejected "solely because he was a Negro," reversed the lower court's decision. After a summer of legal maneuver Justice Hugo Black, an Alabaman, upheld the court of appeals. Governor Ross Barnett of Mississippi promptly declared, "We will not surrender to the evil and illegal forces of tyranny." [5]

Robert Kennedy thereupon phoned the Governor, pointing out that he was proposing to defy a federal court order, and suggested they try to work out a solution together. But Barnett's neo-Confederate rhetoric, echoed by most of the legislature and most of the newspapers of the state, had already incited a wave of panic and hate among his fellow-Mississippians; and this encouraged the Governor in his course. On September 20, when James Meredith, accompanied by federal marshals, presented himself at Oxford for registration, students were marching around the campus singing "Glory, Glory, Segregation." Barnett grandiloquently read aloud a long proclamation rejecting Meredith's application. Concluding, he handed the document to Meredith: "Take it and abide by it."

This action in Oxford gave Washington a new states' rights crisis—and also me a new assignment. Up to this

---

[4] Harry S. Murphy, Jr., a light-skinned Negro, later revealed that he had studied at Ole Miss in 1945–46 as a Navy V-12 student. Doubtless there had been others in the years since the university was founded in 1848.

[5] Walter Lord's *The Past That Would Not Die* (New York, 1965) provides a careful, accurate and lively account of the Meredith affair. See also, for further detail, Michael Dorman, *We Shall Overcome* (New York, 1965), 11–143.

point, though my personal concern was of very long standing, my participation in civil rights matters at the White House had been slight. After Harris Wofford left for the Peace Corps and Ethiopia in the spring of 1962, Lee White, the very capable Associate Special Counsel to the President, took over the civil rights responsibility. Louis Martin of the Democratic National Committee, an able Negro newspaperman in whose judgment the President had confidence, also served as a link between the White House and the Negro leaders. Now both the Mississippi impasse and the impending centennial of the Emancipation Proclamation, set for September 22 at the Lincoln Memorial, drew me into civil rights. This was at first in my capacity as an historian; for Barnett was resting his case on nothing more nor less than the old doctrine of nullification or interposition—that is, the alleged right of state officials "to interpose the State sovereignty and themselves between the people of the State and any body politic seeking to usurp such power." One supposed that this proposition had died with John C. Calhoun; and I was able to recall to the Attorney General that, when South Carolina had claimed the right of interposition 130 years earlier, the Mississippi Legislature of that day had rejected it as "a heresy, fatal to the existence of the Union . . . contrary to the letter and spirit of the Constitution and in direct conflict with the welfare, safety and independence of every state." Consitutional scholarship had evidently languished in Jackson since 1832.

In the meantime, two days after Ross Barnett turned back James Meredith in Oxford, the country marked the first century of the Emancipation Proclamation. The President, in a message to the gathering at the Lincoln Memorial, placed special emphasis on the Negro role in the long fight for equal rights since the abolition of slavery. "The essential effort, the sustained struggle," he said, "was borne by the Negro alone with steadfast dignity and faith. . . . It can be said, I believe, that Abraham Lincoln emancipated the slaves, but that in this century since, our Negro citizens have emancipated themselves." But the task was not finished: "like the proclamation we celebrate, this observance must be regarded not as an end, but a beginning."

Robert Kennedy had already responded to Barnett's defiance by citing the three top officers of the University of Mississippi for contempt of court. Once in the courtroom the academic administrators readily agreed to register

Meredith. But the Governor, furious at this pusillanimity and unimpressed by federal law, told the Attorney General, "I consider the Mississippi courts as high as any other court and a lot more capable. . . . I am going to obey the laws of Mississippi." Robert Kennedy replied, "My job is to enforce the laws of the United States—I intend to fulfill it." The next day he obtained a restraining order from the Fifth Circuit Court enjoining Barnett and other state officials not to interfere with the registration of Meredith. But when Meredith again tried to register, Barnett physically barred his way. As Meredith and the Department of Justice officials departed, the mob surrounding the building shouted, "Communists. . . . Go home, nigger." That night Barnett told Robert Kennedy, "It's best for him not to go to Ole Miss." The Attorney General replied softly, "But he likes Ole Miss."

In the next days the Department of Justice made one more attempt to find a solution. After complicated negotiation through intermediaries, Barnett assured the Attorney General that a sufficient show of federal force—the appearance, for example, of marshals who, when the governor confronted them, would promise to draw their guns—would give him the excuse he needed for retreat. But the state was now aflame, and the excitement was bringing to Oxford country folk from miles around, many armed, all determined to keep the nigger out of Ole Miss. Recruits were on their way even from more distant points. On September 26, General Edwin A. Walker, now of Dallas, who had commanded the federal troops at Little Rock in 1957, repented in a disjointed radio exhortation: "Now is the time to be heard. Ten thousand strong from every state in the Union. Rally to the cause of freedom. The battle cry of the Republic. Barnett, yes; Castro, no. Bring your flags, your tents and your skillets. . . . The last time in such a situation I was on the wrong side. . . . This time I am out of uniform and I am on the right side and I will be there."

As Meredith, flanked by a group of armed marshals, prepared to make his third try, Barnett decided that the situation was too dangerous, the crowd might break out of control. The Attorney General, who had never much liked the play-acting, instructed Meredith and the marshals to pull back. The next day Barnett was found guilty of civil contempt and ordered to purge himself by the following Tuesday or face arrest and a fine of $10,000 a day. The Attorney General had hoped up to this time that civil force would suffice to get Meredith into the university. But Barnett's continued defiance was foreclosing this hope. On Friday, September 28, Robert Kennedy met with General Maxwell Taylor to provide for the necessary troop movements.

Later that afternoon he asked me to come over to the Department of Justice to work on a statement explaining the necessity for federal intervention. Preparations were being made with great secrecy. Edwin Guthman spirited me into the Department through a side entrance and installed me in a room behind the Attorney General's office. In a moment Bobby came in and said he understood better now how Hitler had taken over in Germany. "Everyone in Mississippi is accepting what that fellow is doing," he said. "There are no protests anywhere—from the bar or from professional men or from the professors. I wouldn't have believed it." He described with incredulity the latest proposition from Barnett: that Mississippians would raise money for Meredith to go to any university he desired outside the state if the Attorney General would persuade him to give up on Ole Miss.

The next afternoon, Saturday, September 29, I was called over to the President's office. The Attorney General, Burke Marshall and Kenneth O'Donnell were there. Matters were now rushing to climax. In a final effort to get a peaceful settlement and avert the sending of troops, the President himself had put in a call to Governor Barnett. Awaiting the call, the Kennedys were calm and dispassionate, talking quietly between themselves in fraternal shorthand and, as ever, lightening the tension with jokes. As the phone rang, the President, with the air of a master of ceremonies, announced, "And now—Governor Ross Barnett." Bobby, mocking a prize-fight manager, said, "Go get him, Johnny boy." As if rehearsing to himself, the President went on, "Governor, this is the President of the United States—not Bobby, not Teddy." Then he picked up the receiver. His expression serious, his voice calm, his manner unemotional, he began, "I am concerned about this matter as I know you must be. . . . Here's my problem, Governor. I don't know Mr. Meredith, and I didn't put him in there. But under the Constitution I have to carry out the law. I want your help in doing it." Barnett said that Tom Watkins, the Mississippi lawyer who had served as intermediary in the show-of-force scheme, was ready to come to Washington with a new plan. "The difficulty is this," the President said. "We have two or three problems. First, the Court's order gives you till Tuesday to permit the entry of Mr.

Meredith. What is your position on that? . . . I have my
responsibility as you have yours. The Attorney General can
talk to Mr. Watkins tomorrow. I want to work this out in
an amicable way. I don't want a lot of people down there
to be hurt or killed." There was a long silence while Barnett
spoke. Then the President said, "The Attorney General will
see Mr. Watkins. After that I will be back in touch with
you." Hanging up, he added, "You know what that fellow
said? He said, 'I want to thank you for your help on the
poultry program.' "

As the two brothers discussed the Barnett proposal, they
concluded that there was no point in Watkins's coming to
Washington unless he was prepared to negotiate a change
in Barnett's position. The Attorney General then called
Watkins. He had, he said crisply, two questions: "Will the
Governor defy or follow the order of the Court? If he
means to defy that order will we have a pitched battle
down there when we arrest the Governor?" After a moment, "Is there any possibility of finding out what we need
down there? Must we send an army, a division or what?
This depends on what the Governor will do. We are at
least entitled to know that. If the Governor is going to stand
up and bar the way, that's one situation. If he is going to
tell everyone to go home, that's an entirely different situation." Watkins said his understanding was that Barnett
would physically bar Meredith; he would also try to quiet
the mob. Robert Kennedy: "He can't do that. You can't
tell others to behave if you yourself are obstructing the
order of the court." Watkins went on to say that the situation was explosive; he was not sure the law enforcement
officials could control it. The President whispered to Bobby,
"Will they try?" The Attorney General asked the question
and whispered back, "He doesn't know." Then, before concluding the conversation, he asked Watkins whether Barnett
would take responsibility for maintaining law and order.

They waited for a while to give Watkins a chance to talk
to Barnett. Then the President called Barnett again. For
some reason Watkins had not called the Governor; so the
Attorney General, going to the phone, recapitulated his
conversation with Watkins. "I said that, unless he had concrete proposals which might form a basis for agreement, he
was wasting his time in coming to Washington. These proposals would have to include strong and vocal action on
your part . . . at minimum an order that people could not
congregate in Oxford in groups larger than three or five;
that students who commit disorders are liable for expulsion; that all people carrying guns or clubs in Oxford be

arrested." Barnett then suggested that, while he himself would go with a flourish to Oxford, Meredith should be registered at Jackson, the state capital. Robert Kennedy said, "Sneaking Meredith off to Jackson for registration doesn't meet the problem. It doesn't really make much sense, does it?"

In a minute the President went on the phone. "I know your feeling about the law of Mississippi and the court order," he said. "What we are concerned about is whether you will maintain law and order—prevent the gathering of a mob and action taken by a mob. Can you stop that? What about the Attorney General's proposals to stop a mob?" His voice was dispassionate and stern. Barnett evidently said that he would do his best. The President: "As I understand it, you will do everything you can to maintain order. Next, Governor, *can* you maintain order?" Barnett then suggested a cooling-off period. The President: "Would you undertake to register him in two weeks? Unless we have your support and assurance . . ." The conversation trailed off.

At seven that night there was a third phone call. Barnett brought up again the idea of registering Meredith secretly in Jackson, assuring the President that the state police could keep everything under control. With reluctance, the President decided to accept the subterfuge. Then three hours later Barnett phoned Robert Kennedy canceling the deal. There was now no alternative to a collision between the state of Mississippi and the national government. After midnight the President issued orders federalizing the Mississippi National Guard and sending troops of the United States Army to Memphis. He also requested national television time for Sunday evening.

Mississippi, throbbing with righteous emotion, prepared as if for war. But Barnett, whose rhetoric constantly outran his resolution, drew back once again, calling the Attorney General on Sunday morning with a more elaborate version of the show-of-force proposal, this time a staged capitulation of Mississippi forces to the Army. Robert Kennedy coldly dismissed it as "a foolish and dangerous show." He added that the President planned to report Barnett's repudiation of their earlier agreement in his television speech. Alarmed at this, Barnett quickly came up with a substitute proposal: that Meredith be quietly flown into Oxford that afternoon. He told the Attorney General that the state police would keep outsiders off the campus; and that, while he would have to say that he had yielded to overwhelming force, he would condemn any talk of violence and urge that the fight be carried forward in the courts.

In a few hours Meredith and the federal marshals, led by their brave and humorous chief, James McShane, arrived on the campus in Oxford. While Meredith went off to a dormitory, Deputy Attorney General Nicholas Katzenbach and the federal officials waited in the Lyceum, an imposing ante-bellum building which housed the university's administrative offices. As the sun set, a crowd, without challenge from the state police, began to collect menacingly around the Lyceum: first, "2-4-1-3, we hate Ken-ne-dy"; then a rising growl of taunts and curses—"Kill the nigger-loving bastards"; then, as it grew dark, bottles and bricks. For an hour and a half the marshals, though a number were hurt and bleeding, stood impassively under the attack. But after a time, as the mob, now numbering 2500, began to surge toward the Lyceum, the order was given to respond by tear gas.

In Washington the President, unaware of the troubles in Oxford, had gone on the air to say that Meredith was safely on the campus and explain why the federal government had massed its power to put him there. "If this country," he said, "should ever reach the point where any man or group of men by force or threat of force could long defy the commands of our court and our Constitution, then no law would stand free from doubt, no judge would be sure of his writ, and no citizen would be safe from his neighbors." He concluded with a direct appeal to the students of the university: "The honor of your University and State are in the balance. I am certain that the great majority of the students will uphold that honor."

In Oxford students jeered. A tall figure moved through the crowd with military stride. A student asked where he was from. General Walker replied, "I come from Dallas, Texas." Other outsiders joined the mob, some with shotguns and rifles. At the Lyceum the marshals were running out of tear gas. As Katzenbach heard the sounds of shots through the Confederate howls, he concluded that the time had come to call in the troops. In Washington the President issued the order. A federalized National Guard unit under the command of a cousin of William Faulkner's was summoned from Oxford, while regular units began to move by helicopter from Memphis. Robert Kennedy in Washington asked Edwin Guthman in Oxford how things were going. "Pretty rough," Guthman replied. "This place is sort of like the Alamo." "Well," Bobby said, "you know what happened to those guys." The battle raged on until the troops arrived. Hundreds were wounded, including more than a third of the marshals; two men, one a French reporter, were killed. The President stayed in his office at the other end of the telephone until dawn.

The next morning James Meredith appeared before the registrar in the Lyceum and was duly inducted into the University of Mississippi. A fellow student shouted, "Was it worth two lives, nigger?" For weeks troops stayed on campus, for months marshals accompanied Meredith to classes, reprisals were attempted against his family; but with heroic tenacity he pursued his chosen course. "Having his father's house shot at," Robert Kennedy said in January 1963, "still not accepted by his fellow students, having had 400 or 500 soldiers around and having marshals— well, I, at least, found college tough enough without having all that." Some of the faculty, led by the undaunted historian James W. Silver,[6] gave Meredith support. But it was a long lonely time until he graduated in August 1963.

Yet he had established the principle; and President Kennedy's action had a profound effect around the world, most of all in Africa. As the delegate from Upper Volta put it in the UN General Assembly, segregation unquestionably existed in the United States, but "what is important is that the Government of the United States did not make an institution of this. It does not praise the policy. On the contrary, it energetically fights it. For one small Negro to go to school, it threatens governors and judges with prison . . . it sends troops to occupy the University of Mississippi." Three weeks after Oxford, Sékou Touré and Ben Bella were prepared to deny refueling facilities to Soviet planes bound for Cuba during the missile crisis.

Though some American Negroes felt Kennedy might have acted sooner and did not much like his television appeal to Mississippians to honor their traditions, this was quickly forgotten in the memory of the dispatch of the Army and the admission of Meredith. In the fall elections the Democrats won more Negro votes than ever. Then on November 20 Kennedy finally issued the executive order on housing. While limited to housing owned or directly insured by the federal government and thus covering only 15 per cent of savings and loans residential mortgage holdings, it still marked a new step toward equal opportunity.

In the middle of 1963, when the Louis Harris polling

[6] Whose book *Mississippi: The Closed Society* (New York, 1964) contains an invaluable account of these days as well as of the atmosphere in Mississippi.

organization asked Negroes who had done most for Negro rights, the first three in the judgment of the rank and file were the NAACP, Martin Luther King, Jr., and President Kennedy.

XXXVI

THE NEGRO REVOLUTION

IN THE WINTER OF 1962–63 the civil rights leaders, more bent than ever on legislation, watched the success of the President's strategy with understandable frustration. Martin Luther King, Jr., sorrowfully described 1962 as "the year that civil rights was displaced as the dominant issue in domestic politics. . . . The issue no longer commanded the conscience of the nation." He attributed this to the readiness to accept token victories as evidence of genuine progress. "In fairness," he added, "it must be said that this Administration has outstripped all previous ones in the breadth of its civil-rights activities. Yet the movement, instead of breaking out into the open plains of progress, remains constricted and confined. A sweeping revolutionary force is pressed into a narrow tunnel."

Nor did there seem much they could do about it. In January 1963, when the attempt to amend Senate Rule 22 —the rule which facilitated filibusters—failed, as it had many times before, the civil rights leaders, after trying unsuccessfully to enlist Vice-President Johnson's aid, sat down to discuss strategy in Joseph Rauh's office. Someone suggested that they put out a statement condemning the President. Roy Wilkins replied that he had recently spoken to a Negro group in North Carolina. "I attacked John Kennedy for ten minutes," he said, "and everyone sat on their hands. Then I said a few favorable words about the things he had done, and they clapped and clapped."

1. NEW DIRECTIONS IN LEGISLATION

However, the President, recognizing the discontent and perceiving a need for new action if he were to preserve his control, had decided to seek legislation himself. On February 28, 1963, he sent a message to Congress setting forth in moving detail the national shame of inequality not only in voting and education but in employment and public accommodations. Racial discrimination, he said, hampered our economic growth and our world leadership; it increased the costs of public welfare, crime, delinquency and disorder; it marred the atmosphere of a united and classless society. "Above all, it is wrong." But, after this eloquent start, the actual legislative recommendations disappointed the civil rights leaders—piecemeal improvements in existing voting legislation, technical assistance to school districts voluntarily seeking to desegregate, an extension of the life of the Civil Rights Commission.

The Commission itself, though warmly praised in the President's message, shared this disappointment. It felt that the time was approaching to attack the broad problem of which the housing order had been a symbol: that is, the extent to which federal programs and activities themselves supported the structure of segregation. In August 1961 Roy Wilkins, as chairman of the Leadership Conference on Civil Rights, had given Kennedy a memorandum pointing out that federal grants to the eleven southern states amounted in 1960 to over a billion dollars and constituted from 10 to 22 per cent of all funds expended by state and local government in these states; yet, so long as there was no means of assuring the non-discriminatory use of these grants, federal money became a fund for the preservation of segregation. Now the Commission noted that in 1962 Mississippi had received over $650 million from the national government in a variety of forms—grants, federal programs, defense and construction contracts, civil and military payrolls, social security payments, veterans' benefits. Its members were particularly indignant over a $2 million grant by the Federal Aviation Agency to build a jet airport at Jackson, Mississippi, complete with segregated restaurants and restrooms.

At the same time the Commission was in a wrangle with the Department of Justice on the question whether it should be permitted to hold hearings in Mississippi. The Commission felt that drawing national attention to terror might to some degree deter it. But the Department feared that the hearings would stir local trouble and prejudice its own complicated litigations, especially those arising from the Oxford affair. Accordingly the Attorney General on three occasions asked the Commission to delay its Mississippi hearings. Though in March the President said in a press conference he thought that the Commission should "go ahead and hold . . . any hearing that they feel advances their cause or meets their responsibility," the Attorney General still sought postponement until it would be clear that the hearings would not coincide with a possible jury trial of the criminal contempt charges against Governor Barnett.

But the Commission's statutory existence was running out, and by March it seemed too late to prepare for hearings. When the Commissioners met in Indianapolis at the end of the month, they were in a state of considerable irritation. "A great many very bad things were happening in Mississippi," one of its members, Dean Erwin Griswold of the Harvard Law School, told an interviewer, "and the government was not doing anything appreciable about it. People were being shot at, the home of one of our state advisory committee members was bombed, another member had been jailed, and so on." The members therefore took the unusual step of preparing an interim report. It began by describing the defiance of the Constitution in Mississippi:

> Citizens of the United States have been shot, set upon by vicious dogs, beaten, and otherwise terrorized because they sought to vote. Since October, students have been fired upon, ministers have been assaulted . . . children, at the brink of starvation, have been deprived of assistance by the callous and discriminatory acts of Mississippi officials administering Federal funds.

Given this situation, the Commission (including its southern members) concluded unanimously that "only further steps by the Federal Government can arrest the subversion of the Constitution in Mississippi." In particular, it proposed that the President strengthen the administration's efforts to provide federal protection for the citizens in the exercise of their constitutional rights; that he "consider seriously" the desirability of legislation to "assure that Federal funds contributed by citizens of all States not be made available to any State which continues to refuse to abide by the Constitution," and further that he "explore" his legal authority as chief executive "to withhold Federal funds from the State of Mississippi until the State of Mississippi demonstrates its compliance with the Constitution."

In a few days, Dr. Hannah, as chairman of the Commission, and Berl Bernhard, as director, presented the document to the President. Kennedy asked whether the report was unanimous and whether the Commission was adamant about putting it out. Assured on both points, he said he thought the part about cutting off funds was "subject to misunderstanding. I am not sure it is constructive. . . . I know some of the agencies have been dragging [their feet]. I am doing everything I can to see that they get in line. Your Commission doesn't understand I can't do it

alone. The Commission report would be better directed at
the Congress. That is where the trouble is—appropriations,
etc. As the report reads now, you make it appear that I
have the power to do all these things, and I don't. Such
power might be dangerous. Even if it existed, it would not
be understood." Bernhard said that he gathered the President would prefer that the Commission not publish the
report. "That is correct," Kennedy said. "It will make a lot
of people mad up there and may make my own efforts more
difficult." After some going over of the statistics, he finally
said, "I still don't like it. If the Commissioners have made
up their mind, I presume they will issue the report anyway. I think they are off track on this one, but I wouldn't
try to suppress it. That would be wrong—couldn't do it
anyway. It is independent, has a right to be heard, but I
do wish you could get them to reconsider."

2. FEDERALISM AND FREEDOM

The report of the Civil Rights Commission called attention
to one tragic gap in the administration design: the difficulty
of protecting individuals in the South in the assertion of
their federal rights. For most of the time since Reconstruction this had hardly been a problem; the rights had
not been fully defined by the courts, and in any case the
southern Negro had not protested their denial. Neither
condition prevailed now. Recent events had proved several
things: the readiness of the courts to define the rights, the
unalterable purpose of the Negro to claim them, the brutality with which some southern whites were determined
to withhold them, and, most troubling of all, the evident
intention of local police authority, especially in Alabama
and Mississippi, to support those who would frustrate the
law against those who would fulfill it.

The last phenomenon confronted the Department of Justice with intricate problems of the relationship between national and local jurisdictions under the federal system.
Robert Kennedy could send federal marshals to protect the
freedom riders in Alabama in the spring of 1961 because
the Interstate Commerce Act gave the national government
clear responsibility to safeguard interstate travel. He could
send federal marshals and the Army itself to Mississippi
in the autumn of 1962 because state officials were defying
federal court orders. But what could the Department do
when defiance of the national government was less flagrant
or the breakdown of local law enforcement less manifest?
What could it do in particular with what Burke Marshall
called the "double standard in the daily administration of

law," so deeply imbedded in southern folkways, so routine and so automatic, so pervasively affecting not only the citizens involved but the very concept of government held by the law enforcement officials? How could it prevent what Marshall called "official wholesale local interference with the exercise of federal constitutional rights?" [1]

Shortly after Kennedy came into office, for example, a Negro Air Force captain in a southern city visited the house of a white major with whom he had served; the police, on the complaint of a neighbor, arrested them both for disturbing the peace. In Clinton, Louisiana, twelve Negroes who sent a wholly respectful letter to the mayor asking for the establishment of a biracial committee on community relations were arrested on the charge of intimidating public officials. In addition to cases of this sort there was the normal incidence of police brutality, falling more heavily on Negroes than on any other group in American society. When cases went to trial, it was always before white judges and all-white juries. Often Negroes could not obtain adequate counsel. Often bail was excessive. Yet the double standard, while in many cases "clearly beyond the very large limits of permissibility set by federal constitutional standards," was presently, Marshall said, "almost outside the reach of federal action" except when individuals themselves fought state criminal convictions up to the Supreme Court.

Though William Howard Taft's coarse formula about "the regulation by Southern States of their domestic affairs" was extinct, the Department of Justice felt a responsibility to preserve an appropriate balance between national and state powers in the federal system. This feeling inclined it to question proposals that the national government be given authority to enjoin interference with constitutional protests against racial injustice. The feeling also, in the eyes of some critics, discouraged the Department from using to the hilt laws already on the books (though in the case of sections 332–334 of Title 10, United States Code, conferring on the President power in effect to invade a state whose constituted authorities failed to protect legal rights, the Department considered this a remedy for a major breakdown of civil order, like Birmingham, and not for a sporadic pattern of local police harassment). As for prosecutions of police abuses, the Department feared that, every time a southern grand jury refused to return an indictment requested by a federal attorney, it only invited further police

[1] See Marshall's illuminating Speranza lectures of 1964, *Federalism and Civil Rights* (New York, 1964).

brutality. The Department considered itself, in addition, as Deputy Attorney General Katzenbach put it, "ill-equipped to assume responsibility for the performance of ordinary police functions." Attorneys from Justice recalled that, when the federal marshals went to Montgomery in 1961 to rescue the freedom riders, the chief of police asked sarcastically whether they intended to take over for the traffic cops and the fire department too.

Yet the bitter problem remained. In too many civil rights cases the police themselves were perpetrators of crimes or protectors of criminals. Even when local authorities in the South met their minimum responsibilities for public order, they sometimes refused to give effect to the federal rights at issue, assuming that litigation would be so complex, burdensome and protracted that in the meantime, as Marshall put it, "the federal rights would atrophy." Marshall did not think that the federal system interposed insuperable obstacles to the right to vote; this could be secured "with enough money, enough energy, enough lawyers, and enough months or years." But the abuse of local police power and criminal processes for the purpose of frustrating federal court orders or the purpose of punishing those who agitated against the segregation system (and even those who, without agitation, quietly declined to abide by it) provided, he concluded, "a new test of the ability of the federal system" to meet its responsibilities. "Manipulation of state law for either purpose," he said, "involves dangerous corruption of legal institutions. . . . How long will the inescapable dilemmas of the federal system continue to permit resistance to demands for direct federal controls over local police action?"

Nothing gave Robert Kennedy and Marshall greater distress than their sense of the constitutional impotence of the national government in face of what the Attorney General called "the heartless, organized mistreatment of our fellow Americans who are Negroes." They well understood the fury of Negroes and civil rights workers who, after watching local authorities humiliate, beat and even murder their comrades, unavailingly demanded instant and massive retaliation by Washington. "While federal authority appears powerless to take effective steps," as Marshall put it, "the gulf between Negroes and whites everywhere is widened, and the chances of racial conflict increased. At the least the generation of students which sees this happen are to some extent losing faith in their government, with consequences for the future that cannot be foreseen."

And not just students, though this was important: loss of

faith in government by the Negroes themselves was the overhanging threat. Whites who looked only at the things in American life which had changed in a generation drew one conclusion; Negroes who looked only at the things which were the same drew another. However impressive—however truly unprecedented the achievements of the Kennedy administration between 1961 and 1963, terrible facts remained. Seven and a half years after the school desegregation decision, fewer than 13,000 Negro children in the South were attending school with white children, and more than 2000 southern school districts were still wholly segregated, while the spread of *de facto* segregation (defined by James Baldwin as meaning "that Negroes are segregated but nobody did it") was actually reducing integration in northern schools. The right to vote?—still smothered in litigation and constitutional hair-splitting. Employment? —Negroes, still the last to be hired and the first to be fired, had an unemployment rate two and a half times that of whites. Housing?—still hopeless. The federal government? —still subsidizing discrimination through a wide range of federal programs, and still incapable, short of major outrages like Meredith at Oxford, of protecting Negroes in the exercise of their constitutional rights in the South. The Emancipation Proclamation?—a hundred years gone, and the Negro still in bondage.

3. THE RAGE WITHIN

And more and more Negroes perceived these facts at a time when the sit-in demonstrators and the freedom riders and James Meredith, Roy Wilkins and A. Philip Randolph and Martin Luther King, Jr., had given them a new pride in themselves and a new sense of the power of direct action. The southern penchant for mass jailing had been particularly helpful. "Words cannot express," King wrote, "the exultation felt by the individual as he finds himself, with hundreds of his fellows, behind prison bars for a cause he knows is just." The hoarded anger of generations, so long starved by despair, was now fed by hope.

The whites wondered why, when the Negroes had come so far, they pushed so hard. "For years now I have heard the word 'Wait!'," replied King. "It rings in the ear of every Negro with piercing familiarity. This 'Wait' has always meant 'Never.'" They could wait no longer: each year rotted away more of the Negro future. Boys and girls whose lives had been crippled by ten could not be easily redeemed at twenty. As John Howard Griffin, the white man who had disguised himself as a Negro and rendered an appalled report to his fellow white men in the book *Black Like Me*, asked, why should the Negro "allow his children to go on being dwarfed and deprived . . . so that the whites can indulge themselves in their prejudices for a little longer?"

Martin Luther King, Jr., had called 1961 "a year of the victory of the non-violent method: though blood flowed, not one drop was drawn by a Negro from his adversary." How long could this last? Negro militants were impatient not only of Kennedy and his strategy of executive action but of Roy Wilkins and his strategy of law, soon perhaps of King himself and his strategy of non-violence. Professor Kenneth Clark, a Negro psychologist at the City College of New York, told an interviewer in April 1963 that in 1961 he had been sure the American race problem would be resolved by the Negro's confidence that he was simply seeking his rights as an American citizen; now he anticipated a "total rejection of the American pattern as being incorrigibly hypocritical and corrupt and therefore unworkable in terms of a meaningful change in the status of the Negro." The rise in these years of the Muslims in the steaming black ghettos of the North, where Elijah Muhammad and Malcolm X preached the ineradicable evil of the white man, contained chilling portents for the future. Early in 1963 a book by Robert F. Williams called *Negroes with Guns* argued that armed force in self-defense was the only way to combat the double standard of southern law enforcement. Williams, who fled the United States for Cuba, engaged in anti-American diatribes over the Havana radio. A new generation of extremists, leapfrogging over the sedate Moscow faith of the American Communist party, were approaching a quasi-Maoist belief in the virtues of violence.

And now in April 1963 in Birmingham, Alabama, a new crisis was developing. Under the leadership of Martin Luther King, Jr., the Negroes of Birmingham were launching a great campaign to end discrimination in shops, restaurants and employment. But sit-ins and marches were producing sharp retaliation. When King called for a protest march on Good Friday, April 12, Police Commissioner Eugene Connor obtained an injunction, harassed the marchers with police dogs and arrested King and other leaders. A new and more moderate city administration was about to take office, and the Attorney General three times counseled the Birmingham leaders not to force issues while Bull Connor was still in charge. But the movement by now had a momentum of its own. King told Robert Kennedy that the

Negroes had waited one hundred years and could wait no longer. The demonstrations increased. So did the arrests. On May 2 about 500 Negroes, many of them high school students and younger, were hauled off to jail, some in school buses. The next day more students paraded. This time white bystanders threw bricks and bottles. The police turned fire hoses on the marchers, and Bull Connor released his growling police dogs. On Saturday, May 4, newspapers across the United States and around the world ran a shocking photograph of a police dog lunging at a Negro woman.

That morning the President received an Americans for Democratic Action group. They pressed him hard on civil rights. He said that the picture had made him "sick," but that at this point there was nothing he could constitutionally do. He regretted the fact that the Birmingham demonstrators had not waited for the new city administration to take over. Then he added, "I am not asking for patience. I can well understand why the Negroes of Birmingham are tired of being asked to be patient."

Burke Marshall flew to Birmingham the same day in an effort to compose the situation. Finding total separation between the white and Negro communities, he worked in quiet talks to open up channels of communication. Meanwhile, the President, McNamara and Dillon tried to persuade business leaders with branches in Birmingham to use their influence toward mediation. Washington meanwhile refrained from public comment lest it undercut Marshall's effort. On May 10 an agreement was reached. But Governor George C. Wallace quickly announced that he would not be a party to any "compromise on the issues of segregation." The next night white patriots bombed houses and hotels in the Negro district. Rioting continued until dawn.

Martin Luther King's younger brother, whose house had been bombed, said, "We're not mad at anyone. We're saying, 'Father, forgive them for they know not what they do.'" The mayor of Birmingham, about to retire from office, observed of the Attorney General, "I hope that every drop of blood that's spilled he tastes in his throat, and I hope he chokes on it." As for King, "This nigger has got the blessing of the Attorney General and the White House." In Washington President Kennedy sent federal troops into Alabama and prepared to federalize the state's National Guard.

The events in Birmingham abruptly transformed the mood of the nation. Churchmen, whose piety had studiously overlooked what John Quincy Adams had called the foul stain on the American conscience, idealistic students, recently preoccupied with disarming the United States and leaving the Soviet Union the great nuclear power in the world, ordinary citizens, complacent in their assumptions of virtue, were for a season jerked into guilt and responsibility. Bull Connor's police dogs accused the conscience of white America in terms which could not longer be ignored. But the awakening was so belated that it could hardly claim moral credit. Adam Clayton Powell, the urbane and cynical Negro Congressman from Harlem, stated it with precision from Paris in May: all of a sudden in Birmingham the white man had come face to face with the fact that his numerical superiority and naked power could no longer contain the black mass. "He has seen little children stand up against dogs, pistol-packing policemen and pressure hose, and they kept on coming, wave after wave. So the white man is afraid. He is afraid of his own conscience. . . . Now is the time to keep him on the run."

No one assailed the moral confusion and shame of white America more effectively than the Negro writer James Baldwin. In a long piece for the *New Yorker* in November 1962 called "Letter from a Region of My Mind," later published in the book *The Fire Next Time,* Baldwin evoked with penetrating power the fate of the Negro in white society—the past

> of rope, fire, torture, castration, infanticide, rape; death and humiliation; fear by day and night, fear as deep as the marrow of the bone; doubt that he was worthy of life, since everyone around him denied it; sorrow for his women, for his kinfolk, for his children, who needed his protection, and whom he could not protect; rage, hatred and murder, hatred for white men so deep that it often turned against him and his own, and made all love, all trust, all joy impossible;

and the present of wine-stained and urine-splashed hallways, knife and pistol fights, clanging ambulance bells, helplessness and terror. "For the horrors of the American Negro's life," Baldwin said, "there has been almost no language." Neither civilized reason nor Christian love had persuaded the whites to treat Negroes with decency. The power of the white world was a criminal power; "the Negro's experience of the white world cannot possibly create in him any respect for the standards by which the white world claims to live." Only the fear of retaliation could deter the white man, protect the Negro's dignity and assert his individuality: as Ellison's hero had said, you strike out with your fists, you curse, and you swear to make them recognize you.

Baldwin described meetings with Elijah Muhammad and

Malcolm X; while rejecting their racism, he unwillingly acknowledged their appeal. "Things are as bad as the Muslims say they are—in fact, they are worse, and the Muslims do not help matters—but there is *no* reason that black men should be expected to be more patient, more forbearing, more farseeing than whites; indeed, quite the contrary." The real reason that non-violence was considered a virtue in Negroes was that white men did not want their lives, their self-image or their property threatened. And in the end, Baldwin argued, the white man could save himself, end the joylessness and self-mistrust of his existence, recover the capacity to renew himself at the fountain of his own life, only if he accepted the unconditional freedom of the Negro: "The price of the liberation of the white people is the liberation of the blacks—the total liberation, in the cities, in the towns, before the law, and in the mind." He concluded in the words of an old spiritual: *God gave Noah the rainbow sign. No more water, the fire next time!*

Baldwin was a small, darting man of brilliant articulateness as well as, when he wished, of great charm. His own life had not perhaps been so entirely desperate, externally at least, as his writings sometimes suggested. White society had discerned his gifts early enough to make him in his teens editor of the literary magazine at a high school for bright children in New York City (a predecessor was Paddy Chayefsky, an associate, Richard Avedon) and to turn him into a best-selling author while not very much older. But this was all irrelevant; indeed, Baldwin's own opportunities made him the more sensitive to the fate of his brothers who had never had a chance. He drew into himself the agony he saw around him and charged it with the force of an electric and passionate personality. He had come to the White House for the dinner for the Nobel Prize winners in the spring of 1962. Afterward, when he and others came back to my house, Baldwin suddenly turned on Joseph Rauh, presumably because Rauh was a white leader in the civil rights fight. It was evident that Baldwin could not abide white liberals. In the *New Yorker* piece he referred to their "incredible, abysmal and really cowardly obtuseness," and he seemed to regard them as worse than southern bigots, who at least were honest enough to admit that they, like all white men (by definition), hated the Negro. Now he baited Rauh as if to goad him by sarcasm and insult into confessing that his concern for civil rights was a cover for prejudice. Rauh equably fielded Baldwin's taunts and kept asking him what he would have the government do. Baldwin, who showed little interest in public policy, finally muttered something about bringing Negroes into the FBI.

Then in May 1963 the Attorney General, whose concern for civil rights had steadily deepened as his duties had confronted him with the horror of Negro inequality, sought to extend his contacts with Negro intellectuals. Accordingly he invited Baldwin to breakfast with him in Washington. Baldwin's plane was late; Robert Kennedy had an early engagement; and their talk was cut short. But the meeting was cordial. The Attorney General had asked Baldwin what specific steps the government could take and proposed that they resume the conversation the next day in New York where Baldwin might bring along knowledgeable people with concrete suggestions. The next day Baldwin and a number of Negro writers and show people—Professor Kenneth Clark, Lorraine Hansberry, Lena Horne, Harry Belafonte and others—met Robert Kennedy in his New York apartment.

In the Negro group was also Jerome Smith, a young freedom rider who had recently been savagely beaten in the South. Smith opened the meeting by saying, as the Attorney General understood it, that being in the same room with Robert Kennedy made him feel like vomiting. What Smith was apparently trying to say was that he felt like vomiting to have to plead before the Attorney General for the rights to which he was entitled as an American, but it came through to Kennedy, who had been fighting hard himself for these rights, as a gratuitous expression of personal contempt. The Attorney General showed his resentment; the group rallied around the freedom rider; and from this already low point the conversation went rapidly down hill.

Jerome Smith added that, so long as Negroes were treated this way, he felt no moral obligation to fight for the United States in war. The group applauded this sentiment. Some spoke of sending arms into the South. Baldwin said that the only reason the government had put federal troops in Alabama was because a white man had been stabbed. Burke Marshall, who was present, said that he had consulted with Dr. King about the use of federal troops; the group laughed at him. When Robert Kennedy, recalling his talk with Baldwin the day before, tried to seek their ideas about civil rights policy, they showed no interest. Baldwin was evidently not even aware that the President had given a civil rights message in February. "They didn't know anything," Bobby said to me later. "They don't know what the laws are—they don't know what the facts are—they don't know what we've been doing or what we're trying to do. You couldn't talk to them as you can to Roy Wilkins or Martin Luther King. They didn't want to talk that way. It was all emotion, hysteria. They stood up and orated. They cursed. Some of them wept and walked out of the room." What shocked him most was that, when the meeting broke up after three hours of non-communication, a representative of King's who was present drew the Attorney General aside and said, "I just want to say that Dr. King deeply appreciates the way you handled the Birmingham affair." Kennedy said, "You watched these people attack me over Birmingham for forty minutes, and you didn't say a word. There's no point in your saying this to me now." A Negro singer who had often come for dinner at Hickory Hill similarly approached Kennedy and said, "Of course you have done more for civil rights than any other Attorney General." Kennedy said, "Why do you say this to me? Why didn't you say this to the others?" "I couldn't say this to the others," came the reply. "It would affect my relationship with them. If I were to defend you, they would conclude I had gone over to the other side."

As for Baldwin, he felt that Kennedy was just unable to understand the sense of urgency of the Negro people—and this once again confirmed his thesis about the white man. Kenneth Clark, more thoughtfully, said later, "The fact that Bobby Kennedy sat through such an ordeal for three hours proves he is among the best the white power structure has to offer. There were no villains in that room—only the past of our society."

4. THE PRESIDENT IN COMMAND

On May 18, speaking at Vanderbilt University in Tennessee, the President glanced at the recent events in Birmingham. "No one can deny the complexity of the problems involved in assuring to all of our citizens their full rights as Americans," he said. "But no one can gainsay the fact that the determination to secure these rights is in the highest traditions of American freedom." His remark appeared to acknowledge that the revolution was overflowing its banks and to give non-violent resistance presidential sanction. In any case, the momentum after Birmingham now seemed irresistible. In Nashville, Tennessee, in Raleigh and Greensboro, North Carolina, in Cambridge, Maryland, Albany, Georgia, Selma, Alabama, Negroes marched, prayed, sat in for their rights. During the summer 14,000 demonstrators were arrested in the states of the old Confederacy.

Then on May 21 a federal district judge ruled that the University of Alabama must admit two Negroes to its summer session in June. "I am the embodiment of the sovereignty of this state," Governor George Wallace replied, "and I will be present to bar the entrance of any Negro who attempts to enroll." It looked as if Alabama were going to follow Mississippi down the road of nullification. On June 12 the President instructed Governor Wallace not to try to stop the integration of the university at Tuscaloosa. But on the next morning Wallace personally blocked the entry of the Negro students and federal marshals into the administration building. The President promptly federalized part of the Alabama National Guard. Then when Guardsmen arrived on the campus, Wallace judiciously retreated. That afternoon the students were registered. In the evening—it was the day after the American University speech—Kennedy went on television to discuss civil rights.

After describing the events of the day at Tuscaloosa, the President expressed the hope that every American would examine his conscience. The nation, he said, was founded "on the principle that all men are created equal, and that the rights of every man are diminished when the rights of one man are threatened." It ought to be possible, he said.

> for American students of any color to attend any public institution without having to be backed up by troops. It ought to be possible for American consumers of any color to receive equal service in places of public accommodation, such as hotels and restaurants and theaters and retail stores, without being forced to resort to demonstrations in the street, and it ought to be possible for American citizens of any color to register and to vote in a free election without interference or fear of reprisal. . . . In short, every American ought to have the right to be treated as he would wish to be treated, as one would wish his children to be treated.
>
> But this is not the case.

In burning language he set forth the plight of the American Negro. If the Negro could not enjoy the full and free life which all of us want, "then who among us would be content to have the color of his skin changed and stand in his place? Who among us would then be content with the counsels of patience and delay?" We said to the world and to each other that we were the land of the free; did all we mean was that it was a land of the free except for the Negroes? "that we have no second-class citizens except Negroes; that we have no class or caste system, no ghettos, no master race except with respect to Negroes?"

This was, he said, "a moral issue"—"as old as the scriptures and . . . as clear as the American Constitution."

The time had come for the nation to fulfill its promise. The fires of frustration and discord were burning in every city where legal remedies were not at hand. The moral crisis could not be quieted by token talk or moves; it could not be left to demonstrations in the streets. "A great change is at hand, and our task, our obligation, is to make that revolution, that change, peaceful and constructive for all." Next week, he said, he would ask Congress to make the commitment it has not yet fully made in this century—the commitment to the proposition "that race has no place in American life or law."

It was a magnificent speech in a week of magnificent speeches. Some criticized Kennedy for not having given it earlier. But the timing was a vindication of his approach to mass education. He had prepared the ground for that speech ever since he became President. His actions, his remarks, the concern for Negro rights and scorn for racism implicit in his personality and bearing—all had subtly entered and transformed national expectations and attitudes. He had quietly created an atmosphere where change, when it came, would seem no longer an upheaval but the inexorable unfolding of the promise of American life. Yet he did not call for change in advance of the moment. If he had made his June speech in February, it would have attracted as little attention as his civil rights message that month. But Birmingham and the Negroes themselves had given him the nation's ear.

May and June 1963 were exciting months for an historian. One had seen no such surge of spontaneous mass democracy in the United States since the organization of labor in the heavy industries in the spring and summer of 1937. Characteristically each revolution began with direct local action—one with sit-downs, the others with sit-ins. In each case, ordinary people took things into their own hands, generated their own leaders, asserted their own rights and outstripped not only the government but their own organizations (and, thus far, fewer people had been killed in the Negro than in the labor revolution). Franklin Roosevelt's first response to the labor revolution had been to pronounce a curse on both their houses. Kennedy now responded to the Negro revolution by seeking to assume its leadership.

The night of Kennedy's speech, Medgar Evers of Mississippi, James Meredith's friend and counselor, a brave, gentle and responsible man, was murdered by a white killer in front of his house in Jackson. A week later the President invited his wife, children and brother-in-law, Charles Evers, who was taking Medgar's place as director of the Missis-

sippi NAACP, to the White House. They were an exceptionally attractive family. When they left, I said to the
President, "What a terrible business." He said sadly, "Yes.
I don't understand the South. I'm coming to believe that
Thaddeus Stevens was right. I had always been taught to
regard him as a man of vicious bias. But, when I see this
sort of thing, I begin to wonder how else you can treat
them." Robert Kennedy attended Medgar Evers's funeral
in Arlington Cemetery and, giving Charles Evers his telephone numbers at the office and at home, said to call any
time, day or night, if Negroes were being harassed or intimidated. (Charles Evers said later, "Whenever I had the
need to call him, I've never found it too late or too
early.")

The President had already begun to mobilize leaders of
opinion in a succession of meetings, first with governors
and then with hotel, restaurant and theater owners, labor
leaders, religious leaders, educators, lawyers, women and
with the Business Council. They sat on the gilt chairs in the
East Room of the White House while the President, the
Vice-President and the Attorney General sought in their
various styles to explain the urgency of the situation and
seek their support in meeting the problem—the President
controlled and terse, the Vice-President evangelical and
often very moving, the Attorney General blunt and passionate. These meetings were highly successful, or most of
them were. The White House staff noted with a certain bitterness that the one group which did not rise when the President entered the room—of which, indeed, only two of its
members rose when asking the President questions after the
speech—consisted of the leaders of American business.

On June 19 the President sent his civil rights bill to the
Hill. In addition to his February proposals, he now called
for equal accommodations in public facilities, the grant of
authority to the Attorney General to initiate school desegregation suits, new programs to assure fair employment,
including support of a Fair Employment Practices Commission (though the FEPC as such was not in the administration bill), the establishment of a Community Relations Service, and a provision authorizing the federal government to withhold funds for programs for activities
in which discrimination occurred. These recommendations
did not produce universal satisfaction. The Vice-President
had doubts about sending up any civil rights bill at this
time, at least until the appropriations were passed. The civil
rights leaders, on the other hand, while acknowledging that
this was the most comprehensive civil rights bill ever to re-

ceive serious consideration from the Congress, wanted a more sweeping public accommodations section, immediate first-step school desegregation everywhere, federal registrars to enroll Negro voters, authorization to the Attorney General to bring suit in all situations where people were denied constitutional rights because of race or color and FEPC in the administration bill.

But even the administration bill had no assurance of an easy passage. We were first beginning to hear this summer about the phenomenon of the 'white backlash.' John Bartlow Martin, back on leave from the Dominican Republic, spent a few days in his home in a Chicago suburb. He returned to Washington depressed over the anxiety and even rancor expressed by his neighbors about the pace of integration. James Lanigan, who had been active in New York politics before going to New Delhi with Chester Bowles, brought back a similar report from New York. Politicians, especially those in touch with Polish-American and Irish-American communities, were pessimistic. They described widespread panic in traditional Democratic districts over the prospective inundation of their neighborhoods and schools by Negroes; some thought that civil rights might very well lose the election for Kennedy in 1964. The Louis Harris poll reported in the autumn that the civil rights issue had already turned some 4.5 million white voters against the administration. In the South, of course, bitterness toward the Kennedys reached new heights of virulence. Samuel Lubell, sampling a working class precinct in Birmingham which had given Kennedy a clear majority in 1960, found only one Kennedy supporter left. Others said, "He's cramming the nigger down our throats" or, "If he's re-elected it will be the end of America."

The President never had any illusions about the political advantages of equal rights. But he saw no alternative to leading the fight in order to prevent the final isolation of the Negro leadership and the embitterment of the Negro people. Every day that summer new and ominous tendencies seemed to appear in the colored masses. In a week when Negroes threw eggs at Martin Luther King, Jr., in Harlem and a Negro meeting in Chicago booed not only Mayor Richard Daley but even James Meredith, the President observed gloomily that the progress since Birmingham had been made possible by the awakening of the middle-class white conscience and the belated rallying to the civil rights cause; now the mindless radicalism of the Negro militants might well drive this new middle-class support away and postpone the hope of progress.

5. WE SHALL OVERCOME

Civil rights filled his mind, even in the summer of the test ban treaty. On June 22, the day before he left on his European trip, he invited the civil rights leaders to a meeting in the Cabinet Room to discuss the tactics of the bill now before the Congress. It was the best meeting I attended in my years in the White House.

The President began with a crisp account of the parliamentary situation. If the bill was to pass, he said, it had to reach out beyond the traditional civil rights groups. Senators in the states west of the Mississippi and east of California would tend to be for the bill but against the invocation of cloture to stop a filibuster. This, he said, was on grounds "not at all related to civil rights. They see what has happened to the small states in the House of Representatives, and they believe that unlimited speech is the only protection for small states in the Congress. They remember the use that Borah and Norris made of the filibuster. This is a weapon they are unwilling to surrender." He concluded by saying that, for reasons he well understood, Negro patience was at an end and that substantial progress had to come in 1963.

The civil rights group had been talking about a peaceful march on Washington, like the one A. Philip Randolph had proposed to Franklin Roosevelt twenty years earlier. Whitney Young of the Urban League now said that the President's comments about demonstrations in the streets were being interpreted to mean he was against the march on Washington. "We want success in Congress," Kennedy replied, "not just a big show at the Capitol. Some of these people are looking for an excuse to be against us. I don't want to give any of them a chance to say, 'Yes, I'm for the bill, but I'm damned if I will vote for it at the point of a gun.' It seemed to me a great mistake to announce a march on Washington before the bill was even in committee. The only effect is to create an atmosphere of intimidation—and this may give some members of Congress an out."

A. Philip Randolph, speaking with the quiet dignity which touched Kennedy as it had touched Roosevelt before him, discussed the attempt to shift the civil rights drive from the streets to the courts. "The Negroes are already in the streets," Randolph said. "It is very likely impossible to get them off. If they are bound to be in the streets in any case, is it not better that they be led by organizations dedicated to civil rights and disciplined by struggle rather than to leave them to other leaders who care neither about civil rights nor about non-violence? If the civil rights leadership were to call the Negroes off the streets, it is problematic whether they would come."

The President agreed that the demonstrations in the streets had brought results; they had made the executive branch act faster and were now forcing Congress to entertain legislation which a few weeks before would have had no chance. "This is true. But now we are in a new phase, the legislative phase, and results are essential. The wrong kind of demonstration at the wrong time will give those fellows a chance to say that they have to prove their courage by voting against us. To get the votes we need we have, first, to oppose demonstrations which will lead to violence, and, second, give Congress a fair chance to work its will."

The Vice-President then remarked that many people had wrong ideas about the way Congress made up its mind. "Not many votes are converted in the corridors. Most fellows vote for what they think is right and for what they think their states want. We have about 50 votes for us in the Senate and about 22 against us. What counts is the 26 or so votes which remain. To get those votes we have to be careful not to do anything which would give those who are privately opposed a public excuse to appear as martyrs. We have to sell the program in twelve crucial states—and we have less than twelve weeks."

James Farmer of CORE said, "We understand your political problem in getting the legislation through, and we want to help in that as best we can. But the civil rights forces have their problems too. We would be in a difficult if not untenable position if we called the street demonstrations off and then were defeated in the legislative battle. The result would be that frustration would grow into violence and would demand new leadership."

"It is not a matter of either/or," Martin Luther King, Jr., now said, "but of both/and. Take the question of the march on Washington. This could serve as a means through which people with legitimate discontents could channel their grievances under disciplined, non-violent leadership. It could also serve as a means of dramatizing the issue and mobilizing support in parts of the country which don't know the problems at first hand. I think it will serve a purpose. It may seem ill-timed. Frankly, I have never engaged in any direct action movement which did not seem ill-timed. Some people thought Birmingham ill-timed." The President interjected wryly, "Including the Attorney General."

Someone brought up the question of police brutality. The President said sardonically, "I don't think you should all be totally harsh on Bull Connor." For a moment, there was an audible intake of breath around the cabinet table. "After all," Kennedy went on, "he has done more for civil rights than almost anybody else." He continued: "This is a very serious fight. The Vice-President and I know what it will mean if we fail. I have just seen a new poll—national approval of the administration has fallen from 60 to 47 per cent. We're in this up to the neck. The worst trouble of all would be to lose the fight in the Congress. We'll have enough troubles if we win; but, if we win, we can deal with those. A good many programs I care about may go down the drain as a result of this—we may all go down the drain as a result of this—so we are putting a lot on the line. What is important is that we preserve confidence in the good faith of each other. I have my problems with the Congress; you have yours with your own groups. We will undoubtedly disagree from time to time on tactics. But the important thing is to keep in touch."

In a few moments he excused himself to go to a meeting on his European trip. "What seems terribly important," he said as he left, "is to get, and keep, as many Negro children as possible in schools this fall. It is too late to get equality for their parents, but we can still get it for the children—*if* they go to school, and take advantage of what educational opportunity is open to them. I urge you to get every Negro family to do this at whatever sacrifice."

As the meeting broke up, Roy Wilkins, who, I believe, was the Negro leader whose intelligence and integrity the President particularly respected, whispered to me his sympathy for the President in view of the pressures playing on him, the choices he had to make, the demands on his time and energy. One was impressed by Wilkins's understanding as against the usual view held by petitioners, whether civil rights leaders, businessmen, liberals or foreign statesmen, who generally felt that the President should subordinate everything else to their own preoccupations. Martin Luther King, Jr., on the other hand, gave newspapermen after the meeting the impression that the President had asked the group to call off demonstrations and that he had boldly refused—a posture calculated to improve his standing among Negroes but only tenuously related to what had happened.

The conference with the President did persuade the civil rights leaders that they should not lay siege to Capitol Hill.

Instead, Bayard Rustin, the organizer of the March, made plans for a mass demonstration in front of the Lincoln Memorial. When asked about the march at a press conference in mid-July, Kennedy, noting that the participants intended "a peaceful assembly calling for a redress of grievances" and that it was "not a march on the Capitol," said, "I think that's in the great tradition." A. Philip Randolph outlined the tradition in a moving speech in Washington two days before the March. The event was "an outcry for justice, for freedom." It would serve "as a witness of commitment on the part of Negroes all over America, as well as our white brothers and sisters, in a great moral protest against racial bias." There was no way, he concluded, to stem such demonstrations until Negroes had acquired "the same things that white citizens possess—all their rights. They want no reservations."

A few days before the March the President expressed some concern that it might not be large enough. The leaders had committed themselves to producing 100,000 people. If it fell materially short of this, Kennedy remarked, it might persuade some members of Congress that the demand for action on civil rights was greatly exaggerated. He need not have worried. On August 28, nearly a quarter of a million people, black and white, came to Washington. They arrived by plane and bus and automobile and foot from almost every state in the union. The concern and mutual consideration of the marchers invested everything they did with an immense and lovely dignity. Nothing marred the beauty of the day.

In the afternoon they gathered in front of the Lincoln Memorial. "Even though we still face the difficulties of today and tomorrow," said Martin Luther King, Jr., the last of the speakers, "I still have a dream. . . . I have a dream that on the red hills of Georgia the sons of former slaves and the sons of former slave-owners will be able to sit together at the table of brotherhood. . . . I have a dream that even the state of Mississippi, a state sweltering with the heat of injustice, will be transformed into an oasis of freedom. . . . I have a dream that one day every valley shall be exalted, every hill and mountain shall be made low, the rough places will be made plain, and the crooked places will be made straight, and the glory of the Lord shall be revealed and all flesh shall see it together." The crowd, joining hands, rocking back and forth, cried, almost ecstatically, "Dream some more." Then in the dusk the vast assemblage quietly dispersed. Snatches of the poignant old Baptist hymn the movement had made its own hung in the air.

We shall overcome, we shall overcome,
We shall overcome, some day.
Oh deep in my heart I do believe,
We shall overcome some day.

6. THE REVOLUTION

The President congratulated the leaders at the White House in the evening. Publicly he said, "This nation can properly be proud." But the March, though so splendid an affirmation, worked no miracles on the Hill.

Liberal Democrats in the House, backed by the civil rights leadership, continued to think the administration bill inadequate; for its part, the administration feared a stronger bill would face trouble in the House Rules Committee and later in the Senate. Then the civil rights forces, arguing that the House had to send the Senate the strongest possible bill to give the Senate leaders room for maneuver in face of a filibuster, attracted the support of southerners, who felt that, the stronger the bill was, the less the chance of passage. After long weeks of discussion and infighting, the President called in the House leaders in late October and, with the help of Charles Halleck, the Republican leader, personally worked out a compromise—FEPC was retained with enforcement in the courts; the Attorney General while not given all the authority the civil rights people had proposed, received power to enter any civil rights case in federal courts and to initiate suits to desegregate public facilities; and the bill was strengthened in other ways. Robert Kennedy called the result a "better bill than the administration's." The Judiciary Committee approved it on October 29 and reported it to the House on November 20. The best civil rights bill in American history thus passed the first obstacles on its road to enactment. The House vote in January 1964 was the fulfillment of the agreement the Democratic and Republican leaders had made with Kennedy in the October White House meetings.

Yet, even when enacted, the new program would meet only part of the causes of the growing unrest. Its provisions were designed for the Negroes of the South. To the Negroes of the North the rights it offered were those they nominally possessed already. And to the heart of the now boiling northern unrest—to the frustrations in the black ghettos of the cities—it offered nothing.

Negroes had been moving north in increasing numbers since the First World War. By 1963 probably more than half lived outside the old Confederacy. They had drifted mostly into the great northern cities in search of jobs, hopes, excitement, oblivion. The 1960 census showed Washington more than half Negro, Baltimore and St. Louis a third, Philadelphia and Chicago a quarter, with the proportion steadily growing as the last wave of white immigrants, moving out to the suburbs, left the newcomers the decaying tenements, the filth and rats of the central city.

For the Negro the North was different from the South —more freedom but less purpose. The northern ghettos lacked the institutions which had to some degree stabilized life in the South. Ironically the very rigidity of the Jim Crow system had given a certain awful definition to the life of the southern Negro. "The northern Negro," James Baldwin wrote, "is much more demoralized than the southern Negro is, because, there being no signs ["white" and "colored",] you have to play it by ear entirely. . . . Negroes do, in the north, go mad for just that reason." Moreover, there was still, Baldwin continued, "the Negro family in the south, and there is no Negro family, effectively speaking, in the north." All this was relative; the southern whites in slavery days had done their best to destroy the Negro family, and it was never strong in cities anywhere; but disintegration was taking place much faster in the North. Nearly one-fourth of all Negro children born in the sixties were illegitimate; in Harlem, two-fifths.

The South, moreover, still had the Negro church with its quietist traditions and devout following; it still had preachers like Martin Luther King, Jr. But in the ghettos the old-time religion was losing its potency, at least among the young, or else becoming an instrument for racists or racketeers. And in the South the mass action of 1963—in Birmingham, Nashville, Raleigh, Greensboro, Albany—had nourished Negro self-discipline and given shape to the sense of a Negro community negotiating with a white community to secure Negro rights. But in the North the sense of a united Negro community had perished in the long distances between the Negro upper class, with its prosperous insurance men and bankers and doctors, and the apathetic, despairing mass. The well-to-do Negro could now take advantage of the guilt of white society and enter universities and professions, hotels and golf courses; he could begin to identify himself with prevailing values. But the poor Negro, hedged in by *de facto* segregation in the schools, watching the gap between his own and the white worker's income and employment steadily widen, felt he was falling further and further behind and was losing his remnants of loyalty to the existing order. The angry Negro intellectuals could not hold the northern ghettos together; and the civil rights leaders had few ties to the rootless Negro urban proletariat.

The ghettos thus lacked internal structures of self-discipline and self-help; here they differed from the communities of European immigrants with their strong family ties and their networks of internal organization. They were swamps of incoherent resentment and despair, responding to prophets and demagogues, seeking identity in crime or surcease in a slug or a fix. Civil rights bills had little to say to the unemployed, undereducated, untrained Negroes wandering aimlessly down the gray streets of Harlem or Watts, to boys and girls in their teens abandoned by their fathers and adrift in a desolation of mistrust and corruption, to the hoods and junkies and winos and derelicts.

The fulfillment of the Negro revolution plainly demanded much more than the achievement of the Negroes' legal rights. In April 1963 the unemployment rate for non-whites was 12.1 per cent, for whites, 4.8 per cent. Poverty afflicted half the non-white population, less than one-fifth of the white population. Three out of five non-white families lived in deteriorating or dilapidated buildings or without plumbing. The racial and social problems were inextricably intermingled. As A. Philip Randolph told the AFL-CIO convention in November 1963, "The Negro's protest today is but the first rumbling of the 'under-class.' As the Negro has taken to the streets, so will the unemployed of all races take to the streets. . . . To discuss the civil rights revolution is therefore to write the agenda of labor's unfinished revolution." Bayard Rustin observed that the civil rights movement could not succeed "in the absence of radical programs for full employment, abolition of slums, the reconstruction of our educational system, new definitions of work and leisure." The deeper problems of inequality were "the result of the total society's failure to meet not only the Negro's needs, but human needs generally."

The President was keenly aware of the larger contexts. When civil rights leaders had reproached him in 1961 for not seeking legislation, he told them that an increased minimum wage, federal aid to education and other social and economic measures were also civil rights bills. He knew that a slow rate of economic growth made every problem of equal rights more intractable, as a faster rate would make every such problem easier of solution. In 1963 he counted on his tax cut to reduce Negro unemployment; he reviewed and enlarged his educational program—vocational education, adult basic education, manpower development, youth employment—to help equip Negroes for jobs; and his concern for the plight of the Negro strengthened his campaigns against juvenile delinquency, urban decay and poverty.

The Negro leaders had never doubted that Kennedy was on their side. But they had feared he regarded the civil rights problem as only one among many problems. By the summer of 1963 he had clearly made it the major problem next to the pursuit of peace itself. Martin Luther King, Jr., later spoke of his "ability to respond to creative pressure. . . . He frankly acknowledged that he was responding to mass demands and did so because he thought it was right to do so. This is the secret of the deep affection he evoked. He was responsive, sensitive, humble before the people, and bold on their behalf." Beside him in the affection of many Negroes stood the Attorney General. "He has done more for us personally than any other public official," said Charles Evers, the brother of Medgar Evers. "Had it not been for him, there would have been many more murders and many more beatings than we have had in Mississippi in the last four years. Mr. Kennedy did more to help us get our rights as first-class citizens than all other U. S. Attorney Generals put together."

Every great period of social change in American history has been set off by the demand of some excluded but aggressive group for larger participation in the national democracy: in the age of Jackson by the frontier farmer, the city worker, the small entrepreneur; in the progressive era by the bankrupt farmers of the middle border and the by-passed old upper classes of the cities; in the New Deal by labor in mass-production industries, the unemployed and the intellectuals. The uprising of the Negroes now contained the potentiality of ushering in a new era which would not only win Negroes their rights but renew the democratic commitment of the national community. It also contained the potentiality, if the anger of the Negroes exceeded the will of the government to redress their grievances and the capacity of their own leadership to retain their confidence, of rending and destroying the fabric of American society.

By 1963 the revolution was enlisting the idealism not only of the Negroes but of the universities and churches, of labor and the law. It was also attracting some who, as one put it, if they could not get their places around the table, threatened to knock its legs off. A generation ago Roosevelt had absorbed the energy and hope of the labor revolution into the New Deal. So in 1963 Kennedy moved to incorporate the Negro revolution into the democratic coalition and thereby help it serve the future of American freedom.

XXXVII

AUTUMN 1963

THE SUMMER OF 1963 ended in sadness. In early August Jacqueline gave birth prematurely to a five-pound boy. Young Patrick Bouvier Kennedy came into the world with respiratory troubles. After thirty-nine hours of struggle, the labor of breathing proved too much for his heart, and he died in a Boston hospital. The President's anguish for his wife and their dead son gave August a melancholy cast. Early in September he and Jacqueline quietly observed their tenth wedding anniversary in Newport.

But in public policy the Presidency of John F. Kennedy was coming into its own. He was doing at last in the summer of 1963 what he had been reluctant to do before: putting the office of the Presidency on the line at the risk of defeat. He was staking his authority and his re-election on behalf of equal rights, the test ban, planned deficits in economic policy, doing so not without political apprehension but with absolute moral and intellectual resolve. As he had anticipated, the civil rights fight in particular was biting into his popularity. In November Gallup would report that national approval of his administration was down to 59 per cent. Most of this decline was in the South; there, if the Republicans, as he came to believe they would, nominated Barry Goldwater, Kennedy expected to carry only two or three states. Moreover, this had been the hardest of his congressional sessions. At the end of July, according to the *Congressional Quarterly*, 38 per cent of the administration's proposals had not yet been acted on by either house. Civil rights and tax reduction were making very slow progress. Knives were sharpening for foreign aid. Even routine appropriation bills were held up.

Then Senate ratification of the test ban treaty in September gave his leadership a new access of strength. "There is a rhythm to personal and national and international life," he had said in the winter, "and it flows and ebbs." It had ebbed for many weeks. Now perhaps it was beginning to flow again.

1. JOURNEY TO THE WEST

On the day the Senate ratified the treaty, Kennedy left Washington for a trip to the West. It was ostensibly a non-political tour, its pretext conservation. This was a genuine, if somewhat abstract, concern, and he welcomed the chance to see the condition of the national estate at first hand. But the trip had other motives too. Of the eleven states on his itinerary, he had lost eight in 1960; with the South turning against him, he needed new sources of support. Furthermore, ten had senatorial contests in 1964, and in several the John Birch Society was active. Above all, he considered Washington overexcited in its response to public issues; impressions lasted longer "out there"; and the trip offered him a chance to reestablish contact and purpose with the people.

He conscientiously pursued the conservation theme for several speeches. Then late on the second day, at Billings, Montana, he struck, almost by accident, a new note. Mike Mansfield was present and in his third sentence Kennedy praised the Senate leader for his part in bringing about test ban ratification. To his surprise this allusion produced strong and sustained applause. Heartened, he set forth his hope of lessening the "chance of a military collision between those two great nuclear powers which together have the power to kill 300 million people in the short space of a day." The Billings response encouraged him to make the pursuit of peace increasingly the theme of his trip. In Great Falls, Montana, he discussed the illusions of isolationism. "You must wonder when it is all going to end and when we can come back home," he said. "Well, it isn't going to end. . . . We have to stay at it. We must not be fatigued." The competition with communism would dominate the rest of our lives, but we must not let it become a competition in nuclear violence. Let us, he said, show the world which society could grow faster, which could educate its children better, which could produce more cultural and intellectual stimulus, "which society, in other words, is the happier."

Then to Hanford, Washington, and on September 26 to Salt Lake City, where he defined America's role in the modern world. I had worked on this speech. The President, recalling that the Mormons had started as a persecuted minority, originally thought of it as a discourse on extremism; then, after seeing a draft, he decided that he wanted to concentrate on extremism in foreign policy—a masked comment, in effect, on Goldwater. Though he eventually cut out direct allusions to the 'total victory' thesis, the point of the speech was nonetheless unmistakable; and he delivered it in a city which, because of Ezra Taft Benson and his son as well as Mayor John Bracken Lee, Washington regarded as a stronghold of the radical right.

The President's unusual cordial reception on the streets belied this impression. Then, before an immense crowd at the Tabernacle of the Latter Day Saints, he began his speech. "We find ourselves," he said, "entangled with apparently unanswerable problems in unpronounceable places. We discover that our enemy in one decade is our ally in the next. We find ourselves committed to governments whose actions we cannot often approve, assisting societies with principles very different from our own." It was little wonder that in a time of contradiction and confusion we looked back to the old days with nostalgia. But those days were gone forever; science and technology were irreversible. Nor could we remake the new world simply by our own command. "When we cannot even bring all of our own people into full citizenship without acts of violence, we can understand how much harder it is to control events beyond our borders." Our national interest was "best served by preserving and protecting a world of diversity in which no one power or no one combination of powers can threaten the security of the United States."

The forces of diversity, he added, were "in the ascendancy today, even within the Communist empire itself. . . . The most striking thing about our world in 1963 is the extent to which the tide of history has begun to flow in the direction of freedom. To renounce the world of freedom now, to abandon those who share our commitment, and retire into lonely and not so splendid isolation, would be to give communism the one hope which, in this twilight of disappointment for them, might repair their divisions and rekindle their hope." At the end the audience stood at their seats and cheered for many minutes.

He had hit his stride, reached the deeper concerns of his audience, and the rest of the journey was a triumphal procession. He always found journeys "out there" refreshing, but this time he returned in a state of particular exhilaration. Whatever the stalemate in Congress, he knew now that he had immense resources of affection and strength in the people. He knew too that peace, economic growth and education would be powerful themes for 1964.

Before his departure, when pressed at a news conference about a Goldwater suggestion that the test ban treaty contained secret commitments, he simply denied the assertion; asked then if he cared to comment further on "this type of attack by Senator Goldwater," he said, "No, no. Not yet, not yet." Now the time had come. On his return, discussing a complaint of Eisenhower's that he was unclear where Goldwater stood on issues, Kennedy observed with evident relish that the Arizona Senator was "saying what he thinks as of the time he speaks. . . . I think he has made very clear what he is opposed to, what he is for. I have gotten the idea. I think that President Eisenhower will, as time goes on." Thereafter the inevitable Goldwater question filled each news conference with expectant delight. So, on October 31, when Kennedy was asked to comment on a Goldwater charge that the administration was falsifying the news to perpetuate itself in office, the gleam came into his eye, and he said that Goldwater had had such "a busy week selling TVA, and giving permission to or suggesting that military commanders overseas be permitted to use nuclear weapons, and attacking the President of Bolivia while he was here in the United States, and involving himself in the Greek election. So I thought it really would not be fair for me this week to reply to him." Plainly the President could not wait for 1964. "Politically the country is closely divided," he told Sidey when queried (as a matter of form) whether he planned to run for a second term, "so it will be tough. But then everything is tough."

2. THE VIETNAM QUANDARY

Nothing was tougher at the moment than the situation in South Vietnam, where the abrupt collapse of the hopes of 1962 had provided the unpleasant surprise of 1963.

Our policy in 1962 had been dominated by those who saw Vietnam as primarily a military problem and who believed that its solution required unconditional support of Diem. The reports rendered by Ambassador Frederick Nolting and General Paul Harkins to Washington conveyed the picture of a regime led by an unquestionably difficult but statesmanlike and, in any case, irreplaceable figure making steady progress in winning over the peasants, pacifying the countryside and restoring the stability of government. The local opposition, in this view, consisted of intellectuals, neutralists and agents of the Viet Cong, concerned more with their own petty grievances and ambitions than with winning the war. The only way to improve things, they believed in all sincerity, was to reassure Diem about the constancy of American support.

Through most of 1962 this policy appeared to be producing results. The Saigon government, so near collapse at the end of 1961, had recovered much of its authority. The strategic hamlet program, in the considered judgment of the Departments of State and Defense, was bringing the countryside into firm alliance with the regime. The Viet Cong were presumably making little progress. Indeed, in the spring of 1963 Alexis Johnson claimed that 30,000 casualties had been inflicted on the guerrillas in 1962—a figure twice as large as the estimated size of the Viet Cong forces at the beginning of the year. In the same month Secretary McNamara authorized the Defense Department to announce "we have turned the corner in Vietnam," and General Harkins predicted that the war would be won "within a year." The communists themselves acknowledged 1962 as "Diem's year." The American advisers and the helicopter war had increased the cost of guerrilla action, and the Viet Cong almost reached the point of giving up in the Mekong delta and withdrawing to the mountains.[1] Kennedy, beset by the missile crisis, congressional elections, Skybolt, de Gaulle, Latin America, the test ban negotiations and the civil rights fight, had little time to focus on Southeast Asia. His confidence in McNamara, so wholly justified in so many areas, led the President to go along with the optimists on Vietnam.

Not everyone shared this optimism, and dissent arose first among the American newspapermen in Vietnam.[2] The reporters were bright, inquisitive, passionate young men in their late twenties or early thirties with careers to make— Malcolm Browne of the Associated Press, Cornelius Sheehan of the United Press International, David Halberstam of the *New York Times,* Charles Mohr of *Time,* François Sully of *Newsweek.* They saw Diem not as a selfless national leader but as an oriental despot, hypnotized by his own monologues and contemptuous of democracy and the west.

[1] See the testimony of the Australian Communist writer, W. T. Burchett, in *Vietnam: Inside Story of the Guerilla War* (New York, 1965).

[2] For details, see Malcolm W. Browne, *The New Face of War* (Indianapolis, 1965), David Halberstam, *The Making of a Quagmire* (New York, 1965), John Mecklin, *Mission in Torment* (New York, 1965) and Robert Shaplen, *The Lost Revolution* (New York, 1965).

They detested the Nhus. They considered the strategic hamlet program a fake and a failure; and their visit to dismal stockades where peasants had been herded, sometimes at bayonet point, to engage in forced labor confirmed their worst misgivings. They did not believe Diem's communiqués; and, when Harkins and Nolting insisted they were true, they stopped believing Harkins and Nolting. They had too often heard American advisers in the field sing a bitter little song to the tune of "Twinkle, Twinkle, Little Star":

> We are winning, this we know.
> General Harkins tells us so.
> In the delta, things are rough.
> In the mountains, mighty tough.
> But we're winning, this we know.
> General Harkins tells us so.
> If you doubt this is true,
> McNamara says so too.

In time the disagreement between the officials and the newspapermen hardened into deep antagonism. Nolting, a conscientious Foreign Service officer, honestly saw no alternative to working with Diem. Diem, who supposed that the American press was as controlled as his own, believed, or pretended to believe, that the newspaper stories were expressing the secret views of the United States government and used his fury over lost face as one more excuse for resisting American advice. The reporters, as Nolting and Harkins saw it, were therefore damaging the war effort; instead of making carping criticisms, they ought, as patriotic Americans, to help the Embassy build up Diem and strengthen his national control and international reputation. In their reports to Washington the officials even gave the astonishing impression that there would be no trouble in Vietnam if only the newspaper fellows would follow the line.

As for the newspapermen, they resented the view that their duty was to write stories in support of official policy. They could never get over Admiral Felt's reproach to Malcolm Browne: "Why don't you get on the team?" They angrily refused to become, as they thought, myth-makers and invoked with solemn indignation the traditions of a free press. "The U. S. Embassy," David Halberstam wrote in a characteristic outburst, "turned into the adjunct of a dictatorship. In trying to protect Diem from criticism, the Ambassador became Diem's agent. But we reporters didn't have to become the adjuncts of a tyranny. We are representatives of a free society, and we aren't going to surrender our principles to the narrow notions of a closed society." One encounter after another made the newspapermen more certain that the Embassy was deliberately lying to them. They did not recognize the deeper pathos, which was that the officials really believed their own reports. They were deceiving not only the American government and people but themselves.

Not everyone in Washington, however, was deceived. Averell Harriman as Assistant Secretary for the Far East had long felt, as by the pricking in his thumbs, that we were on the wrong course. Roger Hilsman, as head of the State Department Office of Intelligence and Research, also doubted whether things were really as splendid as they appeared in Embassy dispatches. In the White House Michael Forrestal shared this skepticism. And, as 1962 gave way to 1963, it seemed increasingly evident that, despite the communiqués and the statistics and the dispatches, the Viet Cong were as omnipresent and the Saigon government as ineffectual as ever. The point was made with some vividness on January 2, 1963, at Ap Bac, fifty miles from Saigon, when a considerable force of Diem's regulars encircled a Viet Cong battalion one-tenth its size, declined to close with them and finally permitted the Viet Cong to escape in the night after they had knocked down five American helicopers and killed three American advisers. A senior American adviser present later surmised that the Vietnamese commander was "reluctant to attack for fear he would take casualties, incur the displeasure of political leaders in Saigon and ruin his military career." Though General Harkins tried to claim Ap Bac as a Vietnamese victory, the newspapermen at the scene reported otherwise, and their reports were not implausible.

Those in Saigon and Washington who saw Vietnam as primarily a military problem thought that the answer to Ap Bac was an intensified military effort—more advisers, more helicopters, more mortars, more defoliation spray, more napalm bombs, more three-star generals in Saigon, more visitations by VIPs. After all, the American presence was still negligible—11,000 troops in all and, in the last two years, a total of thirty-two killed in battle and eighty wounded. But the Harriman group now questioned the exclusively military strategy more insistently than ever. "Fighting a guerrilla war in an underdeveloped nation," Hilsman, the veteran of jungle warfare in Burma, had argued the previous September, "requires as much political and civil action as it does military action." There was danger, they thought, in what Hilsman called the "over-militarization" and "over-Americanization" of the war. The Army, after all, had never cared much for counterinsurgency; at one point, of twenty-seven American generals in Saigon, not one had attended the school at Fort Bragg. The more elaborate the American military establishment, the doubters feared, the more it would be overwhelmed by brass, channels and paperwork, the more it would rely on conventional tactics and the more it would compromise the Vietnamese nationalism of Diem's cause. Worse, the growth of the military commitment would confirm the policy of trying to win a political war by military means.

What was lacking, the Harriman group felt, was any consuming motive to lead the South Vietnamese to fight for Saigon. Why, for example, should peasants die for a government which, when it recovered territory from the Viet Cong, helped the local landowners collect their back rent? General Edward Lansdale, whose experience in guerrilla warfare made him suspect in orthodox military circles, did his best to argue the point in Washington. "The great lesson [of Malaya and the Philippines]," he wrote, "was that there must be a heartfelt *cause* to which the legitimate government is pledged, a cause which makes a stronger appeal to the people than the Communist cause. . . . When the right cause is identified and used correctly, the *anti*-Communist fight becomes a *pro*-people fight."

3. THE BUDDHISTS

This was a minority view. The Secretary of State was well satisfied with military predominance in the formation of United States policy toward Vietnam. As late as April 22, 1963, in a speech in New York, Rusk discerned a "steady movement [in South Vietnam] toward a constitutional system resting upon popular consent," declared that "the 'strategic hamlet' program is producing excellent results," added that "morale in the countryside has begun to rise," assured his listeners that "to the Vietnamese peasant" the Viet Cong "look less and less like winners" and concluded, "The Vietnamese are on their way to success" (meaning presumably the South Vietnamese). So too Alexis Johnson, speaking for right-thinking officials, cited the strategic hamlet program as "the most important reason for guarded optimism." "Perhaps the most important result," Johnson declared, "is the intangible knitting together of Government and people."

Intangible the knitting together certainly was. Exactly a

month after this piece of official wisdom and a fortnight after Rusk's assurances a group of Buddhists gathered in Hue to protest a Diem order forbidding them to display their flags on Buddha's 2587th birthday. Diem's troops fired indiscriminately into the crowd, leaving a moaning mass of dead and wounded. Indignation spread through the towns of South Vietnam; and, when Diem proved unyielding and unrepentant, the anger took appalling forms, culminating in the spectacle of Buddhist *bonzes* dousing themselves in gasoline and burning themselves to death.

Though the Buddhists had suffered legal discrimination in South Vietnam, they had not been actively persecuted. The upheaval, while religious in pretext, was social in its origins and quickly became political in its objectives. It went beyond *bonzes* and students to militant young army officers exasperated by the caprice and confusion of Diem's direction of the war. As the protests spread, the Buddhist revolt threatened to become the vehicle by which all those opposed to the regime, including, no doubt, fellow travelers of the Viet Cong, might hope to bring it down. It was at bottom an uprising, wholly unanticipated by American diplomats, against the hierarchical structure of traditional Vietnamese society—against the older generation of Vietnamese nationalists who, like Diem and Nhu, were upper-class, Catholic, French-speaking, in favor of a new nationalist generation, drawn largely from the middle and lower classes, antiwestern, radical, impassioned: it was, in effect, the angry young men massing to throw out the mandarins.

The Buddhists, with their fiery adventures in self-immolation, engaged the sympathy of the American newspapermen and through them of many people in the United States. Diem helped this process by refusing gestures of contrition or conciliation lest, as usual, he lose face. Washington now instructed the Embassy to bring pressure on him to compose the Buddhist quarrel, warning that, if the situation grew worse, the United States might have to disavow his Buddhist policy publicly. In Saigon, Nolting, to Kennedy's irritation, had departed on a long-planned holiday cruise in the Aegean. His absence, however, permitted his able Deputy Chief of Mission, William Trueheart, to state the American position more bluntly than Diem had ever heard it before.

In response, Diem began to make a few nominal concessions, if with visible resentment. The Nhus, who wanted him to crush the uprising altogether, were even more resentful. In the steaming Saigon summer the incipient hysteria in the presidential palace boiled over. Diem and the Nhus saw plots everywhere: the Buddhists were Viet Cong agents; the American reporters were communists or agents of the CIA; the CIA was even collaborating with the Viet Cong. Madame Nhu said gaily that she clapped her hands whenever more *bonzes* "barbecued" themselves and only wished that David Halberstam would follow their example. Nhu told Morris West, the Australian novelist, that the Americans should get out and that he was in touch with some fine nationalist communists in Hanoi. About this time John Mecklin, the USIA chief, had a nightmare about an American diplomatic mission which gradually discovered it was dealing with a government of madmen, whose words meant nothing, where nothing that was supposed to have happened had actually happened; yet there seemed no escape from dealing with the madmen forever.

The paranoia in Saigon strengthened the Harriman position in Washington. Kennedy himself, who had been doubting the official optimism for some time, used to say dourly that the political thing there was more important than the military, and no one seemed to be thinking of that. When Mecklin visited Washington in the spring, the President asked him why there was so much trouble with the reporters and, after hearing the explanation, personally instructed the Saigon Embassy to change its attitude and start taking American newspapermen into its confidence. Now he began to conclude that the new situation required a new ambassador. Six months before, Nolting had asked, for personal reasons, to be relieved; and, after the Buddhist outburst, the President decided (with some reluctance: like F.D.R. he hated to fire people; moreover, he liked Nolting) that the time had come.

I have the impression that he wanted to send next to Saigon Edmund Gullion, from whom he had first learned about Indochina a dozen years before and who had performed with such distinction in the Congo; Gullion was certainly the candidate of at least some at the White House. But Dean Rusk, in a rare moment of self-assertion, determined to make this appointment himself. He did not want Gullion, and his candidate, to the astonishment or dismay of the White House staff, turned out to be Henry Cabot Lodge.

This was not a wholly irrelevant idea. Lodge, who had been a liaison officer with the French Army during the Second World War, spoke fluent French. In his capacity as reserve officer, he had written a paper on Vietnam in the spring of 1962 and had wanted to take his tour of duty in Vietnam. He was a public-spirited man who felt unhappy out of government and who made clear to Rusk and others his interest in serving in a hardship post. Yet as Ambassador to the United Nations in the Eisenhower years he had displayed no great understanding of the third world and no great talent in dealing with the representatives of new nations. The White House staff feared that once in Saigon he would instinctively side with General Harkins and Diem. But the President was attracted by the idea, not only because he considered Lodge an able man but, because the thought of appointing the man whom he had beaten for the Senate in 1952 and who had run on the opposing ticket for Vice-President in 1960 appealed to his instinct for magnanimity, and also no doubt because the thought of implicating a leading Republican in the Vietnam mess appealed to his instinct for politics. So the appointment was made late in June.

Since Lodge could not leave until late August, it was decided to send back Nolting, who had finally arrived in Washington from his holiday, for one last try of the pro-Diem policy. Nolting, angered by Trueheart's forthright representations to Diem in his absence, felt when he got back to Saigon on July 11, that his labor of two years lay in ruins. Nor had the recent troubles altered in the slightest his estimate of the situation. He considered the Buddhists unappeasable, believing their goal to be the overthrow of the regime. He felt American pressure on their behalf, especially any public disavowal of Diem's anti-Buddhist actions, would only incite Diem to more stringent repression or his opponents to a coup. Any effort to divorce Diem from the Nhus would be useless: "trying to separate the members of that family would be like separating Siamese twins." The best course remained unconditional support of Diem. In order to repair relations with Diem, he now even went to the point of defending the regime's record on religious matters.

In Washington, meanwhile, Kennedy sought to put Saigon's problems in perspective by reminding a press conference that Vietnam after all had been at war for twenty years. "Before we render too harsh a judgment on the people, we should realize that they are going through a harder time than we have had to go through." Our goal, he continued, was "a stable government there, carrying on a struggle to maintain its national independence. We believe strongly in that. . . . In my opinion, for us to withdraw from that effort would mean a collapse not only of South Vietnam but Southeast Asia. So we are going to stay there." He then expressed the hope that the regime and the Buddhists could "reach an agreement on the civil disturbances and also in respect for the rights of others." (In Saigon this last sentence was killed by the censorship.)

Neither Nolting's return nor Kennedy's temperate words had much effect, though, before Nolting left in mid-August, Diem did assure him there would be no more attacks on the Buddhists. Then six days later, Diem's troops assaulted the pagodas, arresting hundreds of *bonzes* and seizing the temples of worship in a night of violence and terror. It was, Mecklin wrote later, "ruthless, comprehensive suppression of the Buddhist movement." Madame Nhu described it to a reporter as "the happiest day in my life since we crushed the Binh Xuyen [a private army of brigands] in 1955."

The Americans were caught completely by surprise. General Harkins had noted the Vietnamese troop movements but thought they were being deployed for an attack on the Viet Cong. "We just didn't know," the CIA chief told Halberstam. It was an act of calculated contempt for the Americans. The next evening in the midst of a hot, soggy drizzle of rain Cabot Lodge arrived in Saigon.

4. THE SOUND OF MUTINY

The White House doubters had been mistaken about Lodge. We had forgotten his patrician's preference for fair play and his patriot's pride in the dignity of his country. Both had been considerably affronted as he read through the Saigon cable file in preparation for his mission. Now Diem and Nhu had obviously carried out their attack against the pagodas the day before his arrival in order to present him with a *fait accompli,* expecting that the Americans would give in, as they had always done before. But Lodge in Saigon agreed with Harriman and Hilsman in Washington that, if we were to retain any credibility in Vietnam, we had to stand up this time.

In Vietnam the brutality of the assault sent a shudder even through the Diem regime itself. The foreign minister resigned and, in a gesture of defiance, shaved his head like a *bonze.* Madame Nhu's father resigned as ambassador to Washington with a denunciation of his daughter. Above all, the action crystallized the disaffection of the generals who, in the confusion, had been themselves blamed (by, among others, the Department of State) for the atrocity. Now they began sending clandestine messages to the new ambassador. They first wanted it made clear that they had nothing to do with the raids. Then they inquired with oriental suavity what our attitude would be if they were to take action against the regime, should Nhu, for example, make a deal with Hanoi. Lodge cabled Washington for instructions.

The reply was drafted on August 24. The American government, it suggested, could no longer tolerate the systematic repression of the Buddhists nor the domination of the regime by Nhu. The generals could be told that we would find it impossible to support Diem unless these problems were solved. Diem should be given every chance to solve them. If he refused, then the possibility had to be realistically faced that Diem himself could not be saved. We would take no part in any action; but, if anything happened, an interim anti-communist military regime could expect American support.

August 24 was a Saturday. The President was on Cape Cod; McNamara and Rusk were out of town; McCone was on vacation. The draft was cleared through all the relevant departments but not at the top level. Defense accepted it because it understood that the cable had already gone; McNamara, if he had been consulted, would have opposed it. So also would McCone. No one is sure what Rusk's position would have been. The President saw the draft at Hyannis Port without realizing that the departmental clearances did not signify the concurrence of his senior advisers.

On his return to Washington Kennedy felt rather angrily that he had been pressed too hard and fast. He discussed the situation with Robert Kennedy, who talked in turn with McNamara and Maxwell Taylor. The Attorney General reported back with great concern that nobody knew what was going to happen in Vietnam and that our policy had not been fully discussed, as every other major decision since the Bay of Pigs had been discussed. The President thereupon called a meeting on Vietnam for the following day and asked that Nolting be invited.

The former ambassador gave a dignified and uncritical statement of the case for Diem and expressed doubt whether the generals involved could carry off a coup. He suggested that we should not jump unless we knew where we were jumping. The President agreed and began a process of pulling away from the cable of August 24. Vietnam meetings continued for several days, and messages flashed back and forth between Washington and Saigon. While the talks went on, the coup itself gradually evaporated. Nolting had been right: these generals could not carry it through.

Diem and Nhu proceeded quickly to exploit their victory. There were more arrests, especially among students, thousands of whom, including boys and girls of high school age, were carted off to indoctrination centers. In Washington policy weakly reverted to collaboration with Diem, encouraged by CIA's suggestion that Diem might have been sufficiently alarmed by the coup rumors to do some of the things we wanted. The President, however, did not wish to leave Diem in any doubt about how he felt, especially about Nhu. In a television interview on September 3, he tossed aside a moderate statement his staff had prepared in light of his reaction to the August 24 telegram. Instead, he said:

> I don't think that the war can be won unless the people support the effort and, in my opinion, in the last two months, the government has gotten out of touch with the people.
>
> The repressions against the Buddhists, we felt, were very unwise. . . . It is my hope that this will become increasingly obvious to the government, that they will take steps to try to bring back popular support. . . . With changes in policy and perhaps with personnel I think it can. If it doesn't make those changes, I would think that the chances of winning it would not be very good.

No one could misinterpret the reference to changes in personnel. Kennedy also emphasized that "in the final analysis, it is their war. They are the ones who have to win it or lose it. We can help them, we can give them equipment, we can send our men out there as advisers, but they have to win it, the people of Vietnam."

The contrast between this statement and his reaction to the August 24 cable suggested Kennedy's own perplexity; and, in a new effort to find out what the situation was, he sent another mission early in September. It consisted this time, not of the usual senior officials, but of two old Vietnam hands, General Victor Krulak of the Marines and Joseph Mendenhall of State, a Foreign Service officer. After a frenzied weekend of inspection and interrogation, the two men flew back to Washington. Mecklin, who came back with them, observed that "the general and the FSO not only appeared to dislike each other, but also disagreed on what should be done about Vietnam. On the whole flight they spoke to each other only when it was unavoidable." They reported immediately to the National Security Council. Krulack told the assembled dignitaries the war was going beautifully, that the regime was beloved by the people and that we need have no undue concern even about Nhu. Mendenhall told them that South Vietnam was in a desperate state, that the regime was on the edge of collapse and that Nhu had to go. The President listened politely and finally said, "Were you two gentlemen in the same country?" And so the meetings on Vietnam continued.

INTERLUDE

MINUTES OF THE NEXT HIGH-LEVEL MEETING ON VIETNAM [3]

The Secretary of State opened the meeting, in the absence of the President, by urging that priority be given to the key question of the past thirteen hours, How did we get here, and Where do we go from here?

On the one hand, he said, it was important to keep moving forward. But on the other hand, we must deal with things as they are.

The Secretary of Defense concurred but felt that we must not permit the views of a handful of neurotic Saigon intellectuals to distract us from the major goal, which was to get on with the war. He asked General Krulack to report on his latest sampling of opinion among the trainers of Vietnamese secret police at Fort Belvoir.

General Krulack reported that morale among the trainers at Fort Belvoir was at an all-time high. Many felt that we had turned a corner, and all were intent on moving on with our objectives.

Mr. Hilsman asked if General Krulack had had an opportunity to talk to the Vietnamese at Fort Belvoir as well as the trainers.

Ambassador Nolting interjected the comment that Mr. Hilsman had expressed doubts about the Vietnamese at Belvoir ten months ago. He wondered, in view of this fact, whether Mr. Hilsman's question was relevant.

General Krulack responded that the American trainers had advised him to refrain from talking with the Vietnamese since their views were well known to the trainers, and conversation would distract them from the purpose at hand, i.e., to win the war.

Governor Harriman stated that he had disagreed for twenty years with General Krulack and disagreed today, reluctantly, more than ever; he was sorry to say that he felt General Krulack was a fool and had always thought so.

Secretary Dillon hoped that press leaks on the cost of opinion-sampling at Fort Belvoir would be kept to a minimum as the dollar reserve problem was acute. He, for one, was against moving forward until the risks had been calculated.

General Taylor said that if risks were involved, "you can count me out."

The Secretary of State re-phrased the basic question in terms of Saigon's 897. What were we to do about the 500 schoolgirls who were seeking asylum in the American Embassy?

(At this point, the President entered the room.)

The President said that he hoped we were not allowing our

---

[3] A document produced by a free spirit lodged in the machinery of government eager to spare Bromley Smith of the National Security Council the labor of keeping a record of each separate Vietnam meeting.

policies to be influenced by immature twenty-year-old school-girls, all of whom were foreigners. He felt that we must not lose sight of our ultimate objective, and in no state was the Vietnamese vote worth very much.

The Attorney General said that it was high time to show some guts, and here was a good place to begin. "After all," he said, "I too am a President's brother."

The Secretary of Defense heartily concurred; as a former businessman, he said, he knew the importance of getting on with business as usual.

Mr. Hilsman raised the question of disaffection among ninety percent of the soldiers, as reported in Saigon's 898. Was not an action plan, phase by phase, now clearly necessary?

The Vice President said that he had lived with both affection and disaffection in Texas and the Senate for thirty years, and he felt we could ride this one through. We must not lose our sense of humor, he said.

The President asked that interagency committees be put to work on the nature of our dialogue with Diem, and he suggested that the Ex-Com meet again in a week or so. Next time, he said, he hoped that a good map of South Vietnam might be available.

5. THE FALL OF DIEM

Lodge had begun his Saigon tour with the usual calls on Diem and Nhu. When he got nowhere with them, he stopped calling on them. "They have not done anything I asked," he would explain. "They know what I want. Why should I keep asking? Let them come to ask me." The anti-Diem section of the Embassy and American press in Saigon, enormously cheered, said to each other: "Our mandarin is going to beat their mandarin." Lodge kept cabling Washington that the situation was getting worse and that the time had arrived for the United States to increase its pressure. He recommended in particular the suspension of American aid.

McNamara and Rusk were at first opposed. The suspension of aid, they said, would hurt the war effort. And Lodge did not help his case by a Bostonian high-handedness which not only turned his embassy into a one-man show but also made him uncommunicative and at times almost derisive in response to inquiries from Washington. But Kennedy, I believe, came to the conclusion in mid-September that Lodge, Harriman, Hilsman and Forrestal were right on the question of pressure, though he remained wary of anything which might involve the United States in attempts against the regime. Accordingly he decided to send McNamara and Taylor on one more trip on the Saigon shuttle in the hope that exposure to Lodge and the facts would convince them too that pressure was essential.

In the past, McNamara's susceptibility to quantification had led him to take excessive comfort in General Harkins's statistical optimism, embodied, for example, in tables purporting to correlate government and Viet Cong casualties; and Nolting had done little to assert the importance of things which could not be quantified. In Saigon, as in Washington, the State Department had acquiesced in the theory that Vietnam was basically a military problem. But Lodge considered intangibles like political purpose and popular support as of the highest importance. For a few days after McNamara's arrival, Lodge and Harkins engaged in a quiet duel for the Secretary's ear. In the end Lodge made the political case so effectively that McNamara agreed there was no alternative to pressure; indeed, McNamara returned to Washington doubting whether Diem could last even if he took corrective action. But he also thought that the political mess had not yet infected the military situation and, back in Washington, announced (in spite of a strong dissent from William Sullivan of Harriman's staff who accompanied the mission) that a thousand American troops could be withdrawn by the end of the year and that the major part of the American military task would be completed by the end of 1965.

This announcement, however, was far less significant than McNamara's acceptance of the Lodge pressure program. Some thought had already been given to the problem of picking out of the aid effort the cuts which would do the least harm to the war, and early in October a selective suspension went quietly into effect. It was hoped that the absence of publicity would encourage Diem to do something about the Nhus and the Buddhists without seeming to act under pressure and thereby losing face. But, in due course, the Vietnamese bitterly announced the suspension themselves. Madame Nhu now appeared in the United States to lobby against the new policy; for a moment she won support from right-wing politicans, though in the end her extravagances injured her own cause. In Saigon her husband apparently renewed his efforts to make contact with Hanoi. Speculation bubbled up again about possible successors to Diem. One official, asked about specifications for the new man, replied crisply, "First of all, he should be an only child."

As for Diem, there is some suggestion that the program of pressure, so belatedly adopted, was having effect. "With or without American aid," he said in mid-October, "I will keep up the fight, and I will always maintain my friendship toward the American people." On the last day of the month Diem and Lodge made a trip together to dedicate an experimental reactor at Dalat. Diem for the first time indicated an interest in compromise and asked Lodge what he had to do. Lodge told him to send Nhu out of the country and institute some reforms. Diem, instead of turning this down out of hand, said that he needed a little time to think about it. It was too late. The next day the generals struck. Diem and Nhu were murdered, and the history of Vietnam entered a new phase.

It is important to state clearly that the coup of November 1, 1963, was entirely planned and carried out by the Vietnamese. Neither the American Embassy nor the CIA were involved in instigation or execution. Coup rumors, epidemic in Saigon since 1960, had begun to rise again toward the end of October; and on October 29 the National Security Council met to consider American policy in the event that a coup should take place. The Attorney General characterized the reports as very thin. The President, noting that the pro-Diem and anti-Diem forces seemed about equal, observed that any American action under such conditions would be silly. If Lodge agreed, the President said, we should instruct him to discourage a coup. But Lodge knew little more than he had reported to Washington. Indeed, on the morning of November 1 he actually took Admiral Felt to call on Diem—an incident which alarmed the conspirators who, knowing Diem's gift for long-distance talking, feared he would detain his visitors past one-thirty in the afternoon, when the revolt was scheduled to begin.

What lay behind the coup was not the meddling of Americans, quiet or ugly, but the long history of Vietnamese military resentment against Diem, compounded now by the fear that Nhu, with his admiration for totalitarian methods of organization, might try to transform South Vietnam into a police state. It was almost inevitable that, at one point or another, the generals would turn against so arbitrary and irrational a regime. As Lodge later put it, the coup was like a rock rolling downhill. It could have been stopped only by aggressive American intervention against the army on behalf of Diem and the Nhus. This course few Americans in Saigon or Washington were willing to recommend.

I saw the President soon after he heard that Diem and Nhu were dead. He was somber and shaken. I had not seen him so depressed since the Bay of Pigs. No doubt he realized that Vietnam was his great failure in foreign policy, and that he had never really given it his full attention. But the fact that the Vietnamese seemed ready to fight had made him feel that there was a reasonable chance of making a go of it; and then the optimism of 1962 had carried him along. Yet, with his memory of the French in Indochina in 1951, he had always believed there was a point at which our intervention might turn Vietnamese nationalism against us and transform an Asian civil conflict into a white man's war. When he came into office, 2000 American troops were in Vietnam. Now there were 16,000. How many more could there be before we passed the point? By 1961 choices had already fatally narrowed; but still, if Vietnam had been handled as a political rather than a military problem, if Washington had not listened to General Harkins for so long, if Diem had been subjected to tactful pressure rather than treated with uncritical respect, if a Lodge had gone to Saigon in 1961 instead of a Nolting, if, if, if—and now it was all past, and Diem miserably dead. The Saigon generals were claiming that he had killed himself; but the president, shaking his head, doubted that, as a Catholic, he would have taken this way out. He said that Diem had fought for his country for twenty years and that it should not have ended like this.

6. TROUBLES IN THE HEMISPHERE

Cuba was another unsolved problem. Fidel Castro did not cease to call for revolution in Latin America. "We do not deny the possibility of peaceful transition," he said in January 1963, "but we are still awaiting the first case. . . . That is the duty of leaders and the revolutionary organizations: to make the masses march, to launch the masses into battle. That is what they did in Algeria. And that is what the patriots are doing in South Vietnam." In July he added the hopeful thought that conditions for revolution in many Latin American countries were "incomparably better than those that prevailed in our country."

But Fidel's appeal to the hemisphere had steadily waned. His opposition to the Alliance for Progress had cast doubt on the selflessness of his interest in social betterment. Then the missile crisis displayed him as a rather impotent and ignominious Soviet tool, warned other Latin revolutionists that they could not count on Soviet support once the chips were down and demonstrated to non-communists the danger communist bridgeheads brought to all Latin America. At the same time, Washington pursued its measures of economic, diplomatic and military containment. Kennedy's policy of isolating and ignoring Castro worked well. By 1963 he was hardly even a thorn in the flesh. Once his influence in Latin America was destroyed, the survival of mendicant communist regime in the Caribbean was not important.

As for the future, Kennedy, as usual, refused doctrinaire conclusions in a world where history produced such astonishing and unforeseen reversals. "There are a good many things which have happened in the last three or four years," he said at the end of 1962, "which could not have been predicted in '57 or '58. No one can predict what the exact course of events will be in Cuba, what movement will take place there." He continued to keep the door open to those within the Castro regime itself who might want to return to the hemisphere. "We believe," as Assistant Secretary Martin told a Senate committee in May 1963, "that it would be a serious mistake to give those in Cuba who are struggling against communism the idea that they are being disregarded and that they have no role to play in determining how Cuba will be governed."

I have the impression that in the autumn of 1963 the President was reappraising the Castro problem. When Tito came to the White House in October, Kennedy remarked that he did not know what was going to happen, but, if Cuba rid herself of Soviet influence, perhaps we could deal with a domestic revolutionary regime; on the other hand, if Castro's refusal to sign the test ban treaty meant that China was now playing a role in Cuba, that could hardly be considered a desirable development. Jean Daniel, who saw Kennedy a few days later, reported him as saying, "The continuation of the [economic] blockade depends on the continuation of subversive activities." Daniel was on his way to Cuba to interview Castro, and Kennedy invited him to stop by on his return.

In the meantime, unofficial soundings encountered difficulties on the two points of submission to extra-continental influence and subversion directed at the rest of the hemisphere. On November 18 in a speech at Miami Kennedy sent a message across the water to Cuba. A band of conspirators, he said, had made Cuba the instrument of an effort dictated by external powers to subvert the other American republics. "This, and this alone, divides us. As long as this is true, nothing is possible. Without it everything is possible. Once this barrier is removed, we will be ready and anxious to work with the Cuban people in pursuit of those progressive goals which in a few short years stirred their hopes and the sympathy of . . . the hemisphere."

Two days later Jean Daniel saw Castro in Havana. The Cuban leader expressed feelings of "fraternity and profound, total gratitude" toward the Soviet Union; there was no give here. As for Cuban subversion, Castro predictably denied that it was the cause of revolution on the mainland. He denounced Washington and the CIA. Still, of Kennedy, Castro said he could "be an even greater President than Lincoln. I know, for example, that for Khrushchev Kennedy is a man you can talk with. I have gotten this impression from all my conversations with Khrushchev. . . . Personally, I consider him responsible for everything, but I will say this: he has come to understand many things over the past few months; and then too, in the last analysis, I'm convinced that anyone else would be worse." He concluded: "As a man and as a statesman, it is my duty to indicate what the bases for understanding could be." And so the matter rested, with lines of communication still open.

"Two dikes are needed to contain Soviet expansion," Kennedy had told Daniel: "the blockade on the one hand, a tremendous effort toward progress on the other." He followed the Alliance for Progress with ever watchful eye. The recommendation of the Inter-American Economic and Social Council in 1962 had led to a review of the Alliance by Lleras Camargo of Colombia and Kubitschek of Brazil. "Nothing that needs to be done in Latin America is easy," Lleras said. Yet, while noting the disappointments of the Alliance, he wrote that it had made "an extraordinary impression upon the old, hardened crust of Latin American society. . . . Governments, which had been indifferent to the anxiety of the people, have shown as never before a zeal for economic development." While the two Latin American leaders disagreed on certain issues, they united in recommending the establishment of an inter-American development committee to preside over the Alliance. When the IA-ECOSOC met in November 1963 at São Paulo in Brazil, it established the Inter-American Committee for the Alliance for Progress (CIAP). This body, on which Walt Rostow became the United States representative, marked the 'Latinization' of the Alliance and gave it new coherence and purpose.

But the road to democracy remained hard. On September 25, 1963, the Dominican military overthrew Juan Bosch in the Dominican Republic. A week later another military coup overthrew the regime of Ramón Villeda Morales in

Honduras. Kennedy promptly recalled our ambassadors and economic and military aid chiefs from Santo Domingo and Tegucigalpa. "We are opposed to coups," he said, "because we think they are defeating, self-defeating and defeating for the hemisphere . . . not only because we are all committed under the Alliance for Progress to democratic government and progress but also because of course dictatorships are the seedbeds from which communism ultimately springs up." [4]

Still, despite political setbacks, the Alliance for Progress continued to gain. In 1963 eight countries attained increases in per capita income of nearly 5 per cent—almost twice the target of Punta del Este. In 1964 Latin America as a whole fulfilled the Punta del Este goal. And the rise of new leaders like Eduardo Frei Montalva in Chile and Belaunde in Peru expressed the vitality of the democratic revolution.

The President was more troubled than ever by the organization of Latin American affairs within our own government. Late in October he discussed with Richard Goodwin and me the old problem which Berle had raised in 1961 of an Under Secretaryship of State for Inter-American Affairs, embracing both the Alliance and the political responsibilities of the Assistant Secretary. Kennedy, remarking sharply that he could not get anyone on the seventh floor of the State Department to pay sustained attention to Latin America, dictated a plain-spoken memorandum to Rusk saying that he wanted to create the new Under Secretaryship. "I am familiar," he said, "with the argument

---

[4] Some commented on the apparent contradiction between the willingness of the United States government to recognize a military coup in Vietnam and its reluctance to recognize military coups in Latin America. While a strong case can be made for a policy of automatic recognition of all governments which can maintain internal order and meet international commitments, the United States had special obligations within the western hemisphere to "the consolidation on this continent, within the framework of democratic institutions, of a system of individual liberty and social justice based on respect for the essential rights of man" (Charter of the Organization of American States). This would justify a policy of suspending recognition of western hemisphere regimes which came to power by overthrowing legitimate governments –i.e., governments which were freely elected and which had not denied political opposition normal channels of expression. This test would not prevent recognition of coups against dictatorships, such as those of Castro or Duvalier. At the same time, it would justify the suspension of relations with the Dominican Republic and Honduras until they could take measures to restore legitimacy by reopening the channels of political opposition and pledging free elections, as it would also justify our resumption of relations with the military regime in Peru once it had taken such steps in 1962.

that, if we do this for Latin America, other geographical areas must receive equal treatment. But I have come increasingly to feel that this argument, however plausible in the abstract, overlooks the practicalities of the situation." Historically Latin America was an area of primary and distinctive United States interest; currently it was the area of greatest danger to us; and operationally it simply was not receiving the day-to-day, high level attention which our national interest demanded. "Since I am familiar with the arguments against the establishment of this Under Secretaryship," his memorandum to the Secretary concluded somewhat wearily, "I would like this time to have a positive exploration of its possibilities."

He had in mind for the job Sargent Shriver or perhaps Averell Harriman, whom he had just designated to lead the United States delegation to the São Paulo meeting. We later learned that Rusk sent the presidential memorandum to the Assistant Secretary for Administration, who passed it along to some subordinate, and it took Ralph Dungan's intervention to convince the Secretary that this was a serious matter requiring senior attention. Receiving no response, the President after a fortnight renewed the request.

7. REVOLUTION IN FISCAL POLICY

The year 1963 was one of initiatives not only in the pursuit of peace and in the struggle for equal rights but in national economic policy.

In the autumn of 1962 the administration had quietly committed itself to a radical principle: the deliberate creation of budgetary deficits at a time when there was no economic emergency—when, indeed, the budget was already in deficit and the economy was actually moving upward. This idea was the wildest heresy to those like George Humphrey who used to predict a depression to curl a man's hair if the government did not balance its books. It would have seemed extreme to the contracyclical spenders of the New Deal, who were prepared for deficits in depression in order to offset declines but supposed that the proper policy in prosperity was to keep taxes up and retire the national debt. Kennedy was even moving beyond his own theory in 1961 of a budget balanced "over the years of the economic cycle" when he adopted the theory of deficits at the peak of the cycle so long as unemployment remained high.

Because the principle was so revolutionary, it exacted a price, or rather a series of prices. The first had been the decision to create the deficit through tax reduction rather than through social spending. Kennedy, in spite of his sympathy with the Galbraithian concern for the public sector, simply considered the expenditures route politically impossible and accepted Walter Heller's argument that the increased revenues produced by the tax route would eventually increase public benefits. The second price, not so serious, was the decision to stretch out the projected cut of about $10 billion over three years. The Treasury favored this, the Council of Economic Advisers opposed it, and the President went along with the Treasury, partly because he did not want to jeopardize the tax bill by requesting a rise in the debt limit and partly because he wanted to keep his own deficit under Eisenhower's record peacetime deficit of 1959. The third price was more serious: an assurance to Wilbur Mills that tax reduction would be accompanied by an "ever-tighter rein on Federal expenditures." The President's assumption here, I think, was that, once he had completed the diversification of national defense required by the strategy of flexible response, military spending would level off, and, as the budget grew in pace with growth in population and output, more money would be available for welfare purposes.

A fourth price was the gradual erosion in Congress of most of the tax reforms to which Dillon and Mills had devoted so much attention in the years preceding. The tax reform program, in essence, was an effort to close loopholes in the tax laws in exchange for a reduction in the surtax rates. Galbraith once complained to Kennedy that it was "a commendable program to get greater equity among the rich, but it affects only a small fraction of the population—a comparative handful of affluent Republicans. This reform is not an exercise with any meaning whatever to the people at large." (He added—this was at the end of 1962—that in any case tax reform would not get anywhere: "Depletion allowances, preferential treatment of capital gains, tax exempt securities will all be preserved. . . . Anyone who disagrees with this prediction can reasonably be requested to put it in writing.")

Galbraith was right in the short term, and Kennedy was prepared to pay this price for the tax cut. But the President reserved the problem in his own mind for treatment in the longer run. He was outraged to discover that an oil man reputed to be among the richest living Americans had in certain years paid income taxes of less than $1000; that, of the nineteen Americans with incomes of more than $5 million a year, more than 25 per cent had paid no income tax at all in 1959 and that of the rest not one had paid in the 80 to 85 per cent bracket to which their income nominally consigned them; that in a recent year one American received an income of nearly $20 million and paid no taxes at all.[5] The President and the Attorney General, brooding over these figures, decided to make a major issue of the tax-avoidance spectaculars after the 1964 election.

Even with all these concessions, the principle of the planned deficit remained too startling for easy acceptance. Mythology died hard. In May 1963 President Eisenhower in an agitated magazine article expressed his "amazement" about this "vast, reckless" plan for "a deliberate plunge into a massive deficit." "What can those people in Washington be thinking about? Why would they deliberately do this to our country? I ask myself." The deficit road, the former President grimly warned, "through history has lured nations to financial misery and economic disaster." And in the business community, a number of leaders, while applauding the idea of tax reduction, especially for higher brackets and for corporations, insisted that it be accompanied by a parallel reduction in government expenditures. It required patient explanation before they began to understand that this approach, by taking out of the spending stream with one hand what was being put in by the other, would nullify the stimulative value of the cut.

The bill made slow progress through Congress. Public reaction at first was muted. Kennedy used to inquire of the professors of the Council what had happened to the several million college students who had presumably been taught the new economics. He wrote Seymour Harris, "As a teacher you must be discouraged that none of the obvious lessons of the last thirty years have been learned by those who have the most at stake in a growing prosperous America." The President watched with envy as the British government called for a tax reduction of comparable size in April, then added a large increase in expenditures and had the program in effect by summer. Still, when the House of Representatives passed the tax bill by 271 to 155 on September 25, 1963, the worst was over. Though Senator Byrd showed every intention of dragging out the hearings

[5] These and other atrocities are discussed by Philip M. Stern in *The Great Treasury Raid* (New York, 1964) and by Stewart Alsop in two pieces for the *Saturday Evening Post*, "The Great Tax Myth" and "More on the Great Tax Myth" (November 23 and December 21, 1963). It should be added that the American Congress greeted the Stern-Alsop revelations with curious apathy.

before the Senate Finance Committee, enactment sometime in early 1964 was reasonably assured. The Yale speech had not been in vain; and the American government, a generation after *General Theory*, had accepted the Keynesian revolution.

But a problem remained. The steady increase in national output since the bottom of the 1960-61 recession had not been accompanied by any equivalent lessening of unemployment. The decline in joblessness from 6.7 per cent of the labor force in 1961 to 5.6 per cent in 1962 left the level far above the 4 per cent economists were willing to tolerate; and the re-employment rate was slower than in any comparable post-recession period since the Second World War. Would the tax cut do any better in cutting into chronic unemployment?

This question had worried Kennedy ever since the primaries in the spring of 1960 had carried him into the blasted valleys of West Virginia. In the campaign he derided Nixon's view that conditions in the United States could not be better:

Let them tell that to the 4 million people who are out of work, to the 3 million Americans who must work part time. Let them tell that to those who farm our farms, in our depressed areas, in our deserted textile and coal towns. Let them try to tell it to the 5 million men and women in the richest country on earth who live on a surplus food diet of $20 a month.

"The war against poverty and degradation is not yet over," he said, ". . . As long as there are 15 million American homes in the United States substandard, as long as there are 5 million American homes in the cities of the United States which lack plumbing of any kind, as long as 17 million Americans live on inadequate assistance when they get older, then I think we have unfinished business in this country." Repeatedly through the campaign he called for "an economic drive on poverty."

Now as President he confronted an economic system which seemed to be able to do everything but give all its people jobs and decent lives. Population growth compounded the challenge: according to the Bureau of Labor Statistics in 1962, 2.5 million new young workers would begin their careers each year in the sixties. The progress of automation further complicated the problem by bringing the period nearer when technology would begin to destroy more jobs than it created. How could an increasingly computerized economy, using fewer people to produce more goods, provide useful employment to those displaced by technological change, to those traditionally discriminated against in the labor market and to those entering that market for the first time? This question did not worry him politically, because he was sure the unemployed would never turn to the Republicans to create jobs for them. But it worried him socially. Unemployment was especially acute among young people, and it thereby placed a growing strain on the social fabric.

The President had always regarded as artificial the debate about the character of American unemployment: whether it was primarily the result of economic slowdown and thus to be cured by aggregate fiscal and monetary stimulus, or whether it was primarily structural and thus to be cured by institutional remedies. "Our feeling," as he said in the spring of 1963, "is that the economy, if sufficiently stimulated . . . could reduce unemployment to the figure of about 4 per cent. There will be some hard-core structural unemployment in Eastern Kentucky and West Virginia, particularly the coal and steel centers, which will not be substantially aided by the tax bill or even by the general rise in the economy. I do think, however, that if we could reduce unemployment to four per cent, then those programs which are specifically directed toward these centers of chronic unemployment . . . may be able to make a further dent."

Tax reduction, in short, was the first part of the assault on unemployment. After the artillery barrage, the structural troops were then expected to move in and mop up remaining pockets of resistance. A basis for structural action had already been laid by legislative enactment: the Area Redevelopment Act, passed in 1961 after having been twice vetoed in the Eisenhower administration, and the Accelerated Public Works Act of 1962. Both of these were put under the charge of William L. Batt, Jr., who had been Commissioner of Labor in Pennsylvania and was now head of the Area Redevelopment Administration in the Department of Commerce. In addition, the Manpower Training and Development Act was passed in 1962, and bills for vocational education and youth employment were moving through Congress in 1963.

Progress had also been made in devising regional stragegies. The President directed Batt to work closely with the Conference of Appalachian Governors, organized in 1960 for a multi-state attack on the spreading economic decay in the hills and valleys of the Appalachian mountains. Appalachia, a region as large as Britain, stretching from

northern Pennsylvania into northern Alabama, had been
primarily a coal area. Now the mining towns were crum-
bling away. Unemployment was twice the average for the
nation. The people were sunk in lethargy and squalor.
Those of intelligence and energy, who might have provided
local leadership, fled the region as fast as they could. On
the Cumberland Plateau in eastern Kentucky 19 per cent of
the adults could not read or write. Harry Caudill's *Night
Comes to the Cumberlands* in 1963, with its powerful portrait of life in the southern Appalachians, made the nation
uneasily aware of the horror of underdevelopment it had
hidden in its bosom. Caudill's book came out with a foreword by Stewart Udall and was widely read in New Frontier Washington.

Kennedy, who never forgot West Virginia, followed developments in Appalachia with particular interest. This region,
as he once put it, would be "very hard to reach even if
the economy is going ahead at a strong rate." From the
start, he steered a great variety of government programs—
ARA, highway construction, Army Corps of Engineers,
TVA, food stamp—into Appalachia. In the spring of 1963
he established a joint federal-state Committee on the Appalachian Region and, with nice historical eye, appointed
Franklin D. Roosevelt, Jr., the Under Secretary of Commerce, as chairman. Roosevelt took hold of the project with
ability and energy. It seemed in 1963 that the Appalachia
program might become a model for comparable programs
in other parts of underdeveloped America, such as the
upper Great Lakes region and the Ozarks.

Within the executive branch the President's Committee
on Juvenile Delinquency had been developing under Robert
Kennedy's goading perhaps the most imaginative attack on
the structure of poverty. The Committee decided to use its
funds—$10 million a year—to stimulate cities to come up
with coordinated plans, uniting federal, municipal and private instrumentalities in an effort to help boys and girls in
the slums. When the plans met the Committee's criteria,
more money would be available for their execution. In order to make sure that they would not just be schemes benev-
olently imposed by social workers and welfare agencies,
Robert Kennedy insisted on bringing the poor into planning
and execution—an innovation of great significance, stoutly
resisted in many cases by city administrations. He also
laid emphasis on pre-school education, pointing out that the
formative years of a child's life were before the age of six
or seven and that many children from poor families arrived
in the first grade so far behind that they could never

catch up. The Committee concentrated on sixteen cities in the course of 1963 and approved plans in ten of them. Mobilization for Youth and the Haryou program in Harlem were among the best known. Out of this experience there emerged the concept of 'community action' as a fundamental part of the war against deprivation.

Yet, apart from the Committee on Juvenile Delinquency, none of the structural efforts quite worked. The Area Redevelopment Administration received inadequate appropriations and, because of political pressure as well as human need, had to spread them too thin over too wide an area. After a year and a half, only slightly more than 150,000 were in training under the Manpower Development and Training Act. The youth employment bill, proposing a Youth Conservation Corps, passed the Senate in April 1963 but bogged down in the House. And the Appalachia program threatened to be dominated by the state governors, who flinched from offending the absentee corporate owners of the area and wanted to put the bulk of government funds into highway construction.

8. THE WAR AGAINST POVERTY

As Kennedy reflected on these matters in the spring of 1963, he began to feel that the problem was one not only of greater investment in private industry but of greater investment in public services and human beings, not only of distressed areas but of distressed individuals, not only of vocational training but of elementary education, medical care, civil rights, community action and personal morale. He was reaching the conclusion that tax reduction required a comprehensive structural counterpart, taking the form, not of piecemeal programs, but of a broad war against poverty itself. Here perhaps was the unifying theme which would pull a host of social programs together and rally the nation behind a generous cause.

Kennedy knew that unemployment and poverty were in part separate problems (indeed statistics showed that a majority of the unemployed were not below the poverty line and a majority of the poor were not unemployed; but the problems overlapped in the area of structural remedy. This concern for poverty as a problem distinct from unemployment—for chronic or, in bureaucratese, 'hardcore' poverty—was relatively new. Franklin Roosevelt in his Second Inaugural had spoken of "one-third of a nation ill-housed, ill-clad, ill-nourished . . . lacking the means to buy the products of farm and factory and by their poverty denying work and productiveness to many other millions"; but, in the depression, he had the unemployed primarily in mind. The war made people think of other things. Then in 1949 the Joint Committee on the Economic Report established a Subcommittee on Low-Income Families, which began to demonstrate by statistical analysis the persistence of poverty in the national community. Two old New Dealers, Averell Harriman and Isador Lubin, were quick to see the significance of this work. In 1953, when Harriman became president of the Franklin D. Roosevelt Foundation, he decided to focus its program on the third of the Four Freedoms, Freedom from Want. By 1956, with Harriman now governor of New York and Lubin his labor commissioner, Harriman asked the legislature to set up a commission to study the causes and remedies of poverty. Harriman's message to the Legislature on January 31, 1956, contained the basic elements of the war against poverty begun half a dozen years later. It defined the problem as something separate from unemployment and even from distressed areas, set forth its composition and magnitude and laid emphasis on the need to help the individual make his own escape from poverty through "medical and vocational rehabilitation." Leon Keyserling, another old New Dealer still in Washington, put out a series of well-documented papers discussing what he called "the gaps in our prosperity," and the Joint Economic Committee continued its work on low-income families. But neither the statistics in Washington nor Harriman's little New Deal in Albany had much impact on the comfortable fifties. Indeed, one of Nelson Rockefeller's first acts as governor in 1959 was to abolish Harriman's commission.

It was not till toward the end of the decade—and especially with the publication in 1958 of Galbraith's *The Affluent Society* and its chapter xxiii on "The New Position of Poverty"—that chronic poverty began to impinge on the national consciousness as a distinct issue. Galbraith warned that the poor, unlike the ambitious immigrants of the nineties or the politically aggressive unemployed of the thirties, were now a demoralized and inarticulate minority who in many cases had inherited their poverty and accepted it as a permanent condition. Because of their apathy and invisibility they had ceased to be objects of interest to the politician. Nor would the increase of the gross national product of itself solve their problems. But he insisted that an affluent society, through investment in the public sector, could begin to take measures which might at least keep poverty from being self-perpetuating. Then in 1962 *The Other America,* a brilliant and indignant book by Michael Harrington, translated the statistics into bitter human terms. If Galbraith brought poverty into the national consciousness, Harrington placed it on the national conscience.

Kennedy read both Galbraith and Harrington; and I believe that *The Other America* helped crystallize his determination in 1963 to accompany the tax cut by a poverty program. Galbraith's unremitting guerrilla warfare in support of the public sector against "reactionary" Keynesianism certainly played its part too.[6] The Senate Subcommittee on Employment and Manpower, under the leadership of Joseph S. Clark of Pennsylvania, conducted a series of thoughtful hearings to determine what the proper 'policy mix' should be to achieve full employment. And the Council of Economic Advisers itself, amending its earlier emphasis on aggregate measures, provided a main stimulus to the new structural effort.

In the spring of 1963, Robert Lampman, who had conducted poverty studies for the Joint Economic Committee in 1959 and was now a member of the Council staff, brought his researches up to date. His data, as Heller explained in a memorandum to Kennedy on May 1, underlined the drastic slowdown in the rate at which the economy was taking people out of poverty. In spite of the remarkable increase in the gross national product, the absolute number of the poor appeared to be slightly larger than in 1957 and the proportion only 1 per cent lower. By reasonable definitions —an annual income of $3000 for a family or $1500 for an individual—one-fifth of the nation lived in an underworld of poverty beyond the reach of most government programs, whether housing, farm price supports, social security or tax reduction.

It puzzled Kennedy that the poor were not angrier and more politically demanding. "In England," he said one day

---

[6] It is idle to speculate whether Keynes himself was a "reactionary" or "progressive" Keynesian. He was a political realist and, like Heller and Harris, might well have favored a tax cut in 1963 as the only form of major stimulus acceptable to Congress. On the other hand, those, like Colin Clark and *Business Week*, who claimed him as a conservative, forgot his burning outrage over unemployment, which always seemed to him cruel and senseless human waste. In the thirties, except for a passing reference in *The Means to Prosperity* ("given sufficient time to gather the fruits, reduction of taxation will run a better chance, than an increase, of balancing the budget"), he hardly mentioned tax reduction, arguing instead for public spending. (It should be noted, however, that tax reduction would then have been a feeble weapon in the United States. As late as 1939 there were less than 4 million taxable returns. The Second World War made the income tax a powerful instrument of fiscal policy. By 1945 45 million persons were filing taxable returns.)

in the spring of 1963, "the unemployment rate goes to two per cent, and they march on Parliament. Here it moves up toward six, and no one seems to mind." But, as he said to Heller, the time had come for action. There were doubts in other parts of the government, even in Heller's own staff. Ted Sorensen, however, told Heller, "This is the President's kind of program. Go ahead on it." Early in June Heller circulated a memorandum within the Council asking "what lines of action might make up a practical Kennedy anti-poverty program in 1964?" Through the summer and fall the Council carried on its work. During the cabinet meeting on October 29, 1963, the President scribbled, as usual, on a yellow lined pad; the doodles show the word "poverty" half a dozen times, encircled and underlined. On Armistice Day, 1963, Kennedy told Heller, "First we'll have your tax cut; then we'll have my expenditures program." One day in November, musing about the 1964 State of the Union message, he remarked to me, "The time has come to organize a national assault on the causes of poverty, a comprehensive program, across the board"; this, he suggested, would be the centerpiece in his 1964 legislative recommendations. On November 19 he observed to Heller that the middle class might feel threatened and we would have to do something for the suburbs, but the Council should go full speed ahead to get the program ready for 1964. Between tax reduction and the war against poverty, Kennedy believed that he had finally put together the elements of a total program for economic growth and opportunity.

Already the policies of the Kennedy years had resulted in the longest American peacetime expansion of the economy in the century of recorded business cycle history. The average increase in the gross national product in real terms was 5.6 per cent a year[7]—measurably more than the 5 per cent Kennedy had talked about in the 1960 campaign. Profits, wages and salaries were higher than ever before; yet costs and prices remained stable, and wage rates on the average rose no faster than productivity.

The sources of this triumph can be briefly enumerated. The steady rise in expenditures, averaging over $5 billion a year, contributed basic economic stimulus.[8] The investment tax credit and the liberalized depreciation allowances encouraged investment. The Federal Reserve Board followed

[7] This figure is from the first quarter of 1961 to the third quarter of 1963.

[8] The administrative deficits were $3.9 billion in 1961, $6.4 billion in 1962 and $6.3 billion in 1963.

924 A THOUSAND DAYS

the election returns and, where the balance of payments permitted, pursued a policy of monetary ease. The guideposts and the steel fight restrained the wage-price spiral. Roosa's legerdemain defended the dollar. Neither of the right-wing bogies of the fifties—the passion for a balanced budget or the fear of inflation—was allowed to abort the boom. Then the tax cut promised to infuse the body economic with new energies for consumption and investment and the poverty program to open the gates of escape from deprivation and squalor.

Dillon, describing these years as a "watershed in the development of American economic policy," thus summed up their meaning:

> They have borne witness to the emergence, first of all, of a new national determination to use fiscal policy as a dynamic and affirmative agent in fostering economic growth. Those years have also demonstrated, not in theory, but in actual practice, how our different instruments of economic policy—expenditure, tax, debt management and monetary policies—can be tuned in concert toward achieving different, even disparate, economic goals. In short, those years have encompassed perhaps our most significant advance in decades in the task of forging flexible economic techniques capable of meeting the needs of our rapidly changing economic scene.

It was, indeed, an unprecedented performance in economic management; and its success was due to Heller and Dillon, whose creative debates first illuminated the choices and then led to consensus, and above all to Kennedy, whose political instinct determined the timing of policies and whose intellectual leadership made them acceptable to the country.

The growing accord between Heller and Dillon expressed a convergence of opinion among most economically literate Americans.[9] So *Business Week* suddenly discovered that Keynesianism was not so radical after all; "it is, in fact, a new variety of middle-of-the-road conservatism." Perhaps only a Wall Street banker could have enrolled the leaders of American business in the Keynesian revolution. Like Vandenberg's conversion to internationalism in 1945, Dillon's espousal of Keynesianism (though he did not much like to be called a Keynesian) was one of those timely actions which carried over the line thousands of others, who had too long been suppressing doubts about the laissez-faire verities. When Dillon retired as Secretary of the Treasury in 1965, leaving behind an appeal for tax reductions in the lower brackets, warnings against high interest rates and emphasis on the growing need for public services,

[9] Outside the University of Chicago.

his record and leadership were warmly praised on the floors of Congress by such liberal Democrats as Paul Douglas, Henry Reuss and even that scourge of bankers Wright Patman. Nor had the educational process been all one-way. The liberals learned things too—that measures to induce business investment, price stability and wage restraint, for example, were not all bad. It became a time, as Heller liked to say, of "the decline of the doctrinaire."

The question remained of the extent to which the new ideas were penetrating beyond the still smallish circle of the economically literate. Though Wall Street was coming to accept deficits as a benign invention, Main Street still evidently regarded them as the work of the devil. This mythology about the sinfulness of federal spending and the wickedness of a growing federal debt had deep roots in the folkways. Heller, in a moment he was not soon allowed to forget, attributed this to "the basic Puritan ethic of the American people"; but, if so, it was a very peculiar Puritanism, for it permitted the people to indulge freely in all the vices—to unbalance budgets, to go into debt, to spend more than they earned—they would righteously deny their government. Indeed, consumer debt had increased about 1000 per cent since the war, while the national government's debt had only increased 18 per cent. Perhaps Heller had Mencken's view of Puritanism in mind: "The objection to Puritans is not that they try to make us think as they do, but that they try to make us do as they think." In any case, so long as the national government itself continued to encourage the mythology—even Kennedy, to meet his congressional problems, used occasionally to talk about frugality in government as if the reduction of public spending were per se a good thing—the new economic policy could not be wholly secure.

The job of public education which Kennedy had begun so brilliantly at Yale was yet to be completed. Still, these years equipped the republic with policies which promised to advance economic growth, move toward full employment and relieve the age-old burdens of poverty.

9. ONE ACQUAINTED WITH THE NIGHT

On a beautiful autumn Saturday at the end of October the President flew to Amherst College in Massachusetts to take part in a ceremony in honor of Robert Frost. He had decided to speak about Frost's inaugural theme of poetry and power. When we were talking over what he might say, we had chatted about Frost's poems. He recalled *"I have been one acquainted with the night"* and, "What a terrific line!" Now on Air Force One he worked over the speech some more and then joined Stewart Udall, James Reed, his friend of PT-boat days, now Assistant Secretary of the Treasury, and me in the forward compartment. The President's mood was gay. Udall remarked that he feared a lady of his acquaintance, fanatically anti-Kennedy, might appear and even try to interrupt the ceremony, "so if you see me in the crowd struggling with a woman and rolling on the ground, you will know what is going on." "In any case, Stewart," the President said, "we will give you the benefit of the doubt."

Soon we landed and motored over to the college. It was Indian summer, golden and vivid but with forebodings of winter. "The men who create power," Kennedy told his Amherst audience, "make an indispensable contribution to the nation's greatness, but the men who question power make a contribution just as indispensable . . . for they determine whether we use power or power uses us." Frost, he continued, saw poetry as the means of saving power from itself. "When power leads man toward arrogance, poetry reminds him of his limitations. When power narrows the area of man's concern, poetry reminds him of the richness and diversity of existence. When power corrupts, poetry cleanses."

"I see little of more importance to the future of our country and our civilization," he said, "than full recognition of the place of the artist." And then he offered his vision of the American promise.

I look forward to a great future for America, a future in which our country will match its military strength with our moral restraint, its wealth with our wisdom, its power with our purpose.

I look forward to an America which will not be afraid of grace and beauty, which will protect the beauty of our natural environment, which will preserve the great old American houses and squares and parks of our national past, and which will build handsome and balanced cities for our future.

I look forward to an America which will reward achievement in the arts as we reward achievement in business or statecraft. . . .

I look forward to an America which commands respect throughout the world not only for its strength but for its civilization as well. And I look forward to a world which will be safe not only for democracy and diversity but also for personal distinction.

This was his sense of the future, and he embraced it as if on a rising tide of confidence. A few days later at a press conference someone asked him how he felt about the Presidency. He replied, "I have given before to this group the definition of happiness of the Greeks, and I will define it again: it is full use of your powers along lines of excellence. I find, therefore, the Presidency provides some happiness." For all the congressional problems of 1963, he knew he had had a good year, and he anticipated 1964 with relish. So much beckoned: the enactment of the civil rights and tax reduction bills; the war against poverty; education and Medicare; the pursuit of peace beyond the test ban; the advance of the Alliance for Progress; a visit from de Gaulle in February; a trip with Jacqueline to the Far East in the spring; the presidential election in the fall.

He had little real doubt, I think, that he would win the election with ease, especially against Goldwater. This would give his second term the congressional margin and the popular mandate the first had lacked. He saw his second administration, like Theodore Roosevelt's, as the time of great legislative action, when the seeds planted in the first term would come to fruition. He expected, of course, to make some changes. The conduct of foreign affairs never ceased to bother him. Discussing the de Gaulle visit with Ambassador James Gavin in late October, he said, "In the meantime, though, I must get something done about that State Department." He continued to hope for the best from his Secretary of State; but the frustrations—the Under Secretaryship for Inter-American Affairs was only the most recent and one of the more trivial—were accumulating. He wanted ideas, initiatives and action from State, not cautious adherence to the policies of the past varied by anxious agnosticism in face of new problems—for example, the Bay of Pigs, the missile crisis, Berlin, Vietnam, the Congo, disarmament, Skybolt, de Gaulle, Italy, Latin America, India—on very few of which his Secretary of State vouchsafed a definite view. With reluctance, because he still liked Rusk and thought he had useful qualities, he made up his mind to accept his resignation after the 1964 election and seek a new Secretary. He always had the dream that a McNamara might someday take command and make the Department a genuine partner in the enterprise of foreign affairs (though he also said that he had to have a McNamara at Defense in order to have a foreign policy at all). He planned other changes in his administration, some notable, though none, so far as I know, in the cabinet (unless he could not persuade his brother to stay on as Attorney General). Then after the election, he could not only complete his present program but move forward to new problems—tax evasion was one, an attack on the structure of government subsidies was another, the rationalization of the city, the promotion of the arts and the protection of the natural environment, others. In foreign affairs he looked forward particularly to the possibility, if the *détente* held, of a journey to the Soviet Union.

Sometimes he would muse about life beyond 1968. He had remarked early in his administration that, "whether I serve one or two terms in the Presidency, I will find myself at the end of that period at what might be called the awkward age—too old to begin a new career and too young to write my memoirs." Many thoughts drifted through his mind about the future—publishing a newspaper (he sometimes joked with Ben Bradlee about buying the *Washington Post*), returning to Congress like John Quincy Adams, traveling around the world, writing a book. As the plans for his presidential library at Harvard took shape, he began to visualize the future with more particularity. They would, he thought, live part of each year in Cambridge. Here he could use his offices in the Library, work on the history of his administration, hold seminars and talk to students. He hoped that the Library might become a center where academicians, politicians and public servants could challenge and instruct one another, thereby realizing his old dream of bringing together the world of thought and the world of power.[10]

But 1969 was a long time away, and there remained the hurdle of 1964. The President looked forward with high anticipation to running against Goldwater. I think he felt that this would give him the opportunity to dispose of right-wing extremism once and for all and win an indisputable mandate for his second term. On November 12 he convened his first strategy meeting for 1964—Robert Kennedy, O'Brien, O'Donnell, Sorensen, John Bailey and Richard Maguire of the National Committee, Stephen Smith and Richard Scammon, a political scientist, director of the Census Bureau and a lively expert on voting statistics. They discussed the South and its representation at the national convention, meditated on the suburbs, considered the organization of the campaign, then reverted to the South, where the President was to go in another ten days to carry the fight to Florida and Texas. It was a sanguine meeting, filled with badinage about the future. A notable absentee was the Vice-President of the United States.

10 This intention will now be carried out in the John F. Kennedy Institute of Politics under the direction of his friend Richard Neustadt.

Johnson's absence stimulated a curious story that the Kennedy's intended, in the political idiom, to dump him as the vice-presidential candidate in 1964, as Roosevelt had dumped John Nance Garner in 1940. These stories were wholly fanciful. Kennedy knew and understood Johnson's moodiness in the Vice-Presidency, but he considered him able and loyal. In addition, if Goldwater were to be the Republican candidate, the Democrats needed every possible asset in the South. The meeting on November 12 assumed Johnson's renomination as part of the convention schedule.

It had not been an easy year for Johnson. One saw much less of him around the White House than in 1961 or 1962. He seemed to have faded astonishingly into the background and appeared almost a spectral presence at meetings in the Cabinet Room. Though his fidelity to the President was constant and his self-discipline impressive, the psychological cost was evidently mounting. Theodore White has written, "Chafing in inaction when his nature yearned to act, conscious of indignities real or imagined, Johnson went through three years of slow burn." The Vice-President disagreed with administration tactics in 1963 on a number of points—on the civil rights bill, on the Committee on Equal Employment Opportunity, on selling wheat to the Soviet Union, on Vietnam. He evidently felt he should have been consulted more, especially in legislative matters. Yet about the President himself Johnson always spoke with deep and unaffected admiration. He would mention the grace with which he bore his burdens and say that, when Kennedy went around the room with the question "What would you do?", he would pray that he would not have to answer first.

As 1964 approached, Kennedy looked to Johnson for particular help in the Vice-President's own state. There John Connally, who had resigned as Secretary of the Navy to run successfully for governor, and Senator Ralph Yarborough were engaged in the latest phase of the quarrel which had plagued the Texas Democratic party ever since Garner had opposed a third term for Roosevelt in 1940. The conservative Democrats of Texas were increasingly based on the oil industry, the young suburban businessmen and the rural conservatives, while the liberal Democrats had joined the old populist tradition with the new force of organized labor. The conservatives had won out in the late forties and fifties; this had been reflected in Johnson's own movement from the aggressive young New Dealer to the cautious middle-of-the-roader of the Eisenhower years. Yet, though in the course of this journey he had estranged many

Texas liberals, his heart had remained with the New Deal. Kennedy now looked to him to use his personal influence with Connally and his ideological affinity with Yarborough to end the wracking fight in the Texas Democracy. By going to Texas himself, the President hoped to use the presidential authority to help the Vice-President bring the warring Texans together.

On November 19 he had the usual breakfast with the congressional leaders. Chatting about his trip, he said that the Texas feuds would at least create interest and bring people out. He added, "Things always look so much better away from Washington." The next night was Robert Kennedy's thirty-eighth birthday. At the party at Hickory Hill, Ethel Kennedy, instead of making her usual chaffing toast about her husband, asked us all, with simplicity and solemnity, to drink to the President of the United States. The next morning the President and Mrs. Kennedy flew to Texas, with stops scheduled for San Antonio, Houston, Dallas, Austin.

10. DALLAS

Exactly four weeks before, Adlai Stevenson had gone to Dallas for a meeting on United Nations Day. The National Indignation Convention, still active on the radical right, decided to counter this visit by holding a "United States Day" meeting the previous day with General Edwin A. Walker as the main speaker. Governor Connally, without perhaps knowing the character of the occasion, dismayed the friends of the UN by giving "United States Day" the sanction of an official proclamation. That night General Walker denounced the United Nations. The next day handbills with photographs of the President of the United States—full-face and profile—were scattered around Dallas: "WANTED FOR TREASON. THIS MAN is wanted for treasonous activities against the United States," followed by a scurrilous bill of particulars.

That evening many of Walker's patriots returned to the same auditorium to harass Stevenson. While Adlai spoke, there was hooting and heckling; placards and flags were waved, and noisemakers set off. When the police removed one of the agitators from the hall, Stevenson, with customary poise, said, "For my part, I believe in the forgiveness of sin and the redemption of ignorance." At the close he walked through a jostling crowd of pickets to his car. A woman screamed at him, and he stopped for a moment to calm her down. The mob closed in on him. Another woman crashed a sign down on his head. A man spat at him. As the police broke through to him, Stevenson, wiping his face with a handkerchief, said coldly, "Are these human beings or are these animals?"

The next morning Kennedy read the story in the papers. He considered Stevenson's coolness under fire impressive and particularly admired the presence of mind which produced the line about forgiveness and redemption. "Call Adlai," he instructed m, "and give him my sympathy, and tell him we thought he was great." Stevenson had left Dallas, but I soon tracked him down in Los Angeles and transmitted the President's message. He was pleased, joked a bit about the night before and then said, "But, you know, there was something very ugly and frightening about the atmosphere. Later I talked with some of the leading people out there. They wondered whether the President should go to Dallas, and so do I." After all, the assault on Stevenson was by no means an isolated event. During the 1960 campaign Lyndon Johnson himself, accompanied by his wife, had been hissed and spat upon by a screaming mob in the lobby of the Adolphus Hotel.

Still, Kenneth O'Donnell said later, the President "could not possibly go to Texas and avoid Dallas. It would cause more controversy—and it would not accomplish for us what really was the long-range purpose of the visit." In any case, I was reluctant to pass on Stevenson's message lest it convict him of undue apprehensiveness in the President's eyes. In a day or so Adlai called again to ask whether I had spoken to the President and expressed relief when I said I had not. He said that it would of course be out of character for Kennedy to avoid something because physical danger might be involved. Moreover, he had just received a reassuring letter from a leading Dallas businessman reporting that the outrage had had "serious effects on the entire community. . . . You can feel that your visit has had permanent and important results on the city of Dallas."

Dallas plainly was a peculiar place. It was the newest rich city in the country. As late as 1940, it had been a medium-sized community of less than 300,000 people. But the discovery of the East Texas oil pool was already turning it into the financial capital of East Texas. Its population considerably more than doubled between 1940 and 1960; and now it was dominated by raw new wealth flowing from the oil fields into banking, insurance, utilities and real estate. The manners of the Dallas plutocracy had been somewhat refined by Neiman-Marcus, but its policies had been kept in a primitive and angry state by the *Dallas Morning News*, whose publisher two years before had told Kennedy at the White House that the nation needed a man on horseback while he was riding Caroline's tricycle. A white collar city, it had neither a traditional aristocracy nor a strong labor movement to diversify its opinion or temper its certitudes. The fundamentalist religious background of many of its inhabitants had instilled a self-righteous absolutism of thought; the Dallas Citizens' Council, an organization of leading businessmen, imposed a solid uniformity of values and attitudes; and the whole community, with bank clerks and real estate hustlers sporting Stetsons and sombreros, carefully cultivated the myth of the old Texas and its virile, hard-riding, hard-shooting men taking the law into their own hands.[11] Texas had one of the highest homicide rates in the country—far higher, for example, than New York—and Dallas, which murdered more people some years than England, doubled the national average. By November 1, it had already had ninety-eight murders in 1963. It was a city of violence and hysteria, and its atmosphere was bound to affect people who were already weak, suggestible and themselves filled with chaos and hate.

But not all Texas was in the image of Dallas. San Antonio, where the President stopped early Thursday afternoon, had recently sent Henry Gonzalez, a liberal Democrat, to Congress, and it greeted Kennedy with great enthusiasm. Even conservative Houston was almost as friendly later that same day. Kennedy, delighted by the warmth of his reception, remained, however, in a mood of puzzlement and annoyance over the backbiting of Texas Democratic politics. He had insisted that Senator Yarborough come along; but Governor Connally, it seemed to the White House, despite the presidential wish for reconciliation, was doing all he could to keep Yarborough out of as many things as possible, including even the great reception at the gubernatorial mansion designed to climax the trip Friday evening in Austin. Yarborough, sure that Johnson was siding with his former protégé, declined both in San Antonio and Houston to ride in the same car with the Vice-President.

Kennedy, who thought these disputes childish and un-

11 About this time the December issue of *Redbook* came on the newsstands. An article by Jhan Robbins recorded the impressions of European children about Americans. The first answer to the question "What are Americans like?" was: "The average American is, of course, a Texan. He eats lots of breakfast and gets fat so he has to go on a diet because he likes to look skinny. He calls everyone 'sweetheart' and is bad to colored people. If he doesn't like who is his President, he usually shoots him."

necessary, wanted Yarborough to have the respect due the Democratic Senator of the state; and he counted on Johnson to compose matters. But Johnson had lost much of his standing in Texas: his association with the New Frontier had greatly hurt him with the conservatives, and the liberals had mistrusted him for years. In the limbo of the Vice-Presidency, he was now only a name and a memory. Yarborough and Connally, on the other hand, had their own political bases in Texas, and each was a determined man—the one to uphold the banner of New Frontier liberalism, the other to display his control over the Texas Democratic party. Probably the President overestimated the Vice-President's capacity to deal with the situation. In any case, in a brief but cogent private talk at the Rice Hotel in Houston on Thursday afternoon Kennedy expressed his discontent with the situation.

Later the President spoke to the League of United Latin-American Citizens, recalling the Good Neighbor policy and the Alliance for Progress. Then, "in order that my words may be even clearer," he introduced Jacqueline who said a few words in Spanish. As they left for a dinner in honor of Congressman Albert Thomas, a group of Cuban refuges held signs and shouted slogans. In their midst, Ronnie Dugger of the *Texas Observer* saw one old man waving over his head a small sign: "Welcome Kennedy." [12] At the dinner Kennedy began by saying that, when he heard Thomas was thinking of resigning, "I called him up on the phone and asked him to stay as long as I stayed. I didn't know how long that would be."

Later that night the presidential party went on to Fort Worth. Before breakfast the next morning, Friday, November 22, Kennedy read the *Dallas Morning News*. The day before a sports columnist in the *News* had suggested that the President talk about sailing in Dallas in order to avoid trouble. "If the speech is about boating you will be among the warmest of admirers. If it is about Cuber, civil rights, taxes or Vietnam, there will sure as shootin' be some who heave to and let go with a broadside of grape shot in the presidential rigging." This morning the *News* ran a full-page advertisement headed: WELCOME MR. [sic] KENNEDY TO DALLAS. It claimed to speak for the "American-thinking citizens of Dallas" who still had, "through a Constitution largely ignored by you," the right to disagree and criticize. It then set forth a series of questions: why had Kennedy "scrapped the Monroe Doctrine in favor of the 'Spirit of

---

12 For Dugger's vivid record of the Kennedy trip, see the *Texas Observer*, November 29, 1963; also "Dallas, After All," *Observer*, March 6, 1964.

Moscow' "? why had the foreign policy of the United States "degenerated to the point that the C.I.A. is arranging coups and having staunch Anti-Communist Allies of the U.S. bloodily exterminated"? why had Kennedy "ordered or permitted your brother Bobby . . . to go soft on Communists, fellow-travelers and ultra-leftists in America, while permitting him to persecute loyal Americans who criticize you"? why had Gus Hall, head of the American Communist Party, "praised almost every one of your policies and announced that the party will endorse and support your re-election"? why, why, why—a list designed to suggest that the President was systematically pro-communist if not a traitor. Kennedy pushed the paper aside with disgust. He asked, "How can people write such things?" To Yarborough he said, "Did you see what the *Dallas News* is trying to do to us?" adding that he had "a very strong feeling" about this sort of thing. "He did not say it," Yarborough said later, "in the light bantering manner that he often used when meeting criticism."

But he was light and bantering when he addressed the citizens of Fort Worth a little later in the soft rain in front of the Texas Hotel. "Mrs. Kennedy is organizing herself," he said. "It takes longer, but, of course, she looks better than we do when she does it." Then he went on to speak at a breakfast of the Fort Worth Chamber of Commerce. "No one expects that our life will be easy," he said. ". . . History will not permit it . . . [But] we are still the keystone in the arch of freedom, and I think we will continue to do, as we have done in our past, our duty." At the conclusion the chairman of the meeting presented him with a cowboy hat. The President, who never put on funny hats, looked at it with suspicion and finally said, "I'll put it on at the White House and you can photograph it there." Back at the Texas Hotel, he chatted with Jacqueline and Kenneth O'Donnell about the role of the Secret Service. All they could do, he said, was to protect a President from unruly or overexcited crowds. But if someone really wanted to kill a President, it was not too difficult; put a man on a high building with a telescopic rifle, and there was nothing anybody could do to defend a President's life. O'Donnell said afterward that Kennedy regarded assassination as a risk inherent in a democracy; "it didn't disturb him at all."

During the short trip to Dallas, the men in the plane discussed the city's aberrant atmosphere. The President "seemed puzzled by the prevalent Dallas attitude," Congressman James Wright later recalled, "and asked questions of each of us in an attempt to understand its genesis." Fanaticism was what he detested most—as the reason and poise he incarnated were what distraught and rootless people, drawn to Dallas by the climate of alienation and anger, might find most intolerable. The general conclusion, in Wright's words, was that the real culprit was "the steady drum-beat of ultra right-wing propaganda with which the citizenry is constantly besieged."

When they arrived at Love Field, Congressman Henry Gonzalez said jokingly, "Well, I'm taking my risks. I haven't got my steel vest yet." The President, disembarking, walked immediately across the sunlit field to the crowd and shook hands. Then they entered the cars to drive from the airport to the center of the city. The people in the outskirts, Kenneth O'Donnell later said, were "not unfriendly nor terribly enthusiastic. They waved. But were reserved, I thought." The crowds increased as they entered the city —"still very orderly, but cheerful." In downtown Dallas enthusiasm grew. Soon even O'Donell was satisfied. The car turned off Main Street, the President happy and waving, Jacqueline erect and proud by his side, and Mrs. Connally saying, "You certainly can't say that the people of Dallas haven't given you a nice welcome," and the automobile turning on to Elm Street and down the slope past the Texas School Book Depository, and the shots, faint and frightening, suddenly distinct over the roar of the motorcade, and the quizzical look on the President's face before he pitched over, and Jacqueline crying, "Oh, no, no. . . . Oh, my God they have shot my husband," and the horror, the vacancy.

11. THE DRUMS OF WASHINGTON

On Friday morning I had flown to New York with Katharine Graham, whose husband Philip had died three months before, for a luncheon with the editors of her magazine *Newsweek*. Kenneth Galbraith had come down from Cambridge for the occasion. We were still sipping drinks before luncheon in an amiable mood of Friday-before-the-Harvard-Yale game relaxation when a young man in shirtsleeves entered the room and said, a little tentatively, "I am sorry to break in, but I think you should know that the President has been shot in the head in Texas." For a flash one thought this was some sort of ghastly office joke. Then we knew it could not be and huddled desperately around the nearest television. Everything was confusing and appalling. The minutes dragged along. Incomprehensible bulletins came from the hospital. Suddenly an insane surge of conviction flowed through me: I felt that the man who had survived the Solomon Islands and so much illness and agony, who so loved life, embodied it, enhanced it, could not possibly die now. He would escape the shadow as he had before. Almost immediately we received the irrevocable word.

In a few moments Galbraith and I were on Katharine Graham's plane bound for Washington. It was the saddest journey of one's life. Bitterness, shame, anguish, disbelief, emptiness mingled inextricably in one's mind. When I stumbled, almost blindly, into the East Wing, the first person I encountered was Franklin D. Roosevelt, Jr. In a short time I went with my White House colleagues to Andrews Field to await the return of Air Force One from Texas. A small crowd was waiting in the dusk, McNamara, stunned and silent, Harriman, haggard and suddenly looking very old, desolation everywhere. We watched incredulously as the casket was carefully lifted out of the plane and taken to the Naval Hospital at Bethesda. Later I went to my house in Georgetown. My weeping daughter Christina said, "Daddy, what has happened to our country? If this is the kind of country we have, I don't want to live here any more." The older children were already on their way back from college to Washington.

Still later I went back to the White House to await the last return. Around four in the morning the casket, wrapped in a flag, was brought from the Naval Hospital and placed on a stand in the East Room. Tapers were lit around the bier, and a priest said a few words. Then Jacqueline approached the bier, knelt for a moment and buried her head in the flag. Soon she walked away. The rest of us waited for a little while in the great hall. We were beyond consolation, but we clung to the comradeship he had given us. Finally, just before daybreak, we bleakly dispersed into the mild night.

We did not grieve alone. Though in Dallas school children applauded the news [13] and in Peking the *Daily Worker* ran a savage cartoon entitled "Kennedy Biting the

[13] The children were not responsible; they expressed the atmosphere of the city. What was more shocking was that the Reverend William Holmes, who reported these incidents in a sermon on the following Sunday and said that "the spirit of assassination" had pervaded the city, received such threats that he had to take his own children out of school and go into hiding. The Dallas feeling evidently was that, whether true or false, Holmes's remarks reflected on their city and were therefore unforgivable. Subsequently a Dallas school teacher who asked in a letter to *Time* how her students could be expected to "grow up to be good citizens when the newspapers, their parents and the leaders of their own city preached dissension" was suspended. Judge Sarah T. Hughes of Dallas, who administered the presidential oath to Lyndon

Dust" showing the dead President lying in a pool of blood, his necktie marked with dollar signs, sorrow engulfed America and the world. At Harvard Yard the bells tolled in Memorial Church, a girl wept hysterically in Widener Library, a student slammed a tree, again and again, with his fist. Negroes mourned, and A. Philip Randolph said that his "place in history will be next to Abraham Lincoln." Pablo Casals mused that he had seen many great and terrible events in his lifetime—the Dreyfus case, the assassination of Gandhi—"but in recent history—and I am thinking of my own lifetime—there has never been a tragedy that has brought so much sadness and grief to as many people as this." "For a time we felt the country was ours," said Norman Mailer. "Now it's theirs again." Many were surprised by the intensity of the loss. Alistair Cooke spoke of "this sudden discovery that he was more familiar than we knew." "Is there some principle of nature," asked Richard Hofstadter, "which requires that we never know the quality of what we have had until it is gone?" Around the land people sat desperately in front of television sets watching the bitter drama of the next four days. In Washington Daniel Patrick Moynihan, the Assistant Secretary of Labor, said, "I don't think there's any point in being Irish if you don't know that the world is going to break your heart eventually. I guess that we thought we had a little more time. . . . Mary McGrory said to me that we'll never laugh again. And I said, 'Heavens, Mary. We'll laugh again. It's just that we'll never be young again.'"

In Ireland, "Ah, they cried the rain down that night," said a Fitzgerald of Limerick; he would not come back in the springtime. David Bruce reported from London, "Great

---

Johnson on the plane back to Washington, said, "It could have happened anywhere, but Dallas, I'm sorry to say, has been conditioned by many people who have hate in their hearts and who seem to want to destroy."

On May 29, 1965, the 48th anniversary of Kennedy's birth, the Texas House of Representatives defeated on a record vote of 72–52 (with Governor Connally's brother voting with the majority) a bill passed unanimously in the State Senate proposing to rename the state school for the mentally retarded at Richmond in President Kennedy's honor. One resident of Fort Bend County testified in the House hearings that changing the name of the school might cause local people to withdraw their support. When the *Texas Observer* asked the sponsor of the bill, Representative Neil Caldwell of Alvin, what reasons his colleagues had given him for their no votes, he said, "With most of them it's been the politics of the man—the dead man. They think enough things have been named for him. 'Just wouldn't be popular back home.' 'Not well thought of.' 'Don't want to get hurt politically.' Some of 'em say, 'I didn't like him.'" In the debate Caldwell said that, though memorials had been raised to Kennedy around the world, there were none in Texas. See "And Finally, As to John F. Kennedy," *Texas Observer*, June 11, 1965.

Britain has never before mourned a foreigner as it has President Kennedy." As the news spread around London, over a thousand people assembled before the embassy in Grosvenor Square; they came in endless thousands in the next days to sign the condolence book. That Was The Week That Was on television, unwontedly serious: "the first western politician to make politics a respectable profession for thirty years—to make it once again the highest of the professions, and not just a fabric of fraud and sham. . . . We took him completely for granted." "Why was this feeling—this sorrow—at once so universal and so individual?" Harold Macmillan later asked. "Was it not because he seemed, in his own person, to embody all the hopes and aspirations of this new world that is struggling to merge —to rise, Phoenix-like, from the ashes of the old?" In West Berlin people lighted candles in darkened windows. In Poland there was a spontaneous mass mourning by university students; church bells tolled for fifteen minutes on the night of the funeral. In Yugoslavia Tito, so overcome that he could hardly speak, phoned the American chief of mission; later he read a statement over the state radio and went in person to the embassy to sign the book. The national flag was flown at half-mast, and schools were instructed to devote one full hour to a discussion of the President's policies and significance. In Moscow Khrushchev was the first to sign the book, and the Soviet television carried the funeral, including the service in the church.

Latin America was devastated. Streets, schools, housing projects were named after him, shrines set up in his memory; his picture, torn from the newspaper, hung on the walls of workers' shacks and in the hovels of the *campesinos*. "For Latin America," said Lleras Camargo, "Kennedy's passing is a blackening, a tunnel, a gust of cloud and smoke." Castro was with Jean Daniel when the report came; he said, *"Es una mala noticia"* ("This is bad news"). In a few moments, with the final word, he stood and said, "Everything is changed. . . . I'll tell you one thing: at least Kennedy was an enemy to whom we had become accustomed." In Cambodia Prince Sihanouk ordered court mourning; "a light was put out," he later said, "which may not be re-lit for many years to come." In Indonesia flags flew at half-mast. In New Delhi people cried in the streets. In Algiers Ben Bella phoned Ambassador Porter in tears and said, "I can't believe it. Believe me, I'd rather it happen to me than to him." In Guinea Sékou Touré said, "I have lost my only true friend in the outside world." The embassy reported, "People expressed their grief without restraint,

and just about everybody in Guinea seemed to have fallen
under the spell of the courageous young hero of far away,
the slayer of the dragons of discrimination, poverty, ignorance and war." In N'zérékoré in the back country, where
one would hardly think they had heard of the United
States let alone the American President, a group of natives presented a sum of money to their American pastor to
buy, according to the custom of the Guerze people, a rush
mat in which to bury President Kennedy. In Kampala Ugan-
dans crowded the residence of the American Ambassador;
others sat silently for hours on the lawns and hillsides
waiting. In Mali, the most left-wing of African states, President Keita came to the embassy with an honor guard and
delivered a eulogy. In the Sudan a grizzled old Bisharine
tribesman told an American lawyer that it was terrible
Kennedy's son was so young; "it will be a long time before
he can be the true leader." *Transition,* the magazine of
African intellectuals, said, "In this way was murdered the
first real chance in this century for an intelligent and
new leadership to the world. . . . More than any other person, he achieved the intellectual's ideal of a man in action.
His death leaves us unprepared and in darkness."

In Washington grief was an agony. Somehow the long
hours passed, as the new President took over with firmness
and strength, but the roll of the drums, when we walked to
St. Matthew's Cathedral on the frosty Monday, will sound
forever in my ears, and the wildly twittering birds during
the interment at Arlington while the statesmen of the world
looked on. It was all so grotesque and so incredible. One
remembered Stephen Spender's poem:

I think continually of those who were truly great. . . .
The names of those who in their lives fought for life,
Who wore at their hearts the fire's center.
Born of the sun they traveled a short while towards the sun,
And left the vivid air signed with their honour.

It was all gone now—the life-affirming, life-enhancing zest,
the brilliance, the wit, the cool commitment, the steady
purpose. Richard Neustadt has suggested that two years
are the period of presidential initiation. He had had so
little time: it was as if Jackson had died before the nullification controversy and the Bank War, as if Lincoln had been
killed six months after Gettysburg or Franklin Roosevelt
at the end of 1935 or Truman before the Marshall Plan.[14]

[14] In the summer of 1964 Richard Wilson of *Look* asked congressional
leaders whether Kennedy would have got his legislative programs, especially the civil rights and tax reduction bills, if he had lived. He re-

Yet he had accomplished so much: the new hope for peace on earth, the elimination of nuclear testing in the atmosphere and the abolition of nuclear diplomacy, the new policies toward Latin America and the third world, the reordering of American defense, the emancipation of the American Negro, the revolution of national economic policy, the concern for poverty, the stimulus to the arts, the fight for reason against extremism and mythology. Lifting us beyond our capacities, he gave his country back to its best self, wiping away the world's impression of an old nation of old men, weary, played out, fearful of ideas, change and the future; he taught mankind that the process of rediscovering America was not over. He re-established the republic as the first generation of our leaders saw it— young, brave, civilized, rational, gay, tough, questing, exultant in the excitement and potentiality of history. He transformed the American spirit—and the response of his people to his murder, the absence of intolerance and hatred, was a monument to his memory. The energies he released, the standards he set, the purposes he inspired, the goals he established would guide the land he loved for years to come. Above all he gave the world for an imperishable moment the vision of a leader who greatly understood the terror and the hope, the diversity and the possibility, of life on this planet and who made people look beyond nation and race to the future of humanity. So the people of the world grieved as if they had terribly lost their own leader, friend, brother.

On December 22, a month after his death, fire from the flame burning at his grave in Arlington was carried at dusk to the Lincoln Memorial. It was fiercely cold. Thousands stood, candles in their hands; then, as the flame spread among us, one candle lighting the next, the crowd gently moved away, the torches flaring and flickering, into the darkness. The next day it snowed—almost as deep a snow as the inaugural blizzard. I went to the White House. It was lovely, ghostly and strange.

It all ended, as it began, in the cold.

---

ceived the following answers. Everett Dirksen: "This program was on its way before November 22, 1963. Its time had come." Carl Albert: "The pressure behind this program had become so great that it would have been adopted in essentially the same form whether Kennedy lived or died." Charles A. Halleck: "The assassination made no difference. The program was already made." Mike Mansfield: "The assassination made no real difference. Adoption of the tax bill and the civil-rights bill might have taken a little longer, but they would have been adopted." *Look*, November 17, 1964.